The Professional Pastry Chef

Third Edition

Bo Friberg

VNR **VAN NOSTRAND REINHOLD**
I⊕P™ A Division of International Thomson Publishing Inc.

New York • Albany • Bonn • Boston • Detroit • London • Madrid • Melbourne
Mexico City • Paris • San Francisco • Singapore • Tokyo • Toronto

Charts, Cake Decorating Designs, Chocolate Figurines, Marzipan Designs, and Templates drawn and copyrighted by Bo Friberg

All other illustrations designed by Bo and Amy Friberg and drawn by Joyce Hasselbeck Fowler

All photography produced and copyrighted by Bo Friberg with foodstyling by Bo and Amy Friberg

I(T)P™ A division of International Thomson Publishing, Inc.
The ITP logo is a trademark under license

Printed in the United States of America

For more information, contact:

Van Nostrand Reinhold
15 Fifth Avenue
New York, NY 10003

Chapman & Hall GmbH
Pappelallee 3
69469 Weinheim
Germany

Chapman & Hall
2–6 Boundary Row
London
SE1 8HN
United Kingdom

International Thomson Publishing Asia
221 Henderson Road #05–10
Henderson Building
Singapore 0315

Thomas Nelson Australia
102 Dodds Street
South Melbourne, 3205
Victoria, Australia

International Thomson Publishing Japan
Hirakawacho Kyowa Building, 3F
2-2-1 Hirakawacho
Chiyoda-ku, 102 Tokyo
Japan

Nelson Canada
1120 Birchmount Road
Scarborough, Ontario
Canada M1K 5G4

International Thomson Editores
Campos Eliseos 385, Piso 7
Col. Polanco
11560 Mexico D.F. Mexico

4 5 6 7 8 9 10 COU-WF 01 00 99 98 97

Library of Congress Cataloging-in-Publication Data

Friberg, Bo, 1940–
    The professional pastry chef / Bo Friberg. — 3rd ed.
        p.   cm.
    Includes index.
    ISBN 0-442-01597-6
    1. Pastry.   I. Title.
TX773.F75   1996
641.8′65—dc20   95-33377
                    CIP

To my wife, Amy, without whom this book would not have been possible. Her culinary knowledge, good taste, common sense, and ability to articulate my ideas made it possible to transform my scribblings into usable text. Thank you, Amy, for your fingers on the computer, your advice, encouragement, hard work, and patience.

Contents

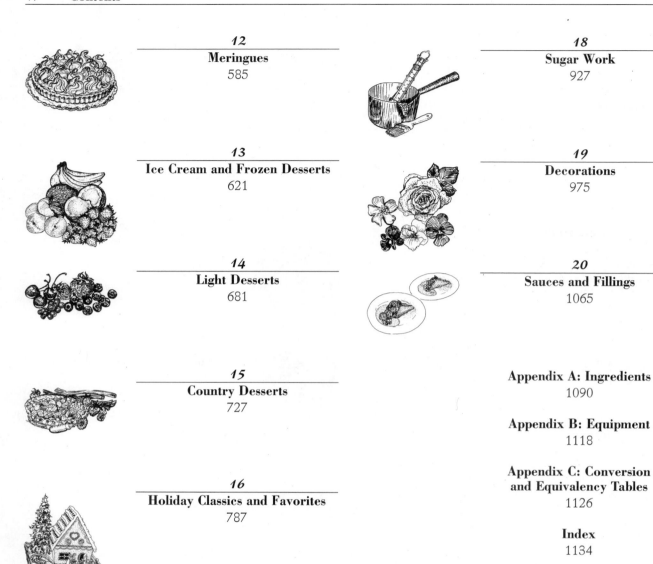

Recipe List

Chapter 11: Charlottes and Bavarois, Custards, Mousses, and Soufflés   **529**

Foreword

This third edition of *The Professional Pastry Chef* offers a comprehensive and logical introduction to various recipes, tools, and innovative applications in the art of baking and pastry.

Through his simple, yet interesting, approach, Chef Friberg has successfully managed to remove much of the mystery of the art. His recipes are appropriately supported by historical aspects, alternatives for ingredients, and techniques.

Chef Friberg's approach to baking and pastry is based on years of experience in both Europe and the United States where he has taught aspiring culinary professionals for over 17 years.

I believe this book to be an invaluable addition to the library of culinary novices, yet it is sophisticated enough to challenge the creativity of accomplished pastry chefs and bakers.

We at The Culinary Institute of America congratulate Master Pastry Chef Friberg on this work.

Ferdinand E. Metz

Foreword

For me, pastry is related to my childhood. My parents had a pastry shop, and pastry is a fundamental part of my life. Some of my fondest early memories are of the aroma of baking throughout the entire house. I would wake up to the pleasing fragrance of croissants, brioche, and gugelhupfs, or the wonderful perfume from an array of freshly baked tarts such as rhubarb, apricot, mirabelle, or cheesecake. How great are these pastry memories!

Therefore, a full knowledge of the classics and a respect for tradition are very important to me; however, the art of pastries cannot and must not live on its past glories. It must continually modernize according to circumstance. This is how I first met Bo Friberg a few years ago and was introduced to his innovative work, through his book *The Professional Pastry Chef.* Bo Friberg is one of the most talented pastry chefs I have ever met. His ability as a teacher is reflected in the pages of his book, and his passion for pastry carries through it. I consider Bo to be an innovator who is enriching the art of pastry as did the great masters of their time, including Rouget, Chiboust, Coquelin, and Bourbonneux.

What I marvel at above all in Bo is the ease with which he adjusts himself to new challenges. What Bo has capitalized on in his latest edition is not only describing and breaking down the recipes into the smallest details but also greatly extending the technical information and explaining any useful hints.

I am sure that all of these recipes will leave the reader with a sweet smile.

Hubert Keller
chef/owner Fleur de Lys Restaurant
San Francisco

Foreword

I never went to school to be trained as a professional chef because my career as a chef began by accident. So, as I ran the kitchen at *Chez Panisse* in Berkeley in the early seventies, I knew my knowledge of the art of pastry making was minimal.

Nevertheless, I read many dessert and pastry books. The ones "for the housewife" were mainly recipe books, so I bought some professional tomes, which were usually a thousand pages long and absolutely frightening. So I was left in a bit of a lurch.

I met Bo Friberg at the California Culinary Academy some years later when I was introduced in the evening dinner classes and slowly wormed my way into his kitchen, out of which emerged each day large quantities of effortlessly made superb pastries, all made by students who, theoretically, had very limited knowledge and expertise.

I quickly became friends with Bo and admired his talent for explaining and producing pastries, from the simplest cakes to the most complicated sugar baskets, all with no worry or panic.

The first two editions of this successful book seemed geared to professionals. This wonderful new third edition has a broader range and appeal, because recipes both simple and complex, from Peach Cobbler with Cinnamon to Individual Baked Alaskas or Triple Chocolate Terrine, are totally accessible. It will further the knowledge and skill of a professional pastry chef, but most of all, it is a book for every cook to work with and enjoy. *The Professional Pastry Chef* will lead you as far as you want to go with pastries, breads, ice creams, candies, and anything to do with sugar.

I salute Bo on his new creation and know that every reader will be eager to use it.

Jeremiah Tower
chef/owner Stars Restaurant
San Francisco

Preface

This third edition of *The Professional Pastry Chef* began over three years ago, and just as was true of the second edition, in the end it virtually became a brand new text. This compendium has now grown to almost 1,200 pages and is presented in a larger, simplified format that will make it much easier to use, whether you are a student, an experienced professional chef, a pastry teacher at the professional level, or a serious amateur chef. Instructions for every recipe have been rewritten in an effort to make them as easy to follow as possible, while maintaining the format of using shorter numbered steps. All of the classics and the recipes that have stood the test of time from the first two editions have been included here along with the latest preparation methods, innovative ideas for impressive plate presentations, and techniques that utilize equipment and tools such as silicone baking mats, stencils, trowels, and acetate or polyurethane strips, to make high-tech, nouvelle creations. There is also a new Country Desserts chapter that features American and European classics, from those that are very simple and unpretentious to some that have been dressed up for restaurant service. The Light Desserts chapter has just about doubled in size in reaction to the public's demand for lighter offerings, and every other chapter has been expanded as well, including the nonrecipe sections. Information on the production of products, which are so important to our industry, such as chocolate, sugar, and wheat flour are covered in depth and are illustrated with tables. Contained here are approximately 500 line drawings and close to 150 color photographs (most of them new to this edition), and nearly all of the over 1,000 recipes feature introductions that discuss the history of the dish, offer an alternate presentation, or offer detailed information on one or more of the ingredients. The number of step-by-step illustrations, tables, and life-size templates and stencils included here has

almost doubled from the previous edition. The yield of the recipes has been streamlined and reduced in some cases to make the book more accessible to a wider range of readers and to both large and small professional operations. Most cake and tart recipes yield two, as before, making it equally convenient for a professional to multiply this amount as needed depending on business demands, or for the home chef to simply divide the ingredients in half to make one birthday cake, for example. Recipes for plated desserts have been changed to yield either sixteen, twelve, or eight, which again makes it easy to divide the ingredients to serve eight, six, or four. In some cases where a recipe was still deemed to be too large for the average non-professional or small restaurant, a smaller version of the same recipe has been provided as well.

This book differs from many other textbooks in some very important ways. My background allows me to approach the subject matter from several different angles. This book is written by a working Certified Master Pastry Chef with over forty years of professional experience in the industry. I have worked in both small shops and large retail and wholesale operations in the United States and in Europe. I worked for the Swedish American Cruise Ship Line, I have demonstrated the art of pastry making in three television shows, and I have spent the last seventeen years teaching all levels of students. In writing this book I have drawn from all of these experiences to try to make this text a guide not only for those who want to make baking and pastry their career and for the teachers who, like me, are guiding their students along this path, but also for working professionals, who are looking for doable recipes for both the basics and the more modern innovations. It seems one is frequently called upon to prepare this or that as a special request or for a particular function or occasion, and it is certainly a great help to have a compendium with a multitude of recipes—which actually work—to draw from.

Both instructors and students will be pleased to note that all of the recipes and procedures in this book have been tested by literally thousands of students in my classes and have been changed and improved as needed. In the instructions I point out typical pitfalls and explain why certain steps must be completed in a particular order or manner. I also offer suggestions for using more than one type of form or mold when applicable, knowing that not only does every operation not have the same equipment, but these items are not always in ready supply when needed. There are also several instances where instructions, complete with illustrations, are given for making your own forms and molds.

Upon leaving any school, it is not enough that a student is simply able to perform, but he or she must also be able to produce at a reasonable speed in order to make a living in this field. Although there are many fine cooking schools that are not set up to actually serve food to the public, these recipes are not in any sense designed just for practice, or for all-day student projects where labor cost is not an issue. These are workable, practical recipes to be used in the real world of pastry and baking production. Students will certainly want to carry this text with them out into the industry after graduation.

Depending on the institution and its curriculum, an instructor may want to use this book in different ways. Although the order of the chapters follows a logical sequence of procedures that is in keeping with students' skill development, it is not necessary to follow this format. It is, however, important that students first learn how to work with basic doughs and ingredients. While the illustrations will be of great help in showing the student the particular steps for a given item, it is still very important that the instructor follow up a lecture on puff pastry, for example, by showing the students how the turns are made, how to roll and cut the dough, how to make bouchées, and so on. While these techniques are explained in this book the way that I do them (and I do from time to time explain a variation), instructors are encouraged to give the students their own input.

I wish every reader—professional, nonprofessional, student, instructor, beginner, or experienced master—great success.

Bo Friberg

Introduction

All of these recipes have two things in common: They have been written so that any person with a basic knowledge of cooking will be able to understand them, and they have all been thoroughly tested, by myself and by my students. I started the first edition of this book fourteen years ago when I came back from a trip to Europe, full of inspirations and new ideas, and began to catalog my new recipes along with the other recipes I was teaching. The second edition of *The Professional Pastry Chef,* written six years ago, incorporated major changes into the recipe format and added technical information and illustrations. This third edition, like the first two, is a little different from some other cookbooks in that it tells you not only what you should do but also what not to do, based on common mistakes I have observed in working with students.

Some of the selections are classic recipes made my way. Some date back to when I was an apprentice. A few I have "borrowed" from restaurants and pastry shops in the United States and around Europe, where I would order something that looked interesting, pick it apart, literally and mentally, and then try to duplicate or even improve it. I developed many of the recipes through knowing what goes well together and what the American customer likes. In addition to the classics, this third edition continues to expand on recipes and techniques that are in keeping with current trends in the industry, such as the offering of lighter or reduced-calorie desserts, the renewed interest in American country-style desserts, and the use of more artistic presentations. An old colleague once said to me, "Don't be concerned about someone stealing your ideas; show them all your cards, but always be working on something new."

Many changes in the pastry field during the last ten years have been influenced by the increased availability of reasonably priced imported produce, such as tropical fruits, excellent quality "halfway" products

from European manufacturers such as gianduja, florentina mix, chocolate shells, praline paste, and truffle fillings, and specialty baking equipment such as silkscreens, silicone baking mats, stencils, and pastry trowels used to create ribbon sponge sheets and the like. The ability to order passion fruit, for instance, at a price that makes it economically feasible to use it, and the opportunity to have plums, peaches, and raspberries, once strictly seasonal, available almost all year round, can allow the pastry chef much more creativity, as can having the aforementioned products and equipment at hand.

Pastry is distinct from other types of cooking because you cannot just stick your spoon (or finger) in for a taste and then add a pinch of this and a pinch of that as you might when making a pot of soup; most ingredients must be measured precisely, and many formulas work on scientific principles. For this reason the pastry chef must learn how different ingredients react with others, and how and why ingredients respond to temperature, friction, and storage. To create new recipes (or sometimes to figure out what you did wrong) you need to know, for example, that baking soda must be mixed with some type of acid to make it react, that gelatin will not work in the presence of an enzyme found in certain fresh tropical fruits, that yeast does not multiply successfully without sugar and how hot it can get before it is killed. You should also know at what temperature sugar will caramelize, what causes air to become trapped in cake batters, and what storage temperatures will destroy the appearance of chocolate products.

To be a first-rate pastry chef, you must have some artistic talent, a good sense of coordination and taste, and a steady hand. You must also possess some people skills and be able to earn the respect of those working with you. You must be able to solve problems and hire the right people. A good chef must be born with at least some of these talents, but keen interest and a lot of practice will improve these skills over the years. A competent chef's most important assets are common sense and self-confidence. These are the two things that cannot be taught. When you love what you are doing, believe in yourself, and believe that you can do the job, you will give everything your best effort. If the result is less than perfect, at least you will have learned something, and the next time you will try a little harder.

My first experiment with cooking took place in my mother's kitchen when I was eleven years old. When I came home from school and found the house empty, I attempted some kind of candy, I guess. I don't remember exactly what it was supposed to be, but I do remember my poor mother had great difficulty cleaning up the sticky pots and pans. We both learned something from this: my mom, to time her trips to the grocery store better; and I, to clean up my messes.

After graduating from school at fourteen, I started as an apprentice at one of the local *konditoris* (pastry shops). It was quite small—just two *commis,* the pastry chef, and myself. I was lucky, without knowing it, to happen to pick the best: my master and teacher for the next five years was a dedicated and skilled craftsman. When I began I was, of course, a young boy who knew everything already. However, I soon found out about the real world, and especially how to take constructive criticism and learn from my mistakes. I remember his words: "One mistake is no mistake. But two mistakes are one too many."

I spent my first six months of training practicing the three Ls: listening, looking, and learning. While I was helping a little here and cleaning up a little there, I saw the breads and pastries being made. I had helped in making the dough for rye bread, but I had not done it on my own from start to finish. One morning when I arrived at work, my master said, "Bo! We are short-handed today. Make up the rye bread!" I was startled and said, "I can't do that!" My master angrily replied, "Do not ever use that word here again! You can do anything you want to do if you want to do it badly enough. The least you can do is give it your very best try." I have always remembered and tried to live by those words. It is one of the philosophies that I try to instill in all of my students.

After I had become a regular on the rye bread, the retired owner of the pastry shop used to come down to check me out. (At that time most bakeries in Sweden were in the cellar with small windows level with the street, so when the bakers looked out all they could see were shoes.) After a few lectures about "loaves that were not perfectly formed," I learned that he would always walk in a straight line from the door to the shelves where the breads cooled and pick up a loaf in the center of one particular shelf to examine. After I started placing the almost-perfect loaves in this place, I could practice and improve in peace. But if I happened to pay too much attention to those shoes outside the windows, I used to hear from across the room, "Bo, throw some sheet pans on the floor." (And I have to admit the first time I did just that!) "I don't see you doing anything, so at least let me hear you!" In the end my "yes-I-know-that" attitude must have improved too, for my master named his first and only son Bo, which I claimed as the ultimate victory. He assured me, however, that naming his son had nothing to do with a certain apprentice. I have a lot to thank John Håkanson for, and later on, Curt Anderson: two great Swedish Master Confectioners who not only had the patience and craft to teach me what they knew of their profession but also taught me a lot about life.

Unfortunately, very few restaurants and bakeries today can afford to completely train an apprentice; it costs too much in both time and materials. Schools such as the Culinary Institute of America now provide the training that small business cannot, and this allows an employer to hire a graduate who has received instructions in the basics and has some experience to build on.

Once you master the basic methods, you can start to create, improve, and put a little bit of yourself and your own style into the dishes you prepare. In our industry today, I am pleased to see more creativity and that "bit of self" going into dessert menus. Even so, too often you still find restaurants where, though the food coming out of the main kitchen is unusual and carefully prepared, the dessert menu offers only a basic chocolate cake with too much sponge and not enough filling, a basic custard, and an overbaked cheesecake. Or the worst offender: plain vanilla or chocolate ice cream, sometimes "creatively" put together in one dish. Most of the time these desserts are not even made on the premises and are a few days old and dry as well as boring.

The first and last impressions of a meal are very important. I do not expect anything of a meal if the

Special Reward Dog Biscuits

thirty 3-by-1¹/₂-inch (7.5-×-3.7-cm) dog biscuits

12 ounces (340 g) whole wheat flour
12 ounces (340 g) bread flour
2 ounces (55 g) wheat germ
1 teaspoon (5 g) salt
2 tablespoons (30 g) brown sugar
3 eggs
1 cup (240 ml) vegetable oil
3 ounces (85 g) powdered dry milk
1 cup (240 ml) water

This is a recipe that doesn't really fit into any particular chapter (or even necessarily into this book for that matter), but it is important to me, and I'm sure that anyone who is fortunate enough to share their life with a dog will understand why I am including it.

Any close reading of this text will soon reveal that I was lucky enough to grow up on a farm; it was rather small, but it still had a nice assortment of animals. The only drawback was that I was never allowed to have a dog because there were always a couple of cats close at hand to keep the mice in check. It wasn't until I was thirty years old that I was ready to settle down and buy a house, but it did not take very long after that for me to get my first Akita puppy. The two Akitas that are presently part of the family—a female named Kuma and her son, Shiro—received a dog-bone cookie cutter as a gift from one of my classes. Anyone who has taken my classes has heard my dog stories "slip out." Now, if given the choice, my dogs will have nothing at all to do with store-bought biscuits! You will probably find the same thing will happen should you decide to reward your best friend.

1. Combine the whole wheat flour, bread flour, wheat germ, salt, and brown sugar in a mixing bowl. Stir in the eggs and the vegetable oil.

2. Dissolve the milk powder in the water and then incorporate the mixture.

3. Mix to form a very firm dough that is smooth and workable. Adjust by adding a little extra flour or water as required.

4. Cover the dough and set it aside to relax for 15–20 minutes.

5. Roll the dough out to ¹/₂ inch (1.2 cm) thick. Cut out biscuits using a bone-shaped cutter 3 inches long by 1¹/₂ inches wide (7.5 × 3.7 cm). Place the biscuits on sheet pans lined with baking paper.

6. Bake at 375°F (190°C) for approximately 40 minutes or until the biscuits are brown and, more importantly, rock-hard. Let the biscuits cool, then store in a covered container five to six feet off the floor. Use as needed to reward your four-legged friends.

kitchen cannot make a decent salad or serve the soup hot. However, even if the meal is mediocre, a dessert that looks and tastes terrific will leave the guest with a positive last impression. I have noted with pleasure the rebirth of interest in great desserts. It is especially rewarding for me when I realize, glancing at a restaurant menu or tasting a dessert, that one of my former students has been in the kitchen.

This book is about making desserts and baked goods that are both good and exciting. It is not meant to impress or to set any particular standards. The methods described and used in the recipes are not the only ones possible or necessarily the best methods. There are different ways to form a loaf of bread, frost a cake, or hold a pastry bag. One way is good for one person, another way better for someone else.

In this book I offer the best of my knowledge and experience, as I give it to my students. It is my hope that this knowledge will be useful to you as you seek to better yourself in our creative and honorable profession.

Before You Use This Book

Certain ingredient information is standard throughout the book. Please note the following conventions:

• Butter is always specified as "unsalted butter." Salted butter can be substituted if the salt in the recipe is reduced by about $^1/_5$ ounce (6 g) for every pound of butter. You cannot substitute salted butter, however, if the recipe contains little salt or if the main ingredient is butter.

• The number of eggs specified in each recipe is based on 2-ounce (55-g) eggs (graded large). If you use eggs of a different size, adjust the number accordingly. For convenience in kitchens where a supply of separated egg yolks and egg whites is on hand, a volume measure is given when yolks or whites are used independently. The quantity of yolks, whites, and whole eggs per cup has been rounded to twelve, eight, and four, respectively, for these measures.

• Yeast is always specified as "fresh compressed yeast." To substitute dry yeast for fresh, reduce the amount called for by half. "Fast rising" yeast should be avoided. It is treated with conditioners that accelerate the yeast, which gives the chef less control and, in most cases, impairs the flavor of the baked goods.

• Gelatin is available in both sheet and powdered form. For the most part, unless you are multiplying the recipe, the same measure of either can be used. Sheet gelatin is more expensive but more convenient. To prepare sheet gelatin, place it in enough cold water to cover the sheets. Within a few minutes it will absorb enough liquid to become soft and spongy. Remove the sheet without squeezing the water out. Sheet gelatin will always absorb the same amount of liquid, so you do not need to soak it in a specified amount of water as you do powdered gelatin. Instructions for calculating the amount of liquid absorbed are given on page 1110.

• Raw eggs: When egg yolks, whites, or whole eggs are included in a recipe in which they are not cooked—in a mousse or gelatin-fortified cake filling, for example—they are first heated to at least 140°F (60°C) to pasteurize them (see Eggs and Sanitation, page 1095). This is done using different procedures, depending on the recipe; often it involves beating a hot syrup into the eggs or whipping the eggs over a bain-marie with another ingredient.

• The unsweetened cocoa powder called for in the recipes in this book refers to the alkalized (Dutch-process) type, preferred for its darker color and smoother flavor, and also because it dissolves more easily. Natural cocoa powder, which is somewhat acidic, may be substituted, provided it is used in a recipe that contains a sweetener, but it should not be used to sift on top of a pastry or to coat a truffle, for example.

• Both metric and U.S. units are given throughout. However, to avoid unmeasurable fractions, metric amounts have been rounded to the nearest even number. The equivalent for 1 ounce, for instance, is given as 30 grams rather than 28.35 grams.

• When 1 ounce or less of an ingredient, dry or liquid, is needed, the quantity is always given in teaspoons or tablespoons and is based on an exact measurement. Hedges like "scant" or "heaping" are not used in this book.

• Avoid the temptation to convert ingredients into cups and tablespoons. Weight measurements are used in professional recipes for better accuracy, and a good scale can be purchased inexpensively. Make certain that your scale (old or new) is properly calibrated.

• In many recipes in this book, instructions are given to spread a batter (most often a sponge batter) over a sheet of baking paper set on the work surface and then to "drag" the paper onto a sheet pan. This is done to facilitate spreading the batter evenly without the sides of the sheet pan getting in the way, since in the United States standard industry sheet pans have 1-inch (2.5-cm) sides. Readers throughout Europe and in many other countries where regular sheet pans contain raised sides only on the short ends may eliminate this step.

• Many recipes in this text include instructions for making templates from thin cardboard. Cardboard is suggested because it is both readily available and easy to work with; however, these cardboard templates are intended for one-time use only. A sturdier and more practical template can be made from $^1/_{16}$-inch (2-mm) plastic. These take a bit more effort to construct, but they can be used over and over. I prefer the laminated type of plastic since it will lay perfectly flat and will not tear (this is the type often used to cover office files or documents), but polyurethane sheets also work well.

• Any recipe in this book can be scaled up or down in direct proportions as long as it is not multiplied or divided by any number greater than four. In calculating ingredients that do not divide straight across—to divide in half a recipe calling for 3 eggs, or 1¹/₃ cups of a liquid, for example—round the number up (using 2 eggs or 5¹/₂ ounces of liquid for the examples given).

• When a weight yield is given for baked goods (for example, four 1-pound, 4-ounce [570 g] loaves), it relates to the product before being baked. As a general rule, 10 percent of the weight is lost in steam during the baking process of any item. When a large amount of liquid is part of the ingredients (such as for bread) up to 2 ounces (55 g) for every pound (455 g) of dough will expire.

• A properly calibrated thermometer is of great importance both for safe food handling, when working with egg-based desserts for example, and also to obtain satisfactory results whenever the precise temperature of the ingredients determines the outcome such as when cooking sugar. Therefore recalibration (or testing) should be done periodically. This can be done using the ice-point method or the boiling-point method. Ice-point calibration is done by immersing the sensor in a 50:50 mixture of ice and water. Once the reading has stabi-

lized it should register 32°F (0°C). To use the boiling-point method, immerse the sensor in boiling water; the stabilized reading should be 212°F (100°C). If the thermometer you are using gives a different reading you must compensate accordingly, up or down, when you use it. If the measure is off significantly, the unit should be replaced. When testing the thermometer, you should also take into consideration that the boiling point for water decreases about 1°F (0.6°C) for every 550 feet (165 meters) above sea level.

• The ingredients and equipment used in the production of the following recipes are discussed in detail in Appendixes A and B, respectively. These sections contain a great deal of useful information, and I strongly urge readers to thoroughly familiarize themselves with the ingredients and equipment utilized in the preparation of a particular item, not simply for the sake of curiosity but to ensure the best possible result in the safest manner.

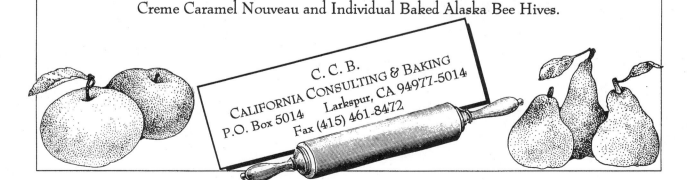

1

Mise en Place

Acidophilus Yogurt	Ricotta Cheese
Almond Paste	Simple Syrup
Beet Juice	Spiced Poaching Syrup
Butter and Flour Mixture	Streusel Topping
Candied Chestnuts	Vanilla Extract
Caramel Coloring	Vanilla Sugar
Cinnamon Sugar	Savory Recipe Variations
Coffee Reduction	Anchovy Sticks
Crepes	Buckwheat Blini
Crystallized Ginger	Cheese Soufflé
Egg Wash	Cheese Straws
Graham Crackers and Crumbs	Cummin Kravatten
Hazelnut Paste	Gougères
Mascarpone Cheese	Ham and/or Cheese Croissants
Plain Cake Syrup	Quiche Lorraine
Praline	Sausage Cuts in Puff Pastry
	Miscellaneous

The literal translation of *Mise en Place* is to "put things in place." In the professional kitchen the term means the things we need to get done ahead of time, or prep work. Preparation is an important factor for the professional pastry chef. In the pastry kitchen many things should be done at the end of the day so they will be ready the next morning, such as making pastry cream and other fillings or removing butter from the freezer so it can thaw and soften.

Advance Planning and Stock Items

Before starting any project the professional will make a "plan of attack," first going through the recipe mentally and making sure all of the ingredients needed to complete it smoothly are at hand, then thinking of how to accomplish the tasks most efficiently. If toasted sliced almonds are needed to decorate the sides of Poppy Seed Cake, they should be prepared first thing so they are cold by the time they are used. If melted chocolate is needed to finish Vanilla Macaroons, it can be placed over hot water and stirred from time to time while the buttercream is being formed on the macaroons. If you need to melt the Butter and Flour Mixture so you can brush it on cake pans, there is no reason to go and put it on the top of the stove if the oven is closer; just put the pot in there for a few seconds.

Items that are used regularly should always be accessible. If you make Croissants every morning, there is no reason to make fresh Egg Wash each day. Instead, make enough to last three or four days and store it covered in the refrigerator (in fact it actually works better if it is a day or more old). When going to the refrigerator for milk to make Pastry Cream, think about what you are making next, and if, for example, that happens to be apple filling, get the apples at the same time instead of making two trips. If you can think one or two steps ahead you will get a lot more done in less time. It is a bit like the old saying "Don't walk across the river to fetch water" or, as my master used to tell me when I was an apprentice "What you do not have in your head, you have to make up for with your feet."

 ## Acidophilus Yogurt

4 cups (960 ml) yogurt

5 cups (1 l, 200 ml) milk, whole or skim
¼ cup (60 ml) unflavored commercial yogurt

NOTE 1: If you do not have a milk thermometer which can be placed in the saucepan, you can make a convenient holder by laying a large spoon across the center of the pan. Place an inverted dinner fork at a 90° angle to the spoon with the tines of the fork balanced on the spoon handle. You can now insert your instant-read pocket thermometer through the tines of the fork and let it hang in the milk.

NOTE 2: In some recipes yogurt can be substituted for sour cream, crème fraîche, or cream cheese to reduce fat and calories. The substitution can be made in an equal quantity in recipes where the ingredient is not cooked, for example Sour Cream Mixture for Piping, Romanoff Sauce, or when crème fraîche is used to accompany a dessert. You will get a better result if you drain some of the liquid out of the

Making your own yogurt will only take about five minutes away from your other work while you monitor the temperature of the milk in step one. The incubation takes care of itself, thanks to the bacteria cultures lactobacillus bulgaricus and/or streptococcus thermophilus. Basically, they consume the lactose as a source of energy, thereby producing lactic acid during the incubation period, which, after the pH has reached 4 to 4.5, sets the liquid.

Fermented milk is nothing new. It was almost certainly consumed in some form as early as 6000 B.C., invented most likely by accident, and then used as a convenient way to preserve milk. Yogurt made its way to Europe as early as the fifteenth century, but it was not until well into the nineteen hundreds that it became fashionable as a health food. Later, plain yogurt was mixed with fruits and flavorings to balance the sourness, and it became a popular commercial product. Today the latest craze is frozen yogurt, which is very similar in texture to soft ice cream but much lower in fat. Just how healthy yogurt is has been the source of debate for a long time. It is no doubt a good source of vitamin B, calcium, and protein, but it is, of course, only low in fat if made from low-fat milk to begin with.

1. In a thick-bottomed saucepan, heat the milk to a simmer, about 185°F (85°C), while stirring frequently. Remove from the heat and let cool to 110°F (43°C) (see note 1).

2. Place the yogurt in a mixing bowl that measures about 9 inches (22.5 cm) in diameter. Gradually stir in the cooled milk, continuing to stir until the mixture is smooth before adding the next portion. Cover the bowl with a plate, wrap two or three towels around the bowl and the lid, and set aside in a warm location to set the yogurt. This usually takes about 5 hours, depending on the temperature in your kitchen. If

yogurt before you use it, as this thickens and improves the texture.

Place the yogurt in a strainer lined with cheesecloth and set the strainer over a bowl to catch the liquid. Refrigerate for 24 hours. Discard the liquid and store the yogurt "cheese" as you would yogurt.

this is not 80°F (26°C) or above, and I sincerely hope that it is not, you should place the bowl in a 90 to 100°F (32 to 38°C) oven. You can usually achieve this temperature by turning the oven off and on a few times during the first hour. Be careful not to let it get too hot or you will kill the bacteria.

3. Remove the towels and the plate and cover the bowl with plastic wrap. Store the yogurt in the refrigerator. Use part of this batch to make the next batch, and so on.

Almond Paste

1 pound, 14 ounces (855 g) paste

10 ounces (285 g) dry blanched almonds
10 ounces (285 g) powdered sugar
1¼ cups (300 ml) Simple Syrup (page 11), approximately

NOTE: If the almonds are not completely dry, you will get a paste at this point rather than a powder. This is fine provided that the paste is smooth.

Although it is simple to make if you have an almond mill (see page 1118), the time involved in producing your own Almond Paste does not justify the cost savings in today's industry, so it is rarely made in the pastry shop nowadays. The only disadvantages to purchasing a commercial brand are that the consistency will vary from one batch to another, and you will need to compensate for that fact in some recipes, and there can also be tiny specks of brown skin from almonds that were not blanched properly in some batches. If you find that you cannot produce the specified powdery consistency in step one, very finely ground almonds will suffice. The quality of the finished product will not be as good, but the only recipe where it will be noticeable is in Marzipan.

1. Place the almonds in a high-speed food processor and process to a powder (see note).

2. Add the powdered sugar; then, with the machine running, gradually add the Simple Syrup until the mixture forms a paste. The amount of Simple Syrup needed will vary depending on how dry the almonds are. Freshly blanched almonds will need less syrup. Store the Almond Paste tightly covered. If kept more than one week, store in the refrigerator.

Beet Juice

NOTE: If you do not have a juice extractor, grate the beets finely and press the juice through a fine sieve. This method is not as desirable, as the yield of juice is much lower.

Beets are one of the few red vegetables. They get their color from a group of pigments called anthocyanins. These are the same elements that are responsible for most of the color in red, purple, and blue fruits and flowers. Extracted Beet Juice can be used to color food products as an alternative to using artificial red dyes. If added to foods that are too alkaline, the color will change from red to purple and begin to fade. Adding an acid will prevent this and will even reverse the effect after it has occurred, changing the purple color back to red.

1. Wash and peel red beets, then process using a juice extractor.

2. Store the juice in a plastic squeeze bottle in the refrigerator. The juice will keep for several months.

Butter and Flour Mixture

2 cups (480 ml)

2 ounces (55 g) bread flour
1 pound (455 g) soft unsalted butter

Using a Butter and Flour Mixture (four parts melted butter and one part bread flour, by volume) is a quick and easy way to prepare cake pans, forms, or molds in a recipe that says to grease and flour the pan. Rather than applying the two separately, brush on the flour at the same time you grease the pan. This method can save a great deal of time when the task is done over and over throughout the day.

1. Combine flour and butter. Heat to melt.
2. Apply the mixture with a brush.

The combination can be left at room temperature for up to one week. If the mixture is refrigerated, warm it before using (but do not boil) and stir to combine.

Candied Chestnuts

1 pound, 4 ounces (570 g)

1 pound (455 g) fresh chestnuts (thirty to thirty-five)
4 cups (960 ml) water
8 ounces (225 g) granulated sugar

Candied Chestnuts are expensive to purchase, so preparing your own can be very economical, assuming you can justify the labor to remove the shells. If you want perfect whole Candied Chestnuts for garnish, start with more than you need, because some will break when you shell them, and don't let the chestnuts boil vigorously in the syrup or all of them will break up into small pieces. Broken pieces can, of course, be used in fillings and for chestnut purée. Pay close attention toward the end of the cooking process, as the thick syrup can burn easily.

1. Cut a small X in the flat side of the shell on each chestnut, using the tip of a paring knife.
2. Place the chestnuts on a sheet pan and roast at 375°F (190°C) for approximately 15 minutes. (Or, place in a saucepan with enough water to cover, simmer for the same length of time, and drain.)
3. While the nuts are still hot, remove the shells and the dark paper-like skin around the meat.
4. Place the chestnuts in a saucepan with the water and sugar. Bring to a boil, stirring gently, and then simmer for approximately 45 minutes or until the liquid has reduced to a thick syrup. Let cool.
5. Store the Candied Chestnuts in the syrup covered in the refrigerator. They will keep for several weeks.

Caramel Coloring

3 cups (720 ml)

2 pounds (910 g) granulated sugar
1/2 cup (120 ml) water
4 drops lemon juice
1 1/2 cups (360 ml) water

This was known as Blackjack when I learned this trade in Europe. It is basically just burned sugar which, when cooked to 392°F (200°C), turns completely black. Once the mixture has cooled, a small amount is used to color baked goods, mainly breads. Caramel Coloring will last indefinitely and does not need to be refrigerated.

I find many students do not cook the sugar long enough, especially when they make Caramel Coloring for the first time. There is probably some guilt involved in burning something intentionally, and no doubt they assume something must have gone wrong when they smell it, since the sugar, when cooked to this extreme temperature, will produce an aroma that should bring any executive chef worth his or her title into your kitchen in a hurry!

1. Combine the sugar, the first measurement of water, and the lemon juice in a heavy saucepan. Cook over medium heat until the sugar turns to caramel, brushing down the sides of the pan with water from time to time. Continue to cook, stirring frequently so that the sugar colors evenly, to 392°F (200°C)—"blackjack" stage. The sugar will be burned, and there will be smoke coming from the pan. Stand back, very carefully pour in the second measurement of water, and stir until the mixture is smooth.

2. Let cool. Pour into a jar and store covered at room temperature.

 ## Cinnamon Sugar

*C*ombine one part ground cinnamon with four to five parts granulated sugar by volume.

 ## Coffee Reduction

*T*his simple method of developing a good strong coffee flavor can, of course, be modified to your own taste. Start with fresh coffee brewed from top quality beans (do not use instant coffee).

1. Make coffee 10 times the normal strength.
2. Bring to a boil in a saucepan and reduce by half.
3. Let cool and use as needed.

Coffee Reduction can be stored at room temperature for a few weeks; it should be refrigerated if it is to be kept any longer.

Crepes

about forty 6-inch (15-cm) crepes

6 ounces (170 g) cake flour
6 ounces (170 g) bread flour
3 ounces (85 g) granulated sugar
2 teaspoons (10 g) salt
6 eggs
6 egg yolks (½ cup/120 ml)
6 ounces (170 g) melted unsalted butter
3 cups (720 ml) warm milk
⅓ cup (80 ml) brandy
clarified unsalted butter

1. Sift the flours together and combine with the sugar and salt in a mixing bowl.

2. Lightly beat the eggs with the egg yolks, just to mix. Gradually stir the eggs into the dry ingredients. Add the melted butter, milk, and brandy. Mix until smooth. If the batter appears broken, the milk was probably too cool. To remedy this, warm the batter over simmering water, stirring constantly, until smooth. Let the batter rest at room temperature for 1 hour.

3. Heat two 6-inch (15-cm) Crepe pans and brush with clarified butter (see note). Do not use a nylon brush. Cover the bottom of the pans with a thin film of batter by quickly tilting and rotating the pan (Figure 1–1). Try to avoid making the batter run up on the sides of the pans. Pour any excess batter back into the bowl. With practice you should be able to add just the right amount of batter each time.

NOTE: If you are using properly seasoned Crepe pans, you probably will only have to grease the pans for the first few Crepes. In any case, avoid using too much butter as this saturates the Crepes and adds excess calories.

FIGURE 1–1   *Rotating the pan to distribute the Crepe batter*

4. Flip the Crepes when the bottoms have a nice golden brown color, using a spatula and the fingers of one hand, or flip them in the air if you have the knack. The second side need only cook for a few seconds, until it is no longer sticky; overcooking the Crepes will make them dry.

5. Slide the Crepes out of the pans and stack them on top of each other on a plate to prevent their drying out as you make the remaining Crepes; cover once you have a large stack. After you have made a few Crepes, adjust the batter, if necessary. If large bubbles form as the Crepe cooks, the batter is probably too thin (or the pan may be too hot). Thicken the batter by whipping in some additional flour. If the batter is too thick (does not pour in a thin film), add milk to thin it. Once you have the batter and the heat adjusted correctly, making a few dozen Crepes is easy. If they will not be used within several hours, wrap and store in the refrigerator. Crepes can also be made up to three days ahead and stored, layered with paper and properly covered, in the refrigerator, or frozen up to one month. Crepes are suitable for use in dishes where they will be served hot but should not be used in a cold dish because they tend to be a bit rubbery. Wipe the Crepe pans clean with a towel; do not use water under any circumstance.

Crystallized Ginger

about 10 ounces (285 g)

1 pound (455 g) fresh ginger root
    (see note)
water
1 pound (455 g) granulated sugar
¹/₃ cup (80 ml) water
granulated sugar

Crystallizing ginger is rarely done in the professional bakeshop, although it is quite easy and not very time-consuming either. As with many home-made foodstuffs, which are free from artificial ingredients such as coloring, bleaching, or preserving chemicals, the finished product will not look like the one you are familiar with buying. This Crystallized Ginger has a much darker color than the golden or tan product produced commercially.

1. Peel the ginger rhizomes and slice ¹/₄ inch (6 mm) thick.

2. Place the slices in a saucepan and add enough water to cover. Simmer over low heat until the ginger is tender, approximately 40 minutes. Drain the ginger, discarding the liquid.

NOTE: Use large rhizomes as much as possible and slice smaller pieces on the bias to make the pieces more uniform.

3. Place 1 pound (455 g) granulated sugar in the empty saucepan. Add ¹/₃ cup (80 ml) water and stir to moisten all of the sugar. Bring to a boil, add the drained ginger slices, and boil gently, stirring frequently, until the ginger looks transparent, about 20 minutes.

4. Reduce the heat and simmer until the syrup is quite thick. The sugar syrup is likely to form lumps if you reduce it too long. This is all right; however, you should remove any large lumps that stick to the ginger pieces.

5. Using two forks, remove the ginger slices from the syrup and toss them in granulated sugar. Place the pieces in a single layer, spaced well apart, on a sheet pan. Let sit overnight in a warm place. Store the ginger in an airtight container for up to six months.

Egg Wash

*E*gg Wash gives a shine to soft breads and rolls, Croissants, and Puff Pastry items. It is also used as a "glue" to hold pieces of dough together, or to make almonds or sugar adhere when sprinkled on a pastry or cookie before baking.

The best shine is obtained from using Egg Wash containing yolks alone, thinned with a little water or milk. This is not really practical unless you have egg yolks sitting around or have a use for the separated whites. It makes more sense to use the whole egg beaten with a little salt (but no water or milk) for everyday use.

Egg Wash for General Use

1 cup (240 ml) egg wash

4 eggs
¹/₂ teaspoon (2.5 g) salt

1. Beat the eggs and salt together until the yolks and whites are combined.

2. Allow the Egg Wash to stand for 30 minutes before using or, preferably, overnight.

3. Store in the refrigerator.

Egg Wash with Yolks Only

³/₄ cup (180 ml)

8 egg yolks (²/₃ cup/160ml)
¹/₂ teaspoon (2.5 g) salt
2 to 3 tablespoons (30 to 45 ml) water
  or milk

NOTE: This Egg Wash might be too strong for items which are baked at temperatures above 400°F (205°C). The color will be too dark, giving the crust an overbaked appearance. If so, thin further or use Egg Wash made from whole eggs.

1. Mix as above.

2. Store in the refrigerator.

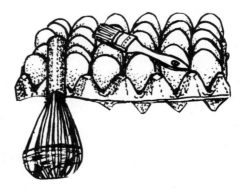

Egg Wash for Spraying

2 cups (480 ml) egg wash

6 eggs
4 egg yolks (¹/₃ cup/80 ml)
¹/₂ teaspoon (2.5 g) salt

Applying Egg Wash with a spray bottle powered by compressed air, electricity, or elbow grease instead of a brush (the more typical and time-consuming method) has been common in European bakeries since the early sixties. The spray technique makes a lot of sense. Not only is it faster, but it also produces a smooth, even application. Moreover, since you do not actually touch the product, you do not risk damaging the soft dough. The only disadvantage is that you will, of course, be applying Egg Wash to the sheet pan or baking paper around the items you are spraying, but this small amount of waste is offset by the advantages. It is a good idea to designate an easy-to-clean area in the kitchen to use for spraying, or be sure to place a few sheets of baking paper around where you are working to aid in cleanup. For the best result, Egg Wash for use in a spray bottle should be prepared a day ahead to give the salt time to make the eggs less viscous.

1. Combine eggs, egg yolks, and salt. Process for 10 to 15 seconds in a food processor. Strain through a fine mesh strainer (*chinois*) to remove the chalazae (the thick white cord attached to the yolk).

2. Cover the mixture and refrigerate for a minimum of 12 hours.

3. Pour the Egg Wash into a spray bottle set to fine mist.

4. Spray the item to be baked, holding the bottle about 10 inches (25 cm) above, and turning the sheet pan as necessary to ensure even coverage on all sides.

5. To achieve the maximum amount of shine, let the Egg Wash dry for a few minutes and then apply a second coat.

Graham Crackers and Crumbs

seventy 2-by-2-inch (5-×-5-cm) crackers or 1 pound, 8 ounces (680 g) graham cracker crumbs

6 ounces (170 g) bread flour
6 ounces (170 g) cake flour
2 ounces (55 g) whole wheat flour
2 ounces (55 g) dark brown sugar
1 teaspoon (4 g) baking soda
1 teaspoon (5 g) salt
3 ounces (85 g) soft unsalted butter
¹/₂ cup (120 ml) or 6 ounces (170 g) honey
1 teaspoon (5 ml) vanilla extract
¹/₃ cup (80 ml) water, approximately

I'm sure many of us have, on occasion, found that the pantry was fresh out of graham cracker crumbs when they were needed for cheesecake. While it is less convenient to make the crackers and crumbs the old-fashioned way, it only sets you back about 30 minutes (in an emergency, keep the dough fairly firm to speed up the baking and drying process), and once you try these I think you will find producing your own to be an advantage both in cost and quality. It is a good idea to keep the crumbs on hand as part of your regular mise en place *so they are available when needed. Graham Cracker Crumbs can be stored for several weeks.*

1. Thoroughly combine the bread flour, cake flour, whole wheat flour, brown sugar, baking soda, and salt in an electric mixer bowl.

2. Using the dough hook attachment, incorporate the butter, honey, vanilla extract, and water. Mix until a smooth and pliable dough has formed, adjusting with additional water if necessary. Do not overmix.

To make crackers

1. Roll the dough out to a 10-by-14-inch (25-×-35-cm) rectangle, using flour to prevent it from sticking. Mark the dough with a docker or the tines of a fork.

2. Cut the rectangle into 2-inch (5-cm) squares.

3. Transfer the squares to a sheet pan lined with baking paper.

4. Bake at 325°F (163°C) for approximately 15 minutes.

5. Store in an airtight container.

To make crumbs

1. Roll the dough out to ¹/₈ inch (3 mm) thick.

2. Cut into small pieces (it is not necessary to measure).

3. Transfer to a sheet pan lined with baking paper.

4. Bake at 325°F (163°C) until dark golden brown.

5. When cold, process the pieces in a food processor to make fine crumbs.

6. Store in an airtight container.

Hazelnut Paste

1 cup (240 ml) paste

8 ounces (225 g) hazelnuts
¹/₃ cup (80 ml) Simple Syrup (page 11), approximately

*T*his product is typically purchased rather than made in most professional operations. The commercial product is more concentrated, so you may need to decrease the amount specified in the recipes if you substitute purchased paste.

1. Toast the hazelnuts and remove the skins (see note on pages 965 and 966 for more information).

2. Process the hazelnuts and Simple Syrup together in a food processor until the mixture becomes a thick paste.

3. Store in an airtight container to use as needed.

Mascarpone Cheese

1 pound, 8 ounces (680 g) cheese

2 quarts (1 l, 920 ml) heavy cream
¹/₂ teaspoon (2.5 ml) Tartaric Acid Solution (page 1115)

*M*ascarpone Cheese is made from fresh cream derived from cow's milk. The cream is reduced to near triple-cream consistency to give the cheese its soft, smooth, rich texture. This Italian cream cheese originated in the Lombardy region of Italy but is now made throughout the country. The flavor of Mascarpone blends beautifully with other food, most especially fruit. Fresh figs with Mascarpone is a classic, although Tiramisu is probably the dessert that most people think of first when it comes to Mascarpone. Uses for Mascarpone are certainly not limited to dessert. A speciality of Trieste, in the northeast corner of Italy, is a mixture of Mascarpone, anchovies, mustard, and spices. Another popular appetizer preparation is a layered torte alternating Mascarpone with pesto or smoked salmon.

Since the cheese is very perishable, and the imported product is quite expensive, the time involved to make it yourself is well worth the effort.

1. Bring the cream to a boil in a thick saucepan and boil over medium heat until reduced by one-third (to about 5¹/₄ cups/1 l, 260 ml). Remove from the heat, place in an ice bath, and stir the reduced cream until it is cold.

2. Stir in the tartaric acid, return the saucepan to the heat, and bring the mixture to 118°F (48°C). Remove from the heat.

3. Line a strainer with a triple layer of cheesecloth. Set the strainer over a bowl or pan to catch the liquid. Pour the cream mixture into the strainer. Place in the refrigerator overnight.

4. Remove the thickened Mascarpone from the cheesecloth and discard the liquid. Store covered in the refrigerator.

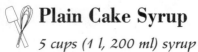

Plain Cake Syrup

5 cups (1 l, 200 ml) syrup

1 quart (960 ml) water
1 pound (455 g) granulated sugar

*P*lain Cake Syrup is basically Plain Poaching Syrup without any citric acid. If you have leftover poaching syrup after cooking fruit, keep that on hand to use as cake syrup instead; the subtle flavor from the fruit is an added bonus. If the liquid has been reduced significantly during the poaching process, add water accordingly before using. Leftover poaching liquid must be stored in the refrigerator. Secondly, if you have Simple Syrup made up you may use that as a substitute for cake syrup as well. Add 1/4 cup (60 ml) of water to 1 cup (240 ml) of Simple Syrup. Dilute only the amount required for each use.

1. Place the water and sugar in a saucepan and bring to a boil. Remove from the heat and let cool.

2. Store covered to use as needed. This syrup does not need to be refrigerated; it can be kept at room temperature for several weeks.

Praline

1 pound (455 g) praline

4 ounces (115 g) hazelnuts
4 ounces (115 g) blanched almonds
corn oil, or other bland oil
8 ounces (225 g) granulated sugar
1 teaspoon (5 ml) lemon juice

*T*his is very hard to work with in a humid climate or in wet weather, since the sugar starts to break down and the Praline becomes very sticky. If this happens, it is suitable to use in making Praline Paste.

1. Toast the hazelnuts and remove the skin (see note on pages 965 and 966). Toast the almonds lightly. Reserve the nuts.

2. Lightly oil a marble slab or sheet pan.

3. Caramelize the sugar with the lemon juice to a light golden color (see page 954).

4. Immediately add the toasted nuts, stir to combine, and pour out onto the oiled marble.

5. Let the Praline cool completely, then crush with a dowel or rolling pin to the desired consistency.

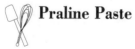

Praline Paste

*T*his is mainly used for making candy and for flavoring cake and pastry fillings. Like Hazelnut Paste, making your own Praline Paste is time-consuming, and you will be hard pressed to achieve the same result as the ready-made commercial product. Commercial Praline Paste is passed through a grinding machine equipped with stone rollers (known as an almond mill), which produces a superior result. This recipe or a purchased paste can be used in the recipes in this book.

1. Crush the praline as fine as possible.

2. Place in a high-speed food processor and process using the metal blade until the mixture becomes a fine paste. If you are preparing a small amount, you can also use a coffee grinder.

Ricotta Cheese

2 pounds (910 g) cheese

6 quarts (5 l, 760 ml) skim milk

6 drops lemon juice

1 pound (455 g) plain, unflavored yogurt

1 tablespoon (15 g) salt

1/2 cup (120 ml) heavy cream

1/2 cup (120 ml) whey (reserved after straining the curds)

Ricotta translates to "recooked" or "cooked again." The name for this wonderful cooking cheese came about because it was originally (and still is in many parts of Italy) made from the whey drained off of cow's, goat's, or ewe's milk after making other cheeses such as mozzarella. Today ricotta is most often made starting with whole or skimmed milk. In addition to numerous applications in the pastry kitchen, ricotta is used in savory dishes such as lasagne and ravioli. Ricotta is easy to make; however, most consumers today prefer to purchase it ready-made. The main drawback in making your own cheese is the time lag between the start and the finished product.

1. Pour the milk into a plastic container and stir in the lemon juice. Cover, and place the mixture in the refrigerator for approximately 24 hours.

2. Stir in the yogurt and the salt using a wooden spoon. Transfer to a heavy-bottomed saucepan. Stirring constantly, bring the mixture to a boil and boil for 2 minutes; a thick layer of curds should form on the top.

3. Remove from the heat and strain through a fine mesh strainer (*chinois*) lined with cheesecloth. Reserve 1/2 cup (120 ml) of the whey (the liquid) and discard the remaining whey.

4. Spread the hot curds out to cool on a sheet pan lined with baking paper. Separate the curds as much as possible by rubbing them between your hands.

5. Once the cheese has cooled, place it in a bowl and stir in the reserved whey and the heavy cream. The Ricotta Cheese will keep for up to two weeks stored covered in the refrigerator.

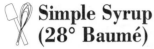

Simple Syrup (28° Baumé)

3 quarts (2 l, 880 ml) syrup

2 quarts (1 l, 920 ml) water

2 pounds, 8 ounces (1 kg, 135 g) granulated sugar

2 cups (480 ml) or 1 pound, 8 ounces (680 g) glucose or light corn syrup (see note 1)

Simple Syrup is a very useful ingredient to have on hand. It keeps indefinitely if proper hygiene is observed during preparation and storage. Besides the everyday uses such as sweetening sorbets and parfaits, it is used to thin fondant to the proper consistency before it is applied and to thicken chocolate for piping. I also use it as a quick cake syrup by adding 1/4 cup (60 ml) of water for every 1 cup (240 ml) of Simple Syrup, plus liqueur or other flavoring if appropriate.

1. Place the water, sugar, and glucose or corn syrup in a saucepan; stir to combine.

2. Heat to boiling and let boil for a few seconds.

NOTE 1: To avoid any mess when measuring glucose or corn syrup, first weigh the sugar and leave it on the scale, then make a well in the sugar (adjust the scale) and pour the corn syrup into the well until you have the right amount. Glucose is too thick to pour but can easily be scooped up using your hand if you wet your hand first. (The glucose or corn syrup is added to prevent the syrup from recrystallizing when stored.) If you are using a small amount of corn syrup in a recipe that does not have any sugar, it may be easier to measure the syrup by volume; both measurements are given throughout the recipes in this text. Converting dry to liquid ounces is simple for corn syrup: Fluid ounces are two-thirds of dry ounces (e.g., 6 ounces by weight = 4 fluid ounces.)

NOTE 2: Since it is impossible to know exactly when the syrup will come to a boil, and hopefully you do not have the time to stand there watching it, do not be concerned about boiling the syrup just a little longer than specified in the recipe; it will not adversely affect the viscosity of the syrup. However, boiling the syrup for as much as 5 minutes longer than the specified time will increase the Baumé to 30°; 10 minutes of boiling will bring it to 34°. Should this happen, let the syrup cool to approximately 60°F (16°C), check the sugar content using the Baumé thermometer, and replace the evaporated water as needed to bring it to 28° Baumé. The water that you add should first be boiled and then cooled to 60°F (16°C) to get an accurate reading and also to sterilize the water so that the syrup can be stored. Although it is simple enough to test the Baumé level, going through this procedure is really only practical if you have a large batch of syrup.

3. Set aside to cool. If any scum has developed on the surface, skim it off before pouring the syrup into bottles. Simple Syrup should be refrigerated if kept for more than two to three weeks.

Spiced Poaching Syrup

5 cups (720 ml) syrup

1 quart (960 ml) water
1 pound (455 g) granulated sugar
one-half lemon, cut into wedges
1 teaspoon (5 ml) vanilla extract
six whole cloves
one cinnamon stick

The basic ratio of water to sugar in poaching liquid is two parts water to one part sugar by weight. This can be modified depending on the desired sweetness of the finished product. However, to keep the fruit firm after being poached, the poaching syrup must have a higher sugar content than the fruit itself. After the first use the syrup can be used again to poach fruit (you may need to replace the evaporated water) or it can be used as a cake syrup. After poaching, any fruit that is susceptible to browning should be kept in the syrup until it is needed to prevent oxidation. Apricots are especially delicate and become brown very quickly. To keep the fruit submerged, place a towel (or sheet of baking paper) on top and place a plate on top of the towels.

1. Combine all of the ingredients in a saucepan and bring to a boil.
2. Proceed as directed in the individual recipes.

VARIATION
Plain Poaching Syrup

NOTE: *Remove peaches after they have cooked for a few minutes, peel off the skin using a small pointed knife, then return them to the syrup and continue cooking until soft. When poaching pears, select firm, unblemished fruit. If poached whole, core from the bottom and leave the stems.*

Follow the preceding recipe but omit the whole cloves and the cinnamon stick.

To poach pears or apples

1. Place a lid or plate that fits down inside the saucepan on top of the fruit to keep it submerged; otherwise the fruit will bob on top of the syrup and the exposed part will oxidize, turn brown, and will not cook.
2. Boil gently for about 5 minutes.
3. Lower the heat and simmer very slowly until the fruit is tender and cooked all the way through. Do not poach the fruit too rapidly or it will become overcooked on the outside and still raw inside. Worse yet, the uncooked part will turn brown.
4. To check if pears or apples are done, pinch gently with your fingers. They should feel soft but not mushy, having about the same amount of resistance as the fleshy part of your hand.

To poach plums, peaches, apricots, cherries, and other fragile fruits

1. Bring the syrup to a boil, add the fruit, and lower the heat immediately to simmer very gently; do not boil.
2. Cook the fruit until it is tender.

To poach or reconstitute dried fruit

Ideally, allow the fruit to soak in cold water overnight, then add the appropriate amounts of sugar and lemon to make a poaching liquid. Poach as directed for fresh fruit.

Streusel Topping

2 pounds, 10 ounces (1 kg, 195 g)

6 ounces (170 g) light brown sugar
6 ounces (170 g) granulated sugar
11 ounces (310 g) unsalted butter
1 tablespoon (5 g) ground cinnamon
2 teaspoons (10 g) salt
1 teaspoon (5 ml) vanilla extract
1 pound, 2 ounces (510 g) bread flour, approximately

 ## VARIATION
Hazelnut Streusel

*T*his topping (as the name might give away) was originally intended for sprinkling on top of the German delicacy Streusel Kuchen; streusel means "to sprinkle" or "to strew" in German. You will find that I have borrowed it for use in a number of recipes throughout the book—Danish pastries, tarts, muffins, and Apple Mazarins to name a few. The crunch of the baked topping adds a nice contrast in each case.

1. Mix the brown sugar, granulated sugar, butter, cinnamon, salt, and vanilla.

2. Stir in the flour. The mixture should be crumbly and should not come together like a dough; you may need to add extra flour.

3. Store covered in the refrigerator to prevent the topping from drying out.

Add 10 ounces (285 g) chopped, or coarsely crushed, untoasted hazelnuts when you add the flour.

 ## Vanilla Extract

1 quart (960 ml)

six long, soft, whole vanilla beans
1 quart (960 ml) good quality vodka
two whole vanilla beans

*M*aking your Vanilla Extract is as easy as one, two, three—it merely requires advance planning on your part. The two whole beans added at the end are purely for decoration, but the extract does make a great place to store them.

1. Split six of the beans lengthwise and then cut into small pieces.

2. Put the pieces and the vodka in a bottle and seal tightly.

3. Let stand in a dark cool place for about one month, shaking the bottle from time to time.

4. Sieve the liquid through a strainer lined with cheesecloth.

5. Clean the bottle and return the vanilla extract to the bottle.

6. Add the two whole vanilla beans. Store tightly sealed.

 ## Vanilla Sugar

*T*here are a number of recipes for making Vanilla Sugar. A simple way, which also protects the beans from drying out when stored, is to place split or whole vanilla beans in a jar of granulated sugar. The jar should be tall enough to hold the beans standing up and allow room for plenty of sugar around them. Make sure the jar is tightly sealed. Shake it once a day to circulate the sugar and increase the fragrance. After one week the Vanilla Sugar is ready to use. As you use up the Vanilla Sugar and the beans, keep adding to the jar. Naturally, the more beans you store in the jar in relation to the amount of sugar, the stronger the flavor or fragrance.

Savory Recipe Variations

The following recipes don't really fit into any of the other chapters in this book. They are included here because in my experience the pastry department is usually called upon to help with the preparation and baking of items such as quiches, cheese puffs, and puff pastries like Ham or Cheese Croissants and Cheese Straws. This of course does make sense since these items are all variations on basic pastry doughs and products, and we usually have much better ovens in which to bake them. Also, in the old classical menus (which typically consisted of as many as fourteen courses, each accompanied by the appropriate wine), a savory dish was always served between the "sweet," which could be just about anything sweet that did not interfere with the dessert, and the actual dessert. Typical favorites for the sweet course were blancmange, Bavarian creams, and ices. Then a savory such as Cheese Straws was served, followed by the final dessert course.

Many of the Puff Pastry hors d'oeuvres in this chapter, such as Anchovy Sticks, Cheese Straws, *Cummin Kravatten,* Ham and/or Cheese Croissants, and Sausage Cuts, can be made up in advance and then frozen to bake as needed.

 Anchovy Sticks

fifty-six 2-inch (5-cm) pieces

1 pound, 10 ounces (740 g) Puff
    Pastry (page 44)
14 ounces (400 g) canned anchovy
    filets
Egg Wash (page 7)

Anchovy Sticks are always included in a European assortment of Puff Pastry hors d'oeuvres together with Cheese Straws, Ham and/or Cheese Croissants, and Cumin Bow Ties. Anchovies should always be used with restraint since their salty flavor is an acquired taste; it almost seems as if you have to be raised in Europe to fully appreciate the fillets of these small silvery fish.

There are many different species of anchovy; they are a member of the herring family and bear a strong resemblance to the English sprat fish; in fact, the Norwegian anchovy is actually a young sprat. The true anchovy is found along the southern European coastline, most abundantly in the Mediterranean. They are most popular in the cuisine of southern Europe; they are a must in such classics as Caesar salad, Salad Nicoise, Pissaladière, *and of course pizza (at least on the pizza of yours truly). Anchovies have also found their way to many other countries; an extremely popular dish in Sweden, for example, is* Janson's Frestelse *(Janson's Temptation), which is a gratin of anchovies and potatoes.*

1. Roll the Puff Pastry out to a 21-by-16-inch (52.5-×-40-cm) rectangle. It may be necessary to do this in two stages, letting the dough relax for 30 minutes in the refrigerator in between, if the dough shrinks back excessively as you roll it.

2. Cut the sheet in half lengthwise to make two 16-by-10$^{1}/_{2}$-inch (40-×-26.2-cm) pieces. Measure and mark (without cutting through the dough) both short ends of one piece every 1$^{1}/_{2}$ inches (3.7 cm). Use the back of a chef's knife to draw lines lengthwise between the marks.

3. Cut the anchovy filets in half lengthwise. Brush Egg Wash over the entire marked sheet of Puff Pastry. Place a row of anchovies lengthwise down the center of each of the seven marked rows.

4. Pick up the second Puff Pastry sheet and place it on top of the anchovy-covered sheet. Using a thin (1/2-to-3/4-inch, 1.2-to-2-cm) dowel, press down between the rows of anchovies, and also on the long edges, to seal the Puff Pastry sheets together.

5. Cut the strips apart with a chef's knife or pastry wheel. Brush Egg Wash over the strips. Transfer the strips to a sheet pan and place in the refrigerator or freezer until the Egg Wash is dry.

6. Score the tops of the strips crosswise every 1/2 inch (1.2 cm) by pressing a serrated knife lightly into the dough. Cut each strip into eight 2-inch (5-cm) pieces. Place the pieces on sheet pans lined with baking paper.

7. Bake at 425°F (219°C) for 8 minutes. Lower the heat to 375°F (190°C) and continue baking approximately 10 minutes longer or until baked through.

Buckwheat Blini

approximately twenty 4 1/2-inch (11.2-cm) blini

1/2 ounce (15 g) or 1 tablespoon (15 ml) fresh compressed yeast

1 1/2 cups (360 ml) milk, at room temperature

5 ounces (140 g) buckwheat flour

2 ounces (55 g) bread flour

1/2 cup (120 ml) buttermilk

1/2 cup (120 ml) beer

3 eggs, separated

1 teaspoon (5 g) salt

1 tablespoon (15 g) granulated sugar

melted unsalted butter

NOTE: The blini should be about 3/8 inch (9 mm) thick. If the batter does not spread out properly, thin it with milk. If you are making a fair amount of these and do not have the benefit of a griddle, try this technique using two skillets: when the first batch of three or four blini are ready to turn, flip them all at once into a

The name blini is a western modification of the Russian word blin, *which means pancake. Although they are enjoyed in Russia all year round, blini are traditionally associated with Maslenitsa, the weeklong, pre-Lenten, "Butter Festival." This is a lively and joyous celebration signifying the end of the long, cold winter and the beginning of spring. As one famous Russian once said, "blini are round and hot and beautiful like a glorious sun." During the festival it is traditional to serve hot, freshly made blini at every meal topped with melted butter, sour cream, and either caviar, salmon, or herring (usually in that order with the toppings becoming a bit more humble as the week goes by).*

These little pancakes can be found in many sizes and variations. An authentic blini pan is slightly over 5 inches (12.5 cm) in diameter. I find this size to be too large in many instances, considering the richness of the toppings and the fact that blini are generally served as an appetizer. I like to make them using the small Swedish pancake iron called plättiron, *which has indentations a little less than 3 inches (7.5 cm) across. It is excellent for this purpose, and it produces blini that are small enough to serve stacked "Napoleon-style," giving some height to the presentation.*

While blini and Beluga caviar are almost synonymous—being a traditional must-order appetizer by tourists in Russia, and a classic part of the Captain's Farewell Dinner on many cruise ships—I have had blini served with many other types of fish eggs in Scandinavia from salmon to whitefish, trout, and herring, usually accompanied by diced onions and/or chives plus sour cream. Regardless of where and with what blini are served, they should always be served warm, shining from melted butter on top.

second hot skillet instead of turning them individually. Pour another three or four pools of batter into the first skillet while the group in the second skillet finishes cooking, and repeat.

1. Dissolve the yeast in the milk. Incorporate the buckwheat flour and mix to form a smooth paste. Cover and set aside in a warm place for 1 hour to rise.

2. Add the bread flour, buttermilk, beer, and the egg yolks, stirring until smooth. Cover and set aside in a warm place for 1 hour to rise again. After the second rising the blini batter may be reserved in the refrigerator for several hours.

3. When you are ready to cook the blini, whip the egg whites with the salt and the sugar to stiff but not dry peaks. Fold into the batter.

4. Generously butter a heavy 10-to-12-inch (25-to-30-cm) skillet (or use a griddle). Heat until it is hot but not smoking. Pour three or four small pools of batter onto the skillet, using slightly less than 1/4 cup (60 ml) of batter for each pancake (see note). Cook for about 4 minutes, then turn and cook approximately 1 minute longer on the second side. You can usually judge when the blini are ready to turn by watching the bubbles as they form on the surface. Brush additional butter on the skillet as you turn the blini if necessary to avoid a dry appearance. Transfer to an ovenproof pan or platter, cover, and keep warm while you cook the remaining blini.

 ## Cheese Soufflé

8 servings

melted unsalted butter

5 ounces (140 g) freshly grated
    Parmesan cheese

3 ounces (85 g) bread flour

3 ounces (85 g) soft unsalted butter

2 cups (480 ml) milk

7 eggs, separated

2 ounces (55 g) grated Gruyère cheese

1/4 teaspoon (1 g) cayenne pepper

1/2 teaspoon (1 g) ground nutmeg

2 teaspoons (10 g) salt

Soufflé is actually a French verb meaning "to blow," "to breathe," or "puffed up." This latter is, of course, how we like to see our finished soufflés. Soufflés should always be made in round forms with straight sides (this goes for the dessert version as well as the savory) to help them rise. Although a savory soufflé will never rise as high as a properly prepared dessert soufflé, it must still be served hot, straight from the oven.

1. Brush melted butter over the insides of eight 5-ounce (150-ml) soufflé molds. Coat with Parmesan cheese; reserve the remaining cheese for the batter. Set the forms aside.

2. Combine the flour and butter.

3. Heat the milk in a saucepan to the scalding point.

4. Whisk in the flour mixture and cook to a thick paste, stirring constantly.

5. Remove from the heat. Mix in the egg yolks a few at a time, continuing to stir constantly so the yolks do not cook. Add the remaining Parmesan, the Gruyére cheese, cayenne, nutmeg, and salt.

6. Whip the egg whites to stiff peaks (be careful not to whip them dry). Gently fold the egg whites into the batter one-third at a time.

7. Fill the prepared forms three-fourths full.

8. Bake immediately at 400°F (205°C) for approximately 15 minutes. Serve at once.

Cheese Straws

sixty-four 3¹/₂ inch (8.7-cm)
hors d'oeuvres

3¹/₂ ounces (100 g) grated Parmesan
   cheese
1 teaspoon (2 g) paprika
1 pound (455 g) Puff Pastry
   (page 44)
Egg Wash (page 7)

In addition to making a nice before-meal snack with your favorite aperitif, Cheese Straws are often served as an accompaniment to soups or salads. As with many puff pastry products, these can be made up in advance and conveniently stored in the freezer, well wrapped, for up to a month. Bake as needed directly from the freezer.

1. Combine the Parmesan and paprika; reserve.

2. Roll out Puff Pastry ¹/₈ inch (3 mm) thick in a rectangle 14 by 10 inches (35 × 25 cm).

3. Brush the entire surface of the dough heavily with Egg Wash.

4. Sprinkle the cheese mixture over half of the dough, starting from one of the long sides.

5. Fold the plain half of the dough over the cheese. Roll the dough to 6 inches (15 cm) in width, sealing and pressing the cheese into the dough at the same time.

6. Place the dough in the refrigerator for 30 minutes to relax and firm up.

7. Cut the dough lengthwise into sixteen strips ³/₈ inch (9 mm) wide. Twist each strip into a spiral as shown in Pretzel Pastries (see Figure 15–8, page 775), stretching the strips to 16 inches (40 cm) at the same time.

8. Place on sheet pans lined with baking paper, securing both ends of each twisted strip to the paper by pressing hard with your thumbs. This will help to keep them straight; they still tend to curl and twist somewhat but can easily be straightened before they are completely baked through. Let rest for at least 30 minutes before baking .

9. Bake at 400°F (205°C) for approximately 15 minutes or until golden brown and done.

10. Immediately cut each strip into four 3¹/₂ inch (8.7-cm) lengths. Cheese Straws are best if served the same day they are baked.

Cummin Kravatten (Cumin Bow Ties)

forty-eight 1¹/₂-by-3-inch (3.7-×
7.5-cm) hors d'oeuvres

1 pound, 10 ounces (740 g) Puff
   Pastry (page 44)
Egg Wash (page 7)
2 tablespoons (14 g) whole cumin
   seed
salt

These little bow ties are part of a long list of Puff Pastry hors d'oeuvres. You might say they come dressed for the occasion, requiring only Egg Wash and a sprinkling of cumin after they are cut, unlike Anchovy Sticks or Ham and Cheese Croissant, which are a bit more involved.

Adjust the amount of cumin used to suit your own preference. The distinctive warm flavor of the seeds blends very well with both Mexican and Middle Eastern dishes. Kravatten should not be restricted to simply a before-dinner tidbit but could be served as an accompaniment or garnish to a curry or lamb dish.

1. Roll out the Puff Pastry, using flour to prevent the dough from sticking, to make a rectangle that is slightly larger than 12 by 18 inches

(30 × 45 cm). Place the dough in the refrigerator to chill and become firm.

2. Trim the sides of the dough to make them even and make the rectangle exactly 12 by 18 inches (30 × 45 cm). Cut four strips lengthwise and then cut across into 1¹/₂-inch (3.7-cm) pieces to make forty-eight 1¹/₂-by-3-inch (3.7-×-7.5-cm) rectangles.

3. Leaving the pieces in place, brush Egg Wash over the dough. Immediately sprinkle the cumin seeds evenly over the cut pieces. Lightly sprinkle salt on top.

4. Twist each piece twice in the center to form a bow tie shape. The side of the dough with the cumin seeds will be facing up on both ends. Place the pieces on sheet pans lined with baking paper.

5. Bake at 400°F (205°C) for approximately 15 minutes or until golden brown and baked through. Let cool completely and then store in a dry place. The *Kravatten* taste best the day they are baked. If needed, you can refresh the hors d'oeuvres by placing them in a hot oven for a few minutes.

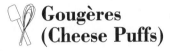

Gougères (Cheese Puffs)

approximately 50 hors d'oeuvres

one-quarter recipe Pâte à Choux (page 36)

5 ounces (140 g) Gruyère or Emmenthaler cheese, finely diced or grated

This savory French speciality from Burgundy makes a quick and easy hors d'oeuvre, excellent with, of course, red wine. They are traditionally piped into a ring shape, but individual Gougères are more common and perhaps more practical. The addition of cheese greatly affects the ability of the paste to puff, so do not expect that these will increase in volume to the extent of profiteroles piped the same size. If you must substitute another cheese for either of the two in the recipe, Parmesan adds a nice flavor, but you probably should not suggest it to a French chef.

1. Draw two 10-inch (25-cm) circles on a sheet of baking paper. Invert the paper on a sheet pan and set aside.

2. Reserve ¹/₄ cup (60 ml) of the cheese. Mix the remaining cheese into the Pâte à Choux. Place in a pastry bag with a no. 6 (12-mm) plain tip.

3. Pipe approximately 25 mounds around each circle to form a ring. If you have Pâte à Choux left over, pipe it into individual mounds inside the ring; do not pipe on top of the ring. Sprinkle the reserved cheese over the Pâte à Choux mounds.

4. Bake immediately at 400°F (205°C) for approximately 25 minutes or until fully baked and golden brown. Gougères should be eaten the same day they are baked.

Ham and/or Cheese Croissants

approximately 50 hors d'oeuvres

6 ounces (170 g) ham and/or Swiss
    cheese
milk
1 pound (455 g) Puff Pastry
    (page 44)
Egg Wash (page 7)

*T*hese hors d'oeuvres can, and often seem to be, made into a full meal. Be
forewarned, you would be wise to bake a few extra since they have a tendency to "disappear." If made ahead and frozen, bake them directly from the
freezer; they will require a slightly longer baking time.

1. Process the ham in a food processor to make a purée (this makes
it easier to roll up the croissants). If using cheese and ham, finely dice
or grate the cheese and mix it with the ham. If using cheese alone, grate
it and mix in enough milk to make a paste or the cheese will just fall off
when you roll up the croissants.

2. Roll out Puff Pastry to a 16-by-18-inch (40-×-45-cm) rectangle,
which should be slightly thinner than ¹⁄₈ inch (3 mm). Let rest, then cut
into four 4-inch-wide (10-cm) strips. Cut 3-inch (7.5-cm) triangles from
the strips.

3. Place a small amount of filling on top of the Puff Pastry at the
wide end of each triangle. Roll up tightly, stretching and pinching the
ends underneath to prevent them from unrolling, and place on sheet
pans lined with baking paper. Shape each one into a crescent as you
place them.

4. Brush with Egg Wash. Bake at 400°F (205°C) for about 20 minutes or until baked through. Serve the same day they are baked.

Quiche Lorraine

two 11-inch (27.5-cm) quiches

one recipe Pie Dough (page 36)
3 cups (720 ml) heavy cream
¹⁄₂ teaspoon (2.5 g) salt (see note)
pinch white pepper
pinch ground nutmeg
12 egg yolks (1 cup/240 ml)
14 ounces (400 g) bacon, cut in small
    pieces, cooked and drained
14 ounces (400 g) diced Gruyère
    cheese

*NOTE: You can substitute diced ham for the
bacon. Adjust the amount of salt according to
the saltiness of the ham or bacon.*

*Q*uiche, which originated in Lorraine, took its name from the German word
Küchen, which means "little cake." Quiches can be loosely defined as
unsweetened custards with various fillings. In some areas of Lorraine any dish
containing custard (eggs and cream), onion, and/or cheese is called a quiche.

1. Roll out Pie Dough ¹⁄₈ inch (3 mm) thick and line two 11-inch
(27.5-cm) false-bottom tart pans (see Figure 2–14, page 56). Prick the
bottom of the shells lightly and let rest for at least 30 minutes.

2. Combine the cream, salt, pepper, nutmeg, and egg yolks; blend
thoroughly. Distribute the bacon and cheese evenly over the bottom of
the shells. Pour the custard on top, dividing it between the two pans.

3. Bake at 375°F (190°C) directly on the bottom of a deck oven or
directly on the oven rack (do not use a sheet pan) for approximately 30
minutes or until the custard is set. Serve warm.

Sausage Cuts in Puff Pastry

54 hors d'oeuvres

1 pound, 8 ounces (680 g) Puff Pastry (page 44)

1/2 teaspoon (1 g) ground oregano

1/2 teaspoon (1 g) ground thyme

1/2 teaspoon (1 g) ground fennel

1/4 teaspoon (.5 g) ground cloves

1/4 teaspoon (.5 g) ground cayenne pepper

three medium-sized cloves of garlic, finely chopped

1 pound, 8 ounces (680 g) ground pork (not too lean)

2 eggs

Egg Wash (page 7)

These great-tasting little tidbits are a welcome addition to an assortment of passed hors d'oeuvres at any gathering. This type of hors d'oeuvre is often referred to as "pigs in a blanket," although the term is probably more commonly used for cocktail sausages wrapped in pastry or for small breakfast sausages wrapped in pancakes. If you make the Sausage Cuts ahead of time, or if you freeze part of the recipe, wait to apply the Egg Wash until you are ready to bake the pastries.

1. Roll the Puff Pastry out to a 13 1/2-by-24-inch (33.7-×-60-cm) rectangle using flour to prevent the dough from sticking. The dough should be about 1/8 inch (3 mm) thick. Refrigerate the sheet to relax and firm the dough.

2. Combine the spices and then thoroughly mix them into the ground pork together with the garlic and the eggs.

3. Cut the Puff Pastry sheet into three 4 1/2-inch (11.2-cm) strips lengthwise. Brush Egg Wash over the strips.

4. Place the pork mixture in a pastry bag with a no. 7 (14-mm) plain tip. Pipe a rope of filling next to one long edge on each strip, dividing the filling evenly between the strips. Roll the dough around the filling enclosing it in a spiral of dough.

5. Place the finished ropes seam-side down on a sheet pan lined with baking paper. Press lightly with the palm of your hand to flatten the ropes slightly. Brush Egg Wash over the tops.

6. Bake at 375°F (190°C) for approximately 35 minutes or until light brown and baked through. Cool slightly and then cut each strip into 18 equal pieces. Serve warm.

Miscellaneous

Filling and Piping with a Pastry Bag

Use a pastry bag that is large enough to allow you to fill the bag only half to two-thirds full. This will prevent the contents from being forced out through both ends.

1. Cut the opening of a new bag so that the point of your largest piping tip just barely shows through; this will ensure that the opening will not be too large for the smaller tips.

2. Fold the top half or one-third of the empty bag open.

3. Place the tip in the bag. Turn the bag upside down and force a small part of it, closest to the tip, inside the tip to lock the bag and prevent the filling from running out (Figure 1–2). This is a good habit all of the time but essential when you are piping a thin or runny filling.

4. Use one hand to hold the bag under the folded section and place the filling in the bag with the other (Figure 1–3).

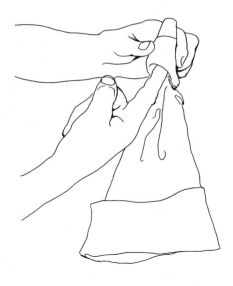

FIGURE 1–2   *Pushing the top of the pastry bag inside the tip to prevent the filling from leaking out as it is added*

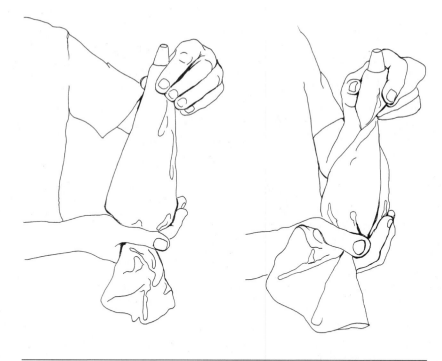

FIGURE 1–4   *Releasing the portion of the bag that was pushed inside after adding the filling; twisting the bag below the tip to temporarily relock the opening*

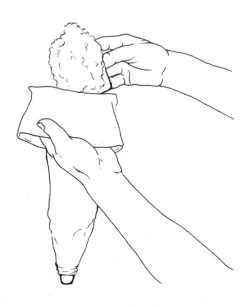

FIGURE 1–3   *Adding the filling to the pastry bag*

5. Straighten out the fold and slide the top of the bag between your thumb and forefinger from the top to where the filing is, on both sides of the bag, to move the filling away from the top and remove any air pockets. Twist the bag closed at the top. Turn the bag upside down and pull the tip up to release the inverted (locked) bag. Twist to temporarily relock it before pointing the bag down to pipe (Figure 1–4).

6. Hold the bag by resting the top between your thumb and fingers and apply pressure to the top of the bag only with the palm of your hand. Use your other hand to guide the tip, or to hold onto the item being filled or decorated; do not apply pressure with this hand.

7. Squeeze out some of the filling back into the bowl to make sure there are no air pockets before piping on the item you are decorating. When you are ready to pipe, untwist to open the flow and then twist again as you move between items so that the filling does not continue to run out (Figure 1–5). This is not necessary with a thick filling that will stay in the bag without running, such as a cookie dough, for example.

FIGURE 1–5   Untwisting the top while piping; twisting again to close and stop the flow while moving between items

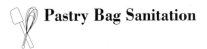 **Pastry Bag Sanitation**

*B*ecause pastry bags are used for so many dairy items—such as buttercream, pastry cream, and whipped cream—that are susceptible to food-borne illness, the bag must be washed after each use in warm soapy water. The piping tip should be removed and washed separately, and the bag should be turned inside out to clean the inside thoroughly. Never wash the bag with the piping tip inside; there is almost always some amount of foodstuff trapped between the tip and the bag. Rinse the bag and wipe dry before turning right-side out and drying the outside of the bag. Hang the bag on a pastry bag rack, or place inverted over a bottle so that air can circulate around the bag until it is completely dry. To sanitize the pastry bags, submerge them in water that is at least 180°F (82°C), or in water containing a chemical sanitizing solution, after washing the bag. While it is not practical to go through this procedure after each use in a busy shop, it is important to do at the end of each workday. Not only are these rules important from a health and safety standpoint, but your bags will last longer if cared for properly.

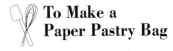 **To Make a Paper Pastry Bag**

NOTE: Moist fillings such as whipped cream, pastry cream, and some jams must be piped out within 5 to 10 minutes after filling the bag or the bag may burst.

*W*hat constitutes a pastry bag versus a piping bag, by definition, is that a pastry bag, being larger, must be held in your hands when piping, while a piping bag is held using the fingers only. Therefore, technically speaking, it is the size that determines the name. However, in general, when someone refers to a pastry bag they are speaking of a reusable bag made of canvas or other material, and a piping bag is usually a one-time-use, handmade paper cone. These directions, combining the two, are for making a disposable pastry bag from

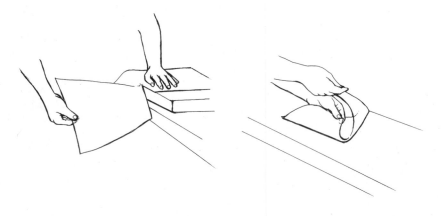

FIGURE 1–6   *Tearing the paper in half; starting to form a disposable pastry bag*

baking paper. It is very fast and easy to do and is a practical solution in many instances. I simply tear a sheet of baking paper in half when I need a bag, but you could certainly cut sheets ahead of time so you always have 12-by-16-inch (30-X-40-cm) pieces handy. In several European countries, including my own, Sweden, professionals are required by law to use disposable pastry bags when working with dairy products.

1. Tear a full sheet (16 × 24 inches/40 × 60 cm) of baking paper in half, crosswise, against the edge of a table. The cut edge will be a bit ragged, but this doesn't matter. Set one piece of paper aside to use another time.

2. Hold the paper so that the rough edge becomes the top (opening of the bag) and fold the paper into a cone as you do to make a piping bag (Figures 1–6 and 1–7).

3. To keep the bag from coming apart, fold up about 2 inches (2.5 cm) of the tip.

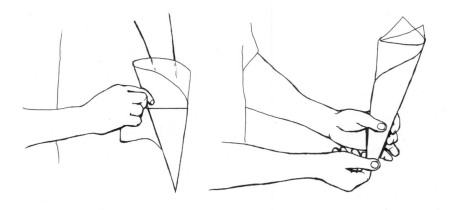

FIGURE 1–7   *Completing the pastry bag; folding the tip to prevent the bag from coming apart*

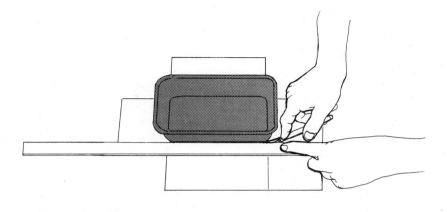

FIGURE 1–8   Cutting baking paper to line the inside of a rectangular pan

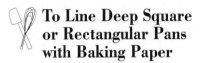

To Line Deep Square or Rectangular Pans with Baking Paper

1. Place the pan in the center of a square or rectangle of baking paper that is large enough that the paper that extends beyond the pan will cover the sides.

2. Place a ruler against one side of the pan and draw a line along the edge next to the pan continuing to the end of the paper. Repeat on all four sides of the pan to create intersecting lines with a box the same size as the bottom of the pan in the center. Take into consideration that you are drawing on the outside of the pan, so make the square or rectangle slightly smaller.

3. Cut away the corner squares (Figure 1–8) leaving a cross-shaped piece of paper (Figure 1–9).

4. Place the paper in the pan.

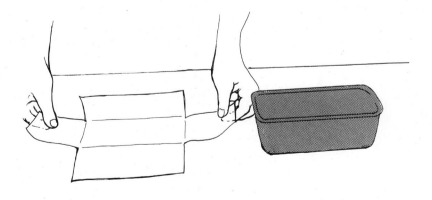

FIGURE 1–9   The paper ready to line the pan

To Line the Bottom of Round Pans with Baking Paper

It is very fast and easy to cut a circle of paper to fit in the bottom of a round pan. Describing it actually takes more time than doing it!

1. Start with a rectangle of baking paper; if you are lining a 10-inch (25-cm) round cake pan, half of a standard sheet of baking paper will suffice. Fold the paper in half by bringing the short sides together and then in half again the same way. Fold the two short folded edges in toward the long folded edge (Figure 1–10). Fold again in the same direction (Figure 1–11). The point of the triangle should be in the center of the original rectangle. You may need to fold one or two more times in the same direction depending on the size of the circle you are creating. The more times you fold the paper, the rounder the finished edge will be because each straight cut you make later will be shorter.

2. Hold the folded cone over the pan with the pointed end in the center and cut the opposite end of the paper even with the edge of the pan.

3. Unfold the paper; you should have a circle the same size as the bottom of the pan (Figure 1–12). If the paper circle is too large, refold and cut again.

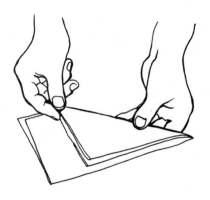

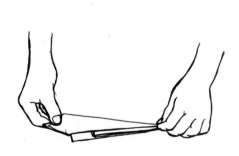

FIGURE 1–10   Folding a rectangle of baking paper to create a circle for lining a cake pan

FIGURE 1–11   Folding again in the same direction

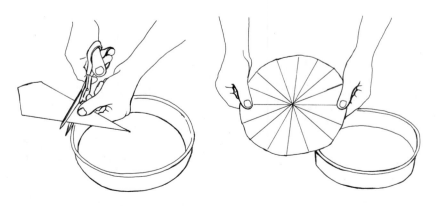

FIGURE 1–12   Cutting the folded paper to make it as long as half the diameter of the pan; the circle after unfolding, ready to place in the pan

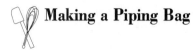

Making a Piping Bag

1. Cut a standard full-size sheet (24 by 16 inches/60 × 40 cm) of baking paper into six 8-inch (20-cm) squares. Fold each square diagonally and cut into two triangles.

2. Start by holding the triangle horizontally in such a way that the longest side is in front of you. Fold into a cone shape so that the long side becomes the tip, and the point of the original triangle (the opposite side) becomes the opening of the cone (Figures 1–13, 1–14, 1–15, and 1–16). Fold the top into the cone to secure the shape (Figure 1–17). Fill the cone only halfway. Close the top securely and cut the tip into the desired size opening.

FIGURES 1–13, 1–14, 1–15, and 1–16
Making a piping bag from baking paper

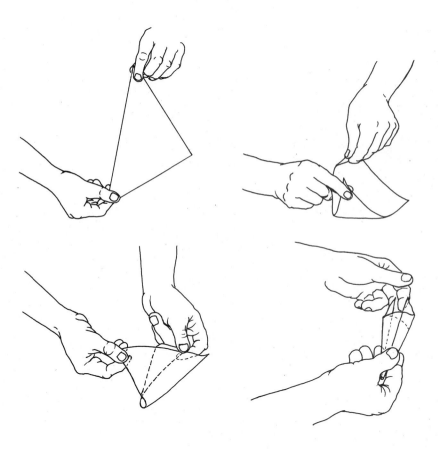

FIGURE 1–17   *Securing the top of the cone inside the bag to prevent the bag from unfolding*

2

Basic Doughs

A mastery of dough making is obviously critical to the success of a professional pastry kitchen. Different techniques are required to create Short Dough, Puff Pastry, choux paste, and perfect Pie Dough. However, in making any basic dough, it is important to use a good, workable recipe and follow the proper procedures for preparation.

Short Dough

Short Dough, along with its many variations, such as Linzer Dough and Cornmeal Crust, is without question the dough used most frequently in the majority of pastry shops. A proficient pastry chef will always keep a supply of Short Dough in the refrigerator ready to use as a base for cakes and pastries, or to line tart pans. Short Dough is also irreplaceable for preparing what I call "nothing-left-in-the-showcase" cookies. With one basic dough, you can make a variety of cookies and pastries quickly and efficiently.

Puff Pastry

Another basic dough used continually in the pastry kitchen is Puff Pastry. It is one of the most exciting, and also one of the most challenging, doughs to work with. The use of Puff Pastry dates back many centuries, and one can find many theories as to its origin in cookbooks and food reference books. It is impossible to say which story is accurate, but one that I particularly like tells of a pastry apprentice in France. The young man was given the responsibility of making up all of the pastry doughs for use the following day. When he was finished, he realized that he had forgotten to add the butter in one of the recipes. Knowing that the master would certainly find out, but not wanting to start over, he quickly mixed in the missing butter, flattening and turning the dough over several times in an effort to hide his mistake. The next day the master let it be known that he intended to have a few words with the apprentice. The apprentice, fearing he was to be scolded for ruining the dough, ran away. When he was found at last

Ingredient Ratios in Basic Doughs Relative to One Pound of Flour				
	PUFF PASTRY	**QUICK PUFF PASTRY**	**SHORT DOUGH**	**PIE DOUGH**
Flour	1 pound (455 g)	1 pound (455 g)	1 pound (455 g)	1 pound (455 g)
Butter (margarine in Danish)	1 pound (455 g)	1 pound (455 g)	14 ounces (400 g)	10 ounces (285 g)
Yeast	0	0	0	0
Sugar	0	0	6 ounces (170 g)	0
Eggs	0	0	1	0
Water	6 1/2 ounces (195 ml)	3 ounces (90 ml)	0	3 ounces (90 ml)
Milk	0	0	0	0
Salt	2 1/2 teaspoons (12.5 g)	2 1/2 teaspoons (12.5 g)	0	2 1/2 teaspoons (12.5 g)
Other	1 1/2 teaspoons (7.5 ml) lemon juice	0	1 teaspoon (5 ml) vanilla extract	3 ounces (85 g) lard
Mixing/ Production Method	The majority of the butter is mixed with the lemon juice and one-third of the flour, and the mixture is formed into a block. The remainder of the flour is mixed with water, salt, and the balance of the butter to form a dough. The butter block is layered with dough. The dough is given four double turns (or six single turns if using the classical French method).	The flour and salt are combined. The butter is cut into large chunks, which are added to the flour mixture but are not fully incorporated. The water is mixed in just until the dough holds together. The dough is given three double turns.	Sugar, soft butter, egg, and vanilla are mixed for a few minutes at low speed. The flour is added, and the dough is mixed only until the flour is fully incorporated.	Flour and salt are combined. The butter and lard are added and mixed until the fat pieces are the size of marbles. Water is added, and the dough is mixed only until it holds together.

FIGURE 2–1   A comparison of basic dough formulas relative to one pound flour

and brought trembling before the master, he was astonished to find out that rather than intending to punish him, the master wanted to praise him and learn the secret of the wonderful new flaky dough he had invented!

Pâte à Choux

Pâte à Choux, also known as éclair paste, is a basic and versatile paste used to make many items in the pastry kitchen, including Cream Puffs or Profiteroles, Swans, Croquembouche, and, of course, Éclairs. Pâte à Choux (like Short Dough) is also used in combination with Puff Pastry to make delicious sweets such as Gâteau Saint Honoré and Choux Surprise. The translation of Pâte à Choux is "cabbage paste," referring to the baked cream puff's resemblance to a small cabbage head.

Ingredient Ratios in Basic Doughs Relative to One Pound of Flour					
	CROISSANT DOUGH	**DANISH DOUGH**	**BASIC BREAD DOUGH**	**PÂTE À CHOUX**	**BRIOCHE DOUGH**
Flour	1 pound (455 g)	1 pound (455 g)	1 pound (455 g)	1 pound (455 g)	1 pound (455 g)
Butter (margarine in Danish)	11 1/2 ounces (325 g)	17 ounces (485 g)	2 ounces (55 g)	6 1/2 ounces (185 g)	5 ounces (140 g)
Yeast	1 1/4 ounces (37 g)	1 1/2 ounces (40 g)	1 ounce (30 g)	0	1 ounce (30 g)
Sugar	7 teaspoons (35 g)	1 1/2 ounces (40 g)	1 ounce (30 g)	0	2 1/2 ounces (70 g)
Eggs	0	2	0	14	4
Water	0	0	0	3 1/3 cups (800 ml)	0
Milk	9 ounces (270 ml)	6 1/2 ounces (195 ml)	8 ounces (240 ml)	0	1 1/2 ounces (45 ml)
Salt	2 1/2 teaspoons (12.5 g)	2/3 teaspoon (3 g)	2 1/4 teaspoons (11.25 g)	1 1/4 teaspoons (6.25 g)	2 teaspoons (10 g)
Other	few drops lemon juice	2/3 teaspoon cardamom	0	0	0
Mixing/ Production Method	Lemon juice, butter and a portion of the flour are formed into a block. The yeast is dissolved in the milk. The sugar, salt, and the balance of the flour are kneaded in with the dough hook. The butter block is layered with the dough. The dough is given three single turns.	The margarine is shaped into a block. The yeast is dissolved in the cold milk and eggs. Salt, sugar, and cardamom are added, and the flour is incorporated to form a dough. The margarine block is layered with the dough. The dough is given four single turns.	The yeast is dissolved in the milk. Salt, flour and sugar are incorporated using the dough hook. Butter is mixed in, and the dough is kneaded for 10 minutes. The dough is proofed, formed, and proofed a second time before baking.	The water, butter and salt are brought to a boil. The flour is stirred in over the heat. The roux is cooked for a few minutes and then cooled slightly. The eggs are incorporated gradually off the heat.	The yeast is dissolved in the milk. The sugar, salt, and eggs are added. The flour, and then the butter, are incorporated. The dough is kneaded with the dough hook and then proofed in the refrigerator. The dough is formed and then proofed a second time prior to baking.

FIGURE 2-1   (Continued)

Rubbed Doughs

Rubbed doughs are made by rubbing the fat into the flour, as in pie dough. The type can vary from mealy to flaky. Flaky dough must have large distinct pieces of shortener in it. Just enough water is then added to bind the dough together. When the fat melts during baking it leaves small pockets of air which expands as the temperature increases, creating a light finished product.

Simple and Decorative Doughs

Pie Dough, Pizza Dough, and Pasta Dough are much quicker and less complicated to master than Puff Pastry or Pâte à Choux. This chapter also contains four recipes for decorative doughs. Of these, only the Whole-Wheat Weaver's Dough is intended for consumption. The Salt Doughs and the Weaver's Dough are used for purely decorative purposes (although technically they are completely edible, you would have to be pretty hungry, or uninformed, to give them a try).

Comparison of Doughs

Figure 2–1 (pages 30 and 31) shows the formulas of some of the doughs in this chapter, as well as other basic doughs throughout the text, relative to 1 pound (455 g) of flour.

Basic Pasta Dough

approximately 1 pound (455 g) dough

12 ounces (340 g) semolina flour
1/2 teaspoon (2.5 g) salt
2 eggs
1 teaspoon (5 ml) olive oil
2 tablespoons (30 ml) water, approximately

I have included a basic pasta recipe not so much because I love pasta but because the bakeshop is often asked to make the dough when a large amount is required. I use semolina flour, which in my opinion produces a far superior product. It gives the dough a much better color, makes it easier to work with, and gives the cooked pasta a slightly chewy bite. You can, however, replace all or part of the semolina flour with bread flour, or even all-purpose flour if desired. Try to use the minimum amount of water possible at the start and then if the dough can not be formed into a ball, add more drop-by-drop. Eggs are considered optional; they give the pasta a more appealing color and a richer texture but can be replaced with an additional 1/4 cup (60 ml) of water. This recipe gives you a fundamental plain pasta dough. Many ingredients such as vegetables or vegetable juices and fresh or dried herbs can be added to change the flavor of the pasta.

To mix using a food processor

1. Combine all of the ingredients in the food-processor bowl with the steel blade. Process until the dough forms a crumbly mass, about 2 or 3 minutes. The dough should hold together when you gather it into a ball with your hands but should not feel sticky. Add more flour or water (only a few drops at a time) if required. It is best to keep the dough as dry as possible while still having it hold together. The texture of a pasta dough made with semolina flour will be coarse and sandy compared to pasta dough made with bread or all-purpose flour.

2. Cover the dough and let it rest for 1 hour before rolling it out.

To mix using an electric mixer

1. Place all of the ingredients in the mixer bowl. Mix at medium speed, using the dough hook, for about 3 minutes. Add more flour or water as required. The dough should form a smooth ball that pulls away cleanly from the sides of the bowl.

2. Cover the dough and let it rest for 1 hour before rolling it out.

To mix by hand

1. Place the dry ingredients on your work surface in a mound and make a well in the center. Pour the remaining ingredients into the well. Working quickly, incorporate the eggs, water, and oil into the flour until the mixture forms a crumbly mass. Then knead the dough against the table until it becomes smooth and pliable, about 6 to 10 minutes.

2. Cover the dough and let it rest for 1 hour before rolling it out.

Cornmeal Crust

4 pounds, 10 ounces (2 kg, 105 g) dough or enough to line six 11-inch (27.5-cm) tart pans

1 pound, 6 ounces (625 g) soft
   unsalted butter
1 pound (455 g) granulated sugar
1 teaspoon (5 g) salt
2 teaspoons (10 ml) vanilla extract
1/4 cup (60 ml) or 3 ounces (85 g)
   honey
6 egg yolks (1/2 cup/120 ml)
grated zest from two lemons
1 pound (455 g) bread flour
1 pound (455 g) cornmeal

One-Half Recipe

*2 pounds, 5 ounces
(1 kg, 50 g) dough*

12 ounces (340 g) soft unsalted butter
8 ounces (225 g) granulated sugar
1/2 teaspoon (2.5 g) salt
1 teaspoon (5 ml) vanilla extract
2 tablespoons (30 ml) honey
3 egg yolks (1/4 cup/60 ml)
grated zest from one lemon
8 ounces (225 g) bread flour
8 ounces (225 g) cornmeal

Yellow cornmeal gives this type of Short Dough a great robust texture and a rich buttery color; it also makes the dough very easy to work with. I use a medium-textured grind in this recipe but fine or coarsely ground cornmeal can be used as well. Very coarsely ground cornmeal (the type used to make polenta) makes the crust very crisp, but some people do not care for it, finding it unpleasant to eat the hard grains. I previously called this recipe Polenta Short Dough until I was informed by an Italian colleague that polenta is the name of the cooked cornmeal mush, not the grain. His exact words were "It isn't polenta until your Italian grandmother stirs it on top of the stove!"

1. Using the dough hook on low speed, thoroughly combine the butter, sugar, salt, vanilla extract, honey, egg yolks, and lemon zest.

2. Blend in the flour and cornmeal, mixing only until the ingredients are combined.

3. Chill the dough before using.

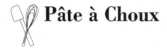 Linzer Dough

*1 pound, 14 ounces
(855 g) dough*

6 ounces (170 g) granulated sugar
8 ounces (225 g) soft unsalted butter
3 egg yolks (¹/₄ cup/60 ml)
8 ounces (225 g) bread flour
2 teaspoons (3 g) ground cinnamon
¹/₂ teaspoon (1 g) ground cloves
6 ounces (170 g) finely ground
    hazelnuts
2 teaspoons (12 g) grated lemon peel

*A*t first glance this dough appears fairly simple, and although that is true for the most part, Linzer Dough is actually a bit deceiving in that it can become unusable if you are not careful. It is critical that the hazelnuts are ground to a fine consistency. (If this is done in a food processor, add half of the sugar to the nuts while grinding, to absorb the oil and keep the nuts from turning into a paste.) When the ground nuts are too coarse it becomes virtually impossible to move a rolled sheet of dough without having it fall apart. Overmixing the dough will cause the same problem, which in that case is a result of incorporating too much air.

In addition to this one, see the recipe for piped Linzer Dough on page 241. The piped method works especially well if you are making a large quantity of tarts.

1. Combine the sugar, butter, and egg yolks in a mixer bowl, using the dough hook on low speed.

2. Sift the flour with the cinnamon and cloves.

3. Add the flour mixture, hazelnuts, and lemon peel to the butter mixture; mix just until all ingredients are incorporated and smooth. Overmixing will make this dough very hard to work with.

4. Cover the dough and refrigerate on a paper-lined sheet pan.

Pâte à Choux

*P*âte à Choux, or choux paste, as the name suggests, is not really a dough in the strictest sense but rather a thick paste that could be described as a roux with the addition of eggs. There are many different recipes and philosophies to choose from when it comes to making this classic pastry. However, the one factor that holds true in each case is that the more eggs you are able to add to the base mixture (without causing it to lose its shape when piped), the higher and lighter your finished product will be, ideally becoming just a hollow shell.

Composition and Preparation of the Batter

Pâte à Choux begins as a cooked mixture of water or milk, fat (usually butter), and flour, with a small amount of salt added if sweet butter is used. The sifted flour is added to the boiling water and fat and stirred in quickly. The resulting roux is then cooked for a few minutes, while stirring constantly, to allow as much liquid as possible to evaporate so that the maximum number of eggs can be incorporated. Although some chefs use a slightly different formula that incorporates a stronger flour (especially for larger items such as Paris-Brest as opposed to profiteroles), I find it quite satisfactory to compromise and use a combination of bread and cake flours (in a sense creating all-purpose flour). You should add as many eggs as the paste can absorb and still stay in a precise shape once it is piped out; the paste will have a slightly shiny appearance if the correct amount of eggs has been added. On the other hand, if not enough eggs are used, the baked pastries will be low and heavy and filled with a gluey mass that must be removed before the pastries can be filled. Add the eggs a few at a time; you can then mix them in more easily and also avoid accidentally adding too many. A small amount of ammonium carbonate is added with the eggs to give an extra lift. The ammonium gas released during baking helps to increase the volume; the strong-smelling gas quickly dissipates as the pastry cools. If you do not have ammonium carbonate it is not necessary to substitute another leavener; simply leave it out.

Using Egg Wash

It isn't necessary to brush Pâte à Choux pastries with Egg Wash before baking; in fact, it is just a waste of time. The Egg Wash usually dries before the pastries have finished expanding, which gives them an unattractive cracked appearance (resembling a dry riverbed!). In most cases the pastries are to be finished with a glaze or powdered sugar on top and, provided that the roux was cooked properly and an adequate number of eggs were added, plain Pâte à Choux (without Egg Wash) will have a shiny surface.

Advance Preparation of Individual Pieces

Pâte à Choux is never prepared ahead of time and refrigerated or frozen in a batter or dough form before being shaped, as you would, for example, with Puff Pastry dough. It must be piped out first, then either baked or frozen immediately, before the paste develops a skin.

Baking

The formed paste is put into a hot (425°F/219°C) oven (directly from the freezer without thawing, if frozen; increase the baking time) to produce the maximum amount of steam, which rapidly expands the paste and leaves a large empty space in the center. The heat coagulates the gluten and proteins that set the structure and make a firm shell. After approximately 10 minutes the heat is reduced (375°F/190°C) to finish baking and allow the shells to become firm and dry, without getting too dark. Simply turning the thermostat control will not lower the heat quickly enough. Open the oven door partway as well to reduce the temperature, but do not open it fully; a sudden drop in temperature at this stage can cause the shells to collapse. As long as you do not let it become too brown, you cannot overbake Pâte à Choux, so make sure that the shells have been baked long enough to hold their shape and not fall. The baked shells, for eclairs and profiteroles for example, can be stored covered for a day or so before being filled, but once filled they should be served the same day.

Pâte à Choux

*2 pounds, 10 ounces
(1 kg, 195 g) paste*

8 ounces (225 g) cake flour
11 ounces (310 g) bread flour
1 quart (960 ml) water
8 ounces (225 g) unsalted butter
1½ teaspoons (7.5 g) salt
1 quart (960 ml) eggs, approximately
1 teaspoon (3.5 g) ammonium
    carbonate

One-Half Recipe

*1 pound, 5 ounces
(595 g) paste*

4 ounces (115 g) cake flour
5½ half ounces (155 g) bread flour
1 pint (480 ml) water
4 ounces (115 g) unsalted butter
½ teaspoon (2.5 g) salt
1 pint (480 ml) eggs, approximately
½ teaspoon (2 g) ammonium
    carbonate

1. Sift the flours together on a sheet of baking paper and reserve.

2. Heat the water, butter, and salt to a full rolling boil, so that the fat is not just floating on the top but is dispersed throughout the liquid.

3. Form the ends of the baking paper into a pouring spout. Then, using a heavy wooden spoon, stir the flour into the liquid, adding it as fast as it can be absorbed. Avoid adding all of the flour at once.

4. Cook, stirring constantly and breaking up the inevitable lumps by pressing them against the side of the pan with the back of the spoon, until the mixture comes away from the sides of the pan, about 2 to 3 minutes.

5. Transfer the paste to a mixer bowl (or, if you are making the small recipe, adding the eggs by hand is quite easy; use the spoon and leave the paste in the saucepan). Let the paste cool slightly so the eggs will not cook when they are added.

6. Mix in the eggs, two at a time, using the paddle attachment on low or medium speed. After the first few eggs are incorporated, add the ammonium carbonate. Add as many eggs as the paste can absorb and still hold its shape when piped.

7. Pipe the paste into the desired shape according to the individual recipe.

8. Bake at 425°F (219°C) until fully puffed and starting to show some color, about 10 minutes. Reduce the heat to 375°F (190°C) and bake about 10 to 12 minutes longer, depending on size.

9. Let the pastries cool at room temperature. Speeding up the process by placing them in the refrigerator or freezer can cause the pastries to collapse.

Pie Dough

*approximately 3 pounds,
4 ounces (1 kg, 480 g) dough*

1 pound, 9 ounces (710 g) bread flour
1 tablespoon (15 g) salt
1 pound (455 g) cold unsalted butter
5 ounces (140 g) cold lard
2/3 cup (160 ml) ice water,
    approximately

NOTE: Unless you are making a large amount, always mix Pie Dough by hand because it is very easy to overmix the dough by machine. The Pie Dough should rest for an additional 30 minutes after it has been rolled out, to prevent shrinkage as it is baked.

Making Pie Dough is quick and easy as long as the ingredients are kept cold and are only mixed until just combined. In a good Pie Dough, most of the fat should still be visible in small separate lumps. Overmixing or using soft fat will make the dough hard to work with, and the baked crust will be crumbly and mealy instead of flaky. While some chefs insist on the exclusive use of lard in their pie crust, I feel that even though it unquestionably produces a beautiful, flaky crust, the flavor of the lard can be overwhelming, especially when the pie has a sweet fruit filling. In my opinion, a compromise using both lard and butter gives the best overall result. Also, the flakiness of the pie crust depends a great deal on the flour-to-fat ratio. As with Short Dough, the more flour in the dough, the harder the finished shell. Therefore, you should use the smallest amount of flour possible when rolling out a Pie Dough. Scraps from Pie Dough should be treated with the same care as Puff Pastry. They should be layered on top of each other to roll out a second time; never knead the scraps together. These precautions will help to keep the dough from becoming rubbery and hard to work with. If you do not have lard, or you prefer not to use it, it is preferable to substitute margarine or vegetable shortening for lard rather than to make the dough with all butter. Because of butter's higher water content and

FIGURE 2–2   Method I: Creating a fluted edge using the knuckle and fingertips

FIGURE 2–3   Method II: Creating a fluted edge by pinching and twisting the dough

Pizza Dough

approximately 1 pound (455 g) dough or enough for two 10-to-12-inch (25-to-30-cm) pizza crusts

$^1/_2$ ounce (15 g) fresh yeast
$^3/_4$ cup (180 ml) water, at room temperature
1 teaspoon (5 g) granulated sugar
2 tablespoons (30 ml) olive oil
1 teaspoon (5 g) salt
1 tablespoon (15 ml) honey
10 ounces (285 g) bread flour

lower melting point, a Pie Dough made using 100 percent butter is very hard to work with, and the texture of the baked crust can be mealy.

1. Combine the flour and salt in a bowl.

2. Add the firm butter and lard and pinch the fat down to the size of hazelnuts with your fingertips.

3. Add the ice water and mix just until the dough comes together; the butter should still be lumpy.

4. Flatten the dough to help it chill faster.

5. Let the Pie Dough rest in the refrigerator covered for at least 30 minutes before using.

To make a decorative fluted edge

Roll the dough out $^1/_8$ inch (3 mm) thick, large enough so that it will extend about 1 inch (2.5 cm) beyond the edge of the pie pan. Roll the dough up on a dowel and unroll over the pan (see Figure 2–14, page 56). Fold the edge under and form it into a $^1/_2$-inch (1.2-cm) lip standing up around the edge of the pan.

Method I: Use the knuckle of your right index finger and the tips of your left thumb and index finger to bend the lip of dough into an evenly spaced fluted design (Figure 2–2).

Method II: Pinch the lip of dough between your thumb and the side of your bent index finger and twist to make the fluted pattern (Figure 2–3).

T he word pizza translates, of course, to "pie." It is unclear exactly where pizza originated, but the similarity of the name and the product to the French pissaladière (a provincial specialty typically topped with olives, onions, and anchovies) would suggest that the Italians may have borrowed the idea they later made so famous, especially in the city of Naples, which is most recognized for popularizing the traditional-style Italian pizza. Another theory says that Italian pizza evolved from Middle Eastern flatbread. Who is to say, really, which came first hundreds, if not thousands, of years ago? One can certainly imagine that the idea of taking some raw dough from the daily bread, flattening it and topping it with whatever was on hand before placing it in the oven, would come naturally. Today, pizza has become a very popular American fast food with so many changes and variations that the Neopolitans might not link it to their original creation.

1. Dissolve the yeast in the water (help it along by squeezing it with your fingers) in a mixer bowl.

2. Mix in the sugar, olive oil, salt, and honey.

3. Add the flour and knead with the dough hook until the dough has a smooth, elastic consistency, about 10 minutes.

4. Place the dough in an oiled bowl, turn to coat both sides with oil, cover, and let rise until slightly less than doubled in volume.

5. Place the dough, covered, in the refrigerator for at least two hours. Bring the dough to room temperature before proceeding.

6. Divide the dough in half. On a floured board, roll and stretch the dough with your hands to make each piece into a 10-to-12-inch (25-to-30-cm) circle.

7. Top as desired and bake at 450°F (230°C) on a heated pizza stone or a thin sheet pan placed in the bottom of the oven to allow the crust to brown on the bottom.

 **Puff Pastry**

The preparation of Puff Pastry demands great care. To produce a light and flaky product, everything must be done properly, start to finish, or the results will be disappointing.

The Dough (Détrempe)

Making the basic dough correctly (the flour and water mixture also commonly referred to as détrempe) is extremely important. If you add too much flour, or you do not work the dough long enough, it does not matter how carefully you roll in the butter; the paste will be glutenous and rubbery, hard to work with, and will shrink when baked. When the dough shrinks to this extent, not only are the texture and appearance affected but the baked dough can taste salty as well since the same amount of salt is now concentrated within a smaller portion of product.

Creating the Layer Structure

Great care must also be taken when rolling in the butter and turning the dough to get the optimum rise, or puff. If rolled in properly, there will be a layer of butter between each layer of dough. In a hot oven the moisture in the dough layers produces steam that, if properly sealed in by the butter, will push up as it evaporates. This is how Puff Pastry rises without the addition of a leavening agent.

Creating an even layer structure can be accomplished only if the butter and the dough have the same consistency, which is why some flour must first be worked into the butter. As in Short Dough, gluten is formed when flour and water (here, the water in the butter) are combined. Although not necessary, adding a small amount of citric acid (lemon juice, for example) to the butter strengthens the gluten and also gives an extra measure of pliability to ensure that the butter will stretch with the dough.

Butter

There are many specially made fats on the market designed for Puff Pastry, but none stands up to butter when it comes to taste. Also, because butter has a much lower melting point, it will not leave an unappetizing film in one's mouth the way some shortening products do.

Number of Layers

There are actually 513 layers of butter and dough in Puff Pastry made with four double turns as directed in the following recipe (Figure 2–4). When the dough is given six single turns, which is the classical French technique, the finished dough will have almost 1,500 layers of dough and butter combined (Figure 2–5). The French word for Puff Pastry is *feuilletage* from *feuilles,* meaning "leaves;" the pastry we call a napoleon is known as *mille feuilles* or "a thousand leaves."

Precautions

Even after you have made perfect Puff Pastry there are many things to watch out for as you work with it:

• Be very careful not to damage the layer structure when rolling the dough. Never let your rolling pin roll over the edge of the dough, which mashes down the sides, and always apply even pressure as you are rolling so that the butter is evenly distributed.

• As a general rule, Puff Pastry dough should rest 5 to 10 minutes between rolling it out and cutting it. It should then rest an additional 15 minutes after it has been made up (for example, into turnovers) before baking to eliminate shrinkage. (If the dough seems particularly rubbery and shrinks back a lot as you roll it, it will need to rest a bit longer.)

• As you cut the dough, hold the knife at a sharp 90° angle so the edges of the dough are perfectly straight. This way the dough will rise straight up in the oven.

• When using Egg Wash on a product made with Puff Pastry dough, take care not to let any drip on the side. This can seal the dough to the pan and prevent it from rising.

• Start baking Puff Pastry in a hot oven; if the oven is not hot enough you will lose the effect of the steam, and the butter will run out of the dough instead.

• Ideally, the following recipe should be ready to use the day after it is started, with all four turns having been made before it is placed in the refrigerator overnight. If the situation demands, the dough can be given two turns only and then finished the following day to be ready for use on day three. Puff Pastry should not be started if there is only time to make one turn before leaving it overnight. The butter layer will be too thick and will break when the dough is rolled out the following day.

Dough
Butter Block
Dough
1
The Puff Pastry Dough and Butter Block before making turns

Dough	Dough
Butter	Butter
Dough	Dough
Dough	Dough
Butter	Butter
Dough	Dough

1 A
The first step of the first
Double Turn
(both ends were folded in to meet in the center)

Dough	Dough
Butter	Butter
Dough	Dough
Dough	Dough
Butter	Butter
Dough	Dough
Dough	Dough
Butter	Butter
Dough	Dough
Dough	Dough
Butter	Butter
Dough	Dough

1 B	**1 C**
After making the first Double Turn: 12 layers... (the folded dough was folded in half again)	**...in actuality, 9 layers as the adjacent dough layers blend forming a single dough layer**

	Dough	Dough
9 Butter and Dough Layers including Dough Layers on the top and bottom	7 layers of Dough and Butter	7 layers of Dough and Butter
	Dough	Dough
9 Butter and Dough Layers including Dough Layers on the top and bottom	Dough	Dough
	7 layers of Dough and Butter	7 layers of Dough and Butter
	Dough	Dough
9 Butter and Dough Layers including Dough Layers on the top and bottom	Dough	Dough
	7 layers of Dough and Butter	7 layers of Dough and Butter
	Dough	Dough
9 Butter and Dough Layers including Dough Layers on the top and bottom	Dough	Dough
	7 layers of Dough and Butter	7 layers of Dough and Butter
	Dough	Dough

2 A	**2 B**	**2 C**
After completing the second Double Turn there are 36 layers... (the dough consisting of 9 layers was folded in four layers)		**...in actuality, 33 layers as the adjacent dough layers blend forming a single dough layer**

FIGURE 2–4   The layer structure in a Puff Pastry dough made with four double turns

33 Butter and Dough Layers including Dough Layers on the top and bottom	Dough	Dough
	31 layers of Dough and Butter	31 layers of Dough and Butter
	Dough	Dough
33 Butter and Dough Layers including Dough Layers on the top and bottom	Dough	Dough
	Dough	Dough
	31 layers of Dough and Butter	31 layers of Dough and Butter
	Dough	Dough
33 Butter and Dough Layers including Dough Layers on the top and bottom	Dough	Dough
	Dough	Dough
	31 layers of Dough and Butter	31 layers of Dough and Butter
	Dough	Dough
33 Butter and Dough Layers including Dough Layers on the top and bottom	Dough	Dough
	Dough	Dough
	31 layers of Dough and Butter	31 layers of Dough and Butter
	Dough	Dough
3 A After completing the third Double Turn there are 132 layers... (the dough consisting of 33 layers was folded in four layers)	**3 B**	**3 C** ...in actuality, 129 layers as the adjacent dough layers blend forming a single dough layer

129 Butter and Dough Layers including Dough Layers on the top and bottom	Dough	Dough
	127 layers of Dough and Butter	127 layers of Dough and Butter
	Dough	Dough
129 Butter and Dough Layers including Dough Layers on the top and bottom	Dough	Dough
	Dough	Dough
	127 layers of Dough and Butter	127 layers of Dough and Butter
	Dough	Dough
129 Butter and Dough Layers including Dough Layers on the top and bottom	Dough	Dough
	Dough	Dough
	127 layers of Dough and Butter	127 layers of Dough and Butter
	Dough	Dough
129 Butter and Dough Layers including Dough Layers on the top and bottom	Dough	Dough
	Dough	Dough
	127 layers of Dough and Butter	127 layers of Dough and Butter
	Dough	Dough
4 A After completing the fourth Double Turn there are 516 layers... (the dough consisting of 129 layers was folded in four layers)	**4 B**	**4 C** ...in actuality, 513 layers as the adjacent dough layers blend forming a single dough layer

FIGURE 2–4   (Continued)

Dough	Dough
Butter	Butter
Dough	Dough
Dough	
Butter	Butter
Dough	Dough
Dough	
Butter	Butter
Dough	Dough
1 A **After making the first** **Single Turn: 9 layers...** **(the dough was folded in thirds)**	**1 B** **... in actuality, 7 layers as the** **adjacent dough layers blend** **forming a single dough layer**

Dough
Butter Block
Dough
1 **The Puff Pastry Dough and Butter Block** **before making turns**

7 Butter and Dough Layers including Dough Layers on the top and bottom	Dough	Dough
	5 layers of Dough and Butter	5 layers of Dough and Butter
	Dough	Dough
7 Butter and Dough Layers including Dough Layers on the top and bottom	Dough	Dough
	5 layers of Dough and Butter	5 layers of Dough and Butter
	Dough	Dough
7 Butter and Dough Layers including Dough Layers on the top and bottom	Dough	Dough
	5 layers of Dough and Butter	5 layers of Dough and Butter
	Dough	Dough
2 A **After completing the second Single Turn there are 21 layers...** **(the dough consisting of 7 layers was folded in thirds)**	**2 B**	**2 C** **...in actuality, 19 layers as the adjacent dough layers blend forming a single dough layer**

19 Butter and Dough Layers including Dough Layers on the top and bottom	Dough	Dough
	17 layers of Dough and Butter	17 layers of Dough and Butter
	Dough	Dough
19 Butter and Dough Layers including Dough Layers on the top and bottom	Dough	Dough
	17 layers of Dough and Butter	17 layers of Dough and Butter
	Dough	Dough
19 Butter and Dough Layers including Dough Layers on the top and bottom	Dough	Dough
	17 layers of Dough and Butter	17 layers of Dough and Butter
	Dough	Dough
3 A **After completing the third Single Turn there are 57 layers...** **(the dough consisting of 19 layers was folded in thirds)**	**3 B**	**3 C** **...in actuality, 55 layers as the adjacent dough layers blend forming a single dough layer**

FIGURE 2–5   *The layer structure in a Puff Pastry dough made with six single turns, the classical French method*

55 Butter and Dough Layers including Dough Layers on the top and bottom	Dough	Dough
	53 layers of Dough and Butter	53 layers of Dough and Butter
	Dough	Dough
55 Butter and Dough Layers including Dough Layers on the top and bottom	Dough	Dough
	53 layers of Dough and Butter	53 layers of Dough and Butter
	Dough	Dough
55 Butter and Dough Layers including Dough Layers on the top and bottom	Dough	Dough
	53 layers of Dough and Butter	53 layers of Dough and Butter
	Dough	Dough
4 A **After completing the fourth Single Turn there are 165 layers...** **(the dough consisting of 55 layers was folded in thirds)**	**4 B**	**4 C** **...in actuality, 163 layers as the adjacent dough layers blend forming a single dough layer**

163 Butter and Dough Layers including Dough Layers on the top and bottom	Dough	Dough
	161 layers of Dough and Butter	161 layers of Dough and Butter
	Dough	Dough
163 Butter and Dough Layers including Dough Layers on the top and bottom	Dough	Dough
	161 layers of Dough and Butter	161 layers of Dough and Butter
	Dough	Dough
163 Butter and Dough Layers including Dough Layers on the top and bottom	Dough	Dough
	161 layers of Dough and Butter	161 layers of Dough and Butter
	Dough	Dough
5 A **After completing the fifth Single Turn there are 489 layers...** **(the dough consisting of 163 layers was folded in thirds)**	**5 B**	**5 C** **...in actuality, 487 layers as the adjacent dough layers blend forming a single dough layer**

487 Butter and Dough Layers including Dough Layers on the top and bottom	Dough	Dough
	485 layers of Dough and Butter	485 layers of Dough and Butter
	Dough	Dough
487 Butter and Dough Layers including Dough Layers on the top and bottom	Dough	Dough
	485 layers of Dough and Butter	485 layers of Dough and Butter
	Dough	Dough
487 Butter and Dough Layers including Dough Layers on the top and bottom	Dough	Dough
	485 layers of Dough and Butter	485 layers of Dough and Butter
	Dough	Dough
6 A **After completing the sixth Single Turn there are 1, 461 layers...** **(the dough consisting of 487 layers was folded in thirds)**	**6 B**	**6 C** **...in actuality, 1, 459 layers as the adjacent dough layers blend forming a single dough layer**

FIGURE 2–5   (Continued)

Freezing Puff Pastry

Puff Pastry freezes very well both as a dough and made up, ready to be baked. However, it should not be stored in the refrigerator for more than one week after it is finished. If held longer than that, the flour and water mixture in the dough will start to ferment, eventually causing the dough to turn gray. It will gradually become darker, and both taste and appearance will suffer. The ideal way to use Puff Pastry, providing you have the freezer space, is to make up as many apple turnovers or Fleurons (or whatever recipes you are using) that you will need for the week and freeze them to take out and bake fresh every day. If this is not practical, freeze the dough, divided into suitably sized pieces, to use as required. Puff Pastry dough must be kept well covered at all times, especially in the freezer, to prevent the top from drying and forming a skin (freezer burn).

Using Scrap Dough

Scraps from rolled Puff Pastry dough (as with any other dough such as Danish, pie, and croissant) will not be as good rolled out the second time, but it can be used successfully in some recipes. Puff Pastry scraps are preferable to fresh dough for pastries that should not puff up as much. Scrap pieces can be frozen until needed, or combined with a fresh dough. Never knead the scraps together to form a larger piece; lay them on top of each other and then roll to retain the layered structure. Scraps from Puff Pastry can also be used for Butter-Wheat Bread (see page 87).

NOTE: In the recipes for Fleurons, Vol-au-vent, and Bouchées, the amount of dough required and the thickness specified for rolling it out assume you are using properly layered, freshly made Puff Pastry dough, following the recipe in this book. If you are using another recipe or a dough that you know (or suspect) is getting old (more than one week in the refrigerator), you may need to adjust the thickness of the dough when rolling it out. Bake a few samples before making a large batch. A good Puff Pastry dough should rise to four times its original height.

Puff Pastry

approximately 11 pounds (5 kg) dough

Butter Block

4 pounds, 6 ounces (1 kg, 990 g) soft unsalted butter

3 tablespoons (45 ml) lemon juice

1 teaspoon (5 g) salt

1 pound, 2 ounces (510 g) bread flour

Dough

1 quart (960 ml) cold water

3 tablespoons (45 g) salt

7 ounces (200 g) soft unsalted butter

14 ounces (400 g) cake flour

2 pounds, 4 ounces (1 kg, 25 g) bread flour, approximately

To make the butter block

1. Work the butter, lemon juice, salt, and bread flour into a smooth paste using the paddle attachment.

2. Shape into a 12-inch (30-cm) square (6-inch/15-cm for the one-quarter recipe) and refrigerate until firm.

The butter should not be so soft that it is hard to handle; you should be able to transfer the finished block from one hand to the other without breaking it. It should not be so firm that it cracks or breaks if you press on it. Ideally, the dough and the butter block should have the same consistency. A dough that is softer than the butter will be forced to the sides by the firmer butter; a dough that is too firm will force the butter out on the sides. Either will result in poor-quality Puff Pastry. Take into consideration that the dough needs to rest for 30 minutes and try to time it so that both the dough and the butter block are ready at the same time.

To make the dough (production method) using a mixer

1. Using the paddle in a mixer on low or medium speed, mix the water, salt, soft butter, cake flour, and enough of the bread flour to form

One-Quarter Recipe

*approximately 2 pounds,
12 ounces (1 kg, 250 g) dough*

Butter Block

1 pound, 2 ounces (510 g) cold
  unsalted butter
2 teaspoons (10 ml) lemon juice
pinch of salt
4½ ounces (130 g) bread flour

Dough

1 cup (240 ml) cold water
2 teaspoons (10 g) salt
2 ounces (55 g) soft unsalted butter
3½ ounces (100 g) cake flour
11 ounces (310 g) bread flour,
  approximately

NOTE: When rolling the smaller amount of dough in the one-quarter recipe to make a double turn, it is difficult to avoid having the dough become so thin that the layer structure is compressed and the dough's ability to rise is significantly decreased. A better option is to give the smaller amount of dough five single turns, since it does not have to be rolled out as large for a single turn as it does for a double turn. The single turns take slightly less time to complete and you can be assured of a high-puffing dough at the end. See pages 159 and 160 for instructions on making a single turn. Start by rolling the dough to 16 by 12 inches (40 × 30 cm) and then make five single turns, resting the dough between each turn (the dough does not have to rest as long as for a double turn, however). When the dough is finished it will have 487 layers of butter and dough, slightly less than with four double turns, but quite adequate.

a soft dough. Avoid overmixing and/or adding too much flour. This will make the dough too glutenous and rubbery.

2. Shape the dough into a tight ball. With a sharp knife, cut a cross halfway into the ball. Let rest for 30 minutes, covered, in the refrigerator.

To make the dough (European style) by hand

In this preparation method the order of the ingredients is reversed. You start by using the full measurement of both flours, and instead of adjusting the consistency of the dough with bread flour, adjust the amount of water added at the end. The butter should be firm rather than soft. The dough is worked much less and when finished should not be soft, smooth, and elastic, but quite the opposite.

1. Sift both flours together onto your work surface (preferably a marble slab or table). Cut the firm butter into chunks, place on top of the flour, and using your fingertips, cut it into the flour, pinching it down until the mixture resembles coarse crumbs.

2. Shape into a mound, make a well in the center, and add the salt and most of the cold water into the well. Gradually mix the flour and butter into the water, using the fingers of both hands. If necessary, gradually add more water to form a dough that will hold together but is fairly sticky and rough looking.

3. Form the dough into a ball, kneading it as little as possible. Flatten the dough a little and cut a cross halfway into the ball. Cover and let rest for 30 minutes in the refrigerator.

To assemble

1. Pull the corners of the cuts out to make the dough square-shaped (Figure 2–6).

2. Roll the opened dough out to a square slightly thicker in the center than on the sides, and slightly larger than the butter block.

3. Place the butter block diagonally within the square so there are four triangles around the sides (Figure 2–7). Fold these dough triangles in so they meet in the center. Pinch the edges together to seal in the butter block (Figure 2–8).

4. Roll the dough into a rectangle ½ inch (1.2 cm) thick. Do not roll the dough wider than a sheet pan is long.

5. Give the dough four double turns (instructions follow), refrigerating it for approximately 30 minutes between each turn. Be sure the dough is well covered at all times.

6. After the last turn, roll the Puff Pastry out to approximately ¾ inch (2 cm) thick. If this is difficult to do, refrigerate the dough for a few minutes to relax the gluten. Place the dough on a sheet pan lined with baking paper, cover, and refrigerate or freeze. Remember that you should not keep Puff Pastry dough in the refrigerator more than one week.

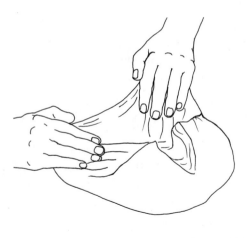

FIGURE 2–6   Opening the cut ball of dough to make it square

To make a double turn

1. Roll the dough to a rectangle 30 by 20 inches (75 × 50 cm) or 15 by 10 inches (37.5 × 25 cm) for the one-quarter recipe (see note on previous page), as carefully and evenly as possible. Arrange the dough with a long side closest to you.

2. Make a vertical mark in the center of the rectangle. Fold both ends of the dough in to this mark (Figure 2–9).

3. Brush away excess flour from the top of the dough and fold once more as if you were closing a book (Figure 2–10). The dough now has one double turn.

4. Carefully place the dough on a sheet pan, cover, and refrigerate for 30 minutes.

5. When you begin the second double turn, place the dough in front of you so that the short ends of the rectangle are on your left and

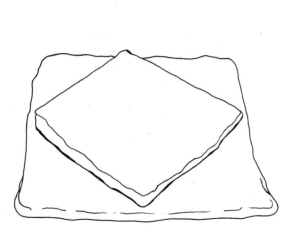

FIGURE 2–7   Positioning the butter block diagonally on the dough square

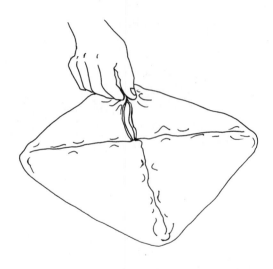

FIGURE 2–8   Sealing the butter block inside the dough

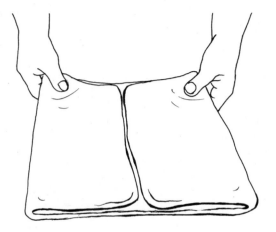

FIGURE 2–9   The first step of a double turn: folding both short edges in to meet in the center

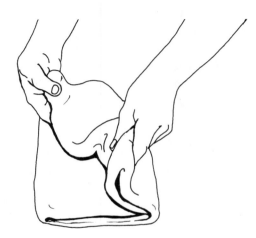

FIGURE 2–10   Completing a double turn: folding the dough in half as if closing a book

right, opposite to the way the dough lay when you "closed the book" with the first turn. Roll out and turn as above; repeat as you make the remaining turns.

Quick Puff Pastry

approximately 11 pounds,
2 ounces (5 kg, 60 g) dough

5 pounds (2 kg, 275 g) bread flour
3 tablespoons (45 g) salt
5 pounds (2 kg, 275 g) cold unsalted
   butter
1 pint (480 ml) cold water,
   approximately

One-Quarter Recipe

approximately 2 pounds,
12 ounces (1 kg, 250 g) dough

1 pound, 4 ounces (570 g) bread flour
2 teaspoons (10 g) salt
1 pound, 4 ounces (570 g) cold
   unsalted butter
1/2 cup (120 ml) cold water,
   approximately

NOTE: This dough does not rest between turns; it is ready to use immediately after the last turn. However, after the dough has been rolled, it must rest 20 to 30 minutes before baking to prevent it from shrinking.

If you do not have time to make traditional Puff Pastry, Quick Puff Pastry is a fast compromise. You will not get the height of the authentic version, but this one can easily be made—from scaling through baking—in two hours. It is perfect for lining tart pans or making Fleurons and napoleons, when the dough must not puff up too much. In Europe this type of dough is known as American Puff Pastry. The name has nothing to do with the lesser quality of dough you get from mixing all of the ingredients together in a rapid fashion but simply came about because this method resembles the technique used to make Pie Dough, and in Europe, pies are synonymous with America.

1. Combine the flour and salt in a mixer bowl.
2. Cut the butter (it should be firm but not hard) into 2-inch (5-cm) pieces (or about half this size for the smaller recipe). Add to the flour mixture on low speed using the dough hook; be careful not to knead.
3. Mix in just enough water so the dough can be handled. Mix carefully and only for a short amount of time so the lumps of butter remain whole; the dough should look like well-made pie dough.
4. Shape the dough into a square. Roll two single and two double turns alternately (see double turn instructions preceding this recipe, and see pages 159 and 160 for single turn instructions). Cover and refrigerate.

Fleurons

28 pieces

1 pound (455 g) Puff Pastry (page 44)
Egg Wash (page 7)
vegetable oil

NOTE: If you are making a great many Fleurons and you are not sure about the quality of the dough, make a few samples so you can adjust the thickness as necessary.

Fleurons are small crescent-shaped Puff Pastry garnishes. They are used in classical French cooking, usually as a garnish with seafood and as an accompaniment to soup.

1. Roll out the Puff Pastry to a 12-by-12-inch (27.5-×-27.5-cm) square about 1/8 inch (3 mm) thick (see note). Prick the dough lightly.
2. Place the dough on cardboard or on an inverted sheet pan. Brush with Egg Wash.
3. Using the back of a chef's knife, mark a diamond pattern in the Egg Wash.
4. Refrigerate or freeze until firm (the Egg Wash will dry slightly). It is much easier to brush on the Egg Wash and mark the dough before you cut than to try to do each Fleuron individually.

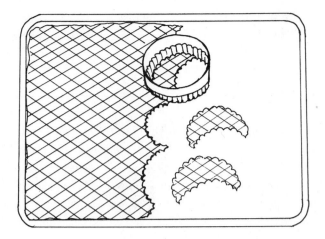 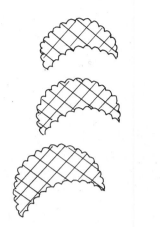 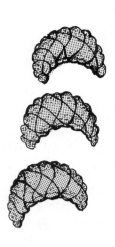

FIGURE 2–11   *Cutting crescents to create Fleurons*   FIGURE 2–12   *The Fleurons before and after baking*

5. Starting from the bottom edge of the square on the left side, cut away a little less than a half circle of dough using a 3-inch (7.5-cm) fluted cookie cutter dipped occasionally in oil. Cut straight down and do not twist the cutter. Make a second cut, parallel to the first and 1¹/₂ inches (3.7 cm) higher, to form a crescent (Figure 2–11). The cut that makes the top of one crescent becomes the bottom of the next one. Continue cutting until you have made the first row of seven Fleurons. Cut three additional rows of seven Fleurons in the same way. The only scraps of dough will be at the beginning and at the end of each row. Place the individual pieces on a sheet pan lined with baking paper.

6. Bake at 400°F (205°C) about 10 minutes. You may need to lower the heat and leave them in a few minutes longer to finish drying (Figure 2–12). Fleurons can be frozen before baking; bake directly from the freezer for about 12 minutes following the same procedure.

Vol-au-vent

one 10-inch (25-cm) pastry shell, 10–12 servings

1 pound, 8 ounces (680 g) Puff Pastry
   (page 44)
Egg Wash (page 7)

*Y*ou *could say that a Vol-au-vent is a big Bouchée or, conversely, that a Bouchée is a small Vol-au-vent; in principle they are the same thing. Vol-au-vent (which literally means "flying in the wind," a reference to the delicate nature of the baked Puff Pastry) were invented by the famous French chef Antonin Caréme, who according to history, is said to have proclaimed "s'envola au vent" referring to the lightness of his creations as he removed them from the oven. These pastry shells can be made anywhere from around 8 to 10 inches (20 to 25 cm) in diameter for multiple servings, to 4 to 5 inches (10 to 12.5 cm) across for individual servings. Ten inches is the largest size shell it is practical to make. If this is not large enough for the number of servings needed, it is best to make two smaller shells.*

1. Roll the Puff Pastry to a square slightly larger than 10 inches (25 cm) and approximately ¹/₂ inch (1.2 cm) thick (see note, page 44).

2. Refrigerate the dough first if it has become soft; then, using a 10-inch (25-cm) template as a guide (a cake pan is a good choice), cut out a circle of dough. Be sure to cut at a 90° angle to prevent the Vol-au-vent from falling to one side as it puffs up in the oven.

3. Place an 8¹/₂-inch (21.2-cm) template in the center of the circle and cut again. Carefully transfer the ring-shaped piece of dough to a sheet pan, cover, and place in the refrigerator.

4. Roll the remaining circle of dough ¹/₈ inch (3 mm) thick and in a shape that will allow you to cut from it one 10-inch (25-cm) circle, which will be the bottom, and one 8¹/₂-inch (21.2-cm) circle to use for the lid of the Vol-au-vent (if desired). Cut out the circles, prick the dough thoroughly, and refrigerate for approximately 30 minutes. (If you have enough scrap dough on hand you can roll and cut these two circles first, then allow them to rest in the refrigerator while you are making the ring.)

5. Take out the 10-inch (25-cm) circle and place it on an even sheet pan.

6. Brush the outer 1 inch (2.5 cm) with Egg Wash and place the chilled ring on top so it sticks to the Egg Wash. Adjust to make the Vol-au-vent perfectly round.

7. With the back side of a knife, mark the Vol-au-vent every 1¹/₂ inches (3.7 cm) around the outside, holding the knife vertically, marking from the bottom to the top, and pushing in just a little to create a scallop pattern (Figure 2–13).

8. Prick the top of the ring and brush lightly with Egg Wash (do not let any drip down the sides).

9. Remove the 8¹/₂-inch (21.2-cm) circle from the refrigerator and place it on the pan next to the Vol-au-vent. Brush the lid with Egg Wash and mark it with a diamond pattern using the back of a chef's knife.

10. Bake at 400°F (205°C), double-panned to prevent the bottom from getting too dark, for about 15 minutes or until puffed. Then reduce the temperature to 375°F (190°C) and continue baking until dry

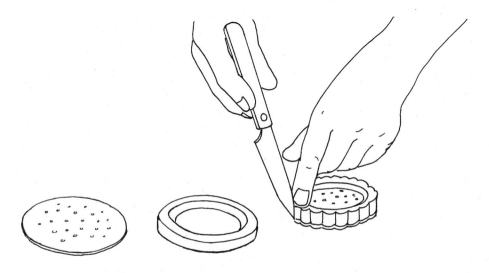

FIGURE 2–13   Pressing the back of a knife into the dough to create vertical marks and a scalloped edge on a Vol-au-vent

and golden, 30 to 35 minutes. If the top gets too dark before it is dried through, cover it with a piece of baking paper or aluminum foil. The lid will, of course, be finished baking long before the case of the Vol-au-vent; remove it carefully.

One of the best ways to keep the sides of a Vol-au-vent from falling in as it puffs up is to arrange a cake cooling rack above the Vol-au-vent on baking forms or coffee cups set at the edges of the baking pan. Place them at a height slightly below the point you expect, or want, the dough to puff. This acts as a mold, preventing the Vol-au-vent from puffing too high and helping to keep the edges straight.

To make a smaller Vol-au-vent, follow the same directions using whatever size is required for the outside template; just use a ring 1 inch (2.5 cm) smaller to create the frame.

Individual Vol-au-vent

fifteen 3¹/₄-inch (8.1-cm) pastry shells

2 pounds (910 g) Puff Pastry (page 44)
vegetable oil
Egg Wash (page 7)

There are two basic ways of making Individual Vol-au-vent: the production method and the classic method. If you use the production method they won't get quite as high, but they can be made very quickly and you can be sure that the sides will not fall in as they bake. The classic method produces higher and more elegant Vol-au-vent, but they take a little longer to finish.

Classic Method

1. Roll the Puff Pastry out to a rectangle measuring 7 by 10 inches (17.5 × 25 cm) and slightly less than ¹/₂ inch (1.2 cm) thick (see note, page 44). Place the dough in the refrigerator for a few minutes to relax and firm up.

2. Using a 3¹/₄-inch (8.1-cm) plain or fluted cookie cutter, cut out fifteen circles of dough. Dip the edge of the cutter in oil periodically and push the cutter straight down without twisting.

3. Using a 2-inch (5-cm) cutter, cut a circle out of each round to form rings. Carefully place the rings on a sheet pan and refrigerate.

4. Layer the scrap dough, including the circles cut out of the centers, and roll it out ¹/₈ inch (3 mm) thick. Prick the dough and place in the refrigerator to firm and relax.

5. Cut out fifteen 3¹/₄-inch (8.1-cm) circles (not rings) from the sheet of dough plus fifteen 2-inch (5-cm) circles to use as lids if desired.

6. Brush Egg Wash on the larger circles and place the reserved rings on top. If you wish, brush the top of the rings with Egg Wash, but be very careful not to let any run down the sides.

7. Bake the Vol-au-vent and the lids at 400°F (205°C) until puffed, about 10 minutes. Reduce the heat to 375°F (190°C) and bake until they are dry enough to hold their shapes, about 30 minutes. (You might have to use a second pan underneath to prevent the bottoms from becoming too dark, and you may need to remove the Vol-au-vent on the edges of the pan if they are done before those in the middle. The lids will finish baking sooner.)

Production method

Follow steps 1 and 2 as in the classic method.

3. Place the circles on a sheet pan about ³/₄ inch (2 cm) apart. Rather than cutting all the way through the dough and removing the 2-inch (5-cm) center, cut only two-thirds of the way through the dough. Do not forget to continue dipping the cutter in oil as you work to produce a clean cut.

4. Thoroughly prick the 2-inch (5-cm) center of the circles.

5. Bake as directed in step 7 for classic Vol-au-vent, increasing the time slightly.

6. When the Vol-au-vent have cooled slightly, lift off the lids and use a fork to scrape out the unbaked dough inside. If necessary, put the shells back in the oven to dry further.

Bouchées

twenty-four 1¹/₂-inch (3.7-cm) pastry shells

2 pounds (910 g) Puff Pastry (page 44)
vegetable oil

Bouchée is a French word which means "mouth-size" or "mouthful." They are usually made with savory fillings and served as hors d'oeuvres. It is best to use the production method described in individual Vol-au-vent to make these petite pastry shells.

Follow the instructions given in the production method for individual Vol-au-vent, using a 1¹/₂-inch (3.7-cm) cutter to cut out 24 circles of dough. Then use a 1-inch (2.5-cm) cutter to cut two-thirds of the way through the center. Continue as directed; these will require a shorter baking time.

Salt Dough

approximately 4 pounds, 6 ounces (1 kg, 990 g) dough

2 pounds (910 g) bread flour
1 pound (455 g) salt
1 pint (480 ml) water, approximately
Egg Wash (page 7)

NOTE: When making large pieces, check to be sure they are dry enough not to break before removing them from the oven. Keep the dough covered at all times while working. Store covered in the refrigerator no longer than three days. For a sturdier dough, use up to a 1:1 ratio of flour and salt. To color the dough see note 2 after the following recipe for Unbaked Salt Dough.

This is an inexpensive and easy-to-make dough used to make bread ornaments, or to practice braiding. Try to keep the dough as firm as possible as there is no gluten structure, and the dough will therefore stretch and fall apart easily if the consistency is too soft. Because of the nonexistent gluten structure, Salt Dough is excellent for patterns that are assembled after they are baked. The pieces will not shrink or change shape.

1. Combine the flour and salt.

2. Mix in just enough water to make a fairly stiff dough.

3. Roll out to the desired thickness—¹/₄ inch (6 mm) for most uses. Should the dough seem to drag as you cut around your templates, refrigerate the dough until it is firm. Dipping the tip of the knife in oil from time to time will also help prevent a ragged finish.

4. Brush the pieces with Egg Wash.

5. Bake at 375°F (190°C) until the pieces have a pleasant, light brown color.

Unbaked Salt Dough

*4 pounds, 5 ounces
(1 kg, 960 g) dough*

9 ounces (255 g) cornstarch
2 cups (480 ml) water, approximately
2 pounds, 12 ounces (1 kg, 250 g)
    popcorn salt (see note 1)

*NOTE 1: Popcorn salt is a very finely ground
salt. If it is not available, use an almond mill to
grind table salt to a very fine consistency. A coffee grinder can also be used, but that is rather
time-consuming.*

*NOTE 2: You can add food coloring to the
dough or apply color to the finished pieces using
a brush or a fixative syringe. If coloring the
dough, try to use natural sources as much as
possible. Ground cinnamon, nutmeg, or
unsweetened cocoa powder make nice shades of
brown; cayenne pepper or paprika are good for
creating russet tones. Avoid harsh or bright
colors.*

Short Dough

*This dough is ideal for small intricate showpieces as it is very pliable and
easy to work with. Figures made with this dough are not baked; they are
left to air dry instead. Typically, pieces take up to three days to dry completely,
so you will have to allow more time than usual to complete your project. If the
figure you are making is more than 1/4 inch (6 mm) thick, it should be made in
layers, letting each layer dry before adding the next, or the dough will shrivel
from the moisture trapped inside. The drying process may be accelerated by
placing the finished pieces in a gas oven using the heat from the pilot light only,
or by placing the pieces outside to dry in the sun.*

*The ingredients in this recipe can alternatively be measured by volume,
using one part each of cornstarch and water and two parts of salt.*

1. Mix the cornstarch and water in a saucepan. Heat the mixture
over medium heat, stirring constantly with a heavy spoon, until it starts
to gelatinize, approximately 10 minutes. As the mixture thickens it will
be rather difficult to stir and you may need to have some help during
the last few minutes.

2. Remove the mixture from the heat and transfer the paste to a
mixer bowl. Using the dough hook on low speed, incorporate the salt
plus 1 or 2 tablespoons (15–30 ml) of additional water as needed to
make a stiff but pliable dough. Mix until the dough is completely
smooth, about 5 minutes. Store the Salt Dough covered in the refrigerator.

*The name Short Dough makes more sense if you realize that "short" refers
to its crumbly quality, produced by the shortening (butter or margarine).*

Butter versus Margarine

Short Dough can be prepared with butter, margarine, or with a combination of the two. Although butter produces the best flavor, it makes the
dough harder to manage. Because the temperature range is so narrow,
when butter is just the right consistency, the butter in the dough will be
rock-hard if the dough is stored in the refrigerator and too soft if the
dough is left at room temperature. Another disadvantage to using butter
is that if too much flour is worked into the dough while it is being rolled
out, the dough will not only crumble and be harder to work with but will
also become rubbery and shrink when it is baked. In cold climates all or
part butter can be used more successfully. A Short Dough made with a
high-quality margarine may not be as tasty, but it is less complicated to
handle. By comparison, if you work too much flour into a dough made
with margarine, the dough will crumble and be hard to work with, but it
will not shrink during baking. Margarine is often a better choice if you
are in a hurry as it may be used straight from the refrigerator, while but-

ter must first be brought to room temperature to soften. A compromise is to use half butter and half margarine to benefit from the advantages they each have. When using both butter and margarine in a Short Dough it is essential that they have the same consistency before mixing the dough. If the butter is harder than the margarine you will end up with small lumps of butter in the finished dough.

Mixing the Dough

If Short Dough is overmixed, mixed using the wrong tool, mixed at the wrong speed, or any combination of these, too much air will be incorporated into the dough. This will result in a very soft product that could very well, in the worst scenario, be piped out using a pastry bag. When this happens, you can imagine the problems and frustrations the baker has attempting to roll the "dough" into a thin sheet to line tart pans, for example. However, trying to compensate for the softness by adding too much flour to the Short Dough, either when making the dough or while rolling it out, will make the baked crust unpleasantly tough and hard instead of crumbly. (The best way to salvage a dough that has been improperly mixed is to combine it with a larger portion of properly prepared dough.)

Being cautious about working in excess flour is especially important when working with a Short Dough made with butter. The toughness that can occur is the result of hydration and the development of insoluble proteins in a gluten-rich flour. The water contained in the butter, together with that in the eggs, forms a gluten structure when combined with flour. The strength of the gluten structure is proportionate to the amount of flour used and the amount of time the dough is worked. A Short Dough in which the gluten structure has been allowed to develop will also shrink when baked. When used properly, the butter (or other fat) will insulate the insoluble proteins and keep them from coming into contact with the water. But if the dough is overmixed or handled in a rough manner, the water is forced through the fat instead.

Working with Short Dough

To work at a reasonable production speed the dough should be somewhat elastic so that it will not break as it is molded and fit into pans, but as previously discussed it should not be too soft. When making the dough use the dough hook at low speed and mix just until combined. Remember, overmixing will incorporate too much air. Before you start working with chilled Short Dough knead it with your hands until it is smooth. This will minimize cracking around the edges when you roll it out, and help to prevent it from breaking as it is shaped. Use bread flour to roll out the dough, but only the minimum amount needed to prevent the dough from sticking to the table. Add new dough, cold and firm from the refrigerator, to the scraps from the batch you are working with, as needed.

Storage

Short Dough can be stored in the refrigerator for several weeks and can be frozen for up to two months if well wrapped.

Baking

A Short Dough that has been made correctly does not need to rest before it is baked, and it should not shrink or puff up during baking as long as the dough has been pricked. Short Dough can be baked at any temperature between 325 and 425°F (163 and 219°C), but 375°F (190°C) is ideal. Short Dough made according to this recipe is one of the few doughs where simply looking at the color of the baked product will tell you if it is done (provided the dough was rolled out to the proper thickness). This is not necessarily true of other Short Dough recipes, some of which might contain a different proportion of sugar. But if you use this recipe and follow the directions as given, you can be certain it is done when the dough turns golden brown.

Short Dough

4 pounds, 14 ounces (2 kg, 220 g) dough; enough to line about ninety 2¹/₂-inch(6.2-cm) tartlet pans or six 11-inch (27.5-cm) tart pans

12 ounces (340 g) granulated sugar
1 pound, 12 ounces (795 g) soft unsalted butter or margarine
2 eggs
2 teaspoons (10 ml) vanilla extract
2 pounds, 2 ounces (970 g) bread flour

One-Half Recipe

2 pounds, 6 ounces (1 kg, 80 g) dough

6 ounces (170 g) granulated sugar
14 ounces (400 g) soft unsalted butter or margarine
1 egg
1 teaspoon (5 ml) vanilla extract
1 pound (455 g) bread flour

NOTE: If overmixed, the dough will be much harder to roll out. This is especially true if you use all butter or a large percentage of butter.

1. Place the sugar, butter or margarine, eggs, and vanilla in a mixing bowl; mix at low speed with the dough hook just until combined.

2. Add the flour and mix only until the dough is smooth.

3. Place the dough on a paper-lined sheet pan; press out as flat as possible so that the dough takes up less space and cools down quickly.

4. Cover and refrigerate until firm enough to work with, about 30 minutes.

Cocoa Short Dough

*4 pounds, 12 ounces
(2 kg, 160 g) dough*

8 ounces (225 g) granulated sugar

1 pound, 12 ounces (795 g) soft
    unsalted butter or margarine

2 eggs

2 teaspoons (10 ml) vanilla extract

2 pounds, 4 ounces (1 kg, 25 g) bread
    flour

1 ounce (30 g) unsweetened cocoa
    powder

One-Half Recipe

*2 pounds, 6 ounces (1 kg, 80 g)
dough*

4 ounces (115 g) granulated sugar

14 ounces (400 g) soft unsalted butter
    or margarine

1 egg

1 teaspoon (5 ml) vanilla extract

1 pound, 2 ounces (510 g) bread flour

2 tablespoons (16 g) unsweetened
    cocoa powder

1. Place the sugar, butter or margarine, eggs, and vanilla in a mixing bowl. Mix on low speed using the dough hook, just until the ingredients are combined.

2. Sift the flour with the cocoa powder; add to the dough and mix only until smooth.

3. Place the dough on a paper-lined sheet pan; press the dough as flat as possible.

4. Cover and refrigerate.

Hazelnut Short Dough

3 pounds (1 kg, 365 g) dough

8 ounces (225 g) granulated sugar

1 pound (455 g) soft unsalted butter or
    margarine

1 egg

1/2 teaspoon (2.5 ml) vanilla extract

1 pound, 2 ounces (510 g) bread flour

4 ounces (115 g) hazelnuts, finely
    ground

1. Place the sugar, butter or margarine, egg, and vanilla in a mixing bowl; mix on low speed using the dough hook, just long enough to incorporate the ingredients.

2. Add the flour and hazelnuts and mix just until the dough is smooth.

3. Place the dough on a paper-lined sheet pan; press out as flat as possible so that the dough takes up less space and cools down quickly.

4. Cover and refrigerate.

Short Dough Cake Bottoms

one 10-inch (25-cm) cake bottom

9 ounces (255 g) Short Dough
    (page 54)

1. Work the Short Dough smooth with your hands, shaping it to a thick circle in the process.

2. Start to roll it out to 1/8 inch (3 mm) thick and slightly larger than the size you need. Sprinkle just enough bread flour on the board to keep it from sticking. Keep moving and turning the dough over as you roll it, first with your hands and then, as the dough gets thinner, by rolling it up on a dowel. Look closely at the dough as you roll it out. If only the edge of the dough is moving and not the middle, the middle is sticking to the table. Try to roll the dough into the general shape of what you plan to make. Trim off the ragged edge that always develops when the dough starts to get thin; this edge often tears away from the dough when you are picking it up or rolling it.

3. When the Short Dough is ¹/₈ inch (3 mm) thick, roll it up on a dowel (avoid using a rolling pin) and place on a sheet pan lined with baking paper.

4. Place a 10-inch (25-cm) cake ring or template on top of the Short Dough and cut around the outside edge; remove the leftover dough. If you cut the dough circle first and transfer it to the pan, you will probably stretch the dough as you move it, resulting in an oval rather than a circle.

5. Prick the dough lightly so that any trapped air can escape.

6. Bake at 375°F (190°C) for about 10 minutes.

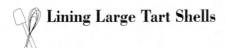 **Lining Large Tart Shells**

*Y*ou will need to start with 12 ounces (340 g) of Short Dough to line an 11-inch (27.5-cm) tart pan.

1. Prepare and roll the dough ¹/₈ inch (3 mm) thick as directed for Short Dough Cake Bottoms, making a circle about 2 inches (5 cm) larger than the tart pan.

2. Roll the dough up on a dowel (not a rolling pin), place the tart pan in front of the dough, and, working as quickly as possible, unroll the dough over the pan (Figure 2–14).

3. Pick up the edges of the dough all around to allow the dough to fall into the pan where the sides meet the bottom. Gently press the dough against the sides and bottom of the pan. Take care not to stretch the dough; it should still be ¹/₈ inch (3 mm) thick when you have finished.

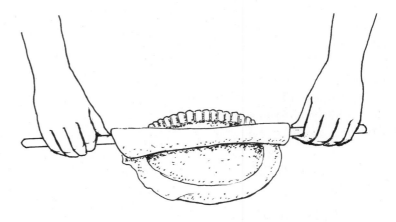

FIGURE 2–14   *Lining a large tart shell with Short Dough by rolling the dough sheet up on a dowel and unrolling it over the pan*

4. Roll your rolling pin over the top edge of the pan to trim away the excess dough.

5. Prick the dough lightly to be sure trapped air can escape.

If the tart shell is to be prebaked (baked blind), line the inside with a circle of baking paper and fill it with dried beans or pie weights; bake as indicated in the recipe. It is not necessary to use pie weights if it does not matter that sides will settle (not shrink) slightly as the crust bakes. The dough settles because it is so thin and the sides of the form are almost completely straight. Lining the forms with a thicker layer of dough will prevent settling, but a thicker crust detracts from the taste.

Lining Small Individual Forms

1. Prepare the dough and roll out as instructed for Short Dough Cake Bottoms, rolling the dough into a rectangle 1/8 inch (3 mm) thick. If you are lining forms that are very small, roll the dough slightly thinner so that there will be room in the forms for the filling.

2. Stagger the forms, 1 to 2 inches (2.5 to 5 cm) apart, in the approximate shape of the dough. The taller the forms, the more space you need to leave between them, so the dough will line the sides.

3. Roll the dough up on a dowel and unroll over the forms (Figure 2–15).

4. Push the forms together with your hands to create enough slack for the dough to fall into the forms without overstretching and breaking (Figure 2–16).

5. Dust the dough lightly with bread flour and, using a ball of dough about the same size as the inside of the forms, gently pound the dough in place (Figure 2–17).

FIGURE 2–15   The first step in lining small forms with Short Dough: rolling the dough up on a dowel and unrolling it over the forms

FIGURE 2–16   Pushing the forms together to make the dough fall into the forms

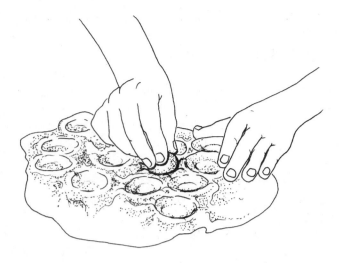

FIGURE 2–17   *Using the ball of dough to press the dough into place*

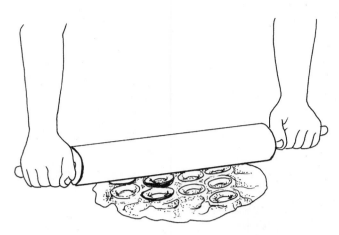

FIGURE 2–18   *Rolling over the top of the lined forms with a rolling pin to trim away the excess dough*

6. When all the air pockets are eliminated, roll the rolling pin over the forms to trim away the excess dough (Figure 2–18). (You can also press down on the forms with the palm of your hand to achieve the same result.)

7. Place the finished forms on a sheet pan. Bake as directed in the individual recipes.

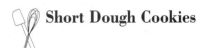

Short Dough Cookies

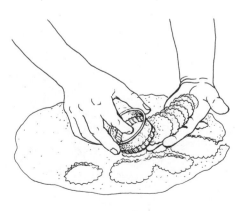

FIGURE 2–19   *Flipping Short Dough Cookies into the palm of the hand as they are cut*

1. Prepare and roll the dough as for Short Dough Cake Bottoms, rolling it into a rectangle ¹⁄₈ inch (3 mm) thick. Make sure the dough does not stick to the table.

2. Cut the cookies with a plain or fluted cutter, holding your other hand next to where you are cutting.

3. As you cut each cookie, flip the dough in one smooth motion into your waiting palm (Figure 2–19). Smaller cookies are the easiest to flip, but with a little practice this method works well with sizes up to 3¹⁄₂ inches (8.7 cm). If you are doing this for a living you simply have to learn this technique to save time.

4. When you have about six cookies in your hand, place them on a sheet pan lined with baking paper. Continue to cut the remaining cookies in the same manner. Stagger the cutting and the placing of the cookies for the least amount of wasted dough and space.

5. Bake the cookies at 375°F (190°C) until golden brown, 10 to 12 minutes depending on size.

Weaver's Dough

*8 pounds, 2 ounces
(3 kg, 695 g) dough*

¹/₄ cup (60 ml) vegetable oil
2 eggs
4 tablespoons (60 g) salt
2 ounces (55 g) granulated sugar
4¹/₂ cups (1 l, 80 ml) water
5 pounds, 12 ounces (2 kg, 615 g)
    bread flour, approximately
Egg Wash (page 7)

Like Salt Dough, Weaver's Dough is used to make ornaments and decorations. But, because Weaver's Dough has some elasticity, it is better suited to long pieces—in making a bread basket for example. Since the dough does not contain yeast, baked ornaments look exactly as you shaped them. For the same reason, the ornaments will be quite hard and not very appetizing and are intended for purely decorative purposes.

1. Add the oil, eggs, salt, and sugar to the water.

2. Incorporate all but a handful of the flour. Knead, using the dough hook for approximately 10 minutes, to make a smooth and elastic dough. Adjust with additional flour as needed.

3. Cover the dough and let it rest for about 1 hour before using. Weaver's Dough can be stored covered in the refrigerator for up to four days without deteriorating and can be kept frozen for months.

4. Shape as desired.

5. Before baking the ornaments, brush with Egg Wash (if you let the first layer dry and then brush a second time you will get the maximum amount of shine on the finished pieces).

6. Bake at 350°F (175°C) until the ornaments have a nice deep-golden color.

Whole-Wheat Weaver's Dough

6 pounds, 2 ounces (2 kg, 785 g) dough

¹/₂ ounce (15 g) fresh compressed
    yeast
1 quart (960 ml) cold water
¹/₂ ounce (15 g) malt sugar
    or
2 tablespoons (30 ml) honey
2 ounces (55 g) granulated sugar
2 tablespoons (30 g) salt
3 pounds, 8 ounces (1 kg, 590 g)
    finely ground whole-wheat flour
6 ounces (170 g) soft unsalted butter
Egg Wash (page 7)

This is another dough intended for ornaments and decorating pieces, but because it contains a small amount of yeast, the baked goods are soft enough to be pleasant to eat. Whole-Wheat Weaver's Dough is especially suitable for rolled, cutout, flat pieces. To make nice clean edges, place the rolled dough in the freezer for a few minutes to harden so that it won't drag as you cut it.

1. In a mixer bowl, dissolve the yeast in the water.

2. Add the malt sugar or honey, sugar, and salt.

3. Incorporate about half of the flour using the dough hook.

4. Add the soft butter, then the remaining flour.

5. Knead until you have a smooth, elastic dough, approximately 8 to 10 minutes. Adjust with additional flour as necessary. Do not overknead the dough because it will become too soft to work with.

6. Cover the dough and let rest for 1 hour in the refrigerator.

7. Punch the dough down and form as desired. If the pieces are to be eaten, allow them to proof (rise) in a warm, draft-free location until slightly less than doubled in volume.

8. Brush the pieces with Egg Wash and bake at 375°F (190°C) until they are golden brown.

🥄 Bread Basket

one basket measuring 15 inches long, 12 inches wide, and 15 inches high (37.5 × 30 × 37.5 cm)

one recipe Weaver's Dough (page 59)
Egg Wash (page 7)
one-half recipe Boiled Sugar Basic
    Recipe (page 936) (see note 4 here)

NOTE 1: If you do not have time to make a border, use the extra dough for two additional strings. Your basket will look just fine.

NOTE 2: Although the Weaver's Dough is very firm, the weight of the top strings tends to flatten and compress the bottom two or three strings as you weave the sides of the basket. To avoid this, place the basket in the freezer after weaving the first two strings long enough for them to firm up. Repeat after weaving two more, and so on. The strings are intentionally rolled out too short. By stretching them and making them stick to the dowels as you weave, they will remain in place. After they are baked, the dowels are easy to pull out because of the aluminum foil.

NOTE 3: Unfortunately, it is impossible to bake the basket handle standing up. Therefore, the side that is against the sheet pan will be flat after baking and is not very attractive. This is fine if the basket is to be displayed in a corner or against a wall, but it doesn't look good if visible from all sides. If this is the case, you can make two thinner handles and glue them together with sugar after baking to achieve a more three-dimensional effect. In steps 17 and 18, divide the 1-pound (455-g) pieces of dough into four pieces each. Roll the pieces out evenly to the same length given but braid the eight pieces into two braids following the instructions for Four-String Braid I instead (see page 80). Bake as directed, cool, then glue the flat sides of the two handles together with boiled sugar or Royal Icing. Attach the handle to the basket.

*T*his decorative woven Bread Basket is ideal for displaying freshly baked rolls or bread on a buffet table, in a shop window, or for a special occasion. This is a big project, but the result is something you can be proud of. It is a good idea to read through all of the instructions before you begin. For a simplified, less time-consuming version, see Simple Bread Basket, page 82.

Before you can make the basket you must make the guide that is used to weave the dough. While making the form does take a little work and requires some special equipment, once you have made it the form will last forever. These instructions will make a medium-sized oval basket with slanted sides. If you wish to make another design, keep in mind that you must have an even number of dowels, and they should be spaced approximately 1½ inches (3.7 cm) apart. If you want to keep the oval shape but would like to make a smaller or larger basket, modify the template to the size desired and increase or decrease the weight and thickness of the dough. If carpentry is not your favorite hobby (as it is mine) or you simply don't have the time or tools to make the form, bread basket forms are available from bakery suppliers.

1. Cut a 14 ½-by-9 ½-inch (36.2-×-23.7-cm) rectangle from ¾-inch (2-cm) particle board.

2. Copy and enlarge the template (Figure 2–20) to make a 12-by-8½-inch (30-×-21.2-cm) oval.

3. Center the drawing on top of the particle board and mark the position of the holes. Remove the paper.

4. Make a pilot hole using a small drill bit, then drill the holes using a ⁵/₁₆-inch (8-mm) drill bit, drilling the holes at a slight outward angle. If you do not have a drill guide to ensure the same angle for all twenty holes, cut a piece of wood to the proper angle and hold this in front of the drill bit. If you try to approximate the angle freehand, you are sure to end up with an uneven circumference in your finished basket.

5. Cut twenty ⁵/₁₆-inch (8-mm) wooden dowels to 6 inches (15 cm) in length.

6. Divide the Weaver's Dough as follows:
—Eight 7-ounce (200-g) pieces for the sides of the basket.
—One 12-ounce (340-g) piece for the bottom. (Form into an oval shape before refrigerating.)
—Two 1-pound (455-g) pieces for the handle.
—Two 10-ounce (285-g) pieces for the border (see note 1).
—Four 1-ounce (30-g) pieces for the dowels.
Leave the eight 7-ounce (200-g) pieces out to work with and refrigerate the remaining pieces covered.

7. Pound and roll each of the 7-ounce (200-g) pieces into strings using the technique described in Braided Bread (see pages 77–78 and Figures 3–3 to 3–5); do not use any flour as you are rolling. As the dough is (and must be) very firm and rubbery (glutenous), the strings can only be rolled out a little at a time, left to relax for a few minutes, then rolled and stretched a bit further. Work on the strings alternately

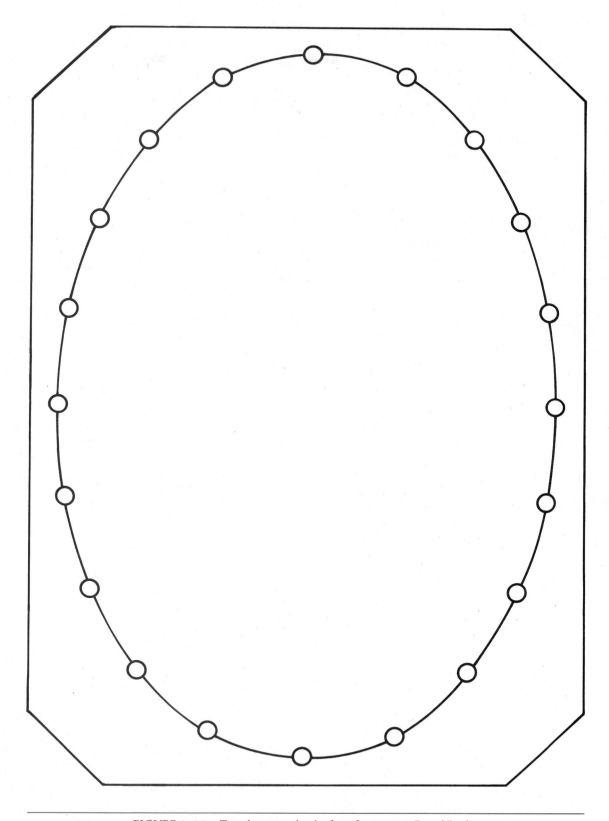

FIGURE 2–20   *Template to make the form for a woven Bread Basket*

NOTE 4: While the bread dough portion of the basket will last almost indefinitely without breaking down, the sugar glue will absorb moisture from the air and will soften and fall apart fairly quickly. To prevent this from occurring, spray or brush the basket with marzipan lacquer and store in an airtight plastic bag. The handle and border can alternatively be attached with royal icing. This will last forever like the bread dough, but the icing will take approximately 24 hours to harden completely. If time permits, this is the practical way of assembling the basket. Hold the handle in place while the icing dries by wrapping plastic wrap over the handle and securing it underneath the basket.

in this way, moistening the palm of your hand with water as needed to prevent the strings from sliding instead of rolling (have a plate with a small amount of water nearby to use as you are working). Keep the strings uniform in thickness and continue rolling until they are 3 feet (90 cm) long. Keep the strings covered with a damp towel during this process.

8. While you are rolling the strings and waiting for them to relax, cover the particle board base with aluminum foil. Press the foil on top of the holes so that you can see their location, then push the wooden dowels through the foil and into the holes. Cover the dowels with aluminum foil. Set the form aside.

9. Use some flour to prevent the dough from sticking and roll out the 12-ounce (340-g) piece of dough into an oval slightly larger than the base of the basket. Reserve covered in the refrigerator.

10. Weave the first string of dough in and out around the dowels on the foil (Figure 2–21). Weave a second string on top of the first, alternating the sequence in front of and behind the dowels. Stretch the strings slightly as you weave (see note 2). Add the remaining strings in the same manner, starting and finishing each of the strings staggered along one long side. Cut the strings to fit where the ends meet and press them together using a little Egg Wash as glue. Because the sides of the basket are slanted, you will have some extra dough left from the lower strings. However, making all of the strings the same length to begin with is the simplest way of ensuring that they all have the same thickness, and that the ones for the top (wider part) of the basket will be long enough. Adjust the strings as you weave them to be sure the height of the basket is even all around.

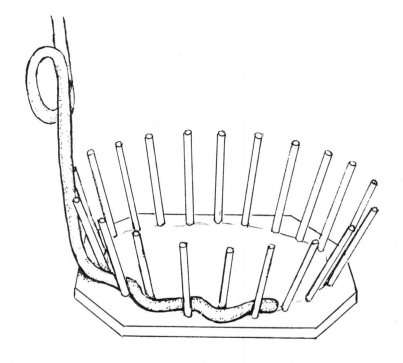

FIGURE 2–21   *Weaving the first dough string around the dowels on the form*

11. Brush Egg Wash over the bottom 1/2 inch (1.2 cm) of the strings inside of the basket. Place the reserved oval piece of dough inside the basket, stretching the dough slightly and pressing it against the Egg Wash. Prick the bottom of the basket thoroughly.

12. Brush Egg Wash on the inside base and on both the inside and outside of the basket. Place the particle board on a sheet pan.

13. Bake the basket at 350°F (175°C) until golden brown, approximately 1 hour and 30 minutes. Let the basket cool completely.

14. Remove the wooden dowels by twisting as you pull them out.

15. Cover the outside of the basket with aluminum foil. Remove from the particle board and place upside down on a sheet pan.

16. Return the basket to the oven and bake until the bottom is golden brown, approximately 30 minutes.

17. While the basket is baking, make the handle (see note 3): Roll each of the two 1-pound (455-g) pieces of dough to 7 feet (2 meters, 10 cm) long, using the same method used to roll the strings for the sides. If you do not have a table long enough to allow for the full length, loosely curl one end of the string as you are working on the other.

18. Braid the strings together in a Two-String Braid (see instructions on page 80). Since it would take a great deal of room to braid the strings at their full length, curl the ends loosely as needed as you place one on top of the other to form the X. The finished braid should be 36 inches (90 cm) long; stretch if necessary.

19. Place the braid on a sheet pan lined with baking paper and form it into a softly curved half-circle measuring 14 inches (35 cm) across the bottom. Bend the lower 5 inches (12.5 cm) of each side inward slightly to conform with the angle of the slanted sides of the basket (Figure 2–22).

20. Brush the handle with Egg Wash. Bake at 350°F (175°C) until golden brown, approximately 1 hour. It is important to bake the handle

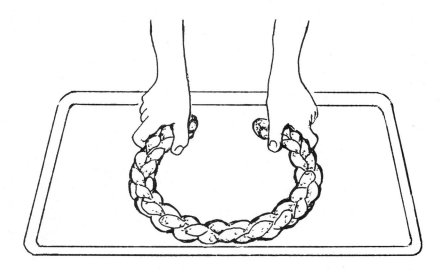

FIGURE 2–22   Bending the lower edges of the handle before baking to make the angle conform to the slanted sides of the Bread Basket

and the basket to the same color or the handle will not look as attractive on the finished basket. Let the handle cool.

21. To make the border: Using the same method as to braid the handle, roll out the two 10-ounce (285-g) pieces of dough to 8 feet (2 meters, 40 cm). Braid the pieces together in a Two-String Braid. Stretch the finished braid to 38 inches (95 cm) long (allow the dough to relax first as needed). Carefully transfer the braid to a sheet pan lined with baking paper and shape into an oval the same size as the top of the baked basket. Press the ends together using a little Egg Wash to make them stick.

22. Brush the oval with Egg Wash. Bake at 350°F (175°C) until golden brown, approximately 35 minutes. (Again, it is important to bake this piece to the same color as the handle and the basket.)

23. Roll each of the remaining four 1-ounce (30-g) pieces of dough to 25 inches (62.5 cm) long. These pieces must be perfectly even in diameter. Let the dough relax, then cut each rope into five 5-inch (12.5-cm) pieces. Place the pieces on a sheet pan lined with baking paper, keeping them perfectly straight.

24. Brush the dough with Egg Wash. Bake at 350°F (175°C) until golden brown, approximately 15 minutes. Let cool.

25. Using a serrated knife, trim both ends of the basket handle flat so they can sit against the bottom of the basket. The dough is very hard so this will take some patience. Trim the sides of the lower part of the handle as needed so they will fit snugly inside. If the handle does not fit correctly, warm it in the oven and then bend it to the proper angle. Plan

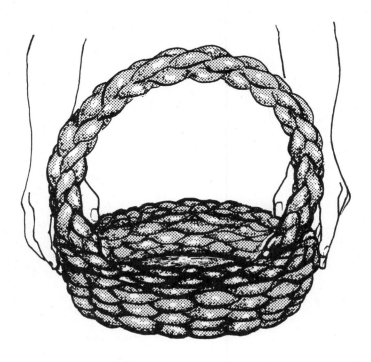

FIGURE 2–23   *Holding the handle in place at the proper angle until the sugar hardens*

to place the handle so that the flat side (the side that was against the sheet pan) is facing the side of the basket where the strings were joined.

26. Insert the bread dough dowels into the holes around the rim of the basket; you may need to trim them a bit using a file or coarse sandpaper.

27. Trim the top of the basket as necessary, using a serrated knife or file, so that the border will lie flat and even on top. Also trim the inside of the border if needed where the handle will be placed inside.

28. Follow the boiled sugar recipe, cooking the syrup to 310°F (155°C); do not add any acid. Let the syrup cool until it is thick enough to be applied with a metal spatula.

29. When the sugar has reached the proper consistency, spread a thin layer in four or five places on the bottom of the border. Immediately press the border in place, placing the seam in the border on the side of the basket where the strings meet.

30. Quickly and carefully apply sugar to the inside of the basket where the handle will sit and to the outside of the handle where it will touch the inside of the basket. Position the handle in the basket and press it into place (Figure 2–23). Hold the handle straight for a few minutes until the sugar is hard.

All that is required now is to bake some rolls and bread knots to fill up the basket. Tying a satin ribbon to the top of the basket handle adds a nice touch.

3

Breads and Rolls

History

The baking of bread dates back to the Stone Age, when people first learned to grind seeds, probably barley and millet, in mills made from stone. It was not a great step from the first porridge to bread. Early bread, heavy and unleavened, was cooked on heated stones (it was not called the Stone Age for nothing). Over the centuries the process of milling the grain was improved. The early Egyptians, with the aid of wind-powered fans and sieves, developed a way to remove parts of the chaff and bran. The Romans and Greeks further advanced cultivation and milling methods and produced different kinds of flour in various stages of refinement.

Baking bread has always had an important place in the European home. Different regions of various countries produce breads that differ not only in

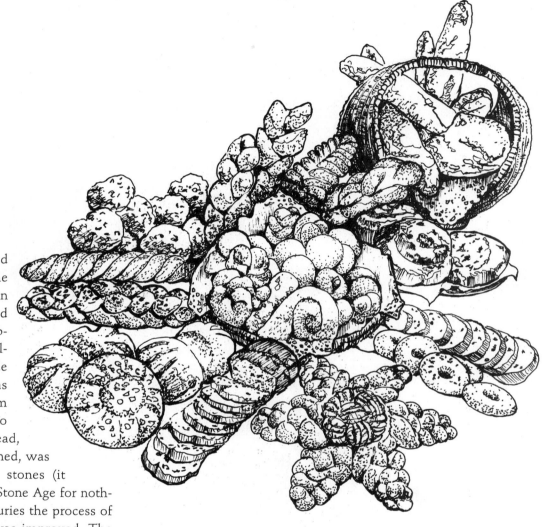

flavor but also in shape. Although today most bread baking is commercial, it is still a favorite hobby of many.

Basically, there are three types of bread products: loaf bread in many shapes; breakfast items, such as Croissant and Danish; and soft cakes such as muffins and doughnuts. Some of these are leavened with baking powder or soda, but most are leavened with yeast.

Effects of Ingredients

Baking with yeast demands that the ingredients be in proper proportion. Yeast needs sugar to grow, but too much sugar can slow the process to the point where it stops altogether. Sugar also colors and flavors the bread. Salt is used in a yeast dough to add color and flavor and to retard the yeast just a little. When I see a loaf of baked bread that is pale instead of a healthy brown color, I know that the loaf was either baked at too low a temperature or that the salt was left out.

Yeast

Yeast fermentation is damaged in temperatures above 115°F (46°C), and the yeast is killed at 140°F (60°C). At the other end of the scale, yeast fermentation is slowed but not damaged at temperatures below 65°F (19°C) and is nonexistent at 40°F (4°C) or lower. In certain types of yeast dough, such as for Danish pastry, Braided White Bread, and Croissant, it is essential that the yeast be kept cold to prevent fermentation while the dough is being shaped.

The easiest bread to make is plain white bread that has all white glutenous flour and only the amount of sugar that is healthy for the yeast. White bread can therefore be made with cold milk, which slows the fermentation long enough to allow time to braid the dough into various shapes. In a bread with a higher proportion of sugar, with a sweet flour such as rye, or with flours that have little or no gluten structure, such as whole wheat, it is very important to keep the dough from getting too cold.

Rising Temperature

The ideal temperature for the yeast to develop is from 78–82°F (25–27°C) with 85 percent humidity. The dough should be kept as close to this temperature as possible by starting with a warm liquid, 105–115°F (40–46°C). However, if the liquid is too hot, the yeast will be damaged or killed. Use a thermometer until you know your judgment is accurate. Take care to keep the dough covered and away from drafts at all times.

Sponge Method

There are two methods of fermenting the yeast (the pre-dough method is listed as a third, but it is basically the same as the sponge). In the sponge method a very soft dough is made using a small amount of flour, water, sugar (although sugar is not necessary if milk is used because milk is naturally sweet), and, most of the time, all of the yeast. This "sponge" rises in a warm place, covered, until it has doubled in volume. The sponge is then mixed with all of the remaining ingredients to make the dough. This method allows the yeast to ferment in peace and develop strength, without interference from other ingredients. The flavor from the alcohol (produced by the fermented yeast) also becomes stronger during the longer time period. In breads with a high sugar content, such as Swedish Orange Rye or the Italian Triestine Bread, the sponge method is essential for a satisfactory result.

Straight-Dough Method

In the straight-dough method, all of the ingredients are mixed together at the beginning and, in most cases, are kneaded to form a gluten structure. The dough is then given one or two periods to rise before being punched down for the last time and made into loaves or rolls.

Pre-Dough Method

A pre-dough is used for primarily the same reasons as the sponge method, but the pre-dough is intentionally made firmer to allow the dough a longer time in which to develop flavor (which comes from the acids and alcohol produced during the rising period) and to soften the gluten, giving the final product increased volume. To make the pre-dough, a small percentage of the yeast is mixed with water and flour to form a stiff, smooth dough. The firmness of the dough will depend on the planned length of time for the rising period and the conditions of where it is left to rise: the stiffer the dough, the longer it will take for the yeast to leaven it. The mixture is then covered and left to rise for 12 to 24 hours before proceeding with the recipe.

Danish Pastry and Croissant Doughs

Danish pastry and Croissant depend on thin layers of butter or margarine to "help" the yeast. The fat particles produce steam when the Danish or Croissant are baked, and that, together with the trapped air and the yeast, gives them their light, flaky consistency.

Proofing

Most bread doughs should rise to double in volume, but this includes the rising that will occur in the oven before the bread reaches 140°F (60°C), when the yeast is killed. Therefore, prior to baking, the bread should rise to just before it has doubled in volume, to allow for the final rise in the oven (there are some exceptions in individual recipes). Test by pressing the dough lightly with your fingertip: a slight indentation should remain. A loaf that has risen too much is very crumbly, dries out faster because of the extra air, and has less flavor because the flavor does not increase with the dough's volume. On the other hand, if the bread is not allowed to rise long enough, the gluten will not have formed all the elasticity it needs to expand and, as a result, the loaf will crack (usually on the side) and will be compact and heavy. Not enough rising time for Danish pastry and Croissant will cause some of the butter to run out onto the pan simply because there is not enough dough volume to absorb it as it melts. This results in a drier and heavier pastry. Last, but certainly not least, it is very important that the proof box (the box where the yeast ferments in a dough in industrial baking) or other rising area is not too hot. Ideally it should be about 80°F (26°C) with 85 percent humidity.

Forming Freestanding Loaves of Bread

To make round or oval loaves of bread, put the required weight of dough on the table in front of you and cup your hand around it. Using primarily the section of your palm at the base of the thumb, knead and move the dough around counterclockwise as you lift one section at a time from the outside, and press it down in the center, forming a tight skin around the dough (Figure 3–1). When you have worked all the way around the circle a few times and the dough is tight, gradually turn it upside-down using the same movements, so that the seam is now on the bottom. Hold the side of your hand against the table and form the loaf round or oval as desired (Figure 3–2). You can form two loaves of bread simultaneously by working a second piece of dough with your other hand in the same way, moving this one clockwise so that the two loaves press up against each other in the center. This is same technique that is used to form and tighten the skin around individual rolls but here the kneading motion is reversed: With rolls, the kneading motion moves clockwise with your right hand and counterclockwise with your left (both hands moving to the outside). With loaves it is the opposite: your hands move in circles toward the center and each other.

Shaping Loaves for Bread Pans

Forming loaves which are to be baked in bread pans is a little different (and much easier) than forming freestanding loaves since the pan helps

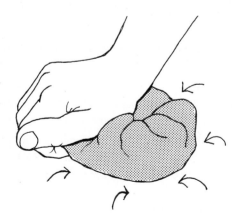

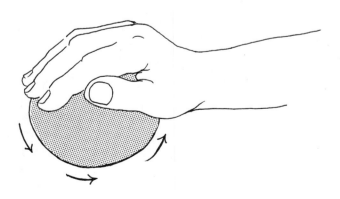

FIGURE 3–1   *Forming a tight skin around the bread dough by lifting the outer edges and pressing them into the center with the palm of the hand*

FIGURE 3–2   *Forming the loaf into a round or oval shape using the palm of the hand, after the dough has been turned seam-side down*

to develop the shape during proofing and baking. To form loaves for baking in pans, start by punching each piece down to flatten it using the heels of both hands. Tuck in stray end pieces and roll the dough against the table to form a tight wrinkle-free cylinder. At the same time stretch the loaf if necessary to make it the same length as the pan. Place seam-side down in the prepared pan.

Slashing

Slashes are cut on the top of breads and rolls before baking, not simply for appearance, but as an aid to relieve pressure. During the oven-spring the product increases in volume at a greatly accelerated speed, which can cause the surface to break or crack at any weak point. By slashing the skin into decorative patterns these points become prede-termined and the expansion is uniform and controlled. In most cases, the cuts should be made just under the skin of the loaf and not deep toward the center. The slashes can be made with small serrated knives made especially for this purpose, or a razor blade works fine as well. Bread will occasionally develop cracks around the base in spite of the fact that the top has been slashed. As stated previously, this is generally related to the bread not having proofed long enough.

The Baking Process

The baking of bread (and of most other yeast-leavened products) is a three-stage process that ultimately transforms the raw dough into a pleasant-to-eat, digestible product. The first part of this process is the rapid rise that takes place when the partially proofed loaf (referred to in this text as slightly less than doubled in volume) is placed into a hot oven, typically 375–425°F (190–219°C). This expansion occurs during the first five minutes or so of baking and stops when the interior of the loaf has reached about 140°F (60°C) and all of the yeast cells are dead. This first stage is commonly referred to as the oven-spring. Because this phenomenon cannot be altered or eliminated it must be anticipated and is the reason that the loaf is only allowed to expand partially dur-ing the proofing stage. The oven-spring is caused by a temporary increase in the production of carbon dioxide as well as the rapid expan-sion of the carbon dioxide that was created during the proofing process.

The baking temperature is an important consideration which must be selected to balance the effects of two different processes taking place within the dough at almost the same time: the expansion of gas cells previously discussed, and the gelatinization of the starch and coagulation of the gluten. If the oven temperature is too low the gas cells, and therefore the loaf, will expand before the gluten and starch are set. Without the necessary structure this loaf will fall. Too high a temperature will cause the outer crust to form prematurely and prevent maximum expansion. As a general rule, doughs with a higher sugar content must be baked at a lower temperature or the surface may become too brown before the interior has gelatinized. In stage two the interior of the loaf reaches its maximum temperature of 212°F (100°C); due to the evaporation of moisture and alcohol this internal temperature is not exceeded, and the starches and gluten complete their coagulations. The coagulating process begins at 140°F (60°C) in the case of the starches and 160°F (71°C) for the proteins and continues until the bread is fully baked. In the final third stage, the crust formed from starch and sugar on the surface of the dough becomes brown due to a chemical reaction. To obtain a surface crust that has a glossy shine in addition to a pleasant color, Egg Wash is applied before baking or moisture is added during the initial phase of the baking process. The starch on the surface, in conjunction with the applied moisture (steam), becomes gelatinized into a glossy thin coat.

When baked loaves of bread are removed from the oven, the composition throughout is far from homogenous: The outside is dry, brown, and close to the temperature of the oven, while the interior is moist and even sticky, and the temperature is about half that of the outside. As moisture from the interior of the loaf escapes, and the room temperature cools the outside, the difference in temperature begins to stabilize, and simultaneously the starches begin to solidify. This is why it is not possible to cut into a loaf of bread to check for doneness, but instead one must rely on feel and the customary method of tapping the bread sharply on the bottom to check for a hollow sound.

Pan breads should be unmolded at once after they are removed from the oven and placed on a cooling rack to allow air to circulate around all sides as they cool. The loaves are still exhausting their moisture as they finish the baking process. If left in the pans the moisture will have nowhere to go, which will result in a wet surface on the loaf.

Baking with Steam

Some of the recipes in this chapter give baking instructions for ovens with steam injectors. Steam creates a moist environment that prevents the dough from forming a crust too soon. After a specified length of time a damper is opened to let the steam out, and the bread finishes baking. The resulting crust is much thinner and crisper, fragile enough to crack and break. The steam also produces a glossy surface. As explained in the baking process, there is sugar present in any bread dough. The moisture from the steam mixes with the sugar on the surface of the dough, which then caramelizes as it bakes. For this reason breads and rolls that are baked with steam need not, and should not, be brushed with Egg Wash. It takes some experimenting with a steam oven to determine the proper length of time for the steam period. If too much steam is used, almost no crust will form at all. If the steam is not left in the oven long enough, you will not achieve the desired effect either. The trick is to use exactly enough steam, for the correct length of time, in combination with the proper temperature, so that the crust that begins to form after the steam is vented out is thick enough to stay crusty and dry after the bread has been removed from the oven but is not so thick that it will not crack from the sudden change in temperature.

Creating Steam without Steam Injectors

If your oven is not equipped with steam injectors, you can keep the bread moist for the prescribed length of time by quickly opening the oven door every 1 or 2 minutes during this period and spraying water into the oven and/or on the bread using a spray bottle. Start baking the loaves at a higher temperature in this case to compensate for the heat lost as you open the door. An alternative method is to place a pan containing four or five ice cubes in the oven and add ice cubes, a few at a time, to create steam during the initial baking period. After the length of time specified in the individual recipe, remove the pan and continue baking as directed.

Staling and Storage

Our common sense might lead us to believe that bread will start to become stale as soon as it has cooled. This is not so; unfortunately, the process is already at work even before the starch has solidified to the point that the bread can be sliced! Exactly how and why bread and other baked goods become stale has been studied by researchers for ages. One study showed that even if bread is hermetically sealed it will still lose moisture (become stale). The crust becomes stale at a different rate than the interior: as moisture from the body of the loaf moves outward it transforms the dry crust into a chewy, leathery and tough skin, far from the crisp texture it had when freshly baked. The interior, or body, of the bread will become dry at a slower rate as it is protected by the crust. If the staling process has not progressed too far, it can be remedied temporarily by reheating the loaf, which will make the body soft and pleasant to eat; the crust, however, will remain tough.

Baked bread is best preserved by freezing. The bread should be properly wrapped and placed in the freezer as soon as possible once it has cooled. Bread that is not to be frozen should be stored wrapped at room temperature. Baked loaves should not be stored in the refrigerator. Wrapped or not, refrigerating the bread will actually expedite the staling process up to six times.

Reducing Staling

Specially formulated emulsifying agents which act as preservatives have been added to bread made by commercial bakers for years. The use of malt sugar or syrup, as well as milk powder and soybean oil, have all been found to retard the staling process. Increasing the fat content is also beneficial but is not possible with certain types of bread. Durham or other high gluten flours will aid in absorbing a larger percentage of moisture during the kneading process, which in turn produces a loaf which will stay moist longer. Lastly, correct proofing is essential: bread that was overproofed or left to dry and form a skin will get "old" much faster than properly fermented and cared-for bread.

If you keep to all of these rules and guidelines, I can assure you that you will be very satisfied with the results of the following recipes.

 # Baguettes

five 13-ounce (370-g) loaves

1¹/₂ ounces (40 g) fresh compressed yeast

3 cups (720 ml) warm water (105–115°F, 40–46°C)

4 teaspoons (20 g) salt

2 ounces (55 g) malt sugar
   or
¹/₃ cup (80 ml) or 4 ounces (115 g) honey

2 pounds, 7 ounces (1 kg, 110 g) bread flour, approximately

cornmeal

One-Half Recipe

three 11-ounce (310-g) loaves

³/₄ ounce (22 g) fresh compressed yeast

1¹/₂ cups (360 ml) warm water (105–115°F, 40–46°C)

2 teaspoons (10 g) salt

1 ounce (30 g) malt sugar
   or
3 tablespoons (45 ml) or 2 ounces (55 g) honey

1 pound, 6 ounces (625 g) bread flour, approximately

cornmeal

NOTE: If your oven is not equipped with steam injectors, see Creating Steam without Steam Injectors, page 73.

*T*he word baguette *literally translates to a "small rod"; however, most people today would immediately identify it as a French type of white bread. Baguettes are far and away the most popular bread in France—or in any other French-speaking country for that matter—currently, about 25 million Baguettes are sold there each day. Baguette loaves are long, thin, and crusty, usually weighing between 10 ounces and 1 pound. Although we certainly make wonderful Baguettes in this country, in my opinion there is nothing here that measures up to what you get in France. When I travel there, a Baguette is always one of the first things I buy after crossing the border. If I am able to buy one freshly baked first thing in the morning at the local* boulangerie *(it seems that even the smallest village in France has a church, a city hall, a* pâtisserie, *and a* boulangerie*), I need nothing else for breakfast but a good cup of coffee.*

As a perfect example of how seriously the French take their Baguettes, a new decree was issued in 1993 that calls for specific labeling of all Baguette loaves sold. A 1912 law states that Baguettes must contain nothing other than flour, water, salt, and yeast. The new decree takes things a step further and states that if the bread is kneaded and baked on the seller's premises it shall be labeled "pain maison" (homemade bread). If it is labeled "de tradition française" (traditional French), this means that no additives were used and the dough was never frozen; however, it may be baked in one location and sold in another.

When you make the smaller (one-half) recipe, follow the instructions as given but scale the dough into 11-ounce (310-g) pieces and roll each piece to 20 inches (50 cm) in length.

1. Dissolve the yeast in the warm water in a mixer bowl. Stir in the salt, malt sugar or honey, and enough of the bread flour to make a fairly firm dough. Knead, using the dough hook at medium speed, until the dough is smooth and elastic. Place the dough in an oiled bowl, turn to coat both sides with oil, cover, and let rise until it has doubled in volume.

2. Punch down the dough. Scale the dough into 13-ounce (370-g) pieces. Roll and pound each piece into a 23-inch (57.5-cm) baguette, using the same method as for forming bread strings (see Figures 3–3, 3–4, and 3–5, pages 77 and 78).

3. Place the baguettes on a sheet pan lined with baking paper. Dust the top of the loaves heavily with cornmeal. Let rise until slightly less than doubled in volume.

4. With a razor blade or a very sharp knife cut deep slits, 4 to 5 inches (10 to 12.5 cm) long, approximately 3 inches (7.5 cm) apart at a sharp angle, on top of each baguette.

5. Bake at 400°F (205°C) with steam, leaving the damper closed for the first 10 minutes. Open the damper and continue to bake approximately 20 minutes longer or until the loaves are golden brown and feel light. Cool on racks. Freeze the loaves if they will not be served the same day.

Black Forest Bread

four 1-pound, 14-ounce (855-g) loaves

10 ounces (285 g) dried cherries (see introduction)

1 cup (240 ml) apple cider

2 ounces (55 g) fresh compressed yeast

3½ cups (840 ml) warm coffee (105–115°F, 40–46°C) (see note 1)

2 tablespoons plus 2 teaspoons (40 g) salt

½ cup (120 ml) or 6 ounces (170 g) molasses

4 eggs

4 ounces (115 g) unsweetened cocoa powder

1 pound, 12 ounces (795 g) high-gluten flour

5 ounces (140 g) whole wheat flour

5 ounces (140 g) pumpernickel flour

5 ounces (140 g) multigrain cereal flour (see note 2)

3 ounces (85 g) cornmeal

¾ cup (180 ml) vegetable oil

1 pound (455 g) high-gluten flour, approximately

Small Recipe

two 1-pound, 8-ounce (680-g) loaves

4 ounces (115 g) dried cherries (see introduction)

½ cup (120 ml) apple cider

1½ ounces (40 g) fresh compressed yeast

1½ cups (360 ml) warm coffee (105–115°F, 40–46°C) (see note 1)

*T*his wholesome multigrain bread takes a little longer to knead than most breads. Also, you may find it difficult to judge when the loaves are baked through since the bread dough is so dark to begin with. If, after removing the loaves from the pans, you find that the bread is still soft on the sides and/or bottom, place the loaves directly on a sheet pan and put them back in the oven for 5 to 10 minutes. If necessary, cover the tops of the loaves with a sheet of baking paper or foil to keep them from getting overbaked. Black Forest Bread can also be made into freestanding loaves (baked without using bread pans). Make a firmer dough in that case to support the shape of the loaves until the crust has formed.

The type of dried cherries I like to use in this bread are the European Montmorency variety, which have a distinctive tart flavor. Unfortunately, I have trouble getting them from the suppliers from time to time. The dried cherries I have found to be readily available commercially are the sweeter variety. These taste and even look like miniature prunes and since they are about three times more expensive than prunes, you might as well just go ahead and use prunes cut into smaller pieces, or try substituting dried cranberries which taste good and are easy to come by.

1. Combine the dried cherries and apple cider and set aside for 30 minutes to soften and plump the cherries. Strain, reserving the cider and cherries separately.

2. Dissolve the yeast in the warm coffee. Add the salt, molasses, reserved apple cider, and the eggs.

3. Thoroughly combine the unsweetened cocoa powder and the first measurement of high-gluten flour. Add to the coffee mixture.

4. Using the dough hook at medium speed, mix in the whole wheat flour, pumpernickel flour, multigrain flour, and the cornmeal. Add the vegetable oil and mix until incorporated.

5. Reserve a few handfuls of the remaining high-gluten flour, then add the rest to the dough. Once it is incorporated, turn to medium speed and knead for about 12 minutes. The dough should be smooth, quite soft, and elastic. Adjust by adding the reserved flour as necessary while kneading (see introduction).

6. Place the dough in an oiled bowl and turn to coat it completely with oil. Cover and let rise in a warm place until doubled in volume.

1 tablespoon (15 g) salt

¼ cup (60 ml) or 3 ounces (85 g)
   molasses

1 egg

1½ ounces (40 g) unsweetened cocoa
   powder

10 ounces (285 g) high-gluten flour

2 ounces (55 g) whole wheat flour

2 ounces (55 g) pumpernickel flour

2 ounces (55 g) multigrain cereal flour
   (see note 2)

1 ounce (30 g) cornmeal

¼ cup (60 ml) vegetable oil

6 ounces (170 g) high-gluten flour,
   approximately

*NOTE 1: It is not necessary to use freshly
brewed coffee in the dough. This is a good way
to utilize leftover coffee (regular or decaf is fine)
that would otherwise be wasted.*

*NOTE 2: This is a special flour containing a
mixture of whole grains. It is often found in
health-food stores. If it is not available, substitute an additional 2½ ounces (70 g) each of
pumpernickel flour and whole wheat flour (1
ounce/30 g each for the small recipe).*

*NOTE 3: For freestanding loaves see Figures
3–1 and 3–2, page 70.*

Braided White Bread

six 18-ounce (510-g) loaves

4 ounces (115 g) fresh compressed
   yeast

1 quart (960 ml) cold milk

2 pounds (910 g) bread flour

2 pounds (910 g) cake flour

3 tablespoons (45 g) salt

4 ounces (115 g) granulated sugar

8 ounces (225 g) soft unsalted butter

Egg Wash (page 7)

poppy or sesame seeds (optional)

7. Knead the reserved cherries into the dough by hand. Let rise again until doubled in volume.

8. Scale the dough into four 1-pound, 14-ounce (855-g) pieces (two 1-pound, 8-ounce/680-g pieces for the small recipe). Form the pieces into rectangular loaves as described in Shaping Loaves for Bread Pans, page 70 (see note 3 here).

9. Place the loaves in oiled bread pans measuring approximately 10 inches long by 4 ½ inches wide and 3 inches tall (25 × 11.2 × 7.5 cm). Let rise until slightly less than doubled in volume.

10. Make three slashes lengthwise in the center of each loaf.

11. Bake at 350°F (175°C) with steam, leaving the damper closed for the first 10 minutes. Open the damper and continue to bake approximately 30 minutes longer, or until baked through. Take the bread out of the pans as soon as possible to prevent the sides and bottom from becoming soggy from trapped moisture. Finish cooling on racks.

*B*raided breads are found all over continental Europe, especially in Germany and Switzerland. There, you can find some version in virtually every bakery and in many pastry shops as well, even those that do not necessarily specialize in bread. These shops usually make a small quantity just to look (and smell) good on display—a form of advertising, you might say. The braids you find most often are the two-string, four-string, and five-string, since they are quick and easy to make but appear just the opposite.

Basically, any firm bread dough that can be made with a cold liquid can be used for braiding. The following recipe is a firmer version of the dough for Milk Rolls and is also used to make Knots; see page 135. Egg Bread and Challah are the types of doughs most commonly used, but try braiding Butter-Wheat or Honey-Wheat as well. For an unusual effect, combine strings of white and wheat breads in the same loaf.

1. Dissolve the yeast in the milk. Add both flours, salt, and the sugar. Mix using the dough hook until the dough forms a ball. Incorporate the butter.

One-Half Recipe

three 18-ounce (510-g) loaves

2 ounces (55 g) fresh compressed
    yeast
1 pint (480 ml) cold milk
1 pound (455 g) bread flour
1 pound (455 g) cake flour
1½ tablespoons (22 g) salt
2 ounces (55 g) granulated sugar
4 ounces (115 g) soft unsalted butter
Egg Wash (page 7)
poppy or sesame seeds (optional)

Instructions for Braided Loaves

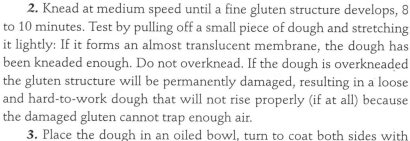

NOTE: Try this for a very pretty and appetizing effect: Egg wash and proof the braids a little less than specified. Egg wash the braids a second time and then place the sheet pan in the freezer long enough for the loaves to become firm on the outside, 15–20 minutes. Bake directly from the freezer. The temperature change from the freezer to the hot oven, combined with the under-proofing, makes the bread develop more oven-spring. This shows up between the strings as a lighter-colored area (without Egg Wash) and gives the pattern more definition.

2. Knead at medium speed until a fine gluten structure develops, 8 to 10 minutes. Test by pulling off a small piece of dough and stretching it lightly: If it forms an almost translucent membrane, the dough has been kneaded enough. Do not overknead. If the dough is overkneaded the gluten structure will be permanently damaged, resulting in a loose and hard-to-work dough that will not rise properly (if at all) because the damaged gluten cannot trap enough air.

3. Place the dough in an oiled bowl, turn to coat both sides with oil, cover, and let rise until doubled in volume.

1. Punch down the dough and divide it into pieces for braiding. The total weight of each braided loaf should be about 18 ounces (510 g). The weight and length of the pieces depend on how many strings are used. For example, if you want three strings per braid, make each piece 6 ounces (170 g); if you want six strings, make each piece 3 ounces (85 g). The length of the strings must be increased as the number of strings used is increased to compensate for the greater number of turns and complexity. Weights and lengths of the strings for each braid are specified in the instructions that follow. Keep the pieces covered to prevent a skin from forming.

2. Form the pieces into strings by repeatedly folding the dough and pounding with the heel of your hand to remove any air bubbles or pockets (Figures 3–3 and 3–4). Then gently roll the string between

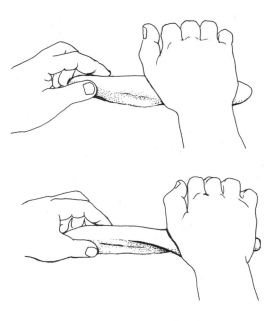

FIGURES 3–3 and 3–4   Forming the dough strings by folding and pounding with the palm of the hand

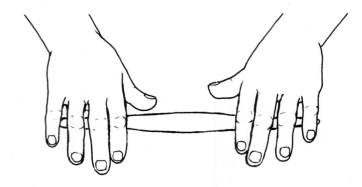

FIGURE 3–5   *Rolling the dough string against the table to create the desired length*

your hands and the table until you have reached the desired length (Figure 3–5).

3. Pound and roll enough pieces for one loaf into tapered strings, thicker at the centers and thinner on the ends. (In most cases it is possible to use strings of a uniform thickness, instead of tapered strings, if you prefer, except when the instructions specify tapered strings). It is better not to roll all the dough into strings at once but to braid each loaf after rolling out one set of strings.

4. Lay the strings in front of you and join them at the top (or for the braids that allow you to do so, it is preferable to start braiding in the center and then turn the loaf 180° to braid the other side). Braid according to the instructions that follow. Take care not to braid too tightly, and try not to stretch the strings any more than is necessary. This is usually a problem only if the dough has been overkneaded.

5. In following the numbers in the instructions for the different braids, count from left to right; when you move string number 1 in a five-string braid over numbers 2 and 3, number 1 becomes number 3 and number 2 becomes number 1 (Figure 3–6). In Figure 3–7, number 5 is being moved over numbers 4 and 3; number 5 becomes number 3, and number 4 becomes number 5. Doing it is not as complicated as reading about it—give it a try!

6. As you come to the end of the braid, pinch the strings together and tuck underneath. When making a braided loaf with a large number of strings it is often necessary to stop braiding before reaching the end because some of the strings may become too short to be usable. If this is the case, trim all of the remaining strings even and tuck the pieces underneath.

7. Place the braided loaves four to a sheet pan. If they have shrunk during the braiding, which will happen in a six- or eight-string braid, gently stretch them to about 14 inches (35 cm) as you put them on the pan. This will give you more attractive, uniform loaves.

8. Brush the loaves with Egg Wash, and let rise until slightly less than doubled in volume (see note). For extra shine, brush the braids

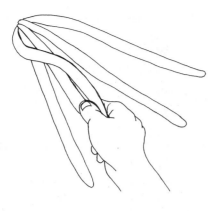

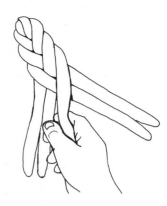

FIGURE 3–6   *Moving string number 1 over string number 2 and string number 3*

FIGURE 3–7   *Moving string number 5 over string number 4 and string number 3*

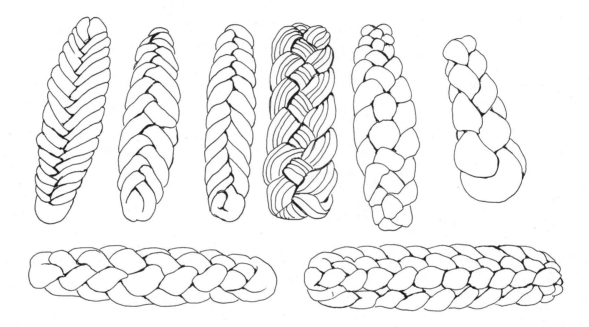

FIGURE 3–8   *The braided breads before baking. Top row from left to right: Seven-String Braid, Five-String Braid, Three-String Braid, a loaf made using the method for forming the center of the Star Braid, Four-String Braid II, and Two-String Braid. Bottom row: Six-String Braid on the left and Eight-String Braid on the right*

with Egg Wash again prior to baking. Sprinkle with poppy or sesame seeds if desired. Figure 3–8 shows some braided breads before baking.

9. Bake at 400°F (205°C) for about 25 minutes. Cool on racks.

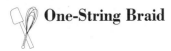 **One-String Braid**

*R*efer to the technique shown for Double-Knots, Figure 3–35, page 136. Because the string used for the One-String Braid is much larger, the loop will be much bigger than shown in the roll illustration, and the twisting motion is repeated several times to make the loaf. These instructions will produce a 12-inch (30-cm) loaf; however, this method can be used with a string as small as a *few inches (as is done to make the Double-Knot roll) up to many feet to produce a wreath, for example.*

1. Weigh the dough into 1-pound, 2-ounce (510-g) pieces.

2. Pound and roll the pieces out to make 28-inch (70-cm) strings that are tapered at both ends.

3. Place one string in front of you vertically.

4. Pick up the end closest to you and, forming a loop to the right, cross it over the top of the string just below the tip, so that one-third of the length is now in a straight line pointing to the left (the loop and the straight piece should be the same length).

5. In one continuous motion, twist the bottom of the loop one-half turn to the right and tuck the opposite end underneath and up through the opening.

6. Twist the bottom of the loop one-half turn to the left and tuck the opposite end underneath and up through the opening.

7. Repeat steps 5 and 6 until the braid is finished.

Two-String Braid

1. Weigh the dough into two 9-ounce (255-g) pieces.

2. Pound and roll the pieces out to make 20-inch (50-cm) strings that are tapered at both ends.

3. Place the strings in a wide X shape in front of you.

4. Pick up the two ends of the bottom string, and move the two ends straight across the other string so they change sides but do not cross over each other.

5. Repeat the procedure with the other string, and continue the sequence until the braid is finished.

Three-String Braid

NOTE: I find it much easier to start this braid in the center, braid the bottom half first, and then flip the loaf over to braid the other half. With any of the braids that use an odd number of strings it is possible to either flip the loaf over in this manner or simply turn the loaf around keeping it right-side up. There is no difference in the outcome.

1. Weigh the dough into three 6-ounce (170-g) pieces.

2. Pound and roll out to make 12-inch (30-cm) strings.

3. Braid 1 over 2. Braid 3 over 2.

4. Repeat braiding sequence.

Four-String Braid I

1. Weigh the dough into four 4½-ounce (130-g) pieces.

2. Pound and roll out to make 12-inch (30-cm) strings.

3. Braid 2 over 3.

4. Braid 4 over 3 and 2.

5. Braid 1 over 2 and 3.

6. Repeat braiding sequence.

Four-String Braid II

1. Weigh the dough into four 4½-ounce (130-g) pieces.

2. Pound and roll out to make 12-inch (30-cm) strings.

3. Line the strings up next to one another and start braiding in the center, working toward you.

4. Braid 4 over 3

5. Braid 2 over 3.

6. Braid 1 under 2.

7. Repeat braiding sequence.

8. Squeeze the ends pieces together and tuck underneath. Turn the braid around on its own axis (keeping it right-side up) and repeat the braiding sequence to braid the other half.

 ### Four-String Braid III

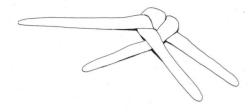

FIGURE 3–9   *The completed fourth step in the Four-String Braid III*

This variation gives you the same pattern as the Four-String Braid I but uses the technique of the Two-String Braid.

1. Weigh the dough into two 9-ounce (255-g) pieces.

2. Pound and roll out to make 24-inch (60-cm) strings that are tapered on both ends.

3. Place the strings in front of you in a + shape with the vertical string underneath the horizontal string. Fold the top vertical string down and place it to the right of the bottom vertical string.

4. Braid 4 (the right horizontal string) over 3 and under 2 (Figure 3–9).

5. Braid 1 under 2.

6. Repeat braiding sequence.

 ### Five-String Braid

1. Weigh the dough into five 3½-ounce (100-g) pieces.

2. Pound and roll out to make 12-inch (30-cm) strings.

3. Braid 2 over 3.

4. Braid 5 over 4, 3, and 2.

5. Braid 1 over 2 and 3.

6. Repeat braiding sequence.

7. When the braid is finished, roll the whole loaf one-quarter turn to the left (on its side) before proofing and baking.

 ### Six-String Braid

1. Weigh the dough into six 3-ounce (85-g) pieces.

2. Pound and roll out to make 14-inch (35-cm) strings.

3. Braid 1 over 2, 3, 4, 5, and 6.

4. Braid 5 over 4, 3, 2, and 1.

5. Braid 2 over 3, 4, 5, and 6.

6. Braid 5 over 4, 3, 2, and 1.

7. Braid 2 over 3 and 4.

8. Repeat from step 4.

 ### Seven-String Braid

NOTE: As with the Three-String and Four-String Braids, the Seven-String Braid not only

1. Weigh the dough into seven 2½-ounce (70-g) pieces.

2. Pound and roll out to make 14-inch (35-cm) strings.

3. Braid 7 over 6, 5, and 4.

4. Braid 1 over 2, 3, and 4.

looks better but is easier to produce if you start braiding from the center. After you braid the first half and flip the loaf over, it is necessary to gently unfold the remaining strings before braiding the second half.

 Eight-String Braid

5. Repeat braiding sequence. This is the same general procedure as is used for the Three-String Braid and can be used for any odd number of strings (5, 7, 9 etc.). Always place the odd string in the center (over half of the remainder) alternating between left and right.

1. Weigh the dough into eight 2-ounce (55-g) pieces.
2. Pound and roll out to make 14-inch (35-cm) strings.
3. Braid 2 under 3 and over 8.
4. Braid 1 over 2, 3, and 4.
5. Braid 7 under 6 and over 1.
6. Braid 8 over 7, 6, and 5.

Repeat braiding sequence.

Simple Bread Basket

one basket approximately 12 inches (30 cm) in diameter and 15 inches (37.5 cm) tall

one recipe Braided White Bread
   dough (page 76) (see step one)
soft unsalted butter
Egg Wash (page 7)
Royal Icing (page 1019)
one-quarter recipe Caramelized Sugar
   for Decorations (page 955)

NOTE 1: It is not absolutely necessary, but a good idea, to have a second larger bowl 15 to 16 inches (37.5 to 40 cm) in diameter available when you invert the partially baked basket just in case it is not ready to stand on its own.

NOTE 2: Because this braid must be started at one end rather than in the center, it takes a little more effort. You must untangle the opposite end as you work.

*T*his basket may appear to be more difficult than the name implies as you first look through the instructions. But when you consider that it does not require that you make a form, and it contains about half as many steps and notes as the elegant but labor-intensive Bread Basket made with Weaver's Dough, you hopefully will agree it is a rather quick and easy project. Of course, it is all a relative matter of opinion and skill level.

Because this basket is made with a yeast dough, the strings will proof as you form and work with them and you must be able to work quickly. You should be fairly proficient in rolling dough out to even ropes to be able to produce a neat and professional-looking finished basket. The yeast does, however, actually make the Braided White Bread dough easier to work with in terms of stretching the strings.

The instructions suggest drying the pieces for one day before assembly. But, by placing the bowl and the other pieces in a low temperature oven for approximately 1 hour after baking, the basket can be finished in one day. In this case, glue the two handle pieces together after drying them in the oven.*

1. Make the braided bread dough using only half the amount of yeast specified in the recipe. Weigh out twelve 3-ounce (85-g) pieces. Divide the remaining dough into 2-ounce (55-g) pieces; you will get about 35. Cover and refrigerate the two groups of pieces separately.

2. Butter the outside of an inverted mixing bowl approximately 12 inches in diameter and 5 inches high (30 by 12.5 cm). Set the bowl aside.

3. Draw a 16-inch (40-cm) circle on a sheet of baking paper. Place inverted on a sheet pan. Draw three additional circles, 1 inch (2.5 cm) larger in diameter than the mixing bowl you set aside (if the bowl is 12 inches the circles will be 13 inches), on three sheets of baking paper. Invert these papers on three separate sheet pans.

4. Pound and roll the 2-ounce (55-g) dough pieces out to 20-inch (50-cm) strings (see Figures 3–3 to 3–5, pages 77 and 78). Do these in sequence by rolling a few out part way, working on the next group, and then returning to the first strings, to allow the gluten to relax and avoid breaking the strings. When about half of the strings have been rolled out to the final length, place them in the refrigerator while you complete the remainder.

5. When you have finished forming the strings, place 20 strings in straight horizontal rows, about ¹/₂ inch (1.2 mm) apart, centered over the 16-inch (40-cm) drawn circle. Fold back up every other horizontal string halfway. Place a vertical string in the center, and cross the folded horizontal strings over the vertical string to start weaving (see Figure 15–6, page 764). Add vertical strings ¹/₂ inch (1.2 mm) apart in the same manner, alternating with every other horizontal string, until the circle is covered with woven strings (see Figure 15–7, page 764). As you come to the edges of the circle you can cut the strings shorter but they should still extend about 2 inches (5 cm) beyond the drawn circle on all sides. Push the ends of the strings together where they extend beyond the circle. Place in the refrigerator for 30 minutes to firm the woven dough.

6. Place the buttered bowl right-side up in the center of the woven circle. Place a sheet of baking paper and a sheet pan on top. Firmly hold on to both sheet pans and invert to transfer the dough to the outside of the bowl. The bowl should now be inverted on a sheet pan lined with baking paper. Adjust the dough as needed to center it over the bowl, and then trim the excess dough around the rim of the bowl. Brush the dough lightly with Egg Wash. If you apply too much, it will accumulate in the dimples between the woven spaces and detract from the finished appearance.

7. It is not necessary to let the dough rise before baking because it will have proofed the small amount that is required during the weaving process. Bake at 375°F (190°C) for approximately 40 minutes or until the crust is a rich, dark brown. Wait until the basket and the bowl are cool enough to pick up with your bare hands, then carefully turn the basket right-side up, place it into a larger bowl to support the outside, and remove the bowl from the interior (see note 1). Place the basket back in the oven for 15 minutes to dry and brown the interior. Set the basket aside to cool.

8. Roll the reserved 12 pieces of dough, four at a time, out to 44-inch (1-m, 10-cm) strings. Braid four of the strings following the instructions for Four-String Braid I on page 80 (see note 2 here). Place the finished braid in a ring on top of one of the reserved circles drawn on baking paper. Join the ends together and pinch to secure.

9. To make the first half of the two-part handle, braid the next set of four strings following the instructions for Four-String Braid II on pages 80 and 81. Place this braid on another of the reserved circles, arranging it so that the ends of the braid are at the widest point of the edges of the circle and the braid forms a handle that is 14 inches (35 cm) tall. Bring both ends to the outside of the circle to widen the base slightly. Place in the refrigerator. Repeat to make an identical handle with the remaining four strings and place on the last drawn circle.

10. Remove the first section of the handle from the refrigerator; it should be firm. Leaving it on the baking paper (and using the paper to lift it), place it on top of the second section and adjust the two pieces to make them the same shape and size. Place the first section back on its sheet pan.

11. Brush Egg Wash over all three of the braided pieces. Refrigerate for 5 minutes, and then brush with Egg Wash a second time.

12. Bake at 400°F (205°C) for approximately 20 minutes or until dark golden brown. Set aside to cool.

13. Place the Royal Icing in a pastry bag with a no. 2 (4-mm) plain tip. Turn one of the cooled handle pieces over and pipe a string of icing, in the center, the full length of the handle. Place the second half of the handle on top and press down firmly so that the pieces are glued together. Reserve the remaining Royal Icing. Set all of the pieces of the basket aside to dry overnight.

14. To assemble the basket: Trim the top of the basket if necessary so that it is even. Cut two notches on opposite sides of the basket the same width as the width of the assembled handle. Adjust the handle to fit by trimming the ends as needed so they are flush with the inside of the bowl. Using a palette knife, spread some caramelized sugar inside, just below the notches, where the ends of the handle will touch the inside of the basket. Quickly put the handle in place, holding it straight and firmly pressing the ends against the inside of the basket. It is helpful to have some assistance at this point. Hold the handle in place until the sugar hardens and the handle can support itself.

15. Place the remaining Royal Icing in a pastry bag with a no. 2 (4-mm) plain tip. Pipe icing around the ends of the handle inside the basket for additional support.

16. Cut the ring braid in half. Trim the ends of each half so that the pieces will fit snugly against the handles when placed on top of the bowl. Attach the pieces to the bowl with Royal Icing.

Star or Sunburst Braid

one loaf

one-half recipe Braided White Bread dough (page 76)
Egg Wash (page 7)
poppy and sunflower seeds (optional)

NOTE: You can use the same method used for forming the center to make a normal-sized loaf: Start with four 4-ounce (115-g) strings for a 1-pound (455-g) loaf. It takes a little extra time,

*T*his bread makes a striking centerpiece for any table. The recipe makes a *star 15 inches (37.5 cm) in diameter and leaves enough dough for one braided loaf. If you want a larger star, increase the weight and length of the pieces. Although you need only know how to make a Four-String Braid to make this loaf, you should not attempt it before you are fairly successful in rolling out and forming the strings. If you take too long, the first string will have risen while you are still shaping the last one. If you are not yet up to speed, or when the weather is very warm, keep the dough in the refrigerator as you are forming the strings. In this case it is also a good idea to place the completed outside of the loaf in the refrigerator while you are braiding the center.*

1. Make the bread dough and weigh out sixteen 2-ounce (55-g) pieces (twelve pieces for the points and four pieces for the center of the star). Keep the pieces you are not working with covered to prevent a skin from forming.

but the finished loaf looks very unusual and few people will know it is only a Four-String Braid. This loaf is shown in Figure 3–8, page 79.

2. Pound and roll twelve pieces into 12-inch (30-cm) strings that are tapered at both ends (see Figures 3–3, 3–4, and 3–5, pages 77 and 78).

3. Bend each string in a upside down U-shape and place them, overlapped, on a paper-lined sheet pan (I find it easier to use an inverted pan) in a wreath shape with the ends pointing out. Space each string one-third of the distance between the two halves of the previous string; when you add the last one, place one side under the first string (Figure 3–10). Place the strings so that you leave a 5-inch (12.5-cm) opening in the center. An easy way to do this is to arrange them around a cookie cutter or other round object of the proper size.

4. Divide into six sections of four strings (Figure 3–11), and form each section in a Four-String Braid II (Figure 3–12): Braid 4 over 3, braid 2 over 3, braid 1 under 2; repeat from the beginning. (For more information on braiding, see pages 77–79.)

5. As you come to the end of each braid, pinch the ends together and tuck underneath. (Figure 3–13). If the opening in the center becomes too large, move the sections closer together after you have finished braiding.

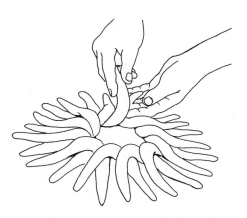

FIGURE 3–10   Positioning the strings for outside of the Star Braid

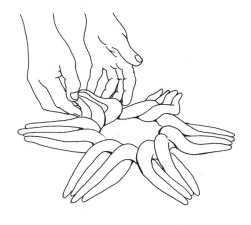

FIGURE 3–11   Dividing the strings into six sections of four strings each

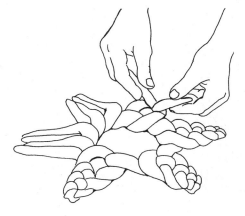

FIGURE 3–12   Braiding each of the six sections, using the Four-String Braid II method

FIGURE 3–13   The outside of the Star Braid before adding the center

6. Pound and roll the remaining four pieces into 30-inch (75-cm) strings. Do this in sequence to give the gluten a chance to relax: Roll each string part way (keeping them in order) and then go back and extend each one a little further and so on.

7. Place them next to each other and cut in half (Figure 3–14).

8. Cut both pieces in half again. The strings will shrink as you do this and probably end up different lengths, but it will not show in the finished shape. You should now have four pieces, each consisting of four strings, approximately 7 inches (17.5 cm) long.

9. Place them next to each other and braid, following the preceding directions for the Four-String Braid II, braiding from the center out to one end (Figure 3–15).

10. Turn the pieces around so the opposite side is facing you and braid from the center again, making sure that the pieces in each group remain together. Leave both ends of the braid open.

11. Pick up the braid with both hands and push the two ends under so that you form a round loaf (Figure 3–16).

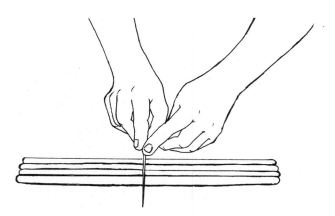

FIGURE 3–14   *Cutting the group of four strings in half to use for braiding the center of the star*

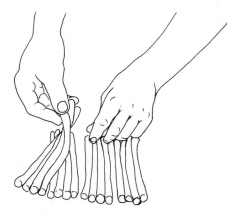

FIGURE 3–15   *Braiding the four groups of four strings each, using the Four-String Braid II method*

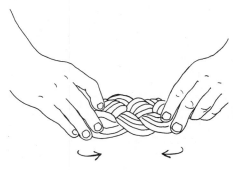

FIGURE 3–16   *Pushing both ends of the braid underneath to form a round loaf for the center of the star*

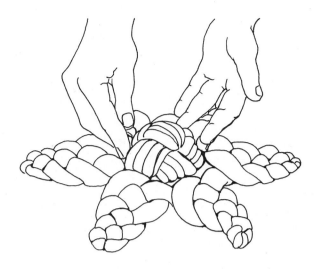

FIGURE 3–17   *Placing the center of the star within the outside frame; the completed Star Braid before baking*

12. Place the loaf in the center opening of the star (Figure 3–17). Brush with Egg Wash.

13. Let rise until slightly less than doubled in volume.

14. For a good shine, brush a second time with Egg Wash; sprinkle with poppy and/or sunflower seeds if you wish.

15. Bake at 375°F (190°C) until golden brown, about 40 minutes.

Butter-Wheat Bread

six 1-pound, 4-ounce (570-g) loaves

3 ounces (85 g) fresh compressed yeast

1 quart (960 ml) warm water (105–115°F, 40–46°C)

1 pound (455 g) whole wheat flour

2 pounds, 8 ounces (1 kg, 135 g) bread flour, approximately

3 tablespoons (45 g) salt

2 pounds (910 g) Puff Pastry, Croissant, or Danish dough scraps (see note)

Egg Wash (page 7)

whole wheat flour

This is a great way to use up Puff Pastry, Croissant, or Danish dough scraps that might otherwise go to waste (you might call it the baker's version of rum balls). I put pieces of scrap dough in the freezer until I have enough scraps to make a batch. The scraps keep fine in the freezer for several weeks. To use this dough for braiding, start with cold water, keep the dough rather firm, and instead of letting it rise until doubled in volume, just let it relax for 10 minutes before you begin to form it.

1. Dissolve the yeast in the warm water. Add the whole wheat and bread flours and mix 3 minutes on medium speed using the dough hook.

2. Add the salt and dough scraps. Knead until the dough is smooth and elastic, about 5 minutes. Add more bread flour if needed to make a medium-firm dough.

3. Place the dough on a sheet pan and let rise in a warm place, covered, until the dough doubles in volume, about 45 minutes.

4. Divide the dough into 1-pound, 4-ounce (570-g) pieces, keeping the pieces covered as you weigh them to prevent a skin from forming.

5. Knead each piece between your palm and the table until the loaf is tight and round, and the dough has enough tension to spring

One-Third Recipe

two 1-pound, 4 ounce (570-g) loaves

1¼ ounces (35 g) fresh compressed yeast

1⅓ cups (320 ml) warm water (105–115°F, 40–46°C)

5 ounces (140 g) whole wheat flour

13 ounces (370 g) bread flour, approximately

1 tablespoon (15 g) salt

11 ounces (310 g) Puff Pastry, Croissant, or Danish dough scraps (see note)

Egg Wash (page 7)

whole wheat flour

NOTE: If you are using all Croissant and/or Danish dough scraps, reduce the amount of yeast in the dough by 10 percent.

FIGURE 3–18 *Slashing the tops of the Butter-Wheat loaves before baking*

back when pressed (see Figures 3–1 and 3–2, page 70). If kneaded too much, the skin will break, giving the loaf a ragged look.

6. Immediately after kneading each loaf, flatten it slightly with your hand, brush with Egg Wash, and invert it in whole wheat flour. Shake off the excess.

7. Place the loaves, flour-side up, on sheet pans, four to a pan.

8. Using a sharp paring knife, cut a flower pattern ⅛ inch (3 mm) deep by first making one vertical slash in the center and then three fanned slashes on either side all joining at the bottom (Figure 3–18).

9. Let the loaves rise until slightly less than doubled in volume.

10. Bake at 400°F (205°C) until the loaves have a healthy brown color and test done (they should feel light when you pick them up and sound hollow when tapped), about 50 minutes. Place on racks to cool.

Challah

five 1-pound, 8-ounce (680-g) loaves

1½ ounces (40 g) fresh compressed yeast

1 quart (960 ml) cold milk

1 tablespoon (15 ml) vanilla extract

3 ounces (85 g) Vanilla Sugar (page 14) (see note)

2 tablespoons (30 g) salt

6 eggs

6 egg yolks (½ cup/120 ml)

4 pounds, 8 ounces (2 kg, 45 g) bread flour, approximately

1 cup (240 ml) olive oil

Egg Wash (page 7)

poppy and/or sesame seeds (optional)

*T*his traditional Jewish egg bread is usually made in a Three-String Braid when served at the Sabbath but is formed into other braids for specific holidays. The large quantity of eggs in this dough provide additional richness, better volume, and a longer shelf life and give the bread a pleasant golden color. Challah dough can be shaped following the instructions given for any of the braids described in the recipe for Braided White Bread, but keep in mind that the Challah dough will rise much faster and therefore tends to dry out faster as well. After applying the Egg Wash, try dusting the center of the loaf with bread flour using a small sifter so that the flour goes only in the center and the rest of the loaf keeps the shine from the Egg Wash. The flour will keep the strings separate during the oven-spring and give the Challah an appetizing rustic look.

1. Dissolve the yeast in the cold milk. Add the vanilla extract, vanilla sugar, salt, whole eggs, and the egg yolks. Mix in all but a few handfuls of the flour using the dough hook.

One-Third Recipe

two 1-pound, 8-ounce (680-g) loaves

1 ounce (30 g) fresh compressed yeast

1 ½ cups (360 ml) cold milk

1 teaspoon (5 ml) vanilla extract

1 ounce (30 g) Vanilla Sugar (page 14) (see note)

1 tablespoon (15 g) salt

2 eggs

2 egg yolks

1 pound, 8 ounces (680 g) bread flour, approximately

⅓ cup (80 ml) olive oil

Egg Wash (page 7)

poppy and/or sesame seeds (optional)

NOTE: If you do not have Vanilla Sugar, substitute granulated sugar and increase the vanilla extract by 1 tablespoon (15 ml) for the large recipe or 1 teaspoon (5 ml) for the small recipe. Traditionally, Challah does not contain vanilla, but I find it gives the bread a more well-rounded flavor with an added depth. To produce an authentic-style bread, use granulated sugar and omit the vanilla extract.

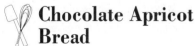

Chocolate Apricot Bread

three 1-pound, 6-ounce (625-g) loaves

2½ cups (600 ml) boiling water

8 ounces (225 g) dried apricots

2 ounces (55 g) fresh compressed yeast

⅓ cup (80 ml) or 4 ounces (115 g) honey

1 pound, 12 ounces (795 g) bread flour, approximately

1 tablespoon (15 g) salt

8 ounces (225 g) sweet dark chocolate, melted

bread flour

2. Add the olive oil and knead the dough on low speed for 15 minutes, adding the reserved flour if necessary to correct the consistency.

3. Cover the dough and let it rise in a warm place until it has doubled in volume.

4. Punch the dough down. Cover and let rise again until the dough doubles in volume a second time.

5. Punch the dough down and weigh it into 8-ounce (225-g) pieces.

6. Using three pieces for each braid, pound and roll the pieces into strings (see Figures 3–3, 3–4, and 3–5, pages 77 and 78) and then braid them following the directions for a Three-String Braid on page 80.

7. Transfer the braids to sheet pans and let them rise until they are one-and-one-half times the original size. Brush with Egg Wash, then sprinkle with poppy and/or sesame seeds if desired.

8. Bake at 350°F (175°C) for approximately 35 minutes. The loaves should be deep golden brown and sound hollow when tapped on the bottom.

Although this may not be the best choice of bread to serve on the dinner table, it is a great addition to a cheese and fruit platter and an ideal selection for a ham and cheese sandwich. Chocolate Apricot Bread is also the ultimate option for Chocolate Bread and Butter Pudding Kungsholm (page 738). Many other dried fruits can be used in combination with the dried apricots or as a substitution; dried pears and cherries are two examples.

This bread is a bit difficult when it comes to judging if it is done, since the color does not give you any clue as it would with a typical lighter-style bread. Instead, you must pick up the loaves to feel for lightness and tap them sharply on the bottom to check for a hollow response.

1. Pour the boiling water over the apricots and set aside for 30 minutes.

2. Drain the apricots, reserving the water in a bowl. Cut the apricots into large chunks. Reserve

3. Make a sponge by dissolving the yeast in the water drained from the apricots (warm it to 105–115°F, 40–46°C, first if it has cooled beyond that point), then mixing in the honey and half of the bread flour until the mixture is smooth. Cover and allow to rise until more than doubled in volume.

4. Place the sponge in a mixer bowl. Add the salt, melted chocolate, and all but a handful of the remaining bread flour. Scrape down the sides of the bowl and knead with the dough hook for 8 to 10 minutes, adjusting the consistency by adding the reserved flour if necessary. The dough should be soft and glutenous. Add the reserved apricots, mixing just long enough to incorporate them.

5. Cover the dough and let it rise in a warm place until it has doubled in volume.

6. Divide the dough into three equal pieces, about 1 pound, 6 ounces (625 g) each. Form the pieces into oval loaves (see Figure 3–24, page 120). Place the loaves on sheet pans lined with baking paper. Brush water lightly over the top of the loaves, then dust with bread flour. Let rise until one-and-one-half times the original size.

7. Make three slashes, lengthwise, on the top of each loaf (see Figure 3–25, page 120). Bake at 375°F (190°C) for approximately 40 minutes or until baked through.

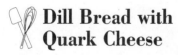

Dill Bread with Quark Cheese

three 1-pound, 8-ounce (680-g) loaves

8 ounces (225 g) fresh yellow onions
3/4 cup (180 ml) olive oil
3 tablespoons (10 g) dry dill weed
5 teaspoons (25 g) salt
1 1/2 ounces (40 g) fresh compressed yeast
1 1/2 cups (360 ml) warm water (105–115°F, 40–46°C)
1 ounce (30 g) granulated sugar
3 eggs
6 ounces (170 g) quark or cottage cheese
2 pounds, 10 ounces (1 kg, 195 g) bread flour, approximately

NOTE: If your oven is not equipped with steam injectors, see Creating Steam without Steam Injectors, page 73.

I was somewhat surprised at the enthusiastic reception this bread received when I first made it with my class. The student who baked the first batch was quite proud when the three loaves he produced disappeared rather quickly!

Dill plays a big role in Scandinavian cooking and, to some degree, in many German-speaking countries as well. It is most often associated with seafood presentations; however, dill is also used in the Swedish kitchen to flavor lamb and veal dishes. Its decorative, feathery green fronds dot the famous Swedish Smörgåsbord, and it is a must when cooking crawfish (crawdads). Here, the crown containing the seeds must also be included to obtain the proper flavor. The popularity of dill in Scandinavia can be compared to that of rosemary in the southern regions of Europe.

As you might guess, this bread is a wonderful accompaniment to fish and is especially good with smoked fish. You may want to adjust the amount of dill used, although the amount in the recipe is actually on the light side.

1. Peel the onions and chop into small pieces. Sauté the onions in a small portion of the olive oil until they are soft. Remove from the heat and add the remaining oil, the dried dill, and the salt. Reserve.

2. In a mixer bowl, dissolve the yeast in the warm water, and then add the granulated sugar, the eggs, and the quark or cottage cheese. Using the dough hook, incorporate enough of the bread flour to form a soft dough.

3. Add the reserved onion mixture and adjust by adding the remaining flour as required to make a fairly firm dough. Knead at medium speed for 8 to 10 minutes; the dough should be elastic and should not be sticky.

4. Cover and set aside in a warm place until doubled in volume.

5. Punch the dough down, cover, and allow to proof a second time until doubled in volume.

6. Divide the dough into three pieces, approximately 1 pound, 8 ounces (680 g) each. Shape the pieces into smooth, round loaves (see Figures 3–1 and 3–2, page 70).

7. Allow the loaves to rise until slightly less than doubled in volume.

8. Bake at 400°F (205°C) using steam for the first 10 minutes. Open the damper to remove the steam and continue baking approximately 20 minutes longer. The loaves should feet light and sound hollow when tapped sharply on the bottom. Let cool completely before slicing.

Epis Baguettes

four loaves, about 1 pound (455 g) each

1¹/₂ ounces (40 g) fresh compressed yeast

2¹/₂ cups (600 ml) ice-cold water

1 pound (455 g) old bread dough (see note 1)

2 pounds, 6 ounces (1 kg, 80 g) bread flour, approximately

5 teaspoons (25 g) salt

1 teaspoon (4 g) ascorbic acid (see note 2)

olive oil

NOTE 1: You can use either dough left over from a previous batch of this recipe or any white bread dough. If you do not have any suitable bread dough scraps, use the following recipe for Epis Baguette *Pre-Dough.*

NOTE 2: Ascorbic acid is pure vitamin C. Although it is eventually destroyed once exposed to high heat in the oven, it is beneficial as the yeast is growing. The microorganisms seem to thrive on it and grow stronger. If you do not have this ingredient on hand, simply leave it out of the recipe; however, the salt must be increased by 1 teaspoon (5g).

NOTE 3: If properly covered, the leftover dough can be stored in the refrigerator for up to three days. If you do not plan to make another batch of Epis Baguettes *within this time, either make a fifth loaf or freeze the dough until needed.*

*I*f you have the opportunity to drive through the farm country in the fall you *may be lucky enough to see the beautiful golden ripe wheat sheaves bending into shallow waves in the wind. This picture-perfect display of nature's bounty is the inspiration for the shape of these loaves—Epis is the French word for an ear of wheat; the top part of the wheat sheaf. Forming the baguettes in this shape is not only fitting but also very attractive. Epis Baguettes add lots of visual appeal to a bread display on a buffet table or in a shop window. The shape is also practical for use in bread baskets since it allows the guests to break off individual rolls as they please. The epis design can be made using any gluten-rich bread dough in this book with excellent results.*

I first came across these shapely baguettes in a small restaurant in Provence which served an individual epis loaf to each diner, placed directly on the table-cloth next to the plate. To make the individual size, divide the dough into 4-ounce (115-g) pieces, shape as described for the larger size, but make them 5 inches (12.5 cm) long. The individual loaves will require less time in the oven.

Although it is not necessary to start this dough with ice-cold water (this is usually done when making a large batch so that the dough will not get too warm from friction during the kneading process), using cold water generates a slower and longer proofing period, which allows the dough to absorb more flavor from the alcohol which is produced by the yeast. This, and the use of "old" bread dough, are what give these baguettes their special taste and character.

1. Dissolve the yeast in the cold water. Add the bread dough scraps and all but a handful of the bread flour. Knead with the dough hook on low speed for 8 minutes, adjusting the consistency if necessary by adding the remaining bread flour. The dough should be soft but not sticky.

2. Incorporate the salt and the ascorbic acid. Knead 4 minutes longer on low speed.

3. Cover the dough and let it rest in a warm place for 30 minutes.

4. Reserve 1 pound (455 g) of dough to use in the next batch (see note 3). Divide the remaining dough into 4 equal pieces, about 1 pound (455 g) each.

FIGURE 3–19   *Cutting the* epis *design in the loaves before baking*

NOTE 4: *If your oven is not equipped with steam injectors, see Creating Steam without Steam Injectors, page 73.*

5. Form the pieces into Baguette loaves 16 inches (40 cm) in length (see Figures 3–3, 3–4, and 3–5, pages 77 and 78). Place on sheet pans that have been lightly greased with olive oil (do not place more than three per full sheet pan).

6. Use scissors held at a 45° angle and cut an *epis* or wheat sheaf design into the loaves alternating left and right (Figure 3–19). Let the loaves rise until doubled in volume.

7. Bake the loaves at 425°F (219°C), using steam for the first 10 minutes. Open the damper (or the oven door) to let all of the moisture out, then continue baking approximately 10 minutes longer or until the baguettes are baked through (see note 4).

Epis Baguette Pre-Dough

1 pound (455 g) pre-dough

10 ounces (285 g) bread flour
1 teaspoon (2 g) cumin powder
1/4 ounce (7.5 g) or 1 slightly rounded
    teaspoon (5 ml) fresh compressed
    yeast
    or
1/2 teaspoon (2.5 ml) dry yeast
3/4 cup (180 ml) warm water

1. Combine all of the ingredients.
2. Cover, and refrigerate overnight.

Farmer's Rye Rings

four 1-pound, 3-ounce (540-g) ring-shaped loaves

2 ounces (55 g) fresh compressed
    yeast
1 quart (960 ml) warm milk
    (105–115°F, 40–46°C)
2 tablespoons (30 ml) white vinegar
3 tablespoons (45 ml) or 2 ounces
    (55 g) honey

As late as just a century ago rye bread was a significant part of the peasant diet in Northern Europe. Not only is rye easier to grow in poor soil than other grains, it retains moisture better (due to the richness of carbon sugar), which made it possible to store the breads longer, and a hearty slice of rye bread blended well with the simple peasant fare. Preparing the loaves in a ring shape had a practical purpose in the old days: The rings could be hung up high on dowels where they stayed dry and were protected from pests. Today the design is more of an aesthetic touch than anything else.

The protein in rye flour forms a very weak gluten structure. Therefore, unless you want a very dense and flat bread, the amount of rye flour in any rye bread dough should not exceed 30 to 35 percent of the total flour weight. The following recipe contains 32 percent rye flour. This lack of gluten-producing

2 tablespoons (30 g) salt

1 pound (455 g) medium rye flour

8 ounces (225 g) whole wheat flour

1 pound, 10 ounces (740 g) bread flour, approximately

water

medium rye flour

NOTE: If your oven is not equipped with steam injectors, see Creating Steam without Steam Injectors, page 73.

help from the rye flour gives extra responsibility to the wheat flour, so it is even more important to pay close attention to the dough's temperature and consistency.

1. Dissolve the yeast in the warm milk in a mixer bowl. Add the vinegar, honey, and salt. Mix in the rye and whole wheat flours using the dough hook.

2. Reserve one handful of the bread flour. Mix in the remainder and knead for 4 to 5 minutes until you have a smooth, elastic dough. Adjust the consistency, if required, by adding the reserved flour.

3. Place the dough in an oiled bowl, turn to coat both sides with oil, cover, and let rise in a warm place until it has doubled in volume.

4. Punch down the dough. Divide into four equal pieces, approximately 1 pound, 3 ounces (540 g) each. Form the pieces into tight, round loaves (see Figures 3–1 and 3–2, page 70). Flatten the loaves.

5. Using a thick dowel, make a hole in the center of each loaf, cutting all the way through the dough. (The original technique for making the holes was to use your bare elbow; try it if it seems appropriate.) Let the rings relax for a few minutes, then widen the holes by placing your fingers in the center and stretching the dough around the holes until the opening is approximately 6 inches (15 cm) in diameter.

6. Place the rings on sheet pans lined with baking paper. Spray or brush with water. Dust the top of the rings with enough rye flour to cover. Let rise until doubled in volume.

7. Using a sharp knife, make three evenly spaced slashes on top of each ring.

8. Bake at 425°F (219°C) with steam, leaving the damper closed for the first 10 minutes. Open the damper and bake approximately 20 minutes longer or until baked through.

Focaccia

one 16-by-24-inch (40-×-60-cm) sheet

Sponge

1½ ounces (40 g) fresh compressed yeast

¾ cup (180 ml) warm water (105–115°F, 40–46°C)

1 tablespoon (15 g) granulated sugar

8 ounces (225 g) high-gluten flour

This Italian flatbread is a close cousin to the better-known pizza and has long been found all over the Italian Riviera; it is said to have originated in Genoa. Focaccia has become a popular bakery offering in both Europe and the United States though sometimes in rather disguised variations. The original version started as a simple unpretentious bread, traditionally flavored using the local herbs and olive oil indigenous to the region where it was made, and topped with olives, sweet onions, potatoes, and/or anchovies. Use your imagination to suit your taste and requirements in choosing flavors and toppings, but keep in mind that without the Herb and Olive Oil Mixture to begin with, you are not making an authentic Focaccia.

Focaccia is good as a snack or an accompaniment to soups or salads. If you prefer to make the Focaccia round, this recipe will yield two circles 14 inches (35 cm) in diameter or fifteen individual 5-inch (12.5-cm) rounds. The individual servings will bake in much less time.

Dough

2 cups (480 ml) warm water
(105–115° F, 40–46°C)

3/4 cup (180 ml) olive oil

3 ounces (85 g) granulated sugar

2 tablespoons (30 g) salt

1 pound (455 g) high-gluten flour

14 ounces (400 g) bread flour,
approximately

Topping

1/4 cup (60 ml) olive oil

Herb and Olive Oil Mixture
(recipe follows)

Potato Topping (instructions follow)
(optional)

1 teaspoon (5 g) salt

1. To make the sponge, dissolve the yeast in the first measurement of warm water. Add the sugar and high-gluten flour, and knead using the dough hook until the dough is smooth and elastic, about 5 minutes.

2. Cover and let rise in a warm place until the sponge starts to fall.

3. Add and mix into the sponge the remaining warm water, the first measurement of olive oil, the sugar, salt, high-gluten flour, and enough of the bread flour to develop a very soft, smooth, yet still elastic, dough.

4. Form the dough into a ball, place on a floured surface, and cut an X halfway through the ball of dough. Pull the cuts out slightly to form a rough square (see Figure 2–6, page 46); this will make it easier to shape the dough into a rectangle later. Cover and let rest for 30 minutes.

5. Use the 1/4 cup (60 ml) of olive oil to generously coat the bottom and sides of a full sheet pan (16 by 24 inches/ 40 × 60 cm) with olive oil (do not use baking paper). Place the dough in the center of the pan. Oil your hands, then stretch the dough out as far as you can. Let rise in a warm place until the dough has doubled in bulk.

6. Use your hands to stretch the dough until it covers the entire sheet pan. As you stretch and form the dough, press your fingertips into the top to mark it with "dimples."

7. Let the dough rise until it is is one-and-one-half times the original size.

8. Using your hand, very gently spread three-quarters of the Herb and Olive Oil Mixture evenly over the surface of the dough. Place the potato slices on top if you are using them. Sprinkle 1 teaspoon (5 g) of salt evenly over the top.

9. Place the bread in an oven preheated to 475°F (246°C). Immediately reduce the heat to 375°F (190°C) and bake for 25 to 30 minutes, or until baked through. Remove from the pan by placing a second sheet pan on top and inverting. This will keep the bottom of the Focaccia from becoming soggy. Place another inverted pan on top and invert again to place the Focaccia on the underside of the sheet pan (so that the sides do not hold in any steam). Immediately brush the remainder of the Herb and Olive Oil Mixture on top. Allow to cool, then cut into the desired sized pieces.

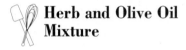

Herb and Olive Oil Mixture

1 ounce (30 g) fresh rosemary

1 ounce (30 g) fresh sage

1 ounce (30 g) fresh basil

1 cup (240 ml) olive oil, heated

two heads garlic, roasted and puréed

1. Finely chop the herbs. Add to the heated olive oil along with the garlic.

2. Let sit for at least 1 hour, or overnight.

Potato Topping

1. To use potatoes as a topping, bake 14 ounces (400 g) of small red potatoes until they are cooked through but still firm. Slice them thinly and add them to the herb and oil mixture.

2. When you are ready to assemble the Focaccia, drain off the oil and reserve it. Brush the oil over the surface of the dough, then distribute the potatoes and herbs evenly on top. Sprinkle the salt over the potatoes.

Garlic Bread

six 1 pound, 2-ounce (510-g) loaves

2 ounces (55 g) minced fresh garlic
   (about ten medium-sized cloves)
olive oil
2 ounces (55 g) fresh compressed yeast
1 quart (960 ml) warm water
   (105–115°F, 40–46°C)
2 egg whites (¹/₄ cup/60 ml)
2 ounces (55 g) soft unsalted butter
2 ounces (55 g) granulated sugar
4 tablespoons (60 g) salt
2¹/₂ tablespoons (15 g) ground, dried
   oregano
2¹/₂ tablespoons (15 g) ground, dried
   basil
4 pounds, 4 ounces (1 kg, 935 g)
   bread flour, approximately
water
whole wheat flour

One-Half Recipe

three 1 pound, 2-ounce (510-g) loaves

1 ounce (30 g) minced fresh garlic
   (about five medium-sized cloves)
olive oil
1¹/₄ ounces (35 g) fresh compressed
   yeast
1 pint (480 ml) warm water
   (105–115°F, 40–46°C)
1 egg white
1 ounce (30 g) soft unsalted butter
1 ounce (30 g) granulated sugar
2 tablespoons (30 g) salt
4 teaspoons (8 g) ground, dried oregano
4 teaspoons (8 g) ground, dried basil
2 pounds, 2 ounces (970 g) bread
   flour, approximately
water
whole wheat flour

*T*his is one of the most popular breads that I make with my students. Everyone loves the wonderful aroma and flavor of garlic. The history of the bulb dates back to ancient times when it was treasured as a medicine and antidote. Garlic was introduced to Europe during the Crusades. Today it is popular all over the world with the major exceptions of Japan, Scandinavia, and, to some degree, England.

California produces 80 percent of the garlic grown in the United States. The annual garlic festival held in Gilroy, California (just south of San Francisco), draws tens of thousands of garlic worshipers eager to sample not only savory dishes but such oddities as garlic ice cream and garlic-flavored chocolate mousse as well!

Fresh garlic is available all year round. It should be stored in a cool, dry place.

1. Sauté the garlic in olive oil to soften the flavor; do not allow the garlic to brown. If the garlic is very strong, reduce the amount.

2. Dissolve the yeast in the warm water. Stir in the egg whites, butter, sugar, salt, oregano, basil, cooked garlic, and all but a few ounces of the bread flour. Using the dough hook on medium speed, knead the dough, adding the reserved bread flour as needed, until the dough is fairly stiff and smooth.

3. Place the dough in an oiled bowl, turn to coat both sides with oil, cover, and let rise for 1 hour.

4. Punch down the dough and divide into six equal pieces (three for the smaller recipe), approximately 1 pound, 2 ounces (510 g) each. Shape each piece into a round loaf. Starting with the loaf formed first, shape each into a tight oval loaf (see Figures 3–1, and 3–2, page 70). The loaves should spring back when pressed lightly.

5. Place the loaves seam-side down on sheet pans lined with baking paper. Brush with water and sprinkle lightly with whole wheat flour. Make diagonal slashes across each loaf, about ¹/₄ inch (6 mm) deep. Let rise until doubled in volume.

6. Bake at 375°F (190°C) for about 30 minutes. Cool on racks.

Honey-Wheat Bread

four 1-pound, 4-ounce (570-g) loaves

1¾ cups (420 ml) milk

4 teaspoons (20 g) salt

1 cup (240 ml) or 12 ounces (340 g) honey

7 ounces (200 g) soft unsalted butter

1 ounce (30 g) fresh compressed yeast

1 cup (240 ml) warm water (105–115°F, 40–46°C)

1 pound, 4 ounces (570 g) medium whole wheat flour

1 pound, 4 ounces (570 g) bread flour, approximately

Egg Wash (page 7)

wheat bran

NOTE: If your oven is not equipped with steam injectors, see Creating Steam without Steam Injectors, page 73.

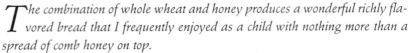

The combination of whole wheat and honey produces a wonderful richly flavored bread that I frequently enjoyed as a child with nothing more than a spread of comb honey on top.

Honey has been used as a sweetener in cooking far, far longer than sugar. Previous to the nineteenth century, sugar was still considered a luxury for the masses and honey was one of the most commonly used substitutes. As is true with molasses and other sweetening agents, the darker the color of the honey the stronger the flavor. There are hundreds of types of honey; most are named for the flower that the honey derives its fragrance from. Two of the most common varieties in this country are clover and orange blossom. Most types of honey are interchangeable, with the exception of some which are very strongly scented.

As a variation, try substituting molasses for the honey in this recipe. It produces a heartier, robust loaf. You can also add one-third of a cup of chopped fresh parsley and one tablespoon of chopped fresh rosemary (with either the honey or molasses variation) for an herb bread that is delicious, especially with lamb dishes.

1. Combine the milk, salt, honey, and butter. Heat to 115°F (46°C), then set aside.

2. In a mixer bowl, dissolve the yeast in the warm water. Add the milk mixture, the whole wheat flour, and all but a handful of the bread flour. Knead, using the dough hook at low speed, until the dough has developed a smooth, elastic, glutinous consistency. Add the reserved bread flour while kneading if necessary.

3. Cover the dough and let rise in a warm place until it has doubled in volume.

4. Punch the dough down, recover, and proof a second time until doubled in volume.

5. Punch the dough down and scale into four equal pieces, approximately 1 pound, 4 ounces (570 g) each.

6. Form each piece into an oval loaf (see Figure 3–24, page 120). Brush Egg Wash on the loaves, then invert them in wheat bran. Place bran-side up on sheet pans.

7. Let the loaves rise until they have slightly less than doubled in volume.

8. Using a sharp knife or a razor blade, slash three deep lines, lengthwise, on each loaf (see Figure 3–25, page 120).

9. Bake at 400°F (205°C), using steam and leaving the damper closed for 10 minutes. Open the damper and continue baking approximately 30 minutes longer, or until dark golden brown and baked through.

Italian Easter Bread
(Columba Pasquale: Easter Doves)

four 1-pound, 2-ounce (510-g) loaves

10 ounces (285 g) whole almonds, blanched and skins removed

2 ounces (55 g) fresh compressed yeast

1¼ cups (300 ml) warm milk (105–115°F, 40–46°C)

1½ tablespoons (22 g) salt

1 pound, 8 ounces (680 g) bread flour, approximately

7 ounces (200 g) soft unsalted butter

10 egg yolks (⅞ cup/210 ml)

½ teaspoon (2.5 ml) *flori de sicilia*, or orange flower water

3 ounces (85 g) granulated sugar

grated zest of one lemon

6 ounces (170 g) Candied Orange Peel (page 978), diced finely

Simple Syrup (page 11)

granulated sugar

powdered sugar

*T*his sweet Italian bread, also called Colomba Pasquale *or* Easter Doves, *is made from a dough very much like panettone; the shape, however, differs a great deal. Veiled with crystallized sugar and studded with whole almonds, these loaves are formed to resemble a dove in flight.*

As is often the case when one travels far back in history (around 1176), there are several different stories regarding the origin of this bread. One places it in Milan (which is where the panettone bread is also said to have originated) and says this bread was created to celebrate the victory over Barbarossa, whose goal was to conquer all of Italy for the Roman Empire. Another story says the Colomba was first made in the nearby city of Pavia during the conquest over Albion: A woman who had been captured made a sweet bread in the shape of a dove to symbolize peace. When the bread was brought to the villain who had abducted her, he was so touched he granted her freedom. Today, this bread is offered in bakeries at Easter. Special baking pans are available to shape the dough into a rounded cross design.

It is important that this bread is allowed to proof long enough to be light and airy; compared to a standard bread it would actually be considered over-proofed.

1. Reserve 32 almonds to use for decoration. Lightly toast the remaining almonds, chop finely, and reserve.

2. Dissolve the yeast in the warm milk (be sure the milk is not too hot). Add the salt and approximately two-thirds of the flour, or enough for a soft, sponge-like consistency. Mix until smooth.

3. Cover the sponge and let rise in a warm place until it has doubled in volume.

4. Mix the butter and the remaining flour into the sponge. Knead with the dough hook at medium speed until the dough is smooth and elastic, approximately 10 minutes.

5. Combine the egg yolks, *flori de sicilia* or orange flower water, and sugar. Incorporate this mixture into the dough in four additions, letting the dough completely absorb each portion before adding the next. Add additional flour if required, to make a fairly soft, but workable dough.

6. Combine the lemon zest and the orange peel with the reserved chopped almonds. Mix into the dough. Place the dough in an oiled bowl, turn to coat both sides with oil, cover, and let rise in a warm place for 1 hour, punching the dough down twice during that period.

7. Divide the dough into eight equal pieces, approximately 9 ounces (255 g) each. Working with two pieces at a time, pound and roll them into 8-inch (20-cm) ropes (see Figures 3–3, 3–4, and 3–5, pages 77 and 78), not tapered on the ends but shaped instead like sausages.

8. Place one piece on a sheet pan lined with baking paper and make an indentation across and slightly off center, using the side of your hand. Place the second piece in the indentation, across the first, and bend both ends back slightly to form the wings of the dove (Figure

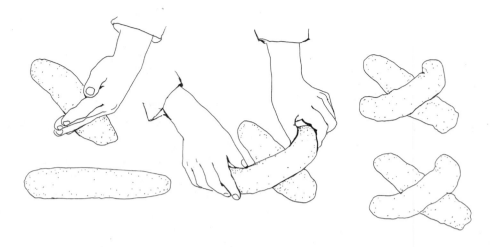

FIGURE 3–20   *Using the edge of the hand to make an indentation across one dough rope; placing the second rope in the indentation and bending the ends back slightly; the formed Easter Doves before baking*

3–20). Repeat with the remaining pieces to form three more loaves. Let the loaves rise until doubled in volume.

9. Brush the top and sides of the loaves with Simple Syrup. Sprinkle with granulated sugar, then dust heavily with powdered sugar. Place eight almonds, evenly spaced, on the top of each loaf, pressing them in so they adhere tightly.

10. Bake at 375°F (190°C) for about 20 minutes or until baked through. Remove the loaves from the pans and allow them to cool on racks.

Joggar Bread

four 1-pound, 7-ounce (655-g) loaves

1 cup (240 ml) warm water
  (105–115°F, 40–46°C)

2 cups (480 ml) warm milk
  (105–115°F, 40–46°C)

2 ounces (55 g) fresh compressed
  yeast

2 eggs

1/4 cup (60 ml) or 3 ounces (85 g)
  honey

1/4 cup (60 ml) or 3 ounces (85 g)
  molasses

2 tablespoons (30 g) salt

3 ounces (85 g) unprocessed wheat
  bran

This is a good example of how the English language is infiltrating Sweden. Joggar is the adopted Swedish word for jogger. I have to admit it sounds more appealing than the proper Swedish word lunka, *meaning "to run slowly at a steady pace."*

This bread is quite appropriately named as it is great-tasting and rich in fiber and carbohydrates, our bodies' preferred energy source.

1. Combine the water and milk in a mixer bowl. Add the yeast and mix to dissolve.

2. Combine the eggs, honey, and molasses. Add to the liquid in the bowl, together with the salt, bran, cornmeal, rolled wheat, and whole wheat flour.

3. Using the dough hook, knead in the butter and the bread flour at medium speed, adjusting the amount of bread flour as necessary for a fairly stiff dough. Continue kneading until the dough is smooth and elastic, approximately 8 minutes.

6 ounces (170 g) cornmeal

4 ounces (115 g) rolled wheat

1 pound (455 g) whole wheat flour

3 ounces (85 g) soft unsalted butter

1 pound, 8 ounces (680 g) bread flour, approximately

water

whole wheat flour

NOTE: If your oven is not equipped with steam injectors, see Creating Steam without Steam Injectors, page 73.

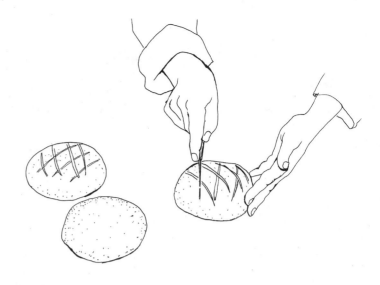

FIGURE 3–21   *Slashing the top of Joggar Bread loaves with two sets of parallel lines to form a diamond pattern*

4. Place the dough in an oiled bowl, turn to coat both sides with oil, cover, and let rise until doubled in volume.

5. Punch the dough down, then cover and let it rise a second time until doubled in volume.

6. Punch the dough down, and divide into four equal pieces, approximately 1 pound, 7 ounces (655 g) each. Form the pieces into round loaves (see Figures 3–1, and 3–2, page 70). Flatten the loaves lightly. Spray or brush with water, then sprinkle enough whole wheat flour over the loaves to cover the tops.

7. Place on sheet pans lined with baking paper. Slash the top of the loaves, cutting just deep enough to penetrate the skin, making a series of parallel lines approximately ¾ inch (2 cm) apart, first in one direction, then at a 45° angle to create a diamond pattern (Figure 3–21). Let rise until slightly less than doubled in volume.

8. Bake at 400°F (205°C), using steam and leaving the damper closed for the first 10 minutes. Open the damper and bake approximately 30 minutes longer, or until the loaves are baked through.

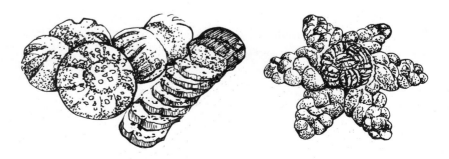

Multigrain Bread with Walnuts

three 1-pound, 10-ounce (740-g) loaves

10 ounces (285 g) walnuts

2 ounces (55 g) fresh compressed yeast

1³/₄ cups (420 ml) warm water (105–115°F, 40–46°C)

4 teaspoons (20 g) salt

4 ounces (115 g) light brown sugar

¹/₃ cup (80 ml) or 4 ounces (115 g) honey

³/₄ cup (180 ml) buttermilk

4 ounces (115 g) rolled oats

4 ounces (115 g) coarse rye flour (pumpernickel flour)

4 ounces (115 g) wheat bran

1 pound, 12 ounces (795 g) high-gluten flour, approximately

olive oil

*T*he toasted walnuts set this bread apart from the run of the mill "health-food" breads that are found everywhere these days (many of which unfortunately sound more interesting—with a long list of good-for-you ingredients—than they taste). The instructions call for making fairly large loaves, so you can still form two normal-sized loaves from half of the recipe. Because of its high sugar content, this bread proofs very slowly; do not worry, just be patient and it will happen. This higher proportion of sugar makes Multigrain Bread a great match for smoked meats and fish.

1. Chop the walnuts coarsely without crushing. Toast lightly and reserve.

2. In a mixer bowl, dissolve the yeast in the warm water. Mix in the salt, brown sugar, honey, and buttermilk. Incorporate the rolled oats, rye flour, wheat bran, and most of the high-gluten flour (reserve a handful or so to add if necessary as you knead the dough). Knead, at low speed using the dough hook, for approximately 10 to 12 minutes, until the dough is smooth and elastic. Halfway through kneading add the chopped walnuts and also the reserved flour, if necessary.

3. Cover the dough and let it rise in a warm place until it has doubled in volume.

4. Scale the dough into three equal pieces, approximately 1 pound, 10 ounces (740 g) each. Form the pieces into round loaves (see Figures 3–1, and 3–2, page 70). Place the loaves on sheet pans and let rise until they have slightly less than doubled in volume.

5. Bake at 375°F (190°C) for approximately 40 minutes or until golden brown and baked through. Brush olive oil over the loaves as soon as they are removed from the oven.

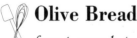

Olive Bread

four 1-pound, 4-ounce (570-g) loaves

Pre-Dough

1¹/₂ ounces (40 g) fresh compressed yeast

1 cup (240 ml) warm water (105–115°F, 40–46°C)

1 tablespoon (15 g) granulated sugar

10 ounces (285 g) high-gluten flour

*O*lives are found all over the Mediterranean; over 90 percent of the world's cultivated olives are grown in that region. The ragged-looking trees are among the most hearty species and can live to be hundreds of years old. Their main harvest, of course, is olive oil, but what would we do without the popular small pitted fruit? It is hard to imagine a salade niçoise without the dark olives from Provence, or a martini without a pimento-stuffed green olive (or my favorite martini olive—stuffed with anchovy). The dozens of different varieties, sizes, and colors have one thing in common: They are all green before they are ripe and turn black when left on the tree to ripen. Either way, when first picked olives are very bitter, and if they are not pressed for oil they are always cured in brine or oil before they can be eaten.

Dough

2¼ cups (540 ml) warm water
   (105–115°F, 40–46°C)

⅓ cup (80 ml) olive oil

2 ounces (55 g) granulated sugar

2 tablespoons (30 g) salt

1 pound (455 g) high-gluten flour

1 pound (455 g) bread flour,
   approximately

1 pound, 8 ounces (680 g) kalamata
   olives, pitted and coarsely chopped

   or

1 pound, 3 ounces (540 g) pitted
   kalamata olives (2¾ cups/660 ml)

olive oil (optional) (see note)

NOTE: Should you prefer not to use steam, or not have a steam oven, baking this bread in a regular "dry heat" oven will produce a very good soft-crust loaf. The baking time will be a little shorter, about 35 minutes. Brush the loaves with olive oil immediately after removing from the oven if you use this method. To add steam, see Creating Steam without Steam Injectors, page 73.

This bread is marbled throughout with the flavorful brine-cured Greek kalamata olives. It goes well with antipasto or carpaccio, or try it toasted, topped with creamy goat's milk cheese and fresh basil, and serve it with a glass of chardonnay. I have not had good results when substituting other olives for the kalamatas. The Greek-style California olives lose all of their flavor after being baked in the bread. If the kalamata olives you are using seem very salty, reduce the amount of salt in the recipe by one or two teaspoons.

Pay close attention when making the dough that you do not add too much flour. If the dough is too firm you will find it hard, if not impossible, to incorporate all of the olives (and kalamata olives are too good, and too expensive, to end up burned on the sheet pan next to the loaves!). If you find it difficult to incorporate the olives into the dough, bake the loaves in greased, paper-lined bread pans instead of on the sheet pans, to avoid losing the olives. Olive Bread will keep fresh for up to one week due to the moisture in the olives.

1. Start the pre-dough by dissolving the yeast in the warm water. Add the sugar and high-gluten flour. Knead for about 5 minutes using the dough hook. Let the pre-dough rise in a warm place just until it starts to fall.

2. Add the remaining warm water, olive oil, sugar, salt, high-gluten flour, and all but a handful of the bread flour to the pre-dough. Knead until the dough is smooth and elastic, adding the last handful of flour if necessary. Cover the dough and let it rise in a warm place until it has doubled in volume.

3. Add the olives to the dough and knead by hand just until they are incorporated. Do not mix so long at this step that the olives break up completely and turn the dough an unpleasant gray color. However, the dough should have a slightly marbled look from the olives. This is not only for appearance but adds to the flavor of the finished bread. Cover the dough and let it rise a second time until it has doubled in bulk.

4. Punch the dough down and divide it into four equal pieces, approximately 1 pound, 4 ounces (570 g) each. Shape the pieces into oval loaves (see Figure 3–24, page 120). Let the loaves rise until they are one-and-one-half times the original size.

5. Bake at 375°F (190°C), using steam and leaving the damper closed for the first 10 minutes. Open the damper, lower the heat slightly, and continue to bake approximately 35 minutes longer, or until baked through.

Onion-Walnut Bread

six 1-pound, 5-ounce (595-g) loaves

8 ounces (225 g) peeled yellow onions, minced

butter or olive oil to sauté onions

2 ounces (55 g) fresh compressed yeast

5 cups (1 l, 200 ml) warm milk (105–115°F, 40–46°C)

2 ounces (55 g) granulated sugar

4 tablespoons (60 g) salt

1 cup (240 ml) olive oil

4 pounds, 6 ounces (1 kg, 990 g) bread flour, approximately

8 ounces (225 g) finely chopped walnuts

whole wheat flour

*T*he Spanish introduced both yellow onions and walnuts to California in the 1700s. Today California produces about 90 percent of the world's supply of the most common commercial walnut, the English variety. Onions are now grown in every part of the world, with the United States being one of the top producers. Onions are sometimes referred to as the King of Vegetables, in part because of their widespread use, versatility, and year-round availability, but also because of their distinctive, pungent, and sometimes overpowering flavor. Because the taste can be so strong (and lingering) it is important to avoid chopping the onions on a board or table where you will be working with other products later. Ideally, designate a cutting board for that use only. This is not so crucial in other kitchens where the next item to be chopped might be carrots for a stock, but in the pastry kitchen or bakeshop where the next task might be chopping chocolate for chocolate chip cookies, it could be a real disaster!

The walnuts, through the interaction of the tannin in their skins with the other ingredients and the metal in the mixing bowl, create a lavender-colored dough. If this is not desired, add the walnuts at the end after most of the kneading is done. A stainless-steel bowl will also minimize the coloring. These loaves are proofed in round bannetons (see page 1119) to mark a ring pattern. In absence of these, follow the alternate directions in the note.

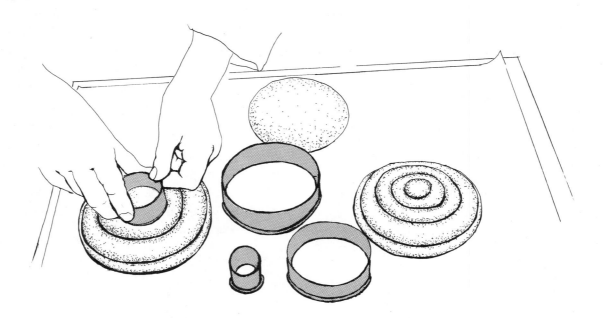

FIGURE 3–22   *Using cookie cutters to mark the top of Onion-Walnut loaves if bannetons are not available*

One-Quarter Recipe

two 1-pound (455-g) loaves

2 ounces (55 g) peeled yellow onions, minced

butter or olive oil to sauté onions

3/4 ounce (22 g) fresh compressed yeast

1 1/4 cups (300 ml) warm milk, 105–115°F, 40–46°C

1 tablespoon (15 g) granulated sugar

1 tablespoon (15 g) salt

1/4 cup (60 ml) olive oil

1 pound (455 g) bread flour, approximately

2 ounces (55 g) finely chopped walnuts

whole wheat flour

NOTE: If you do not have these baskets, you can create the same rustic-looking beehive pattern in the following way: Form the loaves as directed at the start of step six. Instead of placing the loaves in the **bannetons**, *brush with Egg Wash, then invert in whole wheat flour, completely covering the tops of the loaves with flour. Turn right-side up and immediately mark the top with four plain cookie cutters, using the back of the cutters so you can press firmly and leave a distinct mark without cutting the skin of the loaf (Figure 3–22). Start with a 5-inch (12.5-cm) cutter for the outside ring, then mark three additional rings in descending size using cutters approximately 3 3/4, 2 1/2, and 1 1/2 inches (9.3, 6.2, and 3.7 cm) in diameter, depending on the spacing of the particular set of cutters you are using. Let the loaves rise until they have doubled in volume. Bake as directed in step nine.*

1. Sauté the onions in butter or olive oil until golden. Set aside to cool to lukewarm.

2. Use a stainless-steel or other noncorrosive bowl to mix the dough. Dissolve the yeast in the warm milk in the mixer bowl. Stir in the sugar, salt, and olive oil.

3. Mix in half of the flour using the dough hook. Mix in the walnuts and onions. Incorporate enough of the remaining flour to make a quite-firm dough. Knead until smooth, approximately 8 to 10 minutes at low or medium speed.

4. Place the dough in an oiled bowl, turn to coat both sides with oil, cover, and let rise until doubled in volume.

5. Dust the inside of *bannetons* heavily with whole wheat flour; reserve (see note).

6. Divide the dough into six equal pieces, approximately 1 pound 5 ounces (595 g) each (two equal pieces about 1 pound/455 g each if making the smaller recipe). Knead the pieces into firm round loaves (see Figures 3–1, and 3–2, page 70). Place the loaves inverted in the prepared *bannetons* so that the smooth sides of the loaves are against the baskets.

7. Let the loaves rise in the baskets until they have doubled in volume.

8. Invert the loaves onto paper-lined sheet pans, dislodging them carefully from the baskets. Remove the baskets.

9. Bake at 400°F (205°C) for about 35 minutes. Cool on racks.

To form rolls

Although in principal all bread doughs can be made into rolls, this dough makes a particularly pretty and unusual roll when shaped as described below.

1. Divide each 1-pound, 5-ounce (595-g) piece into ten equal pieces.

2. Shape into rolls (see Figure 3–27, page 124) and finish as instructed in the note, using three cutters approximately 2 1/2, 1 1/2, and 3/4 inches (6.2, 3.7, and 2 cm) in diameter to mark the pattern.

3. Bake at 400°F (205°C) for about 20 minutes.

🥄 Pita Bread

sixteen 7-inch (17.5-cm) pita breads

Sponge

½ ounce (15 g) or 2 tablespoons (30 ml) fresh compressed yeast
1 tablespoon (15 g) granulated sugar
1½ cups (360 ml) warm water (105–115°F, 40–46°C)
14 ounces (400 g) bread flour

Dough

1½ cups (360 ml) warm water (105–115°F, 40–46°C)
4 teaspoons (20 g) salt
⅓ cup (80 ml) olive oil
1 pound, 4 ounces (570 g) bread flour

NOTE: *If you are using a noncommercial oven that does not have a hearth, use a "homemade" one (see page 1121), or use a baking stone. Place the stone in the oven well ahead of time so it will be very hot when you are ready to bake the pitas. A nonstick or well-seasoned sheet pan can be used as well in a pinch. When you use sheet pans, the breads will require longer to bake and the pitas will not be as crunchy on the bottom.*

*T*he most widely consumed bread in the Middle East is this classic pita or flatbread, referred to simply as khubz, meaning "bread" in Arabic. It is a bread with very little leavening that puffs up spectacularly, like an odd-looking balloon, after a few minutes in a hot oven. The pocket develops from the rapid conversion of water to steam. Throughout the Middle East they are served whole with meals, cut or broken into wedges for dipping into local dishes such as baba ghanoush or hummus, or the pocket breads themselves are made into a meal by stuffing them with meats, falafel topped with tahini sauce, or other ingredients to create a sandwich.

My first exposure to Pita Bread (although I did not know what it was at the time) was in Cairo, Egypt, where the local pita is known as baladi. As usual, I was ready with my camera looking for unusual local photos (one had to be quick and almost sneaky at times because it seemed people did not like having their pictures taken there). On this occasion, when I saw a man half running down the street with a large board balanced on top of his head that was covered with something that looked like flat loaves of bread, I naturally pointed my camera and shot, and then followed him to see what this was about. After I had run behind him for a few blocks, trying not to lose him in the crowded streets (although the big board on his head did make him pretty easy to spot), he stopped at what was literally a hole in the wall on the outside of a building on a street corner. This turned out to be an extremely hot brick oven and apparently a thriving business someone had set up solely for baking pitas and other types of flatbreads for the locals since most households, I later learned, did not have ovens of their own. The process was quick and simple: A customer would deliver his tray of baladi or other bread dough rounds, which had, shall we say, already gotten a running start as far as proofing, the tray was slid into the oven for just the few minutes required, and the freshly baked pitas were carried back home.

If your baked Pita Breads feel tough and cardboard-like, as so many store-bought pitas do, replace the bread flour with all-purpose flour or use one-third cake flour with two-thirds bread flour to reduce the gluten and make the bread more tender. As a variation, replace up to half of the bread flour with whole wheat flour. In any case it is preferable to use unbleached bread flour.

1. Make the sponge by dissolving the yeast and sugar in the warm water and then adding the first measurement of bread flour. Mix until well blended and smooth, then cover and let stand in a warm place until it has doubled in bulk, approximately 30 minutes.

2. Add the remaining water to the sponge together with the salt, olive oil, and all but a handful of the remaining flour. Knead, using the dough hook on low speed, until the dough forms a smooth and elastic ball, about 8 minutes.

3. Place the dough on a worktable and knead in as much of the reserved flour by hand as needed to prevent the dough from being sticky. Work the dough into a firm ball and place in a lightly oiled bowl, turn to coat all sides with oil, then cover and let proof in a warm place for 1½ hours.

4. Punch the dough down and divide into 16 equal pieces about 4 ounces (115 g) each. Shape the pieces into tight round balls (see Figure

3–27, page 124). Set aside on a floured surface for 30 minutes to let the dough proof and allow the gluten to relax.

5. Before starting to form the breads, preheat the oven to 475°F (246°C). Flatten and roll each ball of dough out to a 7-inch (17.5-cm) disk, using flour to prevent the dough from sticking. There should not be any wrinkles or cuts in the dough that can prevent the pitas from forming pockets as they bake. Lay the dough rounds on floured towels or baking pans after rolling them. Let stand at room temperature until they have puffed slightly.

6. Working with four pitas at a time, and starting with the breads rolled out first, use a floured peel to slide the pitas directly onto the hearth of the oven (see note). Bake for approximately 4 minutes or until light golden brown on the bottom. The breads should puff up halfway through baking. If the breads become too dark on the bottom before they are firm on the top, lower the heat slightly. Place on wire racks to cool. Cover with a dry towel if you would like to keep the crust soft. Bake the remaining Pita Breads in the same way.

7. Once the breads have cooled, wrap them in plastic if they will not be served right away, to keep the pitas flexible. Freeze for longer storage.

Potato Bread

four 1-pound, 2-ounce (510-g) loaves

Sponge

1 cup warm water (105–115°F, 40–46°C)

2 tablespoons (30 ml) or 1¹/₂ ounces (40 g) light corn syrup

¹/₂ ounce (15 g) fresh compressed yeast

8 ounces (225 g) bread flour

Dough

10 ounces (285 g) russet potatoes

2 ounces (55 g) fresh compressed yeast

1 pint (480 ml) warm milk (105–115°F, 40–46°C)

1¹/₂ tablespoons (22 g) salt

1 ounce (30 g) malt sugar
    or
3 tablespoons (45 ml) or
    2 ounces (55 g) honey

6 ounces (170 g) whole wheat flour

1 pound, 14 ounces (855 g) bread flour, approximately

Egg Wash (page 7)

whole wheat flour

*T*his is another typical peasant-style bread; potatoes being one of the staple foods of the Northern European farmer. Potatoes were always readily available, providing a good source of energy, and by adding moist potatoes to the bread dough, the farmers found the baked loaves stayed fresh longer. If you are not in a hurry, try Rosemary Potato Bread on page 110. It requires slow ris-ing—overnight in the refrigerator—but is well worth the wait.

To make the sponge

1. Combine the water and corn syrup and dissolve the yeast in the liquid.

2. Add the bread flour and mix until you have a very soft, smooth sponge.

3. Cover and let rise in a warm place until the sponge starts to fall.

To make the dough

1. Peel, cook, and mash the potatoes. Set aside to cool.

2. Dissolve the yeast in the warm milk. Add the salt, malt sugar or honey, and the whole wheat flour.

3. Mix the mashed potatoes and the sponge into the dough.

4. Reserve a handful of the bread flour, then mix in the remainder. Knead with the dough hook for about 8 minutes at medium speed, then adjust with the reserved flour if necessary. The dough will be smooth and elastic, but not sticky.

5. Cover the dough and let rest for 1 hour in a warm place, punch-ing the dough down after 30 minutes.

NOTE: If your oven is not equipped with steam injectors, see Creating Steam without Steam Injectors, page 73.

6. Divide the dough into four equal pieces, approximately 1 pound, 2 ounces (510 g) each. Pound each piece into a tapered oval loaf about 10 inches (25 cm) long (see Figures 3–3, 3–4, and 3–5, pages 77 and 78). The loaves should be thicker in the center and thinner on the ends.

7. Brush the loaves with Egg Wash, invert in whole wheat flour, and place right-side up on sheet pans lined with baking paper. Let the loaves rise until slightly less than doubled in volume.

8. With a sharp knife, make three slashes at a 45° angle across each loaf. Cut only deep enough to go through the skin.

9. Bake at 400°F (205°C), using steam and leaving the damper closed for the first 10 minutes. Open the damper and continue baking approximately 20 minutes longer.

Pullman Loaves

two 4-by-4-by-16-inch (10-×-10-×-40-cm) loaves or three 4-by-4-by-12-inch (10-×-10-×-30-cm) loaves

Sponge

2 ounces (55 g) fresh compressed yeast
2½ cups (600 ml) warm water (105–115°F, 40–46°C)
1 ounce (30 g) malt sugar
or
3 tablespoons (45 ml) or 2 ounces (55 g) honey
2 pounds (910 g) bread flour
melted unsalted butter

Dough

2 ounces (55 g) dry milk powder
1½ cups (360 ml) warm water (105–115°F, 40–46°C)
2 ounces (55 g) granulated sugar
2 tablespoons (30 g) salt
1 pound, 8 ounces (680 g) bread flour, approximately
3 ounces (85 g) soft unsalted butter

NOTE: Instead of Pullman pans, you can use regular bread pans covering the tops with a flat sheet pan as a lid. Weigh the pan down with a minimum of 16 pounds (7 kg, 280 g) of weight on top to prevent the dough from seeping out

George Pullman, in lending his name to the Pullman railroad car, secondarily inspired the name for this bread due to the bread's resemblance to the car in its long, boxy shape. The basic difference between a regular loaf of bread and a Pullman Loaf is that Pullman Loaves are baked in pans that are enclosed on all sides so the top of the loaf is flat rather than rounded. The top of the pan slides into place after putting the dough inside. Pullman bread pans have a larger capacity than the average bread pan. Pullman Loaves are used primarily for sandwiches or toast in commercial food establishments.

If you do not have pans that are the precise size specified here, adjust the amount of dough used accordingly. Since there is nowhere for the dough to escape in an enclosed pan such as the Pullman, you will be able to determine quite easily if you use too much by the "dead dough" trapped under the lid. This can also happen to a properly scaled loaf during the oven-spring if the bread has been overproofed.

1. To make the sponge, dissolve the yeast in the first measurement of warm water. Add the malt sugar or honey and the first measurement of bread flour. Mix for a few minutes until you have a smooth dough.

2. Cover, and let rise in a warm place until the sponge starts to fall.

3. Butter the inside and the underside of the lids of two 4-by-4-by-16-inch (10-×-10-×-40-cm) or three 4-by-4-by-12-inch (10-×-10-×-30-cm) Pullman pans or other suitable bread pans (see note).

4. To make the dough, dissolve the milk powder in the remaining warm water. Add the granulated sugar, the salt, the prepared sponge, and all but a handful of the remaining bread flour. Incorporate the soft butter. Knead the dough with the dough hook for approximately 8 minutes, adjusting the consistency by adding the reserved flour if necessary, to develop a soft but not sticky dough.

5. Cover and let the dough rise until it has doubled in volume.

6. Divide the dough into two equal pieces, approximately 3 pounds (1 kg, 365 g) each, for the larger loaves or three equal pieces, approximately 2 pounds (910 g) each, for the smaller size loaves. Form

during the oven-spring. (Two 8-pound/3-kg, 640-g) weights from the balance scale are a good choice)

each piece into a tight round loaf (see Figures 3–1 and 3–2, page 70). Allow the loaves to relax on the table for a few minutes.

7. Form the loaves into thick ropes the length of the pans, using the same technique as for shaping Baguettes (see Figure 3–24, page 120; do not taper the ends). Place the ropes in the pans. Slide the tops of the pans in place leaving them partially open so you will be able to check the loaves as they proof. Let proof until doubled in volume (the pans should only be approximately three-quarters full).

8. Close the tops of the pans. Bake the loaves at 400°F (205°C) for 30 minutes. Slide the tops of the pans open partially to allow steam to escape (if the top sticks, bake a few minutes longer), then remove the tops completely (remember that for every 1 pound/455 g of bread dough, 2 ounces /55 g is lost in steam during baking). Continue baking 15 minutes longer or until the loaves are baked through. Turn the loaves out onto a rack to cool. Do not slice before they are completely cool.

🥄 Pumpernickel Bread

four 1-pound, 8-ounce (680-g) loaves

1 ounce (30 g) fresh compressed yeast
3 cups (720 ml) warm water
    (105–115°F, 40–46°C)
2 tablespoons (30 g) salt
⅓ cup (80 ml) Caramel Coloring
    (page 4)
1 pound (455 g) Sourdough Starter
    (page 114)
3 tablespoons (24 g) caraway seeds
1 pound, 12 ounces (795 g) coarse rye
    flour (pumpernickel flour)
2 pounds (910 g) bread flour,
    approximately

This is my version of this well-known German bread. The name pumpernickel comes from two German words. The first, pumper, meaning "to break wind," and the second, which means "demon," are probably both references to the digestive upset that can occur after eating too much of the old-fashioned Pumpernickel Bread, which was unleavened, dense, and slightly sour. The small amount of yeast added to this recipe gives the bread a lighter texture, but it will still take much longer to proof than other breads. Pumpernickel Bread is wonderful with cheese, especially a sharp cheese like stilton or a sharp white cheddar.

1. In a mixer bowl, dissolve the yeast in the warm water. Add the salt and Caramel Coloring and mix to combine.

2. Incorporate the Sourdough Starter, caraway seeds, and rye flour. Reserve a few handfuls of the bread flour and knead in the remaining flour using the dough hook. Continue kneading the dough, adding the reserved flour as required, for approximately 8 minutes. The dough should be smooth, yet somewhat sticky.

3. Place the dough, covered, in a warm place and let it rise until it has doubled in volume.

4. Punch the dough down, cover, and let rise again until it has doubled in volume.

5. Scale the dough into four equal pieces, approximately 1 pound, 8 ounces (680 g) each. Line the insides of four loaf pans (approximately 10 by 4 by 3 inches/25 × 10 × 7.5 cm) with baking paper (see Figures 1–8, and 1–9, page 25), or brush the pans with Butter and Flour Mixture. Fold the dough pieces into tight rectangles that will fit inside the pans. Place the dough in the pans, seam-side down, and let rise until the loaves have doubled in volume.

6. Bake at 350°F (175°C) for approximately 45 minutes or until baked through. The baked loaves should feel light when you pick them up and sound hollow when tapped sharply on the bottom. Turn out onto a cooling rack immediately.

To Make Pumpernickel Bread without a Sourdough Starter

1 ounce (30 g) fresh compressed yeast

1 cup (240 ml) warm water (110–115°F, 40–46°C)

1 teaspoon (5 ml) Caramel Coloring (page 4)

1 teaspoon (5 ml) white vinegar

8 ounces (225 g) bread flour

NOTE: For a much better flavor, start with cold water and let the sponge rise, covered, overnight in the refrigerator.

*S*ubstitute the following for the 1 pound (455 g) Sourdough Starter called for in the recipe. The bread will not have the same flavor but will suffice.

1. Dissolve the yeast in the warm water (see note). Add the Caramel Coloring and the vinegar. Using the dough hook, knead in the bread flour. Continue kneading until the sponge is smooth, approximately 10 minutes. The sponge will be quite soft, which helps the yeast react more rapidly.

2. Place the sponge, covered, in a warm place and let it rise until it bubbles and starts to fall.

Raisin Bread

four 1-pound (455-g) loaves

melted unsalted butter

2 cups (480 ml) warm milk (105–115°F, 40–46°C)

1½ ounces (40 g) fresh compressed yeast

1 tablespoon (15 g) salt

½ cup (120 ml) or 6 ounces (170 g) honey

1 pound, 8 ounces (680 g) bread flour, approximately

2 ounces (55 g) soft unsalted butter

12 ounces (340 g) dark raisins

Egg Wash (page 7)

Cinnamon Sugar (page 5)

One-Half Recipe

two 1-pound (455-g) loaves

melted unsalted butter

1 cup (240 ml) warm milk (105°–115°F, 40°–46°C)

¾ ounce (22 g) fresh compressed yeast

1½ teaspoons (8.g) salt

¼ cup (60 ml) or 3 ounces (85 g) honey

*T*he addition of raisins to any baked good will retard staling since raisins, which are high in sugar, retain moisture. I do not soften the raisins before adding them to the dough because I have found that very soft raisins tend to crush or mash, leaving unpleasant dark streaks in the dough. However, if the raisins you are using are dry and hard, soak them in warm water for about 30 minutes and then drain well before adding them to the dough. Try thick slices of Raisin Bread toasted at breakfast or use Raisin Bread to make French Toast.

1. Butter the inside of bread pans measuring 8 by 4 by 2½ inches (20 × 10 × 6.2 cm). Reserve.

2. Dissolve the yeast in the warm milk. Stir in the salt and the honey. Reserve a few ounces of the bread flour, then add the remainder. Mix in the butter.

3. Knead using the dough hook for 8 to 10 minutes to make a smooth, soft dough. Adjust by adding the reserved bread flour if necessary. Do not overknead or tighten the dough or it will be difficult to work the raisins in later.

4. Place the dough, covered, in a warm place and let it rise until it has doubled in volume, about 1 hour.

5. Turn the dough out onto the workbench but do not punch it down. Incorporate the raisins by hand. Let the dough rest, covered, for 10 minutes.

6. Divide the dough into eight equal pieces (four for the smaller recipe), approximately 8 ounces (225 g) each. Keep the pieces covered. Starting with the first one weighed, pound and roll each piece into a

12 ounces (340 g) bread flour,
    approximately
1 ounce (30 g) soft unsalted butter
6 ounces (170 g) dark raisins
Egg Wash (page 7)
Cinnamon Sugar (page 5)

NOTE: Due to the large amount of sugar in this bread, you must protect the dough from cooling below 75°F (24°C) or the capability of the yeast will be severely reduced.

10-inch (25-cm) string (see Figures 3–3, 3–4, and 3–5, pages 77 and 78); do not taper the ends.

7. Twist two strings together loosely and place in one of the prepared pans. Repeat with the remaining strings.

8. Brush the loaves with Egg Wash and sprinkle quite heavily with Cinnamon Sugar. Let the loaves rise until just under doubled in volume.

9. Bake at 375°F (190°C) for about 40 minutes. Unmold and cool on racks.

Rosemary Bread

six 1-pound (455-g) loaves

2 ounces (55 g) fresh compressed yeast
3 1/2 cups (840 ml) warm water
    (105–115°F, 40–46°C)
2 ounces (55 g) granulated sugar
1 cup (240 ml) olive oil
3 tablespoons (45 g) salt
6 tablespoons (30 g) fresh rosemary,
    finely chopped
3 pounds, 12 ounces (1 kg, 705 g)
    bread flour, approximately
Egg Wash (page 7)

One-Third Recipe

two 1-pound (455-g) loaves

3/4 ounce (22 g) fresh compressed yeast
1 1/4 cups (300 ml) warm water
    (105–115°F, 40–46°C)
2/3 ounce (20 g) granulated sugar
1/3 cup (80 ml) olive oil
1 tablespoon (15 g) salt
2 tablespoons (10 g) fresh rosemary,
    finely chopped
1 pound, 4 ounces (570 g) bread flour,
    approximately
Egg Wash (page 7)

*T*he flavor of this bushy herb, native to the Mediterranean where it grows wild, is a mixture of lemon and pine. While rosemary is used in many types of cooking, I think you will find its flavor especially pleasing in this classic Italian bread. Try reserving some Rosemary Bread dough to use for a pizza crust. The bread dough can be stored in the freezer for several weeks if it is well wrapped.

1. Dissolve the yeast in the warm water. Stir in the sugar, oil, salt, rosemary, and enough of the flour to make a smooth, nonsticky dough.

2. Knead using the dough hook at medium speed for 6 to 8 minutes to develop the gluten structure. The dough will get a little looser as it becomes smoother.

3. Place the dough in an oiled bowl and turn to coat both sides with oil. Cover and let rise for 30 minutes.

4. Punch down the dough, then let it rise 30 minutes longer.

5. Punch the dough down again and divide into six equal pieces (two pieces for the smaller recipe) approximately 1 pound (455 g) each. Shape the pieces into tight oval loaves (see Figures 3–1 and 3–2, page 70). The loaves should be tight enough to spring back when lightly pressed, but not so tight that the skin on the dough breaks. Place the loaves on sheet pans lined with baking paper.

6. Brush Egg Wash over the loaves. Let rise until slightly less than doubled in volume.

7. Using a serrated knife, cut halfway into each loaf at a 45° angle, starting in the center.

8. Bake at 400°F (205°C) until the loaves sound hollow when tapped, about 35 minutes. Place the loaves on racks to cool.

VARIATION
Crisp Bread

12 pieces

1. Weigh the dough into 8-ounce (225-g) pieces and form into round loaves. Let stand a few minutes to relax the dough.

2. Starting with the loaf you formed first, roll each one out to a 10-inch (25-cm) circle. If the dough is still rubbery, let it rest some more by rolling all the circles halfway then coming back to finish.

3. Cut a 3-inch (7.5-cm) hole in the center of each circle.

4. Place the rings and the cutouts on sheet pans, rub with olive oil, and sprinkle lightly with kosher salt. Let rise until one-quarter larger in size.

5. Bake at 375°F (190°C) for about 30 minutes.

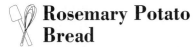

Rosemary Potato Bread

five 1-pound, 10-ounce (740-g) loaves

Sponge

1 ounce (30 g) malt sugar
   or
3 tablespoons (45 ml) or 2 ounces (55 g) honey
1 cup (240 ml) warm water (105–115°F, 40–46°C)
2 ounces (55 g) fresh compressed yeast
12 ounces (340 g) high-gluten flour

Dough

2 pounds (910 g) red potatoes
1 quart (960 ml) cold water
3 pounds (1 kg, 365 g) bread flour
12 ounces (340 g) high-gluten flour
1 teaspoon (4 g) ascorbic acid (see note 2 on page 91, in the recipe for *Epis* Baguettes)
4 tablespoons (60 g) salt
1½ ounces (40 g) fresh rosemary, finely chopped
1 cup (240 ml) olive oil

Two-Loaf Recipe

two 1-pound, 12-ounce (795-g) loaves

Sponge

2 tablespoons (18 g) malt sugar
   or

*P*otatoes are not high on the list of culinary ingredients associated with Italy; however, they are plentiful all over the southern region (Puglia and Basilica in particular), and while it is certainly more common to find a baker in Northern or Eastern Europe adding this popular vegetable to their bread, it is done in Italy as well. This tuber, which is a member of the same family as tomatoes and eggplants, is added to the bread not for flavoring but to retain moisture. The starch released by the potato helps trap liquid, producing in turn a soft, moist, longer-lasting bread. One caution, however, because of the high starch content, the bread will brown quickly and requires close attention during baking. For a traditional potato bread, omit the rosemary or try the recipe on page 105.

If you can not wait until the following day to bake (and taste) this absolutely delicious bread, you can treat it as you would any other bread dough, in other words let it rise in a proof box, but the bread will not have the desired unusual-looking cross section when sliced. When the uncovered loaves are allowed a long slow rising in the refrigerator overnight, the outside forms a crust. Once the loaves have proofed to their maximum potential, the interior "falls" and partially detaches itself from the top crust. This creates the large irregular air pockets that give this bread its characteristic rustic appearance. The large air pockets under the top crust will also be lost if the dough is too firm when it is shaped into loaves.

1. To start the sponge, add the malt sugar or honey to the warm water. Dissolve the yeast in this mixture. Add the high-gluten flour and mix with the dough hook until the sponge is smooth, about 5 minutes.

2. Cover and let rise in a warm place until doubled in bulk.

3. Wash the potatoes, then arrange in a single layer on a sheet pan or hotel pan (cut any large potatoes in half). Cover with foil and bake at 400°F (205°C) for approximately 30 minutes or until somewhat softened. Do not overbake. Once they have cooled, cut the potatoes into olive-sized chunks. Do not cut the pieces too small; they will become smaller as they are worked into the dough. Reserve.

4. Add the cold water, both flours, ascorbic acid, salt, rosemary, and olive oil to the sponge. Knead for 6 minutes using the dough hook at low speed. Scrape down the bowl, knead 6 minutes longer, then incorporate the potatoes. Knead just long enough to mix in the potato chunks.

1 tablespoon plus 2 teaspoons (25 ml)
   honey

1/2 cup (120 ml) warm water
   (105–115°F, 40–46°C)

1 ounce (30 g) fresh compressed yeast

4 ounces (115 g) high-gluten flour

Dough

12 ounces (360 g) red potatoes

1 1/2 cups (360 ml) cold water

1 pound (455 g) bread flour

10 ounces (285 g) high-gluten flour

1/2 teaspoon (2 g) ascorbic acid
   (see note 2 on page 91, in the
   recipe for *Epis* baguettes)

1 tablespoon (15 g) salt

1/2 ounce (15 g) fresh rosemary, finely
   chopped

1/3 cup (80 ml) olive oil

NOTE 1: This Italian country-style bread dough will be soft and may seem too sticky at first. After the resting and punching down periods it will firm up considerably as the gluten matures.

NOTE 2: If your oven is not equipped with steam injectors, see Creating Steam without Steam Injectors, page 73.

🥄 Russian Rolled-Wheat Bread

four 1-pound, 4-ounce (570-g) loaves

2 cups (480 ml) water

1/2 cup (120 ml) or 6 ounces (170 g)
   light corn syrup

9 ounces (255 g) rolled wheat

2 cups (480 ml) warm water
   (105–115°F, 40–46°C)

2 1/2 ounces (70 g) fresh compressed
   yeast

5 teaspoons (25 g) salt

2 ounces (55 g) soft unsalted butter

8 ounces (225 g) whole wheat flour

2 pounds (910 g) bread flour,
   approximately

Egg Wash (page 7)

rolled wheat

Do not mash them into the dough (whole pieces of potato should be visible in the finished bread).

5. Cover the dough and let it rest in a warm place for 30 minutes.

6. Punch the dough down, then let it rise again for 30 minutes.

7. Punch the dough down and weigh into five equal pieces approximately 1 pound, 10 ounces (740 g) each or two pieces approximately 1 pound 12 ounces (795 g) each for the smaller recipe. Form the pieces into tight round loaves (see Figures 3–1, and 3–2, page 70). Place on sheet pans and leave in the refrigerator overnight to rise and form a natural crust.

8. Remove the loaves from the refrigerator. They should be one-and-one-half times the original size. Let rise further at room temperature if necessary.

9. Bake at 475°F (246°C), directly on the floor of a deck oven or otherwise on the bottom rack, using steam for the first 10 minutes. Open the damper to remove the steam and lower the temperature to 375°F (190°C) (see note 2). Continue baking 20 to 25 minutes longer, or until the bread is baked through and has a dark golden crust.

*T*his robust Russian peasant bread is one of my personal favorites, probably because it is one of the breads I ate while I was growing up. We called it Ryskt Matbröd, and it was very popular in Sweden at that time. Try serving Russian Rolled-Wheat Bread spread with sweet butter and topped with Swedish herrårdost (roughly translated, "estate or mansion cheese") or with Swedish fontina cheese.

This bread is made using the scalding method: Boiling water is poured over the grain, and the mixture is left to sit overnight. This allows the grain to absorb the maximum amount of moisture possible and ensures the bread will stay moist longer.

A special cutter is available to mark the decorative pattern on the top of the loaves. It can be purchased from bakery suppliers.

1. Heat the first measurement of water and the corn syrup to boiling; pour over the rolled wheat. Do not stir. Let stand overnight.

2. Pour the warm water into a mixer bowl, add the yeast, and mix to dissolve. Add the rolled-wheat mixture, salt, butter, whole wheat flour, and all but a handful of the bread flour. Knead the mixture with the dough hook at medium speed for 6 to 8 minutes, adding the

Two-Loaf Recipe

two 1-pound, 4-ounce (570-g) loaves

1 cup (240 ml) water

¹/₄ cup (60 ml) or 3 ounces (85 g) light
    corn syrup

4¹/₂ ounces (130 g) rolled wheat

1 cup (240 ml) warm water
    (105–115°F, 40–46°C)

1¹/₂ ounces (40 g) fresh compressed
    yeast

2 teaspoons (10 g) salt

1 ounce (30 g) soft unsalted butter

4 ounces (115 g) whole wheat flour

1 pound (455 g) bread flour,
    approximately

Egg Wash (page 7)

rolled wheat

*NOTE: This bread can be made with very good
results even if the resting time for step one is
reduced to 3 or 4 hours. The loaves will just not
be as moist as they will be if the rolled wheat is
given the full length of time to absorb the maximum amount of liquid.*

FIGURE 3–23   *Slashing lines on the top of Russian Rolled-Wheat loaves before
baking*

reserved handful of bread flour if needed to make a smooth, elastic
dough.

3. Let rest, covered, in a warm place for 30 minutes.

4. Divide the dough into four equal pieces (two for the smaller
recipe), approximately 1 pound, 4 ounces (570 g) each. Shape each
piece into a smooth, round loaf (see Figures 3–1 and 3–2, page 70). Flatten lightly with your hand. Place the loaves on sheet pans lined with
baking paper.

5. Brush Egg Wash over the loaves and sprinkle rolled wheat on
top. Using a 3-inch (7.5-cm) plain cookie cutter, cut a circle ¹/₈ inch (3
mm) deep in the center of each loaf. Cut about ten slashes to the same
depth radiating out from the circle (Figure 3–23). Let the loaves rise
until they are slightly less than doubled in volume.

6. Bake at 400°F (205°C) for approximately 35 minutes. Place on
racks to cool.

Sicilian White Bread

*four 1-pound, 6-ounce (625-g)
loaves*

2 ounces (55 g) fresh compressed
    yeast

1 quart (960 ml) warm water
    (105–115°F, 40–46°C)

2 tablespoons (18 g) malt sugar
    or

¹/₄ cup (60 ml) or 3 ounces (85 g)
    honey

1 pound (455 g) bread flour

¹/₄ cup (60 ml) olive oil

3 tablespoons (45 g) salt

*This gluten-rich bread from Italy brings back memories of my first visit to the
spectacular island of Sicily. I was in my early twenties and working in the
pastry department on board the Swedish American Lines proud ship MS
Kungsholm. Having never been to that part of the world before, my palate was
quite unaccustomed to tasting bread without any salt (what I referred to with the
arrogance of youth as "tasteless bread"). I also had the misfortune of gulping
down my first espresso like a regular cup of coffee not knowing such strong coffee even existed! I later learned that the bakers of Sicily have a very good reason for not adding salt to some of their breads: the milder taste complements the
richly-flavored, often spicy cuisine, and I have since come to truly enjoy a
slightly milder version of espresso.*

*Yes, there is salt in this bread, and I have added garlic for more flavor (the
garlic can, of course, be omitted if you want). This dough makes up well into
traditional baguette-shaped loaves, scaled half of the normal size. The gluten
generates a very pronounced oven-spring which is attractive on the slashed*

4 teaspoons (12 g) garlic powder
   or
2 tablespoons (30 ml) puréed fresh
   garlic
2 pounds, 8 ounces (1 kg, 135 g) finely
   milled Durham wheat (semolina)
   flour, approximately

Two-Loaf Recipe

two 1-pound, 6-ounce (625-g) loaves

1 ounce (30 g) fresh compressed yeast
2 cups (480 ml) warm water
   (105–115°F, 40–46°C)
1 tablespoon (9 g) malt sugar
   or
2 tablespoons (40 g) honey
8 ounces (225 g) bread flour
2 tablespoons (30 ml) olive oil
4 teaspoons (20 g) salt
2 teaspoons (6 g) garlic powder
   or
1 tablespoon (15 ml) puréed fresh
   garlic
1 pound, 6 ounces (625 g) finely
   milled Durham wheat (semolina)
   flour, approximately

NOTE: *If your oven is not equipped with steam injectors, see Creating Steam without Steam Injectors, page 73.*

baguettes and also on rolls formed as for Rustica rolls (page 134). With the rolls, try proofing them in fine or medium semolina flour instead of bread flour. The appearance and flavor are wonderful.

1. Dissolve the yeast in the warm water. Using the dough hook, mix in the malt sugar or honey, bread flour, olive oil, salt, garlic powder or puréed garlic, and all but a handful of the semolina flour. Once the ingredients have formed a dough, continue kneading for about 10 minutes, adding the remaining semolina flour as necessary to form a smooth, soft dough.

2. Cover the dough and let it rise in a warm place until it has doubled in volume.

3. Punch the dough down. Let rise again until it has doubled in volume a second time.

4. Divide the dough into four equal pieces (two for the smaller recipe), approximately 1 pound, 6 ounces (625 g) each. Shape the pieces into round loaves (see Figures 3–1, and 3–2, page 70).

5. Let the loaves rise until they are one-and-one-half times the original size.

6. Bake at 410°F (210°C), using steam for the first 10 minutes, until the loaves are golden brown and baked through, about 40 minutes total.

Sourdough Bread

Although making sourdough bread using your own starter is a lengthy and sometimes frustrating procedure, that can make it all the more rewarding to sample the finished product when you have been successful. Sourdough starters provide a unique flavor as they leaven the bread. The starter, a fermented flour and water mixture, is used to trap the natural wild yeast present in the air. Natural airborne yeast is abundant in a kitchen or bakery where bread has been baked for many years. To assure a predictable result, especially in a kitchen where these organisms are not so plentiful, a small amount of fresh yeast is used to help the starter develop. Even then the performance of the starter will be affected by temperature and climate, and it requires careful tending to achieve the desired result. Making bread with a sourdough starter, as you will see, is not completed in a few hours like most other types of bread. Instead, it requires several days while the starter (affectionately referred to as the mother) ferments. You may replace the water called for in the starter recipe with water left after boiling potatoes; the starch and sugar from the potatoes can enhance the starter's development.

If you are a purist who refuses to use anything other than natural wild yeast in your sourdough, you can try making the natural starter (directions follow), but unfortunately that is the one recipe in this book I cannot guarantee will work every time. However, if you have the time and patience, and you are up for a real challenge—give it a try. As a third option, commercial starters are available to make life a little easier; just follow the directions on the package.

Using the Sourdough Starter alone to leaven the bread will produce a reasonably good but fairly dense product. It will take much longer to proof than other breads, making it impractical, especially in a commercial operation. Therefore, we again help the starter along by including fresh or dry yeast in the recipe to guarantee a light and flavorful bread.

Sourdough Starter

approximately 3 pounds (1 kg, 365 g) starter

1¹/₂ ounces (40 g) fresh compressed yeast
3 cups (720 ml) water, at body temperature
1 ounce (30 g) granulated sugar
1 pound, 8 ounces (680 g) unbleached bread flour

NOTE: Care of your starter: The starter should always be replenished after each use. And even if not used, it must be fed every ten days or so. If left alone too long it will perish in its own residue. To feed the Sourdough Starter, add half as much flour and water as in the original recipe, relative to the amount of starter you are feeding. As an example: if the full amount of the recipe above was left unused and had to be fed, you would add 12 ounces (340 g) of unbleached bread flour and 1¹/₂ cups (360 ml) of water and stir until completely smooth again. If you are replenishing the starter after using about half of it for the sourdough bread recipe, you would add ³/₄ cup (180 ml) of water and 6 ounces (170 g) of flour. Let the starter proof,

1. In a plastic or crockery container with a large opening and plenty of room for expansion, dissolve the yeast in the water, then add the sugar. Stir in the flour using a wooden spoon; keep stirring until you have a smooth paste.

2. Cover loosely to allow gases to escape, and let stand at approximately 80°F (26°C) for at least two to three days, preferably a little longer. The mixture should bubble and have a strong sour smell. Stir the starter down once a day during the time it is fermenting, also stirring in any crust that forms on top. After that, the starter should be stored in the refrigerator (see note). The starter, or part of it, may also be frozen; before using, allow it to slowly thaw and start to bubble again at room temperature.

loosely covered, in a warm place for 24 hours before refrigerating again.

If you are not using the starter very often, replenishing may present a small problem as the volume grows with each feeding. A way around this is to remove the starter from its container, discard half (or give it to a friend—one who will appreciate it and not think it is some kind of bad joke!), wash and rinse the container, place the remaining starter back inside, and feed as directed.

Natural Sourdough Starter

approximately 3 pounds (1 kg, 365 g) starter

3 cups (720 ml) milk, at body
    temperature
2 ounces (55 g) granulated sugar
1 pound, 8 ounces (680 g) bread flour

$\mathcal{R}$*emember, this will not work unless there is natural yeast present in the air of your kitchen from recent bread baking.*

   1. Follow the preceding directions for Sourdough Starter.
   2. When ready to replenish, add 1 cup (240 ml) warm milk, 8 ounces (225 g) bread flour, and 1 ounce (30 g) granulated sugar.

San Francisco Sourdough Loaves

four 1-pound, 2-ounce (510-g) loaves

1 ounce (30 g) fresh compressed yeast
2 cups (480 ml) warm water
    (105–115°F, 40–46°C)
2 tablespoons (30 g) salt
2 tablespoons (18 g) malt sugar
    or
1/4 cup (60 ml) or 3 ounces (85 g)
    honey
1 pound, 4 ounces (570 g) Sourdough
    Starter (page 114)
2 pounds, 6 ounces (1 kg, 80 g) bread
    flour, approximately
cornmeal

NOTE: Sourdough bread is also typically made in a very large, flat round shape in San Francisco. Scale the dough into two equal pieces, approximately 2 pounds, 4 ounces (1 kg, 25 g) each, then form the pieces into tight round

$\mathcal{P}$*roducing a bread with a sour flavor was long looked upon as a serious fault—a bread fit only for peasants (whose rye bread commonly had a sour taste and not necessarily by choice). While sourdough bread is still regarded as a country-style bread, its characteristic flavor is now very popular in Scandinavia and other parts of Europe, made from either rye or wheat; in France they call their wheat sourdough bread "pain de Campagne."*

It was first the pioneers and later on the gold miners of California and the Yukon (whose sharing of the sourdough starter was considered the ultimate act of friendship) that made sourdough bread popular in this country. As there was little access to any fresh supplies, and certainly not to yeast, they utilized the method of including a piece of leftover dough to start a new fermentation. The leftover "starter" became known as the mother dough.

Much has been written about the renowned San Francisco sourdough bread; many say it simply can not be made to taste the same (read: as good) anywhere else. The famous fog in San Francisco is given the credit by some. The basic explanation is this: since the yeast present in the starter is dependent on the type or characteristic of the microflora of any one area, and as this, of course, will not be the same in, for instance, New York as in San Francisco, even if the starter is transferred to another part of the country, the bread naturally will not taste the same baked in one area as it does in another. This is the reason the bakers in San Francisco get away with saying that their bread can not be duplicated. I say they also have a few tricks up their sleeve that they are not telling. Although, to be fair, while I haven't really tried that hard, I must admit I can't copy that wonderful aroma and I live and work in the San Francisco Bay Area!

loaves (see Figures 3–1, and 3–2, page 70). Let relax for a few minutes, then flatten them to approximately 9 inches (22.5 cm) in diameter. Proof and spray as for the long loaves. Dust with bread flour (quite heavily so that it shows after baking). Slash the tops of the loaves first in a series of parallel lines, then with additional parallel lines at a 45° angle to the first set to form a diamond pattern (see Figure 3–21, page 99). Bake as directed in step six for approximately 35 minutes.

1. In a mixer bowl, dissolve the yeast in the warm water. Add the salt, malt sugar or honey, and the Sourdough Starter. Kneading with the dough hook at low speed, incorporate enough of the bread flour to make a quite firm, not sticky dough. Continue kneading at medium speed for about 8 minutes until the dough is elastic and pliable.

2. Place in a lightly oiled bowl and turn the dough so that the top will be oiled as well. Cover and let rise in a warm place for 2 hours.

3. Punch the dough down and scale into four equal pieces, approximately 1 pound, 2 ounces (510 g) each.

4. Pound and roll each piece into a 16-inch (40-cm) loaf (see Figures 3–3 and 3–4, page 77; also see note).

5. Let rise until slightly less than doubled in volume. Be patient here; the loaves will take quite a bit longer to rise than regular bread. While proofing, spray the loaves with water to prevent a crust from forming on the top. Before baking, spray the loaves again, then dust with cornmeal. Slash the tops of the loaves using a sharp serrated knife or razor blade, cutting lengthwise at a slight angle as for Baguettes.

6. Bake at 425°F (219°C) with steam, leaving the damper closed for the first 10 minutes. Open the damper and bake approximately 30 minutes longer, or until done. Allow the bread to cool on a rack. If your oven is not equipped with steam injectors, see Creating Steam without Steam Injectors, page 73.

Southwestern Corn and Cheese Bread

six 1-pound, 8-ounce (680-g) loaves

1 cup (240 ml) warm water
   (105–115°F, 40–46°C)
2 cups (480 ml) warm buttermilk
   (105–115°F, 40–46°C)
2 ounces (55 g) fresh compressed
   yeast
2 eggs
6 ounces (170 g) granulated sugar
10 ounces (285 g) cornmeal
12 ounces (340 g) bread flour
2 teaspoons (4 g) ground paprika
2 teaspoons (4 g) cumin seed
2 teaspoons (4 g) ground cumin
2 tablespoons (10 g) garlic powder
4 teaspoons (20 g) salt
1/2 cup (120 ml) olive oil
2 pounds (910 g) bread flour
1 pound, 2 ounces (510 g) blanched
   fresh corn kernels

To prepare the fresh corn kernels for this recipe, remove the corn husks and then cut the kernels away from the cob using a serrated knife. Blanch the kernels in boiling water (to cook the starch) for approximately 1 minute, refresh under cold water, and dry on paper towels. You will need approximately five ears of fresh corn. When corn is not in season, substitute thawed frozen corn kernels. You may want to consider sprinkling the peppers over one half of the dough only, so that you will have some cheese bread for those who would prefer it less spicy.

1. Combine the warm water and buttermilk in a mixer bowl. Dissolve the yeast in this mixture. Add the eggs, sugar, cornmeal, first measurement of bread flour, paprika, cumin seed, ground cumin, garlic powder, salt, and olive oil. Mix until well blended, about 2 minutes.

2. Reserve a few handfuls of the second measurement of bread flour. Add the remainder and knead with the dough hook for 6 to 8 minutes. While kneading, add as much of the remaining bread flour as required to make a smooth and elastic dough. Add the corn kernels and mix just until incorporated.

3. Form the dough into a ball. It will be a little sticky at this point; use flour as necessary. Cut an X halfway through the ball of dough using a sharp knife. Pull the cuts out a little to make a rough square (see Figure 2–6, page 46); this will make it easier to roll the dough into a rectangle later. Cover the dough and let rest for 30 minutes.

Egg Wash (page 7)

4 ounces (115 g) minced jalapeño
   peppers

1 pound, 6 ounces (625 g) cheddar
   cheese, cut in ¹/₂-inch (1.2-cm)
   cubes

*NOTE: Just like a cinnamon roll, the finished
appearance of these loaves depends on how
tightly you roll the log to begin with. If they are
rolled up tightly as instructed, the oven-spring
will force the center of the coil up and into an
attractive peak. If rolled too loose, they will flatten as they bake with the energy directed outward instead.*

Sun-Dried Tomato Bread with Onion

*four 1-pound, 6-ounce (625-g)
loaves*

8 ounces (225 g) moist or
   reconstituted sun-dried tomatoes
   (see note)

¹/₂ cup (120 ml) olive oil

2 ounces (55 g) fresh compressed
   yeast

2¹/₂ cups (600 ml) warm water
   (105–115°F, 40–46°C)

1 tablespoon (15 ml) minced fresh
   garlic (about five medium-sized
   cloves)

5 ounces (140 g) finely chopped
   yellow onion

2 tablespoons (30 g) salt

3 pounds (1 kg, 365 g) bread flour,
   approximately

*NOTE: In addition to oil-packed dried toma-
toes, there are two types of plain dried tomatoes: the moist type (like dried fruit) are generally sold in a sealed package. The others are
completely dried through and crisp, and are
often available in bulk at a lower cost. The latter must be reconstituted before using; you will
only need 6 ounces (170 g) for this recipe. Soak
the tomatoes in about 3 cups (720 ml) of hot
water (but no vinegar as is used to make the
oil-packed tomatoes). When they are soft, drain
the tomatoes and save the water to use as part
or all of the warm water called for in the recipe.*

4. Roll the dough into a 15-by-20-inch (37.5-×-50-cm) rectangle. Brush Egg Wash over the dough. Sprinkle the minced jalapeño peppers and cubed cheddar cheese evenly over the top. Roll the dough into a tight log starting from the top (see note).

5. Cut the dough into six equal slices. Place the pieces on two paper-lined sheet pans cut-side down. Using your fingers, spread the spirals apart, pushing down and out, to open up the loaves. Let proof until one-and-one-half times the original size.

6. Brush the loaves with Egg Wash.

7. Bake at 375°F (190°C) for approximately 30 minutes.

---

*T*his is a wonderfully unique bread. It gets a tang and meatiness from the *tomato pieces that is incomparable. Unfortunately, their terrific flavor does not come cheap. I have reduced the expense a bit by using plain sun-dried tomatoes rather than the purchased oil-packed variety. If cost is not an issue, or if you already have oil-packed sun-dried tomatoes on hand, skip the ingredients and procedure in step one and use 12 ounces (340 g) of oil-packed tomatoes (including some of the oil) instead. If you have the time and space and use a lot of these, drying your own tomatoes in the oven makes a lot of sense. Directions follow the recipe.*

To prepare sun-dried tomatoes in oil for part of your regular mise en place: Soak the dried tomatoes (either the moist or completely dry variety; see note) in a mixture of equal parts white vinegar and water, long enough for the tomatoes to become perfectly soft; about one hour. Drain the liquid and discard. Pat the tomatoes dry on paper towels. Place in a jar, add a few bay leaves and add enough olive oil to cover. They will keep for many weeks stored covered in the refrigerator.

If you prefer not to use steam when baking (or you do not have a steam oven and do not want to fuss with spray bottles and ice cubes), forego the steam and brush the loaves with olive oil left from the saucepan when they come out of the oven.

1. Cut the sun-dried tomatoes into ¹/₂-inch (1.2-cm) pieces. Combine with the olive oil in a saucepan. Bring to a boil, remove from the heat, and set aside. When cool, strain and reserve the oil and tomatoes separately.

2. Dissolve the yeast in the warm water. Add the garlic, onion, salt, the strained oil from the tomatoes, and all but a handful of the bread flour. Mix on low speed, using the dough hook, for about 1 minute.

3. When the flour has been incorporated, turn the mixer to medium speed and knead for approximately 6 minutes, adjusting with additional flour if required (turn the mixer back to low speed before adding any flour). The dough should be smooth and elastic. Incorporate the reserved tomatoes on low speed.

4. Place the dough in an oiled bowl and turn the dough to cover it completely with oil. Cover and let rise in a warm place until doubled in volume.

5. Turn the dough onto a lightly floured workbench (do not punch it down first). Divide into four equal pieces, about 1 pound, 6 ounces (625 g) each.

6. Shape the pieces into round loaves (see Figures 3–1 and 3–2, page 70). Place on a sheet pan lined with baking paper.

7. Let proof in a warm place until just doubled in volume. Use a serrated paring knife or a razor blade and cut decorative slashes on top of the loaves.

8. Bake at 400°F (205°C) using steam for the first 10 minutes. Open the damper to remove the steam, and continue baking approximately 20 minutes longer. Let the loaves cool completely before slicing.

Oven-Dried Tomatoes

approximately 4 ounces (115 g) if dried through or 8 ounces (225 g) if left moist

6 pounds (2 kg, 730 g) plum (Roma) tomatoes
2 tablespoons (30 g) salt (optional)

There is no excuse for not drying your own tomatoes since, after you have spent a few minutes slicing and sprinkling them with salt, they need very little attention other than turning the pans from time to time and making sure the oven does not creep over 200°F (94°C). If you have a food dehydrator you won't even have to worry about that. In a professional kitchen, the sliced tomatoes can be dried under the heat lamp when the space is not being occupied by plates waiting to be delivered to the dining room. This is probably the next best thing to utilizing the hot sun since, just as out in the open, this shelf provides for plenty of air circulation. You may have seen pictures from various areas around the Mediterranean showing clusters of tomatoes hanging outside to dry slowly in the sun. But even if you live in Florida or the southwest it will take much longer due to the cooler and sometimes damp nights. If you want to try it, arrange them just as you would for drying inside, but you must cover the tomatoes with netting to prevent insects from landing on them. I dry my homegrown Italian prune plums this way in wooden frames covered with plastic screening (the same material used for screen doors) made to fit the size of a full sheet pan.

1. Wash the tomatoes. Dry them thoroughly. Remove the core and stem if necessary.

2. Slice the tomatoes in half lengthwise. Arrange cut-side up on wire racks set on three half-size sheet pans (you will be able to fit this amount onto one full-size pan if you crowd them at the beginning). Lightly sprinkle salt over the tomatoes, if desired. The salt helps to draw moisture out of the tomatoes.

3. Place the tomatoes in a 170–200°F (77–94°C) oven; a convection oven is preferable. If you are using a conventional oven without the air vent found in commercial ovens, prop the door ajar slightly with a wooden spoon to increase air circulation.

4. The amount of time necessary to dry the tomatoes will vary considerably depending on the oven, the relative humidity, and how dry you want them. This quantity of tomatoes should take 12 to 20 hours to dry. If you plan to store the tomatoes for any length of time they must be completely dry, actually brittle, or they can mold. If you will be using the tomatoes fairly soon, dry them just until leathery and then pack in olive oil to store. The tomatoes will become much darker in color after drying.

Swedish Limpa Rye

four 1-pound, 4-ounce (570-g) loaves

1½ ounces (40 g) fresh compressed yeast

1½ cups (360 ml) warm water (105–115°F, 40–46°C)

8 ounces (225 g) medium rye flour

1 tablespoon (6 g) fennel seed

1 tablespoon (6 g) caraway seed

4 teaspoons (8 g) anise seed

1½ cups (360 ml) warm milk (105–115°F, 40–46°C)

½ cup (120 ml) or 6 ounces (170 g) molasses

¾ cup (180 ml) vegetable oil

1 tablespoon (15 g) salt

4 ounces (115 g) light brown sugar

grated zest of two oranges

2 pounds (910 g) bread flour, approximately

rye flour

NOTE: Use a mortar and pestle to crush the spices. If one is not available, wrap the spices in a towel and crush them with a rolling pin.

*T*he Swedish word limpa *refers to a loaf of bread that is formed into an oblong shape, slightly tapered at the ends, and baked free-form without a bread pan. (This recipe may alternatively be baked in a conventional rectangular bread pan if you prefer.) Limpa breads usually contain spices and rye flour. This particular limpa is flavored with the popular Scandinavian spices fennel, anise, and caraway, as well as orange peel. For a lighter taste (and color) you can replace the molasses with an equal amount of either light corn syrup or golden syrup, or you can replace both the molasses and brown sugar with 1 cup (240 ml) or 12 ounces (340 g) of either light corn syrup or golden syrup. The golden syrup produces a very authentic Swedish limpa.*

1. Dissolve the yeast in the warm water. Add the rye flour and mix to make a smooth, sticky paste. Cover and let stand in a warm place until the sponge has doubled in bulk.

2. Crush the fennel, caraway, and anise seeds (see note).

3. Place the sponge in a mixer bowl and mix in the milk, molasses, vegetable oil, salt, brown sugar, and orange zest using the hook attachment at low speed.

4. Add the crushed spices and enough of the bread flour to form a dough. Knead for 8 to 10 minutes, adding the remaining flour as necessary, to make a smooth and elastic, yet fairly stiff, dough.

5. Place the dough in a lightly oiled bowl and turn the dough so it is coated with oil on both sides. Let rise in a warm place until it has doubled in bulk.

6. Divide the dough into four equal pieces, approximately 1 pound, 4 ounces (570 g) each. Do not punch the dough down first. Pound and form each piece into an oval limpa loaf, slightly tapered on both ends (Figure 3–24). Place the loaves on a sheet pan lined with baking paper. Let the loaves rise until they have slightly less than doubled in volume.

7. Spray or brush the loaves with water. Dust heavily with rye flour. Use a razor blade or a small serrated knife and score the loaves lengthwise down the center (Figure 3–25).

8. Bake at 375°F (190°C) for approximately 35 minutes or until baked through. When the loaves are done they will sound hollow when tapped on the bottom. Let cool, then store the loaves covered.

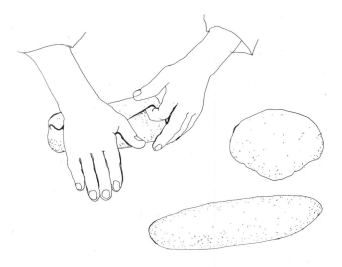

FIGURE 3–24   *Shaping slightly tapered oval loaves for Swedish Limpa Rye by folding and pounding the dough; the final shape after rolling the dough against the table*

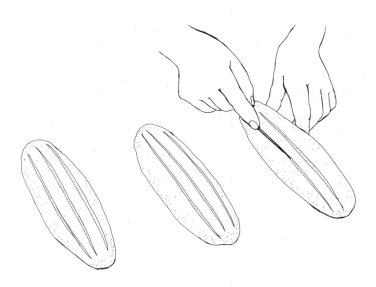

FIGURE 3–25   *Slashing the tops of Swedish Limpa Rye loaves before baking, making three cuts lengthwise*

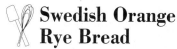

Swedish Orange Rye Bread

six 1-pound, 2-ounce (510-g) loaves

1½ cups (360 ml) or 1 pound, 2 ounces (510 g) molasses

3¾ cups (900 ml) hot water (130°F, 54°C)

2½ ounces (70 g) fresh compressed yeast

3 ounces (85 g) medium rye flour

1 pound, 8 ounces (680 g) bread flour

7½ ounces (215 g) Candied Orange Peel (page 978)

12 ounces (340 g) medium rye flour

1 pound, 4 ounces (570 g) bread flour, approximately

2 tablespoons (30 g) salt

1½ ounces (40 g) unsalted butter

vegetable oil

One-Third Recipe

two 1-pound, 2-ounce (510-g) loaves

½ cup (120 ml) or 6 ounces (170 g) molasses

1¼ cups (300 ml) hot water (130°F, 54°C)

1 ounce (30 g) fresh compressed yeast

1 ounce (30 g) medium rye flour

8 ounces (225 g) bread flour

2½ ounces (70 g) Candied Orange Peel (page 978)

4 ounces (115 g) medium rye flour

7 ounces (200 g) bread flour, approximately

2 teaspoons (10 g) salt

½ ounce (15 g) unsalted butter

vegetable oil

*I*t is very important that the temperature of this dough does not fall below 75°F (24°C). Because of the high amount of sugar in the recipe, the yeast needs a warm dough in order to work properly. This bread differs from most in that the dough is not kneaded to develop the gluten. Do not be tempted to add extra flour. Just keep your hands and the table well floured and the dough will be manageable. Because the dough is so soft, I bake the loaves in bread pans. They can be baked free-form as limpa-style loaves, but they will be a little flat. The reduced flour and gluten structure make for a very tender and moist bread with a distinctive flavor combining molasses, orange, and rye.

1. Combine the molasses and hot water in a mixer bowl. Add the yeast, the first measurement of rye flour, and the first measurement of bread flour. Mix to form a smooth sponge.

2. Cover and let rise in a warm place until the sponge just starts to fall, about 1 hour.

3. Chop the orange peel to the size of currants and then add it to the sponge along with the remaining rye flour, as much of the remaining bread flour as is necessary to be able to form the dough into a loaf, the salt, and the butter. Mix using the dough hook, just until the ingredients are incorporated and you have a smooth dough; do not overmix. The dough should be sticky and will not come away from the side of the bowl. Let dough rest, covered, for 10 minutes.

4. Butter the inside of rectangular bread pans 8 by 8 by 4 inches (20 × 20 × 10 cm). Reserve.

5. Divide the dough into six equal pieces (two for the smaller recipe) approximately 1 pound, 2 ounces (510 g) each. Roll each piece into a tight circle and form into an oval loaf (see Figures 3–1 and 3–2, page 70). The dough should spring back when pressed lightly. Place the loaves in the prepared pans. Let rise until doubled in volume.

6. Bake at 375°F (190°C) for about 45 minutes. You may need to protect the loaves from overbrowning by placing a second pan underneath, or by covering the tops with baking paper. Brush the loaves with vegetable oil as soon as they come out of the oven. Unmold and cool on racks.

Swedish Peasant Bread

six 1-pound, 8-ounce (680-g) loaves

3 cups (720 ml) water

1½ tablespoons (22 g) salt

9 ounces (255 g) whole wheat flour

9 ounces (255 g) medium rye flour

2 tablespoons (30 ml) white vinegar

1 cup (240 ml) or 12 ounces (340 g) light corn syrup

2½ cups (600 ml) warm water (105–115°F, 40–46°C)

2½ ounces (70 g) fresh compressed yeast

1 ounce (30 g) malt sugar
or
3 tablespoons (45 ml) or 2 ounces (55 g) honey

6 ounces (170 g) soft unsalted butter

2 tablespoons (12 g) ground cumin

2 tablespoons (12 g) ground fennel

4 pounds (1 kg, 820 g) bread flour, approximately

Egg Wash (page 7)

whole wheat flour

One-Third Recipe

two 1-pound, 8-ounce (680-g) loaves

1 cup (240 ml) water

1½ teaspoons (8 g) salt

3 ounces (85 g) whole wheat flour

3 ounces (85 g) medium rye flour

2 teaspoons (10 ml) white vinegar

⅓ cup (80 ml) or 4 ounces (115 g) light corn syrup

¾ cup (180 ml) warm water (105–115°F, 40–46°C)

1 ounce (30 g) fresh compressed yeast

1 tablespoon (9 g) malt sugar
or
2 tablespoons (40 g) honey

2 ounces (55 g) soft unsalted butter

2 teaspoons (4 g) ground cumin

2 teaspoons (4 g) ground fennel

*B*reads using the scalding method have been made for centuries by peasant farmers all over Europe. The shape, texture, and taste of the bread would differ within as well as between countries, making the breads representative of a particular region. The common characteristics were that the breads were always robust multigrain loaves made to last for several weeks. This was necessary as freezing food as we know it today was not an option. The peasant bread was stored in the bread chest that was central to every farmer's kitchen. Swedish Peasant Rings were threaded onto sticks and stored hung from the rafters.

1. Heat the first measurement of water to boiling. Add the salt, whole wheat flour, and rye flour. Mix until smooth and let stand, covered, for 1 hour.

2. Combine the vinegar, corn syrup and the remaining warm water in a mixer bowl. Add the yeast and mix to dissolve. Stir in the flour-water mixture, malt sugar or honey, butter, and spices.

3. Reserve a few ounces of the bread flour, add the remainder, and knead for about 2 minutes, using the dough hook at medium speed. Adjust with the reserved bread flour as required to make a dough that is not sticky. Knead until smooth, 2 to 4 minutes longer.

4. Turn the dough onto a floured table and let rest, covered, for 10 minutes.

5. Divide the dough into six equal pieces (two for the smaller recipe), approximately 1 pound, 8 ounces (680 g) each. Roll each piece into a firm round loaf (see Figures 3–1 and 3–2, page 70). The formed loaves should spring back immediately when you press lightly.

6. Using the side of your hand, press down on the center of each loaf and roll the loaf back and forth until you have almost severed the two halves (Figure 3–26).

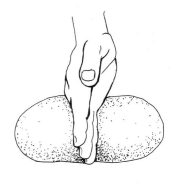

FIGURE 3–26   *Using the side of the hand to form Swedish Peasant Bread loaves in a double rounded shape; the loaves after slashing the tops*

1 pound, 4 ounces (570 g) bread flour,
approximately
Egg Wash (page 7)
whole wheat flour

 **VARIATION**
Swedish Peasant Rings

three ring-shaped loaves

7. Brush the loaves with Egg Wash, invert in whole wheat flour, and place flour-side up on sheet pans lined with baking paper. Slash a few lines across the top of each loaf with a sharp knife. Let rise until doubled in volume.

8. Bake at 375°F (190°C) for about 35 minutes. Cool on racks.

1. Scale the small recipe into three equal pieces, approximately 1 pound (455 g) each.

2. Form round loaves, then flatten the loaves by rolling them to 9-inch (22.5-cm) circles. Cut a 3-inch (7.5-cm) hole in the center of each circle.

3. Brush the rings and the cutouts with Egg Wash, invert in whole wheat flour, and place flour-side up on sheet pans lined with baking paper. Prick all over with a docker. Proof as above.

4. Bake the rings and the cutouts at 400°F (205°C) for approximately 25 minutes. The cutouts will be done a little sooner than the rings.

Rolls

With a few exceptions, virtually any bread dough can be made into rolls or knots and, conversely, the opposite is also true. Rolls can be defined simply as bread dough that is portioned into individual servings, usually around 2 ounces (55 g) each, before it is baked. Rolls (especially knots) take longer to form than loaves, but fortunately the results are worthwhile. Rolls look much more elegant served in a bread basket on the lunch or dinner table than do slices of bread, and rolls do not become stale as quickly. In many European countries a Kaiser Roll or other type of crusty roll is considered an absolute must at breakfast.

To Form Rolls

Forming a perfectly round, smooth, tight roll with the palm of your hand is very easy if you use the right technique. As when forming bread loaves, your objective is to form a tight skin around the mass of dough. Place two balls of dough on the table with your hands cupped on top, fingers clenched like claws. Press down fairly hard on the dough as you move both hands simultaneously in tight circles. Move your left hand counterclockwise and your right hand clockwise, so both are moving toward the outside (Figure 3–27). As you press down, forming the dough into a tight round ball, let the dough stick to the table just a little or it will not form a skin. For this reason, as little flour as possible should be used, and if the dough just slides and doesn't stick at all, try rubbing the table with a wet towel. If you are making oval rolls, such as the Milk Rolls, first roll the dough round. Then, without lifting your hands (keeping them cupped around the dough) move them away and back toward you a few times in a straight line.

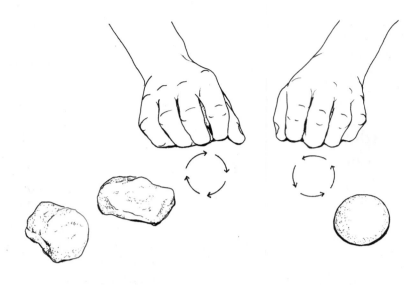

FIGURE 3–27   *Forming rolls by moving the hands in circular directions, at the same time pressing the balls of dough against the table*

An easier instructional method is to practice with just one hand: Use the palm of your left hand (if you are right-handed) as the tabletop, holding it flat, and work the dough into a round ball by cupping your right hand on top and moving it in a circle.

Bagels

36 bagels

1¹/₂ ounces (40 g) fresh compressed yeast

1 quart (960 ml) warm water (105–115°F, 40–46°C)

2 tablespoons (30 g) salt

3 tablespoons (45 ml) or 2 ounces (55 g) honey

2 ounces (55 g) sugar

4 pounds, 4 ounces (1 kg, 935 g) high-gluten flour, approximately

Poaching Liquid for Bagels (recipe follows) (see note 1)

Egg Wash (page 7) (optional)

poppy, sesame, or caraway seeds, kosher salt or chopped onion (optional) (see note 2)

NOTE 1: This may seem like a lot of water and honey to use for poaching the Bagels only 2 minutes. The large quantity is necessary to be

*T*he name bagel ("beygel" in Yiddish) comes from the German word "boug," meaning ring. These doughnut-shaped bread rolls are poached in a sweetened water solution before they are placed on sheet pans and baked in the oven. This reduces the starch which, in combination with the gluten-rich flour and the absence of fat, gives the Bagels their characteristic chewy texture. Poaching also contributes to the Bagel's glossy finish. Bagels are a traditional Jewish breakfast food served topped with cream cheese and smoked salmon (lox). Smaller cocktail-sized Bagels are becoming popular for hors d'oeuvres and snacks. Egg Bagels are less chewy and are not poached prior to baking. They have a lighter texture which is similar to challah bread. Egg Bagels are often topped with poppy, sesame, or caraway seeds, kosher salt, or chopped onions (after they are fully proofed) before being placed in the oven. As a variation with either type of bagel, replace one-third of the flour with whole wheat or rye flour.*

1. Dissolve the yeast in the warm water. Mixing with the dough hook, add the salt, honey, sugar, and enough of the flour to make a stiff, smooth dough.

2. Cover tightly to prevent a skin from forming, then let the dough relax in a warm place for about 1 hour.

3. Punch down and divide the dough into three equal pieces, approximately 1 pound, 14 ounces (855 g) each. Roll each piece into a 16-inch (40-cm) rope. Do not use any flour while forming the ropes. The dough should be stiff and elastic enough to form without flour.

able to poach a greater number at the same time or the bagels "waiting their turn" would overproof. If kept in the refrigerator, the poaching liquid can be used over again many times.

NOTE 2: Chop the onion fine, blanch in boiling water, then pat dry with paper towels.

Poaching Liquid for Bagels

1 gallon (3 l, 840 ml) water
1¹/₂ cups (360 ml)
   or
1 pound, 2 ounces (510 g) honey

Egg Bagels

24 bagels

1 ounce (30 g) fresh compressed yeast
1¹/₂ cups (360 ml) warm water
   (105–115°F, 40–46°C)
2 ounces (55 g) granulated sugar
1 tablespoon (15 g) salt
¹/₄ cup (60 ml) olive oil
1 pound, 12 ounces (795 g) high-gluten flour, approximately
1 egg
1 egg yolk
Egg Wash (page 7)
caraway, sesame, or poppy seeds, kosher salt, or chopped onion (optional) (see note)

NOTE: Chop the onion fine, blanch in boiling water, then pat dry with paper towels.

4. Cut twelve pieces from each rope. Form and roll each of the smaller pieces into ropes about 9 inches (22.5 cm) long. Overlap the ends of the ropes about ¹/₂ inch (1.2 cm) and press them together firmly against the table, rocking the dough back and forth with your palm to seal the edges together. Try to make the rings a uniform thickness throughout.

5. Place the Bagels on a sheet pan lined with cloth; canvas is ideal. Let the Bagels rise until they have slightly less than doubled in volume.

6. Bring the poaching liquid to a boil, reduce the heat to a simmer, then carefully drop the Bagels into the liquid. Poach for approximately 2 minutes. Remove the Bagels using a slotted spoon or skimmer and place them 1¹/₂ inches (3.7 cm) apart on sheet pans lined with baking paper. If desired, brush with Egg Wash and top with poppy, sesame, or caraway seeds, kosher salt or chopped onion.

7. Bake at 450°F (230°C) until the Bagels are light brown, approximately 12 minutes. Flip the Bagels over, and continue baking about 10 minutes longer.

1. Combine the water and honey in a large pan and bring to a boil.
2. Reduce the heat to a simmer to use for poaching.

1. Dissolve the yeast in the warm water. Add the sugar, salt, and olive oil. Mix in enough of the flour to form a pasty dough. Mix in the egg and egg yolk separately, mixing well after each. Incorporate all but a few handfuls of the remaining flour.

2. Knead for about 8 minutes, using the dough hook at medium speed and adding the reserved handfuls of flour if necessary, to make a stiff yet smooth dough.

3. Place the dough in an oiled bowl and invert it to coat both sides with oil. Cover and leave in a warm place until doubled in volume, about 40 minutes.

4. Divide the dough into two equal pieces, approximately 1 pound, 8 ounces (680 g) each.

5. Proceed as directed in traditional Bagels, omitting the poaching step and placing the Bagels directly on paper-lined sheet pans as you form them. Let the Bagels rise until one-and-one-half times the original size.

6. Brush the Bagels with Egg Wash. Sprinkle with caraway seeds, poppy seeds, kosher salt, or chopped onion as desired.

7. Bake as directed in the main recipe.

Bread Sticks

twenty-four 16-inch (40-cm) bread sticks

1 ounce (30 g) fresh compressed yeast
2½ cups (600 ml) warm water
 (105–115°F, 40–46°C)
1 ounce (30 g) malt sugar
 or
3 tablespoons (45 ml) or 2 ounces
 (55 g) honey
1 tablespoon (15 g) salt
2 pounds, 4 ounces (1 kg, 25 g) bread
 flour, approximately
¼ cup (60 ml) olive oil
sesame seeds or semolina flour

Bread Sticks are a popular addition to a bread basket and also make a great snack. They are known as grissini in Italy, where they seem to be included on the table at almost every meal. Instead of sesame seeds, try coating the dough with chopped fresh rosemary, fennel seeds, poppy seeds, cracked black pepper, or use a combination. For a more nutritious Bread Stick, use the Swedish Whole Grain Crisp Rolls dough, formed and baked as directed here.

1. In a mixer bowl, dissolve the yeast in the warm water. Add the malt sugar or honey and the salt. Incorporate about three-quarters of the flour. Add the olive oil and knead the dough for 6 to 8 minutes, using the dough hook and adding as much of the reserved flour as required to make a smooth and elastic dough.

2. Place the dough in a bowl oiled with olive oil and turn the dough to coat both sides with the oil. Cover and let rise in a warm place until doubled in volume.

3. Punch the dough down and form it into a 10-by-6-inch (25-×-15-cm) rectangle using your hands. Cover the dough and let it relax for 30 minutes.

4. Cut the dough in half lengthwise. Cut each half, lengthwise, into 12 equal pieces.

5. Pound and roll the pieces into strings (see Figures 3–3, 3–4 and 3–5, pages 77 and 78) without using any flour. Roll and stretch the strings to make them 16 inches (40 cm) long.

6. Line the pieces up and spray lightly with water. Sprinkle sesame seeds or semolina flour on top, then roll each piece a half turn and sprinkle again to cover them on all sides. (If you want the Bread Sticks heavily coated with sesame seeds, place the seeds on a sheet pan and roll the bread strings on top.)

7. Place the Bread Sticks on sheet pans lined with baking paper, spacing them a few inches apart.

8. Bake immediately (without allowing the Bread Sticks to rise first) at 425°F (219°C) for approximately 10 minutes or until golden brown. They will still be soft inside. To dry them completely, reduce the oven temperature to 300°F (149°C) and bake about 20 minutes longer. Stored in airtight containers, the Bread Sticks will stay fresh and dry for several weeks.

Hamburger Buns

24 hamburger buns or 36 hot dog buns

1½ ounces (40 g) fresh compressed
 yeast
1 quart (960 ml) warm low-fat milk
 (105–115°F, 40–46°C)

The name hamburger steak, or hamburger as it has been abbreviated, comes from the city of Hamburg, Germany. The small grilled or fried beef patty we are so familiar with today became firmly established and synonymous with American fast food at the 1904 St. Louis World's Fair, and America never looked back—the fast-food chains made sure of that. Enclosing the cooked meat between two toasted bun halves was popularized around 1940 with the birth of what is currently the oldest and largest of these establishments.

1 ounce (30 g) granulated sugar

3 tablespoons (27 g) malt sugar

or

3 tablespoons (45 ml) or 2 ounces
(55 g) honey

2 pounds, 2 ounces (970 g) bread flour

1 pound, 4 ounces (570 g) bread flour,
approximately

2 tablespoons (30 g) salt

1/3 cup (80 ml) vegetable oil

poppy or sesame seeds

Today hamburgers are enjoyed virtually throughout the entire industrialized world, however, this phenomenon had not reached Sweden when I was an apprentice. Then, the sausage or hot dog was king of what was the equivalent of today's take-out or fast-food outlets. Every village in Scandinavia and the German-speaking countries of the continent (especially Germany itself, which is unsurpassed when it comes to making delicious wurst or frankfurters) had a hot dog stand which was a mini street kitchen serving various sausages and other quickly made specialities. The hot dog stand in the small village where I did my apprenticeship usually received its hot dog buns from the local bakery but would, in an emergency, order a hundred or so from the pastry shop where I was one of several young trainees. Reporting to work and being told that part of your job was to make hot dog buns (and this is still vivid in my memory after all these years) was considered just about as low as you could sink. One would of course respectfully reply "Yes, chef!" but at the same time try to figure out what you had done wrong to be handed this degrading task!

This recipe for Hamburger (or hot dog) Buns is not for the most common type, but I personally like these better. If you yearn for tradition, make the buns from the Milk Roll dough instead (page 129), following these instructions, but omitting the steam during baking.

1. Start making the sponge by first dissolving the yeast in the warm milk. Using the dough hook, mix in the granulated sugar, the malt sugar or honey, and the first measurement of flour. Continue mixing until the sponge has a smooth, paste-like consistency, about 2 to 3 minutes. Cover and let rise in a warm place for 1 to 2 hours.

2. Reserve two handfuls of the second measurement of flour. Mix the salt with the remainder of the flour and add this to the sponge. Knead for a minute or so to combine well. Add the oil and continue kneading for 8 to 10 minutes, adjusting the consistency by adding the reserved flour as required to make a medium-stiff dough that is smooth and elastic.

3. Place the dough in a lightly oiled bowl. Turn the dough to coat both sides with oil, place a damp towel on top, and set aside to rise in a warm location until the dough has doubled in volume.

4. Punch the dough down, cover, and let rise a second time until doubled in volume.

5. Divide the dough into three equal pieces approximately 2 pounds, 4 ounces (1 kg, 25 g) each (do not punch the dough down or otherwise tighten the gluten). Form the pieces into even strings.

6. Cut each string into eight equal pieces. Form the pieces into round rolls (see Figure 3–27, page 124). Set the rolls on sheet pans lined with baking paper, leaving about 3 inches (7.5 cm) between them.

7. Set the rolls aside in a warm place until the dough has relaxed and they have just started to rise, about 10 minutes.

8. Using a flat, round object about 4 to 6 inches (10 to 15 cm) in diameter, flatten the rolls to make them 4 inches (10 cm) in diameter. Spray or brush with water and then sprinkle poppy or sesame seeds over the tops. Let rise until slightly less than doubled in volume.

9. Bake at 400°F (205°C) for approximately 15 minutes or until baked through and done.

- Cut each of the three strings into twelve equal pieces instead of eight.
- Pound and form each of the small pieces into 6-inch (15-cm) ropes, using the same technique as for baguettes (see Figures 3–3, 3–4, and 3–5, pages 77 and 78).
- Continue as directed.

To Form Hot Dog Buns

Kaiser Rolls

72 rolls, approximately 2 ounces (55 g) each

1 quart (960 ml) warm water (105–115°F, 40–46°C)
2 ounces (55 g) fresh compressed yeast
3 tablespoons (45 g) salt
2 ounces (55 g) malt sugar
or
⅓ cup (80 ml) or 4 ounces (115 g) honey
3 ounces (85 g) soft unsalted butter
Kaiser Roll Pre-Dough (recipe follows) (see note 1)
3 pounds, 5 ounces (1 kg, 505 g) bread flour, approximately
poppy seeds (optional)

NOTE 1: To make Kaiser Rolls without pre-dough, increase the yeast to 2½ ounces (70 g) and decrease the salt to 2 tablespoons (30 g). This will yield forty-five rolls.

NOTE 2: If your oven is not equipped with steam injectors, see Creating Steam without Steam Injectors, page 73.

The Kaiser, Emperor of Austria from 1804 to 1918 (and of Germany from 1871 to 1918), has lent his name to many culinary creations, including the desserts Kaiser Schmarren and Franz Joseph Torte, as well as Kaiser Rolls, which are also known as Vienna rolls. Although they can be formed by hand, most commercial operations mark the pattern on top using a special cutter with a fan-shaped blade, or they use a Kaiser Roll machine. You cannot have missed these great-looking crusty rolls if you have traveled in Germany or Austria. They are always on the breakfast table with cheese, cold cuts, and marmalade—what a way to start the day! I like them best the way they are made in Europe: with plenty of poppy seeds on top.

1. Dissolve the yeast in the warm water. Mix in the salt and the malt sugar or honey. Add the butter and the pre-dough. Using the dough hook on low to medium speed, mix in enough of the bread flour to form a dough. Knead until smooth and elastic, 10–15 minutes.

2. Place the dough in an oiled bowl. Turn to coat both sides of the dough with oil, cover, and let rise for 30 minutes.

3. Punch the dough down to remove all air. Cover and let rise an additional 30 minutes.

4. Divide the dough into three equal pieces approximately 2 pounds (910 g) each. Form each piece into an even rope about 24 inches (60 cm) long, and then cut each rope into 24 equal pieces. Form the small pieces into round rolls (see Figure 3–27, page 124). Place the rolls on sheet pans lined with baking paper. Sprinkle with poppy seeds if desired.

5. Mark the rolls with a kaiser cutter, or cut an X on the tops using a razor blade. Let the rolls rise until slightly less than doubled in volume.

6. Bake the rolls at 400°F (205°C), with steam, leaving the damper closed for the first 10 minutes. Open the damper and continue baking approximately 10 minutes longer or until done.

Kaiser Roll Pre-Dough

2 pounds, 12 ounces (1 kg, 250 g) dough

¹/₂ ounce (15 g) fresh compressed yeast
1 teaspoon (5 g) granulated sugar
1 pint (480 ml) cold water
1 pound, 12 ounces (795 g) bread flour

NOTE: For quick pre-dough, use warm water (105–115°F, 40–46°C) and 1 ounce (30 g) of yeast and let rise in a warm place until the dough begins to bubble and fall.

Milk Rolls

48 rolls, approximately 2 ounces (55 g) each

4 ounces (115 g) fresh compressed yeast
1 quart (960 ml) cold milk
2 pounds (910 g) bread flour
1 pound, 10 ounces (740 g) cake flour
3 tablespoons (45 g) salt
4 ounces (115 g) granulated sugar
8 ounces (225 g) soft unsalted butter
Egg Wash (page 7)
poppy seeds (optional)

1. Dissolve the yeast and the sugar in the water (see note).

2. Add all of the bread flour at once, mixing with the dough hook on low speed. Knead until the dough has developed a smooth consistency, about 10 minutes. The dough will be quite firm, which makes the yeast react more slowly and allows the dough to develop properly.

3. Cover the dough and leave at room temperature overnight.

*P*lain white bread and rolls seem to have been ranked with secondary status lately, given the current favor toward whole grain and multigrain supposed health breads. Whole grain purists refuse to eat white bread, rationalizing that the nutritious part of the wheat kernel has been milled out, and there is some truth to that argument. There are times, however, when only buttery white bread or rolls will do. It may go against today's trend for the rustic and hearty types, but I feel that plain white bread rolls—with a hard crust like Kaiser Rolls, or these softer Milk Rolls—will never go out of style. They make such a good accompaniment to a meal because their flavor doesn't compete with other dishes, and what could be better for mopping up that last bit of gravy?

This basic recipe can be formed into several of the classic American dinner roll shapes, such as Cloverleaf, Butterflake, and Parkerhouse, enabling you to easily offer an assortment in the bread basket. Soft crust rolls are always a better choice if you plan to make the rolls ahead of time to freeze. If properly thawed and warmed before service, it becomes almost impossible to tell them from freshly baked. Rolls with a hard crust, on the other hand, tend to become a bit chewy after freezing because there is little or no fat in the dough.

1. Dissolve the yeast in the milk. Add the bread and cake flours, salt, and sugar. Mix using the dough hook until the dough forms a ball. Incorporate the butter.

2. Knead the dough for 6 to 8 minutes until it is smooth and elastic.

3. Place the dough, covered, in a warm place and let it rise until it has doubled in volume.

4. Punch the dough down and let rise until it has doubled a second time.

5. Divide the dough into four equal pieces, approximately 1 pound, 10 ounces (740 g) each. Pound and roll each piece into an 18-inch (45-cm) rope. Cut each rope into twelve equal pieces. Form the pieces into oval rolls (see Figure 3–27, page 124).

6. Place the rolls on sheet pans lined with baking paper. Let the rolls rise until slightly less than doubled in volume.

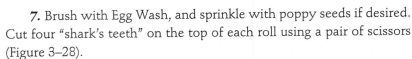

7. Brush with Egg Wash, and sprinkle with poppy seeds if desired. Cut four "shark's teeth" on the top of each roll using a pair of scissors (Figure 3–28).

8. Bake the rolls at 425°F (219°C) for approximately 12 minutes.

FIGURE 3–28   Cutting the "shark's tooth" design on the top of the Milk Rolls before baking

 **VARIATIONS**

Cloverleaf Rolls

1. Brush melted butter over the inside of forty-eight cups in standard-sized muffin tins.

2. Follow the recipe for Milk Rolls through step four.

3. After dividing the dough into forty-eight pieces in step five, divide each piece again into three equal pieces. Roll the small pieces into smooth round balls.

4. Cluster three balls in each cup of the muffin tins.

5. Proof, brush with Egg Wash, and bake as directed in the main recipe.

Butterflake Rolls

1. Brush melted butter over the inside of forty-eight cups in standard-sized muffin tins.

2. Follow the recipe for Milk Rolls through step four. Divide the dough into four pieces as directed in step five, but do not form the pieces into ropes.

3. Roll each of the four pieces of dough into a 14-by-18-inch (35-×-45-cm) rectangle approximately ¹/₈ inch (3 mm) thick, using flour to prevent the dough from sticking. Transfer each rectangle to a sheet pan and place in the refrigerator while you are working on the next one.

4. Cut the sheet of dough that was rolled out first in half lengthwise. Brush melted butter over one half. Place the other half on top. Cut the stacked sheet lengthwise into three equal strips. Brush butter on top of two strips and stack again, placing the unbuttered piece on the top (the dough stack should now have six layers and measure 18 inches long and a little over 2 inches wide (45 × 5 cm).

5. Cut the strip across into twelve equal pieces. Place the pieces in the prepared muffin pans with the cut edges facing up.

6. Repeat steps four and five with the remaining three dough rectangles.

7. Proof and bake as directed for Milk Rolls but do not use Egg Wash. Instead, brush the tops of the rolls with butter as soon as they come out of the oven.

Parkerhouse Rolls

1. Brush melted butter over the inside of forty-eight cups in standard-sized muffin tins.

2. Follow the recipe for Milk Rolls through step four. After dividing the dough into forty-eight pieces in step five, roll each piece into a ball and set the pieces aside to relax for a few minutes on a lightly floured area of your worktable.

3. Using a dowel, press down on the center of each round and roll it into a 4-inch (10-cm) oval, keeping the ends thick and shaping the middle section flat.

4. Brush melted butter over the tops of the ovals. Fold one thick edge on top of the other, placing the top edge slightly behind the bottom edge (see example in the recipe for Stollen, Figure 16–1, page 793. The shape here is not curved, however.) Press lightly with your palm to make the edges adhere.

5. Proof and bake as directed for Milk Rolls, brushing the rolls with melted butter rather than Egg Wash prior to baking.

Pretzels

thirty 3-ounce (85-g) traditional pretzels, or sixty 8-inch (20-cm) twisted pretzel sticks

1 ounce (30 g) fresh compressed yeast
1 quart (960 ml) warm water
  (105–115°F, 40–46°C)
4 teaspoons (20 g) salt
2 tablespoons (30 g) granulated sugar
1 ounce (30 g) caraway seeds (optional)
3 pounds, 12 ounces (1 kg, 705 g)
  bread flour, approximately
melted butter
Baking Soda Solution (recipe follows;
  see note 2)
coarse salt
caraway seeds for topping (optional)

NOTE 1: *Since this no-butter, no-egg dough can be very rubbery and hard to work with, a good method is to roll one-third (ten) of the strings out partially and then go back and finish stretching them to their full length, working on*

*Y*ou would be hard pressed to find another single shape that could symbolize the baker's art better than the Pretzel. The name comes from a Germanic word meaning bracelet. Some information says this twisted knot dates back to the sixth century, and others suggest that the Pretzel goes back to the Romans. I particularly like the story which tells of the heroic bakers of Vienna. While the city was held under siege by the Turks during the Ottoman reign, this group, upon seeing the enemy's flag raised above the cathedral, battled their way to the top and put their own flag in its place. With the Turkish flag torn down, the Viennese defenders gained new strength, rallied, and saved the city. The Emperor rewarded these brave bakers with the royal coat of arms. The pretzel (which was the symbol of the bakers' guild) had been incorporated into the design.

Pretzels are made in two variations, both from the same dough. The thicker, soft Pretzels are boiled before baking (in the same way as Bagels), which kills the yeast immediately and eliminates any oven-spring. This, in combination with the fact that the dough is not proofed very much, produces a fairly dense and chewy Pretzel, the type that are typically sold garnished with mustard by street vendors, especially in cities on the East Coast. The other Pretzel, the hard type, is proofed and baked in the oven just like any ordinary bread. These are generally made much smaller than the chewy Pretzels and are a popular snack to accompany drinks. Both varieties are formed in both the traditional Pretzel shape or in sticks. Due to the absence of fat in the Pretzel dough, the finished Pretzels will keep fresh for many weeks.

the strings in the same order. This will allow the gluten time to relax and make the job easier. Repeat this procedure twice with the remaining dough. It should not be necessary to use any flour in shaping the strings and Pretzels. If you find you must use flour, this indicates the dough is too soft.

NOTE 2: Pretzels are traditionally dipped in a 5 percent solution of sodium hydroxide (caustic soda) and water. Follow the instructions with the following changes:

- in step 3, brush the butter on 3 baking papers instead of directly onto the sheet pans
- in step 6, omit the baking soda solution and boiling
- instead, dissolve 1 1/2 ounce (40 g) sodium hydroxide U.S.P.-N.F. in 1 quart (960 ml) warm water
- dip the pretzels into this solution wearing latex food-handling gloves for protection
- transfer pretzels to the reserved sheet pans

Warning: sodium hydroxide is harmful when not properly diluted and baked. Store in a safe place.

If you do not need or wish to make this number of Pretzels or sticks at one time, the dough can be divided and frozen for several weeks if properly wrapped. Thaw the dough as needed and shape as desired.

1. Dissolve the yeast in the warm water. Add the salt, the sugar, and the caraway seeds if desired. Gradually mix in enough of the bread flour to make a stiff dough. Knead at medium speed with the dough hook, adding the remaining flour if necessary, until the dough is smooth and elastic, about 8 minutes.

2. Place the dough in a well-buttered bowl. Turn the dough to butter both sides. Cover and set aside in a warm place until doubled in volume, approximately 45 minutes.

3. Brush melted butter over three full-size sheet pans; reserve.

4. Punch down the dough and divide it into three equal pieces, approximately 1 pound, 12 ounces (795 g) each. Roll each piece into a rope 20 inches (50 cm) long. Cut each rope into ten equal pieces.

5. Pound and roll each of the smaller pieces into a 20-inch (50-cm) tapered string as instructed for Braided Bread (see Figures 3–3, 3–4 and 3-5, pages 77 and 78). Form the strings into twisted Pretzel shapes (Figures 3–29 and 3–30) and place them on a lightly floured board or sheet pan. Let the gluten in the Pretzels relax for 1 or 2 minutes, then stretch each one to make it approximately 7 by 4 inches (17.5 × 10 cm) (Figure 3–31).

6. Bring the Baking Soda Solution to a boil. Drop two or three Pretzels at a time into the liquid and boil for 1 minute after they float to the surface. Remove them carefully with a slotted spoon and transfer to the buttered sheet pans.

7. As each sheet pan is filled, sprinkle coarse salt (and caraway seeds if desired) over the Pretzels.

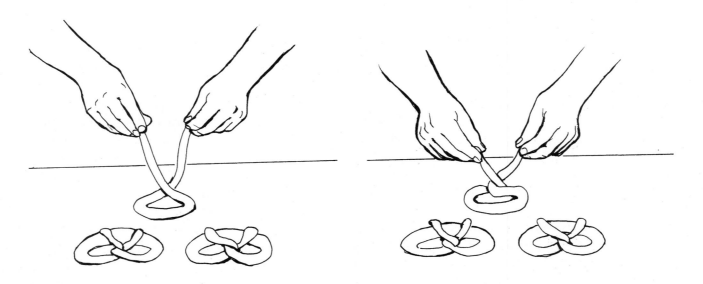

FIGURE 3–29   *Starting the Pretzel shape by crossing and twisting the string*

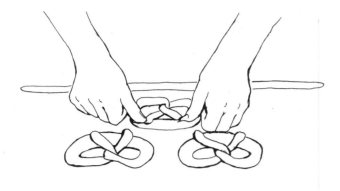

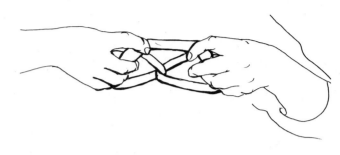

FIGURE 3–30   Pressing the ends of the string firmly into the dough

FIGURE 3–31   Stretching the Pretzel after the gluten has relaxed

8. Bake at 475°F (246°C) until dark brown, approximately 20 minutes. Remove from the baking sheets and let cool on racks. The Pretzels will keep for several weeks stored in an airtight container.

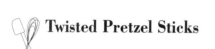
Twisted Pretzel Sticks

1. Follow the instructions in the main recipe through step four. However, cut each of the three ropes into twenty pieces rather than ten.

2. Pound and roll each of the small pieces into a 16-inch (40-cm) tapered string (Figures 3–3, 3–4, and 3–5, pages 77 and 78). Work in batches to allow the gluten to relax (see preceding note).

3. Fold the strings in half. Hold the thicker folded end steady with one hand, and then use the other hand to roll and twist the bottom of the stick (Figures 3–32 and 3–33).

4. Place on sheet pans lined with baking paper, pinching the ends together firmly as you place them to prevent the Pretzels from unwinding.

5. Poach and bake as directed in the main recipe.

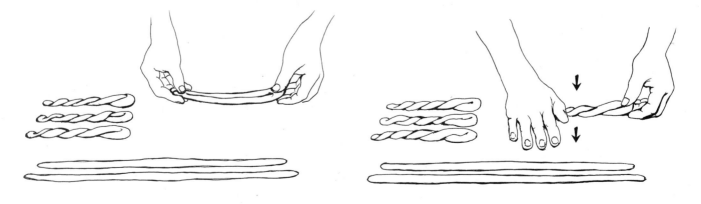

FIGURES 3–32 and 3–33   Forming Twisted Pretzel Sticks by holding the folded end of the string steady while twisting the opposite end with the other hand

Baking Soda Solution

2 quarts (1 l, 920 ml) water
3 tablespoons (36 g) baking soda
1 tablespoon (15 g) salt

1. Bring all of the ingredients to a boil in a 10-to-12-inch (25-to-30-cm) saucepan or sauté pan.

2. Use as directed in the Pretzel recipe.

Rustica

36 rolls, approximately 2 ounces (55 g) each

¹/₂ ounce (15 g) fresh compressed yeast
2 cups (480 ml) warm water (105–115°F, 40–46°C)
2 tablespoons (30 g) salt
1¹/₂ ounces (40 g) malt sugar
  or
¹/₄ cup (60 ml) or 3 ounces (85 g) honey
one-half recipe Kaiser Roll Pre-Dough (page 129)
1 pound, 14 ounces (855 g) bread flour, approximately
3 tablespoons (45 ml) olive oil
olive oil
water
bread flour

NOTE: If your oven is not equipped with steam injectors, see Creating Steam without Steam Injectors, page 73.

*C*hances *are good that you will be served these homey-looking rolls in any small village in Switzerland; there they are known as Schlumbergerli. I make them from the Tessiner Rolls dough. Rustica are simple to make, do not require any special cutter or form, and the finished rolls have a very appetizing appearance. Because they are rolled in olive oil, the dough does not seal completely; consequently, the oven-spring causes the rolls to open up slightly as they bake. The contrast between the newly revealed crust and the flour-coated top looks great. Like most things, it may take some practice before you are able to form the rolls so they open up just right. Generally, if too much oil is used in shaping the rolls they will open up too far. If not enough oil is used, or if you overwork the dough as you form them, they will stay closed.*

1. Dissolve the yeast in the warm water. Mix in the salt, malt sugar or honey, and pre-dough. Incorporate approximately three-quarters of the flour. Mix in the olive oil together with most of the remaining flour. Knead using the dough hook on low speed for 8 to 10 minutes, adding the reserved flour if necessary for a smooth and elastic dough.

2. Place the dough in an oiled bowl, turn the coat both sides with oil, and allow to rise in a warm location until the dough has doubled in volume.

3. Punch down the dough and divide into two equal pieces, approximately 2 pounds, 6 ounces (1 kg, 80 g) each.

4. Roll each piece into a rope approximately 24 inches (60 cm) in length, then cut each rope into eighteen equal pieces.

5. Lightly oil the area of the worktable where you are forming the rolls. Roll them into round rolls (see Figure 3–27, page 124). Keep the table oiled as needed so that the rolls do not stick to the table and therefore do not close completely on the bottom.

6. Place the rolls bottom (wrinkled) side up on the table next to you and spray the rolls lightly with water.

7. Fill two sheet pans almost to the top with bread flour. Invert the rolls into the flour, leaving enough room around them for expansion. Let the rolls rise in the flour until slightly less than doubled in volume.

8. Gently transfer the rolls, inverting each one flour-side up, to a sheet pan.

9. Bake at 400°F (205°C), using steam and leaving the damper closed for 10 minutes. Open the damper and continue baking approximately 10 minutes longer or until baked through.

Single-Knots, Double-Knots, and Twisted Knots

twenty-seven 2-ounce (55-g) rolls

one-half recipe Braided White Bread dough (page 76)
Egg Wash (page 7)

*K*nots, also called twisted rolls, always start out in the form of a string, which is then crossed or twisted in a wide variety of ways. (Simply joining the two ends of the string would not be considered a knot, but the simplest form of a loop—a circle—which is known scientifically as an unknot.) The Single-Knot shown here is the fastest, easiest knot one can make. It is basically a circle that winds through itself making three crossings along the way. I call these production knots because they can be formed quickly in midair on their way down to the sheet pan. Single-Knots are the most likely choice when you have to produce several hundred. There are many more elaborate choices available if you are making a fairly small quantity. These fancier shapes are not necessarily more complicated; they are just more time-consuming since they must be formed on the tabletop after the string has been rolled out. Whichever shape you choose, a knot will always take more time than a plain round or oval roll since you can only produce one knot at a time, in contrast to the rolls which are made two at at time using both hands (see page 124). A nice assortment of Knots in a bread basket, shining from the Egg Wash, always makes an impressive addition to a buffet table or display case. If you think any of these knots look complicated, consider this: Knot theorists have determined that there are almost 13,000 different knots which contain twelve or fewer crossings!

Single-Knots

1. Punch the dough down and divide it into 2-ounce (55-g) pieces. Keep the pieces you are not using covered to prevent a skin from forming.

2. Working with one piece at a time, roll into a 9-inch (22.5-cm) rope, and tie the rope into a loose knot so that the ends protrude out just slightly beyond the body of the roll (Figure 3–34).

3. Place the knots on a sheet pan lined with baking paper.

4. Let the knots rise until slightly less than doubled in volume.

5. Brush with Egg Wash and bake at 400°F (205°C) for approximately 15 minutes.

FIGURE 3–34   Forming a Single-Knot

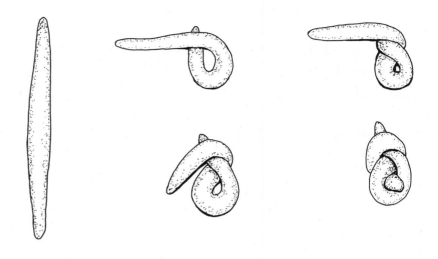

FIGURE 3–35   Forming a Double-Knot

Double-Knots

1. Punch dough the down and divide it into 2-ounce (55-g) pieces. Keep the pieces you are not using covered to prevent a skin from forming.

2. Working with one piece at a time, roll into an 11-inch (27.5-cm) rope and place it in front of you vertically.

3. Pick up the end closest to you and, forming a loop on the right, cross it over the top of the rope just below the tip, so that one-third of the length is now in a straight line pointing to the left.

4. In one continuous motion, twist the bottom of the loop one-half turn to the right and tuck the top end underneath and up through the opening (Figure 3–35).

5. Place the knots on a sheet pan lined with baking paper.

6. Let the knots rise until slightly less than doubled in volume.

7. Brush with Egg Wash and bake at 400°F (205°C) for about 15 minutes.

Twisted Knots

1. Punch the dough down and divide it into 2-ounce (55-g) pieces. Keep the pieces you are not using covered to prevent a skin from forming.

2. Working with one piece at a time, roll into a 16-inch (40-cm) rope and place it in front of you in a U shape, with the inner edges touching.

3. Fold the bottom up to about ³/₄ inch (2 cm) from the top.

4. Using both hands, twist the sides in opposite directions as if you were opening a book. Repeat this motion (Figure 3–36).

5. Place the knots on a sheet pan lined with baking paper.

6. Let the knots rise until slightly less than doubled in volume.

7. Brush with Egg Wash and bake at 400°F (205°C) for approximately 15 minutes.

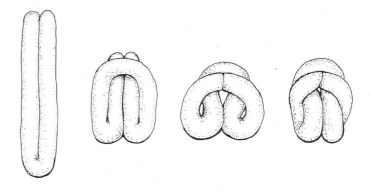

FIGURE 3–36   *Forming a Twisted Knot*

 Swedish Thin Bread (Knäckebröd)

one hundred and twelve 2-by-3-inch (5-×-7.5-cm) crackers

4 ounces (115 g) vegetable shortening
2 ounces (55 g) soft unsalted butter
2 ounces (55 g) granulated sugar
6 ounces (170 g) rolled oats
1 pound, 5 ounces (595 g) bread flour, approximately
1 teaspoon (5 g) salt
1 teaspoon (4 g) baking soda
1½ cups (360 ml) buttermilk

NOTE: If you do not need the full amount of crackers all at once, place the extra dough pieces in the freezer after step four. They will keep for several weeks.

*T**his type of bread or cracker—hard, crisp, and healthy—is included in the daily diet of the majority of Scandinavians. The crackers are delicious eaten plain as a quick snack, or they can be cut into a larger size before baking and served topped with cheese or pâté as an appetizer.*

1. Cream the shortening, butter, and sugar, using the paddle until the mixture is light and fluffy.

2. Combine the rolled oats, flour, salt, and baking soda.

3. On low speed, incorporate the dry ingredients into the butter mixture in two additions alternating with the buttermilk. Do not over-mix; the dough will be fairly sticky. Adjust with a little additional flour if necessary to be able to roll the dough out very thin; however, keep in mind that the softer the dough, the crisper the finished product.

4. Divide the dough into four 12-ounce (340-g) pieces. Cover and place three pieces in the refrigerator (see note).

5. Roll the remaining piece into a 14-by-12-inch (35-×-30-cm) rectangle, using flour to prevent the dough from sticking. The dough will be very thin.

6. Mark the top of the rolled sheet with a waffle roller or, if not available, prick well.

7. Roll the dough up on a dowel and transfer to a sheet pan lined with baking paper. Score the top, cutting approximately halfway through, marking twenty-eight 2-by-3-inch (5-×-7.5-cm) rectangles (seven on the long side by four on the short side).

8. Repeat steps five, six, and seven with the three remaining pieces of dough.

9. Bake at 325°F (163°C) for approximately 30 minutes or until completely dry. Let the crackers cool on the pan. Break apart on the scored lines. Stored in airtight containers, the crackers will stay fresh and crisp for several weeks.

Swedish Whole Grain Crisp Rolls

120 crackers

1 cup (240 ml) boiling water

8 ounces (225 g) cracked wheat

1½ ounces (40 g) fresh compressed yeast

1 pint (480 ml) warm milk (105–115°F, 40–46°C)

2 tablespoons (30 ml) or 1½ ounces (40 g) honey

1 tablespoon (15 g) salt

4 ounces (115 g) bread flour

1 pound (455 g) whole wheat flour, approximately

3 ounces (85 g) soft lard

Wheat Crisp Rolls

120 crackers

1½ ounces (40 g) fresh compressed yeast

1 pint (480 ml) warm milk (105–115°F, 40–46°C)

4 ounces (115 g) granulated sugar

2 tablespoons (30 g) salt

1 tablespoon (6 g) ground cardamom

1 pound, 14 ounces (855 g) bread flour

2 ounces (55 g) soft lard

*C*risp rolls, or Skorpor *as they are called in Scandinavia, are a delicious and hearty snack eaten plain, dipped in coffee or tea, or topped with butter, cheese, or marmalade. They are a type of cracker and should not be mistaken for dried, leftover rolls. The characteristic fragile and crunchy texture, which is the trademark of a real crisp roll, is only obtained by making sure the dough as been prepared and proofed properly.*

1. Pour the boiling water over the cracked wheat and stir to combine. Cover and set aside until soft: 2 to 3 hours or, preferably, overnight.

2. Dissolve the yeast in the warm milk. Mix in the honey and salt, then incorporate the bread flour, half of the whole wheat flour, and the reserved cracked wheat. Add the lard, and knead, using the dough hook, for 6 to 8 minutes at low to medium speed, adding enough of the remaining whole wheat flour to make a fairly firm and elastic dough.

3. Place the dough in an oiled bowl, turn to coat both sides with oil, cover, and let rise in a warm place until doubled in volume.

4. Punch the dough down, and repeat step three twice.

5. After the third rising, punch the dough down and divide it into two equal pieces, approximately 1 pound, 14 ounces (855 g) each. Roll each into a 30-inch (75-cm) string and cut the strings into thirty equal pieces each. Form the pieces into 3-inch (7.5-cm) ovals, slightly tapered at the ends (see Figure 3–27, page 124).

6. Place the rolls on sheet pans lined with baking paper and let rise until doubled in volume.

7. Bake at 400°F (205°C) until light brown and baked through, approximately 15 minutes. Let cool.

8. Break the rolls in half horizontally in the traditional way, using a large fork, or cut them in half with a serrated knife. Return the pieces to the sheet pans, cut-side up.

9. Toast the roll halves at 400°F (205°C) until they have browned lightly. Reduce the oven temperature to 300°F (149°C) and leave the rolls in the oven until they are completely dried through. If stored in airtight containers, these crackers will keep fresh for many weeks.

1. Dissolve the yeast in the warm milk. Add the sugar, salt, and cardamom.

2. Incorporate about two-thirds of the flour.

3. Add the lard and knead, using the dough hook for approximately 6 minutes, adding enough of the remaining flour to make a smooth and elastic dough.

4. Proceed with the directions for Swedish Whole Grain Crisp Rolls, steps three through nine, shaping the rolls round instead of oval.

Tessiner Rolls

60 rolls, approximately 2 ounces (55 g) each

3 cups (720 ml) warm water (105–115°F, 40–46°C)

3 cups (720 ml) warm beer (105–115°F, 40–46°C)

1 ounce (30 g) fresh compressed yeast

2 tablespoons (30 g) salt

3 ounces (85 g) malt sugar

or

1/2 cup (120 ml) or 6 ounces (170 g) honey

one recipe Kaiser Roll Pre-Dough (page 129)

3 pounds,12 ounces (1 kg, 705 g) bread flour, approximately

6 tablespoons (90 ml) olive oil

NOTE: If your oven is not equipped with steam injectors, see Creating Steam without Steam Injectors, page 73.

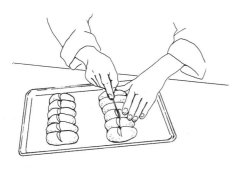

FIGURE 3–37 Cutting a deep slash in the top of Tessiner Rolls before baking

*T*hese unusual Swiss pull-apart rolls borrowed their name from the Italian-influenced region (or canton as it is called there) of Tessin (Ticino in Italian), which is located in the southern part of Switzerland at the Italian border. The restaurants in Tessin serve a whole "loaf" of these rolls in their bread baskets, which not only looks interesting but keeps the rolls from drying out.

Malt, which is extracted from barley, in addition to being used by the brewing industry, is used as a powerful food for the yeast in a bread dough. It adds flavor to the finished product and additional color to the crust. Replacing part of the liquid in this recipe with beer, in combination with the use of malt sugar, amplifies this effect. Should you feel this is a waste of beer and that you would rather use it in another manner (preferably cold I would think), substituting water will work fine.

1. Combine the water and beer. Dissolve the yeast in the warm liquid. Mix in the salt, malt sugar or honey, and pre-dough. Incorporate approximately three-quarters of the flour. Mix in the olive oil together with most of the remaining flour, and knead with the dough hook at low to medium speed for 8 to 10 minutes, adding the remaining flour as needed for a smooth, elastic dough.

2. Place the dough in an oiled bowl, turn to coat all sides with oil, cover, and let rise in a warm place for 30 minutes.

3. Punch the dough down to remove all air, then let rise again for 30 minutes.

4. Punch the dough down and divide it into three equal pieces, approximately 2 pounds, 8 ounces (1 kg, 135 g) each. Roll these out to 24-inch (60-cm) strings and cut each string into twenty equal pieces.

5. Form the pieces into round balls, then roll into tapered ovals 3 inches (7.5 cm) long (see Figure 3–27, page 124).

6. Place in rows of six, with the long sides touching, on sheet pans lined with baking paper. Let rise until slightly less than doubled in volume.

7. Using a sharp, thin knife or a razor blade, make a cut down the full length of each loaf (six rolls). Start the cut at one-third of the width of the rolls, cutting at an angle 1/2 inch (1.2 cm) deep toward the center of each loaf (Figure 3–37).

8. Bake at 400°F (205°C) with steam, leaving the damper closed for 10 minutes. Open the damper and continue baking approximately 10 minutes longer or until done.

Zwieback

about seventy 5-by-2½-by-¾-inch (12.5-×-6.2-×-2-cm) crackers

Sponge

2 ounces (55 g) fresh compressed
    yeast
2 cups (480 ml) warm milk
    (105–115°F, 40–46°C)
14 ounces (400 g) bread flour

Dough

1 cup (240 ml) warm milk
    (105–115°F, 40–46°C)
3 ounces (85 g) granulated sugar
1 tablespoon (15 g) salt
3 eggs
2 pounds, 6 ounces (1 kg, 80 g) bread
    flour, approximately
5 ounces (140 g) unsalted butter
Potato Starch Solution (recipe follows)

*C*risp rolls, wheat rusks, Zwieback (and its many variations, such as Melba Toast), all have one common denominator: They are baked twice, which produces a pleasant dry and crunchy texture. When I was growing up, Zwieback were made not only in factories and larger bakeries but even the smallest pastry shop typically produced its own version of this cracker. Today, with few exceptions, Zwieback are mass-produced exclusively in factories.

Literally translated from German, zwieback means "two times baked." It is basically a breakfast bread dough, similar to the one used for Cinnamon Twists, which, instead of being filled, is baked, cut in half or sliced, and toasted until dry.

There are many ways to vary this basic recipe. By increasing or decreasing the amounts of sugar and/or eggs, you can produce differing flavors and textures. Zwieback are also made with a special highly nutritious flour for those on special diets, and for infants and toddlers; these are especially popular for youngsters who are teething. My mother was a great believer in the theory that hard or stale bread was good for children (although all through my early childhood I personally felt it was just an excuse to use up old bread).

The dessert version of Zwieback often contains raisins, almonds, or hazelnuts, the most well known of these being the Italian biscotti. Others are glazed, dipped in chocolate, or decorated with various ingredients. Generally, these are made with a cookie dough rather than a yeast-based dough, but the baking, slicing, and toasting is done in the same way.

To achieve the desired texture in the finished cracker, it is crucial to keep the dough a little firmer than you might expect and to take the time to allow the dough to mature fully, punching it down and letting it proof three times. Use a low oven for the final toasting to dry the crackers all the way through.

1. To make the sponge, dissolve the yeast in the warm milk and then stir in the flour, mixing until you have a smooth paste.

2. Cover and let stand in a warm place until the sponge has risen to its maximum volume: When the sponge is fully mature it first begins to bubble on the surface and then gradually starts to fall, this takes approximately 30 minutes.

3. Incorporate the remaining milk, the sugar, salt, and eggs. Hold back a handful of the remaining flour and incorporate the rest. Knead in the butter and enough of the reserved flour to make a quite firm dough. Continue to knead on low speed until the dough is smooth and elastic, about 6 minutes.

4. Place the dough in a lightly oiled bowl, turn the dough over to coat both sides with oil, cover, and let rise in a warm place until doubled in volume.

5. Punch the dough down, then cover and let it rise again until doubled in volume.

6. Punch the dough down and let it rise once more for a total of three risings.

7. Divide the dough into three equal pieces, approximately 1 pound, 10 ounces (740 g) each. Pound and roll each piece into a 16-inch (40-cm) rope (see Figures 3–3, 3–4, and 3–5, pages 77 and 78).

8. Cut each rope into twelve equal pieces. Form the small pieces into mini loaves. Place the pieces side by side on sheet pans lined with baking paper as shown for Tessiner Rolls (see Figure 3–37, page 139; do not cut these as shown in the drawing). Let rise to just under one-and-one-half times the original size. Do not overproof. Brush the Potato Starch Solution over the loaves.

9. Bake at 400°F (205°C) for approximately 25 minutes or until completely baked through. Remove from the oven and brush again with the Potato Starch Solution. Set the Zwieback loaves aside at room temperature until the following day.

10. Cut the loaves lengthwise into ³/₄-inch (2-cm) thick slices. Place the slices cut-side down on sheet pans lined with baking paper.

11. Toast the slices at 325°F (163°C) until they are light golden brown on top, about 20 minutes. Turn the slices over and continue baking for about 20 minutes longer, or until golden brown on the second side as well. Adjust the oven temperature if necessary: if the oven is too hot the Zwieback will not have a chance to dry properly in the center by the time they are brown on the outside, which will cause them to become chewy after just a few days of storage. Properly baked and stored in airtight containers, they will stay crisp for many weeks. Zwieback make great croutons for soups, salads, or canapes.

 Potato Starch Solution

1 cup (240 ml) cold water
4 tablespoons (32 g) potato starch

1. Stir the water into the potato starch.
2. Heat, stirring constantly to just under boiling.

 **VARIATION**
Melba Toast

This is the lesser known of the culinary creations named for the opera singer Nellie Melba, the most famous being the dessert Peach Melba, which is accompanied by Melba Sauce. All were composed in her honor by the great chef Auguste Escoffier. History has it that having returned from a tour exhausted and in poor health, Nellie Melba was put on a strict diet, which included thin slices of toasted bread. Chef Escoffier's plain dried bread then became known as Melba Toast.

Although any rich bread can be and often is used, Zwieback is ideal due to its fine, crumbly texture. To make Melba Toast, slice the baked Zwieback loaves 1/4 inch (6 mm) thick. Cut the slices into rounds, triangles, or squares as desired. Toast the slices as instructed in the main recipe; however, the thinner Melba Toasts will only require about 10 minutes on each side.

4

Breakfast Breads
and Pastries

Apple Turnovers
Berliners
Brioche
Butter Gipfels
Cherry Crossover Strip
Choux Surprise
Cinnamon Snails
Croissants
English Muffins
Gosen
Gugelhupf
Honey-Pecan Sticky Buns
Hot Cross Buns
Hungarian Twists
Parisiennes
Puff Pastry Diamonds
Scones
Swedish Lenten Buns
Wales Strips
Danish Pastries
    Danish Pastry Dough

Danish Fillings
Bear Claws
Butterhorns
Danish Cinnamon Wreath
Danish Twists
Double Curls
Envelopes
Honey Raisin Snails
Mayor's Wreath
Sister's Pull-Apart Coffee
    Cake
Sugar Buns
    Muffins

Apple-Pecan Buttermilk
    Muffins
Blueberry Ginger Muffins
Chocolate Cherry Muffins
Chocolate Chip Muffins
Chocolate Honey Muffins
Honey-Bran Muffins
Nutmeg Muffins
Oat Bran-Yogurt Muffins
Pumpkin Muffins
Zucchini-Walnut Muffins

Unfortunately, breakfast for a lot of us simply means a cup or two of coffee, gulped down while we dress, or shave, or drive to work. This habit really is a shame because a good hearty breakfast is the most important meal of the day. Because our bodies have been without food for 10 hours or so, our brains need sugar. Breakfast can be a welcome opportunity to enjoy sweets, whether they be in the form of fruit, Oat-Bran Muffins for the health-conscious, or the delicious indulgence of a pastry.

I grew up eating a big breakfast. There were always two or three different types of home-baked bread on the table: rye, a whole grain, and white bread to toast (try toasting the Raisin Bread on page 108!). We spread the bread with fresh sweet butter and piled on an abundance of other wonderful things like ham, cheeses, and smoked fish.

Although a good old-fashioned breakfast is still available in many countries, travelers, unfortunately, often end up with the so-called continental breakfast, which does not provide much opportunity to try the local specialties. The typical restaurant breakfast in

Scandinavia is served on a large buffet and contains everything from scrambled eggs to herring, caviar, and pâtés. It also includes, of course, the famous *Wienerbröd,* known in this country as "Danish pastries" (the actual translation of *Wienerbröd* is "bread from Vienna," but it has come to mean any fine or delicate bread). In Germany you can have a breakfast sweet very familiar to Americans: doughnuts. Called Berliners, German doughnuts have a different round shape and no hole, but basically they are the same thing. While traveling in Switzerland, don't miss having coffee and Gipfels (what we call croissants) at a *Konditorei,* or café—a delicious experience. And in France you will naturally want to try the baguettes. Fresh out of the oven their taste and crispness are found nowhere else, and when topped with sweet butter and marmalade they are a wonderful breakfast treat.

In the United States, the muffin has been gaining in popularity as a breakfast item in the last few years as people have become more concerned about nutrition. Many types of muffins are both lower in calories and higher in fiber than Danish pastries or croissants, and the aroma of a freshly baked bran or zucchini muffin is just as good as the muffin is good for you.

Apple Turnovers

20 pastries

2 pounds, 8 ounces (1 kg, 135 g) Puff Pastry (page 44)
Egg Wash (page 7)
1 pound (455 g) Chunky Apple Filling (page 1085)
Cinnamon Sugar (page 5)
sanding sugar
crushed, sliced almonds
Simple Syrup (page 11)

NOTE: *Apple Turnovers are excellent to make up ahead and freeze. When needed, bake them directly from the freezer. Cherry Filling (page 1084) can be substituted for the Chunky Apple Filling.*

*T*hese are the classic Puff Pastry breakfast treat; few pastries can compete with a well-made Apple Turnover to go with morning coffee. Ideally, turnovers should have a slightly tart, moist filling surrounded by very flaky Puff Pastry. The key is to have the Puff Pastry as dry and crumbly as possible (no one will care that some of the crumbs inevitably end up on the one who is eating it). If the dough is rolled too thick, or if the oven temperature is too high, you may very well produce a tall, golden brown pastry that looks great on the outside, but the inside will contain a thick layer of heavy, unbaked dough. Some is impossible to avoid due to the moisture in the apples, but the proper dough thickness and oven temperature will minimize the problem. Another more labor-intensive solution is to fold the Puff Pastry squares into triangles and prebake them (bake blind without the filling) until they are almost done. Remove them from the oven, carefully lift up or cut off the top of each shell, and add the filling. Continue baking until done. Turnovers also make a lovely simple dessert served with Vanilla Ice Cream or Sauce Anglaise. For variation, try the Sour Apple and Cheese Turnovers on page 781.*

1. Roll out the Puff Pastry to ⅛ inch (3 mm) thick, 22½ inches (56.2 cm) long, and 18 inches (45 cm) wide. Let it rest 5 to 10 minutes to relax.

2. Cut the dough into five rows of four squares each, making twenty 4½-inch (11.2-cm) squares.

3. Brush two adjoining sides of each square with Egg Wash.

4. Pipe a mound of apple filling in the center of each, dividing it evenly, and sprinkle Cinnamon Sugar on the apple filling.

5. Fold the upper part of the squares onto the part brushed with Egg Wash to make triangles (make sure apple filling does not get on the Egg Wash). Press the edges together with your fingers.

6. Mix equal amounts of sanding sugar and almonds. Brush the tops of the triangles with Egg Wash, invert into the sugar mixture, then place the turnovers sugar-side up on sheet pans. Do not put more than sixteen turnovers per full-sized pan, 24 by 16 inches (60 × 40 cm).

7. Cut a small slit in the center of each turnover.

8. Bake at 375°F (190°C) until golden and completely baked through, about 25 minutes. You may need to use a second pan underneath and/or baking paper on the top to prevent the turnovers from overbrowning.

9. Brush the pastries lightly with Simple Syrup as soon as they come out of the oven.

Berliners

40 buns

Sponge

1½ cups (360 ml) warm milk (105–115°F, 40–46°C)

2 ounces (55 g) fresh compressed yeast

12 ounces (340 g) bread flour

Dough

½ cup (120 ml) warm milk (105–115°F, 40–46°C)

1½ ounces (40 g) fresh compressed yeast

4 ounces (115 g) granulated sugar

1 teaspoon (5 g) salt

grated rind of one-half lemon

6 egg yolks (½ cup/120 ml)

4 ounces (115 g) soft unsalted butter

1 pound, 2 ounces (510 g) bread flour, approximately

vegetable oil for frying

Cinnamon Sugar (page 5)

Chunky Apple or Cherry Filling (pages 1085 and 1084), puréed

A Berliner is simply a doughnut without the cut-out hole. But unlike traditional American-style doughnuts, which are always cooked first if they are to be filled, Berliners can be filled before or after cooking. The latter is more practical for commercial operations. The trademark for a perfectly prepared Berliner is a lighter colored ring around the center where the dough was not in the oil as long. In addition to adding to the overall appearance, it shows that the oil was hot enough to make them rise up high before the yeast was killed (the same as oven-spring for baked yeast products). If the oil temperature is too low, the Berliners absorb oil which makes them heavy and unable to spring up.

1. To make the sponge, dissolve the yeast in the warm milk, then add the flour and mix to a smooth consistency. Let the sponge rise, covered, in a warm place until it starts to fall.

2. Start making the dough by dissolving the yeast in the warm milk in a mixer bowl. Add the sponge and start kneading with the dough hook.

3. Add the sugar, salt, lemon rind, egg yolks, and butter as you continue to knead the dough. Knead in enough of the bread flour to make a medium-soft dough, kneading for a total of 5 to 10 minutes. The dough should not be too firm, so do not add all the flour at once.

4. Refrigerate the dough, covered, for 1 hour to relax it.

5. Divide the dough into four equal pieces, approximately 14 ounces (400 g) each. Roll each piece into a rope, then cut each rope into ten equal pieces.

6. Roll the small pieces into smooth round buns (see Figure 3–27, page 124). Place them on a sheet pan covered with a cloth or towel. Try not to use any flour at all when working with Berliners as it will burn when they are fried, making the outside too dark.

7. Let the buns rise in a warm place, around 80°F (26°C), until slightly less than doubled in volume (this will happen fairly quickly due to the softness of the dough).

8. Preheat the frying oil to 350°F (175°C). Use a frying thermometer to test the temperature, and try to time it so the oil is ready when the Berliners have risen. You should have at least 4 inches (10 cm) of oil. Use a good quality vegetable oil or, better yet, an oil specifically made for deep-frying. It is very important that the oil is at the correct temperature. If it is not hot enough, the buns will absorb too much oil and be heavy and unappetizing. If the oil is hotter than it should be, the Berliners will brown before they are cooked through, the flavor will not be as good, and the oil will darken so that you will not be able to use it a second time.

9. Pick the Berliners up one at a time and quickly add them to the oil, seam-side up. Do not fill up the pan completely, because the Berliners will increase in volume as they cook.

10. When they are golden brown, about 5 minutes, turn them over and cook about 4 minutes longer on the other side. Try to turn them all over at about the same time so they are uniform in color.

11. As you remove the Berliners from the frying pan, place them on a rack or paper towels to drain.

12. While the buns are still hot, roll them in Cinnamon Sugar.

13. After the Berliners have cooled down a bit, inject them with Chunky Apple or Cherry Filling, using a special plain pastry bag tip made for that purpose, pushing the sharp end of the tip halfway into the side of the Berliner. If you do not have a tip made for filling, use a no. 3 (6-mm) plain tip and be careful not to make the opening in the bun any larger than necessary. Berliners should be served the day they are made.

 **VARIATION**
Klenäter

thirty-six 1¹/₄-by-4-inch (3.1-×-10-cm) pastries

K̲nown as Schüferli in Germany and Switzerland, these pastries are very popular there and are considered a must at Christmas time in Sweden. They are traditionally leavened with baking powder rather than yeast, but are even better made with the Berliner dough.

1. Make a half recipe of Berliners, preparing the dough through step four with the following changes:

• Replace the ¹/₄ cup (60 ml) of milk in the dough (not the sponge) with an equal amount of brandy.
• Add ¹/₂ teaspoon (1 g) of cardamom with the flour.
• Omit Chunky Apple or Cherry Filling.

2. Roll the dough to a rectangle 12 by 16 inches (30 × 40 cm), using as little flour as possible. (Let the dough relax for a few minutes as

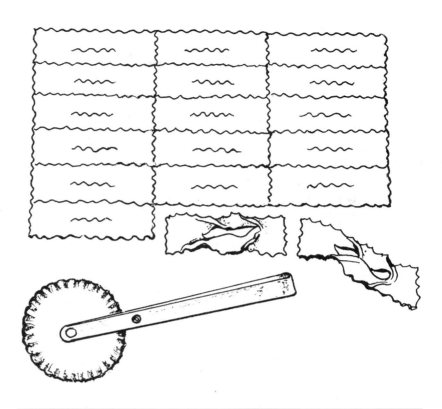

FIGURE 4–1　The dough for Klenäter after cutting the strips with a fluted pastry wheel; one piece turned inside-out; a piece after stretching the diagonal corners

needed to keep it from shrinking.) Brush off any excess flour from the top and the bottom.

3. Preheat the frying oil to 350°F (175°C).

4. Cut the dough into three 4-inch (10-cm) strips, using a fluted pastry wheel. Leave the strips in place. Using the same tool, cut crosswise, cutting twelve pieces, approximately 1¼ inches (3.1 cm) wide, in each strip. Cut a 2-inch (5-cm) slit, lengthwise, in the center of each piece.

5. Pick up one piece and pull one end of the strip through the slit. Then, holding the rectangle by two diagonal corners, stretch lightly so it takes on a slight diamond-shape (Figure 4–1).

6. Repeat with the remaining pieces and place them on a sheet pan covered with a cloth or towel (they are ready to cook immediately; they do not require additional proofing).

7. Pick up the pieces one at time and drop them carefully into the hot frying oil. Cook approximately 2 minutes or until nicely browned, then turn and cook about 1 minute longer on the other side.

8. Remove from the oil with a slotted spoon or skimmer and place on paper towels or napkins for a few seconds to drain.

9. While still warm, turn in Cinnamon Sugar to coat thoroughly.

Brioche

36 brioche, approximately 2 ounces (55 g) each or four 1-pound, 3-ounce (540-g) loaves

Sponge

2 ounces (55 g) fresh compressed yeast

1 cup (240 ml) warm milk (105–115°F, 40–46°C)

1/4 cup (60 ml) or 3 ounces (85 g) honey

8 ounces (225 g) bread flour

Dough

4 teaspoons (20 g) salt

4 ounces (115 g) granulated sugar

8 eggs

1 pound (455 g) cake flour

1 pound (455 g) bread flour, approximately

8 ounces (225 g) soft unsalted butter

Egg Wash (page 7)

This light French speciality, so rich in butter and eggs, is said to have gotten its name from the French word brier, *which means "to pound." I assume this relates to the dough's lengthy kneading process, which long ago, before electric mixers, simply meant pounding the dough until it reached the desired consistency.*

The most typical shape for Brioche is a round fluted base with slightly sloping sides and a round knot on top. This shape can be used for individual servings up to larger sizes equivalent to a standard loaf. For this shape the dough is baked in brioche molds which can be made of metal or ceramic, the latter being mostly for the larger sizes. Brioche can also be made into rectangular loaves. Brioche dough is very versatile and is used frequently for encasing other foods: it can be wrapped around a wheel of cheese, it is used for Beef en croûte, *and in the Russian classic* Kulebiaka *(often known by the French spelling* Coulibiac*) where the dough is filled with layers of salmon, rice, eggs, and herbs. Individual baked Brioche are sometimes hollowed out and filled with savory stews or with fruit and cream for dessert.*

1. To make the sponge, dissolve the yeast in the warm milk in a mixer bowl and then add the honey and bread flour on low speed. Mix until soft and smooth. Cover the sponge and let it rise until it has doubled in volume.

2. Add the salt, granulated sugar, and eggs to the sponge. Mix in the cake flour and all but a handful of the bread flour. Gradually mix in the butter, adding it in small pieces.

3. Knead with the dough hook until the dough forms a ball. Adjust the consistency by adding the reserved bread flour if necessary. The dough should not stick to the sides of the bowl and should have a slightly shiny appearance.

4. Cover the dough and refrigerate 5 to 6 hours. During this time the dough should double in size. If you are not going to shape the dough within a few hours after it has risen, freeze it so that the large amount of yeast does not make the dough sour.

5. Punch down the dough.

6. To make loaves, divide the dough into four equal pieces, approximately 1 pound, 3 ounces (540 g) each. Pound the pieces into tight loaves (see Figure 3–24, page 120) and place in buttered or paper-lined loaf pans 8 by 4 by 4 inches (20 × 10 × 10 cm). Let rise until doubled in volume. Bake the loaves at 375°F (190°C) until they have a healthy brown color and are baked through, about 40 minutes. Unmold and let cool on racks.

7. To make Brioche, divide the dough into three equal pieces, approximately 1 pound, 8 ounces (680 g) each. Roll each piece into a 16-inch (40-cm) rope, then cut each rope into twelve equal pieces. Roll each piece into a firm ball (see Figure 3–27, page 124); set the balls to the side in order so you can form them in the same order they were rolled.

8. Starting with the ball of dough you rolled first, place it in front of you and hold your hand above it with your fingers held tightly together and your hand completely vertical, press down on the ball at one-third of the width, and move your hand back and forth in a sawing motion until you almost sever the ball into two portions (Figure 4–2).

9. You should now have two round balls of dough, one twice the size of the other, connected by a very thin string of dough. Gently pinch the connecting string between the thumbs and index fingers of both hands and, still holding on to it, force your thumbs and fingers straight down into the top of the larger ball, all the way to the bottom. Open your fingers slightly to create a hole, and let the smaller ball drop into it (Figure 4–3). Be sure the smaller ball of dough sits well inside the larger, or it can fall off as the dough expands in the proof box, and later in the oven. Form the remaining Brioche in the same way.

10. Place the Brioche into buttered forms (Figure 4–4) and let them rise until slightly less than doubled in volume.

11. Brush the Brioche with Egg Wash being careful not to let any drip between the dough and the form, as this will make it difficult to remove the Brioche after baking.

12. Bake at 400°F (205°C) for about 18 minutes. Unmold before completely cool and finish cooling on racks. A faster cooling method, and one that is more typically used in the industry, is to quickly turn the Brioche on its side, leaving it in the form; this allows air to circulate underneath.

FIGURE 4–2   Using the side of the hand with a sawing motion to form two connected balls of dough for Brioche

FIGURE 4–3   Pushing the smaller ball of dough inside the larger one

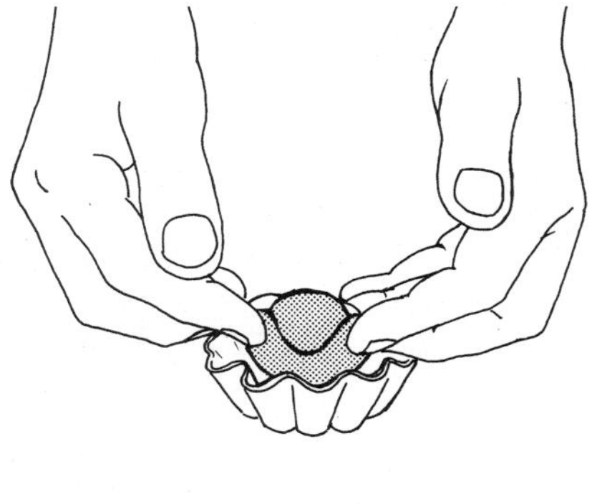

FIGURE 4–4   Placing the Brioche into the baking form

Butter Gipfels

48 gipfels,
about 3¹/₂ ounces (100 g) each

8 ounces (225 g) unsalted butter

2 pounds, 4 ounces (1 kg, 25 g) soft
unsalted butter

5 ounces (140 g) lard

4 ounces (115 g) bread flour

4 teaspoons (20 ml) lemon juice

3 ounces (85 g) fresh compressed
yeast

3 cups (720 ml) cold water

2 ounces (55 g) malt sugar
or

¹/₃ cup (80 ml) or 4 ounces (115 g)
honey

4 tablespoons (60 g) salt

6 ounces (170 g) granulated sugar

4 eggs

3 pounds, 6 ounces (1 kg, 535 g)
bread flour, approximately

Egg Wash (page 7)

NOTE: If your oven is not equipped with steam
injectors, see Creating Steam without Steam
Injectors, page 73.

A version of Croissants made in Germany and Switzerland, Butter Gipfels have a more pronounced crescent shape (almost circular), which requires a different, slightly slower, rolling technique. Although the fat content is almost the same as Croissants, Gipfels are lighter in texture due to the much thinner, and greater number of, layers, produced by stretching the dough while rolling up the triangles. Another contributing factor, and one that is quite unusual with a laminated dough, is that the Gipfels are baked using steam at the beginning. This gives a more rapid oven-spring. The Gipfels may also be baked without steam (as is typical for Croissants) with excellent results.

1. Melt the 8 ounces (225 g) of butter and brown lightly (*buerre noisette*). Remove from the heat and set aside to cool to room temperature.

2. Combine the remaining soft butter, lard, 4 ounces (115 g) bread flour, and lemon juice.

3. Shape the mixture into a rectangle, 14 by 12 inches (35 × 30 cm), on a sheet of baking paper and reserve (place in the refrigerator if necessary).

4. Dissolve the yeast in the cold water in a mixer bowl. Add the malt sugar or honey, salt, granulated sugar, eggs, and browned butter. Reserve a handful of the remaining bread flour and add the rest. Mix for approximately 1 minute until you have a smooth soft dough. Adjust by adding the reserved flour as needed.

5. Cover the dough and place in the refrigerator for 30 minutes.

6. Roll the dough out to a 14-by-18-inch (35-×-45-cm) rectangle.

7. Place the butter block on top of the dough covering two-thirds of the rectangle. The butter block should have the same consistency as the dough.

8. Fold the uncovered third of the dough over half of the butter block. Fold the remaining butter-covered piece on top of the dough (Figure 4–5).

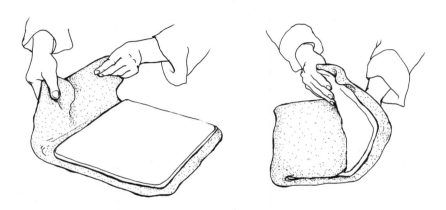

FIGURE 4–5   Folding the butter block into the Gipfel dough: the butter is positioned to cover two-thirds of the dough; the dough is folded in thirds, folding the uncovered portion first

9. Roll the dough out to a rectangle ¹/₂ inch (1.2 cm) thick. Give the dough one single turn (see Figures 4–15 and 4–16, page 160).

10. Cover and refrigerate for 30 minutes.

11. Make two additional single turns, refrigerating the dough for 30 minutes between them.

12. After completing the third turn, roll the dough out to the size of a full sheet pan, 16 by 24 inches (40 × 60 cm) (refrigerate to relax the dough first if necessary).

13. Cover the dough and place in the refrigerator or freezer for at least 2 to 3 hours or, preferably, overnight.

14. Cut the dough in half crosswise. Roll one piece at a time to a rectangle 16 by 42 inches (40 cm × 1 m, 5 cm) about ¹/₁₆ inch (2 mm) thick.

15. Let the dough relax for a few minutes (roll the second piece in the meantime), then cut the dough lengthwise into two strips, each 8 inches (20 cm) wide.

16. Cut each strip into 12 triangles, 7 inches (17.5 cm) across the base.

17. Cut a slit in the center of the base of each triangle as for Croissants (see Figure 4–14, page 159).

18. Roll the triangles tightly by holding the pointed end still with one hand while using the palm of the other hand to curl up the dough, lightly stretching it as you roll (Figure 4–6).

19. Roll each piece between your palms and the table to make it about 9 inches (22.5 cm) long and very tapered at the ends.

20. Place on sheet pans lined with baking paper, and curl each Gipfel into a full circle so that the ends meet. Pinch the ends together. Let the Gipfels rise until slightly less than doubled in volume.

21. Brush with Egg Wash.

22. Bake at 400°F (205°C) with steam, leaving the damper closed for 5 minutes. Open the damper and continue baking approximately 10 minutes longer, or until baked through.

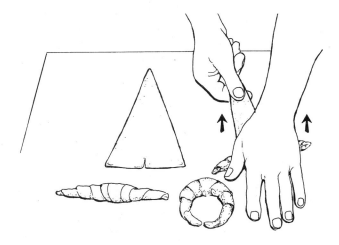

FIGURE 4–6   *Forming Gipfels by holding the tip of the triangle steady and stretching the dough, while rolling the wide end toward you with the other hand*

Cherry Crossover Strip

*two 24-inch (60-cm) strips or
16 pastries*

2 pounds (910 g) Puff Pastry
  (page 44)
2 pounds (910 g) Cherry Filling
  (page 1084)
sanding sugar
crushed, sliced almonds
Egg Wash (page 7)
Simple Syrup (page 11)
Simple Icing (page 1020)

Back in the mid-sixties when I worked on cruise ships, we used to make these with apple filling and call them strudel. The crossover strips were faster to assemble, and we got away with it since they resemble the German apple strudel. Try making them with Chunky Apple Filling (page 1085); sprinkle some Cinnamon Sugar (page 5) on the filling before braiding the top. Crossover strips freeze very well; bake as needed directly from the freezer.

1. Roll the Puff Pastry dough out to $^1/_8$ inch (3 mm) thick, 23 inches (57.5 cm) long, and 16 inches (40 cm) wide. Cut the dough in half to make two strips 23 inches by 8 inches (57.5 × 20 cm) each.

2. Fold each strip lengthwise over a 1-inch-wide (2.5-cm) dowel so that the long cut edges meet and are closest to you. (The dough should be firm for easy handling; reserve the second strip in the refrigerator while you are working on the first if necessary).

3. Using the back of a chef's knife, lightly mark, but do not cut, a line about 2 inches (5 cm) away from and parallel to the cut edges.

4. With the sharp edge of the knife, cut $^1/_4$-inch (6-mm) strips, up to the mark, along the entire length of the dough, leaving the folded edge uncut (Figure 4–7).

5. Use the dowel to lift the strip and place it on an inverted sheet pan lined with baking paper (two strips will fit on one pan). Remove the dowel carefully and separate the fringed edges so that the dough lies flat and open. Repeat with the second strip.

6. Place the Cherry Filling in a pastry bag with a no. 8 (16-mm) plain tip. Pipe the filling down the uncut center of the strips. If needed, spread it out with a spatula to the edge of the cuts.

7. Fold the left and right strips alternately over the filling, using both of your hands in an even rhythm (Figure 4–8). Make sure each left strip is folded on top of the right, and each right is folded on top of the left, and so on so that they lock each other in place.

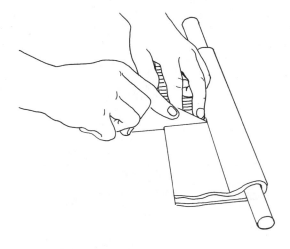

FIGURE 4–7   *Cutting the two short edges of the dough into $^1/_4$-inch (6-mm) wide strips*

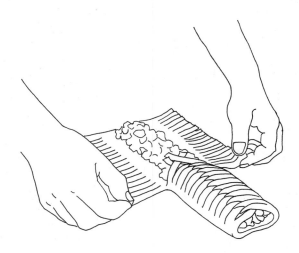

FIGURE 4–8   *Alternating the left and right strips over the filling*

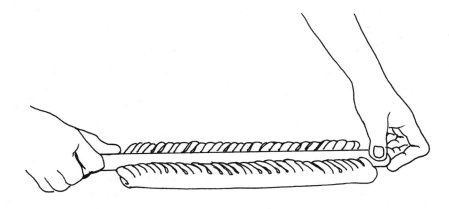

FIGURE 4–9 *Pressing a dowel lengthwise in the center of the assembled Cherry Crossover Strip to prevent the woven strips from unfolding*

8. Place the dowel in the middle of one finished strip and press down hard enough to be sure the strips will not unfold in the oven (Figure 4–9). You will leave a small indentation, but you do not want to press the filling out. Repeat with the second strip.

9. Mix equal amounts of sugar and almonds. Brush the pastries lightly with Egg Wash, then sprinkle the sugar and almond mixture on top.

10. Bake double-panned at 375°F (190°C) for about 35 minutes. You may need to protect the top with baking paper to give the dough time to bake through completely.

11. Brush the crossover strips with Simple Syrup as soon as they come out of the oven. When cool, ice with Simple Icing. Slice each strip into eight pieces at an angle.

Choux Surprise

24 pastries

2 pounds, 4 ounces (1 kg, 25 g) Puff Pastry (page 44)

10 ounces (285 g) Pâte à Choux (page 36)

Egg Wash (page 7)

sanding sugar

crushed, sliced almonds

6 ounces (170 g) Pastry Cream (page 1088)

Simple Syrup (page 11)

Simple Icing (page 1020)

These delicious pastries rank very high on my list of favorites, not only because of the wonderful combination of the three main ingredients—Puff Pastry, Pâte à Choux, and Pastry Cream—but also for their practicality. Choux Surprise can be fully assembled and frozen, then plunged directly into a pre-heated oven (not only is it not necessary to thaw them, it is preferable not to do so). So in less than half the time it takes to proof and bake some of the more common breakfast pastries such as Danish and Croissant, Choux Surprise are ready to eat.

In Sweden we call these breakfast treats Franska Wienerbröd, *which translated into English means "French Danish" and gets pretty confusing! The French elements of course are the Puff Pastry and the Pâte à Choux. As with most baked goods that are comprised of a combination of doughs, Choux Surprise can be a little tricky to bake correctly. In general, it is better to let them get a bit dark than to underbake them. When underbaked, the pastries become doughy and heavy.*

NOTE: It is important that you press firmly when you make the indentation for the Pastry Cream. You want to push all the Pâte à Choux underneath out of the way. Otherwise, as it bakes, the Pâte à Choux will puff up and force the Pastry Cream off the pastry and onto the pan.

1. Roll the Puff Pastry dough to a rectangle measuring 22½ by 15 inches (56.2 × 37.5 cm) and ⅛ inch (3 mm) thick. Cut into twenty-four 3¾-inch (9.3-cm) squares (four strips cut into six pieces each).

2. Pipe a small mound of Pâte à Choux, about the size of a prune, in the center of each square. Brush the sides of each square with Egg Wash. Fold the points in to meet in the center like an envelope. With your thumb, press firmly, all the way down to the pan, in the spot where the points come together (see note).

3. Mix equal amounts of sugar and almonds. Brush the squares with Egg Wash, invert onto the sugar mixture, then place right-side up on a sheet pan lined with baking paper.

4. Pipe a small amount of Pastry Cream in the indentation left by your thumb.

5. Baked double-panned at 375°F (190°C) for about 40 minutes. Be certain that the pastries are done. If the Pâte à Choux inside is not thoroughly baked, the pastries will collapse, becoming heavy and dense.

6. Brush the pastries with a small amount of Simple Syrup as soon as they come out of the oven. When cool, spread Simple Icing on top.

Cinnamon Snails

thirty 2½-ounce (70-g) pastries

---

2 ounces (55 g) fresh compressed yeast

1 pint (480 ml) warm milk (105–115°F, 40–46°C)

3 ounces (85 g) granulated sugar

1 tablespoon (15 g) salt

2 tablespoons (12 g) ground cardamom

4 eggs

2 pounds, 10 ounces (1 kg, 195 g) bread flour, approximately

7 ounces (200 g) soft unsalted butter

1 pound, 8 ounces (680 g) Danish Filling II (page 175)

Cinnamon Sugar (page 5)

Egg Wash (page 7)

sanding sugar

sliced almonds

*T*hese are made with a not too sweet, butter-enriched egg bread dough, which complements the filling nicely. To avoid ending up with dry snails, make sure the dough is not too firm, add all of the filling, use a heavy hand with the Cinnamon Sugar (no one buys a Cinnamon Snail if they don't like cinnamon anyway), and finally, make certain that the oven is hot. In the second variation the loaves and wreaths are baked at a lower temperature because of their larger size.

1. In a mixer bowl, dissolve the yeast in the warm milk. Add the sugar, salt, cardamom, and eggs. Reserve a few ounces of the flour and mix in the remainder. Mix in the butter (it is important that the butter does not come in contact with the yeast before the yeast has had a chance to start expanding).

2. Using the dough hook, knead the dough for a few minutes and then adjust by adding the reserved flour, if required, to make the dough firm enough to roll out. Continue to knead until the dough is smooth and elastic, approximately 6 minutes. Cover and let rest 10 minutes.

3. Roll the dough into a rectangle 14 by 36 inches (35 × 90 cm). Spread the Danish Filling over the dough, leaving a 1-inch (2.5-cm) strip uncovered along the bottom (long) edge. Sprinkle Cinnamon Sugar heavily over the filling. Roll up the rectangle, from the top toward you, making a tight rope.

4. Cut the rope evenly into thirty slices. Place on paper-lined sheet pans, cut side up, tucking the ends underneath to prevent the snails from unrolling as they expand. Let rise until slightly less than doubled in volume.

5. Brush the snails with Egg Wash. Sprinkle with a mixture of equal parts sanding sugar and sliced almonds.

6. Bake at 410°F (210°C) for approximately 15 minutes or until golden brown and baked through. Use a second pan underneath to prevent them from becoming too brown on the bottom.

1. Roll the dough out to the same size but spread the filling over the left half only. Sprinkle Cinnamon Sugar over the filling.

2. Brush Egg Wash over the uncovered side of the dough and fold over the filling. The dough should now measure 14 by 18 inches (35 × 45 cm).

3. Roll out to a 16-by-24-inch (40-×-60-cm) rectangle (dust with flour underneath to prevent sticking). Cut into thirty 16-inch (40-cm) strips.

4. One at a time, place each strip in front of you horizontally. With one hand on top of each end of the strip, quickly move one hand up and the other hand down simultaneously to twist the strip (Figure 4–10). Wind the twists into a knot shape in the same way you would roll up a ball of yarn; each turn should cross over the previous one and hold it in place (Figure 4–11). As you finish each knot, tuck the end underneath (Figure 4–12) and place it on a sheet pan lined with baking paper. Let the knots rise until slightly less than doubled in volume.

5. Brush with Egg Wash and sprinkle with the sugar and almond mixture. Follow baking instructions above, increasing the time a few minutes.

VARIATION I
Cinnamon Knots

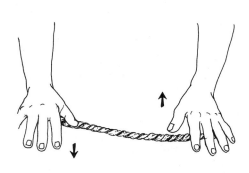

FIGURE 4–10   Twisting the strip of filled dough by quickly moving the hands in opposite directions

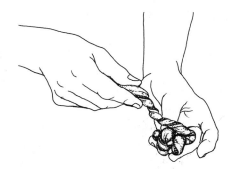

FIGURE 4–11   Winding the twisted strip into a ball

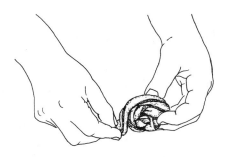

FIGURE 4–12   Tucking the end underneath the assembled Cinnamon Knot

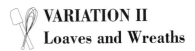

VARIATION II
Loaves and Wreaths

1. Increase Danish Filling II to 2 pounds, 10 ounces (1 kg, 295 g).

2. To make loaves, divide the dough into six pieces approximately 12 ounces (340 g) each and roll each piece into a 12-by-12-inch (30-×-30-cm) square. To make wreaths, divide the dough into four pieces and roll each piece into an 8-by-22-inch (20-×-55-cm) rectangle.

3. Divide the filling equally between the pieces and spread out, leaving ½ inch (1.2 cm) uncovered on one edge (choose a long edge on the rectangles). Sprinkle Cinnamon Sugar over the filling. Brush Egg Wash on the uncovered strips. Roll the dough toward you to make tight ropes.

4. Place the ropes seam-side down, then cut in half lengthwise using a knife or pastry wheel. Turn the pieces so the cut sides face up.

5. Braid two pieces together by alternating one on top of the other, keeping the cut sides facing up the entire time. Pinch the ends together. If making wreaths, form each one into a circle and join the ends together. Try to disguise the seam as well as possible. Place on sheet pans lined with baking paper and let the loaves and wreaths rise until slightly less than doubled in volume.

6. Brush with Egg Wash and sprinkle with the sugar and almond mixture.

7. Bake at 375°F (190°C) for approximately 25 minutes or until light brown and baked through, using a second pan underneath to protect the bottom of the pastries.

Croissants

44 croissants, approximately 3 ounces (85 g) each

2 teaspoons (10 ml) lemon juice

3 pounds, 4 ounces (1 kg, 480 g) bread flour

2 pounds, 8 ounces (1 kg, 135 g) chilled unsalted butter

3 ounces (85 g) fresh compressed yeast

1 quart (960 ml) cold milk

3 ounces (85 g) granulated sugar

1 ounce (30 g) malt sugar
    or

3 tablespoons (45 ml) or 2 ounces (55 g) honey

3 tablespoons (45 g) salt

Egg Wash (page 7) or milk

There is a popular, romantic story which tells how a group of bakers working late into the night in 1886 heard the ominous sound of tunneling under their bakery. They were able to alert the authorities in time to save their city from the subterranean invaders and consequently became heroes. There seems to be some question as to whether the city in the story was Vienna or Budapest, but in either case, the Turks were beaten and the bakers were rewarded with the privilege of creating a commemorative pastry. The pastry was shaped in a crescent, the same symbol which appeared on the Islamic flags, including those of the Turks. At the outset the crescent was simply made from a rich bread dough. It was not until half a century later that the creative French bakers (Croissant literally means crescent *in French) began to make the pastry with a dough similar to Puff Pastry, and the Croissant as we know it was born.*

Today Croissants are one of the most popular yeast-leavened breakfast pastries anywhere in the world south of Scandinavia (there the wienerbröd *or Danish pastry still reins). In addition to the classic plain Croissant, the French also bake them filled with chocolate, soft Almond Paste, or Pastry Cream. Instead of curving these pastries into the crescent shape, they are often left straight to signify that they are filled. In Austria, Germany, and Switzerland, they make a pastry called Plunder, which is sort of a cross between a Croissant and a Danish pastry. The main distinction between Plunder, filled Croissants, and Danish pastries is the amount of fat rolled into the dough. A genuine Danish pastry dough contains*

One-Quarter Recipe

about fifteen 2-ounce (55-g) croissants

few drops of lemon juice

12 ounces (340 g) bread flour

10 ounces (285 g) chilled unsalted butter

1 ounce (30 g) fresh compressed yeast

1 cup (240 ml) cold milk

4 teaspoons (20 g) granulated sugar

2¼ teaspoons (7 g) malt sugar

   or

1 tablespoon (15 ml) honey

2 teaspoons (10 g) salt

Egg Wash (page 7) or milk

about twice as much fat as a Croissant dough, and about twice as much fat as what I call the American-style Danish pastry. Most American-made Danish pastries are actually closer to Plunder than to the Scandinavian version of Danish. Another difference between these three is that a true Croissant dough does not contain eggs as a Danish pastry or Plunder dough does.

Forming Croissants; production schedule

Croissant dough is easier to work with if it is allowed to rest several hours between giving the dough three single turns and forming the Croissants. Because you generally want to bake Croissants early in the morning, here are two possible game plans, neither of which requires starting in the middle of the night. Make the dough in the morning, leave it to rest until early afternoon, form the Croissants, leave them overnight in the refrigerator, then proof and bake the next morning. An even better method is to prepare the dough in the afternoon, let the dough rest overnight in the refrigerator, then form, proof, and bake the Croissants in the morning. If your refrigerator does not keep a consistent temperature below 40°F (4°C) (in other words, there is a lot of traffic in and out), store the dough in the freezer instead. This is important to keep the yeast dormant; otherwise the dough will start to proof in the refrigerator, lowering the quality of the finished product and possibly making the dough taste sour.

The instructions that follow assume that you will be making up all of the dough at once. If this is not the case (if you want to freeze part of the dough to use later), roll the amount you are working with into a strip 9 inches (22.5 cm) wide, ⅛ inch (3 mm) thick, and as long as needed. After the dough has relaxed, cut triangles every 4½ inches (11.2 cm).

1. Work the lemon juice and 4 ounces (115 g) of the flour (1 ounce/30 g for the one-quarter recipe) into the chilled butter by kneading it against the table, or in a bowl, with your hand. Do not use a mixer.

2. Shape the butter into a 10-inch (25-cm) square (5-inch/12.5-cm for the one-quarter recipe). Place the butter on a piece of baking paper and set aside. If the room is warm, place it in the refrigerator, but do not let it get too firm. If this happens, rework and reshape the butter back to the original consistency.

3. Dissolve the yeast in the cold milk. Add the granulated sugar, malt sugar or honey, and the salt. Mix for a few seconds using the dough hook, then start adding the remaining flour. Mix in enough flour to make a dough that is slightly firm but not rubbery. Take care not to mix any longer than necessary.

4. Place the dough on a table dusted lightly with flour; roll it out to a 14-inch (35-cm) square (7-inch/17.5-cm for the one-quarter recipe).

5. Check the butter to be sure that it is smooth and at the same consistency as the dough, and adjust if necessary. Place the butter square on the dough diagonally so that there are four triangles on the sides, fold in the sides, and seal in the butter (see Figures 2–7 and 2–8, page 46).

6. Give the dough three single turns (directions follow). Refrigerate, covered, for at least 2 hours.

7. Roll the dough into a rectangle 49½ by 20 inches (123.7 × 50 cm), slightly thinner than ¼ inch (6 mm) and as even as possible. (If you are making the quarter recipe, roll out the dough following the instructions given after the recipe.) Let the dough rest 5 minutes so that it will not shrink when you cut it, then cut it lengthwise into two 10-inch (25-cm) wide strips.

8. On the bottom edge of the strip closest to you, start at the left corner and make a mark every 4½ inches (11.2 cm). Do the same on the top edge of the top strip.

9. Place a ruler from the lower left corner up to the first mark on the top strip (4½ inches/11.2 cm from the left edge) and cut the dough, using a knife or pastry wheel, following the ruler through the top strip. Then cut from the first mark on the bottom strip (4½ inches/11.2 cm from the left edge) to the second mark (9 inches/22.5 cm from the left edge) on the top strip. Repeat, cutting every 4½ inches (11.2 cm) for the length of the dough.

10. Beginning on the opposite end, follow the same pattern and cut from right to left (Figure 4–13). Pick away the scrap dough and save for the next batch of Butter-Wheat Bread (see page 87).

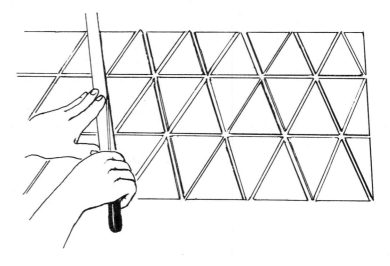

FIGURE 4–13   Cutting the dough into triangles for Croissants

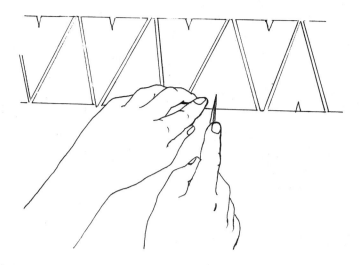

FIGURE 4–14   *Cutting a small slit in the base of each dough triangle. (Because the dough is elastic, the slit opens up into a wedge-shape)*

11. Make a ¹/₂-inch (1.2-cm) cut in the center of the short side on each Croissant (Figure 4–14). Pull the cuts apart a little, then form the Croissants by rolling the triangles toward you. Roll them up tightly, but do not stretch the dough too much.

12. Form each one into a crescent shape as you place them on sheet pans lined with baking paper. The tip of the Croissant should be inside the center curve and tucked underneath so that the Croissant do not unroll. Do not put more than sixteen to eighteen on a full-sized pan, to ensure that they bake evenly. If too crowded, they will get overdone on the ends before they are fully baked in the middle.

13. Let the Croissants rise until slightly less than doubled in volume in a 78–82°F (25–27°C) proof box with 80 percent humidity. If the proof box gets too hot, the butter will start to leak out. (This can also happen while they are baking if they have not proofed enough.)

14. Brush the Croissants with Egg Wash (or use milk, which is typical in France).

15. Bake at 425°F (219°C) until golden and baked through, about 25 minutes.

To form Croissants using the one-quarter recipe

1. Roll the dough out to 18 by 31¹/₂ inches (45 × 78.7 cm) and ¹/₈ inch (3 mm) thick. Let the dough relax for a few minutes, then cut in half lengthwise to make two strips 9 inches (22.5 cm) wide.

2. Continue as directed in main recipe.

Instructions for single turn

1. Roll the dough into a rectangle ¹/₂ inch (1.2 cm) thick, as carefully and evenly as possible.

2. Divide the rectangle crosswise into thirds by sight alone, or mark the dough lightly with the edge of your hand.

FIGURE 4–15   *The first step in making a single turn: folding one-third of the dough toward the center*

3. Fold one-third of the dough over the middle section (Figure 4–15), then fold the remaining one-third over both of them (Figure 4–16), brushing away the excess flour from the inside as you fold. The dough now has one single turn.

4. Refrigerate, covered, for 30 minutes.

5. Position the dough so that the long sides run horizontally, roll the dough to the same size rectangle as before, and make the second single turn.

6. Chill the dough, covered, for 30 minutes; then make the last single turn.

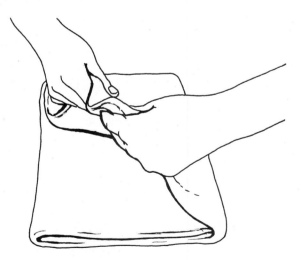

FIGURE 4–16   *Completing the single turn: folding the remaining one-third over the folded section*

English Muffins

twenty-five 3¹/₂-inch (8.7-cm) muffins

1 ounce (30 g) fresh compressed yeast

1¹/₂ cups (360 ml) warm water
  (105–115°F, 40–46°C)

2 ounces (55 g) granulated sugar

2 teaspoons (10 g) salt

1 egg

1 pound, 8 ounces (680 g) bread flour,
  approximately

3 ounces (85 g) soft unsalted butter

cornmeal

NOTE 1: If you do not have crumpet rings or other suitable rings, you can make the muffins without them. They will not be quite as high, nor will they be perfectly round, but the taste will be the same.

NOTE 2: Although English Muffins should be baked on a griddle, they can, if necessary, be baked in the oven. Leave the muffins on the sheet pan after proofing. Bake at 450°F (230°C) for 2 minutes on each side. Remove the rings and lower the oven temperature to 400°F (205°C). Bake approximately 14 minutes longer or until done.

*E*nglish Muffins are a breed apart from the sweet, cupcake-like American muffin traditionally baked in a paper cup: English Muffins are flat, barely sweetened yeast-leavened buns, very closely resembling crumpets. Both English Muffins and crumpets are baked on a griddle on top of the stove within small ring forms, usually about 3 inches (7.5 cm) in diameter. Crumpets are made with a softer dough—almost a batter—which cannot be rolled out and is instead poured into the rings. The softer dough produces larger air pockets (holes) in the baked crumpets.

Try making half of the dough into loaf bread. It is great sliced and toasted (although it challenges the rule that says an English Muffin must be pierced with a fork and pulled apart) and certainly convenient to make. The full recipe will yield two large loaves about 1 pound, 6 ounces (625 g) each before baking. Grease the inside of 10-by-4-by-2¹/₂-inch (25-×-10-×-6.2-cm) bread pans, form the dough to fit, let proof until doubled in volume, then bake at 375°F (190°C) until golden and baked through. Let cool slightly before unmolding.

1. In a mixer bowl, dissolve the yeast in the warm water. Add the sugar, salt, and the egg. Incorporate about two-thirds of the flour and mix with a wooden spoon to form a smooth paste.

2. Cover and let the sponge rise in a warm place until it has reached its maximum size and starts to fall.

3. Mix in the butter and the remaining flour, using the dough hook or paddle. Adjust with additional flour if necessary; the dough should be soft and smooth, but, because it is not kneaded, it will remain slightly sticky.

4. Cover the dough and let rise in a warm place until doubled in volume.

5. Punch the dough down and let it rest for 10 minutes.

6. Roll the dough out to ¹/₄ inch (6 mm) thick, using flour to prevent it from sticking.

7. Cut out 3¹/₂-inch (8.7-cm) circles using a plain cookie cutter. If the dough shrinks as you cut the first few, let it relax for a few minutes before continuing or you will end up with ovals instead of circles.

8. Line a sheet pan with baking paper. Sprinkle cornmeal lightly over the paper. Grease the inside of 3¹/₂-inch (8.7-cm) crumpet rings (see note 1) and place the rings on the cornmeal. Place the dough rounds inside the rings.

9. Stack the dough scraps, then roll out and cut more rounds until all of the dough is used.

10. Let the muffins rise until doubled in volume.

11. Use a metal spatula to transfer the muffins (including the rings) to a hot, greased griddle (see note 2). Remove the rings and cook the muffins for 2 minutes. Turn them over and cook for 2 minutes on the other side. Lower the heat and continue cooking for approximately 12 minutes or until done, turning the muffins again halfway through cooking. Carefully transfer the muffins to a cake rack to cool.

12. To split the muffins, pierce them horizontally all around the sides with a large fork, then break the two halves apart. You should never cut an English Muffin in half with a knife. Not only will they no longer look the way they are supposed to, they will not be as crisp after they are toasted.

13. Store leftover muffins in the freezer. The muffins will start to taste like the store-bought variety after a few days in the refrigerator.

Gosen

36 pastries approximately
2 ounces (55 g) each

Dough

1½ ounces (40 g) fresh compressed yeast

1 cup (240 ml) cold milk

3 eggs

3 ounces (85 g) granulated sugar

2 teaspoons (10 g) salt

1 pound, 8 ounces (680 g) bread flour

10 ounces (285 g) soft unsalted butter

Filling

10 ounces (285 g) soft unsalted butter

6 ounces (170 g) light brown sugar

6 ounces (170 g) granulated sugar

4 ounces (115 g) toasted hazelnuts, finely ground

1½ tablespoons (7 g) ground cinnamon

Topping

5 ounces (140 g) unsalted butter

2 tablespoons (30 ml) heavy cream

4 ounces (115 g) granulated sugar

2 tablespoons (30 ml) or 1½ ounces (40 g) light corn syrup

2 ounces (55 g) coarsely chopped or crushed hazelnuts

I have not been successful in finding out how and where Gosen got their name. I acquired the recipe from an old (or so he seemed at the time) Danish pastry chef when I was a young apprentice. The only reference I have been able to find for the word gosen is the biblical land of Goshen. (This may or may not be where the name originated, but they do taste heavenly.) The pastries are made with a soft Brioche dough, a cinnamon-hazelnut filling, and are topped with a florentina-type mixture before baking. Gosen are baked in muffin cups so that none of the goodies are lost on this very special breakfast pastry.

To make the dough

1. Dissolve the yeast in the milk; stir in the eggs, sugar, and salt.

2. Mix in enough of the flour, using the dough hook or the paddle, to make a sponge with the consistency of soft butter, then mix in the remaining flour and the butter. This method ensures that you will not get lumps of butter from adding it to a cold dough. Mix the dough until smooth; it will be very soft and will not come away from the sides of the bowl.

3. Spread the dough out evenly on a sheet pan and refrigerate (or freeze if you are in a hurry) until dough is firm enough to roll out.

To make the filling

1. Cream the butter with both sugars.

2. Add the hazelnuts and cinnamon.

3. If the filling is left overnight, the nuts will absorb much of the moisture and it may be necessary to soften the filling to a spreadable consistency by adding some Pastry Cream or an egg.

To make the topping

1. Place the butter and cream in a saucepan over low heat. When the butter starts to melt, add sugar and corn syrup.

2. Boil to 215°F (102°C), then add the hazelnuts.

3. Boil 5 minutes longer over medium heat. The hotter the sugar mixture gets (as it is being reduced), the smaller and slower the bubbles will become; with some experience you will be able to judge the temperature by the appearance.

4. Remove the topping from the heat and let cool until it is firm enough to be spread with a spatula. If the topping becomes too hard, or if it is made ahead, you will need to reheat it. When you reheat it the butter will separate; stir in 1 tablespoon (15 ml) of heavy cream to bring it back together.

Assembly

1. Roll the dough to 14 inches (35 cm) wide, 3 feet (90 cm) long, and ¹/₈ inch (3 mm) thick.

2. Spread the filling evenly over the dough. If you are not making the spirals in paper cups, leave a ¹/₂-inch (1.2-cm) strip at the bottom without filling, and brush it with Egg Wash; this will prevent the spirals from unrolling as they rise.

3. Roll the strip up tightly, starting from the top edge.

4. Cut the roll into thirty-six equal pieces. An easy way to ensure that the pieces will be uniform is to cut the roll into quarters and then cut each quarter into nine pieces.

5. Place the spirals level in muffin-size paper cups; you can place the paper cups in muffin pans to keep the spirals from spreading too flat if desired.

6. Let the spirals rise until slightly less than doubled in volume; be careful not to let them rise too long or when they expand in the oven a lot of the topping will fall off onto the sheet pan and be lost.

7. Spread the topping on the spirals using a small spatula.

8. Bake at 375°F (190°C) until golden brown, about 40 minutes.

Gugelhupf

four 15-ounce (430-g) loaves

6 ounces (170 g) dark raisins
¹/₄ cup (60 ml) dark rum
³/₄ ounce (22 g) fresh compressed yeast
1 cup (240 ml) warm water
   (105–115°F, 40–46°C)
¹/₂ ounce (15 g) malt sugar
   or
2 tablespoons (30 ml) honey
8 ounces (225 g) bread flour
forty whole blanched almonds
³/₄ cup (180 ml) warm milk
   (105–115°F, 40–46°C)
1 tablespoon (15 g) salt
4 ounces (115 g) granulated sugar
4 ounces (115 g) soft unsalted butter
2 eggs
finely diced zest of one lemon
1 pound (455 g) bread flour,
   approximately
powdered sugar

*T*here are a number of rather interesting stories that credit people from Austria to France with the invention of this yeasted coffee cake. One theory says it was first made in Vienna in the seventeenth century and was modeled after the headdress (turban) of a sultan to celebrate Austria's defeat of the Turkish invaders. The cake is also closely associated with the French Alsace region. There it is called Kugelhopf from two German words: kugel *meaning ball and* hopf, *which translates to hump. Both are references to the rounded, fluted bundt pan that the cakes are baked in. In addition to being good as a snack or with a coffee break, Gugelhupf slices are excellent toasted. See also Chocolate Gugelhupf on page 282.*

1. Macerate (soak) the raisins in the rum.

2. Dissolve the yeast in the warm water in a mixer bowl. Add the malt sugar or honey and 8 ounces (225 g) of flour. Mix with a wooden spoon to make a smooth sponge. Cover and let rise in a warm place until doubled in volume.

3. Grease four 1-quart (960-ml) Gugelhupf forms or other similar molds. Place the whole almonds in the bottom of the forms, spacing them evenly around the rings, using ten per form.

4. Incorporate the milk, salt, and sugar into the sponge using the paddle attachment. Mix in the butter, eggs, and lemon zest.

5. Hold back a handful of the second measurement of bread flour, mix the remainder into the dough, then adjust the consistency as needed with the reserved flour to make a smooth soft dough.

6. Cover and let rise in a warm place for 1 hour, punching the dough down once during that time.

7. Knead in the raisin and rum mixture by hand.

8. Divide the dough into four equal pieces, approximately 15 ounces (430 g) each. Form the pieces into round loaves (see Figures 3–1 and 3–2, page 70).

9. Let the loaves relax for a few minutes, then use a thick dowel to punch a hole in the center of each loaf.

10. Place the loaves in the reserved pans, pressing the dough firmly into the forms. Let rise until slightly less than doubled in volume.

11. Bake at 375°F (190°C) for approximately 20 minutes or until baked through. Invert immediately onto a cake rack and remove the forms. When cool, dust very lightly with powdered sugar.

Honey-Pecan Sticky Buns

16 individual buns or two 9-inch (22.5-cm) pull-apart cakes

Honey Glaze (recipe follows)
3 ounces (85 g) coarsely chopped pecans
one-half recipe Cinnamon Snails dough (page 154)
one-third recipe or 8 ounces (225 g) Gosen Filling (page 162)

NOTE: You should use up all of the glaze when you coat the pans. If you do, however, have any leftover, spread (or brush) it over the dough before topping with the filling.

These sticky, gooey, and highly-caloric-but-irresistible buns are deeply ingrained in American history. It is said that they originated in Philadelphia during the nineteenth century. They seem to bring back happy childhood memories for anyone who grew up in this country. Not having done so, I must admit that I didn't think too much of sticky buns the first time I tried one. To me, they were overly sweet and besides that, having the chewy sugar stick to your teeth didn't appeal to me either. Well, this was a long time ago and I have since softened up on the issue (or perhaps I have become a bit Americanized) but I would still say hold the glaze, given the choice. I make my version (which does not claim to be anywhere near the authentic Philadelphia bun) with the Cinnamon Snails dough, but Croissant or Danish dough works fine as well. The crucial parts here are the filling and, of course, the topping. If you can't invert the baked buns immediately, put the pan back in the oven to reheat the glaze before doing so, or the sticky part of their name will have a whole new meaning!

1. Brush the Honey Glaze on the inside of sixteen large muffin tins or two 9-inch (22.5-cm) cake pans. Be sure the glaze is not too cold (thick) or you risk losing bristles from your pastry brush. Most of the glaze will settle at the bottom—this is okay. Sprinkle the pecans evenly over the glaze. Reserve.

2. Roll the Cinnamon Snails dough into an 18-by-15-inch (45-×-37.5-cm) rectangle, using the minimum amount of flour needed to prevent it from sticking. Spread the filling evenly over the dough. Starting from the top, roll lengthwise into a tight rope. Roll the rope against the table, stretching it at the same time, to make it 24 inches (60 cm) long.

3. With the seam underneath, cut the rope into sixteen equal pieces. Place the pieces cut-side up in the prepared muffin tins or cake pans. Let rise until slightly less than doubled in volume.

4. Bake at 375°F (190°C) for approximately 35 minutes for the individual buns, or 45 minutes for the cake pans. The top and bottom should have a pleasant brown color. Since the top will brown faster than the bottom, which is moist with glaze, use a fork to lift one of the buns out of the pan to check.

5. Remove from the oven, place a sheet pan large enough to cover over the top, and immediately invert. Be very careful of the hot glaze which should run down the sides of the buns but could also end up on your hands. Use a palette knife to scoop up any excess glaze or nuts that fall onto the sheet pan and place back on the buns. Let the sticky buns cool for about 10 minutes. The glaze will set up quite fast on the outside but any that has seeped inside can easily burn a too-eager taster.

Honey Glaze for Sticky Buns

2 cups (480 ml) glaze

4 ounces (115 g) unsalted butter
10 ounces (285 g) light brown sugar
3 tablespoons (45 ml) or 2 ounces (55 g) honey
¼ cup (60 ml) or 3 ounces (85 g) light corn syrup
2 tablespoons (30 ml) water

1. Combine all of the ingredients in a heavy-bottomed saucepan. Stir over medium heat until the mixture just comes to a boil.
2. Cool to thicken slightly before using.

Hot Cross Buns

36 buns, approximately 2 ounces (55 g) each

2 cups (480 ml) warm milk (105–115°F, 40–46°C)
1½ ounces (40 g) fresh compressed yeast
1 tablespoon (15 g) salt
½ cup (120 ml) or 6 ounces (170 g) honey
2 pounds (910 g) bread flour, approximately
2 teaspoons (3 g) ground cinnamon
1½ teaspoons (3 g) ground nutmeg
½ teaspoon (1 g) ground cloves
2 ounces (55 g) soft unsalted butter
12 ounces (360 g) dried currants
finely chopped peel from two lemons
Egg Wash (page 7)
12 ounces (360 g) or one-half of the small recipe Pastry Cream (page 1088)
vanilla extract
Simple Icing (page 1020)

The custom of serving Hot Cross Buns at Easter, specifically on Good Friday, was institutionalized by the English at the beginning of the 1700s. These lightly spiced buns, filled with currants and sometimes dried fruit, are slashed on top in the outline of a cross. Don't forget—they should be served hot.

By spacing the buns just ½ inch (1.2 cm) apart, they will push up next to one another once they are fully proofed and baked, creating a different look and a slightly moister bun. This alternative is helpful when making a large quantity, since you are not only able to fit more buns on each pan but it also speeds up the process of cutting the crosses and piping on the Pastry Cream, as both can be done in straight lines across the pan instead of working on each bun individually.

1. In a mixer bowl, dissolve the yeast in the warm milk. Stir in the salt and the honey.
2. Combine the flour with the spices. Mix into the yeast and milk mixture, using the dough hook at low speed. Incorporate the soft butter.
3. Knead at medium speed for 8 to 10 minutes, adding additional bread flour if necessary. The dough should be smooth and soft. Do not overknead the dough or it will be difficult to incorporate the fruit later.
4. Place the dough, covered, in a warm place and let it rise until it has doubled in volume, about 1 hour.
5. Knead in the currants and lemon peel by hand, kneading until the dough is smooth and glutenous. Let the dough rest, covered, for 10 minutes.

6. Divide the dough into two equal pieces approximately 2 pounds (910 g) each. Roll the pieces into 18-inch (45-cm) ropes, and then cut each rope into eighteen equal pieces. Roll the small pieces against the table into tight round buns (see Figure 3–27, page 124). Place approximately 1½ inches (3.7 cm) apart on sheet pans lined with baking paper (see introduction).

7. Using a sharp knife or razor blade, cut a cross on top of each bun just deep enough to penetrate the skin. Let the buns rise until slightly less than doubled in volume.

8. Brush the buns with Egg Wash.

9. Place the Pastry Cream in a pastry bag with a no. 3 (6-mm) plain tip. Pipe a cross of Pastry Cream in the opened cut on top of each bun.

10. Bake at 400°F (205°C) for approximately 20 minutes or until done. Let cool slightly.

11. Flavor the Simple Icing with vanilla extract. Use a spatula to drizzle the icing on the buns.

Hungarian Twists

four 1-pound, 14-ounce (855-g) loaves

2 ounces (55 g) fresh compressed yeast
1 pint (480 ml) cold milk
1 ounce (30 g) malt sugar
   or
3 tablespoons (45 ml) or 2 ounces (55 g) honey
3 ounces (85 g) granulated sugar
2 pounds, 4 ounces (1 kg, 25 g) bread flour, approximately
2 tablespoons (30 g) salt
grated zest of one lemon
1 teaspoon (5 ml) vanilla extract
2 eggs
5 ounces (140 g) unsalted butter
1 ounce (30 g) unsweetened cocoa powder
⅓ cup (80 ml) water
Orange Almond Filling (recipe follows)
Egg Wash (page 7)
sliced almonds

*T*his recipe was given to me by a Hungarian colleague from Budapest. I don't really know if this Brioche-like dough stuffed with orange filling is authentically Hungarian or not. I haven't seen this particular shape anywhere else, though the idea of braiding or twisting plain and chocolate doughs, batter, or sponges for contrast is nothing new. Hungarian Twists will keep fresh for several days.

1. In a mixer bowl, dissolve the yeast in the cold milk. Add the malt sugar or honey and the granulated sugar. Reserve a few ounces of the flour and mix the remainder into the milk mixture.

2. Combine the salt, lemon zest, vanilla, and eggs. Add to the dough. Mix in the butter.

3. Knead the dough 8 to 10 minutes, using the dough hook. Halfway through the kneading add more flour, if necessary, to make a fairly soft and elastic dough.

4. Divide the dough into two parts, with one part 4 ounces (115 g) lighter than the other.

5. Combine the cocoa powder and the water and add to the lighter piece of dough, mixing well so it is uniform in color.

6. Cover both pieces of dough and let them rest for approximately 10 minutes.

7. Divide the chocolate dough and the light dough into four equal pieces (approximately 9 ounces/255 g) each. Form each piece into a rectangle without kneading or overworking it; cover the pieces.

8. Starting with the piece you formed first, roll each piece out to approximately 15 by 4 inches (37.5 × 10 cm).

9. Spread the filling out evenly over the eight rectangles leaving a ½-inch (1.2-cm) border on the bottom long sides.

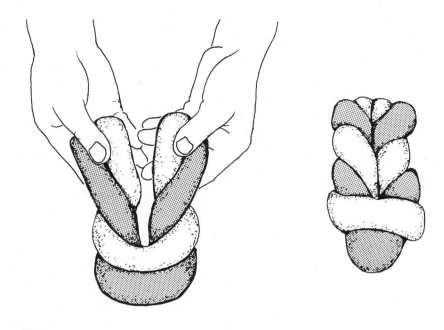

FIGURE 4–17   Twisting the filled ropes of light and chocolate dough together to form Hungarian Twists

10. Brush the borders with Egg Wash and roll the dough toward you (starting from the top long side) in a very tight spiral. Press the egg-washed border on the outside to seal the rolls.

11. Roll each rope between your hands and the table to make it 20 inches (50 cm) long.

12. Place a plain and a chocolate rope next to each other in an upside down U shape, with the light piece on the inside. "Braid" by twisting each side of the U four times toward the outside (Figure 4–17) (hold the pair of ropes on each side of the U in your hands and turn your hands as if you are opening a book). Make sure the chocolate and the light dough line up evenly in the finished twist.

13. Place the twists on sheet pans, brush with Egg Wash, and sprinkle lightly with sliced almonds. Let rise until slightly less than doubled in volume.

14. Bake double-panned at 375°F (190°C) for about 40 minutes.

 Orange Almond Filling

5 ounces (140 g) Almond Paste (page 3)

8 egg whites (1 cup/240 ml)

1 pound, 6 ounces (625 g) blanched almonds or hazelnuts, finely ground

8 ounces (225 g) granulated sugar

5 ounces (140 g) Candied Orange Peel (page 978), chopped fine

1. Incorporate the egg whites into the Almond Paste, adding them gradually so you do not get lumps.

2. Add the nuts, sugar, and orange peel.

3. If the filling feels too firm to spread (this will usually be the case if it is left overnight since nuts absorb moisture), add enough additional egg whites to give it a spreadable consistency.

Parisiennes

24 pastries

12 ounces (340 g) Quick Puff Pastry
or Puff Pastry (pages 47 or 44)

1 pound, 2 ounces (510 g) Pastry
Cream (page 1088)

2 pounds, 8 ounces (1 kg, 135 g)
Danish Pastry Dough (page 174)

8 ounces (225 g) Danish Filling II
(page 175)

1¹/₂ ounces (40 g) sliced almonds

Simple Syrup (page 11)

Simple Icing (page 1020)

NOTE: When you cut the sheet after it is baked you will appreciate the fact that you lined the pastries up evenly. The round snails will rise and bake together into squares. When you cut them apart you should be able to cut straight lines that fall between the pastries without cutting into the snails. If they are not spaced evenly to begin with, the cut pieces will be different sizes and you will have to cut into some snails to cut straight lines. If you have trouble, try this: Mark the Pastry Cream into twenty-four even squares before you add the snails and then center a snail in each square.

*P*arisiennes cannot be produced as quickly as some of the more common-place breakfast pastries such as Bear Claws or cheese Danish, but they allow you to offer something that will not be found in every other pastry shop in town. These pastries are also an excellent way to use up good Puff Pastry scraps; however, this only makes sense if you have the scrap dough stored in the refrigerator or freezer previously rolled out and ready to use, since freshly rolled or sheeted scrap dough must be left to relax at least several hours, or better still until the following day, to avoid having the dough shrink. Parisiennes can also be made by substituting Croissant dough for the Danish dough to add more variety.

1. Roll the Puff Pastry out to a rectangle 12 by 16 inches (30 × 40 cm) and about ¹/₈ inch (3 mm) thick. Place in the bottom of a half-sheet pan lined with baking paper. Prick the dough well and allow it to rest for at least 30 minutes in the refrigerator.

2. Bake the Puff Pastry sheet at 400°F (205°C) until light brown and baked through, approximately 20 minutes. Let cool.

3. Spread 12 ounces (340 g) of the Pastry Cream on top of the Puff Pastry sheet (leaving the sheet in the pan).

4. Roll the Danish dough out to a rectangle 12 by 18 inches (30 × 45 cm). Spread the Danish filling over the dough. Starting from the long edge away from you, roll the dough toward you to make a tight rope. Cut the rope into twenty-four equal slices.

5. Arrange the slices, evenly spaced, cut-side up, in straight rows over the Pastry Cream, placing four across and six lengthwise (see note). As you place each slice, tuck the end piece of the dough underneath. Using your thumbs and index fingers on both hands, spread the top of each pastry apart a little (Figure 4–18).

FIGURE 4–18   Using the thumb and index finger on both hands to open up the spirals by pushing the dough gently to the outside

6. Let the pastries rise until they have slightly less than doubled in volume.

7. Place the remaining 6 ounces (170 g) of Pastry Cream in a pastry bag with a no. 3 (6-mm) plain tip. Pipe about 1 tablespoon (15 ml) of Pastry Cream in the center of, and partially inside, each pastry. Sprinkle the sliced almonds over the pastries.

8. Bake double-panned at 400°F (205°C) for about 35 minutes or until rich golden brown and baked through. Immediately brush Simple Syrup over the pastries. Let cool, then ice with Simple Icing. Cut the sheet into 24 pastries.

Puff Pastry Diamonds

20 pastries

2 pounds (910 g) Puff Pastry
   (page 44)
Egg Wash (page 7)
14 ounces (400 g) Pastry Cream
   (page 1088)
fresh fruit
one recipe Apricot Glaze (page 1016)

NOTE: Puff Pastry Diamonds can be prepared up to the point of baking, and then frozen to bake and decorate as needed; bake directly from the freezer.

This is a great versatile pastry shell for a breakfast treat, dessert, or to use with a savory filling. I have used this shape many times instead of individual Vol-au-vents for large banquets (or when a customer's taste exceeded their budget). The diamonds are less costly to produce since you can just about eliminate any scrap dough and, being much faster to assemble, your labor cost is lower. Since they look good on top of all that—why not!

Instead of decorating with fresh fruit after baking, the pastries can be baked topped with apples or pears (follow the directions in Fruit Waffles, page 392, to prepare the fruit; top with Cinnamon Sugar before baking). Or bake the pastries with fresh apricots or plums. Cut the fruit in half, remove the pits, slice, and fan the fruit over the Pastry Cream. Bake and glaze as directed in the recipe.

1. Roll out the Puff Pastry to ⅛ inch (3 mm) thick and into a rectangle measuring 16 by 20 inches (40 × 50 cm). Refrigerate covered for a few minutes to firm and relax the dough.

2. Cut into four 4-inch (10-cm) wide strips lengthwise, then cut across the strips every 4 inches (10 cm) making twenty 4-by-4-inch (10-×-10-cm) squares. Refrigerate the dough again if necessary. Do not attempt to cut and fold the squares when the dough is soft.

3. Fold the firm squares into triangles with the folded side in front of you. Cut through ¼ inch (6 mm) from the edge on both the left and right sides, ending the cuts ¼ inch (6 mm) from the top (Figure 4–19). Do not cut all the way to the top so you cut the sides off; the dough should still be in one piece.

FIGURE 4–19   The folded square of Puff Pastry dough after making two cuts starting from the folded edge

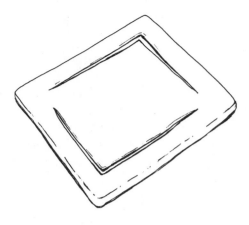

FIGURE 4-20   *The square after unfolding*

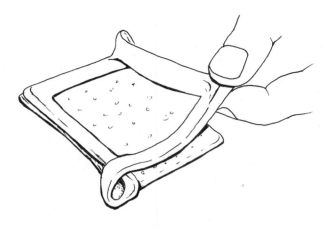

FIGURE 4-21   *After moving the right cut edge to the left side, crossing the left cut edge over the top to form a frame*

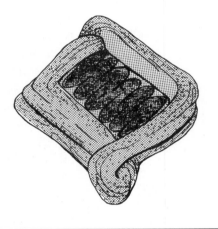

FIGURE 4-22   *A Puff Pastry Diamond after baking*

4. Unfold the triangles; the square will now have an L shape on each side (Figure 4-20). Brush Egg Wash over the squares. Prick the center of each square.

5. Cross the right L to the left side and the left L to the right side to form a frame (Figure 4-21). Brush Egg Wash lightly over the top of the frame, being careful not to get any on the sides.

6. Using a no. 4 (8-mm) plain tip, pipe an even layer of Pastry Cream on the inside of the frame.

7. Bake at 400°F (205°C) for about 20 minutes or until baked through and golden brown (Figure 4-22). Let the diamonds cool completely.

8. Decorate the Pastry Cream, staying inside the frame, with fresh fruit (see note with Fruit Tartlets, page 391). Brush the entire pastry with Apricot Glaze.

Scones

16 scones

6 ounces (170 g) currants or dark raisins

6 ounces (170 g) Candied Orange Peel (page 978), cut into raisin-sized pieces

1 pound, 12 ounces (795 g) bread flour

3 ounces (85 g) granulated sugar

3 tablespoons (36 g) baking powder

1 teaspoon (5 g) salt

3½ cups (840 ml) heavy cream

⅓ cup (80 ml) or 4 ounces (115 g) honey

granulated sugar

U se any combination of dried fruit you wish, such as cherries and apricots or cranberries and pears. The finished size suggested here gives you a rather large Scone; you can certainly decrease the size for a larger yield. The Scones can be made up ready-to-bake and then refrigerated overnight with excellent results. Alternatively, the formed dough can be frozen for longer storage. Thaw the Scones before baking them. If making ahead, do not brush with cream or invert the Scones in sugar until ready to bake.

1. Combine the currants or raisins and the orange peel. Add a handful of the flour and mix to coat the fruit pieces with flour and prevent them from sticking together. Set aside.

2. Combine the remaining flour, 3 ounces (85 g) granulated sugar, the baking powder and the salt in a mixing bowl. Reserve approximately ¼ cup (60 ml) of the cream. Add the remainder of the cream, together with the honey and the reserved fruit, to the dry ingredients. Mix only until the ingredients come together in a smooth dough. Do not overmix.

3. Gently form the dough (do not knead it) into a round disk. Cover the dough and set aside to relax for 5 minutes.

4. Cut the disk of dough in half horizontally (as you would a sponge cake) to form two equal pieces. Knead each piece of dough into a round loaf to tighten the gluten (see Figure 3–1 and 3–2, page 70). Press or pat the pieces out to form 10-inch (25-cm) circles.

5. Cut each dough circle into eight wedges. Brush the top of each wedge with some of the reserved cream. Invert the pieces in granulated sugar. Place sugar-side up on sheet pans lined with baking paper.

6. Bake at 425°F (219°C) for approximately 15 minutes.

Swedish Lenten Buns (*Fastlags Bullar*)

32 buns

one recipe Cinnamon Snails dough
(page 154)
12 ounces (340 g) Almond Paste
(page 3)
2 ounces (55 g) Pastry Cream
(page 1088) (see note 2)
3 cups (720 ml) heavy cream
4 teaspoons (20 g) granulated sugar
powdered sugar
warm milk (optional)
Cinnamon Sugar (page 5) (optional)

NOTE 1: *To be at their best,* Fastlags Bullar *should be served the same day they are baked, but they can be stored, covered, in a cool place (but not refrigerated) until the next day before they are filled. If they are then served with warm milk, none of their appeal will be lost.*

NOTE 2: *The amount of Pastry Cream required depends on the starting consistency of the Almond Paste. If you do not have Pastry Cream on hand, you can soften the Almond Paste to a spreadable consistency with water. Conversely, if you do not care for Almond Paste, using all Pastry Cream tastes good, combined with the roll and the whipped cream.*

These cream-filled buns were originally created for Fat Tuesday, the day before Ash Wednesday when fasting for Lent begins. Fat Tuesday is the day people traditionally eat large quantities of the goodies which will be off limits until Easter. In the old days Fastlags Bullar *("fasting buns") were always made in the Swedish pastry shops beginning a few weeks before Lent. Then, year by year, they became available a little earlier (and of course once one shop started making them, the others had to follow suit) until today when you can enjoy these delicacies when the Christmas decorations have barely left the store windows!*

Although they are filled with whipped cream, Fastlags Bullar *are traditionally eaten with your hands as you would a Danish pastry or a cinnamon roll. The way I remember eating them with my friends as a child is first using the lid to scoop out some of the cream before biting into the rest of the bun. Even so, we would usually end up with a mustache from the remaining cream. A conventional presentation on Fat Tuesday (Fet Tisdag) is to serve a bun in a deep bowl with Cinnamon Sugar and warm milk.*

If you didn't grow up with these treats, your first reaction may be the same as that of my students, who asked "what's so special about these?" But that was only before they tasted them—the buns might seem simple, but they are simply delicious!

1. After it has rested, divide the Cinnamon Snails dough into two pieces, about 2 pounds, 4 ounces (1 kg, 25 g) each. Form each piece into a rope about 20 inches (50 cm) long. Cut each rope into sixteen pieces. Form the pieces into round rolls (see instructions on page 123 and in Figure 3–27, page 124).

2. Place the rolls, staggered, on sheet pans lined with baking paper. Let rise until doubled in volume.

3. Bake at 400°F (205°C) until brown and baked through, about 15 minutes. Set aside to cool.

4. Soften the Almond Paste by gradually mixing in the Pastry Cream; the mixture should be spreadable.

5. Whip the heavy cream and the granulated sugar until stiff peaks form. Place in a pastry bag with a no. 7 (14-mm) star tip.

6. Using a serrated knife, slice the top 1/2 inch (1.2 cm) off the buns, leaving a flat even surface. You can also use scissors held at a 45° angle to remove the top of the buns in a triangular-shaped cut. Point the scissors toward the center of the bun and cut about 3/4 inch (2 cm) deep. Spread the Almond Paste mixture over the cut surface. Pipe a ring of the whipped cream around the edge, on top of the Almond Paste. Replace the tops of the rolls, setting them on the whipped cream ring. Sift powdered sugar lightly over the buns. Serve with warm milk and Cinnamon Sugar if desired. Refrigerate until needed if the buns are not served as soon as they are assembled.

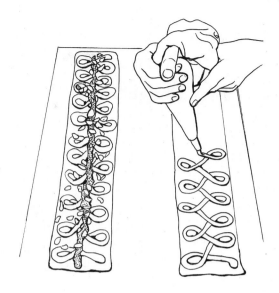

FIGURE 4–23   *Piping the Pâte à Choux over the Puff Pastry dough in a figure-eight pattern. The strip on the left shows the jam and sliced almonds added.*

Wales Strips

two 24-by-4-inch (60-×-10-cm) strips

1 pound (455 g) Puff Pastry
   (page 44)

10 ounces (285 g) Pastry Cream
   (page 1088)

1 pound (455 g) Pâte à Choux
   (page 36)

4 ounces (115 g) raspberry jam

sanding sugar

sliced almonds

Simple Syrup (page 11)

Simple Icing (page 1020)

*W*ales Strips, like Choux Surprise, are nice light pastries to try as a change of pace from the usual Danish or cinnamon rolls. How they got their name I really don't know for sure, but one has to assume that it has something to do with the country of Wales, a division of the United Kingdom in southwest England. Wales Strips provide an excellent use for leftover scrap Puff Pastry dough. If you are using virgin Puff Pastry, be sure to prick the dough well or it will puff too high.

1. Roll out the Puff Pastry dough to a 24-by-8-inch (60-×-20-cm) strip. Let the Puff Pastry rest for a few minutes to avoid shrinkage, then cut into two 4-inch (10-cm) wide strips.

2. Place the strips on a sheet pan lined with baking paper. Spread the Pastry Cream out evenly on top of the strips, spreading it almost all the way to the edges.

3. Place the Pâte à Choux in a pastry bag with a no. 3 (6-mm) plain tip. Pipe the Pâte à Choux in a figure-eight pattern, with the loops of the eights touching the long sides, to cover each strip (Figure 4–23).

4. Place the jam in a pastry bag with a no. 3 (6-mm) plain tip. Pipe the raspberry jam in one line, lengthwise, down the center of each strip. Combine equal amounts of sanding sugar and almonds, and sprinkle on top.

5. Bake double-panned at 375°F (190°C) for about 45 minutes. Be sure the Pâte à Choux is baked through or it will fall after the pastries have been removed from the oven. Immediately brush Simple Syrup over the top of the strips. Let cool.

6. Ice with Simple Icing, then cut into the desired number of pieces.

Danish Pastries

Danish Pastry Dough

*12 pounds, 8 ounces
(5 kg, 680 g) dough or about
ninety 3-ounce (85-g) pastries*

1 quart (960 ml) cold milk

8 eggs

5 pounds (2 kg, 275 g) cold margarine
    or unsalted butter (see introduction)

5 ounces (140 g) fresh compressed
    yeast

6 ounces (170 g) granulated sugar

1 tablespoon (15 g) salt

1 tablespoon (6 g) ground cardamom

4 pounds, 8 ounces (2 kg, 45 g) bread
    flour, approximately

One-Third Recipe

*4 pounds, 3 ounces (1 kg, 905 g)
dough or about thirty 3-ounce
(85-g) pastries*

1⅓ cups (320 ml) cold milk

3 eggs

1 pound, 10 ounces (740 g) cold
    margarine or unsalted butter (see
    introduction)

2 ounces (55 g) fresh compressed
    yeast

2 ounces (55 g) granulated sugar

1 teaspoon (5 g) salt

1 teaspoon (2 g) ground cardamom

1 pound, 8 ounces (680 g) bread flour,
    approximately

NOTE 1: If you are working in an air-conditioned kitchen, the refrigeration time in step one can be shortened or possibly even eliminated.

NOTE 2: If the dough does not seem to be rubbery aftr making the first turn, it does not have to rest between the first turn and the second turn. This is such a soft dough it has less gluten structure and is therefore more pliable.

*I*n making Danish dough, it is crucial that all of the ingredients are cold. On very hot days you may want to decrease the amount of yeast slightly so that the dough does not rise too fast. Due to the limited amount of sugar, and the soft consistency of the dough, these precautions keep the yeast from "taking over" before you have a chance to roll in the margarine. Margarine is used for this dough because it remains firm at a higher temperature than butter, due largely to its hydrogenated nature. Unsalted butter may be substituted if it is stabilized with the addition of lard, using 75 percent butter and 25 percent lard, well blended. You must also increase the salt to a total of 3 tablespoons for the full recipe or 1 tablespoon for the one-third recipe. The salt measurement may require adjustment when using margarine as well.

1. Mix the milk and the eggs, then refrigerate the mixture, and the flour, for at least 1 hour before making the dough (see note 1).

2. Shape the cold margarine into a 10-inch (25-cm) square (5-inch/12.5-cm for the one-third recipe) and place in refrigerator. It should be firm and smooth, but not hard, when the dough is ready.

3. Dissolve the yeast in the milk and egg mixture (use your hand to speed this up since yeast dissolves slowly in cold liquid). Stir in the sugar, salt, and cardamom.

4. Reserve a handful of the flour and mix in the remainder. Add enough of the reserved flour to make a soft, sticky dough.

5. Place the dough on a floured table and shape it into a 14-inch (35-cm) square (7-inch/17.5-cm for the one-third recipe).

6. Place the chilled margarine square diagonally on the dough so that there are four dough triangles showing. Fold the triangles in toward the center and seal in the margarine (see Figures 2–7 and 2–8, page 46).

7. Roll the dough as carefully and evenly as possible into a rectangle, 30 by 20 inches (75 × 50 cm) (12 by 8 inches/30 × 20 cm for the one-third recipe). Use plenty of flour to prevent the dough from sticking to the table and the rolling pin.

8. Give the dough one single turn (see Figures 4–15 and 4–16, page 160) (see note 2). Cover and refrigerate 30 minutes.

9. Roll the dough to the same size as before and make three additional single turns, resting the dough in the refrigerator for 30 minutes in between.

10. Roll the dough out to about ½ inch (1.2 cm) thick, cover with plastic wrap, and place it in the refrigerator or freezer, depending on how hot the room is where you are working and when you are going to make up the Danish. In either case the dough should chill at least 30 minutes.

11. Make up the Danish according to the individual recipes and let the pieces rise until slightly less than doubled in volume. Watch carefully to check on their rising: if they rise too long they will lose their flakiness and get spongy; if they do not rise enough, the fat will run out when they are baked. Individual pieces of formed Danish and Danish dough can be prepared ahead and stored in the freezer (unbaked) with excellent results. However, the pieces should never be frozen after baking. To use frozen Danish made up in individual pieces, let them thaw slowly, preferably in the refrigerator, before placing them in the proof box to rise. Use frozen dough as soon as it has thawed enough, in the refrigerator or at room temperature, to be workable.

12. Do not brush the Danish with Egg Wash before baking unless you are covering them with a nut or streusel topping. Instead, brush the pastries with Simple Syrup as soon they are removed from the oven, then let cool completely and ice lightly with white Fondant or Simple Icing.

Danish Filling I

5 pounds (2 kg, 275 g) filling

1 pound, 4 ounces (570 g) cake or
  cookie scraps (see note 1)
³/4 cup (180 ml) water, approximately
2 pounds (910 g) Almond Paste
  (page 3)
8 ounces (225 g) granulated sugar
1 pound (455 g) soft unsalted butter

NOTE 1: Use any non-chocolate sponge cake, coffee cake, or cookie scraps that do not contain any perishable filling or decoration.

NOTE 2: This filling will keep fresh at room temperature for several days. If stored longer, it should be refrigerated.

1. Place the scraps in a mixer bowl and start mixing using the paddle. Mix in just enough water to make a firm paste and continue mixing until smooth.

2. Add the Almond Paste and sugar.

3. Incorporate the butter gradually and beat until smooth.

Danish Filling II

3 pounds (1 kg, 365 g) filling

10 ounces (285 g) soft unsalted butter
2 pounds (910 g) Almond Paste
  (page 3)
4 ounces (115 g) finely ground
  hazelnuts
6 ounces (170 g) Pastry Cream,
  approximately (page 1088)

1. Mix the butter into the Almond Paste, adding it gradually to avoid lumps. Mix in the hazelnuts.

2. Stir in enough Pastry Cream to reach the desired consistency. If the filling is to be piped on the dough, it needs to be a little firmer than if it is to be spread; for spreading you want it loose enough that you can apply it easily.

3. Store in the refrigerator.

Cream Cheese Filling for Danish

*2 pounds, 9 ounces
(1 kg, 165 g) filling*

1 pound, 6 ounces (625 g) soft cream cheese

3½ ounces (100 g) sugar

3½ ounces (100 g) soft unsalted butter

3 eggs

1½ ounces (40 g) bread flour

½ teaspoon (2.5 ml) vanilla extract

4 ounces (115 g) dark raisins

¼ cup (60 ml) milk, approximately

1. Place the cream cheese and sugar in mixer bowl. Combine, using the paddle at medium speed. Add the butter gradually and mix until smooth.

2. Mix in the eggs and flour; then add the vanilla, raisins, and enough milk so that the mixture can be piped.

3. Store in the refrigerator.

Bear Claws

30 pastries

4 pounds, 3 ounces (1 kg, 905 g) or one-third recipe Danish Pastry Dough (page 174)

1 pound (455 g) Danish Filling I, approximately (page 175)

Egg Wash (page 7)

12 ounces (340 g) sliced almonds

Simple Syrup (page 11)

Simple Icing (page 1020)

NOTE 1: If you do not have a Bear-Claw cutter, use a multiple pastry wheel, with the wheels pushed together. If you do not have either of these tools, a chef's knife will do; it just takes a little longer. Make cuts ¾ inch (2 cm) long and ¼ inch (6 mm) apart along the length of each strip.

NOTE 2: The quantity of sliced almonds is specified because it is a fairly large amount. However, a faster and more practical method in a professional kitchen is to work with a greater amount of almonds, sprinkle them on top, and simply return the leftovers to the almond supply.

*T*hese are by far the most well-known and probably the most popular of all the Danish pastry varieties. In Scandinavia these pastries are called Kamm, *which translates to "comb" and refers to a cock's comb (the fleshy red decoration on the head of a rooster), not the type you use on your hair. The method for making the pastries is different in Scandinavia as well. There the slits are cut with a special knife instead of the rolling cutter used in this country.*

1. Roll the dough into a rectangle measuring 55 by 12 inches (1 m, 37.5 × 30 cm) and approximately ⅛ inch (3 mm) thick. Allow the dough to relax for a minute or so, then cut lengthwise into three 4-inch (10-cm) strips. Leave the strips in place.

2. Place the Danish Filling in a pastry bag with a no. 6 (12-mm) plain tip. Beginning ¼ inch (6 mm) down from the top edge, pipe a ribbon of filling along the complete length of each strip.

3. Brush Egg Wash on the entire lower part of each strip below the filling. Fold the top edge down, over, and past the filling, and press the ¼-inch (6-mm) borders into the Egg Wash, just below the filling, to seal.

4. Fold the lower part of the strip up past the sealed point to just below the filling so the seam is in approximately the center of the strip, and press again to secure (Figure 4–24). Lightly flatten and shape the strips with your palm.

5. Roll a Bear-Claw cutter (see note 1), which looks like a miniature waterwheel with a handle, along the unfilled edge to create the typical claw pattern (Figure 4–25). Be careful not to cut into the filling or it will leak out. Turn the filled strips over so that the seams are underneath.

6. Push the strips together next to each other with a ruler or a dowel.

7. Brush the strips with Egg Wash and sprinkle generously with sliced almonds. If you are making only one strip, it is more convenient to do this before cutting the claws as shown in the illustration.

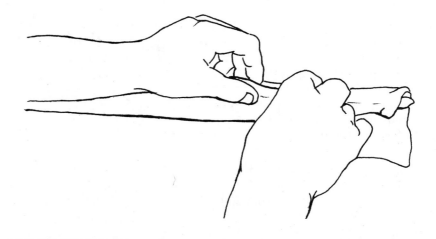

FIGURE 4–24   *Folding the lower edge of the dough strip up to seal in the filling*

FIGURE 4–25   *Rolling the Bear-Claw cutter along the unfilled edge of the strip*

8. Cut each strip into ten pieces 5½ inches (13.7 cm) long. The pieces will weigh approximately 3 ounces (85 g) each.

9. One at a time, pick up the Bear Claws, shake off any almonds that are not stuck to the Egg Wash, stretch the pastries slightly, and place them on paper-lined sheet pans, bending each strip into a half-circle so that the cuts open up. Let rise until slightly less than doubled in volume.

10. Bake at 410°F (210°C) for about 15 minutes. Brush the pastries with Simple Syrup as soon as you remove them from the oven. Let cool completely, then ice lightly with Simple Icing.

Butterhorns

about 30 pastries

4 pounds, 3 ounces (1 kg, 905 g) or
   one-third recipe Danish Pastry
   Dough (page 174)
Egg Wash (page 7)
6 ounces (170 g) Cinnamon Sugar
   (page 5)
1 pound, 5 ounces (595 g) or one-half
   recipe Streusel Topping (page 14)
Simple Icing (page 1020)

This pastry is the one that my students seem to have the most success with when making Danish pastries for the first time. (Maybe this is the reason it is the teacher's favorite.) Since Butterhorns do not have any filling in the conventional sense, be sure you apply plenty of Egg Wash—enough so the dough is quite wet—and use all of the Cinnamon Sugar. When the sugar melts and mixes with the Egg Wash as the pastries bake, it creates a moist interior. The Streusel Topping contributes not only to the taste but also gives the Danish a nice finished appearance.

1. Roll the dough into a rectangle measuring 24 by 14 inches (60 × 35 cm) and approximately ¼ inch (6 mm) thick. If necessary, trim the edges of the strip to make them even.

2. Brush the entire surface of the dough heavily with Egg Wash. Sprinkle the Cinnamon Sugar over the dough.

3. Fold the long sides in to meet in the center; brush again with Egg Wash, then fold in half in the same direction (double turn). Even the top by gently rolling with a rolling pin.

4. Cut the folded strip into pieces ¾ inch (2 cm) wide, and at the same time use the knife to turn them over a quarter-turn so that the cut sides are up (Figure 4–26).

5. Brush the top (cut sides) of the pieces with Egg Wash and sprinkle the Streusel Topping over them. Press the Streusel with the palm of your hand to help keep it in place.

6. Carefully place the pieces on sheet pans and let rise until slightly less than doubled in volume.

7. Bake at 425°F (219°C) until golden brown, about 15 minutes. Let the pastries cool completely, then spread a small amount of Simple Icing on top.

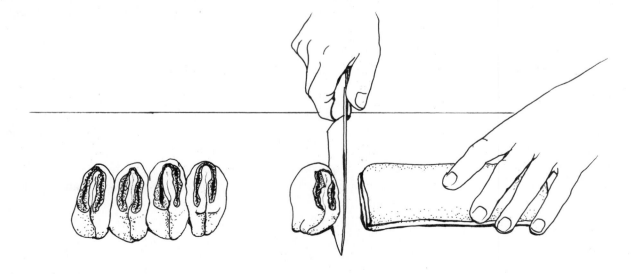

FIGURE 4–26   Slicing the Butterhorns and turning each piece cut-side up at the same time

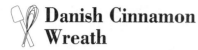 **Danish Cinnamon Wreath**

one 12-inch (30-cm) wreath

1 pound (455 g) Danish Pastry Dough (page 174)

6 ounces (170 g) Danish Filling I or II (page 175)

4 tablespoons (48 g) Cinnamon Sugar (page 5)

Egg Wash (page 7)

sliced almonds

Simple Syrup (page 11)

Simple Icing (page 1020)

Making breads and pastries in a wreath shape is very popular in Scandinavia. It makes sense for the customer who wants more than half a dozen Danish or rolls at the same time, and since it is faster for the baker than making individual pieces, it becomes less expensive. A wreath also looks good displayed alone or on a tray with other rolls or pastries. The epis (wheat sheaves) design is definitely the most common. This shape can be made very quickly and looks so appealing.

1. Roll the dough into a strip 22 inches (55 cm) long, 7 inches (17.5 cm) wide, and approximately 1/8 inch (3 mm) thick.

2. Spread the Danish Filling over the dough. (It is a common misconception that spreading on a little extra filling will make the wreath especially tasty, but this is not so! The filling will overpower the dough in the flavor of the baked wreath, and part of the filling will run out and burn on the sheet pan while the wreath is baking.)

3. Sprinkle Cinnamon Sugar over the filling, and roll the strip into a tight string, starting from the top.

4. Roll the coiled string between your palms and the table to make it even and about 24 inches (60 cm) in length.

5. Place the string on a sheet pan lined with baking paper and shape it into a ring 10 inches (25 cm) in diameter, making sure the seam is on the bottom. Seal the ends by pushing one inside the other.

6. Holding scissors at a 45° angle from the wreath, make cuts 1/2 inch (1.2 mm) wide, cutting almost to the bottom of the wreath. As you cut, use your free hand to turn these cuts to the side (Figure 4–27), alternating between left and right.

7. Brush with Egg Wash and sprinkle lightly with sliced almonds. Let the wreath rise until slightly less than doubled in volume.

8. Bake at 400°F (205°C) for about 30 minutes. Brush with Simple Syrup immediately after removing the wreath from the oven. Let the wreath cool completely, then spread Simple Icing lightly over the top.

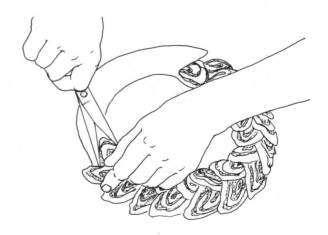

FIGURE 4–27   *Cutting the filled coil of dough and turning each cut piece to the side to form the Danish Cinnamon Wreath*

Danish Twists

about 30 pastries

4 pounds, 3 ounces (1 kg, 905 g) or
  one-third recipe Danish Pastry
  Dough (page 174)
1 pound (455 g) Pastry Cream
  (page 1088)
  or
1 pound (455 g) apricot jam
  or
1 pound (455 g) Cherry Filling
  (page 1084)
Simple Syrup (page 11)
Simple Icing (page 1020)

*T*his is a very simple and quickly made Danish pastry. It does, however, require a carefully rolled and well-chilled dough in order to achieve the characteristic crispness on the top. The crispness is also lost if the dough is rolled too thin, if the strips are cut too wide, or if the Danish are left to rise too long before baking. Choose a good piece of dough (avoid end pieces). If you accidentally roll the dough too thin, make Envelopes or turnovers from that piece and start over with a fresh piece of dough.

1. Roll the dough into a rectangle measuring 14 by 12 inches (35 × 30 cm) and approximately ³/₈ inch (9 mm) thick.

2. Chill the dough if needed; it should still be firm before going to the next step.

3. Cut the dough lengthwise into ³/₈-inch (9-mm) strips, using a sharp knife or pastry wheel and a ruler as a guide.

4. Twist the strips tight, stretching them slightly at the same time (see Figure 4–10, page 155).

5. Shape into Cherry Twists, Singles, or Figure Eights (Figures 4–28 and 4–29) instructions follow. Check to make sure the pieces weigh about 2¹/₂ ounces (70 g), which will make the finished pastries about 3 ounces (85 g) each. If any are too heavy, cut a piece off the end before you shape it; if too light, conceal a scrap piece under the pastry after forming it.

6. Let the pastries rise until slightly less than doubled in volume.

7. Bake at 425°F (219°C) until golden brown, about 15 minutes. Brush the pastries with Simple Syrup as soon as they are out of the oven. Let them cool completely, then ice with a small amount of Simple Icing.

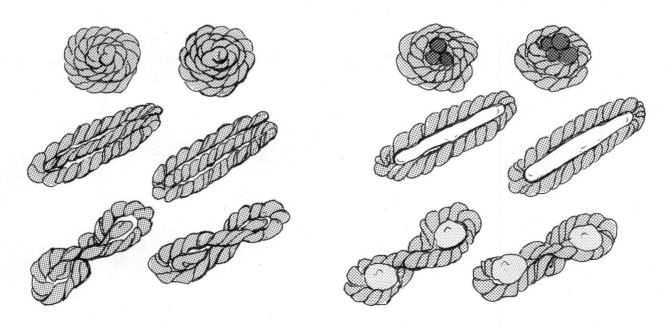

FIGURES 4–28 and 4–29   *Top to bottom: Cherry Twists, Singles, and Figure Eights, before and after the toppings are added*

 **Cherry Twists**

*T*wist the strips and shape into loose spirals. Secure the end piece underneath as you place each one on paper-lined sheet pans. Pipe a small amount of Cherry Filling (a generous tablespoon/15 ml) onto the center of each twist.

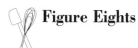 **Figure Eights**

*T*wist the strips and fold them in thirds as in a single turn. Place them on paper-lined sheet pans, and at the same time tuck the end piece underneath. Pipe a ribbon of Pastry Cream lengthwise down the center of each Danish.

 Singles

*T*wist the strips and form into figure-eight shapes. Overlap both end pieces enough to protrude into the center and cover the openings in the eight. Invert onto paper-lined sheet pans. Pipe a dot of apricot jam into both indentations on the eight.

 Double Curls

30 pastries

4 pounds, 3 ounces (1 kg, 905 g) or one-third recipe Danish Pastry Dough (page 174)

1 pound, 4 ounces (570 g) Danish Filling I (page 175), softened

Egg Wash (page 7)

12 ounces (340 g) Pastry Cream (page 1088)

sliced almonds

Simple Syrup (page 11)

Simple Icing (page 1020)

*T*hese pastries are known as Glasögon *in Swedish, which translates to "glasses" in English. Interestingly, they are fashioned after the distinctive marking—a double spiral design—found on the head of a cobra. This pattern resembles a pair of eyeglasses. For a different twist (literally) on this shape, omit brushing the Egg Wash between the two cylinders after rolling them. After slicing the pieces, turn one curl on each piece over to make an "S" shape as you place them on the pan.*

1. Roll the Danish Pastry Dough out, using flour to prevent the dough from sticking, to make a rectangle 36 by 18 inches (90 × 45 cm); the dough should be about 1/8 inch (3 mm) thick.

2. Check the consistency of the filling to be certain it is soft enough to spread easily and then spread the filling evenly over the surface of the dough.

3. Starting with the long side farthest away from you (the top), roll the dough toward you forming a tight spiral; stop when you reach the center of the dough. Repeat the procedure with the bottom half of the dough, rolling it away from you toward the center, until it meets the other coil. Stretch the ropes as needed so that they are the same length and thickness. Brush Egg Wash on the dough where the two coils meet and push them together firmly.

4. Place the double rope at the edge of the table keeping it right-side up. Using a sharp knife, cut thirty equal pieces, each about 1 1/4 inches (3.1 cm) wide. The individual pieces should weigh 3 ounces (85 g). Place the pastries cut-side up on sheet pans lined with baking paper.

5. Pipe two dots of Pastry Cream on each pastry, placing them in the center of each spiral. Sprinkle sliced almonds lightly over the pastries. Let rise until slightly less than doubled in volume.

6. Bake the Double Curls at 425°F (219°C) for about 15 minutes or until golden brown. Brush Simple Syrup over the pastries immediately after removing them from the oven. After the Danish have cooled, spread a small amount of Simple Icing over the tops.

Envelopes

30 pastries

4 pounds, 3 ounces (1 kg, 905 g) or one-third recipe Danish Pastry Dough (page 174)

Egg Wash (page 7)

8 ounces (225 g) Danish Filling I, II, or Cream Cheese Filling (pages 175 and 176)

8 ounces (225 g) Pastry Cream (page 1088)

or

apricot jam

sliced almonds

Simple Syrup (page 11)

Simple Icing (page 1020)

*C*alled Kuverts *in Sweden and* Spandaurs *in Denmark, Envelopes are one of the best and most convenient ways to enclose a filling. They are fast to produce, and since you start by cutting squares, you don't have any scrap dough. Try these two variations on the same theme: Fold two opposite corners into the center and leave two flat. Or, fold as directed in the recipe, but invert the pastries as you place them on the sheet pans, and pipe the jam or Pastry Cream on top of the bottom (so to speak).*

1. Roll the dough into a rectangle measuring 21 by 17¹/₂ inches (52.5 × 43.7 cm) and approximately ¹/₄ inch (6 mm) thick.

2. Let the dough rest for a few minutes before you cut the squares so that they will not shrink and become rectangles. Mark and cut the dough into 3¹/₂-by-3¹/₂-inch (8.7-×-8.7-cm) squares, using a ruler as a guide, or use a multiple pastry wheel adjusted to 3¹/₂ inches (8.7 cm). The pieces will weigh approximately 2¹/₂ ounces (70 g) each.

3. Lightly brush Egg Wash along the cuts to cover all four edges of each square.

4. Place Danish or Cream Cheese Filling in a pastry bag. Pipe a dot of filling the size of a cherry in the center of each square.

5. Fold the four corners of each square in to meet in the center. Press the center down firmly with your thumb, pushing all the way down to the pan, to prevent the dough from unfolding.

6. Place the Envelopes on sheet pans lined with baking paper. Pipe a dot of either Pastry Cream or jam, the size of a cherry, on top of the pastries in the indentation created by your thumb. Or, if you used Cream Cheese Filling inside the Envelopes, you can use it for the top as well, to indicate what is inside.

7. Lightly sprinkle sliced almonds on the pastries; they will stick to the topping. Let rise until slightly less than doubled in volume.

8. Bake at 425°F (219°C) until golden brown, about 15 minutes. Brush the pastries with Simple Syrup immediately after removing them from the oven. When the Envelopes have cooled, spread a small amount of Simple Icing on top.

Honey Raisin Snails

30 pastries

4 pounds, 3 ounces (1 kg, 905 g) or one-third recipe Danish Pastry Dough (page 174)

Honey Butter (recipe follows)

2 pounds (910 g) dark raisins, soaked in water then well drained

6 ounces (170 g) Cinnamon Sugar (page 5)

Simple Syrup (page 11)

Simple Icing (page 1020)

*B*rushing the Honey Butter over the dough gives these snails a distinctive taste. Do not skimp on the raisins—no one likes a raisin snail when they can count the raisins using the fingers on one hand! Although you can use regular dry raisins in the snails, the soaked raisins provide additional moisture for the pastries, which lack any filling. The raisins should soak until they are nice and plump, several hours or, preferably, overnight. You can speed up the process by starting with hot water.

1. Roll the dough into a rectangle measuring 48 by 14 inches (1 m, 20 cm × 35 cm) and approximately 1/8 inch (3 mm) thick.

2. Brush the surface of the dough with the Honey Butter leaving a 1-inch (2.5-cm) strip uncovered along the bottom edge. Evenly distribute the soft raisins over the Honey Butter; do not discriminate against the ends. Sprinkle the Cinnamon Sugar on top. Roll over the top with a rolling pin to make the raisins stick to the dough.

3. Starting at the top, roll the dough up evenly, stretching it if necessary, to make a tight rope. Place the rope at the edge of the table with the seam underneath.

4. Using a sharp knife, cut the rope into thirty pieces weighing approximately 3 1/2 ounces (100 g) each.

5. Place the snails on paper-lined sheet pans, cut sides up, tucking the ends underneath so they will not unroll while baking. Let rise until slightly less than doubled in volume.

6. Bake at 425°F (219°C) until golden brown, about 15 minutes. Brush the pastries with Simple Syrup immediately after removing them from the oven. When the snails have cooled, spread a small amount of Simple Icing on the top of each one.

Honey Butter for Raisin Snails

6 ounces (170 g) unsalted butter

2 ounces (55 g) light brown sugar

1/3 cup (80 ml) or 4 ounces (115 g) honey

1/2 cup (120 ml) half-and-half

1. Combine all of the ingredients in a heavy-bottomed saucepan. Stir over medium heat until the mixture comes to a boil. Remove from the heat.

2. Cool before using.

Mayor's Wreath

one 12-inch (30-cm) wreath

1 pound (455 g) Danish Pastry Dough
   (page 174)
6 ounces (170 g) Danish Filling II
   (page 175)
Egg Wash (page 7)
sliced almonds
Simple Syrup (page 11)
Simple Icing (page 1020)

*T*he name suggests that this wreath is something special, and I think you will agree after your first bite. But there is a price to pay: The filling is made with a high percentage of Almond Paste and the braiding is very labor-intensive. However, the elegant appearance and great taste have always made it very popular, especially with anyone who doesn't care for cinnamon, as this is one of the few Danish without it.

1. Roll the dough out to a strip 8 inches (20 cm) wide, 18 inches (45 cm) long, and 1/8 inch (3 mm) thick. Cut the strip lengthwise into three equal pieces.

2. Check the Danish Filling to be sure it is not too soft, as the strips will be braided later; adjust if needed. Place the filling in a pastry bag with a no. 3 (6-mm) plain tip. Pipe a ribbon of filling along the entire length of each strip approximately 1/2 inch (1.2 cm) from the top.

3. Brush Egg Wash along the bottom of the strips, and then roll each one into a spiral, rolling from the top to the bottom.

4. Roll each coiled strip out to 20 inches (50 cm) in length by rolling it between your palms and the table.

5. Place the three strings, seam-side down, next to each other on the table. Braid them into a Three-String Braid (see page 80), starting from the middle and working to each end to avoid stretching the dough any more than necessary.

6. Carefully place the braided loaf on a sheet pan lined with baking paper. If necessary, stretch the braid slightly to make it 24 inches (60 cm) in length.

7. Shape into a ring that is 10 inches (25 cm) in diameter. Fold the ends together so that the seam shows as little as possible.

8. Brush with Egg Wash and sprinkle lightly with sliced almonds. Let rise until slightly less than doubled in volume.

9. Bake at 375°F (190°C) about 30 minutes. Brush with Simple Syrup immediately after removing the wreath from the oven. Let cool completely, then lightly spread Simple Icing over the top.

Sister's Pull-Apart Coffee Cake

one 10-inch (25-cm) cake

1 pound, 4 ounces, (570 g) Danish
   Pastry Dough (page 174)
6 ounces (170 g) Danish Filling I or II
   (pages 175)
6 ounces (170 g) Pastry Cream
   (page 1088)

*I*f you are wondering about this title, there is an explanation: In Sweden whenever you pay a visit you are always served coffee with some kind of coffee cake or Danish and also cookies. During one of my frequent visits to my sister's house I jokingly said "Isn't this the same type of coffee cake you served last time and the time before that? I hope it's not the same one!" She said since this cake has always turned out great every time she has made it, she figured why take a chance when her critical and always hungry brother was invited! This cake is traditionally known simply as Buttercake.

1. Roll the dough into a strip 22 inches (55 cm) long, 7 inches (17.5 cm) wide, and 1/8 inch (3 mm) thick. Cut a 7-inch (17.5-cm) square from one end, and set this piece aside.

sliced almonds
Simple Syrup (page 11)
Simple Icing (page 1020)

2. Spread the Danish Filling over the larger piece of dough.

3. Roll up the strip into a tight string, starting from the top. Roll the string between your palms and the table to make it even. Cut the strip into 12 equal pieces.

4. Roll and shape the reserved square of dough into a 10-inch (25-cm) circle. Place it on a sheet pan lined with baking paper.

5. Put about one-third of the Pastry Cream in a pastry bag with a no. 3 (6-mm) plain tip. Set aside. Using a metal spatula, spread the remainder of the Pastry Cream over the dough, covering the entire surface. Place a 10-inch (25-cm) adjustable cake ring around the dough (or use the ring from a springform pan).

6. Arrange the twelve pieces, cut-side up, on the cream. Press them in lightly with your knuckles. Pipe a dot of Pastry Cream, about the size of a hazelnut, on top and partially inside each piece. Sprinkle with sliced almonds. Let the cake rise until slightly less than doubled in volume.

7. Bake at 375°F (190°C) for about 35 minutes. Brush the cake with Simple Syrup as soon as you remove it from the oven. When the cake has cooled, remove the ring, and ice lightly with Simple Icing.

Sugar Buns

30 pastries

4 pounds, 3 ounces (1 kg, 905 g) or one-third recipe Danish Pastry Dough (page 174)
Egg Wash (page 7)
1 pound (455 g) Pastry Cream (page 1088)
melted unsalted butter
granulated sugar

*T*his is my number one favorite Danish pastry. One good reason I never get tired of Sugar Buns is that I so seldom get to enjoy one, since this is not a pastry that you are likely to find at most bakeries. They are a little delicate and time-consuming to produce, but you are guaranteed plenty of favorable comments when you make them. The Pastry Cream inside bubbles up as the pastries bake, coating the inside of the shell and leaving the center hollow. The initial sensation of biting into thin air is fabulous.

1. Roll the dough into a rectangle measuring 24 by 20 inches (60 × 50 cm) and approximately 1/8 inch (3 mm) thick.

2. Mark and cut the dough into 4-inch (10-cm) squares, using a ruler as a guide, or use a multiple pastry wheel adjusted to 4 inches (10 cm). The pieces will weigh approximately 2 1/2 ounces (70 g) each.

3. Lightly brush Egg Wash along the cuts to cover all four edges of each square.

4. Place the Pastry Cream in a pastry bag. Pipe a mound of Pastry Cream about the size of an unshelled walnut in the middle of each square. (If you use too much Pastry Cream, it will be difficult to seal the pastries; if you use too little, it will be absorbed into the dough and leave the inside dry.)

5. Pick up the corners, stretch them if necessary to cover the filling, and fold in to meet in the center. Pinch the seams closed so the Pastry Cream will not leak out.

6. Place the buns, seam-side down, on sheet pans lined with baking paper. Let rise in a warm place until slightly less than doubled in volume.

7. Bake at 400°F (205°C) until golden brown, about 20 minutes. Because of the Pastry Cream inside, the buns will puff up as high as a large Profiterole, so they must bake long enough to hold their shape once removed from the oven. Let the buns cool completely.

8. Brush the tops and sides of the buns with melted butter. Fill a bowl with enough sugar to make a well in it deep enough to fit a bun without flattening it. Dip each bun into the sugar well; the sugar should stick to the melted butter.

Muffins

The word muffin is derived from the Germanic word *muffe,* which is the name for a type of cake. Muffins are always baked in forms and, like tea cakes, the batter almost always contains some type of addition such as chopped fruit or nuts. Muffins are not iced or decorated in any way after they are baked.

Although really quite simple, muffins are finicky by nature—they can be extremely good or just plain bad. The secret to success lies in how you add and trap the moisture. If you overmix the batter, add too much leavening (both of which add air), overbake, or store the muffins improperly, you can end up with a dry product. When the recipe calls for beating or creaming the ingredients, always use the paddle attachment rather than the whip which again can incorporate excess air. Mix at low to medium speed, depending on the variety and the amount of batter (a small batch can easily be mixed up with a spoon), and don't overdo it.

Lining the muffin tins with paper cups helps keep the muffins from drying out and tasting stale, but if you prefer your muffins with a crust all around, omit the paper cups and grease the inside of the tins instead. As soon as you remove the muffins from the oven, quickly turn them on their sides in the pans to allow air to circulate underneath. The best way to store baked muffins is not to, which is to say that ideally muffins should be eaten the same day they are baked. You can keep muffin batter in the refrigerator for several days, or in the freezer for up to two weeks, with no loss in quality. Another solution is to freeze the batter preportioned in the muffin cups. Thaw overnight in the refrigerator and they are ready to bake in the morning; saving time when you often need it the most.

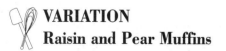

Apple-Pecan Buttermilk Muffins

thirty 4-ounce (115-g) muffins

Butter and Flour Mixture (page 4)
1 pound (455 g) soft unsalted butter
1 pound (455 g) light brown sugar
1 cup (240 ml) or 12 ounces (340 g)
   honey
6 eggs
1 teaspoon (5 ml) vanilla extract
1 teaspoon (5 g) salt
4 teaspoons (16 g) baking powder
4 teaspoons (16 g) baking soda
1 pound, 8 ounces (680 g) cake flour
1 tablespoon (5 g) ground cinnamon
1 teaspoon (2 g) ground nutmeg
6 ounces (170 g) whole wheat flour
1¼ cups (300 ml) buttermilk
³/₄ cup (180 ml) half-and-half
one recipe Chunky Apple Filling
   (page 1085)
8 ounces (225 g) pecans, coarsely
   chopped
Streusel Topping (page 14)

NOTE: If you want the batter to stay within the paper cups, use 3 ounces (85 g) of batter per muffin (it is not necessary in that case to skip any spaces or grease the top of the pan).

These muffins combine the moist goodness of apples and buttermilk with a crunchy Streusel Topping. The recipe is very adaptable: You can use unflavored yogurt in place of the buttermilk, and you can substitute any other nuts you have on hand for the pecans. If you're in a hurry and don't have Streusel Topping, sprinkle additional chopped nuts on top instead.

1. Line muffin pans with paper cups, skipping every other space because this amount of batter will make the muffins "mushroom" out on top of the pan as they bake. Grease the top of the pan around each cup with Butter and Flour Mixture; set aside (see note).

2. Cream the softened butter with the brown sugar and honey to a light and fluffy consistency. Mix in the eggs and the vanilla.

3. Sift together the salt, baking powder, baking soda, cake flour, cinnamon, and nutmeg. Stir the whole wheat flour into the sifted ingredients. Add to the batter in three segments alternating with the buttermilk and half-and-half.

4. Add the Chunky Apple Filling to the batter together with the pecans.

5. Use an ice-cream scoop to portion 4 ounces (115 g) of batter into each muffin cup, then sprinkle Streusel Topping lightly on top of the batter.

6. Bake at 400°F (205°C) for about 30 minutes or until the muffins spring back when pressed lightly in the middle. Remove from the pans as soon as they are cool enough to handle, to prevent the muffins from becoming wet on the bottom.

VARIATION
Raisin and Pear Muffins

Substitute eight pears, poached and chopped into ¹/₂-inch (1.2-cm) chunks, for the Chunky Apple Filling. Replace the pecans with raisins.

Blueberry Ginger Muffins

thirty 4-ounce (115-g) muffins

Butter and Flour Mixture (page 4)

14 ounces (400 g) light brown sugar

14 ounces (400 g) soft unsalted butter

1/2 cup (120 ml) or 6 ounces (170 g) molasses

2/3 cup (160 ml) or 8 ounces (225 g) honey

6 eggs

1 teaspoon (5 ml) vanilla extract

2 teaspoons (10 g) salt

1 tablespoon (12 g) baking powder

1 tablespoon (12 g) baking soda

1 teaspoon (2 g) ground ginger

1 pound (455 g) cake flour

14 ounces (400 g) bread flour

1 cup (240 ml) buttermilk

1 pound, 8 ounces (680 g) fresh or frozen blueberries (if frozen, do not thaw)

If you like blueberry muffins, these are the very best. The ginger adds an extra zing, but if it doesn't appeal to you, just leave it out. When using frozen blueberries, do not thaw them first before adding them to the batter. If thawed they will break up, turn the batter light blue, and also make the batter too thin. Also, do not fold them in until you are ready to portion the muffins; if left to stand the batter will "set up," making it very difficult to work with. A former student of mine learned the hard way (if you will pardon the pun) that if you multiply the recipe, and use frozen berries, you had better not be the only one with an ice-cream scoop! He was working in a Seattle restaurant that did a brisk business in blueberry muffins each Sunday brunch, and he was making ten times this recipe for each batch. This worked out fine until the fresh blueberry season was over, and he added 15 pounds of frozen blueberries to all of that batter, which caused it to set up just like cement!

1. Line muffin pans with paper cups, skipping every other space because the muffins will "mushroom" out on top as they bake. Grease the top of the pan around each cup with Butter and Flour Mixture; set aside.

2. Cream together the brown sugar and butter until light and fluffy. Mix in the molasses, honey, eggs, and vanilla.

3. Combine the dry ingredients and mix into the sugar mixture in three segments, alternating with the buttermilk.

4. Stir in the blueberries gently so that the berries do not break and turn the batter blue.

5. Place the batter in a pastry bag with a large plain tip. Pipe the batter in a dome shape slightly above the rim of each cup, using 4 ounces (115 g) of batter per muffin. If the batter is firm enough to allow you to do so, use an ice-cream scoop to portion them out instead. (If you use frozen berries, you will have no choice but to use an ice-cream scoop.)

6. Bake at 375°F (190°C) until brown and baked through, about 35 minutes.

VARIATION
Banana Muffins

Replace the blueberries with bananas chopped into 1/2-inch (1.2-cm) cubes. Increase bread flour by 2 ounces (55 g) and omit the ground ginger.

Chocolate Cherry Muffins

twenty-six 4-ounce (115-g) muffins

Butter and Flour Mixture (page 4)

6 eggs

These rich, dark muffins have a distinctive slightly bitter chocolate taste that is sweetened by the cherries and honey. The beets too add sugar to the muffins (although these are not the well-known sugar beets), and they contribute to the intense dark color, which could otherwise be achieved only by adding an overpowering amount of chocolate. These muffins are not only tasty, they are great keepers as well, since both the beets and the cherries are instrumental in retaining moisture. The batter for these, as with many muffins con-

1 pound, 6 ounces (625 g) granulated
  sugar

1½ cups (360 ml) buttermilk

1½ cups (360 ml) sour cream

⅓ cup (80 ml) or 4 ounces (115 g)
  honey

1 pound, 8 ounces (680 g) bread flour

4 ounces (115 g) unsweetened cocoa
  powder

1 tablespoon (12 g) baking soda

1 tablespoon (12 g) baking powder

10 ounces (285 g) finely ground
  almonds

12 ounces (340 g) melted unsalted
  butter

3 ounces (85 g) or ½ cup (120 ml)
  grated beets

1 pound (455 g) fresh or canned
  cherries (see note 1)

NOTE 1: If you use fresh cherries, stem them, remove the pits, and cut into quarters. Drain canned cherries, pat dry, then cut into quarters as well.

NOTE 2: It is no doubt a lot more convenient to line the pans with paper cups instead of using the Butter and Flour Mixture; however, the latter contributes to a more attractive appearance and a better volume. The batter tends to stick to the paper cups, thereby inhibiting a proper rise from the eggs and the chemical leavening agents. This results in a cracked and peaked muffin, something which is not necessarily bad in other cases, but undesirable in a mushrooming-type muffin.

VARIATION
Chocolate Cherry Coffee Cakes

taining both baking powder and baking soda, can be prepared the day before baking without any ill side effects and stored overnight, covered in the refrigerator, either preportioned in muffin cups or in bulk. Freeze the batter for longer storage. If you have a craving for another fruit, or you just don't have cherries on hand, either cubed poached pears or whole fresh raspberries make great substitutes.

1. Brush Butter and Flour Mixture over the inside of muffin pans. Skip every other space because the muffins will "mushroom" out on top as they bake. Grease the top of the pan around each cup as well (see note 2). Reserve.

2. Beat the eggs and sugar together just long enough to break up the eggs; do not overmix. Stir in the buttermilk, sour cream, and honey.

3. Sift together the flour, cocoa powder, baking soda, and baking powder. Add to the batter together with the ground almonds and mix until completely incorporated. Stir in the melted butter, grated beets, and the cherries.

4. If necessary, refrigerate the batter until it is firm enough to scoop, then portion 4 ounces (115 g) of batter into each of the greased muffin cups using an ice-cream scoop of the appropriate size. Alternatively, you can pipe the batter into the pans right away using a pastry bag with a no. 8 (16-mm) plain tip.

5. Bake at 375°F (190°C) for approximately 25 minutes or until the tops of the muffins spring back when you press lightly with your finger.

The batter can be made into coffee cakes without any alteration.

1. Butter six 1-quart (960-ml) Gugelhupf or tube pans and coat the pans lightly with dry cake crumbs or finely ground almonds or hazelnuts.

2. Divide the batter between the pans and bake as directed, increasing the time by about 15 minutes.

Chocolate Chip Muffins

twenty-eight 4-ounce (115-g) muffins

Butter and Flour Mixture (page 4)

14 ounces (400 g) sweet dark chocolate

8 ounces (225 g) walnuts

10 ounces (285 g) soft unsalted butter

10 ounces (285 g) light brown sugar

3/4 cup (180 ml) or 9 ounces (255 g) honey

4 eggs

1 teaspoon (5 ml) vanilla extract

1 tablespoon (12 g) baking powder

4 teaspoons (16 g) baking soda

1 pound, 12 ounces (795 g) bread flour

2 ounces (55 g) unprocessed wheat bran

1 1/4 cups (300 ml) buttermilk

1 1/2 cups (360 ml) half-and-half

8 ounces (225 g) dark raisins

NOTE: If you want the batter to stay within the paper cups, use 3 ounces (85 g) of batter per muffin. It is not necessary in that case to skip any spaces or to grease the top of the pan.

These are gooey and delicious and, like Chocolate Chip Cookies, are especially so right out of the oven when the chocolate chunks are still runny. Take care not to overbake or they can go from fabulous to dry and boring.

1. Line muffin pans with paper cups, skipping every other space because the muffins will "mushroom" out on top as they bake. Grease the top of the pan around each cup with Butter and Flour Mixture; set aside (see note).

2. Chop the chocolate and walnuts into raisin-sized pieces; set aside.

3. Beat the butter and brown sugar until fluffy. Add the honey, eggs, and vanilla.

4. Sift the baking powder, baking soda, and flour together. Add the bran.

5. Add the dry ingredients to the butter mixture in three parts, alternating with the buttermilk and half-and-half. Stir in the raisins, chocolate, and walnuts.

6. Use an ice-cream scoop to portion 4 ounces (115 g) of batter into each muffin cup.

7. Bake at 375°F (190°C) for about 25 minutes or until brown and baked through. To check if the muffins are done, press down in the center; they should spring back. As soon as they can be handled, either remove the muffins from the pans or tilt them in the pans to allow air underneath; this will keep them from getting wet on the bottom.

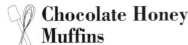

Chocolate Honey Muffins

thirty 4-ounce (115-g) muffins

Butter and Flour Mixture (page 4)

6 ounces (170 g) walnuts

7 ounces (200 g) sweet dark chocolate

7 ounces (200 g) white chocolate

10 ounces (285 g) soft unsalted butter

10 ounces (285 g) light brown sugar

1 cup (240 ml) or 12 ounces (340 g) honey

1/4 cup (60 ml) or 3 ounces (85 g) molasses

6 eggs

Good looking and great tasting. Honey adds a rounder, deeper flavor and contributes to the moist texture. Chunks of both dark and white chocolate give these muffins lots of visual appeal.

1. Line muffin pans with paper cups, skipping every other space because the muffins will "mushroom" out on top of the pan as they bake. Grease the top of the pan around each cup with Butter and Flour Mixture; set aside (see note).

2. Chop walnuts, dark chocolate, and white chocolate to raisin-sized pieces; set aside.

3. Cream together the butter and brown sugar until light and fluffy. Add the honey, molasses, eggs, and vanilla.

4. Sift together salt, baking powder, baking soda, bread flour, cake flour, and cocoa powder. Add to the butter mixture in three parts, alter-

1 teaspoon (5 ml) vanilla extract

1 teaspoon (5 g) salt

4 teaspoons (16 g) baking powder

2 teaspoons (8 g) baking soda

14 ounces (400 g) bread flour

10 ounces (285 g) cake flour

2 ounces (55 g) unsweetened cocoa powder

1³/₄ cups (420 ml) half-and-half

2¹/₄ cups (540 ml) buttermilk

6 ounces (170 g) dark raisins

NOTE: If you prefer a smaller muffin, use 3 ounces (85 g) of batter per muffin. It is not necessary in that case to skip any spaces or to grease the top of the pan.

Honey-Bran Muffins

thirty-five 4-ounce (115-g) muffins

1³/₄ cups (420 ml) water

1 pound, 3 ounces (540 g) unprocessed wheat bran

4 ounces (115 g) wheat germ

Butter and Flour Mixture (page 4)

12 ounces (340 g) soft unsalted butter

1 pound, 5 ounces (595 g) light brown sugar

1 cup (240 ml) or 12 ounces (340 g) molasses

1 cup (240 ml) or 12 ounces (340 g) honey

6 eggs

1 teaspoon (5 ml) vanilla extract

1 pound, 12 ounces (795 g) bread flour

2¹/₂ teaspoons (10 g) baking powder

2 tablespoons (24 g) baking soda

1 teaspoon (5 g) salt

1³/₄ cups (420 ml) half-and-half

2¹/₄ cups (540 ml) buttermilk

6 ounces (170 g) dark raisins

NOTE: If you want the batter to stay within the paper cups, use 3 ounces (85 g) of batter per muffin. It is not necessary in that case to skip any spaces or to grease the top of the pan.

nating with the buttermilk and half-and-half. Add the raisins, walnuts, and chocolate.

5. Use an ice-cream scoop to portion 4 ounces (115 g) of batter into each muffin cup.

6. Bake at 400°F (205°C) for about 30 minutes or until the muffins spring back when pressed lightly in the center. Remove from the pans as soon as they are cool enough to handle, to prevent the muffins from becoming wet on the bottom.

This healthy muffin can stand in as a light breakfast all by itself. If the muffins seem heavy and do not "mushroom out" much as they bake, you may need to increase the water a little. The consistency of the batter will vary with the type of bran used; smaller pieces absorb more liquid.

1. Bring the water to a boil and pour over the bran and wheat germ. Mix to combine and set aside to cool.

2. Line muffin pans with paper cups, skipping every other space because this amount of batter will make the muffins "mushroom" out on top of the pan as they bake. Grease the top of the pans around each cup with Butter and Flour Mixture; set aside (see note).

3. Cream together the butter and brown sugar until fluffy. Combine the molasses, honey, eggs, and vanilla; add to the butter mixture. Fold in the soaked bran and wheat germ.

4. Sift together the bread flour, baking powder, baking soda, and salt. Add to the batter in three parts, alternating with the half-and-half and the buttermilk. Stir in the raisins.

5. Use an ice-cream scoop to portion 4 ounces (115 g) of batter into each muffin cup.

6. Bake at 375°F (190°C) for about 25 minutes or until dark brown and baked through. To check if the muffins are done press down in the center, they should spring back. As soon as the muffins can be handled, either remove them from the pans or tilt them in the pans to allow air underneath; this will keep the muffins from getting wet on the bottom.

Nutmeg Muffins

eighteen 4-ounce (115-g) muffins

Butter and Flour Mixture (page 4)

10 ounces (285 g) bread flour

12 ounces (340 g) cake flour

2 tablespoons (24 g) baking powder

1 teaspoon (4 g) baking soda

2 tablespoons (15 g) freshly grated nutmeg, about two medium-sized pods (see note 1)

4 eggs

1½ teaspoons (7.5 g) salt

8 ounces (225 g) granulated sugar

½ cup (120 ml) or 6 ounces (170 g) honey

½ cup (120 ml) buttermilk

1½ cups (360 ml) half-and-half

8 ounces (225 g) melted unsalted butter

6 ounces (170 g) fresh or frozen cranberries (see note 2)

4 ounces (115 g) cashew nuts, finely chopped

NOTE 1: *Grate the nutmeg using a nutmeg grinder. Avoid using a box grater since it is almost impossible to grate the whole (end of the) nut without including part of your fingers.*

NOTE 2: *If using frozen cranberries, do not thaw; keep them in the freezer until you are ready to add them to the batter. If thawed, they may break and discolor the batter.*

*T*his recipe was given to me by one of my students after she learned of my love for nutmeg. In the original version, the wonderful taste and aroma that is only obtained from freshly grated nutmeg was there all right, but the remaining ingredients needed some tender loving care. For one thing, the muffins were very plain looking: pale yellow like the type of muffin you find in a six-pack at your local supermarket. The addition of a little baking soda darkens them a bit, the cranberries give the muffins color and a slight tang without taking away from the nutmeg taste, and the nuts on top add some visual appeal as well.

Due to my passion for nutmeg, you might find the flavor a little too strong for some tastes, in which case you may want to reduce the quantity accordingly. Please do not attempt this recipe with commercial pre-ground nutmeg. The flavor simply isn't there, and increasing the amount does not help because the taste then becomes bitter. Instead, try substituting cardamom pods—another of my favorite spices—for the nutmeg. Crush the pods fine in a mortar and use the same amount. The cranberries can be left out of either variation if you wish.

1. Line muffin pans with paper cups, skipping every other space to allow the batter to "mushroom" out on top of the pan as the muffins bake. Grease the top of the pans around each cup with Butter and Flour Mixture; set aside.

2. Sift together the bread flour, cake flour, baking powder, and baking soda. Add the nutmeg and reserve.

3. Combine the eggs, salt, and granulated sugar. Beat rapidly for 2 minutes. Gradually stir the egg mixture into the reserved dry ingredients. Mix in the honey, buttermilk, and half-and-half, stirring until the batter is smooth. Stir in the melted butter, cranberries, and half of the cashew nuts.

4. Use an ice-cream scoop to portion the batter into the prepared pans. (If the batter seems too soft to use a scoop, you probably had the butter too hot. Refrigerate the batter until it firms up a bit, or use a pastry bag to pipe the batter into the pans.) Sprinkle the remaining cashew nuts on top of the muffins.

5. Bake at 375°F (190°C) for approximately 20 minutes or until the muffins spring back when pressed lightly on top. Let cool slightly, then remove from the pans.

Oat Bran-Yogurt Muffins

thirty-five 4-ounce (115-g) muffins

Butter and Flour Mixture (page 4)

12 ounces (340 g) soft unsalted butter

1 pound, 6 ounces (625 g) light brown sugar

1 cup (240 ml) or 12 ounces (340 g) molasses

1 cup (240 ml) or 12 ounces (340 g) honey

12 eggs

2 teaspoons (10 ml) vanilla extract

1 pound, 12 ounces (795 g) bread flour

2 tablespoons (24 g) baking powder

4 teaspoons (16 g) baking soda

1 teaspoon (5 g) salt

1 pound, 10 ounces (740 g) unprocessed oat bran

1¹⁄₂ cups (360 ml) half-and-half

2¹⁄₄ cups (540 ml) Acidophilus Yogurt (page 2), made with low-fat milk

8 ounces (225 g) dark raisins

NOTE: For a smaller muffin, use 3 ounces (85 g) of batter per muffin. It is not necessary in that case to skip any spaces or to grease the tops of the pans.

*T*his is a variation of the Honey-Bran Muffin recipe. Oat Bran-Yogurt Muffins provide an alternate way to enjoy the goodness of oats at breakfast instead of the usual oatmeal. For a long time oats were used only as animal feed and were considered a weed when they sprouted up in wheat fields. It has been only relatively recently that oats have received due credit for their high content of soluble fiber as well as vitamins E and B. Oat bran does not contain any gluten, and in baking the oat bran must be always be combined with another flour that does have gluten.*

1. Line muffin pans with paper cups, skipping every other space because this amount of batter will make the muffins "mushroom" out on top of the pans as they bake. Grease the top of the pans around each cup with Butter and Flour Mixture; set aside.

2. Cream the butter and brown sugar until fluffy. Combine the molasses, honey, eggs, and vanilla; add to the butter mixture.

3. Sift together flour, baking powder, baking soda, and salt. Stir in the oat bran and reserve.

4. Stir the half-and-half into the yogurt. Add the dry ingredients to the batter in three parts, alternating with the yogurt mixture. Stir in the raisins.

5. Portion 4 ounces (115 g) of batter per muffin into the muffin cups, using an ice-cream scoop.

6. Bake at 375°F (190°C) for about 25 minutes or until brown and baked through (the muffins should spring back when pressed lightly in the center). As soon as they can be handled, either remove the muffins from the pans or tilt them in the pans to allow air underneath and prevent the muffins from getting wet on the bottom as they cool.

Pumpkin Muffins

twenty-five 4-ounce (115-g) muffins

Butter and Flour Mixture (page 4)
1 pound (455 g) soft unsalted butter
13 ounces (370 g) light brown sugar
4 eggs
½ cup (120 ml) or 6 ounces (170 g) molasses
½ cup (120 ml) or 6 ounces (170 g) honey
1 teaspoon (5 g) salt
1 teaspoon (2 g) ground ginger
1 teaspoon (1.5 g) ground cinnamon
1 teaspoon (2 g) ground allspice
½ teaspoon (1 g) grated nutmeg
1 tablespoon (12 g) baking powder
1 tablespoon (12 g) baking soda
2 pounds (910 g) bread flour
8 ounces (225 g) dark raisins
1 teaspoon (5 ml) vanilla extract
1½ cups (360 ml) buttermilk
1½ cups (360 ml) pumpkin purée

NOTE: For a smaller muffin, use 3 ounces (85 g) of batter per muffin. It is not necessary in that case to skip any spaces or to grease the tops of the pans.

*T*his is a versatile recipe that can be made any time of the year, although we seem to associate pumpkin mostly with the holiday season. Many other types of cooked and puréed winter squash (except spaghetti squash), such as acorn, butternut, or Hubbard, can be substituted in equal amounts. Or, try using cooked sweet potato purée instead of the pumpkin purée. Another option, as suggested in the variation, is persimmon purée (unfortunately, you only find persimmons during the last three months of the year, but the purée freezes quite well). The batter can also be baked in loaf pans or ring forms to create tea cakes, which are convenient to have on hand for a quick snack.*

1. Line muffin pans with paper cups, skipping every other space because this amount of batter will make the muffins "mushroom" out on top of the pans as they bake. Grease the tops of the pans around each cup with Butter and Flour Mixture; set aside.

2. Cream together the butter and brown sugar. Mix in eggs, molasses, and honey; reserve.

3. Sift together the salt, ginger, cinnamon, allspice, nutmeg, baking powder, baking soda, and flour. Mix in the raisins, coating them with flour to prevent them from sinking to the bottom of the batter; reserve.

4. Combine the vanilla, buttermilk, and pumpkin. Add the pumpkin mixture to the butter mixture in two portions, alternating with the dry ingredients.

5. Place the batter in a pastry bag with a no. 8 (16-mm) plain tip. Pipe the batter into the prepared pans, slightly above the rim of each cup, using 4 ounces (115 g) of batter per muffin. Or, use an ice-cream scoop to fill the pans.

6. Bake at 375°F (190°C) until the crust is brown, about 35 minutes. The muffins should spring back when pressed lightly in the center.

VARIATION
Persimmon Muffins

*D*elete the raisins and pumpkin purée. Add instead 8 ounces (225 g) of dates chopped to the size of raisins, 1¼ cups (300 ml) persimmon purée, and 8 ounces (225 g) persimmon chunks, also chopped into raisin-sized pieces.*

Zucchini-Walnut Muffins

thirty 4-ounce (115-g) muffins

Butter and Flour Mixture (page 4)

8 eggs

1 pound, 12 ounces (795 g) granulated sugar

1 pound, 4 ounces (570 g) grated zucchini (skin on)

10 ounces (285 g) grated carrots

2 cups (480 ml) vegetable oil

1 teaspoon (5 g) salt

1 pound, 12 ounces (795 g) bread flour

4 teaspoons (16 g) baking powder

1 tablespoon (12 g) baking soda

1 tablespoon (5 g) ground cinnamon

2 teaspoons (4 g) ground allspice

1 teaspoon (2 g) grated nutmeg

8 ounces (225 g) unprocessed wheat bran

10 ounces (285 g) chopped walnuts

finely chopped walnuts

light brown sugar

NOTE: *For a smaller muffin, use 3 ounces (85 g) of batter per muffin. It is not necessary in that case to skip any spaces or to grease the tops of the pans.*

 ## VARIATION
Zucchini-Fig Muffins

My personal favorite and a hearty good-for-you muffin. As with Pumpkin Muffins, you can experiment by substituting other summer squash varieties-crookneck, for example—for the zucchini. However, the green zucchini skin really looks good and adds a nice texture to the finished product. You can certainly use whatever type of nuts you have on hand, and you can replace the wheat bran with oat bran. With all of that flexibility, there is just no excuse not to try this recipe. A particular type or brand of bran may absorb more moisture than is desirable, resulting in a heavy, dense muffin. If so, increase either the zucchini or carrots a little.

1. Line muffin pans with paper cups, skipping every other space because the muffins will "mushroom" out on top of the pans as they bake. Grease the top of the pans around each cup with Butter and Flour Mixture; set aside.

2. Beat the eggs and sugar just to combine. Stir in zucchini, carrots, oil, and salt.

3. Sift the flour with the baking powder, baking soda, and spices. Add to the egg mixture.

4. Stir in the bran and the 10 ounces (285 g) walnuts.

5. Use an ice-cream scoop to portion 4 ounces (115 g) of batter into each muffin cup.

6. Mix equal parts of finely chopped walnuts and brown sugar and sprinkle on top of the muffins.

7. Bake at 400°F (205°C) for approximately 35 minutes. Remove the muffins from the pans as soon as they are cool enough to touch to prevent them from becoming wet on the bottom.

Reduce the amount of zucchini to 8 ounces (225 g). Add 12 ounces (340 g) dried figs. Soften the figs in hot water for 30 minutes. Drain, and chop into raisin-sized pieces. Add the figs to the batter together with the walnuts.

5

Cookies

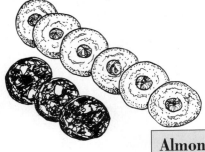

Almond Macaroon Cookies	Macadamia Nut Cookies
Almond Shortbread	Madeleines
Biscotti	Oat and Date Chews
Brownies	Oat Flakes
Brysselkex Cookies	Orange Macaroons
Chewy Trail Mix Cookies	Palm Leaves
Chocolate Chip Cookies	Peanut Butter Cookies
Chunky White-Chocolate-Chip Cookies	Pirouettes
Cocoa Cuts	Raspberry Turnovers
Coconut Haystack Cookies	Rugelach
Coconut Macaroons	Sesame Seed Cookies
Florentinas	Spritz Rings
Gingersnaps	Strassburger Cookies
Hazelnut Butter Cookies	Traditional Shortbread
Hazelnut-Almond Squares	Triple-Chocolate Indulgence
Heide Sand Cookies	Vanilla Dreams
Honey Oatmeal Cookies	Walnut Bars

It is a tradition in Sweden to serve cookies and coffee at 3 o'clock each afternoon: the Swedish equivalent of English afternoon tea. There should be seven kinds of cookies, neatly lined up on trays. If it is not possible to have seven different types, the custom is to serve an odd number of varieties. When someone dropped by to visit during the day, we always

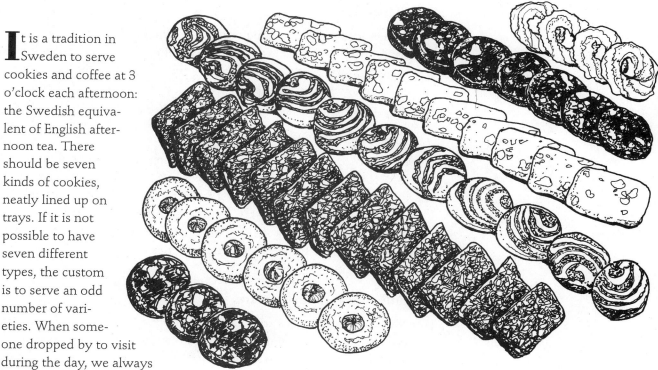

served coffee and cookies automatically. Cookies are also great for after-dinner treats. It has become popular in some restaurants to serve a platter of assorted small cookies when the check is presented, perhaps to cushion the shock a little.

The word cookie comes from the Dutch word *koekje,* which translates to "small cake," as do both the Swedish name for cookies, *småkakor,* and the

German *klein gebäck.* In England cookies are known, of course, as biscuits. There are more varieties of these small irresistible little sweets than any other baked good—due largely to the fact that so many variations in shape, flavor, texture, and size fall under this one heading. There are drop cookies, refrigerator cookies, meringue-type cookies, petit four sec, bar cookies, piped cookies, cookie-cutter cookies, cake-like cookies, twice-baked varieties such as biscotti, et cetera. Add to each of those seasonal and international modifications, and the list goes on indefinitely!

Texture

Certain cookies are intentionally made soft and/or chewy (all chewy.cookies are soft, but not all soft cookies can be considered chewy), but in other recipes this would be considered a serious flaw. Some cookies should spread out flat during the baking process, while this, too, could be a disaster in another variety. In order to produce the desired texture, to correct mistakes, or to modify cookie recipes, it is of the utmost importance that you have an understanding of the role played by each ingredient.

Chewy Texture

A chewy cookie needs a high moisture content, which is provided by eggs and other liquids. In comparison to other recipes, the eggs must be in higher proportion to the other ingredients, while the fat content must be lower. You should use a high-gluten flour and be certain that there is some gluten development when mixing the dough.

Crisp Texture

For a cookie to be crisp, the dough must be relatively low in moisture to begin with. The cookies should be small and thin to allow them to dry properly as they bake. Most importantly, these cookies must be high in both fat and sugar. Crisp cookies can become soft if stored improperly, especially if they contain hygroscopic ingredients that absorb moisture from the air. Crisp cookies must be stored in an airtight container.

Soft (Cake-Like) Texture

Naturally, soft cookies are found at the opposite end of the scale from crisp cookies, and therefore they require a dough with a high proportion of liquid, and a low sugar and fat content. A soft cookie is generally thick and comparatively large, which allows the cookie to retain the additional moisture during baking. They usually contain either corn syrup, honey, or molasses, which are hygroscopic (moisture-absorbing) sweeteners. Soft cookies should be slightly underbaked and must be stored in a covered container or they will dry out. Storing moist or chewy cookies in the same container with a few slices of apple or quince will greatly prolong their shelf life.

Altering the Shape in the Baking Process

Within any of the previous texture traits, you may want the cookies to spread out flat during baking, or it may be highly undesirable for the cookie to change shape at all. When the latter is preferable, the cookie dough generally will not contain any chemical leavening agent, and the dough should be mixed only until the ingredients are well incorporated. Beating or creaming will incorporate air and cause the cookies to puff and fall as they bake. Using a chlorinated flour will also reduce spreading. Granulated sugar acts as an aid to incorporating air into fat, so a high sugar content can contribute to spreading when combined with overmixing. If the sugar and fat are mixed to a paste without incorporating air, however, it will not have the same effect. In general, the higher the sugar content, the more the cookies will spread. Using powdered sugar, or even a very fine granulated sugar such as castor sugar, will reduce this tendency. Additional sugar will also make the baked cookies harder. An overgreased baking pan and/or a soft dough will further cause the cookies to spread.

If the cookies are intended to spread out, the dough will contain baking soda, baking powder, ammonium carbonate, potash, or a combination of these leaveners. Increased spread is also obtained by the addition of tenderizers such as fat, honey, molasses, or corn syrup. These can have an adverse effect if used in a quantity that disrupts the balance of the strengtheners (also called the binding ingredients) in the recipe: the eggs and flour.

Appearance

Cookies should look as good as they taste. You want to create petite, bite-sized morsels that your guests just can't resist, even if they are not hungry! With few exceptions, cookies should be small and uniform in size and thickness. Not only will they bake more evenly, your cookies will create an elegant presentation when displayed on a tray or mirror. Pay special attention when the following recipes call for chilling the dough at various stages in the preparation; skipping this important step will result in misshapen, unprofessional-looking cookies.

Decorating

Cookies can be decorated, and made more delicious, with jam piped on top, dipped in chocolate (completely or in part), sandwiched together with preserves or buttercream, dipped in fondant, or topped with sifted, powdered sugar or an icing.

Forming

Shaping the cookie dough is done in several ways. Some cookies, such as Coconut Macaroons and Spritz Rings, are piped out into shapes using a pastry bag with a specific tip. In other recipes the dough is divided into equal portions; each portion is then rolled into a rope of uniform thickness and cut into cookies. These are known as icebox cookies, and this technique is used with Macadamia Nut, Hazelnut, and all variations of Brysselkex cookies. This production method not only gives you cookies of uniform size but also makes storage easier: If well wrapped, the logs can be kept in the refrigerator for days, or in the freezer for weeks. The cookies can be baked and finished as needed, allowing you to produce fresh cookies with a minimum of effort. A third way of forming cookies is to spread the dough in sheets on a pan, or roll it into ropes and press these on the pan. The cookies are cut to size as soon as the baked dough comes out of the oven. This procedure is used for Cocoa Cuts and Hazelnut-Almond Squares.

Baking

Most cookies have a high sugar content, which makes them susceptible to overbrowning. It is usually a good idea to bake them double-panned to prevent them from becoming too dark on the bottom before they have a chance to reach an appetizing golden brown color on the top. Generally cookies should be baked around 375°F (190°C), except macaroons, which need high heat, 425°F (219°C), to ensure softness.

Storage

In most instances there is no reason to use anything but butter in cookie doughs. The buttery flavor is irreplaceable, and cookies baked with butter will taste fresh at least three to four days if they are stored properly. Cookies baked with jam stay at their best for the shortest amount of time, as the jam tends to become rubbery. To keep cookies crisp, store them in a jar with a little air for circulation; or keep the cover on loosely (although this might be taken as an invitation for munching by your coworkers or friends). If cookies become soft anyway, due to high humidity or rain, dry them in a cool 200°F (94°C) oven, providing they are not dipped or filled. Other cookies, such as macaroons, need to be kept soft; store these in an airtight container. If they get a little dry, take them out of the container and place them on a sheet pan in the refrigerator overnight. The old-fashioned method mentioned previously of putting a few apple or quince slices in the jar is helpful with macaroons as well.

The table shown in Figure 5–1 categorizes the cookie recipes throughout this book by texture, production method, and storage capability.

Cookies Categorized by Texture, Production Method, and Storage Capability

Holiday Cookies ✤

SOFT COOKIES	CHEWY COOKIES	CRISP COOKIES	FANCY COOKIES	PIPED COOKIES	ICEBOX COOKIES	GOOD FOR LONG STORAGE
Almond Macaroons	Almond Macaroons	Almond Shortbread	Almond Doubles	Almond Macaroons	Almond Shortbread	Biscotti
Brownies	Chewy Trail Mix Cookies	Biscotti	Brandy Pretzels	Chocolate-Filled Macadamia Morsels	Brysselkex Cookies	Brysselkex Cookies
Chewy Trail Mix Cookies	Chocolate Snow Hearts ✤	Brysselkex Cookies	Chocolate-Filled Macadamia Morsels	Cocoa Strassburger Cookies	Chewy Trail Mix Cookies	Cocoa Cuts
Chocolate Chip Cookies	Chocolate Orange Pillows ✤	Christmas Cookie Ornaments ✤	Christmas Cookie Ornaments ✤	Coconut Haystack Cookies	Chocolate Chip Cookies	Date Bars
Chocolate Snow Hearts ✤	Chunky White-Chocolate Chip Cookies	Cocoa Cuts	Hazelnut Flowers	Coconut Macaroons	Chunky White-Chocolate Chip Cookies	Florentinas
Chunky White-Chocolate Chip Cookies	Cinnamon Stars ✤	Florentinas	Macaroon Candies	Hazelnut Flowers	Hazelnut Butter Cookies	Gingerbread Cookies ✤
Cinnamon Stars ✤	Coconut Haystack Cookies	Gingerbread Cookies ✤	Palm Leaves	Oat Flakes	Heide Sand Cookies	Hazelnut Squares
Coconut Haystack Cookies	Coconut Macaroons	Hazelnut Squares	Pirouettes	Spritz Rings	Macadamia Nut Cookies	Heide Sand Cookies
Coconut Macaroons	Gingersnaps	Heide Sand Cookies	Raspberry Cutouts	Strassburger Cookies	Oat and Date Chews	Honey Oatmeal Cookies
Gingersnaps	Macaroon Candies	Honey Oatmeal Cookies	Raspberry Turnovers		Peanut Butter Cookies	Lebkuchen Bars ✤
Lebkuchen Bars ✤	Oat and Date Chews	Palm Leaves	Spritz Rings		Sesame Seed Cookies	Lebkuchen Hearts ✤
Lebkuchen Hearts ✤	Orange Macaroons	Peanut Butter Cookies	Strassburger Cookies		Walnut Bars	Madeleines
Macadamia Nut Cookies		Pirouettes	Strawberry Hearts			Sesame Seed Cookies
Madeleines		Sesame Seed Cookies				Springerle ✤
Oat and Date Chews		Springerle ✤				Traditional Shortbread
Orange Macaroons		Traditional Shortbread				Walnut Bars
Raspberry Turnovers		Vanilla Dreams				
Rugelach		Walnut Bars				
Triple-Chocolate Indulgence						

BAR COOKIES

Hazelnut Squares	Brownies
Lebkuchen Bars ✤	Date Bars
Meyer Lemon Bars	
Traditional Shortbread	

FIGURE 5–1 Cookie recipes throughout the text categorized by texture, production method, and storage capability

Almond Macaroon Cookies

about sixty 2-inch (5-cm) cookies

2 pounds (910 g) Almond Paste (page 3)
1 pound (455 g) granulated sugar
6 egg whites (³/₄ cup/180 ml), approximately

These small cookies, crunchy on the outside and soft inside, can be positively addictive! They originated in Venice, Italy, during the Renaissance and are popular today all over Europe. Numerous varieties are made—flavored with chocolate or liqueur, two cookies may be sandwiched together with Ganache, buttercream, or jam, and one variety of Almond Macaroon is sold still attached to its baking paper (an edible rice paper known as oblaten*). A version of tiny macaroons was my favorite candy as a kid. They were made about the size of a quarter coin and sold in cellophane bags to prevent them from drying out.*

1. Place the Almond Paste and sugar in a mixing bowl. Combine, using the paddle at low speed.

2. Blend in one egg white at a time, being careful not to get any lumps in the batter. Add as many egg whites as the batter will absorb without getting runny; this will vary depending on the firmness of the Almond Paste and, to some degree, the size of the egg whites.

3. Beat for a few minutes at high speed to a creamy consistency.

4. Place the batter in a pastry bag with a no. 6 (12-mm) plain tip. Pipe the batter in 1¹/₂-inch (3.7-cm) mounds onto sheet pans lined with baking paper. They will bake out slightly, so do not pipe them too close together.

5. Bake the cookies, double-panned, at 410°F (210°C) for about 10 minutes or until light brown.

6. Let the macaroons cool attached to the baking paper. To remove them from the paper, turn them upside down and peel the paper away from the cookies, rather than the cookies off the paper (Figure 5–2). If

FIGURE 5–2   *Peeling the baking paper away from the baked Almond Macaroon Cookies with the cookies turned upside down*

they are difficult to remove, brush water on the back of the papers, turn right-side up, and wait a few minutes; then try again. For long-term storage, place the cookies in the freezer still attached to the baking paper. Macaroons can be served as is or dipped in melted coating chocolate.

VARIATION
Macaroon Decorating Paste

*M*ake the recipe above, keeping the paste a bit firmer by using fewer egg whites. The paste should be soft enough that you can pipe it out without a monumental effort, but it should not change shape at all when it is baked. It should always be baked it a hot oven; follow directions in the individual recipes in which the paste is used.

Almond Shortbread

32 cookies

2 eggs

7 ounces (200 g) Almond Paste (page 3)

14 ounces (400 g) soft unsalted butter

7 ounces (200 g) granulated sugar

1/2 teaspoon (2 g) ammonium carbonate (see introduction)

1 tablespoon (15 ml) vanilla extract

1 pound, 2 ounces (510 g) bread flour

4 ounces (115 g) smooth strawberry jam

*J*ust about everyone loves shortbread cookies—the buttery taste and crumbly texture are all but irresistible. In this recipe, a portion of the butter has been replaced with Almond Paste, which makes it possible to roll the dough into logs and slice into cookies before baking, unlike the traditional bar-type of shortbread cookies, in which the dough is rolled out flat, scored, baked, and then cut into individual pieces after baking. Keep the logs of dough in the refrigerator and finish the cookies as needed. The baked cookies will stay fresh for several days, but unfortunately, as the moisture dissipates the jam becomes chewy and dry. If you do not have ammonium carbonate substitute a mixture of baking powder and baking soda (in equal amounts).

1. Mix the eggs into the Almond Paste one at a time to avoid lumps. Incorporate the butter, sugar, ammonium carbonate, and vanilla. Add the flour and mix only until combined. Refrigerate the dough until it is workable.

2. Divide the dough into two equal pieces, about 1 pound, 8 ounces (680 g) each. Roll each piece into a 12-inch (30-cm) rope and cut sixteen equal slices from each. Refrigerate the ropes first if necessary to keep the slices round and even.

3. Place the slices on sheet pans lined with baking paper. Make an indentation in the center of each cookie using your thumb or an appropriate tool. If the dough cracks when you do this, let it soften at room temperature for a short time and then continue.

4. Place the strawberry jam in a disposable pastry bag made from a half sheet of baking paper (see Figures 1–6 and 1–7, page 24). Pipe the jam into the indentation on each cookie.

5. Bake at 375°F (190°C) for approximately 30 minutes or until golden brown.

Biscotti

about 120 cookies

1 pound, 4 ounces (570 g) bread flour

4 teaspoons (16 g) baking powder

12 ounces (340 g) granulated sugar

6 ounces (170 g) white bread crumbs

8 ounces (225 g) whole almonds with skin

8 ounces (225 g) whole hazelnuts with skin

1 teaspoon (5 ml) orange flower water

1 teaspoon (5 ml) vanilla extract

¼ cup (60 ml) orange juice

5 eggs

Egg Wash (page 7)

sanding sugar

dark coating chocolate, melted

NOTE: If making more cookies than you will use within one week, it is better to store some of the uncut baked ropes in the refrigerator (covered) to slice and dry as needed.

*T*his Italian specialty is part of an international group of cookies and crackers that are baked twice: The French biscotte, the German zwieback, and Swedish skorpor, which are known in America as rusks. Some of these are unsweetened or, in the case of Biscotti, sweetened and flavored with nuts. If you like anise flavor, substitute three tablespoons of lightly crushed anise seed for the orange flower water (you can also add some anisette liqueur).

1. Sift the flour with the baking powder. Add the sugar and bread crumbs, and combine using the dough hook at low to medium speed. Mix in the almonds and hazelnuts.

2. Combine the orange flower water, vanilla, orange juice, and eggs. Gradually add the liquid to the dry ingredients and mix for approximately 1 minute until you achieve a firm dough.

3. Divide the dough into four equal pieces; they will weigh about 15 ounces (430 g) each. Roll each piece into a uniform rope 16 inches (40 cm) long. Place the ropes on sheet pans lined with baking paper. Brush Egg Wash on top of the ropes, then sprinkle with sanding sugar.

4. Bake at 350°F (175°C) for about 25 minutes or until golden brown. Let cool for at least 1 hour or, preferably, overnight.

5. Slice ropes diagonally into cookies ⅜ inch (9 mm) thick. Place the slices cut-side down on sheet pans lined with baking paper.

6. Bake at 375°F (190°C) until the cookies start to turn golden brown around the edges, approximately 15 minutes.

7. When the cookies have cooled completely, dip them halfway into melted dark coating chocolate. Store in airtight containers.

Brownies

one 16-by-12-inch (40-×-30-cm) sheet

14 ounces (400 g) walnuts

1 pound, 8 ounces (680 g) sweet dark chocolate

1 pound (455 g) unsalted butter

1 pound, 12 ounces (795 g) granulated sugar

8 eggs

1 teaspoon (5 ml) vanilla extract

1 pound (455 g) bread flour

½ teaspoon (2 g) baking powder

6 ounces (170 g) dark raisins (optional)

I certainly cannot call myself an expert on Brownies, which are very much an American delicacy. They seem to come in all varieties, from fudgy and chewy to very cake-like, and from tiny cookie-sized pieces to big squares. It is up to you how to portion the baked sheet. These Brownies hold together well if you are cutting them small. I happen to like raisins, so in the previous edition of this book I added 6 ounces (170 g) of raisins mixed in with the nuts. I have not gotten into so much trouble since I used someone's sewing scissors to cut paper! The word I get from my students and the customers at the school is that adding raisins to Brownies is un-American. So, the raisins are gone and are now just a (humble) option.

1. Chop the walnuts into raisin-sized pieces and set aside.

2. Cut the chocolate into chunks, place in a bowl with the butter, and melt together over simmering water. Set aside to cool.

3. Line the bottom of a half-sheet pan (16 by 12 inches /40 × 30 cm) with baking paper.

4. Whip the sugar, eggs, and vanilla at high speed until light and fluffy. Fold into the cooled chocolate mixture.

5. Sift the flour with baking powder and stir into the chocolate. Add 12 ounces (340 g) of the walnuts (and the raisins if you are using them).

6. Spread the batter evenly in the prepared pan. Sprinkle the remaining 2 ounces (55 g) of walnuts over the top.

7. Bake at 400°F (205°C) for about 30 minutes or until the cake is completely set but still slightly soft. Cool and slice into pieces of the desired size.

 # Brysselkex Cookies

Brysselkex Dough

1 pound, 11 ounces (765 g) unsalted butter
1 teaspoon (5 ml) vanilla extract
10 ounces (285 g) powdered sugar
2 pounds, 3 ounces (1 kg) bread flour
1 ounce (30 g) unsweetened cocoa powder

 ## Vanilla Brysselkex

about 100 cookies

one recipe Brysselkex Dough (omit cocoa powder)
pale pink decorating sugar (see note, page 216)

These are also known as sablés *in parts of Europe and as Dutch biscuits in others. It reminds me of the Swedish saying "kärt bain har många namn," which means "a loved child has many names." Many varieties of cookies can be made from this one basic dough; the most common are Vanilla, Marble, and Checkerboard. Like most cookies that are divided into pieces from ropes, these can be refrigerated or frozen, well wrapped, then sliced and baked as needed.*

1. Using the dough hook at low to medium speed, mix the butter, vanilla, sugar, and flour until smooth.

2. Divide the dough in half. Mix the cocoa powder into one half.

3. Refrigerate the dough if necessary until it has a workable consistency.

1. Divide the dough into three equal pieces, about 1 pound, 8 ounces (680 g) each. Refrigerate if needed.

2. Roll each piece into a rope 2 inches (5 cm) in diameter.

3. Brush excess flour from the ropes and roll in sugar to coat.

4. Transfer the ropes to a sheet pan; roll them so they are even and just slightly thinner. Refrigerate until firm.

5. Cut the ropes into ¼-inch (6-mm) slices. Place the cookies on sheet pans lined with baking paper.

6. Bake at 375°F (190°C) until golden brown, about 15 minutes.

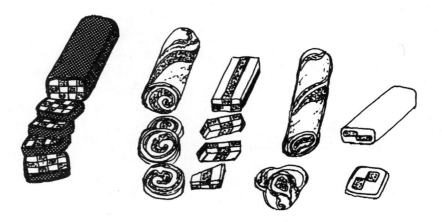

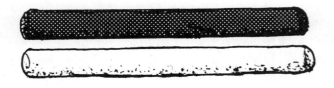

FIGURE 5–3   A plain rope and a chocolate rope in one group

FIGURE 5–4   One pair of ropes cut into thirds

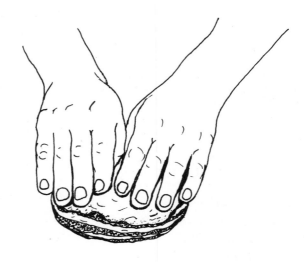

FIGURE 5–5   Alternating 3 pieces of plain dough with 3 pieces of chocolate dough from one group, to form a stack

FIGURE 5–6   Starting to roll the stacked pieces of dough into a log

Marble Brysselkex

about 100 cookies

one recipe Brysselkex Dough

1. Divide the plain and chocolate doughs into three portions each; this can be done by eye, as the pieces need not be exactly equal.

2. Roll all six pieces, separately, into ropes about 10 inches (25 cm) long.

3. Arrange the ropes in three groups with one plain and one chocolate rope in each (Figure 5–3). Cut each pair into thirds so you now have three small chocolate and three small plain in each group (Figure 5–4).

4. Working with one group at a time, gently press the six pieces on top of one another, alternating plain and chocolate (Figure 5–5); keep each group separate.

5. Roll each group of stacked dough into a log 1³/₄ inches (4.5 cm) in diameter (Figure 5–6), twisting the logs as you form them to create the marbled effect (Figure 5–7).

6. Carefully transfer the logs to a sheet pan and refrigerate until firm. Slice and bake as directed for Vanilla Brysselkex.

Checkerboard Brysselkex

about 150 cookies

one recipe Brysselkex Dough

2 pounds, 10 ounces (1 kg, 195 g)
Short Dough or Cocoa Short Dough
(see pages 54 and 55)

Egg Wash (page 7)

1. Roll the plain and chocolate doughs into rectangles of equal size, 5/8 inch (1.5 cm) thick.

2. Brush Egg Wash on the chocolate dough and place the plain dough on top.

3. Refrigerate until firm.

4. Cut the rectangle into 5/8-inch (1.5-cm) strips (Figure 5–8). Lay half of the strips on their sides; brush with Egg Wash.

5. Arrange the remaining strips on top of the egg-washed strips, stacking them so that the chocolate dough is on top of the plain dough and vice versa, to create the checkerboard effect.

6. Roll out Short Dough 1/8 inch (3 mm) thick and the same length as the strips.

7. Brush the Short Dough with Egg Wash.

8. Place one of the stacked cookie strips on top, and roll to enclose all four sides in Short Dough. Cut away the excess dough. Repeat with the remaining strips. You can omit wrapping the logs in Short Dough, or stack three or four strips together to create different patterns and sizes (Figures 5–9 and 5–10).

9. Refrigerate the logs until firm.

10. Slice and bake as instructed in Vanilla Brysselkex.

FIGURE 5–7   *The marbled log after rolling while twisting*

FIGURE 5–8   *Slicing the stacked rectangle of plain and chocolate doughs into strips, and laying half of the strips on their sides*

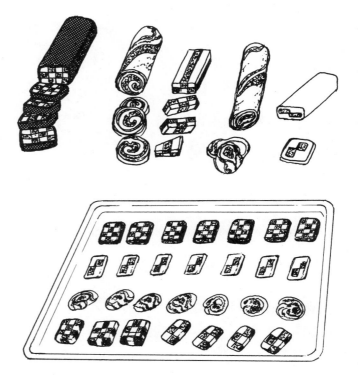

FIGURES 5–9 and 5–10   *Examples of Marble and Checkerboard Brysselkex Cookies*

Chewy Trail Mix Cookies

64 cookies

6 ounces (170 g) cashew nuts

6 ounces (170 g) walnuts

14 ounces (400 g) soft unsalted butter

12 ounces (340 g) light brown sugar

12 ounces (340 g) granulated sugar

½ cup (120 ml) or 6 ounces (170 g) honey

4 eggs

1 tablespoon (15 ml) vanilla extract

1 pound, 8 ounces (680 g) bread flour

2 teaspoons (7 g) ammonium carbonate (see note)

2 teaspoons (8 g) baking soda

1 teaspoon (1.5 g) ground cinnamon

2 teaspoons (10 g) salt

12 ounces (340 g) pumpkin seeds

6 ounces (170 g) sunflower seeds

8 ounces (225 g) rolled oats

1 pound, 8 ounces (680 g) moluka raisins (see note)

NOTE: *If you are not able to locate the large juicy moluka raisins, use any other dark seedless raisin such as Thompson. If ammonium carbonate is not available substitute a mixture of baking powder and baking soda (in equal amounts).*

These cookies are a favorite of many—colorful, crunchy and chewy at the same time. They make a great snack with a glass of cold milk, even if you are not out hiking in the woods but just moving along in the kitchen or around the house. As with most refrigerator-type cookies these are very practical, so I suggest that you don't bother to cut down the recipe even if you do not need the full amount of cookies immediately. The dough will keep fine in the refrigerator for weeks and in the freezer for much longer. Use any nuts or seeds that you like instead of the varieties specified if you want to vary the flavor. Or, try omitting the salt in the recipe and substitute lightly salted pumpkin seeds or cashew nuts. If the unthinkable should happen and the cookies become overbaked and dry, place them in a covered container with an apple (or better yet, if you have one, a quince) cut into wedges and the cookies will become soft and chewy again overnight. Happy Trails!

1. Chop the cashews and walnuts into raisin-sized pieces and reserve.

2. In a mixing bowl with the paddle attachment, mix the butter, the brown sugar, the granulated sugar, and the honey until combined. Do not overmix or cream. Incorporate the eggs two at a time. Add the vanilla extract.

3. Sift together the flour, ammonium carbonate, baking soda, cinnamon, and salt. Mix into the batter together with half of the pumpkin seeds (reserve the other half for decorating), the sunflower seeds, cashews, and walnuts. Incorporate the rolled oats and the raisins, mixing until just combined. Place the dough on a sheet pan lined with baking paper and refrigerate until firm.

4. Divide the dough into four equal pieces; they will weigh about 2 pounds (910 g) each. Roll each piece into an 18-inch (45-cm) rope, using flour to prevent the dough from sticking. Cut each rope into sixteen slices and roll the pieces into round balls. Place the balls of dough on top of the reserved pumpkin seeds. Flatten the cookies lightly with the palm of your hand. Place the cookies seed-side up, staggered, on sheet pans lined with baking paper. Flatten the cookies slightly with the palm of your hand to secure the seeds on top.

5. Bake at 300°F (149°C) for approximately 20 minutes or until the cookies are light brown and done.

Chocolate Chip Cookies

60 cookies

6 ounces (170 g) light brown sugar

6 ounces (170 g) granulated sugar

These all-American favorites were invented by a woman in Philadelphia who had the brilliant idea of mixing small chunks of chocolate into her cookie dough. They are irresistible when eaten warm, fresh out of the oven, the way you get them at those little hole-in-the-wall cookie shops in the shopping centers (the ones that lure you in with their enticing aroma to make you an easy target!). Chocolate Chip Cookies should be slightly underbaked so they stay soft and chewy. While that would be a sign of a stale or improperly stored butter cookie,

9 ounces (255 g) soft unsalted butter

2 eggs

1 teaspoon (5 ml) vanilla extract

13 ounces (370 g) bread flour

1 teaspoon (5 g) salt

1 teaspoon (4 g) baking soda

6 ounces (170 g) chopped walnuts

12 ounces (340 g) large dark chocolate
   chips

these are the exception to the rule. To make the currently popular "giant" choco-late chip cookies, use a 2-ounce ice-cream scoop to portion the dough, placing twelve cookies (evenly spaced) on a full-sized sheet pan. Bake at 350°F (175°C) for approximately 15 minutes. This recipe will make 24 giant cookies.

1. Beat the butter and sugars together, using the dough hook at medium speed. Add the eggs and vanilla.

2. Sift the flour, salt, and baking soda together; mix into batter. Stir in the walnuts and chocolate chips.

3. Divide the dough into three equal pieces, approximately 1 pound, 2 ounces (510 g) each. Roll the pieces into ropes and cut each rope into twenty equal pieces.

4. Place the pieces, cut-side up (it is not necessary to roll the pieces round), on sheet pans lined with baking paper; stagger the cookies so they do not bake together.

5. Bake the cookies at 375°F (190°C) until just done, about 10 minutes. The cookies should still be a bit sticky in the middle and just slightly brown on the edges.

Chunky White-Chocolate-Chip Cookies

60 cookies

14 ounces (400 g) white chocolate

12 ounces (340 g) walnuts

6 ounces (170 g) granulated sugar

8 ounces (225 g) light brown sugar

8 ounces (225 g) soft unsalted butter

1 teaspoon (5 g) salt

3 eggs

¼ cup (60 ml) or 3 ounces (85 g)
   honey

2 teaspoons (10 ml) vanilla extract

1 pound, 2 ounces (510 g) bread flour

1½ teaspoons (6 g) baking soda

*T*his variation tastes distinctively different from regular Chocolate Chip Cookies, and the chunks of melted white chocolate on top give the cookies lots of visual appeal. Every once in a while one of my students will produce a batch of (unfortunately) familiar-looking white-chocolate-chip cookies. These always appear normal going into the oven, but they come out extremely flat with no visible chunks of chocolate left. What invariably causes this mysterious disappearance is that the student chops up chunks of cocoa butter instead of white chocolate (in all fairness, they do look very much alike since "white" chocolate is actually an ivory color) and, of course, the cocoa butter just melts away in the oven. This reinforces the doctrine we teachers preach over and over: Always taste to be sure!*

1. Chop the white chocolate and the walnuts into raisin-sized pieces and set aside.

2. Using the dough hook at low to medium speed, mix together the sugars, butter, and salt until well combined. Add the eggs, honey, and vanilla.

3. Sift together the flour and baking soda. Add to the butter mixture. Stir in the walnuts and white chocolate. Chill the dough if it is too soft to form.

4. Divide the dough into three equal pieces; they will weigh approximately 1 pound, 9 ounces (710 g) each. Roll each piece into a 20-inch (50-cm) rope; use flour as needed to prevent the dough from sticking.

5. Cut each rope into twenty pieces and place them, staggered, on sheet pans lined with baking paper.

6. Bake the cookies at 350°F (175°C) just until they start to color, about 15 minutes. They taste best if still somewhat soft in the center.

Cocoa Cuts

about 60 cookies

12 ounces (340 g) soft unsalted butter
8 ounces (225 g) granulated sugar
14 ounces (400 g) bread flour
2 tablespoons (16 g) unsweetened
  cocoa powder
½ teaspoon (2 g) ammonium
  carbonate
Egg Wash (page 7)
sanding sugar
sliced almonds

These are a typical Swedish cookie. I like to include them on cookie trays because their unusual shape adds some contrast to all of the other round cookies. Another plus is that they can be produced very quickly, since they are not shaped individually. If you do not have ammonium carbonate, use twice as much baking soda instead.

1. Using the dough hook at medium speed, beat the butter and sugar together until well combined.

2. Sift the flour, cocoa powder, and ammonium carbonate together and blend into the butter mixture. Mix until smooth.

3. Divide the dough into four equal pieces, about 8 ounces (225 g) each. Refrigerate the dough if necessary to make it easier to handle.

4. Roll each piece of dough into a 20-inch (50-cm) rope. Transfer the ropes to full-sized sheet pans lined with baking paper (the cookies will bake out slightly, so do not put more than three ropes on a pan if you are increasing the recipe).

5. Roll the ropes on the pans to make them the full length of the pan, 24 inches (60 cm). Flatten the ropes slightly, using the palm of your hand.

6. Brush Egg Wash over the dough.

7. Combine equal parts of sanding sugar and sliced almonds. Sprinkle the mixture over the cookie dough.

8. Bake at 375°F (190°C) for about 12 minutes or until baked through. Since it is harder to judge when chocolate dough is baked (because of the color), look at the almonds: when they start to turn light brown the cookies should be almost done.

9. As soon as the cookies come out of the oven, cut them, at a slight angle, into 1¼-inch (3.1-cm) strips using a metal dough scraper (Figure 5–11). If you are making several pans of these cookies, stagger the baking so you will have time to cut each pan before the cookies become crisp.

FIGURE 5–11   Using a metal dough scraper to cut Cocoa Cuts while they are soft right after baking

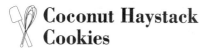

Coconut Haystack Cookies

36 cookies

12 ounces (340 g) unsalted butter

1 pound (455 g) granulated sugar

6 eggs

1 pound, 2 ounces (510 g) dessicated coconut (see note with Coconut Macaroons)

Simple Syrup (page 11)

dark coating chocolate, melted (optional)

*T*here is only one thing that could possibly prevent you from gulping down these old-fashioned and absolutely delicious chewy cookies: Not liking coconut at all!

In the mid 1950s when I was starting out as an apprentice, coconut was just becoming available again after a long drought that followed World War II. Consequently, when we began making these cookies as well as the macaroon version that follows, they seldom made it as far as the showcase—they were usually sold right from the sheet pan in the bakery to customers who had been without these treats for a long time.

1. Place the butter and sugar in a saucepan and heat to 150°F (65°C) while stirring constantly. Remove from the heat and beat in the eggs a few at a time. Stir in the coconut.

2. Return to the stove and cook, stirring constantly, until the mixture comes away from the sides of the pan. Let the batter cool to room temperature.

3. Place the cookie batter in a pastry bag with a no. 9 (18-mm) plain tip. Pipe out thirty-six tall mounds of dough shaped like large chocolate kisses on a sheet pan lined with baking paper.

4. Bake, double-panned, at 425°F (219°C) for approximately 15 minutes. Brush Simple Syrup over the cookies as soon as they come out of the oven. If you would like to dress them up a bit, dip the bottom of the cookies into melted chocolate, coating them halfway up the sides (see Figures 9–27 to 9–31, page 428), or streak melted chocolate over the top of the cookies. Allow the cookies to cool completely before applying the chocolate.

Coconut Macaroons

forty 2-inch (5-cm) cookies

6 ounces (170 g) Almond Paste (page 3)

2 egg whites (¼ cup/60 ml)

5 ounces (140 g) unsalted butter

7 ounces (200 g) granulated sugar

12 ounces (340 g) dessicated coconut (see note)

3 eggs

1 pound (455 g) Short Dough (page 54)

6 ounces (170 g) raspberry jam

Simple Syrup (page 11)

dark coating chocolate, melted

*T*hese cookies may be too labor-intensive for some operations. They are actually something in between a fancy cookie and a simple pastry. But (semantics aside) you can make a simplified version by omitting the Short Dough bottom and piping the batter directly onto paper-lined sheet pans, either in a star shape as specified or in small rosettes using a no. 6 (12-mm) star tip. In that case also omit dipping the baked cookies in chocolate. Coconut Macaroons taste best when they are freshly baked and still soft inside, so rather than baking more cookies than you can use right away, store the batter covered in the refrigerator for up to one week, and bake fresh macaroons as needed. Bring the batter to room temperature before piping it out.*

1. Soften the Almond Paste by mixing in the egg whites; reserve.

2. Melt the butter in a saucepan. Add the sugar and bring to a boil.

3. Transfer to a mixing bowl and combine with the coconut. Gradually blend in the eggs and the Almond Paste mixture; stir until smooth. Let the batter rest for a few minutes.

NOTE: Dessicated coconut is ground, dried coconut. It is sometimes called macaroon coconut and is available from baking suppliers. The coconut is dried and processed to a texture similar to that of coarse polenta. If substituting flaked or shredded coconut, dry it by spreading a thin layer on a sheet pan and leaving it at room temperature for a few days. Or, dry the coconut in a very low oven, but be sure not to toast (brown) the coconut. Chop the dried coconut very fine or grind in a food processor. If you substitute sweetened coconut, decrease the sugar in the recipe.

4. Roll out the Short Dough 1/8 inch (3 mm) thick. Cut out forty cookies, using a 2-inch (5-cm) fluted cookie cutter. Place the cookies on a sheet pan lined with baking paper.

5. Place the reserved coconut mixture in a pastry bag with a no. 8 (16-mm) star tip. Pipe the coconut batter onto the Short Dough, holding the bag straight up above the cookies to make a star design. If the batter seems difficult to pipe or is too runny, adjust with an additional egg or extra ground coconut.

6. Make a small indentation in the top of the coconut batter. Put the raspberry jam into a piping bag and pipe it into the indentations.

7. Bake the cookies at 400°F (205°C) until the top of the coconut batter starts to brown and the Short Dough is golden, about 15 minutes.

8. Brush Simple Syrup over the pastries as soon as they come out of the oven, taking care not to soak them. Let cool completely.

9. Hold on to the baked coconut topping, and dip the Short Dough, including the top of the Short Dough cookie, into melted dark coating chocolate. Allow the excess to drip back into the bowl, scrape the bottom against the side of the bowl, and place the cookies on baking paper.

10. Move the cookies on the paper once or twice before the chocolate sets up completely to remove excess chocolate. If you have trouble with this dipping method, set the cookie on top of a dipping fork as you immerse it in the chocolate, to prevent it from breaking and falling in the chocolate.

11. Store Coconut Macaroons covered, in a cool dry place.

Florentinas

35 cookies

Florentina Batter (recipe follows)
bittersweet chocolate, tempered
  (see note 2)

NOTE 1: To make a simplified Florentina cookie, just drop small portions of batter directly onto the baking paper and flatten the batter slightly before baking. Don't bother with drawing the circles, cutting the baked cookies, or coating them with chocolate. Do not bake more than you can use in one day, however, because the cookies will become soft after one day without the chocolate coating.

NOTE 2: If you do not have time to temper the chocolate, use dark coating chocolate instead.

You will find these classic irresistible cookies in just about every pastry shop in continental Europe and Scandinavia, often with the addition of chopped candied fruit (see note 3). The cookies can be left flat or molded into a curved shape made by draping the soft cookies over a rolling pin and leaving them to set up. Most often they are about 3 inches (7.5 cm) in diameter, round, and flat with chocolate on one side combed into a wavy pattern. The chocolate is added not only because it looks and tastes good but also because it helps to prevent the cookies from becoming soft. Florentinas are also made into cookie shells shaped in the manner of pirouettes or in cones and are used in many types of elegant desserts and filled pastries.

The name Florentina implies that these cookies originated in Italy, but if the city of Florence had anything to do with the title I have not been able to find it documented. However, strangely enough, I have found references to these cookies as an Austrian invention. The term à la florentine is used in savory cooking, usually with egg, fish, or white meat dishes, and suggests the dish contains spinach and often a gratinéed white sauce.

The method used here for making the Florentinas perfectly round is practical only if you are making a small quantity and you have a use for the scrap pieces (although unless you hide them they will be nibbled away in record time).

Add enough Simple Syrup (see page 11) to the coating chocolate to thicken it to the consistency of tempered chocolate so the combed pattern will hold its shape.

NOTE 3: To prepare Florentinas with candied fruit, add up to 6 ounces (170 g) of diced candied and/or dried fruit at the end of step 2 in the Florentina Batter recipe after removing the batter from the heat, and omit the rolled oats. A colorful combination is Candied Orange Peel, candied angelica, and dried or candied cherries.

To produce these cookies in a large quantity and/or on a regular basis, you should purchase special Florentina baking sheets. These are silicone coated with very shallow round indentations in which the batter spreads out into perfect circles. Special sheets are also available for forming the chocolate coating. These pans have round indentations with the same diameter as the cookie pans, but the indentations are even thinner and have the classic wavy pattern on the bottom. Chocolate is spread in the indentations, left to harden in the refrigerator, and then the chocolate discs and the cookies are sandwiched together with a little additional melted chocolate. If the chef is using this method he or she is probably using one of the convenient (and foolproof) Florentina mixes that are also available.

1. Draw thirty-five 3¼-inch (8.1-cm) circles on baking paper, using a plain cookie cutter as a guide. Invert the papers, place them on sheet pans, and set aside while you make the batter.

2. Using two spoons, divide the Florentina Batter between the circles, flattening and spreading it to within ¼ inch (6 mm) of the drawn lines. Wet the spoons to keep the batter from sticking.

3. Bake at 375°F (190°C) for about 8 minutes or until light brown. Stagger the baking so you will have time to trim the edges of the cookies immediately as you take each pan from the oven.

4. If the cookies are just a little uneven, place a cookie cutter that is slightly larger than the baked cookie around the cookie (not on top). Using a circular motion, push the soft cookie into a nice even round shape. If the cookies are very uneven, or have spread too far beyond the lines, transfer the baking paper with the baked cookies on it to a piece of cardboard, or an even tabletop. Use a 3¼-inch (8.1-cm) cookie cutter to cut out the center of the cookie to the correct size. Pull the baking paper back on the pan, let the cookies cool, then break off the excess from the outside (Figure 5–12).

5. When the cookies are cold, brush a thick layer of bittersweet chocolate on the bottom (flat) side. For the classic Florentina look, comb the chocolate into a wavy pattern, using a cake-decorating comb, before the chocolate hardens. Do not refrigerate Florentinas.

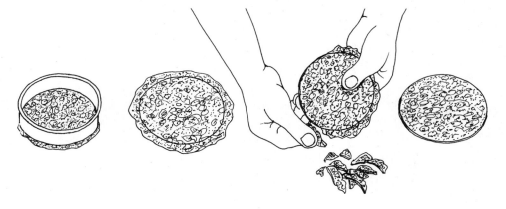

FIGURE 5–12   Cutting Florentinas while they are still soft to even the edges; breaking off the uneven edges after they have hardened; a finished cookie with a clean edge

Florentina Batter

7 ounces (200 g) unsalted butter
6 ounces (170 g) granulated sugar
3 tablespoons (45 ml) or 2 ounces (55 g) glucose or corn syrup
¼ cup (60 ml) heavy cream
7 ounces (200 g) sliced almonds, lightly crushed
2 ounces (55 g) rolled oats

1. Combine the butter, sugar, glucose (or corn syrup), and cream in a saucepan; bring to a boil.

2. Add the almonds and oats and cook over medium heat for 2 to 3 minutes. Remove the batter from the heat.

3. Try baking a small piece of batter as a test. If the batter spreads out too thin, cook the batter in the saucepan a little longer. Conversely, if the batter does not spread enough, add a little more cream and test again; you will need to warm the batter to mix in the cream. Although Florentina Batter does not have to be baked immediately, it is easier to work with if it is spread into the desired shape as soon as possible. If the batter has set up and is too firm to spread, you will need to reheat it. Reheating may cause the butter to separate, but mixing in a small amount of cream will remedy this.

Gingersnaps

120 cookies

8 ounces (225 g) soft unsalted butter
1 pound, 6 ounces (625 g) granulated sugar
3 eggs
1 cup (240 ml) or 12 ounces (340 g) molasses
2 tablespoons (30 ml) white vinegar
1 pound, 12 ounces (795 g) bread flour
2 tablespoons (24 g) baking soda
4 teaspoons (8 g) ground ginger
1 teaspoon (1.5 g) ground cinnamon
1 teaspoon (2 g) ground cloves
1 teaspoon (2 g) ground cardamom
granulated sugar

NOTE: These are great refrigerator cookies. Form the dough into ropes; then slice and bake as needed.

As the name implies, these cookies should be dry and crisp. Nonetheless, I actually prefer them soft and chewy, which is what happens when they are left uncovered overnight. Be careful to mix the butter and sugar together just to combine. If you cream or beat them together you will incorporate too much air, which causes the cookies to spread out too far as they bake, making them thin and unpleasant looking.

1. Using the dough hook at low speed, mix the butter and measured sugar together until well combined. Incorporate eggs, molasses, and vinegar.

2. Sift together the flour, baking soda, ginger, cinnamon, cloves, and cardamom. Add to the butter mixture and mix on low speed just until combined. Refrigerate.

3. Divide the dough into four equal pieces, approximately 1 pound, 2 ounces (510 g) each. Roll each piece into a rope and cut each rope into thirty pieces.

4. Form the pieces into round balls and roll the balls in granulated sugar to cover. Place the cookies on sheet pans lined with baking paper.

5. Bake at 375°F (190°C) until light brown on top but still soft in the center, approximately 10 minutes.

Hazelnut Butter Cookies

approximately 110 cookies

1 pound, 5 ounces (595 g) soft unsalted butter
11 ounces (310 g) granulated sugar

One of my own favorites, and the cookie most begged for among my colleagues. A word of warning: Be sure to press the hazelnuts all the way to the bottom of the pan or they will bake loose in the oven and fall off. I got into a little trouble with these cookies myself as an apprentice. My boss told me that half of the cookies in the showcase had just an empty hole in the center! He instructed me to "push the nuts down firmly," so I did. A few days later it was the same story all over again, except this time, naturally, my boss was a bit angry. Since I knew for certain that I pressed those nuts down all the way to the

12 ounces (340 g) hazelnuts, finely
    ground

1 pound, 5 ounces (595 g) bread flour

1/2 teaspoon (2 g) baking soda

whole hazelnuts, lightly toasted, skins
    removed

NOTE: *This recipe can be made with walnuts,
cashews, or pecans; you can also combine different types of nuts.*

*metal (yes, I'm afraid there was no baking paper way back then), I got a little
suspicious and decided to conduct an investigation. The next time I made the
cookies I walked up to the shop a few moments after the prep girl had picked up
the sheet pan and peeked around the corner. Sure enough, while transferring the
cookies to the showcase tray, she was picking the nuts off and eating them as
fast as she could chew!*

1. Using the dough hook at low to medium speed, mix the butter
and sugar together. Add the ground nuts.

2. Sift the flour with the baking soda. Blend into the butter mixture
on low speed, mixing only until just combined. Refrigerate the dough if
necessary.

3. Divide the dough into three pieces (this can be done by eye; it
need not be exact) and roll each piece into a rope 1 1/2 inches (3.7 cm) in
diameter. Refrigerate the ropes until firm.

4. Slice the ropes into 3/8-inch (9-mm) cookies. Place the cookies,
staggered, on sheet pans lined with baking paper. Leave the cookies at
room temperature until they are fairly soft.

5. Push a hazelnut, point up, into the center of each cookie. Push
the nut all the way down to the sheet pan so it will not fall off after the
cookies are baked (if you try to do this while the dough is still firm it
will crack).

6. Bake at 375°F (190°C) for about 12 minutes or until the cookies
are golden brown. Store the Hazelnut Butter Cookies in airtight containers to prevent softening.

Hazelnut-Almond Squares

ninety-six 2-inch (5-cm) cookies

6 ounces (170 g) hazelnuts

15 ounces (430 g) granulated sugar

10 ounces (285 g) soft unsalted butter

3 eggs

1 teaspoon (5 ml) vanilla extract

8 ounces (225 g) bread flour

2 tablespoons (16 g) unsweetened
    cocoa powder

1 tablespoon (12 g) baking powder

1 1/2 ounces (40 g) sliced almonds

*Another of my favorites, partly because I don't get to have them very often. I
think you too will find it impossible to eat just one cookie, but I try not to feel
guilty, because at least the cookies are small and thin. Although not the best production cookie, since you have to stand by and cut them as soon as the sheet
comes out of oven, these are a good choice when you want an unusual addition
to your assortment.*

1. Toast the hazelnuts and remove the skin (see note on pages 965
and 966). Crush coarsely, using a rolling pin, and reserve.

2. Beat the sugar and butter together until light and creamy, using
the paddle at medium speed. Add the eggs and vanilla.

3. Sift the flour, cocoa powder, and baking powder together. Mix
into the batter together with the reserved hazelnuts.

4. Spread the batter evenly over a 24-by-16-inch (60-×-40-cm)
sheet of baking paper. You will have to spread back and forth a few
extra times to fill in the lines made by the crushed nuts as you drag
them across. Sprinkle the sliced almonds over the batter.

5. Drag the baking paper onto a sheet pan (see Figure 16–15,
page 842).

6. Bake at 375°F (190°C) for about 20 minutes. When the sliced almonds on top start to brown, it is a pretty good indication that the cookies are done.

7. Cut the sheet into 2-inch (5-cm) squares as soon as it comes out of the oven. Store the cookies in airtight containers so that they remain crisp.

 Heide Sand Cookies

75 cookies

1 pound, 10 ounces (740 g) bread flour
7 ounces (200 g) powdered sugar
1 pound, 5 ounces (595 g) soft unsalted butter
a few drops of lemon juice
½ teaspoon (2.5 ml) vanilla extract
pale pink decorating sugar (see note)
8 ounces (225 g) smooth apricot jam

NOTE: To make the decorating sugar, add drops of red food coloring to granulated sugar and rub between the palms of your hands to mix the color into the sugar. Add more color gradually until the desired shade has been achieved.

I have not been able to find out how these cookies got their curious name. Perhaps a Frau Heide used to make them at one time and the cookies were named after her. Heide Sand Cookies are made throughout the German-speaking part of Europe and in Scandinavia as well. After forming the ropes, you can store the dough in the freezer, or for up to one week in the refrigerator, to slice and bake as needed. Leave the ropes at room temperature for about five minutes before rolling them in decorating sugar.

1. Sift the flour with the powdered sugar. Place in a mixing bowl with the butter, lemon juice, and vanilla. Mix, using the dough hook at low speed, until smooth. Refrigerate the dough if necessary to make it easier to handle.

2. Divide the dough into three pieces, about 1 pound, 4 ounces (570 g) each. Roll the pieces into ropes, pressing the dough together to compact it. The ropes should be about 10 inches (25 cm) long. Do not use any flour as you roll, as it will prevent the colored sugar from sticking.

3. Place the ropes in the colored sugar and roll to make them 12 inches (30 cm) long. Remove the ropes from the sugar.

4. Using the palm of your hand, flatten the side nearest you to form a smooth teardrop shape (Figure 5–13). Refrigerate the ropes until firm.

5. Cut each rope into twenty-five slices. Arrange the pieces on sheet pans lined with baking paper. Let the cookie slices sit at room temperature until softened.

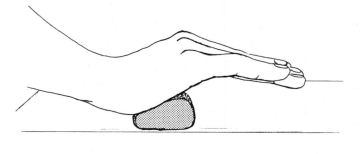

FIGURE 5–13   *Using the palm of the hand to flatten one side of the cookie dough rope to form Heide Sand Cookies into a teardrop shape*

6. Make an indentation in the wider part of the cookies and fill it with apricot jam.

7. Bake at 375°F (190°C) for about 15 minutes or until the cookies are golden brown. Store the baked cookies in airtight containers to keep them crisp.

Honey Oatmeal Cookies

80 cookies

1 pound, 3 ounces (540 g) soft unsalted butter

8 ounces (225 g) granulated sugar

9 ounces (255 g) dark raisins

8 ounces (225 g) rolled oats

1 teaspoon (5 ml) vanilla extract

3/4 cup (180 ml) or 9 ounces (255 g) honey

1 teaspoon (4 g) baking soda

1 pound, 5 ounces (595 g) bread flour

While American kids grow up with peanut butter and chocolate chip cookies, their counterparts in Sweden enjoy oatmeal cookies with the same degree of enthusiasm. These cookies continue to be irresistible to me. The baked cookies don't really spread out much; they hold their shape and are crisp like shortbread. For a soft oatmeal cookie, try the recipe for Chewy Trail Mix Cookies or Oat and Date Chews.

1. Beat the butter and sugar together lightly. Add the raisins, rolled oats, vanilla, and honey; mix until combined.

2. Sift the baking soda with the flour; mix into the batter. Refrigerate the dough if necessary.

3. Divide the dough into four equal pieces, about 1 pound (455 g) each. Roll each piece into a rope 16 inches (40 cm) long. Refrigerate the ropes until firm.

4. Cut each rope into twenty pieces. To save time, try placing two ropes together and cut them simultaneously.

5. Place the slices, staggered, cut-side down, on sheet pans lined with baking paper. Use a fork to flatten and mark the cookies.

6. Bake at 375°F (190°C) until golden brown, about 15 minutes. Keep the baked cookies in airtight containers to prevent them from getting soft.

Macadamia Nut Cookies

80 cookies

14 ounces (400 g) granulated sugar

3 ounces (85 g) light brown sugar

12 ounces (340 g) soft unsalted butter

3 eggs

1 teaspoon (5 ml) vanilla extract

1 pound, 3 ounces (540 g) bread flour

1/2 teaspoon (2 g) baking soda

9 ounces (255 g) chopped macadamia nuts

9 ounces (255 g) shredded coconut

Unfortunately, the scarcity of macadamia nuts keeps the price high; sometimes as much as three times that of walnuts, almonds, and hazelnuts. You can substitute any of those for the macadamias in this recipe (chop or crush them coarsely), but what I prefer as an alternate are pine nuts. Leave them whole and toast them before mixing into the dough.

1. Using the dough hook at low to medium speed, cream the granulated sugar, brown sugar, and butter together until light and fluffy. Mix in the eggs and vanilla.

2. Sift the flour with the baking soda and incorporate into the batter on low speed, together with the nuts and the coconut.

3. Divide the dough into four equal pieces; they will weigh about 1 pound, 2 ounces (510 g) each. Roll each piece into a rope 2 inches (5 cm) thick.

4. Cut each rope into twenty equal pieces. Stagger the pieces on sheet pans lined with baking paper.

5. Bake at 375°F (190°C) until the cookies are just starting to color at the edges, about 12 minutes. Like Chocolate Chip Cookies, these cookies taste best if they are a little chewy.

 ## Madeleines

sixty 2¹/₂-by-1¹/₂-inch (6.2-×-3.7-cm) cookies

Butter and Flour Mixture (page 4)
9 ounces (255 g) granulated sugar
4 ounces (115 g) bread flour
4 ounces (115 g) cake flour
4 ounces (115 g) finely ground
    blanched almonds
6 eggs
1 teaspoon (5 g) salt
9 ounces (255 g) noisette butter, at
    room temperature (see note 1)
2 teaspoons (10 ml) orange blossom
    water
2 teaspoons (10 ml) vanilla extract
powdered sugar

NOTE 1: Noisette butter, or beurre noisette, *is the French term for "brown butter." Noisette is the French word for hazelnut, and the term refers to both the color and fragrance of the butter after browning. To prepare* beurre noisette, *cook the butter over low heat until it reaches a light brown color and is fragrant. Be careful not to burn the butter. The word* noisette *is also used in cooking to refer to small (round) medallions of lamb or veal.*

NOTE 2: For lemon-flavored Madeleines replace the orange blossom water with the grated zest of two lemons.

*T*hese small scallop-shaped sponge cakes were made immortal by the French writer Marcel Proust around 1912 in his celebrated Remembrance of Things Past. *Here Proust recalls the taste of a Madeleine dunked in lime blossom tea, given to him by his aunt. I particularly like what A. J. Liebling had to say about the connection: "In the light of what Proust wrote with so mild a stimulus, it is the world's loss he did not have a heartier appetite; with a full meal he might have written a masterpiece."*

Legend has it that these little cakes were named for their inventor, a French pastry chef from Commercy, which is a small town in Lorraine. Madeleines are served much as any fancy cookie or petite four sec, with the exception that dipping them in coffee or tea is more socially acceptable; after all, Proust did so.

1. Brush the Butter and Flour Mixture on the inside of sixty Madeleine forms. Reserve.

2. Sift the sugar and flours together. Mix in the ground almonds.

3. Whip the eggs and salt at high speed until foamy, about 2 minutes. Add the flour mixture in two parts alternating with the noisette butter. Mix in the orange blossom water and vanilla.

4. Cover the batter and let it rest in the refrigerator for 1 hour.

5. Place the batter in a pastry bag with a no. 5 (10-mm) plain tip. Pipe the batter into the prepared forms filling them to just below the rim.

6. Bake at 450°F (230°C) for approximately 8 minutes or until the tops are until golden brown and spring back when pressed lightly in the center. Unmold and sprinkle powdered sugar lightly over the tops.

 ## Oat and Date Chews

64 cookies

12 ounces (340 g) pitted dates
12 ounces (340 g) light brown sugar
12 ounces (340 g) granulated sugar

*T*hese are easy-to-make, wholesome cookies without any fussy techniques— in fact, you don't even have to soften and cream the butter; it is actually preferable if a few small lumps of butter remain in the dough. Try using soft Medjool dates, which are available in most grocery or health-food stores. You will have to pit them, but their flavor is well worth the extra effort. Lacking Medjool, use any packaged dates that are convenient or, for a change, replace

1 pound (455 g) firm unsalted butter

½ cup (120 ml) or 6 ounces (170 g) honey

5 eggs

2 tablespoons (30 ml) vanilla extract

1 pound, 8 ounces (680 g) bread flour

2 teaspoons (7 g) ammonium carbonate

2 teaspoons (8 g) baking soda

1 pound (455 g) rolled oats

12 ounces (340 g) dark raisins

1 pound, 8 ounces (680 g) chopped walnuts

the dates with dried cherries or dried cranberries. Cranberries not only provide color, they give the cookies a great tangy flavor.

1. Chop the dates into raisin-sized pieces and reserve.

2. Combine the brown and granulated sugars in a mixing bowl. Add the firm butter, cut into chunks, and the honey. Mix with the paddle attachment until combined. Do not cream the mixture together; small lumps of butter should remain.

3. Beat the eggs with the vanilla extract in a separate bowl. Add to the sugar mixture and mix to combine.

4. Sift together the flour, the ammonium carbonate, and the baking soda. Incorporate into the dough without overmixing. Mix in the oats and then the raisins, dates, and half of the walnuts, reserving the remainder for decorating. Refrigerate the dough until it is firm enough to work with.

5. Divide the dough into four equal pieces, approximately 1 pound, 14 ounces (855 g) each. Roll each piece into a 16-inch (40-cm) log, and cut each log into sixteen equal slices. Roll the pieces into balls and then roll the balls lightly in the reserved chopped walnuts. Place the cookies on sheet pans lined with baking paper.

6. Bake at 350°F (175°C) for approximately 25 minutes.

Oat Flakes

approximately one hundred 2½-inch (6.2-cm) cookies

9 ounces (255 g) melted unsalted butter

8 ounces (225 g) rolled oats

3 eggs

12 ounces (340 g) granulated sugar

1 ounce (30 g) bread flour

3 tablespoons (36 g) baking powder

dark coating chocolate, melted

Oat Flakes are a peasant-style Florentina cookie: less expensive oats replace the almonds. Keep the batter in the refrigerator and, ideally, bake only as many cookies as you will serve the same day. They taste great plain if they are freshly baked. The oats continue to absorb moisture even after the cookies have been baked, which causes them to become soft rather quickly. For longer storage, the chocolate coating helps to keep them crisp.

Another way to form these cookies is to pipe the batter on the bottom of small, buttered half-sphere forms, about 2 inches (5 cm) in diameter. The batter will climb up the sides of the forms as it bakes, the same as if you had lined the inside of the form. Mazarin forms may also be used with this method. Serve the baked cookies inverted.

Oak Flakes batter should be made the day before it is used to allow the oats time to absorb moisture, which in turn helps to prevent the cookies from spreading too much. If time does not permit you to start one day in advance, allow the batter to rest for a minimum of 4 hours.

1. Combine the butter and oats. Blend in the eggs and sugar. Mix the flour and baking powder together; then incorporate into the batter. Refrigerate overnight.

2. Place the batter in a pastry bag with a no. 6 (12-mm) plain tip. Pipe into cherry-sized cookies on sheet pans lined with baking paper; do not crowd the cookies, as they will spread out quite a bit.

3. Bake at 375°F (190°C) about 8 minutes; the whole surface of the cookies should be golden brown, not just the edges.

4. When the cookies have cooled completely, brush melted dark coating chocolate on the back. For a variation, you can sandwich two cookies together before the chocolate hardens. Store the cookies in an airtight container; they become soft easily.

Orange Macaroons

96 cookies

1 pound, 8 ounces (680 g) blanched almonds

1 pound, 6 ounces (625 g) granulated sugar

11 ounces (310 g) Candied Orange Peel (page 978)

1 pound, 6 ounces (625 g) powdered sugar

4 ounces (115 g) bread flour

½ teaspoon (2.5 ml) orange flower water

8 egg whites (1 cup/240 ml)

powdered sugar

ninety-six whole almonds with skin

This variety of macaroon cookie is convenient to keep in mind if you do not have Almond Paste on hand. It is a good idea to bake a few test cookies to make sure they spread out properly before rolling all of the dough; they should spread out flat like Chocolate Chip Cookies. If the cookies do not spread out enough, add more egg white; if they spread too thin add a small amount of flour.

1. Grind the blanched almonds and granulated sugar to a coarse consistency. Add the orange peel and continue grinding to a very fine consistency; transfer to a mixing bowl.

2. Add the measured powdered sugar, flour, orange flower water, and egg whites. Blend until all of the ingredients are incorporated.

3. Divide the dough into six equal pieces, approximately 1 pound (455 g) each. Roll each piece into a rope 16 inches (40 cm) long, using powdered sugar to prevent the dough from sticking.

4. Cut each rope into sixteen pieces. Roll the small pieces into balls, then roll the balls in powdered sugar to coat them completely. Place on sheet pans lined with baking paper.

5. Flatten the cookies just enough so that they do not roll. Press a whole almond on top of each cookie in the center.

6. Bake at 325°F (163°C) for approximately 12 minutes or until very lightly browned. When cool, store covered to prevent the macaroons from drying out.

Palm Leaves

about forty-five 3-inch (7.5-cm) cookies

2 pounds (910 g) Puff Pastry (page 44)

8 ounces (225 g) granulated sugar, approximately

dark coating chocolate (optional)

Vanilla Buttercream (page 978) (optional)

These are most often known by their French name, Palmier, *which literally translates to "palm tree." The distinctive shape of the baked cookies resembles the leaves of a palm. It is not documented who first came up with the idea of rolling Puff Pastry out in sugar and then giving it what amounts to a double-double turn in the wrong direction, but research shows the cookies were invented in the beginning of the twentieth century.*

The granulated sugar not only takes the place of flour to prevent the dough from sticking but it also makes the Palm Leaves crisp, shiny, and sweet, as the sugar caramelizes while the cookies are baking. You may not use up all of the sugar in the recipe, but the more sugar you can roll into the Puff Pastry the better. Should you fail to roll enough sugar into the dough, the cookies will not only be less sweet, they could spread out too far and lose their special shape.

1. Roll out the Puff Pastry in the granulated sugar to make a 24-by-12-inch (60-×-30-cm) rectangle about ⅛ inch (3 mm) thick. If the dough is uneven or too large on any side, trim it to the proper dimen-

NOTE: Palm Leaves can be served as is, or you can dip the tip of each cookie into melted dark coating chocolate. Two cookies (with or without chocolate) can also be sandwiched together with buttercream.

FIGURE 5–14   Slicing Palm Leaves

sions. Keep turning and moving the dough as you roll it out, spreading the sugar evenly underneath and on top of the Puff Pastry at the same time, to keep the dough from sticking to the table.

2. Place the dough in front of you horizontally. Fold the long sides of the rectangle in toward the center leaving a ¹/₂-inch (1.2-cm) opening between them.

3. Fold in half in the opposite direction (crosswise) to bring the two short sides together at the right side.

4. Using a dowel about 1 inch (2.5 cm) in diameter, make a shallow indentation horizontally down the center of the folded dough. Do not press too hard or the Puff Pastry will become too thin and the cookies will break apart as they expand in the oven. Fold in half again on this line (the indentation makes it possible to fold the dough again and still have the edges line up squarely). Refrigerate the strip until firm.

5. Cut the folded strip into slices ¹/₈ inch (3 mm) thick (Figure 5–14). Place the slices cut-side up, on sheet pans lined with baking paper. Keep in mind as you place them on the pans that they will spread to about three times as wide while baking.

6. Bake at 425°F (219°C) until the sugar starts to caramelize and turn golden on the bottoms, about 8 minutes.

7. Remove the pan from the oven and quickly turn each cookie over on the pan using a spatula or metal scraper. Return the cookies to the oven and bake for a few minutes longer or until as much sugar as possible has caramelized on the tops. Let the cookies cool.

Peanut Butter Cookies

60 cookies

8 ounces (225 g) soft unsalted butter
8 ounces (225 g) granulated sugar
6 ounces (170 g) light brown sugar
9 ounces (255 g) chunky peanut butter
2 eggs
2 teaspoons (10 ml) vanilla extract
13 ounces (370 g) bread flour
4 teaspoons (16 g) baking powder
¹/₂ teaspoon (3 g) salt
2 ounces (55 g) sweet dark chocolate, finely chopped
4 ounces (115 g) toasted peanuts, coarsely chopped
6 ounces (170 g) currants or raisins

*T*hese cookies are always a big hit with kids. Instead of currants or raisins, try adding dates chopped to the same size. And for something really special, dip the baked and cooled cookies halfway into melted dark coating chocolate.

1. Using the paddle attachment, cream the butter, both sugars, and the peanut butter until fluffy. Add the eggs and vanilla extract.

2. Sift together the bread flour, baking powder, and salt. Add to the butter mixture along with the chocolate, peanuts, and currants or raisins, mixing at low speed only until the ingredients are combined. Chill the dough until firm.

3. Divide the dough into three equal pieces, about 1 pound, 2 ounces (510 g) each. Roll each piece into a rope and cut the ropes into twenty pieces each.

4. Place the small pieces on sheet pans lined with baking paper. Flatten each cookie with a fork.

5. Bake at 375°F (190°C) for about 10 minutes.

Pirouettes

about eighty 3-inch (7.5-cm) cookies

8 ounces (225 g) granulated sugar
3½ ounces (100 g) cake flour
½ cup (120 ml) heavy cream
½ teaspoon (2.5 ml) vanilla extract
4 egg whites (½ cup/120 ml), at room temperature
4 ounces (115 g) melted unsalted butter
unsweetened cocoa powder (optional)

Pirouette *is a ballet term that means "a rapid spin of the body on the point of the toe." Here, it refers to the way the just-baked cookie wafers are curled around a dowel, which also must be done rapidly. Pirouettes can be served plain or with the ends dipped into melted coating chocolate. They may also be filled and served as a pastry. Additionally, a portion of the batter can be colored with unsweetened cocoa powder at the rate of 1 teaspoon (2.5 g) per 2 tablespoons (30 ml) of batter. Use a piping bag with a very small opening to decorate the batter with spirals or parallel lines after you have spread it within the template. Bake as directed. Roll the striped cookies so that the lines run diagonally rather than horizontally or vertically.*

1. Combine 2 ounces (55 g) of the sugar with the flour. Gradually stir in the cream and vanilla, and mix until smooth Set aside to rest for about 30 minutes.

2. While the batter is resting, make a round 3-inch (7.5-cm) template from cardboard that is ¹/₁₆ inch (2 mm) thick. Grease and flour the back of (inverted) even sheet pans (or use silicone mats which do not need to be greased and floured).

3. Whip the egg whites to a foam. Gradually add the remaining 6 ounces (170 g) of sugar and whip to soft peaks. Fold the reserved batter into the egg whites. Fold in the melted butter.

4. Using the template, spread out thin wafers on the prepared sheet pans (see method shown in Figures 19–55 and 19–56, pages 1046 and 1047) or silicone mats.

5. Bake at 400°F (205°C) until light brown in a few spots (this will ensure that the cookies are cooked enough to become crisp when cold), about 5 minutes.

6. Immediately roll the hot wafers around a dowel that is just large enough in diameter to allow the ends of the wafer to meet and overlap very slightly. Press the edges together to make them stick. Push each finished Pirouette to the opposite end of the dowel and leave it there until it is firm. Continue forming the remaining wafers in the same way. If the cookies become too brittle to bend easily, reheat until soft. Store the Pirouettes in airtight containers to keep them crisp and brittle.

Raspberry Turnovers

24 cookies

1 pound, 2 ounces (510 g) Short Dough (page 54)
5 ounces (140 g) raspberry jam
Egg Wash (page 7)
sanding sugar
sliced almonds, crushed

These little Swedish cookies can double as a simple pastry. Use fresh Short Dough that has not been rolled out previously; the dough will break when folded if too much flour has been mixed into it. The jam should be fairly thick so it will not run when you pipe it. The turnovers taste best if served the same day they are baked; the jam tends to dry out a little after a day or so. Raspberry Turnovers can be made up in large batches and stored in the refrigerator or freezer. Bake as needed directly from the freezer.

1. Roll out the Short Dough ⅛ inch (3 mm) thick. Cut out twenty-four cookies using a 3-inch (7.5-cm) fluted cookie cutter.

2. Place the raspberry jam in a disposable pastry bag made from a half sheet of baking paper (see Figures 1–6 and 1–7, page 24). Pipe the jam onto each circle, slightly off center and toward you, dividing it evenly between the cookies.

3. Brush Egg Wash on the lower edge of the dough. Fold the top over the jam and onto the lower half. Press the edges together with your fingers.

4. Combine equal parts of sugar and almonds. Brush the tops of the turnovers with Egg Wash, then invert them into the almond and sugar mixture. Be sure not to get any Egg Wash or sugar on the bottom of the turnovers or it will burn. Place the turnovers, right-side up, on sheet pans lined with baking paper.

5. Bake at 375°F (190°C) until golden brown, about 10 minutes.

Rugelach

48 cookies

Dough

12 ounces (340 g) soft unsalted butter
12 ounces (340 g) soft cream cheese
6 ounces (170 g) granulated sugar
1 teaspoon (5 g) salt
2 teaspoons (10 ml) vanilla extract
4 egg yolks (1/3 cup/80 ml)
1 pound (455 g) bread flour

Apricot Filling

3 ounces (85 g) walnuts
2 ounces (55 g) granulated sugar
1/2 teaspoon (.75 g) ground cinnamon
12 ounces (340 g) smooth apricot jam
Egg Wash (page 7)

Rugelach (also spelled Rugalach) are cookies from eastern Europe whose name derives from the Yiddish word rugel, *translating to "royal." They are also known as* kipfel *and in this country cheese* bagelach *(it seems the cream cheese was an American addition). Good Rugelach should be more chewy than flaky, so it is important not to make the dough too short. The cookies are made with several types of fillings, including various jams, poppy seed paste, and chocolate. To replace the apricot filling with chocolate filling for this recipe, combine 6 ounces (170 g) grated sweet dark chocolate, 2 ounces (55 g) grated unsweetened chocolate (or use a total of 8 ounces/225 g semisweet chocolate), 1 egg, 2 ounces (55 g) granulated sugar, and 8 ounces (225 g) AA confectioners' sugar, mixing to form a paste. If necessary, add one more egg (or part of one) to make the paste spreadable.*

1. Using the ingredients listed for the dough, combine the butter, cream cheese, sugar, and salt in a mixing bowl. Beat until light and fluffy. Incorporate the vanilla and the egg yolks. Gradually add the flour and mix until just combined. Transfer the dough to a lightly floured baking table and knead gently until the dough is smooth.

2. Divide the dough into three equal pieces, form them into rounds, cover, and refrigerate for approximately 2 hours to relax the gluten.

3. To make the filling, place the walnuts, sugar, and cinnamon in a food processor and process until the walnuts are finely chopped. Reserve.

4. Roll one of the dough rounds into a 14-inch (35-cm) circle, using flour to prevent the dough from sticking. Spread one-third of the jam over the dough. Sprinkle one-third of the nut mixture evenly over the jam.

5. Use a plain pastry wheel or a chef's knife to cut the circle into sixteen equal wedges. Dip either tool into water from time to time to keep it from skicking. Starting at the wide end, roll each wedge up to the point as you would a Croissant. Place the Rugelach on sheet pans lined with baking paper, placing them straight (do *not* bend them into half-circles like Croissant).

6. Repeat steps 4 and 5 with the remaining dough, jam, and nut mixture.

7. Brush Egg Wash lightly over the tops of the cookies. Bake, double-panned, at 350°F (175°C) for approximately 30 minutes or until golden brown and baked through.

Sesame Seed Cookies

50 cookies

10 ounces (285 g) granulated sugar
1 pound (455 g) soft lard (do not substitute another fat)
3 eggs, at room temperature
1 pound (455 g) bread flour
1 teaspoon (3.5 g) ammonium carbonate (see note)
sesame seeds

NOTE: *Make sure your oven is not too hot, or the cookies will flatten and become too dark around the edges. If ammonium carbonate is not available substitute a mixture of baking powder and baking soda (in equal amounts).*

This simple recipe was given to me by an old Chinese baker in the small village of Qufu, which is located northeast of Shanghai, off the main road, on the way to Beijing. The village is famous as the birthplace of Confucius. It was certainly the highlight of my trip during a three-week culinary exchange I was invited to participate in together with Jacques Pepin and Cindy Pawlcyn. We taught the Chinese chefs Western cooking, and they showed us their tricks. With all of the many Chinese delicacies, and their sometimes (to us from the West) unusual way of preparing them, on the whole they do not fancy dessert much. We were generally served litchi fruit, oranges, or cookies such as almond or these sesame cookies. When I questioned (through an interpreter) the use of lard in this recipe, I was told very firmly that under no circumstances should any fat other than lard be used! Lard is what gives the cookies their special character. Through my students I have found that the average American does not care for this refined pork fat; however, when given a cookie to try they rarely wrinkle their noses.

1. Place the granulated sugar and the lard in a mixing bowl and beat until creamy. Mix in the eggs one at a time.

2. Sift the bread flour and the ammonium carbonate together. Add to the lard mixture and blend until incorporated.

3. Place the dough on a sheet pan lined with baking paper. Refrigerate until well chilled.

4. Divide the dough into two pieces, 1 pound, 4 ounces (570 g) each. Roll the pieces out to 16-inch (40-cm) ropes, using flour to prevent the dough from sticking.

5. Cut each rope into twenty-five equal pieces. Roll the small pieces between your hands to form balls. Roll the balls in sesame seeds, coating all sides.

6. Place the cookies 1 inch (2.5 cm) apart on sheet pans lined with baking paper. Press down on the top of each cookie just enough so that it will not roll.

7. Bake at 350°F (175°C) for about 20 minutes or until golden brown.

Spritz Rings

about 100 cookies

1 pound, 5 ounces (595 g) unsalted
  butter, at room temperature
10 ounces (285 g) powdered sugar
3 egg yolks (¼ cup/60 ml)
1 teaspoon (5 ml) vanilla extract
1 pound, 11 ounces (765 g) bread
  flour
raspberry jam (optional)

These are considered an absolute must on an assorted cookie tray in Scandinavia. While basically a plain sugar and butter cookie, it is the ring shape that makes these so pretty and decorative. If you are making lots of Spritz Rings all the time, a fast and easy production method is to pipe out several long strips of dough, parallel to one another, on top of the table. Cut through the strips every 6 or 7 inches (15 to 17.5 cm), then pick up the short pieces one at a time and quickly twist them into a circle around two fingers as you move them to the sheet pan.

1. The butter must be quite soft or you will have trouble piping out the dough. Beat the butter and sugar for a few minutes with the paddle at medium speed. Mix in the egg yolks and vanilla. Add the flour and mix until you have a smooth, pliable dough.

2. Place the dough in a pastry bag with a no. 4 (8-mm) star tip. Do not put too much dough in the bag at one time or it will be much more difficult to pipe out. Pipe out 2-inch (5-cm) rings, or 2½-inch (6.2-cm) **S** shapes, on sheet pans lined with baking paper. If you make the **S** shape, the ends should curl in and close.

3. Make an indentation in each curled part of the **S**. Place the jam in a disposable pastry bag and pipe a small amount into the indentations.

4. Bake at 375°F (190°C) until golden brown, about 15 minutes. Store Spritz Rings in airtight containers to keep them crisp.

Strassburger Cookies

about 80 cookies

1 pound, 8 ounces (680 g) soft
  unsalted butter
1 pound (455 g) powdered sugar
6 eggs
3 egg yolks (¼ cup/60 ml)
2 teaspoons (10 ml) vanilla extract
2 pounds, 8 ounces (1 kg, 135 g) cake
  flour
2 teaspoons (4 g) ground cardamom
dark coating chocolate, melted

This is one of the most common cookies found in Europe, and also one of the most versatile. Strassburger Cookies can be piped out in an array of different shapes, and two cookies may be sandwiched together with jam or another filling before they are dipped in chocolate.

1. Beat the butter and sugar together, using the paddle attachment at medium speed until light and creamy, approximately 5 minutes. Mix in the eggs and egg yolks a few at a time. Add the vanilla. Add the flour and cardamom and stir on low speed until well combined.

2. Place the cookie dough (a portion at a time) in a pastry bag with a no. 6 (12-mm) star tip. Pipe the dough into one of the following shapes on sheet pans lined with baking paper (Figure 5–15). Attach the paper to the pan with a pea-sized piece of dough in each corner to keep the paper from moving as you pipe, and draw parallel lines on the paper (invert the paper before before attaching it to the pan) to serve as a guide in making the cookies the correct size.

3. Bake the cookies at 375°F (190°C) for approximately 12 minutes.

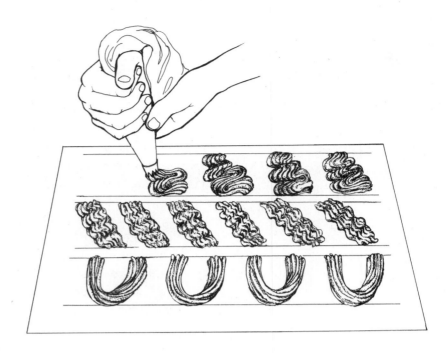

FIGURE 5–15   *Piping Strassburger Cookies into (top to bottom) Cones, Pleated Ribbons, and Horseshoes*

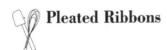 **Pleated Ribbons**

*P*ipe the cookies in 3¹/₂-inch (8.7-cm) flattened ribbons, holding the pastry bag close to the sheet pan so that the width of the dough is piped out flatter than the width of the tip. As you pipe, wiggle the tip back and forth a little so the dough forms pleats, or gathers. Bake and cool the cookies, then dip one-half into melted coating chocolate.

 **Horseshoes**

*P*ipe half circles that are 3 inches (7.5 cm) tall. Bake and cool, then dip both ends in melted coating chocolate.

 Cones

*P*ipe out 2¹/₂-inch (6.2-cm) long cone-shaped cookies (wider at the top and narrowing down to a point at the bottom). Bake and cool, then dip the tips of the cookies into melted coating chocolate.

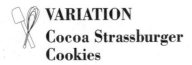 **VARIATION**
Cocoa Strassburger Cookies

*R*eplace 2 ounces (55 g) of cake flour with an equal amount of unsweetened cocoa powder.

Assorted Breakfast Pastries

Assorted Breads and Rolls

Rhubarb Meringue Tart, Swedish Hazelnut Tart, Clafoutis with Cherries, Walnut-Caramel Tart

Italian Pear, Almond, and Cranberry Tart

Chestnut Puzzle Cake

Zuger Kirsch Cake

Cappuccino Mousse with Sambuca Cream in a Chocolate Coffee Cup

Caramelized Apple Galette in Phyllo Dough with Kumquat

Blueberry Pirouettes

Florentina Cones with Seasonal Fruit

Marjolaine

Blueberry Soufflé

Chianti Poached Figs with Lavender Mascarpone

Chocolate and Frangelico Mousse Cake

Caramel Cake

Blancmange with Florentina Halos, Dried Kumquats, and Kumquat and Pear Sauces

Caramel Boxes with Caramel-Macadamia Nut Mousse

Red Currant Sorbet in Magnolia Cookie Shells (variation)

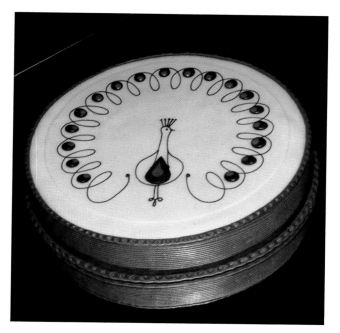

Marzipan Covered Cake with Peacock Design

Cupid's Treasure Chest

Chocolate Rum Pudding with Chocolate Beetles

Triple Chocolate Terrine

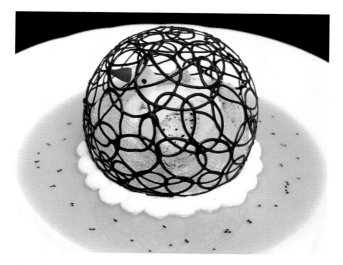

Snowbird in a Chocolate Cage

Diplomat Cake

Chocolate Decadence

Peach and Berry Crisp

Queen's Apple

Gâteau Moka Carousel

Chocolate Mint Torte with a Golden Touch

Swedish Profiteroles

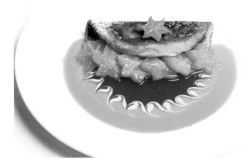

*Omelette Pancake with Sautéed Starfruit,
Pomegranate Sauce, and Mango Coulis*

Traditional Shortbread

*twenty 3¹/₄-by-3-inch
(8.1-×-7.5-cm) pieces*

1 pound, 2 ounces (510 g) soft
   unsalted butter
1 tablespoon (15 ml) vanilla extract
6 ounces (170 g) powdered sugar
12 ounces (340 g) bread flour
6 ounces (170 g) rice flour
¹/₂ teaspoon (2.5 g) salt

This delicious and delicate cookie is made from a mixture of sugar and flour that has been "shortened" (made soft and crumbly) by the addition of fat. In this case butter is used, but lard, margarine, or oil would have the same effect—although they would not produce the same wonderful flavor: These cookies are the epitome of "buttery."

Scotland is probably the country that is best known for its Shortbread. There, the cookies are traditionally made around the Christmas and New Year's holidays. The dough is typically baked in a round, shallow, ovenproof form, 8 to 10 inches in diameter. After baking, the circle is inverted and the round is cut into wedges. The problem with this method is that it makes for a lot of broken pieces, due to the fragile nature of the cookie. A more practical alternative is to cut the cookies into squares, which are more durable.

The addition of rice flour gives this cookie a special crispness. If you do not have rice flour, cake flour can be substituted with a good result. You would be hard put to improve on these cookies, but if you like, try adding nuts or candied ginger to the dough. Traditional Shortbread makes a perfect accompaniment to ice cream, especially vanilla.

1. Place the soft butter, vanilla, and powdered sugar in a mixing bowl. Beat with the paddle attachment until creamy. Incorporate the bread flour, rice flour, and salt on low speed. Place the dough in the refrigerator until firm.

2. Briefly work the dough with your hands to make it pliable, then roll it out to a 16-by-12-inch (40-×-30-cm) rectangle, using flour to prevent it from sticking. Roll the dough up on a dowel and transfer it to a half-sheet pan lined with baking paper. Adjust the size of the rectangle as needed if it becomes stretched in the moving process.

3. Mark the top of the dough with a pattern of wavy lines, using a fork. If the dough sticks to the fork, dip the fork into vegetable oil as you work.

4. Bake at 400°F (205°C) for approximately 30 minutes or until the top is golden brown. While the sheet is still warm, cut it into four strips lengthwise and then five across. Allow the Shortbread to cool completely before removing the pieces from the pan. Store in airtight containers. Do not stack too high since the pieces are quite fragile.

Triple-Chocolate Indulgence

80 cookies

6 ounces (170 g) unsweetened chocolate

1 pound (455 g) sweet dark chocolate

3 ounces (85 g) unsalted butter

5 eggs

14 ounces (400 g) granulated sugar

½ teaspoon (3 g) mocha paste
or

2 tablespoons (30 ml) Coffee Reduction (page 5)

1 teaspoon (5 ml) vanilla extract

3 ounces (85 g) cake flour

2 teaspoons (8 g) baking powder

1 teaspoon (5 g) salt

8 ounces (225 g) dark chocolate chips

8 ounces (225 g) white chocolate, coarsely chopped

6 ounces (170 g) chopped walnuts

powdered sugar

These are the ultimate chocolate cookie. They are something like a fudgy brownie in the shape of a cookie. And, just like brownies, it can be tricky to know when to remove them from the oven the first time you try the recipe. Since looking at the color of a chocolate cookie doesn't tell you anything (unless they are burned!), you must rely on the oven temperature and the approximate baking time given, and then touch the cookies to judge if they are baked. The edges should just feel firm and the center should stay soft and gooey. Be careful not to overbake or you lose the fudgy quality.

1. Place the unsweetened and dark chocolates in a bowl with the butter. Melt together over simmering water. Reserve.

2. Whip the eggs and granulated sugar on high speed until light and fluffy. Add the mocha paste or Coffee Reduction and the vanilla. Mix the egg mixture into the melted chocolate.

3. Combine the flour, baking powder, salt, chocolate chips, chopped white chocolate, and walnuts. Add to the chocolate and egg mixture and stir just until combined. Refrigerate the dough until it is firm enough to handle.

4. Divide the dough into four equal pieces, approximately 1 pound, 2 ounces (510 g) each. Roll each piece into a rope 16 inches (40 cm) long, using powdered sugar to prevent the dough from sticking. Refrigerate the ropes until they are firm.

5. Cut each rope into twenty equal pieces. Using a serrated knife makes it much easier to cut the slices, keeping them round instead of pressing into ovals. Place the cookies, cut-side down, on sheet pans lined with baking paper.

6. Bake the cookies, double-panned, at 400°F (205°C) for about 10 minutes.

Vanilla Dreams

75 cookies

1 pound, 10 ounces (740 g) granulated sugar

1 pound (455 g) soft unsalted butter

2 teaspoons (10 ml) vanilla extract

1 pound (455 g) bread flour

1 teaspoon (3.5 g) ammonium carbonate

I suspect that these simple but unusual cookies got their name because they have a mysterious hollow center, and not because cookie lovers can't get them out of their thoughts, although this would certainly be easy to understand. I loved to eat these cookies when I was a kid: We would dip the cookies in milk (or even water) so that the hollow space would fill up with liquid. The surrounding cookie, because of its high sugar content, would remain crisp, allowing us to suck the milk or water out of the center before we ate the cookie (it did not take very much to entertain kids in those days).

Ammonium carbonate, while not readily available in your local supermarket, can be obtained from the pharmacist. These cookies can alternatively be made using a mixture of baking powder and baking soda in equal amounts, but the cookies will be a lot less "dreamy" with only a tiny hollow center.

NOTE: The ammonium carbonate causes the cookies to puff up, which creates a hollow space in the center, but they will fall easily if they are removed from the oven before they are done, or if the oven door is opened early while they are baking.

1. Combine the sugar, butter, and vanilla, mixing until well blended.

2. Sift the flour with the ammonium carbonate and incorporate into the butter mixture.

3. Divide the dough into three 18-ounce (510-g) pieces. Roll each piece into a 20-inch (50-cm) rope. Cut each rope into twenty-five equal slices and roll the slices into round balls.

4. Place the balls of dough on sheet pans lined with baking paper. Flatten each piece slightly using the palm of your hand.

5. Bake at 300°F (149°C) until the cookies are light, golden brown, about 30 minutes.

 ## Walnut Bars

90 cookies

1 pound, 12 ounces (795 g) soft unsalted butter

1 pound (455 g) granulated sugar

1 tablespoon (15 ml) vanilla extract

1 teaspoon (5 g) salt

1 pound, 12 ounces (795 g) bread flour

12 ounces (340 g) walnut halves or pieces

It doesn't get much easier than this! The few ingredients (which only by coincidence are all measured using the numerals 1 or 2) are a cinch to remember, and there is just one step involved to combine them. How you shape the dough and the size you slice the cookies are both fairly flexible. The size given here produces a relatively small butter cookie, which is probably just as well, since it is hard to stop eating these crumbly little morsels. Walnut Bars are one of the few cookies that can be baked at any temperature between 325 and 425°F (163–219°C). You can gauge when they are done simply by looking at the color. The only difference is that they will take a little longer at a lower temperature. Keep the bars of dough wrapped in the refrigerator to slice and bake as needed. The dough must be firm when it is sliced so that you can cut cleanly through the walnuts without dragging them through the dough.

1. Cream the butter, sugar, vanilla, and salt together using the paddle. Mix in the flour and then the walnuts.

2. Press the dough into a one-quarter sheet pan (12 by 8 inches/30 × 20 cm). It should be approximately 1 inch (2.5 cm) thick. Chill until firm.

3. Cut the dough into three strips lengthwise. Slice each strip across into thirty pieces. Place the cookies cut-side down on sheet pans lined with baking paper.

4. Bake at 375°F (190°C) for approximately 15 minutes or until golden brown.

6

Tarts

Apple Tart Parisienne

Apricot and Fig Tart
  with Prickly Pear Sorbet

Cherry Meringue Tart
  with Rhubarb Sauce

Chocolate Pine Nut Tart

Clafoutis with Cherries

Cointreau Tart with Apple,
  Pear, or Rhubarb

Italian Pear, Almond,
  and Cranberry Tart

Linzer Tart

Mandarin Tart with Armagnac

Mandarin Tarts with Cointreau
  Custard

Nectarine Meringue Tart
  with Rhubarb

Pecan-Whiskey Tart

Pink Grapefruit and Orange
  Tart

Quince Custard Tart

Raspberry-Lemon Tart

Strawberry-Kiwi Tart

Strawberry-Rhubarb Tart

Swedish Apple Tart

Swedish Hazelnut Tart

Tart Hollandaise

Tart Tatin

Walnut-Caramel Tart

It is a common misconception that a tart is a European type of pie, or nothing more than a pie with a fancy name. Pies and tarts do have some similarities: they are both made of a crust and a filling, and they are usually baked in a metal tin. However, the baking pan itself sets the two apart: tart pans are not as deep as pie pans so they hold less filling, they have almost straight sides, the sides are usually fluted, and the pans have no lip. A tart is removed in one piece from the baking pan. A pie, on the other hand, is cut and served from the baking pan; it cannot be unmolded because of its fragile crust and large, mounded filling. Since a pie will fall apart if you try to take it out of the pan whole, pie pans have slanted sides to make serving easier. In most cases a pie is made with a double crust, and a tart with a single, but actually both can be made either way.

The tart pan most often used professionally is an 11-inch (27.5-cm) round, but tarts are also made in square or rectangular shapes. Tart pans can be one solid piece, or two-piece "false bottom" pans; the latter make removing the baked tart easier. The tart pan is usually lined with a short-type dough

(Pie Dough or Puff Pastry are also used for some recipes). You will have a small piece of dough leftover after lining the tart pans when using the amount called for in the individual recipes since it is unrealistic to work with precisely the amount of dough required and some must be trimmed from the edges after it is fitted in the pans. In a professional kitchen the doughs that are needed are kept as part of the regular mise en place, and the chef will simply take an approximate amount and return the leftover to the supply.

Since a tart pan is only about 1 inch (2.5 cm) deep, it is important that the dough is not rolled out any thicker than $1/8$ inch (3 mm) to allow sufficient space for the filling. The shells are sometimes "baked blind," which means the shell is lined with baking paper or aluminum foil, filled with dried beans or pie weights to prevent the dough from puffing or distorting, and fully or partially baked, depending on the filling used. As a rule, the less time it takes to bake the filling, the longer the shells need to be prebaked. In the case of a custard filling, the shells must be completely baked through before the custard is added, even though they will go back in the oven later, since the custard is baked at such a low temperature. For tarts that are assembled and finished in a completely baked crust, you may want to "waterproof" the crust by coating the inside with a thin film of apricot glaze or melted coating chocolate. A thin layer of Sponge Cake or some leftover Ladyfingers can also be placed in the bottom to absorb excess juices from fruits or moisture from the filling.

When making tarts with Pie Dough or Puff Pastry, allow a sufficient amount of resting time before baking the shells to keep the crust from shrinking. With Short Dough the beans or weights are not used to prevent puffing but to keep the sides straight. If you want the sides absolutely straight, place a circle of baking paper in the bottom of the pan only, so the beans come in contact with the dough on the sides. However, the beans tend to stick to the crust so you must carefully pick them out with a fork.

If you need to freeze unbaked tart shells, you can either store them frozen in the pans, or freeze them in the pans and then remove the shells once they are solid. In either case, if they are properly covered, they can be frozen for four to six weeks. Make sure the coating has not worn off if the pans are made of sheetmetal (which they usually are), as the metal will stain the dough if left too long.

To remove a tart from a false-bottom tart pan, first make sure the sides are not stuck anywhere. Use the tip of a paring knife, if needed, to loosen the edge, but never run the knife around the sides. Remove the fluted ring by pushing the tart straight up while holding on to the ring. Run a thin knife all around between the crust and the metal bottom, then slide the tart onto a serving platter or cardboard cake circle; do not attempt to lift it. If you use a one-piece pan, treat the sides in the same manner, then place a cardboard circle over the top, hold the tart with both hands, invert it to unmold, place your serving platter or a second cardboard circle on top (which is the bottom of the tart), and invert again. With either type of pan the dough has a tendency to stick when cold, because the butter acts as a sort of glue. To remedy this, place a hot sheet pan, or hot damp towels, on the outside of the pan to warm the butter and help loosen the crust.

In addition to being delicious, a freshly made tart looks beautiful, arranged perhaps with an assortment of fresh, colorful, glazed fruit shining on top. A tart is elegant, which makes it appropriate for almost any occasion: as a luncheon dessert, as one of the selections on a buffet (where a fruit tart not only adds color but offers a choice for the customer who wants something light), or even served after dinner, perhaps dressed up with a sauce and decoration. With the exception of custard fillings, which should be chilled, a tart may be served warm or at room temperature but should never be served cold.

 Apple Tart Parisienne

two 11-inch (27.5-cm) tarts

1 pound, 8 ounces (680 g) Short Dough (page 54)

3 pounds (1 kg, 365 g) Granny Smith or Pippin apples (about eight medium-size)

3 ounces (85 g) granulated sugar

2 ounces (55 g) unsalted butter

4 ounces (115 g) smooth apricot jam

Calvados Custard (recipe follows)

Cinnamon Sugar (page 5)

powdered sugar

Crème Fraîche (page 1073)

fanned strawberry halves

A blowtorch can be used to brown the tarts, but be very careful in directing the flame and stand back far enough that you can control the browning process. Although it usually is not necessary to use dried beans or pie weights with Short Dough, in this recipe you want to make sure the sides do not settle during the prebaking, or you will risk having the custard run between the crust and the pan.

1. Roll the Short Dough to ⅛ inch (3 mm) thick and use it to line two 11-inch (27.5-cm) tart pans (see Figure 2–14, page 56). Line with baking paper, then fill with dried beans or pie weights.

2. Bake at 400°F (205°C) for about 12 minutes or until the dough is set, but not colored. Do not use a double pan; set the pans directly on the oven rack. Set the shells aside to cool.

3. Peel, core, and cut the apples into ten wedges each.

4. Sauté the apples with the sugar and butter in a large skillet over medium heat, until they begin to soften, 10 to 15 minutes. If you do not have a skillet that is large enough to allow you to cook the apples no more than two or three layers deep in the pan, cook them in two batches. Set the cooked apples aside.

5. Remove the dried beans or pie weights from the cooled tart shells.

6. Divide the apricot jam between the shells and spread over the bottom. Arrange the apple wedges in concentric circles on top of the jam. Pour the Calvados Custard over the apples. Sprinkle lightly with Cinnamon Sugar.

7. Bake the tarts at 350°F (175°C) for about 35 minutes or until the custard is set.

8. Let the tarts cool, then sift powdered sugar over the tops. Place the tarts under a salamander or hot broiler just long enough to caramelize the sugar on the apples. Be careful not to overbrown. Cut the tarts into the desired number of servings.

9. Presentation: Place a slice of tart, off-center, on a dessert plate. Spoon a small amount of Crème Fraîche in front of the slice and place a fanned strawberry on the plate behind the tart.

1. Combine the flour and sugar. Mix in the eggs and stir to make a smooth paste.

2. Scald the half-and-half with the vanilla bean, if used. Remove the bean and add the Calvados and vanilla extract, if used.

3. Gradually whisk the half-and-half into the egg mixture.

Calvados Custard

about 5 cups (1 l, 200 ml) custard

3 ounces (85 g) bread flour
7 ounces (200 g) granulated sugar
6 eggs
2¹/₂ cups (600 ml) half-and-half
one vanilla bean, split
    or
1 teaspoon (5 ml) vanilla extract
¹/₄ cup (60 ml) Calvados

Apricot and Fig Tart with Prickly Pear Sorbet

16 servings

1 pound, 8 ounces (680 g) Short
    Dough (page 54)
1 pound, 6 ounces (625 g) Mazarin
    Filling (page 1088)
1 pound, 4 ounces (570 g) Lemon
    Cream (page 1087) (approximately
    one-third recipe)
sixteen medium-sized fresh apricots
fourteen Brown Turkey or large Black
    Mission figs
granulated sugar
powdered sugar
eight prickly pears
dark coating chocolate, melted
sixteen mint sprigs
one recipe Prickly Pear Sorbet
    (page 653)

NOTE: To prevent the sorbet from melting prematurely, place the prickly pear shells in the freezer for a few minutes before you fill them but do not freeze them solid or it will detract from the presentation.

*T*his tart contains a potpourri of palatable combinations: slightly tart apricots paired with sweet figs, almond Mazarin Filling, and Lemon Cream. You will be pleasantly surprised at how well they all come together with the Prickly Pear Sorbet. If you can not obtain prickly pears (also known as cactus pears), try serving Passion Fruit Ice Cream Parfait (see page 673) in a passion fruit shell.

1. Roll the Short Dough out to ¹/₈ inch (3 mm) thick and use it to line eight tart pans 4¹/₂ inches in diameter by ³/₄ inch high (11.2 × 2 cm) (see Figures 2–15 through 2–18, pages 57 and 58).

2. Place the Mazarin Filling in a pastry bag with a no. 5 (10-mm) plain tip. Pipe the filling into the shells, dividing it evenly; they should be about two-thirds full. Top with a ¹/₈-inch (3-mm) layer of Lemon Cream. Reserve the remaining Lemon Cream.

3. Reserve eight good-looking apricots as well as six of the figs. Cut the remaining apricots in half, remove the stones, then cut each half again to make quarters. Cut the remaining eight figs into quarters lengthwise.

4. Alternate four wedges of fig and four wedges of apricot on the top of each tart, placing the fruit skin-side down with the pointed ends directed toward the center and the outside like a fan. Press the fruit lightly into the filling. Sprinkle just enough granulated sugar over the tarts to cover.

5. Bake at 375°F (190°C) for 20 minutes. Sift powdered sugar lightly over the tarts, then continue baking until they are dark golden brown and baked through, about 20 minutes longer. Let cool completely, then unmold.

6. Cut the prickly pears in half crosswise. Use a small spoon to scoop out the flesh (reserve to make the sorbet). Cut a small sliver off the bottom of the shells so they stand upright.

7. Cut the tarts in half so that each piece contains two wedges of apricot and two wedges of fig. Set aside.

8. Place melted coating chocolate in a piping bag and cut a small opening. Decorate sixteen dessert plates (or as many as you will need) by piping the chocolate in a free-form design. Reserve.

9. Cut the reserved apricots in half, remove the pits, and cut in half again to make quarters. Cut three round slices from the sides of each fig, making pieces that are rounded on the skin side and flat on the flesh side. Ideally cut just as many apricot and fig pieces as you will need right away so that the pieces of fruit do not dry up.

10. Presentation: Place one tart half on one of the decorated plates, arranging it so that the cut side is in the center of the plate. Pour a small pool of Lemon Cream on the right corner of the tart and onto the plate. Arrange one fig slice and two apricot pieces in the sauce. Set a mint sprig next to the fruit. Place a scoop of Prickly Pear Sorbet in one of the prepared shells (see note) and set on the left side of the tart. Sift powdered sugar over the plate in back of the dessert. Serve immediately.

Cherry Meringue Tart with Rhubarb Sauce

16 servings

1 pound, 8 ounces (680 g) Short
    Dough (page 54)
3 ounces (85 g) smooth apricot jam
12 ounces (340 g) fresh cherries,
    pitted (10 ounces/285 g pitted)
Almond Kirsch Filling (recipe follows)
Apricot Glaze (page 1016)
one-quarter recipe Italian Meringue
    (page 591) (see note 3)
Rhubarb Sauce (page 1080)
about seventy fresh cherries, stems
    attached

NOTE 1: Leave the fresh cherries used for garnish unpitted for a more attractive look, but cut one in half to expose the pit. It looks good, but more importantly, it alerts the guest to the fact that the garnish cherries (unlike the cherries in the tart) contain pits.

NOTE 2: The tarts can be prepared through step three one or two days in advance and stored in the refrigerator. Bake and top with meringue the day they are to be served. Reserve

This is truly a case of the whole being greater than the sum of its parts—the relatively few ingredients come together delectably. If you serve this dessert in late spring/early summer when the first fresh cherries become available, I guarantee rave reviews.

Preparing the tarts in 4½-inch forms and serving a half-tart per person allows you to expose the filling in the presentation, which would not be the case if you made individual tarts and served a whole tart to each guest. The other typical alternative, making standard 11-inch tarts and serving a wedge on each plate, shows off the filling but is more commonplace. See note 2 for other presentation ideas.

1. Roll the Short Dough out to ⅛ inch (3 mm) thick and use it to line eight tart pans 4½ inches in diameter by ¾ inch high (11.2 × 2 cm) (see Figures 2–15 through 2–18, pages 57 and 58). Pipe the apricot jam into the bottom of the shells, dividing it equally between them. Spread the jam out to cover the base of the shells.

2. Cut the cherries into halves and quarters. Divide them evenly over the bottom of the shells.

3. Place the Almond Kirsch Filling in a pastry bag with a no. 4 (8-mm) plain tip. Pipe the filling on top of the cherries, dividing it evenly between the tarts.

4. Bake the tarts at 375°F (190°C) for approximately 25 minutes or until light brown and baked through. Let the tarts cool completely.

5. Remove the tarts from the forms. Brush Apricot Glaze over the tops.

6. Place the meringue in a pastry bag with a no. 4 (8-mm) plain tip. Pipe a spiral of meringue covering the top of each tart. Start the first ring about ⅛ inch (3 mm) from the outside edge and overlap each pre-

*at room temperature after browning the
meringue. For a different presentation bake the
tarts in sixteen 3¹/₂-inch (8.7-cm) fluted tart
pans (false-bottom or solid) and use a whole tart
for each serving. Present the tart cut in half garnished with five or six fresh cherries (one cut to
expose the pit) arranged between the two pieces.
The recipe can also be used to make one 11-
inch (27.5-cm) tart (you may use a false-bottom
or solid tart pan). The larger tart will require
about 15 minutes longer baking time. When cutting the large tart into the desired number of
serving pieces, do not forget to dip your knife in
hot water before each cut so as to be able to slice
cleanly through the meringue.*

*NOTE 3: It is important to use a small pan
when making only a quarter recipe of Italian
Meringue, or it becomes almost impossible to get
an accurate reading from the sugar thermometer
because there is so little syrup in the pan.*

Almond Kirsch Filling

*1 pound, 10 ounces (740 g)
filling*

5 ounces (140 g) soft unsalted butter
4 ounces (115 g) granulated sugar
2 egg yolks
¹/₄ cup (60 ml) kirschwasser
2 ounces (55 g) cornstarch
6 ounces (170 g) finely ground
    almonds
8 ounces (225 g) Pastry Cream
    (page 1088), strained

*NOTE: If the Pastry Cream is cold (which it
usually is since it must be stored in the refrigerator) the filling will break when it is added. To
avoid this, warm the Pastry Cream over a bain-
marie, stirring constantly. If you add cold Pastry Cream and the filling breaks, warm the
entire filling up in the same manner. Be careful
not to overheat or cook either mixture.*

vious ring halfway to mound the meringue slightly higher in the center. Brown the meringue under a hot broiler or salamander, or by very care-fully using a blowtorch.

7. Presentation: Cover the base of a dessert plate with Rhubarb Sauce. Cut a tart in half using a thin, sharp knife dipped in hot water to keep the meringue from sticking to the knife. Place one half in the cen-ter of the plate. Place four or five fresh cherries next to the cut side of the tart (see note 1). Serve immediately to prevent the bottom of the crust from becoming soft from the sauce.

1. Mix the butter and sugar together. Incorporate the egg yolks and kirschwasser. Beat at medium speed until the mixture is light and fluffy.

2. Combine the cornstarch and ground almonds. Add to the butter mixture. Stir in the Pastry Cream.

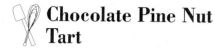

Chocolate Pine Nut Tart

two 11-inch (27.5-cm) tarts

1 pound, 8 ounces (680 g) Short Dough (page 54)

12 ounces (340 g) sweet dark chocolate

3 ounces (85 g) unsweetened chocolate

8 ounces (225 g) unsalted butter

grated rind of two oranges

6 ounces (170 g) toasted pine nuts

6 ounces (170 g) granulated sugar

6 egg yolks (½ cup/120 ml)

¼ cup (60 ml) orange liqueur

6 egg whites (¾ cup/180 ml)

1 teaspoon (5 g) salt

4 ounces (115 g) smooth apricot jam

8 ounces (225 g) Ganache (page 1086)

1 cup (240 ml) heavy cream

2 teaspoons (10 g) granulated sugar

Orange Sauce (page 1077)

Chocolate Sauce for Piping (page 1072)

Instead of making tarts, you can use this filling to make delicious, gooey, Brownie-like bars. Pour the filling into a half-sheet pan lined with baking paper and spread it out evenly. Bake at 375°F (190°C) for about 35 minutes, let cool, then cut into the desired size pieces. It is a good alternative and a change of pace from regular Brownies.

1. Roll out the Short Dough to ⅛ inch (3 mm) thick and use it to line two 11-inch (27.5-cm) tart pans (see Figure 2–14, page 56). Reserve in the refrigerator.

2. Place the dark chocolate, unsweetened chocolate, butter, and orange rind in a bowl. Melt together over simmering water. Set aside but keep warm.

3. Reserve 2 ounces (55 g) of the pine nuts for garnish. Grind the remainder with 3 ounces (85 g) of the sugar to a fine flour-like consistency (be careful not to grind beyond this point or you will get an oily paste).

4. Whip the egg yolks to the ribbon stage. Add the orange liqueur.

5. Whip the egg whites and the salt to a foam. Gradually add the remaining 3 ounces (85 g) of sugar and whip to soft peaks. Do not over-whip or the additional air will cause the tart to crack while baking.

6. Combine the nut mixture with the chocolate. Add the egg yolks, then carefully fold in the egg whites.

7. Spread the apricot jam over the bottom of the two lined pans. Divide the chocolate filling between them.

8. Bake at 350°F (175°C) for approximately 35 minutes. Let the tarts cool.

9. Carefully remove the tarts from the pans. Warm the Ganache until it is melted and liquid, then spread it quickly over the top of the tarts. Before it starts to set up, sprinkle the reserved pine nuts on top. Chill briefly to set the Ganache.

10. Slice the tarts into the desired number of pieces. Whip the heavy cream with the 2 teaspoons (10 g) of sugar to stiff peaks. Place in a pastry bag with a no. 7 (14-mm) star tip and reserve in the refrigerator.

11. Presentation: Pour a round pool of Orange Sauce on one side of a dessert plate. Pipe a pea-sized dot of whipped cream on the opposite side of the plate, and set a tart slice on the whipped cream (to prevent it from sliding) so that the tip is in the sauce. Pipe a large rosette of whipped cream on the wide end of the tart. Decorate the Orange Sauce with the Chocolate Sauce for Piping as shown on pages 998 to 1006).

Clafoutis with Cherries

two 11-inch (27.5-cm) tarts

1 pound, 8 ounces (680 g) Short
   Dough (page 54)
1 ounce (30 g) flour
12 ounces (340 g) granulated sugar
6 eggs
1 cup (240 ml) heavy cream
1½ cups (360 ml) milk
1 pound, 4 ounces (580 g) cherries,
   pitted and halved
Romanoff Sauce (page 1081)
whole cherries with stem

NOTE: It is best to place the tart shells next to the oven before you pour in the custard, so you will be moving them as little as possible after filling. If the custard runs between the crust and the pan, the tarts will be difficult to remove later. One method that works well is to fill the shells only partway with custard, set them in the oven, then "top off" with the remaining custard. Since all custards shrink as they are baked, the tarts should be filled as close to the top as practical without overflowing.

Cointreau Tart with Apple, Pear, or Rhubarb

two 11-inch (27.5-cm) tarts

1 pound, 8 ounces (680 g) Short
   Dough (page 54)

*C*lafoutis is a derivative of the word clafir, which translates to "fill." The dessert is famous in the Limousin region of central France where it origi-nated. Clafoutis is actually a type of fruit pancake and does not normally have a Short Dough crust. I have added a crust to make it more practical to cut and serve, and to improve the taste by providing a contrasting texture. While cher-ries are the most commonly used fruit for Clafoutis, other fruits that are suitable for baking, such as apricots, blueberries, or plums, can be substituted. Regard-less, this tart should be served the same day it is baked, and there is really no reason not to since it is so simple and quick to make, especially if the shell is prepped ahead. Both the cherries and the blueberries will bleed and stain the custard around them if the tarts are left overnight.

1. Roll out the Short Dough ⅛ inch (3 mm) thick and use it to line two 11-inch (27.5-cm) tart pans (see Figure 2–14, page 56). Prick the dough lightly and place a piece of baking paper in each of the shells.

2. Fill the pastry shells with dried beans or pie weights and prebake at 375°F (190°C) for approximately 10 minutes. Remove the paper and the weights and continue to bake about 2 minutes longer. The dough should be set and golden but not browned.

3. Combine the flour and sugar. Mix in the eggs and cream with a whisk.

4. Scald the milk, then gradually whisk the hot milk into the first mixture. Reserve.

5. Divide the cherries between the two shells, arranging them cut-side up on top of the crust. Gently pour the custard over the cherries (see note).

6. Bake the tarts at 350°F (175°C) for approximately 30 minutes or until the custard is set. Cool at room temperature.

7. Remove the tarts from the pans and cut into desired size serving pieces, using a serrated knife to cut through the cherries.

8. Presentation: Place a slice of Clafoutis on a dessert plate. Pour Romanoff Sauce over one-third of the tart on the narrow end. Set two or three whole cherries next to the slice (see note 1 following Cherry Meringue Tart with Rhubarb Sauce, page 235). Serve at room temperature.

*T*his delicious but delicate tart can be quite a handful. Take great care when removing the beans after the blind baking. Too much patching of the dough while lining the pans, or overbaking the shells, will make the dough susceptible to cracks where the thin custard can run out during baking. If you do need to make repairs, dab a little egg white over the crack and then press some fresh Short Dough on top before you arrange the fruit or add the custard (see note fol-lowing Clafoutis with Cherries above).

1 pound, 8 ounces (680 g) apples or
   pears (about six medium-sized of
   either)
   or
1 pound, 4 ounces (570 g) rhubarb
   stalks
Cointreau Custard (recipe follows)
Cinnamon Sugar (page 5) for
   apples and pears
   or
granulated sugar for rhubarb
Apricot or Pectin Glaze
   (pages 1016 and 1017)
whipped cream, optional

For the crust

1. Line two 11-inch (27.5-cm) false-bottom tart pans with Short Dough rolled 1/8 inch (3 mm) thick (see Figure 2–14, page 56). Prick the dough lightly with a fork, line the bottom and sides of the shell with baking paper, and fill with dried beans or pie weights.

2. Bake at 375°F (190°C) just until golden, about 12 minutes. Let cool, then remove the paper and the weights.

Apple or Pear Tarts

1. Peel and core the apples or pears; place them in acidulated water to prevent them from becoming brown (oxidizing). If they are not quite ripe enough, poach in Plain Poaching Syrup (page 13) for a few minutes to soften them.

2. When you are ready to assemble the tarts, cut each apple or pear in half lengthwise, then cut crosswise into thin slices. Arrange the sliced fruit in concentric circles over the crusts, starting at the outside edge.

3. Gently pour the Cointreau Custard over the fruit, dividing it evenly between the two shells.

4. Sprinkle Cinnamon Sugar over two or three circles of the fruit, creating alternating rings.

5. Bake at 350°F (175°C) until the custard is set, about 30 minutes.

6. When the tarts have cooled enough so that they will not break when you handle them, remove them from the pans and glaze with Apricot or Pectin Glaze. Slice and serve at room temperature. If you like, pipe whipped cream at the edge of each slice.

Rhubarb Tarts

1. Cut rhubarb stalks into 2-by-1/2-inch (5-✕-1.2-cm) pieces. Place them in a stainless-steel or other noncorrosive pan, and sprinkle granulated sugar on top to draw out some of the juice.

2. Bake covered at 375°F (190°C) until slightly softened, about 8 minutes. If overcooked the rhubarb will turn into a purée. Arrange the rhubarb in the shells and proceed as in Apple or Pear Tart, but use granulated sugar instead of Cinnamon Sugar on top.

 ## Cointreau Custard

5³/₄ cups (1 l, 380 ml) custard

12 egg yolks (1 cup/240 ml)
7 ounces (200 g) granulated sugar
4 cups (960 ml) heavy cream
1/4 cup (60 ml) Cointreau

1. Beat the egg yolks and sugar by hand for a few seconds, just to combine.

2. Add the cream and Cointreau and blend thoroughly.

Italian Pear, Almond, and Cranberry Tart

two 11-inch (27.5-cm) tarts

12 medium-sized pears
  (approximately 4 pounds/
  1 kg, 820 g)
1 tablespoon (15 ml) whole black
  peppercorns
one and one-half recipes Spiced
  Poaching Syrup (page 13)
2 pounds, 12 ounces (1 kg, 250 g)
  Cornmeal Crust (page 33)
1 pound, 12 ounces (795 g) Mazarin
  Filling (page 1088)
3 ounces (85 g) dried cranberries
powdered sugar
one-half recipe Cranberry Coulis
  (page 1073)
1 ounce (30 g) pistachio nuts,
  blanched, skins removed, and
  coarsely chopped
edible flowers

NOTE: You may need to refrigerate the tart shells before placing the baking paper and adding the pie weights, depending on the texture of your dough.

The Cornmeal Crust gives this tart a distinctive taste and provides a nice contrast to the soft, juicy pears inside. If you do not plan to serve the tarts the same day they are baked, eliminate the top crust; the pears will cause it to become soggy if left overnight. Alternatively, you can prep the tarts ahead of time through step six and then bake them a few hours before they are to be served. If you opt to leave off the top crust, slice the pear halves lengthwise and fan them slightly as you place them on the filling. Sprinkle the cranberries between the pears. Let the baked tarts cool completely, then brush Apricot or Pectin Glaze (see pages 1016 and 1017) over the tops before slicing.

1. Peel the pears and cut them in half. Place the pears in acidulated water as you work to keep them from browning (oxidizing).

2. Crush the peppercorns and add them to the Poaching Syrup. Add the pear halves and poach until they begin to soften, but do not cook them all the way through. Remove from the heat and set aside to steep for at least 30 minutes.

3. Roll a portion of the Cornmeal Crust to 1/8 inch (3 mm) thick and use it to line two 11-inch (27.5-cm) tart pans (they do not need to be false-bottom) (see Figure 2–14, page 56). Reserve the leftover dough.

4. Remove the pear halves from the poaching liquid. Remove the cores (I use a mellon-ball cutter for this) and at the same time look for and discard any peppercorns that are stuck to the pears. Blot the pears dry.

5. Divide the Mazarin Filling between the two tart shells and spread it out evenly. Sprinkle the dried cranberries over the filling. Arrange ten pear halves, cut-side down, in a circle on each tart. The stem end of the pears should point to the center of the circle, and the pears should be close, but don't force them together. Place the four remaining pear halves, two per tart, arranged in the center of the circles with the stem end of one half next to the bottom end of the other.

6. Roll the remaining Cornmeal Crust to 1/8 inch (3 mm) thick. Drape it over the top of the tarts and press the edges together to make them adhere firmly. Cut away any excess dough from the edges.

7. Bake the tarts at 375°F (190°C) directly on the oven rack (do not use a sheet pan), for about 30 minutes or until they are light brown on top. Let cool to room temperature. Remove from the pans, then cut into the desired number of pieces.

8. Presentation: Sift powdered sugar lightly over a tart slice and place in the center of a dessert plate. Pour a pool of Cranberry Coulis in front, and sprinkle pistachio nuts on top of the sauce. Place an edible flower on the plate next to the tip of tart.

Linzer Tart

two 11-inch (27.5-cm) tarts

1 pound, 6 ounces (625 g) soft unsalted butter

1 pound, 4 ounces (570 g) granulated sugar

3 eggs

1 tablespoon (8 g) unsweetened cocoa powder

2 teaspoons (3 g) ground cinnamon

1 teaspoon (2 g) ground cloves

1 pound (455 g) cake flour

1 pound, 6 ounces (625 g) finely ground hazelnuts

1 tablespoon (18 g) grated lemon zest

2 ounces (55 g) cake flour

1 pound, 4 ounces (570 g) raspberry preserves

powdered sugar

2 ounces (55 g) pistachios, blanched, skins removed, and finely chopped

*T*he descent of this famous tart is somewhat obscure, but one can generally assume that it originated in the town of Linz, which is located in upper Austria on the banks of the river Danube. The Danube, which has inspired so many great pieces of music, majestically flows eastward traveling through the birthplaces of two other well-known pastry creations: Vienna, home of the Sacher Torte, and then on to Budapest where the Dobos Torte was introduced.

Ground nuts, spices, citrus peels, and jam magically combine in the irresistible Linzer Tart. I use hazelnuts, but almonds, and even walnuts, are featured in many recipes. Nothing but a high quality raspberry jam will do, however.

The Linzer Dough used in the recipe for Individual Linzer Tartlets on page 396 is very fragile, and the pans must be lined one at a time. When making full-sized tarts the piped method used here is much more practical. Either way Linzer Tarts are great for making ahead and can be refrigerated or frozen either baked or before baking. It is actually preferable to bake the tarts the day before they are to be served, because the nuts in the crust, being hygroscopic, will not only absorb moisture from the air but also from the jam, making the pastry more moist the next day.

If you experience the problem of the jam filling boiling over on the sides and then burning and looking messy, the best remedy (assuming you are not using too much jam) is to simply lower the heat so that the jam does not boil so vigorously.

1. Cream the butter and granulated sugar together until the mixture is light and fluffy. Add the eggs one at a time.

2. Sift together the cocoa powder, spices, and first measurement of cake flour. Mix in the ground hazelnuts and the lemon zest and then incorporate this mixture into the butter mixture. Weigh out 2 pounds, 4 ounces (1 kg, 25 g) of the dough and into that thoroughly mix in the remaining 2 ounces (55 g) of cake flour. Reserve this portion of the dough at room temperature.

3. Place the remaining dough (without the extra flour) in a pastry bag with a no. 3 (6-mm) plain tip. Pipe the dough over the bottom of two 11-inch (27.5-cm) tart pans, starting at the outside edge and making concentric circles to cover the pans; use all of the paste (see Figure 12–2, page 592, as an example).

4. Bake at 375°F (190° C) for approximately 15 minutes or until the crust just starts to color. Remove from the oven and cool slightly.

5. Divide the raspberry preserves evenly between the two pans and spread over the crust leaving a ¼-inch (6-mm) border around the outside.

6. Place the reserved dough in the pastry bag with the no. 3 (6-mm) plain tip. Pipe straight parallel lines, ½ inch (1.2 cm) apart, across each tart. Then pipe a second set of parallel lines at a 45° angle to the first set. Lastly, pipe a pearl pattern (see Figure 19–6, page 983) around the border of the tarts. Adjust the pattern to the amount of paste you have left; if necessary, stretch the piping a bit.

7. Bake at 375°F (190°F) for approximately 25 minutes or until the tarts have a pleasant brown color on top. Cool.

8. Center a 9-inch (22.5-cm) cardboard cake circle on top of one tart. Sift powdered sugar over the exposed edge of the tart. Remove the cardboard and sprinkle the chopped pistachio nuts around the inside edge of the powdered sugar. Repeat with the second tart.

VARIATION
Linzer Bars

one 12-by-16-inch (30-×-40-cm) sheet or forty-eight 4-by-1-inch (10-×-2.5-cm) bars

Follow the recipe and instructions above with the following changes:

• Use only 1½ ounces (40 g) of additional flour instead of 2 ounces (55 g) and add it to only 2 pounds (910 g) of the dough.

• Pipe the remaining dough over the bottom of a half-sheet pan (12 by 16 inches/30 × 40 cm) lined with baking paper, piping it in straight lines lengthwise to cover the entire pan.

• After baking the crust, spread the jam over the whole surface (do not leave a ¼-inch/6-mm border uncovered).

• Do not pipe a pearl pattern border around the edge.

• Bake the sheet 5 to 10 minutes longer than the tarts.

• Omit the pistachios.

• When cool, trim the edges and cut into forty-eight individual pieces.

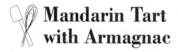

Mandarin Tart with Armagnac

two 11-inch (27.5-cm) tarts

one-third recipe High Ratio Sponge Cake batter (page 274)

1 pound, 8 ounces (680 g) Hazelnut Short Dough (page 55)

one recipe Red Currant Glaze (page 1017)

1 pound, 8 ounces (680 g) Pastry Cream (page 1088)

¼ cup (60 ml) Armagnac

⅓ cup (80 ml) mandarin or orange juice

twelve Satsuma mandarins, approximately

Raspberry Sauce (page 1080)

Sour Cream Mixture for Piping (page 1081)

NOTE 1: If you know the number of servings you will be cutting the tarts into, mark the top of the custard accordingly, then arrange the fruit

*T*his is a tart that I make during the winter months when fresh berries are scarce and expensive, but citrus fruits are plentiful, juicy-good, and reasonably priced. Because this recipe uses a thin layer of Sponge Cake, it is a sensible choice should you have leftover sponge from another project, such as Puzzle Cake or Chocolate and Frangelico Mousse Cake. But don't wait for that to try this refreshing combination.

The High Ratio Sponge Cake is very quick to make, so rather than just making the amount needed for the tarts, it would be a good idea to make the full recipe and freeze the extra. It will keep for several weeks if properly covered, and it is always good to have handy. I have, on many occasions, found myself out of Armagnac and have substituted cognac (or even brandy) without much noticeable difference in flavor, but perhaps the name should be changed.

1. Line the bottom of a 10-inch (25-cm) cake pan with a circle of baking paper. Pour the sponge batter into the pan and spread it out evenly. (The diameter of the sponge will be a little smaller than that of the tarts, but it is insignificant.)

2. Bake at 400°F (205°C) for about 10 minutes. Reserve.

3. Roll out the Hazelnut Short Dough to ⅛ inch (3 mm) thick and use it to line two 11-inch (27.5-cm) tart pans (see Figure 2–14, page 56). Cover the dough with baking paper, and fill with dried beans or pie weights.

on top within the lines. This allows you to avoid having to cut through the fruit or possibly push it into the custard as you cut the tarts.

NOTE 2: *If mandarins are not available, substitute oranges; you will need about eight. For a quick and colorful fruit tart, arrange other assorted fresh fruits (including some mandarins as desired) in concentric circles on top of the Pastry Cream; brush with glaze as directed.*

4. Bake at 375°F (190°C) for approximately 18 minutes or until the edges are golden brown. Immediately remove the paper and weights, then return to the oven to finish baking the bottom if necessary. Let the shells cool.

5. Brush Red Currant Glaze over the base, and slightly up the sides, of the cooled shells; reserve the remaining glaze.

6. Place one-fourth of the Pastry Cream in each of the shells and spread it out over the glaze, covering the bottom of the shells.

7. Slice the cake into two layers horizontally. Place one sponge in each tart shell on top of the Pastry Cream.

8. Combine the Armagnac with the mandarin or orange juice. Brush the juice over the sponges. Spread the remaining Pastry Cream evenly on top.

9. Peel and section the mandarins, taking great care to remove all of the white membrane. Separate the segments by hand instead of cutting them out with a knife as you would oranges. Make concentric circles of fruit starting at the edge of the tarts (see note 1).

10. Warm the reserved Currant Glaze (stir in a little water it if seems too thick), and brush on top of the mandarin segments. Cut the tarts into the desired number of slices.

11. Presentation: Place a tart slice off-center on a dessert plate. Pour a pool of Raspberry Sauce in front of the slice, and decorate the sauce with the Sour Cream Mixture for Piping (see pages 998 to 1006).

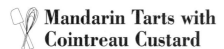

Mandarin Tarts with Cointreau Custard

twelve 4¹/₂-inch (11.2-cm) tarts

2 pounds (910 g) Short Dough (page 54)

six medium-sized Satsuma mandarins, peeled, seeded, and sectioned (see introduction)

one-half recipe Cointreau Custard (page 239)

twelve fresh or frozen cranberries

Apricot Glaze (page 1016)

Piping Chocolate (page 904), melted

Cranberry Coulis (page 1073)

Sour Cream Mixture for Piping (page 1081)

twelve small mint leaves

T hese little mandarin tarts are irresistible and a great alternative to tarts using berries during the winter months when berries are out of season and so expensive. Satsuma mandarins are my favorite not only for eating out of hand but also for pastries since they are virtually seedless and have the distinctive "zipper skin" (which pulls away easily) revealing the easy-to-separate segments. There is no such thing as a mandarin that is always completely seedless, but Satsuma and also Clementines can have few or none. I have found, however, that the Clementines can be quite unreliable.

As good as mandarins are, try replacing the mandarin segments with a poached and fanned pear half (see Small Pear Tartlets with Caramel Sauce, page 494). The Cranberry Coulis is a fitting compliment to the pears as well. When plums and apricots come into season they are also a great choice. By substituting fresh cherries for the mandarin segments, you are basically making my version of Clafouti.

Because of their small size, the tart shells do not need to be blind baked initially, but it is important that they receive proper bottom heat.

1. Line twelve 4¹/₂-inch (11.2-cm) false-bottom tart pans with Short Dough rolled ¹/₈ inch (3 mm) thick (see Figures 2–15 to 2–18, pages 57 and 58).

2. Arrange five mandarin segments in a fan shape in the bottom of each form. Skim the foam from the top of the Cointreau Custard and then divide the custard between the forms, filling them almost to the top. Place a cranberry in the center of each tart.

3. Carefully place the tarts in a 350°F (175°C) oven and bake for approximately 35 minutes or until the custard is set and the Short Dough is light brown on the top and around the perimeter. Remove them from the oven and let cool.

4. Brush a thin layer of Apricot Glaze over the tops of the cooled tarts.

5. Decorate the number of dessert plates you anticipate needing by piping four straight lines of Piping Chocolate, ¹/₂ inch (1.2 cm) apart, across the center of each plate.

6. Presentation: Place the Cranberry Coulis in a piping bottle. Cover the lower half of one of the prepared plates with sauce, being careful not to get any sauce beyond the chocolate border (do not cover the chocolate lines with sauce). Place the Sour Cream Mixture for Piping in a piping bag and pipe three or four lines in the Cranberry Coulis parallel to the chocolate lines. Pull a small wooden skewer through the lines at a 90° angle to make a wavy pattern (see Figure 19–23, page 1001). Place a tart above the sauce on the chocolate lines. Decorate with a mint leaf.

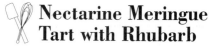

Nectarine Meringue Tart with Rhubarb

12 servings

1 pound, 8 ounces (680 g) Hazelnut Short Dough (page 55)

one-half recipe Apricot Glaze (page 1016)

1 pound, 12 ounces (795 g) fresh rhubarb stalks

1 tablespoon (8 g) cornstarch

¹/₄ cup (60 ml) cold water

4 ounces (115 g) granulated sugar

one-half recipe Italian Meringue (page 591)

six medium-sized ripe nectarines (approximately 1 pound, 12 ounces 795 g)

Piping Chocolate (page 904), melted

Raspberry or Strawberry Sauce (pages 1080 and 1081)

edible flowers

NOTE: Because nectarines are not a freestone fruit, cut them in the following manner to produce precise, attractive wedges with clean

*H*ere the word tart, *which has two meanings—referring either to a type of pie or a sour flavor—applies both ways. The slightly acidic, sour taste of rhubarb combines beautifully with sweet Italian Meringue, providing the base for this refreshing dessert. Since nectarines have a fairly short season, try replacing them with either plums or peaches when they are not available. My preference is to leave the skin on fruit whenever possible to provide color and since most commercial peaches are gently scrubbed to remove their unwanted fuzz before they are shipped, chances are you will not have to blanch them and remove the skin. When none of the above are available, another excellent choice are strawberries, which are a classic accompaniment to rhubarb. If you do not have rectangular tart forms use two 9-inch (22.5-cm) round false-bottom pans instead.*

1. Line two 14-by-4¹/₂-inch (35-×-11.2-cm) false-bottom tart pans with Hazelnut Short Dough rolled ¹/₈ inch (3 mm) thick (see Figure 2–14, page 56). Cover the bottom and sides of pans with baking paper. Fill the pans with dried beans or pie weights.

2. Bake the tart shells at 375°F (190°C) until the dough starts to firm up and feel done, approximately 15 minutes. Remove the paper and the beans. If necessary, return the shells to the oven and continue baking until the bottom of the shells are baked through.

3. Remove from the oven and let cool. Remove the shells from the pans. Brush Apricot Glaze over the insides of the shells. Reserve the leftover glaze.

4. Wash the rhubarb and trim both ends off each stalk. Chop the stalks into small pieces and place in a saucepan. Dissolve the cornstarch

edges. Start by cutting the two halves away from the center of the fruit by making two cuts about ¹/₄ inch away from and parallel to the natural crease in the center. This will leave the stone and the surrounding fruit in a separate third piece. Trim the fruit away from the stone and use it for ice cream, sorbet, or nectarine-plum crisp. The half-rounds can then be set flat-side down and cut into attractive wedges (do not make slices).

in the cold water and add it to the rhubarb along with the sugar. Cook over medium heat until the rhubarb falls apart and the mixture thickens to a jam-like consistency. This will take about 45 minutes; you should be left with 1³/₄ to 2 cups (420–480 ml) of reduced rhubarb.

5. Divide the rhubarb mixture between the tart shells. Spread the Italian Meringue in an even layer over the rhubarb. Use a serrated scraper or decorating comb to decorate the meringue, forming a wavy pattern.

6. Brown the meringue lightly under a broiler or salamander. Cut each tart across into six slices. Dip the knife in water before each cut to keep the meringue from sticking to the knife.

7. Cut the nectarines in half (see note). Cut each half into five or six small, neat wedges. Arrange the wedges at an angle on top of each tart slice, using one nectarine half per serving. Brush the remaining Apricot Glaze over the nectarine wedges.

8. Presentation: Place the Piping Chocolate in a piping bag and pipe chocolate in a zigzag pattern over one half of the base of a dessert plate. Place a tart slice in the center of the plate so that half of it is on the piped lines. Pour a pool of Raspberry or Strawberry Sauce on the undecorated part of the plate. Place edible flowers next to the sauce.

 Pecan-Whiskey Tart

two 11-inch (27.5-cm) tarts

1 pound, 8 ounces (680 g) Short Dough (page 54)
Pecan Filling (recipe follows)
dark coating chocolate, melted
1 pint (480 ml) heavy cream
1 tablespoon (15 g) granulated sugar
2 tablespoons (30 ml) whiskey
pecan halves
mint sprigs

This is basically an American pecan pie "dressed up" a little for restaurant service. It is fabulous served warm with a scoop of Vanilla Ice Cream, but being one of my favorites, I wouldn't turn a piece down at any temperature. If you prefer not to use alcohol, substitute orange juice for the whisky.

1. Line two 11-inch (27.5-cm) tart pans with Short Dough rolled ¹/₈ inch (3 mm) thick (see Figure 2–14, page 56). Reserve the shells in the refrigerator while you make the filling.

2. Divide the Pecan Filling evenly between the shells.

3. Bake at 350°F (175°C) for approximately 35 minutes or until the filling is firmly set. Let cool completely.

4. Unmold the tarts. Place a small amount of melted coating chocolate in a piping bag (see page 27) and cut a very small opening. Decorate the tarts by streaking the chocolate across in thin parallel lines. Turn the tart 90° and repeat the procedure to create lines going in the opposite direction (Figure 6–1). As you streak the chocolate across the tarts, move quickly, alternating left to right and right to left, overlapping the edge of the tart on both sides. Cut the tarts into the desired number of pieces.

5. Whip the cream, sugar, and whiskey to very soft peaks; reserve in the refrigerator.

6. Presentation: Place a tart slice on a dessert plate. Spoon a small mound of cream onto the plate next to the slice. Stand a pecan half in the cream and place a mint sprig next to it.

FIGURE 6–1   *Streaking chocolate over Pecan-Whiskey Tart by quickly moving back and forth across the top in both directions, overlapping the edges, to create decorative lines*

 **Pecan Filling**

*enough for two 11-inch
(27.5-cm) tart shells*

8 eggs

13 ounces (370 g) light brown sugar

$^1/_2$ cup (120 ml) or 6 ounces (170 g)
   light corn syrup

$^1/_2$ cup (120 ml) or 6 ounces (170 g)
   molasses

1 teaspoon (5 g) salt

1 teaspoon (5 ml) vanilla extract

$^1/_4$ cup (60 ml) whiskey

3 ounces (85 g) melted unsalted butter

1 pound, 4 ounces (570 g) pecans,
   roughly chopped

1. Whisk the eggs just to break them up, about 1 minute.

2. Mix in the brown sugar, corn syrup, molasses, salt, vanilla, and whiskey.

3. Stir in the melted butter and the pecans.

 **Pink Grapefruit
and Orange Tart**

two 11-inch (27.5-cm) tarts

1 pound, 8 ounces (680 g) Cornmeal
   Crust (page 33)

Orange Custard Filling (recipe
   follows)

segments from four pink grapefruits
   (see Figure 12–5, page 596)

*C*itrus *is an excellent (and often times necessary) choice when making a fresh fruit tart during the early months of the year. In most establishments strawberries are the only berry affordable (or available at all), and many times their quality is way below par. Pink grapefruit, which can be found in the market just about all year round, not only looks good but is very good for you, providing one of nature's best sources of vitamin C with very few calories. (I must point out, however, to get the maximum amount of vitamins you must eat the whole grapefruit segment, including the membrane, which is removed in this recipe.) Look, or perhaps I should say feel, for grapefruits which are heavy and*

segments from six oranges (see Figure
12–5, page 596)
Pectin or Apricot Glaze
   (pages 1017 and 1016)
dark coating chocolate, melted
Lime Cream (page 1088)
long strips of lime zest for garnish

_firm to the touch, with smooth-textured skin. I prefer the Star Ruby to the March
Pink or Ruby Red. They are all pretty much free of seeds, but the Star has a
deeper red (pink) flesh and the reddish-gold peel is also very attractive. Bear in
mind that, just as with blood oranges, the color of the peel is not an indication of
the color or ripeness of the interior flesh in any of the grapefruit varieties._

_Regular Short Dough can be used instead of the Cornmeal Crust, and if
you have Pastry Cream sitting around with nowhere to go, stir orange liqueur
into this and use it instead of the Orange Custard._

1. Line two 11-inch (27.5-cm) false-bottom tart pans with Cornmeal Crust rolled $^{1}/_{8}$ inch (3 mm) thick (see Figure 2–14, page 56). Prick
the dough lightly over the bottom of the pans. (If the dough has
become soft at this point, place the shells in the freezer for a few minutes until firm.) Place a circle of baking paper in each one to cover the
bottom and the sides of the crust. Fill with dried beans or pie weights.

2. Bake the shells at 375°F (190°C) until the edges are golden, about
12 minutes. Remove the baking paper and the weights. Place the shells
back in the oven and continue baking for approximately 10 minutes or
until the bottom is set.

3. Divide the Orange Custard Filling evenly between the shells.
They should be about two-thirds full.

4. Bake at 350°F (175°C) until the custard is set, about 30 minutes.
Let cool completely.

5. Remove the tarts from the pans and set them on cardboard cake
circles. Cut or mark into the desired number of serving pieces. Arrange
the grapefruit and orange segments on the tarts, placing the fruit at an
angle within the marks for each slice. Brush Pectin or Apricot Glaze
over the fruit.

6. Presentation: Place melted dark coating chocolate in a piping
bag and streak lines of chocolate over the upper half of a dessert plate.
Place a tart slice on the other side of the plate at a 45° angle to the lines,
with the tip of the tart on the first few lines. Pour a small pool of Lime
Cream to the left of the tart. Twist a strip of lime zest into a spiral and
set it on the cream.

 Orange Custard Filling

_4$^{1}/_{2}$ cups (1 l, 80 ml)_

12 egg yolks (1 cup/240 ml)
6 ounces (170 g) granulated sugar
3$^{1}/_{3}$ cups (800 ml) heavy cream
3 tablespoons (45 ml) orange liqueur

1. Beat the egg yolks and sugar together to combine.
2. Mix in the cream and liqueur.

Quince Custard Tart

two 11-inch (27.5 cm) tarts

1 pound, 8 ounces (680 g) Short
   Dough (page 54)
2 pounds, 10 ounces (1 kg, 195 g)
   quince (about six medium-size)
one recipe Plain Poaching Syrup
   (page 13)
$^1/_2$ teaspoon (1 g) ground nutmeg
$^1/_2$ teaspoon (.75 g) ground cinnamon
2 ounces (55 g) bread flour
2 ounces (55 g) melted unsalted butter
2 teaspoons (10 ml) lemon juice
6 egg yolks ($^1/_2$ cup/120 ml)
4 ounces (115 g) granulated sugar
2 cups (480 ml) half-and-half
one-quarter recipe Italian Meringue
   (page 591) (see note 3, page 236)

*I*t did not take me long to realize that most Americans do not care all that much for quince. Part of the reason, I think, is that they have never been exposed to this fruit. When I talk about quince at school, the majority of my students look somewhat bewildered as if they are trying to figure out what it is I said (they probably think they missed something because of my accent). I am hoping that if nothing else your curiosity will tempt you to try this great dessert. The slightly tart custard filling contrasts perfectly with the sweet meringue, and if you are like me, a scoop of Vanilla or Caramel Ice Cream completes the picture beautifully.

As an alternative to a dressed-up tart, quince can also be enjoyed baked or caramelized as a simple country-style dessert. To bake, peel and core two quince and cut each one into six wedges. Arrange in a single layer in a small baking dish. Add $^1/_2$ cup (120 ml) of orange juice and 1 ounce (30 g) of melted butter. Sprinkle 5 ounces (140 g) of granulated sugar on top. Bake at 375°F (190°C) for about 40 minutes or until tender. For caramelized quince, cut in half lengthwise after peeling and coring, then slice across $^1/_4$ inch (6 mm) thick. Place the slices in a skillet with 5 ounces (140 g) of granulated sugar, 1 ounce (30 g) of butter, and $^1/_2$ cup (120 ml) of heavy cream. Cook over medium heat, turning the fruit frequently, until the quince is tender and the liquid has been reduced to a caramel. Enjoy baked or caramelized quince with your favorite ice cream.

1. Roll out the Short Dough to $^1/_8$ inch (3 mm) thick and line two 11-inch (27.5-cm) false-bottom tart pans (see Figure 2–14, page 56). Reserve.

2. Peel, core, and quarter the quince. Poach in the Poaching Syrup until tender. Remove the fruit from the liquid and reserve the poaching liquid for another use, such as cake syrup. Purée the cooked quince; you should have about 2 cups (480 ml). Add the nutmeg, cinnamon, bread flour, melted butter, and lemon juice to the purée.

3. Whip the egg yolks with the sugar until thick and foamy. Stir into the quince mixture together with the half-and-half. Divide the filling between the two prepared tart shells.

4. Bake at 425°F (219°C) for 10 minutes. Reduce the heat to 350°F (175°C) and continue baking until the custard is set, approximately 30 minutes. Remove from the oven and set aside to cool.

5. Divide the Italian Meringue evenly between the two tarts. Spread it out to cover the filling, making swirls and tips by moving your spatula up and down. Brown the meringue using a salamander, broiler, or blowtorch.

6. Cut the tarts into the desired number of pieces, using a thin chef's knife. Dip the knife in hot water to keep the meringue from sticking.

Raspberry-Lemon Tart

two 11-inch (27.5-cm) tarts

1 pound, 8 ounces (680 g) Short Dough (page 54)
one recipe Lemon Cream (page 1087)
1 dry pint (480 ml) fresh raspberries
softly whipped cream
thin strips of lemon zest

This is a very pretty tart; do not miss out on trying it when fresh raspberries are plentiful and inexpensive. Fresh blueberries, ripe and bursting with flavor, also make a great substitute. For a very colorful presentation, use a combination of the two. When using blueberries alone, reserve ¼ cup (60 ml) of the Lemon Cream and brush it over the top of the baked and cooled tarts before adding the blueberries or they have a tendency to roll off.

1. Line two 11-inch (27.5-cm) false-bottom tart pans with Short Dough rolled ⅛ inch (3 mm) thick (see Figure 2–14, page 56). Place a circle of baking paper in each pan to cover the bottom and sides and fill with dried beans or pie weights.

2. Bake at 375°F (190°C) to a light golden, not brown, color, about 12 minutes. Cool to room temperature.

3. Remove the paper and weights from the cooled tart shells. Divide the Lemon Cream evenly between the shells.

4. Bake at 375°F (190°C) until the filling is just set, about 15 minutes (the filling will set a little more as it cools).

5. Let the tarts cool completely, then remove them from the pans and slide onto cake cardboards. Cut (or mark if presenting whole) into the desired number of pieces.

6. Arrange the raspberries on the surface of each slice, placing them within the markings for each piece so that they will not be cut when the tart is sliced. To preserve the natural satin look of the raspberries, do not rinse or glaze them.

7. Presentation: Place a tart slice in the center of a dessert plate. Spoon softly whipped cream over the tip of the slice and onto the plate. Place two or three strips of lemon zest on the cream.

VARIATION
Fig Tart

1 pound, 8 ounces (680 g) Short Dough (page 54)
three-quarter recipe Lemon Cream (page 1087)
twenty-four fresh (green or black) figs, cut in quarters, lengthwise
softly whipped cream

NOTE: This is a refreshing and striking alternative: Follow the directions for the Raspberry-Lemon Tart through step 5, but do not cut the tarts. Slice the figs crosswise and use to cover the lemon filling. Brush with Pectin Glaze (page 1017). Allow it to set before cutting.

1. Follow the preceding directions in steps one, two, and three.

2. Arrange the figs on top of the Lemon Cream, cut-side up, making concentric circles and spacing the fig quarters about ¼ inch (6 mm) apart.

3. Bake as instructed for Raspberry-Lemon Tart.

4. Presentation: Place a tart slice in the center of a dessert plate. Spoon softly whipped cream over the tip of the slice and onto the plate.

Strawberry-Kiwi Tart

two 11-inch (27.5-cm) tarts

1 pound, 8 ounces (680 g) Short Dough (page 54)

Apricot Glaze (page 1016)

3 pounds, 14 ounces (1 kg, 765 g) or two-thirds recipe Pastry Cream (page 1088)

four kiwis, peeled and thinly sliced crosswise (instructions follow)

twenty strawberries (approximately) cut in half lengthwise

I made a version of this tart on the PBS series "Cooking at the Academy," using a rainbow of fresh seasonal fruit. I could have kicked myself later for not remembering to caution about the different ways of arranging fruit on a tart, taking into consideration whether the tarts would be cut and plated or presented whole. I often observe students arranging the fruit in a beautiful pattern without realizing what is going to happen to that so-carefully-assembled creation once the tart is cut into twelve (or worse, sixteen) pieces, which is a typical buffet portion. Although it may not pose a problem to cut through the thin slices of kiwi in this tart, it is always a good idea to plan ahead, and this extra step does not take much time or effort. It is especially important when working with fruit that should not be cut, such as raspberries, blackberries, or blueberries. First, mark the top of the custard into the number of slices desired. It is then easy to arrange the fruit within the marks so that you can later cut the tart without cutting into, or ruining, the design.

To mark sixteen servings from an 11-inch (27.5-cm) round tart, begin by marking a circle in the center of the tart using a 5-inch (12.5-cm) plain cookie cutter. Next mark the tart (including the center circle) into quarters. Lastly, mark each of the quarters around the outside ring (excluding the circle) into three equal pieces. You now have sixteen pieces which, being shorter and wider, are easier to decorate. When you are ready to cut the tart, use the cookie cutter as a guide for your paring knife to cut the center.

1. Line two 11-inch (27.5-cm) false-bottom tart pans with Short Dough rolled ⅛ inch (3 mm) thick (see Figure 2–14, page 56). Line with circles of baking paper to cover the bottom and sides, then fill with dried beans or pie weights.

2. Bake at 375°F (190°C) until light golden, about 12 minutes. Remove the paper and the weights. Place the shells back in the oven for about 6 to 8 minutes longer or until they are pale brown on the bottom. Let cool.

3. Brush Apricot Glaze over the bottom and sides of the cooled shells. Reserve the remaining glaze to use later. Divide the Pastry Cream equally between the two tart shells and spread it out evenly. If possible, it is best to make the Pastry Cream fresh so you can pour it into the shells while it is still warm (not hot). It will adhere to the sides of the crust nicely. If you do use it warm, let the Pastry Cream cool before adding the fruit.

4. Remove the tarts from the pans and place on serving platters or on cardboard rounds for support. Arrange sliced kiwis in the center and the strawberries around the edge. Reheat the Apricot Glaze (you may need to add a small amount of water). Brush the Apricot Glaze over the top of the tarts. Cut the tarts into the desired number of slices.

Instructions for Peeling Kiwifruit with a Spoon

A great way to peel kiwis and still retain their oval shape is to use an oval soup spoon, preferably one with a thin sharp edge. For this to work properly, the fruit must be ripe but not soft. Cut off the top and

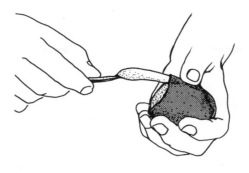

FIGURE 6–2   *Inserting a spoon between the skin and the flesh of a kiwi*

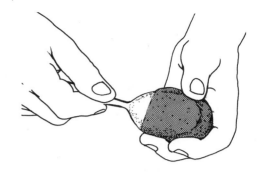

FIGURE 6–3   *Gradually pushing the spoon to the bottom of the kiwi while turning the kiwi at the same time*

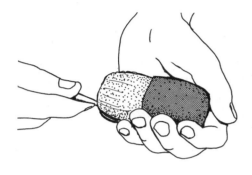

FIGURE 6–4   *After twisting the spoon all the way around inside the skin, pulling out the spoon to remove the peeled kiwi*

bottom of the kiwi. Carefully, and gradually, insert the spoon between the skin and the flesh (Figure 6–2). Holding the kiwi in your palm, gradually slide the spoon all the way around between the skin and the flesh, making two or three turns, while pushing the spoon through to the bottom of the kiwi (Figure 6–3). Pull the spoon out (Figure 6–4). You will have a perfectly smooth kiwi with its natural shape and a minimum of wasted fruit instead of a kiwi that resembles a potato peeled with a large knife.

Strawberry-Rhubarb Tart

two 11-inch (27.5-cm) tarts

4 pounds (1 kg, 820 g) rhubarb stalks

3 tablespoons (24 g) cornstarch

1 pound (455 g) granulated sugar

2 pounds, 14 ounces (1 kg, 310 g) Short Dough (page 54)

5 ounces (140 g) apricot jam

Egg Wash (page 7)

twenty medium-sized fresh strawberries

Apricot Glaze (page 1016)

Romanoff Sauce or Crème Fraîche (pages 1081 and 1073)

This classic combination of tangy rhubarb and sweet strawberries is not only delicious but the tarts look very pretty framed with Short Dough strips in a diamond pattern. Unfortunately, this tart is not a good keeper; it has a tendency to become moist on the bottom after one day. The best solution is to prep the baked shells and the cooked rhubarb ahead (a few days is okay) and then quickly assemble and finish the tarts as needed.

1. Trim off the top and bottom of the rhubarb stalks and discard. Cut the stalks into 1/2-inch (1.2-cm) cubes.

2. Stir the cornstarch into the sugar, add the rhubarb cubes, and mix well. Set aside for about half an hour to draw some of the juice out of the rhubarb.

3. Transfer the rhubarb, and the accumulated juice, to a saucepan. Cook over low heat until soft but not falling apart. Strain off the liquid; you may save the liquid to make the sauce for a variation of this recipe (instructions follow), use it for cake syrup, or discard it.

4. Roll out a portion of the Short Dough 1/8 inch (3 mm) thick, and use it to line two 11-inch (27.5-cm) tart pans (see Figure 2–14, page 56); reserve the remaining dough. Line the pans with baking paper and fill with dried beans or pie weights.

5. Bake at 375°F (190°C) until the Short Dough is set but has not yet started to brown, approximately 8 minutes.

6. Remove the paper and the weights. Allow the shells to cool slightly, then divide the jam between them and spread out over the bottom of the shells. Return to the oven and continue baking until the crust is just done. Divide the rhubarb evenly between the two tart shells and continue baking until the shells begin to turn golden brown, approximately 10 minutes. Do not overbake. Cool slightly.

7. Roll the remaining Short Dough into a rectangle 11 inches (27.5 cm) wide and ¹/₈ inch (3 mm) thick. Cut twenty-four ³/₈-inch (9-mm) strips, using a fluted pastry wheel. It is usually a good idea to transfer the dough to a sheet pan or a sheet of cardboard and chill it before cutting the strips.

8. Brush Egg Wash lightly around the edge of the baked tarts.

9. Twist the Short Dough strips one at a time into a corkscrew shape (see Figure 4–10, page 155). Arrange twelve strips, evenly spaced, on top of each tart, first placing six in one direction, then six on top at a 45° angle to the first set, to form a diamond pattern (see Figure 9-32, page 429). Brush Egg Wash on the first layer of strips before placing the second layer on top. Then brush additional Egg Wash on the second layer.

10. Return the tarts to the oven and bake at 375°F (190°C) until the Short Dough strips are golden brown, approximately 10 minutes. Let the tarts cool to room temperature.

11. Rinse the strawberries, trim off the tops (a melon-ball cutter is excellent for this), and slice them lengthwise into six pieces each. Place the strawberry slices in the diamonds between the Short Dough strips.

12. Brush the tops of the tarts with Apricot Glaze to preserve the fresh look of the berries. Cut the tarts into the desired number of serving pieces.

13. Presentation: Place a tart slice in the center of a dessert plate. Spoon Romanoff Sauce or Crème Fraîche over the tip of the slice and let some run onto the plate. Serve at room temperature.

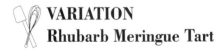

VARIATION
Rhubarb Meringue Tart

*T*opping *fruit desserts with Italian Meringue is classic in Europe. The meringue gives the dessert a clean finished look, and the sweet flavor contrasts beautifully with acidic fruits, especially rhubarb. Browning the meringue adds to the visual appeal. Do not pipe and brown the meringue more than three hours prior to serving; ideally it should be done to order—à* la minute. *If you are presenting the tarts whole, glaze the rhubarb with Apricot Glaze and then pipe rosettes of meringue using a no. 6 (12-mm) star tip around the perimeter only, so the rhubarb remains visible. Serve Rhubarb Meringue Tart warm or at room temperature.*

1. Follow the directions for Strawberry-Rhubarb Tart through step six, using only 1 pound, 8 ounces (680 g) of Short Dough.

2. Make one-quarter recipe of Italian Meringue (see page 591) (see note 3, page 236).

3. Cut or mark the tarts into serving pieces.

4. Using a pastry bag with a no. 3 (6-mm) star tip, pipe the meringue on top of the rhubarb, within the markings for each slice, starting at the tip of the slice and piping the strips of meringue next to each other in a zigzag design (piping left to right then right to left) to the edge (see Figure 8–16, page 348, as an example).

5. Caramelize (brown) the meringue in a salamander, a very hot oven (450°F/230°C), or use a propane torch.

6. Adjust the sweetness of the reserved rhubarb juice by adding either sugar or water as necessary. Thicken with 1 tablespoon (8 g) cornstarch per pint (480 ml) of liquid.

7. **Presentation:** Place the tart slice off-center on a dessert plate. Pour a pool of sauce on the larger exposed part of the plate.

Swedish Apple Tart

two 11-inch (27.5-cm) tarts or 16 individual tarts

4 pounds, 8 ounces (2 kg, 45 g) Red Delicious apples (approximately twelve medium-sized)
one-half recipe Spiced Poaching Syrup (page 13)
1 pound, 8 ounces (680 g) Short Dough (page 54)
1 cup (240 ml) lingonberry jam
one-half recipe Swedish Hazelnut Filling (page 255)
8 ounces (225 g) Pastry Cream (page 1088)
1 ounce (30 g) thinly sliced natural almonds
powdered sugar
1 cup (240 ml) heavy cream
1 teaspoon (5 ml) vanilla extract
Florentinas (page 212), cut in half
edible flowers

This is my version of a popular Swedish country-style apple tart. My mom made this often enough when I was a kid that I should have remembered it (unfortunately, my excuse is that it has been quite awhile since then), but I had forgotten this recipe until a few years back when I was served a variation of it at Operakällaren, an old and well-known restaurant in Stockholm. Prepared lingonberries are a staple found in every Swedish pantry. You can substitute cranberry jam if you wish or use the recipe for Cranberry Purée on page 300. If you use purchased cranberry jam, do not put any on top of the apples. The type of jam sold commercially dries out instead of soaking into the fruit. Another way to modify this recipe is to use poached pears instead of apples. They too taste great baked in the nut filling.

This recipe can be used to make sixteen individual tarts by making the following changes: Use eight small apples rather than twelve medium, double the amount of Short Dough, and increase the amount of lingonberry jam slightly. Follow the directions using tart pans that measure 4¹/₂ inches (11.2 cm). The individual tarts take about 15 minutes to bake.

1. Peel, core, and cut the apples in half. Place the apples in a saucepan together with the Poaching Syrup and simmer until the apples are soft. Remove from the heat and reserve.

2. Line two 11-inch (27.5-cm) false-bottom tart pans with Short Dough rolled ¹/₈ inch (3 mm) thick (see Figure 2–14, page 56). Spread half of the lingonberry jam over the bottom of the tart shells.

3. Combine the Swedish Hazelnut Filling with the Pastry Cream. Divide between the shells.

4. Cut the apples into thin slices cutting from the round side without cutting all the way through (leave the slices attached on the flat sides). Divide the apples evenly between the two tarts, placing them on the filling flat-side down, leaving a ¹/₂-inch (1.2-cm) space between them. Press the apples down to fan the cuts out. Using all of the remaining jam, spoon a small dot of jam on each apple. Sprinkle sliced almonds around the apples.

5. Bake at 375°F (190°C) for 20 minutes. Remove from the oven and sift powdered sugar over the tops of the tarts. Place the tarts back in the oven and bake until cooked through, about 15 minutes longer. Let cool. Remove the tarts from the pans and cut into the desired number of serving pieces.

6. Whip the heavy cream and the vanilla until stiff peaks form. Place in a pastry bag with a no. 7 (14-mm) star tip. Reserve in the refrigerator.

7. Presentation: Place a tart slice in the center of a dessert plate. Pipe a rosette of cream on the plate next to the tart and stand a Florentina cookie in the cream. Place an edible flower next to the cookie.

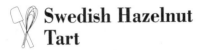 **Swedish Hazelnut Tart**

two 11-inch (27.5-cm) tarts

1 pound, 8 ounces (680 g) Short
 Dough (page 54)
5 ounces (140 g) apricot jam
Swedish Hazelnut Filling
 (recipe follows)
powdered sugar
Ganache (page 1086)
fresh orange slices for decoration

NOTE: To get a precise and sharp contrast, use a plain cookie cutter as a guide for the center circle when you cut your template, then place the cutter in the opening to act as a seal while you sift the powdered sugar. Remove the cutter and the template carefully.

*T*his tart is a perennial favorite and very adaptable: You may substitute any other nut in place of the hazelnuts, or you can use a combination of several varieties. I have even made this recipe without the Candied Orange Peel, substituting grated orange rind, Pastry Cream, and even apricot jam with excellent results. Another great thing about this recipe is that the baked tarts keep exceptionally well and taste even better, or I should say moister, after a few days in the refrigerator. (Nuts tend to absorb moisture in baked goods; many times this works to our disadvantage, as in cookies, but they are working with us here.) This tart has been a real lifesaver for large banquet functions. You can easily make small, pretty buffet-size pieces by covering the bottom only of a paper-lined sheet pan with Short Dough. Spread apricot jam over the Short Dough and then add the filling. The filling recipe makes enough for one half-sheet pan. Bake the sheet a little longer than the round tarts. Cool and cut into the desired size and shape pieces. Decorate each piece with a rosette of Ganache and a small orange wedge or strip of orange peel.*

1. Line two 11-inch (27.5-cm) tart pans (false-bottom or solid) with Short Dough rolled ⅛ inch (3 mm) thick (see Figure 2–14, page 56). Place the lined pans in the refrigerator to firm the dough.

2. Soften the jam by working it in a bowl with a spoon until smooth. (You may need to add a small amount of water if the jam is too firm.) Divide the jam between the shells and spread out in a thin film on the bottom of each tart. Return the pans to the refrigerator while you make the filling.

3. Divide the filling between the tart shells and spread it out, mounding it just slightly higher in the center.

4. Bake the tarts at 350°F (175°C) until the filling is firm in the middle and the shells are golden brown, about 35 minutes. Let the tarts cool completely, then unmold.

5. Make a template that is ½ inch (1.2 cm) smaller than the tarts and has a 4-inch (10-cm) circle cut out of the center. Place the template on the tarts, one at a time, and sift powdered sugar on top. Slice the tarts into the desired number of servings.

6. Warm the Ganache until it develops a slight shine. Place in a pastry bag with a no. 4 (8-mm) plain tip. Pipe the Ganache in a heart design at the edge of each slice; decorate with a small slice of fresh orange. (Unfortunately, the oranges will only look fresh for a few hours, so do not decorate more tarts or slices than you will use within that time.)

Swedish Hazelnut Filling

3 pounds (1 kg, 365 g) Filling

12 ounces (340 g) hazelnuts
5 ounces (140 g) Candied Orange Peel
   (page 978)
12 ounces (340 g) granulated sugar
12 ounces (340 g) soft unsalted butter
3 eggs
4 egg yolks (1/3 cup/80 ml)
1 1/2 teaspoons (7.5 ml) vanilla extract

1. Grind the hazelnuts, orange peel, and 6 ounces (170 g) of the sugar very finely, until almost a paste.

2. Cream the butter with the remaining 6 ounces (170 g) of sugar. Gradually mix in the whole eggs, egg yolks, vanilla, and the nut mixture. Be careful not to overmix; if too much air is incorporated, the tarts will puff up while baking and then fall in the center, giving them an unattractive finished appearance.

Tart Hollandaise

two 11-inch (27.5-cm) tarts

1 pound, 12 ounces (795 g) Puff
   Pastry or Quick Puff Pastry
   (pages 44 and 47)
5 ounces (140 g) apricot jam
3 pounds (1 kg, 365 g) Mazarin Filling
   (page 1088)
2 ounces (55 g) sliced almonds
1 pound 6 ounces (625 g) Short Dough
   (page 54)
Egg Wash (page 7)
powdered sugar

NOTE: It takes more Puff Pastry than Short Dough, rolled out to the same thickness, to line two tart pans. The reason is this: after rolling out the Short Dough to line one pan, I can reroll the scraps to line the second pan; with Puff Pastry this is not practical since the dough scraps would have to rest before being rolled out again.

*T*his old-fashioned Dutch tart features Puff Pastry, Short Dough, and almonds, which combine so well and appear in many European pastries. You can easily adapt this recipe to make a wonderful apple or pear tart: Use a little less Mazarin Filling (make only a half-recipe, 2 pounds, 5 ounces/1 kg, 50 g) and press poached pears or apples halfway into the Mazarin Filling before baking. Sprinkle almonds over the fruit (plus some Cinnamon Sugar if you like) and eliminate the Short Dough strips.*

1. Cut the Puff Pastry in half. Roll out 1/8 inch (3 mm) thick and line two 11-inch (27.5-cm) tart pans (false-bottom or solid). Using your thumbs, press the dough up about 1/4 inch (6 mm) above the edge of the pans to allow for shrinkage. Place a circle of baking paper in each pan to cover the bottom and sides, fill with dried beans or pie weights, and let rest for at least 30 minutes in the refrigerator.

2. Bake the shells at 375°F (190°C) for about 10 minutes. Let them cool until they can be handled, then remove the paper and the weights.

3. Spread the jam in a thin layer on the bottom of each shell. Place the Mazarin Filling in a pastry bag with a no. 6 (12-mm) plain tip. Pipe the filling into the tarts shells in an even layer. Sprinkle sliced almonds evenly over the tops.

4. Roll out the Short Dough into a rectangle 11 inches (27.5 cm) wide and 1/8 inch (3 mm) thick. Refrigerate the dough to make it easier to handle. Cut into 1/4-inch-wide (6-mm) strips, using a fluted pastry wheel.

5. Arrange the dough strips 1/4 inch (6 mm) apart over the almonds; then arrange strips on top in the other direction so they form a diamond pattern (see example Figure 9–32, page 429). Press the strips lightly with your hand as you place them to make sure they stick together. Carefully brush the strips with Egg Wash.

6. Bake the tarts at 375°F (190°C) until golden brown, about 45 minutes. Let cool to room temperature.

7. Remove the tarts from the pans. Slice into the desired number of serving pieces, and sift powdered sugar lightly over the tops. Serve warm or at room temperature.

 ## Tart Tatin

one 9-inch (22.5-cm) tart

6 ounces (170 g) Puff Pastry, Quick Puff Pastry, or scraps) (pages 44 and 47)
6 pounds (2 kg 730 g) Red or Golden Delicious apples (approximately twelve medium-sized)
3½ ounces (100 g) unsalted butter
7 ounces (200 g) granulated sugar
1½ cups (360 ml) Crème Fraîche (page 1073), approximately
Cinnamon Sugar (page 5)
strawberry halves

NOTE 1: A skillet that measures 10 inches across the top with 2-to-2½-inch sides sloping down to 9 inches across the bottom is ideal (25 × 5 to 6.2 × 22.5 cm). If you use a larger skillet, place an adjustable ring made of stainless steel (the anodized metal type will stain the apples) adjusted to 10 inches (25 cm) in the skillet, or use the ring from a 9-inch (22.5-cm) springform unclamped. The ring will sit high on the sides of the skillet, but as the apples cook and compact, you can adjust it. I prefer to use a copper skillet lined with stainless steel (the French make one designed specifically for Tart Tatin), but any heavy skillet will do as long as the handle is heatproof so that the skillet can be placed in the oven.

NOTE 2: This tart is best served warm from the oven. If you must, serve it at room temperature, but never cold. Tart Tatin should be served the same day it is made. If necessary it can be made up to 24 hours ahead, provided the tarts are cooled completely and then refrigerated after baking and are reheated in a low oven

*T*his fabulous French upside-down apple tart was first made by the sisters demoiselles Tatin at their restaurant in the Loire Valley over one hundred years ago. And still standing across from the station house in the little railroad junction of Lamotte-Beuvron is the Hotel Tatin, where you can enjoy a warm slice of their famous caramelized apple tart. I have seen many shortcut versions in which baked Puff Pastry and cooked apples (and in some extreme cases, even a separate caramel sauce) are individually prepared ahead of time, and the dessert (I cannot call it Tart Tatin) is assembled to order. This may taste good in some instances, but the result is an entirely different dessert from a genuine Tart Tatin. The only way you can achieve the true caramelized apple flavor is to cook the apples and sugar together, creating a natural phenomenon in which the apple halves release their juice into the sugar and butter mixture flavoring and diluting the liquid, and at the same time keeping it from caramelizing too fast, which in turn allows the apples to become partially cooked before the liquid is reduced and caramelized. Your job is to oversee the process, making sure there are no hot spots and the heat is not too high.*

The ingredients specify Red or Golden Delicious apples, and I mean it! I have not found any other apples that will not fall apart into applesauce using this cooking method. (Red and Golden Delicious have a higher starch content.) While I am sure there are other varieties that will work, do not try substituting any of the standard green cooking apple variations.

1. Roll the Puff Pastry into a square approximately 10 by 10 inches (25 × 25 cm) and slightly thinner than ⅛ inch (3 mm) thick. Place on a sheet pan, prick well, and reserve in the refrigerator.

2. Peel, core, and cut the apples in half lengthwise.

3. Put the butter in a 9-inch (22.5-cm) skillet (see note 1) and melt over medium heat. Sprinkle the sugar evenly over the melted butter. Quickly arrange as many of the apples as possible in the skillet, standing them on their stem ends and packing them tightly. You will not be able to fit all of the pieces in the pan at the beginning, but as the apples cook, release their juice, and shrink, you will be able to squeeze in the remainder. It is important that the apples form a tight layer in the pan or they will not hold together when the tart is inverted later.

4. Cook over medium heat, shaking the skillet gently to make sure the apples do not stick to the bottom and pressing lightly on the top to form a compact layer. As the apples in the skillet shrink, add the apple pieces that you were not able to fit in at the start. Continue cooking, still shaking the skillet and pressing the apples together, until the sugar turns a dark golden brown, about 30 minutes depending on the type of

just before inverting and serving. Crème Fraîche is the classical accompaniment to Tart Tatin, but Chantilly Cream (see page 1083) will do as well, if you sweeten it less than is called for in the recipe; there is plenty of sugar from the caramel in the tart. Or, serve Tart Tatin the way I like it with Vanilla Ice Cream, either the old-fashioned version or a slightly acid yogurt-based ice cream.

skillet and the temperature of the stove. Remove from the heat and let cool for 10 minutes.

5. Cut a 10-inch (25-cm) circle from the reserved Puff Pastry square (save the scraps for another use). Cover the apples with the Puff Pastry, tucking the dough between the apples and the skillet (or the apples and the ring).

6. Bake at 375°F (190°C) for about 30 minutes or until the Puff Pastry is baked through. Let the tart cool until the caramelized sugar has thickened to a syrup. If it cools to the point that the apples are stuck on the bottom, place the skillet on the stove and warm slightly.

7. Invert a platter on top of the tart and flip them over together to unmold the tart onto the platter. Be careful of the hot caramel as you do this. Cut the tart into the desired number of slices.

8. Presentation: Place a tart slice on a dessert plate, spoon Crème Fraîche over the tip of the tart, and sprinkle Cinnamon Sugar lightly over the top. Fan a strawberry half and set on the plate next to the Crème Fraîche.

Walnut-Caramel Tart

two 11-inch (27.5-cm) tarts

2 pounds, 14 ounces (1 kg, 310 g) Short Dough (page 54)
Caramel Filling (recipe follows)
Egg Wash (page 7)
10 ounces (285 g) Ganache (page 1086)
5 ounces (140 g) walnuts, finely chopped
Orange Sauce (page 1077)
Chocolate Sauce for Piping (page 1072)
raspberries

NOTE: Walnut-Caramel Tart must be served at room temperature because the caramelized sugar becomes too hard if refrigerated.

You could argue that this is a candy disguised as a tart, but whatever you want to call it, it is a very rich, delicious combination of buttery chewy caramel with walnuts in a crisp Short Dough crust; who could resist?

Keep a watchful eye on the caramel as you make the filling and have the cream ready. If you let it get too dark, don't waste the cream and the butter—just start over. Not only will the filling be bitter if the caramel is overcooked, but it will set up hard enough to pull the fillings right out of your teeth! At the same time, keep in mind that if you play it too safe and do not caramelize the sugar enough, the filling will not harden sufficiently.

1. Roll out a portion of the Short Dough 1/8 inch (3 mm) thick and use it to line two 11-inch (27.5-cm), tart pans (see Figure 2–14, page 56). These do not have to be false-bottom pans. Reserve the remaining dough. Place circles of baking paper in the pans to cover the bottom and sides, and fill with dried beans or pie weights.

2. Bake at 375°F (190°C) until set but not brown, about 12 minutes.

3. Remove the paper and weights from the partially baked shells. Divide the Caramel Filling evenly between the shells.

4. Roll out the remaining Short Dough 1/8 inch (3 mm) thick.

5. Brush the edge of the baked shells with Egg Wash, then cover with the dough. Press the edges together to seal, and trim away any excess dough. Prick the top lightly to let air escape.

6. Bake the tarts at 350°F (175°C) until golden brown, about 30 minutes. If the pastry bubbles, press it down with the bottom of a cake pan or any other flat object while the tart is still hot from the oven. Let the tarts cool to room temperature.

7. Remove the tarts from the pans. Warm the Ganache to a soft, but not runny, consistency; it should have a nice shine.

8. Spread a thin even layer of warm Ganache on top of one tart. Place a 5-to-6-inch (12.5–15-cm) plain cookie cutter (or anything with a rim around it so it will not damage the Ganache) in the center of the tart. Sprinkle the chopped walnuts around the ring before the Ganache hardens, taking care not to spill any in the middle. (Sprinkle the walnuts lightly; you should still be able to see as much uncovered Ganache as you do nuts.) Remove the cookie cutter and refrigerate the tart to firm the Ganache. Repeat with the remaining tart.

9. Cut the tarts into the desired number of slices using a sharp knife dipped in hot water.

10. Presentation: Place a slice of Walnut-Caramel Tart slightly off-center on a dessert plate. Pour a pool of Orange Sauce in the larger space, and decorate the sauce with Chocolate Sauce for Piping (as shown on pages 998 to 1006). Place three raspberries on the opposite side of the plate.

Caramel Filling

4 pounds, 3 ounces (1 kg, 905 g) filling

2 pounds (910 g) granulated sugar

4 teaspoons (20 ml) lemon juice

1 cup (240 ml) heavy cream, at room temperature

10 ounces (285 g) unsalted butter

1 pound (455 g) walnuts, coarsely chopped

NOTE: If made ahead, you may need to warm the filling before spreading it in the tart shells.

1. Caramelize the sugar with the lemon juice in a heavy-bottomed saucepan (see page 954).

2. Cook, stirring constantly with a wooden spoon, until the mixture reaches a light brown color, 335°F (168°C). Remove from the heat.

3. Quickly add the cream and swirl it around to mix.

4. Stir in the butter, then the walnuts.

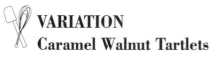

VARIATION
Caramel Walnut Tartlets

30 pastries

1 pound, 8 ounces (680 g) Short Dough (page 54)

one-half recipe Caramel Filling, walnuts chopped fine rather than coarse

powdered sugar

6 ounces (170 g) soft Ganache (page 1086)

thirty small walnut quarters for decorating

Be forewarned that these are addictive! They are basically like eating a piece of walnut toffee wrapped in Short Dough. If you do not have Ganache on hand, omit the powdered sugar, dip the top of the tartlets into melted dark coating chocolate instead, and place a walnut half in the center before the chocolate hardens.

1. Line 30 tartlet forms with Short Dough (see Figures 2–15 to 2–18, pages 57 and 58), rolling the Short Dough 1/16 inch (2 mm) thick and reserving the remaining Short Dough rather than rolling it out again. Prick the bottom of the shells with a fork.

2. Bake the shells at 375°F (190°C) for approximately 12 minutes or until they start to brown lightly. Remove from the oven and let cool for a few minutes.

NOTE: Do not bake the tartlets in a hotter oven or longer than necessary or you risk having the filling boil over in the forms, making the tartlets impossible to remove from the forms.

3. Warm the Caramel Filling if necessary to soften it. Place in a pastry bag with a no. 7 (14-mm) plain tip. Pipe the filling into the shells. Flatten the top of the filling if necessary. Push the forms as close together as possible.

4. Roll the reserved Short Dough out to ¹/₁₆ inch (2 mm) thick, roughly in the same shape as the forms on the sheet pan. Roll the dough up on a dowel and unroll over the top of the tartlets. Press down on the top of each one with the palm of your hand to trim the short dough around the sides of the forms. Cover the scrap dough and save for another use. Spread the tartlets out over the pan. Use a fork to prick the top of the dough.

5. Bake the tartlets at 325°F (163°C) for approximately 12 minutes or until the tops are baked (they should not brown; see note). Let the tartlets cool.

6. Unmold and sift powdered sugar lightly over the tops. Place the Ganache in a pastry bag with a no. 5 (10-mm) star tip. Pipe a small rosette of Ganache in the center of each pastry. Place a walnut quarter on the Ganache.

Walnut-Topped Spanish Rum Torte

two 10-inch (25-cm) tortes

Butter and Flour Mixture (page 4)

1 pound, 8 ounces (680 g) soft unsalted butter

1 pound, 8 ounces (680 g) granulated sugar

2 tablespoons (30 ml) vanilla extract

5 eggs, at room temperature

1 pound, 4 ounces (570 g) cake flour

1 tablespoon (12 g) baking powder

1 teaspoon (5 g) salt

¹/₄ cup (60 ml) dark rum

1 pound (455 g) Pastry Cream (page 1088)

2 ounces (55 g) finely crushed walnuts

powdered sugar

*T*his simple and delicious torte is also known as a Basque Cake. It is really a type of pound cake or coffee cake filled with a vanilla custard. This is certainly not all that unusual, except that here, the filling is added before the tortes are baked. This step allows the vanilla and rum plenty of time to fully flavor the torte. Adjust the amount of rum to suit your own taste should the flavor seem too strong. The custard layer in the center helps to make this torte a great keeper. Stored covered in the refrigerator, it will keep fresh up to one week.

1. Grease the inside of two 10-inch (25-cm) cake pans using the Butter and Flour Mixture. Reserve.

2. Cream together the butter, sugar, and vanilla until light and fluffy. Add the eggs one at a time.

3. Sift together the flour, baking powder, and salt. Gradually incorporate the dry ingredients into the butter mixture.

4. Place the batter in a pastry bag with a no. 5 (10-mm) plain tip. Pipe the batter in a spiral over the bottom of one of the prepared cake pans, starting in the center. Pipe an additional ring of batter on top of the largest ring against the inside perimeter of the pan. Repeat with the second cake pan; you will not use all of the batter.

5. Stir the rum into the Pastry Cream. Divide the Pastry Cream between the two pans, on top of the batter within the extra rings piped around the perimeter, and spread it out evenly. Pipe the remaining batter in a spiral on top of the Pastry Cream in each pan. Sprinkle the walnuts over the top of each.

6. Bake at 350°F (175°C) for approximately 50 minutes. Allow to cool in the pans. Remove the tortes from the pans and dust powdered sugar lightly over the tops. Cut into the desired number of servings.

7

Sponge Cakes and Tea Cakes

Sponge Cakes and Other Cake Batters	Tea Cakes
Sponge Cake	Apple Cinnamon Cake
Chocolate Sponge Cake	Banana Bread
Almond Sponge	Chocolate Crisp Cake
Angel Food Cake	Chocolate Gugelhupf
Chiffon Sponge Cake	Lingonberry Cake
Devil's Food Cake Layers	Raisin Cake
Dobos Sponge	Soft Gingerbread Cake
Hazelnut-Chocolate Sponge	Streusel Kuchen
High-Ratio Sponge Cake	Swedish Jam Roll
Ladyfingers	Tiger Cake
Othello Sponge	
Ribbon Sponge Sheets	

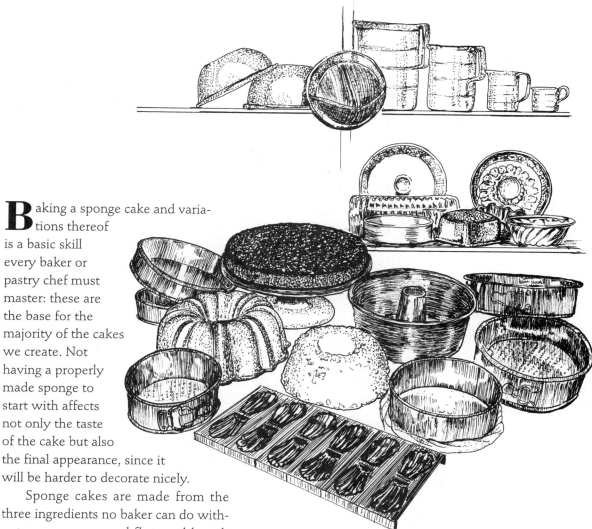

Baking a sponge cake and variations thereof is a basic skill every baker or pastry chef must master: these are the base for the majority of the cakes we create. Not having a properly made sponge to start with affects not only the taste of the cake but also the final appearance, since it will be harder to decorate nicely.

Sponge cakes are made from the three ingredients no baker can do without—eggs, sugar, and flour—although some sponges also contain butter. Sponge cakes do not contain baking powder or baking soda—their volume and light texture come solely from the air whipped into the eggs.

Formula Balance

An extremely heavy, or rich, sponge contains equal parts eggs, sugar, and flour. In other words, for every 8 ounces (225 g) of eggs (approximately four) there are 8 ounces (225 g) of sugar and 8 ounces (225 g) of flour. This ratio is actually the formula for a standard pound cake. A medium-bodied mixture will contain 5 ounces (140 g) each of flour and sugar, for the same quantity (8 ounces/225 g) of eggs. In the lighter and most common type of sponge cake, the sugar and flour weights are 3 ounces (85 g) each, per 8 ounces (225 g) of eggs. The sugar and flour ratio can be altered to a small degree in individual formulas such as 3 ounces (85 g) of sugar and 4 ounces (115 g) of flour, or vice versa. If butter is used, the amount is generally about half of the weight of the sugar or flour and it is added at the end.

Eggs

In any sponge formula the weight of the eggs is always used as the basis for determining the quantity of the remaining ingredients. Whole eggs, entirely or in part, may be replaced with egg yolks or egg whites. More egg yolks will result in a denser sponge with finer pores. Increasing the amount of egg whites produces a lighter sponge with a larger pore structure. Increasing the yolk content in an already heavy sponge cake can have a detrimental effect. The yolks will reduce the available water content, making it difficult for all of the sugar to dissolve. The eggs should be broken as close as possible to the time of making the sponge. Eggs that have been broken and left overnight should not be used for this purpose.

Sugar

Granulated sugar, or even better the finer grade, castor sugar, should always be used in a sponge cake to ensure that the sugar dissolves easily. The proper amount in relation to the other ingredients is also important as discussed above. Too little sugar, in addition to affecting the taste and color, can make the cake tough by throwing the formula off balance: in actuality you now have too much flour. It will also cause the crust to darken unfavorably and will give the sponge a dense texture.

Flour

The flour used in a sponge cake must have a good ratio between starch and protein. Some gluten (for instance, bread flour) is necessary to bind and hold the structure, but too high a percentage makes the batter rubbery and hard to work with and results in a tough and chewy sponge. A flour with too much starch, such as cake flour, will produce a light and tender sponge, but the structure will collapse partially when baked. It is best to adjust this ratio yourself in individual recipes by combining both bread and cake flours in the proper proportions as opposed to using premixed all-purpose flour.

Pure starches such as potato or cornstarch can be used to weaken the gluten, but no more than half of the weight of the flour should be replaced. Cocoa powder, which also does not contain any gluten, is usually added for flavor rather than as a means to reduce the gluten strength.

Flour for sponge cakes should always be sifted. If you use unsweetened cocoa powder or any other dry ingredient, sift it in with the flour. You must be very careful when adding the flour to the batter not to break the air bubbles that you just whipped in. Fold in the flour with a rubber spatula or your hand, and turn the mixing bowl slowly with your other hand at the same time to combine the ingredients evenly. Never stir the flour into the batter or add it using the mixer.

Butter

Butter is added to a sponge cake not only for flavor but to improve the quality of the finished sponge. The cake will have a finer pore structure as the batter becomes heavier, and butter also extends the shelf life.

Butter can be added to a sponge in an amount up to two-thirds of the weight of the sugar. The butter should be melted but not hot. It is always added last, after the flour has been completely incorporated. Otherwise, the butter will surround any small lumps of flour and you won't be able to break them up without losing volume.

Nuts, Nut Paste, and Candied Fruit

Chopped nuts or chopped candied fruit may be added to a sponge cake without changing the formula, provided it is a fairly heavy sponge (the pieces will settle on the bottom in a very light sponge batter). Chopped nuts do not absorb much moisture and therefore do not have the same effect on the batter that ground nuts do. Almond or hazelnut paste may also be added without any reformulating; however, in this case, the butter is generally left out. The almond paste is first softened and worked free of lumps by incorporating egg white. The egg yolks are whipped as directed in the recipe and can then be folded into the almond paste mixture quickly and smoothly without causing lumps or losing volume.

Ideally, ground almonds or hazelnuts should be of such a fine consistency that they can be sifted with the flour. The flour must be reduced accordingly, since the fine structure of the nuts will absorb moisture. Decrease the weight of the flour by 1 ounce (30 g) for every 3 ounces (85 g) of ground nuts added. Further, the quantity of ground nuts added cannot be higher than the weight of the sugar in the recipe.

Unsweetened Cocoa Powder, Unsweetened Chocolate, and Sweet Chocolate

Unsweetened cocoa powder may be substituted for cake flour in an equal weight. No more than 3 ounces (85 g) of cocoa powder should be used for every one pound (455 g) of flour. Sift the cocoa powder in with the flour. Unsweetened chocolate can be added (not substituted) at a ratio of no more than 5 ounces (140 g) per pound (455 g) of flour. Sweet chocolate may be added at the same rate, but the sugar should be decreased by 2 ounces (55 g) for this amount. Fold the chocolate into a small amount of the batter to temper it, and then fold this into the remaining batter. This works best with sponges containing a chemical leavening agent.

Warm-Method Sponge (Genoise)

There are two basic ways to make a classic sponge cake: the warm method and the cold method. In the warm method, eggs and sugar are mixed over simmering water (while stirring constantly so that the eggs do not cook) to about 110°F (43°C) or until the sugar has dissolved completely. This improves the emulsifying properties of the eggs. Test to be certain that the sugar is completely dissolved by rubbing a little of the mixture between your thumb and forefinger. The mixture is removed from the heat, placed in a mixing bowl, and whipped at high speed until creamy and light in color. It is then whipped at a lower speed for about 5 minutes longer to stabilize the batter. Sifted flour is folded in, followed by the melted butter.

Cold-Method Sponge

In the cold method the eggs are first separated; the yolks are whipped with part of the sugar to a light and fluffy consistency, and the whites and the remaining sugar are whipped to soft peaks. The yolks are gradually folded into the whites, then the sifted flour and any other ingredients are folded in, and last the melted butter if used. The cold method produces a somewhat lighter sponge than the warm method. Due to the lightness of the cake, the cold-method sponge tends to shrink away from the sides of the pan more than is desirable. For this reason, it is best not to grease the sides of the cake pan. Instead, cut the baked sponge free using a sharp, thin knife.

Note that in many recipes a combination of the warm and cold methods is used with or without the addition of baking powder. Baking powder can be added to either the cold- or warm-method sponge if you must use eggs which have been broken the previous day, or if for any other reason you are concerned about the outcome. Use 2 teaspoons (8 g) baking powder for every 12 eggs in the recipe, sifted in with the flour.

Emulsifier-Method Sponge

A third method, and probably the most common in the baking industry today, is the emulsifier method; it is quick, convenient, and almost foolproof. Emulsifiers have been used by professional bakers for about 40 years. The emulsifier is basically a whipping agent, which contains a molecule that preserves the emulsion of lipids (fat) and water. By keeping the ingredients suspended and preventing separation, emulsifiers allow the batter to hold the air that has been whipped in without falling. In the emulsifier-method sponge, all ingredients, including the flour, are whipped together with the emulsifier for a specified time. The emulsifier method uses baking powder and does not rely on air as a leavening agent, so the sponge does not need to be baked immediately but can "wait its turn for the oven" just as any plain cookie—a big advantage in a busy bakery. Emulsifiers are available primarily through suppliers to the professional baking industry. Emulsifiers are used in recipes specifically formulated by the manufacturer, but they can be altered using the general guidelines outlined here.

Ladyfinger Sponge

Another sponge variation is the ladyfinger sponge, also known as a "piped sponge," which is used not only for cookies but also for several classical desserts such as Tiramisu, Charlotte Russe, and Gâteau Malakoff. In this method, more air is whipped into the batter so that it can be piped into various shapes without running. Ladyfinger sponges are meant to be very dry after baking but will easily absorb moisture from fillings or syrup.

Othello Sponge

Othello sponge is comparable to the ladyfinger sponge, and the two are easily interchangeable. The othello sponge has a lighter structure, due to less flour and more egg white. The batter should immediately be piped out and baked as soon as it is finished, as the mixture becomes tough if left to stand too long.

Baking Pans

The sponge cake batter should be divided into prepared pans and baked immediately or the air bubbles will start to break. Pans should be buttered and floured using a combination of four parts melted butter to one part flour, by volume. By brushing this mixture on the pans you only have to handle them once. With some lighter mixtures, such as two-way or chiffon, it is advantageous to butter and flour only the bottom of the pan, or line it with a circle of baking paper, allowing the sponge to stick to the sides and thereby preventing it from shrinking as it bakes.

Baking

The oven should be around 400°F (205°C) for a typical 10-by-2-inch (25-×-5-cm) cake pan or cake ring. The deeper and wider your cake pan, the lower you should have the heat. On the other end of the scale, if you are baking a ¼-inch (6-mm) roulade, the oven should be at 425°F (219°C) or the roulade will dry out as it bakes and be difficult (or impossible) to roll. To test a sponge for doness, gently press down in the center with your finger; the sponge should spring right back and not leave any indentation.

Storage

Do not unmold any sponge before it has cooled completely. Store it covered or wrapped in plastic. If you do not need to reuse the pans, leave the cakes in the pans, turn them upside down to store, and unmold as needed. When sponge cakes or sheets are refrigerated, the skin on top of the cakes becomes soft. It must be removed before the layers are used. Sponge cake freezes exceptionally well, even for weeks if wrapped properly; both the professional baker and the home cook should always have some sponge cake in the freezer for creating a last-minute dessert.

Cake Mixtures Other Than Sponge Cakes

These mixtures are divided into two general groups: heavy mixtures, which include cakes made using the creaming method and the high-ratio method, and light mixtures, which include two-stage method cakes, angel-food method cakes, and chiffon method cakes. Each of these uses a different technique to accomplish the same goal: Combining the ingredients into a smooth and homogenous batter, while at the same time developing and incorporating air pockets, or cells, which give the finished product its proper texture.

Two of these ingredients, fat and water (including the water in the eggs), are by nature incompatible—they will not mix together. A smooth and uniform substance made up of two unmixable foods is known as an emulsion. Cake batters which are properly mixed—emulsified—contain microscopic droplets of water surrounded by fat and other ingredients. The emulsion will become broken if the fat can no longer surround and hold the water. One reason this can occur is if the wrong type of fat is used. Butter, although it contributes a superior flavor, has poor emulsifying abilities and also contains about 20 percent water. Butter, therefore, may not be substituted in a recipe that specifies shortening. It will be even less positive in a recipe that is designed to use high-ratio shortening, which contains an added emulsifier to enable it to hold a larger quantity of water without curdling. If the ingredients are too cold, most importantly the fat and/or eggs, this can also effect the ability of the batter to form an emulsion; 70°F (21°C) is the ideal temperature. If the fat is not soft, it can not be creamed properly at the beginning, and it will not develop the structure necessary to hold and contain the tiny water droplets. This factor is amplified if the liquid to be incorporated is added too quickly and not, as it should be, in several small portions.

Creaming Method

This is the conventional method used for many different butter cakes. The following rules must be observed for a good result: The ingredients should be at room temperature, approximately 70°F (21°C). The fat must be beaten until it is light and fluffy. The eggs must be added in small portions, with each one fully absorbed before the next is added. The dry and liquid ingredients should be added alternately, starting and finishing with the dry to ensure that the batter can absorb all of the liquid, which would be impossible without the assistance of the flour.

High-Ratio Method

This is a simple, foolproof way of mixing a cake base, using very few steps in the process. This method was developed using the modern high-ratio shortening, therefore butter or margarine may not be substituted. The same rules discussed in the creaming method should be followed. When using the high-ratio method, it is important to pay attention to the length of time specified in the mixing steps and to scrape the sides and the bottom of the bowl several times during the mixing process to produce a smooth and homogenous batter.

Two-Stage Method

This method is used for both cold-method genoise-type sponge cakes and baking-powder cake bases. The eggs are separated and the yolks are first whipped with a small amount of the sugar. The egg whites are whipped separately. Because the fat (the egg yolks) has been removed, it is possible to whip the egg whites to stiff peaks, which produces a cake with a lighter texture.

Angel-Food Method

This type of cake does not contain any fat and relies solely on stabilized egg-white foam for leavening. The foaming power of the egg whites results from a combined effort of various proteins which increase the thickness (viscosity) of the albumen and produce a fine mesh of foam

FIGURES 7–2 and 7–3   *Folding the flour
into a Sponge Cake batter by hand, by moving the hand around the sides of the bowl
and also lifting the mixture from the bottom
of the bowl to the top as the flour is incorporated*

(tiny bubbles) that will hold together for a period of time if properly combined with the sugar. Angel-food batters have a much higher sugar content than any other sponge or butter cake. Although sugar has a mixed influence in the whipping stage, where it acts to delay the foaming of the whites, it stabilizes the foam once it is whipped, especially in the oven where sugar is necessary to prevent a total collapse. It does this by forming hydrogen bonds and delaying evaporation. Mixing and baking an angel food cake successfully is a delicate procedure.

Chiffon Method

This method has some similarities to the angel-food-cake method in that the light and airy texture is derived from whipped egg whites. Chiffon cakes are much easier to make, however, since they contain baking powder and do not depend exclusively on the air whipped into the egg whites for leavening. Also, here the whipped whites are folded into a batter containing yolks, oil, water, and flour, as opposed to the angel food cake where part of the sugar is mixed with the flour and this is then folded into the whipped whites. Chiffon cakes using baking powder are the most common variety; there are also some that use emulsifiers.

The table in Figure 7-1 compares the various sponge recipes in this text.

Sponge Cakes and Other Cake Batters

 ## Sponge Cake

*two 10-by-2-inch
(25-×-5-cm) cakes*

Butter and Flour Mixture (page 4)

12 eggs

2 egg whites (¼ cup/60 ml)

10 ounces (285 g) granulated sugar

1 teaspoon (5 g) salt

6 ounces (170 g) cake flour

6 ounces (170 g) bread flour

5 ounces (140 g) melted unsalted
    butter

1. Brush Butter and Flour Mixture over the inside of two 10-inch (25-cm) cake pans. Reserve.

2. Place the whole eggs, egg whites, sugar, and salt in mixer bowl. Heat over simmering water to about 110°F (43°C), whipping continuously. Remove from the heat and whip at high speed until the mixture has cooled and is light and fluffy.

3. Sift the flours together and fold into the batter by hand (Figures 7–2 and 7–3). Fold in the melted butter. Divide the batter between the prepared pans.

4. Bake immediately at 400°F (205°C) for approximately 15 minutes. Let the sponges cool before removing them from the pans.

Sponge Cake Formulas Relative to One Pound, Eight Ounces (12 Whole) Eggs

	SPONGE CAKE (GENOISE)	ALMOND SPONGE	ANGEL FOOD CAKE	CHIFFON SPONGE CAKE	DOBOS SPONGE	OTHELLO SPONGE	HIGH-RATIO SPONGE CAKE	LADYFINGERS
Eggs	12 whole plus 2 whites	12 separated plus 2 whites	24 whites	12 separated	12 separated	12 separated plus 2 whites	12 whole	12 separated
Sugar	10 ounces (285 g)	10 ounces (285 g)	1 pound, 8 ounces (680 g)	1 pound, 5 ounces (595 g)	12 ounces (340 g)	6 ounces (170 g)	13 1/2 ounces (385 g)	12 ounces (340 g)
Flour	12 ounces (340 g)	7 ounces (200 g)	8 ounces (225 g)	1 pound, 5 ounces (595 g)	8 ounces (225 g)	5 ounces (140 g)	13 1/2 ounces (385 g)	8 ounces (225 g)
Butter	5 ounces (140 g)	0	0	0	12 ounces (340 g)	0	0	0
Other Ingredients	salt	almond paste, vanilla extract	cream of tartar, vanilla extract, lemon juice, lemon zest, salt	vegetable oil, water, salt, vanilla extract, baking powder	vanilla extract, salt, lemon zest, ground almonds	cornstarch, cream of tartar	baking powder, high-ratio shortening, milk, vanilla extract	cornstarch, lemon juice or tartaric acid
Production Method	Warm Method	Cold Method	Angel-Food Method	Chiffon Method	Creaming Method	Two-Way Method	High-Ratio Method	Cold Method
Characteristics	Somewhat crumbly; light and airy texture	Moist, flexible, not very crumbly	Light, moist; cholesterol- and fat-free	Few crumbs; moist; easy to make	Dense; little or no crumbs	Dry and crumbly; can be stored for several weeks	Not very flexible, breaks easily	Dry; holds its shape when piped or spread
Uses	Multipurpose cake base	Roulades and sheets	Light desserts	Multipurpose cake base	Petits fours; uses when crumbs are detrimental	Pastry shells and in desserts	General cake base	As a cookie by itself; in dessert preparations

FIGURE 7–1 Comparison of Sponge Cake formulas relative to 1 pound, 8 ounces (or twelve whole) eggs

Chocolate Sponge Cake

two 10-by-2-inch (25-×-5-cm) cakes

Butter and Flour Mixture (page 4)

12 eggs

2 egg whites (¹/₄ cup/60 ml)

10 ounces (285 g) granulated sugar

1 teaspoon (5 g) salt

4 ounces (115 g) cake flour

6 ounces (170 g) bread flour

2 ounces (55 g) unsweetened cocoa powder

5 ounces (140 g) melted unsalted butter

1. Brush Butter and Flour Mixture over the inside of two 10-inch (25-cm) cake pans. Reserve.

2. Place the whole eggs, egg whites, sugar, and salt in mixer bowl. Heat over simmering water to about 110°F (43°C), whipping continuously. Remove from the heat and whip at high speed until the mixture has cooled and is light and fluffy.

3. Sift the flours and cocoa powder together and fold into the batter by hand. Fold in the melted butter. Divide the batter between the prepared pans.

4. Bake immediately at 400°F (205°C) for approximately 15 minutes. Let the sponges cool before removing them from the pans.

Almond Sponge

two ¹/₄-by-14-by-24-inch (6-mm-×-35-×-60-cm) sheets, or two 10-by-2-inch (25-×-5-cm) layers

2 egg whites (¹/₄ cup/60 ml)

10 ounces (285 g) Almond Paste (page 3)

12 eggs, separated

10 ounces (285 g) granulated sugar

1 teaspoon (5 ml) vanilla extract

7 ounces (200 g) cake flour

NOTE: If the oven is not hot enough, or if the sheets are overcooked (and therefore dried out) the sponge will not bend without breaking. To remedy this, place a damp towel on a sheet pan and place the sponge on top with the paper next to the towel. Invert a second sheet pan on top as a lid. Place in the oven (400°F/205°C) for 5 to 10 minutes to soften. If the sponge is to be used the next day, repeat the process as above but soften in the refrigerator instead of in the oven.

1. Gradually mix the 2 egg whites into the Almond Paste to soften it.

2. Whip the egg yolks with 3 ounces (85 g) of the sugar to the ribbon stage. Add the vanilla. Very gradually, add the yolk mixture to the Almond Paste mixture; if you try to add it too fast, you are sure to get lumps.

3. Whip the egg whites to a foam. Gradually add the remaining 7 ounces (200 g) of sugar and whip to stiff peaks.

4. Sift the flour (and the cocoa powder, if making the variation). Carefully fold the egg whites into the yolk mixture. Fold in the dry ingredients.

To make sheets

Immediately spread the batter on paper-lined sheet pans to 14 by 24 inches (35 × 60 cm), taking care not to overwork the sponge. Bake at 425°F (219°C) for approximately 8 minutes or until just done.

To make layers

Line the bottoms of two 10-inch (25-cm) cake pans with baking paper (see Figures 1–10 to 1–12, page 26), or grease and flour, but do not grease and flour the sides. Divide the batter between the pans and bake at 375°F (190°C) for about 25 minutes or until the sponge springs back when pressed lightly in the middle. When cold, cut the sponge away from the side of the pan with a thin sharp knife.

VARIATION
Cocoa Almond Sponge

*T*o make Cocoa Almond Sponge, delete 3 ounces (85 g) of flour and substitute 3 ounces (85 g) of unsweetened cocoa powder sifted with the remaining flour.

Angel Food Cake

one 10-by-4-inch (25-×-10-cm) tube pan

4 ounces (115 g) cake flour, sifted
12 ounces (370 g) granulated sugar
12 egg whites (1½ cups/360 ml)
1 teaspoon (2 g) cream of tartar
pinch of salt
2 teaspoons (10 ml) vanilla extract
grated zest of one lemon
2 teaspoon (10 ml) lemon juice

*T*his feather-light sponge cake uses only the air incorporated into stiffly beaten egg whites as a leavener; it contains no egg yolks or other fat and no chemical leavening agent. The one complaint I used to have about this completely cholesterol-free cake was that I found it too sweet. Additional sugar is needed to support and stabilize the albumen in the whipped egg whites, in part due to the lack of fat. After some experimenting I managed to decrease the sugar to a level that supports the egg whites without being cloying. Because of its sweet flavor, Angel Food Cake is especially nice paired with fruit. Adding unsweetened cocoa powder to make Chocolate Angel Food Cake (see page 263) also brings the sweetness to a more acceptable level.

Due to the tender and light structure of this cake, it is of the utmost importance that the ingredients are measured precisely and the directions followed exactly. It is also essential to use a tube pan to produce the traditional look and light composition (you can bake the cake in two 9-inch [22.5-cm] regular cake pans with a fairly good result, but the cakes will not have the same airiness). The tube pan can be false-bottom or not, and it does not have to have legs. The legs allow you to invert the baked cake so that it cools without falling and, at the same time, they allow air to circulate around the entire cake as it cools. Hanging the inverted cake on the neck of a bottle works just as well.

1. Line the bottom of a 10-inch (25-cm) tube pan with a ring of baking paper (see Figures 1–10 to 1–12, page 26; refold and use the same technique to cut out the center).

2. Combine the flour with half of the granulated sugar. Reserve.

3. Whip the egg whites with the cream of tartar and salt at high speed until they have tripled in volume. Gradually add the remaining sugar and continue whipping until the whites hold soft peaks. Remove from the mixer.

4. Place the flour and sugar mixture in a sifter. (Set the sifter on a piece of baking paper so you do not lose any of the mixture.) Sift the flour-sugar mixture over the whipped egg whites a little at a time and gently fold it in together with the vanilla, lemon zest, and lemon juice. Place the batter in the prepared tube pan. Tap the pan firmly against the table a couple of times to release any large air pockets.

5. Bake at 325°F (163°C) for approximately 55 minutes or until the cake is golden brown on top and springs back when pressed lightly. Invert the pan onto its legs or over the neck of a bottle to allow air to circulate underneath as it cools upside down.

 Chiffon Sponge Cake

two 10-by-2-inch (25-×-5-cm) cakes

⅔ cup (160 ml) vegetable oil
8 egg yolks (⅔ cup/160 ml)
1 cup (240 ml) water, at room temperature
1 tablespoon (15 ml) vanilla extract
14 ounces (400 g) cake flour
14 ounces (400 g) granulated sugar
4 teaspoons (16 g) baking powder
1 teaspoon (5 g) salt
8 egg whites (1 cup/240 ml)

1. Line two 10-inch (25-cm) cake pans with circles of baking paper, or grease and flour, but do not grease and flour the sides.

2. Whip the vegetable oil and the egg yolks together just until combined. Stir in the water and the vanilla extract.

3. Sift together the cake flour, one-third of the sugar, the baking powder, and the salt. Stir this into the egg yolk mixture, then whip at high speed for 1 minute. Reserve.

4. Whip the egg whites to a foam. Gradually add the remaining sugar and continue whipping until stiff peaks form.

5. Carefully fold the meringue into the reserved batter. Divide the batter between the prepared pans.

6. Bake at 375°F (190°C) for approximately 25 minutes or until the cakes spring back when pressed lightly in the center.

7. Invert the pans on a rack and allow the cakes to cool in the pans before unmolding.

 VARIATIONS
Chocolate Chiffon Sponge Cake

Decrease the cake flour by 3 ounces (85 g) and replace with 3 ounces (85 g) of unsweetened cocoa powder sifted with the remaining flour.

 Lemon Chiffon Sponge Cake

Replace ½ cup (120 ml) of the water with ½ cup (120 ml) of lemon juice. Add the grated zest of 3 lemons together with the water-juice mixture.

 Devil's Food Cake Layers

two 10-inch (25-cm) cake layers

1 pound, 4 ounces (570 g) granulated sugar
4 ounces (115 g) unsweetened cocoa powder

The word devil, or deviled, is applied to a number of savory culinary dishes, most notably stuffed eggs, fried oysters, and ham sandwich spread. It suggests that they have a spicy flavor, generally originating from such "devilish" ingredients as cayenne, tabasco sauce, or paprika. Devil's Food Cake, however, has been spared this peppery fate. This dense, deeply-chocolate American hallmark is found at the opposite end of the spectrum from the airy, white, nonfat, low-calorie, low-cholesterol Angel Food Cake. Devil's Food Cake is dramatically dark with a reddish tint that is produced from the alkalizing effect of the

8 ounces (225 g) bread flour

8 ounces (225 g) cake flour

2 teaspoons (8 g) baking soda

2 teaspoons (8 g) baking powder

6 eggs

2 cups (480 ml) buttermilk

2 cups (480 ml) sour cream

12 ounces (340 g) melted unsalted butter

8 ounces (225 g) finely grated raw zucchini or beet

NOTE: This is a very moist cake that is excellent layered with whipped cream, Italian Cream (see page 1087), Crème Parisienne (see page 1086), or just as is with a dusting of powdered sugar. A variation of this batter is used in the recipe for Chocolate Cherry Muffins on page 188.

🥄 Dobos Sponge

one 16-by-24-inch (40-×-60-cm) sheet or six 10-inch (25-cm) rounds, ¼ inch (6 mm) thick

12 ounces (340 g) soft unsalted butter

12 ounces (340 g) granulated sugar

12 egg yolks (1 cup/240 ml), at room temperature

1 teaspoon (5 ml) vanilla extract

1 teaspoon (5 g) salt

grated zest of one lemon

12 egg whites (1½ cups/360 ml), at room temperature

8 ounces (225 g) sifted cake flour

5 ounces (140 g) finely ground almonds (almond meal; see note 1)

NOTE 1: If you do not have almond meal or do not have the proper equipment to make it, add part of the granulated sugar from the recipe (taking it away from the amount used in step one) to blanched (dry) almonds and process to a fine consistency in a food processor. The sugar will absorb some of the oil released by the almonds and prevent the mixture from caking.

baking soda on cocoa amplified even further by the red tint of the beets when used. A finished Devil's Food Cake is generally tall, filled and frosted country-style with a fudge-type of icing. I prefer the cake as is or, as suggested below, with a slightly lighter filling.

1. Cover the bottom of two 10-inch cake pans with rounds of baking paper. Reserve.

2. Sift together the granulated sugar, cocoa powder, bread flour, cake flour, baking soda, and baking powder. Set aside.

3. Beat the eggs for 1 minute. Stir in the buttermilk and the sour cream. Add the reserved dry ingredients, mixing until well combined and smooth. Mix in the melted butter and the grated zucchini or beets.

4. Divide the batter between the two prepared pans. Smooth the top of the cakes to make them level.

5. Bake at 350°F (175°C) for approximately 40 minutes or until the cakes spring back when pressed lightly in the center. Allow the cakes to cool completely before unmolding.

---

1. Cream the butter with half of the sugar to a light and fluffy consistency. Beat in the egg yolks a few at a time. Mix in the vanilla, salt, and lemon zest (see note 2).

2. Whip the egg whites until foamy. Gradually add the remaining sugar and whip until soft peaks form. Carefully fold the whipped egg whites into the yolk mixture.

3. Combine the sifted flour (and cocoa powder if making the variation) with the ground almonds. Gently fold the flour and almond mixture into the egg mixture.

4. Immediately spread the batter evenly over a 16-by-24-inch (40-×-60-cm) sheet of baking paper. Drag the paper onto a sheet pan (see Figure 16–15, page 842).

5. Bake at 425°F (219°C) for about 10 minutes or until baked through.

NOTE 2: If the egg yolks are not approximately the same temperature as the butter and sugar emulsion, the mixture will break when they are added. If this happens, warm the broken mixture over a bain-marie, stirring constantly, before folding in the egg whites.

NOTE 3: To make round layers, see Dobos Torte, page 328.

 VARIATION
Cocoa Dobos Sponge

*F*or Cocoa Dobos Sponge, delete 2 ounces (55 g) of the cake flour, and replace with 2 ounces (55 g) of unsweetened cocoa powder sifted with the remaining flour.

 **Hazelnut-Chocolate Sponge**

two 10-inch (25-cm) cakes

Butter and Flour Mixture (page 4)
14 eggs
12 ounces (340 g) granulated sugar
1 teaspoon (5 ml) vanilla extract
1 teaspoon (5 g) salt
8 ounces (225 g) bread flour
6 ounces (170 g) hazelnuts, toasted and finely ground (see note)
3 ounces (85 g) sweet dark chocolate, grated
4 ounces melted unsalted butter

NOTE: Add about one-quarter of the sugar to the nuts if you are using a food processor to grind them. The sugar will absorb the oil released by the nuts due to heat produced by the friction.

1. Brush Butter and Flour Mixture inside two 10-inch (25-cm) cake pans. Reserve.

2. Combine the eggs, sugar, vanilla, and salt in a mixer bowl. Heat over simmering water until the mixture reaches about 110°F (43°C), whipping continuously. Remove from the heat and whip at high speed until the mixture has cooled and has a light and fluffy consistency.

3. Sift the flour. Mix in the hazelnuts and chocolate, then carefully fold into the batter by hand. Fold in the melted butter. Divide the batter between the prepared pans.

4. Bake immediately at 400°F (205°C) until the cake springs back when pressed lightly on top, approximately 15 minutes. Allow the sponges to cool completely before removing them from the pans.

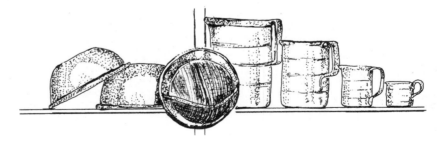

 **High-Ratio Sponge Cake**

two 10-by-2-inch (25-×-5-cm) cakes

Butter and Flour Mixture (page 4)
14 eggs, at room temperature

1. Brush Butter and Flour Mixture over the inside of two 10-inch (25-cm) cake pans. Reserve.

2. Place the eggs, granulated sugar, cake flour, and baking powder in a mixer bowl. Stir on low speed, using the whip attachment, until the mixture forms a paste. Add the shortening and whip at high speed for 2 minutes, scraping down the sides of the bowl as needed. Lower the speed and incorporate the milk and vanilla. Continue whipping one minute longer.

1 pound (455 g) granulated sugar

1 pound (455 g) cake flour

2 tablespoons (24 g) baking powder

10 ounces (285 g) soft high-ratio shortening

1 cup (240 ml) milk, at room temperature

2 teaspoons (10 ml) vanilla extract

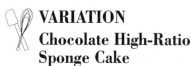

VARIATION
Chocolate High-Ratio Sponge Cake

Ladyfingers

about one hundred and eighty 2-inch (5-cm) cookies

3 ounces (85 g) cornstarch

4 ounces (115 g) bread flour

6 eggs, separated

6 ounces (170 g) granulated sugar

a few drops of Tartaric Acid Solution (page 1115) or lemon juice

3. Divide the batter evenly between the prepared pans.

4. Bake at 375°F (190°C) for approximately 20 minutes or until the cake springs back when pressed lightly in the center.

*R*eplace 4 ounces (115 g) of the cake flour with 4 ounces (115 g) of unsweetened cocoa powder.

---

*T*his light and delicate sponge has many uses. Ladyfingers are served as an accompaniment to ice cream and are an integral part of several classic desserts, such as Tiramisu and Gâteau Malakoff. The cookies are either soaked in a liqueur or other flavoring before or after they are added to the dessert. Ladyfingers are also used to line the sides of several varieties of Charlotte, including Royal and Charente. Ladyfinger sponge batter contains a little more flour in relation to sugar than the usual 50:50 ratio. This, combined with the method of whipping the egg yolks and whites separately, makes the batter thick enough to hold its shape. Ladyfinger cookies are similar in shape to Cat's Tongues cookies—Langues-de-chat—which are usually sandwiched together with nougat. The name lady's fingers is also used for the vegetable okra.

1. Sift together the cornstarch and flour (with the cocoa powder if making the variation), and reserve.

2. Whip the egg yolks and 2 ounces (55 g) of the sugar at high speed until they are light and creamy; reserve.

3. Add 2 ounces (55 g) of the remaining sugar, along with the tartaric acid or lemon juice, to the egg whites. Whip the egg white mixture at high speed until it is foamy and has tripled in volume, about 2 minutes.

4. Gradually add the last 2 ounces (55 g) of sugar and whip to stiff peaks.

5. Fold in the reserved egg yolk and sugar mixture, and then fold in the flour and cornstarch mixture. (Follow the instructions in a particular recipe if not making individual Ladyfingers.)

6. Place the batter in a pastry bag with a no. 5 (10-mm) plain tip. Pipe 2-inch-long (5-cm) cookies onto sheet pans lined with baking paper.

7. Bake at 425°F (219°C) for about 8 minutes or until golden brown. Ladyfingers will keep for weeks if stored in a dry place.

VARIATION
Chocolate Ladyfingers

*D*elete 1 ounce (30 g) of the cornstarch and replace with 1 ounce (30 g) of unsweetened cocoa powder.

Othello Sponge

approximately one hundred 2-by-³/₄-inch (5-×-2-cm) pastry shells

6 ounces (170 g) granulated sugar
6 ounces (170 g) cornstarch
5 ounces (140 g) bread flour
12 egg yolks (1 cup/240 ml)
14 egg whites (1³/₄ cups/420 ml)
1 teaspoon (2 g) cream of tartar

1. Combine half of the sugar with half of the cornstarch. Set aside.

2. Sift the remaining cornstarch with the flour. Set aside.

3. Whip the egg yolks with the remaining sugar until the consistency is light and fluffy. Reserve.

4. Whip the egg whites and cream of tartar for a few minutes until they have quadrupled in volume, lower the mixer speed, and gradually add the sugar and cornstarch mixture. Increase the speed and whip to stiff but not dry peaks. Carefully fold half of the egg whites into the whipped egg yolks. Fold in the flour mixture, then fold in the remaining whites. Use immediately.

Ribbon Sponge Sheets

two 23-by-15-inch (57.5-×-37.5-cm) sheets

14 ounces (400 g) or one-half recipe Chocolate Tulip Paste (page 1047)
Ribbon Sponge Base I or II (recipes follow)
4 ounces (115 g) cocoa butter, melted (see note 1)

NOTE 1: *The amount of cocoa butter specified in the ingredient list is far more than you will need if you use a brush to apply it. However, if you use a spray bottle, the additional liquid is required for the sprayer to work well.*

NOTE 2: *To use a silkscreen to transfer an image to the sponge sheet, make a cocoa paste by gradually adding approximately ³/₄ cup (180 ml) of water to 2 ounces (55 g) of sifted unsweetened cocoa powder. Stir until you have a smooth, thin paste; it should be just pourable, but not runny. If necessary, pass the paste through a fine mesh strainer. Let sit at room temperature for 30 minutes, then add more water if needed. Place the silkscreen on top of a silicone mat and pour a line of paste along the top edge of the screen. Using the specially made*

*T*hin, elegant, and decorative Ribbon Sponge Sheets can be made very easily using imported European silicone baking mats along with a special scraper-like tool that is made to fit the mats and has interchangeable blades (typically made of rubber) with notched edges in various sizes. Silicone mats are now readily available and relatively inexpensive, and they are a tool that no professional (or serious amateur) should be without today, especially since the mats have so many other uses in addition to making sponge sheets. The custom-made scrapers or decorating combs that cover the length or width of a mat in one pass are not only a necessity if you are producing Ribbon Sponge Sheets in a great quantity, but since they are available with so many different patterns and are becoming much more affordable in this country, they are something a smaller restaurant or shop should consider as well. However, as an alternative, in paint or home improvement stores you can purchase a trowel that is designed for spreading adhesive when installing tiles and other floor covering. These are made of plastic and, like the bakery tool, are available with notches in various sizes and widths. The depth of the notches for use in this recipe should be ¹/₁₆ inch (2 mm). File the notches down to ¹/₁₆ inch or, as a temporary solution, tape over the base of the notches next to the tool to bring them to the right depth. This "substitute" tool is not wide enough to cover the silicone mats in one pass, so you will have to go over the sheet more than once, as shown in the illustrations.

In addition to making straight lines lengthwise, crosswise, or diagonally, try using the trowel to make curved or wavy lines (to create a wood grain pattern, see note 2 on page 899). To create a colorful Ribbon Sponge, substitute Vanilla Tulip Paste for the chocolate paste and color it as desired to create special effects. Or, color the Ribbon Sponge Base to contrast with either plain or chocolate lines. There are many possible combinations and the results can be stunning, but use restraint: colors that are too bright or combinations using too many colors can turn out garish. You do not have to limit these impressive sponge sheet designs to ribbons either: a wide variety of decorative metal and plastic grills, made to fit the silicone mats, are available (although they are not cheap) in patterns such

rubber trowel (squeegee), spread the cocoa paste across the mat in one smooth motion moving toward yourself from top to bottom. Remove the silkscreen; the design will appear on the silicone mat. Follow the procedure in steps two through five to finish making the sponge sheet. A silkscreen can also be used to apply contrasting colors of chocolate to sheets of acetate or polyurethane when making *Molded Chocolate Strips* (see page 916). Let the chocolate design harden before applying the contrasting color of chocolate as described in steps six through nine on page 899.

NOTE 3: *To prevent the silicone mat and/or ruler from sliding when you put pressure on the trowel, it is helpful to have two extra hands helping at this point.*

as diamond, herringbone, and polka dot, to name just a few. Another option is to use silkscreens which can be even more impressive as these leave a picture-like image on top of the baked sponge (see note 2).

The two recipes for *Ribbon Sponge Base* are fairly similar and can be used interchangeably. *Sponge Base II* takes a bit longer to make but is a better choice if you plan to add coloring to the base portion. With either recipe be sure to keep the whipped egg whites and sugar very soft, because a thinner batter will flow out and fill in much more tightly between the *Tulip Paste* lines. Being careful not to overwhip the egg whites will also help to prevent air bubbles in the finished sponge sheets that will detract from the appearance.

1. Spread the Chocolate Tulip Paste evenly over two full-size silicone baking mats, covering them completely; the paste should be approximately $1/16$ inch (2 mm) thick. Use a decorating comb or trowel with square notches spaced $1/8$ inch (3 mm) apart to remove half of the paste in straight lines lengthwise (Figure 7–4) on each sheet. When using a trowel you must make several passes over the sheet. An easy way to keep the lines straight as you do this is to place a ruler balanced on top of two pieces of wood (or any suitable objects about 1 inch/2.5 cm high) positioned at each of the short ends of the silicone mat. Use the ruler as a guide for the trowel (Figure 7–5) (see note 3).

2. Lift up the silicone mats by the edges (Figure 7–6), place them on top of inverted sheet pans, and place in the freezer to firm the Tulip Paste while you make the Ribbon Sponge Base. If you are not proceeding to the next step immediately, the prepped silicone mats can be left at room temperature for several hours. Place them in the freezer for a few minutes to firm the paste when you are ready to resume.

3. Leave the mats in place on the inverted pans. Divide the Ribbon Sponge Base between the two mats, spreading it out evenly on top of the chocolate lines. Tap the pans quite firmly against the table to set the batter and remove air bubbles.

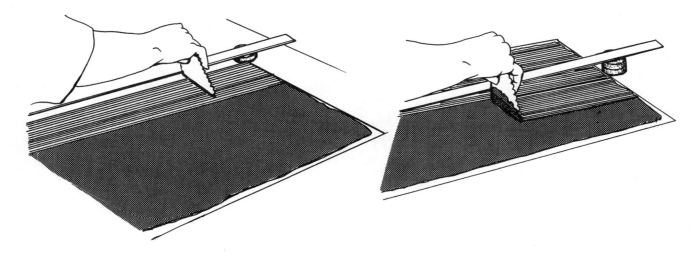

FIGURE 7–4   *Preparing to make the second pass with the trowel to remove the Chocolate Tulip Paste in straight lines for Ribbon Sponge Sheets*

FIGURE 7–5   *Using a ruler balanced at either end of the silicone mat as a guide to create straight lines*

FIGURE 7–6   *Lifting up the silicone mat after forming the Chocolate Tulip Paste lines*

FIGURE 7–7   *Peeling the silicone mat away from the baked Ribbon Sponge Sheet*

4. Bake immediately at 550°F (288°C) for approximately 4 minutes or until the sponge begins to color slightly.

5. Dust flour lightly over the top of the sponge sheets. Invert them onto sheets of baking paper and let cool for 2 minutes. Carefully peel away the silicone mats (Figure 7–7). Spray or brush melted cocoa butter over the patterned side of the sheets. The cocoa butter will help keep the sheets flexible and at the same time, prevent them from sticking to the forms or rings when the sheets are used in assembling cakes or other desserts. Cover the Ribbon Sponge Sheets with plastic wrap and store in the refrigerator for up to one week, or in the freezer for up to one month, until needed.

 **Ribbon Sponge Base I**

5 eggs

4 egg yolks (¹⁄₃ cup/80 ml)

7 ounces (200 g) granulated sugar

7 ounces (200 g) blanched almonds, finely ground (or almond meal; see note)

2 ounces (55 g) bread flour, sifted

4 egg whites (¹⁄₂ cup/120 ml)

2 ounces (55 g) melted unsalted butter

NOTE: *The almonds should be ground to a consistency as fine as granulated sugar to compensate for the reduced flour in the sponge. You can purchase the same product, known as almond flour or almond meal, from bakery sup-*

1. Place the whole eggs, egg yolks, and half of the sugar in a bowl. Set the bowl over simmering water. Heat the mixture to 120°F (49°C) while stirring constantly. Remove from the heat and whip at high speed for 1 minute.

2. Thoroughly combine the ground almonds and flour. Reserve.

3. Whip the egg whites with the remaining sugar until they have the appearance of snow (the egg whites should be very thick and foamy but should not hold a peak).

4. Stir the reserved almond mixture into the whipped whole egg mixture. Stir in the melted butter. Gradually fold the egg whites into this mixture.

pliers. If this is not available and you must use a food processor to grind the nuts, add most of the sugar used in step one (saving a few table-spoons to whip with the eggs) to the almonds when you grind them. The sugar will absorb oil and prevent the mixture from caking.

Ribbon Sponge Base II (Joconde)

8 ounces (225 g) blanched almonds, finely ground (or almond meal; see note)
6 ounces (170 g) powdered sugar
2 ounces (55 g) bread flour
8 eggs
2 egg yolks
6 egg whites (³⁄₄ cup/180 ml)
2 ounces (55 g) granulated sugar
2 ounces (55 g) melted unsalted butter

NOTE: If almond meal is not available and you must grind the almonds in a food processor, add 3 ounces (85 g) of granulated sugar to the nuts when you grind them and decrease the amount of powdered sugar in the recipe by 3 ounces (85 g). The granulated sugar will absorb the oil released by the almonds during processing and prevent the mixture from cak-ing. The almonds should be ground to a consis-tency as fine as granulated sugar.

1. Place the ground almonds, powdered sugar, bread flour, and half of the eggs into a mixer bowl. Beat with the paddle attachment for 5 minutes at high speed, scraping down the sides of the bowl once or twice.

2. Gradually incorporate the remaining eggs and egg yolks, mixing at medium speed until well combined. Set aside.

3. Whip the egg whites with the granulated sugar until they just barely hold a soft shape. Fold half of the meringue into the egg mixture. Stir in the melted butter, followed by the remaining meringue.

Tea Cakes

Several years ago I was asked to judge a decorated cake contest in San Francisco. My two fellow judges were Jeremiah Tower and another local celebrity chef who is also a well-known food show host. After seeing the large array of cakes, we decided that we should each sepa-rately pick what we thought were the top five and then together pick the winner and runners-up from this pool. When we told each other our choices my unnamed colleague had picked one tea cake among his five. Although the cake was iced and decorated, it had been baked in a tube pan and had not been split and filled. I agreed that it did taste good but said I had disqualified this one as not being a legitimate decorated cake. We had a heated debate on the issue. My point was this: If I order a decorated cake at the local bakery, this is not the type of cake I expect to receive. I ended up winning the argument, but I realized later that in fact we both were right. There certainly is a gray area dividing dressed-up tea cakes and simple decorated cakes.

Tea cakes are generally made from a richer and heavier batter than sponge cakes and therefore require a leavening agent such as baking powder or baking soda. Rather than adding the filling after the cake is baked, a flavoring or filling is added directly to the batter. For example, chopped nuts, sliced apples, chocolate chips, raisins, bananas, and spices are used to flavor the tea cakes in this chapter. Because the cakes are heavier, they are baked in a tube pan, loaf pan, or other narrow form so they bake evenly. The decoration (if any) on a tea cake is usually kept very simple, often just a sprinkling of powdered sugar or a plain glaze. This makes tea cakes quick and easy to prepare. Tea cakes will remain fresh for several days in the refrigerator and actually become more moist after a few days. Sliced tea cakes are always included along with an assortment of petits fours or cookies at the traditional three o'clock coffee break in Sweden.

Apple Cinnamon Cake

four 1-pound, 5-ounce (595-g) cakes

melted unsalted butter

finely ground bread crumbs

2 pounds (910 g) Golden Delicious, pippin, or Granny Smith apples (approximately four medium-size)

one-half recipe Plain Poaching Syrup (page 13)

Cinnamon Sugar (page 5)

1 pound (455 g) granulated sugar

6 eggs, at room temperature

1 teaspoon (5 ml) vanilla extract

1 pound (455 g) bread flour

2 tablespoons (24 g) baking powder

1 teaspoon (1.5 g) ground cinnamon

1 teaspoon (2 g) ground cardamom

1 teaspoon (5 g) salt

12 ounces (340 g) melted unsalted butter

1¼ cups (300 ml) half-and-half, at room temperature

Try the following delicious variation on this classic tea cake: Instead of poaching the peeled and cored apples, cut them into wedges and set aside. Place 2 ounces (55 g) of unsalted butter and 5 ounces (140 g) of granulated sugar in a skillet. Heat stirring constantly until the mixture begins to bubble. Add the apple wedges and cook, stirring frequently, until the apples are soft. Add half of the batter to the tube pans, sprinkle cinnamon on top, arrange the apples over the batter, and top with the remaining batter.

1. Brush melted butter on the inside of four 1-quart (960-ml) tube-style cake pans. Coat the pans with bread crumbs. Set aside.

2. Peel and core the apples. Poach them in the syrup until soft, about 15 minutes, remove from the liquid, and let cool. Slice the apples into ½-inch (1.2-cm) wedges. Toss the wedges in Cinnamon Sugar to coat, and arrange them evenly over the bottoms of the forms.

3. Whip the sugar, eggs, and vanilla together until light and foamy.

4. Sift together the flour, baking powder, cinnamon, cardamom, and salt. Fold into the egg mixture.

5. Combine the 12 ounces (340 g) of melted butter with the half-and-half. Add to the batter slowly. Divide the batter between the prepared cake pans, filling them no more than halfway.

6. Bake at 350°F (175°C) for about 45 minutes or until baked through.

7. Unmold the cakes and let them cool on a cake rack.

8. When completely cool, cover the cakes and refrigerate.

Banana Bread

three 1-pound, 5-ounce (595 g) cakes

Butter and Flour Mixture (page 4)

10 ounces (285 g) unsalted butter

1 pound, 2 ounces (510 g) granulated sugar

3 eggs, at room temperature

1 teaspoon (5 ml) vanilla extract

1 pound, 5 ounces (595 g) puréed bananas, somewhat overripe

1 pound, 2 ounces (510 g) bread flour

2 teaspoons (10 g) salt

2 teaspoons (8 g) baking soda

9 ounces (255 g) coarsely chopped walnuts

While this American favorite with the confusing name may have limited use in sandwich making, it ranks high on my list for a good wholesome snack. The misnomer probably came about because Banana Bread falls into the category of what are called quick breads. In the previous edition I changed the name to banana tea cake, and this proved even more confusing because no one knew what it really was. So, do not throw out those overripe bananas, just place them in the refrigerator to stop the ripening process until you are ready to make your Banana Bread.

1. Brush Butter and Flour Mixture over the inside of three 1-quart (960-ml) gugelhupf forms or other molds with the same capacity.

2. Melt the butter and add the sugar. Beat together for a few minutes. Stir in the eggs, vanilla, and puréed bananas.

3. Mix together the flour, salt, baking soda, and walnuts. Stir into the butter mixture.

4. Spoon the batter into the prepared forms. If you are using small forms, fill them only three-quarters full.

5. Bake at 350°F (175°C) for about 45 minutes or until baked through. You may need to use a second pan underneath to ensure that the cakes do not get too dark on the bottom while baking.

6. Unmold the cakes as soon as possible and let cool on a cake rack (they will get wet if left to cool in the pans).

Chocolate Crisp Cake

four 1-pound, 5-ounce (595-g) cakes

Butter and Flour Mixture (page 4)

12 ounces (340 g) soft unsalted butter

12 ounces (340 g) granulated sugar

8 eggs, at room temperature

1 teaspoon (5 ml) vanilla extract

1 pound, 5 ounces (595 g) bread flour

1 tablespoon (12 g) baking powder

7 ounces (200 g) sweet dark chocolate, chopped

8 ounces (225 g) hazelnuts, toasted and crushed

grated zest of one orange

1¼ cups (300 ml) milk, at room temperature

Although these cakes taste great as is (especially if you age them a few days in the refrigerator), you can also dress them up a bit by first brushing Apricot Glaze over the top and sides and then covering the glaze with a thin layer of melted coating chocolate. Place an icing rack on a sheet pan lined with baking paper, place the cakes on the rack, and slowly pour or spoon the melted chocolate over the top. Remove the cakes from the rack before the chocolate hardens. Slice the cakes using a heated serrated knife in a sawing motion to prevent cracking the glaze.

1. Brush Butter and Flour Mixture on the insides of four 1-quart (960-ml) rectangular, fluted forms.

2. Beat the softened butter with the sugar until fluffy. Add the eggs one at a time. Mix in the vanilla.

3. Sift the flour with the baking powder. Combine the chopped chocolate, hazelnuts, and orange zest with the flour. Mix into the butter mixture in two additions, alternating with the milk. Divide the batter between the prepared pans.

4. Bake at 350°F (175°C) for about 50 minutes or until baked through.

5. Unmold as soon as possible and let the cakes cool on a cake rack.

6. When cooled, wrap the cakes and store in the refrigerator.

Chocolate Gugelhupf

four 1-pound, 4-ounce (570-g) cakes

melted unsalted butter

finely crushed almonds

8 ounces (225 g) soft unsalted butter

1 pound, 2 ounces (510 g) granulated sugar

1½ teaspoons (7.5 ml) vanilla extract

6 eggs, at room temperature

11 ounces (310 g) potatoes, boiled and mashed

15 ounces (430 g) cake flour

1½ ounces (40 g) unsweetened cocoa powder

1½ tablespoons (18 g) baking powder

½ teaspoon (3 g) salt

8 ounces (225 g) blanched almonds, finely ground (see note)

1¼ cups (300 ml) heavy cream, at room temperature

NOTE: If you do not have almond meal or do not have the proper equipment to make it, add part of the granulated sugar from the recipe to the blanched (dry) almonds and process to a fine consistency in a food processor. The sugar will absorb some of the oil released by the almonds and prevent the mixture from caking.

This coffee cake version of the classic Gugelhupf (see page 163 for more information), gets a unique flavor bonus from the addition of potatoes, which also add moisture and shelf life (although I don't think you will have to worry about leftovers). This batter can be used to make a good muffin as well; they are especially nice with the addition of dried cranberries and/or pears. Reconstitute the fruit before adding it to the batter at the end of the recipe. Portion 4 ounces (115 g) of batter for each muffin. Bake at 375°F (190°C) for approximately 25 minutes. You will get about twenty muffins.

1. Brush melted butter on the inside of four gugelhupf forms or other 1-quart (960-ml) tube pans. Coat with crushed almonds.

2. Beat the soft butter with the sugar until light and fluffy. Add the vanilla to the eggs, then gradually add the eggs to the butter. Mix in the mashed potatoes.

3. Sift together the flour, cocoa powder, baking powder, and salt. Mix in the ground almonds. Add to the butter mixture in two additions, alternating with the cream. Divide the batter between the prepared forms. If you are using small forms, do not fill them more than two-thirds full.

4. Bake at 350°F (175°C) for about 50 minutes or until baked through.

5. Immediately unmold and let the cakes cool on a cake rack.

6. When completely cold, wrap in plastic and refrigerate.

Lingonberry Cake

four 1-pound, 8-ounce (680-g) cakes

melted unsalted butter

finely ground bread crumbs

12 ounces (340 g) black or English walnuts

1 pound, 2 ounces (510 g) granulated sugar

2 teaspoons (10 g) salt

8 ounces (225 g) soft unsalted butter

You can easily substitute cranberry jam for the lingonberries (which are a member of the cranberry family) if lingonberries are unavailable. This tea cake provides a nice change of pace, as the lingonberries add a special slightly tart flavor and also keep the cake moist. I am the first to admit that I have a passion for these small northern berries. They grow wild in many sunny openings within the Scandinavian forest (as well as in many other northern regions and countries) and I would probably love any recipe that featured them.

1. Brush melted butter inside four 1-quart (960-ml) rectangular, fluted cake pans. Coat the pans with bread crumbs and set aside.

2. Chop the walnuts into raisin-sized pieces, toast them lightly, then set aside to cool.

1 pound (455 g) cake flour

2 teaspoons (4 g) ground cardamom

1 teaspoon (2 g) ground nutmeg

1 teaspoon (4 g) baking soda

1 teaspoon (4 g) baking powder

1¼ cups (300 ml) heavy cream, at room temperature

1 cup (240 ml) buttermilk, at room temperature

5 eggs, at room temperature

1 pound (455 g) lingonberry jam

3. Beat together the sugar, salt, and soft butter for a few minutes until well combined.

4. Sift together the flour, cardamom, nutmeg, baking soda, and baking powder.

5. Combine the heavy cream, buttermilk, and eggs.

6. Incorporate the dry ingredients into the butter mixture in two additions, alternating with the cream mixture. Mix at medium speed for 4 to 5 minutes.

7. Stir the toasted walnuts into the batter. Stir in the jam.

8. Divide the batter between the prepared cake pans. If using smaller pans, do not fill them more than two-thirds full.

9. Bake at 375°F (190°C) for approximately 35 minutes or until the top springs back when pressed lightly in the center.

10. Unmold immediately and let the cakes cool.

11. Store the cakes wrapped in plastic in the refrigerator. This cake will stay fresh for at least a week if stored properly, and it actually becomes more moist after a few days in the refrigerator.

Raisin Cake

four 1-pound, 7-ounce (655-g) cakes

melted unsalted butter

finely ground bread crumbs

1 pound, 8 ounces (680 g) soft unsalted butter

1 pound, 8 ounces (680 g) granulated sugar

1 teaspoon (5 ml) vanilla extract

10 eggs, at room temperature

13 ounces (370 g) bread flour

10 ounces (285 g) cornstarch

1½ tablespoons (18 g) baking powder

8 ounces (225 g) dark raisins

NOTE: This batter can also be baked in muffin pans: portion 4 ounces (115 g) of batter for each small cake. Bake at 400°F (205°C) for about 25 minutes or until the cake springs back when pressed lightly.

You will love this Swedish version of traditional pound cake unless, of course, you do not like raisins. Raisins are popular in many Swedish recipes and, as you may have already noticed if you have used this book for awhile, my recipes are no exception. Raisins not only add flavor and texture to the cakes but they also help keep them fresh. Raisin Cake is terrific right out of the oven, or it can be used to make a quick, country-style dessert after the cakes have been in the refrigerator for a day or two, by serving the sliced cake with whipped cream and fresh strawberries.

1. Brush melted butter inside of four gugelhupf forms, or other tube pans with a 1-quart (960-ml) capacity. Coat the forms thoroughly with the bread crumbs.

2. Beat the softened butter, sugar, and vanilla together until creamy. Mix in the eggs a few at a time.

3. Sift the flour with the cornstarch and baking powder. Add the raisins and mix to coat them with the flour. Stir the flour into the butter mixture, taking care not to incorporate too much air by overmixing. Divide the batter equally between the prepared pans. If you use small pans, do not fill them more than two-thirds full.

4. Bake at 375°F (190°C) until the cake springs back when pressed lightly, about 30 minutes.

5. Unmold and cool the cakes on a cake rack.

6. When cool, wrap and store in the refrigerator.

Soft Gingerbread Cake

four 17-ounce (485-g) cakes

Butter and Flour Mixture (page 4)
1 pound (455 g) light brown sugar
6 eggs, at room temperature
1 pound (455 g) bread flour
2 tablespoons (24 g) baking powder
1 teaspoon (4 g) baking soda
4 tablespoons (20 g) ground cinnamon
2 teaspoons (4 g) ground ginger
1 teaspoon (2 g) ground cloves
2 teaspoons (4 g) ground cardamom
1 teaspoon (5 g) salt
12 ounces (340 g) melted unsalted
    butter
1¼ cups (300 ml) half-and-half, at
    room temperature
powdered sugar

NOTE: This batter can also be baked in muffin tins. Line every other space of muffin pans with paper cups, and grease the top of the pan around the cups with Butter and Flour Mixture. Pipe the batter into the cups using a no. 6 (12-mm) plain tip in your pastry bag. Bake at 375°F (190°C) for about 30 minutes or until baked through. Makes about sixteen 4-ounce (115-g) muffins.

Mjuk Pepparkaka is one of the family recipes in this book; it was a standard coffee cake in my home. In Scandinavia gingerbread cakes are a traditional must-have for the holidays, but this cake is really too good to ignore for a year at a time. My sister and I used to have big arguments over whose turn it was to scrape the last of the batter from the mixing bowl. It was, in our opinion, every bit as good raw as it would be when baked! For a more elegant presentation, try Brandied Gingerbread Cake on page 800.

1. Brush Butter and Flour Mixture on the insides of four 1-quart (960-ml) rectangular, fluted cake pans.

2. Whip the brown sugar and eggs together to a foamy consistency.

3. Sift together the flour, baking powder, baking soda, cinnamon, ginger, cloves, cardamom, and salt. Add to the egg mixture.

4. Combine the melted butter with the half-and-half. Add to the batter slowly. Divide the batter between the prepared pans.

5. Bake at 350°F (175°C) for about 45 minutes or until the cakes spring back when pressed lightly in the center.

6. Unmold the cakes and cool on a cake rack.

7. When the cakes have cooled completely, wrap in plastic and refrigerate. When ready to serve, place a 1-inch-wide (2.5-cm) strip of baking paper, lengthwise, on top of the cakes. Sift powdered sugar over the cakes. Remove the paper template, and slice into the desired size pieces.

Streusel Kuchen

24 pieces approximately 2 by 4 inches (5 × 10 cm) each

unsalted melted butter
⅔ ounce (20 g) fresh compressed
    yeast
1 cup (240 ml) warm milk
    (105–115°F, 40–46°C)
2½ ounces (70 g) granulated sugar
½ teaspoon (3 g) salt
3 egg yolks (¼ cup/60 ml)
1 teaspoon (5 ml) vanilla extract

Streusel is a German word which means "sprinkled" or "strewn together." Kuchen, of course, translates to "cake" or "pastry." Streusel Kuchen dates back to the famous city of Leipzig—home of Johann Sebastian Bach—which is in the former kingdom of Saxony; the early Saxons were well known for their cakes and pastries.

Streusel Kuchen is a staple German coffee cake, typical of good home cooking. It is traditionally served at an afternoon coffee break either with a cream-type filling, as in my version, or with various sweet toppings. One such variation is known as bien stick *("bee sting" in English): the baked cake is topped with a coarse florentina batter and then returned to the oven to cook the topping as is done with Tosca pastries. To make Streusel Kuchen without a filling, follow the instructions through step five, brushing 2 ounces (55 g) of melted butter on the dough before applying the Streusel. Let cool slightly before cutting into serving pieces.*

1 pound (455 g) bread flour,
  approximately
2 ounces (55 g) soft unsalted butter
Egg Wash (page 7)
14 ounces (400 g) Streusel Topping
  (page 14)
1 pound (455 g) Quick Bavarian
  Cream (page 1089)
powdered sugar

1. Brush melted butter over the bottom and sides of a half-sheet pan (16 by 12 inches/40 × 30 cm). Lay a piece of baking paper in the bottom and reserve.

2. In a mixer bowl dissolve the yeast in the warm milk. Add the sugar, salt, egg yolks, and vanilla. Incorporate approximately half of the flour, using the dough hook. Add the soft butter and the remaining flour, and mix until you have a very soft smooth dough, approximately 5 minutes. Mix in additional flour if necessary while mixing. Place the dough in an oiled bowl, cover, and let rise in a warm place until doubled in volume.

3. Punch the dough down. Roll and stretch it to fit, and place the dough in the reserved buttered sheet pan. Let rise again until slightly less than doubled in volume.

4. Brush the dough with Egg Wash. Sprinkle the Streusel Topping over the dough.

5. Bake at 400°F (205°C) for about 10 minutes. Let cool.

6. Cut around the edges of the pan if necessary to loosen the cake. Invert the cake onto a sheet pan and peel away the baking paper. Invert again to turn the cake right-side up on an inverted sheet pan or cardboard. Slice the cake into two equal layers horizontally. Spread Bavarian Cream on the bottom layer, then replace the top. Refrigerate to set the cream, approximately 1 hour.

7. Trim the sides of the cake. Cut into three equal strips lengthwise. Cut each strip into eight equal pieces. Sift powdered sugar lightly over the cut pieces.

Swedish Jam Roll (*Rulltårta*)

two 11-inch (27.5-cm) rolls

Roulade Batter (recipe follows)
granulated sugar
12 ounces (340 g) smooth strawberry
  or raspberry jam

This is a simple and delicious tea cake that can be made in a very short amount of time and does not even require any particular cake pan. Rolled cakes (roulades) are popular all over Europe since, in addition to being quick to make, they can be made ahead and sliced to order, which keeps the servings from becoming dry. Roulades are made with many different fillings—Citrus Roulade and Kirsch Roulade being two old favorites. They can also be iced and decorated to use as part of a pastry display. The following recipe is a typical Scandinavian version.

1. Spread the Roulade Batter evenly over a sheet of baking paper that is 16 by 24 inches (40 × 60 cm), leaving approximately ¹/₂ inch (1.2 cm) of paper uncovered along all four sides. Drag the paper onto a sheet pan (see Figure 16–15, page 842).

2. Bake immediately at 425°F (219°C) for about 10 minutes or until just done. Transfer the sponge to a second (cool) sheet pan after removing it from the oven so it will not dry out. Let the sponge sheet cool, then store it covered in the refrigerator if it is not to be rolled right away. If the sponge seems too dry to roll, follow the instructions given in the note on page 270 to soften it.

3. Sprinkle granulated sugar over a sheet of baking paper. Invert the sponge sheet on top. Peel the paper off the back. Trim the sheet to 15 by 22 inches (37.5 × 55 cm).

4. Spread the jam evenly over the entire surface of the sponge.

5. Pick up the two upper corners of the paper and roll the cake into a tight log, starting from the top long edge and rolling toward you, using the paper underneath the help you form the roll (see Figure 12–3, page 595).

6. Leaving the paper in place around the cake, hold the bottom of the paper still with your left hand, and push a dowel or ruler against the roll with your free hand. The paper will wrap around the roll and tighten it (see Figure 16–5, page 810).

7. Cut the roll into two 11-inch (27.5-cm) pieces. Wrap them in plastic and place seam-side down on a sheet pan lined with baking paper. Refrigerate until ready to serve. The Jam Rolls can be kept in the refrigerator up to one week at this point.

 Roulade Batter

one 16-by-24-inch (40-×-60-cm) sheet or one 10-inch (25-cm) layer

8 eggs
2 egg whites (¹⁄₄ cup/60 ml)
6 ounces (170 g) granulated sugar
grated zest of one-half lemon
4 ounces (115 g) cake flour
4 ounces (115 g) bread flour
1 teaspoon (4 g) baking powder
3 ounces (85 g) melted unsalted butter

NOTE: To make a 10-inch (25-cm) layer, pour the batter into a prepared cake pan and bake at 375°F (190°C) for about 18 minutes.

1. Place the whole eggs, egg whites, sugar, and lemon zest in a mixer bowl.

2. Heat over simmering water, whipping constantly, until the mixture reaches approximately 110°F (43°C). Remove from the heat and whip at high speed until the mixture has cooled completely and is light and fluffy.

3. Sift the flours with the baking powder. Fold the flour into the batter by hand. Fold in the melted butter by hand.

 Tiger Cake

four 17-ounce (485-g) cakes

melted unsalted butter
finely ground bread crumbs
8 eggs, at room temperature
1 pound, 2 ounces (510 g) granulated sugar
³⁄₄ cup (180 ml) milk, at room temperature

*T*his is the designer version of coffee cake—no two patterns of the light and dark batters ever turn out quite the same. Very popular all over Europe, these cakes are also known as marble cakes. Alternatively, this recipe makes a very nice pound cake with a hint of lemon if you leave out the cocoa powder altogether. If you would like to make two plain cakes and two Tiger Cakes, divide the batter in half and add the zest of one lemon and half of the vanilla to one portion of the batter. Divide the lemon batter evenly between two pans. Add ¹⁄₂ ounce (15 g) of unsweetened cocoa powder to one-third of the remaining batter, and the zest of one lemon plus the remaining vanilla to the remaining plain batter. Proceed as directed to make the tiger pattern. To make any variation of this

1 pound, 6 ounces (625 g) melted
   unsalted butter

14 ounces (400 g) cake flour

1 tablespoon (12 g) baking powder

1 ounce (30 g) unsweetened cocoa
   powder

grated zest of two lemons

1 teaspoon (5 ml) vanilla extract

(three plain, one tiger, etc.) use 1 tablespoon of unsweetened cocoa powder per cake, mixed into one-third of the batter for one cake.

1. Brush the inside of four 1-quart (960-ml) gugelhupf forms with melted butter and coat with the bread crumbs.

2. Separate the eggs. Whip the egg yolks with 9 ounces (255 g) of the sugar until light and fluffy. Add the milk and the melted butter (the butter should not be hot).

3. Sift the flour with the baking powder, then mix into the butter mixture.

4. Whip the egg whites until foamy; gradually add the remaining 9 ounces (255 g) sugar and whip to stiff peaks. Carefully fold the butter mixture into the whipped egg whites by hand.

5. Sift the cocoa powder into a bowl; gradually add one-third of the batter and mix to combine. Mix the lemon zest and the vanilla into the remaining two-thirds of the batter.

6. Starting and finishing with the white batter, spoon three or four alternating layers of white and chocolate batters into the prepared forms. If you are using small forms, fill each one only two-thirds full.

7. Bake immediately at 375°F (190°C) for about 40 minutes or until the cake springs back when pressed lightly.

8. Unmold onto a cake rack to cool.

9. When the cakes have cooled completely, wrap in plastic and store in the refrigerator.

8

Decorated Cakes

Apple Wine Cake

Apricot Cream Cake

Black Currant Cake

Black Forest Cake

Boston Cream Pie

Caramel Cake

Carrot Cake

Cheesecakes

    Cheesecake, New York Style

    Cheesecake, West-Coast Style

    Cheesecake with Caramelized Apples

Chestnut Puzzle Cake

Chocolate and Frangelico Mousse Cake

Chocolate Decadence

Chocolate Ganache Cake

Chocolate Hazelnut Cake

Chocolate Mint Torte with a Golden Touch

Chocolate Mousse Cake with Banana

Chocolate Truffle Cake with Raspberries

Diplomat Cake

Dobos Torte

Gâteau Istanbul

Gâteau Lugano

Gâteau Malakoff

Gâteau Moka Carousel

Gâteau Pithiviers

Gâteau Saint-Honoré

Harlequin Cake

Lemon Chiffon Cake

Mocha Cake

Pariser Chocolate Cake

Poppy Seed Cake

Princess Cake

Queen of Sheba Cake

Raspberry Cake

Sacher Torte

Sicilian Macaroon Cake

Strawberry Kirsch Cake

Sugar Kirsch Cake

Swedish Chocolate Cake

Tropical Mousse Cake

White Chocolate Pumpkin Cheesecake

The term *decorated cake* is generally used to describe a cake that has been filled, iced, and has some type of finishing touch on the icing. Whether or not the cake is decorated attractively can influence your sales to a great degree. The decoration should tempt the customer to try the product, and at the same time it should suggest the flavor and texture of the cake and filling. The decoration is the final wrapping, or packaging, designed to market your product.

The degree of complexity of the cake decorations in this chapter range from Princess Cake, which traditionally has only a thin sheet of Marzipan encasing the whole cake and a dusting of powdered sugar on top, to the more involved Lemon Chiffon Cake. The latter is iced with whipped cream, the surface of the cake is covered with lemon glaze or chocolate shavings, the side of each serving is decorated with a thin handmade chocolate square, and last, rosettes of whipped cream are piped around the edge and are topped with a small wedge of lemon. In some cases, instead of being added later, the decoration is inherent to the cake itself: The Chocolate Ganache Cake is made with a showy Ribbon Sponge Sheet perimeter; Chestnut Puzzle Cake is assembled with its many sponge layers going in several intriguing directions; and the West-Coast Style Cheesecake has a simple piped decoration baked on top.

Cutting or Marking Portions

Most of the cakes in this chapter are decorated after being marked or cut into serving pieces. This enables you to decorate each serving identically. If you are displaying the cakes in a pastry case, the servings will still look attractive even if only a few remain. Precut or marked slices can save time for the waitperson or retail clerk, and it is also a good idea for the chef to designate the portion size from the standpoint of cost control. If you do choose to cut the pieces rather than mark them, you may want to cover the cut sides of each slice with small sheets of paper to prevent the cake from drying out. The slices should then be reassembled into the original shape for display. Any of the cakes in this chapter can also be decorated before cutting using the techniques and special-occasion designs described in the chapter on Decorations.

Cutting Sponge Layers

Before you can assemble and decorate the cake, it is usually necessary to cut a baked sponge into two or three layers and alternate these layers with the filling. Cutting and moving thin sponge layers is often a more challenging skill for students to master than some of the decorating procedures. Use a serrated knife to slice the layers and hold the blade of the knife parallel to the tabletop. Place your left hand flat on top of the cake (if you are right-handed) and turn the cake counterclockwise as you cut. Do not move the knife from side to side; hold it level and only move it away and toward you as you turn the cake into the knife's path. Start by cutting the skin off the top of the cake and cutting the top flat at the same time if necessary (Figure 8–1). Then cut the desired number of layers, starting from the top and removing each layer before cutting the next. After completing the cut for the first layer, leave the layer in place on the cake (Figure 8–2). Carefully slide a cardboard cake round into the cut, easing it in by wiggling it up and down a bit instead of just pushing it into the cut, which can break the cake, then simply pick up the cardboard to move the layer to the side. Repeat to cut the remaining layers. It becomes more difficult to cut thin, even layers as the size of the sponge increases in circumference, but use the same technique for all sizes. Assuming the sponge was made correctly, you should be able to move the layers of a standard (10-by-2-inch/25-x-5-cm) sponge using your hand, or by lifting the cake with the knife used for slicing, rather than using a cardboard as shown in Figures 8–3 and 8–4. However, with a more fragile sponge, or when working with a half or full sheet of sponge, the cardboard technique becomes essential.

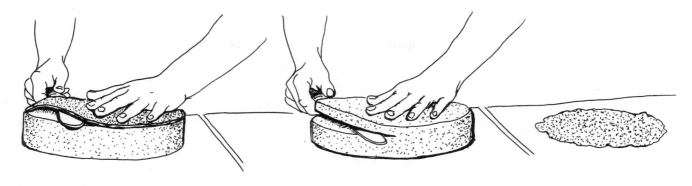

FIGURE 8–1 Cutting the skin from the top of the sponge cake and cutting the top level at the same time if necessary

FIGURE 8–2 Cutting the first cake layer

FIGURES 8–3 and 8–4 Using the slicing knife to transfer the cut layers of sponge

When you are ready to stack the layers, pick up the cardboard and hold the layer just above the cake where you want to place it. Slide the layer off the cardboard and onto the cake, guiding it into place with your free hand as you pull the cardboard away from the bottom (see Figure 8–17, page 353, as an example).

Gelatin in Cake Fillings

Note that many of the cakes in this chapter use unflavored gelatin powder to thicken the filling so that the cakes can be cut attractively (for information on substituting sheet gelatin see page 1110). Gelatin powder is first softened by sprinkling it over a cold liquid, usually water, and allowing it to stand two or three minutes (the surface area of the liquid must be large enough for all of the gelatin to become wet). Do not stir at this point or the gelatin will lump. The mixture is then heated until the gelatin has dissolved completely. This actually occurs at 86°F (30°C), but it is necessary to heat it above this temperature, to about 100°F (43°C), or it would set up almost immediately. If you do not have a thermometer, or you are unsure of the temperature, heat the mixture until it is warm to the touch—just a little higher than body temperature.

It is not necessary to heat gelatin to any particular temperature in order for it to work properly; the gelatin must simply be dissolved in the liquid. However, depending on its use, and more specifically how it will be mixed with the other ingredients, a higher or lower temperature can be preferable. In the glaze on the Black Currant Cake, for example, the dissolved gelatin can be heated to a fairly low temperature. The glaze does not contain any whipped cream, so it can be reheated if it should set up too soon, and you want the gelatin to start setting up fairly quickly so that the glaze can be spread over the cakes. The other ingredients in the glaze are stirred into the dissolved gelatin in this case because a relatively small amount of gelatin is used, and it is important that none of it is left clinging to the sides of the bowl or pot that it was dissolved in. Again, because there is no cream in the glaze, it is not necessary to temper the heated gelatin before mixing it with the remaining ingredients. On the other hand, in the recipe for Chocolate Cognac Cream, you will see that the instructions call for quickly mixing the dissolved gelatin into a small portion of the filling to temper it before adding this to the remaining filling. In this instance, the gelatin should be heated until it is a bit warmer. It is added to a large amount of cold whipped cream, and you will need time to mix the gelatin in thoroughly before it sets up. If the dissolved gelatin were added directly to the cold cream it might start to set up (lump) before it could be completely incorporated. And, because of the cream, you would not be able to reheat the filling to melt the lumps as you can with the glaze. In this particular filling melted chocolate, which is a thickening agent in itself, is added at the same time; this causes the filling to set up more rapidly.

Adding gelatin that is too hot to a filling containing whipped cream can cause the cream to melt partially, which will decrease the volume of the filling and result in an overly firm, dense finished product. Although it is better to heat gelatin a little too hot than to have the filling lump because the gelatin was too cold, in most instances any temperature above 130°F (54°C) is considered too hot. If you are unsure and do not have a thermometer available, put your finger into the liquid: if you cannot keep it there comfortably, the liquid is too hot and must be allowed to cool before it is used. If the gelatin mixture is accidentally heated close to the boiling point, it is best to discard it and start over. Gelatin that boils will form a skin and will also lose some of its ability to thicken.

The same problems that occur when adding gelatin that is too hot to a cream filling will take place if a whipped cream filling containing gelatin must be reheated due to the gelatin lumping or setting prematurely: The cream will melt and deflate, and the filling will lose volume. Since there will still be the same amount of gelatin in less filling, the texture will be too firm and much less appealing. It is therefore very important that the forms that will be used to contain the filling are prepared before the filling is made, or at least before the gelatin is added. Stainless-steel cake rings, either solid or adjustable, are ideal, although plastic strips such as acetate or polyurethane may be used instead in most cases. You will need a 34-inch (85-cm) strip to make a 10-inch (25-cm) round frame. If you use cake rings that are not made from stainless steel, line them with strips of plastic or baking paper.

Bloom

The term *bloom* scientifically refers to the strength of the set gelatin which is measured using a gellometer (see page 1110). This term comes from the French scientist named Bloom who invented the gellometer. Some people also use the word *bloom* to describe the process of softening the gelatin in a cold liquid before it is dissolved. These are two distinct meanings.

Apple Wine Cake

two 10-inch (25-cm) cakes

one recipe Almond Sponge batter
   (page 270)

3 pounds, 8 ounces (1 kg, 590 g)
   Golden Delicious, pippin, or
   Granny Smith apples (about eight
   medium-sized)

3 cups (720 ml) muscat or riesling
   wine

1 tablespoon (15 ml) lemon juice

one cinnamon stick

²/₃ cup (160 ml) Calvados

4 ounces (115 g) dark raisins

two 10-inch (25-cm) Short Dough
   Cake Bottoms (page 55)

4 ounces (115 g) apricot jam

Calvados Wine Filling (recipe follows)

8 ounces (225 g) smooth raspberry
   jam

1 cup (240 ml) heavy cream

2 teaspoons (10 g) granulated sugar

one recipe Apricot Glaze (page 1016)

6 ounces (170 g) sliced almonds,
   toasted and lightly crushed

one recipe Mousseline Sauce
   (page 1076)

¹/₄ cup (60 ml) Calvados

mint sprigs

*I*f the twenty-one steps involved in making this cake are more than you want to tackle, try this variation instead; both are unusual and refreshing. To make the variation, omit the jelly rolls; use all four sponge layers; and double the amounts of apples, raisins, and poaching liquid. Divide the fruit mixture in half after cooking, reserving the most attractive apple wedges for decorating the cakes. Assemble the cakes as described in the main recipe, placing the second sponges on top of the cream filling and brushing them lightly with some of the poaching liquid before refrigerating the cakes. Decorate the tops of the cakes with the reserved apple wedges and raisins (instead of jelly roll slices), arranging the apples in concentric circles as in the layer inside. Brush the apple wedges with Apricot Glaze, and continue as in the main recipe.*

1. Line the bottom of a 10-inch (25-cm) cake pan with baking paper (or grease and flour, but do not grease and flour the sides).

2. Pour a little more than half of the sponge batter into the pan and spread to even the surface.

3. Pour the remainder of the batter onto a sheet of baking paper and spread it into a 20-by-15-inch (50-×-37.5-cm) rectangle. Drag the paper onto a sheet pan (see Figure 16–5, page 842).

4. Bake both sponges at 400°F (205°C). The sheet will take approximately 8 minutes to bake, and the round cake will take about 18 minutes; the tops of the cakes should spring back when pressed lightly in the center.

5. Immediately transfer the thin sheet to a second (cool) sheet pan. Let both sponges cool completely.

6. Peel the apples, core, and cut into ¹/₂-inch (1.2-cm) thick wedges (not slices). To prevent oxidation, keep the apples in acidulated water as you are working.

7. Combine the wine, lemon juice, cinnamon stick, and ²/₃ cup (160 ml) of Calvados in a saucepan. Heat the liquid to boiling, then add the raisins and the apple wedges. Simmer until the apples are soft but not falling apart. Set the apples and raisins aside to cool in the liquid.

8. Cut the skin from the top of the round sponge cake. Slice the cake into four thin layers, and reserve two of the layers for another project or use them to make the variation of this recipe (see introduction).

9. Place the Short Dough Cake Bottoms on cardboard cake rounds for support. Divide the apricot jam between them and spread out evenly. Place one sponge layer on each.

10. Remove the cinnamon stick from the apples and raisins and discard it. Strain off the liquid. Reserve 1 cup (240 ml) of the poaching liquid to use in making the filling, and brush some of the remainder over the sponge cakes to soak them lightly. Discard the remainder of the liquid unless you are making the variation.

11. Remove about half of the raisins from the apple-raisin mixture and reserve them to use in the presentation. Divide the remaining apple-raisin mixture between the two cakes, arranging the apple wedges in concentric circles on top of the sponge.

12. Place 10-inch (25-cm) stainless-steel cake rings snugly around each sponge. (If cake rings are not available, secure strips of acetate or polyurethane around the sponges instead.)

13. Divide the Calvados Wine Filling between the two cakes. The filling should be just starting to thicken when you pour it into the rings. Refrigerate the cakes until the filling is set, approximately 2 hours.

14. Invert the thin sponge sheet onto a sheet of baking paper, then peel the paper off the back of the sponge. (If the sponge has been made ahead and refrigerated, carefully scrape the skin off the top of the sponge before inverting it.) Cut the sponge in half lengthwise and transfer one half to a second sheet pan. Spread the raspberry jam over the entire surface of both sponges. There should be just enough jam to make the surface sticky. Roll the sponge sheets lengthwise following the instructions for Yule Logs (see Figure 12–3, page 595, and Figure 16–5, page 810). Place the jelly rolls in the freezer to make them firm and easier to cut.

15. Remove the cake rings or plastic strips from the two round cakes. Trim away any excess Short Dough to even the sides of the cakes (see Figure 8–11, page 325).

16. Whip the heavy cream and the sugar to stiff peaks. Ice the tops and sides of the cakes with a thin layer of whipped cream.

17. Cut the jelly rolls into thin slices, approximately 1/8 inch (3 mm) wide. Starting at the edge of the cakes, arrange the slices in concentric circles covering the tops of the cakes. Place the rounds in each circle between those in the previous row to cover as much of the surface as possible.

18. Brush the jelly rolls with Apricot Glaze.

19. Cover the sides of the cakes with sliced almonds (see Figure 8–5, page 296).

20. Cut the cakes into the desired number of servings. Flavor the Mousseline Sauce with the remaining 1/4 cup (60 ml) of Calvados.

21. Presentation: Place a slice of cake off-center on a dessert plate. Pour a pool of Mousseline Sauce in front of the dessert. Sprinkle some of the reserved raisins over the sauce and place a sprig of mint next to the sauce.

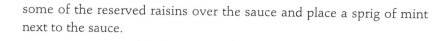

Calvados Wine Filling

3 pounds, 8 ounces
(1 kg, 590 g) filling

2 tablespoons (18 g) unflavored
   gelatin powder
1 cup (240 ml) strained liquid from
   poaching the apples, chilled
4 egg yolks (¹/₃ cup/80 ml)
¹/₄ cup (60 ml) or 3 ounces (85 g) light
   corn syrup
5 cups (1 l, 200 ml) heavy cream
¹/₄ cup (60 ml) Calvados

NOTE: Because you cannot reheat this filling to soften it, do not make it until you are ready to assemble the cakes.

1. Sprinkle the gelatin over the poaching liquid and set aside to soften.

2. Beat the egg yolks lightly just to combine them.

3. Heat the corn syrup to boiling. Whip the corn syrup into the egg yolks and continue whipping until the mixture is light and fluffy.

4. Whip the cream to soft peaks. Combine the cream with the yolk mixture.

5. Add the Calvados to the softened gelatin mixture. Place over a bain-marie and heat until the gelatin is dissolved; do not overheat.

6. Rapidly mix the gelatin into a small part of the cream mixture; then, still working quickly, mix this into the remainder.

Apricot Cream Cake

two 10-inch (25-cm) cakes

two 10-inch (25-cm) Short Dough
   Cake Bottoms (page 55)
4 ounces (115 g) smooth apricot jam
one 10-inch (25-cm) Chiffon Sponge
   Cake (page 272)
Apricot Whipped Cream
   (recipe follows)
1¹/₂ cups (360 ml) heavy cream
1 tablespoon (15 g) granulated sugar
6 ounces (170 g) sliced almonds,
   toasted and lightly crushed
dark chocolate shavings
apricot wedges
Apricot Sauce (page 1068)
mint sprigs

*T*his is a great tasting dessert to keep in mind during peak apricot season. It is perfect when you need something you can prep ahead, since the cakes can be made through step three, covered, and then refrigerated for up to five days, or frozen for two to three weeks. While Cointreau can be relatively expensive, and in many instances it wouldn't matter if you used a less expensive orange liqueur, in this filling you can tell the difference so do not substitute unless you must.

1. Place the Short Dough Bottoms on cardboard cake rounds for support. Divide the jam between them and spread it out evenly.

2. Cut the skin from the top of the Sponge Cake, cutting the top level at the same time. Cut the sponge into four thin layers. Place one layer on top of each Short Dough Bottom. Place 10-inch (25-cm) stainless-steel cake rings around each sponge, setting them on top of the Short Dough. If cake rings are not available, secure strips of acetate or polyurethane around the sponges.

3. Divide the Apricot Whipped Cream between the two rings and spread it out evenly. Place the remaining cake layers on top of the filling. Refrigerate the cakes for at least 2 hours to set the filling.

4. Whip the heavy cream and granulated sugar to stiff peaks.

5. Remove the rings or plastic strips from the cakes. Trim the Short Dough around the base of the cakes to make the sides even (see Figure 8–11, page 325).

6. Ice the top and sides of the cakes with the whipped cream; use just enough of the cream to cover the sponge. Place the remaining whipped cream in a pastry bag with a no. 6 (12-mm) plain tip and reserve in the refrigerator.

FIGURE 8–5   Pressing crushed almonds onto the side of the Apricot Cream Cake

7. Cover the sides of the cakes with the crushed sliced almonds (Figure 8–5).

8. Cut a 6-inch (15-cm) circle out of the center of a 10-inch (25-cm) cardboard circle. Place the doughnut-shaped template on top of one of the cakes. Sprinkle the shaved chocolate over the top to cover the center of the cake. Carefully remove the template and repeat with the second cake.

9. Cut or mark the cakes into the desired number of pieces. Pipe a rosette of the reserved whipped cream at the edge of each slice; top each rosette with an apricot wedge.

10. Presentation: Place a slice of cake off-center on a dessert plate. Pour a small pool of Apricot Sauce in front of the slice. Place a mint sprig next to the sauce.

 Apricot Whipped Cream

4 pounds (1 kg, 820 g)

1 pound, 4 ounces (570 g) ripe
    apricots
6 egg yolks ($\frac{1}{2}$ cup/120 ml)
$\frac{1}{2}$ cup (120 ml) or 6 ounces (170 g)
    light corn syrup
2 tablespoons (18 g) unflavored
    gelatin powder
$\frac{1}{2}$ cup (120 ml) cold water
3 cups (720 ml) heavy cream
$\frac{1}{2}$ cup (120 ml) Cointreau
$\frac{1}{4}$ cup (60 ml) apricot juice
2 ounces (55 g) apricot purée

1. Wash and stone the apricots, then cut them into $\frac{3}{4}$-inch (2-cm) chunks. If you must use apricots that are not fully ripe, poach them first in Plain Poaching Syrup (see page 13).

2. Whip the egg yolks until they are broken up and combined.

3. Bring the corn syrup to a boil and then whip the hot syrup into the egg yolks, continuing to whip until the mixture has cooled and has reached a light and fluffy consistency.

4. Sprinkle the gelatin over the cold water and set aside to soften.

5. Whip the cream until soft peaks form. Fold the cream into the yolk mixture.

6. Add the Cointreau and the apricot juice to the softened gelatin mixture. Place over a bain-marie and heat until the gelatin is dissolved; do not overheat.

7. Remove about one-fourth of the cream mixture and rapidly mix the gelatin into it. Working quickly, add this to the remaining cream. Fold in the apricot purée and chunks.

8. If the filling has not started to set up, wait a few minutes and mix again before using in the cakes to prevent the apricot chunks from sinking to the bottom of the filling.

 **VARIATION**

*B*y making just a few changes you can give the Apricot Cream Cake a more modern look (as shown in the color insert) by replacing the crushed almonds on the sides of the cakes with Ribbon Sponge Sheets.

Omit the Short Dough Cake Bottoms, apricot jam, and sliced almonds from the ingredient list. Replace them with one Ribbon Sponge Sheet (see page 276), making the chocolate ribbons in a wavy pattern lengthwise. You will have quite a bit of Ribbon Sponge left over, but it is not practical to make less than one sheet at a time. Leftover sponge can be kept for several weeks in the freezer if wrapped well.

1. Cut 2-inch (5-cm) wide strips lengthwise from the Ribbon Sponge Sheet. Place two 10-inch (25-cm) cake rings on cardboard cake circles (or use 10-inch/25-cm) cake pans if cake rings are not available). Line the inside of the rings or pans with strips of acetate, polyurethane, or baking paper. Line the sides with the Ribbon Sponge Strips, placing the striped side against the plastic or paper.

2. Cut the skin from the top of the Chiffon Sponge Cake and then cut it into into four layers. Place one layer of sponge inside each ring, making sure it fits snugly against the Ribbon Sponge (trim to fit as needed, or if the sponge is too small, make a cut from the outside about halfway toward the center and open the sponge up to make it larger so it fits tight against the sides).

3. Divide the Apricot Whipped Cream between the two rings and spread it out evenly. Place the two remaining cake layers on top of the cream filling. Refrigerate the cakes for at least 2 hours to set the filling.

4. Continue as directed in the main recipe except do not ice the sides of the cakes in step six, and omit step seven.

Black Currant Cake

two 10-inch (25-cm) cakes

two 10-inch (25-cm) Short Dough
  Cake Bottoms (page 55)

4 ounces (115 g) smooth apricot jam

one 10-inch (25-cm) Cocoa Almond
  Sponge (page 271)

¼ cup (60 ml) Black Currant Purée
  (recipe follows)

¼ cup (60 ml) crème de cassis

Black Currant Mousse (recipe follows)

Black Currant Glaze (recipe follows)

reserved black currants (see purée
  recipe)

granulated sugar

Apricot Sauce (page 1068)

Chocolate Sauce for Piping
  (page 1072)

fanned fresh apricot halves or other
  fruit in season

mint sprigs

*T*his is one of the cakes to choose when you're looking for something special and out of the ordinary. It is not the quickest, I admit, but the results are certainly worthwhile. The black currants give the filling a rich, dark, purple color and impart their distinctive tangy flavor, which is not found in any other fruit.

Black currants are quite obscure in this country where, when people speak of currants, it is usually the dried Zante grape they are referring to. In fact, it has happened at the school a couple of times over the years that students unfamiliar with black currants have attempted to make the purée for this recipe using the small, almost black, dried grapes. They usually catch on in step three, however, when they try to pass it through a strainer!

1. Place the Short Dough Cake Bottoms on cardboard cake rounds for support. Divide the jam between them and spread it out evenly.

2. Cut the skin off the top of the sponge cake, cutting the cake even at the same time. Slice into two layers and set them on the jam.

3. Combine the Black Currant Purée with the crème de cassis. Brush the mixture over the sponges, allowing all of the liquid to soak in.

4. Place 10-inch (25-cm) stainless-steel cake rings around the sponge layers, setting them on top of the Short Dough. If cake rings are not available, secure strips of acetate or polyurethane around the sponges instead. Divide the Black Currant Mousse between the two cakes. Refrigerate for at least 2 hours to set the filling.

5. When the cakes are completely set, carefully run a thin knife dipped in hot water around the inside of the rings, then remove the rings or simply peel away the plastic. Trim away any Short Dough that protrudes outside the sponge to make the sides even (see Figure 8–11, page 325).

6. Pour half of the Black Currant Glaze on one cake and quickly spread it out with a metal spatula to cover the whole surface. Repeat with second cake. Be sure that the glaze is not too hot or it can melt the filling. Also, do not pour it straight down in one spot or it will make a hole.

7. Refrigerate the cakes for a few minutes to set the glaze. If any glaze has run down the sides, cut it away with a knife. Warm a metal spatula and use it to smooth the sides of the cakes.

8. Slice the cakes into the desired number of serving pieces, using a thin knife dipped in hot water (let the warm knife melt through the glaze, then cut).

9. Roll the reserved black currants in granulated sugar to coat them. Place one at the edge of each slice. If necessary, attach them to the cake by touching a hot metal skewer or heated knife-tip to the glaze to melt it, then set the currant on top.

10. Presentation: Place a slice of cake off-center on a dessert plate. Pour a pool of Apricot Sauce in front of the slice and decorate it with Chocolate Sauce for Piping (see pages 998 to 1006). Place a fanned apricot half on the opposite side of the plate and place a mint sprig next to the apricot.

Black Currant Mousse

4 pounds (1 kg, 820 g)

3 cups (720 ml) heavy cream

2 tablespoons (18 g) unflavored
gelatin powder

³/₄ cup (180 ml) cold water

6 egg whites (³/₄ cup/180 ml)

6 ounces (170 g) granulated sugar

8 ounces (225 g) white chocolate,
melted

1¹/₂ cups (360 ml) Black Currant
Purée (recipe follows)

NOTE: *Because it will set fairly quickly, do not make this filling until you are ready to use it.*

1. Whip the cream to soft peaks. Reserve in the refrigerator.

2. Sprinkle the gelatin over the water and set aside to soften.

3. Combine the egg whites and sugar. Heat the mixture over simmering water until it reaches 140°F (60°C), whipping constantly to prevent the egg whites from cooking on the bottom. Remove from the heat and immediately continue whipping until the mixture is cold and has formed stiff peaks.

4. Stir the white chocolate into the Black Currant Purée.

5. Place the softened gelatin mixture over a bain-marie and heat until dissolved. Do not overheat.

6. Rapidly add the gelatin mixture to the Currant Purée (be sure that the purée is not any cooler than room temperature). Gradually fold this mixture into the reserved meringue. Fold into the reserved whipped cream.

Black Currant Glaze

enough to cover the tops of two 10-inch (25-cm) cakes

1 tablespoon (9 g) unflavored gelatin
powder

¹/₄ cup (60 ml) cold water

¹/₂ cup (120 ml) Simple Syrup
(page 11)

¹/₄ cup (60 ml) Black Currant Purée
(recipe follows)

1. Sprinkle the gelatin over the water and let sit until softened. Place the gelatin mixture over a bain-marie and heat until dissolved. Do not overheat.

2. Stir in the Simple Syrup and the Currant Purée and use as soon as the glaze shows signs of thickening. Should the glaze thicken too much before it can be applied, reheat to ensure a smooth glaze on the cakes.

Black Currant Purée

approximately 2 cups (480 ml) purée

2 pounds (910 g) fresh or frozen black
currants (see note)

1 cup (240 ml) water

4 ounces (115 g) granulated sugar

NOTE: *If using black currants in heavy syrup, strain and reserve the syrup before weighing the currants. Substitute 2 cups (480 ml) of the syrup for the granulated sugar and the water.*

1. Reserve one whole black currant to decorate each serving of cake. Combine the remaining currants with the water and granulated sugar in a skillet.

2. Cook over low heat until the currants start to soften, about 5 minutes.

3. Purée the mixture, then pass the purée through a strainer. Divide as follows:

- ¹/₄ cup (60 ml) to use in assembling the cakes
- ¹/₄ cup (60 ml) to use in the glaze
- remainder, approximately 1¹/₂ cups (360 ml), to use in the mousse

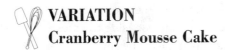

VARIATION
Cranberry Mousse Cake

If black currants are not available, or if you want to make a dessert especially suitable for the holiday season, you can alter the recipe in the following ways:

- Substitute Cranberry Purée for the Black Currant Purée (directions follow).
- Use whole cranberries instead of currants to decorate.
- Replace the crème de cassis with cranberry juice.
- Serve the cake with Cranberry Coulis (see page 1073) instead of Apricot Sauce.

Cranberry Purée

approximately 2 cups (480 ml) purée

1 pound (455 g) fresh or frozen
   cranberries
¹/₂ cup (120 ml) water
6 ounces (170 g) granulated sugar

1. Set aside the number of berries you need for decoration if applicable.

2. Combine the remaining cranberries, the water, and the granulated sugar in a saucepan.

3. Cook over low heat until the berries start to soften and split open, about 5 minutes.

4. Purée the mixture and use as directed.

Black Forest Cake

two 10-inch (25-cm) cakes

one recipe Chocolate Sponge Cake
   batter (page 270)
³/₄ cup (180 ml) kirschwasser
¹/₂ cup (120 ml) Simple Syrup
   (page 11)
1 quart (960 ml) heavy cream
Black Forest Cherry Filling
   (recipe follows)
2 cups (480 ml) heavy cream
1 tablespoon (15 g) granulated sugar
Dark Chocolate Squares (page 890)
dark chocolate shavings
powdered sugar
fresh cherries

NOTE: If fresh cherries are not available, substitute a chocolate figurine for decoration or leave the rosettes plain rather than using canned (or worse yet the infamous maraschino) cherries.

This is one of the Western world's most popular cakes, and for good reason. Schwartzwalder Kirsch Torte is as delicious as the Black Forest (in the Swabia region of Germany for which it is named) is beautiful. If you do not find one of these cakes in any pastry shop there, it's a good bet that they have just run out! Each shop seems to make its own particular version: some add rum to the cherry filling, others use a light sponge cake instead of chocolate, and another interpretation uses chocolate whipped cream. The four basic building blocks are chocolate, cherries, kirsch liqueur or kirschwasser, and whipped cream. Sour cherries such as Montmorency or Morello are always used in the classic rendition. I think you will also enjoy my own hybrid, the Meringue Black Forest cake on page 608. Whichever version you make, do not skimp on the cherries: this exquisite cake should be moist and bursting with cherry flavor.

1. Divide the Chocolate Sponge Cake batter between two greased and floured 10-inch (25-cm) cake pans. Bake at 400°F (205°C) for approximately 12 minutes. Set aside to cool.

2. Combine the kirschwasser and Simple Syrup. Reserve.

3. Whip 1 quart (960 ml) of heavy cream with about one-third of the kirschwasser mixture to stiff peaks. Reserve in the refrigerator.

4. Unmold the cooled Sponge Cakes and cut them into three layers each. Place the two bottom layers on your work surface, saving the two best sponges for the tops if there seems to be any difference. Brush the bottom sponge layers with some of the remaining kirschwasser mixture.

5. Place one-fourth of the Cherry Filling on each of the bottom layers and spread it out carefully. Top each layer with one-fourth of the whipped cream and spread it out evenly on top of the Cherry Filling. Place the middle sponge layers on top of the cream. Brush some kirschwasser mixture over the sponges. Divide the remaining Cherry Filling on top and spread out evenly. Divide the remaining whipped cream on top of the filling and spread it evenly as well. Place the top sponge layers on the cream, making sure the cakes are level. Brush the remainder of the kirschwasser mixture over the sponges.

6. If you plan to precut the cakes into serving pieces, you should cover them at this point and place them in the freezer until they are frozen solid. This will enable you to cut cleanly through the cream and the cherries without dragging one into the other.

7. Remove the cakes from the freezer.

8. Whip the remaining heavy cream with the granulated sugar to stiff peaks. Spread enough of the cream over the top and sides of the cakes to cover the sponge.

9. When the cakes have thawed halfway (if the inside feels too hard, wait a little longer), cut them into the desired number of pieces. Put the remaining whipped cream in a pastry bag with a no. 6 (12-mm) star tip and pipe a rosette at the edge of each slice. Place a chocolate square on the side of each slice. Sprinkle the shaved chocolate over the top of the cake, inside the piped rosettes. Sift powdered sugar lightly over the shavings. Place a cherry on each whipped cream rosette. Be certain that the cake is fully thawed before serving.

1. Macerate the cherries in the kirschwasser for at least 2 hours or, preferably, overnight.

2. Strain the kirschwasser from the cherries and add enough of the cherry juice to the kirschwasser to make 2¹/₂ cups (600 ml) of liquid. Dissolve the cornstarch in the raspberry juice. Mix the pectin powder into the granulated sugar. Add to the cherry liquid along with the cornstarch-juice mixture.

3. Bring to a boil and cook for a few seconds to eliminate the cornstarch flavor.

4. Remove from the heat and carefully stir in the cherries without breaking them. Cool completely before using the filling.

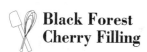

Black Forest Cherry Filling

6 cups (1 l, 440 ml) filling

2 pounds (910 g) well-drained, canned sour cherries (see note)

¹/₂ cup (120 ml) kirschwasser

2 cups (280 ml) juice from canned cherries, approximately

2 ounces (55 g) cornstarch

¹/₄ cup (60 ml) strained raspberry juice

2 tablespoons (18 g) pectin powder

10 ounces (285 g) granulated sugar

NOTE: *If you must substitute sweet canned cherries, cut them in half before macerating (do not chop) and decrease the sugar in the recipe to 3 ounces (85 g).*

Boston Cream Pie

two 10-inch cakes

two 10-inch (25-cm) Boston Cream
   Pie Cake Bases (recipe follows)
Rum Syrup (recipe follows)
1 cup (240 ml) heavy cream
2 tablespoons (30 ml) dark rum
one-quarter recipe or 1 pound, 8
   ounces (680 g) Pastry Cream
   (page 1088) (see note)
one-half recipe Chocolate Glaze
   (page 1016)
unsweetened cocoa powder
powdered sugar

*NOTE: Replace the milk with half-and-half
when preparing the Pastry Cream.*

*T*his, of course, is not a pie at all but a cake disguised by a misnomer. The
first reference to this dessert dates back to 1855 when a New York newspaper published a recipe for a "pudding pie cake." That recipe was similar to
Boston Cream Pie as we know it, but it had a powdered sugar topping. A year
later Harvey D. Parker opened his Parker House Restaurant in Boston (this
restaurant was also the birthplace of the famous Parker House rolls) and featured a version of the pudding pie cake on his menu. Parker's cake was topped
with a chocolate glaze. How the cake became known as Boston Cream Pie is not
entirely clear, but it seems likely that the name stems from the original title combined with the reference to Boston as the place where the cake became well
known.

It was common for New England colonists to bake cakes in pie tins, as they
were more likely to have a baking pan for a pie than for a cake, if they did not
have both.

1. Cut the skin and as much of the top as necessary off of the cake
bases to make the tops level. Invert so that the flat part becomes the
bottom and cut them into two layers each.

2. Brush Rum Syrup on both bottom layers, paying special attention to the edges.

3. Whip the heavy cream to stiff peaks.

4. Stir the rum into the Pastry Cream. Stir about $^1/_2$ cup (120 ml) of
the mixture into the whipped cream. Divide the remainder evenly
between the bottom layers and spread it out evenly. Place the top cake
layers on the custard. Press down lightly to secure and to force the custard to the edges of the cake. Brush the remaining Rum Syrup over the
top of the cake layers. Divide the whipped cream mixture between the
cakes and spread it over the tops and sides.

5. Place the cakes on a cake rack set over a clean sheet pan. Pour
half of the Chocolate Glaze on top of one cake (you may have to reheat
the glaze to get it to a spreadable consistency). Use a spatula to carefully push some of glaze from the top to the edges, letting it run down
to cover the sides of the cake as well. Repeat the procedure with the
second cake and the remaining glaze. Transfer the cakes to cardboard
cake circles. Refrigerate until the glaze is set, then cut the cakes into the
desired number of servings, using a knife dipped in hot water.

6. Presentation: Lightly sift cocoa powder over the base of a
dessert plate, using a small, fine mesh strainer. Lightly sift powdered
sugar on top of the cocoa powder, with or without the use of a template (see page 1040). Place a slice of cake on top of the design.

Boston Cream Pie Cake Base

two 10-inch (25-cm) cake layers

Butter and Flour Mixture (page 4)
4 egg whites (½ cup/120 ml)
1¼ cups (300 ml) half-and-half, at
    room temperature
1 pound (455 g) cake flour
1 pound (455 g) granulated sugar
4 teaspoons (16 g) baking powder
½ teaspoon (2.5 g) salt
2 teaspoons (10 ml) vanilla extract
12 ounces (340 g) melted unsalted
    butter
1 egg

1. Brush the Butter and Flour Mixture over the inside of two 10-inch (25-cm) pie pans. Reserve.

2. Stir together the egg whites and one third of the half-and-half. Reserve.

3. Sift together the cake flour, granulated sugar, baking powder, and salt. Add the vanilla, melted butter, the remaining half-and-half, and the whole egg. Beat at high speed for a few minutes. Gradually stir in the reserved egg white mixture and mix until combined. Divide between the two prepared pie pans.

4. Bake at 350°F (175°C) for approximately 40 minutes or until the center springs back when you press the cakes lightly with your finger. Invert on a sheet pan lined with baking paper. Let cool.

Rum Syrup

¾ cup (180 ml)

¼ cup (60 ml) dark rum
¼ cup (60 ml) water
¼ cup (60 ml) Simple Syrup (page 11)

1. Combine all ingredients.
2. Use as directed.

Caramel Cake

two 10-inch (25-cm) cakes

one 10-inch (25-cm) Almond Sponge
    (page 270)
one 10-inch (25-cm) Cocoa Almond
    Sponge (page 271)
two 10-inch (25-cm) Short Dough
    Cake Bottoms (page 55)
4 ounces (115 g) smooth apricot jam
¾ cup (180 ml) Plain Cake Syrup
    (page 10)
Caramel Cream (recipe follows)
1½ cups (360 ml) heavy cream
1 tablespoon (15 g) granulated sugar
6 ounces (170 g) sliced almonds,
    toasted and lightly crushed
dark chocolate shavings
Caramel Sauce II (page 1071)
Chocolate Sauce for Piping
    (page 1072)
Sour Cream Mixture for Piping
    (page 1081)

Simply switching the sponges around a little makes this cake interesting and unusual. If you do not already have the sponges on hand, instead of making two separate sponges, make the full Almond Sponge recipe, divide the batter in half, and add 1½ ounces (40 g) of unsweetened cocoa powder to one half.

For a refreshing variation, try serving this cake with Calvados Sauce (page 1070) instead of the sweeter (but oh-so-good) Caramel Sauce.

1. Cut the skin and ⅛ inch (3 mm) off the tops of the Almond and Cocoa Sponges, cutting them even at the same time; cut each sponge into two layers.

2. Using a 5½-inch (13.7-cm) plain cookie cutter, cut a circle from the center of all four layers. Place the center circles from the light sponge inside the rings from the dark sponge and vice versa.

3. Place the Short Dough Bottoms on cake cardboards for support. Spread the apricot jam evenly on top. Place one of the dark rings with a light center on top of the jam on each cake. Brush the sponges with half of the Cake Syrup. Place stainless-steel cake rings around both cakes, fitting them snugly around the sponge layer and setting them on top of the Short Dough. If cake rings are not available, use strips of acetate or polyurethane to make a frame around the sponges.

4. Divide the Caramel Cream between the two cakes and spread it out evenly. It should have a thick enough consistency that it will hold its shape as you spread it. If not, wait until the cream thickens a little more before using. Place the remaining sponge layers on top of the cream. Brush the remaining Cake Syrup over the sponges.

5. Refrigerate the cakes for about 2 hours to set the cream.

6. Whip the heavy cream and sugar to soft peaks. Remove the cake rings or plastic strips. Trim away any excess Short Dough from the bottom of the cakes to make the sides even (see Figure 8–11, page 325). Ice the top and sides of the cakes with the whipped cream.

7. Cover the sides of the cakes with the sliced almonds (see Figure 8–5, page 296).

8. Place the 5¹/₂-inch (13.7-cm) cookie cutter in the center of one of the cakes and sprinkle the shaved chocolate around the outside of the cake. Repeat with the second cake. Cut the cakes into the desired number of slices.

9. Presentation: Place a slice of cake off-center on a dessert plate. Pour a pool of Caramel Sauce in front of the slice. Decorate the sauce with Chocolate Sauce for Piping and Sour Cream Mixture for Piping (see pages 998 to 1006).

1. Caramelize the sugar to a light golden color (see note following, and directions on page 954). Add the hot water and cook out any lumps. Cool completely. If you evaporate too much water while cooking the caramel, it will be too thick when it is cold to be able to combine it with the cream. In this case, add just enough water to bring it back to a syrupy consistency.

2. Sprinkle the gelatin over the cold water and set aside to soften.

3. Whip the cream to soft peaks. Fold in the cooled caramel.

4. Place the softened gelatin mixture over a bain-marie and heat until dissolved. Do not overheat. Rapidly mix the gelatin into a small portion of the cream, then quickly add that mixture to the remainder of the cream.

Caramel Cream

3 pounds, 2 ounces
(1 kg, 420 g)

12 ounces (340 g) granulated sugar
1 cup (240 ml) hot water
4 teaspoons (12 g) unflavored gelatin
    powder
¹/₃ cup (80 ml) cold water
3¹/₂ cups (840 ml) heavy cream

NOTE: It is important to caramelize the sugar dark enough not only to color the filling but also to give it a caramel flavor.

 Carrot Cake

two 10-inch (25-cm) cakes

Carrot Sponges (recipe follows)
Cream Cheese Filling (recipe follows)
8 ounces (225 g) Vanilla Buttercream
    (page 978)
hazelnuts, toasted and finely crushed
10 ounces (285 g) Marzipan
    (page 1022), untinted
powdered sugar
dark coating chocolate, melted
Marzipan Carrots (page 1026)

*T*he Carrot Sponge is very adaptable: It can be baked in a tube pan and served plain as a coffee cake; it makes great muffins; and the batter can also be baked in sheets, cut into small squares, and topped with a rosette of Cream Cheese Filling to use as a simple buffet item or snack cake. When the sponges are made into decorated layer cakes it is necessary to level the tops before assembling. Baking powder and baking soda stop working at approximately 170°F (77°C); the batter next to the side of the pan will reach that temperature first (in part due to the hot metal), so a heavy sponge like this one always bakes higher in the middle. This will not occur to the same extent when making sheets, since they are not as thick and the batter responds more evenly. I'm sure you will have plenty of help getting rid of the scraps!

The following is a very elegant but also very time-consuming finish. For a quick and easy alternative, follow the instructions through step three only, icing the tops and sides of the cakes with Cream Cheese Filling instead of buttercream. Using a star tip, pipe additional Cream Cheese Filling around the outside edge of the cakes making a simple border design (see Figure 19–6, page 983).

1. Cut the tops off the Carrot Sponges to make them level. Cut both sponges in half to make two layers each.

2. Divide the Cream Cheese Filling between the bottom sponge layers; spread it out evenly. Place the top layers on the filling.

3. Ice the tops and sides of the cakes with a thin layer of Vanilla Buttercream. Cover the sides of the cakes with the crushed hazelnuts (see Figure 8–5, page 296).

4. Roll out the Marzipan, using powdered sugar to prevent it from sticking, to 1/8 inch (3 mm) thick. Cut out two circles the same size as the tops of the cakes. Place them on the cakes.

5. Place a cardboard circle on each cake and invert the cakes onto the cardboards. Place in the refrigerator (upside down) to flatten the tops and firm the filling (do not leave the cakes like this for more than 2 hours or the moist air will make the Marzipan wet).

6. Turn the cakes right-side up and cut them into the desired number of serving pieces. Sift powdered sugar very lightly over the cakes. Pipe a dime-sized dot of melted coating chocolate on each slice, 1/2 inch (1.2 cm) away from the edge. Before the chocolate hardens, place a Marzipan Carrot on top.

Carrot Sponge

two 10-by-2-inch (25-×-5-cm) cake layers

8 eggs

1 1/2 cups (360 ml) vegetable oil

1 pound, 12 ounces (795 g) granulated sugar

1 teaspoon (5 g) salt

1 pound, 2 ounces (510 g) bread flour

3 tablespoons (15 g) ground cinnamon

1 1/2 teaspoons (6 g) baking soda

1/2 teaspoon (2 g) baking powder

2 pounds (910 g) peeled carrots, shredded or grated finely

5 ounces (140 g) walnuts, chopped

1. Whip the eggs at high speed to a light and frothy consistency. Reduce the mixer speed to medium and gradually add the oil. Turn the mixer speed to low and mix in the sugar and salt.

2. Sift together the flour, cinnamon, baking soda, and baking powder. Add to the egg mixture. Fold in the carrots and walnuts, evenly distributing them in the batter.

3. Divide the batter between two greased and floured 10-inch (25-cm) cake pans.

4. Bake at 375°F (190°C) for about 50 minutes or until the cakes spring back when pressed lightly in the center.

Cream Cheese Filling

1 pound, 10 ounces (740 g) filling

14 ounces (400 g) cream cheese, at
    room temperature
4 ounces (115 g) soft unsalted butter
1 teaspoon (5 ml) vanilla extract
8 ounces (225 g) powdered sugar,
    sifted

1. Soften the cream cheese, using the paddle attachment of an electric mixer, without beating in any air.

2. Add the butter gradually, blending until the mixture is smooth. Add the vanilla and powdered sugar.

3. Mix until smooth and spreadable, but do not overmix.

Cheesecakes

Cheesecakes have been made in Europe and other places around the world since the fifteenth century. They are created in many variations from light and fluffy to dense and rich. Virtually any region that has a dairy industry will produce some version of cheesecake using their local product. In the United States the main ingredient is usually cream cheese, but ricotta and cottage cheeses are used in some cases to produce a lighter-style or lower-fat alternative. Ricotta cheesecakes are very popular in Italy; Germany uses a soft fresh cheese called quark in their rendition, and in parts of Sweden (especially so where I grew up in *Småland*), in addition to using quark, they make cheesecakes with milk that has been coagulated, using a small amount of rennet. Actually these are more of a tart, they are very special and always served with—you guessed it—lingonberries!

The cheesecake recipe that I call West-Coast Style, for lack of a better name, is the type of cheesecake that many people are probably the most familiar with. Here the cream cheese is thickened with eggs (and heat) and topped with a sweetened sour cream mixture containing the desired flavoring. The cakes are baked again just long enough to set the sour cream. In the case of a fresh fruit topping, the sour cream is sweetened but not flavored, and the fruit is added after the final baking.

The problem I see all too often when it comes to beginners making cheesecake are lumps in varying degrees of seriousness. Lumps are caused by adding the eggs to the cream cheese mixture too fast, not scraping the bottom of the mixing bowl properly, or both. The problem is often exaggerated by using cream cheese straight out of the refrigerator (which can be done, but you must be even more careful). Unless there are only a few small lumps, the batter must be made smooth before it is poured into the forms. The best way to accomplish this is to use a food processor. You can't avoid incorporating more air than is desirable, but it is the lesser of the two evils.

Cheesecake is considered a plain, country-style dessert in Europe, but it can (as you will see by some of the recipes in this book) be presented in a very elegant manner. Each of the following cheesecakes has a graham cracker crust. Because some graham crackers contain more moisture than others, the measurement given for the melted butter in the crust is always approximate. Adjust the amount of butter you add accordingly so that the crumbs are moist enough to hold together well when the crust is pressed into place. You may want to experiment with using thin, rigid wire (such as piano-wire) to cut cheesecakes neatly.

The following cheesecake recipes were developed using the block-style cream cheese, which contains gum and stabilizing agents. Substituting the softer product, usually sold in a log-shape and labeled natural cream cheese, will not produce a good result.

Cheesecake, New York Style

two 10-inch (25-cm) or four 7-inch (17.5-cm) cakes

1 pound, 6 ounces (625 g) Graham Cracker Crumbs (page 8)

8 ounces (225 g) melted unsalted butter

3 pounds (1 kg, 365 g) cream cheese, at room temperature

1 pound (455 g) granulated sugar

2 ounces (55 g) cornstarch

finely grated zest of one lemon

4 teaspoons (20 ml) vanilla extract

4 eggs, at room temperature

8 egg yolks (⅔ cup/160 ml)

6 ounces (170 g) sour cream

*T*he main difference between the New York style cheesecake and the west-coast version is that, here, the sour cream is part of the filling and is mixed with the other ingredients at the beginning. In the other cake the sour cream is added as a topping after the cream cheese filling is partially baked. Secondly, in the west-coast recipe the ratio of sour cream to cream cheese is just about equal, while here, only a small amount of sour cream is used by comparison. Lastly, the New York cheesecake contains approximately half again as much egg.

1. Combine the Graham Cracker Crumbs and the melted butter. Divide the crumb mixture between two 10-inch (25-cm) or four 7-inch (17.5-cm) cake pans. Press evenly over the bottoms and sides of the pans using your hands. Reserve.

2. Mix the cream cheese and granulated sugar together on low speed, using the paddle attachment until completely smooth. Mix in the cornstarch, lemon zest, and vanilla. Mix until smooth, scraping down the sides and the bottom of the bowl. Add the eggs and egg yolks a few at a time, blending thoroughly after each addition. Incorporate the sour cream.

3. Divide the batter evenly between the prepared pans.

4. Place the cake pans inside hotel pans or other suitable pans, adding hot water around the pans to reach about halfway up the sides. Bake at 350°F (175°C) until set, approximately 50 minutes (35 minutes for the small size). Cool completely, and then chill before removing the cakes from the pans. Decorate the tops of the cakes with thinly sliced fresh fruit, serve fruit on the plate next to a slice of cake, or serve the cheesecake with a thick fruit sauce such as Blueberry Sauce (see page 1069).

Cheesecake, West-Coast Style

*two 10-inch (25-cm) or
four 7-inch (17.5-cm) cakes*

1 pound (455 g) Graham Cracker
  Crumbs (page 8)
6 ounces (170 g) melted unsalted
  butter, approximately
3 pounds, 7 ounces (1 kg, 565 g)
  cream cheese, at room temperature
7 eggs, at room temperature
1 pound (455 g) granulated sugar
3 pounds (1 kg, 365 g) sour cream
7 ounces (200 g) granulated sugar
flavoring (choices follow)

This recipe, as simple as it is, has been highly praised for years by cheese-cake lovers. It was given to me by default many years ago, by a young lady who had a summer job in my kitchen. She kept asking me to make cheesecakes, saying that many customers had requested them. My consistent reply was that I didn't have time to add another item, and besides that, I didn't even have a good recipe. Not one to give up, she said her mother had a great recipe and she could even make the cheesecakes herself on Friday afternoons after I went home, so we would have them for the weekend. I finally decided it was worth a try, and sure enough we began selling more and more of her cheesecakes as the summer went on. I must admit my feelings were hurt a few times when people would say to me (after learning of my association with their favorite pastry shop), "Oh, I just love that bakery; they have the best cheesecake!" So when the young lady went back to school in the fall, I had no choice but to continue making her cheesecake!

1. Mix the Graham Cracker Crumbs with the melted butter. Divide the crumbs between two 10-inch (25-cm) or four 7-inch (17.5-cm) springform pans, covering the bottom of the pans, and pat the crumbs even with your hands.

2. Soften the cream cheese in a mixer on low speed using the paddle attachment, or stir by hand, until it has a smooth consistency. Take care not to incorporate too much air or you will end up with a dry and crumbly cheesecake.

3. Lightly mix the eggs and 1 pound (455 g) of sugar, stirring them together by hand. Gradually add the egg mixture to the cream cheese, scraping the bottom and sides of the mixing bowl frequently to avoid lumps. Divide the batter between the prepared pans and spread out evenly.

4. Bake at 375°F (190°C) until just done, about 35 minutes (slightly less for the smaller version). The filling should move in one mass inside the forms when shaken gently. If it moves more in the center than on the sides, continue baking. The cakes will become firmer once they have cooled, so do not overbake them "just to play it safe," or the cakes will crack on the surface and taste dry and stale.

5. Mix the sour cream with the remaining 7 ounces (200 g) of sugar. Divide the mixture between the baked cakes. (You can do this as soon as they are baked, but be careful not to damage the tops of the cakes when you pour on the sour cream mixture.)

6. Place the flavoring in a pastry bag with the piping tip indicated in the flavoring instructions. Pipe the flavoring in a spiral pattern on top of each cake, starting in the center. Drag the back of a paring knife through the spiral starting in the center and pulling toward the edge of the pan to make a spiderweb pattern. See the example in Figure 19–24, page 1001).

7. Bake the cakes at 375°F (190°C) for 8 minutes to set the sour cream (5 minutes for the small size). The sour cream will still look liquid but will set as it cools.

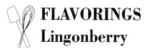

FLAVORINGS
Lingonberry

Lingonberries are an expensive Scandinavian delicacy that look like small cranberries but taste sweeter. They are available as a preserve in most grocery stores. Pipe lingonberry jam in a spiral pattern using a no. 4 (8-mm) plain tip (you may need to crush the berries to ensure that they will go through the tip).

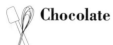

Chocolate

Reserve ¼ cup (60 ml) of the sour cream mixture per cake. Flavor the remainder with 2 tablespoons (16 g) unsweetened cocoa powder per cake (add a little sour cream to the cocoa powder to make a paste before mixing with the remainder to avoid lumps). Top the baked cheesecake with the cocoa-flavored sour cream and use the reserved plain sour cream mixture to pipe the spiral pattern on top, using a no. 2 (4-mm) plain tip.

Strawberry

Use good quality strawberry preserves. If the preserves have large chunks of purée or fruit, break up the chunks with a spoon. Pipe the preserves onto the cakes in a spiral pattern using a no. 2 (4-mm) plain tip. For a fresh strawberry topping, bake the sour cream mixture plain. Top the cooled cakes with strawberries cut into thin slices lengthwise. Brush the strawberries with Apricot Glaze (page 1016).

Lemon

Add 2 teaspoons (12 g) of grated lemon zest per cake to the cream cheese batter (not the sour cream topping) before baking the cake. Pipe Lemon Curd (page 1087) into a spiral pattern on top of the sour cream mixture using a no. 2 (4-mm) plain tip.

Cheesecake with Caramelized Apples

*two 10-inch (25-cm) or four 7-inch
(17.5-cm) cakes*

1 pound, 6 ounces (625 g) Graham
    Cracker Crumbs (page 8)

8 ounces (225 g) melted unsalted
    butter, approximately

4 ounces (115 g) walnuts, chopped
    fine

5 pounds (2 kg, 275 g) Red Delicious
    apples (approximately fourteen
    medium-sized)

8 ounces (225 g) unsalted butter, cut
    into chunks

12 ounces (340 g) granulated sugar

1¼ cups (300 ml) heavy cream, at
    room temperature

two lemons

1 pound (455 g) cream cheese, at
    room temperature

8 ounces (225 g) granulated sugar

4 eggs, at room temperature

1 pound (455 g) sour cream

1 tablespoon (15 ml) vanilla extract

1 pound, 8 ounces (680 g) sour cream

4 ounces (115 g) granulated sugar

4 ounces (115 g) dried cranberries cut
    into small pieces

Marzipan Apples (page 1023)

It seems entirely appropriate that this cross between a New York style cheese-cake and the west coast version should contain apples, since the city of New York is known as The Big Apple. This cake is so moist it does not require any sauce or garnish, but if you want to dress up the plate a little, Cranberry Coulis (see page 1073) would be an excellent choice.

1. Combine the Graham Cracker Crumbs and the melted butter. Mix in the walnuts and additional melted butter if necessary for the mixture to hold together. Divide the crumb mixture between two 10-inch (25-cm) or four 7-inch (17.5-cm) springform pans. Press evenly over the bottoms and halfway up the sides of the pans using your hands. Cut the top edge of the crumbs even. Reserve.

2. Peel, core, and slice the apples into ¼-inch (6-mm) wedges.

3. Place the butter chunks and 12 ounces (340 g) of granulated sugar in a large skillet over medium heat. Stir together and bring to a rapid boil. Add the apple wedges and cook, turning the apples frequently so that they cook evenly. (If you don't have a large enough skillet, you may need to start cooking in two batches. Once the apples start to soften and reduce in size you can combine them.) When the liquid in the skillet has reduced and caramelized to light brown, and the apples are soft but not mushy, remove the skillet from the heat. Add the warm cream, stirring it in carefully so that it does not splatter. Set the apple mixture aside to cool.

4. Finely grate the zest from the lemons. Juice the lemons and combine the strained juice and zest. Reserve.

5. Mix the cream cheese and 8 ounces (225 g) of granulated sugar on low speed, using the paddle, just until smooth. Beat in the eggs one at a time. Mix in 1 pound (455 g) of sour cream, the lemon juice and zest, and the vanilla. Scrape the sides and bottom of the bowl frequently while mixing to avoid lumps.

6. Divide the apple mixture between the two prepared forms in an even layer on top of the crumbs. Divide the cream cheese mixture between the forms on top of the apples. Spread the tops level.

7. Bake at 350°F (175°C) for about 35 minutes (a bit less for the smaller cakes) or until the filling is set. Let cool for at least 10 minutes.

8. Mix together the remaining 1 pound, 8 ounces (680 g) sour cream and 4 ounces (115 g) of granulated sugar. Divide the mixture evenly between the cooled cakes and spread the tops level. Sprinkle the dried cranberries on top of the sour cream.

9. Bake the cakes at 375°F (190°C) for 8 minutes (5 minutes for the small version). Let the cheesecakes cool for at least 6 hours or, preferably, refrigerate overnight.

10. Run a knife around the inside perimeter of the cakes where the cake touches the pan; do not disturb the crust. Release the springforms and remove the cakes. Cut into the desired number of servings and decorate each slice with a Marzipan Apple.

Chestnut Puzzle Cake

two 10-inch (25-cm) cakes

3 pounds (1 kg, 365 g) Vanilla
 Buttercream (page 978)

8 ounces (225 g) unsweetened
 chestnut purée

1 ounce (30 g) unsweetened
 chocolate, melted

8 ounces (225 g) sweet dark
 chocolate, melted

two 10-inch (25-cm) Chiffon Sponge
 Cakes (page 272) (see note 1)

two 10-inch (25-cm) Chocolate
 Chiffon Sponge Cakes (page 272)

1/2 cup (120 ml) Frangelico liqueur

1/4 cup (60 ml) water

6 ounces (170 g) sliced almonds,
 toasted and lightly crushed

8 ounces (225 g) light chocolate
 shavings

Piping Chocolate (page 904), melted

Strawberry Sauce (page 1081)

Candied Chestnuts (page 4), (optional)

Miniature Tulip Crowns (page 1058),
 (optional)

wild strawberries or small
 strawberries

NOTE 1: If you are making only one cake, you can speed things up by making one recipe of Chiffon Sponge Cake and baking one-third of the batter in a prepared 10-inch (25-cm) cake pan. Sift 1 1/2 ounces (40 g) of unsweetened cocoa powder over the remaining batter, carefully fold it in, and bake in a second prepared pan. Cut the plain sponge into two layers and the cocoa sponge into three layers, after cutting the tops even. Working the cocoa batter twice means you will get less volume and a slightly denser sponge, but you will save time.

NOTE 2: If you are having second thoughts about cutting the cone out of the cakes as described, try placing an instant-read meat thermometer or a metal skewer in the center of the cake, sticking it into the cardboard. Use it to guide the tip of your knife evenly around the

*T*his was one of the desserts that I made on the PBS television series "Cooking at the Academy." Unfortunately, I think I made it look too easy. Do not feel bad if your cake does not look like the photograph on your first try. Just as some of the viewers learned the hard way—this cake takes practice before you can complete it comfortably. Perhaps I should have asked for a warning, "For professionals only. Do not try this at home." I received numerous letters, not to mention the phone calls, from people trying to find their way out of the puzzle. They, however, did not have this book.

This is the showy kind of dessert that will have your customers and friends "oohing and aahing," even before they have discovered how delicious it is, trying to figure out how you managed to get the cake layers going in alternate directions! With this reward in mind it is well worth the effort to make two different sponges, two flavors of buttercream, and go through all of the various steps.

1. Flavor 1 pound, 12 ounces (795 g) of the Vanilla Buttercream with the chestnut purée. Flavor the remaining buttercream with the melted unsweetened and dark chocolates. Set the buttercream aside.

2. Cut about one-third off the top of both plain sponges and reserve for another use (such as the refreshing Mandarin Tart with Armagnac on page 242). Slice the remaining two-thirds of each plain sponge in half.

3. Cut just enough off the top of the chocolate sponges to make the tops even. Then cut the sponges into three layers each. (You need five 1/4-inch (6-mm) layers of sponge cake, three chocolate and two plain, for each cake.) Cover two of the chocolate layers and reserve.

4. Place two of the remaining chocolate layers on cardboard cake rounds for support. Combine the Frangelico and the water; brush or spray some of this mixture over the layers.

5. Reserve 6 ounces (170 g) of the chestnut buttercream to use for decoration. Spread a 1/8-inch (3-mm) layer of the remaining chestnut buttercream evenly over each of the layers on the cardboards.

6. Place a plain sponge on the buttercream on each cake, brush or spray the Frangelico mixture on top. Spread another 1/8-inch (3-mm) layer of the chestnut buttercream on top.

7. Continue layering, alternating one more chocolate and plain layer on each cake, brushing or spraying each sponge with the Frangelico mixture before spreading a 1/8-inch (3-mm) layer of chestnut buttercream on top. You should end with plain sponges as the top layers. Do not brush these with the Frangelico mixture. Place the cakes in the refrigerator until the buttercream is completely set.

8. Using a serrated knife dipped in hot water, cut a cone-shaped piece from each cake, 8 inches (20 cm) in diameter at the top of the cake and approximately 2 inches (5 cm) in diameter at the bottom (Figure 8–6). Place one hand flat on the cake and, using the knife or a spatula to help you, remove the cone by inverting it onto your hand. Place the cone flat-side down on a cardboard. Repeat with the second cake.

bottom. You will not get the desired 2-inch (5-cm) hole in the bottom, but you will at least get an evenly cut cone.

9. Ice the inside of the "crater" and the remaining top edge of each cake with a ¼-inch (6-mm) layer of chocolate buttercream (Figure 8–7).

10. Place the reserved chocolate sponges flat on top of each cake. Place cardboard cake rounds on top and invert the cakes so the uncut chocolate layers are now on the bottom.

11. Gently press the top around the hole in and down, so it touches the bottom of the cake, and you have a cone-shaped crater again (Figure 8–8). Repeat with the second cake.

12. Ice the new craters with a ¼-inch (6-mm) layer of chocolate buttercream. Replace the cones in the craters.

13. Trim the sides of the cakes to make them even. Ice the tops and sides of the cakes with just enough chocolate buttercream to cover the sponge. Cover the sides of the cakes with the crushed almonds (see Figure 8–5, page 296).

14. Use a 5-inch (12.5-cm) plain cookie cutter to mark a circle in the center of each cake. Place the reserved chestnut buttercream in a pastry bag with a no. 3 (6-mm) plain tip. Pipe a spiral on top of each cake, inside the circle only, starting in the center and piping the rings next to one another (see example in Meringue Noisette, Figure 12–2, page 592).

15. Sprinkle shaved chocolate around the piped circles on top of the cakes. Refrigerate the cakes until the buttercream is firm. Cut the cakes into the desired number of serving pieces.

16. Place the Piping Chocolate in a piping bag and pipe a scalloped line of chocolate across the lower part of as many dessert plates as you expect to need. Reserve the plates until time of service.

17. Presentation: Place a slice of cake off-center on one of the prepared dessert plates. Pipe Strawberry Sauce on the plate, filling in the chocolate border. Place a Candied Chestnut in a Tulip Crown if you are using them, and place in front of the cake slice. Arrange a few strawberries in the sauce and next to the chestnut. Or simplify the presentation by omitting the berries, the Tulip, and the chestnut, and instead decorate the sauce with Sour Cream Mixture for Piping (see pages 1081 and 998 to 1006). Try to serve the cake at room temperature; buttercream tastes much better this way.

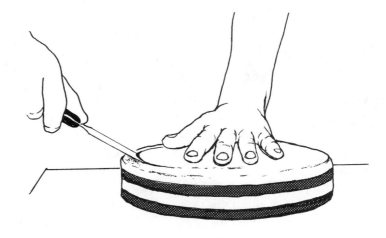

FIGURE 8–6   Cutting a cone-shaped piece from the layered sponges

FIGURE 8–7   Icing the inside and the top edge after removing the cone-shaped piece

FIGURE 8–8   Pushing the ring of chocolate sponge down and inside the cake to create a new cone-shaped crater, after inverting the cake so that the uncut sponge layer is on the bottom

Chocolate and Frangelico Mousse Cake

two 10-inch (25-cm) cakes

one 10-inch (25-cm) Sponge Cake (page 268)

two 10-inch (25-cm) Short Dough Cake Bottoms (page 55)

4 ounces (115 g) red currant jelly

1/3 cup (80 ml) Plain Cake Syrup (page 10)

Dark Chocolate Cream (recipe follows)

Frangelico Cream (recipe follows)

light chocolate shavings

1 1/4 cups (300 ml) heavy cream

1 teaspoon (5 g) granulated sugar

1-inch (2.5-cm) Chocolate Rounds (page 890)

one-half recipe Mousseline Sauce (page 1076)

2 tablespoons (30 ml) Frangelico liqueur

one-half recipe Chocolate Sauce (page 1072)

seasonal fruit

mint sprigs

*T*his cake has something in common with the previous recipe, which is that the layered filling does not conform to the flat, horizontal norm. In addition to the unusual look of the cut slices, the combination of hazelnuts and chocolate is a tried and true palate pleaser. I have made this cake on many occasions in a slightly simplified (and lighter) version, replacing the Chocolate Rounds with fresh raspberries and substituting Raspberry Sauce for the Mousseline and Chocolate Sauces. It is not as rich, and it's a time-saving alternative when raspberries are in season. A second variation with a contemporary finish follows the recipe.

1. Slice the sponge into three layers. Reserve the top layer for another use such as Mandarin Tart with Armagnac, page 242.

2. Place the Short Dough Bottoms on cardboard cake circles for support. Divide the red currant jelly between them and spread out evenly. Place the sponge layers on top of the jelly. Brush the Cake Syrup on top.

3. Check the Dark Chocolate Cream. If it seems too thin to hold its shape, stir until thickened. Divide the Chocolate Cream equally between the two cakes and spread it into a high dome shape.

4. Place 10-inch (25-cm) stainless-steel cake rings snugly around the sponges. If you do not have cake rings, secure strips of acetate or polyurethane around the sponges. Place the cakes in the refrigerator while you make the Frangelico Cream.

5. Divide the Frangelico Cream between the cakes and spread it out evenly on the top of the chocolate dome so the cakes are now level (Figure 8–9). Refrigerate the cakes until the fillings are set, about 2 hours. Also refrigerate the chocolate shavings to make them easier to put on the cakes.

6. Whip the heavy cream and sugar to stiff peaks.

7. Remove the rings or plastic strips from the cakes. Trim any Short Dough that protrudes outside the sponge layer to make the sides

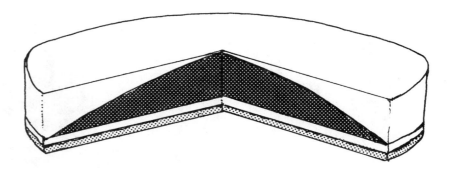

FIGURE 8–9   *The configuration of the two fillings in the Chocolate and Frangelico Mousse Cake*

of the cakes even (see Figure 8–11, page 325). Ice the sides of the cakes with a thin layer of whipped cream. Place the remaining whipped cream in a pastry bag with a no. 6 (12-mm) plain tip and reserve in the refrigerator.

8. Place a 7-inch (17.5-cm) round template on the top of one of the cakes in the center. Use a spatula to pick up and gently pat the chilled chocolate shavings onto the side of the cake. Still using the spatula, sprinkle additional shavings over the top of the cake (if you were to use your hands the shavings would melt as you touched them). Carefully remove the template and repeat with the second cake.

9. Mark or cut the cakes into the desired number of serving pieces. Pipe a cherry-size mound of the reserved whipped cream on each slice, on the exposed cream just next to the shaved chocolate. Place a Chocolate Round on each mound.

10. Flavor the Mousseline Sauce with the Frangelico liqueur.

11. Presentation: Place a slice of cake in the center of a dessert plate. Pour pools of Chocolate Sauce and Mousseline Sauce next to each other in front of the dessert. Swirl the sauces together where they meet (see photo in color insert). Place a small piece of fruit and a mint sprig behind the cake.

Dark Chocolate Cream

*2 pounds, 6 ounces
(1 kg, 80 g) cream*

2¹/₂ teaspoons (8 g) unflavored gelatin
   powder
¹/₄ cup (60 ml) cold water
3 cups (720 ml) heavy cream
one-quarter recipe Swiss Meringue
   (page 592)
¹/₃ cup (80 ml) water
¹/₄ cup (60 ml) crème de cacao liqueur
4 ounces (115 g) sweet dark
   chocolate, finely chopped

1. Sprinkle the gelatin over the cold water and set aside to soften.

2. Whip the cream to a very soft consistency; it should fall in soft mounds, not peaks, when dropped from the whisk. If overwhipped, it is likely to break when you add the rest of the ingredients. Fold the cream into the meringue.

3. Place the softened gelatin mixture over a bain-marie and heat until dissolved. Do not overheat. Stir in the second measurement of water, the crème de cacao, and the chocolate. Keep stirring until all of the chocolate is melted.

4. Rapidly add this mixture to a small amount of the cream mixture. Then, still working quickly, add back to the remaining cream mixture. If the filling is not thick enough to hold its shape, just mix a little longer.

Frangelico Cream

*2 pounds, 10 ounces
(1 kg, 195 g) cream*

4¹/₂ teaspoons (14 g) unflavored
   gelatin powder
¹/₂ cup (120 ml) cold water
3¹/₂ cups (840 ml) heavy cream
2 ounces (55 g) granulated sugar
¹/₂ cup (120 ml) Frangelico liqueur

1. Sprinkle the gelatin over the cold water and set aside to soften.

2. Whip the cream and sugar to very soft peaks.

3. Place the softened gelatin mixture over a bain-marie and heat until dissolved. Do not overheat. Add the liqueur. Rapidly stir the gelatin into a small part of the whipped cream. Then, still working quickly, add this mixture to the remaining cream.

VARIATION

To produce a striking nouvelle finish using Ribbon Sponge Sheets to cover the sides of the cakes instead of sliced almonds, follow the recipe and instructions with the following changes:

• Omit the Short Dough Cake Bottoms and the currant jelly and replace with one Ribbon Sponge Sheet (see page 276). You can form the ribbons in whatever direction you wish: horizontal, vertical, diagonal, or curved. One Ribbon Sheet is actually enough to use for up to six cakes, but it is not practical to make a partial sheet, and the extra can be frozen for another use.

• Slice the Sponge Cake into two layers rather than three in step one. Place the cake layers on cardboard circles for support. Brush with syrup and spread the Chocolate Cream on top as directed. Wrap strips of acetate or polyurethane (or use adjustable stainless-steel cake rings) loosely around the sponge cakes. Cut 2-inch (5-cm) wide strips from the Ribbon Sheet and place them with the striped side against the plastic or cake rings. Tighten the plastic collars or cake rings so that they fit snugly.

• Continue as directed (there will not be any Short Dough crust to trim in step seven), omitting icing the sides of the cakes and covering them with chocolate shavings.

Chocolate Decadence

two 10-inch (25-cm) cakes

melted unsalted butter

12 ounces (340 g) sweet dark chocolate

14 ounces (400 g) unsweetened chocolate

1¼ cups (300 ml) water

12 ounces (340 g) granulated sugar

1 pound, 2 ounces (510 g) soft unsalted butter

12 eggs

6 ounces (170 g) sugar

3 cups (720 ml) heavy cream

2 tablespoons (30 g) granulated sugar

light chocolate shavings

Chocolate Solution for Spraying (page 921)

Raspberry Sauce (page 1080)

Sour Cream Mixture for Piping (page 1081)

raspberries for decoration

mint leaves

This sumptuous chocolate and cream combination became the rage about fifteen years ago. It is the ultimate chocolate-lover's dream cake—actually much closer to a baked chocolate truffle than to a cake. Some versions are known by the straight-to-the-point name of Flourless Chocolate Cake. Chocolate Decadence is a very easy cake to make (basically it's a brownie without the flour and nuts), and it's quite practical since the cakes can be stored unfinished in the refrigerator for weeks, or in the freezer for many months, ready to complete quickly as needed. I always have some in the refrigerator to ice and use as a backup if we run out of any of the desserts on the menu. When the guests are offered Chocolate Decadence as an alternative to their first choice, they seldom decline.

The richness of this cake contrasts beautifully with a fresh fruit sauce. Raspberry Sauce is traditional and the color looks great next to the dark chocolate, but don't miss trying either Bitter Orange Sauce or Bijou Coulis (a tangy combination of cranberry and raspberry).

One dictionary defines decadence as "falling into an inferior condition or state; moral decay; self indulgence." In this case I think we can get away with it quite nicely!

In the photograph of Chocolate Decadence cake in the color insert, I used a white dessert plate sprayed with Chocolate Solution. The base of the plate was covered with a template before spraying, in this case an aluminum screen purchased at the hardware store, but you can make your own custom patterns from cardboard such as a company logo or a heart or star for a holiday or special occasion. Simply spraying the entire plate with a light coating of chocolate also

NOTE: Chocolate Decadence must be cut when it is chilled, but it should be served at room temperature. Because of the fragile consistency of this cake (due in part to the fact that it does not contain flour), it should be handled as little as possible. You cannot pick the cake up to move it as you would a sponge cake. Instead, leave it on the 10-inch cardboard cake circle and set this on a larger cake cardboard and/or doily, depending on the situation. If this is not appropriate, invert the cake onto a platter instead. Of course, if you have prepared the cakes ahead of time and they are frozen, you will be able to move them around quite easily before you decorate them.

looks (and smells) good and is very easy. If your dessert plates have a decorative border, spray the base of the plate only, using an aluminum pie tin frame to protect the edges, with or without a template (see page 1040). If you do not have a power sprayer, make the Cocoa Solution for Manual Spray Bottle on page 475.

1. Brush melted butter over the insides of two 10-inch (25-cm) cake pans. Place rounds of baking paper in the bottoms and butter the papers. Set the pans aside.

2. Cut the dark chocolate and unsweetened chocolate into small pieces.

3. Bring the water and 12 ounces (340 g) of sugar to a boil. Remove from the heat and add the chocolate; stir until the chocolate is melted and completely incorporated. Add the butter, in chunks, and stir until melted. Set aside at room temperature.

4. Whip the eggs with the 6 ounces (170 g) of sugar at high speed for about 3 minutes. The mixture should be light and fluffy. Do not whip to maximum volume as you would a sponge cake; incorporating too much air will make the finished cakes crumbly and difficult to work with. Very gently, fold the melted chocolate into the egg mixture. The chocolate may be warm, but it must not be hot.

5. Divide the batter between the two prepared pans. Place the pans in a water bath.

6. Bake immediately at 350°F (175°C) for approximately 40 minutes or until the top feels firm. Refrigerate the cakes for at least 2 hours or, preferably, overnight. The chocolate must be completely set before you unmold or finish the cakes.

7. Unmold the cakes by briefly warming the outside bottom of the pans (moving them over a gas or electric burner just until the cake moves freely inside the pan), and invert them onto 10-inch (25-cm) cardboard circles (see note). Peel the circles of baking paper off the tops of the cakes.

8. Whip the cream with the 2 tablespoons (30 g) of sugar to just under stiff peaks. Place the whipped cream in a pastry bag with a no. 4 (8-mm) plain tip. Mark the top of the cakes into quarters to easily locate the exact center. Starting at this point, pipe a spiral of whipped cream, with each circle touching the last one, over the entire top of each cake. Cut the cakes into the desired number of servings using a thin knife dipped in hot water. Sprinkle the chocolate shavings lightly over the top.

9. Decorate as many dessert plates as you will need with Chocolate Solution, following the instructions in Spraying with Chocolate, page 919. After decorating the plates, be very careful as you handle them not to leave any fingerprints in the chocolate.

10. **Presentation:** Place a cake slice off-center on a prepared dessert plate. Pour a round pool of Raspberry Sauce in front of the slice. Decorate the sauce using the Sour Cream Mixture for Piping (see pages 998 to 1006). Place three raspberries with a mint leaf next to each one, on the left side of the plate.

Chocolate Ganache Cake

two 10-inch (25-cm) cakes

one-half recipe Baked Chocolate
    Sheet batter (page 570)
    (see step two)
1 ounce (30 g) bread flour
one 15-by-22-inch (37.5-×-55-cm)
    Ribbon Sponge Sheet (page 276)
    made with diagonal stripes
Chocolate Ganache Filling (recipe
    follows)
unsweetened cocoa powder
twenty-eight Cookie Butterflies
    (page 1052)
edible flowers

*NOTE: If you do not have cake rings for bak-
ing the chocolate sheet batter, bake it in two 10-
inch (25-cm) cake pans instead. The cake pans
can also be used for assembly instead of rings.
Line the sides of the pans with strips of acetate
or baking paper. Invert the cakes to unmold,
being extremely careful not to damage the tops.*

*W*hen you read through this book you will find that I use this versatile
    Chocolate Ganache Filling in half a dozen different recipes, changing the
shade, flavor, and shape. The filling is quick and easy to prepare, and any leftover can be stored in the refrigerator for weeks. Using the surplus filling is actually how I first starting making this cake: When preparing Honey Truffle Symphony in large quantities for banquets, I would omit both the chocolate sheet
and the Ribbon Sponge and simply pour the Ganache Filling straight into a pan
2 inches deep (such as a sheet pan with a frame set on top). The next day we
would cut out rounds, decorate them with cocoa powder, a chocolate fan, and a
butterfly, and there you have it—a very tasty, elegant dessert mass-produced.
However, I had all of that leftover Ganache to deal with (the part that was left
after cutting out the rounds). By warming the filling until it has a thick mousse-
like consistency I was able to put it to good use as the filling for this cake; dressing it up, of course, with the Ribbon Sponge and Cookie Butterflies.

To make two smaller 7-inch (17.5-cm) cakes, make half the quantity of
both filling and chocolate sheet batter. Spread the batter into two 7-inch (17.5-
cm) circles.

1. Set a 10-inch (25-cm) stainless-steel cake ring on a sheet of baking paper. Fold the edges of the paper in while turning the ring to secure
the paper on the bottom of the ring (Figure 8–10). (This is the same
method of fastening the paper that is used in savory cooking for baking
in parchment.) Repeat with a second ring (see note).

2. Make the Chocolate Sheet batter, sifting the additional 1 ounce
(30 g) of bread flour into the batter at the end when folding in the egg
white. Divide the batter evenly between the cake rings. Bake immedi-

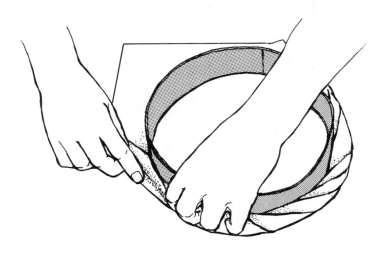

*FIGURE 8–10   Securing a base of baking paper on a cake ring by pleating the
paper tightly against the sides of the ring*

ately at 375°F (190°C) for approximately 12 minutes or until baked through. Let cool.

3. Cut 1³/₄-inch (4.5-cm) strips, lengthwise, from the Ribbon Sponge. The ribbons will run diagonally on the cakes.

4. Run a knife around the inside of the chocolate cakes to loosen them, then remove the cake rings. Clean the rings and place them on cardboard cake circles for support. Line the inside of the rings with strips of acetate or baking paper. Place the Ribbon Sponge strips inside the rings so that the striped side is against the acetate or baking paper. Peel the baking paper from the chocolate sponge layers (trim to fit if needed) and place one layer inside each ring.

5. Divide the Ganache Filling between the two cake rings (reserving a small amount to use in attaching the butterflies, if desired) and smooth the tops to make them even. Take extra care here, because the cakes will not be iced but simply dusted with unsweetened cocoa powder to finish. Place cardboard circles on top of the rings to cover the cakes. Chill in the refrigerator for a minimum of 2 hours to set the filling.

6. Remove the cake rings and peel away the plastic or paper strips. Sift cocoa power lightly over the tops of the cakes. Cut each cake into fourteen servings, using a knife dipped in hot water. Wipe the knife clean and dip it into hot water after each cut. Place a Butterfly at the edge of each slice, pressing them into the cake gently so they stick (or pipe small dots of the reserved filling on top of the cake before placing the butterflies, to hold them at a slight angle).

7. Presentation: Make a stencil with a 6-inch (15-cm) round opening and attach it to a bottomless pie tin (see page 1040 for instructions). Place the stencil against the base of a dessert plate. Sift unsweetened cocoa powder lightly over the stencil. Carefully remove the stencil. Place a slice of cake in the center of the cocoa round. Place an edible flower on the cocoa next to the slice.

Chocolate Ganache Filling

10 cups (2 l, 400 ml) filling

1 pound, 12 ounces (795 g) sweet dark chocolate

6 ounces (170 g) unsweetened chocolate

5 cups (1 l, 200 ml) heavy cream

8 egg yolks (²/₃ cup/160 ml)

3 ounces (85 g) granulated sugar

¹/₂ cup (120 ml) or 6 ounces (170 g) honey

¹/₃ cup (80 ml) Frangelico liqueur

1. Chop the sweet and unsweetened chocolates into small chunks. Place in a bowl set over simmering water and melt together. Set aside, but keep warm.

2. Whip the heavy cream until soft peaks form. Reserve.

3. Whip the egg yolks with the sugar for about 2 minutes; the mixture should be light and fluffy. Bring the honey to a boil, and gradually pour it into the egg yolks while whipping. Continue whipping until cold. Fold in the reserved chocolate and the Frangelico liqueur. Quickly stir in the whipped cream.

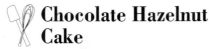

Chocolate Hazelnut Cake

two 10-inch (25-cm) cakes

one recipe Chiffon Sponge Cake batter (page 272)

1 ounce (30 g) unsweetened cocoa powder

6 ounces (170 g) whole hazelnuts, toasted

4 pounds (1 kg, 820 g) Vanilla Buttercream (page 978)

3 ounces (85 g) Hazelnut Paste (page 9)

6 ounces (170 g) sweet dark chocolate, melted

Chocolate Rounds (page 890)

dark coating chocolate, melted

NOTE: The decorating instructions assume that you will be cutting the cakes into a typical number of slices, about 12. If you will be cutting a significantly larger number of pieces (making the servings much smaller), pipe only one or two chocolate lines, omit the chocolate circles, and place the hazelnut directly on the buttercream line(s).

*T*his is another cake that, like Chocolate and Frangelico Mousse Cake, Gâteau Istanbul, and Chestnut Puzzle Cake, features the classic combination of chocolate and nuts. Although the presentation is a bit more humble than the other three, the great flavor is there, and this cake is fast and easy to make. If you are really pressed for time, eliminate the decoration in step eight and instead, after you have cut or marked the cakes into slices, pipe a rosette of buttercream at the end of each slice using a no. 6 (12-mm) star tip. Place a hazelnut on each rosette, then sprinkle light chocolate shavings over the center of the cakes.

1. Cover the bottom of two 10-inch (25-cm) cake pans with rounds of baking paper. Add slightly more than half of the batter to one of the pans. Level the top of the batter. Sift the cocoa powder over the remaining portion of batter and fold it in carefully. Place the cocoa batter in the other pan and level the top of the batter. Bake the sponges at 375°F (190°C) for approximately 20 minutes or until they spring back when pressed lightly in the center; the cocoa sponge will be done a little sooner than the plain sponge. Allow the cakes to cool in the pans before unmolding.

2. Remove as much of the skin from the hazelnuts as possible (see note on pages 965 and 966). Set aside enough of the best-looking nuts to use one on each slice of cake. Crush the remaining nuts.

3. Flavor 1 pound, 8 ounces (680 g) of the Vanilla Buttercream with the Hazelnut Paste. Flavor the remaining buttercream with the melted sweet dark chocolate.

4. Cut the skin from the top of both Sponge Cakes, cutting the tops level at the same time. Cut the cocoa sponge into two layers. Cut the plain sponge into four thin layers.

5. Place the cocoa layers on cardboard cake rounds and spread a ¹/₈-inch (3-mm) layer of hazelnut buttercream on each. Place one of the plain layers on top of each and spread a layer of hazelnut buttercream on top.

6. Add the remaining plain layers, layering with hazelnut buttercream between each in the same way. Use all of the hazelnut buttercream.

7. Reserve 6 ounces (170 g) of chocolate buttercream. Divide the remainder between the two cakes and spread it in a thin layer over the top and sides. Cover the sides of the cakes with the reserved crushed hazelnuts (see Figure 8–5, page 296). Refrigerate the cakes until the buttercream is set.

8. Place one of the reserved whole toasted hazelnuts in the middle of each Chocolate Round, securing it with the melted coating chocolate. Make one decoration for each serving.

9. Cut or mark the cakes into the desired number of serving pieces. Place the reserved chocolate buttercream in a pastry bag with a no. 1 (2-mm) plain tip. Pipe two straight lines of buttercream, next to each other, in the center and down the length of each slice, starting about one-third from the center of the cake. Pipe a third line, slightly longer, in between and on top of the first two. Place a Chocolate Round at a slight angle on top of the three lines at the end of each slice.

Chocolate Mint Torte with a Golden Touch

two 10-inch (25-cm) tortes or 16 servings

Butter and Flour Mixture (page 4)

1 ounce (30 g) fresh mint leaves

1/3 cup (80 ml) water

10 ounces (285 g) sweet dark chocolate

6 ounces (170 g) soft Almond Paste (page 3)

10 eggs, at room temperature

4 ounces (115 g) bread flour

2 ounces (55 g) unsweetened cocoa powder

4 ounces (115 g) finely ground almonds

10 ounces (285 g) soft unsalted butter

1 pound (455 g) granulated sugar

Chocolate-Mint Glaze (recipe follows)

one-half recipe Mousseline Sauce (page 1076)

Mint Pesto (recipe follows)

three sheets (3½ by 3½ inches/8.7 × 8.7 cm) gold leaf

lavender or other edible fresh flowers

This dessert was born of necessity: I was trying to find something to do with the large outer mint leaves that are left once all of the small leaves and sprigs have been pinched off and used for garnish (another good use is Mint and Parsley Ice Cream, page 634). This torte is also quite practical since it can be stored covered in the refrigerator for two to three days. The glaze tends to become a bit dull, but it can be brought back to life by carefully applying indirect heat from above using a broiler or, better yet, a blowtorch. If you want to simplify the torte and/or the presentation, omit the gold leaf and the Mint Pesto. Decorate the slices instead with a small edible flower or a single petal from a larger one. Add 2 tablespoons (30 ml) of mint liqueur to the Mousseline Sauce when the sauce is finished.

1. Brush the Butter and Flour Mixture over the inside of two 10-inch (25-cm) cake pans. Set aside.

2. Finely chop the mint and place it in a small pan with the water. Bring to a boil. Set aside to steep for at least 30 minutes or, ideally, complete this step a day ahead.

3. Melt the chocolate in a bain-marie over simmering water. Add the mint-flavored water and mint leaves and stir to combine. Keep the chocolate warm.

4. Soften the Almond Paste by mixing in the white from one of the eggs. Reserve.

5. Sift the bread flour and cocoa powder together. Mix in the ground almonds. Set aside.

6. Beat the butter and sugar together until creamy. Add the soft Almond Paste, and beat until smooth. Add the eggs in four additions. Blend in the chocolate mixture and then the flour mixture, mixing until thoroughly combined. Divide the batter between the two prepared cake pans.

7. Bake at 350°F (175°C) until baked through but still moist, about 30 minutes. Let cool completely.

8. Remove the cracked skin from the top of the tortes as necessary. Carefully unmold by inverting the cakes onto cardboard cake circles. Turn right-side up and slide onto a cake rack. Ice the top and sides with the Chocolate-Mint Glaze. Allow the glaze to set up, refrigerating if necessary.

9. Using a warm, thin, sharp knife, cut the tortes into eight pieces each.

10. Presentation: Place a slice of torte off-center on a dessert plate. Pour a pool of Mousseline Sauce in front. Place 1 tablespoon

(15 ml) of Mint Pesto in the Mousseline Sauce. Transfer a small piece of gold leaf (about the size of a quarter coin) to each slice, placing it in the center at the wide end of each slice (see page 1017 for more information). Place a second piece of gold leaf the same size on the pesto. Decorate the other side of the plate with lavender or other edible flowers.

 ## Chocolate-Mint Glaze

4 cups (960 ml)

1 pound (455 g) sweet dark chocolate, chopped

10 ounces (285 g) soft unsalted butter

$^{1}/_{2}$ cup (120 ml) or 6 ounces (170 g) light corn syrup

4 teaspoons (20 ml) mint liqueur

1. Melt the chocolate over hot water. Remove from the heat, add the butter, and stir until fully incorporated.

2. Stir in the corn syrup and the liqueur. Cool until the glaze has a spreadable consistency, stirring occasionally.

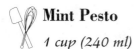 ## Mint Pesto

1 cup (240 ml)

2$^{1}/_{2}$ ounces (70 g) fresh mint leaves without stems

2 ounces (55 g) blanched almonds, finely ground (see note)

3 tablespoons (45 ml) Simple Syrup (page 11), approximately

NOTE: If ground almonds are not available use any type of blanched almond for processing.

1. Place the mint leaves and the almonds in a food processor with the metal blade. Process on and off until the mixture is puréed.

2. With the machine running, add enough Simple Syrup to make a loose paste. The pesto should be used immediately. If necessary it may be stored in the refrigerator for several days; however, the outside will oxidize and turn dark and should not be used. The interior portion will still be bright green.

 ## Chocolate Mousse Cake with Banana

two 10-inch (25-cm) cakes

one 10-inch (25-cm) Cocoa Almond Sponge (page 271)
     or
one 10-inch (25-cm) Chocolate Chiffon Sponge Cake (page 272)

two 10-inch (25-cm) Short Dough Cake Bottoms (page 55)

4 ounces (115 g) red currant jelly

$^{1}/_{2}$ cup (120 ml) Plain Cake Syrup (page 10)

five medium-sized ripe yellow bananas

Chocolate Cognac Cream (recipe follows)

*T*his is another great do-ahead cake. Although the cakes cannot be frozen because of the bananas, they can be refrigerated for up to three days after completing step five. Finishing each cake as needed goes very quickly after that point. Chocolate Mousse Cake with Banana makes an elegant substitute for the ordinary chocolate mousse station at a brunch or luncheon buffet. The banana flavor combines well with chocolate, and the banana looks interesting in the cut slice. Alternatively, I have made this cake several times without bananas (when I found out that the bananas I intended to use were more suitable for Banana Bread), and it is delicious that way as well. If you have a little more time, or have a Ribbon Sheet in the freezer, try the variation.

1. Cut the skin from the top of the Cocoa Almond (or Chocolate Chiffon) Sponge, cutting it level at the same time. Slice the cake into two layers.

2. Place the Short Dough Bottoms on cake cardboards for support. Spread the jelly thinly and evenly on top.

1½ cups (360 ml) heavy cream
1 tablespoon (15 g) granulated sugar
6 ounces (170 g) sliced almonds,
   toasted and lightly crushed
Dark Chocolate Figurines (page 906)

3. Place the sponge layers on the jelly. Brush the Cake Syrup over the sponges. Place stainless-steel cake rings snugly around the sponge cakes. If cake rings are not available, secure strips of polyurethane or acetate around the sponges.

4. Peel the bananas and slice in half lengthwise. Bend the halves carefully to accentuate the natural curve (they will break slightly, but it will not show in the finished cakes) and make two circles of banana on each cake, placing them with the cut sides against the sponge. Make the first circle close to the edge and the second, smaller, circle about 2 inches (5 cm) toward the center.

5. Spread the Chocolate Cognac Cream smoothly and evenly on top of the cakes. Refrigerate the cakes until the cream is set, 1 to 2 hours.

6. Whip the heavy cream with the sugar until stiff peaks form.

7. Remove the rings or plastic strips. Spread a thin layer of whipped cream on the sides of the cakes. Cover the sides with the almonds (see Figure 8–5, page 296). Cut or mark the cakes into desired number of serving pieces.

8. Place the remaining whipped cream in a pastry bag with a no. 7 (14-mm) plain tip. Pipe a mound of whipped cream at the edge of each slice. Decorate each mound with a Chocolate Figurine.

 VARIATION

two 10-inch (25-cm) cakes

one sheet (one-half recipe) Ribbon
   Sponge Sheet (page 276) (see note)
one 10-inch (25-cm) Cocoa Almond
   Sponge Cake (page 271)
      or
one 10-inch (25-cm) Chocolate
   Chiffon Sponge Cake (page 272)
Plain Cake Syrup (page 10)
five medium-sized ripe bananas
Chocolate Cognac Cream (recipe
   follows)
1 cup (240 ml) heavy cream
1 tablespoon (15 g) granulated sugar
Dark Chocolate Figurines (page 906)

NOTE: To create different patterns, try dragging the trowel in a wavy pattern when you make the Ribbon Sheet, or use a wide-notched trowel and drag it crosswise instead. When the strips are cut lengthwise, the stripes will appear vertically on the cakes.

The elegant look of this finished cake makes it well worth the extra steps. One Ribbon Sheet is enough to make up to six cakes, but it doesn't make sense to make less than one-half of the recipe at a time. Besides, the leftover sheet can be stored in the freezer, well covered, for weeks and can be used for so many other projects. If the tops of the cakes do not look presentable left uncovered as instructed in the recipe, finish them with a spiral of whipped cream piped to cover the entire top, as is done with Chocolate Decadence cake. Decorate with shaved chocolate instead of Chocolate Figurines. You will need double the amounts of cream and sugar.

1. Place 10-inch (25-cm) stainless-steel cake rings on top of two 12-inch (30-cm) cardboard cake circles. Cut 2-inch (5-cm) wide strips, lengthwise, from the Ribbon Sheet (see note) and line the inside of the cake rings with the strips. (It is always a good idea, although not absolutely necessary, to line the inside of the rings with strips of baking paper or acetate first to prevent the Ribbon Sponge from sticking to the rings.)

2. Cut the skin from the top of the sponge and slice the cake into two layers. Place one layer inside each of the rings (adjust the rings or trim the cakes as needed for a snug fit). Brush Cake Syrup over the top of each sponge.

3. Continue with steps four and five in the main recipe.

4. Remove the cake rings and the paper or acetate strips if used. Cut or mark the cakes into the desired number of servings.

5. Whip the heavy cream and the sugar to stiff peaks. Place in a pastry bag with a no. 7 (14-mm) plain tip. Pipe a large mound of whipped cream at the end of each slice. Decorate each mound with a Chocolate Figurine.

 ### Chocolate Cognac Cream

9 cups (2 l, 160 ml)

4¹/₂ teaspoons (14 g) unflavored gelatin powder

¹/₂ cup (120 ml) cold water

3 cups (720 ml) heavy cream

one-quarter recipe Swiss Meringue (page 592)

¹/₂ cup (120 ml) water

¹/₄ cup (60 ml) cognac

6 ounces (170 g) sweet dark chocolate, melted

NOTE: Do not make this filling until you are ready to use it.

1. Sprinkle the gelatin over the cold water and set aside to soften.

2. Whip the cream to a very soft consistency. Fold the cream into the Swiss Meringue.

3. Place the softened gelatin mixture over a bain-marie and heat until dissolved. Do not overheat. Stir in the second measurement of water, the cognac, and the melted chocolate.

4. Rapidly add this mixture to a small amount of the cream mixture. Then, still working quickly, add back to the remaining cream mixture.

Chocolate Truffle Cake with Raspberries

two 10-inch (25-cm) cakes

one-half recipe Japonaise Meringue Batter (page 591)

one-half recipe Chocolate Sponge Cake batter (page 270)

4 pounds (1 kg, 820 g) Ganache (page 1086)

¹/₂ cup (120 ml) brandy

¹/₄ cup (60 ml) Simple Syrup (page 11)

two 10-inch (25-cm) Short Dough Cake Bottoms (page 55)

5 pints (2 l, 400 ml) raspberries

dark coating chocolate, melted

Raspberry Sauce (page 1080)

Sour Cream Mixture for Piping (page 1081)

mint sprigs

*A*t first glance, Chocolate Truffle Cake with Raspberries may appear too rich, too expensive, and too time-consuming for anything other than a very special occasion. But if you consider that this dessert will keep fresh for up to four days, and that each 10-inch cake can be cut into sixteen servings, you will certainly be able to justify the time and expense. Also, the number of steps can be decreased by omitting the chocolate collar and leaving the sides of the cake plain (take extra care when icing the sides in this case). If you make the cakes more than one day ahead, do not put the raspberries on the top until you are ready to serve or display the cakes. Before you add the raspberries, use a torch to carefully soften the Ganache so that they stick.

1. Pipe the Japonaise Meringue Batter into two 10-inch (25-cm) circles, using the procedure for Meringue Noisette (see Figure 12–2, page 592). Bake at 300°F (149°C) for approximately 30 minutes or until golden.

2. Divide the Chocolate Sponge Cake batter between two greased and floured 10-inch (25-cm) cake pans. Bake at 375°F (190°C) for about 15 minutes or until the cake springs back when pressed lightly in the middle. Set aside to cool.

3. Warm the Ganache to soften it to a thick, sauce-like consistency.

4. Combine the brandy and Simple Syrup.

5. Spread a thin layer of Ganache over the Short Dough Bottoms and place the Japonaise circles on top. Spread another thin layer of Ganache over the Japonaise.

6. Cut the top of the Sponge Cakes to make them level, then cut them horizontally into two layers about ¼ inch (6 mm) thick each. Place one sponge layer on each cake, on top of the Ganache. Brush with the syrup mixture. Arrange one-fourth of the raspberries evenly over each sponge.

7. Place 10-inch (25-cm) cake rings around each sponge, or make collars out of acetate or polyurethane strips. Don't worry if the Short Dough Bottom and the Japonaise are larger; you will trim them later.

8. Reserve 1 pound (455 g) of the Ganache and pour the remainder evenly over the raspberries (you may have to rewarm the Ganache slightly to pour it).

9. Place the second sponge layers on top of the Ganache and press down gently so they stick. Brush the cakes with the remaining syrup mixture. Refrigerate to set.

10. Remove the cake rings or plastic collars and trim the Short Dough and Japonaise as needed to make the sides even (Figure 8–11).

11. Rewarm the reserved Ganache to give it a nice shine. Ice the top and sides of the cakes with the Ganache. Immediately, while the Ganache is still sticky, arrange the remainder of the raspberries on top of the cakes, starting at the edge and making concentric circles next to each other.

12. Measure and cut out two strips of baking paper or acetate as wide as the cakes are high and the exact length of the circumference of the cakes. Place one of the strips on a flat surface and spread evenly with just enough of the dark coating chocolate to cover the paper. (Since this has to be done quickly, it is impossible to do without spreading some of the chocolate outside the paper.)

13. Before the chocolate has time to harden, pick up both ends of the chocolate-covered paper and position it around the cake so that the

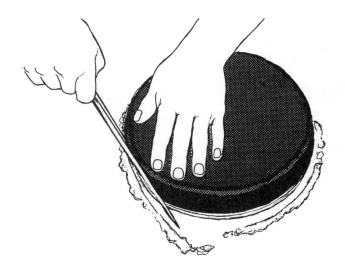

FIGURE 8–11   *Trimming the excess Short Dough and Japonaise from the base of the Chocolate Truffle Cake to make the sides even*

chocolate sticks to the cake. Repeat with the second cake. Refrigerate the cakes for a few minutes.

14. Carefully pull the paper away from the chocolate. Cut the cakes into the desired number of pieces by first melting through the chocolate layer with a hot knife.

15. **Presentation:** Place a cake slice in the center of a dessert plate. Pour a pool of Raspberry Sauce on the plate at the tip of the slice, and pipe the Sour Cream Mixture into the sauce to decorate (see pages 998 to 1006). Place a mint sprig next to the cake.

 # Diplomat Cake

two 10-inch (25-cm) cakes

two 10-inch (25-cm) Sponge Cakes (page 268)
  or
two 10-inch (25-cm) Chiffon Sponge Cakes (page 272)

³/₄ cup (180 ml) Plain Cake Syrup (page 10)

6 ounces (170 g) smooth strawberry jam

2 pounds, 7 ounces (1 kg, 110 g) Pastry Cream (page 1088)

6 ounces (170 g) sliced almonds, lightly crushed (untoasted)

1 pound (455 g) Macaroon Decorating Paste (page 203)

Almond Paste (page 3) as needed, see step four

fresh fruit

Apricot or Pectin Glaze (pages 1016 and 1017)

*T*he light, fresh taste of this traditional Swedish cake is always welcome, and its colorful appearance makes a great addition to a buffet table. I make Diplomat wedding cakes by piping the Macaroon Paste into four hearts on the top of each cake, with the points of the hearts meeting in the center. After the cakes are baked, the hearts are filled with fresh raspberries. Again, very colorful and certainly unique. The French version of Diplomat Cake, Gâteau Senator, is basically made the same way except that there, raspberry and apricot jams are piped within the Macaroon Paste rings before the cake is baked. The variation is also very pretty but is much sweeter than the Diplomat Cake's fresh fruit topping. Truthfully, I do not know which cake is the original and which is the variation.*

1. Slice the Sponge Cakes level and then into three layers each.

2. Brush the two bottom layers lightly with Cake Syrup. Divide the jam between the two and spread it out evenly. Place the middle layers on the jam and brush them with Cake Syrup. Spread a ¼-inch (6-mm) layer of Pastry Cream on the middle layers. Place the top layers on the Pastry Cream and brush them with Cake Syrup. Spread another layer of Pastry Cream, ⅛ inch (3 mm) thick, on the top and sides of the cakes. Cover the sides of the cakes with crushed almonds (see Figure 8–5, page 296).

3. Place the cakes on a sheet pan lined with baking paper. Mark the cakes into desired size serving pieces (this design does not look good with more than fourteen pieces per cake).

4. Place the Macaroon Paste in a pastry bag with a no. 3 (6-mm) plain tip. The Macaroon Paste should be firm enough that it will not run when it is baked. Add some additional Almond Paste if necessary; it will be somewhat difficult to pipe out. Pipe a flower design on the top of each cake, just inside the marks for the individual pieces, forming one petal on each slice (Figure 8–12).

5. Bake the cakes at 425°F (219°C), double-panned, for about 10 minutes or until the Macaroon Paste is light brown and the sliced almonds are toasted. Let the cakes cool completely.

6. Decorate the cakes with two or three different kinds of fruit on each slice, using the Macaroon Paste as a frame. Use small, soft fruits that can be cut into thin slices, such as kiwi, strawberries, plums, or

FIGURE 8–12   *Piping the Macaroon Decorating Paste on the top of the Diplomat Cake*

apricots (read the instructions for decorating Fruit Tartlets in the note on page 391 for more information). Make the same design on each slice to create a uniform and elegant look. Brush Apricot or Pectin Glaze over the fruit and the baked Macaroon Paste. Cut the cakes following the marks between each flower petal.

1. Omit the fresh fruit and Apricot or Pectin Glaze . Replace with 4 ounces (115 g) of raspberry jam, 4 ounces (115 g) of apricot jam, and Simple Syrup (see page 11). Follow steps one and two in the main recipe.

2. Place the cakes on a sheet pan lined with baking paper. Place the Macaroon Paste in a pastry bag with a no. 3 (6-mm) plain tip. Starting at the edge of the cakes, pipe five concentric rings, spaced about 1 inch (2.5 cm) apart, on the top of each cake. If you are making a large number of cakes you can make this easier by marking the Pastry Cream with the appropriate sized rings first.

3. Put the two varieties of jam into disposable pastry bags made from baking paper (see Figures 1–6 and 1–7, page 24). Pipe the jam into the space between the Macaroon Paste, alternating raspberry and apricot. Do not overfill; the jam will bubble up when the cakes are baked and can boil over the Macaroon Paste.

4. Bake at 425°F (219°C) for approximately 10 minutes or until the Macaroon Paste is light brown and the almonds on the sides are toasted (see note). As soon as the cakes come out of the oven, carefully brush Simple Syrup over the Macaroon Paste without disturbing the jam. Let the cakes cool completely.

5. Cut the cakes into the desired number of servings using a serrated knife to saw through the macaroon rings.

VARIATION
Gâteau Senator

NOTE: If the cakes will be cut the same day they are baked, press the back of a knife dipped in water through the Macaroon Paste to mark the slices before the cakes are baked. This will allow you to cut clean precise slices without breaking the firm Macaroon Paste.

Dobos Torte

one 10-inch (25-cm) cake

Butter and Flour Mixture (page 4)

one recipe Dobos Sponge batter
(page 273)

³/₄ cup (180 ml) Plain Cake Syrup
(page 10)

¹/₄ cup (60 ml) Frangelico liqueur

1 pound, 6 ounces (625 g) Chocolate
Buttercream (page 977)

6 ounces (170 g) granulated sugar

¹/₂ ounce/1 tablespoon (15 g/45 ml)
unsalted butter

*NOTE: Spread a small amount of vegetable oil
on top of some baking paper and set it next to
your work area. This is a great help (and a
must if you are making two cakes) to allow you
to quickly re-oil the knives as you spread the
caramel and cut the top sponge layer.*

*T*his rich and delectable cake is loved all over the world by the consumer and
the pastry chef alike. For the chef, Dobos Torte is a great showcake:
Spreading hot sugar over a thin sponge layer is impressive in itself, but cutting
the layer into precise pieces before the sugar hardens and cracks is even more of
an accomplishment. Dobos Torte is not a very practical cake, however, since you
must make many thin sponges. I use only six, but Hungarian cookbooks refer to
anywhere from eight to twelve. Also, the caramelized sugar topping will not look
as good the next day, which is why this recipe only makes one cake. If you need
two cakes, it is possible to prepare two caramelized tops at once, provided you
are fairly experienced. Spread the sugar out over both pieces before cutting the
first one.

Back when a group of Eastern European countries were referred to as being
"behind the Iron Curtain," Hungary was the most accessible of the lot and the
one suffering the least from the communist grasp. Budapest in particular has
always been famous for both its architecture and its culinary achievements,
being influenced by nearby Vienna. József C. Dobos was born in Hungary in
the mid-nineteenth century, and his father was also an accomplished chef, pre-
siding in the kitchen of Count Rákóczi. József Dobos opened a gourmet deli-
catessen in Budapest where he imported and sold previously unheard of
gourmet products such as special cheeses and champagne known only to the
"capitalist westerners." He invented the showy Dobos Torte in 1887 and found
a way to package and ship the cake to foreign countries. The Millennium Expo-
sition in 1896 featured a Dobos Pavilion where his creation was baked and
served to the crowds. Dobos published the original recipe for his torte in 1906;
by this time, of course, many had copied his idea. Before his death in 1924,
Dobos published a total of four cookbooks, the most well known being The
Hungarian-French Cookbook. *In 1962 the Hungarian Chef's and Pastry
Chef's Association held a celebration to commemorate the seventy-fifth anniversary of the creation of the Dobos Torte, and a six-foot Dobos Torte was paraded
through the streets of Budapest.*

1. Invert three perfectly even, clean sheet pans. Brush the Butter
and Flour Mixture over the back of the pans.

2. Mark two 10-inch (25-cm) circles on each pan, using a cake pan
or ring. Divide the sponge batter equally between the six circles. Spread
the batter out flat and even within the markings.

3. Bake immediately at 425°F (219°C) for approximately 8 minutes
or until just baked through. Remove the sponge layers from the sheet
pans and let cool.

4. Trim all six sponge layers to 10 inches (25 cm) in diameter (they
usually spread out in the oven) and cut the tops level if necessary. Place
the best-looking layer on a cardboard cake round and set it aside to use
as the top.

5. Combine the Cake Syrup and Frangelico liqueur (this amount of
syrup and liqueur will be sufficient if applying with a brush, but you
will need to double both to use a spray bottle effectively). Place one of

the five remaining sponge layers on a cardboard cake circle. Brush or spray some of the Cake Syrup mixture on top.

6. Reserve 2 ounces (55 g) (about ¹/₂ cup/120 ml) of the Chocolate Buttercream. Using some of the remaining buttercream, spread a ¹/₈-inch (3-mm) layer on top of the sponge layer with Cake Syrup. Continue layering the remaining four sponges, brushing or spraying them with the Cake Syrup mixture and spreading a ¹/₈-inch (3-mm) layer of buttercream between each layer. Use all of the buttercream but take care not to get any on the sides of the cake; instead, spread the buttercream just to the edge each time; the sides of the cake are not iced, to expose the many thin layers. Refrigerate the cake until the buttercream is set.

7. Cook the sugar to the amber stage: just before it turns light brown or caramelizes. Remove from the heat and quickly stir in the butter. Immediately spread the caramel over the top of the reserved sponge layer using an oiled palette knife (see note). Quickly, before the caramel hardens, cut the sponge into the desired number of servings, using a thin, oiled knife.

8. Cut the cake into the same number of servings as the caramelized top. Place the reserved buttercream in a pastry bag with a no. 3 (6-mm) plain tip. Pipe a rope of buttercream along one cut edge of each slice (see Figure 8–22, page 363). Place one caramelized sponge triangle on each slice of cake, arranging them at an angle on top of the buttercream lines, in a fan pattern.

Gâteau Istanbul

two 10-inch (25-cm) cakes

two 10-inch (25-cm) Cocoa Almond
   Sponges (page 271)
   or
two 10-inch (25-cm) Chiffon Sponge
   Cakes (page 272)
two 10-inch (25-cm) Short Dough
   Cake Bottoms (page 55)
Nougat Butter (recipe follows)
¹/₂ cup (120 ml) Plain Cake Syrup
   (page 10)
Hazelnut Cream (recipe follows)
1¹/₂ cups (360 ml) heavy cream
1 tablespoon (15 g) granulated sugar
6 ounces (170 g) sliced almonds,
   toasted and lightly crushed
unsweetened cocoa powder
Chocolate Crescent Cookies
   (recipe follows)

A few years ago this cake was a regular feature on the dessert buffet prepared by my students. In addition to being much requested, Gâteau Istanbul often aroused the curiosity of our guests, many of whom are very interested in cooking and know quite a bit about it. The puzzle was this: How is it possible to make a clean precise cut through the whole hazelnuts in the middle of the soft cream filling? The answer, as you will see when you read the recipe, is that the cakes are frozen, then finished and sliced when they are half-thawed.

1. Cut the skin from the tops of the sponge cakes and trim the tops to make them even if necessary. Cut each sponge into two layers.

2. Place the Short Dough Bottoms on cardboard cake circles for support. Divide the Nougat Butter between them and spread it out evenly. Place a sponge layer on top of each one, and brush the sponges lightly with the Cake Syrup.

3. Spread the Hazelnut Cream evenly over the first sponge layers. Place the second sponge layers on the cream and press down lightly to even the tops. Brush again with Cake Syrup.

4. Place the cakes in the freezer, covered, until completely frozen (this is not necessary if you plan to present the cakes whole rather than cut into serving pieces).

5. Trim away any Short Dough that protrudes outside the sponge to make the sides even (see Figure 8–11, page 325).

6. Whip the cream and the sugar to stiff peaks. Ice the tops and sides of the cakes with a thin layer of whipped cream. Reserve the remaining cream.

7. Cover the sides of the cakes with crushed almonds (see Figure 8–5, page 296).

8. Place a 10-inch (25-cm) round template with a 6-inch (15-cm) hole cut out of the center on one of the cakes. Sift cocoa powder over the cake to cover the whipped cream. Remove the template carefully. Repeat with the second cake.

9. When the cakes have thawed halfway, cut them into the desired number of serving pieces. (Do not allow the cakes to thaw completely, or you will push the nuts in the filling into the cake rather than slicing through them.)

10. Place the remaining whipped cream in a pastry bag with a no. 7 (14-mm) plain tip. Pipe a mound of whipped cream the size of a cherry at the edge of each slice. Place a Chocolate Crescent Cookie on each mound.

Nougat Butter

2 ounces (55 g) soft unsalted butter
2 ounces (55 g) Hazelnut Paste
    (page 9)

1. Gradually work the soft butter into the Hazelnut Paste to make a smooth, lump-free mixture.

2. Use at room temperature.

Hazelnut Cream

8 ounces (225 g) toasted hazelnuts
1 quart (960 ml) heavy cream
6 ounces (170 g) Hazelnut Paste
    (page 9)

1. Rub the nuts between your palms to remove as much skin as possible. Do not attempt to remove all of it; it is just too time-consuming.

2. Very gradually mix enough of the cream into the Hazelnut Paste to make it soft and similar in consistency to lightly whipped cream. Whip the remaining cream to soft peaks.

3. Fold the cream into the Hazelnut Paste together with the toasted nuts. If the cream is overwhipped, it can break when the rest of the ingredients are added. If it is not whipped enough and the filling seems too runny, just mix a little longer.

Chocolate Crescent Cookies

24 cookies

5 ounces (140 g) Cocoa Short Dough
    (page 55) (or flavor regular Short
    Dough with some unsweetened
    cocoa powder)

1. Roll out the Short Dough ⅛ inch (3 mm) thick.

2. Using a ¾-inch (2-cm) plain cookie cutter, cut out crescents as described in making Fleurons (see Figure 2–11, page 48).

3. Bake the cookies at 375°F (190°C). Let them cool completely before placing them on the whipped cream.

Gâteau Lugano

two 10-inch (25-cm) cakes

two 10-inch (25-cm) Cocoa Almond
   Sponges (page 271)
   or
two 10-inch (25-cm) Chocolate
   Chiffon Sponge Cakes (page 272)
3 pounds (1 kg, 365 g) Vanilla
   Buttercream (page 978)
¹/₂ cup (120 ml) arrack or dark rum
¹/₃ cup (80 ml) Plain Cake Syrup
   (page 10)
6 ounces (170 g) sliced almonds,
   toasted and lightly crushed
unsweetened cocoa powder
small strawberries

I found the recipe for this cake in a German cooking magazine many years ago; the following is my version. I do not know how it came to be named for the city of Lugano, which is near the Italian border in Switzerland. I once had a student from Lugano and she did not know either, nor had she ever heard of or seen this cake before learning the recipe in my class—and she had previously lived in Lugano all of her life! So much for my assumption that this was a specialty of that Swiss town. Regardless, Lugano is a beautiful city, well worth a trip, and Gâteau Lugano is a very pretty cake, well worth trying and very practical. You can make the cakes up to four days ahead and store them well-covered in the refrigerator. Add the cocoa powder and strawberry decorations the same day the cakes are to be served.

1. Cut the two sponge cakes into three layers each. Use a 6-inch (15-cm) round template or plain cookie cutter to cut both top layers into 6-inch (15-cm) circles. Cut them level and trim off the skins if necessary. Save the doughnut-shaped rings that are left for another use. (The middle and bottom layers remain whole.)

2. Flavor the buttercream with half of the arrack or rum. Add the remainder of the arrack or rum to the Cake Syrup. Brush the bottom sponge layers lightly with Cake Syrup. Spread a ¹/₄-inch (6-mm) layer of buttercream on each of the two bottom sponge layers. Place the middle layers on top and brush again with Cake Syrup.

3. Ice the top and sides of both the 10-inch (25-cm) base cakes and the 6-inch (15-cm) sponge cakes with buttercream. Reserve the remaining buttercream for decoration. Cover the sides of both the larger and small cakes with the crushed almonds (see Figure 8–5, page 296).

4. Refrigerate the four iced sponges until the buttercream is firm.

5. Place a stencil with parallel striped openings similar to a cake cooler or aspic rack over the 6-inch (15-cm) layers. Sift cocoa powder through a fine sieve on top. Be very careful as you remove the stencil so that you do not disturb the pattern.

6. Set one of the 6-inch (15-cm) layers in the center of each of the 10-inch (25-cm) layers. Cut or mark the cakes into the desired number of pieces.

7. Place the remaining buttercream in a pastry bag with a no. 6 (12-mm) plain tip; pipe a mound of buttercream, the size of a Bing cherry, at the edge of each piece.

8. Remove the stems from the strawberries and cut them in half lengthwise. Place one half, cut-side up, on each buttercream mound. Although this cake looks best if cut while the buttercream is cold, it should be eaten when the buttercream is at room temperature.

Gâteau Malakoff

two 10-inch (25-cm) cakes

one-half recipe Ladyfingers batter
  (page 275)

two 10-inch (25-cm) Short Dough
  Cake Bottoms (page 55)

5 ounces (140 g) smooth strawberry
  jam

two 10-inch (25-cm) Cocoa Almond
  Sponges (page 271)

³/4 cup (180 ml) Plain Cake Syrup
  (page 10)

³/4 cup (180 ml) Simple Syrup
  (page 11)

¹/2 cup (120 ml) light rum

Maraschino Cream (recipe follows)

8 ounces (225 g) Ganache (page 1086)

whipped cream

*T*he name Malakoff is given to various culinary items, including a type of neufchâtel cheese. The best known of the sweets is the Charlotte Malakoff. There is conflicting data on the background of this title. Some research indicates that it was a Russian noble family who lent their name to these creations, but others say that the name Malakoff comes from the town of the same name in north central France. The French town of Malakoff was named for the fortress of Malakhov captured by the French during the Crimean War. A third possibility is that the French general, duc de Malakoff, took a liking to this pretty, maraschino-flavored dessert and it was named for him.

In any event, this cake is a variation of the classic Charlotte Malakoff recipe. I have added rum and left out the nuts which are traditionally included in the filling.

1. Place the Ladyfingers batter in a pastry bag with a no. 4 (8-mm) plain tip. Pipe out batter 1¹/2 inches (3.7 cm) long on sheet pans lined with baking paper, making approximately 120 Ladyfingers. Bake as directed in the recipe and reserve.

2. Place the Short Dough Cake Bottoms on cardboard cake circles for support. Spread the jam evenly on top.

3. Cut the skin and about ¹/4 inch (6 mm) from the top of the sponge cakes. (Use the scraps for Rum Balls, page 417.) Slice each cake into two layers. Place one layer of sponge on each Short Dough Cake Bottom. Brush the sponges with some of the Cake Syrup. Place a stainless-steel cake ring snugly around each sponge (or make collars from strips of polyurethane or acetate if cake rings are not available).

4. Combine the Simple Syrup and rum. Reserve 72 of the most attractive Ladyfingers to use in decorating. Place the remaining Ladyfingers in the Simple Syrup mixture and let them soak about 5 minutes to fully absorb the liquid.

5. Top each of the sponge cakes with one-quarter of the Maraschino Cream and spread it out evenly within the rings.

6. Arrange the soaked Ladyfingers flat-side down on the cream, with the long sides touching, making a circle 1 inch (2.5 cm) from the edge of the cake. Work quickly so that the filling does not set up.

7. Divide the remaining Maraschino Cream between the cakes and spread it out evenly on top of the Ladyfingers. Place the remaining sponge layers on top of the cream and press down gently to even the tops. Brush the sponges with the remaining Cake Syrup.

8. Refrigerate the cakes at least 2 hours to set the filling.

9. Run a thin knife around the inside of the rings to free the cakes and then remove the rings, or simply peel away the plastic strips.

10. Heat the Ganache until liquid and very glossy. Spread Ganache over the top of the cakes, using just enough to cover the sponge. As soon as the Ganache starts to harden, score lines every ¹/2 inch (1.2 cm) using the back of a chef's knife, turn the cake 45°, and repeat to create a diamond pattern.

11. Cover the sides of the cakes with whipped cream. Cut each cake into twelve servings. Stand three Ladyfingers upright on the side of each slice. If the Ladyfingers are taller than the cake, trim one end and place the cut end at the base of the cake.

1. Sprinkle the gelatin over the cold water and set aside to soften.

2. Whip the cream to soft peaks. Reserve in the refrigerator.

3. Whip the egg yolks and sugar until just combined. Whip in the wine and maraschino liqueur. Place over simmering water and heat to about 140°F (60°C), whipping the mixture to a thick foam in the process. Remove from the heat and continue whipping until cold. Fold the yolk mixture into the reserved whipped cream.

4. Place the softened gelatin over simmering water and heat to dissolve. Working quickly, add the gelatin to a small portion of the cream mixture, and then rapidly mix this into the remaining cream mixture.

Maraschino Cream

7 cups (1 l, 680 ml) filling

4 teaspoons (12 g) unflavored gelatin
    powder
¹/₃ cup (80 ml) cold water
5 cups (1 l, 200 ml) heavy cream
4 egg yolks (¹/₃ cup/80 ml)
3 ounces (85 g) granulated sugar
¹/₂ cup (120 ml) dry white wine
¹/₃ cup (80 ml) maraschino liqueur
    (or kirschwasser)

NOTE: Because you can not reheat this filling to soften it, do not make it until you are ready to use it in the cakes.

Gâteau Moka Carousel

two 10-inch (25-cm) cakes

one-half recipe Japonaise Meringue
    Batter (page 591)
one recipe Cocoa Almond Sponge
    batter (page 271)
8 ounces (225 g) Ganache (page 1086)
Mocha Whipped Cream
    (recipe follows)
¹/₄ cup (60 ml) Plain Cake Syrup
    (page 10)
2¹/₂ cups (600 ml) heavy cream
5 teaspoons (25 g) granulated sugar
ground coffee
Marzipan Coffee Beans (page 1029)
    or
candy coffee beans
one recipe Mousseline Sauce
    (page 1076)
¹/₄ cup (60 ml) Kahlua liqueur
fanned apricot halves
mint leaves

*A*ny variation on traditional horizontal cake layers makes for an impressive, professional-looking presentation. Other examples of this are Chocolate Triangles and Chestnut Puzzle Cake. To achieve the desired outcome with any of these pastries, it is extremely important that the sponges are thin and are cut precisely. The narrow strips used for this cake must be placed on top of the Ganache while it is still sticky so that they will adhere and remain straight when the filling is added. It is a good idea to fill all of the sponge circles partway before filling the outside circle to the top, to help prevent the strips from sliding. If the vertical layers lean every which way in the set filling when the cake is sliced and served, it greatly diminishes the original intention to create something distinctive and elegant.

1. Draw two 10-inch (25-cm) circles on baking paper. Invert the paper on a sheet pan. Place the Japonaise Meringue Batter in a pastry bag with a no. 3 (6-mm) plain tip. Pipe the batter in a spiral within each of the circles as described in Meringue Noisette (see Figure 12–2, page 592). Bake at 275 to 300°F (135–149°C) until golden brown, about 35 minutes.

2. Line the bottom of a 10-inch (25-cm) cake pan with baking paper (or grease and flour but do not grease and flour the sides). Pour about one-third of the cocoa sponge batter into the pan and spread it out evenly.

3. Pour the remaining batter onto a sheet of baking paper and spread it out to slightly less than 24 by 16 inches (60 × 40 cm) leaving a border approximately ¹/₄ inch (6 mm) all around. Drag the paper onto a sheet pan (see Figure 16–15, page 842). Immediately bake both

FIGURE 8–13   *Piping the Mocha Whipped Cream between the sponge rings in the Gâteau Moka Carousel*

sponges at 400°F (205°C). The round cake will take about 15 minutes; the sheet will take about 10 minutes. Let the sponge cakes cool completely. Cut the thin chocolate sheet lengthwise into strips 1 inch (2.5 cm) wide. Reserve.

4. Warm the Ganache to soften it. Place the Japonaise bottoms on cardboard cake rounds for support, divide the Ganache between them, and spread it out evenly. Place 10-inch (25-cm) stainless-steel cake rings on the Ganache. Do not be concerned about Japonaise that protrudes outside the rings; it will be trimmed later.

5. Stand the sponge strips up on the Ganache in five evenly spaced concentric circles, starting at the outside against the ring on each cake.

6. Place the Mocha Whipped Cream in a pastry bag with a no. 6 (12-mm) plain tip. Pipe the cream between the circles (Figure 8–13). Spread the excess evenly over the top with a spatula.

7. Cut the skin off the top of the 10-inch (25-cm) chocolate sponge, cutting the top even at the same time if necessary. Slice the sponge into two layers. Place one on top of each cake and press gently to be sure they are sticking to the Mocha Cream. Brush the sponges with the Cake Syrup. Refrigerate the cakes until the cream is set, about 2 hours.

8. Remove the cake rings. Trim away any excess Japonaise that protrudes outside the sponge to make the sides even (see Figure 8–11, page 325).

9. Whip the heavy cream and sugar to stiff peaks. Ice the top and sides of the cakes with a thin layer of the cream. Place a portion of the remaining whipped cream in a pastry bag with a no. 6 (12-mm) flat, plain, tip. Pipe vertical lines on the sides of the cakes, working from the bottom to the top and placing the lines next to one another. Use a palette knife to even the top edge all around each cake.

10. Mark or cut the cakes into the desired number of pieces. Place the remaining whipped cream in a pastry bag with a no. 6 (12-mm) star tip. Pipe a rosette of cream at the edge of each slice. Sprinkle ground coffee very lightly on the whipped cream inside the piped rosettes. Place Marzipan or candy coffee beans on the rosettes.

11. Flavor the Mousseline Sauce with the Kahlua.

12. Presentation: Place a slice of cake in the center of a dessert plate. Pour a pool of sauce on one side of the dessert and use the back of a spoon to shape it into a half-circle. Sprinkle ground coffee in a narrow band along the round edge of the sauce. Place a fanned apricot half and a mint leaf on the other side of the cake.

Mocha Whipped Cream

3 pounds, (1 kg, 365 g) cream

4¹/₂ teaspoons (14 g) unflavored
    gelatin powder
¹/₂ cup (120 ml) dry white wine
4 egg yolks (¹/₃ cup/80 ml)
¹/₂ cup (120 ml) or 6 ounces (170 g)
    light corn syrup
1 quart (960 ml) heavy cream
¹/₃ cup (80 ml) Kahlua liqueur
¹/₄ cup (60 ml) Coffee Reduction
    (page 5)
    or
1 teaspoon (4 g) mocha paste

NOTE: Do not make this filling until you are ready to use it.

1. Sprinkle the gelatin over the wine and set aside to soften.

2. Beat the egg yolks just until combined. Heat the corn syrup to boiling and whip the hot syrup into the yolks, continuing to whip until the mixture has cooled and has a light and fluffy consistency.

3. Whip the cream to soft peaks and combine with the yolk mixture.

4. Add the Kahlua and Coffee Reduction to the softened gelatin mixture. Place over a bain-marie and heat until dissolved. Do not overheat. Rapidly combine this mixture with a small amount of the yolk and cream mixture. Still working quickly, combine with the remaining cream.

Gâteau Pithiviers

two 10-inch (25-cm) cakes

2 pounds, 12 ounces (1 kg, 250 g)
   Puff Pastry (page 44)
1 pound (455 g) Mazarin Filling
   (page 1088)
6 ounces (170 g) Pastry Cream
   (page 1088)
¼ cup (60 ml) light rum
Egg Wash (page 7)

*T*his very famous classical French almond cake takes its name from the small town of Pithivier (pronounced pa-tiv-e-ay) outside Orléans near Paris. If you are in the neighborhood and have a few days to spare, keep going southwest along the Loire River and if at all possible do not end your journey until you get to Tours. It is fabulous country there, and everywhere you go, at any time you want, they will be happy to serve you a slice of Pithivier with your afternoon coffee or for dessert with caramel or vanilla ice cream à la mode.

The Puff Pastry on top of the cakes is always scored in a fan-shaped pattern using a small sharp knife before the cakes are baked. They can be refrigerated at this point for a few days, or frozen for much longer, to bake as needed. This makes Pithivier a practical (and not so commonplace) choice as an addition to a buffet table. If the cakes are to be presented whole, you may want to dress up the tops by glazing them in the following manner: Bake the cakes at 400°F (205°C) for the first 25 minutes (rather than 12 minutes at 450°F/230°C). Quickly sift a thin layer of powdered sugar on top using a fine mesh sieve. Return the cakes to the oven, lower the oven temperature to 375°F (190°C) (leaving the oven door ajar while you sift the sugar will take care of this), and continue baking approximately 20 minutes longer or until the sugar has melted and beautifully glazed the tops. This cake is best served warm or at least at room temperature and should be enjoyed the same day it is baked. Any leftovers should be heated slightly before serving.

1. Divide the Puff Pastry into two equal pieces. Divide each of these 1-pound, 6-ounce (625-g) pieces in half again, making one piece in each group 3 to 4 ounces (85 to 115 g) heavier than the other.

2. Roll out the two smaller pieces of dough into 11-inch (27.5-cm) squares, approximately ¹/₁₆ inch (2 mm) thick. These squares will be used for the base of the cakes. Place the squares on a sheet pan brushed lightly with water. Place in the refrigerator.

3. Roll the two remaining (larger) pieces of dough into squares the same size as the first two; these should be about ⅛ inch (3 mm) thick. Place these dough squares on a sheet pan lined with baking paper and refrigerate.

4. Combine the Mazarin Filling, the Pastry Cream, and the rum. Set aside.

5. When the Puff Pastry has relaxed for at least 30 minutes and is firm, cut all four squares into 11-inch (27.5-cm) circles, leaving the dough in place on the pans.

6. Divide the filling evenly between the two base circles (the circles on the sheet pan brushed with water), spreading it out to 1½ inches (3.7 cm) from the edge. Brush Egg Wash on the uncovered edges. Place the remaining dough circles on top of the filling, then use your thumbs to press the edges together and make a tight seal.

7. Using a Pithivier ring, a 10-inch (25-cm) flan ring, or the frame of a 10-inch (25-cm) springform pan, one at a time press the ring into the top of the cakes hard enough to mark a distinctive border 1 inch (2.5 cm) from the edge. Leave the ring in place and cut the border in

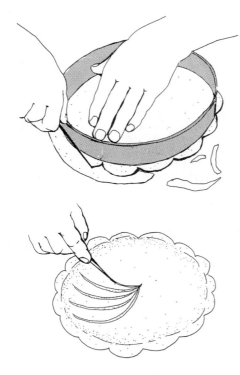

FIGURE 8–14   Using a cake ring as a guide while cutting the edge of the Puff Pastry in a scalloped pattern; scoring the Puff Pastry on top of Gâteau Pithiviers in a fan pattern

scallop pattern (Figure 8–14). If the dough has become soft at this point, refrigerate before proceeding.

8. Brush Egg Wash over the entire top of each cake. Score slightly curved, faint lines on top of the cakes using the tip of a paring knife. Cut from the center to the edge of the cakes without cutting through the dough, as shown in the illustration.

9. Bake at 450°F (230°C) for 12 minutes. Lower the heat to 375°F (190°C) and continue baking approximately 35 minutes longer or until baked through. Cool to room temperature, then cut the cakes into the desired number of serving pieces.

Gâteau Saint-Honoré

two 11-inch (27.5-cm) cakes

1 pound (455 g) Puff Pastry
  (page 44)
one-half recipe Pâte à Choux
  (page 36)
Bavarian Rum Cream (recipe follows)
1 pound (455 g) granulated sugar
1 cup (240 ml) heavy cream
2 teaspoons (10 g) granulated sugar
light chocolate shavings

This cake is far more attractive than it is practical. It was named for Saint Honorius, the Bishop of Amiens in the sixth century and the French Patron Saint of Pastry Cooks. You will also find a street in Paris which bears his name; it is the Rue du Faubourg Saint Honoré. Unfortunately this absolutely delicious and unusual-looking cake must be served the same day it is finished. If not, two of its components—Puff Pastry and Pâte à Choux—become soggy and less appetizing. The cake can, however, be prepared through step four and then frozen for several weeks until needed. Place the sheet pan in the freezer for 10 minutes before wrapping in plastic to keep the plastic from sticking to the Pâte à Choux.

Gâteau Saint-Honoré was the "show-me-what-you-can-do" cake back when I was starting out. This cake was a good test to see what a prospective employee could actually produce on the bench under a time constraint. Completing this cake successfully would prove you had mastered the three P's—Puff Pastry, Pâte à Choux, and Pastry Cream (obviously you could not actually make the Puff Pastry needed for the cake; this was given to you. But you had to make a new dough to replace what you used, showing the chef that you had planned your work so that all the turns were completed in the four hours or so you were usually given to finish the full project). You then had to make Italian Meringue for the Cream Chiboust and delicately combine it with the hot Pastry Cream, testing more of your skills. This mixture was piped on the cake in a symmetrical pattern using a special Saint-Honoré tip (the pattern looks very much as though you used a large spoon to place oval dollops of cream all over the cake), which would show how well you did with a pastry bag. But you were not finished yet; you still had to caramelize sugar and dip the top and sides of the small profiteroles in the hot sugar syrup before placing them around the perimeter of the Saint-Honoré. All in all a rather exhaustive test in one dessert!

Today, with few exceptions, the somewhat tricky Cream Chiboust is no longer used for this cake.

1. Roll the Puff Pastry out to ⅛ inch (3 mm) thick, 23 inches (57.5 cm) long, and 12 inches (30 cm) wide. Place on a sheet pan lined with baking paper. Refrigerate covered at least 20 minutes.

2. While the Puff Pastry is resting, make the Pâte à Choux and place it in a pastry bag with a no. 4 (8-mm) plain tip. Reserve.

3. Leaving the Puff Pastry in place on the sheet pan, cut two 11-inch (27.5-cm) fluted circles from the dough and remove the scraps. (An easy way to cut them is to use an 11-inch/27.5-cm tart pan as a "cookie cutter.") Prick the circles lightly with a fork.

4. Pipe four concentric rings of Pâte à Choux on each circle. Pipe out 24 Pâte à Choux profiteroles the size of Bing cherries onto the paper around the cakes (Figure 8–15) (see introduction).

5. Bake the Puff Pastry circles and the profiteroles at 400°F (205°C) until the Pâte à Choux has puffed, about 10 minutes. Reduce the heat to 375°F (190°C) and bake until everything is dry enough to hold its shape, about 35 minutes longer for the cake and about 8 minutes longer for the profiteroles. (Just pick the profiteroles up and take them out as they are done.)

6. Place approximately 6 ounces (170 g) of the Bavarian Rum Cream in a pastry bag with a no. 2 (4-mm) plain tip. Use the pastry bag tip or the tip of a paring knife to make a small hole in the bottom of each profiterole. Pipe the cream into the profiteroles to fill them. Refrigerate the filled profiteroles.

7. Divide the remaining filling evenly between the two cakes, spreading it into a dome shape. Refrigerate the cakes for at least 2 hours to set the cream.

8. Caramelize the first measurement of sugar (see page 954). Dip the filled profiteroles into the hot caramel, using two forks to avoid burning your fingers. Place them on a sheet pan. The caramel must be hot enough to go on in a thin layer. Reheat if necessary as you are dipping, stirring constantly to avoid darkening the caramel any more than necessary. Also, avoid getting any Bavarian Cream mixed in with the caramel while dipping as the cream can cause the sugar to recrystallize.

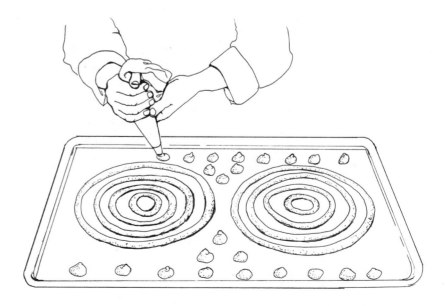

FIGURE 8–15   *Piping the Pâte à Choux in rings on top of the Puff Pastry circles, and into profiteroles around the circles on the pan, for Gâteau Saint-Honoré*

9. Whip the heavy cream and remaining sugar to stiff peaks. Place the whipped cream in a pastry bag with a no. 5 (10-mm) star tip. Pipe a border of whipped cream around the top of the cakes. Arrange the profiteroles, evenly spaced, on top of the filling next to the cream. Sprinkle the chocolate shavings over the center of the cakes inside the profiteroles. If the cakes are to be sliced and not presented whole, slice them after piping the whipped cream, before adding the profiteroles.

1. Sprinkle the gelatin powder over the rum. Set aside to soften.

2. Whip the heavy cream and vanilla to stiff peaks. Fold the whipped cream into the Pastry Cream. Fold in the Italian Meringue.

3. Place the softened gelatin mixture over a bain-marie and heat to dissolve. Do not overheat. Place one-third of the cream mixture in a separate bowl and rapidly stir in the dissolved gelatin. Still working quickly, mix this into the remaining cream mixture.

Bavarian Rum Cream

6 cups (1 l, 440 ml)

4 teaspoons (12 g) unflavored gelatin powder

¹/₃ cup (80 ml) light rum

2 cups (480 ml) heavy cream

2 teaspoons (10 ml) vanilla extract

8 ounces (225 g) Pastry Cream (page 1088) (see note)

one-quarter recipe Italian Meringue (page 591)

NOTE: If you do not have Pastry Cream already made up, make it far enough in advance that it is thoroughly chilled before combining it with the whipped cream. If the Pastry Cream is warm, the whipped cream will break.

Harlequin Cake

two 10-inch (25-cm) cakes

one Ribbon Sponge Sheet (page 276)

one 10-inch (25-cm) Devil's Food Cake Layer (page 272)

White Chocolate Bavarian Filling (recipe follows)

one-half recipe Chocolate Cognac Cream (page 324)

¹/₂ cup (120 ml) heavy cream

10 ounces (285 g) Marzipan (page 1022), untinted or chocolate-flavored

powdered sugar

dark coating chocolate, melted

Piping Chocolate (page 904), melted

candied violets

Raspberry Sauce (page 1080)

Orange Sauce (page 1077)

Sour Cream Mixture for Piping (page 1081)

*T*he name Harlequin, or Arlequin in French, is given to many culinary specialities as well as some living creatures such as birds, snakes, and the so appropriately named Harlequin Cabbage Bug. Harlequin entitled food items range from canapés to roasts, casseroles, and an abundance of sweets. They are so named either for being very colorful or for having a marked contrast of two colors, most often black and white. The original Harlequin was one of the principal characters in the Italian Commedia Dell' Arte *(a comic theater), which was popular throughout Europe from the mid-sixteenth through the eighteenth century. Harlequin's earliest costume had colorful rags and patches on his peasant shirt and trousers, and his role was that of a wild and comic servant. Later, as the character developed, he became a faithful valet noted for his patience and good spirits, and Harlequin's costume became a tight-fitting one-piece suit decorated with triangular or diamond shapes both in bright multicolors or in just black and white, and he wore a black half mask. The most famous among the sweets named for Harlequin is the classical Soufflé Harlequin, which contains vertical layers of chocolate and vanilla. Other pastries are made up of bits and pieces, which signify the patches on Harlequin's early costume.*

1. Place two 10-inch (25-cm) stainless-steel cake rings on a sheet pan lined with baking paper. (If cake rings are not available, line the sides of two cake pans with strips of polyurethane or acetate.) Cut

NOTE 1: You will have quite a bit of Ribbon Sponge left over after lining the rings; reserve in the freezer (well wrapped) for another project.

NOTE 2: If the cakes are not to be precut, the chocolate Marzipan tops should be cut the same size as the cakes and placed on the top whole.

2-inch (5-cm) wide strips, lengthwise, from the Ribbon Sponge Sheet and place them inside the rings with the striped side against the ring.

2. Cut the skin from the top of the Devil's Food Cake to make it level. Cut the cake into two layers. Trim the sides to fit, and then place the layers inside the cake rings.

3. Divide the White Chocolate Bavarian Filling between the cakes and smooth the top level. Place the cakes in the refrigerator while making the Chocolate Cognac Cream.

4. Divide the Chocolate Cognac Cream between the cakes, on top of the Bavarian Filling, and spread the top level. Refrigerate to set, approximately 2 hours.

5. When the fillings are completely set, remove the rings from around the cakes (or invert the cakes to remove them from the cake pans, turn right-side up, and remove the plastic strips.) Whip the cream to stiff peaks and ice the tops of the cakes.

6. Divide the Marzipan into two pieces. Roll them out one at a time, using powdered sugar to prevent them from sticking, into circles about 12 inches (30 cm) in diameter and $1/16$ inch (2 mm) thick. Place the Marzipan rounds on cardboard cake circles and spread a thin layer of melted dark coating chocolate on top. Use just enough to cover the circles evenly.

7. Using a guide, trim each round into an even circle slightly smaller than the top of the cakes (save the trimmings for Rum Balls or chocolate-flavored Marzipan).

8. Cut the Marzipan circles into the same number of slices you will be cutting the cakes (see note 2). Slide the cuts (chocolate-side up) all at once onto the top of the cakes (as shown in Figure 8–17, page 353), or pick the pieces up one at a time and reassemble on the cakes.

9. Cut between the Marzipan pieces and slice the cakes into serving pieces. Be sure to clean the knife after each cut. Pipe the melted Piping Chocolate decoratively on top of each slice (see Figure 17–21, page 908, designs in the third row). Place a small piece of candied violet at the wide end of each piece.

10. Presentation: Place a slice of cake off-center on a dessert plate. Pour small pools of Raspberry Sauce and Orange Sauce next to each other in front of the slice. Pipe a line of Sour Cream Mixture where the two sauces meet. Using a wooden skewer, swirl the three together in a circular pattern (see Figure 19–31, page 1005).

White Chocolate Bavarian Filling

4¹/₂ cups (1 l, 80 ml)

1¹/₂ cups (360 ml) heavy cream
1 tablespoon (9 g) unflavored gelatin
   powder

*T*his delightful silky-smooth filling is easy to make, provided you observe the following two warnings: Whip the cream only until soft peaks form, and do not overheat the white chocolate. To ensure that the chocolate does not get too hot, do not walk away when melting it, stay with it and stir it constantly to speed up the process. Remove the chocolate from the bain-marie while there are still some unmelted chunks left and stir these out off the heat. The chocolate should be warm but not hot. Not heeding these cautions will cause the filling to separate and become grainy, and you will have no recourse but to start over.

¼ cup (60 ml) cold water

1½ tablespoons (14 g) pectin powder (see note)

4 ounces (115 g) granulated sugar

4 egg whites (½ cup/120 ml)

6 ounces (170 g) white chocolate, melted

2 ounces (55 g) pistachio nuts, blanched, skins removed, chopped

NOTE: Use regular canning pectin. If it is unavailable, increase the gelatin by 1 teaspoon, for a total of 1 tablespoon plus 1 teaspoon. Increase the cold water by 1 tablespoon, and the granulated sugar by 1 ounce.

Lastly, do not make the filling until you are ready to use it because it will thicken quite fast.

1. Whip the heavy cream to soft peaks. Do not overwhip. Reserve in the refrigerator.

2. Sprinkle the gelatin over the cold water and set aside to soften.

3. Combine the pectin powder and granulated sugar in a mixing bowl. Stir in the egg whites. Place the bowl over simmering water and heat, stirring constantly with a whisk, to 140°F (60°C). Remove from the heat and immediately whip the mixture until it has cooled completely and has formed stiff peaks.

4. Place the gelatin mixture over a bain-marie and heat until dissolved. Quickly stir the gelatin into the melted white chocolate, then quickly stir the chocolate mixture into one-third of the meringue mixture to temper it. Still working quickly, add this to the remaining meringue. Stir in the reserved whipped cream. Fold in the chopped nuts.

Lemon Chiffon Cake

two 10-inch (25-cm) cakes

1¼ cups (300 ml) lemon juice

½ cup (120 ml) Plain Cake Syrup (page 10)

5 teaspoons (30 g) finely grated lemon zest

one 10-inch (25-cm) Sponge Cake (page 268)

6 egg yolks (½ cup/120 ml)

¾ cup (180 ml) or 8 ounces (225 g) light corn syrup (see note)

2 tablespoons (18 g) unflavored gelatin powder

½ cup (120 ml) cold water

3 cups (720 ml) heavy cream

Tartaric Acid Solution (page 1115) (optional)

1 quart (960 ml) heavy cream

2 tablespoons (30 g) granulated sugar

⅔ cup (160 ml) Pectin Glaze (page 1017)
    or

Lemon Glaze (recipe follows)

Dark Chocolate Squares (page 890)

lemon slices

Piping Chocolate (page 904), melted

Raspberry Sauce (page 1080)

lemon mint sprigs

*T*his cake comes from one of my very first notebooks, which I still refer to from time to time. The book is starting to show its age after all these years by getting a little rough around the edges, but so, I might add, is the author of this book! Back then one had to earn the right to copy a particularly good recipe or a certain shop speciality like Lemon Chiffon Cake. To obtain a really top-secret recipe, some of the apprentices would try to figure it out one ingredient at a time, observing closely, checking the scale after the boss was through, or even counting the eggshells in the garbage! Usually there was simply nothing written down to copy; it was all memorized. And even in the cases where the recipe was on paper, one ingredient was often intentionally left out or changed in such a way that the recipe would only work if you knew the code. Well, as I started to use the recipes from my old notebook I even fooled myself half the time, since I couldn't remember what kind of tricks I had been up to when I made my notes. I found I had no choice but to use trial and error in some cases.

I often tell my students that if they were to take with them just one recipe from my class it should be the Lemon Chiffon Cake. Not only is this cake very inexpensive to produce, it can be made up in advance through step seven and stored for several days in the refrigerator (or for weeks in the freezer), so it is perfect for large banquets. Its refreshing light taste makes it appropriate for use on a lunch or brunch buffet and, with the addition of a sauce, it can be transformed into an elegant plated dessert. The chiffon filling is simplicity itself to make. It is important to use finely grated lemon zest, since it will give the filling a better flavor and texture than coarsely grated or, worse, zested lemon zest. If you prefer a less tart filling, increase the light corn syrup a bit (step 3).

If you do not have time to make either of the glazes, substitute shaved chocolate sprinkled lightly within the rosettes of whipped cream.

NOTE: *You may substitute ⅓ cup (80 ml) of water and 4 ounces (115 g) of granulated sugar, boiled to 230°F (110°C), for the corn syrup.*

1. Add ¼ cup (60 ml) of the lemon juice to the Cake Syrup. Add the grated lemon zest to the remaining juice. Set both mixtures aside.

2. Cut the skin from the top of the Sponge Cake and cut the top of the cake level if necessary. Slice the cake into two layers. Place the layers on cardboard cake circles for support. Brush the lemon-flavored Cake Syrup over the sponges. Place a 10-inch (25-cm) stainless-steel cake ring snugly around each sponge or secure strips of polyurethane or acetate around them to form a collar.

3. Start whipping the egg yolks on medium speed in a mixer. Place the corn syrup in a small saucepan and bring to a boil. Lower the mixer speed and pour the hot syrup into the whipped egg yolks in a steady stream. Increase the mixing speed and continue whipping until the mixture is light and fluffy.

4. Sprinkle the gelatin over the cold water and set aside to soften.

5. Whip the 3 cups (720 ml) of heavy cream to soft peaks. Combine the egg yolk mixture, whipped cream, and lemon juice with zest.

6. Place the gelatin mixture over a bain-marie and heat until dissolved. Do not overheat. Place about one-fourth of the cream mixture in a separate bowl and rapidly mix in the dissolved gelatin; quickly mix this into the remaining cream mixture. Add a few drops of Tartaric Acid Solution, if desired, to neutralize the gelatin flavor.

7. Divide the lemon filling between the two prepared Sponge Cake halves. Spread out evenly within the rings. Cover the cakes and refrigerate until the filling is set, about 2 hours.

8. Remove the cake rings or plastic strips. Whip the remaining cream and sugar to stiff peaks. Spread a ¾-inch (2-cm) layer of cream on the top of the cakes, and just enough on the sides to cover the sponge. Reserve the remaining cream in the refrigerator.

9. Cover the top of the cakes with a thin layer of Pectin or Lemon Glaze. When the glaze has set up, cut or mark the cakes into the desired number of pieces. Place a Chocolate Square on the side of each slice; it should stick to the cream.

10. Place the remaining whipped cream in a pastry bag with a no. 6 (12-mm) star tip. Pipe a rosette of cream at the edge of each slice. Place a small wedge of sliced lemon on each rosette.

11. Pipe a large S of Piping Chocolate on the base of as many dessert plates as you will need.

12. Presentation: Place a portion of the Raspberry Sauce in a piping bottle. Pipe enough sauce into the bottom loop of the S on one of the prepared plates to fill it. Place a slice of cake in the top loop next to the sauce. Decorate the plate with a sprig of lemon mint.

Lemon Glaze

1 cup (240 ml)

1 tablespoon (9 g) gelatin powder

¼ cup (60 ml) cold water

½ cup (120 ml) strained lemon juice

¼ cup (60 ml) Simple Syrup
(page 11)

¼ teaspoon (1.25 ml) Tartaric Acid
Solution (page 1115)

NOTE: This glaze can be made in a larger quantity as a mise en place item; just melt the amount needed each time.

 VARIATION

one Ribbon Sponge Sheet (page 276)

2 cups plus 2 tablespoons (510 ml)
lemon juice

¼ cup (60 ml) Plain Cake Syrup
(page 10)

3 tablespoons (55 g) finely grated
lemon zest

one 10-inch (25-cm) Sponge Cake
(page 268)

12 egg yolks (1 cup/240 ml)

1 cup (240 ml) or 12 ounces (340 g)
light corn syrup

4 tablespoons (36 g) unflavored
gelatin powder

1 cup (240 ml) cold water

6 cups (1 l, 400 ml) heavy cream

Tartaric Acid Solution (page 1115),
(optional)

fresh fruit

Pectin Glaze (page 1017)

1. Sprinkle the gelatin over the cold water and let sit until softened. Place the gelatin mixture over a bain-marie and heat until dissolved. Do not overheat.

2. Stir the lemon juice, Simple Syrup, and Tartaric Acid Solution into the gelatin mixture.

3. Use the glaze on the cakes as soon as it shows signs of thickening. If the glaze should thicken too much before it can be applied, reheat before using to avoid ruining the appearance of the cakes.

*Y*ou can produce an entirely different finish and a refreshing, less rich cake by omitting the whipped cream, Lemon Glaze, and Chocolate Squares, and instead decorating the sides of the cakes with Ribbon Sponge Sheets and the tops with a colorful arrangement of fresh fruit. You can cut the Ribbon Sheets so that they cover the entire side of each cake or so that they come only halfway up the sides as shown in the color photograph. You will not need a full Ribbon Sponge Sheet, but it is not practical to make less than a full one a one time. Use a leftover partial sheet if you have it on hand.

1. Place two 10-inch (25-cm) stainless-steel cake rings on cardboard cake circles for support, or use 10-inch (25-cm) cake pans instead. Line the sides of either with 1¾-inch (4.5-cm) strips of Ribbon Sponge or strips cut about half as wide if you only want the sponge to cover half of the filling.

2. Add 2 tablespoons (30 ml) of the lemon juice to the Cake Syrup. Combine the grated lemon zest with the remaining juice.

3. Cut the skin from the top of the Sponge Cake and cut the top level at the same time. Cut the sponge into four thin layers. Reserve two layers for another use. Place each of the remaining layers in the bottom of the lined cake rings or pans, trimming as needed so that they fit snugly. Brush the Cake Syrup over the sponges.

4. Follow steps three, four, five, and six in the main recipe.

5. Divide the filling between the cake rings or cake pans. Cover the cakes and refrigerate until the filling is set, about 2 hours.

6. Remove the cake rings or invert to remove from the cake pans and then turn right-side up. Decorate the tops of the cakes with fresh fruit. Brush the Pectin Glaze over the fruit and the top of the cakes.

Mocha Cake

two 10-inch (25-cm) cakes

2 pounds, 12 ounces (1 kg, 250 g)
   Vanilla Buttercream (page 978)
1 tablespoon (15 ml) mocha extract
   or
3 tablespoons (45 ml) Coffee
   Reduction (page 5)
one 10-inch (25-cm) Chiffon Sponge
   Cake (page 272)
one 10-inch (25-cm) Chocolate
   Chiffon Sponge Cake (page 272)
1/2 cup (120 ml) coffee liqueur
1/4 cup (60 ml) water
4 ounces (115 g) sliced almonds,
   toasted and lightly crushed
Chocolate Figurines (page 906)
espresso coffee powder
Mango Coulis (page 1075)

NOTE 1: If you are making only one cake and you do not have sponges on hand, rather than making two different kinds you can save time by doing the following: Make one-half recipe of the plain sponge batter and pour half of it into a prepared 10-inch (25-cm) cake pan. Sift 3 tablespoons (24 g) of unsweetened cocoa powder over the remaining batter and fold it in very carefully. Place this batter in a second prepared pan, and bake the sponges as directed. After they have cooled, cut each sponge into two layers. Since you are working the chocolate sponge batter twice, it will be a little denser and lower in volume. Be careful when slicing it in half, as it may be quite thin.

NOTE 2: It is impossible to press the top part of the cakes into the bottom without deforming, and possibly even cracking, the sides of the cakes. Consequently, the finished cakes will probably be closer to 9 1/2 inches (23.7 cm) rather than 10 inches (25 cm) in diameter.

I always try to make a new and impressive dessert for each student graduation luncheon. These celebrations occur every two months and total about three hundred students and guests, so the possibilities can be somewhat limited. A few times I have simply created a different, more showy presentation of an old favorite, as was the case with the Cappucino Mousse in Chocolate Cups and the Strawberries Romanoff. This time the students requested a classic Mocha Cake. While it certainly is a good old-fashioned cake, I felt it needed a face-lift.

As you look through this recipe you may figure out that it is actually a scaled-down version of the infamous Chestnut Puzzle Cake, using one less sponge layer and a simplified cut to remove the center. You must still make both a chocolate and plain sponge, but at least you only have to worry about one flavor of buttercream. The presentation used here can be replaced with Chocolate Sauce or Mousseline Sauce flavored with a hint of cinnamon if you wish.

To make the classical version of a Mocha Cake, cut a vanilla sponge into three or four layers. Follow the directions given below to assemble the cake through step three. Use all of the sponge layers. Ice the top and sides of the cake in the conventional fashion. Cover the sides with toasted sliced almonds. Chill the cakes to set the buttercream before cutting the cake into the desired number of pieces. Place the reserved buttercream in a pastry bag with a no. 7 (14-mm) star tip. Pipe a rosette of buttercream at the end of each slice and decorate each one with a Chocolate Figurine. Sprinkle ground coffee lightly over the center of the cakes within the rosettes.

1. Flavor the buttercream with the mocha extract or Coffee Reduction. Reserve 4 ounces (115 g) to use later in decorating. Set the buttercream aside.

2. Cut the skin from the top of both Sponge Cakes, cutting the tops even at the same time. Cut each sponge into four thin layers. Place two of the chocolate layers on a cardboard cake circle, cover, and set aside.

3. Place a plain layer on each of two cardboard cake circles. Combine the coffee liqueur and the water. Brush or spray some of this mixture on top of the sponge layers. Spread a thin (approximately 1/8-inch/3-mm) layer of buttercream evenly over each sponge. Place the two remaining chocolate sponges on top. Brush or spray with the liqueur mixture, then top each with another thin layer of buttercream. Top with plain sponge layers. Press the assembled cakes together lightly. Brush or spray the liqueur mixture over the cakes. Place in the refrigerator until the buttercream is set.

4. Dip a sharp pointed knife (a cake knife or an 8-to-10-inch/20-to-25-cm chef's knife) into hot water. Holding the knife at a 45° angle, cut a circle around the perimeter of one cake about 1/2 inch (1.2 cm) away from the side at the top, angling down to about 2 inches (5 cm) from the side at the bottom (see Figure 8–6, page 313). Move the knife up and down as you cut and dip the knife back into the hot water if you feel any resistance. Remove the cut piece by lifting it out with the knife and inverting it onto your hand. The inverted piece should be approximately 6 inches at the top and 9 inches at the bottom (15 × 22.5 cm). Place this piece on a cardboard cake circle. Repeat with the second cake.

5. Ice the flat ring around the top of each cake and the area inside the cut with a ¹/₈-inch (3-mm) layer of buttercream (see Figure 8–7, page 313).

6. Place the reserved chocolate sponge layers flat on top of each cake. Place a cardboard cake circle on top of each one. Invert the cakes so that the new chocolate layer is on the bottom.

7. Gently press the cut ring in and down so that it touches and adheres to the bottom of each cake (see Figure 8–8, page 313).

8. Ice the newly formed craters with a ¹/₈-inch (3-mm) layer of buttercream. Set the cutout pieces inside the craters. Trim the sides of the cakes to make them even (see note 2).

9. Ice the top and sides of the cakes with just enough buttercream to cover.

10. Lightly mark the top of the cakes in quarters to identify the centers. If necessary, stir the reserved 4 ounces (115 g) of buttercream to make it smooth. Place in a pastry bag with a no. 3 (6-mm) plain tip. Starting in the center of one cake (where the lines cross) pipe a 5-inch (12.5-cm) spiral of buttercream in the center of the cake, with each ring of buttercream touching the previous one. (You can first mark the tops with a 5-inch 12.5-cm cookie cutter if you are not sure where to stop, or just count seven to eight rings.)

11. Cover the sides of each cake, and the undecorated part of the tops, with crushed almonds (see Figure 8–5, page 296). Refrigerate the cakes until the buttercream is set, approximately 1 hour.

12. Cut the cakes into the desired number of serving pieces. Use a small skewer to make a small indentation in the center of the almond-covered portion of each slice and then insert a Chocolate Figurine.

13. Make the template on page 507 and attach it to a paper plate or a disposable pie tin that fits within the base of your serving plates (see page 1040 for more information). Position the template over the base of each dessert plate and sift coffee powder over the top. Decorate as many plates as you expect to need.

14. Presentation: Place a slice of cake on one of the prepared plates, positioning it so the wide end of the cake is inside the curve of the coffee decoration and angled far enough away from the wide part of the decoration to leave room for the sauce. Using a piping bottle, pipe five or six dots of Mango Coulis, each about the size of a quarter coin, around the point of the cake slice.

✎ Pariser Chocolate Cake

two 10-inch (25-cm) cakes

³/₄ cup (180 ml) light rum

¹/₄ cup (60 ml) Simple Syrup (page 11)

one recipe Crème Parisienne (page 1086)

two 10-inch (25-cm) Hazelnut-Chocolate Sponges (page 274)

dark chocolate shavings

¹/₄ cup (60 ml) Frangelico liqueur

one recipe Mousseline Sauce (page 1076)

Chocolate Sauce for Piping (page 1072)

fresh fruit

*T*his is an extremely light, delicious chocolate and nut combination. It is inexpensive and quick to produce, but it does require advance planning since the Crème Parisienne must be made one day ahead in order to whip properly. In cases of "miscommunication" substitute Chocolate Cream (see page 1084). Make two times the recipe and heed the caution about overwhipping the cream. The same consideration applies to some degree when working with the Crème Parisienne. You must take into account the fact that as the cream is spread back and forth while icing the cakes, the friction continues the whipping process (the same phenomenon occurs as you force whipped cream through the small tip of a pastry bag). If the cream is whipped too much initially, it will be impossible to achieve a smooth attractive finish.

1. Combine the rum and the Simple Syrup. Reserve.

2. Whip the Crème Parisienne to stiff peaks. Reserve.

3. Cut the skin off the top of the sponges and cut the tops level if necessary. Slice the sponges into three layers each. Brush the bottom layers with one-third of the syrup mixture. Spread a ¹/₄-inch (6-mm) thick layer of Crème Parisienne on top. Place the second layers on the cream. Repeat the procedure adding more syrup, filling, and the remaining sponge layers. Brush the remaining rum syrup on the top of the cakes. Ice the tops and sides of the cakes with a thin layer of Crème Parisienne. Place the cakes on cardboard cake rounds for support.

4. Place about half of the remaining cream in a pastry bag with a no. 6 (12-mm) flat star tip (see Figure 19–1, page 980). Pipe vertical strips on the sides of the cakes, next to each other, working from the bottom to the top. Smooth the top edge all around the cakes with a spatula.

5. Place the remainder of the Crème Parisienne in a second pastry bag with a no. 4 (8-mm) plain tip (unfortunately, you can not put a round tip on the outside of a flat one as would otherwise be the sensible thing to do). Pipe lines ¹/₂ inch (1.2 cm) apart on the tops of the cakes, first in one direction, then at a 45° angle, to create a diamond pattern.

6. Cut the cakes into the desired number of servings. Sprinkle chocolate shavings lightly over the tops of the cakes and place in the refrigerator until needed. Combine the Frangelico liqueur and the Mousseline Sauce. Reserve the sauce in the refrigerator.

7. Presentation: Place a slice of cake in the center of a dessert plate. Pour a pool of Mousseline Sauce at the tip of the slice so that the sauce runs out evenly on either side. Decorate the sauce with Chocolate Sauce for Piping (see pages 998 to 1006). Place a piece of seasonal fruit on the side.

Poppy Seed Cake

two 10-inch (25-cm) cakes

Poppy Seed Cake Base (recipe follows)

1 quart (960 ml) heavy cream

2 tablespoons (30 g) granulated sugar

12 ounces (340 g) medium-size stemmed strawberries, thinly sliced (about twenty)

6 ounces (170 g) sliced almonds, toasted and lightly crushed

Piping Chocolate (page 904), melted

strawberry wedges

NOTE: If you do not have time to pipe the chocolate design, pipe the rosettes and then sprinkle dark chocolate shavings on top of the cakes within the rosettes.

*T*he speckled cake layers, dotted with orange zest, and separated by white cream and red strawberries, make this cake as visually appealing as it is delicious.

The batter for the *Poppy Seed Cake Base* is very adaptable: To make a fabulous coffee cake, make one-half the recipe with an additional 2 ounces (55 g) of bread flour and bake in a 10-inch (25-cm) tube pan. If a tube pan is not available, use a loaf pan. Use a cake tester to be certain that the cake is baked in the center because this is a very moist cake and it is easy to underbake. A simple Orange Glaze is all that is needed to finish the coffee cake; make the full recipe on page 1016. Pour the glaze over the top of the cake, letting it run down the sides evenly. The same batter (with the additional flour) also makes great muffins. The full recipe will yield eighteen 4-ounce (120-ml) muffins.

Be careful not to overmix the batter regardless of what you are using it for. Overmixing can cause what is known as a tunnel effect: Long, worm-shaped holes are found throughout the baked cake.

The quantity of poppy seeds can be scaled up or down to suit your individual taste.

1. Cut the skin from the tops of the cakes and even the tops if necessary. Cut the cakes into three layers each.

2. Whip the cream and sugar to stiff peaks. Spread a thin layer of cream, 1/8 inch (3 mm) thick, on the bottom cake layers. Cover the cream with a single layer of strawberry slices. Spread another thin layer of cream on top of the strawberries. Place the second cake layers on top of the cream and repeat the procedure. Add the top cake layers.

3. Ice the top and sides of the cakes with a thin layer of whipped cream. Use just enough to cover the sponge; you should have some left for decorating.

4. Cover the sides of the cakes with the crushed almonds (see Figure 8–5, page 296).

5. Cut or mark the cakes into the desired number of serving pieces. Decorate the top of each slice with the Piping Chocolate (Figure 8–16). Place the reserved whipped cream in a pastry bag with a no. 4 (8-mm) star tip. Pipe a rosette at the edge of each slice. Place a small strawberry wedge on each rosette.

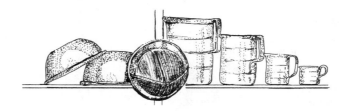

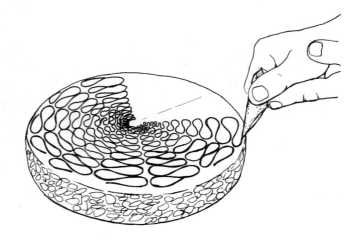

FIGURE 8–16   *Decorating the top of the Poppy Seed Cake with a design made from Piping Chocolate*

Poppy Seed Cake Base

two 10-inch (25-cm) cake layers

Butter and Flour Mixture (page 4)
8 ounces (225 g) bread flour
8 ounces (225 g) cake flour
1¹/₂ teaspoons (6 g) baking soda
1 teaspoon (4 g) baking powder
5 ounces (140 g) poppy seeds
2 tablespoons (36 g) grated or finely chopped orange zest (about two medium oranges)
1 pound (455 g) soft unsalted butter
1 pound, 8 ounces (680 g) granulated sugar
10 egg yolks (⁷/₈ cup/210 ml), at room temperature
1 tablespoon (15 ml) vanilla extract
12 ounces (340 g) sour cream
12 egg whites (1¹/₂ cups/360 ml)
¹/₂ teaspoon (2.5 g) salt
¹/₂ teaspoon (1 g) cream of tartar

1. Brush the Butter and Flour Mixture over the inside of two 10-inch (25-cm) cake pans. Set aside.

2. Sift the flours, baking soda, and baking powder together. Mix in the poppy seeds and the orange zest.

3. Cream the butter. Add 1 pound, 4 ounces (570 g) of the sugar and beat until light and fluffy. Add the egg yolks and vanilla. Mix for two minutes.

4. Mix in half of the dry ingredients on low speed. Add the sour cream and mix until just combined. Mix in the remaining dry ingredients.

5. Whip the egg whites, salt, and cream of tartar to a foam. Gradually add the remaining 4 ounces (115 g) of sugar and whip to soft peaks. Fold the whites into the batter one-quarter at a time. Divide the batter between the reserved cake pans.

6. Bake at 350°F (175°C) for approximately 35 minutes or until the cake springs back when pressed lightly in the center.

Princess Cake

two 10-inch (25-cm) cakes

two 10-inch (25-cm) Sponge Cakes (page 268)
    or
two 10-inch (25-cm) Chiffon Sponge Cakes (page 272)
³/₄ cup (120 ml) Plain Cake Syrup (page 10)
6 ounces (170 g) smooth strawberry jam

*W*hy is the Marzipan on top of a Princess Cake traditionally colored green? This is a question I have been asked time after time, and I am slightly embarrassed to admit that I do not have a definite answer. Believe me, I have tried to find out! I have consulted with many pastry chefs both in Europe and in the United States and, in fact, during the course of writing this book I made a research trip to Europe and while in Sweden I tried again, but no one seems to have a sure explanation. It would at least make more sense to me if the cake was flavored with mint or pistachios.

Princess Cakes are often made in other colors: The Marzipan is left its natural off-white hue and the cakes are sometimes made with pale pink Marzipan

1 pound, 4 ounces (570 g) Quick
   Bavarian Cream (page 1089)
5 cups (1 l, 200 ml) heavy cream
2 tablespoons (30 g) granulated sugar
1 pound, 4 ounces (570 g) Marzipan
   (page 1022), tinted light green
powdered sugar
Strawberry Sauce (page 1081)
Piping Chocolate (page 904)

*NOTE: The Marzipan may alternatively be
textured with a tread roller or waffle roller
before it is placed on the cake. If you plan to
decorate the cakes, sift the powdered sugar over
the top after adding the decoration. Princess
Cake is an excellent choice for a cake to make
up ahead because the Marzipan keeps the cake
fresh for days if well-covered and refrigerated.
To protect the Marzipan from becoming wet
from the whipped cream, brush or spread a thin
layer of Vanilla Buttercream on the bottom side
of the Marzipan before placing it on the cake.
You then have to invert the Marzipan onto the
cake and will not be able to avoid getting some
buttercream on your hands, so be sure to clean
them before smoothing the Marzipan onto the
cake.*

*for special occasions; however, pale green is the norm. Regrettably, not everyone
remembers the pale part. Food colorings come in different strengths, and once
you have added too much it might be too late (unfortunately, there isn't a natural green coloring agent that can be added to Marzipan). When tinting the
Marzipan bear in mind that this is a Swedish cake, not an Irish one!*

*The smooth Marzipan covering on the Princess Cake makes an ideal sur-
face on which to pipe a design in chocolate such as "Happy Birthday" or a mes-
sage to acknowledge any special occasion. Otherwise, the only decoration
required is a light dusting of powdered sugar. In the color photograph of this
cake I added a small pink Marzipan Rose, an optional decoration that is often
used and adds a nice touch (see page 1034 for instructions).*

1. Cut the skin from the top of the two cakes, cutting the tops level
at the same time if necessary. Cut the cakes into three layers each.

2. Brush Cake Syrup over the two bottom layers. Divide the jam
between the bottom layers and spread out evenly. Place the middle
cake layers on top of the jam. Brush Cake Syrup over the middle layers.
Divide the Bavarian Cream between the middle layers and spread out
evenly. Place the top cake layers on the Bavarian Cream.

3. Whip the heavy cream and granulated sugar to stiff peaks.
Divide the cream between the two cakes. Spread just enough cream on
the sides of the cakes to cover them. Spread the remaining cream into
a dome shape on the tops, about ³/₄ inch (2 cm) thick in the center.

4. Divide the Marzipan into two pieces. Roll them out one at a
time into circles ¹/₈ inch (3 mm) thick and about 15 inches (37.5 cm) in
diameter, using powdered sugar to prevent the Marzipan from sticking.

5. Roll one circle onto a dowel and unroll over one of the cakes.
Smooth the Marzipan onto the cake with your hands, keeping the
dome shape on top. Pay special attention to the sides to be sure the
Marzipan is not wrinkled. Trim the Marzipan around the base of the
cake to make it even. Repeat the procedure to cover the second cake.

6. Cut or mark the cakes into the desired number of serving pieces.
Cut from the edge of the cake toward the center to prevent the Marzipan from being pushed into the whipped cream. If you have problems,
cut through the Marzipan layer first before cutting the cake. Sift powdered sugar lightly over the cakes.

7. Put a portion of the Strawberry Sauce into a piping bottle. Place
a small amount of melted Piping Chocolate in a piping bag and decorate the base of as many dessert plates as you anticipate needing by
piping a zigzag pattern on the top half of the plates, ending with a large
loop on the bottom half. Set the plates aside.

8. Presentation: Sift powdered sugar over the base of one of the
prepared plates. Place a slice of cake crosswise on top of the zigzag
lines of chocolate. Pipe Strawberry Sauce inside the piped chocolate
loop. Place a Marzipan Rose on top of the cake slice at the wide end, if
using, securing it with a drop of Piping Chocolate.

Queen of Sheba Cake

two 10-inch (25-cm) cakes

4 ounces (115 g) Short Dough
   (page 54)

dark coating chocolate, melted

Queen of Sheba Cake Base (recipe
   follows)

$^1/_2$ cup (120 ml) orange juice

3 tablespoons (45 ml) orange liqueur

2 pounds (910 g) Ganache
   (page 1086)

14 ounces (400 g) Vanilla Buttercream
   (page 978)

hazelnuts, toasted and crushed

10 ounces (285 g) Marzipan
   (page 1022), untinted

powdered sugar

*T*here are countless variations of this classic French chocolate cake, but you would be hard put to find Reine de Saba in a French pastry shop or on a restaurant menu; it is more of a homemaker's speciality there.

How the name Sheba became associated with this cake is a mystery. Or, should I say more specifically, why the Queen of Sheba would be linked to something made of chocolate is the real question. Although there is documentation that cocoa was known prior to the seventh century A.D., it is a big jump back to the tenth century B.C. when Sheba (the Hebrew spelling of Saba) was a thriving kingdom in southwest Arabia in approximately the same location as present-day Yemen. Sheba is known historically for the biblical visit of the Queen of Sheba to King Solomon in Israel. The queen was sent to test the young king's legendary wisdom. King Solomon, the third king of Israel, successor to King David and his son by Bathsheba, proved that there was no reason to doubt his abilities: During his rein he masterfully and relentlessly eliminated all threats to his rule, leaving him free to develop the economy of his kingdom. He used the wealth for many building projects; the most famous was the Temple in Jerusalem.

1. Roll out the Short Dough to $^1/_8$ inch (3 mm) thick. Cut out cookies using a 1-inch (2.5-cm) fluted cookie cutter. Place the cookies on a sheet pan lined with baking paper. Cut three holes in each cookie using a no. 2 (4-mm) plain pastry tip. Bake the cookies at 375°F (190°C) until golden brown, about 10 minutes. Let the cookies cool, then place them next to each other and streak in one direction with melted coating chocolate (see Figure 6–1, page 246, for example).

2. Cut the skins from the cake bases and at the same time cut the tops even. Slice each cake into two layers. Combine the orange juice with the orange liqueur. Brush some of the mixture over the bottom cake layers.

3. Reserve 10 ounces (285 g) of the Ganache and mix the remainder with the buttercream. Spread a $^1/_4$-inch (6-mm) layer of the Ganache mixture on the bottom cake layers. Invert the remaining two cake layers and place one on top of each Ganache layer. Brush the remainder of the orange juice mixture over the top cake layers. Ice the top and sides of the cakes with the Ganache mixture, using just enough to cover the sponge. Reserve the remainder for decorating. Cover the sides of the cakes with crushed hazelnuts (see Figure 8–5, page 296).

4. Roll out half of the Marzipan to a $^1/_{16}$-inch (2-mm) thick circle, slightly larger than 10 inches (25 cm) in diameter. Use powdered sugar to prevent it from sticking. Place the Marzipan on a 12-inch (30-cm) cardboard cake circle, or any size slightly larger than the cakes. Use a 10-inch (25-cm) guide and cut out a circle the same size as the tops of the cakes, leaving the Marzipan in place on the cardboard. Carefully slide the Marzipan circle onto the top of one of the cakes (see Figure 8–17, page 353). Place the cardboard circle on top of the cake and invert. Press down firmly to even the top of the cake. Repeat the entire procedure to make a Marzipan circle for the second cake.

5. Warm the reserved Ganache until liquid. Turn the cakes right-side up again and spread Ganache on top of the Marzipan just thick enough to cover. Let the Ganache sit for a few minutes to set up, then use the back of a chef's knife to mark a diamond pattern in the Ganache. Make parallel marks every ¹/₂ inch (1.2 cm), then turn the cake a quarter-turn and repeat. Refrigerate the cakes until the Ganache and buttercream are firm.

6. Mark or cut the cakes into the desired number of serving pieces. Place the remaining Ganache and buttercream mixture in a pastry bag with a no. 6 (12-mm) plain tip. Pipe a small mound, the size of a cherry, at the edge of each slice. Place one of the cookies at an angle on each mound. This cake should be cut while chilled, but it tastes better if served at room temperature.

Queen of Sheba Cake Base

two 10-inch (25-cm) cake layers

1 pound (455 g) sweet dark chocolate

¹/₂ cup (120 ml) dark rum

1 pound (455 g) soft unsalted butter

1 pound (455 g) granulated sugar

12 eggs, separated and at room temperature

8 ounces (225 g) Almond Paste (page 3)

10 ounces (285 g) bread flour

7 ounces (200 g) hazelnuts, toasted and finely ground

1. Line the bottom of two 10-inch (25-cm) cake pans with baking paper (or grease and flour but do not grease and flour the sides).

2. Melt the chocolate. Stir in the rum and set aside, but keep warm.

3. Beat the butter with 8 ounces (225 g) of the sugar until light and fluffy.

4. Gradually mix the egg yolks into the Almond Paste. You must mix them in a few at a time or you will get lumps. Stir the yolk mixture into the butter mixture. Add the melted chocolate rapidly and mix until completely incorporated.

5. Whip the egg whites to a foam; gradually add the remaining 8 ounces (225 g) sugar, and whip to stiff peaks. Carefully fold the egg whites into the chocolate mixture in three segments.

6. Sift the flour and mix with the nuts. Fold into the batter. Divide the batter equally between the prepared pans.

7. Bake at 350°F (175°C) for about 50 minutes, making sure the cakes are baked through. Let the cakes cool completely. Cut around the sides with a thin knife and unmold.

Raspberry Cake

two 10-inch (25-cm) cakes

two 10-inch (25-cm) Chiffon Sponge
Cakes (page 272)

two 10-inch (25-cm) Short Dough
Cake Bottoms (page 55)

4 ounces (115 g) raspberry jam

¹/₂ cup (120 ml) Plain Cake Syrup
(page 10)

Raspberry Cream (recipe follows)

2 dry pints (960 ml) raspberries

8 ounces (225 g) Vanilla Buttercream
(page 978)

5 ounces (140 g) sliced almonds,
toasted and lightly crushed

8 ounces (225 g) Marzipan
(page 1022), untinted

powdered sugar

dark chocolate shavings

I use this great-looking cake primarily as a buffet item, since the flower design of the Marzipan looks so much more impressive presented whole. To serve Raspberry Cake as a plated dessert, use the presentation suggested for either Lemon Chiffon or Princess Cake (pages 341 and 348). Raspberry Cake tastes good with a number of fruit sauces; using Raspberry and Lemon Sauces together is an especially nice combination.

In addition to this cake you will find several others in this text that start with a thin Short Dough or meringue layer on the bottom; this is a very traditional European method. The contrast between the crisp, dry base and the soft sponge and cream filling is very palate pleasing. A classic example is the famous Swiss speciality, Sugar Kirsch Torte.

On the other hand, for a more modern version, as shown in the color insert, you can give the cakes a contemporary air by using Ribbon Sponge Sheets on the sides and leaving out the Short Dough bases. If you have a partial Ribbon Sheet left over from another project it makes it even easier. One sheet is enough to cover the sides of approximately six cakes, so if you make a sheet specifically for this recipe you will have quite a bit left. You can use the extra for the variations of Apricot Cream Cake, Chocolate Mousse Cake with Banana, or Lemon Chiffon Cake.

To make the variation, omit the Short Dough Cake Bottoms, raspberry jam, and the toasted almonds from the ingredient list. Place the stainless-steel cake rings around the cakes directly on top of cardboard cake circles for support instead of the Short Dough bases in step two (or make 10-inch [25-cm] collars from strips of acetate or polyurethane). Cut 2-inch (5-cm) wide strips, lengthwise, from the Ribbon Sponge and place them inside the rings or collars with the striped side facing out. Trim the Sponge Cake layers so that they fit snugly inside the rings. Place one layer of sponge inside each ring and continue as directed, cutting the top sponge layers thin enough so that they fit just below the top edge of the Ribbon Sponge. (Do not ice the sides of the cakes in step six.)

1. Cut the top of the Sponge Cakes to make them level, then slice into two layers each.

2. Place the Short Dough Cake Bottoms on cardboards for support. Divide the jam between them and spread it out evenly. Place one layer of Sponge Cake on each jam-covered base. Brush Cake Syrup over the layers. Place stainless-steel cake rings around the cakes, setting them on top of the Short Dough. If cake rings are not available, secure strips of acetate or polyurethane around the cakes.

3. Pour one-fourth of the Raspberry Cream on each cake. Spread it out evenly within the rings.

4. Arrange whole raspberries, stem-side down, in three concentric circles spaced evenly over the cream. Start the first circle about ¹/₂ inch (1.2 cm) from the cake ring. Use both hands to put the berries on the cakes quickly, before the remaining cream sets up.

5. Divide the remaining cream filling between the cakes, pouring it over the raspberries; spread out evenly. Place the remaining two cake layers on top of the cream and press down lightly to make the tops level. Brush the remaining Cake Syrup over the top cake layers. Refrigerate the cakes until the filling is set, about 2 hours.

6. Remove the rings or plastic strips. Trim away any Short Dough that protrudes outside of the cake layers, to make the sides even (see Figure 8–11, page 325). Spread a thin layer of buttercream over the top and sides of each cake. Cover the sides of the cakes with crushed almonds, gently pushing them into the buttercream (see Figure 8–5, page 296).

7. Roll out the Marzipan to ¹/₁₆ inch (2 mm) thick, using just enough powdered sugar to prevent it from sticking. Make sure there is no powdered sugar underneath when you finish, as part of the bottom side will be visible in the final presentation. Texture the Marzipan with a waffle roller.

8. Cut out two circles of Marzipan the same size as the tops of the cakes. Place the Marzipan circles on cardboard rounds and cut 3-inch (7.5-cm) circles out of the centers. Reserve the centers for another use.

9. Mark the Marzipan rings into the desired number of slices for each cake. Cut through the marks, cutting from the center of the rings and stopping 1 inch (2.5 cm) from the edge so that the pieces remain attached at the outside edge of the rings. Roll back the cut edge of each Marzipan wedge toward the outside of the rings.

10. Carefully slide the rings onto the tops of the cakes (Figure 8–17). Cut the cakes into serving pieces, cutting between the rolled Marzipan pieces. Cover the exposed center of the cakes with the shaved chocolate. Place the remaining buttercream in a pastry bag with a no. 6 (12-mm) plain tip. Pipe a small mound of buttercream on the flat part of the Marzipan at the edge of each piece. Top each mound with a raspberry.

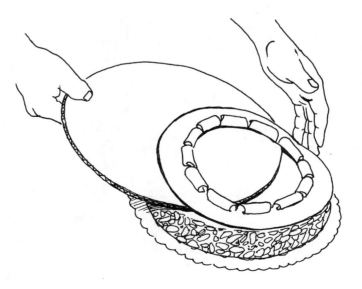

FIGURE 8–17 Sliding the Marzipan ring into place on top of the Raspberry Cake

Raspberry Cream

3 pounds (1 kg, 365 g)

5 teaspoons (15 g) unflavored gelatin
   powder
½ cup (120 ml) cold water
3 cups (720 ml) heavy cream
3 egg yolks (¼ cup/60 ml)
2 eggs
3 ounces (85 g) granulated sugar
½ cup (120 ml) dry white wine
¼ cup (60 ml) raspberry liqueur
½ cup (120 ml) strained raspberry
   purée

*NOTE: Do not make the filling until you are
ready to use it in the cakes.*

VARIATION
Blackberry Cake

*NOTE: Puréed blackberries are not used in the
filling because they turn the filling an unappetizing color.*

1. Sprinkle the gelatin over the cold water and set aside to soften.

2. Whip the cream to soft peaks. Reserve in the refrigerator.

3. Whip the egg yolks, whole eggs, and sugar until just combined. Add the wine and liqueur and whip over simmering water until the mixture reaches 140°F (60°C). Remove from the heat and continue whipping until the mixture has cooled and has a light and fluffy consistency, about 15 minutes.

4. Fold the yolk mixture into the reserved whipped cream. Stir in the raspberry purée.

5. Place the gelatin mixture over a bain-marie and heat until dissolved. Do not overheat. Quickly add the gelatin to a small portion of the cream mixture. Then, still working quickly, stir this mixture into the remaining cream.

*Substitute whole blackberries for the raspberries inside the cakes and in the
decoration. In the cream filling, substitute ½ cup (120 ml) heavy cream for
the raspberry purée, and Chambord liqueur for the raspberry liqueur.*

Sacher Torte

two 10-inch (25-cm) cakes

Sacher Biscuits (recipe follows)
3 cups (720 ml) Apricot Glaze
   (page 1016)
1½ cups (360 ml) Chocolate Glaze
   (page 1016)
dark or light Piping Chocolate
   (page 904), melted

*In the nineteenth century, Vienna was the undisputed capitol of the confec-
tioner's art. Among all of the calorie-rich, cholesterol-saturated offerings, none
was more famous than the Sacher Torte. Franz Sacher was the head pastry
cook of Prince Metternich and part of the famous Viennese hotel and restaurant
family. He invented the Sacher Torte for the congress of Vienna (1814–1815).
Long after Sacher's death there was a great controversy with many in Vienna
divided into two groups: the descendants of Franz Sacher who proclaimed that
the cake must consist of two layers with jam in the center rather than, as the
other side led by Edouard Demel of the famed Demel's Patisserie insisted, only
one layer with jam spread on top (a recipe he claimed was authorized by
Sacher's grandson). A court battle went on for six years before it was won by the
Hotel Sacher family.*

*I have come across many recipes (and also chefs) that specify raspberry jam
rather than apricot. This recipe was given to me by an Austrian konditor
named Manfred with whom I worked back in the sixties. Recently this Sacher*

Torte was on the menu and received what the server described as "the ultimate accolade." One of his guests, a tourist from Vienna, told him to send word to the kitchen that this was the best Sacher Torte she had ever tasted! (Of course, who knows how long she had been away from home.)

A slice of Sacher Torte mit schlag—which means "with cream" (the cream contrasts with the richness of the cake, so go for it even though you can order a slice without "ohne")—and a good cup of coffee are a must during a visit to Vienna. If you have the opportunity to enjoy this treat on the terrace of the Sacher Hotel, across from the opera, while writing "grüsse von Wien" on postcards picturing St. Stephen's church, you "have arrived" in this famous city!

1. Cut the skins from the tops of the Sacher Biscuits (even the tops, if necessary) and cut each cake into two layers.

2. Heat the Apricot Glaze until completely melted and smooth. Place one-fourth on each of the two bottom cake layers and spread it out quickly, forcing it into the cake before it has a chance to form a skin. Add the second cake layers and press them into the glaze. Use the remaining Apricot Glaze to ice the tops and sides of the cakes.

3. Move the cakes to a cake cooler or aspic rack with a sheet pan underneath. Be careful not to disturb the Apricot Glaze once it has started to form a skin. Spread a thin layer of Chocolate Glaze on the tops and sides of the cakes. It should be just thick enough to mask the Apricot Glaze underneath. Leave the cakes on the rack for a few minutes, then move them to cardboard cake circles before the glaze is completely set.

4. When the glaze is firm enough to be cut without running, mark or cut the cakes into the desired number of servings. Place light or dark Piping Chocolate in a piping bag and pipe a large **S** on each slice.

 Sacher Biscuit

two 10-inch (25-cm) biscuits

14 eggs, separated

12 ounces (340 g) granulated sugar

6 ounces (170 g) bread flour

3 ounces (85 g) cake flour

3 ounces (85 g) unsweetened cocoa powder

3 ounces (85 g) hazelnuts, finely ground

3 ounces (85 g) sweet dark chocolate

7 ounces (200 g) unsalted butter

1. Whip the egg yolks with 5 ounces (140 g) of the sugar until light and fluffy.

2. Sift the flours and cocoa powder together; mix in the ground nuts.

3. Melt the chocolate and butter together. Keep warm.

4. Whip the egg whites to a foam. Gradually add the remaining 7 ounces (200 g) of sugar and whip to stiff peaks. Fold the yolk mixture into the egg whites, then fold in the dry ingredients. Fold in the chocolate mixture. Divide the batter evenly between two greased and floured 10-inch (25-cm) cake pans.

5. Bake at 375°F (190°C) for about 20 minutes. Let the cakes cool completely before using them in the recipe.

Sicilian Macaroon Cake

two 10-inch (25-cm) cakes

one-half recipe Japonaise Meringue Batter (page 591)

1 tablespoon (5 g) ground cinnamon

one-half recipe Almond Sponge batter (page 270) (see step two)

dark coating chocolate, melted

two 10-inch (25-cm) Cocoa Short Dough Cake Bottoms (page 55)

4 ounces (115 g) red currant jelly

Macaroon-Maraschino Whipped Cream (recipe follows)

1/4 cup (60 ml) orange juice

2 tablespoons (30 ml) Maraschino liqueur

3/4-to-1-inch (2-to-2.5-cm) Almond Macaroon Cookies (page 202)

2 cups (480 ml) heavy cream

1 tablespoon (15 g) granulated sugar

5 ounces (140 g) sliced almonds, toasted and lightly crushed

dark chocolate shavings

*T*he prospect of making Short Dough, meringue, and sponge layers might give you second thoughts about the practicality of this cake. True, there are plenty of "slice-and-fill" type cakes that can be prepared in less than half the time, but if you are looking for something special, Sicilian Macaroon Cake is both unusual and delicious.

Now, what does Sicily have to do with this cake, you may wonder. After all, the majority of almonds in Italy are grown in the north, especially in the Piedmont-Lombardy region, which is famous for its almonds, amaretti cookies, and the well-known almond liqueur Amaretto di Saronno. Nor is it the Maraschino liqueur that is Sicilian: Maraschino liqueur is made from the marasca cherry, which is grown primarily in the Trieste area, in the northeast corner of Italy. How this cake came to have the Sicilian name goes way back in history. Sicily has, at one time or another, been home to every one of the great civilizations of the Mediterranean region: the Greeks, Romans, Arabs, Vikings, and more recently the French and Spanish have all laid claim at one time or another. In fact, this beautiful and much sought after island has only belonged to Italy for a little more than a century. All of these cultures contributed to what are now indigenous foods of Sicily. The Greeks planted olive trees and grape vines, and when the Romans took charge they introduced wheat, corn, and a multitude of other grains. The fertile soil in the valleys gave Sicily the title of Grain Bowl of the Roman Empire. When the Arabs conquered the island, they introduced rice, planted citrus trees and date palms, but, much more importantly, they brought with them their spices—saffron, cloves, and cinnamon—the latter influencing the name of this cake. These spices were very important to trade at the time and helped to make Sicily and seaports such as Palermo and Catania notable trade centers.

1. Draw two 10-inch (25-cm) circles on baking paper and invert the paper on a sheet pan. Place the Japonaise Meringue Batter in a pastry bag with a no. 4 (8-mm) plain tip. Pipe the batter in a spiral within each of the circles as described in Meringue Noisette (see Figure 12–2, page 592). Bake at 300°F (149°C) until the meringue is dry, about 45 minutes.

2. Line the bottom of a 10-inch (25-cm) cake pan with baking paper (or grease and flour but do not grease and flour the sides). Sift the ground cinnamon with the flour when you make the sponge batter. Pour the batter into the pan. Bake at 400°F (205°C) for about 15 minutes or until done.

3. Brush melted coating chocolate on one side of the Japonaise bottoms. Place the Short Dough Bottoms on cardboard cake circles for support. Divide the red currant jelly between the Short Dough Bottoms and spread it out evenly. Place the Japonaise bottoms on top, with the chocolate side up.

4. Put 10-inch (25-cm) stainless-steel cake rings on top of the Japonaise and press lightly to seal. If you must use rings that are not stainless steel, line the inside with baking paper, acetate, or polyurethane strips to prevent the metal from staining the filling. As soon as it begins to thicken, divide the Macaroon-Maraschino Whipped Cream filling equally between the two cakes.

5. Cut the top of the sponge even, then cut it into two layers. Place the layers on top of the cream on each cake. Combine the orange juice and Maraschino liqueur. Brush the mixture over the sponge layers. Refrigerate the cakes until the cream is set, about 2 hours.

6. While the cakes are chilling, dip the macaroons halfway in melted dark coating chocolate.

7. Remove the cake rings and paper or plastic strips. Trim the sides of the cakes so that the Short Dough and Japonaise are even with the filling (see Figure 8–11, page 325). Whip the heavy cream and sugar to stiff peaks. Ice the top and sides of the cakes with a thin layer of the cream, saving some for decoration.

8. Cover the sides of the cakes with the crushed almonds (see Figure 8–5, page 296). Place a 6-inch (15-cm) plain cookie cutter in the center of the cakes. Sprinkle chocolate shavings inside the cutter, just thick enough to cover the cream. Mark or cut the cakes into the desired number of servings.

9. Place the remaining whipped cream in a pastry bag with a no. 5 (10-mm) plain tip. Pipe a small mound of cream at the edge of each slice. Place a macaroon on each whipped cream mound.

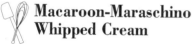

Macaroon-Maraschino Whipped Cream

3 pounds, 12 ounces (1 kg, 705 g) filling

10 ounces (285 g) dry Almond
    Macaroon Cookies (page 202)
¹/₂ cup (120 ml) Maraschino liqueur
2¹/₂ tablespoons (23 g) unflavored
    gelatin powder
¹/₂ cup (120 ml) cold water
1 quart (960 ml) heavy cream
6 egg yolks (¹/₂ cup/120 ml)
3 ounces (85 g) granulated sugar
¹/₃ cup (80 ml) milk

*T*his is a good opportunity to use up some leftover or dry Macaroon Cookies. If you make them fresh just for this recipe, bake the macaroons at a lower temperature until they are dried all the way through to prevent them from falling apart when they are mixed with the cream.

1. Cut the macaroons into ¹/₂-inch (1.2-cm) pieces. Place in a bowl and add the Maraschino liqueur, tossing the pieces to coat evenly. Set aside.

2. Sprinkle the gelatin over the cold water and set aside to soften.

3. Whip the heavy cream to soft peaks and reserve in the refrigerator.

4. Whip the egg yolks and sugar just to combine. Add the milk, set the bowl over a bain-marie, and continue to whip until the mixture reaches 140°F (60°C) and is light and fluffy. Remove from the heat and whip until completely cooled. Fold the yolk mixture into the reserved whipped cream.

5. Place the gelatin mixture over a bain-marie and heat to dissolve. Rapidly add the gelatin to a small portion of the cream. Still working quickly, add this mixture to the remaining cream. Fold in the soaked macaroon pieces.

Strawberry Kirsch Cake

two 10-inch (25-cm) cakes

one 10-inch (25-cm) Chiffon Sponge
  Cake (page 272)
two 10-inch (25-cm) Short Dough
  Cake Bottoms (page 55)
4 ounces (115 g) strawberry jam
1/3 cup (80 ml) Simple Syrup
  (page 11)
1/4 cup (60 ml) kirschwasser
  (see note 1)
2 pounds (910 g) medium-sized
  stemmed strawberries (about fifty)
Kirsch Whipped Cream
  (recipe follows)
Vanilla Buttercream (page 978)
5 ounces (140 g) sliced almonds,
  toasted and finely crushed
10 ounces (285 g) Marzipan
  (page 1022), untinted
powdered sugar
Piping Chocolate (page 904), melted
Strawberry Sauce (page 1081)
Sour Cream Mixture for Piping
  (page 1081)
small mint sprigs

NOTE 1: I have seen the word kirschwasser
*incorrectly used on products which are actually
a liqueur. True kirschwasser is a spirit and is
not sweet. If you substitute a kirsch liqueur,
replace the Simple Syrup with water.*

*NOTE 2: This cake should not be frozen
because the strawberries will lose their texture
and become unpleasant-looking when thawed.*

*T*his cake signifies the arrival of spring in many European countries. Or I
*suppose I should say it did in the past: This has changed in recent years as
the cost of flying in fresh strawberries from the other side of the equator during
our winter months has become less expensive. I suppose this is a change for the
better, but it sure takes some of the romance out of many pastries. It used to be
that we would get the first fresh strawberries (usually from Italy) in April, and
then as the spring oh-so-slowly made its way north, our strawberries were ready
to pick in Sweden at the end of June—just in time for the midsummer festivities.
As soon as this cake was put into the display case, all the customers would
change their mind from whatever they had come into the* konditori *to buy in the
first place. Some shops made the cakes in long (1 to 2 meter) strips that were
displayed whole in a showy fashion. These were then cut to order and priced by
the centimeter. In the case of the long strips, the buttercream and almonds were
omitted from the sides. You may want to leave them off of the round cakes as
well to save time and effort. If so, pay extra attention to the edges of the sponge
when brushing or spraying with the kirsch syrup.*

1. Cut the skin from the top of the Sponge Cake, cutting it even at
the same time. Slice the sponge into four thin layers.

2. Place the Short Dough Cake Bottoms on cardboard cake circles
for support. Divide the jam between them and spread it out evenly.
Place one of the sponge layers on the jam on each cake bottom. Combine the Simple Syrup with the kirschwasser. Brush or spray some of
the mixture over the sponge layers. Place a 10-inch (25-cm) stainless-
steel cake ring snugly around each cake. If you must use rings that are
not stainless steel, line them with strips of acetate, polyurethane, or
baking paper to prevent the metal from discoloring the filling.

3. Cut enough strawberries in half lengthwise (pick the nicest looking ones) to line the inside of each ring (you will need approximately 32
halves per cake). Place them stem-end down with the cut side against
the rings. Divide the remaining whole strawberries between the cakes,
placing them evenly over the sponges, points up (Figure 8–18).

4. Divide the Kirsch Whipped Cream between the cakes. The
cream should be just starting to set up before you pour it over the
strawberries or it will run between the cut strawberries and the ring
ruining the appearance of the cakes. Place the remaining two sponge
cake layers on top of the cream filling. Brush or spray the remaining
Simple Syrup mixture over the sponge layers. Refrigerate the cakes
until the filling is set, at least 2 hours.

5. Remove the rings and the paper or plastic strips. Trim away any
excess Short Dough to make the sides of the cakes even (see Figure
8–11, page 325). Cut two new strips of baking paper, wide enough to
cover the strawberries on the sides of the cakes, leaving the top and
bottom sponges exposed. Wrap the paper strips around the strawberry
layers, making sure you are not covering the sponge on the top or the
bottom. Make a mark on the cardboards where the ends of the paper
meet so you will be able to find them easily later.

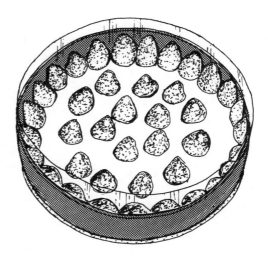

FIGURE 8–18   *Strawberry halves placed on top of the sponge cake with the cut sides against the cake ring and whole strawberries arranged in the center for Strawberry Kirsch Cake*

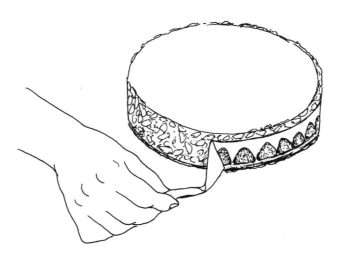

FIGURE 8–19   *Removing the strip of baking paper after icing the sides of the cake to reveal the cut strawberries and the filling layer in the center of the cake*

6. Ice the tops and the sides of the cakes, including the protective paper, with a thin layer of Vanilla Buttercream. Cover the the sides of the cakes with crushed almonds (see Figure 8–5, page 296), getting as few as possible on the paper strips. Carefully pull off the paper strips (Figure 8–19). Do not refrigerate the cakes before removing the paper.

7. Roll out half of the Marzipan ⅛ inch (3 mm) thick, using powdered sugar to prevent it from sticking. Place the Marzipan on a cake cardboard and cut out a circle the same size as the top of the cake. Repeat to make a Marzipan circle for the second cake. Carefully slide the circles onto the tops of the cakes (see example at Figure 8–17, page 353).

8. Cut or mark the cakes into the desired number of serving pieces. Decorate the top of each slice with the Piping Chocolate (see Figure 17–21, page 908; the designs in the third row would be the most appropriate).

9. Presentation: Place a slice of cake off-center on a dessert plate. Pour or pipe a round pool of Strawberry Sauce next to the slice. Use a spoon or the piping bottle to form the sauce into a strawberry shape. Decorate the sauce with the sour cream mixture (see pages 998 to 1006). Place a mint sprig at the "stem end" of the sauce.

Kirsch Whipped Cream

7 cups (1 l, 680 ml) filling

2 tablespoons (18 g) unflavored
    gelatin powder
1 cup (240 ml) dry white wine
5 cups (1 l, 200 ml) heavy cream
4 egg yolks (¹/₃ cup/80 ml)
4 ounces (115 g) granulated sugar
¹/₄ cup (60 ml) kirschwasser

NOTE: Do not make the filling until you are ready to use it.

1. Sprinkle the gelatin over half of the wine and set aside to soften.

2. Whip the cream to soft peaks and reserve in the refrigerator.

3. Whip the egg yolks and sugar until just combined. Add the remaining wine and the kirschwasser and whip over a bain-marie until the mixture reaches 140°F (60°C) and is light and fluffy. Remove from the heat and whip until cold. Fold the yolk mixture into the reserved whipped cream.

4. Place the gelatin mixture over a bain-marie and heat until dissolved. Do not overheat.

5. Rapidly mix the gelatin into a small part of the cream and egg yolk mixture. Still working quickly, mix this into the remaining cream.

Swiss Kirsch Cake (*Zuger Kirsch Torte*)

two 10-inch (25-cm) cakes

one recipe Japonaise Meringue Batter
    (page 591)
1¹/₄ cups (300 ml) Simple Syrup (page
    11)
³/₄ cup (180 ml) kirschwasser
¹/₂ teaspoon (2.5 ml) Beet Juice
    (page 3)
one-half recipe or 2 pounds, 10
    ounces (1 kg, 195 g) Vanilla
    Buttercream (page 978)
one 10-inch (25-cm) Chiffon Sponge
    Cake (page 272)
powdered sugar
Cherry Cookies (instructions follow)
Cherry Compote (page 452)
    (see note 2)

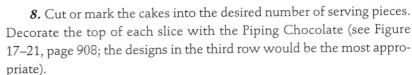

*Z*uger Kirsch Torte, also known simply as Zug Torte, was named after the medieval Swiss town of Zug located near the northern end of the Zuger Sea (perhaps a bit too near, as part of the town sank in 1435, 1594, and again in 1887). A wonderful time to visit this area is in the early spring when the cherry trees are in bloom and the tourist season hasn't officially started. You can hardly find a konditori in this region, or for that matter Switzerland, that does not have some version of this diet busting dessert with its delicious combination of kirschwasser-soaked sponge, thin crisp layers of meringue, and a covering of kirsch-flavored buttercream. Add to that the practicality of this cake, which can be made several days ahead and then finished quickly, and it is not hard to understand why Zuger Kirsch Cake is a hit with both the consumer and the konditor.

1. Pipe the Japonaise Meringue Batter into four 10-inch (25-cm) circles, following the instructions for Meringue Noisette (see Figure 12–2, page 592). Bake at 300°F (149°C) for approximately 30 minutes or until dry and golden. Set aside to cool.

2. Combine the Simple Syrup and kirschwasser. Add half of the mixture, together with the Beet Juice, to the buttercream. Stir until completely incorporated. Reserve the remaining syrup mixture.

3. Cut the skin from the top of the Sponge Cake and cut the top even at the same time. Cut the cake into two layers.

NOTE 1: *This is an excellent cake to prepare ahead, as it can be stored covered in the refrigerator for up to four days. However, do not add the powdered sugar and cookie decoration until the day the cakes will be served.*

NOTE 2: *Omit the ground black pepper from the Cherry Compote recipe.*

FIGURE 8–20   *Using a serrated cake-decorating comb to mark horizontal lines on the sides of Swiss Kirsch Cake, by holding the comb against the cake while rotating the cake-decorating turntable*

4. Place two of the Japonaise circles on cardboard cake rounds for support. Spread a ¹/₄-inch (6-mm) layer of buttercream on each one. Brush some of the reserved syrup mixture over the two sponge layers, then invert them syrup-side down, onto the buttercream. Press down lightly so they adhere. Brush as much of the remaining syrup as needed over the top and sides of the sponges so that the syrup throughly penetrates the cake. Spread a ¹/₄-inch (6-mm) layer of buttercream over the sponges. Place the remaining Japonaise circles on top of the buttercream layer flat-side up. Refrigerate the cakes until the buttercream is firm.

5. Trim any Japonaise that protrudes outside the sponge on the sides of the cakes to make the sides even (see Figure 8–11, page 325). Ice the top and sides of the cakes with a thin layer of buttercream, using just enough to cover the sponge. You should have a small amount of buttercream left to use in decorating. Mark the sides of the cakes with horizontal lines using a serrated cake-decorating comb (Figure 8–20). Mark the tops of the cakes in a diamond pattern, using either a diamond template or by using the back of a long knife to mark parallel lines every ¹/₂ inch (1.2 cm), first in one direction, and then again at a 45° angle. Refrigerate the cakes to set the buttercream.

6. Sift powdered sugar lightly over the tops of the cakes. Cut or mark the cakes into the desired number of servings. Place the remaining buttercream in a pastry bag with a no. 4 (8-mm) plain tip. Pipe a small dot of buttercream at the wide end of each slice. Place a Cherry Cookie on the buttercream dots (see note 1). Serve with Cherry Compote if using as a plated dessert.

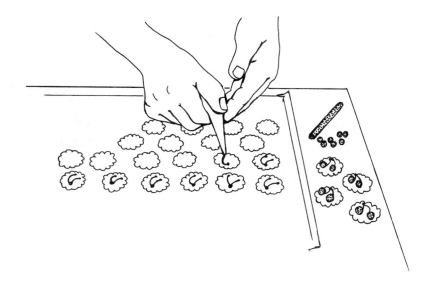

FIGURE 8–21   Piping cherry stems on the Short Dough cookies to decorate the Swiss Kirsch Cake; the completed cookies after adding the Marzipan cherries on the right

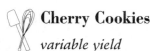 **Cherry Cookies**

variable yield

2 ounces (55 g) Short Dough (page 54)

1 ounce (30 g) Marzipan (page 1022), colored red

Piping Chocolate (page 904), melted

1. Roll the Short Dough out to ¹/₈ inch (3 mm) thick, using flour to keep it from sticking. Cut out one cookie for each serving of cake, using a 1¹/₄-inch (3.1-cm) fluted round cookie cutter. Place the cookies on a sheet pan lined with baking paper.

2. Bake at 375°F (190°C) until golden brown, approximately 10 minutes. Let the cookies cool completely.

3. Roll the Marzipan into a ¹/₄-inch (6-mm) rope. Slice the rope into pea-sized pieces, making two for each cookie. Roll the pieces into round balls and set aside.

4. Place the Piping Chocolate in a piping bag and cut a small opening. Pipe two cherry stems on each cookie. Pipe the lines so that the stems are attached at the top, curve toward the outside, and are separate at the bottom (Figure 8–21). Place one of the reserved Marzipan cherries at the end of each stem before the chocolate sets up. If you are making a large number of these decorations, pipe all of the stems, then go back and add a tiny drop of chocolate at the bottom to attach the cherries. Store the cookies covered in a dry place until needed.

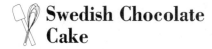 **Swedish Chocolate Cake**

two 10-inch (25-cm) cakes

two 10-inch (25-cm) Chocolate Sponge Cakes (page 270)

³/₄ cup (180 ml) Plain Cake Syrup (page 10)

T his is one of the recipes from the konditori *where I was an apprentice. It is simply the way a chocolate layer cake was made in my hometown. And for good reason, it would seem, because I have received compliments from customers and guests over the course of many years wherever I have made it. The main difference between this cake and the multitude of other chocolate cakes around to choose from is that this one is not overbearingly rich. The Pastry Cream, in addition to adding a pleasant moist flavor, offsets the Chocolate Buttercream, making it less overwhelming, especially to those who are watching their diet.*

1 pound, 12 ounces (795 g) Pastry
 Cream (page 1088)

2 pounds, 10 ounces (1 kg, 195 g)
 Chocolate Buttercream (page 977)

dark curled chocolate shavings

Chocolate Squares (page 890)

4-by-1-inch (10-×-2.5-cm) Chocolate
 Rectangles (page 890)

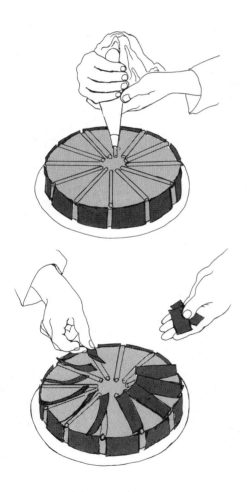

Probably the ultimate kudo I received for this cake came to me indirectly from the guests of a large hotel in Oslo, Norway. One of my former students, a Norwegian woman who apprenticed under me here in the United States and then moved back to Norway, returned for a visit and proudly told me that she was now in charge of the desserts in one of the hotel's restaurants. She said she was featuring, among other things, my Swedish Chocolate Cake and that it was a big hit. Taking into consideration the well-known (but not too serious) old feud between the two countries, I said I was surprised she could even sell one slice. She responded with a sly smile saying "No offense Chef Bo, but I left the Swedish part out of the title!"

1. Cut the skin off the chocolate sponges, cutting the tops even at the same time. Cut each into three layers. Use the bottom layers as the base for each cake.

2. Brush some of the Cake Syrup over the bottom cake layers. Place half of the Pastry Cream on each one and spread out evenly. Place the second cake layers on the cream and brush with Cake Syrup. Spread a ¼-inch (6-mm) layer of Chocolate Buttercream on the second cake layers. Place the remaining cake layers on top and brush with Cake Syrup.

3. Ice the top and sides of the cakes with Chocolate Buttercream, spreading it just thick enough to cover the sponge. Reserve some buttercream for decoration. Refrigerate the cakes until the buttercream is firm so that the cakes will slice cleanly.

4. Put the reserved buttercream in a pastry bag with a no. 4 (8-mm) plain tip. Making one decoration for each serving of cake, pipe a small mound of buttercream, about the size of a cherry half, onto a sheet pan lined with baking paper. Cover the mounds with curled chocolate shavings. Refrigerate the decorations until they are firm.

5. Cut the cakes into the desired number of slices. Place a Chocolate Square on the side of each piece. Pipe a straight line of buttercream next to one cut side on the top of each piece (Figure 8–22). Place a Chocolate Rectangle standing at an angle on each slice, supported by the buttercream lines and angled slightly toward the center of the cake, as shown in the illustration. Place one of the reserved decorations at the end of each slice.

FIGURE 8–22 Piping Chocolate Buttercream lines on top of Swedish Chocolate Cake; placing the Chocolate Rectangles at an angle against the buttercream lines

Tropical Mousse Cake

16 servings

Passion Fruit Jelly (recipe follows)

one-third recipe Cocoa Almond Sponge batter (page 271)

Passion Fruit Mousse Filling (recipe follows)

2 tablespoons (30 ml) light rum

¼ cup (60 ml) papaya or other tropical fruit juice

Strawberry Sauce (page 1081)

sixteen strawberry halves, fanned

thirty-two mint sprigs

Sour Cream Mixture for Piping (page 1081)

*T*he small black seeds in passion fruit are completely edible, although they are a little harder than what we are used to eating when compared with other fruits such as raspberries, strawberries, and the one I use in the variation of this recipe, kiwi (see page 366). You may be tempted to strain them out of the Passion Fruit Jelly, as is done when making the filling. This is up to you; they are left in as a purely decorative measure so the only impact will be to give the final product a less interesting appearance.

This recipe can alternatively be made into two 7-inch (17.5-cm) round cakes. Line the round cake pans with baking paper and divide the sponge batter between them. Bake a little longer than directed for the sponge sheet. Cut the skin from the top of the sponges and cut the tops even at the same time. Slice each sponge into two layers. For the jelly, stretch heavy plastic wrap tightly around two 10-inch (25-cm) cardboard cake rounds. Place 7-inch (17.5-cm) stainless-steel cake rings on top. Seal by pressing a thin rope of Short Dough (or whatever you have on hand) around the outside edge. Assemble the cakes as described in the main recipe. After the cakes have set and are unmolded, whip 1 cup (240 ml) of heavy cream with 1 teaspoon (5 g) of granulated sugar and finish the cakes by piping the whipped cream on the sides, using either a flat ¾-inch (2-cm) tip or a no. 4 (8-mm) plain tip.

1. Stretch a sheet of plastic wrap tightly over a sheet of corrugated cardboard or an inverted sheet pan (make sure the sheet pan has an even surface). Make a frame by first cutting two strips of corrugated cardboard 2 inches wide by 20 inches long (5 × 50 cm). Then cut a straight line halfway through the cardboard in the center across the width of each strip, bend the strips from the uncut side at a 90° angle, and tape the corners together to form a 10-inch (25-cm) square. Place the frame on top of the plastic sheet. If the bottom of the frame does not sit tight against the plastic, the jelly will run out, so weigh it down by placing a heavy object on the corners. Or, better yet, roll some Short Dough or nontoxic modeling clay into a rope and press it against the outside bottom edge of the frame to seal. Set the frame aside.

2. Make the Passion Fruit Jelly, let it start to thicken slightly, then pour it over the bottom of the frame. Chill in the refrigerator until set, about 30 minutes.

3. Make the sponge batter. Immediately spread the batter into a 12-by-22-inch (30-×-55-cm) rectangle. Bake at 400°F (205°C) for about 10 minutes or until just done. Let the sponge sheet cool. Cut in half crosswise and trim the pieces to fit inside the frame.

4. Spread half of the mousse filling evenly on top of the jelly. Top with one of the sponge sheets. Combine the rum and fruit juice and brush half of the mixture over the sponge. Spread the remaining mousse filling on top of the sponge, then set the second sponge sheet on the filling. Brush the remaining fruit juice mixture over the sponge. Refrigerate for at least 3 hours to set the filling.

5. Place a sheet pan or a sheet of cardboard on top of the frame and then invert the cake. Remove the other sheet pan or cardboard and the plastic wrap. Using a thin, sharp knife dipped in hot water, cut around the inside of the frame and remove the frame. Trim the sides if necessary, and then cut the cake into four equal strips approximately 2¼ inches (5.6 cm) wide. Cut each strip into four squares.

6. **Presentation:** Place a serving in the center of a dessert plate. Pipe Strawberry Sauce around the dessert to cover the plate. Place a fanned strawberry half and two mint sprigs in front of the cake. Decorate the Strawberry Sauce with the Sour Cream Mixture for Piping (see pages 998 to 1006), making a half circle behind the cake.

Passion Fruit Jelly

1 cup (240 ml)

1½ teaspoons (5 g) unflavored gelatin powder

½ cup (120 ml) papaya or other tropical fruit juice

⅓ cup (80 ml) passion fruit pulp

1½ ounces (40 g) granulated sugar

NOTE: If you do not want the seeds in the jelly, strain the mixture before adding the gelatin.

1. Sprinkle the gelatin over half of the fruit juice and set aside to soften.

2. Stir the passion fruit pulp into the remaining fruit juice. Add the sugar and bring to a full boil in a saucepan.

3. Remove from the heat, add the softened gelatin, and stir until the gelatin is dissolved. Skim any foam from the surface. Cool until the mixture just begins to thicken before using.

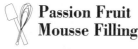 Passion Fruit Mousse Filling

10 cups (2 l, 400 ml)

2½ tablespoons (23 g) unflavored gelatin powder

2 cups (480 ml) papaya or other tropical fruit juice

1 pound (455 g) passion fruit (about eighteen medium-sized)

one-quarter recipe Italian or Swiss Meringue (pages 591 and 592)

2½ cups (600 ml) heavy cream

1 cup (240 ml) unflavored yogurt

1. Sprinkle the gelatin over ½ cup (120 ml) of the fruit juice to soften.

2. Cut the passion fruits in half and scoop out the pulp and seeds to make ¾ cup (180 ml). Stir in the remaining 1½ cups (360 ml) of fruit juice. Bring to a full boil. Remove from the heat and strain to remove the seeds.

3. Add the softened gelatin to the hot liquid and stir until dissolved. Set aside.

4. Make the meringue and set aside.

5. Whip the cream to soft peaks. Fold into the yogurt. Fold the yogurt and cream into the reserved meringue. Make sure it is not too warm or the cream will break, then quickly add the gelatin mixture to a small amount of the cream mixture, and then add this back to the remainder, still mixing rapidly. If necessary, cool the mousse until it starts to thicken before using, but do not make the mousse until you are ready to use it in the cake.

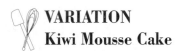

VARIATION
Kiwi Mousse Cake

Although passion fruit is certainly more tropical and unusual, its season is rather short. By substituting kiwis when passion fruit is not in season, you can make this delicious cake any time of the year. You will need one regular-sized kiwi to make the jelly and four for the filling (you should have 1 cup/240 ml of kiwi pulp for the mousse filling). Use only fully ripe kiwis. Remove the skin, purée or mash the fruit, and use as directed in the recipes. Using blood orange juice instead of papaya or tropical fruit juice produces a very attractive color when used with either kiwi or passion fruit in both the jelly and the mousse filling.

White Chocolate Pumpkin Cheesecake

two 10-inch (25-cm) or four 7-inch (17.5-cm) cakes

Crust

12 ounces (340 g) Graham Cracker Crumbs (page 8)

4 ounces (115 g) finely ground almonds

1 teaspoon (2 g) ground ginger

1 teaspoon (1.5 g) ground cinnamon

6 ounces (170 g) melted unsalted butter, approximately

Filling

2 pounds, 6 ounces (1 kg, 80 g) cream cheese, at room temperature

1 pound (455 g) white chocolate, melted

6 eggs

¼ cup (60 ml) pure maple syrup

¼ cup (60 ml) brandy

2 teaspoons (4 g) ground ginger

2 teaspoons (3 g) ground cinnamon

1 teaspoon (2 g) ground nutmeg

1½ cups (360 ml) canned or freshly cooked pumpkin purée (page 809)

Topping

2 pounds, 8 ounces (1 kg, 135 g) sour cream

6 ounces (170 g) granulated sugar

2 tablespoons (30 ml) pure maple syrup

2 tablespoons (30 ml) brandy

2 tablespoons (30 ml) pumpkin purée

This delicious cheesecake almost didn't make it into the second edition of this book due to a misunderstanding and too much assumption on my part. As we were in the very final stages of sending the galleys back and forth between my home and the person doing the page layout in Boston, I asked my wife, Amy, to print a copy of the Pumpkin Cheesecake recipe from the manuscript. To my horror, she responded by saying, "I don't think it's in there; I thought you wanted to leave it out." I explained that this terrific hybrid descendant of my basic cheesecake was an absolute must and that we had to try hard to get it included. After conferring with the editor we were told the typesetting was done and that it was too late to change anything. There was no way to place the recipe in its proper alphabetical order (after Princess Cake); however, by pure luck, there was an extra one and one half pages at the end of the cake chapter and the recipe could be placed there. This is where the idea for the addition of white chocolate was born. By adding the white chocolate, making a few other changes, and renaming the cake, it not only kept the recipes in the right order, it improved an already great dessert! I make this cake all year round as a nice change of pace from time to time, but it is at the holidays that it really stands out as a welcome alternative to the more traditional offerings. The smaller 7-inch (17.5-cm) size often makes sense since cheesecakes are not only rich and filling they are expensive to produce.

1. Combine all of the ingredients for the crust. Divide the mixture between two 10-inch (25-cm) or four 7-inch (17.5-cm) springform pans. Use your hands to pat the crumbs in place covering the bottom of the pans. Set the pans aside.

2. Place the cream cheese in a mixer bowl and soften it by stirring on low speed with the paddle. Be careful not to overmix and incorporate too much air, as this will result in a dry and crumbly cheesecake. Stir the white chocolate into the cream cheese, then add the eggs gradually. Scrape the sides and bottom of the mixing bowl frequently to avoid lumps. Combine the maple syrup, brandy, spices, and pumpkin purée. Add this mixture to the cream cheese mixture, stirring only long enough to combine. Divide the batter between the prepared pans and spread it out evenly.

3. Bake at 325°F (163°C) for approximately 40 minutes (slightly less for the small cakes) or until the filling is set. The filling should

NOTE: For an elegant holiday presentation, make individual White Chocolate Pumpkin Cheesecakes using the template and instructions for Lingonberry Cheese Pudding (page 553). Bake at 375°F (190°C) as specified in the recipe for Lingonberry Cheese Pudding; the pumpkin cheesecakes will take slightly less time. Be careful not to overbake. Follow the presentation instructions in step twelve of Lingonberry Cheese Pudding, substituting Cranberry Coulis (page 1073) for the Lingonberry Sauce.

move in one mass inside the forms when shaken gently. If it moves more in the center than on the sides, continue baking. The cakes become firmer once they have cooled, so do not overbake or the cakes will crack on the surface and taste dry.

4. Combine all of the topping ingredients except for the pumpkin purée. Reserve 1/4 cup (60 ml) of the mixture and divide the remainder between the baked cakes. This can be done as soon as they come out of the oven if necessary, but pour the topping gently around the outside edges of the cakes to avoid denting the softer centers.

5. Combine the reserved sour cream mixture with the remaining 2 tablespoons (30 ml) of pumpkin purée and place in a pastry bag with a no. 2 (4-mm) plain tip. Pipe the decoration in a spiral pattern on the top of each cake, starting in the center. Run the back of a paring knife through the spiral starting in the center and pulling toward the edge of the pan to make a spiderweb pattern (see Figure 19–24, page 1001).

6. Bake the cakes at 400°F (205°C) for 8 minutes to set the topping. The topping will still look liquid but will set as it cools.

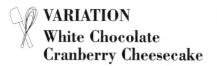

VARIATION
White Chocolate
Cranberry Cheesecake

*F*ollow the recipe and instructions for White Chocolate Pumpkin Cheesecake with the following changes:

- Omit the maple syrup
- Substitute 2 cups (480 ml) of canned puréed cranberry sauce (the thick type) or one recipe Cranberry Purée (page 300) for the pumpkin purée. Force 1/2 cup (120 ml) through a fine mesh strainer and stir into the reserved sour cream for the topping. Use the remaining 1 1/2 cups (360 ml) in the cake filling.

9

Individual Pastries

Almond Truffles	Lemon-Almond Tartlets	Hazelnut Flowers
Angelica Points	Linzer Tartlets	Macaroon Candies
Apple Mazarins	Macaroon Bananas	Miniature Palm Leaves
Battenburg	Mazarins	Strawberry Hearts
Chocolate Éclairs	Noisette Rings	Three Sisters
Chocolate Macaroons	Orange Truffle Cuts	Viennese Petits Fours
Chocolate Triangles	Othellos	Polynées
Citrons	Paris-Brest	Princess Pastries
Conversations	Petits Fours Glacé	Rainbow Pastries
Cream Horns	and Petits Fours	Rum Balls
Diplomats	Petits Fours Glacé	Sarah Bernhardts
Florentina Noisettes	Petits Fours	Small Saint-Honoré
Florentina Surprise	Petits Fours Sec	Swans
Fruit Tartlets	Almond Doubles	Swedish Napoleons
Fruit Waffles	Brandy Pretzels	Tosca
Hazelnut Nougat Slices	Chocolate-Filled	Trier Squares
Kirschwasser Rings	Macadamia Morsels	Walnut-Orange Tartlets
	Hazelnut Cuts	

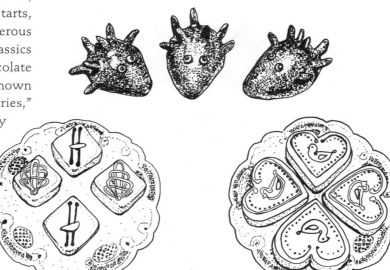

The term *pastries* includes small, decorated cuts of cakes or tarts, fancy individual pieces in numerous shapes, and the much larger classics such as Napoleons and Chocolate Éclairs. They are perhaps best known in this country as "French pastries," which is actually a misnomer (they are called *les petit gâteaux,* or "small cakes," in France), as they are tremendously popular all over Europe, and many other countries in Europe and elsewhere make elegant pastries which rival or surpass any made in France.

European Pastries

Each country in Europe has pastry specialties that vary in flavor and style. The variations are influenced to some degree by the climate: It is much easier to work with chocolate and whipped cream (and more pleasant to eat them) in the cooler northern part of Europe than in the heat of the Mediterranean. In southern France or Italy you will find a tendency (too often in my opinion) to use Fondant, candied fruits, and apricot glaze, which make the pastries very sweet. In the Scandinavian countries of northern Europe many pastries are made from almond, chocolate, and/or fresh fruit. Pastries topped with fresh fruit are typically covered with Pectin Glaze (a sugar syrup that develops a pleasant tart flavor when tartaric acid is added to it), which compliments the fruit nicely. A similar style is popular in Germany, Switzerland, and Austria.

When you enter a European pastry shop, called a *konditori* in Scandinavia, a *konditorei* in Austria, Germany, and Switzerland, and a *pâtisserie* in France, you see an amazing selection of pastries. They range from simple Mazarins and apple tartlets to the elegant Petits Fours Glacé. Certain larger pastries are intended for a single serving and require a fork or spoon to eat; examples of these are babas, cream puffs, and apple strudel. Many in this category can be offered as a plated dessert, in which case they are served with an appropriate sauce and garnish. Other pastries are small enough that you can consume two or three without guilt or calling attention to yourself. These are appropriately eaten with the fingers and include Petits Fours Sec and Petits Fours Glacé. In the same way that many Petits Fours can be made into larger single-portion pastries, many larger pastries can double as Petits Fours by simply cutting them into smaller pieces and perhaps enhancing the decoration a bit. A Petit Four by definition should be bite-size and elegantly decorated.

The pastries in this chapter are quite varied. Some must be started a day in advance of serving, while others can be made on the spur of the moment. Some have a plain finish, although many others require a bit of artistic ability. All of these recipes have proven to be very popular in this country, as I can attest from watching customers delight in my students' creations.

Final Steps

There is no question that individual pastries represent some of the most labor-intensive items in the bakeshop (although suggestions are given throughout to maximize your efforts whenever possible) and use primarily expensive ingredients such as Almond Paste, chocolate, nuts, and candied fruits. This makes it all the more critical to finish and store the pastries properly. It is a shame to go through the necessary steps to create perfect Florentina Surprise pastries, for example, and then dip them improperly so they end up with unprofessional looking rings of chocolate all around the bottom, or to create lovely little Petits Fours and then coat them with thick Fondant so that the multiple layers are obscured. Another step where it is important to pay close attention to the instructions is when pastries are sliced into individual pieces. Always use a sharp knife held at a 90° angle to achieve straight sides and uniform pieces. In some cases the directions call for cutting the pastry sheet upside down when it is topped with Marzipan, for example. This allows you to cut cleanly through the topping without marring the edges. Always be certain you invert the sheet onto a clean surface.

Temperature for Coating Chocolate

The final step in the majority of the following recipes calls for covering the finished pastries partially, or completely, with melted chocolate. Although in each case the instructions specify the use of coating chocolate, which simply has to be melted and does not require tempering, it is still critical to work with the chocolate at the proper temperature or you can ruin your efforts. The chocolate should generally be between 100 and 110°F (38–43°C), depending on the brand you are using. If the melted chocolate is too cold and therefore too thick, the result will be a clumsy looking, heavy coating which will not drape and conform to the shape of the pastry as it should, and your cost will be higher because you will be using more product. Conversely, coating chocolate that is too hot will lose its satin shine and will set up with a dull, somewhat lackluster finish instead. If the chocolate is too hot when dipping a pastry topped with buttercream, such as Chocolate Macaroons, part of the buttercream will melt, ruining both the shape of the pastry and the supply of chocolate.

Dipping Pastries in Chocolate

Whether you use coating chocolate or tempered chocolate to cover the pastries, you should create an organized and efficient workstation for dipping. If you are right-handed, always work from left to right: the undipped pastries on the left followed by the melted chocolate, a sheet of baking paper, and finally a sheet pan lined with baking paper to hold the finished pastries. Your left hand should pick up an undipped pastry as your right hand sets the dipped item down on the tray. When using a dipping fork, as is done with Tosca and Almond Truffles, the tool is inserted into the side of the pastry. After the item is dipped into the chocolate, it is moved up and down over the bowl of chocolate to force as much chocolate as possible off of the pastry to eliminate what are known as "feet"; excess chocolate that floats out around the pastry after it has been placed on the pan. After moving up and down, the bottom of the pastry is scraped against the side of the bowl and then blotted on the sheet of baking paper in a further effort to remove excess chocolate before finally setting it on the tray. When you remove the dipping fork from either of the two pastries mentioned you will leave a mark; this is unavoidable. As you remove the fork from the Tosca pastry you can use your free hand to hold the pastry in place if necessary since there is no chocolate on the top. This is not possible with the Almond Truffles since the entire pastry is covered with chocolate. Instead, press the bottom of the pastry firmly against the sheet pan as you pull the fork out. Sarah Bernhardts and Chocolate Macaroons, in which only the top part of the pastry is dipped in chocolate, require just a few up and down motions and perhaps a small scrape against the side of the bowl; they are not blotted on the paper. When the pastry is held with your fingers, as is the case with these two, it is very important not to leave fingerprints, which will happen if you hold on to the pastry too close to the chocolate. This is even harder to avoid with small, thin pastries such as Citrons. If you have trouble holding the pastry with your fingers, try using a dipping fork, or even a paring knife, inserted into the bottom of the barquette at an angle. This will provide a convenient handle, making them easier to manage. Simply pull the knife or fork out after setting the Citron chocolate-side up on the tray. You may need to use a finger on your free hand to steady the pastry as you pull out the knife or dipping fork; do not press down to free the tool as directed for Almond Truffles or you will break the crust.

Display

When preparing pastries to serve buffet-style, the items should be small enough that the guests can enjoy a variety. Most of the recipes in this chapter are portioned accordingly, but in some cases you may want to make them a little smaller either by piping or rolling them smaller to begin with—in the case of Othellos or Rum Balls, for example—or simply by cutting the pieces smaller for pastries such as Orange Truffle Cuts or Trier Squares. When creating a pastry display it is important to give some thought to your design as you choose the pastries to be prepared. Consider contrast of color, texture, flavor, and shape. Secondly, plan your arrangement before you start to place the items on the trays or mirrors to avoid moving them, which mars both the item and the display surface. Start to arrange the items as close as possible to serving time. U.S. Public Health Service guidelines require that highly perishable foodstuffs such as Pastry Cream and other dairy-based items are not kept at a temperature above 45°F (6°C) or below 140°F (60°C) for more than four hours. Two hours is about the maximum time for most pastries before they start to deteriorate in quality. If your buffet service is longer than two hours, you should plan to replenish the pastries during service.

The pastries should be displayed in rows, one item per row, evenly spaced, on a clean mirror or tray. Cut slices look best displayed in an angled row rather than parallel to one another. When using a round or oval mirror or tray, consider that you will need much more of the item placed around the outside edge when arranging the items in concentric circles, or of the item used in the center row when making straight lines across the diameter. In both instances this pastry will be the focal point of the platter, so plan to use something colorful and eye-catching. It is a good idea to wear food-handling latex gloves to avoid leaving fingerprints on chocolate-covered pastries as you move them. If you are creating a buffet for a small number of guests but must use a large table (in other words, the table might hold three mirrors but you only need to put out enough pastries for two), it looks better to use more trays and space the pastries further apart on each one, than to have a lot of empty tablecloth showing. Use care when transporting the assembled trays from the kitchen to the dining room. In some cases it makes sense to have an extra person walk ahead of you as a "lookout." The assembled trays or mirrors should be arranged on the table at varying heights and/or should be angled slightly by placing a few plates or another object under the edge farthest from the guest to avoid a flat table display.

If the guests will be helping themselves, it is a good idea to place the pastries in small paper cups. Known as petits fours cups, these containers are usually round but should be altered to fit individual shapes

FIGURE 9–1 Using a cookie cutter with the desired shape and diameter as a guide to mold paper petits fours cups

for the most finished appearance. This can be done by pressing a stack of cups with the appropriate size and shape of cookie cutter to enlarge the bottom (Figure 9–1) or by bending the sides to create a new bottom edge with your hands. If there is a server at the buffet table (or when a dessert tray is presented to the table after a meal), it is not necessary to use paper cups as the server should place the selection on the plate using a cake spatula or tongs.

Storage

Pastries based on Pâte à Choux or Puff Pastry, or those with a dairy-based filling, must be made up fresh every day. Other varieties that are covered wholly, or partially, with chocolate, Fondant, or Marzipan will keep fresh much longer and can be made once or twice a week, provided you have a storage area with the proper conditions. Storing some of the following pastries can present a problem at times if you have no other choice than the refrigerator, because of hot climate or lack of an alternate cold storage area. The moist air in the refrigerator will leave tiny droplets or a moist film on top of chocolate if the item is refrigerated for more than a few hours, and when the moisture dries it leaves an unpresentable finish. Pastries which are iced with Fondant, dipped in caramelized sugar, or covered with Marzipan do not develop the same unseemly spots that occur on chocolate, but the dampness causes the sugar or Marzipan to melt and become soggy. If you cannot store these pastries at cool room temperature, they should be stored unfinished in the refrigerator or freezer to decorate as needed. If this is not feasible, placing the pastries in a box before refrigerating will protect them from the moist air; you will still have to contend with the condensation that occurs after they are removed, but the appearance will be acceptable.

 Almond Truffles

30 pastries

10 ounces (285 g) Short Dough (page 54)

2 ounces (55 g) smooth apricot jam

2 pounds, 4 ounces (1 kg, 25 g) soft Mazarin Filling (page 1088)

12 ounces (340 g) Ganache (page 1086)

dark coating chocolate, melted

light coating chocolate, melted

candied violets (optional)

blanched pistachios (optional)

These are one of the best production-oriented pastries in this book. The chocolate coating seals in the moisture of the two fillings—the Ganache and the almond cake—which combine with the crisp Short Dough to make a very pleasing tidbit indeed.

You might want to consider doubling the recipe, since making a half-sheet really doesn't take much longer and, due to the magic of numbers, the larger size pan produces 70 pieces, giving you a bonus of 10 pastries. Cut the half-sheet into ten strips lengthwise in step five and cut each strip into seven equal slices in step seven.

Almond Truffles can be kept for one week with no loss of quality if stored covered in a cool location. If you must refrigerate them, it would be best to finish the pastries through step six only. They can then be refrigerated, well-wrapped, without any side effects or frozen for several weeks to finish as needed.

1. Roll the Short Dough out ⅛ inch (3 mm) thick. Line the bottom of a quarter-sheet pan (8 by 12 inches/20 × 30 cm) with baking paper.

Place the dough in the pan and trim the edges so only the bottom of the pan is covered. Save the Short Dough scraps for another use.

2. Spread the jam evenly over the dough, then spread the Mazarin Filling evenly on top.

3. Bake the sheet at 375°F (190°C) for about 30 minutes or until the filling is baked through.

4. When completely cold, preferably the next day, cut around the inside edge of the pan to loosen the cake, and then cut off the skin and even the top. It is easiest to do this by leaving the sheet in the pan and cutting the top using a serrated knife held parallel to the top of the cake; use the edge of the pan as a guide for your knife. Unmold onto an inverted sheet pan or cardboard. If the sheet does not separate easily from the pan, do not force it. Instead, place a hot sheet pan on the outside of the inverted pan and wait a few seconds. The heat will soften the fat in the Short Dough, which is making it stick, and the pan can then easily be removed.

5. Invert the sheet again so it is now right-side up. Trim one long side. Measure from this edge and cut into six equal strips lengthwise; they should be approximately 1¹/₄ inches (3.1 cm) wide. Separate the strips slightly.

6. Soften the Ganache, if necessary, and place in a pastry bag with a no. 8 (16-mm) plain tip. Pipe the Ganache in a long rope down the center of each strip. The Ganache should be soft enough to stick to the Mazarin but still hold its shape. Refrigerate until the Ganache is firm.

7. Trim the short ends and then cut each strip into five equal slices, approximately 2¹/₄ inches (5.6 cm) long, using a thin, sharp knife. Dip each slice into melted dark coating chocolate as described in the instructions for Tosca (see Figures 9–27 through 9–31, page 428), but unlike Tosca, dip the entire pastry in chocolate.

8. Streak thin lines of light coating chocolate over the tops for decoration. A small piece of candied violet or a half of a blanched pistachio is nice on top as further decoration. Attach these with a small dot of chocolate.

Angelica Points

45 pastries

1 pound, 5 ounces (595 g) Short
   Dough (page 54)

4¹/₂ ounces (130 g) smooth strawberry
   jam

6 ounces (170 g) candied angelica
bread flour

4 pounds, 10 ounces (2 kg, 105 g)
   Mazarin Filling (page 1088)

*M*any different small, simple pastries can be made up starting with the same base of Mazarin Filling baked on a Short Dough crust; each is then topped and decorated in its own way. Almond Truffles, Tosca, and Christmas Tree Pastries are a few examples in this text. If you do not need the full yield of this recipe, rather than dividing it in half, make the full amount and use the extra for another variation or freeze it to use next time.

If you have not cut this triangle shape before I recommend that you measure, mark, and cut as directed to get the proper angle. Attempting it freehand is unlikely to produce precise, professional-looking pastries.

1. Line the bottom of a half-sheet pan (16 by 12 inches/40 × 30 cm) with baking paper. Roll the Short Dough out to ¹/₈ inch (3 mm) thick

2 ounces (55 g) Vanilla Buttercream
(page 978)

1 pound (455 g) Marzipan (page 1022),
untinted

dark coating chocolate, melted

Piping Chocolate (page 904), melted

and slightly larger than the bottom of the pan, and place in the pan. Trim the edges so only the bottom of the pan is covered. Cover and save the scraps for another use. Spread the jam over the Short Dough. Reserve enough of the nicest-looking angelica pieces to make forty-five small decorations. Chop the remainder of the angelica into small pieces. Toss with a little bread flour to prevent them from sticking together and then mix into the Mazarin Filling. Spread the Mazarin Filling out evenly over the jam.

2. Bake at 375°F (190°C) until baked through, about 40 minutes. Cool to room temperature; then refrigerate.

3. When the Mazarin sheet is cold (preferably the day after baking), cut off the skin and even the top of the sheet. To do this, leave the Mazarin sheet in the pan and cut with a serrated knife held parallel to the top of the cake, using the edge of the pan as a guide for your knife. Run the tip of the knife around the inside edge of the pan and then invert the sheet to unmold. If the bottom of the sheet sticks to the pan do not force it. Instead, place a hot sheet pan on the outside for a few seconds to soften the fat in the Short Dough, and then try again. Remove the sheet pan and the baking paper and turn the sheet right-side up. Spread a thin film of buttercream on top of the Mazarin Filling.

4. Roll the Marzipan out to ⅛ inch (3 mm) thick; it should be slightly larger than the Mazarin sheet. Texture the Marzipan with a waffle roller. Roll it up on a dowel and unroll on top of the buttercream. Place a clean cardboard on top and invert. With the pastry upside down, trim away the excess Marzipan. Refrigerate until the buttercream is firm, but no longer than a few hours or the Marzipan will become sticky.

5. Still working with the pastry upside down, trim both long sides and then cut the sheet lengthwise into five strips, holding the knife at a 90° angle so that the edges are straight; a serrated knife or the very tip of a sharp chef's knife works best.

6. Trim the left short end of one strip to make it even. To achieve the correct angle in cutting the triangles mark the strip in the following manner: Beginning ⅞ of an inch (2.1 cm) to the right of the top left corner, mark the strip alternating every ¾ inch (2 cm) and 2½ inches (6.2 cm) for the length of the strip. Next make a mark 2½ inches (6.2 cm) away from the bottom left corner and alternate marking every ¾ inch (2 cm) and 2½ inches (6.2 cm) again along the bottom. Cut nine triangles from the strip following your marks. The triangles will be ¾ inch (2 cm) wide at the top and 2½ inches (6.2 cm) wide along the bottom. The trimmings can be saved to use in Rum Ball Filling. Repeat with the remaining strips.

7. Dip each triangle into melted dark coating chocolate, coating the bottom and sides up to the Marzipan (see Figures 9–27 through 9–31, page 428).

8. Place the Piping Chocolate in a piping bag. Pipe a figurine on top of each pastry as shown in the photograph of assorted individual pastries in the color insert pages.

9. Cut the reserved angelica into decorations in the same shape as the pastries (see photo in color insert). The angelica may be sticky enough to adhere to the pastries as is; if not, attach on top with a tiny bit of Simple Syrup. Do not attach by piping a dot of chocolate underneath because it will show through. Angelica Points will remain fresh for up to one week stored in a cool place but should not be refrigerated. If you must refrigerate them, they should be boxed and well wrapped to prevent the Marzipan from becoming wet.

Apple Mazarins

35 pastries

1 pound, 14 ounces (855 g) Short Dough (page 54)

one-third recipe Chunky Apple Filling (page 1085)

1 pound (455 g) Mazarin Filling (page 1088), soft

1 pound, 8 ounces (680 g) Streusel Topping (page 14)

powdered sugar

These are unpretentious, country-style pastries—a cross between Streusel Kuchen and, as the name suggests, Mazarins—they taste like a good wholesome slice of Swedish-style pie. The tops of the pastries are misted with water before baking to keep the Streusel from falling off as they are unmolded. Placing them in the refrigerator overnight will also help to hold the topping in place.

1. Line mazarin forms with Short Dough rolled to ⅛ inch (3 mm) thick (see Figures 2–15 through 2–18, pages 57 and 58). Cover the Short Dough scraps and save for another use.

2. Place the apple filling in a pastry bag with a no. 6 (12-mm) plain tip. Pipe the filing into the forms, filling them halfway.

3. Place the Mazarin Filling in the same pastry bag used for the apple filling, and pipe over the apple filling to the rim of the forms.

4. Top the pastries with a small mound of the Streusel (it is a good idea to prepare the Mazarins on one sheet pan and then transfer them to another, because it is impossible not to spill the Streusel around the forms). Spray the pastries with a fine mist of water.

5. Bake at 375°F (190°C) until golden brown, about 25 minutes. Let cool to room temperature.

6. When the pastries have cooled, carefully unmold each one while cupping your hand over the Streusel to hold it in place. Sift powdered sugar very lightly over the tops.

Battenburg

48 pastries

2 pounds, 5 ounces (1 kg, 50 g) or one-half recipe Mazarin Filling (page 1085)

red, yellow, and green food coloring

4 ounces (115 g) Vanilla Buttercream (page 978)

8 ounces (225 g) Marzipan (page 1022), untinted

I dug out this old-fashioned classic to add a bit of extra color to the buffet table. The idea is similar to Rainbow Pastries, another old-timer that never seems to go out of style, but here the color is added to the Mazarin Filling rather than to the buttercream. Battenburg pastries are quick and easy to prepare and can be kept for up to one week if stored well covered in the refrigerator. In this case, wrap Marzipan around only as many strips as you will need within a day or so, as the Marzipan gets soft and sticky from the moist air in the refrigerator (and the condensation after it is removed) even when well covered. Battenburg may be served standing up or laying flat, depending on your needs, but avoid placing the slices in paper cups since this will mask some of the colorful pastry.

1. Line two half-sheet pans (16 by 12 inches/40 × 30 cm) with baking paper. Cut two strips of corrugated cardboard 12 inches long by 1 inch wide (30 × 2.5 cm); the pieces should fit snugly crosswise in the pans. Wrap the cardboard strips in aluminum foil. Place the strips in the center of the pans, dividing each one in half. Set aside.

2. Divide the Mazarin Filling into three equal portions. Tint the portions pale pink, pale green, and pale yellow. Spread the batter perfectly even within three of the four sections of the prepared pans. (There will be one empty section; place a small weight in this section against the cardboard strip to hold the cardboard in place.)

3. Bake at 400°F (205°C) for approximately 20 minutes or until the center of the cakes springs back when pressed lightly. Let the cakes cool completely.

4. Carefully remove the cardboard dividing strips. Run a knife around the inside edge of the pans to loosen the sheets. Place a sheet pan or sheet of cardboard over the tops, then invert the pans to unmold the Mazarin sheets. Peel away the baking papers. Cut the skin from the tops and cut them even at the same time if necessary.

5. Reserve one-third of the buttercream. Spread half of the remaining buttercream on top of the pink cake; it should be about $^{1}/_{8}$ inch (3 mm) thick. Top with the yellow cake. Spread the remaining buttercream over the yellow cake. Place the green cake on top. Press down firmly to secure. Place the assembled 8-by-12-inch (20-×-30-cm) cake in the refrigerator. Chill until the buttercream is firm.

6. Trim one long side of the cake to make it even. Starting from this side, cut the cake into four $1^{3}/_{4}$-inch (4.5-cm) strips lengthwise.

7. Roll the Marzipan out to $^{1}/_{8}$ inch (3 mm) thick and as wide as the length of the strips, using powdered sugar to prevent it from sticking. Mark the top of the Marzipan with a waffle or ribbon roller. Trim the short side nearest you to make it even. Invert the Marzipan. Spread a thin film (not a layer) of the reserved buttercream on the back (now top) of the Marzipan. Place one of the cake strips at the trimmed edge and roll the strip 360° to encase it in Marzipan. Cut the strip free, and repeat to encase the other three cakes. Re-roll the Marzipan as needed. Refrigerate the strips just long enough to firm the buttercream.

8. Trim the short ends and then cut each strip of cake into 12 slices. Store the finished pastries tightly wrapped in a cool place. They will keep for two to three days. Do not refrigerate once you have enclosed the cakes in Marzipan.

Chocolate Éclairs

30 pastries

one-half recipe Pâte à Choux
(page 36)
Apricot Glaze (page 1016)
Chocolate Glaze (page 1016)
8 ounces (225 g) smooth strawberry
jam
one-half recipe Crème Parisienne
(page 1086)
    or
one-half recipe Chocolate Cream
(page 1084)

NOTE: If you are planning to freeze the éclairs before baking and you are making a large quantity, pipe them as close together as possible to conserve freezer space. If well covered they can be frozen for weeks without losing quality. Bake as needed without thawing.

If you have piped the éclairs next to one another as suggested, a good way to respace them on the sheet pan is this: Tap the pan firmly against the table to loosen the frozen éclairs. Place a second paper-lined pan next to you and quickly, using both hands, pick up every other éclair and transfer to the second pan. You must do this quickly because the Pâte à Choux will become sticky very fast. This technique can also be used with frozen Pâte à Choux piped for profiteroles.

É*clair literally means "lightening" in French. I don't know if this is a reference to the speed with which one will consume these irresistible filled choux pastries, or if it has to do with the reflection of light from the glaze on top. Unlike their equally well-known and popular close relative the cream puff, or profiterole, éclairs should always be topped with a sweet, shiny icing, typically Fondant, corresponding to the flavor of the filling. In the case of the best-known variety, Chocolate Éclairs, the tops are usually decorated with a rich Chocolate Glaze.*

The classical style of éclairs uses a plain tip when piping the Pâte à Choux. I was taught to use a star tip and, being stubborn, continue to do so. Use either according to your preference.

1. Place the Pâte à Choux in a pastry bag with a no. 8 (16-mm) star tip. Pipe out 4½-inch (11.2-cm) strips onto sheet pans lined with baking paper. Do not put more than 20 éclairs on a pan, because there must be enough space around them to bake thoroughly (see note).

2. Bake the éclairs at 425°F (219°C) until puffed and starting to color, about 10 minutes. Reduce the heat to 375°F (190°C), and continue baking until the éclairs are dry enough to hold their shape when you remove them from the oven, about 12 minutes longer. Let the éclairs cool.

3. Cut off the top third of each éclair and place on a separate sheet pan. Brush Apricot Glaze over the tops. Heat the Chocolate Glaze to make it fairly thin. When the Apricot Glaze has formed a skin (the one you brushed first should be ready by the time you finish the last one), dip the Apricot-Glazed side of the tops into the Chocolate Glaze. Reserve in the refrigerator.

4. Place the strawberry jam in a pastry bag with a no. 5 (10-mm) plain tip. Pipe a small ribbon of jam in the bottom of each éclair. Place the Crème Parisienne or Chocolate Cream in a pastry bag with a no. 6 (12-mm) plain tip. Pipe a coil of cream on top of the jam (Figure 9–2).

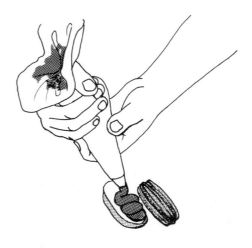

FIGURE 9–2 Piping chocolate filling in a coil shape over the base of an éclair shell

The coil shape makes the cream more visible in the final presentation. It should be at least a ¹/₂ inch (1.2 cm) higher than the base of the éclair.

5. Set the glazed tops on the cream at an angle so the filling shows nicely. Serve the éclairs as soon as possible, as the Pâte à Choux will become soggy and rubbery if left to stand too long. Try not to fill any more éclairs than you will serve within the next few hours.

Chocolate Macaroons

30 pastries

one-half recipe Almond Macaroon Cookies batter (page 202), see step one

1 ounce (30 g) cocoa powder

egg white, if necessary

1 pound, 12 ounces (795 g) Chocolate Buttercream (page 977)

dark coating chocolate, melted

thirty whole hazelnuts, toasted and skins removed

The word macaroon *derives from the French* macaron, *which in turn came from the Italian* maccarone, *used to describe a small cake containing almonds. History tells us that macaroons were made in France as early as the middle of the sixteenth century. They were probably introduced by Catherine de Médicis of Italy, who in 1533, when she was only fourteen years old, married the French Duke of Orléans, who later (in 1547) became King Henry II.*

The Almond Macaroon Cookies used as a base for these simple little pastries are the most common type of macaroon among the dozens of variations. All types of macaroons are made up of three primary ingredients: finely ground almonds (or other nuts including coconut), sugar, and egg whites. The ratio of almonds to sugar is usually 2:1, although a good quality and chewy texture can still be achieved with up to a 1:1 ratio. Macaroons made with a higher proportion of sugar will be lighter and will also be dry and crumbly unless the oven temperature is high enough so that they become baked on the outside while remaining slightly underdone (chewy) inside. Macaroons can be made up, baked, and frozen, still attached to their baking papers, for several weeks. They should be well wrapped. Placing the cookies in the freezer for a few minutes is also a quick and easy way to remove them cleanly from the baking paper if they stick and is a lot less messy than brushing the back of the paper with water.

These pastries are easy to vary: for example, instead of Chocolate Buttercream, flavor an equal amount of Vanilla Buttercream with ¹/₄ cup (60 ml) each of Grand Marnier and kirsch liqueurs. Mix in 2 ounces (55 g) of chopped Candied Orange Peel. Dip the finished pastries in light coating chocolate and decorate with a small piece of Candied Orange Peel. There are many other possible variations. Chocolate Macaroons can be kept in a cool place (ideally not the refrigerator) for up to one week. They must be well covered if they are refrigerated.

1. Sift the cocoa powder over the macaroon batter. Stir until well incorporated. Add egg white if the batter seems too firm. Place the batter (paste) in a pastry bag with a no. 8 (16-mm) plain tip. Line a sheet pan with baking paper and fasten the paper to the pan using a small dab of batter in the corners. Pipe the batter onto the paper making cookies that are 2¹/₂ inches (6.2 cm) long. As you pipe the cookies, hold the tip of the pastry bag close enough to the pan that the batter flattens slightly (becomes wider and lower than the size of the tip) rather than making ropes.

2. Bake immediately, following the instructions for Almond Macaroon Cookies, page 202.

FIGURE 9–3 Piping two pointed mounds of Chocolate Buttercream onto a Macaroon Cookie base for Chocolate Macaroons.

3. Let the cookies cool, then invert the paper and peel it away from the cookies. Arrange the cookies in rows on a sheet pan flat-side up. Press down lightly, if necessary, to flatten the tops (now the bottoms) so that the cookies do not wobble.

4. Place the Chocolate Buttercream in a pastry bag with a no. 7 (14-mm) plain tip. Pipe two small mounds on each cookie, wide enough to cover most of the surface and about ¹/₂ inch (1.2 cm) high (Figure 9–3). Refrigerate until the buttercream is firm.

5. Hold a cookie upside down touching only the edges of the macaroon, and dip it into melted dark coating chocolate, covering the buttercream mounds and the flat side of the macaroon. Move the cookie up and down a few times over the bowl to allow as much of the excess chocolate as possible to drip off, then place it (chocolate-side up) on a sheet pan. Repeat with the remaining cookies. Set a hazelnut between the buttercream mounds before the chocolate hardens.

 Chocolate Triangles

about 25 pastries

one ¹/₄-by-14-by-24-inch
    (6-mm-✕-35-✕-60-cm) Cocoa
    Almond Sponge (page 271)
    (see note)
1 cup (240 ml) Plain Cake Syrup
    (page 10)
1 pound, 6 ounces (625 g) Chocolate
    Buttercream (page 977)
10 ounces (285 g) Marzipan
    (page 1022), untinted
dark coating chocolate, melted
light coating chocolate, melted

NOTE: Ideally, the sponge sheet should be made ahead and either frozen or refrigerated to allow you to easily brush or scrape the skin from the top. This is very important and should be done before you cut the sponge strips or the skin will come away from the sponge after layering the sheets with buttercream, ruining your pastries. If the sponge is freshly baked, use a serrated knife to carefully cut the skin from the top.

*C*hocolate Triangles, or Chocolate Points as they are also known, are a must in any well-rounded European pastry selection. Not only does their radical change of layer direction make them eye-catching, the shape is also interesting, and they add height to the display. The size of the finished triangles is really an optical illusion, as I show in one of my demonstrations. I leave one strip of cake as it appears at the end of step three (before cutting in half diagonally) and finish it in the same way as the triangle, icing this piece with buttercream, covering it with Marzipan, and applying the coating chocolate. When the two strips are later sliced and displayed next to one another, the students can not believe that they started out (and actually are) the same size, except that they watched it happen! While the flat rectangular shape is not as intriguing as the triangle, it too is a classical French pastry configuration and can be made up using various flavors of sponge and filling.

You should not expect the triangles to come out exactly as you would hope for on your first try, since there is more than one thing that can go wrong. First and most important, the batter for the sponge sheet must be spread out thin and evenly, and the sponge strips must be layered with the buttercream in the same way. Keep in mind that the finished pastry will be the same height as the width of the strips before making the diagonal cut, and the base will be twice as wide as the height of the strip. Therefore, if the layers are too thick, the pastries will be large and awkward looking. Next, if the triangles are too cold when you apply the chocolate, it will set up too quickly leaving an uneven surface, and the coating will also be too thick, making it difficult to slice the pastries without breaking the chocolate.

1. When the sponge sheet is cold, cut it into four equal strips crosswise, leaving the baking paper attached. Invert one sponge strip and peel the paper from the back. Brush or spray some of the Cake Syrup over the sponge. Spread a ¹/₈-inch (3-mm) layer of buttercream on top.

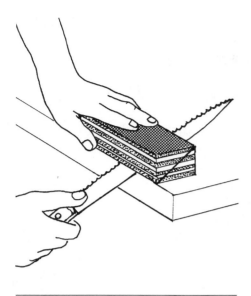

FIGURE 9–4 *Cutting the layered sponge and buttercream rectangle into two triangles*

2. Pick up a second sponge sheet, holding it by the paper, and invert it on top of the buttercream, lining up the edges evenly on one long side. Peel the paper from the back. Brush or spray with Cake Syrup and spread a layer of buttercream on top.

3. Add the remaining two sponge sheets in the same way, layering buttercream between them. Refrigerate until the buttercream is firm.

4. Trim the uneven long side of the layered sponge sheets. Cut in half lengthwise to create two strips, 14 inches (35 cm) long and approximately 2³/₄ inches (6.8 cm) wide.

5. Place one of the strips at the very edge of the table with the layers running horizontally. Using a long, serrated knife dipped in hot water, with the table edge as your guide, cut the strip in half diagonally, making two triangles (Figure 9–4).

6. Move the cut strip away from the edge and tilt the top piece toward you (Figure 9–5). Tilt the bottom piece in the opposite direction so both pieces have their layers running vertically (Figure 9–6). Turn the piece closest to you 180° so that the two uncut long sides are back to back. Place a dowel about 2 inches (5 cm) behind the strips and tilt the back piece onto the dowel.

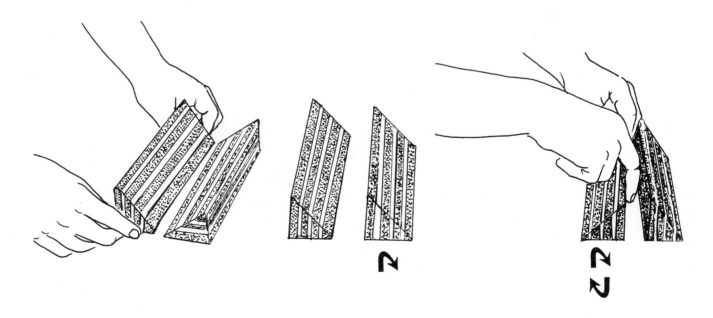

FIGURES 9–5, 9–6, and 9–7 *Arranging the triangles so that the sides which were on the top and bottom of the rectangle before it was cut become back to back, and the layers now run vertically instead of horizontally*

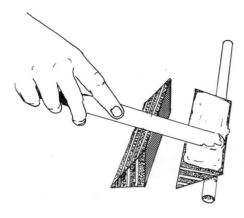

FIGURE 9–8 *Spreading a layer of butter-cream over one of the triangle halves after resting the piece on a dowel*

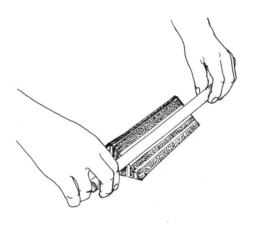

FIGURE 9–9 *Using the dowel to return the iced piece to its original position*

7. Spread a ¼-inch (6-mm) layer of buttercream on the back piece (Figure 9–8). Use the dowel to pick that piece up and put it back into place with the buttercream in the middle (Figure 9–9). Lightly press the two pieces together with your hands (Figure 9–10). Transfer the cake to one side of an inverted sheet pan topped with baking paper.

8. Repeat steps five through seven with the second cake, placing the finished triangle on the same sheet pan.

9. Ice the two exposed sides of the triangles with a thin film of buttercream.

10. Roll out the Marzipan (using powdered sugar to prevent it from sticking) to ¹/₁₆ inch (2 mm) thick, approximately 7 inches (17.5 cm) wide, and twice as long as one strip. Cut in half crosswise.

11. Roll one piece of Marzipan up on a dowel and unroll it over one of the strips. Press the Marzipan in place with your hands. Trim the excess Marzipan even with the bottom of the cake on the long sides (do not worry about covering the ends or trimming the Marzipan on the ends at this time). Cover the second cake with Marzipan in the same way.

12. Working on one cake at a time, spread a layer of melted dark coating chocolate over the Marzipan just thick enough to prevent the Marzipan from showing through (if the chocolate layer is too thick it will be difficult to cut the cake). Keep spreading the chocolate back and forth until it starts to set up. Repeat with the second cake.

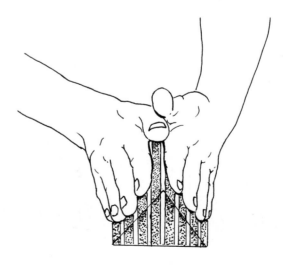

FIGURE 9–10 *Lightly pressing the two halves together*

13. Decorate both cakes by streaking light coating chocolate, crosswise, over the dark chocolate (see example in Figure 6–1, page 246).

14. Refrigerate the cakes just until the buttercream is firm (if you need to refrigerate them longer, make sure they are well covered).

15. Trim the ends and cut into 1-inch (2.5-cm) slices using a thin, sharp (or serrated) knife dipped in hot water.

Citrons

forty-five 3-inch (7.5-cm) pastries

---

1 pound, 8 ounces (680 g) Short Dough (page 54)

4 ounces (115 g) smooth strawberry jam

1 pound, 2 ounces (510 g) Mazarin Filling (page 1088), soft

granulated sugar

12 ounces (340 g) Vanilla Buttercream (page 978)

3 ounces (85 g) Lemon Curd (page 1087)

dark coating chocolate, melted

Marzipan (page 1022), colored yellow

Piping Chocolate (page 904), melted

NOTE: Citrons keep well for several days at normal room temperature; they should be well covered if refrigerated.

*T*his is just one of the many small boat-shaped pastries that are made using barquette molds. In other variations, the buttercream may be flavored with rum or praline. The tops are then dipped in appropriately flavored Fondant, and the pastries are decorated by artistically piping the name or flavor on top of the Fondant, or by attaching chocolate figurines. The same writing technique can be applied to the Citrons instead of writing on the strips of Marzipan; it is not as difficult as you might think to pipe directly on top of these crested pastries. Or do as one of my students: he wrote the word "lemon" instead, explaining that it had one less letter to worry about!

There is a good chance that the buttercream will break when you incorporate the Lemon Curd. To repair it, stir the mixture over hot water just until it is smooth again. When glazing these pastries, either with chocolate or with Fondant, it is easy to leave fingerprints while holding on to the base. This can be avoided by inserting the tip of a paring knife into the bottom of the pastry at a 45° angle and using this as a handle as you dip the top.

1. Line forty-five barquette forms, 3 inches long by ³/₄ inch high (7.5 × 2 cm), with Short Dough rolled to ¹/₈ inch (3 mm) thick (see Figures 2–15 through 2–18, pages 57 and 58). Cover the scrap dough and reserve for another use.

2. Make a disposable pastry bag from baking paper (see page 23). Place the jam in the cone and pipe a ribbon of jam in each form.

3. Place the Mazarin Filling in a pastry bag with a no. 6 (12-mm) plain tip. Pipe the filling into the forms on top of the jam, filling each two-thirds full.

4. Bake at 400°F (205°C) until golden brown, about 10 minutes.

5. As soon as you remove the tartlets from the oven, immediately sprinkle sugar over the tops, then turn the forms upside down on the pan so they will become flat on the top. Cool completely (upside down), then remove the forms.

6. Combine the buttercream and Lemon Curd. Place the mixture in a pastry bag with a no. 5 (10-mm) plain tip. Turn the barquettes right-side up and pipe a rope of buttercream straight down the center of each pastry. With a small metal spatula, spread both sides of the buttercream into a ridge in the center about ¹/₂ inch (1.2 cm) high (Figure 9–11). Refrigerate until the buttercream is firm.

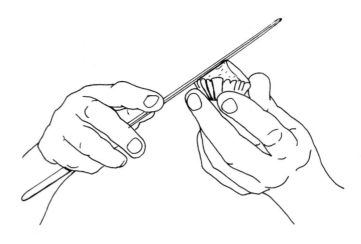

FIGURE 9–11 Using a small metal spatula to shape a piped rope of buttercream into a triangular ridge that will cover the top of a Citron pastry

7. Dip the tops of the pastries (the buttercream) into melted dark coating chocolate.

8. Roll out yellow Marzipan to ¹/₁₆ inch (2 mm) thick. Cut out 45 strips, 1³/₄ by ³/₈ inch (4.5 cm × 9 mm). Put the Piping Chocolate in a piping bag and use it to write "citron" on each strip. Pipe a thin diagonal line of chocolate on each pastry and place a Marzipan strip on top.

Conversations

40 pastries

1 pound, 12 ounces (795 g) Puff
  Pastry (page 44)
4 ounces (115 g) smooth apricot jam
Conversation Filling (recipe follows)
one-quarter recipe Royal Icing
  (page 1019) (see note)

NOTE: Make the Royal Icing without lemon juice and add 1 teaspoon (2.5 g) of cornstarch to the quarter recipe. Avoid overmixing the icing.

*T*hese pastries have an interesting and unusual appearance and an equally peculiar name—one I'm sure you will find they live up to. Curiosity gets the better of most people and they simply have to stop and ask "What are those pastries?" Before you know it, you're having a "conversation"!

If you do not have Puff Pastry on hand, substitute Pie Dough. The decorative strips on top will not have the same dramatic lift, but the overall effect is still good. The Royal Icing should be soft enough to spread easily but not at all runny. If it is too thin it will run between the dough and the form, ruining the appearance of the crust and making it very difficult to remove the pastries.

1. Roll the Puff Pastry out to a rectangle approximately 18 by 24 inches (45 × 60 cm); it should be slightly thinner than ¹/₈ inch (3 mm). Refrigerate the dough to relax and firm it.

2. Cut a 6¹/₂-inch (16.2-cm) strip from one short end of the chilled dough. Reserve this piece in the refrigerator. Use the remaining dough to line forty mazarin forms (see Figures 2–15 to 2–18, pages 57 and 58). Cover the scrap dough and reserve for another use.

3. Place the apricot jam in a disposable pastry bag made from baking paper (see page 23). Pipe the jam into the forms, dividing it evenly between them.

4. Place the Conversation Filling in a pastry bag with a no. 7 (14-mm) plain tip. Pipe the filling on top of the jam, filling the forms almost to the top. If the surface of the filling is not flat, use a small palette knife dipped in water to make it level. Place the forms in the freezer for 30 minutes to firm the top of the filling.

5. Cut the reserved Puff Pastry into three 2-inch-wide (5-cm) strips lengthwise. Leaving them in place on a sheet of cardboard, cut each strip across into ¹/₄-inch (6-mm) pieces. You need a total of 160—four per pastry. Place the cut pieces in the refrigerator.

6. Spread a thin layer of Royal Icing on top of the chilled filling. Decorate with the Puff Pastry strips, placing two parallel strips across the top, close to the edges of the form, and then two additional strips, at a 90° angle to the first set, forming a square in the center. Let sit at room temperature until the Royal Icing has formed a crust.

7. Bake at 400°F (205°C) for approximately 15 minutes.

1. Finely chop the orange peel and the angelica. Combine with the lemon zest and toss with a small amount of bread flour to keep the pieces from sticking together. Reserve.

2. Beat the egg yolks into the Almond Paste a few at a time to avoid lumps. Stir in the water and the reserved fruit mixture. Adjust the consistency as needed by adding water: the filling should be just soft enough to become level when it is piped into the forms.

Conversation Filling

*approximately 3 pounds
(1 kg, 365 g)*

3 ounces (85 g) Candied Orange Peel (page 978)
3 ounces (85 g) candied angelica
grated zest of one lemon
bread flour
8 egg yolks (²/₃ cup/160 ml)
2 pounds (910 g) Almond Paste (page 3)
¹/₄ cup (60 ml) water, approximately

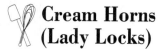

Cream Horns (Lady Locks)

20 pastries

1 pound, 8 ounces (680 g) Puff Pastry (page 44) (see note 1)
water for brushing
granulated sugar
5 ounces (140 g) strawberry jam
1¹/₂ cups (360 ml) heavy cream
1 tablespoon (15 g) granulated sugar
powdered sugar

NOTE 1: Ideally Quick Puff Pastry or Puff Pastry scraps should be used for Cream Horns. A dough with too much rise accentuates the problems described in note 2. If you do not have any dough scraps on hand, be sure to roll the dough thin.

C ream Horns, together with Cream Puffs, Chocolate Éclairs, and Napoleons, have been standard fare in pastry shops throughout Europe for many years. The ability to produce a properly baked and formed Cream Horn was one of the skills that had to be mastered before a young apprentice could even think about passing the all-so-important konditor's test when I was learning.

In addition to sometimes having to literally glue the Puff Pastry strips to the forms as discussed in note 2 it is important to roll the tip of the strips fairly loose. If too tight they will crack and break along the side. The same thing can happen if the dough is not allowed to rest sufficiently before baking. Be certain the oven is hot enough so the sugar will melt and caramelize on top. Unfilled baked shells can be stored covered in a dry place for several days. Reheating the shells (and then cooling them before adding the filling) will ensure a fresh-tasting pastry.

1. Roll the Puff Pastry out to a ¹/₈-inch (3-mm) thick rectangle measuring 16 by 18 inches (40 × 45 cm). Cover the dough and place it in the refrigerator to rest for a few minutes.

2. Prepare (clean) twenty Cream Horn cones. Use the larger size: 5 inches (12.5 cm) long with a 2-inch (5-cm) opening. Set aside.

3. Make sure the dough is well rested, then cut the Puff Pastry crosswise into twenty ³/₄-inch-wide (2-cm) strips. Brush the strips lightly with water. Wind the dough strips around the prepared cones

NOTE 2: *The coiled Puff Pastry strips have a tendency to slide off of the forms during baking, curling into various interesting, but not very presentable, shapes. There are a number of tricks for keeping the Puff Pastry on the molds; freezing them before baking or brushing the strips with water both work well. You must remove the forms just before the pastries have finished baking (as soon as you can handle them after removing from the oven) if you use water. Stick a chef's knife (one you are not too fond of) into the opening of the metal cone, and twist to remove the cone. Return the pastries to the oven to dry the inside as needed. If you let them cool completely before removing the cones the pastries will break into little pieces. This will also happen if the cones are not cleaned properly, or if too much water is used. Another way to prevent the strips from sliding off the cones is to place the tip of the cones against the edge of the baking sheet so that the dough has nowhere to go.*

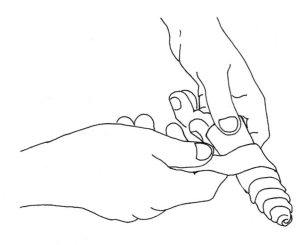

FIGURE 9–12 *Winding a strip of Puff Pastry around a cone-shaped mold for Cream Horns*

(do not stretch them), placing the side brushed with water against the form, starting at the narrow end, and overlapping each previous strip halfway as you go (Figure 9–12). Line them up next to each other on the table as you cover the remaining molds.

4. Brush the top and sides of the pastries with water. Invert onto granulated sugar to coat the top and sides. Roll them back and forth to get sugar on the sides but do not get any on the bottom. Place sugar-side up on sheet pans lined with baking paper.

5. Bake at 400°F (205°C) for about 45 minutes (removing the forms as described in note 2). Allow to cool completely.

6. Place the strawberry jam in a disposable pastry bag made from baking paper (see page 23). Pipe a thin string of jam along the inside of each horn.

7. Whip the cream and 1 tablespoon (15 g) sugar to stiff peaks. Place the cream in a pastry bag with a no. 5 (10-mm) star tip and pipe into the horns, filling them completely.

8. Lightly sift powdered sugar over the pastries.

Diplomats

45 pastries

one recipe Chiffon Sponge Cake batter (page 272)

³/₄ cup (180 ml) Plain Cake Syrup (page 10)

7 ounces (200 g) smooth strawberry jam

1 pound, 6 ounces (625 g) Pastry Cream (page 1088)

This individual version of the cake by the same name will make a refreshing and colorful addition to your pastry display, so many of which tend to be top-heavy with chocolate and/or Fondant-glazed pastries. The Macaroon Paste must be soft enough to stick to the sponge when it is piped on top; however, if the paste is too soft it will change shape when it bakes, creating a less attractive finished pastry. This can also occur if the oven temperature is too low.

For something a little more unique, make the Diplomats in a teardrop shape. If you do not have a tear-shaped cutter, use a 2-inch (5-cm) wide oval cutter and cut one end of each pastry into a point. This method, or using an oval cutter, will create fewer pastries than the round version, and while both the round and teardrop pastries are appealing, they take longer to produce, and cre-

sliced almonds, lightly crushed

one-quarter recipe or 14 ounces (400 g) Macaroon Decorating Paste (page 203)

strawberries

Pectin or Apricot Glaze (pages 1017 and 1016)

ate more scrap pieces, than the traditional rectangles cut from strips (see variation following this recipe).

1. Line the bottom of a half-sheet pan (16 by 12 inches/40 × 30 cm) with baking paper. Fill the pan with the sponge batter, spreading it out evenly.

2. Bake immediately at 400°F (205°C) for about 15 minutes or until the cake springs back when pressed lightly in the center. Let cool completely.

3. Cut around the inside edge of the pan and invert to remove the sponge. Peel the paper from the back and turn right-side up. Cut away the skin and at the same time even off the top to make it level if necessary. Cut into two layers horizontally.

4. Brush half of the Cake Syrup over the bottom cake layer. Spread the strawberry jam evenly on top. Place the top layer on the jam. Brush the remaining Cake Syrup over the top layer.

5. Cut out forty-five 2-inch (5-cm) rounds, using a plain cookie cutter. You will need to keep the cuts close together and stagger the rows to get 45 pieces. Reserve the leftover cake scraps for another use, such as Rum Balls (see page 417).

6. Spread a thin layer of Pastry Cream on the sides of each pastry (you will not use all of it). Roll the sides of the pastries in crushed almonds. Place the cakes on a sheet pan lined with baking paper.

7. Place the Macaroon Decorating Paste in a pastry bag with a no. 3 (6-mm) plain tip. Pipe a ring of paste at the edge of each cake.

8. Place the remaining Pastry Cream in a pastry bag with a no. 4 (8-mm) plain tip. Pipe the Pastry Cream in a spiral, inside the Macaroon Paste border, to cover the sponge on the top of each cake.

9. Bake the cakes, double-panned, at 425°F (219°C) for about 8 minutes or until the Macaroon Paste is light brown. Let the cakes cool completely.

10. Cut the strawberries across to get round slices. Place a slice in the center of each cake. Glaze the tops of the cakes with Apricot or Pectin Glaze.

VARIATION
Senator Cuts

36 pastries

NOTE 1: It is not necessary to mark the tops before baking if the pastries will not be cut until the following day. The Macaroon Paste will soften sufficiently after being refrigerated overnight.

*T*hese are great production pastries with a minimum of scrap pieces. Both the Diplomat pastries and the Diplomat Cake are known as Senator when jam is substituted for the fresh fruit topping. You will need 2 ounces (55 g) of strained apricot preserves and 4 ounces (115 g) of strained strawberry preserves instead of the fresh strawberries, only 12 ounces (340 g) of Macaroon Paste, and a small amount of Simple Syrup (see page 11).

1. Follow the previous instructions through step four.

2. Trim one long side of the sheet. Measure and cut into three 3 1/2-inch (8.7-cm) wide strips lengthwise. Save the trimmings for another use. Ice the top and long sides of each strip with Pastry Cream. Cover

NOTE 2: To make Diplomat Cuts, omit the jam and decorate with fresh fruit between the macaroon borders when cold. Glaze before slicing.

the long sides with crushed almonds and transfer the strips to a sheet pan lined with baking paper.

3. Place the Macaroon Paste in a pastry bag with a no. 3. (6-mm) star tip. Pipe four evenly spaced lines of paste lengthwise on each strip, starting and ending at the long edges. Pipe apricot preserves between the two center lines of paste and strawberry preserves between the frames on either side. Use a knife dipped in water to cut through the Macaroon Paste borders, marking the top of the strips crosswise in 1¼-inch (3.1-cm) pieces. This will make it easier to cut the pastries after baking (see note 1). Do not disturb the jam.

4. Bake as directed for Diplomat pastries. Brush Simple Syrup over the macaroon borders as soon as the pastries come out of the oven. Let cool completely.

5. Cut each strip into 12 slices following the markings.

Florentina Noisettes

30 pastries

1 pound, 10 ounces (740 g) or one recipe Florentina Batter (page 214)
dark coating chocolate, melted
1 pint (480 ml) heavy cream
1 tablespoon (15 g) granulated sugar
one-half recipe Hazelnut Paste (page 9)
or
2 ounces (55 g) commercial hazelnut paste
Hazelnut Cookies (recipe follows)

NOTE: Some of the Florentinas may roll to the side a bit, which can take away from the finished appearance by smearing the cream after they have been filled. A simple solution is to place the culprits in the refrigerator after you have finished the dipping process. Place a small amount of melted chocolate in a piping bag and pipe a small pea-sized dot of chocolate on a baking paper. Immediately set a chilled cookie shell on top holding the cookie straight. The chocolate will set up fairly soon after it touches the cold cookie and will act as a small base to hold it straight; the rolling problem will be eliminated.

*T*hese small pastries and the variations that follow are ideally suited for a buffet or other assorted pastry display; they demonstrate the versatility of Florentina Batter. Florentinas in one form or another should be a standard component of a dessert buffet. It seems almost impossible to make enough of these popular pastries; one reason is that nobody takes just one. Their popularity is evident beginning in the kitchen: The scrap pieces left after trimming the cookies make a great addition to Rum Ball Filling but, mysteriously, they rarely make it that far (in fact sometimes my students are able to produce perfectly trimmed cookies with no scrap pieces whatsoever!). I must admit this is one sweet I have trouble staying away from myself. I enjoy Florentina pastries the most once they start to get a little soft and chewy; however, they are a bit difficult to handle and serve at that point. Although planning ahead usually makes this a moot point, the one drawback to Florentinas in a production kitchen is that they will not keep to the following day once filled. Unfilled shells, on the other hand, can be stored for several weeks well covered in a dry location.

The shapes and fillings used in the variations are all interchangeable: you can fill the cones with the noisette or coconut filling, pipe Chantilly Cream in the tube shapes, and so on. If you use the coconut filling in the cone shape, dip the entire opening into coating chocolate to cover the filling. For yet another filling option, see the introduction to Florentina Cones with Seasonal Fruit on page 469.

1. Draw thirty 3½-inch (8.7-cm) circles on baking paper. Invert the papers and place on sheet pans. Divide the Florentina Batter between the circles, spread out, bake, and trim as instructed in the recipe for Florentinas.

2. Return the cookies to the oven, a portion at a time, for a few minutes until soft. Immediately roll each cookie, top-side out, around a ¾-inch (2-cm) thick dowel so that the ends of the cookie overlap slightly. Push the ends together between the dowel and the table to

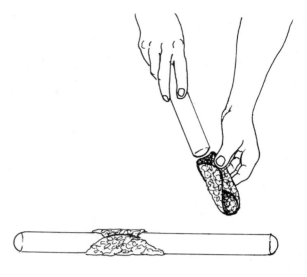

FIGURE 9–13 A Florentina cookie wrapped around a dowel to form a tube; sliding the cookie off of the dowel after it has hardened

make sure they stick. Turn the cookie a half turn so it will not stick to the dowel as it cools. Let each Florentina roll cool completely before sliding it off the dowel (Figure 9–13).

3. Dip both ends of each Florentina ¹/₈ inch (3 mm) into melted coating chocolate and immediately place seam-side up on a sheet pan lined with baking paper (see note).

4. Whip the cream and sugar to soft peaks. Add a small amount of the cream to the Hazelnut Paste and mix until softened; add back to the remaining cream and whip to stiff peaks.

5. Place the cream in a pastry bag with a no. 4 (8-mm) star tip. Fill each Florentina with the cream mixture by piping it into both ends. Attach a Hazelnut Cookie to the top with a dot of coating chocolate. Do not fill any more Florentinas than you plan to serve the same day; they will become soft since they must be stored in the refrigerator once filled.

Hazelnut Cookies

30 cookies

3 ounces (85 g) Short Dough
  (page 54)
dark coating chocolate, melted
thirty whole hazelnuts, toasted and
  skins removed

1. Roll the Short Dough out to ¹/₁₆ inch (2 mm) thick. Cut out thirty ³/₄-inch (2 cm) cookies using a fluted cutter. Cover the dough scraps and reserve for another use. Place the cookies on a sheet pan lined with baking paper and bake at 375°F (190°C) for approximately 8 minutes or until golden brown. Let cool.

2. Pipe a pea-sized dot of coating chocolate in the center of each cookie. Place a hazelnut, pointed-end up, on each chocolate dot. The chocolate should spread out a little to show all around the nut on the top of the cookies.

VARIATION I
Florentina Cones with Chantilly Cream

30 pastries

1 pound 10 ounces (740 g) or one recipe Florentina Batter (page 214)

dark coating chocolate, melted

one recipe Chantilly Cream (page 1083)

edible flowers or fresh raspberries or blueberries

NOTE: If you do not have appropriate-sized molds you can make then easily by cutting them out of styrofoam and then covering the styrofoam with foil.

VARIATION II
Coconut-Filled Florentinas

30 pastries

1 pound, 10 ounces (740 g) or one recipe Florentina Batter (page 214)

10 ounces (285 g) Vanilla Buttercream (page 978)

one-half recipe Coconut Haystack Cookies batter (page 211)

dark coating chocolate, melted

Florentina Surprise

45 pastries

1 pound, 8 ounces (680 g) Short Dough (page 54)

one-half recipe Florentina Batter (page 214)

1 pound, 5 ounces (595 g) Vanilla Buttercream (page 978)

5 ounces (140 g) Hazelnut Paste (page 9)
  or

1. Draw thirty 3¹/₂-inch (8.7-cm) circles on baking paper. Invert the papers on sheet pans. Divide the Florentina Batter between the circles, spread out, bake, and trim as directed in the recipe for Florentinas.

2. Place the trimmed cookies, a few at a time, back in the oven for a few minutes to soften. Place the cookies top-side down on the table and immediately roll around cream horn molds or other cone-shaped molds (see Figure 10–19, page 469); you should have three or four molds to work efficiently (see note). Press the seam together between the mold and the table to be sure they stick. Allow to cool sufficiently before removing the forms so the Florentina cones do not collapse.

3. Dip the open end of each cone ¹/₄ inch (6 mm) into melted coating chocolate. Place seam-side up on a sheet pan lined with baking paper (see note following Florentina Noisette, page 388).

4. Whip the Chantilly Cream to stiff peaks and place in a pastry bag with a no. 7 (14-mm) star tip. Pipe the cream into the cones, filling them just to the edge. Place an edible flower (a small flower such as Borage or Johnny Jump-up looks best) or a berry on the cream. Store in the refrigerator. The filled pastries will stay crisp for a few hours but should not be left overnight.

1. Follow the main recipe through step two.

2. Stir the buttercream into the coconut batter; the cookie batter must be throughly cooled before the buttercream is mixed in. Place the filling in a pastry bag with a no. 6 (12-mm) plain tip. Pipe the filling into both ends of the Florentina shells, piping it flush with the opening on each end; do not fill the entire shell.

3. Dip both ends of each pastry into melted chocolate just deep enough to cover the coconut filling. Store in a cool, dry place; do not refrigerate. Although these pastries have a much longer shelf life than the Noisettes, you should still try to fill only as many as will be needed within one day. The empty shells can be kept for weeks if stored in an airtight container.

*F*lorentina Surprise *pastries contain a medley of flavors—chocolate, nuts, rum, and caramelized sugar—which blend together well, and these pastries give my students an opportunity to work with a broad range of techniques in their preparation. The surprise part of the name refers to the Ganache which is hidden underneath the Florentina cookie. The name is also fitting when, as it happens from time to time, someone forgets to include the filling, leaving the inside hollow! If you want to dress these up, add a Chocolate Beetle and a green Marzipan leaf (see pages 885 and 1038) attached to the top of the Florentina cookie with a tiny bit of melted chocolate.*

1. Roll the Short Dough out to ¹/₈ inch (3 mm) thick. Cut out forty-five 2-inch (5-cm) cookies, using a plain cutter. Cover the dough scraps

2½ ounces (70 g) commercial hazelnut paste

10 ounces (285 g) Ganache (page 1086)

¼ cup (60 ml) light rum

dark coating chocolate, melted

and reserve for another use. Bake the cookies at 375°F (190°C) for about 10 minutes or until light brown. Set aside to cool.

2. Draw forty-five 2-inch (5-cm) circles on baking papers, using a cookie cutter as a guide. Invert the papers and place them on sheet pans. Divide the Florentina Batter between the circles, spread out, bake, and trim the cookies according to the instructions on page 213.

3. Flavor the buttercream with the Hazelnut Paste and place in a pastry bag with a no. 5 (10-mm) plain tip. Pipe a ring of buttercream on each of the Short Dough cookies just inside the edge.

4. Flavor the Ganache with rum. Place it in a pastry bag with a no. 4 (8-mm) plain tip. Pipe a small mound of Ganache inside the buttercream rings. Refrigerate until the buttercream is firm.

5. Holding a cookie upside down, dip the buttercream, Ganache, and the top part of the Short Dough cookie into melted coating chocolate. Gently shake off as much excess chocolate as possible by moving the cookie up and down a few times over the bowl so that the chocolate does not run out around the pastries before it hardens. Place the cookies on paper-lined sheet pans.

6. Before the chocolate hardens, place a Florentina on top of each pastry and press gently to make it level. Do not refrigerate Florentina Surprise pastries.

Fruit Tartlets

thirty 2-inch (5-cm) pastries

1 pound (455 g) Short Dough (page 54)

dark coating chocolate, melted

14 ounces (400 g) Quick Bavarian Cream (page 1089)

fresh fruit

Apricot or Pectin Glaze (pages 1016 and 1017)

NOTE: Choose fruit that is in season. Use small fruits if possible, such as raspberries, blackberries, strawberries, kiwis, figs, plums, and blueberries. Leave the skin on when it is edible and adds to the appearance (figs and plums, for example). Cut the fruit into small pieces or thin slices to make it look more appealing: a whole or half strawberry may look good on a large tart, but on a small tartlet it looks clumsy and is too plain. The same is true for an apricot half or a single round slice of kiwifruit covering the top. A nice idea is to use

*N*o pastry tray or pastry display should be without some form of fruit pastry. Fruit adds color and offers an alternative for the customer or guest who cannot, or prefers not to, eat overly rich or chocolate-filled pastries. The tart shells can be baked several days in advance and then coated, filled, and decorated as needed. I brush the inside with melted chocolate, but Apricot Glaze will suffice as well. Both are used to protect the crust against absorbing moisture from the custard and becoming soft. I feel the dark color of the chocolate provides a better contrast as a background for the fruit.

1. Line thirty 2-inch (5-cm) tartlet pans with Short Dough rolled to ⅛ inch (3 mm) thick (see Figures 2–15 to 2–18, pages 57 and 58). Cover and reserve the dough scraps for another use. Prick the shells lightly with a fork and bake at 375°F (190°C) until light golden brown. Unmold while still warm, then cool the shells completely.

2. Brush melted dark coating chocolate (or Apricot Glaze) on the inside of each shell so that the filling will not soften them.

3. Place the Bavarian Cream in a pastry bag with a no. 6 (12-mm) plain tip. Pipe the cream into each shell, up to the rim, in a nice mound.

4. Decorate the tartlets with the fresh fruit (see note).

5. Brush Apricot or Pectin Glaze on the fruit. Refrigerate if not serving immediately. Use these tarts the day they are made; the fruit tends to bleed into the filling and they usually look a bit wilted the second day. If they are not refrigerated (such as when displayed on a buffet), the tarts must be served within one to two hours.

a very small melon-ball cutter to cut out balls of honeydew melon. These arranged with thin slices of mango and strawberry, for example, make for a nice color contrast. The entire top of the tartlet should be covered with fruit in a simple pattern; do not get too complicated.

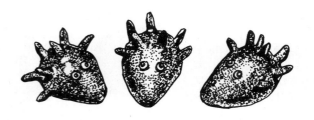

 # Fruit Waffles

30 pastries

3 pounds (1 kg, 365 g) Pippin or
  Granny Smith apples
  (approximately seven
  medium-sized)

one-recipe Plain Poaching Syrup
  (page 13)

1 pound (455 g) Puff Pastry
  (page 44)

flour

granulated sugar

8 ounces (225 g) Pastry Cream
  (page 1088)

Cinnamon Sugar (page 5)

one recipe Apricot or Pectin Glaze
  (pages 1016 and 1017)

NOTE: Because these waffles, like all Puff Pastry goods, should be baked fresh every day, it is a good idea to make a large number to freeze and bake as needed. You can stack six layers of waffles (rolled in sugar), separated with baking paper, per sheet pan.

*T*he waffle part of this title derives from the traditional method of making these pastries, which left a waffle-like pattern on top of the Puff Pastry. This was done either by rolling the dough against a waffle board (an aluminum board with a small raised waffle pattern) or by using a studded rolling pin. The latter is a tool which looks very much like the waffle roller used to texture Marzipan, but it has a larger pattern.

The waffles can also be baked without the apples (but with the Pastry Cream), reducing the baking time to 15 minutes. After they have cooled completely, decorate by placing seasonal fresh fruit on top of the Pastry Cream, and then glaze as directed.

1. Peel and core the apples, cut them in half, and poach in the Poaching Syrup until soft. Remove from the heat and set aside to cool in the syrup. Cut the apples into small wedges and reserve.

2. Roll the Puff Pastry out to a 9-by-11-inch (22.5-×-27.5-cm) rectangle; it will be about ¼ inch (6 mm) thick. Cut out thirty circles using a fluted cookie cutter approximately 1¾ inches (4.5 cm) in diameter. Stagger the cuts to get the full amount of circles. Press the scrap pieces together, cover, and reserve in the refrigerator or freezer for another use. Place the cut circles in the refrigerator to firm up if necessary.

3. Set up your workstation efficiently: If you are right-handed, place some flour in a pie tin on your left, granulated sugar directly on the table in front of you, and sheet pans lined with baking paper on your right.

4. Place a few of the Puff Pastry circles on top of the flour. One at a time, pick up a circle, invert it (flour-side up) onto the sugar in front of you, and use a dowel to roll it in the sugar, making an oval about 4 inches (10 cm) long. If the dough sticks to the dowel, turn the Puff Pastry back over in the flour again, but do not get any sugar on the flour side or it will burn when the pastries bake. Place each rolled pastry sugar-side up on the sheet pan.

5. Place the Pastry Cream in a pastry bag with a no. 3 (6-mm) plain tip. Pipe a small oval of cream in the center of each pastry oval, leaving a ¼-inch (6-mm) border of Puff Pastry uncovered.

6. Arrange five or six apple wedges at an angle in the Pastry Cream. Sprinkle Cinnamon Sugar over the apples.

7. Bake at 400°F (205°C) just until the sugar caramelizes, about 20 minutes. Cool completely.

8. When the pastries have cooled, brush Apricot or Pectin Glaze over the tops. The waffles should be served the same day they are made.

VARIATION
Parisian Waffles

15 pastries

1 pound (455 g) Puff Pastry
   (page 44)

flour

granulated sugar

1 tablespoon (15 ml) arrack or rum

7 ounces (200 g) Vanilla Buttercream
   (page 978)

2 ounces (55 g) strawberry jam

These golden Puff Pastry ovals, sandwiched together with various flavors of buttercream, are also known as Parisian Tongues—a name, no doubt, that has to do with their long oval shape. Parisian Waffles are a good illustration of the principle that one should not judge a book by its cover: Though rather plain and humble looking, they have a wonderful crisp texture and unusual taste, and they are somewhat of a novelty today among the other showy and fancier pastry selections.

1. Follow the directions in steps two, three, and four for Fruit Waffles.

2. Make three angled ¹/₄-inch (6-mm) cuts, lengthwise, down the center of the ovals. Let the dough rest for at least 30 minutes. Bake at 425°F (219°C) until they are golden and the sugar begins to caramelize, about 12 minutes. After they have cooled completely, turn half of the ovals upside down and set the remaining ovals aside to use as the tops.

3. Flavor the buttercream with arrack or rum and pipe a border around each bottom waffle using a no. 3 (6-mm) plain tip in your pastry bag. Pipe a small ribbon of strawberry jam lengthwise in the center.

4. Place the reserved waffles on top and press lightly into the buttercream so they adhere.

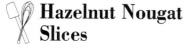

Hazelnut Nougat Slices

thirty 4-by-1¹/₂-inch (10-×-3.7-cm) pastries

one-third recipe Chiffon Sponge Cake
   batter (page 272)

one-half recipe Pâte à Choux
   (page 36)

¹/₄ cup (60 ml) Plain Cake Syrup
   (page 10)

¹/₄ cup (60 ml) Frangelico liqueur

5 ounces (140 g) smooth apricot jam

Hazelnut Nougat Cream
   (recipe follows)

1¹/₂ cups (360 ml) heavy cream

1 tablespoon (15 g) granulated sugar

powdered sugar

Take great care when cutting these pastries. The familiar cautions to use a steady hand, a good knife, and to watch what you are doing certainly apply here. Hazelnut Nougat Slices are fairly tall pastries, which look very elegant if cut precise and even with straight sides, but, if the pastries are cut at an angle, not only will they look clumsy and amateurish, they may even fall over! To cut cleanly through the Pâte à Choux screen, use a thin, sharp chef's knife. Dipping the knife into hot water between strokes will warm the knife, making it slice through the cream easier, and it will also ensure that you do not leave any residue on the Pâte à Choux. Hazelnut Nougat Slices can double as a plated dessert: Cut into 2-by-2¹/₂-inch (5-×-6.2-cm) squares and serve with a fruit sauce such as Strawberry or Orange.

1. Line the bottom of a half-sheet pan (16 by 12 inches/40 × 30 cm) with baking paper. Spread the Sponge Cake batter evenly on top. Bake at 400°F (205°C) about 10 minutes or until the cake springs back when pressed lightly in the center. Reserve.

2. Cut a piece of baking paper the same size as the Sponge Cake. Draw lines the length of the paper ¹/₂ inch (1.2 cm) apart. Draw a second set of lines diagonally to create a diamond pattern. Turn the paper upside down on a sheet pan.

3. Place the Pâte à Choux in a pastry with a no. 1 (2-mm) star tip. Pipe the Pâte à Choux onto the paper following the lines.

4. Bake at 400°F (205°C) until the Pâte à Choux is golden brown and dry enough to hold its shape once removed from the oven, about 15 minutes.

5. Cut the reserved sponge free from the sides of the pan, invert onto a cake cardboard, remove the baking paper, and turn it right-side up. Cut off the skin and cut the top even at the same time if necessary. Slice the sponge into two layers horizontally.

6. Combine the Cake Syrup and the Frangelico. Brush half of the mixture over the bottom sponge layer. Spread the apricot jam on the bottom layer. Place the top layer on the jam, then brush the remainder of the Cake Syrup mixture over the top layer.

7. Cover the top of the cake with the Hazelnut Nougat Cream. Refrigerate until the cream is set, about 2 hours.

8. Whip the heavy cream and granulated sugar to stiff peaks. Spread the cream evenly on top of the hazelnut cream. Place the Pâte à Choux screen on top of the whipped cream; lightly press it into place.

9. Trim the two long sides of the sheet to make them even. Use a thin, sharp knife to cut the sheet into three strips lengthwise. Cut each strip into pieces 1½ inches (3.7 cm) wide. Sift powdered sugar lightly over the slices.

Hazelnut Nougat Cream

10 cups (2 l, 400 ml)

4 teaspoons (12 g) unflavored gelatin powder
⅓ cup (80 ml) cold water
5 cups (1 l, 200 ml) heavy cream
1 teaspoon (5 ml) vanilla extract
one-half recipe Hazelnut Paste (page 9)
    or
4 ounces (115 g) commercial hazelnut paste
10 ounces (285 g) Pastry Cream (page 1088)

1. Sprinkle the gelatin over the cold water and set aside to soften.

2. Whip the heavy cream and vanilla to soft peaks.

3. Combine the Hazelnut Paste and the Pastry Cream by gradually adding a small amount of Pastry Cream to the Hazelnut Paste to soften it before mixing with the remaining Pastry Cream. Mix into the whipped cream.

4. Place the gelatin mixture over a bain-marie and heat until dissolved. Do not overheat. Rapidly add the gelatin to a small part of the cream mixture, then quickly mix this combination into the remaining cream. Allow the filling to thicken slightly before using.

Kirschwasser Rings

twenty-five 3½-inch (8.7-cm) pastries

melted unsalted butter
sliced almonds, lightly crushed
4 ounces (115 g) granulated sugar

You can create a quick and delicious light dessert from these tasty almond rings by serving them with a fresh fruit sauce and a dollop of Italian Cream (see page 1087) or a scoop of frozen yogurt. For buffet service, cut the rings in half and dip ¼ inch (6 mm) of each end into melted dark coating chocolate. This gives the pastries some color contrast and at the same time keeps the cut edges from drying out.

11 ounces (310 g) Almond Paste
     (page 3)
6 ounces (170 g) soft unsalted butter
3 eggs, at room temperature
1 tablespoon (15 ml) kirschwasser
3 ounces (85 g) bread flour
¼ teaspoon (1 g) baking powder
flour
powdered sugar

1. Grease twenty-five 3½-inch (8.7-cm) savarin forms with melted butter, coat with crushed almonds, and place the forms on a sheet pan.

2. Place the sugar and Almond Paste in a mixing bowl. Blend in the butter gradually, making sure there are no lumps. Add the eggs, one at a time, and then the kirschwasser.

3. Sift the flour and baking powder together and stir it into the batter. Take care not to overwhip the mixture at this time, or you will incorporate too much air and the finished product will be dry and crumbly.

4. Place the batter in a pastry bag with a no. 6 (12-mm) plain tip. Pipe the batter into the forms, filling each two-thirds full.

5. Bake at 400°F (205°C) for about 20 minutes or until baked through and golden brown on the bottom as well as the top (unmold one to check). Dust flour lightly over the pastries (leaving them in the forms) and then invert and let cool completely.

6. Remove the forms from the pastries. Sift a small amount of powdered sugar over the tops. Kirschwasser Rings will keep for a week if stored covered in the refrigerator. Allow them to reach room temperature before dusting with powdered sugar or the sugar will quickly disappear.

Lemon-Almond Tartlets

45 tartlets

2 pounds (910 g) Short Dough
     (page 54)
1 pound, 10 ounces (740 g) Mazarin
     Filling (page 1088), soft
bread flour
Apricot Glaze (page 1016)
sliced almonds, toasted and crushed
one-half recipe Lemon Curd
     (page 1087)
powdered sugar

When I was in the retail end of the business we used to line and fill a week's worth of mazarin forms for both Lemon-Almond Tartlets and Mazarins at the same time. After baking we would store them in the freezer and/or refrigerator to remove each morning and finish with either toasted almonds and Lemon Curd or Apricot Glaze and Fondant. It was an easy and productive way to quickly have two pastries, similar in shape, yes, but distinctively different in taste, ready to display and sell.

1. Line mazarin forms (see page 398) with Short Dough rolled to ⅛ inch (3 mm) thick (see Figures 2–15 to 2–18, pages 57 and 58). Cover the leftover dough and reserve for another use.

2. Place the Mazarin Filling in a pastry bag with a no. 6 (12-mm) plain tip. Pipe the filling into the lined pans, filling them two-thirds full.

3. Bake at 400°F (205°C) until golden brown, about 12 minutes.

4. As soon as you remove the tartlets from the oven, dust the tops lightly with bread flour and immediately turn them upside down on the pan to make the tops flat and even.

5. When the tartlets have cooled, brush Apricot Glaze over the tops and dip the tartlets into the almonds to coat.

6. Cut out the center of each tartlet using a 1-inch (2.5-cm) plain cookie cutter. Do not cut through the crust. Reserve the centers.

7. Place the Lemon Curd in a pastry bag made from baking paper (see page 23). Pipe the curd into the holes, filling them to the top. Sift powdered sugar lightly over the pastries. Replace the cutouts on top of the Lemon Curd. Store the pastries, covered, in the refrigerator.

Linzer Tartlets

*forty-five 2-inch (5-cm)
pastries or one 11-inch (27.5-cm)
tart*

one recipe Linzer Dough (page 34)
   (see note 1)
Butter and Flour Mixture (page 4)
1 pound, 4 ounces (570 g) smooth
   raspberry jam
powdered sugar

*NOTE 1: To make the dough easier to work
with, prepare it at least one day in advance and
be certain that the nuts are ground very finely.*

*NOTE 2: To remove the forms, tap them gently
against the table. If this does not work (or if
you forgot to grease them), invert the forms,
place a damp towel on top, and put into a hot
oven for a few minutes.*

*L*inzer Tartlets should be made with only the highest quality raspberry jam
available. The forms must be lined one at a time due to the softness and
composition of the dough; however, the tender and fragile crust is one of the
things that makes this specialty from the town of Linz in Austria so delicious.

1. Roll out 10 ounces (285 g) of the Linzer Dough ¹/₈ inch (3 mm)
thick and as square as possible. Reserve in the refrigerator.

2. Brush Butter and Flour Mixture on the inside of 45 shallow tartlet forms about 2 inches (5 cm) in diameter and ¹/₂ inch (1.2 cm) high.

3. Roll out the remaining Linzer Dough to ¹/₄ inch (6 mm) thick. Cut
out 2¹/₂-inch (6.2-cm) cookies. Gently press the cookies into the buttered forms, then cut away any excess on the tops to make them even.

4. Place the raspberry jam in a pastry bag with a no. 5 (10-mm)
plain tip. Pipe the jam into the forms, filling them halfway.

5. Using a fluted pastry wheel, cut the reserved piece of dough into
¹/₄-inch (6-mm) strips. Place two strips on top of each tartlet in an X,
pressing the ends into the dough on the sides.

6. Bake at 350°F (175°C) for about 15 minutes or until golden
brown on top. Let cool completely before unmolding (see note 2). Sift
powdered sugar lightly over the tartlets. Linzer Tartlets taste best if
they are served the same day they are baked; the jam tends to get dry
and rubbery after that.

Macaroon Bananas

20 pastries

one-half recipe Almond Macaroon
   Cookies batter (page 202)
6 ounces (170 g) Vanilla Buttercream
   (page 978)
4 ounces (115 g) smooth red currant
   jelly
ten ripe red bananas or large ripe
   finger bananas
dark coating chocolate, melted
Piping Chocolate (page 904), melted

*NOTE: If you do not have time to write on each
pastry, simply streaking either dark or light
coating chocolate crosswise over the pastries is
another attractive decoration.*

I am somewhat surprised that I do not see these pastries much in shops or in
other cookbooks. They were a standard item in many German pastry shops
when I first picked up the idea back in the sixties. With a stylishly scripted
"banana" on top, Macaroon Bananas can compete with the best in any fancy
French pastry assortment. They are a great, non-messy pastry to pick up and
eat with your hands for a quick snack, and they taste even better one or two
days after they are made when the macaroon has absorbed some moisture from
the banana. If you can not obtain red or finger bananas, use small yellow
bananas cut to size. You may have to do some mitering in this case.

1. Place the Macaroon Cookie batter in a pastry bag with a no. 8
(16-mm) plain tip. Use a small amount of batter to fasten a sheet of baking paper to a sheet pan so the paper will not move as you pipe. Pipe
the batter into 20 slightly curved cookies 4 inches (10 cm) in length,
holding the pastry tip close to the paper so that the batter comes out
flatter and wider than the opening of the tip.

2. Bake immediately, following the instructions for Almond Macaroon Cookies. Let the cookies cool completely.

3. Invert the paper and peel the paper away from the cookies as shown in the Almond Macaroon Cookies recipe. Place them flat-side up on a sheet pan. Press down lightly, if necessary, to flatten the cookies so they do not wobble.

4. Place the buttercream in a pastry bag with a no. 2 (4-mm) plain tip. Pipe a border of buttercream, ⅛ inch (3 mm) from the edge, around the cookies.

5. Place the red currant jelly in a pastry bag made from baking paper (see page 23). Pipe a small line of jelly inside the frame of buttercream.

6. Peel the bananas and cut them in half lengthwise (do not use overripe or bruised bananas).

7. Place a banana, flat-side down, on each of the cookies, bending it slightly to fit the curve of the cookie if necessary (Figure 9–14). Press the banana down lightly to be sure it is firmly attached. There should not be any banana protruding outside of the macaroon. If there is, trim the banana to fit. Refrigerate just until the buttercream is firm.

8. Place a cake-cooling rack over a sheet pan lined with baking paper. Arrange the pastries on the rack in straight rows, curved-side toward you.

9. Spoon the melted coating chocolate over the bananas starting with the one in the upper right-hand corner, and working right to left, back to front, to avoid dripping chocolate on the bananas once they are coated (Figure 9–15). Be sure each pastry is completely covered in chocolate. When the chocolate has hardened, use a thin, sharp knife to cut the pastries off the rack.

10. Place the Piping Chocolate in a piping bag and cut a very small opening in the tip. Write the word "banana" on each pastry. Macaroon Bananas will keep for a few days covered in a cool place, and for up to one week if refrigerated. To protect the chocolate from moisture, they should be wrapped in a box if refrigerated.

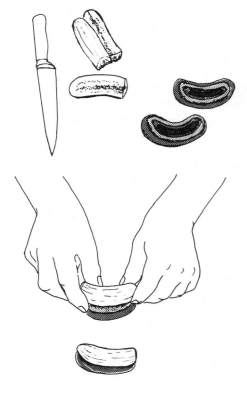

FIGURE 9–14 *Placing the cut bananas on top of the inverted Macaroon Cookies after piping buttercream and red currant jelly on the cookies*

FIGURE 9–15 *Coating the Macaroon Banana pastries with melted chocolate*

Mazarins

50 pastries

2 pounds (910 g) Short Dough
  (page 54)
2 pounds (910 g) Mazarin Filling
  (page 1088), soft
bread flour
Apricot Glaze (page 1016)
Simple Icing (page 1020)

NOTE: Before they are glazed, Mazarins will keep fresh for up to one week stored covered in the refrigerator. Glaze and ice as needed.

Mazarins are popular in most Scandinavian pastry shops, especially in Sweden where they are referred to as a "man's pastry" because they are not too fancy or fussy. When I was in the retail pastry business there was a woman working behind the counter who always suggested the Mazarin pastries whenever a male customer asked for a suggestion, giving the explanation that "the chef refers to these as a man's pastry." I learned that the typical response upon hearing this was (with a smile and a bit of bravado), "In that case I'll take two." Traditional mazarin pans are small, round, plain (not fluted) forms, about 1¼ inches (3.1 cm) high and 2½ inches (6.2 cm) across the top, sloping down to about 1½ inches (3.7 cm) across the bottom.

1. Line mazarin forms with Short Dough rolled to ⅛ inch (3 mm) thick (see Figures 2–15 to 2–18, pages 57 and 58). Cover the leftover dough and reserve for another use.

2. Place the Mazarin Filling in a pastry bag with a no. 7 (14-mm) plain tip. Pipe the filling into the shells almost to the top of the forms.

3. Bake at 400°F (205°C) for about 20 minutes or until filling springs back when pressed gently.

4. As soon as you remove the Mazarins from the oven, dust flour lightly over the tops, then quickly invert them on the sheet pan to make the tops flat and even (a fast way to do this is to place an inverted sheet pan on top of the pastries and flip the whole thing at once). Allow them to cool upside down.

5. When cold, remove the forms and turn the pastries right-side up on a paper-lined sheet pan. Refrigerate briefly until firm.

6. Glaze the tops of the Mazarins with a thin layer of Apricot Glaze, applying it with a brush. Ice with a thin layer of Simple Icing by dipping the top surface of the pastries into the icing and removing the excess with a spatula.

Noisette Rings

35 pastries

1 pound, 4 ounces (570 g) Short
   Dough (page 54)

8 ounces (225 g) hazelnuts, toasted,
   skins removed, and coarsely
   crushed

1 pound (455 g) Almond Paste
   (page 3)

1/4 cup (60 ml) dark rum

1/4 cup (60 ml) water, approximately

dark coating chocolate, melted

soybean oil or a commercial thinning
   agent

The combination of rum-flavored Almond Paste and crunchy hazelnuts on a Short Dough cookie tastes as good as it is simple. The size of the rings is easily adjustable to make a smaller buffet-sized serving, or simply cut these in half before dipping. Keep in mind that there is no decoration other than the crushed nuts so it is essential that they are coarse enough to stand out under the chocolate coating, and it is equally important that the chocolate is thinned sufficiently for the same reason. Thinning the chocolate also keeps its flavor from becoming overpowering.

1. Roll out the Short Dough to 1/8 inch (3 mm) thick. Cut out thirty-five 2³/₄-inch (6.8-cm) cookies using a fluted cutter. Place the cookies on paper-lined sheet pans. Cut a circle out of the center of each cookie using a 1-inch (2.5-cm) fluted cutter. Remove the small circles of dough, cover, and reserve for another use together with the other leftover dough pieces. Bake the cookies at 375°F (190°C) for about 10 minutes or until light brown. Set aside to cool.

2. Sift the crushed nuts to remove the powder and any very small pieces. Save these for another use and reserve the coarse pieces.

3. Add the rum and enough water to the Almond Paste to make it just soft enough to pipe; the amount needed will vary depending on the consistency of the Almond Paste. Place the mixture in a pastry bag with a no. 6 (12-mm) plain tip. Pipe a ring of Almond Paste onto each cookie, holding the bag straight above the cookie to avoid making the cookie slide sideways as you pipe. If you have trouble with the cookies sliding, the Almond Paste is probably too firm.

4. As soon as you finish piping the paste, invert the cookies into the crushed hazelnuts and press gently to make the nuts stick and to flatten the Almond Paste slightly (do not wait too long to do this or the Almond Paste will form a skin and the nuts will not stick). Reshape the Almond Paste circles so they are even.

5. Thin the coating chocolate with enough soybean oil that the hazelnuts will show through the coating: approximately two parts chocolate to one part oil by volume.

6. One at a time, hold a cookie upside down and dip it into the chocolate to cover all of the Almond Paste as well as any Short Dough that is visible on the top. Move it up and down a few times above the bowl to allow as much chocolate as possible to fall back in the bowl to prevent the chocolate from running out around the pastry before it hardens. Place the dipped pastries on paper-lined pans. Noisette Rings should not be refrigerated, but if you have no choice, be sure they are well wrapped.

Orange Truffle Cuts

60 pastries

one-half recipe Japonaise Meringue
Batter (page 591)

one-half recipe Chocolate Chiffon
Sponge Cake batter (page 272)

$^1/_3$ cup (80 ml) Simple Syrup
(page 11)

$^1/_2$ cup (120 ml) Grand Marnier
liqueur

3 pounds (1 kg, 365 g) soft Ganache
(page 1086)

unsweetened cocoa powder

sixty Marzipan Oranges (page 1030)

one large stalk candied angelica

*Y*ou will need to start these rich, creamy, and crunchy chocolate cuts the day
before serving them to give yourself enough time to assemble, ice, cut, and
finish them in a practical manner. Should sixty pastries be too many, rather than
going through all of the steps to make a small yield, follow the instructions for
the full recipe through step six, cut the assembled sheet in half or quarters, and
then cover and place the portion you do not need in the freezer. It will keep for
up to four weeks.

I have been forced to omit either the Marzipan Oranges or icing the long
sides of the cut strips on occasion to save time. The pastries still look great with
the meringue and Ganache layers exposed all around, but by covering the sides
with Ganache, the strips (before you slice them) can be left covered in the refrigerator for many days. When needed, sift cocoa powder over the top, mark the
pattern, and cut them into slices.

1. Spread the Japonaise Meringue Batter into a 16-by-12-inch (40-
×-30-cm) rectangle on a sheet of baking paper. Slide the paper onto a
sheet pan (see Figure 16–15, page 842) and bake at 300°F (149°C) until
golden brown and dry, about 30 minutes. Set aside to cool.

2. Line the bottom of a half-sheet pan (16 by 12 inches/40 × 30
cm) with baking paper. Spread the chocolate sponge batter evenly on
top. Bake immediately at 400°F (205°C) for about 12 minutes or until
the cake springs back when pressed lightly in the center.

3. Flavor the Simple Syrup with about one-fourth of the Grand
Marnier. Add the remaining Grand Marnier to the Ganache.

4. Remove the chocolate sponge from the pan by cutting around
the edge and inverting. Peel the paper from the back and turn right-side
up again. Slice into two layers horizontally. Place the bottom layer on a
cardboard or inverted sheet pan. Brush some of the Simple Syrup mixture on top.

5. Reserve 1 pound, 8 ounces (680 g) of the Ganache. Spread half
of the remaining Ganache on top of the sponge. Place the Japonaise
layer upside down on the Ganache; peel the paper from the back.
Spread the other half of the Ganache over the Japonaise.

6. Top with the second sponge layer and press down to even the
sheet. Brush the remaining Simple Syrup mixture over the sponge.
Refrigerate until the Ganache is firm.

7. Trim the two long sides of the assembled sheet. Cut the sheet
into four strips lengthwise. Ice the top and long sides of each strip with
the reserved Ganache (soften first to spread easily, if necessary) dividing it equally between the strips.

8. Sift cocoa powder over the top of the strips to cover the
Ganache. Using the back of a chef's knife, lightly press straight down to
mark the cocoa powder with diagonal lines in both directions, creating
a diamond pattern.

9. Cut each strip into fifteen 1-inch (2.5-cm) pieces, using a thin
knife dipped in hot water. Drill a small hole in the center of each pastry
with the tip of a paring knife. Place a Marzipan Orange on the hole.

10. Select a good-looking stalk of angelica and cut it into ¹/₂-inch (1.2-cm) wide strips lengthwise. Trim the strips at the thicker (bottom) end of the stalk. Cut ¹/₂-inch (1.2-cm) pieces at a 45° angle, making diamond shapes. Make a small cut next to each Marzipan Orange and place an angelica "leaf" in the cut.

🥄 Othellos

twenty-five 2-inch (5-cm) pastries

---

melted unsalted butter
bread flour
one-half recipe Othello Sponge batter (page 276)
1 pound (455 g) Pastry Cream (page 1088)
one recipe Apricot Glaze (page 1016)
one recipe Chocolate Glaze (page 1016)
dark or light Piping Chocolate (page 904), melted

NOTE 1: Alternatively, draw 2-inch (5-cm) circles on sheets of baking paper and invert the papers on sheet pans. Or, better yet, if you are making these on a regular basis, you can obtain special pans made specifically for Othello shells. The pans have shallow round indentations with a protruding center that creates a pocket in the baked shells and eliminates the need to hollow them out.

NOTE 2: Once filled, the Othellos should be glazed right away, as the Pastry Cream begins to soften the shells rather quickly, making them hard to work with if you wait.

*O*thellos are a classical pastry that borrow their name from the Shakespearean tragedy in which the title character, a Moor, is made mad with jealousy by the evil Iago and subsequently kills his loving and faithful wife, Desdemona. The brown glaze symbolizes the color of Othello's skin; in fact, these pastries are known as mohrenkopf in most parts of Europe, which translates to "Moor's head." Although the following version is the most common, Othello has also lent his name to a rich Danish layer cake that somewhat resembles a large Othello pastry—it consists of Pastry Cream between two layers of Othello Sponge all iced with chocolate. Individual pastries with different fillings and icings have been named for the other main characters in the play as well.

Othello pastries are also often made to resemble peaches, plums, or potatoes. In this case, the shells are filled with flavored Pastry Cream and then covered with Marzipan, shaped and colored like the appropriate fruit or vegetable. The shells for any and all of these Othello variations can be made in advance and kept covered in a dry place until needed. The filling should always be Pastry Cream or at least contain Pastry Cream as the base. The shells absorb moisture from the cream giving them a soft pleasant consistency. With this in mind, it is important that the Pastry Cream not be too firm, or the pastries will be dry.

1. Butter and flour two full-size sheet pans. Use a 2-inch (5-cm) plain cookie cutter to mark 25 circles on each pan (see note 1). Place the Othello batter in a pastry bag with a no. 7 (14-mm) plain tip. Pipe the batter onto the sheet pans in mounds about ³/₄ inch (2 cm) high within the circles.

2. Bake immediately at 450°F (230°C) for approximately 10 minutes or until golden brown. Let cool completely.

3. Use a melon-ball cutter to make a hole the size of a cherry in the bottom of each pastry shell. Divide the shells into two equal groups as you make the holes, with the better looking shells (to be used for the tops) in one group. Flatten the round side of the other group of shells (the bases) just enough to make them stand straight, using a knife or a grater. Arrange both groups of shells with the holes facing up.

4. Place the Pastry Cream in a pastry bag with a no. 6 (12-mm) plain tip. Pipe the cream into all of the shells. Sandwich the shells together in twos, enclosing the cream. Place right side up. Brush Apricot Glaze over the tops of the pastries.

5. Place the Othellos on an aspic rack or cake cooler with a sheet pan underneath. Cover the tops and sides of the pastries with Chocolate Glaze, following the instructions on pages 1014 and 1015 for Glazing or Icing with Fondant (see Figures 19–36 and 19–37, with the instructions).

6. Place light or dark Piping Chocolate in a piping bag and cut a small opening. Pipe a spiral design on the top of each pastry starting in the center.

7. Store the finished Othellos in the refrigerator, placed in a box to protect the Chocolate Glaze from the moist air.

Paris-Brest

30 individual pastries or two 11-inch (27.5-cm) rings

one-half recipe Pâte à Choux
   (page 36)
2 ounces (55 g) sliced almonds
one-quarter recipe or 4 ounces (115 g)
   Praline (page 10), finely crushed
one recipe Italian Cream (page 1087)
powdered sugar

*T*his delightful Pâte à Choux dessert was created by a French pastry chef named Pierre Gateau (no kidding). His shop was located in a suburb of Paris on the route of the famous bicycle race from Paris to Brest (a town in Brittany) and back. In 1891 he decided to honor the race (and at the same time hopefully increase his business a little) by creating a cake that resembled the wheel of a bicycle.

Paris-Brest is traditionally filled with a very rich Praline-flavored mixture of Pastry Cream, Buttercream, and Italian Meringue (there is also a variation of the dessert called Paris-Nice, which is filled with St. Honoré Cream). In this version I use Italian Cream to lighten the filling. The Praline can be left out if you wish.

1. Draw thirty 3-inch (7.5-cm) circles on sheets of baking paper. Invert the papers on sheet pans. (You can alternatively butter and flour the sheet pans and use a 3-inch [7.5-cm] cake ring or cookie cutter to mark outlines on the pan.)

2. Place the Pâte à Choux in a pastry bag with a no. 6 (12-mm) star tip. Pipe the paste into rings on top of the outlines. Spray water lightly over the rings and sprinkle sliced almonds on top.

3. Bake at 400°F (205°C) until the Pâte à Choux is puffed, then reduce the heat slightly and continue baking approximately 25 minutes or until baked through. Let cool completely.

4. Slice each ring horizontally, removing about one-third as a lid.

5. Combine the Praline and Italian Cream. Place in a pastry bag with a no. 6 (12-mm) star tip. Pipe a ring of filling on top of each Pâte à Choux bottom ring. Place the lids on top of the filling. Sift powdered sugar lightly over the tops.

To make the larger rings

Follow the directions above with the following changes:

• Draw or mark two 10-inch (25-cm) circles.

• Instead of piping the paste into rings on top of the lines, pipe it in a corkscrew pattern, letting the paste fall within the circles (Figure 9–16). Another method is to pipe two rings, one on either side of the lines, and then finish with a third ring piped on top of the other two as shown in the second example in the illustration. If you choose this

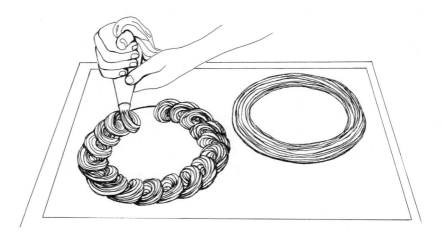

FIGURE 9–16 *Two methods of piping the Pâte à Choux to make the larger version of Paris-Brest*

method, use a slightly larger pastry tip and start each ring in a different place to avoid a noticeable seam and to make the rings stronger.

- Bake at 375°F (190°C). The larger rings will need about 40 minutes after you reduce the heat. Be certain they are baked through; if they start to fall after being removed from the oven it will be too late.

- Use the same corkscrew pattern when piping the filling onto the bottom rings.

- If the rings are to be cut into serving pieces within a few hours, cut the tops into the appropriate sized pieces and reassemble them on top of the filling. This will allow you to cut the pastry cleanly and avoid mashing the top and forcing the filling out. Several hours after assembly the Pâte à Choux will have softened sufficiently to make pre-cutting unnecessary.

Petits Fours Glacé and Petits Fours

Petit four literally translates to "small oven." The name is said to have originated from the practice of cooking small pastries *"a petit four,"* that is to say, in a low-temperature oven. The designation Petits Fours is applied to a myriad of small sweets including chocolate covered and plain candied fruits and elegant bite-sized cakes. The latter are produced in many shapes containing various layered cake mixtures and fillings. Although Petits Fours Glacé are generally either glazed with Fondant or dipped in chocolate before the final decoration is added, the term *glacé* is also used to indicate any iced pastry, such as a small tartlet or those made from Pâte à Choux or meringue, provided they are small enough to be consumed in one or two bites. Small almond cakes may also be wrapped in Marzipan or Modeling Chocolate and served as

Petits Fours, and in the case of miniature Marjolaine or Orange Truffle Cut pastries, they are simply cut into small fancy shapes, leaving the sides uncovered to expose the layer structure. This category of small, fancy treats also includes the more elaborately finished Viennese Petits Fours. Petits Fours are typically served at the end of a meal with coffee or tea as a separate dessert course, or they may be used to garnish or accompany another dessert, a parfait or ice cream bombe, for example. The French terms *friandise* and *mignardise* are also used to describe all of the items mentioned previously, and this category can further include chocolate candies, nougats, fruit jellies, and more.

Petits Fours Glacé

about 80 pieces

one 16-by-24-inch (40-×-60-cm)
   Petits Four Sponge (recipe follows)
1 pound, 4 ounces (570 g) soft
   Ganache (page 1086)
1½ ounces (40 g) Vanilla Buttercream
   (page 978)
8 ounces (225 g) Marzipan
   (page 1022), untinted
powdered sugar
one recipe Fondant (page 1011)
   (see note 2)
Simple Syrup (page 11)
Piping Chocolate (page 904), melted

NOTE 1: If the Petits Four Sponge has been stored for a day or more the skin on top will probably be loose. If this is the case, remove as much of it as will come away easily before using the sheet.

NOTE 2: If you are making Fondant only for this recipe of Petits Fours Glacé, and you have no other use for it, you can probably get away with making just three-quarters of the Fondant recipe, provided you keep it free of crumbs and mix the colors carefully. However, since Fondant will keep for many months if stored properly, in most cases it makes sense to make the full batch.

Should you not need the full yield of Petits Fours from this recipe, make the full recipe through step two, then wrap and freeze what you do not need and finish another time. Although it is easy enough to divide the recipe in half, this makes more sense from a practical standpoint and the quality will not suffer. The layered Petits Fours sheet can also be made into European pastries by cutting the pieces larger—portion size rather than bite-size.

1. Unmold and cut the sponge sheet crosswise into three equal pieces, leaving the baking paper attached (see note 1). Each sheet should be approximately 16 by 8 inches (40 × 20 cm).

2. Place one sheet (paper-side down) on an inverted sheet pan or a cake cardboard. Top with half of the Ganache and spread it out evenly. Invert a second sheet onto the Ganache and peel the paper from the back. Spread the remaining Ganache on the second sheet. Top with the third sheet and press the top with a baking pan to make sure the Ganache and sheets are firmly attached. Peel away the baking paper.

3. Spread the buttercream in a thin film over the top of the sheet.

4. Roll out the Marzipan (using powdered sugar to prevent it from sticking) to a rectangle just slightly large than the stacked sponge sheets and ⅛ inch (3 mm) thick. Roll the Marzipan up on a dowel and then unroll it over the buttercream. Invert the cake onto a clean sheet pan or cardboard and peel the paper off the top. Trim away any Marzipan protruding outside the cake. Refrigerate (upside down) until the Ganache is firm, about 1 hour.

5. Leave the cake upside down and cut out shapes as desired (Figure 9–17). Keep all of the shapes around 1¼ inches (3.1 cm) in size; in other words, make the rectangles longer than the squares but not quite as wide, and so on, so that all the pieces will look uniform. Keep in mind that cutting squares, rectangles, and diamond shapes will give you more Petits Fours and less waste than cutting them into circles or hearts.

6. Place the Petits Fours, Marzipan-side up, on an aspic or cooling rack set over a clean sheet pan. Space them at least 1 inch (2.5 cm) apart.

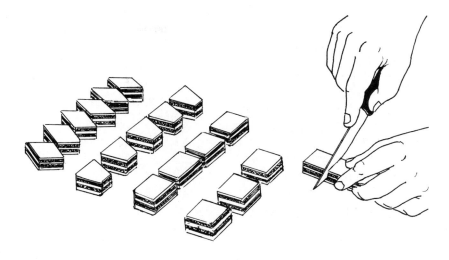

FIGURE 9–17 Cutting the layered sponge cake and Ganache into various small shapes for Petits Fours Glacé

7. Warm the Fondant, stirring constantly, over simmering water to around 100°F (38°C). Do not get it too hot or it will lose its shine when it dries. Thin to the proper consistency with Simple Syrup. Test the thickness by coating one or two pastries: you should be able to clearly see the layers on the sides through the Fondant.

8. Coat the Petits Fours with Fondant by either piping it on using a pastry bag with a no. 3 (6-mm) plain tip or pouring it from a saucer (see Figures 19–36 and 19–37, pages 1014 and 1015). Always start with the pastry farthest away from you so you will not drip over the pastries once you have coated them. Continue to warm the Fondant as needed throughout the coating process so it is always at the correct temperature. If a skin forms on top of the Fondant supply while you are working with it, cover it with hot water for a few seconds, then pour off, stir, and continue. The Fondant that drips onto the sheet pan under the pastries can, of course, be warmed and used again. If you wish to tint the Fondant, see steps four and five, page 1015. When all of the Petits Fours are coated, let the Fondant set completely before moving them.

9. Decorate the tops of the Petits Fours with Piping Chocolate, using the designs shown in Figures 17–20 and 17–21, pages 907 and 908. You can enhance the decoration by piping a small buttercream rosebud on top, placing a small piece of candied violet or pistachio nut on the Petits Fours, or by filling in part of your design with strained strawberry jam or preserves or light sweet chocolate. The finished Petits Fours Glacé can be stored at room temperature for a day or two. They will keep fresh and shiny for up to five days if refrigerated in a covered box.

Petits Four Sponge

one 16-by-24-inch (40-×-60-cm) sheet

14 ounces (400 g) Almond Paste (page 3), at room temperature

12 egg yolks (1 cup/240 ml), at room temperature

7 ounces (200 g) granulated sugar

4 eggs, at room temperature

1 teaspoon (5 ml) vanilla extract

1 teaspoon (5 g) salt

grated zest from one lemon

5 ounces (140 g) cake flour

1. Using the paddle attachment on the mixer, soften the Almond Paste by adding the egg yolks one at a time to avoid lumps. Incorporate the sugar and then gradually add the whole eggs. Mix in the vanilla, salt, and lemon zest. Beat the batter until it is light and fluffy, approximately 5 minutes. Stir in the cake flour.

2. Spread the batter evenly over a 16-by-24-inch (40-×-60-cm) sheet of baking paper. Drag the paper onto a sheet pan (see Figure 16–15, page 842).

3. Bake at 400°F (205°C) for approximately 20 minutes or until baked through.

Petits Fours

about 35 petits fours

10 ounces (285 g) Short Dough (page 54)

2 ounces (55 g) smooth strawberry jam

2 pounds, 5 ounces (1 kg, 50 g) Mazarin Filling (page 1088)

2 pounds (910 g) Marzipan (page 1022), untinted

powdered sugar

Vanilla Buttercream (page 978)

2 pounds, 4 ounces (1 kg, 25 g) Ganache (page 1086)

one small stalk candied angelica

NOTE: If you do not have a quarter-size sheet pan, divide a half-sheet pan in half across the width using a strip of corrugated cardboard wrapped in aluminum foil, or double the recipe and use the other half of the sheet for another project. The baked sheet will keep fresh in the freezer for up to four weeks if wrapped tightly.

1. Line the bottom of a quarter-sheet pan (12 by 8 inches/30 × 20 cm) with baking paper (see note). Roll the Short Dough out to 1/8 inch (3 mm) thick and place it in the pan. Trim the edges so the dough covers only the bottom of the pan and not the sides. Cover the dough scraps and reserve for another use. Spread the jam over the dough in the pan in a thin layer. Spread the Mazarin Filling evenly over the top.

2. Bake at 375°F (190°C) until baked through, about 25 minutes. Let cool to room temperature.

3. When the Mazarin sheet has cooled completely (preferably the day after baking), cut off the skin and even off the top. Use a plain cookie cutter approximately 1 1/2 inches (3.7 cm) in diameter to cut out rounds (or follow the suggestions for cutting the shapes in Petits Fours Glacé, step five).

4. Roll the Marzipan out to 1/8 inch (3 mm) thick and into a rectangle approximately 5 1/2 inches wide (13.7 cm), using powdered sugar to prevent it from sticking. Brush any powdered sugar off of the top. Texture the Marzipan by rolling a waffle roller down the length of the strip (do not roll it across the width, or the strip will become too wide). Invert the Marzipan sheet so that the plain side is facing up.

5. Measure and trim the long edges so that the width of the Marzipan strip is the precise size of the circumference of the cutouts. Next measure the height of the cutouts and then cut across the Marzipan strip, making the pieces 1/4 inch (6 mm) wider than your measurement (if the cutouts are 1 1/4 inches/3.1 cm high you will cut the Marzipan strips 1 1/2 inches/3.7 cm wide).

6. One at a time, pick up a Mazarin sheet cutout, spread a thin film of buttercream on the cut sides, and roll the cutout along a Marzipan strip so that the Marzipan sticks and wraps around it. Start with the Short Dough side even with one edge of the Marzipan so that the opposite side of the Marzipan extends 1/4 inch (6 mm) above the Mazarin side. Place the pastries standing up on their Short Dough ends.

7. Soften the Ganache to a pipeable consistency. Place in a pastry bag with a no. 7 (14-mm) star tip. Pipe a rosette of Ganache on top of each cutout (if you are using shapes other than rounds, pipe the Ganache appropriately to cover the entire top within the Marzipan frame).

8. Decorate each Petit Four with a diamond-shaped piece of candied angelica.

Petits Fours Sec

The French word *sec* translates to "dry" in English, which doesn't sound too appealing and might lead you to believe that these small bite-sized pastries are unfilled or unadorned. In reality, a small amount of Ganache, buttercream, or jam is used either to sandwich the pastries together or to decorate the tops, and they are often dipped in chocolate. They are delicious, elegant, miniature creations, far from dry. The decorated cookies look beautiful lined up on silver trays to be served with afternoon tea, or as an accompaniment to after-dinner coffee. Petits Fours Sec can also be used to garnish ice cream coupes, or any dessert for which the serving dish is placed on a plate with a doily. Many of the cookies and pastries in this book can be used as Petits Fours Sec by simply making them smaller and in some cases enhancing the decoration, just as many of the following recipes can be made into traditional pastries or cookies by cutting or making them larger.

Almond Doubles

eighty-five 2-inch (5-cm) cookies

2 pounds (910 g) Short Dough (page 54)

1 pound, 12 ounces (795 g) or one-half recipe Macaroon Decorating Paste (page 203)

10 ounces (285 g) smooth raspberry jam

10 ounces (285 g) smooth apricot jam

Simple Syrup (page 11)

dark coating chocolate, melted (optional)

Of all of these miniature creations, Almond Doubles are probably the one most frequently found as a larger pastry—usually about 3 inches in diameter—in European pastry shops. They are something of a cross between a fancy cookie and a simple pastry.

1. Roll the Short Dough out to ⅛ inch (3 mm) thick. Cut out eighty-five 2-inch (5-cm) cookies, using a fluted cookie cutter. Place them on a sheet pan lined with baking paper. Cover the dough scraps and save for another use.

2. Place the Macaroon Paste in a pastry bag with a no. 3 (6-mm) plain tip. Pipe the paste onto the cookies by first going all the way around the edge, and then straight across the middle in one unbroken line.

3. Make two pastry bags from baking paper (see page 23) and fill one with the raspberry jam and the other with the apricot jam. Pipe the jam within the macaroon frame, filling one side with each flavor.

4. Bake the cookies at 400°F (205°C) for about 12 minutes or until golden brown.

5. As soon as the cookies come out of the oven, brush Simple Syrup on the macaroon border without disturbing the jam.

6. For a fancier look (and taste), dip the base of the cookie into melted coating chocolate: Hold a dipping fork under the cookie and press lightly into the melted chocolate, coating the bottom and the sides up to the macaroon. Drag off the excess chocolate on the rim of the bowl, and place the cookies on sheet pans lined with baking paper (see Figures 9–27 to 9–31, page 428).

Brandy Pretzels

72 cookies

6 ounces (170 g) granulated sugar
10 ounces (285 g) soft unsalted butter
¼ cup (60 ml) brandy
1 teaspoon (5 ml) vanilla extract
1 pound, 2 ounces (510 g) bread flour
dark coating chocolate, melted
soybean oil or a commercial thinning
   agent

*F*or an easy variation, make Sugared-Brandy Pretzels: After forming the pretzels, invert them in granulated sugar. Place sugar-side up on sheet pans and bake as directed. Omit dipping in chocolate.

1. Combine the sugar and butter. Add the brandy and vanilla. Incorporate the flour and mix to form a smooth dough. Refrigerate if the dough is too soft to work with.

2. Divide the dough into four 9-ounce (255-g) pieces. Roll into ropes and cut each of the four ropes into eighteen small pieces. Roll each of the small pieces into a string 8 inches (20 cm) long and slightly tapered at the ends, using little or no flour. Form the strings into pretzels (see Figure 3–29, page 132). Place on sheet pans lined with baking paper.

3. Bake at 375°F (190°C) for about 8 minutes or until light golden brown and baked through. Let cool completely.

4. Dip the baked pretzels into dark coating chocolate thinned with soybean oil or a commercial thinning agent. (Use approximately two parts chocolate to one part oil by volume.) Add two or three at a time to the bowl of melted chocolate, then remove them one at time using a dipping fork. Scrape each cookie against the side of the bowl as you remove it to eliminate as much excess chocolate as possible.

Chocolate-Filled Macadamia Morsels

50 filled cookies

melted unsalted butter
bread flour
10 ounces (285 g) unsalted
   macadamia nuts
8 ounces (225 g) granulated sugar
6 ounces (170 g) soft unsalted butter
4 egg whites (½ cup/120 ml)
6 ounces (170 g) bread flour
6 ounces (170 g) Ganache (page 1086)
dark coating chocolate, melted

*U*se a 1-inch (2.5-cm) cookie cutter to mark rings in the flour on the prepared sheet pan. This is a convenient way to gauge the size as you pipe and ensures that the cookies will be uniform. Do not use baking paper or the cookies will spread and become too flat. If you do not have macadamia nuts on hand, make these cookies with pine nuts instead; they are equally delicious.

1. Lightly grease sheet pans with melted butter. Place a band of bread flour at the edge on one long side, then tilt the pan to cover it with flour. Tap the sheet pan against the table to remove any excess.

2. Grind the macadamia nuts and sugar together in a food processor to a very fine consistency. Reserve.

3. Beat the soft butter until light and creamy. Add the ground nut mixture. Mix in the egg whites one at a time and beat until smooth. Mix in the flour.

NOTE: Instead of streaking chocolate over the cookies, you can dip the entire top cookie into melted chocolate before sandwiching the cookies together.

4. Place the batter in a pastry bag with a no. 6 (12-mm) plain tip. Pipe out 100 mounds 1 inch (2.5 cm) wide and about ¹/₂ inch (1.2 cm) high onto the prepared pans.

5. Bake at 325°F (163°C) until deep golden brown around the edges, approximately 12 minutes. Let the cookies cool completely.

6. Turn half of the cookies upside down. Warm the Ganache to a soft, paste-like consistency and place it in a pastry bag with a no. 5 (10-mm) plain tip. Pipe a small amount of Ganache on the inverted cookies. Place the remaining cookies on top, pressing lightly to sandwich the two flat sides together and squeeze the Ganache to the edge of the cookies.

7. Place the melted dark coating chocolate in a piping bag and pipe straight lines close to each other (streak) across the cookies (see Figure 6–1, page 246, but pipe in one direction only). Store in airtight containers to keep the cookies crisp.

 Hazelnut Cuts

about 80 cookies

8 egg whites (1 cup/240 ml)
12 ounces (340 g) granulated sugar
14 ounces (400 g) hazelnuts, ground fine
2 ounces (55 g) cornstarch
dark coating chocolate, melted

*F*or a less time-consuming alternative, you can simply pipe the ropes of meringue in pairs with the long sides touching. Omit joining the pieces together, and dip the cut pieces a little further into the melted chocolate.

1. Combine the egg whites and sugar in a mixer bowl, place over hot water, and heat to 110°F (43°C) while whipping constantly. Remove the bowl from the pan and continue whipping until the mixture is cold and stiff peaks have formed.

2. Combine the hazelnuts with the cornstarch and fold into the meringue by hand.

3. Place the meringue in a pastry bag with a no. 5 (10-mm) plain tip. Pipe out ropes of meringue, 1 inch (2.5 cm) apart, the full length of the sheet, onto sheet pans lined with baking paper.

4. Bake at 300°F (149°C) for approximately 25 minutes or until very light brown. Do not dry the meringue completely or it will break when you cut the cookies.

5. Before the meringue is completely cold (while still soft), cut the ropes into 2-inch (5-cm) pieces. Let cool completely.

6. Sandwich the flat sides of the pieces together with coating chocolate by dipping only the surface of one piece into the chocolate and then placing a plain piece on top. After joining all of the pieces, dip both ends of the pastries into chocolate to coat them about ¹/₈ inch (3 mm) on each end. Set on a sheet pan lined with baking paper, placing the pastries on their sides so the chocolate in the center is visible on top.

Hazelnut Flowers

about seventy-five 2-inch (5-cm) cookies

2 pounds (910 g) Hazelnut Short
    Dough (page 55)
14 ounces (400 g) or one-quarter
    recipe Macaroon Decorating Paste
    (page 203)
seventy-five whole hazelnuts, lightly
    toasted, skins removed
Simple Syrup (page 11)

If you don't want to use hazelnuts for decoration, make an indentation in the center using your index finger (use some water to keep it from sticking) and pipe a little apricot jam in the hollow before baking.

1. Roll out a piece of the Short Dough ¹⁄₈ inch (3 mm) thick. Cut out star-shaped cookies using a cutter approximately 2 inches (5 cm) in diameter. Place the cookies on sheet pans lined with baking paper. Repeat with remaining dough and scraps until you have used all of it.

2. Place the Macaroon Decorating Paste in a pastry bag with a no. 2 (4-mm) plain tip. Pipe the paste onto the cookies in a series of small teardrop shapes, starting at the end of each point of the star and ending in the center to form a flower pattern (see step two in Strawberry Hearts, page 412). Place one hazelnut, pointed end up, in the center of each cookie.

3. Bake at 400°F (205°C) for about 12 minutes. Brush the cookies lightly with Simple Syrup as soon as they come out of the oven.

Macaroon Candies

about 70 cookies

3 pounds, 8 ounces (1 kg, 590 g) or
    one recipe Macaroon Decorating
    Paste (page 203) (see note 1)
food colorings
almonds, blanched and skins removed
pistachios
raisins or currants
Candied Orange Peel (page 978)
granulated sugar
Simple Syrup (page 11)
dark coating chocolate, melted

NOTE 1: Leave out more egg white than usual when you make the Macaroon Decorating Paste. The paste will be too firm to pipe, but using the warming method to soften it, rather than adding egg whites, will keep the cookies from spreading while they bake.

NOTE 2: This paste can be used to make figures such as chickens, ducks, and rabbits, as shown in Figure 9–18 (the chicken's tail is Candied Orange Peel, the duck's beak is a pine nut, and the rabbit's ears are made of sliced almonds).

This type of cookie is very popular in Europe, and even though it is not really a Petits Fours Sec, the color can really enliven the cookie tray. Macaroon Candies are often referred to as Almond Paste Petits Fours. You can delay the staling process with the addition of invert sugar, adding 5 percent of the sugar weight, and by piping the paste into high shapes rather than flat.

1. Warm the Macaroon Paste in a saucepan over low heat, stirring constantly, until it is soft enough to pipe without effort. If you want to color the paste, use pale shades.

2. Pipe the paste in various shapes onto sheet pans lined with baking paper, using a no.-4-to-no.-6 (8-to-10-mm) pastry bag with a plain or star tip, separately or in combination. Use your imagination and creativity but keep the shapes 1¹⁄₂ to 2 inches (3.7 to 5 cm) in size.

3. Decorate with whole or slivered almonds, pistachios, raisins, and Candied Orange Peel. Granulated sugar can be sprinkled over the tops, but this should be done immediately after the cookies are piped and decorated, before a skin forms on the top. Set the cookies aside at room temperature overnight to allow them to dry slightly before baking.

4. Bake the cookies, double-panned, at 425°F (219°C) for about 8 minutes or until they just start to show color. Brush with Simple Syrup as soon as they come out of the oven. Let cool completely before attempting to remove them from the paper. If they stick, follow the directions in Almond Macaroon Cookies on page 202. Dip some of the cookies partially into melted coating chocolate for a nice contrast. Store in airtight containers. Macaroon Candies may be frozen but should not be dipped in chocolate in that case.

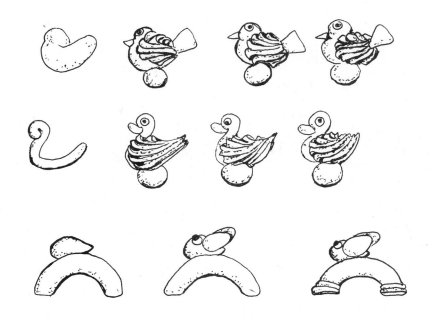

FIGURE 9–18 Bird and animal shapes made from Macaroon Decorating Paste for a variation of Macaroon Candies

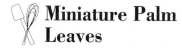 **Miniature Palm Leaves**

about forty-five 2-inch (5-cm) cookies

12 ounces (340 g) Puff Pastry
    (page 44)
4 ounces (115 g) granulated sugar,
    approximately
dark coating chocolate, melted

NOTE: The cookies can also be served without chocolate, or sandwiched together as described in the recipe for the larger Palm Leaves, depending on what other selection of Petits Fours Sec you are serving.

*I*t is of the utmost importance that the Puff Pastry be rolled out as thin as specified when making Miniature Palm Leaves. If the folded layers are too thick, the cut cookies will be too wide and the layers will rip apart as they expand in the oven. An easy way around this, but one which produces a less intricate cookie, is to omit folding the strip in half crosswise, which gives you just a double turn instead. You should still make the indentation before folding the strip in half lengthwise.

Cut and bake only as many Palm Leaves as you will be serving within one or two days. The unsliced folded dough can be refrigerated for one day or frozen to use later.

1. Roll out the Puff Pastry in the granulated sugar to make a strip 20 by 8 inches (50 × 20 cm) and about $1/16$ inch (2 mm) thick, following the directions for rolling out the sheet in Palm Leaves on page 220.

2. Fold the long sides in to meet in the center. Fold the strip in half crosswise so it is now 10 inches (25 cm) long. Use a thin dowel to make a light indentation lengthwise down the center of the strip. Fold in half on this mark. Refrigerate until firm.

3. Slice and bake following the directions for Palm Leaves but allow only 6 minutes before turning the cookies and be very careful not to burn them after they are turned over.

4. When they have cooled completely, dip the wider end of each cookie into melted coating chocolate.

Strawberry Hearts

eighty 2-inch (5-cm) cookies

2 pounds (910 g) Short Dough
   (page 54)
1 pound, 12 ounces (795 g) or one-
   half recipe Macaroon Decorating
   Paste (page 203)
12 ounces (340 g) smooth oven-stable
   strawberry jam
Simple Syrup (page 11)
dark coating chocolate, melted

I often make these using the next larger size cutter as a quick and colorful addition to a buffet table. They are especially appropriate for a Mother's Day celebration or as a complimentary treat at the end of the meal on Valentine's Day.

1. Roll out half of the Short Dough to ⅛ inch (3 mm) thick. Cut out heart-shaped cookies using a cutter approximately 2 inches (5 cm) across the top. Place the cookies on sheet pans lined with baking paper. Repeat with the remaining dough and scraps until you have cut eighty hearts. Cover and save any leftover dough for another use.

2. Place the Macaroon Decorating Paste in a pastry bag with a no. 3 (6-mm) plain tip. Pipe a border of paste around each heart. The paste should be just soft enough to stick to the dough; if it is too soft it will run when it bakes. (If the cookies keep moving as you try to pipe the paste, place them in a warm oven for about 30 seconds, which will make them stick to the paper.)

3. Place the jam in a disposable pastry bag made from baking paper (see page 23). Pipe just enough jam inside the macaroon border to cover the Short Dough.

4. Bake the cookies at 400°F (205°C) until golden brown, about 12 minutes. Brush Simple Syrup on the macaroon border as soon as the cookies come out of the oven, taking care not to smear the jam. Let the cookies cool completely.

5. Place the melted coating chocolate in a piping bag and cut a very small opening. Streak the chocolate over the cookies as explained for Pecan Whiskey Tart (see Figure 6–1, page 246) but pipe the lines in one direction only, diagonally, across the cookies.

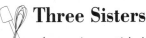

Three Sisters

about ninety 1¾-inch (4.5-cm) cookies

2 ounces (55 g) bread flour
one recipe Spritz Rings dough
   (page 225)
12 ounces (340 g) smooth raspberry
   jam
powdered sugar

You can obtain a special cutter for these cookies that will cut out the three holes at the same time that you cut out the cookie itself, which is helpful if you are making a large quantity. To make the variation known as Bull's Eyes, cut out one large hole in the center of half of the cookies, instead of three small ones. The end result is a cookie that looks something like a flat, raspberry-filled bouchée. If you have Short Dough (made with butter) on hand you can use that instead of the Spritz Rings dough; it is not necessary in that case to add the extra flour. The cookies will not be quite as tender but certainly acceptable.

1. Add the additional flour to the Spritz Rings when making the dough. Mix on low speed only until smooth. Refrigerate the dough if it is too soft to work with.

2. Roll out a piece of dough to ⅛ inch (3 mm) thick. Cut out round cookies using a 1¾-inch (4.5-cm) fluted cutter. Place the cookies on sheet pans lined with baking paper. Repeat with remaining dough and scraps until all the dough is used. Cut three small holes in half of the cookies using a no. 4 (8-mm) plain piping tip.

3. Bake the cookies at 400°F (205°C) until they are golden, about 10 minutes. Let the cookies cool completely.

4. Place the jam in a disposable pastry bag made from baking paper (see page 23). Pipe a dot of jam on top of the plain cookies. Place the cut cookies on the jam and press down lightly. Sift powdered sugar lightly over the tops.

 Viennese Petits Fours

about 85 pieces

1 pound, 6 ounces (625 g) Short Dough (page 54)
or
1 pound, 6 ounces (625 g) Hazelnut Short Dough (page 55)
or
1 pound, 6 ounces (625 g) Linzer Dough (page 34)
6 ounces (170 g) Almond Paste (page 3), approximately
4 ounces (115 g) soft unsalted butter, approximately
2 tablespoons (30 ml) dark rum
8 ounces (225 g) Ganache (page 1086)
2 tablespoons (30 ml) orange liqueur
6 ounces (170 g) Vanilla Buttercream (page 978)
1 tablespoon (15 ml) cherry or mint liqueur
dark or light coating chocolate, melted
Apricot Glaze (page 1016)
or
Red Currant Glaze (page 1017)
slivered almonds
pistachios
hazelnuts
Candied Orange Peel (page 978)
candied violets
Chocolate Figurines (page 906)

There is nothing more elegant to serve with afternoon tea or at the end of dinner with cordials than a tray of Viennese Petits Fours, arranged perhaps with some Macaroon Candies. To produce the best look and variety in this type of Petits Fours you need an assortment of individual small molds, 1¹/₂ inches (3.7 cm) in diameter and ¹/₂ inch (1.2 cm) high or, better yet, rows of molds fastened to a metal strip. The individual molds can be purchased in sets containing six to eight different shapes, but using the forms attached to a strip greatly speeds up the production process. To produce a very precise and professional looking finish, line only half of the molds (of each shape) at one time. Use the back of a knife to trim the dough even with the edge of the molds instead of using your palm or thumb. Place the remaining empty molds on top and press them lightly into the dough. Bake the shells this way until they are almost done. Quickly remove the empty molds on top, and continue to bake a few minutes longer until the shells are light brown inside. You cannot use this method for molds attached to a strip unless you also have individual molds that are identical in shape to those on the strip.

1. Line the molds with Short Dough, Hazelnut Short Dough, or Linzer Dough (or use a combination) rolled ¹/₁₆ inch (2 mm) thick (see Figures 2–15 to 2–18, pages 57 and 58). Cover and reserve the dough scraps for another use. Prick the shells, then bake at 375°F (190°C) for about 8 minutes. Let the shells cool and then carefully remove from the molds.

2. Fill and decorate the shells. Here is a good chance to use your imagination as well as your good taste. You might, for example:

• soften the Almond Paste to a pipeable consistency with butter and flavor it with rum;
• add orange liqueur to the Ganache; or
• flavor Vanilla Buttercream with cherry or mint liqueur.

The amounts given in the ingredients list are based on using three separate fillings. If you wish to use just one or two fillings, adjust the quantities accordingly. Pipe the fillings into the shells in the shape of a mound or rosette.

3. Dip the tops of the pastries in melted coating chocolate or brush them with Apricot or Currant Glaze.

4. Decorate with slivered almonds, pistachios, hazelnuts, Candied Orange Peel, candied violets, or Chocolate Figurines.

Polynées

40 pastries

2 pounds (910 g) Short Dough
(page 54)

6 ounces (170 g) smooth strawberry
jam

one recipe Almond Macaroon Cookies
batter (page 202)

3 egg whites (³/₈ cup/90 ml),
approximately

powdered sugar

*H*ow these rather plain and typically Scandinavian pastries came to be named after such an exotic place as the tropical Polynesian Islands (a group of French territorial islands in the South Pacific, Tahiti being the most well known) is unclear. Perhaps the French, who have been responsible for naming so many culinary creations, had something to do with these as well. Polynées are basically an Almond Macaroon Cookie wrapped in Short Dough. They are somewhat similar to the pastry known as Conversation, the main difference being that there, the forms are lined with Puff Pastry instead of Short Dough, and the Almond Paste is thinned with egg yolks. The Polynées filling should puff up around the Short Dough cross. If it does not, the batter was too firm or the oven wasn't hot enough.

1. Roll out one-third of the Short Dough to ¹/₈ inch (3 mm) thick and reserve in the refrigerator. Roll out the remaining dough to ¹/₈ inch (3 mm) thick and use it to line forty mazarin forms (see page 398) or other forms of similar size (see Figures 2–15 to 2–18, pages 57 and 58). Cover the scrap dough and save for another use.

2. Make a pastry bag from a half sheet of baking paper (see page 23) and fill it with the strawberry jam. Pipe the jam into the forms, dividing it evenly.

3. Add one to three egg whites to the macaroon batter, beating it to a soft, creamy, yet still pipeable consistency. It should be liquid enough to flatten when piped. Place the batter in a pastry bag with a no. 4 (8-mm) plain tip. Pipe the batter into the forms on top of the jam, almost filling the forms.

4. Cut the reserved Short Dough into ¹/₄-inch (6-mm) wide strips. Place two strips on top of each form, crossing them at a 90° angle and pinching the ends to the dough lining the sides. Add the scraps to the others reserved earlier.

5. Bake the pastries at 400°F (205°C) until golden brown, about 20 minutes. Let cool slightly and then remove the forms. Very lightly sift powdered sugar over the tops. Polynées will keep fresh for up to one week if stored, covered, in the refrigerator.

Princess Pastries

45 pastries

one recipe Chiffon Sponge Cake batter
(page 272)

8 ounces (225 g) smooth strawberry
jam

2 pounds (910 g) Marzipan
(page 1022), colored light pink

powdered sugar

*T*hese pretty, petite, Princess Pastries are a staple in many pastry shops across Europe, with variations in fillings, sometimes disguised by other names, and with different textures on the Marzipan; both basketweave and ruffled designs look great. The Marzipan rings can be made ahead and used to frame other pastries as well. Follow the procedure in step five, cutting the Marzipan strips to fit the circumference of the item you are going to make. Once the strips have been cut, brush a little water on one short end, then, using an appropriately sized plain cookie cutter as a guide, roll the strip around the cutter and press the ends together. Carefully place the Marzipan frames standing upright on a paper-lined sheet pan. Allow the rings to dry overnight at room

10 ounces (285 g) Vanilla Buttercream
(page 978)

1 pound, 8 ounces (680 g) Pastry
Cream (page 1088)

1 quart (960 ml) heavy cream

2 tablespoons (30 g) granulated sugar

fresh cherries or strawberries

forty-five Chocolate Figurines
(page 906)

NOTE: You can pick up each strip of Marzipan and press it in place with your hand, or simply leave the strips in place on the table, pick up each cake instead and roll the side of the cake along the strip so that the buttercream flattens and glues the Marzipan to the cake.

FIGURE 9–19 The progression in piping the whipped cream on top of Princess Pastries

temperature before using. The Marzipan rings can be used to create many quick pastries. For example, cut circles of sponge to fit within the rings (they need to fit snugly so they don't fall out), fill with Pastry or Bavarian Cream, arrange fresh fruit on top, and brush some Apricot Glaze over the fruit. There are many other uses, depending on the ingredients you have on hand.

1. Line the bottom of a half-sheet pan (16 by 12 inches/40 × 30 cm) with baking paper. Fill the pan with the Sponge Cake batter, spreading it out evenly. Bake immediately at 400°F (205°C) for about 15 minutes or until the cake springs back when pressed lightly in the center. Let cool completely.

2. Cut around the side of the pan and invert to remove the sponge. Peel the paper from the back and turn right-side up. Cut the skin from the top and cut the top level at the same time. Cut into two layers horizontally.

3. Spread the strawberry jam over the bottom layer, then place the top layer on the jam.

4. Cut out forty-five 2-inch (5-cm) rounds using a plain cookie cutter. To get the full number you will need to keep the cuts close together and stagger the rows. Save the scraps for a trifle or for Rum Ball Filling.

5. Roll half of the Marzipan out to ⅛ inch (3 mm) thick, in a rectangle approximately 7½ by 16 inches (18.7 × 40 cm), using powdered sugar to prevent it from sticking. Roll a waffle roller lengthwise over the strip to texture the top. The Marzipan should increase in size as you do this. Invert the strip and trim it to 7¼ inches (18.1 cm) wide. Cut the strip across into 1½-inch-wide (3.7-cm) pieces. Repeat with the remaining Marzipan to make 45 pieces total. Cover and save the leftover Marzipan for another use.

6. Place the buttercream in a disposable pastry bag made from baking paper (see page 23). Pipe a rope of buttercream lengthwise in the center of each Marzipan strip. Fasten a strip around the side of each cake, so that the buttercream sticks to the sponge and the bottom long edge of the Marzipan is even with the bottom of the sponge cake (see note). The strips should overlap just slightly so you can press them together.

7. Place the Pastry Cream in pastry bag with a no. 4 (8-mm) plain tip. Pipe the cream on the tops of the cakes in a spiral pattern, covering the sponge completely

8. Whip the heavy cream and granulated sugar to stiff peaks. Place in a pastry bag with a no. 3 (6-mm) star tip. Pipe the whipped cream decoratively on top of the Pastry Cream, within the Marzipan border, making loops left to right and right to left (Figure 9–19).

9. Pit and cut the cherries in half or cut the strawberries into small wedges. Stand a Chocolate Figurine in the whipped cream in the center of each pastry. Place a cherry half or strawberry wedge next to the figurine. Princess Pastries should be served the same day they are finished. If they must be kept overnight they should be boxed and refrigerated.

Rainbow Pastries

40 pastries

1 pound, 13 ounces (825 g) or one-third recipe Mazarin Filling (page 1088)

1 pound, 8 ounces (680 g) Vanilla Buttercream (page 978)

2 ounces (55 g) strawberry jam or preserves, strained

1 teaspoon (5 ml) Beet Juice (page 3) (see note)

2 ounces (55 g) Lemon Cream or Lemon Curd (page 1087)

2 ounces (55 g) sweet dark chocolate, melted

one recipe Chocolate Glaze (page 1016)

NOTE: You may want to adjust the amount of Beet Juice used or omit it all together, depending on the jam or preserves you are using.

*T*his old-fashioned recipe is not quite as practical as it is elegant. Although Rainbow Pastries can be prepared through step five and kept covered in the refrigerator for a few days to be completed as needed, once they are iced and cut they are easily smeared and damaged. On a positive note, they add a nice splash of color to your pastry selection. You can use this basic idea and instructions to create other combinations. Try replacing the lemon buttercream with buttercream flavored with praline or coffee, and the strawberry with buttercream flavored with rum or arrack. These flavors compliment the chocolate nicely.

The glazed pastries must be refrigerated before they can be cut; this will dull the Chocolate Glaze quite alarmingly. Therefore, the pastries should always be left at room temperature long enough for the shine to return before they are served. The buttercream is also more pleasant to eat when it is not cold and hard.

1. Spread the Mazarin Filling out within a quarter-sheet pan (8 by 12 inches/20 × 30 cm) lined with baking paper. If you do not have this size pan, use a half-sheet pan and stand a strip of corrugated cardboard wrapped in foil against the exposed long side of the filling to prevent it from spreading.

2. Bake at 400°F (205°C) for about 15 minutes or until the cake is baked through. Allow to cool completely, preferably overnight in the refrigerator, covered.

3. Run a knife along the edge of the cake to loosen it from the pan. Invert and then peel the baking paper from the back. Turn right-side up and cut the top level if necessary. Cut the cake lengthwise into four 2-inch (5-cm) strips. Place each strip on a rectangular piece of cardboard.

4. Divide the buttercream into three equal portions. Flavor one with the strawberry jam or preserves and add the Beet Juice for color. Flavor one portion of buttercream with the Lemon Cream or Curd. Flavor the remaining one-third of the buttercream with the melted chocolate.

5. Place the lemon-flavored buttercream in a pastry bag with a no. 8 (16-mm) plain tip. Pipe a rope of buttercream 1/4 inch (6 mm) from one long side on all four Mazarin strips. Squeeze out any buttercream left in the bag (there should not be much, if any) and fill the pastry bag with the strawberry-flavored buttercream. Pipe a rope of strawberry-flavored buttercream next to the lemon buttercream on each Mazarin strip. This should leave an equal amount of space on the opposite long side (the two ropes should be centered on the Mazarin strip). Squeeze out any leftover strawberry buttercream and fill the bag with the chocolate buttercream. Pipe a rope of chocolate buttercream, in the center, on the top of the first two buttercream ropes (Figure 9–20). Refrigerate the Mazarin strips until the buttercream is firm.

6. Place the strips on a icing rack or cake-cooling rack set over a sheet pan lined with baking paper. Warm the Chocolate Glaze to the proper temperature so that it will easily coat the pastries: If the glaze is too cool (thick) the chilled surface of the buttercream will cause it to set up before it has floated down to cover the pastry. On the other hand, if

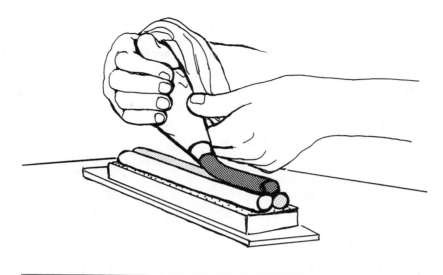

FIGURE 9–20 *Piping a rope of chocolate-flavored buttercream on top of the lemon- and strawberry-flavored buttercream ropes for Rainbow Pastries*

the glaze is too warm, it can melt the buttercream on contact. Anything above body temperature is considered too warm. Make a test before you attempt to glaze an entire strip. Use a spoon to apply the glaze to one strip at a time in smooth, even strokes (see Figure 9–15, page 397). Immediately go back and cover any bare spots on the sides before moving on. Waiting even a minute will leave a mark after the glaze has hardened. Wait until the glaze has run off completely so that none is dripping from the sides, and then carefully transfer the strips to a sheet pan lined with baking paper. Place in the refrigerator until the glaze is firm to the touch.

7. Trim the short ends. Slice each strip into 10 pieces at a 45° angle, using a sharp chef's knife dipped in hot water to heat and clean the knife between each cut. The warm knife will smear the different colors of buttercream into one another as you slice. To repair this, gently run the edge of the knife from the bottom up to the top immediately after making each cut. Store covered in the refrigerator.

Rum Balls

60 pastries

Rum Ball Filling (recipe follows)
powdered sugar
2 pounds (910 g) melted dark or light coating chocolate, approximately
4 teaspoons (20 ml) Simple Syrup (page 11), approximately

*R*um Balls *are an excellent way of recycling good leftover pastries, end pieces, scraps, and other preparations, just as vegetable trimmings, bones, and some types of leftover sauces go into the stock pot in the hot kitchen. However, the Rum Ball bucket should not be mistaken for a garbage can: Only those scraps that will not spoil within a week or so should be added. No Pastry Cream or whipped cream should be used, and buttercream or buttercream-filled items should be used only if they are no more than one day old. The best kinds of scraps to use are slightly stale cookies, meringues or macaroons, Florentinas, Ladyfingers, pastries such as Tosca or Polynées that do not contain buttercream, light or dark sponge cake, and baked Short Dough cookies or cake bottoms.*

NOTE 1: *I generally do not specify the amount of melted chocolate where the item is simply to be dipped in or decorated with chocolate. Most pastry kitchens have a supply of chocolate on hand, either melted or ready to melt, for this purpose. Also, the amount of chocolate the chef needs to work with is always quite a bit more than is actually used on the finished pastries, and the size of the bowl used to hold the melted chocolate will make a big difference as well. I am specifying an amount in this recipe to emphasize that a fairly large amount is needed.*

NOTE 2: *The first coating is necessary to seal the surface of the Rum Balls before they are rolled in thick chocolate. This makes it possible to roll the Rum Balls in thick chocolate at room temperature without having them fall apart. Simply firming them in the refrigerator will produce small cracks in the chocolate coating as the filling expands when it reaches room temperature.*

Danish or other yeast-dough pastries should not be used in a quality Rum Ball mixture but can be recycled as part of a Bear Claw filling.

The technique used for coating Rum Balls with chocolate is a little more complicated than the dipping technique used in many of the other recipes. However, because Rum Balls are so simple and inexpensive to make, there is no need to speed up the finishing process by simply dipping them or, worse yet, rolling them in chocolate sprinkles. I prefer to use light chocolate for coating Rum Balls, as so many of the other pastries look better with dark chocolate, but of course they are interchangeable.

1. Divide the Rum Ball Filling into five pieces a little over 1 pound (455 g) each. Roll each piece into a 12-inch (30-cm) rope, using powdered sugar to prevent the filling from sticking to the table. Cut each rope into 12 equal pieces. Roll the small pieces into round balls and place the balls on sheet pans lined with paper. Refrigerate until firm.

2. The temperature of the coating chocolate should be between 100 and 110°F (38 to 43°C). Cover the Rum Balls with a thin layer of melted chocolate by picking up some chocolate with your fingers and rolling a Rum Ball between your palms to coat. Place them back on the pans and reserve at room temperature.

3. Weigh out 1 pound, 8 ounces (680 g) of the remaining chocolate (add more chocolate if necessary, depending on the amount used to coat the Rum Balls the first time, or remove some for another use). Bring the chocolate back to the proper working temperature. Stir in the Simple Syrup. You may need to increase the amount of syrup added depending on the brand of chocolate you are using. The chocolate should thicken to the consistency of mayonnaise.

4. Pick up some of the thickened chocolate with your fingers and roll each rum ball between your palms as before, but this time cover them with a thick layer of chocolate, with spikes and tails of chocolate standing up (Figure 9–21). You must work quickly or the heat from

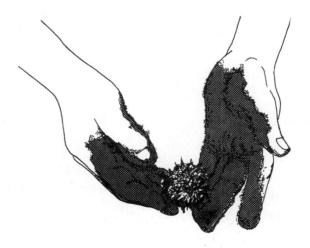

FIGURE 9–21 *Coating Rum Balls with thickened melted chocolate by rolling them between your palms to produce a spiked surface*

your hands will melt the chocolate and you will not be able to achieve the rough texture; the finished pastry should be full of ridges and points like a properly rolled truffle.

5. Replace the Rum Balls on the pans and store in a dry box or covered in the refrigerator.

1. Heat the rum and raisins slightly, and macerate for a few hours.

2. Place the scraps and water in a mixer bowl and mix with a paddle to a smooth consistency. You may have to adjust the amount of water, depending on how many dry items you are using. Mix until you have a very firm, smooth dough, approximately 10 minutes. Add the crushed nuts and the chocolate and mix until combined. Incorporate the rum and raisin mixture.

3. Place on a sheet pan lined with baking paper. Refrigerate until the filling is firm before shaping. If the mixture is too soft to work with, add some additional scraps from dry items, finely ground, to absorb moisture. If the filling is dry and crumbly, mix in enough buttercream or Ganache to bring it to a workable consistency.

1. Divide the Rum Ball Filling into two equal pieces. Roll each piece into a 16-inch (40-cm) rope, using powdered sugar to prevent the filling from sticking to the table. Cut each rope into fifteen equal pieces.

2. Roll the small pieces into round balls. Keeping the ball between your hands, taper one end to make a small cone, rounded at the wide end. To be sure the pastries will resemble porcupines (and not look like some strange rodent instead), make the cones only about 2 inches (5 cm) long, with a definite point at the narrow end. Place the cones on sheet pans lined with baking paper and press lightly, just enough to keep them from rolling. Refrigerate until firm.

3. If you are using whole blanched almonds, cut them into pointed strips (which is easiest to do while the almonds are still soft from blanching). Dry the almond strips in the oven until hard.

4. Push seven almond strips or slivers into the top of the wide portion of each Rum Ball cone (Figure 9–22).

5. Bring the Porcupines close to room temperature if they have been chilled. One at a time, set the Porcupines on a dipping fork, and dip into melted coating chocolate, covering them completely. As you remove each Porcupine, move it up and down over the bowl of chocolate a few times to remove as much of the excess chocolate as possible. Place the Porcupines on sheet pans lined with baking paper.

6. Check the Royal Icing to be sure it is thick enough not to run after it is piped. Put the Royal Icing in a piping bag and cut a very small opening. Pipe two dots (the size of white peppercorns) on each Porcupine for eyes. Place melted dark coating chocolate in a second piping bag and pipe a smaller dot of chocolate on the Royal Icing, making pupils in the eyes. Store the finished Porcupines in a dry box or well covered in the refrigerator.

 Rum Ball Filling

about 5 pounds, 10 ounces (2 kg, 560 g) filling

³/₄ cup (180 ml) dark rum

6 ounces (170 g) dark raisins

4 pounds (1 kg, 820 g) scraps (see introduction)

¹/₄ cup (60 ml) water, approximately

5 ounces (140 g) nuts, any variety, crushed fine

12 ounces (340 g) dark or light sweet chocolate, melted

Porcupines

30 pastries

2 pounds, 12 ounces (1 kg, 250 g) or one-half recipe Rum Ball filling (this page)

powdered sugar

3 ounces (85 g) whole almonds, blanched and skins removed

or

2 ounces (55 g) blanched, slivered (not sliced) almonds

dark coating chocolate, melted

Royal Icing (page 1019)

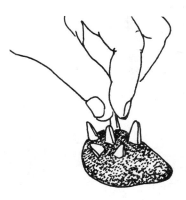

FIGURE 9–22 *Pushing slivered almonds into shaped Rum Ball Filling to make Porcupines*

Rum-Chocolate Spools

40 pastries

2 pounds, 12 ounces (1 kg, 250 g) or
  one-half recipe Rum Ball Filling
  (page 419)

powdered sugar

1 pound, 2 ounces (510 g) Marzipan
  (page 1022), untinted

2 ounces (55 g) Vanilla Buttercream
  (page 978)

dark coating chocolate, melted

1. Divide the Rum Ball Filling into four equal pieces, about 11 ounces (310 g) each. Roll each piece into a rope 20 inches (50 cm) long, using powdered sugar to prevent the filling from sticking to the table. Set the ropes aside on a sheet pan lined with baking paper.

2. Roll out a portion of the Marzipan to $1/8$ inch (3 mm) thick; the width of the strips should be the same as the length of the ropes (use powdered sugar to keep it from sticking also). Trim one short side to make it even and straight. Turn the Marzipan upside down and spread a thin film of buttercream over it.

3. Set one of the Rum Ball ropes at the trimmed edge of the Marzipan sheet and roll up one full turn to encase it completely; the edges should line up, not overlap. Cut the rope away from the Marzipan sheet (Figure 9–23).

4. Roll the covered rope against the table until it is 24 inches (60 cm) long, making it even at the same time. Carefully transfer the rope back to the sheet pan. Cover the remaining ropes, rolling out additional Marzipan as needed. Refrigerate the ropes, covered, until they are firm.

5. Trim the ends and then cut each rope into ten equal pieces, about $2 1/4$ inches (5.6 cm) long.

6. Dip $1/8$ inch (3 mm) of both ends of each pastry into melted dark coating chocolate. Place the Rum-Chocolate Spools back on sheet pans with paper, arranging them seam-side down in straight rows.

7. Place a small amount of the melted chocolate in a piping bag (see page 27). Pipe a small dot of chocolate, the size of a pea, in the center of each pastry. Store as directed in Rum Balls.

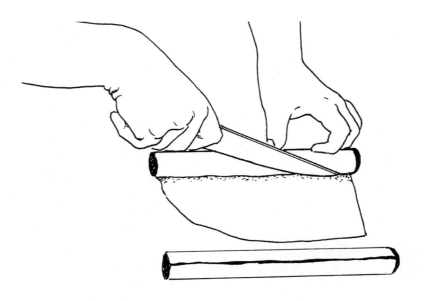

FIGURE 9–23 Cutting away the excess Marzipan sheet after rolling the Marzipan around a rope of Rum Ball Filling for Rum-Chocolate Spools. The edges of the Marzipan just meet but do not overlap.

Sarah Bernhardts

30 pastries

thirty Almond Macaroon Cookies
(page 202)
1 pound (455 g) Vanilla Buttercream
(page 978) (see note)
¹/₂ teaspoon (2.5 ml) mocha paste
or
2 tablespoons (30 ml) Coffee
Reduction (page 5)
dark coating chocolate, melted
thirty candy or Marzipan Coffee Beans
(page 1029)

NOTE: An equal amount of Ganache, flavored with Coffee Reduction or mocha paste, can be substituted for the buttercream. Spread the Ganache into a point rather than a dome.

These pastries are named for Henrietta Roslin Bernhardt, whose personality, emotion, and command of voice made her famous as one of the greatest tragediennes of all times. She was enormously popular as a comedienne as well before her death in 1923 at the age of 79. My version of this classical pastry uses a macaroon base topped with mocha-flavored buttercream, but Japonaise crowned with Ganache and iced with either Chocolate Glaze or mocha-flavored Fondant is also very common. In any case, Sarah Bernhardts should be small, simple, and elegant, just like their namesake.

1. Remove the cookies from the baking paper as instructed and shown in the recipe. Arrange them in rows, flat-side up. Press down lightly to flatten the cookies so they do not wobble.

2. Soften the buttercream as needed and flavor it with the mocha paste or Coffee Reduction. Place the buttercream in a pastry bag with a no. 6 (12-mm) plain tip. Pipe a mound of buttercream, the size of a large egg yolk, onto each cookie. Use a soup spoon to smooth and shape the buttercream into an even mound about ¹/₂ inch (1.2 cm) thick in the center, tapering down to the sides of the cookie (Figure 9–24). Refrigerate until the buttercream is firm.

3. Holding a pastry upside down, insert a dipping fork at an angle into the base. Dip the buttercream mound into the melted dark coating chocolate. Hold the dipped pastry over the bowl of chocolate for a few moments, moving it up and down to allow as much of the excess chocolate as possible to fall back into the bowl. Place the cookies on a sheet pan in straight rows chocolate-side up.

4. Put a small amount of melted coating chocolate in a piping bag. Cut a small opening in the tip. Use the chocolate to attach a coffee bean in the center on top of each pastry. Sarah Bernhardts will keep for up to one week stored in a cool location. If you must store them in the refrigerator, they should be boxed to protect the chocolate.

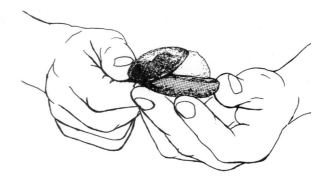

FIGURE 9–24 Using a spoon to mold the buttercream in a smooth mound that covers the flat side of a macaroon cookie for Sarah Bernhardts

Small Saint-Honoré

45 pastries

3 pounds (1 kg, 365 g) Puff Pastry (page 44) or good scrap Puff Pastry

or

1 pound, 10 ounces (740 g) or one-half recipe Pie Dough (page 36) (see introduction)

one-quarter recipe Pâte à Choux (page 36)

one recipe Bavarian Rum Cream (page 339)

one-half recipe Caramelized Sugar, Dry Method (page 954)

1¹/₃ cups (320 ml) heavy cream

1 teaspoon (5 g) granulated sugar

These will stand out on a dessert tray amid the typical assortment of European pastries such as Napoleons, Éclairs, and the many variations of chocolate pastries that are cut into different shapes from layered sheets of cake. Sure, we need all of those too (so many are easily done way ahead), but the following are a sure bet when you or your customer are looking for something out of the ordinary. The small caramel-dipped profiteroles make the whole pastry tray shine and come alive. If you are short on time, you can simplify Small Saint-Honoré without sacrificing any of the taste or appeal. Because of its nature, lining small forms with Puff Pastry can be time-consuming. By substituting Pie Dough, although not faithful to the classical rendition, lining the forms becomes quick and effortless. (You will only need about half as much Pie Dough, since the scraps can be rerolled right away.) Another shortcut is to eliminate filling the profiteroles and simply divide the Bavarian Rum Cream between the shells; the small profiteroles do not hold very much filling anyway. However, do not in any case omit dipping the profiteroles in caramel, since this is what makes these pastries so unusual and pretty.

1. Roll out the Puff Pastry or Pie Dough to ¹/₁₆ inch (2 mm) thick. Prick well and then let the dough rest for a minimum of 30 minutes in the refrigerator.

2. Line forty-five mazarin forms (or other forms of approximately the same size) with the Puff Pastry or Pie Dough (see Figures 2–15 to 2–18, pages 57 and 58). Reroll the Pie Dough scraps as needed to line all of the forms. Cover any leftover dough and save for another use. Fill the forms with dried beans or pie weights.

3. Bake at 375°F (190°C) for approximately 15 minutes or until they are golden brown and baked through. Let the shells cool.

4. Using a fork, scrape all of the beans out of the shells and at the same time remove the shells from the forms. Reserve.

5. Place the Pâte à Choux in a pastry bag with a no. 5 (10-mm) plain tip. Pipe out small mounds, about the diameter of a quarter coin, on a sheet pan lined with baking paper (use up all the choux paste; you should get about fifty to sixty mounds, which gives you a few extra for insurance). Bake at 425°F (219°C) until light brown and baked through, about 10 minutes. Set aside to cool.

6. Using the tip of a paring knife, make a small hole in the bottom of each profiterole. Place a small amount of the Bavarian Rum Cream in a pastry bag with a no. 2 (4-mm) plain tip. Pipe the cream into the profiteroles and place in the refrigerator. Place the remaining Rum Cream in a pastry bag with a no. 5 (10-mm) plain tip. Pipe the cream into the reserved Puff Pastry or Pie Dough shells, dividing it evenly and forming a smooth mound on each, just slightly above the rim. Place the pastries in the refrigerator to allow the filling to set.

7. Follow the directions for caramelizing the sugar, cooking it to a light caramel color. Dip the tops and sides (do not dip the bottom) of each filled profiterole into the caramel, using a two- or three-pronged dipping (or table) fork inserted into the side. Use a second fork to push the profiterole off onto a sheet pan lined with baking paper, caramel-side up. Return to the refrigerator.

8. Whip the heavy cream and granulated sugar until stiff peaks form. Place in a pastry bag with a no. 5 (10-mm) plain tip. Pipe a cross of cream on the top of each pastry. Place one of the reserved caramelized profiteroles on the top in the center. These pastries should be stored in the refrigerator and served the same day they are assembled.

Swans

approximately 50 pastries

one recipe Pâte à Choux (page 36)

6 ounces (170 g) smooth strawberry jam

two recipes Chantilly Cream (page 1083)

dark coating chocolate, melted

powdered sugar

NOTE: If you are making a small batch of Swans, or if it just makes more sense space-wise, it is fine to pipe both the bodies and the necks on the same sheet pan. If you do simply remove the necks individually as they are done.

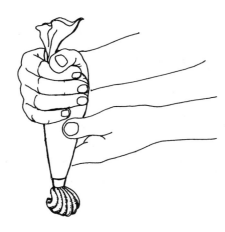

FIGURE 9–25 *Starting to pipe the bodies for Swans, using an up-and-over motion to make the wide end of the Pâte à Choux cones higher than the narrow end*

*S*wans *are a natural for buffet displays. They are light and delicious, and they look very elegant presented on mirrors. I have occasionally run out of Swans at the end of service and have had customers expressing their disappointment close to the point of crying and/or wanting their money back! It doesn't seem to matter to the untrained eye that there are times when the student's creations more closely resemble certain scavenger birds, or pelicans (from piping the beak too large), than Swans. There is something magical about these winged pastries that makes people fall in love with them. Depending on the other pastries you are offering, you may want to add a small wedge of strawberry placed on top of the whipped cream at the back end of each Swan to add some color.*

1. Reserve about 1 cup (240 ml) of the Pâte à Choux to make the Swan necks (cover tightly so it doesn't form a skin). Place the remaining paste (a portion at a time) in a pastry bag with a no. 7 (14-mm) star tip. Pipe the paste in cone shapes 3 inches (7.5 cm) long and 1³/₄ inches (4.5 cm) wide, on sheet pans lined with baking paper. Start by making the wide end of the cone, piping in an up-and-over motion (Figure 9–25), then relax the pressure on the bag and end in a narrow point. It is important that the wide end be quite a bit higher than the narrow end for nice-looking Swans.

2. Place the reserved Pâte à Choux in a pastry bag with a no. 1 (2-mm) plain tip. To pipe out the head and neck pieces, start by piping a ¹/₄-inch (6-mm) strip (the beak), moving quickly so the flow of paste is actually thinner than the pastry tip; pause for a second so you get a lump for the head, then continue in the shape of a question mark, forming the long curved neck with the flow of paste the same thickness as the pastry tip for this section (Figure 9–26). You should make quite a few extra head and neck pieces so you will be able to pick and choose during the assembly and also to allow for breakage.

3. Bake the bodies and the head and neck pieces at 400°F (205°C). The bodies will take about 20 minutes and the neck pieces about half as long. Let cool completely.

4. Cut the top third off the bodies; then cut the top piece in half lengthwise to create two wings (scissors work best). Place two wings on either side of each body, lining the pastries up for assembly.

FIGURE 9–26 The piped Pâte à Choux Swan bodies and head-neck pieces before baking

5. Pipe a thin ribbon of strawberry jam in the bottom of each shell.

6. Whip the Chantilly Cream to stiff peaks and place in a pastry bag with a no. 6 (12-mm) star tip. Pipe the cream into the shells using the same up-and-over motion you used to pipe the shells, coming to a point at the narrow end (which will be the tail).

7. Arrange the wings in the whipped cream pointing upward and meeting at the top. Dip the bottom of each neck in coating chocolate to prevent the whipped cream from softening it and causing it to fall (this is not necessary if you assemble the Swans to order). Push the necks into the whipped cream so they lean back slightly between the wings.

8. Sift a little powdered sugar over the top of the pastries. Place in the refrigerator. As with all Pâte à Choux products, Swans should be served the same day they are assembled.

VARIATION
Courting Swans

16 servings

1 pound, 5 ounces (595 g) or one-half recipe Pâte á Choux (page 36)

3 ounces (85 g) smooth strawberry jam

one recipe Chantilly Cream (page 1083)

dark coating chocolate, melted

one-half recipe Chocolate Sauce (page 1072)

one-half recipe Raspberry Sauce (page 1080)

The ever-elegant Swans really make this very simple plated dessert stand out. Courting Swans makes a good choice when you need a dessert that can be served without a lot of finishing touches, or for a very large party, as they can be assembled hours ahead and it takes a minimum of time to complete the presentation. Do keep in mind that the Swans should be small. If either the head and neck portion or the bodies are piped out too large, or are misshapen, you will end up with ugly ducklings instead of Swans!

This amount of Pâte á Choux will make a few more Swans than you need for sixteen servings which allows you to pick and choose a bit during the assembly.

1. Place 1 cup (240 ml) of the Pâte á Choux in a separate bowl. Cover and reserve.

2. Place the remaining paste in a pastry bag with a number 6 (12-mm) star tip. Pipe the paste in small cone shapes (the wide end should

Sour Cream Mixture for Piping
(page 1081)

powdered sugar

be about the size of an unshelled walnut) onto sheet pans lined with baking paper, following the instructions in the main recipe for Swans. You are making them the correct size if you have used half of the paste after making about twenty (there are two Swans per serving).

3. After piping the bodies, replace the star tip with a no. 1 (2-mm) plain tip and place the reserved Pâte á Choux in the bag. Pipe out the head and neck shapes (see preceding illustration and instructions). You should be able to pipe out quite a few extras so you will have a choice and will not have to worry about breakage. Bake the bodies and necks and assemble the Swans with jam and Chantilly Cream as instructed in the main recipe.

4. Presentation: Adjust the consistency of the Chocolate and Raspberry Sauces, if necessary, so they are thick enough not to run on the plate when piped out. Place a portion of each sauce in a piping bottle. Pipe the sauces onto the base of a dessert plate in a yin-yang pattern, covering the base of the plate. Hold the plate in one hand and tap it with the palm of your other hand to flatten and smooth the surface of the sauces. Place the Sour Cream Mixture in a piping bag and pipe a line following the border where the sauces come together in the center. Use a wooden skewer to blend the sour cream with the two sauces (see photo in color insert). Sift powdered sugar lightly over two Swans. Place one in each pool of sauce, arranging them so they face each other. Serve immediately.

Swedish Napoleons

15 pastries

1 pound, 8 ounces (680 g) Puff Pastry (page 44) or scrap Puff Pastry

5 ounces (140 g) smooth red currant jelly

3 ounces (85 g) Fondant or Simple Icing (pages 1011 and 1020)

Simple Syrup (page 11)

2 cups (480 ml) heavy cream

1 tablespoon (15 g) granulated sugar

NOTE: A good production method for Napoleons, or anytime you need thin baked sheets of Puff Pastry, is to roll out the dough sheets and place them covered in the freezer to bake as required. When I was in the retail business we always rolled out a week's worth at one time and then baked the sheets fresh every morning. Alternatively, storing baked

*N*apoleon is the adopted name for the classical French pastry Mille-Feuille. *My version, Swedish Napoleons, is a little different in that they do not contain Pastry Cream and they have a colorful pink icing on top. Instructions for Mille-Feuille follow this recipe.*

The name Napoleon is a little confusing. People widely assume an association to the infamous corpulent general Napoleon Bonaparte who proclaimed himself Napoleon I in 1804. Although he stands out as one of the most brilliant military leaders in history, he has nothing to do with this pastry other than the fact that both are from France. The name Napoleon is instead a reference to the layer structure stemming from the Neapolitan style of making pastries.

1. Roll the Puff Pastry out to a 24-by-14-inch (60-×-35-cm) rectangle; it should be approximately ⅛ inch (3 mm) thick. Place the dough on an even, paper-lined sheet pan. Prick the dough well and let it rest in the refrigerator for at least 30 minutes (see note).

2. Cover the dough with a second sheet of baking paper and place a second flat and even sheet pan on top. Bake at 375°F (190°C) for 15 minutes. Remove the top sheet pan and baking paper and continue baking approximately 15 minutes longer or until golden brown and completely baked through. Let cool.

sheets well covered overnight is certainly acceptable. It is very important that the Puff Pastry sheets are baked properly to be dry and crisp; this not only makes the Napoleons taste better but makes them much easier to cut after they are assembled.

3. Cut three strips from the pastry sheet, the full length of the sheet and 4 inches (10 cm) wide for regular servings or 3 inches (7.5 cm) wide for buffet servings.

4. Select the nicest strip for the top and turn it upside down. Spread a very thin film of red currant jelly, just enough to color it, over the top of this strip. Spread a slightly thicker layer of jelly on one of the remaining strips, which will become the bottom.

5. Thin the Fondant or Simple Icing to an easy-to-spread consistency with Simple Syrup. Carefully spread a thin film on top of the jelly, blending the two together just enough to produce a pretty marbled surface. Set the top strip aside for about 30 minutes or until a crust has formed on the top of the icing. If you are in hurry you can speed this up by placing the iced strip in a warm oven for 30 seconds; take care not to melt the icing.

6. Whip the heavy cream and sugar to stiff peaks; place in a pastry bag with a large plain tip. Place the middle strip on the bottom strip. Pipe the whipped cream on top of the middle strip in a 1-inch (2.5-cm) layer.

7. Cut the glazed top layer crosswise into 1¹/₂-inch (3.7-cm) pieces. Reassemble the top strip on top of the whipped cream. Using the top pieces as a guide, cut through the other layers. Napoleans must be served the same day they are made.

VARIATION
Mille-Feuille

15 pastries

1 pound, 8 ounces (680 g) Puff Pastry (page 44) or scrap Puff Pastry

4 ounces (115 g) Fondant or Simple Icing (pages 1011 and 1020)

Simple Syrup (page 11)

2 tablespoons (16 g) cocoa powder (see note)

2 pounds (910 g) Pastry Cream (page 1088)

1 tablespoon (15 ml) kirshwasser

NOTE: If using Simple Icing, you will need only half as much cocoa powder. Also, it is not necessary to use Simple Syrup to thin the cocoa icing in this case; water will do.

Mille-Feuille *means "a thousand leaves" and refers to the multiple strata of the classical French Puff Pastry dough, which is given a greater number of turns (six single turns, preferably over a three-day period) than the more practical, and more commonly used, dough included in this text (see Figures 2–4 and 2–5, pages 40 to 43). It is something of a misnomer to call these pastries by their French name when using this Puff Pastry recipe since the dough falls short of 1,000 layers. A way to make up for it is to take finished Puff Pastry made according to the directions in this book and give the dough a half-turn: roll the dough out as you would to make a double-turn and then fold it in half. The dough will then have just over 1,000 layers. However, if you are not such a stickler for accuracy, don't worry.*

You may want to increase the cornstarch in the Pastry Cream by 1 ounce (30 g) per full recipe. The firmer Pastry Cream will make it easier to slice and handle the assembled Napoleons. It is important not only to have the cocoa icing made, but it should also be in the piping bag since the marbling must be done quickly before the icing starts to set.

1. Follow the instructions in the recipe for Swedish Napoleons through step three. Select the best of the strips and turn it upside down. Soften the Fondant to a spreadable consistency by adding Simple Syrup. Remove about 2 tablespoons (30 ml) of the Fondant or Simple Icing and thoroughly mix the cocoa powder into it. Add enough Simple Syrup to the cocoa icing to bring it to the same consistency as the white icing. Place the cocoa icing in a piping bag. Spread the white icing over the inverted strip. Immediately, pipe 8 to 10 thin straight lines of cocoa icing lengthwise on top. Draw a knife across every 1¹/₂ inches (3.7 cm) in one direction and then go back and draw a line in the opposite direction between each of the first lines to create a fishbone pattern. Set the strip aside.

2. Flavor the Pastry Cream with the kirschwasser. Spread half of it on top of one of the remaining Puff Pastry strips. Top with the second strip and spread the remaining Pastry Cream on top.

3. Cut the glazed top layer crosswise into 1¹/₂-inch (3.7-cm) pieces (check first to be sure a skin has formed on the icing). Reassemble the top strip on top of the Pastry Cream. Using the top pieces as a guide, cut through the other layers. Mille-Feuille must be served the same day they are assembled.

Tosca

48 pastries

1 pound, 5 ounces (595 g) Short Dough (page 54)

4¹/₂ ounces (130 g) smooth strawberry jam

4 pounds, 10 ounces (2 kg, 105 g) Mazarin Filling (page 1088)

one-half recipe or 13 ounces (370 g) Florentina Batter (page 214)

dark coating chocolate, melted

NOTE: If you must refrigerate Tosca, they should be boxed and well wrapped to prevent the Florentina topping from getting wet and sticky.

*P*uccini's *famous opera by the same name, which was first performed in Rome in 1900, probably has nothing to do with these pastries other than it is very Italian and so is the Florentina topping. As mentioned in the other recipes, the base for Tosca can used to make several pastries in the book, so it is a good idea to keep a baked sheet on hand in the freezer to create one or more of the variations such as Angelica Points and Almond Truffles.*

1. Line the bottom of a half-sheet pan (16 by 12 inches/40 × 30 cm) with baking paper. Roll out the Short Dough to ¹/₈ inch (3 mm) thick and place in the pan. Trim the edges so only the bottom of the pan is covered with dough. Cover the dough scraps and reserve for another use. Spread the jam in a thin layer over the dough. Spread the Mazarin Filling evenly on top.

2. Bake at 375°F (190°C) until baked through, about 35 minutes (keep in mind that the pastry will be baked an additional 5 minutes with the topping). Let cool to room temperature, then refrigerate.

3. When the Mazarin sheet is cold (preferably the day after baking), cut off the skin and even the top. To do this, leave the Mazarin sheet in the pan and cut with a serrated knife held parallel to the top of the cake, using the edge of the pan as a guide for your knife.

4. Spread the Florentina Batter over the Mazarin using a spatula dipped into hot water to make it slide more easily. Place the Mazarin sheet, still in its original pan, onto a second pan the same size (double-panning).

5. Bake at 425°F (219°C) until the Florentina topping begins to bubble and turn golden brown, about 5 minutes. Let cool to room temperature.

6. Cut the sheet loose from the sides of the pan; place a cake cardboard on top, invert, and unmold onto the cardboard. Refrigerate (upside down) until cool.

FIGURE 9–27 Inserting a dipping fork partway into the side of a Tosca pastry

7. While still upside down, trim both long sides of the sheet and then cut lengthwise into four equal strips slightly less than 3 inches (7.5 cm) wide. Cut each strip across into twelve pieces. Hold the knife at a 90° angle so that the edges are straight. Turn the cut pieces over so that the florentina faces up.

8. Dip the bottom and sides, but not the top, of each pastry into dark coating chocolate, using a dipping fork inserted partway into the pastry. Carefully move the pastry up and down over the bowl a few times to allow as much excess chocolate as possible to fall back into the bowl. Drag the bottom against the side of the bowl. Blot the pastry on a piece of baking paper to remove more chocolate. Place the slices in straight rows on sheet pans lined with baking paper (Figures 9–27 through 9–31). Store the finished pastries in a cool place; they will keep for up to one week.

FIGURE 9–28 Letting the excess chocolate drip back into the bowl after dipping the bottom and sides of the pastry into the melted chocolate

FIGURE 9–29 Scraping the pastry against the side of the bowl to remove excess chocolate from the bottom

FIGURE 9–30 Blotting the pastry on a piece of baking paper

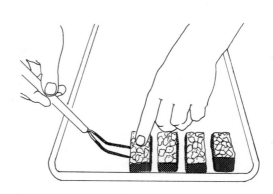

FIGURE 9–31 Removing the dipping fork after placing the dipped pastry on a paper-lined sheet pan, touching the Florentina topping if needed to steady the pastry rather than the chocolate coating

Trier Squares

forty-eight 2-inch (5-cm) square pastries

2 pounds, 3 ounces (1 kg) Short
   Dough (page 54)
4¹/₂ ounces (130 g) smooth apricot jam
Trier Filling (recipe follows)
Egg Wash (page 7)

These pastries are named for the ancient town of Trier located on the banks of the Mosel River in southwestern Germany. I based my version on a recipe I found in a German cookbook from the turn of the century. The town itself dates back much longer than that; in fact, it was founded by the Roman Emperor Augustus in 15 B.C. and named Treveri. Although heavily damaged in World War II, there are still many Roman ruins standing and, of more recent fame, the house where Karl Marx was born.

1. Line the bottom of a half-sheet pan, 16 by 12 inches (40 × 30 cm), with baking paper. Roll a portion of the Short Dough out to ¹/₈ inch (3 mm) thick, roll it up on a dowel, and unroll over the pan. Trim the edges to cover just the bottom of the pan and place the pan in the refrigerator. Add the scraps to the remaining Short Dough and roll to the same thickness and about 16 inches (40 cm) in length. Place on a sheet of cardboard or on an inverted sheet pan and place in the refrigerator until firm as well.

2. Spread the jam in a thin layer over the Short Dough in the pan. Top with the Trier Filling and use a palette knife to spread it out evenly.

3. Cut the reserved dough lengthwise into ¹/₄-inch-wide (6-mm) strips, using a fluted or plain pastry wheel.

4. Brush the top of the Trier Filling with Egg Wash. Arrange the dough strips diagonally, ¹/₄ inch (6 mm) apart, over the filling. Then arrange strips diagonally in the other direction so they form a diamond pattern (Figure 9–32). Press the strips lightly with your hand as you place them to make sure they stick. Trim the edges around the pan and cover the dough trimmings to save for another use. Brush the strips with Egg Wash.

5. Bake at 375°F (190°C) until golden brown and baked through, about 40 minutes. Let the pastry cool completely, preferably overnight.

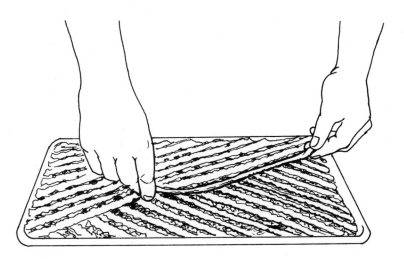

FIGURE 9–32 Arranging strips of Short Dough diagonally to form a diamond lattice pattern on the top of Trier Squares

Cut around the inside edge of the pan and invert the sheet. Remove the pan and the baking paper. Turn right-side up. Trim the long edges. Measure and cut into six equal strips the long way and cut each strip into eight equal pieces. Use a serrated knife with a sawing action to minimize breaking the Short Dough.

1. Combine the almonds, sugar, and milk.

2. Melt the butter and allow it to brown slightly; add to the almond mixture.

3. Mix in the raisins, lemon juice, lemon zest, and cinnamon.

Trier Filling

*2 pounds, 13 ounces
(1 kg, 280 g)*

15 ounces (430 g) sliced almonds
14 ounces (400 g) granulated sugar
1/2 cup (120 ml) milk
5 ounces (140 g) unsalted butter
6 ounces (170 g) golden raisins
1/4 cup (60 ml) lemon juice
grated zest of one lemon
1 tablespoon (5 g) ground cinnamon

Walnut-Orange Tartlets

30 pastries

1 pound, 6 ounces (625 g) Short
 Dough (page 54)
6 ounces (170 g) Almond Paste
 (page 3)
2 ounces (55 g) granulated sugar
4 ounces (115 g) soft unsalted butter
3 eggs, at room temperature
1 ounce (30 g) bread flour
grated zest of one lemon
2 ounces (55 g) Candied Orange Peel
 (page 978), finely chopped
4 ounces (115 g) walnuts, finely
 chopped
1 1/4 cups (300 ml) or one-quarter
 recipe Royal Icing (page 1019)
 (see note)
thirty small walnut halves (or large
 quarters) for decorating

*NOTE: Omit the cream of tartar and add 1
teaspoon (2.5 g) of cornstarch to the quarter
recipe of Royal Icing. Do not overwhip.*

*M*ost of us are more accustomed to using Royal Icing for piping decorative patterns for showpieces or wedding cakes, and for decorating cookies and holiday specialities, than the way it is used in this recipe. Spreading Royal Icing over a pastry prior to baking, however, is an old trick. Other recipes in this text that utilize this method are Cinnamon Stars and Conversations. Here is another variation you might want to try for an easy and unusual treat: Roll out 6 ounces (170 g) of Puff Pastry into an 8-by-12-inch (20-×-30-cm) rectangle; it should be a little thinner than 1/8 inch (3 mm). Refrigerate until firm and then spread a thin film of Royal Icing on top. The icing should be thin enough to spread easily but should not be runny. Freeze partially. Cut in half lengthwise and then cut each piece across into ten rectangles, using a knife dipped in water to keep it from sticking. Allow the icing to dry until a skin has formed. Bake at 400°F (205°C) until baked through, approximately 15 minutes. The sweet, crisp icing complements the unsweetened flaky Puff Pastry beautifully (it is sort of a reduced-calorie Napoleon).

It is important not to use any acid, such as tartaric acid, cream of tartar, or lemon juice, when making the Royal Icing but to use a small amount of cornstarch instead. This will prevent the icing from browning excessively during baking. In addition, the icing should only be whipped for a short time.

1. Roll the Short Dough 1/8 inch thick and use it to line 30 plain (not fluted) round tartlet pans 1 1/4 inches (3.1 cm) high and 2 1/2 inches (6.2 cm) across the top (see Figures 2–15 to 2–18, pages 57 and 58). (Mazarin pans will also work fine.) Combine the Short Dough scraps and roll the dough again to 1/8 inch (3 mm) thick. Place the lined forms and the rolled sheet in the refrigerator.

2. Place the Almond Paste and the sugar in a mixing bowl. Add the butter gradually while mixing on low speed using the paddle. Mix only until the ingredients are combined and smooth. Add the eggs one at a time. Combine the flour, lemon zest, orange peel, and walnuts. Add the flour mixture to the Almond Paste mixture.

3. Place the filling in a pastry bag with a no. 7 (14-mm) plain tip. Pipe the filling into the lined forms, filling them almost to the top. Use the rounded end of a small spatula to spread the filling evenly to the edge all around the forms, making it slightly concave in the center. Place the filled shells back in the refrigerator long enough to firm the filling.

4. Spread a thin layer of Royal Icing on top of the filling. If the icing is too thick to spread easily, thin with a little egg white. Place a walnut half in the center of each pastry on top of the icing.

5. Cut the reserved Short Dough sheet into strips ¼ inch (6 mm) wide, using a fluted pastry wheel. Center one small strip on either side of, and parallel to, the walnut on each pastry. Use your thumbs to sever the ends of the strips against the sides of the forms to remove the excess dough and also to secure the strips to the sides. Cover the scrap dough and save for another use. Set the forms aside until the icing has formed a crust on top, about 30 minutes.

6. Bake the tartlets at 400°F (205°C) for about 15 minutes or until baked through. Let cool before unmolding.

7. Stored in a cool, dry place, Walnut-Orange Tartlets will stay fresh for up to three days. The tartlets may also be stored uncooked in the refrigerator or freezer for up to one week. Before baking, let them sit at room temperature until the icing has formed a crust.

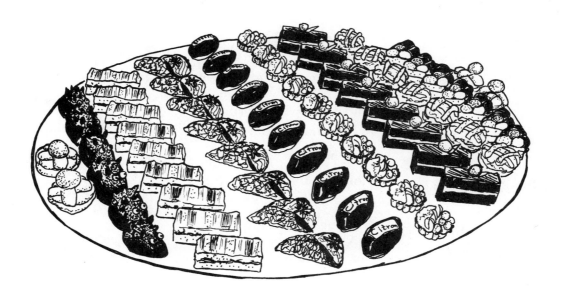

10

Desserts for Plated Presentation

Almond Wafers

Apple Strudel, German Style

Baklava with Mascarpone Bavarian and Cherry Sauce

Blueberry Pirouettes

Caramel Boxes with Caramel-Macadamia Nut Mousse

Caramelized Apple Galette in Phyllo Dough with Kumquat

Cherry Baskets with Cherry Compote and Black Pepper Frozen Yogurt

Chestnut-Rum Cream Cakes

Chianti Poached Figs with Lavender Mascarpone

Chocolate Ganache Towers

Chocolate Marquise

Crepes Suzette

Date-Stuffed Poached Pears in Phyllo Crowns

with Brandied Mousseline Sauce

Dessert Sampling Platter

Florentina Cones with Seasonal Fruit

Forbidden Peach

Honey Truffle Symphony

Hot Chocolate Truffle Cake

Individual Croquembouche

Marco Polo with Spiced Ganache and Tea Ice Cream

Pears Belle Hélène

Pineapple Fritters with Gingered Pineapple Frozen Yogurt

Plum Fritters

Puff Pastry with Fruit and Champagne Sabayon

Raspberry Wafers

Red Banana Truffles in Phyllo Dough

Rhubarb-Meringue Napoleons

Rum Babas

Savarin

Small Pear Tartlets with Caramel Sauce

Small Swedish Pancakes

Strawberries Romanoff

Strawberry Pyramids

Swedish Pancakes Filled with Apples

Swedish Profiteroles

Tiramisu with Fresh Fruit

Trio of Cannolis

Trio of Chocolates with Marzipan Parfait

Triple Treat

Tropical Surprise Packages

Valentine's Day Hearts

White Chocolate Citrus Roulade

Wild Strawberries Romanoff in Caramel Boxes

Wine Foam and Blackberry Bavarian Greystone

For many hundreds of years, sweet and elegant desserts have been a favorite way to reward ourselves and those who are special to us. They are a small luxury that, even though not an essential part of one's everyday diet, has played an important role in cultural history. From the first sweets, which were probably nothing more than a plate of fruit topped with honey, cooking and baking have developed into a creative and sophisticated art. This is especially evident in dessert presentations, which are often a meaningful part of celebrations and special occasions.

Some of the more elaborate recipes in this chapter require time and patience, but they yield breathtaking results. However, any of these desserts, even the quickest and most humble, should be presented in its own elegant way, served on an attractive plate, and accompanied by an appropriate sauce and/or garnish. Even the simple and homey-looking Rum Babas can be dressed up with a little effort, although this type of dessert is not meant to compete with the artistry and complexity of, for example, Tropical Surprise Packages or Marco Polo with Spiced Ganache and Tea Ice Cream.

The size of the serving plate alone can make a big difference in a dessert's appearance. The dessert should not touch the rim of the plate; so for most items, it is essential to use a 10-to-12-inch plate to display the pastry, sauce, and garnish without crowding. All of the presentation instructions in this chapter are based on using plates of this size that have a minimum of a 7-inch-diameter base. It is best to use plates with little or no pattern on the surface and with just a simple design on the rim so as not to detract from the dessert. This is especially important if decorating with two or more sauces, or the result can look like a bad example of modern art. Keep in mind that the serving plate, sauce, and garnish are there to enhance the dessert, not compete with it. Strive for a well-balanced presentation.

Many of the pastries in this chapter would be suitable for the showcase in a pastry shop or for a dessert buffet, instead of plate service, just by leaving out the sauce and garnish. Tiramisu, Baklava, Swedish Profiteroles, and White Chocolate Citrus Roulade are examples. Conversely, some of the pastries found in the preceding chapter—Chocolate Éclairs, Swedish Napoleons, and Orange Truffle Cuts, for example—can easily be turned into elegant plated desserts by serving with a sauce and garnish.

In either case, whether you serve an elegant petits fours tray or an artistically decorated serving of Caramel Boxes with Caramel-Macadamia Nut Mousse, when your customers are finished they should agree that, "It was worth every calorie."

Almond Wafers

16 servings

one recipe Raspberry Wafer Batter
    (page 488) (see step one)
4 ounces (115 g) pistachios
3 ounces (85 g) walnuts
powdered sugar
dark coating chocolate, melted
4 cups (960 ml) heavy cream
2 tablespoons (30 g) granulated sugar
one-quarter recipe Raspberry Sauce
    (page 1080)
one recipe Orange Sauce (page 1077)

NOTE: If you do not have time to make the template, dust powdered sugar over the entire top wafer.

*T*his elegant and delicious dessert was born over a cup of coffee with a colleague who needed a "nutty" dessert for a special function. The original name on the menu was Trio of Nuts, but I have since decided on a more conservative title. I'm using slightly modified versions of the Raspberry Wafers batter and template. The template used to decorate the top wafers has been borrowed from Benedictine Soufflé Glacé.

The fragile wafers literally fall apart in your mouth and also, unfortunately, in your hands if you are not careful during the assembly. The recipe will give you about ten extra wafers, and you will probably need some of them. If any are left over, they can be stored in an airtight container for up to one week. If you must start assembly ahead of time, heed the warning in step five: the wafers will absorb moisture very quickly and become soggy. Part of the appeal of this dessert comes from the contrast in textures between the crisp wafers and the rich cream filling.

You can easily simplify and reduce the calories in this dessert by eliminating both types of nuts, the heavy cream, and the sugar from the ingredients. Instead, substitute one recipe of Italian Cream (page 1087) flavored with Amaretto de Saronno, Frangelico, or another nut-flavored liqueur.

1. Follow the recipe and instructions for Raspberry Wafers (see pages 484 and 485) through step three, substituting almonds for the hazelnuts in the water batter, and using the template marked B in Figure 10–24 with that recipe. You will need four wafers per serving, but make a few extra since they break easily.

2. Blanch the pistachios using a pinch of salt in the blanching water to bring out the green color. Remove the skin and set the nuts aside to dry. (You can speed up the drying process by placing the nuts in a very low oven. Do not toast them, however.) Reserve sixteen good-looking pistachios, or pistachio-halves, to use for garnish. Crush the remainder finely and set aside. Finely chop the walnuts and set aside separately.

3. Select the sixteen best-looking wafers to use on the tops of the desserts. Make the template used for Benedictine Soufflé Glacé, Figure 13–4, page 663 (see note). One at a time, set the template on top of these wafers and sift powdered sugar over the template. Remove the template very carefully so you do not disturb the powdered sugar. Place a small amount of melted chocolate in a piping bag. Pipe a small dot of chocolate in the center of each of the decorated wafers and place one of the reserved pistachios on top. Do not decorate more tops than you expect to use the same day. Set the tops aside. Pipe lines of melted chocolate in a spoke pattern over the entire base of as many dessert plates as you made tops. Reserve.

4. Whip the heavy cream with the granulated sugar to soft peaks. Divide the cream into two portions, one slightly larger than the other. Flavor the smaller portion with the chopped walnuts and place in a pastry bag with a no. 6 (12-mm) plain tip. Flavor the larger portion with the crushed pistachios and place in a second pastry bag with a no. 6 (12-mm) plain tip.

5. The wafers should be assembled to order, or no more than 15 minutes prior to serving. Pipe small mounds of pistachio cream on each of the petals on one wafer. Top with a second wafer and press down very lightly. Pipe mounds of walnut cream on the second wafer in the same manner. Top with the third wafer, press down lightly, and pipe mounds of pistachio cream on top. Place the Raspberry Sauce in a piping bottle with a small opening and reserve.

6. Presentation: Pour a pool of Orange Sauce in the center of one of the decorated plates, then tilt the plate to cover the base entirely. Pipe four small dots of walnut cream in the center of the plate. Place an assembled dessert on top. Carefully top with one of the decorated top wafers. Pipe small dots of Raspberry Sauce in the Orange Sauce between the chocolate lines all around the dessert. Serve immediately.

Apple Strudel, German Style

16 servings

12 ounces (340 g) Short Dough
(page 54)

1 pound (455 g) Puff Pastry or Quick
Puff Pastry (pages 44 and 47)

one ¼-by-14-by-24-inch (6-mm-×-
35-×-60-cm) Almond Sponge
(page 270)

2 pounds (910 g) Granny Smith,
pippin, or, when available,
Gravenstein apples, peeled and
cored (approximately five
medium-sized)

Spiced Poaching Syrup (page 13)

6 ounces (170 g) walnuts

8 ounces (225 g) dark raisins

1 ounce (30 g) Cinnamon Sugar
(page 5)

3 ounces (85 g) Pastry Cream
(page 1088)

3 ounces (85 g) apricot jam

Egg Wash (page 7)

Apricot Glaze (page 1016)

Simple Icing (page 1020)

Simple Syrup (page 11)

sixteen medium-sized strawberries

one-half recipe Vanilla Custard Sauce
(page 1082) (see note)

*NOTE: You can omit the Vanilla Custard
Sauce and serve the warm strudel with Vanilla
Ice Cream instead. As the ice cream melts you
actually get to enjoy both accompaniments.*

*Y*ou can find this appetizing pastry in many German konditoreis *for sale
both in individual portions and in larger pieces, which will serve ten to
twelve people (something like buying a rectangular apple pie). German Apple
Strudel is refreshing and not too filling as a luncheon dessert, served perhaps
with your favorite ice cream instead of the custard sauce in warm weather. If you
do not have Pastry Cream already made up, and do not need it for anything
else, you can easily substitute apricot jam. Along the same lines, this is a good
recipe in which to use up leftover sponges and sponge pieces. If they feel a bit
dry, dab some poaching liquid on top before using.*

1. Roll out the Short Dough into a strip ⅛ inch (3 mm) thick and
the length of a full sheet pan (24 inches/60 cm). Trim the edges to make
the dough strip 4 inches (10 cm) wide. Refrigerate.

2. Roll out the Puff Pastry to ⅛ inch (3 mm) thick, 8 inches (20 cm)
wide, and as long as the Short Dough. Refrigerate. Cover and reserve
the scraps from both pieces of dough for another use.

3. Cut a strip from the sponge sheet 3½ inches (8.7 cm) wide and
as long as the Short Dough. Tear the remainder of the sponge sheet into
small pieces and reserve.

4. Poach the apples in the Spiced Poaching Syrup for 10 to 15 minutes. They should give when pressed lightly. Remove from the liquid,
let cool, then cut the apples into ½-inch (1.2-cm) slices.

5. Chop the walnuts to the size of the raisins. Mix thoroughly with
the apple slices, raisins, Cinnamon Sugar, and Pastry Cream. Add the
reserved sponge cake pieces.

6. Spread the apricot jam on the Short Dough, leaving ¼ inch
(6 mm) of the dough exposed on the long sides. Place the sponge cake
strip on top of the jam. Use your hands to place the filling on top of the
sponge cake, shaping the apple mixture so that it is slightly rounded,
and leaving a ¼-inch (6-mm) edge of Short Dough exposed on each
long side.

7. Fold the Puff Pastry lengthwise over a dowel, positioning the
dowel 2 inches (5 cm) away from the fold. With the back of a chef's
knife (using the dowel as a guide), lightly mark (do not cut) a line parallel to the fold and approximately 1½ inches (3.7 cm) away from it
toward the dowel. Cut through the fold, up to the mark, at ¼ inch (6
mm) intervals (Figure 10–1).

8. Brush Egg Wash on the exposed Short Dough borders. Move the
dowel to the fold of the Puff Pastry, and use the dowel to lift the Puff
Pastry and unfold it over the strudel (Figure 10–2), positioning it so that
the slits are centered over the filling. Fasten the Puff Pastry to the Short
Dough with your thumbs. Trim the excess from the sides (do not
worry about sealing the short ends). Brush with Egg Wash.

9. Bake at 375°F (190°C) until golden brown, about 45 minutes.
You may need to place a second pan underneath to prevent the bottom
from becoming too dark. Let cool.

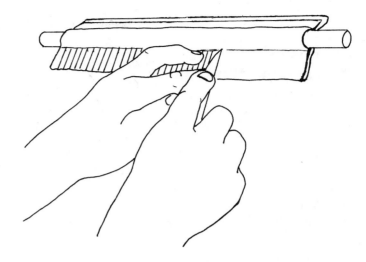

FIGURE 10–1   Cutting slits on the folded side of the Puff Pastry sheet with a dowel between the top and bottom layers, to create the top for Apple Strudel, German Style

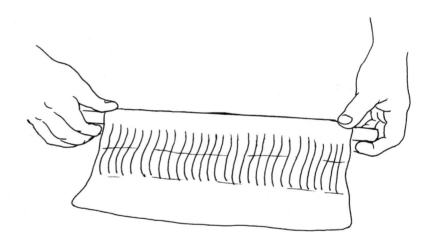

FIGURE 10–2   Using the dowel to lift the dough and unfold it over the strudel filling

10. Glaze the strudel with Apricot Glaze, then brush with Simple Icing that has been thinned enough with Simple Syrup to look transparent. Do not just warm the icing to make it thin enough to use, or the glaze will be too thick when it sets. Cut the strudel into sixteen slices approximately 1½ inches (3.7 cm) wide. Wash the strawberries, pat dry, and reserve.

11. Presentation: Pour 1½ ounces (45 ml) of Vanilla Custard Sauce on a dessert plate, making a round pool, off-center. Place a slice of strudel in the middle of the plate next to the sauce. Fan a strawberry and place the berry behind the strudel on the opposite side. The strudel can be served hot or cold.

Baklava with Mascarpone Bavarian and Cherry Sauce

12 servings

eighteen stemmed fresh cherries, cut
   in half and pitted
Cherry Sauce (page 1071)
Mascarpone Bavarian (recipe follows)
Baklava (recipe follows)
powdered sugar
twelve Caramel Fences (page 961)

*B*aklava is a popular phyllo-dough pastry most commonly associated with Greece, although Baklava is actually a Turkish word, and the confection is popular throughout the eastern part of the Mediterranean and the Near East. Any combination of nuts may be used, but traditionally nuts indigenous to the Middle East, such as walnuts, almonds, hazelnuts, or pistachios, are included. My version of Baklava is paired with a Mascarpone Bavarian and Cherry Sauce. Orange Sauce or any other slightly acidic fruit sauce would make a nice accompaniment as well. If you do not have time to make the sugar screens, stand a fresh cherry (with the stem attached) on a whipped cream rosette; cut the cherry to expose or remove the pit. Baklava can alternatively be offered as an individual pastry instead of a plated dessert. Well covered in the refrigerator, Baklava will stay fresh for up to one week.*

1. Coat the cherry halves with some of the Cherry Sauce so they do not become dry. Reserve.

2. Presentation: Place a Mascarpone Bavarian in the center of a dessert plate. Arrange three pieces of Baklava evenly spaced around the Bavarian with a flat side of each triangle parallel to the sides of the Bavarian. Sift powdered sugar lightly over the Baklava and the plate. Place the Cherry Sauce in a piping bottle with a small opening. Pipe three large dots of sauce on the plate, in between the pieces of Baklava. Pipe a zigzag design of sauce on top of the Bavarian. Place a cherry half, cut-side up, on each dot of sauce. Place a Caramel Fence standing upright on the Bavarian. Serve immediately.

Mascarpone Bavarian

5¹/₂ cups (1l, 320 ml)

1¹/₃ cups (320 ml) heavy cream
12 ounces (340 g) Mascarpone Cheese
   (page 9)
1 tablespoon (9 g) unflavored gelatin
   powder
¹/₃ cup (80 ml) cold water
2 tablespoons (18 g) pectin powder
   (see note 2)
5 ounces (140 g) granulated sugar
6 egg whites (³/₄ cup/180 ml)
4 ounces (115 g) white chocolate,
   melted

NOTE 1: To make the rings, cut strips of acetate or polyurethane 9¹/₂ inches long by 1¹/₄ inches wide (23.7 × 3.1 cm). Overlap the ends

*T*his is a variation of the White Chocolate Bavarian Filling and the same cautions apply: Do not overwhip the cream or overheat the white chocolate. The chocolate should be warm to aid in incorporating the gelatin, but it must never be left unattended while melting. If the chocolate gets too hot, the filling will break and become gritty. Unfortunately, at that point there is nothing to do but start over. To avoid having the filling set prematurely, it should not be made until you are ready to use it.*

1. Place twelve six-sided or round rings 3¹/₄ inches in diameter by 1¹/₄ inches high (8.1 × 3.1 cm) on a sheet pan lined with baking paper. If you do not have rings you can make them easily (see note 1) or you may simply divide the filling between twelve 3-inch (7.5-cm) diameter ramekins instead.

2. Whip the heavy cream to soft peaks; do not overwhip. Gradually fold the cream into the Mascarpone Cheese. Reserve in the refrigerator.

3. Sprinkle the gelatin over the cold water and set aside to soften.

4. Combine the pectin powder and granulated sugar in a mixing bowl. Stir in the egg whites. Place the bowl over simmering water and

¹/₄ inch (6 mm) and tape together. Use an appropriately sized cookie cutter as a guide as you tape the strips: Wrap the strips around the outside of the cutter to make certain that all the rings will be the same size. At the same time, place the plastic flush with the edge of the cutter to ensure that the rings will stand straight and even.

NOTE 2: Use regular canning pectin; pure USP grade pectin is too strong. If pectin is unavailable, increase the gelatin powder by 1 teaspoon (3 g) for a total of 4 teaspoons (12 g).

Baklava

40 pieces

6 ounces (170 g) pistachios
6 ounces (170 g) pecans
6 ounces (170 g) walnuts
4 ounces (115 g) light brown sugar
1 teaspoon (1.5 g) ground cinnamon
¹/₂ teaspoon (1 g) ground cloves
grated zest of two small oranges
¹/₂ cup (120 ml) water
¹/₄ cup (60 ml) or 3 ounces (85 g) honey
¹/₄ cup (60 ml) orange juice
7 ounces (200 g) granulated sugar
twelve sheets phyllo dough, approximately 8 ounces (225 g) (see note 1)
8 ounces (225 g) melted unsalted butter

NOTE 1: This recipes assumes that standard-size phyllo sheets, measuring approximately 12 to 14 by 16 to 18 inches (30 to 35 × 40 to 45 cm), are used.

NOTE 2: The instructions are based on using a standard industry half-sheet pan with ³/₄-inch (2-cm) sides. If you have a one-quarter size sheet pan, use that instead to avoid the need to make the cardboard support frame.

heat, stirring constantly with a whisk, to 140°F (60°C). Remove from the heat and immediately whip the mixture until it has cooled completely and has formed stiff peaks.

5. Place the gelatin mixture over a bain-marie and heat until dissolved. Do not overheat.

6. Quickly stir the gelatin into the melted white chocolate. Then quickly stir the chocolate mixture into one-third of the meringue mixture to temper it. Still working quickly, add this to the remaining meringue. Stir in the reserved whipped cream and cheese mixture.

7. Immediately divide the filling between the prepared rings or forms. Spread the tops even and refrigerate for at least two hours to set. The Bavarian may be kept in the refrigerator for three to four days. Unmold as needed.

1. Blanch the pistachios in water with a pinch of salt to make the green color more vivid. Remove the skins and dry the nuts.

2. Place the pistachios, pecans, walnuts, and brown sugar in a food processor and grind finely. Mix in the ground cinnamon, ground cloves, and half of the orange zest. Reserve.

3. Place the water, honey, orange juice, the remaining orange zest, and the granulated sugar in a heavy-bottomed saucepan. Bring to a boil over medium heat and boil until the mixture becomes syrupy, about 5 minutes. Add about one-third of the syrup to the nut mixture (or just enough to bind it) and mix throughly. Reserve the remaining syrup and the nut mixture separately.

4. Unroll the phyllo sheets and keep them covered with a damp towel as you work. Place a sheet of baking paper larger than the phyllo sheets on your work surface. Layer the phyllo sheets on top of the paper, brushing each one lightly with melted butter before topping it with the next layer. Brush the top sheet with butter as well.

5. Trim one long edge of the phyllo stack, then cut the stack in half crosswise, cutting through the baking paper at the same time. Lift up one stack of phyllo and slide it off the paper into a half-sheet pan. Place the phyllo sheets in the corner of the pan so that two cut (even) edges touch two sides of the pan (see note 2).

6. Spread the nut mixture evenly on top of the phyllo layer in the pan and press it down lightly. Slide the second stack of phyllo sheets on top of the nut mixture, aligning the trimmed edges with those underneath. Trim the two remaining sides, cutting through both layers.

7. Cut the top layer of phyllo dough into five strips lengthwise, then cut four times across to make twenty small rectangles. Cut diagonally across each rectangle (from corner to corner) to make forty triangles. Cut only through the top layer; do not cut through the nut filling and the bottom layer of dough. It will be easier to make precise cuts if you chill the Baklava first.

8. Cut strips of cardboard about 1 inch (2.5 cm) wide and long enough to cover the exposed sides of the Baklava. Place the strips

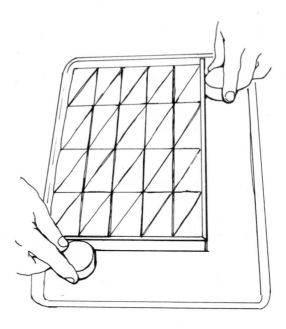

FIGURE 10-3   *Placing weights against two cardboard strips to create a frame to hold Baklava during baking*

against the exposed sides and then place weights against the cardboard to hold it in place (Figure 10-3).

9. Bake at 325°F (163°C) for approximately 45 minutes or until dark golden brown. Reheat the remaining syrup and pour it evenly over the Baklava immediately after removing it from the oven.

10. After the Baklava has cooled completely, cut again following the previous cuts, but this time go all the way through the bottom layer of phyllo dough. Cover the Baklava carefully to avoid crushing the phyllo dough and store it in the refrigerator. Baklava tastes best one or two days after it is baked, once the nuts have absorbed moisture. While it should be stored in the refrigerator, the flavor is improved by letting it come to room temperature prior to serving.

 Blueberry Pirouettes

16 servings

one recipe Vanilla Tulip Paste (page 1047)
1 teaspoon (2.5 g) unsweetened cocoa powder
dark coating chocolate, melted
6 ounces (170 g) shelled pistachios

*L*ike lingonberries, blueberries grow wild on sunny hillsides and in sunny patches of the forest all over Scandinavia and in the northern United States and Canada. When I was a child my Mom and Dad would keep a close eye on their secret (or so they hoped) blueberry patches in the early fall, since the berries had to be picked as soon as they turned from a reddish shade to that beautiful blue color. The trouble was that their secret was often the secret of someone else as well. If you didn't get there first you were out of luck! The blueberries were harvested in the same way as lingonberries, using a small, handheld screened box with a device on the front that would strain out the leaves and twigs, letting the berries fall down into the box. This was pushed through the top of the blue-

2 cups (480 ml) heavy cream

8 ounces (225 g) Pastry Cream
    (page 1088)

one recipe Blueberry Sauce
    (page 1069)

forty-eight Caramel Corkscrews
    (page 960)

berry bushes in a scooping motion. We kids always had to pick our share before we were allowed to go and play. At first there was much more eating than picking, which was evidenced by our blue-stained teeth. The small wild blueberry that grows in Scandinavia is blue throughout, unlike the cultivated variety, and would temporarily give ample proof of where the majority of the picked berries were being stored.

Blueberries contain a large amount of pectin, which gives the sauce in this recipe a lustrous shine and an easily controllable consistency. Fresh blueberries should be stored in a single layer if possible. In this manner they will keep for a week or more in the refrigerator. During the off-season I have, on occasion, used frozen blueberries instead, which works better than you might think given the fact that it is the colorful (and tasty) sauce that really makes this presentation stand out.

1. Grease and flour the back of clean, even sheet pans or, if you have silicone mats, use those instead. Make the template shown in Figure 10–4. The template as shown is the correct size for use in this recipe. Copy or trace the drawing and then cut the template out of ¹/₁₆-inch (2-mm) thick cardboard. Cake boxes are a good choice for this.

2. Place 2 tablespoons (30 ml) of the Tulip Paste in a small cup. Stir in the cocoa powder, mixing until it is thoroughly incorporated. Spread the remaining Tulip Paste on the sheet pans or silicone mats within the template (see Figures 19–55 and 19–56, pages 1046 and 1047). You need to make thirty-two cookies for this recipe, but you should make a few extra since some will break or bake too dark.

3. Place the cocoa-colored Tulip Paste in a piping bag and cut a very small opening. Pipe three diagonal lines on each cookie, close together, in the center.

4. Bake at 425°F (219°C) until the cookies just start to turn light brown in spots. Immediately wrap each one around a 1-inch (2.5-cm) dowel, placing the cookie lengthwise on the dowel so that the finished pirouette will be about 4 inches (10 cm) tall, and press the seam against the table to weld the edges together. Set aside to cool. When cool, dip both ends of each pirouette ¹/₈ inch (3 mm) into melted dark chocolate.

5. Blanch the pistachios and remove the skins. Chop the nuts into small pieces and reserve.

6. Whip the heavy cream until stiff peaks form. Fold in the Pastry Cream and one-half of the pistachio nuts. Place the mixture in a pastry bag with a no. 6 (12-mm) plain tip. Fill both ends of the tubes with the cream mixture reserving about ¹/₃ cup (80 ml). Dip each end into the remaining chopped pistachio nuts. Ideally this should be done to order but certainly no longer than 30 minutes before serving.

7. **Presentation:** Pipe or spoon a raspberry-sized dollop of the reserved cream in the center of a dessert plate (the cream is there to prevent the pirouettes from rolling on the plate, but it should not show in the final presentation). Place two filled pirouettes on top of the cream, leaning one against the other at an angle. Spoon Blueberry Sauce across the center, using enough so that it forms a small pool on each side of the plate. Decorate with three Caramel Corkscrews.

FIGURE 10–4   *The template used to form the Tulip Paste cookies in* Blueberry Pirouettes *and* Crème Caramel Nouveau

Caramel Boxes with Caramel-Macadamia Nut Mousse

16 servings

dark coating chocolate, melted

sixteen Caramel Boxes and Squares (recipe follows)

one-third recipe Chocolate Mint Torte (page 321) (see note 1)

Caramel-Macadamia Nut Mousse (recipe follows)

Caramel Corkscrews (page 960)

Caramel Dipped Macadamia Nuts (page 965)

light chocolate curls

one-quarter recipe Caramel Sauce II (page 1071)

NOTE 1: Follow the recipe and directions for the Chocolate Mint Torte through step seven with the following changes:

- *Omit the mint*
- *Use warm water instead of bringing the water to a boil*
- *Bake the batter in a greased and floured 9-inch (22.5-cm) cake pan. When cold, cut the cake into 1³⁄₄-inch (4.5-cm) squares. Cover and reserve.*

NOTE 2: This dessert tastes best when the boxes are crisp. While it is possible to fill the boxes with mousse and hold them in the refrigerator for up to 2 hours before serving, if necessary, ideally, each box should be filled and decorated to order. This also allows you to keep any unfilled boxes to use later.

Caramel, chocolate, and nuts—if you love this combination, and who doesn't, this is the dessert for you. Making the boxes and decorations may appear intimidating at first but, as you will find out, the Caramel Glass Paste is actually quite easy to work with. Also, unfilled boxes can be stored for up to ten days in an airtight container so you can start well ahead. To simplify, you can omit one of the caramel decorations (using either the corkscrews or the caramelized nuts instead of both) without sacrificing any of the elegance of the presentation. Please do not leave off both decorations however; they are really so easy, well worth the time and effort, and guests always love fancy sugar decorations, especially so these, standing tall and glorious. I have intentionally excluded fruit, mint sprigs, or edible flowers from the presentation to accentuate the subtle gold and brown shades of the caramel, chocolate, and macadamia nuts. For a more colorful presentation featuring the Caramel Boxes, see Wild Strawberries Romanoff in Caramel Boxes, page 526. You may substitute any rich moist chocolate cake (including brownies) for the altered Chocolate Mint Torte.

1. Place a small amount of melted coating chocolate in a piping bag. Cut a very small opening and pipe seven or eight straight lines across the center over the base portion of dessert plates. Let cool.

2. Dip the top edge of as many Caramel Boxes as you will be serving ¹⁄₄ inch (6 mm) into the same chocolate. Dip the same number of small squares halfway into the coating chocolate diagonally. Set aside for the chocolate to harden.

3. Place a square of chocolate torte in the bottom of as many Caramel Boxes as you expect to serve (pick up the square with the tip of a paring knife then lower it down). Place the caramel nut filling in a pastry bag with a no. 6 (12-mm) plain tip. Pipe the filling into the boxes, filling them to just below the rim. Reserve in the refrigerator (see note 2).

4. Presentation: Decorate the top of a filled box with a chocolate dipped Caramel Square, caramelized macadamia nuts, and Caramel Corkscrews. Push the corkscrews into the filling slightly to make them stand at the angle desired, but be careful not to break them. Use the tip of a paring knife to press the bottom of the corkscrew into the filling instead of pushing it down from the top. Spoon chocolate curls on top of the box around the other decorations. Pipe a small dot of filling in the center of one of the decorated plates. Place the filled and decorated box on top, placing it at an angle to the piped chocolate lines. Pipe Caramel Sauce on the plate around the box in large teardrop shapes. Decorate the plate in front of the box with two caramelized macadamia nuts attached with a little chocolate.

Caramel Boxes and Squares

16 boxes and square decorations

Caramel Glass Paste (recipe follows)

NOTE 1: You can make the molding blocks used for shaping the Glass Paste out of styrofoam and wrap them with aluminum foil or, for sturdier forms that will last forever, cut the shapes out of hard wood (or have them made). Smooth the long edges with sandpaper. Screw a small round-headed screw partway into the center of one short end. The screw can be used as a handle to facilitate lifting the block out of the Caramel Box.

NOTE 2: If necessary, you can weld together a number of smaller pieces if you don't have large enough scraps to make the decorations. Overlap the edges and heat until the pieces melt together.

1. Cut a template from sturdy cardboard measuring 4¼ inches by 8½ inches (10.6 × 21.2 cm).

2. Make two rectangular molding blocks 1⅞ inches square and 3 inches long (4.7 cm × 7.5 cm) (see note 1).

3. Place 8 ounces (225 g) (one-fourth) of the Caramel Glass Paste on a sheet of baking paper. Spread it out to a 9-by-20-inch (22.5-×-50-cm) strip. Transfer the paper to a perfectly flat sheet pan. Repeat three times with the remaining paste.

4. Bake one sheet at a time at 350°F (175°C) for approximately 12 minutes or until light brown. Remove the sheet from the oven carefully: a jarring movement will ripple the soft, thin surface. Let the sheet cool for a few seconds, then, still working carefully, transfer it to the tabletop or, better yet, to a full sheet-sized cardboard set on the table. Using the template as a guide, cut the sheet into four pieces with a chef's knife. Set the cut sheet aside to cool while you bake and cut the remaining sheets in the same manner.

5. Break away the scrap pieces around the edges of all sixteen rectangles. Place the larger scrap pieces (slightly apart so they do not touch) on a sheet pan lined with baking paper (see note 2). Place back in the oven until soft. Remove from the oven and cut about twenty 1¾-inch (4.5-cm) squares out of the softened scraps. Reserve the squares to use in serving. The remaining scrap pieces can be used in Rum Ball or Danish Pastry fillings (or eaten).

6. Reheat the large rectangular pieces, four at a time, until they are soft enough to bend yet still firm enough to pick up from the pan. Working at a table close to the oven, invert one rectangle onto the table and place the molding block in the corner of one short end. Quickly wrap the glass sheet around the block, pressing down firmly at the end to weld the edges together. Still working quickly, fold the protruding edges against the end of the block as if you are wrapping a package (Figure 10–5). Stand the box upright and press down hard again to weld the bottom together (Figure 10–6). Leave the block inside the box and form the next one. (You may need to warm the pieces again to prevent breaking them.) Carefully pull out the first block; if it sticks, insert a small paring knife between the block and the box (Figure 10–7). Form the remaining boxes (leaving one block in place while you use the other one) in the same way (Figure 10–8). You can expedite the molding process by keeping the paring knife chilled in ice water: the cold knife in contact with the sides of the box will make it harden more quickly, and you will be able to pull the building block out sooner.

7. If you will not be serving the boxes right away, store them in an airtight container (together with the square decorations) until needed. They can be kept for up to 10 days.

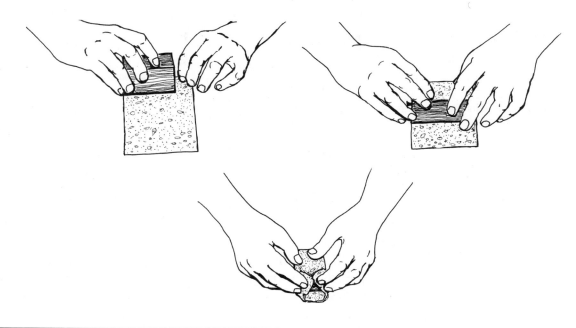

FIGURE 10–5   Wrapping the soft Caramel Glass Paste around a wooden molding block and then folding the bottom edges against the end of the block as if wrapping a package

FIGURE 10–6   Pressing the folded bottom edges firmly against the table to weld the bottom of the box together

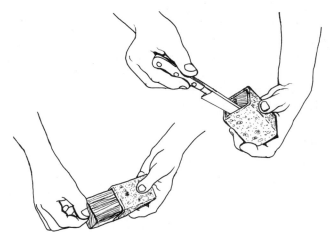

FIGURE 10–7   Removing the Caramel Box once it has hardened; inserting a small paring knife to loosen the sides if they stick

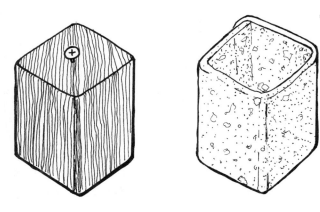

FIGURE 10–8   The wooden molding block and a Caramel Box

Caramel Glass Paste

approximately 2 pounds (910 g)

11 ounces (310 g) soft unsalted butter
11 ounces (310 g) powdered sugar
1/4 cup (60 ml) or 3 ounces (85 g) glucose or light corn syrup
6 ounces (170 g) bread flour

This versatile paste can be used to make tulips to hold ice cream or sherbets. However, unlike Tulip Paste, this batter will not stay in the precise shape you create but instead will float out slightly as it bakes.

If you use baking paper, spread the Caramel Glass Paste out as soon as you portion it onto the paper. Portioning all of the paste out and then going back to spread it into the desired shape will cause the paper to become wet and wrinkled and make the paste difficult to shape. The paste should be soft enough to spread easily. If it has been stored, even at room temperature, you may need to warm it gently over a bain-marie to soften the butter and make it workable.

1. Cream the soft butter with the sugar. Add the glucose or corn syrup and mix to combine, scraping the sides of the bowl. Incorporate the flour.

2. Use as directed in the individual recipes. The paste can be stored at room temperature for two or three days. Refrigerate for longer storage.

Caramel-Macadamia Nut Mousse

6 cups (1 l, 440 ml)

2 cups (480 ml) heavy cream
1 tablespoon (9 g) unflavored gelatin powder
1/3 cup (80 ml) cold water
10 ounces (285 g) granulated sugar
3/4 cup (180 ml) hot water
4 eggs
4 ounces (115 g) unsalted macadamia nuts, toasted and coarsely crushed

NOTE: It is important to caramelize the sugar dark enough, not only to color the filling, but also to give it a caramel flavor.

1. Whip the cream to soft peaks. Set aside in the refrigerator.

2. Sprinkle the gelatin over the cold water and set aside to soften.

3. Caramelize the sugar to a light brown color (see note following this recipe and also page 954). Add the hot water and cook out any lumps. Set aside off the heat.

4. Whip the eggs for about 3 minutes at high speed. Lower the speed and pour the hot caramel into the eggs in a steady stream. Turn back to high speed and continue whipping until the mixture is cold and forms soft peaks. Fold in the reserved whipped cream.

5. Place the gelatin mixture over a bain-marie and heat until dissolved. Do not overheat. Rapidly mix the gelatin into a small portion of the cream, then quickly add that mixture to the remainder of the cream. Fold in the macadamia nuts.

Caramelized Apple Galette in Phyllo Dough with Kumquat

16 servings

twenty-four sheets of phyllo dough (a 1 pound/455 g package)
2 ounces (55 g) melted unsalted butter
1 pound (455 g) Pastry Cream (page 1088)
2 ounces (55 g) sweet dark chocolate
2 ounces (55 g) toasted hazelnuts, skins removed

Galettes are possibly the oldest of all pastries and can be traced back to the Neolithic period. Generally speaking, a galette is a round cake made out of flaky pastry dough. The most celebrated version (which resembles a Pithiviers) is the Galette des Rois, a pastry served during the Twelfth Night celebration in France. The Twelfth Night is the eve of Epiphany (January 6), the close of the Christmas Festivities. Traditionally, the cake would contain a small porcelain doll or a single bean, and the person who found the doll or bean in their serving would proclaim himself King for the night and could then name his Queen. The name galette is also used for many savory tarts that are topped with meat and cheese and for other items such as fried potato cakes and certain pancakes. Given this rather loose interpretation of the word, I do not feel it is out of place here, even though a true galette (whatever that is now), besides being round, should be rather flat. In this dessert I have shaped the crust into a bas-

5 pounds (2 kg, 275 g) Red Delicious
    apples (approximately twelve
    medium size)
4 ounces (115 g) unsalted butter
6 ounces (170 g) granulated sugar
1/3 cup (80 ml) heavy cream
one-half recipe Chantilly Cream
    (page 1083)
one recipe Kumquat Sauce (page 1075)
eight whole kumquats, cut in half
sixteen small mint leaves
lavender sprigs

NOTE 1: Use 7-ounce (210-ml) individual pie forms with slanting sides that measure 4¹/₂ inches in diameter across the top, 2³/₄ inches in diameter across the bottom, and are 1¹/₂ inches tall (11.2 × 6.8 × 3.7 cm). If this size is not available, it is preferable to use slightly smaller forms rather than larger ones.

NOTE 2: To do this without first piping a frame (as described in Honey Truffle Symphony), pipe a circle slightly smaller than the desired finished size, then use the tip of the piping bottle to push the edge of the sauce out to create the fluted pattern.

ket to give it some height and make it look more appealing, and I have placed the fruit on top of phyllo dough instead of the more traditional Puff Pastry. To make a classical galette, see the variation following this recipe.

This is a very quick and easy pastry to produce. If necessary, the apples can be prepared one or two days ahead, as can the phyllo shells. It is then quite simple to assemble and bake the galette. Orange Sauce can be used as a substitute for the Kumquat Sauce if kumquats are unavailable. Don't give up too easily, however, as the wonderful unique flavor of this small citrus fruit is well worth the effort to find, and the peel gives the sauce such a deep vibrant color; the Orange Sauce actually looks faded and plain by comparison.

1. Cut a 5¹/₂-inch (13.7-cm) diameter round template from cardboard or have a lid or plate of the same size handy. Unwrap and unroll the phyllo dough and cut the stacked phyllo sheets in half lengthwise. Cut across in thirds, dividing each sheet of dough into six pieces. Place the pieces in two stacks and cover one with a lightly dampened cloth. Place a piece from the remaining stack on the table in front of you. Brush some of the melted butter in a 4-inch (10-cm) circle in the center of the dough. Place a second piece of dough on top and brush butter on it in the same way. Continue layering and brushing with butter until you have used eight pieces of phyllo. Do not butter the top of the stack.

2. Place the template on top of the stack. Cut around the template with a paring knife and remove the scraps. Brush butter over the top layer of the circle. Carefully press the stack of dough into a small individual pie form (Figure 10–9) (see note 1). If the circle does not form an

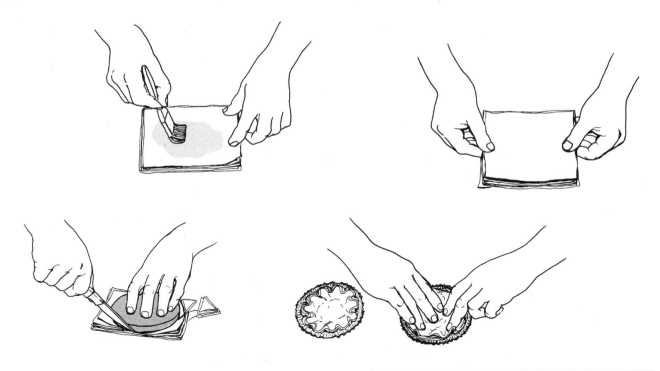

FIGURE 10–9   Brushing butter over a phyllo sheet before placing the next sheet on top; using a template as a guide to cut the layered sheets into a circle; placing the stacked sheets inside an individual pie form so the phyllo dough forms a fluted edge

evenly fluted edge, shape it with your hands. Repeat to form the remaining fifteen phyllo dough shells. Place the lined forms on two sheet pans. Discard any leftover phyllo dough.

3. Place the Pastry Cream in a disposable pastry bag made from a half-sheet of baking paper (see page 23). Pipe the cream into the shells, dividing it evenly.

4. Chop the chocolate and the nuts into raspberry-size pieces. Sprinkle the chocolate and nuts evenly over the Pastry Cream.

5. Peel, core, and cut the apples in quarters lengthwise.

6. Place the 4 ounces (115 g) of butter in a 10-inch (25-cm) (or larger) skillet. Melt the butter over medium heat. Sprinkle the sugar evenly over the melted butter. Place an 11-inch (27.5-cm) adjustable ring (or you can use the ring from a 10-inch/25-cm springform pan, unclamped) in the skillet and quickly arrange the apples inside the ring, standing them on the stem end and packing them as tightly as possible. (The ring may sit high on the sides of the pan at first, but as the apples cook and become smaller, you can adjust it.) Cook the apples over medium heat, shaking the skillet gently to ensure that the apples do not stick and pressing lightly on the top to compact them every few minutes. As the apples shrink, tighten the ring around them. Continue cooking the apples in this manner until enough of the apple liquid has evaporated to allow the sugar to turn dark golden brown (caramelize), about 45 minutes. Remove the skillet from the heat and let the apples cool for a few minutes.

7. Place the apples on a sheet pan lined with baking paper; reserve the syrup in the skillet. Cut each apple quarter in half lengthwise. Place six pieces of apple on top of the Pastry Cream in each phyllo shell, arranging the wedges so that the rounded sides face up.

8. Add the heavy cream to the sugar syrup remaining in the skillet. Bring to a boil while stirring constantly. Strain the sauce, then spoon it over the apples in each form.

9. Bake the galettes at 400°F (205°C) for approximately 15 minutes. Cool slightly, then remove the desserts from the forms.

10. Whip the Chantilly Cream until stiff peaks form. Place in a pastry bag with a no. 6 (12-mm) star tip and reserve in the refrigerator.

11. Presentation: Using a piping bottle, pipe a fluted circle of Kumquat Sauce covering most of the base of a dessert plate (see note 2). Place an Apple Galette in the center of the sauce. Pipe a rosette of Chantilly Cream on top. Decorate the top with a kumquat half and a mint leaf. Arrange sprigs of lavender around the galette in the sauce.

 **VARIATION**
Classic Galette

16 servings

Omit making the phyllo dough baskets. Instead, roll out 3 pounds, 12 ounces (1 kg, 705 g) Puff Pastry to ⅛ inch (3 mm) thick. Refrigerate the dough until it is firm. Using a sharp knife, cut out sixteen 6-inch (15-cm) circles. Divide the Pastry Cream, chopped chocolate, and chopped nuts between the circles, leaving a ¹/₂-inch (1.2-cm) border uncovered. Arrange the apples on top. Do not spoon the sugar sauce over the apples. Bake as directed. Brush the sugar sauce on top as soon as the desserts are removed from the oven.

Cherry Baskets with Cherry Compote and Black Pepper Frozen Yogurt

16 servings

one recipe Vanilla Tulip Paste (page 1047)

2 teaspoons (5 g) cocoa powder

one-half recipe Angel Food Cake (page 271) (see note 1)

one recipe Honey-Vanilla Frozen Yogurt (page 645), unfrozen (see step eight)

1 tablespoon (6 g) coarsely ground black pepper

2 pounds, 4 ounces (1 kg, 25 g) Bing cherries (see note 2)

one-half recipe Italian Cream (page 1087)

Cherry Compote (recipe follows)

NOTE 1: You can make the full recipe of Angel Food Cake in a tube pan as directed, slice the baked cake in half horizontally, and reserve one half for another use. In this case you may have to utilize some scrap pieces for the last one or two baskets. Or, make a half-recipe of batter and pour it into a paper-lined 12-inch (30-cm) cake pan or cake ring. It will bake in slightly less time than directed in the recipe.

NOTE 2: Since the cherry season is short and unpredictable, try using raspberries instead. They both look and taste great as a substitute.

These impressive looking baskets are made even more so by their towering handles. This is a lighter version of an Easter basket dessert typically made for that holiday in Sweden many years ago. Instead of cherries, however, the baskets were filled with small handmade marzipan Easter eggs. For most Europeans marzipan is a must at Easter in the form of rabbits, chickens, and, of course, the aforementioned Easter eggs. Try using these templates and instructions to create basket desserts at Easter, filling them with chocolate or marzipan eggs on top of the cream. If calories are not a concern you may want to fill the baskets with sweetened whipped cream rather than the lighter Italian Cream.

Both the basket shells and the handles can be made several weeks ahead of time as long as they are placed in an airtight container and stored in a warm location. Although the baskets should be filled and assembled to order, it is possible to add the cake, cream filling, and cherries up to 30 minutes in advance if necessary. The cookie shells will get a little soft but will still be fully acceptable. Or, in a case where you must put the desserts together that far ahead of time, you might want to consider the Vineyard Barrels (see page 722) instead. The barrels are a variation of this dessert but are a little quicker to assemble because the handles are built in, and they're also easier to move after they have been sitting because they are made with a bottom.

1. Make the templates for the Cherry Basket and the basket handle (Figure 10–10). The templates as shown are the correct size for the recipe; however, due to the size of these particular templates, it is only possible to show half of each one on the page. Trace as shown, invert your paper, match the dotted line in the center, and trace the other half of each template so that they look like the small examples shown. Cut both templates out of ¹/₁₆-inch (2-mm) thick cardboard (cake boxes work fine for this). Save the solid rectangle cut from the center of the basket template. Overlap the short edges of this piece ¹/₄ inch (6 mm) and tape together to form a round tube. Compress the tube slightly to shape it oval instead of round. Have a short dowel or cannoli tube available.

2. If you do not have silicone mats (which do not need to be greased and floured), lightly grease the back of eight even sheet pans, coat with flour, and then shake off as much flour as possible.

3. Remove 3 tablespoons (45 ml) of the Tulip Paste and stir the cocoa powder into it. Put a portion of it into a piping bag, cut a small opening, and reserve.

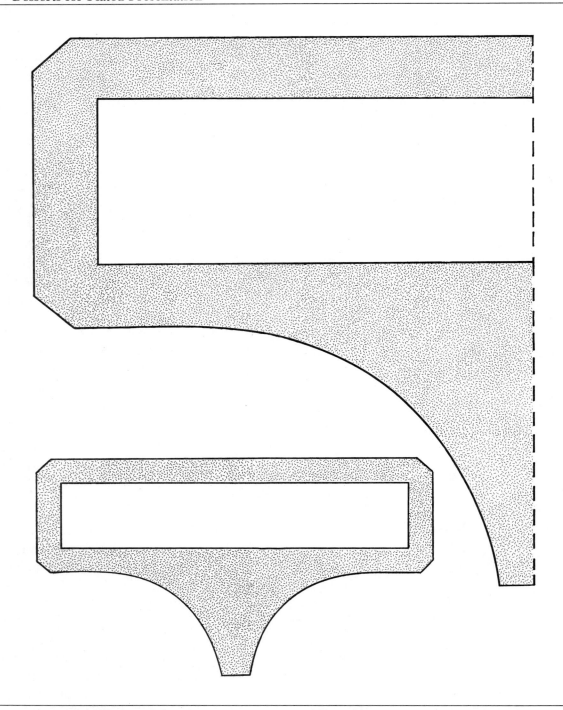

FIGURE 10–10   The templates used to form the cookie basket shells and handles for Cherry Baskets

4. Place the basket template on one of the prepared sheet pans. Spread some of the plain Tulip Paste smoothly and evenly inside the template (see Figures 19–55 and 19–56, pages 1046 and 1047). Make four rectangles on each of four pans. Pipe two lines of cocoa Tulip Paste the length of each basket rectangle, evenly spaced across the width.

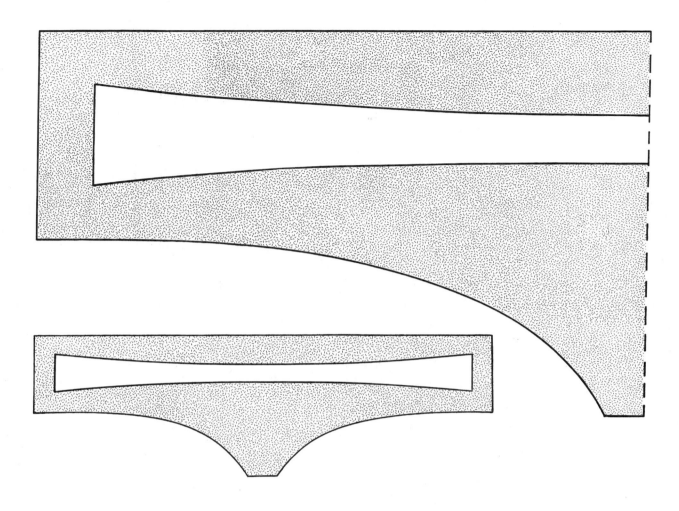

5. Bake one pan at a time at 425°F (219°C) for approximately 6 minutes or until the first strip begins to show light brown spots. Leave the pan in the oven with the door open. With the cardboard mold standing up and working quickly, pick up the strip with the most brown color using your fingers and place it inside the mold topside against the cardboard, overlapping the ends. Place the dowel or cannoli tube inside and use it to press hard on the overlapped edges, pressing them against your fingers on the other side to weld the edges together. Remove the dowel, slide the basket off of the mold, and set it aside standing up. Quickly repeat with the next most browned strip and continue baking and forming the ovals until you have made sixteen baskets. Set the baskets aside.

6. Place the handle template on one of the four remaining prepared sheet pans or on a silicone mat. Spread plain Tulip Paste evenly inside, making five handles per sheet pan. This will give you a few extra since they break easily. Pipe a line of cocoa Tulip Paste, the full length of the strip, in the center of each handle. Place a rolling pin that is 4 inches (10 cm) in diameter on a sheet pan or on your worktable. Raise both ends of the rolling pin a few inches off the table and anchor the pin so that it will not roll; a little Short Dough or a similar material can be used to do both. Bake the handle strips, one pan at a time, for about 4 minutes. As they begin to color, remove the handles and drape them over the rolling pin. Hold the ends against the pin for a few seconds until firm. Carefully pull the handles off. Repeat baking and forming the remaining handles. Reserve.

7. Cut out oval pieces of Angel Food Cake that will fit snugly inside the baskets. Cover and reserve.

8. Prepare the recipe for Honey-Vanilla Frozen Yogurt through step four. Stir in the black pepper and then process in an ice-cream freezer following the manufacturer's directions. Reserve covered in the freezer.

9. Wash, stem, and pit the cherries. Cut the cherries in half. Try to do this as close as possible to serving time to avoid oxidation. If you must prepare the cherry halves in advance, toss them in a little lemon juice.

10. Place the Italian Cream in a pastry bag with a no. 6 (12-mm) plain tip. Reserve in the refrigerator.

11. Presentation: Place a cake oval in the bottom of a cookie basket. Pipe Italian Cream on top, filling the basket to within ¼ inch (6 mm) of the rim. Transfer the basket to the center of a dessert plate. Place a handle on the basket, carefully pushing the ends into the cream to secure. Top the cream with cherry halves. Spoon Cherry Compote in an irregular pattern around the basket on the base of the plate. Place four small scoops of peppered frozen yogurt, evenly spaced around the dessert, on the base of the plate. Serve immediately.

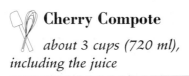

Cherry Compote

*about 3 cups (720 ml),
including the juice*

2 pounds (910 g) Bing cherries

½ cup (120 ml) port wine

1 tablespoon (15 ml) lemon juice

⅛ teaspoon (.5 g) freshly ground
   black pepper

2 tablespoons (18 g) pectin powder

6 ounces (170 g) granulated sugar

1. Wash, stem, and pit the cherries.

2. Combine the port, lemon juice, and black pepper in a saucepan. Thoroughly mix the pectin powder and granulated sugar, then add to the mixture in the saucepan. Bring to a boil, add the cherries, and simmer, stirring frequently for 10 to 12 minutes or until the cherries are very soft but have not fallen apart.

3. Remove from the heat and allow to cool to room temperature. If the liquid seems too thin, strain the cherries and reduce it further. The compote will thicken further if refrigerated.

◍ Chestnut-Rum Cream Cakes

16 servings

one-third recipe Chocolate Chiffon
    Sponge Cake batter (page 272)

$^{1}/_{2}$ cup (120 ml) Plain Cake Syrup
    (page 10)

Chocolate-Rum Cream (recipe
    follows)

Chestnut-Mascarpone Cream
    (recipe follows)

one recipe Mousseline Sauce
    (page 1076)

$^{1}/_{4}$ cup (60 ml) dark rum

1 cup (240 ml) heavy cream

2 teaspoons (10 g) granulated sugar

light chocolate shavings

Chocolate Sauce for Piping
    (page 1072)

sixteen Candied Chestnuts (page 4)

three sheets gold leaf (optional)
    (see note)

NOTE: To use the optional gold leaf decoration, cover half of each Candied Chestnut with $^{1}/_{6}$ of a gold leaf sheet. See page 1017 for more information on working with gold leaf.

*T*he spectacular European sweet chestnut tree (not to be confused with the American variety, which produces a much smaller nut) is a great ornamental and shade tree growing up to one hundred feet tall. They are part of the landscape all over Northern Europe. In the springtime the trees are covered with clusters of yellowish flowers, which later become spiny burrs, each containing up to three nuts. The chestnuts that are sold for cooking, either fresh in the fall and winter, or canned in sugar syrup or water throughout the year, are the European variety. For some reason chestnuts are utilized much more in cooking all across Europe than here in the U.S. where they still seem a bit underrated (with the exception of a brief burst of popularity around the holidays).

In this recipe the puréed fruit (chestnuts are actually classified as a fruit rather than a nut since they contain a greater amount of starch than oil) is delicious mixed with cream, flavored with a hint of rum, and paired with chocolate. If you use canned chestnut purée, which you must do most of the year, be very careful to work it completely smooth before mixing in the Mascarpone Cheese. Because of the high starch content, the purée is quite firm and will give new meaning to the word lumpy if you fail to do so.

1. Line the bottom of a 10-inch (25-cm) cake pan with baking paper. Add the sponge batter and spread the top even. Bake at 425°F (219°C) for approximately 15 minutes or until baked through. The cake should spring back when pressed lightly in the center. Set aside to cool.

2. Place sixteen 3-inch (7.5-cm) cake rings on a sheet pan lined with baking paper. If you do not have cake rings, cut sixteen strips from acetate 10 inches long and $1^{1}/_{2}$ inches high (25 × 3.7 cm), overlap the short ends, and tape them together to make rings that are 3 inches (7.5 cm) in diameter.

3. Run a knife around the edge of the pan to release the cooled Sponge Cake and unmold the sponge. Remove the skin from the top of the cake. Slice the cake horizontally to make two layers. Brush the layers with Cake Syrup, using it all up. Cut sixteen circles from the two layers using a 3-inch (3.7-cm) plain cookie cutter (you will have to piece the last two together). Place a sponge circle in the bottom of each ring.

4. Place the Chocolate-Rum Cream in a pastry bag with a no. 3 (6-mm) plain tip. Pipe the filling on top of the sponge circles, dividing it evenly between the rings. Be careful not to get any filling on the sides of the ring above the cream. Refrigerate while making the Chestnut-Mascarpone Cream.

5. Place the Chestnut-Mascarpone Cream in a pastry bag with a no. 5 (10-mm) plain tip. Pipe the filling on top of the chocolate cream, dividing it evenly between the rings. Use a spatula to even the tops. Refrigerate the cakes until set, at least 2 hours or, preferably, overnight.

6. Flavor the Mousseline Sauce with the rum. Reserve in the refrigerator.

7. Whip the heavy cream with the sugar until stiff peaks form. Place in a pastry bag with a no. 6 (12-mm) star tip.

8. No more than one hour before serving, remove the metal rings or acetate strips from as many cakes as you plan to serve. Pipe a whipped cream rosette in the center on top of each one. Cover the top around the whipped cream with shaved chocolate. Place the decorated servings back in the refrigerator. The undecorated servings can be kept in the refrigerator, covered and left in the rings, for several days.

9. Presentation: Pour approximately ⅓ cup (80 ml) of Mousseline Sauce off-center on a dessert plate. Use the back of a spoon to shape the sauce into a round pool about 5 inches (12.5 cm) in diameter. Place a small amount of Chocolate Sauce for Piping in a piping bag. Pipe a rounded zigzag pattern, about 1 inch (2.5 cm) wide, around the perimeter of the sauce. Pull a small wooden skewer through the center of the zigzag (see Figure 19–32, page 1006). Place a serving of cake behind the sauce with about one-fourth of the cake in the sauce pool. Decorate with a Candied Chestnut on top of the whipped cream rosette.

Chocolate-Rum Cream

3½ cups (840 ml)

3 ounces (85 g) unsweetened chocolate

7 ounces (200 g) sweet dark chocolate

1¾ cups (420 ml) heavy cream

3 egg yolks (¼ cup/60 ml)

¼ cup (60 ml) or 3 ounces (85 g) honey

2 tablespoons (30 ml) dark rum

NOTE: If the filling thickens too much before you are ready to use it, soften it by warming very slightly over a bain-marie, stirring constantly with a whisk or a spoon.

1. Chop both chocolates into small pieces. Melt in a bowl set over simmering water. Set aside but keep warm.

2. Whip the heavy cream until soft peaks form. Reserve.

3. Whip the egg yolks by hand until light and fluffy, about 2 or 3 minutes. Bring the honey to a boil and gradually add it to the egg yolks. Add the dark rum and continue to whip rapidly until the mixture has cooled completely.

4. Mix in the melted chocolate. Quickly fold in the whipped cream.

Chestnut-Mascarpone Cream

4½ cups (1 l, 80 ml)

10 ounces (285 g) Chestnut Purée (page 802)

or

unsweetened canned chestnut purée

8 ounces (225 g) Mascarpone Cheese (page 9)

1½ cups (360 ml) heavy cream

5 teaspoons (15 g) unflavored gelatin powder

⅓ cup (80 ml) cold water

1. Work the chestnut purée until it is smooth. Mix in the Mascarpone Cheese gradually to avoid lumps.

2. Whip the heavy cream until soft peaks form; do not overwhip. Mix the cream into the chestnut mixture. Reserve in the refrigerator.

3. Sprinkle the gelatin over the cold water and set aside to soften.

4. Combine the sugar and egg whites in a mixer bowl. Set the bowl over simmering water and heat, stirring constantly with a whisk, to 140°F (60°C). Remove from the heat and whip immediately until the meringue is cold and has formed stiff peaks.

5. Place the softened gelatin over a bain-marie and heat to dissolve. Do not overheat. Place a small amount of the chestnut mixture in a

6 ounces (170 g) granulated sugar

4 egg whites (¹/₂ cup/120 ml)

NOTE: Do not make this filling until you are ready to use it.

Chianti Poached Figs with Lavender Mascarpone

12 servings

thirty Brown Turkey figs, ripe but firm

5 cups (1 l, 200 ml) Chianti wine

4 ounces (115 g) granulated sugar

one recipe Caramelized Sugar for Decorations (page 955)

8 ounces (225 g) Mascarpone Cheese (page 9)

lavender petals

Caramel Sauce II (page 1071)

crushed toasted hazelnuts

twelve sprigs of flowering lavender

NOTE: If the caramelized figs do not stand straight or steady enough, they can be fixed easily: Place a sheet pan lined with baking paper in the freezer while you melt a small amount of piping or coating chocolate. One at a time, pipe dime-sized dots of chocolate on the chilled pan, set a fig on top, and hold straight for a few seconds.

bowl. Quickly stir in the gelatin and then, continuing to work quickly, add this to the remaining chestnut cream. Fold in the meringue.

Brown Turkey figs, also known as Black Spanish figs, are large, beautiful-looking fruit, with an exceptional mahogany brown skin tinged with purple. The first crop of the year is always particularly eye-catching. (In addition to the unique fact that figs produce fruit without flowering, they are also unusual in that they provide two crops annually.)

This recipe utilizes the classic technique of poaching figs in wine and reducing the liquid to use as a sauce. The lightly cooked fruit is paired with Mascarpone Cheese and Caramel Sauce—a traditional and fabulous combination. The only time-consuming step here is caramelizing the figs, which can easily be omitted if necessary. Instead, poach the reserved figs lightly (less than 5 minutes) after removing the first eighteen from the poaching liquid. Stand the second group of figs on end and allow them to drain throughly. Cut a cross on top of each one, cutting halfway through the fruit, so that the figs open up like flowers. Place in the center of the sauce when serving.

1. Select twelve of the nicest figs and reserve for decoration.

2. Combine the Chianti and the granulated sugar in a large saucepan. Bring to a boil and add the remaining eighteen figs. Adjust the heat so that the liquid is just simmering, and poach the figs for 5 minutes. Depending on the size of your pan, you may need to poach the figs in two batches. Gently remove the figs and stand them upright on a sheet pan lined with baking paper. Boil the poaching liquid until it is reduced to 1³/₄ cups (420 ml) and the consistency is that of a thick syrup. Set aside to cool.

3. Caramelize the twelve reserved figs in the Caramelized Sugar for Decorations following the instructions on page 964.

4. Cut the poached figs in half lengthwise, cutting evenly through the stem as well. Place them back on the sheet pan, cut-side up. Soften the Mascarpone Cheese and place in a pastry bag with a no. 4 (8-mm) plain tip. Pipe the cheese in a pearl pattern down the center of each fig. Sprinkle lavender petals on top of the Mascarpone. Reserve the decorated figs in the refrigerator.

5. Place the Caramel Sauce in a piping bottle and set aside. Carefully twist the caramelized figs off of the skewers (wear a latex glove on the hand that touches the fruit to avoid fingerprints on the caramel). Place the figs standing upright on a sheet pan (see note).

6. **Presentation:** Pour a small pool of the reduced poaching syrup in the center of a dessert plate. Place a caramelized fig in the center of the sauce. Sprinkle crushed hazelnuts on the sauce around the fig. Place three prepared fig halves evenly spaced around the sauce with the stem ends pointing out. Pipe random teardrops of Caramel Sauce around the fig halves. Garnish with a lavender sprig.

Chocolate Ganache Towers

16 servings

one-third recipe Baked Chocolate
   Sheet batter (page 570)
Dark Chocolate Tower Filling
   (recipe follows)
Light Chocolate Filling (recipe
   follows)
unsweetened cocoa powder
powdered sugar
1½ cups (360 ml) heavy cream
2 teaspoons (10 g) granulated sugar
sixteen Chocolate Monarch Butterfly
   Ornaments (page 910)
sixteen edible fresh flowers

NOTE: *This dessert can be left at room temperature (after peeling off the plastic strips) for up to 30 minutes prior to serving. The flavor is actually improved; however, you may need to adjust the consistency of the fillings; see note following Dark Chocolate Filling.*

*E*ven with the help of polyurethane or acetate strips and the support frame, this elegant and showy dessert is still time-consuming. To speed things up you can make the Chocolate Ganache Towers up to one week ahead, and certainly the presentation can be simplified. The more elaborate chocolate butterfly can be replaced with one made from Tulip Paste, as in Chocolate Ganache Cake, or a simple Chocolate Figurine as described in the Tiramisu featured in Triple Treat. If you have forms or rings that are 2 inches in diameter, or if you have made the support frame (directions follow), it is not necessary to tape the plastic strips together. Just overlap the ends and set them inside the forms or box frame; they will not unroll.

1. Spread the Chocolate Sheet batter into a 6-by-23-inch (15-×-57.5-cm) strip (just short of the full length of a sheet pan, but only 6 inches/15 cm wide). Bake immediately at 375°F (190°C) for about 12 minutes or until baked through. Set aside to cool.

2. Cut sixteen strips, 2½ inches wide and 7¼ inches long (6.2 × 18.1 cm), from a sheet of polyurethane or acetate. Overlap the ends and tape them together to make tubes that are 2 inches (5 cm) in diameter and 2½ inches (6.2 cm) high. Stand the tubes on end on a paper-lined sheet pan or in the support frame (see closeup of Figure 10–11 below left) (directions follow to make the frame). If you want to make the filling set up diagonally as shown in the color insert, you must use the frame and set it on the angled base (Figure 10–11).

3. Invert the cooled Chocolate Sheet and peel the paper from the back. Cut out sixteen 2-inch (5-cm) rounds. Place one in the bottom of each tube. Set the tubes aside.

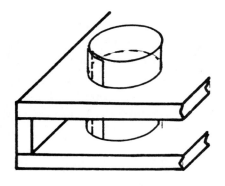

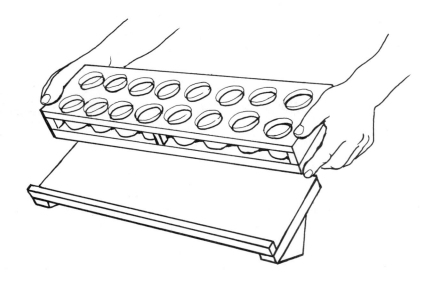

FIGURE 10–11   *Closeup of a plastic tube in the support frames; placing the support frame on an angled base before adding the Dark Chocolate Filling to make the filling set up on an angle in Chocolate Ganache Towers*

4. Pipe the Dark Chocolate Tower Filling into the reserved plastic tubes on top of the sponge rounds. Be very careful not to get any filling on the inside of the tubes above the filling. If you do, remove it carefully or it will detract from the finished appearance. Place the tubes in the refrigerator (leaving them at an angle on the stand if using; see the cutaway closeup of Figure 10–12, top left).

5. If you are making horizontal layers, you can add the Light Chocolate Filling as soon as you have made it. If you are making diagonal layers, wait until the dark chocolate layer is set enough not to move, and then remove the support frame from the angled base and set the frame flat on the table before adding the light chocolate layer. Pipe the Light Chocolate Filling into the tubes on top of the Dark Chocolate Tower Filling (Figure 10–12). Place the tubes in the refrigerator until set.

6. Make the templates shown in Figure 10–13. The templates as shown are the correct size for use in this recipe. Trace the drawings, then cut the templates out of ¹/₁₆-inch (2-mm) thick cardboard (cake boxes work well for this). You will need all of the pieces—A, B, and C. You will also need an aluminum pie tin with the bottom removed (see Figures 19–50 to 19–53, pages 1041 to 1043). Be sure the pie tin will sit flat against the base of your serving plates and is large enough to cover most of the rim of the plates. Place template A with C in place on the base of the inverted pie tin and secure with tape. (Check to be sure the pie tin is not covering any of the template.) Place the pie tin right-side up on top of a dessert plate. Sift cocoa powder lightly over the top, using a fine mesh strainer or sifter. Remove very carefully. Repeat on as many plates as you will be serving. Dust off the pie tin and remove template C. Loosely tape template B in place, creating a smaller circle slightly offset to the first one. Tape three toothpicks on the bottom of

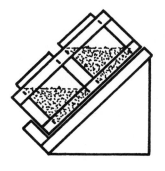

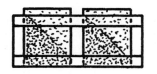

FIGURE 10–12   Cutaway drawings of the support frame before and after piping the light chocolate filling; piping the Light Chocolate Filling on top of the dark filling after removing the support frame from the angled base and placing it flat on the table

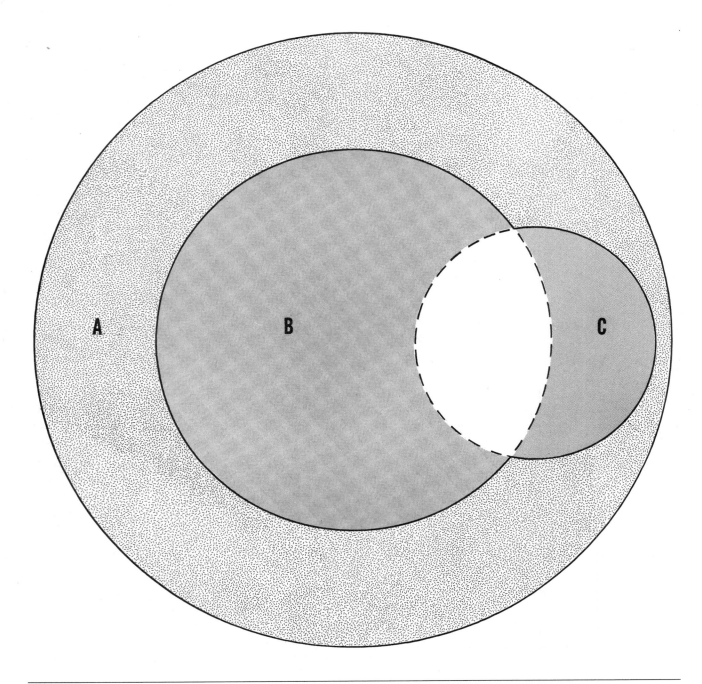

FIGURE 10–13   *The templates used to create overlapping circles of cocoa powder and powdered sugar on the serving plate in the presentation of Chocolate Ganache Towers*

the pie tin at the edge of the cardboard. Carefully place the pie tin on top of one of the plates with cocoa powder. The toothpicks will keep the tin from damaging the cocoa powder design. Lightly sift powered sugar over the new opening. Remove the template carefully and repeat on the other plates. Set the plates aside where they will not be disturbed.

7. Whip the heavy cream and granulated sugar to stiff peaks. Place in a pastry bag with a no. 8 (16-mm) star tip. Reserve in the refrigerator.

8. Remove the polyurethane or acetate strip from as many desserts as you have decorated plates. The remaining desserts can be kept, with the plastic attached, in the refrigerator for several days; they should be covered tightly. (If the plastic strips do not peel away easily, place the desserts in the freezer for 30 minutes first.)

9. Presentation: Pipe a large rosette of whipped cream on the top of a tower, covering it completely. Set the dessert in the center of the cocoa powder circle on one of the prepared dessert plates. Carefully, but firmly, place a chocolate butterfly at an angle on the whipped cream. Place an edible flower on the side.

Dark Chocolate Tower Filling

4 cups (960 ml)

8 ounces (225 g) sweet dark chocolate

3 ounces (85 g) unsweetened chocolate (see note)

2 cups (480 ml) heavy cream

2 egg yolks (save the whites for the light filling)

1 ounce (30 g) granulated sugar

¹/₄ cup (60 ml) or 3 ounces (85 g) honey

NOTE: *Depending on the percentages of cocoa solids and sugar in the brand of sweet chocolate you are using, you may need to adjust the amount of unsweetened chocolate slightly (up or down) to achieve the desired consistency and/or flavor in the filling.*

1. Cut the dark and unsweetened chocolates into small pieces. Melt together in a bowl set over simmering water. Set aside but keep warm.

2. Whip the heavy cream to soft peaks. Reserve in the refrigerator.

3. Whip the egg yolks and sugar until light and fluffy, approximately 3 minutes. In the meantime, bring the honey to a boil. Gradually pour the honey into the egg yolks. Continue to whip until the mixture has cooled completely.

4. Working quickly, incorporate the reserved melted chocolate by hand. Rapidly stir in the reserved whipped cream.

Light Chocolate Filling

4¹/₂ cups (1 l, 80 ml)

2 teaspoons (6 g) unflavored gelatin powder

¹/₄ cup (60 ml) cold water

1³/₄ cups (420 ml) heavy cream

8 ounces (225 g) sweet light chocolate

1 ounce (30 g) unsweetened chocolate

2 egg whites (¹/₄ cup/60 ml) (reserved from dark filling)

¹/₄ cup (60 ml) Simple Syrup (page 11)

1. Sprinkle the gelatin over the cold water and set aside to soften.

2. Whip the heavy cream to a very soft consistency. The cream should collapse when dropped from the whip. If overwhipped, it is likely to break when the remaining ingredients are added. Reserve in the refrigerator.

3. Melt both chocolates together over simmering water. Set aside but keep warm.

4. Combine the egg whites and Simple Syrup. Heat to 140°F (60°C) over simmering water while stirring constantly. Remove from the heat and whip until stiff peaks form. Fold into the reserved whipped cream.

5. Heat the softened gelatin mixture to dissolve. Take care not to overheat.

6. Quickly stir the gelatin mixture into the melted chocolate. Still working rapidly, add a small portion of the cream mixture to temper the chocolate. Then quickly add this to the remaining cream. If the filling is too thin to hold its shape, mix a little longer.

Support Frame for Acetate Strips

1. Refer to Figure 10–14 in constructing the frame. Cut two pieces of ¹/₂-inch (1.2-cm) thick plywood (good on both sides) 5¹/₂ inches wide and 21¹/₂ inches long (13.7 × 53.7 cm). Align the pieces precisely, one on top of the other, and clamp them together. Draw a line on each short end of the top piece 1 inch (2.5 cm) away from the edges leaving a 19¹/₂-inch (48.7-cm) space between the lines.

2. Starting next to the line on one short end, and ¹/₂ inch (1.2 cm) from one long edge, drill eight 2-inch (5-cm) holes, ¹/₂ inch (1.2 cm) apart. Drill a second row of eight 2-inch (5-cm) holes, ¹/₂ inch (1.2 cm) away from the opposite long edge, leaving a ¹/₂-inch (1.2-cm) space in the center between the two rows. Remove the clamps.

3. Cut two pieces of wood (plywood or pine) ¹/₂ inch thick, 1¹/₄ inches wide, and 5¹/₂ inches long (1.2 × 3.1 × 13.7 cm). These pieces will be used on the ends of the frame.

4. Cut two pieces of ¹/₂-inch (1.2-cm) wooden dowel 1¹/₄ inches (3.1 cm) long.

5. Sand all of the wooden pieces smooth (including the two pieces with the drilled holes), using 150-grade sandpaper. Pay special attention to the cut edges.

6. Align the two large pieces with holes, lining up the holes exactly even. Clamp the two end pieces in place between them. Drill, countersink, and screw the end pieces in place, using small brass screws. Remove the clamps.

7. Attach the dowel pieces opposite each other in the center of the box, using screws the same way you attached the ends.

8. The frame is now ready to use. Place a piece of cardboard covered with baking paper under the frame before placing the acetate

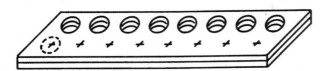
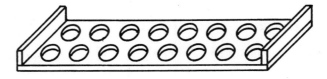
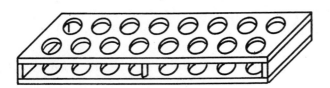
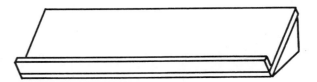

FIGURE 10–14   The sequence in making the support frame; the optional angled base

strips inside. If you are using the frame to support the acetate tubes at an angle, you will probably need to tape the bottom in place, depending on how you are supporting the frame.

Chocolate Marquise

16 servings

one 23-by-15-inch (57.5-×-37.5-cm)
    Ribbon Sponge Sheet (page 276)

¹⁄₄ cup (60 ml) light rum

¹⁄₄ cup (60 ml) Plain Cake Syrup
    (page 10)

Chocolate Marquise Filling (recipe
    follows)

Piping Chocolate (page 904), melted

1 cup (240 ml) heavy cream, whipped

sixteen Marzipan Forget-Me-Not
    Flowers (page 1030)

sixteen Tulip Leaves
    (page 1049)

one-half recipe Raspberry Sauce
    (page 1080)

sixteen mint sprigs

This is a classic recipe that I dusted off and dressed up a little. Marquise can be made in many shapes and forms and can also refer to a fruit ice and cream combination if you do not specify Chocolate Marquise. The following is a very elegant presentation. If necessary, it can be simplified by omitting certain steps or making a few changes. For example, if you do not have a silicone mat to make the Ribbon Sponge Sheet, you can substitute one-half recipe of Cocoa Dobos Sponge batter (page 274). Spread the batter into a 16-inch (40-cm) square and bake as directed. Another way to save time is to use fresh fruit as a garnish rather than the Marzipan Flowers and Tulip Leaves. It is best to serve the scaled-down version in one slice rather than cutting it on the diagonal as described below.

1. Line the bottom and the long sides of two bread pans that are 3¹⁄₂ by 3¹⁄₂ by 8 inches (8.7 × 8.7 × 20 cm) with baking paper. Or make forms this size out of cardboard, following the instructions given in White Chocolate and Pistachio Pâte page 830. Set the forms aside.

2. Trim one short end of the Ribbon Sponge Sheet to make it even, if necessary. Cut crosswise to make two 8-by-14-inch (20-×-35-cm) strips with the ribbons now running across (Figure 10–15). (You will have a little less than one-third of the sheet left over for another use). Combine the rum with the Cake Syrup. Carefully brush some of the mixture on the back (plain side) of the two sponge sheets. Do not soak the sponge sheets or they will fall apart.

FIGURE *10–15   Cutting the Ribbon Sponge Sheet to create two pieces for lining the forms; the piece on the left side will be reserved for another use*

3. Place the sponge sheets in the forms with the striped side against the baking paper and one short side of each sponge flush with one long top edge of each form so that the stripes run lengthwise. Support the pieces that extend outside each form with a rolling pin or more bread pans. If the top edge that is flush with the pan falls in, hold it in place against the form with two paper clips until you add the filling.

4. Divide the Marquise Filling evenly between the pans (Figure 10–16). Tap the forms sharply to settle the filling, then smooth the tops to make them level. Fold the sponges over the top of the filling (Figure 10–17). Press lightly to make sure they stick. Trim away any excess sponge.

5. Place the forms in the refrigerator for at least 4 hours or, preferably, overnight.

6. Decorate the number of dessert plates you will be needing with Piping Chocolate by first placing four pieces of wide masking tape on the rim of the plate on the four opposite sides (noon, three, six, and nine o'clock) to protect it from chocolate. Pipe three parallel lines in the center of the base of the plate and then three more at a 90° angle to the first set. Peel off the tape. Set the plates aside. Place the whipped cream in a pastry bag with a no. 6 (12-mm) star tip. Reserve in the refrigerator.

7. Remove each Chocolate Marquise from its form. Trim the short ends, then use a thin, sharp knife heated in either hot water or on the stove, to cut each one into eight slices (if you will not be serving the full amount right away, cut only the number required). The slices will be slightly wider than 3/4 inch (2 cm). Do not force the knife as you cut but instead let it melt through the chocolate. Wipe the knife clean and reheat it for each cut so you do not mar the sponge. Place the slices back in the refrigerator.

8. Presentation: Cut a slice of Chocolate Marquise in half diagonally, cutting from the corner with the seam to the opposite diagonal corner so the seam does not show. Arrange the two wedges in the center of one of the prepared dessert plates with one piece leaning against the other and the sponge facing out. Pipe a rosette of whipped cream on the plate to the right of the dessert. Set a Marzipan Flower and a Tulip Leaf on the cream. Pour a small pool of Raspberry Sauce on the left side of the Marquise. Place a mint sprig next to the sauce and serve immediately.

FIGURE 10–16   Adding the filling to the form after lining it with Ribbon Sponge, with the piece of sponge that extends beyond the form being supported by a rolling pin

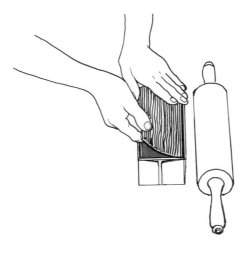

FIGURE 10–17   Folding the extended piece of Ribbon Sponge over the filling

Chocolate Marquise Filling

9 cups (2 l, 160 ml)

1 pound, 8 ounces (680 g) sweet dark
    chocolate
4 ounces (115 g) unsweetened
    chocolate
3 cups (720 ml) heavy cream
6 egg yolks (¹/₂ cup/120 ml)
3 eggs
1 ounce (30 g) granulated sugar
¹/₃ cup (80 ml) or 4 ounces (115 g)
    honey
¹/₄ cup (60 ml) chartreuse

1. Chop the sweet and unsweetened chocolates into small chunks. Place in a bowl set over simmering water and melt together. Set aside, but keep warm.

2. Whip the heavy cream until soft peaks form. Reserve.

3. Whip the egg yolks, eggs, and sugar for about 3 minutes at high speed; the mixture should be light and fluffy. Bring the honey to a boil and gradually pour it into the egg mixture while whipping. Continue whipping until cold. Fold in the reserved chocolate and the chartreuse liqueur. Quickly stir in the whipped cream.

Crepes Suzette

4 servings

two oranges
one lemon
6 ounces (170 g) granulated sugar
6 ounces (170 g) soft unsalted butter
¹/₄ cup (60 ml) orange liqueur
    (Cointreau or Grand Marnier)
twelve Crepes (page 5)
¹/₂ cup (120 ml) cognac or brandy

NOTE: Instead of heating the cognac in the pan with the Crepes, you can pour the cognac into a ladle (move the pan of Crepes to the side) and warm the cognac over the flame. Return the pan to the stand, ignite the cognac in the ladle, and pour it flaming over the Crepes.

*T*his is the most famous of all Crepe recipes. It is usually prepped by the pastry department and prepared tableside on a gueridon by the server. The Crepe sauce can also be prepared in the kitchen and then flambéed at the table. The dessert is generally made for two to four people at a time. For larger servings Crepes Suzette should be prepped in the kitchen, or two gueridons should be used, as it is not practical to heat more than twelve Crepes in one chafing dish or sauté pan. (You can stretch this a little by serving two Crepes per serving rather than the usual three.)

Dining Room Method

1. Arrange your *mise en place* neatly and in sequence on the *gueridon*. Grate the zest of one orange and half the lemon; reserve. Juice the oranges, strain and reserve the juice (do not mix with the zest).

2. Place the sugar in the chafing dish (or a copper sauté pan). Squeeze and strain the juice from the lemon into the sugar.

3. Adjust the flame to medium. Heat the sugar, stirring constantly, until all of the sugar is melted and it just starts to caramelize.

4. Add half of the orange juice and the grated zest and blend thoroughly. Incorporate the butter and stir for a few seconds until the sauce is smooth. Stir in the orange liqueur.

5. Reduce the flame. Add a Crepe to the pan with the best side facing up. Wait a few seconds, then use a fork and spoon to turn it over to ensure that both sides are well coated with the sauce, and the Crepe is hot. Fold the Crepe into quarters and move it to the side of the chafing dish.

6. Add the remaining Crepes in the same way, arranging them in an overlapping circle around the edge of the pan after coating them with the sauce. (If the chafing dish is too small to hold all of the sauced Crepes while you are working, transfer part of them to a side dish while finishing the remainder, then heat them up in the sauce before flaming.) If necessary, thin the sauce with the remaining orange juice during this process.

7. Move the Crepes to the center of the pan. Add the cognac and allow it to warm up for a few seconds, but do not stir to mix it with the sauce.

8. Turn up the flame and tilt the pan to ignite the cognac. Turn the Crepes over in the flambéed sauce, then serve immediately, using the spoon and fork to arrange three Crepes per serving on warm dessert plates. Top each with a portion of the sauce.

Kitchen Method

1. Grate the zest of one orange and half of the lemon. Juice the oranges and the lemon and combine with the grated zest.

2. Cream the butter and sugar until fluffy. Add the lemon juice, orange juice, and grated zest. Stir to combine. (If the butter or juice is cold the mixture might separate; this will not make any difference except for the appearance, but it is a good idea to warm the mixture until it is homogenized.)

3. Give this mixture, together with the Crepes, orange liqueur, and cognac to the server. The server should heat the sauce mixture in the chafing dish until it starts to bubble, then allow it to simmer for a minute or two to ensure that the sugar is melted. The orange liqueur is then added, and the Crepes and cognac are introduced in the same way as described in the preceding method.

Date-Stuffed Poached Pears in Phyllo Crowns with Brandied Mousseline Sauce

12 servings

twelve small Bosc pears with stems
two recipes Spiced Poaching Syrup (page 13)
sixteen sheets phyllo dough (approximately 10 ounces/285 g)
4 ounces (115 g) melted unsalted butter

*P*ears have been popular with gourmands for a very long time. The Romans had pear trees in virtually every garden, which they tended with the utmost of care. In fact, during the time of the Roman Empire the number of pear varieties cultivated grew from as few as six to nearly sixty. The half-dozen or so recipes using pears in this text in no way begin to cover the possibilities; one could easily write a cookbook on this fruit alone. An excellent pear dessert that certainly doesn't require a recipe is simply a perfectly ripe pear served with blue cheese or mascarpone cheese, toasted pecans or hazelnuts, and a glass of port—fabulous!

1. Peel the pears, keeping the stems intact, and place them into acidulated water to prevent oxidation as you are working. Poach the pears in the Poaching Syrup, following the instructions on page 13, until they are just soft to the touch. Be especially careful not to overcook the fruit because it is presented later standing on end. Let the

twelve fresh dates

Almond Filling (recipe follows)

one recipe Mousseline Sauce
(page 1076)

¹/₄ cup (60 ml) brandy

Raspberry Sauce (page 1080) or
other red fruit sauce

powdered sugar

pears cool in the liquid. Ideally, to absorb as much flavor as possible from the spices, leave the pears to cool overnight.

2. Trace the template (Figure 10–18) and cut it out of thin cardboard such as a cake box.

3. Layer eight sheets of phyllo dough, brushing each with some of the melted butter as you stack them. Use the template as a guide and cut out six stars from the layered sheets using a sharp paring knife.

4. Gently guide the phyllo stars (using an empty form to push them down) into 7-ounce (210-ml) individual pie forms measuring 4¹/₂ inches

FIGURE 10–18   *The template used when cutting the stacked phyllo dough sheets for Date-Stuffed Poached Pears*

NOTE: *This dessert should be served while it is still warm from the oven. It may be served at room temperature but should never be served chilled.*

in diameter across the top, 2³/₄ inches in diameter across the bottom, and 1¹/₂ inches tall (11.2 × 6.8 × 3.7 cm). Repeat with the remaining eight sheets of phyllo to make six more crowns. The phyllo shells can be refrigerated in the forms for several days provided they are well covered.

5. Remove the pears from the poaching liquid and pat them dry with paper towels. Reserve the liquid. Using the tip of a paring knife, make a horizontal cut beginning no more than ¹/₂ inch (1.2 cm) below the stem, cutting three-fourths of the way through each pear, leaving the stems attached. Cut just enough from the bottom of each pear to allow it to stand straight up. Push an apple corer up through the bottom of the pears, to the horizontal cut, and remove the cores. If you do not have a corer, this step can be completed with a melon-ball cutter. In this case omit the horizontal cut and proceed with care.

6. Make a cut lengthwise in each date and remove the pits. Push a date into each pear from the bottom. Stand the pears straight up. Using a paring knife, score vertical lines, about ³/₈ inch (9 mm) apart, cutting from the bottom to the top of the pears, making softly curved cuts without cutting all the way through to the date. Wrap aluminum foil around the pear stems to keep them from getting too dark while they bake.

7. Place the Almond Filling in a pastry bag and pipe it into the phyllo shells, dividing it evenly. Place a pear in each shell and press it down firmly.

8. Bake at 400°F (205°C) until the phyllo dough and the Almond Filling are dark golden brown, approximately 15 minutes. Allow the pastries to cool slightly before unmolding and unwrapping the stems.

9. Presentation: Flavor the Mousseline Sauce with the brandy. Cover the base of a dessert plate with some of the sauce. Place a small amount of Raspberry Sauce in a piping bag. Pipe a ring of Raspberry Sauce about ³/₄ inch (2 cm) in from the perimeter of the Mousseline Sauce. Use the blunt edge of a small wooden skewer to blend the sauces together by moving the skewer back and forth in a wavy pattern as shown in Figure 19–29, page 1004. Brush a little Poaching Syrup over one of the pears (do not brush the stem). Sift powdered sugar over the entire pastry and then set in the center of the decorated plate. Serve at once.

Almond Filling

approximately 1 pound, 2 ounces (510 g)

6 ounces (170 g) Almond Paste (page 3)
8 ounces (225 g) granulated sugar
4 egg whites (¹/₂ cup/120 ml), approximately

1. Combine the Almond Paste, the granulated sugar, and 1 egg white, using the paddle attachment in the mixer or by hand with a spoon.

2. When completely smooth add the remaining egg whites one at a time, again mixing until smooth after each addition to avoid lumps. The mixture should be fairly thin, almost runny. It is not possible to specify the exact number of egg whites needed as this varies depending on the texture of the Almond Paste.

Dessert Sampling Platter

16 servings

sixteen Chocolate Fans (page 892)
sixteen Tulip Cookie Wedges
    (page 1049)
unsweetened cocoa powder
one-half recipe Caramel Sauce II
    (page 1071)
sixteen Miniature White Chocolate
    Marquise (instructions follow)
sixteen Miniature Marco Polo
    (instructions follow)
sixteen Miniature Florentina Cones
    (page 515)
sixteen Miniature Tiramisu (page 515)
Piping Chocolate (page 904), melted
sixteen mint leaves
sixteen Chocolate Figurines
    (page 906)

*A*ssorted dessert platters are generally created using items already on the menu that are made into smaller portions either by dividing a single portion in half or simply by making a miniature version along with the standard-sized servings. This tasting platter is intended to serve as a single dessert although, depending on the number of courses served prior, it could easily be stretched to serve two guests by adding some fresh fruit and/or by using the extra Marquise and portioning two triangles per plate. Another option would be to include or substitute a Miniature Triple Chocolate Terrine from the Triple Treat dessert on page 514.

The inspiration for this particular presentation was born from having left-over Tiramisu and Florentina Cones (unfilled) from the Triple Treat dessert which we had served at the graduation gala a few days earlier. I mention this to demonstrate the fact that such an elegant array of shapes and flavors can each be prepped up to a point even more than a week ahead of time to finish as needed. This not only serves to utilize any kitchen downtime, it also ensures that there will not be any waste since it is difficult to predict exactly how many orders will be required.

These desserts are all miniatures of existing recipes with a few hybrids. The Miniature Marquise, for example, uses the filling from the Chocolate Chalet wrapped up in the Ribbon Sponge like the regular Marquise, and borrows its shape from the White Chocolate Bavarian-Style Tri-Color Mousse.

1. Just prior to serving, place as many Chocolate Fans and Tulip Wedges as you expect to need in the refrigerator.

2. Presentation: Using a fine mesh sifter, lightly sift cocoa powder over the base of a dessert plate. Place the Caramel Sauce in a piping bottle and pipe quarter-coin-sized dots of sauce, about 1 inch (2.5 cm) apart, around the perimeter of the plate on top of the cocoa powder. Arrange one each of the four miniature desserts, evenly spaced, in the center of the plate. Place a small amount of Piping Chocolate in a piping bag and cut a small opening. Pipe a small dot of chocolate behind the White Chocolate Marquise and attach a Chocolate Fan, standing straight up, in the Piping Chocolate. Attach a Tulip Wedge to the Marco Polo using the same technique. Decorate the Florentina Cone with a mint leaf and place a Chocolate Figurine on top of the Tiramisu. Serve immediately.

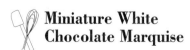

Miniature White Chocolate Marquise

two 16-by-2¹/₂-inch (40-×-6.2-cm) triangular cakes

one-quarter recipe Ribbon Sponge
    Sheet (page 276) (see note)
one-half recipe White Chocolate and
    Pistachio Pâte (page 830)

*T*his recipe will make twice as much Marquise as you need for this dessert but it is really not practical to make less and since it does not take much longer, and it will keep for weeks in the freezer, you may as well make the extra.

1. You will need two triangular forms 16 inches long by 2¹/₂ inches across the top (40 × 6.2 cm). If you do not have forms close to this size, you can make them quickly and easily by following the instructions on

NOTE: When the making the quarter-recipe of Ribbon Sponge you will need a half-size (16-by-12-inches/40-×-30-cm) silicone mat in order to follow the directions as given. If you have only the full-size (16 by 24 inches/40 × 60 cm), use only half of the mat and make the chocolate lines run crosswise instead of lengthwise as directed in the recipe. If your freezer space allows it, make a half recipe (one sheet) and save half of the sheet for another use.

 ## Miniature Marco Polo

16 pieces

one-quarter recipe Devil's Food Cake Layers batter (page 272)
one-third recipe Spiced Ganache Filling (page 479)
white coating chocolate, melted
dark coating chocolate, melted

NOTE: You can also use ABS or PVC pipe, cut to the same width as the plastic strips, to hold the filling. It is unlikely you will find the pipe in the exact diameter specified but that is okay. Line the inside of the pipe rings with the plastic strips; the ends do not need to be taped together but should overlap slightly.

page 502 in the recipe for Strawberry Pyramids. Alter the instructions to make the forms the size given here.

2. Cut two pieces from the Ribbon Sponge Sheet 4½ inches wide by 16 inches long (11.2 × 40 cm), with the ribbons running lengthwise. Arrange the sponge sheets in the forms so that the stripes are against the form. Divide the filling between the forms and spread it out evenly. Cover and place in the freezer for at least 4 hours or, preferably, overnight.

3. Unmold one Marquise and cut into sixteen slices while still frozen. Reserve the other Marquise for another use. Place the slices in the refrigerator until time of service. Be certain that the filling has thawed before serving.

1. Pour the cake batter into a 10-inch (25-cm) square or a 12-inch (30-cm) round cake pan, lined with baking paper. Bake at 375°F (190°C) for approximately 20 minutes or until baked through. Allow to cool completely.

2. Measure the outside circumference of a plain cookie cutter that is 2¼-inches (5.6-cm) in diameter. Cut sixteen 1-inch (2.5-cm) wide strips of acetate or polyurethane that are ¼ inch (6 mm) longer than the circumference measurement (about 7½ inches/18.7 cm). Form the strips into rings, using the cookie cutter as a guide (see note 2, page 478), or just overlap the ends ¼ inch (6 mm) and tape the rings together. Place the rings on a sheet pan lined with baking paper (see note).

3. Cut sixteen rounds from the baked Devil's Food Cake, using the same cookie cutter used to form the rings. Cut each cake round into two layers. Place one cake layer in each of the plastic rings. Divide the Spiced Ganache Filling between the rings. Place the remaining cake layers on top of the filling. Press lightly to make the tops even. Refrigerate for 2 hours to set the filling.

4. Remove the plastic strips and return the desserts to the refrigerator. Wash and dry the plastic strips. Place melted white coating chocolate in a piping bag. Place a plastic strip on a piece of baking paper and pipe chocolate across the plastic strip at an angle, first in one direction and then in the opposite direction. Pick up the plastic strip and place it on a sheet pan lined with baking paper. Repeat with the remaining strips. Place in the refrigerator for a few minutes to set the white chocolate.

5. Spread melted dark coating chocolate over the plastic strips and attach the strips to the cake rounds following the directions in the Marco Polo recipe at the end of step eight, page 478.

Florentina Cones with Seasonal Fruit

16 servings

1 pound, 2 ounces (510 g) or two-thirds recipe Florentina Batter (page 214)

1 pound, 6 ounces (625 g) or two-thirds recipe Quick Bavarian Cream (page 1089)

½ cup (120 ml) heavy cream, whipped to stiff peaks

two recipes Bitter Orange Sauce (page 1078)

2 pounds, 8 ounces (1 kg, 135 g) prepared fresh fruit, approximately (see note)

Sour Cream Mixture for Piping (page 1081)

Strawberry or Raspberry Sauce (pages 1081 and 1080)

NOTE: Use four or five different kinds of fruit for a colorful presentation. Cut the fruit into raspberry-sized chunks. If you use peaches or apricots, leave the skin on. Take care to make nice uniform cuts rather than just chopping the fruit up. Do not use apples or pears unless they have been poached. Apricots, peaches, blueberries, raspberries, and strawberries work well. Add either kiwi or honeydew melon for contrasting color. Leave the varieties separate, waiting to combine them until serving, to protect the fruits from "bleeding" and staining each other.

*T*his colorful dessert is an excellent choice when you need to do most of the work ahead and you want a minimum of last-minute finishing touches to worry about at serving time. You can pipe the Bavarian Cream into the cones and set them aside in the refrigerator for up to four hours. With the sauces and the fruit mixture ready, the final assembly and presentation will go quickly.

For a quick elegant individual pastry, make smaller cones as described in Florentina Cones with Chantilly Cream (see page 390). Flavor and sweeten whipped cream with a good-quality strawberry jam. Pipe this into the cones to within ⅛ inch (3 mm) of the top using a pastry bag with a no. 6 (12-mm) plain tip. Stem, clean, and cut as many small strawberries in half as you will need, allowing one-half per pastry. Dip the open end of the filled cones about ¼ inch (6 mm) into melted dark coating chocolate, fully covering the cream filling. Before the chocolate hardens, place a strawberry half on top, point up, with the cut side against the chocolate. Refrigerate until needed. The pastries should be served the same day they are filled since the cream will soften the Florentina shell.

1. Draw eighteen 4¾-inch (11.8-cm) circles on baking paper using a plain cookie cutter as a guide (you only need sixteen, but there is always the risk of breakage). Invert the papers on sheet pans. Divide the Florentina Batter between the circles. Spread out, bake, and trim the cookies as directed in the recipe for Florentinas.

2. Reheat the trimmed cookies until they are soft enough to bend. Immediately form them into cones by wrapping them, top-side out, around a cone-shaped object. Press the edges together where they meet so the cone will hold together (Figure 10–19). If you do not have an appropriate-sized form, you can make one by cutting it out of styrofoam and covering it with aluminum foil. The cone should be about 4

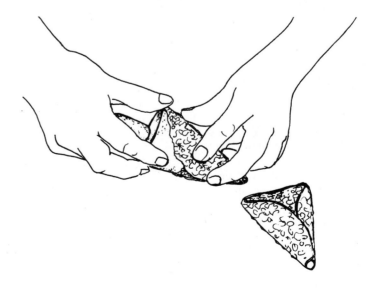

FIGURE 10–19   Wrapping a soft Florentina cookie around a cone-shaped object and pressing the edges together where they overlap

inches (10 cm) long and 2¹/₂ inches (6.2 cm) across at the base. If the cookies become too firm to bend easily, just reheat them. Reserve the finished cones, covered, in a dry place. They can be kept for several days at this point.

3. Place the Bavarian Cream in a pastry bag with a no. 5 (10-mm) star tip. Fill as many cones as you expect to serve within a few hours halfway with the filling. Place the filled cones and any remaining Bavarian Cream in the refrigerator. Place the whipped cream in a pastry bag with a no. 4 (8-mm) star tip. Reserve in the refrigerator. Place a portion of the Orange Sauce in a piping bottle and reserve.

4. Presentation: Pipe a rosette of whipped cream in the center of a dessert plate. Pipe Bitter Orange Sauce on the lower part of the plate. Combine about ¹/₂ cup (120 ml) of the fruit mixture. Hold one of the filled cones vertically and fill with the fruit on top of the Bavarian Cream. Gently place the cone (on its side) on the whipped cream rosette with the wide end in the Orange Sauce. Part of the fruit should fall out onto the Orange Sauce naturally. Decorate the sauce using the Strawberry or Raspberry Sauce and the Sour Cream Mixture (see pages 998 to 1005). Serve immediately.

Forbidden Peach

12 servings

5 ounces (140 g) or one-sixth recipe
   Caramel Glass Paste (page 446)

six dry Almond Macaroon Cookies
   (page 202) (see note 1)

six large perfectly ripe peaches
   (see note 2)

¹/₄ cup (60 ml) amaretto liqueur

one-quarter recipe Italian Meringue
   (page 591)

one recipe Caramel Sauce I
   (page 1070)

edible fresh flower petals such as
   Johnny-jump-up or pansy

twelve Caramel Cages (page 957)
   (see note 3)

one-half recipe Cashew Nut Ice
   Cream (page 628), (optional)

NOTE 1: If you do not have Almond Macaroon Cookies on hand, you can substitute purchased amaretto cookies, which are readily available.

*T*his dessert is a refreshing summer treat with lots of visual appeal, and it is simplicity itself—that is, once you have mastered the Caramel Cages. I have had many students accuse me (with a smile) of withholding some secret when it comes to making these fragile decorations. It looks easy enough when they watch my demonstration, but they have all kinds of problems when they first try to make the cages themselves. Well, as a colleague of mine writes in his book, "It is a little difficult to master at first, but you can have lots of fun practicing." Which is true provided you have the time and patience. Probably the most common mistake, and one I see all too often, involves cooking the sugar. Typically, the first time a student makes the caramel they burn it, either as a result of not getting it into the water bath quickly enough when it reaches the correct color, or because they don't realize how fast it can go from caramelized to burned. Then the next time, because they are understandably afraid of burning it again, they make the mistake of not cooking the sugar long enough. This makes the caramel too soft and causes the cage to either stick to the ladle or collapse soon after it is removed. Properly cooked caramel will appear quite dark in the pan as compared with the thin threads of sugar in the finished cage. You may need to make it a few times before you learn the exact moment to remove it from the heat. It is a good idea to pour a small amount of caramel onto an oiled surface to check the color, especially if you are using a copper pan since the dark color of the pan makes it even more difficult to judge the color of the caramel.

Since the Caramel Cages are what make this dessert so decorative, you can't really leave them out altogether. However, should the standard Caramel Cages prove too demanding, try making the simplified version. The effect is just as dramatic, although perhaps not as professional looking, as the real thing, and while you are making the easier cages you (hopefully) won't curse the author of this book either.

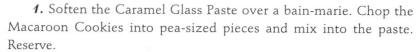

NOTE 2: Use a freestone variety such as Fay Alberta or Hale Haven; both have large fruit with little or no fuzz. Or try the delectable white-fleshed peach.

NOTE 3: Follow the instructions on page 957, making the cages about 6 inches (15 cm) in diameter and at least 2½ inches (6.2 cm) tall.

NOTE 4: This can be done up to one hour ahead. You can finish as many peaches as you will serve within that time if your situation necessitates it.

1. Soften the Caramel Glass Paste over a bain-marie. Chop the Macaroon Cookies into pea-sized pieces and mix into the paste. Reserve.

2. Remove the stems from the peaches and cut each one in half along the natural crease. Remove the stones. Use a melon-ball cutter to make the hollow left by the stones a little larger. If necessary, cut a small slice from the round side of each half so they will stand up straight. Divide the Caramel Glass Paste mixture between the peach halves, placing it loosely in the hollows left by the stones.

3. Brush the amaretto liqueur over the cut surface of the peaches, dabbing some on the filling as well. Place the peaches on a sheet pan lined with baking paper.

4. Bake at 400°F for approximately 15 minutes; the filling should be a rich brown color. Remove from the oven and brush additional amaretto over the tops.

5. Presentation: Place a large spoonful of Italian Meringue on a peach half. Spread out to the edges, covering the entire top of the peach in a rustic-looking dome shape. Use a broiler, salamander, or blowtorch to brown the meringue (see note 4). Cover the base of a dessert plate with Caramel Sauce (do not use too much or it will interfere with the garnish later). Place the peach in the center of the sauce. Arrange flower petals around the peach on top of the sauce. Carefully position a Caramel Cage over the peach. Serve immediately. For a special treat serve the peach with Cashew Nut Ice Cream in a separate dish on the side.

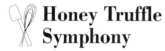

Honey Truffle Symphony

16 servings

one 23-by-15-inch (57.5-×-37.5-cm) Ribbon Sponge Sheet (page 276) (see note 1)

Wild Honey Truffle Cream (recipe follows)

5 ounces (140 g) strained strawberry preserves

1½ cups (360 ml) heavy cream

2 teaspoons (10 g) granulated sugar

one recipe Raspberry Sauce (page 1080)

Sour Cream Mixture for Piping (page 1081)

forty-eight Chocolate Cigars (page 887) (see note 2)

sixteen edible fresh flowers

*Y*ou *may have already spotted the similarity between this dessert and Chocolate Ganache Towers on page 456. The garnish and presentations are easily interchangeable. Also, if wild honey is not available for the Truffle Cream, you may use regular honey. While it does not have the same bite, it still combines with the Gianduja to produce a distinctive flavor. Honey Truffle Symphony is as practical as it is elegant, since any desserts which are not needed the day they are made can be kept in the refrigerator for several days, or may be frozen for weeks, provided they are well covered.*

1. If you do not have plastic tubes of this size, make sixteen acetate tubes that are 2 inches (5 cm) in diameter and 2½ inches (6.2 cm) tall (see instructions in Chocolate Ganache Towers, page 456).

2. Measure and cut sixteen 2½-by-6¼-inch (6.2-×-15.6-cm) strips from the Ribbon Sponge Sheet as shown in Figure 10–20. You will actually get eighteen (three rows lengthwise by six crosswise), plus a narrow end piece, so you will have a little extra during assembly. Save any leftover for other uses. Line the plastic forms with the strips, placing the striped ribbon side against the forms. For the best-looking finished product, the short ends of the sponge sheets should line up against each other (Figure 10–21).

NOTE 1: *When you make the Ribbon Sponge Sheet, make the chocolate lines run diagonally rather than lengthwise as directed in the recipe. If you already have regular Ribbon Sponges on hand, you may cut diagonally to get the same effect, as shown in the illustration; however, this method will not produce as many pieces. To get the full number of pieces from regular Ribbon Sponge Sheets, cut so that the ribbons run horizontally (Figure 10–22).*

NOTE 2: *Make three distinctively different sizes of cigars, 2, 3, and 4 inches (5, 7.5, and 10 cm). Start by making the taller cigars; if some of them do not measure up, you may be able to use them for one of the smaller sizes.*

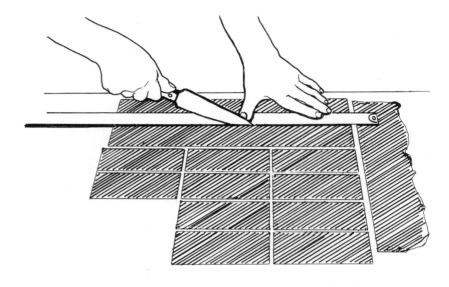

FIGURE 10–20   *Cutting pieces of Ribbon Sponge for Honey Truffle Symphony*

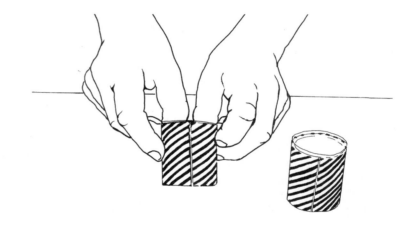

FIGURE 10–21   *The pieces of Ribbon Sponge placed in the plastic tubes so that the edges and the ribbon stripes line up evenly*

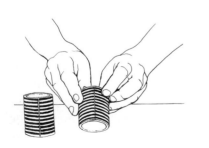

FIGURE 10–22   *Cutting diagonal pieces from a Ribbon Sponge made with horizontal stripes, so the stripes run diagonally on the desserts; cutting the pieces so that the stripes run horizontally to get more usable pieces from the sheet*

3. Check the consistency of the Wild Honey Truffle Cream. If it is too firm to pipe, soften it carefully over a bain-marie. Pipe the cream into the forms, filling them completely. Smooth the tops to make them flat. Cover and refrigerate for at least 4 hours or, preferably, overnight.

4. Make the large tulip template shown in Figure 19–54, page 1045. Place the strawberry preserves in a pastry bag with a no. 1 (2-mm) plain tip. Place the template in the center of a dessert plate. Pipe a thin string of jam on the plate, following the inside edge of the template. Remove the template. Repeat on as many plates as you expect to need for service and set them aside.

5. Whip the heavy cream and sugar to stiff peaks. Place in a pastry bag with a no. 8 (16-mm) star tip and reserve in the refrigerator. Place a portion of the Raspberry Sauce in a piping bottle. Remove the plastic strips from as many desserts as you plan to serve.

6. Presentation: Fill the center of one of the prepared dessert plates with Raspberry Sauce, carefully pushing the sauce out to, but not over, the jam border. Decorate the edge of the sauce with dots of Sour Cream Mixture swirled into hearts (see Figure 19–25, page 1002). Pipe a large rosette of whipped cream to cover the entire top of one dessert. Gently press one of each size of the Chocolate Cigars straight into the cream (use a latex glove on the hand that touches the chocolate to protect it against fingerprints). Place a small edible flower next to the cigars. Set a dessert in the center of the sauce. Serve immediately.

1. Chop the sweet dark chocolate, unsweetened chocolate, and Gianduja into small pieces. Combine in a bowl and melt over simmering water. Set aside but keep warm.

2. Whip the heavy cream to soft peaks. Reserve.

3. Whip the egg yolks and granulated sugar until they are light and fluffy, about 3 minutes by hand.

4. Bring the honey to a boil. Gradually pour the honey into the yolk mixture, and continue whipping the mixture until it is completely cold. Quickly stir in the reserved melted chocolate and the Frangelico liqueur. Still working quickly, fold in the reserved whipped cream.

 Wild Honey Truffle Cream

6 cups (1 l, 440 ml)

10 ounces (285 g) sweet dark chocolate

3 ounces (85 g) unsweetened chocolate

3 ounces (85 g) Gianduja (page 922)

2¹/₂ cups (600 ml) heavy cream

6 egg yolks (¹/₂ cup/120 ml)

2 ounces (55 g) granulated sugar

¹/₃ cup (80 ml) or 4 ounces (115 g) wild honey

2 tablespoons (30 ml) Frangelico liqueur

 Hot Chocolate Truffle Cake

16 servings

Butter and Flour Mixture (page 4)

Chocolate Solution for Spraying (page 921) (see note 1)

Piping Chocolate (page 904), melted

one recipe Vanilla Ice Cream (page 640)

Chocolate Truffle Cake Batter (recipe follows)

one-half recipe Raspberry Sauce (page 1080)

sixteen Tulip Flower Petals (see note 4)

powdered sugar

one dry pint raspberries

sixteen small mint sprigs

NOTE 1: If you do not have access to a power sprayer, and therefore cannot use the Chocolate

*T*his sinfully rich dessert has become the decadence cake of the nineties. It is currently featured on the menu of all of the "in" restaurants, especially so in New York where half of the chefs serving it seem to have laid claim to its invention! There are as many versions and titles as there are makers: warm Valrhona chocolate velvet, hot chocolate soufflé cake, chocolate budino, and, of course, this one: Hot Chocolate Truffle Cake. They all have, or should have, one thing in common—a liquid center that is held in place by a just-baked-enough crust so that the center oozes out onto the plate the moment the customer inserts a fork and doubles as a thick, delicious sauce.

When I first introduced this recipe at school, I was afraid we were going to have some desserts sent back to the kitchen for not being thoroughly cooked (since the waitstaff are also students, they sometimes forget to properly describe the item). Well, it turned out I was only partially right. One young student came to me rather embarrassed and said that one of the customers at her table had brought to her attention that the Truffle Cake was not cooked all the way through. But "it was so good" that his friend wanted to order one as well and had asked if his could also be "undercooked"!

Making the batter is very easy. The only difficult part of this recipe (perhaps aside from finding the right cake rings) is judging the precise baking time. You should have it down after a few practice attempts. If part of the batter seeps out from under the rings at the start of baking, roll out Short Dough (cocoa or plain, you will need about 6 ounces/170 g for sixteen servings) to ¹/₈ inch

Solution to decorate the plates, you can still make a marbleized pattern using a manual spray bottle and the alternate Cocoa Solution (recipe follows). With this technique it is not possible to use a template, however.

NOTE 2: If this size cake ring is not available, any size that is close will do; adjust the paper strips accordingly. If all else fails you can use 3¼-inch (8.1-cm) diameter ramekins (omit the paper and just grease the ramekins) and serve the dessert in its baking dish.

NOTE 3: To prevent the bottom from becoming too dark, you may need to place a second pan underneath during baking. This will not be necessary if you use ramekins instead of cake rings. You will have to adjust the baking temperature and time to suit your oven and the thickness of the cake rings. If the dessert falls apart when you pull off the ring, you must bake it a little longer. Conversely, if a portion of the center is not liquid enough to run out as soon as a spoon or fork is inserted into the dessert, it is over-baked. This will also happen if the dessert cools too long before it is served.

NOTE 4: Follow the recipe and instructions for making the petals in Rainbow of Summer Sorbets in a Cookie Flower, steps one, two, and three, page 713. You will need one-half recipe of Vanilla Tulip Paste and 1 teaspoon (2.5 g) of unsweetened cocoa powder. Make about twenty petals to allow for breakage.

(3 mm) thick, using flour to prevent it from sticking. Cut out sixteen cookies, using one of the cake rings that will be used to bake the desserts. Place the Short Dough cookies inside the cake rings after they have been lined.

Hot Chocolate Truffle Cake is meant to be served in a simple, unpretentious way accompanied by ice cream and/or fresh berries. I have dressed up the plates a bit in this presentation, but you can very well leave out spraying the plates, piping the heart, and using the cookie flower petal. Instead, pipe the Raspberry Sauce in a zigzag pattern over the base of the plate. Place the ice cream scoops on very thin 1-inch (2.5-cm) sponge rounds to prevent them from sliding on the plates.

1. Cut sixteen strips of baking paper 9½ inches long by 3 inches wide (23.7 × 7.5 cm). Brush both sides of each strip with Butter and Flour Mixture and use the strips to line the insides of sixteen cake rings that are 2¾ inches in diameter by 2 inches high (6.8 × 5 cm) (see note 2). Reserve.

2. Make the free-form heart template (Figure 10–23). The template as shown is the correct size to use in this recipe. Trace the drawing and then cut it out of 1/16-inch (3-mm) cardboard such as the type used for cake boxes. Attach a loop of tape to the top to facilitate lifting the template from the plate. Place the template off-center and to the right, on the base of a dessert plate. Weigh it down with a small heavy object (I use a couple of bolts wrapped in aluminum foil). Spray the entire plate with the Chocolate Solution (see Spraying with Chocolate, page 919). Carefully remove the template and repeat with as many plates as you expect to need. Handle the plates carefully so you do not leave fingerprints, and set the plates aside to dry.

3. Place Piping Chocolate in a piping bag. Pipe chocolate around the heart design tracing the perimeter of the design. Reserve the plates.

4. Using a 2-ounce (60-ml) ice-cream scoop, place as many scoops of Vanilla Ice Cream as you anticipate needing on a paper-lined half-sheet pan. Reserve in the freezer.

5. Approximately 20 minutes before serving, place as many prepared rings as needed on a perfectly even inverted sheet pan lined with baking paper. (If you are only firing a few servings at a time, an inverted pie tin or cake pan works fine.) Pipe or scoop the Chocolate Truffle Cake Batter into the rings, filling them two-thirds full.

6. Bake at 375°F (190°C) for approximately 15 minutes (see note 3).

7. Presentation: Place the Raspberry Sauce in a piping bottle and pipe sauce onto as many of the reserved plates as you have desserts in the oven, filling in the heart outline. Place a Tulip Flower Petal, standing on end, to the right of the heart at the bottom of the plate(s). After removing the dessert(s) from the oven, sift powdered sugar lightly over the top. Wait about 30 seconds, then take hold of a cake ring with a pair of tongs. Slide a palette knife underneath, lift the dessert using both tools, and set off-center on one of the plates. Gently slide the knife out and then lift off the ring using the tongs. Peel the paper away from the dessert if necessary. Place one of the prepared ice-cream scoops on the base of the cookie. Arrange raspberries and a mint sprig below the cake and *serve immediately.*

FIGURE 10–23 The template for the Hot Chocolate Truffle Cake presentation

Cocoa Solution for Manual Spray Bottle

¹/₄ cup (60 ml) light corn syrup

3 cups (720 ml) warm water

2 ounces (55 g) unsweetened cocoa powder

Chocolate Truffle Cake Batter

2 quarts (1 l, 920 ml)

12 ounces (340 g) sweet dark chocolate

4 ounces (115 g) unsweetened chocolate

12 ounces (340 g) unsalted butter

6 tablespoons (48 g) cornstarch

1 pound, 4 ounces (570 g) granulated sugar

8 eggs

8 egg yolks (²/₃ cup/160 ml)

1 tablespoon (15 ml) orange liqueur

*T*his will make a medium-dark spray. Add more cocoa powder if a darker color is desired.

1. Stir the corn syrup into the water.

2. Place the cocoa powder in a bowl. Add just enough of the water mixture to make a smooth paste. Gradually mix in the remaining water. Store in the refrigerator.

1. Cut the chocolates into small pieces. Place in a bowl with the butter and set over simmering water to melt. Do not overheat.

2. Use a whisk to mix the cornstarch into the granulated sugar in an oversize bowl. Stir in the melted chocolate mixture. Add the eggs, yolks, and orange liqueur, stirring just until the mixture has developed a smooth consistency, about 2 minutes.

3. Cover and refrigerate for at least 8 hours, preferably overnight.

🥄 Individual Croquembouche

16 servings

one-half recipe Pâte à Choux
　　(page 36)
one recipe or 2 pounds (910 g) Quick
　　Bavarian Cream (page 1089)
Caramelized Sugar with Water
　　(page 955)
1 cup (240 ml) heavy cream
1 teaspoon (5 g) granulated sugar
one recipe Strawberry Sauce
　　(page 1081)
Sour Cream Mixture for Piping
　　(page 1081)
candied violets and/or edible fresh
　　flowers

There is no direct English translation of croquembouche *given in the French dictionary, but the literal meaning is "crunch in the mouth," from the two words* croquem *and* bouche. *This ancient, elaborate French speciality consists of small custard-filled cream puffs (profiteroles) that are glazed with caramelized sugar. In this recipe the cream puffs are assembled into individual servings, but in the classic version they are formed into a large cone-shaped confection that is typically made up of around two hundred small profiteroles stacked one on top of the other around a metal cone as they are dipped in caramel. Once the sugar hardens, the Croquembouche is lifted off the form, placed on a base made of nougatine, and decorated with spun sugar, candied violets, and marzipan or pulled sugar flowers. The classic Croquembouche is traditionally featured as a centerpiece (pièce monté) at French weddings, first-communion celebrations, and opulent Christmas buffets.*

1. Place the Pâte à Choux in a pastry bag with a no. 5 (10-mm) plain tip. Pipe out cherry-sized profiteroles on sheet pans lined with baking paper. You need 128 for this recipe, but you should get about 140. Bake at 400°F (205°C) for about 20 minutes. Be sure they have baked long enough to hold their shape. Let cool completely.

2. Make a small hole in the bottom of each profiterole. Fill them with Bavarian Cream, using a pastry bag with a no. 2 (4-mm) plain tip.

3. Dip the top and sides of the profiteroles in the Caramelized Sugar, using two forks. Place them on paper-lined sheet pans, bottom (undipped-side) down. Reserve in the refrigerator until serving time.

4. Whip the heavy cream and granulated sugar to stiff peaks. Place in a pastry bag with a no. 4 (8-mm) star tip. Reserve in the refrigerator. Place a portion of the Strawberry Sauce in a piping bottle.

5. Presentation: Arrange four profiteroles in a square in the center of a dessert plate. Pipe a large dot of whipped cream in the middle to hold them together. Place three profiteroles on top, centered on the bottom layer. Pipe a second dot of cream in the middle of these, and top with a single profiterole to make a pyramid. Cover the base of the plate around the Croquembouche with Strawberry Sauce. Decorate the Strawberry Sauce with the Sour Cream Mixture (see pages 998 to 1006). Decorate the dessert with candied violets and/or fresh edible flowers.

Marco Polo with Spiced Ganache and Tea Ice Cream

16 servings

one-third recipe Devil's Food Cake
  Layers batter (page 272)
one 23-by-15-inch (57.5-×-37.5-cm)
  Ribbon Sponge Sheet (page 276)
  (see note 1)
Spiced Ganache Filling (recipe
  follows)
dark coating chocolate, melted
Florentina Cookies for Marco Polo
  (page 1009)
unsweetened cocoa powder
one-half recipe Chocolate Sauce
  (page 1072)
one-half recipe Caramel Sauce II
  (page 1071)
powdered sugar
Piping Chocolate (page 904), melted
one recipe Sun-Brewed Jasmine Tea
  Ice Cream (page 639)
thirty-two Curly Cues (page 1055)

NOTE 1: Follow the directions for making the Ribbon Sponge Sheet, but do not use a ruler as a guide to make straight lines in the Chocolate Tulip Paste. Instead, move the trowel side-to-side in a zigzag pattern to create a softly curved design. The back-and-forth motion tends to create small air bubbles in the baked sheet, which is unavoidable. If you are using a small trowel, which requires that you make several passes over the sheet, hold the trowel at an angle rather than perpendicular to the edges of the sheet to avoid creating a buildup of batter along the edge of each pass.

*M*arco Polo was a Venetian merchant and explorer who, along with his father and uncle, is given much of the credit for opening the trade route to China, especially the all-important spice trade. The Polos ventured to China for the first time in the mid-thirteenth century. When Marco returned to Italy in 1295, after spending twenty years roaming through China in service to the Mongolian emperor (who had taken a liking to him), he dictated an account of his experience. His report was not given much credit at the time but rather was looked upon in disbelief. It was not until the beginning of the seventeenth century that Jesuit missionaries verified his incredible stories. Among these were the fact that pasta in various forms was eaten in China long before it became synonymous with Italy. Marco Polo also spoke of tea (a drink not encountered in the West until the beginning of the seventeenth century) and the great teahouses in China. But, most interestingly, Marco Polo's journal tells of a device used to fabricate ice creams and sorbets. As we know, just as salt raises the boiling point of water, it also lowers the freezing point. Having observed the practice of the Chinese pouring snow and saltpeter over containers filled with syrup, he brought the secret back to Italy, a country which much later was to become known as much for its wonderful ices as for pasta.

For a mint-flavored variation, substitute twice as much mint liqueur for the orange liqueur in the chocolate filling and leave out the ginger and cloves, use Mint Ice Cream rather than Tea, and decorate with a mint sprig. I went one step further for a St. Patrick's day special and colored the stripes of the Ribbon Sponge pale green as well.

1. Place a cardboard strip across a sheet pan lined with baking paper to make a section of the pan 7½ by 16 inches (18.7 × 40 cm). Spread the Devil's Food Cake batter out within the sectioned area of the pan. Bake at 375°F (190°C) for approximately 15 minutes or until done. Let the cake cool completely.

2. Measure the outside circumference of a plain cookie cutter that is approximately 3½ inches (8.7 cm) in diameter. Cut sixteen strips of acetate or polyurethane 1¼ inches wide (3.1 cm) and ¼ inch (6 mm) longer than the circumference measurement, about 11¾ inches (29.5 cm). Join and tape the ends together to form rings, using the cookie cutter as a guide (see instructions in note 2) or just overlap the end ¼ inch (6 mm) and tape together. Place the rings on a sheet pan lined with baking paper (see note following Miniature Marco Polo, page 468).

3. Using the same cookie cutter, cut eight rounds from the Devil's Food sheet. Cut each one in half horizontally. Place these inside the plastic rings.

NOTE 2: This is necessary if you are making a large quantity but also helpful for just sixteen rings. If you use the cutter as a guide, each of the rings will be the same size and they will sit flat and level. To make the rings, first cut the plastic strips and have small pieces of tape ready. Place the cookie cutter against the work surface, top (thicker) edge down. Attach a small piece of tape to one end of a plastic strip. Place the opposite end of the strip against the outside of the cutter. Holding that end in place, wind the plastic around the cutter, pushing the bottom of the plastic flush against the edge of the cutter. The end must overlap about 1/4 inch (6 mm). Tape in place, and pull the ring off of the cutter.

4. Using the same cutter, cut sixteen rounds from the Ribbon Sponge Sheet. You will have approximately one-third of the sheet left for another use.

5. Reserve about 1/2 cup (120 ml) of the Ganache Filling to use in the presentation. Place the remainder in a pastry bag with a no. 6 (12-mm) plain tip. Pipe the filling into the rings on top of the sponge circles dividing it evenly. The top of the filling should be slightly below the top of the rings.

6. Place the Ribbon Sponge rounds on top of the filling, striped-side up, and press down lightly to make the tops level. Refrigerate for at least 2 hours to set the filling.

7. Remove the tape and peel the plastic strips away from the pastries. Return the pastries to the refrigerator. Wash and dry the plastic strips.

8. Place a plastic strip on a piece of baking paper. Spread a thin layer of melted coating chocolate on top (to cover the strip completely it is necessary to spread a little chocolate onto the baking paper all around the plastic). Carefully lift up one end of the strip by sliding the tip of a paring knife underneath. Hold the strip by one short end and run the thumb and index finger of your other hand down the long edges to remove excess chocolate and give the strip a cleaner look. Position the strip with the chocolate against the side of one of the pastries and gently push it against the pastry all around. The strip will be just a little too long. Do not overlap the ends and press together but instead, allow the extra piece to stick out. Cover the sides of the remaining pastries with chocolate in the same fashion. Place the pastries in the refrigerator for a few minutes before removing the plastic strips or until time of service.

9. Place as many Florentina Cookies as you expect to need into the refrigerator, allowing one large and one small cookie per serving.

10. Presentation: Sift cocoa powder lightly over the rim of a dessert plate. Place the Chocolate Sauce in a piping bottle. Place the Caramel Sauce in a second piping bottle. Pipe a zigzag design of Chocolate Sauce over the base of the plate. Pipe random dots of Caramel Sauce, making various sizes, around the chocolate piping. Pipe a dot of the reserved Ganache Filling off-center on the plate. Place a Marco Polo standing on its side, seam-side down, on top of the Ganache. Sift powdered sugar lightly over the top of the pastry. Pipe a dot of Piping Chocolate directly to the right of the Marco Polo. Pipe a second dot a few inches in front of the first one. Quickly, secure a large Florentina Cookie on the back dot, arranging it so that the Florentina curls over the pastry. Place a small cookie on the other dot. Hold both cookies in place for a few seconds until the chocolate hardens (this happens quickly since the cookies are cold from the refrigerator). Place a small scoop of tea ice cream on the base of the small cookie. Place two Curly Cues leaning on the ice cream. Serve immediately.

Spiced Ganache Filling

7¹/₂ cups (1 l, 800 ml)

15 ounces (430 g) sweet dark
    chocolate

3 ounces (85 g) unsweetened
    chocolate

2³/₄ cups (660 ml) heavy cream

3 egg yolks (¹/₄ cup/60 ml)

1¹/₂ ounces (40 g) granulated sugar

¹/₄ cup (60 ml) or 3 ounces (85 g)
    honey

2 tablespoons (30 ml) orange liqueur

2 teaspoons (4 g) ground cloves

2 teaspoons (4 g) ground ginger

1. Chop both chocolates into small chunks. Place in a bowl set over simmering water and melt together. Set aside and keep warm

2. Whip the heavy cream until soft peaks form. Reserve.

3. Whip the egg yolks with the sugar for about 2 minutes; the mixture should be light and fluffy. Bring the honey to a boil and gradually pour it into the yolks while whipping. Continue whipping until the mixture has cooled completely. Fold in the reserved chocolate, the orange liqueur, ground cloves, ground ginger, and the reserved whipped cream.

Pears Belle Hélène

16 servings

sixteen Bosc pears with stems
    attached

three recipes Plain Poaching Syrup
    (page 13)

Sponge Cake (page 268) (see note)

one recipe Chocolate Sauce
    (page 1072)

one-half recipe Vanilla Custard Sauce
    (page 1082)

one recipe Vanilla Ice Cream
    (page 640)

NOTE: You only need a ¹/₄-inch (6-mm) thick layer from a 10-inch (25-cm) Sponge Cake, either plain or chocolate (a leftover piece of Ribbon Sponge could be used as well). If you don't have it on hand, you can make a full cake and save the unused portion for another use, or you can make a quarter recipe of Roulade Batter (page 286) and spread it into a 10-inch (25-cm) square, in which case you will not have any left over.

Jacques Offenbach was responsible for the popularity of the light comic operetta. His most ingenious was La Belle Hélène, *a burlesque about the Trojan War, written in 1864. The name Helen or Hélène became popular on menus at this time, inspiring many dishes by Parisian restaurateurs who were eager to take advantage of Offenbach's success. Among the savory creations named for Hélène were renditions of salad, sole, chicken supremes, tournedos, and even a roast.*

In Greek mythology Helen was the daughter of Leda and Zeus, who was the "God of the Gods." Leda, whose parents were Thestius, the King of Aetolia, and Eurthemis, drew the attention of Zeus because of her great beauty. Zeus disguised himself as a swan and ravished Leda who, according to one of several conflicting versions of the story, later laid two blue eggs. When the eggs hatched, Helen and her sister Clytemnestra emerged from one of them and Pollux and Castor, also known as the divine twins, came from the other. Helen grew up to become the most beautiful and sought-after woman in Greece. She married Menelaus, King of Sparta, and had a daughter named Hermione. A Trojan prince named Paris fell in love with Helen and kidnapped her while Menelaus was away. This was the start of the Trojan War, which lasted ten years.

In classical French cooking a savory dish proclaimed Belle Hélène, or Hélène style, always includes asparagus and truffles in some form. As you might expect, the truffles and asparagus have been left out in the dessert interpretations of which Poire Belle Hélène is the most famous. The dish instead consists of a poached pear or pear half—typically French Butter or Anjou—served on a scoop of vanilla ice cream accompanied by chocolate sauce. This dish is often mistakenly credited to Escoffier; however, Escoffier's version came later and was dedicated to yet another Helen, the Duchess D'Acosta, who was the sister of the Duke d'Orleans. In Escoffier's interpretation the dessert is topped with candied violets. I use Bosc pears in my version of this simple and delightful oldtimer because of the pear's elegant stretched neck and the long stems which seem to stay on better than other varieties. Be certain that the pears are fully poached, not only because the flavor is improved, but an underpoached pear will be hard and brittle and may break when being prepared for this presentation.

1. Peel the pears and place them in the Poaching Syrup as they are peeled. Poach the pears in the syrup until they are tender (see page 13). Remove from the heat and set aside to cool in the liquid.

2. Use a 1½-inch (3.7-cm) plain cookie cutter to cut out sixteen rounds from the Sponge Cake. Cover the rounds and reserve.

3. Remove the cooled pears from the syrup and pat as dry as possible. Hold a pear upside down in your hand and make a cut in the center from the bottom about two-third of the length to the top. Make a second cut, the same length as the first, at a 90° angle. The stem and neck of the pear should remain intact, and the bottom two-thirds should be cut into quarters. Keeping the pear in your cupped hand, carefully use a melon-ball cutter to remove the core and at the same time hollow out the base of the pear slightly. Repeat with the remaining pears. Pat the pears dry again. Reserve in the refrigerator.

4. Check the consistency of both sauces to be sure they are thick enough to hold their shape when piped; however, they should still level out and create a smooth surface. Place the sauces in piping bottles.

5. Presentation: Place a sponge round in the center of a dessert plate. Pipe Chocolate Sauce in a 4-inch (10-cm) diameter circle around the sponge. Pipe a 1-inch (2.5-cm) ring of Vanilla Custard Sauce around the Chocolate Sauce (or to the edge of the base of the plate). Use a wooden skewer to blend the sauces together decoratively where they meet (see Figure 19–31, page 1005). Place a scoop of Vanilla Ice Cream on top of the Sponge Cake. Working quickly, stand a pear on top, straddling the quarters evenly around the ice cream. Pipe Chocolate Sauce on each quarter of the pear, starting close to the stem and letting it run down into the Chocolate Sauce pool on the plate. Serve immediately.

Pineapple Fritters with Gingered Pineapple Frozen Yogurt

12 servings

two medium-sized pineapples, approximately 3 pounds, 12 ounces (1 kg, 705 g) each, before trimming
one recipe Spiced Poaching Syrup (page 13)
vegetable oil for deep frying
bread flour
one recipe Fritter Batter (page 483)
one-half recipe Gingered Pineapple Frozen Yogurt (page 644)
dark coating chocolate, melted

This is a very pretty, healthier-than-many, dessert that I hope you will try. It is not a good choice for preparing ahead of time because the fritters should be served while they are still warm from frying to taste their best. If you would rather leave out the Tulip cups, serve a larger scoop of Pineapple Yogurt. In that case, set the yogurt scoop on a thin round of Sponge Cake (see note that follows the previous recipe), cut slightly smaller than the scoop size, to keep the yogurt from sliding on the plate. You will still have a very pretty presentation, not quite as elegant, but the important thing is that the shortcut doesn't alter the taste.

1. Cut the top and bottom off of each pineapple. Trim off the skin, making certain that you remove all of the "eyes." Cut the pineapple into ½-inch (1.2-cm) slices, then remove the core using an appropriately sized plain, round cookie cutter. Reserve the trimmings and the core (see recipe following). Cut each pineapple ring in quarters.

2. Poach the pineapple pieces in simmering Poaching Syrup for about 5 minutes. The pieces should yield easily to pressure. Set aside and let cool in the liquid for at least 30 minutes to infuse. Remove the pieces and drain on paper towels.

one-half recipe Raspberry Sauce
 (page 1080)
powdered sugar
twelve Miniature Tulips (page 1058)
forty-eight thin julienne strips
 Crystallized Ginger (page 6)
 (approximately 1 ounce/30 g)

3. Heat the oil to 375°F (190°C). Pat the poached pineapple pieces dry if necessary and then coat with bread flour to help the batter adhere. Dip them into the Fritter Batter and carefully drop them into the oil. Do not add too many pieces at one time or the fat will cool rapidly and the fritters will become greasy and heavy from absorbing the oil. Fry for about 5 minutes or until golden brown, turning the fritters in the oil so that they brown evenly.

4. Remove the fritters with a slotted spoon or skimmer and place them on paper towels to drain. Keep the fritters warm as you fry the remaining pieces.

5. Use a 1½-ounce (45-ml) ice cream scoop (size 20 in the U.S.) to portion out twelve servings of Gingered Pineapple Frozen Yogurt onto a chilled paper-lined sheet pan. Streak fine lines of melted dark chocolate in one direction over the scoops. Reserve in the freezer. Place a portion of the Raspberry Sauce in a piping bottle.

6. Presentation: Pipe a 3-inch (7.5-cm) circle of Raspberry Sauce in the center of a dessert plate. Dust four warm fritters generously with powdered sugar. Arrange them on the plate, evenly spaced around the sauce. Place a scoop of yogurt in one of the Miniature Tulips and place this in the center of the sauce. Place a strip of ginger between each of the fritters. Serve immediately.

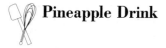 **Pineapple Drink**

I mentioned to one of my students, who was doing her externship with me and on this particular day was working the pineapple fritters station, that she might need go to the storeroom for more pineapple juice. She indicated that we had plenty, explaining that she had made some from the pineapple skin and core that "you throw out anyway, Chef." She said this with a slightly guilty look of "sorry for not checking with you first" on her face. Well shame on me! All this time I have simply discarded the pineapple skin and core. This young lady, from the island of Trinidad, went on to explain that she was taught never to waste anything, and besides, it gets very hot where she lives and the pineapple skin makes a refreshing drink. Here is her recipe for Pineapple Drink. Thank you, Alana.

1. Wash the pineapple, peel, and place the peel in a saucepan along with any other trimmings such as the core. Add enough water to just cover the peel.

2. Bring to a boil and simmer until the liquid is reduced by half. Strain. Adjust by adding sugar or water to taste.

3. Store in the refrigerator and serve chilled. This procedure can be used with other tropical fruits such as papaya or mango as well.

Plum Fritters (Beignets)

16 servings

twenty-four medium-sized whole
  plums (see note)
one recipe Spiced Poaching Syrup
  (page 13)
one and one-half recipes Apricot
  Sauce (page 1068)
vegetable oil for deep frying
bread flour
Fritter Batter (recipe follows)
Cinnamon Sugar (page 5)
powdered sugar

*NOTE: Depending on the time of year and the
variety of plums used, you may need to adjust
the number, cutting a smaller variety into halves
rather than quarters for frying. Conversely, use
only a quarter plum to make each garnish if the
plums are large. Be sure to use a sharp knife
that will cut through the skin cleanly, allowing
you to make thin, elegant slices. Instead of
using fanned plums as a decoration, it looks
very nice to make a rose out of plum peel as is
often done in the garde-manger department
using tomato peel.*

The French words fritter *and* beignet *refer to food, both savory and sweet, that is coated with a batter and deep-fried either whole or in portions, depending on the item. In Japan the equivalent is known as tempura. In the savory renditions of fritters various kinds of seafood are most commonly used (fish and chips are probably the most well-known, with soft-shell crabs counting among the more exclusive offerings), but all kinds of vegetables, as well as certain cheeses, are prepared this way as well. In this country fritters are often associated with New Orleans, where they are most definitely called beignets and where the dessert version is synonymous with that city's dark, rich café au lait.*

Fruits, and even flowers, fried in a batter coating make an especially delicious and very common sweet, from a simple quarter-inch apple ring sprinkled with cinnamon sugar after frying, to fresh cherries, pitted and fried on the stem in pairs or trios. The flowering heads of the elderberry shrub can also be dipped into batter and deep fried. They should not be washed first because this will remove most of their fragrance. Instead, check them carefully for insects which might lurk inside. The fried clusters of flowers are absolutely spectacular. Served with cream, they are a delicious speciality of the Bavarian region of Germany where elderberries seem to grow in almost every garden. The pretty white flowers are available only in the beginning of summer when the shrubs are in full bloom. Elderberry shrubs are also found in the western part of the United States, where the small black berries are used in pies and breads and for making wine and jelly.

1. Select and reserve eight good-looking plums for the garnish (see note). Cut the remaining plums into quarters and remove the pits. Poach the plum quarters gently in the Poaching Syrup for about 5 minutes. They should be soft but not mushy. Remove and set aside to drain on paper towels. Place a portion of the Apricot Sauce in a piping bottle. Reserve it and the remaining sauce at room temperature.

2. Heat the frying oil to 375°F (190°C). Coat the poached plums with bread flour to help the batter adhere. Dip them into the Fritter Batter and carefully drop them into the oil. Do not add too many pieces at one time or the fat will cool rapidly and the fritters will become greasy and heavy from absorbing the oil. Fry for about 5 minutes or until golden brown, turning the fritters in the oil so they will color evenly.

3. Remove the fritters with a slotted spoon or skimmer and place them on paper towels or napkins to drain. Sprinkle Cinnamon Sugar lightly over the fritters and keep them warm as you fry the remaining pieces.

4. Presentation: Cut one of the reserved plums in half, fan it quickly and place in the center of a dessert plate. Pipe Apricot Sauce to cover the lower half of the base of the plate in front of the plum (be sure the sauce is at room temperature or it will cool off the fritters as they are eaten together). Sift powdered sugar over four warm fritters and arrange them on the opposite side of the plate. Serve immediately.

Trio of Chocolates with Marzipan Parfait

Gâteau Saint-Honoré

Rhubarb-Meringue Napoleons

Wine Foam and Blackberry Bavarian Greystone

Chocolate Bread Pudding with Cookie Citrus Rind

Cherry Baskets with Cherry Compote and Black Pepper Frozen Yogurt

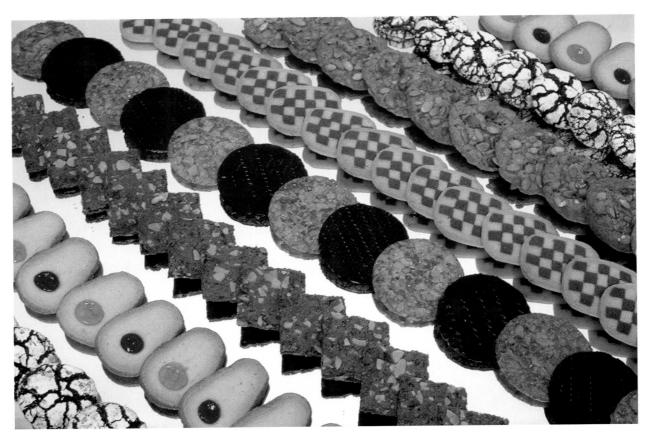

Assorted Cookies

Assorted Cookies

Clockwise from top, variations of Lemon Chiffon Cake. Apricot Crteam Cake, Chocolate Mousse Cake with Bannana, and Rasperry Cake.

White Chocolate Bavarian-Style Tri-Color Mousse

Courting Swans

Chocolate Marquise

Lemon Chiffon Pouches

Princess Cake

Date-Stuffed Poached Pears in Phyllo Crowns with Brandied Mousseline Sauce

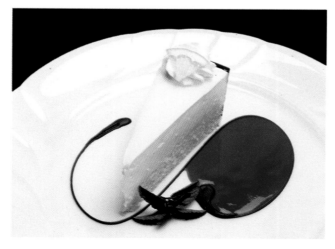

Lemon Chiffon Cake

Puff Pastry with Fruit and Champagne Sabayon

Cherry Meringue Tart with Rhubarb Sauce

Individual Baked Alaska Beehives

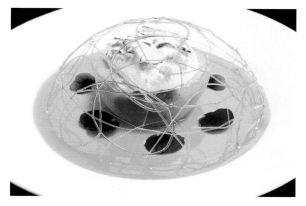

Forbidden Peach

Pineapple Fritters with Gingered Pineapple Frozen Yogurt

Apricot and Fig Tart with Prickly Pear Sorbet

Apricot Cream Cake

Lemon Pudding Cake

Tiramisu with Fresh Fruit

Italian Cheese and Cranberry Strudel

Pears Belle Hélène

Wild Strawberry Parfait

Raspberry Wafers

White Chocolate Citrus Roulade

Cassata Parfait with Meringue

Small Pear Tartlets with Caramel Sauce

Chestnut-Rum Cream Cakes

Fritter Batter

2³/₄ cups (660 ml)

5 ounces (140 g) bread flour
¹/₂ teaspoon (3 g) salt
2 egg yolks
4 ounces (115 g) granulated sugar
finely grated peel of one lemon
1 cup (240 ml) sweet white wine
1 teaspoon (5 ml) vanilla extract
2 egg whites (¹/₄ cup/60 ml)

1. Sift the flour and salt together.

2. Beat the egg yolks, 2 ounces (55 g) of the sugar, and the lemon peel just to combine. Add the wine and vanilla. Gradually stir this mixture into the dry ingredients and mix until completely smooth. Refrigerate for about 30 minutes.

3. Just before the batter is to be used, whip the egg whites with the remaining 2 ounces (55 g) of sugar until stiff peaks form. Gradually fold the reserved batter into the egg whites. For the best result, the batter should be used within 30 minutes. If you know you will not be able to use all of the batter right away, whip just one egg white with 1 ounce (30 g) of sugar and add this to half of the reserved batter.

VARIATION
Fritters with Fresh Berry Sauce

*T*ry this delicious combination when fresh blackberries, or any of the hybrids such as boysenberries or loganberries, are available.

1. Follow the recipe and instructions for Plum Fritters, using fresh peaches or nectarines instead of plums. Cut the fruit into ³/₄-inch (2-cm) wedges and allow five pieces per serving. Substitute Blackberry Sauce (see note with Raspberry Sauce, page 1080) for the Apricot Sauce.

2. **Presentation:** Arrange five warm fritters in a half circle on one side of a dessert plate. Pour a small pool of Blackberry Sauce in front and decorate the sauce with Sour Cream Mixture for Piping (see page 1081 for the recipe and pages 998–1006 for decorating instructions). Serve immediately.

Puff Pastry with Fruit and Champagne Sabayon

16 servings

2 pounds (910 g) Puff Pastry
    (page 44)
Egg Wash (page 7)
2 pounds (910 g) prepared fresh fruit,
    approximately
powdered sugar
one and one-half recipes Cold
    Sabayon (page 719), made with
    champagne
one-half recipe Italian Cream
    (page 1087)
sixteen mint sprigs
Chocolate Sauce for Piping
    (page 1072)

*T*his dessert can be as light and refreshing as a breath of fresh air, or just as easily, the Puff Pastry can become heavy, chewy, and very unappetizing. To begin with, it is crucial to use well-made, rested, and chilled Puff Pastry. The dough should never be cut with a pastry wheel or a dull knife; either one will press the layers near the edge together, reducing the dough's ability to expand in the oven. The Puff Pastry shells should ideally be assembled to order. If this is not possible, assemble them no more than 30 minutes ahead or the Puff Pastry will start to become soggy. Unfilled shells can be stored in a dry location for a maximum of three days, but if stored for more than one day, they should be refreshed by heating them in the oven and letting them cool before using.

1. Roll the Puff Pastry out to a square slightly larger than 14 inches (35 cm); it will be about ¹/₄ inch (6 mm) thick. Refrigerate the dough for 30 minutes to firm and relax it.

2. Trim the edges to make an even 14-inch (35-cm) square. Cover the scraps and reserve for another use. Cut the Puff Pastry into sixteen 3¹/₂-inch (8.7-cm) squares. Brush the squares with Egg Wash, being careful not to let any Egg Wash drip down the sides, which can keep

NOTE: Take care to make nice uniform pieces instead of just chopping the fruit up. Use at least four different varieties with contrasting colors. Leave the skin on apricots or peaches if you use them and try to include either kiwi or honeydew melon (use a small melon-ball cutter for the honeydew). Keep each variety separate until serving time to make the fruit look more attractive and prevent the colors from bleeding together.

the dough from puffing. Lightly score the tops with parallel lines, marking diagonally in both directions.

3. Place the squares on sheet pans lined with baking paper. Bake at 425°F (219°C) for 12 minutes. Lower the heat to 375°F (190°C) and continue baking until dark golden brown and dried all the way through. Set aside to cool.

4. Cut the fresh fruit into pieces the size of raspberries (see note).

5. Cut off the top third of the baked pastry squares. Place the "lids" next to the bottoms and sift powdered sugar lightly over the lids.

6. One-half hour before serving, make the Sabayon and reserve in the refrigerator.

7. Place the Italian Cream in a pastry bag with a no. 4 (8-mm) plain tip. Reserve in the refrigerator.

8. Presentation: Pour approximately ⅓ cup (80 ml) of Sabayon in the center of a dessert plate. Use the back of a spoon to gently shape the sauce into a large even circle without covering the entire base of the plate. Pipe lines of Italian Cream back and forth next to one another on a bottom Puff Pastry square. Pipe a small dot of cream on the plate next to the sauce circle at the top of the plate. Using approximately ½ cup (120 ml) of fruit mixture per serving, arrange a portion of it on the cream on top of the Puff Pastry. Place the Puff Pastry square on the plate on top of the dot of cream, arranging it diagonally so that the bottom corner of the square is in the center of the Sabayon pool. Drizzle a little additional Sabayon over the fruit inside the pastry. Sprinkle additional fruit on the sauce in front of the pastry. Place the lid on top at an angle so you can see the fruit inside. Place a mint sprig so it is sticking out from under the lid. Place the Chocolate Sauce in a piping bag. Pipe two lines of chocolate near the edge of the sauce extending from one edge of the Puff Pastry square to the other so they form two half-circles. Drag a wooden skewer through the lines toward the edge of the sauce every ½ inch (1.2 cm). Serve immediately.

 Raspberry Wafers

16 servings

Butter and Flour Mixture (page 4)
Raspberry Wafer Batter (recipe
    follows)
powdered sugar
5 ounces (140 g) strained strawberry
    jam or preserves
one recipe Raspberry Sauce
    (page 1080)
2 cups (480 ml) heavy cream
2 teaspoons (10 g) granulated sugar

*T*he technique used to create and present Raspberry Wafers is one of the quickest and easiest ways of making a special and impressive dessert. This ideal summer offering can be assembled in just a few minutes provided the components are at hand: whipped cream in a pastry bag, raspberries sorted, and sauce in a piping bottle. The batter will yield a few extra wafers so you can afford to break some during the assembly. This is almost unavoidable since they are so fragile, but their delicacy is part of the dessert's appeal. If it is not possible to assemble each serving à la minute, the assembly should be completed no more than fifteen minutes prior to serving, or the wafers will become soft and unappetizing. It is also important to keep in mind that, just as with other fruits and berries, there are small, medium, and large raspberries. Mixing them up within the same serving will probably result in the layers leaning to one side.

2 dry pints (960 ml) raspberries, approximately (see note)

sixteen small mint leaves

Sour Cream Mixture for Piping (page 1081)

NOTE: If at all possible, try to work with a few extra pints of raspberries so you can choose the best-looking and most evenly sized berries to use in the desserts. Leftover raspberries can be used in part to make the sauce.

1. Make the Raspberry Wafer template marked A in Figure 10–24. The template as shown is the correct size required for this recipe. Trace the drawing, then cut the template out of $^1/_{16}$-inch (2-mm) thick cardboard (cake boxes work fine for this). Make a second solid template that is 2 inches (5 cm) larger than the first one (1 inch/2.5 cm on each of the 8 sides) and reserve this template for the presentation. Brush the Butter and Flour Mixture on the back of clean, even sheet pans, or use silicone mats instead if you have them (in that case it is not necessary to use the Butter and Flour Mixture)

2. Spread the batter onto the prepared sheet pans (or silicone mats), spreading it flat and even within the template (see Figures 19–55 and 19–56, pages 1046 and 1047). You will need three wafers per serving.

3. Bake at 410°F (210°C) until slightly brown in places, approximately 5 minutes. Allow the wafers to cool before removing them from the pans.

4. Place the reserved solid template in the center of a dessert plate. Sift powdered sugar over the remaining exposed plate including the rim. Remove the template (this is easier to do if you make a handle from a piece of tape and attach it to the template). Place strawberry jam or preserves in a piping bag and cut a larger than normal opening. Pipe a line of jam following the perimeter of the powdered sugar octagon. Prepare as many remaining plates as you expect to need in the same way. Set the plates aside. Place a portion of the Raspberry Sauce in a piping bottle and reserve.

5. Whip the heavy cream with the granulated sugar to stiff peaks. Place in a pastry bag with a no. 6 (12-mm) plain tip. Reserve in the refrigerator.

6. **Presentation:** Pipe Raspberry Sauce within the octagonal jam outline, filling in all but a space in the center that is slightly smaller than the size of the wafers. Pipe a small mound of whipped cream at every other point on each of two wafers. Place five raspberries on top of each, arranging four of them between the mounds of cream and one in the center. Stack one wafer on top of the other, placing the second wafer so that the cream and berries that are visible on the sides are alternated. Top the stack with a plain wafer. Hold a no. 4 (8-mm) star tip in place over the plain tip on the pastry bag with whipped cream (see Figures 12–6 and 12–7, page 602). Pipe a small rosette of cream in the center of the top wafer. Sift powdered sugar lightly over the top wafer. Place a raspberry and a small mint leaf on the cream. Place the assembled stack of wafers in the center of the sauce with the edges of the sauce and wafer parallel. Pipe dots of Sour Cream Mixture in the sauce around the wafers at each point of the octagon. Drag a wooden skewer through the dots toward the dessert to create teardrops. Clean the tip of the skewer, then dip it into Raspberry Sauce and decorate each sour cream teardrop with a tiny dot of Raspberry Sauce. Serve immediately.

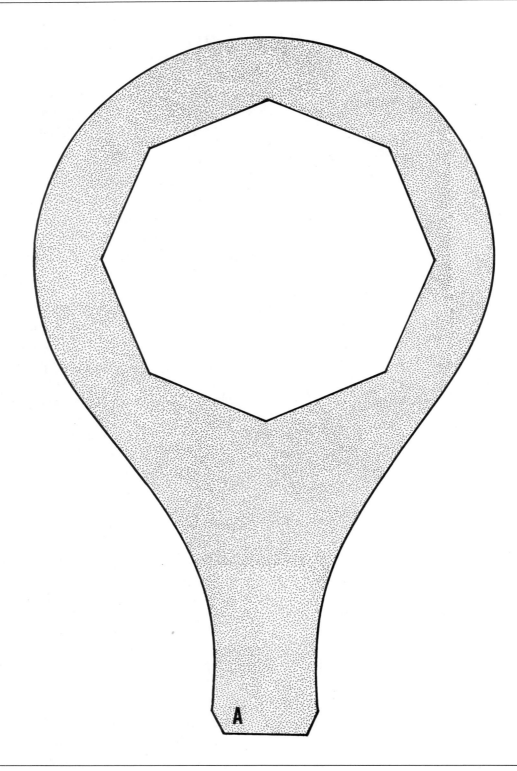

FIGURE 10–24 (A)   *The template for Raspberry Wafers*

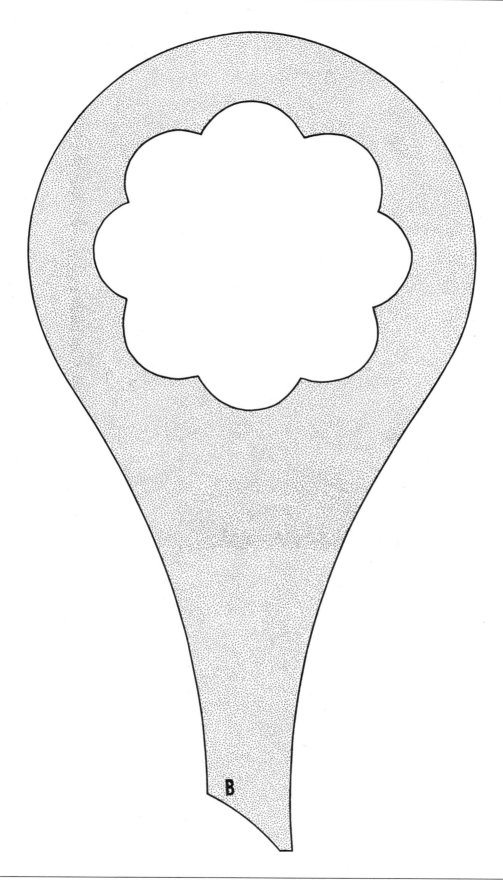

FIGURE 10–24 (B)   The template for Almond Wafers

Raspberry Wafer Batter

2 cups (240 ml)

5 ounces (140 g) toasted hazelnuts

5 ounces (140 g) granulated sugar

4 ounces (115 g) soft unsalted butter

1/2 teaspoon (3 g) salt

1/3 cup (80 ml) heavy cream

2 egg whites (1/4 cup/60 ml)

1 tablespoon (15 ml) Frangelico liqueur

3 ounces (85 g) bread flour

Red Banana Truffles in Phyllo Dough

16 servings

sixteen medium-sized ripe red bananas

6 ounces (170 g) Ganache (page 1086)

5 ounces (140 g) pistachio nuts, blanched, skins removed, dried and finely crushed (see note 1)

thirty-two sheets phyllo dough (about 1 pound, 6 ounces/625 g)

4 ounces (115 g) melted unsalted butter, approximately

Piping Chocolate (page 904), melted

one-half recipe Raspberry Sauce (page 1080)

powdered sugar

1 pound (455 g) prepared fresh fruit, approximately (see note 2)

1/4 cup (60 ml) orange liqueur

NOTE 1: Crush the pistachio nuts into medium-sized pieces. In this process you will get both smaller and larger pieces. Reserve the larger pieces (about one-third of the total) and use the remaining smaller pieces when assembling the bananas.

NOTE 2: Use four kinds of fruit cut into distinct pieces; not chopped or sliced. Place each variety in a separate bowl. Pour a little orange liqueur into each bowl and toss gently to coat.

1. Rub the toasted hazelnuts between your hands to remove some, but not all, of the brown skin. Grind them with half of the sugar to a fine consistency. Cream the butter with the remainder of the sugar, then mix in the ground nuts, salt, and heavy cream.

2. Add the egg whites and Frangelico. Sift the flour and incorporate it into the batter. Let the batter rest for 1 hour.

This is the epitome of a good-tasting, good-looking dessert that can be prepped ahead, with a minimum of time required for last-minute assembly. If you are really pressed for time when serving, eliminate the chocolate piping on the plate and pour the Raspberry Sauce into a pool in the center of the plate instead (be sure that the Raspberry Sauce is thick enough not to run on the plate). Arrange the cut Banana Truffle pieces on top of the sauce. Sift powdered sugar over the entire plate, then arrange the fruit in a circle around the sauce on top of the powdered sugar (do not move it once you set it down). Sprinkle pistachio nuts sparingly on top of the sauce. It's a very pretty presentation and over all a little quicker, which is helpful if you have to assemble quite a few of these desserts and, based on my experience, chances are you will. If red bananas are not available, use eight medium-sized yellow bananas instead. Cut them in half lengthwise and then (keeping the halves together) cut in half again crosswise to make thirty-two pieces.

1. Peel the bananas. Cut the pointed tip off each end and then cut them in half lengthwise. Turn each piece so that the flat (cut) side is facing up.

2. Place the Ganache in a pastry bag with a no. 5 (10-mm) plain tip. Pipe a rope of Ganache on the flat side of half of the banana pieces. Working with the remaining banana pieces (without Ganache), one at a time, pick one up, dip the cut side into the crushed pistachio nuts (pressing firmly so they adhere) then sandwich together with a Ganache-topped banana piece. Reserve.

3. Unwrap and unroll the phyllo dough. Keep the stack of dough covered with a slightly damp (not wet) towel as much as possible as you are working. Place one sheet in front of you and brush it lightly with butter, fold in half lengthwise, and brush lightly with butter again. Repeat buttering and folding with a second sheet and place this on top of the first so that the stack has four layers of phyllo. Place one of the prepared bananas at the short end of the phyllo stack. Bring the sides in on top of the banana, then roll up lengthwise. Place seam-side down on a sheet pan lined with buttered baking paper. Repeat with the remaining pieces.

4. Bake at 375°F (190°C) for approximately 25 minutes or until golden brown and baked through. Let cool to room temperature.

5. Place the Piping Chocolate in a piping bag and cut a small opening. Pipe a narrow elongated X shape, in the center over the entire plate, on as many dessert plates as you anticipate needing. Set the plates aside. Place a portion of the Raspberry Sauce in a piping bottle. Reserve it and the remainder of the sauce until time of service.

6. Presentation: Pipe Raspberry Sauce inside both sides of the chocolate X on one of the prepared plates, covering only the inside portions of the X that are on the base of the plate. Using a serrated knife, carefully cut a banana package in half diagonally and arrange the pieces in the center of the plate. Sift powdered sugar lightly over the whole plate, including the rim. Place seven or eight pieces of prepared fruit on each side of the banana pieces, on top of the powdered sugar. After you set the fruit on the plate, do not move it or you will disturb the powdered sugar. Sprinkle some of the reserved pistachio nuts on top of the sauce.

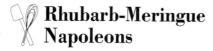

Rhubarb-Meringue Napoleons

16 servings

1 pound, 8 ounces (680 g) Puff Pastry (page 44)

1 pound, 8 ounces (680 g) granulated sugar

2 pounds (910 g) fresh rhubarb stalks

2 cups (240 ml) water

cornstarch

one-quarter recipe Italian Meringue (page 591)

sixteen small stemmed strawberries

NOTE 1: If you increase or decrease the size of this recipe, always roll the sheet(s) out to a size that is slightly larger than a multiple of three inches (7.5 cm) so that after trimming the sheets you can cut 3-inch (7.5-cm) squares.

NOTE 2: The second pan is placed on top of the Puff Pastry sheet to prevent it from puffing too much, which would make the finished sheet uneven and impossible to cut into neat squares.

NOTE 3: The Napoleons should be assembled to order. If you need to expedite several orders

I have wondered lately what the great Carême would make of the current trend in the food industry to borrow the name of his famous dessert and use it for all manner of layered creations. His original pastry was not named Napoleon out of respect for the notorious general, but in reference to the Neopolitan way of making sweets and glazes with layers of varying colors and textures. The title does seem to be a good way to designate that a dish has more than one layer, but I can't help but feel the rationale is being stretched too far when I see a dish of layered vegetables or fish labeled Napoleon of this or that. Perhaps I'm just prejudiced, but I feel the name belongs to the original dessert, or at least to the pastry department! Having said all that, my justification for applying it here is that at least I am using it for a dessert containing Puff Pastry.

1. Divide the Puff Pastry into two equal pieces. Roll each piece out in part of the sugar (about one-third of the sugar will be sufficient to work with at this point) to a rectangle 13 by 19 inches (32.5 × 47.5 cm) (see note 1). The sheets should be about ⅛ inch (3 mm) thick. As you roll the sheets, sprinkle sugar on top of the dough and turn the dough over frequently so that the sugar is preventing the dough from sticking and, at the same time, the sugar is rolled into the Puff Pastry. Add the leftover sugar to the rest of the sugar.

2. Place the Puff Pastry sheets on perfectly flat, even, paper-lined sheet pans. Prick the dough well. Refrigerate for at least 30 minutes so the dough can relax.

3. Place a sheet of baking paper on top of each Puff Pastry sheet. Top each with another flat, even sheet pan (see note 2). Bake the sheets at 400°F (205°C) for 12 minutes. Remove the top sheet pans and the sheets of baking paper. Continue baking until the sugar in the dough

together, the meringue can be piped onto the middle and top layers up to 30 minutes ahead of time, and then each dessert can be assembled with the rhubarb as you are ready to serve.

begins to caramelize and the sheets are deep golden brown, approximately 10 minutes longer. Let the sheets cool.

4. Using a serrated knife, trim the edges of the Puff Pastry sheets as necessary to make them straight and even. Measure and carefully cut each sheet into twenty-four 3-inch (7.5-cm) squares. Set the squares aside. Discard the scrap pieces.

5. Trim the top and bottom of the rhubarb stalks (do not peel them). Cut the stalks into 3-inch (7.5-cm) long pieces. Cut these pieces lengthwise so they are about ¹/₂ inch (1.2 cm) wide. Arrange the pieces in rows in a hotel pan or on a half-sheet pan. Sprinkle the reserved sugar over the rhubarb pieces, then pour the water over the sugar. Set the rhubarb aside for about 30 minutes.

6. Cover the rhubarb with foil or with an inverted sheet pan. Bake at 400°F (205°C) for about 8 minutes or until the rhubarb is just soft. (Watch carefully here: Rhubarb will go from soft to mushy and then literally disintegrate in about 1 minute. If this happens, save it to make sauce and start over.) Let the rhubarb cool in the liquid.

7. Remove the rhubarb pieces from the liquid and set them aside.

8. Strain the rhubarb cooking liquid. Thicken it with cornstarch, using 2 teaspoons (5 g) cornstarch per pint (480 ml) of liquid. Reserve the sauce.

9. Reserve the sixteen best-looking Puff Pastry squares to use for the top layers.

10. Place the Italian Meringue in a pastry bag with a no. 3 (6-mm) plain tip.

11. Presentation: Arrange four or five pieces of rhubarb on top of a Puff Pastry square. Place a second square on top. Pipe meringue back and forth diagonally over the second square, each line touching the previous one, and also over half of one of the reserved Puff Pastry squares in the same pattern (do not place the top piece on the pastry). Lightly brown the meringue on both pieces by placing them under a salamander or use a blowtorch very carefully. Pipe a small dot of meringue in the center of a dessert plate. Place the assembled dessert on top. Pour just enough rhubarb sauce around the Napoleon to cover the base of the plate. Place the top Puff Pastry square leaning against the side of the pastry. Place a strawberry on top of the Napoleon.

 **Rum Babas**

16 servings

Butter and Flour Mixture (page 4)
Baba Dough (recipe follows)
Rum Baba Syrup (recipe follows)
Apricot Glaze (page 1016)

*T*his light yeast cake, studded with raisins and soaked in rum syrup, originated in seventeenth-century Poland where, as the story goes, King Stanislas Leczyinski, finding his gugelhupf too dry, moistened it with syrup. He named his invention Ali Baba after the character in his favorite story, the classic

one recipe Cold Sabayon (page 719)
1 pound, 8 ounces (680 g) fresh
   cherries (see note)

*NOTE: Pick out nice-looking cherries with the
stems attached. When cherries are out of season,
substitute raspberries.*

Thousand and One Nights. *When the dessert was later introduced to the West, apparently by a French pâtissier who came across it among members of the Polish court who were visiting France, it became especially popular and was dubbed simply Babas. The classic baba is baked in a tall cylindrical mold, but the cake is also typically made into individual pastries in timbales about 3 inches deep and 1³⁄₄ inches wide. A variety of other shapes and sizes can also be used, including the brioche mold used in my version. When the Baba Dough is baked in a ring mold, the dessert is known as Savarin. Babas are still very popular in France, and it seems they are part of almost every pastry assortment: sumptuous, soaked in rum syrup, glazed with apricot, and decorated with the infamous maraschino cherry. If you like to enjoy a baba handheld on the go, as I often do, be sure to lean forward as you bite into it or the syrup will run down the front of you the same as if you were eating a fresh ripe peach!*

1. Brush the Butter and Flour Mixture on the inside of sixteen standard-size brioche molds: 3¹⁄₄ inches across and 1¹⁄₂ inches deep (8.1 × 3.7 cm). Reserve.

2. Place the Baba Dough in a pastry bag with a no. 7 (14-mm) plain tip. Pipe the batter into the forms, dividing it evenly; they will be about half full. Let the babas rise until they fill the forms. Make sure they have proofed enough or the baked babas will not be able to absorb enough syrup.

3. Bake at 400°F (205°C) until golden brown and baked through, about 20 minutes. Remove from the forms as soon as possible and let cool.

4. Cut the crust from the top of the babas, making them flat at the same time.

5. Heat the Rum Baba Syrup to scalding and remove from the heat. Place a few babas at a time in the hot syrup. Push them down and let them soak long enough to absorb as much of the syrup as they can. Cut partway into one pastry to see if the syrup has soaked all the way through. Carefully remove the babas from the syrup and place them inverted (cut-side down) on a cooling rack set over a sheet pan to drain. Reheat the syrup, if necessary, while you soak the remaining babas.

6. Brush the sides and the top of each baba with Apricot Glaze. Reserve in the refrigerator until time of service.

7. Presentation: Place a Rum Baba off-center on a dessert plate. Spoon Sabayon over part of the cake and let it flow into a pool on the base of the plate. Place a few fresh cherries next to the sauce. Cut one cherry in half to expose the pit (which will let the guest know that the cherries are not pitted).

Baba Dough

2 pounds (910 g)

1 tablespoon (15 ml) fresh compressed
  yeast
1/2 cup (120 ml) warm milk
  (105–115°F, 40–46°C)
4 ounces (115 g) bread flour
4 eggs
1 teaspoon (5 ml) vanilla extract
1/2 teaspoon (3 g) salt
6 ounces (170 g) soft unsalted butter
8 ounces (225 g) cake flour
2 ounces (55 g) dark raisins

1. Dissolve the yeast in the warm milk. Stir in the bread flour and mix until you have a smooth, soft sponge. Let rise, covered, in a warm place until the sponge starts to bubble and fall.

2. Mix the eggs, vanilla, salt, and butter into the sponge. Add the cake flour and mix until it becomes a soft, smooth paste. Incorporate the raisins.

 Rum Baba Syrup

6 cups (1l, 440 ml)

4 cups (960 ml) water
1 pound, 8 ounces (680 g) granulated
  sugar
one unpeeled orange, quartered
3/4 cup (180 ml) light rum

1. Place the water, sugar, and orange pieces in a saucepan. Bring to a boil and cook for about two minutes, or until all of the sugar has dissolved.

2. Remove from the heat, strain, and add the rum.

Savarin

*16 individual pastries or 2
Savarin rings serving 8 to 10 each*

Butter and Flour Mixture (page 4)
one and one-half recipes Baba Dough
  (this page), made without raisins
Maraschino Syrup (recipe follows)
Apricot Glaze (page 1016)
1/2 cup (120 ml) heavy cream
1 teaspoon (5 g) granulated sugar
1 pound, 4 ounces (570 g) fresh red
  currants (see note)

NOTE: Reserve sixteen attractive clusters of red currants on the stem to use in the presentation. Remove the stems from the remainder and reserve the individual currants separately. If red currants are unavailable, try using wild strawberries or another small berry instead.

Savarins are simply Babas made in a different shape, and without raisins. They are formed as either a large ring-shaped cake serving eight to ten people, or as individual doughnut-like pastries. In both cases the dessert is moistened with maraschino or other kirsch-flavored syrup. Savarin is named after the French gourmet and writer Antoine Brillat-Savarin who, in 1825, just a year before his death, authored The Physiology of Taste, *which was to become a classic culinary text.*

1. Brush the Butter and Flour Mixture on the inside of sixteen ring molds 3 1/4 inches in diameter and 1 1/2 inches tall (8.1 × 3.7 cm) or two 10-inch (25-cm) diameter ring molds.

2. Place the Baba Dough in a pastry bag with a no. 7 (14-mm) plain tip. Pipe the dough into the forms dividing it equally; the forms will be about half full. Let the Savarins rise until they have doubled in volume.

Do not take a short cut here: A Savarin that has not been left to proof properly will not be able to absorb enough syrup and will be dense and unpleasant to eat.

3. Bake at 400°F (205°C) until golden brown and baked through, about 20 minutes (40 minutes for the larger size). Remove from the forms as soon as possible and let cool on a cooling rack.

4. Cut the crust from the top of the Savarins, making them flat at the same time.

5. Heat the Maraschino Syrup to scalding and remove from the heat. Place a few Savarins at a time in the hot syrup, push them down into the syrup, and let them soak long enough to absorb as much of the syrup as they can before carefully removing them. Place them cut-side down on a cooling rack set over a sheet pan to drain. Reheat the syrup, if necessary, while you soak the remaining Savarins. (If you are making the larger Savarin, place it directly on the cooling rack after trimming the crust and spoon the hot syrup evenly over the top until you are sure it has penetrated all the way through. Let the Savarin drain, then use two metal spatulas to carefully place it on a serving platter.) Strain the remaining syrup through cheese cloth. Place a portion of the syrup in a piping bottle and reserve for the presentation. Brush Apricot Glaze over the top and sides of either the large or individual size Savarins.

6. Whip the heavy cream and sugar to stiff peaks. Place in a pastry bag with a no. 7 (14-mm) star tip. Reserve in the refrigerator.

7. Presentation: Place an individual Savarin (flat-side down) slightly off-center on a dessert plate. Pipe a rosette of whipped cream on the plate next to the pastry. Fill the center with loose red currants and decorate the cream with one of the reserved clusters of berries. Pipe a small amount of syrup on top of the Savarin and onto the plate. Serve the large-size ring from the serving tray in the dining room or at the buffet table, cutting eight to ten portions from each ring, spooning some currants in front of the slice on each plate and adding some of the whipped cream and reserved syrup.

1. Place the water, sugar, and orange pieces in a saucepan. Bring to a boil and cook for about two minutes or until all of the sugar has dissolved.

2. Remove from the heat, strain, and add the maraschino liqueur.

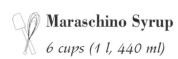

Maraschino Syrup

6 cups (1 l, 440 ml)

4 cups (960 ml) water
1 pound, 8 ounces (680 g) granulated
   sugar
one unpeeled orange, quartered
3/4 cup (180 ml) maraschino liqueur

Small Pear Tartlets with Caramel Sauce

12 to 16 servings

six small to medium-size pears
(see step one)

one recipe Spiced Poaching Syrup
(page 13)

2 pounds, 12 ounces (1 kg, 250 g)
or one-quarter recipe Puff Pastry
(page 44)

4 ounces (115 g) Pastry Cream
(page 1088)

4 ounces (115 g) Almond Macaroon
Cookies batter (page 202)

Cinnamon Sugar (page 5)

Apricot Glaze (page 1016)

one to one and one-half recipes
Caramel Sauce II (page 1071),
at room temperature

Chocolate Sauce (page 1072)

Sour Cream Mixture for Piping
(page 1081)

Raspberry Sauce (page 1080)

twelve or sixteen fresh edible flowers

Pear-Shaped Tarts

12 servings

NOTE: If you want to present the tarts with a pear stem (which looks nice), you will have to do a little pirating in your pear supply since you get only one stem per pear but two servings.

There are many ways to make and present these tarts, which have the unbeatable flavor combination of crisp, flaky Puff Pastry topped with a creamy almond filling and refreshing poached pear, all surrounded by a rich Caramel Sauce that tastes like liquid candy. And, as if that were not enough, serving the tarts with ice cream will really bring on the accolades! The three versions presented here all stand out in their own way. Both the round and pear-shaped patterns lend themselves to elegant presentations. The drawbacks are that these take longer to cut out if you do not have an appropriate cutter, and you end up with fewer tarts and a lot more scrap pieces of dough left over. The latter is no problem provided you have a use for the scraps. If not, or if you need to make a large quantity of tarts (these are a very practical banquet dessert since they can be made ahead and then baked off just before plating; they should be served warm), you will appreciate the simplicity and speed of the rectangular version, which leaves close to zero scraps. Using a combination of Almond Macaroon Cookies batter and Pastry Cream provides the best tasting filling, but in a pinch I have made the tarts using either one alone (twice the amount) with no problem.

1. Try to use French Butter pears or Anjou pears. If the pears are too large, try to peel them to size or use the round tart presentation. If using the pear-shaped presentation, choose pears which have the stem intact. Use a vegetable peeler to peel the pears and then cut them in half; be careful not to damage the stems. Place the pears in acidulated water as you work to prevent them from browning.

2. Poach the pear halves in Poaching Syrup until soft. Take care not to overcook or they will become difficult to work with. If time permits, allow the pears to cool in the syrup.

1. Make the pear-shaped template (Figure 10–25). The template as shown is the correct size for use in this recipe. Trace the drawing, then cut the template out of 1/16-inch (2-mm) cardboard (cake boxes are ideal for this purpose).

2. Roll out the Puff Pastry to make a rectangle measuring 22 by 16 inches (55 × 40 cm). Place the dough in the refrigerator or freezer long enough to completely relax and firm the dough.

3. Using a sharp knife and the template as your guide, cut out twelve pear-shaped pieces of Puff Pastry (Figure 10–26). Place them on a sheet pan lined with baking paper as you cut each one. Gather the scrap pieces, cover, and reserve for another use in the refrigerator or freezer. Prick the top of the dough pieces well, leaving a 1/2-inch (1.2-cm) border unpricked all around.

4. Combine the Pastry Cream and the macaroon batter. Place in a paper pastry bag (see page 23). Cut a small opening in the bag and pipe a layer of filling over the pricked part of the Puff Pastry pieces.

5. Remove the pear halves from the poaching liquid. Remove the stems and reserve (see note). Core the pears using a melon-ball cutter.

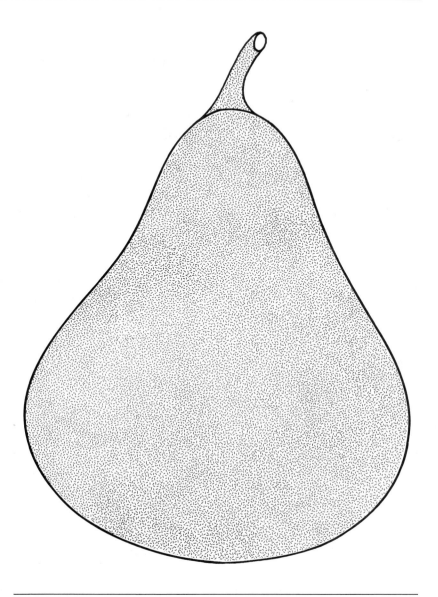

FIGURE 10–25   *The template for making the pear-shaped version of Small*
Pear Tartlets with Caramel Sauce

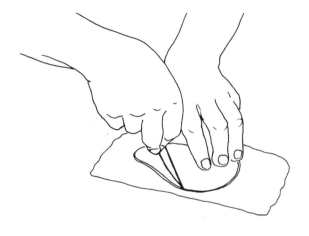

FIGURE 10–26   *Cutting the pear-shaped pieces of Puff Pastry*

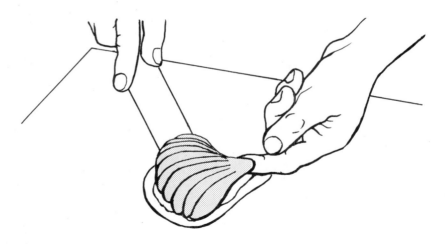

FIGURE 10–27   Placing the pears on top of the filling

Slice the pears lengthwise starting just below the neck of the pear, keeping the slices attached at the top. Fan the slices slightly and place on top of the cream (Figure 10–27). Sprinkle Cinnamon Sugar lightly over the pears.

6. Bake at 375°F (190°C) for about 35 minutes or until the Puff Pastry is golden brown. Melt the Apricot Glaze and brush lightly on top of the fruit and the crust.

7. Place a portion of the Caramel Sauce in a piping bottle (adjust the consistency first if necessary) and set aside at room temperature. Place a portion of each of the Chocolate Sauce, Sour Cream Mixture, and Raspberry Sauce into three piping bags. Reserve.

8. Presentation: Pipe Caramel Sauce in a thin layer to cover the base of a dessert plate. Hold the plate in one hand and tap the rim sharply with your other hand to even the surface of the sauce. Place a tart in the center of the plate. Pipe a ring of Chocolate Sauce on top of the Caramel Sauce close to the edge of the Caramel Sauce. Pipe a ring of Sour Cream Mixture just inside the Chocolate Sauce ring. Pipe dots of Raspberry Sauce, spaced 1 inch (2.5 cm) apart, in a circle about halfway between the other sauce rings and the tart. Drag a small wooden skewer through each dot in a clockwise direction to form teardrops. Then drag the skewer through the other two sauce rings every 1 inch (2.5 cm) from the edge toward the center of the plate. Place an edible flower on the tart and push a reserved pear stem into the pear neck. Serve immediately.

Round Tarts

12 servings

1. Poach pears as directed above. Trace and cut out the inside fluted circle from the large Tulip template Figure 19–54, page 1045). Follow the procedure for rolling out and cutting the dough in the Pear-Shaped Tarts, using the fluted circle template as your guide. Cover the scrap pieces and reserve in the refrigerator or freezer for another use.

2. Use a smaller plain cookie cutter, approximately 4 inches (10 cm) in diameter, to cut halfway through the dough, making a border as you would to make a production style Bouchée. Prick the dough well inside the circle.

3. Pipe the macaroon mixture over the inside circle. Slice the cored pear halves across into thin slices and arrange in overlapping concentric circles, starting at the outside edge and building slightly higher in the center. Use one pear half per serving. Sprinkle Cinnamon Sugar over the fruit, bake and glaze as directed above.

4. Follow the presentation directions above, omitting the raspberry dots and the pear stem. Place an edible flower in the center of the tart.

Rectangular Tarts
16 servings

1. Use eight pears, one and one-half recipes of poaching liquid, half as much macaroon mixture, and 2 pounds (910 g) of Puff Pastry. Poach the pears as directed above.

2. Roll the Puff Pastry to a rectangle slightly larger than 14 by 20 inches (35 × 50 cm). Refrigerate to relax and firm the dough.

3. Use a ruler as a guide and trim one long and one short side of the dough to make them even. Measure and cut four 5-inch (12.5-cm) strips starting at the even short side. Measure and cut these into 3¹/₂-inch (8.7-cm) wide rectangles starting from the even long side. Place the 3¹/₂ by 5 inch (8.7 × 12.5 cm) pieces on sheet pans lined with baking paper.

4. Use a plain, oval cookie cutter that will leave an approximately ¹/₂-inch (1.2-cm) border to cut halfway through the dough pieces. If you do not have an oval cutter you can bend a round cutter to the correct size. Prick the dough well inside the oval.

5. Pipe the macaroon mixture over the ovals. Slice and arrange the pear halves as directed in the Pear-Shaped version, using one pear half per serving. Sprinkle Cinnamon Sugar over the fruit, bake and glaze as directed above.

6. Follow the presentation directions for the Pear-Shaped Tarts, omitting the raspberry dots and the pear stem. You might want to use only one type of sauce for the decoration and/or swirl the circles into the sauce instead (see Figure 19–26, page 1002). Place an edible flower in the center of the tart.

Small Swedish Pancakes (*Plättar*)

16 servings

³/₄ cup (180 ml) heavy cream
1 teaspoon (5 g) granulated sugar
Small Swedish Pancakes Batter (recipe follows)
powdered sugar
8 ounces (225 g) cloudberry jam (see note)
sixteen edible fresh flowers

*T*hese *delicious little pancakes are so tender that they seem to just dissolve on your tongue as you eat them. Being so delicate, they would be impossible to handle if they were made the same size as a regular pancake.* Plättar *are traditionally enjoyed in Sweden after the yellow pea soup on Thursdays. Served warm, dusted with powdered sugar, and topped with cloudberries, they make an unusual light dessert, or try them on your breakfast or brunch table.*

I remember how the American passengers fell in love with Swedish pancakes when I was working on the Swedish American Lines cruise ships in the sixties. One woman in particular was so enamored that she asked the kitchen to make her a special order so she could attach them to her dress and go to the masquerade ball as a Small Swedish Pancake!

Plättar *should, if at all possible, be made to order. If you must make them ahead, you can keep them covered in a low oven (200°F/94°C) for a short time.*

NOTE: If cloudberry jam is unavailable, lingonberry jam makes an excellent substitute.

1. Whip the heavy cream and the sugar to stiff peaks. Place in a pastry bag with a no. 6 (12-mm) star tip. Reserve in the refrigerator.

2. Heat the *plättiron* (the traditional Swedish sectional pancake pan; see page 1124), or a pancake griddle or cast-iron skillet large enough to accommodate at least six 3-inch (7.5-cm) pancakes, until it is hot enough that a small drop of water evaporates instantly when it touches the surface.

3. Stir the rested pancake batter thoroughly. Pour 1 ounce (30 ml) of the batter into each depression in the pan. The iron does not need to be greased because of the large amount of butter in the batter (if you are using a skillet, it may need to be greased for the first batch). Turn the pancakes using a narrow metal spatula as soon as they become light brown on the bottom, about 1 minute. Cook for approximately 1 minute longer to brown the other side. Turning the pancakes takes some practice: It has to be done very rapidly as the batter is not completely set at this point and the pancakes are very tender.

4. Quickly transfer the pancakes to a warm plate and keep them warm if it is necessary to make additional *Plättar*. Make sure the iron does not get too hot or you will risk burning the last few pancakes. This recipe requires quick action even with the iron at the correct temperature. Try the technique of stacking two or three pancakes before removing them from the pan.

5. **Presentation:** Arrange six *Plättar* in a circle on a warm dessert plate overlapping them just enough to leave a small opening in the center. Sift powdered sugar on top of the pancakes and over the exposed part of the plate. Spoon a small dot of cloudberry jam, the size of a hazelnut, in the center of each pancake. Pipe a rosette of whipped cream in the center of the plate. Decorate with an edible flower and serve immediately.

 Small Swedish Pancakes Batter

about 100 pancakes

8 eggs
2 ounces (55 g) granulated sugar
1¹/₃ cups (320 ml) heavy cream
10 ounces (285 g) cake flour
4¹/₂ cups (1 l, 80 ml) milk
1¹/₂ teaspoons (7.5 g) salt
1¹/₂ teaspoons (7.5 ml) vanilla extract
8 ounces (225 g) clarified unsalted butter, melted

NOTE: Be sure to stir the batter every few minutes as you cook the pancakes, and also before you start, to prevent the flour from sinking to the bottom of the thin batter.

1. Beat the eggs and sugar for about 2 minutes to blend well.

2. Mix in the heavy cream and the flour to make a smooth paste.

3. Warm the milk to body temperature and gradually add to the egg mixture along with the salt, vanilla, and butter. The batter will be quite thin. Let the batter rest at room temperature for one hour.

Strawberries Romanoff

16 servings

4 pounds (1 kg, 820 g) small, ripe strawberries

¹/₂ cup (120 ml) Grand Marnier liqueur

¹/₂ cup (120 ml) Simple Syrup (page 11), approximately

powdered sugar

unsweetened cocoa powder

2 cups (480 ml) heavy cream

1 tablespoon (15 ml) Grand Marnier liqueur

Orange Custard (recipe follows)

sixteen Chocolate Goblets (page 894)

sixteen mint sprigs

sixteen Tulip Cookie Spoons (page 1048)

NOTE 1: If you are unable to find small strawberries, cut larger berries in half lengthwise, then cut each half into three or four pieces. Ideally, all of the pieces should be about the same size and shape for the nicest presentation.

NOTE 2: Be very careful not to get fingerprints on the Chocolate Goblets when you handle them. The easiest way to prevent this is by wearing gloves made for food handling.

*S*erving strawberries with cream is nothing new and undoubtedly we will never know who thought of the delectable combination in the first place. This rendition, where the berries are first macerated in liqueur, takes its name from the famous Russian family that dominated the history of that country for more than 300 years. The bona fide version is neither served in a Chocolate Goblet nor with Orange Custard, and the strawberries and cream (quite a bit more cream than I am using, so you can certainly add more if you like without it being overpowering) are mixed together. Tasty, but it doesn't make for a very appealing presentation. If you do not have time to make the Chocolate Goblets, serve this refreshing dessert in silver goblets or saucer-type champagne glasses and omit the Orange Custard.

1. Rinse the strawberries and remove the hulls, using a small melon-ball cutter. Cut the berries into halves or quarters depending on size (see note 1). Toss the strawberries gently with the first measurement of Grand Marnier and the Simple Syrup. Adjust the amount of Simple Syrup in accordance with the ripeness of the fruit and strength of the liqueur flavor desired. Let the strawberries macerate in the liquid for at least 30 minutes. Do not leave the fruit to macerate too long, and definitely not overnight, because it will become too soft and the color will fade.

2. Make the presentation template (Figure 10–28). The template as shown is the correct size for use in this recipe. Trace the drawing and then cut the template out of ¹/₁₆-inch (2-mm) cardboard. Tape the template to an appropriately sized bottomless pie tin (see page 1040). The pie pan is used to protect the rim of the plate when sifting cocoa powder on top, and it also serves as a handle, making it easier to remove the template from the plate. Sift powdered sugar over the base of as many plates as you need. Tape three toothpicks to the bottom of the template to elevate it just enough to prevent it from disturbing the powdered sugar design. One a time, place the pie pan on the dessert plates and sift cocoa powder over the top. Set the decorated plates aside.

3. Whip the heavy cream with the remaining Grand Marnier until stiff peaks form. Place the cream in a pastry bag with a no. 7 (14-mm) star tip. Reserve in the refrigerator. Cut eight rounds from each pan of Orange Custard, using a 3-inch (7.5-cm) plain, round cookie cutter. Reserve in the refrigerator.

4. Presentation: Place a piece of Orange Custard in the bottom of a goblet. Top with approximately ³/₄ cup (180 ml) of the strawberry mixture, including some of the liquid (see note 2). Set the goblet in the center of a prepared dessert plate. Pipe a rosette of whipped cream on top of the strawberries. Top the cream with a mint sprig. Place a Cookie Spoon to the right of the cocoa (shadow) spoon on the plate.

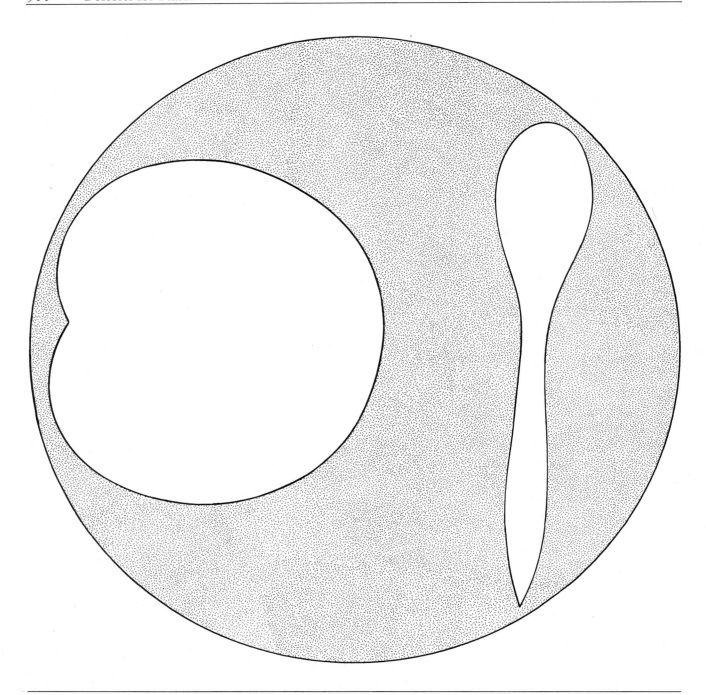

FIGURE 10–28   The template used for the Strawberries Romanoff presentation

 Orange Custard

two 10-inch (25-cm) pans

2 quarts (1 l, 920 ml) half-and-half

finely grated zest from two oranges

3½ cups (840 ml) whole eggs
(approximately fourteen)

1 pound (455 g) granulated sugar

1. Bring the half-and-half and the orange zest to the scalding point in a heavy saucepan.

2. Whisk the eggs and sugar together just to combine. Add the hot half-and-half mixture to the egg mixture while whisking constantly.

3. Divide the custard between two 10-inch (25-cm) cake pans. Place the pans on an even full-size sheet pan and place in a 350°F (175°C) oven. Add enough hot water to the sheet pan to come halfway up the sides of the sheet pans. Bake for approximately 40 minutes or until the custard is set. Let cool completely. Refrigerate until needed.

Strawberry Pyramids

16 servings

granulated sugar

one 14-by-24-inch (35-×-60-cm) Almond Sponge (page 270)

twenty-five to thirty medium-size strawberries

one-half recipe Kirsch Whipped Cream (page 360)

one recipe Strawberry Sauce (page 1081)

Sour Cream Mixture for Piping (page 1081)

sixteen fanned strawberry halves

sixteen mint sprigs

*T*his version of the popular Strawberry Kirsch Cake requires some advance planning since you will first need to make a triangular form before you can prepare the pyramids. If the garde-manger department (the pantry or cold kitchen) has a form that is approximately 3¹/₂ inches deep and 3¹/₂ inches across the top (8.7 × 8.7), and they are willing to part with it, you are in luck! If not, you can make one out of cardboard very quickly; directions follow. The form is similar to, but a little larger than, the one used to make the Chocolate Chalet. If the sponge sheet has been refrigerated overnight, you would be wise to place it in the oven for a minute or so to dry the top. The moist air in the refrigerator tends to make the sponge sticky, which can cause the skin to adhere to the form and possibly pull off when you remove the pastries.

1. Sprinkle granulated sugar lightly on top of the Almond Sponge. Pick the sponge up by the paper and invert on top of another piece of baking paper. Carefully peel the paper from the back of the sponge and trim it to 12 inches (30 cm) wide. Again, picking up the sponge by the paper, place it inside the triangular mold with the paper against the mold and one long edge even with one long edge of the form. Support the top one-third of the sponge that is outside of the form with a rolling pin or some cans (see Figure 10–16, page 462). If necessary, add a piece of sponge at the end to line the full 24 inches (60 cm) of the form.

2. Clean the strawberries and cut off both the stem ends and approximately ¹/₄ inch (6 mm) of the tips (save the tips for sauce). Line the strawberries up end-to-end on their sides next to the form to determine how many you need and to make the assembly go more quickly.

3. Pour the Kirsch Whipped Cream into the sponge-lined form to fill halfway. Quickly place the strawberries on the cream (end-to-end with the cut sides touching). Top with the remaining cream. You may have a small amount of the cream left over depending on the thickness of the sponge and the size of the strawberries: Do not overfill the form. Fold the supported sponge over the top and trim off any excess. Refrigerate for at least 2 hours.

4. Cut the ends loose from the mold, unmold the pyramid onto a cardboard or inverted sheet pan, and remove the paper. Slice into sixteen servings. Arrange the pastries standing up, seam-side down. Heat a metal skewer by holding it against an electric burner or in a gas flame. Quickly use the skewer to mark four horizontal lines on both sides of each pastry by caramelizing the sugar. Place a portion of the Strawberry Sauce in a piping bottle and reserve.

5. Presentation: Place a slice, off-center, in the upper half of a dessert plate (standing on end). Pipe a circle of Strawberry Sauce in front on the larger uncovered space. Decorate the sauce with the Sour Cream Mixture (see pages 998 to 1006). Place a fanned strawberry half and a mint sprig behind the dessert.

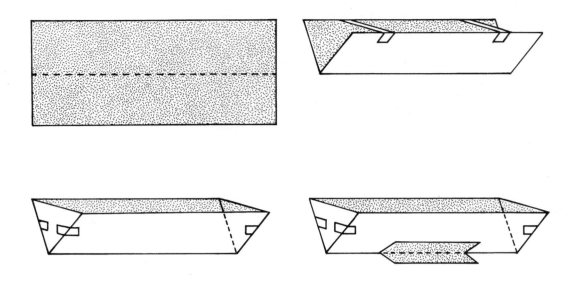

FIGURE 10–29   *Making a triangular cardboard form*

Making a Triangular Cardboard Form

1. See Figure 10–29. Cut a sturdy piece of cardboard 24 inches by 7 inches (60 × 17.5 cm). Score (cut halfway through the thickness of the cardboard) a line lengthwise down the center to make it easier to bend the cardboard. Turn the cardboard sheet upside down so that the cut is on the bottom, then bend the cardboard along the line and tape the top so that the opening is 3¹/₂ inches (8.7 cm) wide.

2. Cut out two triangles of cardboard 3¹/₂ inches (8.7 cm) on all sides. Tape the triangles to the ends of the form, then remove the tape on the top.

3. Cut out two pieces of cardboard 12 inches (30 cm) long and 4 inches (10 cm) wide. Score a cut in the center (lengthwise) on each piece; turn upside down and fold. Tape the folded pieces to the sides of the form for support.

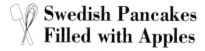 **Swedish Pancakes Filled with Apples**

12 servings

5 pounds (2 kg, 275 g) cooking apples (approximately twelve medium size)

6 ounces (170 g) unsalted butter

8 ounces (225 g) granulated sugar

¹/₂ cup (120 ml) Calvados

one recipe Small Swedish Pancakes Batter (page 498) (see note)

I'm not sure what my Mom would say if she could see what I have done to her pancake recipe! But since they are so flat on the plate ("flat as a pancake," as the saying goes) and rather uninteresting visually (even after folding), adding some height to the presentation could possibly be used to justify what I think she would consider a lot of unnecessary fuss.

Pancakes can be defined as flat round cakes of varying thickness that are cooked on both sides which implies, of course, that they must be turned. Any

1 cup (240 ml) heavy cream

1 teaspoon (5 g) granulated sugar

one-quarter recipe Raspberry Sauce
(page 1080)

one-half recipe Caramel Sauce II
(page 1071)

powdered sugar

twelve Tulip Leaves (page 1049)

twelve edible fresh flowers

*NOTE: Make the pancake batter using ¹/₂ cup
(120 ml) less milk than called for in the recipe.
This will make it possible to turn the larger
sized pancakes.*

*chef worth his or her title will accomplish this by flipping the pancakes in the air
and catching them in the pan on the way down—especially if someone is watching. Pancakes date back to the fifteen hundreds; countless variations, from
sweet to savory and from tiny and petit to big and thick, can be found served
with different toppings and fillings. Pancakes are offered as a main course for
breakfast, as an appetizer at lunch or dinner, and, obviously, for dessert. Each
country has its own speciality when it comes to this popular country fare: there
are small Swedish* plättar, *the French have their paper-thin* crepes, *you can
find Hungarian* palatschinken (palacsinta), *which are sort of a large-size
crepe, the Germans make a souffle or omelette pancake, the Russians are
famous for their* blini, *and let's not forget American hot cakes or flapjacks: a
thick breakfast pancake often enjoyed with maple syrup.*

1. Peel, core, and cut the apples in half. Cut each half into ¹/₄-inch
(6-mm) wedges.

2. Melt the butter in a skillet and stir in the first measurement of
sugar and the apple wedges. Cook over medium heat, stirring occasionally, until the apples are soft and the sugar is close to caramelizing
(just starting to turn light brown). As the apples cook, they will release
more juice than will be evaporated. Pour or spoon the liquid off as it
accumulates and discard or use as cake syrup. Deglaze the pan with the
Calvados. Set the apple mixture aside but keep very warm.

3. Once the pancake batter has rested, stir well and then make at
least thirty-six pancakes using a crepe pan. Make them just slightly
thicker than a standard crepe (see page 5).

4. Whip the heavy cream with the remaining sugar until stiff peaks
form. Place in a pastry bag with a no. 6 (12-mm) star tip. Reserve in the
refrigerator.

5. Presentation: Place a small amount of the warm apple filling on
the lower half of three pancakes. Fold the tops over the filling, then fold
in half again, making quarters. Using plastic piping bottles, pipe the
Raspberry and Caramel Sauces randomly in small dots and teardrops
on the base of a dessert plate. Brush a thick layer of Caramel Sauce on
top of the filled pancakes. Quickly place the pancakes in a hot skillet,
sauce-side down, to crisp and caramelize the tops. Place the filled pancakes on top of the sauce on the prepared plate, arranging them sauce-
side up, evenly spaced, with the points toward the center of the plate.
Sift powdered sugar lightly over the entire plate including the rim. Pipe
a large rosette of whipped cream in the center of the plate. Place a Tulip
Leaf standing upright in the cream then set an edible flower next to the
leaf. Serve immediately.

Swedish Profiteroles

16 servings; about 55 profiteroles

1¹/₂ ounces (40 g) granulated sugar

4 ounces (115 g) Short Dough (page 54)

one-half recipe Pâte à Choux (page 36)

one recipe Quick Bavarian Cream (page 1089)

Piping Chocolate (page 904), melted

3 tablespoons (45 ml) strained strawberry preserves, approximately

1 cup (240 ml) heavy cream

1 teaspoon (5 g) granulated sugar

one recipe Nougat Sauce (page 1077)

powdered sugar

sixteen Curly Cues (page 1055)

NOTE: The profiteroles can be frozen after they have been piped out and topped with the cookies. Bake straight from the freezer without thawing. I try to place them in the freezer long enough to harden even when they are to be baked right away because they seem to puff up better if baked frozen.

*T*he French word profiterole *derives from the word* profit *according to etymology (the study of the origin of words) and means a small profit or gain. One theory supposes that the name may stem from these pastries being "something extra" the chef or servant could make for themselves from leftover batter as they prepared the food for their employer. Profiteroles are simply miniature cream puffs, usually piped out using a plain tip in the pastry bag, filled with either a savory or a sweet mixture after baking. The former are used as hors d'oeuvres or appetizers, and the latter are most commonly filled with a Bavarian Cream and served with chocolate sauce. The most ambitious and famous dessert prepared with these diminutive pastries is the* croquembouche. *Here, the top and sides of each profiterole are dipped into caramel and the pieces are compiled into a large conical* pièce monté.

The following variation serves as a prime example of the old adage that one should never judge a book by its cover. Their appearance may be somewhat plain, but if you factor in the degree of difficulty, practicality, and popularity as you evaluate them, you will rank these right up there with the most elaborately decorated desserts. As the Swedish Profiteroles bake, the expanding Pâte à Choux forces the Short Dough cookie stuck on top to break into tiny pieces. The sweet crunchy cookie makes a perfect match to the Bavarian Cream inside (and actually, the unfilled puffs are pretty good au naturelle *too). Swedish Profiteroles are something I always keep on hand in the freezer for an emergency. They are a cinch to bake, cool, fill, and dust with powdered sugar, and then they're ready to serve.*

1. Mix the first measurement of granulated sugar into the Short Dough. Roll the dough to ¹/₁₆ inch (2 mm) thick and cut out about fifty-five circles using a 1¹/₂-inch (3.7-cm) plain or fluted cookie cutter. Set aside. Discard the scrap pieces.

2. Place the Pâte à Choux in a pastry bag with a no. 4 (8-mm) plain tip. Pipe out fifty-five mounds onto sheet pans lined with baking paper, making them the same diameter as the cookies. The profiteroles should be about the size of golf balls when baked. Immediately place a Short Dough circle on each mound and press lightly with your fingers to be sure they stick (see note).

3. Bake the profiteroles at 400°F (205°C) until puffed, about 10 minutes. Reduce the heat to 375°F (190°C), and bake until they will hold their shape, about 10 minutes longer. Let the puffs cool completely.

4. No longer than one hour before serving, make a small slit in the bottom of each puff just large enough to insert the pastry tip. Put the Bavarian Cream in a pastry bag with a no. 3 (6-mm) plain tip and pipe into the profiteroles. Reserve the profiteroles in the refrigerator.

5. Place the Piping Chocolate and the strained preserves into piping bags and cut small openings in the bags. Pipe three chocolate figurines on the base of as many dessert plates as you anticipate needing. Pipe the designs so that the figurines begin in the center of the plate and end next to the edge of the base, are evenly spaced, and provide enough room to place a profiterole between them (see photo in color insert). Fill the loops of the chocolate figurines with the strained preserves. Set the plates aside.

6. Whip the heavy cream and the remaining sugar to stiff peaks. Place in a pastry bag with a no. 7 (14-mm) star tip and reserve in the refrigerator. Place a portion of the Nougat Sauce in a piping bottle and reserve in the refrigerator with the remaining sauce.

7. Presentation: Pipe three small round pools of Nougat Sauce between the chocolate figurines on one of the prepared plates. Sift powdered sugar over three filled profiteroles and place one on each pool of sauce. Pipe a rosette of whipped cream in the center of the plate. Stand a Curly Cue upright in the cream. Serve immediately.

VARIATION
Marie Puffs

35 individual pastries

5 ounces (140 g) Short Dough
(page 54)
2 ounces (55 g) granulated sugar
one-half recipe Pâte à Choux
(page 36)
one and one-half recipes Quick
Bavarian Cream (page 1089)
powdered sugar

*T**he Swedish Profiteroles recipe evolved from a popular Swedish pastry known as Maria Bollar, or "Maria Balls," strictly translated. One of the many pastries made with Pâte à Choux, these are not as well known as éclairs, Cream Puffs, profiteroles, or Paris-Brest. The unusual-looking cracked surface on top makes people want to try them and then it's too late—they're hooked! As described in the preceding introduction, the soft filling coupled with the sweet crunchy topping makes an irresistible combination.*

Follow the Swedish Profiteroles recipe through step four with the following changes:

- Use a 2¹⁄₂-inch (6.2-cm) cookie cutter and cut out 35 cookies.
- Pipe out thirty-five mounds of Pâte à Choux, using a no. 6 (12-mm) plain tip in the pastry bag. The mounds should have the same diameter as the cookies.
- These will take a little longer to bake than the others.
- After completing step four, dust lightly with powdered sugar and refrigerate until needed.

Maria Puffs are best eaten as soon as possible after they are filled and should not be served the following day.

Tiramisu with Fresh Fruit

16 servings

two recipes Ladyfingers batter
    (page 275)
6 cups (1 l, 440 ml) strong coffee
    (use a good quality coffee brewed
    double strength)
Mascarpone Filling (recipe follows)
unsweetened cocoa powder
dark chocolate shavings
sixteen Marzipan Coffee Beans
    (page 1029)
1 pound (455 g) prepared fresh fruit,
    approximately (instructions follow)
1/4 cup (60 ml) orange liqueur
small mint sprigs

NOTE: If you are preparing the desserts with the intention of serving them the following day, reserve one-quarter of the Mascarpone Filling and leave the top cookies bare. Just before serving, pipe the reserved Mascarpone over the assembled desserts and decorate with cocoa powder as directed.

Tiramisu, *which literally means "pick me up," is also known as Mascarpone a la Venetian, in honor of the Italian city where it is a popular favorite. The dessert was invented only about twenty years ago at El Touga, a restaurant in Treviso. It has become a regular feature on many restaurant menus in the last few years. My interpretation, in which the servings are put together individually, is a little more time-consuming, but much more elegant than the conventional way of assembling and presenting this dessert. To convert the recipe to the traditional Tiramisu presentation, see the instructions following the recipe. The fabulous (and expensive) Mascarpone Cheese from Lombardo can be replaced with a combination of three parts soft cream cheese to one part sour cream by weight. Or, you can make the cheese yourself with the recipe on page 9.*

1. Place the Ladyfingers batter in a pastry bag with a no. 3 (6-mm) plain tip. Pipe out circles 2 1/2 inches (6.2 cm) in diameter on sheet pans lined with baking paper, making at least sixty-four (see Figure 12-2, page 592).

2. Bake the cookies at 400°F (205°C) for approximately 10 minutes or until they are golden brown. Set aside to cool.

3. If necessary, use a 2 1/2-inch (6.2-cm) plain cookie cutter to trim the baked cookies and make them uniform.

4. Dip sixteen of the cookies in the strong coffee, then place them on a sheet pan lined with baking paper. Test a couple first to be sure the coffee has soaked all the way through, then place the mascarpone mixture in a pastry bag with a no. 3 (6-mm) plain tip. Pipe a spiral of Mascarpone Filling on top of the dipped cookies using the same technique as before. Sift cocoa powder over the filling. Dip sixteen additional cookies in the coffee, placing them on top of the filling after you dip each one. Pipe Mascarpone Filling onto the cookies, then sift cocoa powder over the top. Repeat two more times making stacks with four coffee-dipped cookies each, separated by Mascarpone Filling topped with cocoa powder. Do not sift cocoa powder on the top (Mascarpone) layer. Refrigerate the desserts for a minimum of 30 minutes or, preferably, overnight to ensure that the coffee has fully penetrated the cookies (see note).

5. Make the template (Figure 10–30). The template as shown is the correct size for this recipe. Trace the drawing, then cut the template out of 1/16-inch (2-mm) thick cardboard. Cake boxes work well for this. Tape the template to a bottomless pie tin (see page 1040 for instructions).

6. Presentation: Place the template so the exposed portion is on the left side of the dessert plate. Sift cocoa powder over the template. Remove the template carefully. Sift cocoa powder over one of the assembled Tiramisu. Place shaved chocolate on top. Transfer the Tiramisu to the dessert plate placing it within the curve of the cocoa powder design. Place a Marzipan Coffee Bean in the center of the round part of the cocoa powder design. Arrange eight to ten pieces of

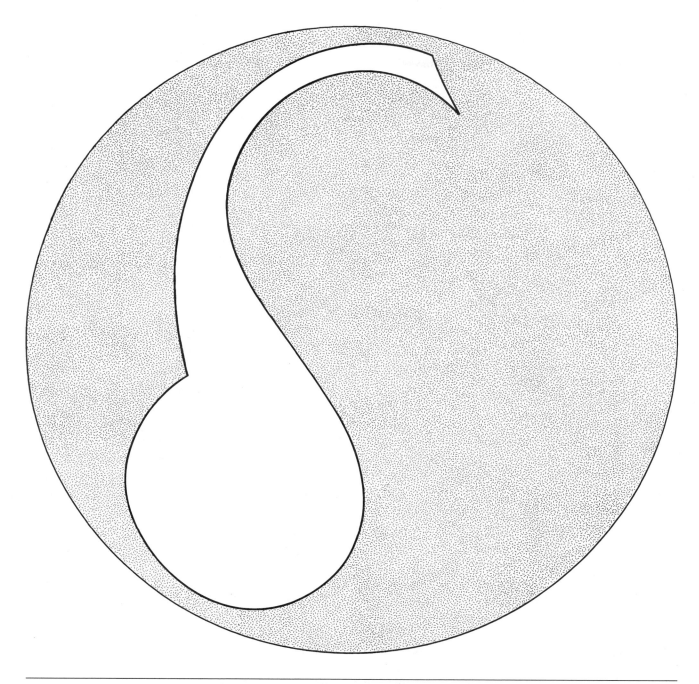

FIGURE 10–30   The template used for the presentation in Tiramisu with Fresh Fruit

fresh fruit on the bottom right side of the plate. Decorate with a few small mint sprigs. Serve immediately.

To prepare the fresh fruit

Although you are limited, of course, to whatever fresh fruit is in season in your area, try to use three or four different kinds for a nice color contrast. Cut the fruit into equal-sized pieces about the size of a raspberry, keeping each variety separate until serving time. Then combine the fruit gently and add the orange liqueur. Fold the liqueur in carefully so you do not bruise the fruit. If you are using a red fruit or any fruit that tends to "bleed," add it at the last moment and only to the amount you are serving right away.

Mascarpone Filling

2 quarts (1 l, 920 ml)

2 eggs
³/₄ cup (180 ml) or 9 ounces (255 g) light corn syrup
3 cups (720 ml) heavy cream
1 pound (455 g) Mascarpone Cheese (page 9), at room temperature

1. Whip the eggs at high speed until they begin to foam, about 30 seconds. Bring the corn syrup to boiling and gradually pour it into the eggs while whipping constantly. Continue whipping until the mixture has cooled completely.

2. Whip the heavy cream to stiff peaks and reserve.

3. Gradually stir the egg mixture into the soft Mascarpone Cheese. Stir in the whipped cream.

4. Refrigerate until needed; use within four days.

Traditional Tiramisu Presentation

16 servings

one and one-half recipes Ladyfingers batter (page 275)
3 cups (720 ml) strong coffee (such as espresso)
one recipe Mascarpone Filling (preceding recipe)
unsweetened cocoa powder

NOTE: Due to the thicker sponge layer in this version, and the fact that you cannot dip the sponge in the coffee, it is a good idea to brush the bottom of the sponge before placing it in the sheet pan, and to brush the bottom of the second sheet before placing it on the filling as well.

1. Spread the Ladyfingers batter out evenly over a full sheet pan lined with baking paper. Bake at 400°F (205°C) for about 30 minutes or until baked through and dry. Let the sheet cool.

2. Invert the baked sheet and remove the baking paper from the back. Cut in half to make two pieces, each 16 by 12 inches (40 × 30 cm). Turn the sheets right-side up and cut the tops even if necessary. Place one of the sheets on a half-sheet pan, trimming to fit as needed.

3. Brush strong coffee heavily over the sheet (see note). Spread half of the Mascarpone Filling on top. Sift cocoa powder over the filling. Top with the second sheet. Brush strong coffee generously on top. Spread the remaining Mascarpone Filling on top. Cover the cake and refrigerate for at least 3 hours or, preferably, overnight.

4. Sift cocoa powder over the sheet. Trim one long and one short side, using a sharp knife dipped in hot water. Starting from the trimmed sides, measure and cut sixteen equal pieces.

Trio of Cannolis

16 servings

2 cups (480 ml) warm white wine (110°F, 43°C)
2 tablespoons (30 g) granulated sugar
3 ounces (85 g) fresh compressed yeast
¹/₄ cup (60 ml) olive oil
1 teaspoon (2 g) ground anise seed
¹/₂ teaspoon (2.5 g) salt
1 pound, 8 ounces (680 g) bread flour
Egg Wash (page 7)

Most Italian grandmothers would probably scoff at this filling and my updated presentation of this traditional Italian cheese-filled pastry. But they would have to agree that it is refreshingly different. As long as the shells are cooked through and crisp, they can be prepared one day ahead and stored covered in a dry place. Any unfilled leftover shells also make great and unusual cookies. Instead of the Jasmine Rice Pudding try filling the Cannoli shells with Vanilla Bavarian Cream mixed with chopped candied fruit and chocolate. You will come very close to the original Cannoli filling.

1. Combine the wine and granulated sugar. Dissolve the yeast in the liquid. Add the oil, anise seed, and salt. Incorporate two-thirds of the flour and mix, using the dough hook, for 3 minutes. Add the remaining flour and continue mixing until the dough forms a smooth ball.

vegetable oil for deep frying

granulated sugar

1 cup (240 ml) heavy cream

1 teaspoon (5 ml) vanilla extract

one-half recipe Jasmine Rice Pudding
(page 777)

one recipe Cranberry Coulis
(page 1073)

2 ounces (55 g) pistachios, blanched,
skins removed, dried, and coarsely
chopped

2. Place the dough in a lightly oiled bowl and turn it to coat the entire dough with oil. Cover and let rise in a warm place until doubled in volume.

3. Punch the dough down and divide it into two equal pieces. Form the pieces into round loaves (see Figures 3–1 and 3–2, page 70). Cut an X in the top of each loaf, then leave the dough to relax for about 5 minutes. Pull the corners of the cut X out to form squares (see Figure 2–6 , page 45). Roll the pieces one at a time into rectangles the size of a full sheet pan (16 by 24 inches/40 × 60 cm) and ⅛ inch (3 mm) thick. Should the dough shrink too much as you work with it, roll each piece halfway, allow it to relax in the refrigerator for 30 minutes, then finish rolling. Refrigerate the rectangles for 30 minutes.

4. Trim one long and one short side of each sheet of dough. Cut each sheet into four 3½-inch (8.7-cm) strips lengthwise starting at the trimmed side. Cut across to make a total of at least sixteen 4-inch strips, sixteen 3-inch strips, and sixteen 2-inch strips (you should get about nine of each size from each piece of dough giving you a few extras) (Figure 10–31).

5. Wrap the dough sheets around Cannoli tubes. Brush Egg Wash on one edge and press the edges together to seal. Place the Cannoli in the refrigerator until you are ready to fry them.

6. Heat the vegetable oil to 375°F (190°C). Fry the Cannolis, a few at a time, until they start to brown. Remove the tubes from the oil with

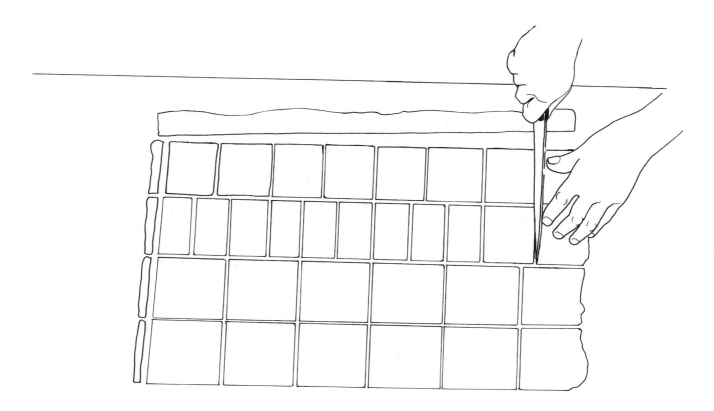

FIGURE 10–31   *Cutting half of the dough for Trio of Cannolis to get small, medium, and large rectangles for the different finished sizes*

a slotted spoon or by inserting a metal skewer into the tube. Pull the Cannoli shells off the metal tubes. Place the shells back in the oil and continue frying until the shells are golden brown and crisp. Remove from the oil with a slotted spoon and drain on paper towels. Gently roll the Cannoli shells in granulated sugar.

7. Use a serrated knife to trim one end of each Cannoli shell, as necessary, so that the tubes will stand straight on end. As you trim them, place one of each size in sixteen groups of three to facilitate serving.

8. Whip the heavy cream with the vanilla until it forms stiff peaks. Fold the cream into the Rice Pudding. Place the Rice Pudding mixture in a pastry bag with a no. 6 (12-mm) plain tip. Place the Cranberry Coulis in a piping bottle and reserve.

9. Presentation: Pipe the pudding into one group of Cannoli shells, filling them to the top. Sprinkle pistachio nuts over the top of the pudding. Pipe Cranberry Coulis in an uneven pool in the center of a dessert plate. Place the filled Cannolis, standing on end, in the center of the coulis. Sprinkle pistachio nuts lightly on the plate around the coulis. Serve immediately.

Trio of Chocolates with Marzipan Parfait

16 servings

Roux Batter (recipe follows)
2 tablespoons (30 ml) Chocolate Tulip Paste (page 1047)
Piping Chocolate (page 904), melted
one 10-inch (25-cm) Sponge Cake (page 268)
½ cup (120 ml) amaretto liqueur
Marzipan Parfait (recipe follows)
unsweetened cocoa powder
Ganache (page 1086) (or Piping Chocolate)
sixteen each Dark and White Chocolate Truffles (page 925)
thirty-two Light Chocolate Truffles (page 925)
sixteen edible fresh flowers

Your initial reaction will probably be that this pretty little box is too labor-intensive for a menu application, but this is not so. True, you must work carefully and deliberately when cutting and assembling the boxes. But, considering that you can assemble, fill, and reserve the boxes in the freezer—days ahead if well covered—and you can always purchase the Truffles instead of making them yourself, it is really not all that difficult to produce this dessert. The average guest does not know about any of these shortcuts, and this is one of those items that always makes the customer happy: They not only get an unusual and tasty dessert, they also feel that they got their money's worth. When wild strawberries are available, or if you can get cloudberries (you will probably have to settle for frozen since fresh cloudberries are very rare), fill the box with either Wild Strawberry Parfait or Gooseberry Ice Cream, omit the Truffles, and decorate with the respective berry.

1. Copy the templates in Figure 10–32. The templates as shown are the correct size to use in this recipe. Using the templates as guides, cut two long side pieces (A), two short side pieces (B), and two bottom pieces (C), out of corrugated cardboard. Set aside one bottom piece. Tape the remaining pieces together to make a rectangular form (see note).

2. Spread the Roux Batter (it must still be warm) evenly into a 16-inch (40-cm) square on a sheet of baking paper. Work quickly as you do this because the batter becomes difficult to work with as it cools. Place a portion of the Chocolate Tulip Paste in a piping bag and cut a small

NOTE: *Corrugated cardboard varies in thickness. Try to use the double-lined ¼-inch (6-mm) thick variety if possible. After taping the longer side pieces against the sides of the bottom piece (do not tape them on top of the bottom piece), adjust the shorter side pieces to fit according to the thickness of the cardboard used. The important thing is that the inside of the box measures 2 by 2¾ inches (2.5 × 6.8 cm).*

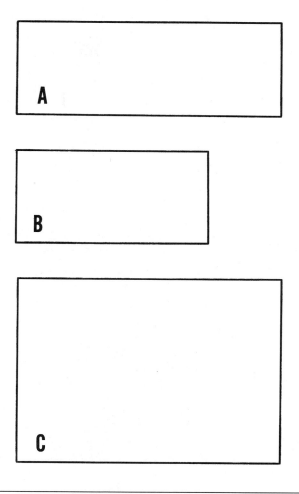

FIGURE 10–32   *The templates used to make the container in Trio of Chocolates with Marzipan Parfait*

opening. Pipe parallel lines every ½ inch (1.2 cm) across and then lengthwise covering the sheet.

3. Bake at 350°F (175°C) for approximately 12 minutes or until light brown. Let cool.

4. Invert the sheet and remove the baking paper. Turn right-side up. Using a serrated knife and the reserved bottom piece of the template, cut sixteen pieces to be used as lids. Cut the remaining sheet into 1-inch (2.5-cm) strips. Cut the strips into thirty-two long side pieces, 2¾ inches (6.8 cm), and then cut thirty-two short side pieces that will fit inside the boxes after the longer side pieces are in place. Before cutting all of the pieces it is a good idea to cut one set, place the pieces inside the form, and then adjust the templates if necessary before cutting the remainder.

5. Place the four side pieces for one box inside the cardboard form with the chocolate lines against the form. Weld the pieces together by piping chocolate along the seams. Place in the freezer for a few seconds to set the chocolate. Remove the set box frame and repeat the process to make the remaining boxes.

6. Cut the Sponge Cake ¹/₄ inch (6 mm) thick and into pieces that will fit snugly inside the frames. Brush the sponge pieces with amaretto liqueur and place inside the frames.

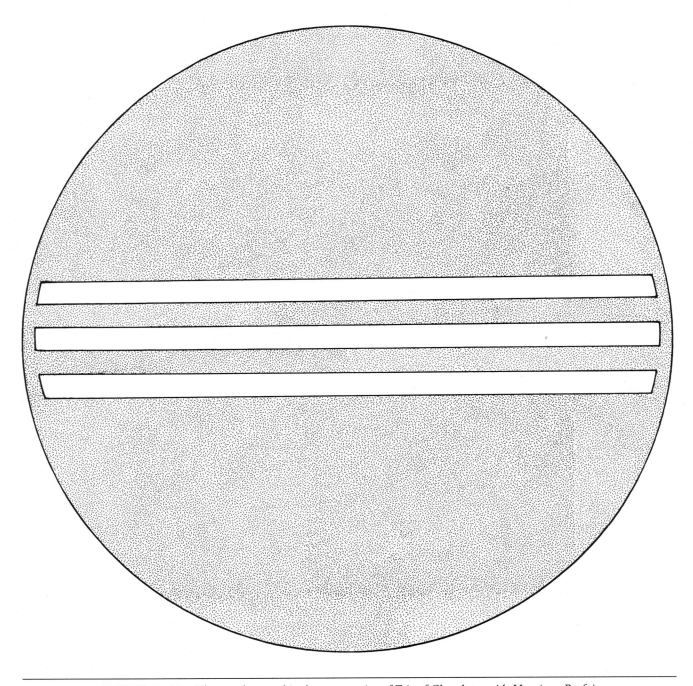

FIGURE 10–33   *The template used in the presentation of Trio of Chocolates with Marzipan Parfait*

7. Stir the Marzipan Parfait to make it smooth. Spoon the parfait into the boxes, filling them almost completely. Use a small spatula to smooth the tops. Reserve in the freezer.

8. Make the template shown in Figure 10–33. The template as shown is the correct size required for this recipe. Trace the drawing, then cut the template out of 1/16-inch (2-mm) thick cardboard (cake boxes work fine for this). Tape the template to the outside of a disposable pie tin with the bottom removed (see page 1040). Place the pie tin template on the base of a dessert plate. Sift cocoa powder on top. Remove the template carefully. Decorate as many plates as you expect to need in the same manner.

9. **Presentation:** Pipe a dot of Ganache or Piping Chocolate in the center of one of the decorated plates. Place a parfait-filled box on top, placing it at an angle perpendicular to the cocoa powder lines. Place one each of the three types of Truffles on top of the parfait in the box. Place one Milk Chocolate Truffle on the plate in front of the box, attached with a little Ganache or Piping Chocolate. Place the lid on top of the box, at an angle and slightly ajar. Decorate with an edible flower. Serve immediately.

 Roux Batter

3 cups (720 ml)

6 ounces (170 g) clarified unsalted butter
6 ounces (170 g) cake flour
1 pound (455 g) granulated sugar
3 ounces (85 g) bread flour
6 egg whites (3/4 cup/180 ml)

1. Melt the butter in a saucepan. Stir in the cake flour and cook over low heat, stirring constantly, for about 5 minutes. Do not allow the mixture to brown. Remove from the heat.

2. Stir in the sugar, bread flour, and egg whites. Use immediately.

 Marzipan Parfait

6 cups (1 l, 440 ml)

8 ounces (225 g) Marzipan (page 1022), untinted
2 tablespoons (30 ml) kirschwasser
3 ounces (85 g) granulated sugar
4 egg yolks (1/3 cup/80 ml)
2 1/2 cups (600 ml) heavy cream

1. Soften the Marzipan by mixing in the kirschwasser. Add the sugar and egg yolks and place over simmering water. Whip until the mixture is light and fluffy. Remove from the heat, then continue whipping until cool.

2. Whip the cream to soft peaks. Fold the cream into the Marzipan mixture.

3. Place in the freezer for at least two hours or, preferably, overnight.

Triple Treat

16 servings

1 cup (240 ml) heavy cream

unsweetened cocoa powder

Caramel Sauce II (page 1071)

sixteen Miniature Triple Chocolate Terrine (recipe follows)

sixteen Cookie Butterflies (page 1052)

sixteen Miniature Florentina Cones (recipe follows)

sixteen Miniature Tiramisu (recipe follows)

sixteen Chocolate Figurines (page 906)

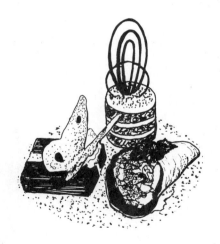

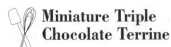

Miniature Triple Chocolate Terrine

two 12-by-2¼-inch (30-×-5.6-cm) terrines

one-third recipe Baked Chocolate Sheet batter (page 570) (see note 1)

2 tablespoons (16 g) bread flour

two-thirds recipe Triple Chocolate Terrine Filling (page 570)

*T*his is the last of six desserts I created especially for the graduation luncheons at the school during the course of working on this edition of this book. Because the junior class is responsible for the dessert preparation on these momentous occasions, they rightfully expect that when their turn comes, the dessert that is selected by their class will be presented in a way that gives full credit to their own special day. In this instance, the graduating seniors voted for a trio of desserts to be served to about 325 guests at their celebration. By making miniature versions of Tiramisu, Triple Chocolate Terrine, and Florentina Cones, there were three distinctive shapes on the plate with the very compatible flavors of coffee, chocolate, and nuts. Paired with Caramel Sauce, these desserts were a vision. This was also one of the easiest desserts to prepare and plate since most of the work could be completed the day before the event. The Chocolate Terrines were finished and left in the freezer, ready to be sliced. The Tiramisu was soaking in the refrigerator needing only to be cut and topped with Mascarpone cream. We then filled the Florentina Cones first thing in the morning, which allowed the cream to begin to soften the shell just a little (if you only fill the number of cones you will need within a few hours this dessert can actually be utilized over several days). Plating the three items with whipped cream rosettes, Cookie Butterflies, and Chocolate Figurines was done quickly and efficiently in an assembly-line fashion.

1. Whip the heavy cream to stiff peaks. Place in a pastry bag with a no. 6 (12-mm) star tip and reserve in the refrigerator.

2. Presentation: Sift cocoa powder very lightly over the base of a dessert plate; wipe off any from the rim of the plate. Place the Caramel Sauce in a piping bottle and pipe dime-sized dots of sauce, 1 inch (2.5 cm) apart, around the perimeter of the base of the plate. Place a slice of Miniature Triple Chocolate Terrine off-center on the plate. Pipe a rosette of whipped cream on one corner of the slice and a second rosette of cream on the plate a few inches away. Place a Cookie Butterfly on the rosette on the corner of the terrine. Place a Miniature Florentina Cone on the second rosette. Place a Miniature Tiramisu in the remaining open space on the plate. Top the Tiramisu with a Chocolate Figurine. The dessert can be set aside at this point for up to 30 minutes before serving under normal conditions.

1. This recipe will yield twice as much terrine as is needed for sixteen servings. However, since the procedure is rather time-consuming and the extra will keep well wrapped in the freezer for up to a month, it does not seem practical to make a smaller quantity. You will need two forms 2¼ inches wide by 2¼ inches tall by 12 inches long (5.6 × 5.6 × 30 cm). If you do not have forms this size you can spread the Chocolate Sheet batter into a different size rectangle to correspond to the forms you have, or you can make a form very easily from corrugated cardboard following the directions on page 830 (see note 2). Line the long sides of the forms with strips of acetate or baking paper. Reserve.

NOTE 1: Follow the instructions as given for making the Chocolate Sheet batter, adding the extra 2 tablespoons of bread flour sifted on top as you fold in the egg whites.

NOTE 2: To obtain the proper size when making the cardboard forms, start with two pieces of corrugated cardboard cut 12 inches long by 7 inches wide (30 × 17.5 cm). Score (cut halfway through) two lines lengthwise to divide the width into three sections: one 2¹/₄ inches (5.6 cm) wide in the center, with two sections, each 2³/₈ inches (5.9 cm) wide, on either side. Fold the outside sections up and continue as directed on pages 830 and 831.

2. Spread the Chocolate Sheet batter into a 10-by-12-inch (25-×-30-cm) rectangle on a sheet pan lined with baking paper. Bake at 375°F (190°C) for about 12 minutes or until the sponge feels firm on the top. Allow to cool completely.

3. Invert the sponge sheet and peel the baking paper from the back. Cut the sheet into four strips 12 inches long by 2¹/₄ inches wide (30 × 5.6 cm). Place one sponge strip in the bottom of each of the reserved forms.

4. Add the three chocolate filling layers on top of the sponge layers as directed in the main recipe for Triple Chocolate Terrine; however, because this miniature version does not have sponge layers between the filling layers, it is necessary to quickly place the terrines in the freezer to partially set each layer before adding the next, or the layers may run together. After adding the final layer (dark chocolate), place the two remaining sponge strips on top. Cover and place the terrines in the freezer.

5. When the terrines are firm, preferably the following day, remove one from the freezer leaving the other for another use. Remove the form and the baking paper or acetate strips. Place the terrine so that the layers run vertically. Using a thin chef's knife dipped in hot water, cut the terrine into sixteen ³/₄-inch (2-cm) slices (if you do not expect to need all sixteen servings the same day, cut only the number you need). Place the slices, cut-side down, on a sheet pan lined with baking paper. Reserve in the refrigerator until time of service.

Miniature Florentina Cones

16 pieces

---

2 ounces (55 g) toasted hazelnuts
sixteen Florentina Cones (page 390)
dark coating chocolate, melted
1¹/₂ cups (360 ml) heavy cream
one-third recipe Hazelnut Paste
    (page 9)
    or
commercial hazelnut paste to taste

1. Remove as much of the skin as possible from the hazelnuts. Crush the nuts coarsely and reserve.

2. Dip the top of as many cones as you expect to serve ¹/₄ inch (6 mm) into melted coating chocolate.

3. No more than 3 to 4 hours prior to service, whip the heavy cream to soft peaks. Add a small amount of the cream to the Hazelnut Paste and mix to soften the paste. Add back to the remaining cream. Place the crushed hazelnuts in a sifter and sift the small pieces into the cream mixture. Continue whipping the hazelnut cream until stiff peaks form. Place in a pastry bag with a no. 6 (12-mm) star tip. Pipe the cream into the Florentina Cones, filling them to the top. Sprinkle the crushed hazelnuts on the exposed cream at the ends. Reserve the cones in the refrigerator until time of service.

Miniature Tiramisu

16 pieces

---

one-half recipe Ladyfingers batter
    (page 275)
3 cups (720 ml) strong coffee,
    approximately
one-half recipe Mascarpone Filling
    (page 508)
unsweetened cocoa powder

1. Spread the Ladyfingers batter into a 16-by-14-inch (40-×-35-cm) rectangle on a sheet pan lined with baking paper. Bake at 400°F (205°C) for approximately 20 minutes or until baked through and light brown on top. Let cool.

2. Invert the sheet, peel the baking paper from the back, and then cut it lengthwise into three strips, each approximately 4¹/₂ inches (11.2 cm) wide. Brush one sheet generously with coffee. Top with one-third of the Mascarpone Filling. Sift cocoa powder over the filling. Generously brush a second Ladyfinger sheet with coffee, place coffee-side down on the cocoa powder, and brush coffee on the other side. Top with half of the remaining filling and sift additional cocoa powder on top. Brush the last sponge sheet with coffee and place coffee-side down on top. Brush coffee generously on the other side. Place the remaining filling in a pastry bag with a no. 2 (4-mm) plain tip and reserve in the refrigerator. Cover and place the assembled sheet in the refrigerator for at least 4 hours or, preferably, overnight.

3. Using a 2-inch (5-cm) plain round cookie cutter dipped in hot water, cut sixteen portions from the assembled sheet. Dip the cutter in water between each cut. Pipe a spiral of Mascarpone Filling over the top of each portion of Tiramisu. Sift cocoa powder over the Mascarpone Filling. Reserve in the refrigerator until time of service.

Tropical Surprise Packages

16 servings

Tamarind Parfait (recipe follows)
one recipe Vanilla Tulip Paste (page 1047)
1 teaspoon (2.5 g) unsweetened cocoa powder
sixteen medium-sized kiwifruit, ripe but firm
one-half recipe Mango Coulis (page 1075)
pomegranate seeds
powdered sugar

NOTE: If the wrappers are left in the oven too long, because you either overbaked them or baked them at too low a temperature, they will crumble and fall apart before you have had a chance to cover the parfait. The best method is to only bake two or three wrappers at a time so you can form them quickly while they are still warm. If properly baked, the wrappers may be returned to the oven to soften if they should cool off before you can form them.

Wrapping a frozen filling inside a hot cookie is not as far-fetched as it might appear if you follow the directions. However, it does take its toll on your fingers, especially if you are not (as I strongly recommend) using silicone mats, because with sheet pans you have the addition of the hot fat as well as the hot cookie. I got the idea for this rather daring and unusual combination from the presentation of a dessert served in a well-known restaurant not far from London. There, it was prepared with a lemon mousse filling and served with strawberry sauce. When I had my version on the menu a few years ago, a server came to me and said that one of his guests, a Londoner in San Francisco for a holiday, "would die" for the recipe! Although, as is true of most chefs, I am not in the habit of giving out recipes to the guests, I did not have the heart to say no since he had come so far (for something so near, had he only known)!

The content of the package is easy to vary, the only requirement is to keep the size the same so it will fit the wrapper. For a chocolate version make one-half recipe of Chocolate Ganache Filling (see page 319). For a lighter option use one and one-third recipes of Lemon Chiffon Filling (see page 701). Change the sauce in the presentation to suit the filling used and, of course, change the name of the dessert accordingly.

1. Make a 9-inch (22.5-cm) square frame from cardboard cut into 1¹⁄₂-inch (3.7-cm) wide strips. Tape the strips together at the corners. Place the frame on a sheet pan or a sheet of cardboard, and line the bottom and sides with plastic wrap.

2. Pour the Tamarind Parfait into the frame and place it in the freezer to harden.

3. Make the template (Figure 10–34) from ¹⁄₁₆-inch (2-mm) thick cardboard (cake boxes are ideal for this). The template as shown is the correct size for use in this recipe. However, due to the size of this template it is possible to show only half of it on the page. Trace the template as shown, then turn your paper over, match the dotted lines in the

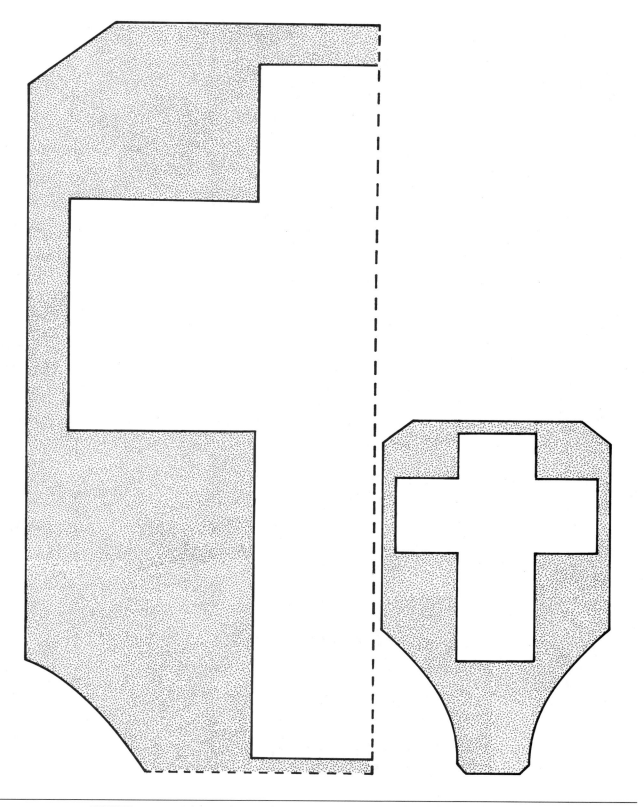

FIGURE 10–34   The template used to make the wrappers for Tropical Surprise Packages

center, and trace the other half to make the shape shown in the illustration. If you do not have silicone mats, lightly grease and flour the back of even sheet pans. Reserve.

4. Color 2 tablespoons (30 ml) of the Tulip Paste with the cocoa powder. Set aside.

5. Spread the remaining paste on silicone mats, or on the reserved sheet pans, using the template as a guide, spreading the paste thin, flat, and even within the template (see Figures 19–55 and 19–56, pages 1046 and 1047). Do not spread more than three per sheet pan. Place the cocoa-colored paste in a piping bag. Pipe a design (which will look like ribbons tying the package closed) on each one by first piping lines in the center, the full length of the cross in both directions, then piping a bow where the lines meet. Reserve in the refrigerator. You can prepare the "wrappers" up to this point several hours ahead of time if desired.

6. Once the Tamarind Parfait has frozen firm, cut it into 2¹/₄-inch (5.6-cm) squares, using a knife dipped in hot water. Place the squares back in the freezer and remove them individually as you are ready to wrap the packages.

7. Bake one pan of prepared Tulip Paste at a time at 400°F (205°C) until the wrappers start to turn golden brown at the edges, approximately 5 minutes. Do not overbake (see note). Remove from the oven and quickly turn them, individually, upside down onto the table. Place a reserved parfait square in the center of a cookie. Quickly wrap the three short sides around the square, then fold the long side on top of these. Place the wrapped packages back in the freezer and continue to assemble the remainder in the same way. If necessary, the wrapped packages will stay crisp in the freezer for a few days if kept well covered.

8. Peel one kiwifruit for each dessert you anticipate serving, using a spoon to retain the natural shape of the fruit (see page 251). Place the peeled kiwis on their sides, cut off the narrow ends, and then cut each fruit into thin round slices; you should get seven to eight slices from each one. Keep the slices and end pieces from each fruit together, cover, and reserve. Place the Mango Coulis into a piping bottle and reserve.

9. Presentation: Arrange a ring of slightly overlapping kiwi slices (from one fruit) in the center of a dessert plate. Place the end pieces in the center of the ring and flatten them slightly so they are level (be sure to remove the small hard portion from the stem end first if present). Place a Tropical Surprise Package on top of the kiwi end pieces, centered on the ring of kiwi slices. Pipe large teardrops of Mango Coulis on the base of the plate around the kiwi slices. Place a pomegranate seed on each teardrop of sauce. Sift powdered sugar lightly over the seeds. Serve immediately.

Tamarind Parfait

5 1/2 cups (1 l, 320 ml)

10 ounces (285 g) tamarind pods
　or
5 ounces (140 g) tamarind paste (see note)
1¼ cups (300 ml) hot water
8 egg yolks (²/₃ cup/160 ml)
2 ounces (55 g) granulated sugar
¼ cup (60 ml) or 3 ounces (85 g) honey
1½ cups (360 ml) heavy cream

NOTE: If you use the more convenient tamarind paste, which saves you the tedious labor of peeling the tamarind pods, follow the recipe and directions as given but reduce the sugar by about half as the paste is usually prepared with sugar. The amount varies by brand.

1. Peel the tamarind pods and remove the seeds and the stringy membranes from the flesh. Cut the flesh into chunks and place in a bowl. Cover with the hot water and leave to soak for a few hours or, if possible, overnight.

2. Transfer the mixture to a saucepan and cook over low heat until it reaches a fairly thick consistency, approximately 10 minutes. Press as much as possible through a fine sieve and set it aside to cool. Discard the contents of the sieve.

3. Whip the egg yolks and sugar until light and fluffy. Bring the honey to a boil in a heavy saucepan. Lower the mixer speed and gradually pour the hot honey into the yolk mixture. Whip at medium speed until cold.

4. Whip the heavy cream to soft peaks. Add the cooled tamarind purée to the yolk mixture. Gradually fold this combination into the whipped cream.

Valentine's Day Hearts

16 servings

one-half recipe Baked Chocolate Sheet batter (page 570) (see step 1)
1 ounce (30 g) bread flour
Red Currant Bavarian Cream (recipe follows)
Piping Chocolate (page 904), melted
8 ounces (225 g) Marzipan (page 1022), tinted red
powdered sugar
Red Currant Coulis (page 1080)
fresh red currants
Sour Cream Mixture for Piping (page 1081)

*A*s Valentine's Day draws close, one may imagine Cupid flying about aiming his arrow at unsuspecting suitors, red roses, heart-shaped boxes filled with chocolate candies and, of course, the all-important Valentine card. Most people are completely unaware of how this holiday, which is celebrated on February 14 in so many countries of the world, came to be. There are several different stories to consider. The first is a fable of a priest named Valentine who was imprisoned by the Roman Emperor Claudius II. The priest had disobeyed the emperor's order which forbade young men to marry (the theory being that unmarried men made better warriors) and had secretly performed many wedding ceremonies. While he was in jail he blessed and restored sight to the jail keeper's blind daughter (with whom he had also fallen in love), and in the wake of all of this, scores of people were supposedly converted to the Christian faith. Enraged, Claudius II ordered him executed on the sixteenth day before March—February 14, A.D. 269. As the story goes, the priest sent a letter to his new love just before he was beheaded and signed it "your Valentine."

Another story associates the holiday with the Feast of St. Valentine of Terni, an old and established celebration of choosing a mate that apparently came about based on a belief that birds choose their mates in the spring, specifically on February 14. There is much controversy surrounding this theory: Many argue that while not really springtime in most of the world, February 14 represents a feeling of spring in one's heart, inspired by the romancing birds. Others

NOTE: *If you do not have a pan this size, you can make a frame from corrugated cardboard or you can "shorten" a half-sheet pan in the following manner. Cut a strip of corrugated cardboard 12 inches long by 2 inches wide (30 × 5 cm). Cut halfway through (score) the cardboard lengthwise down the center. Bend the strip along the cut at a 90° angle. Place this piece against one short end of the half-sheet pan. Line the pan with a sheet of lightly oiled baking paper, placing the end of the paper against the cardboard brace.*

say that February 14 differs little or not at all from winter, and it is simply too early and too cold for either man or bird to develop spring fever.

Even if we can't agree on a connection between the mating of birds and St. Valentine's Day, most people do enjoy the mythological idea of a mischievous, naked, winged boy named Cupid, the Greek Eros, son of Venus. The legend of Cupid says that anyone shot with Cupid's arrow would fall in love with the next person they saw.

The current practice of sending Valentine's Day cards to friends and loved ones is also attributed to the Duke of Orleans who, when imprisoned in the Tower of London, is said to have sent his wife letters filled with love poems. This custom had become commercially popular by the seventeenth century in Europe and was brought to the United States by European immigrants. Whatever the true origin, and there may be more than one, this is a big holiday for our business with all of the emphasis on dining out and giving heart-shaped candies, pastries, and cakes as gifts.

1. Prepare the batter for the Baked Chocolate Sheet, adding the bread flour to the whipped egg yolk and sugar mixture. Spread the batter out into a 12-by-15-inch (30-×-37.5-cm) rectangle on a sheet of baking paper. Bake as directed in the recipe and set aside to cool.

2. Line an adjustable frame, or a cake pan, measuring 12 by 15 inches (30 × 37.5 cm) with baking paper (see note). Pour the Red Currant Bavarian Cream into the frame and spread it out evenly. Invert the chocolate sheet on top of the bavarian, leaving the baking paper attached on the back. Cover and refrigerate for at least 2 hours or, preferably, overnight.

3. Place some Piping Chocolate in a piping bag and cut a small opening. Using Figure 10–35 as a guide, pipe out figurines to use in decorating (see pages 906 to 909 for more instruction). Make a few more than you will need to allow for breakage. Reserve.

4. Remove the baking paper from the back of the Baked Chocolate Sheet. Run a knife around the edge of the pan to loosen the bavarian. Place a sheet of baking paper and a cardboard sheet (or an even sheet pan) on top and invert. Remove the pan or frame from around the bavarian. Peel the baking paper from the bavarian. Using a heart-shaped cookie cutter measuring 3½ inches (8.7 cm) across, cut out sixteen hearts (or as many as you expect to serve) from the bavarian sheet and place them, cake-side down, on a sheet pan lined with baking paper. Dip the cutter in hot water as you work.

5. Roll out the red Marzipan to ⅛ inch (3 mm) thick, using powdered sugar to prevent it from sticking. Mark the top of the Marzipan with a waffle or ridge roller. Cut out the same number of Marzipan hearts, using the same cutter used to cut the bavarian hearts. It is necessary to knead the scraps together and roll out again to get sixteen. Mask one side (lengthwise) of a Marzipan heart. Sift powdered sugar over the exposed side. Place the Marzipan heart on top of one of the bavarian hearts. Repeat with the remaining hearts. Reserve in the refrigerator for no longer than 4 hours.

FIGURE 10–35   The template used as a guide in piping the chocolate figurines to decorate Valentine's Day Hearts

6. Make the template shown in Figure 10–36. The template as shown is the correct size for use in this recipe. Trace the drawing and then cut the template out of ¹/₁₆-inch (2-mm) thick cardboard (cake boxes work very well for this). Place the template off-center, to the right, on a dessert plate, with the more tapered end closest to you. Put Piping Chocolate in a piping bag and, using the template as a guide, pipe the shape on the same number of dessert plates as you have finished desserts. Place the figurines prepared in step three in the refrigerator. Place a portion of the Red Currant Coulis in a piping bottle.

7. Presentation: Place a bavarian heart on the left side of a plate so that the right side of the heart fits just inside the top left side of the chocolate piping. Fill the inside of the piped design with Red Currant Coulis. Place a row of fresh currants along the left straight side of the heart. Place the Sour Cream Mixture in a piping bag. Pipe small dots on top of the coulis along the right side of the heart. Run the tip of a wooden skewer through the dots to create hearts (see Figure 19–25, page 1002). Using the tip of a paring knife, make two small horizontal cuts in the round part of the heart, spacing them the width of the base of the figurines. Pipe a drop of Piping Chocolate in the cuts. Quickly and carefully place one of the chilled figurines in the cuts. Tilt it back slightly and hold for a few seconds until the chocolate is set (this happens quickly since the figurine has been chilled). Serve immediately.

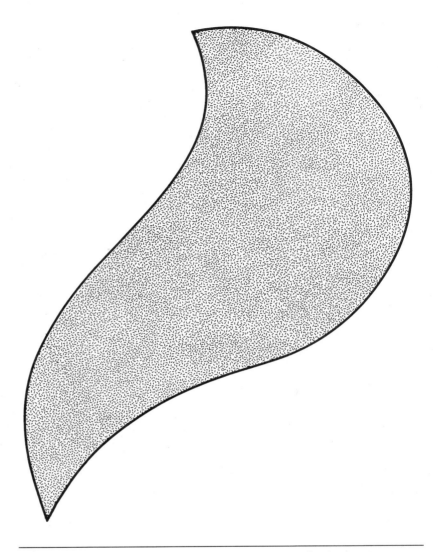

FIGURE 10–36   *The template used in the presentation of Valentine's Day Hearts*

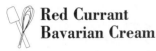 **Red Currant Bavarian Cream**

2¹/₂ quarts (2 l, 400 ml)

1 pound, 6 ounces (625 g) fresh or frozen red currants (see note)

2¹/₄ cups (540 ml) dry champagne

2 cups (480 ml) heavy cream

3 tablespoons plus 1 teaspoon (30 g) unflavored gelatin powder

6 egg yolks (¹/₂ cup/120 ml)

2 ounces (55 g) granulated sugar

one-quarter recipe Swiss Meringue (page 592)

*D*o not make this filling until you are ready to use it.

1. Place the red currants and 1¹/₂ cups (360 ml) of the champagne in a saucepan. Heat to scalding; do not boil. Purée and strain through a *chinois.* Discard the solids in the strainer. Set the liquid aside to cool.

2. Whip the heavy cream to soft peaks. Reserve in the refrigerator.

3. Sprinkle the gelatin over ¹/₂ cup (120 ml) of the remaining champagne. Set aside to soften.

4. Whip the egg yolks and the granulated sugar to combine. Add the remaining ¹/₄ cup (60 ml) of champagne. Heat the mixture over simmering water, whipping constantly, until it reaches 140°F (60°C) and has thickened. Remove from the heat and continue whipping until cold. Stir in the reserved red currant purée, the Swiss Meringue, and the whipped cream.

NOTE: *If you use fresh currants in this recipe, remove the stems before weighing the berries. If you use frozen berries they should be the I.Q.F. type (without sugar). Do not use sweetened red currants in this recipe.*

5. Heat the gelatin mixture to dissolve. Temper by adding the gelatin to about one-fourth of the currant mixture and then quickly incorporate this into the remainder. Use immediately.

White Chocolate Citrus Roulade

16 servings

granulated sugar
Citrus-Almond Sponge
 (recipe follows)
White Chocolate Bavarian Cream
 (recipe follows)
one recipe Raspberry Sauce
 (page 1080)
Sour Cream Mixture for Piping
 (page 1081)
eighty small pink grapefruit segments
 (see note 1)

NOTE 1: *You will need about five medium-size grapefruits. Cut large segments into two or three slices if they are too thick.*

NOTE 2: *The granulated sugar is used to prevent the skin on the sponge from sticking to the paper. The sugar also adds a nice color as it caramelizes when the roulades are decorated with the hot skewer.*

NOTE 3: *For a different presentation, slice the cut roulades in step four on the bias and arrange the pieces on top of the sauce leaning against each other as in Red Banana Truffles in Phyllo Dough (page 488). If you are making quite a few of these, or just want them all to look the same in the presentation, cut a 6-inch (15-cm) circle out of cardboard and attach a looped piece of tape in the center that will act as a handle and allow you to lift the template straight up. Place a small amount of strained strawberry jam (you will need about 5 ounces/140 g total) in a piping bag. Place the template in the center of a dessert plate (you must use a plate large enough so that the tem-*

This would make a light and refreshing dessert to prepare for a summer luncheon. All of the preparation steps can be completed ahead of time, making the presentation quick and easy. Fill and roll the sponge sheets as soon as possible after they are baked, certainly the same day. If they are made ahead and refrigerated before filling, the skin becomes moist and parts of it will come off as you fill and roll the sheets, making the roulade very unattractive, if not unusable. To prevent this, place the sheets in the oven for a minute or so to dry the skin, but don't overdo it.

1. Sprinkle a little granulated sugar over two sheets of baking paper (see note 2). Invert the sponge sheets on top. Peel the baking paper off the back of the sponges. Do this by tearing the top long side of the paper, then, using both hands, pull down and toward the short ends at the same time (Figure 10–37). This will prevent the thin sponge sheets from breaking as you remove the paper. An alternate method is to hold a dowel against the paper and sponge with one hand as you pull the paper away with your other hand; move both hands together in an

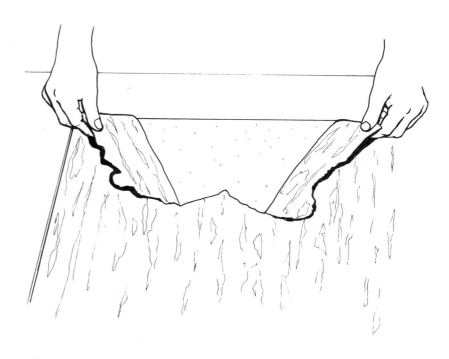

FIGURE 10–37 *Using both hands to remove the baking paper from a thin sponge sheet by starting in the center and working toward each end to prevent tearing the sponge*

plate lies flat). Sift powdered sugar over the exposed part of the plate including the rim. Remove the template carefully by pulling it straight up, using the tape handle. Pipe a thin string of jam on the plate next to the powdered sugar, following the outside edge of the template. Fill the inside of the jam pattern with the Raspberry Sauce.

even speed, working from one end of the sponge to the other (Figure 10–38). The dowel prevents the sponge from pulling up with the paper and tearing. Trim the long edges if necessary and cut the sheets in half lengthwise to make four narrow pieces.

2. Divide the Bavarian Cream filling equally between the sponge sheets and spread it out evenly. The filling should be just starting to thicken when you use it. Place the sheets in the refrigerator until the filling feels firm but still sticky, 5 to 10 minutes.

3. Roll each sheet into a roulade: start by folding the top edge into the filling, then pick up the paper underneath and use it to guide the sponge sheet as you roll it toward you (see Figure 12-3, page 595). Place the roulades seam-side down on a sheet pan lined with baking paper and refrigerate for one to two hours.

4. Trim the ends of the roulades. Cut each roulade into four slices, approximately 4 inches (10 cm) long. Use a hot metal skewer to "brand" each serving, marking four parallel lines at an angle on the top of each pastry. Fill a piping bottle with a portion of the Raspberry Sauce and reserve.

5. Presentation: Pipe a large, approximately 6-inch (15-cm) circle of Raspberry Sauce in the center of a dessert plate (see note 3). Place a roulade serving in the center of the sauce. Pipe small dots of Sour Cream Mixture 1 inch (2.5 cm) apart, all around the perimeter of the sauce. Drag a wooden skewer through the dots, in one motion without lifting the skewer, to make a string of hearts (see Figure 19–22, page 1000). Place five thin grapefruit segments on the plate between the sauce and the edge of the plate. Serve immediately.

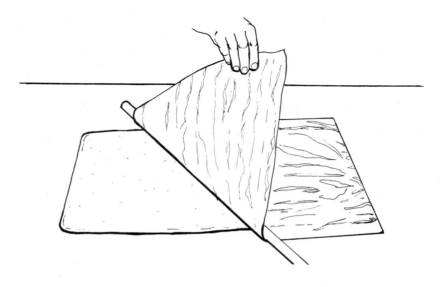

FIGURE 10–38   *A second method of removing the baking paper: holding a dowel against the baking paper and sponge to prevent the sponge from pulling up with the baking paper and tearing as the paper is pulled away with the other hand*

Citrus-Almond Sponge

*two 15-by-18-inch
(37.5-×-45-cm) sheets*

2 egg whites (¹/₄ cup/60 ml)
8 ounces (225 g) Almond Paste
  (page 3)
8 eggs, separated
8 ounces (225 g) granulated sugar
1 teaspoon (5 ml) vanilla extract
finely grated rind from two lemons
  (see note)
5 ounces (140 g) cake flour

*NOTE: After grating the rind, juice the lemons
for the White Chocolate Bavarian Cream.*

1. Gradually mix the 2 egg whites into the Almond Paste to soften it.

2. Whip the egg yolks with 2 ounces (55 g) of the sugar to the ribbon stage. Add the vanilla. Very gradually blend the yolk mixture into the Almond Paste. Do not try to do this too fast or the mixture will become lumpy.

3. Whip the 8 egg whites until foamy. Gradually add the remaining 6 ounces (170 g) of sugar and continue whipping until stiff peaks form.

4. Sift the cake flour. Carefully fold the reserved egg yolk mixture into the whipped egg whites together with the lemon rind. Fold in the flour. Divide the batter between two sheets of baking paper and spread it out evenly into 15-by-18-inch (37.5-×-45-cm) sheets; they should be about ¹/₄ inch (6 mm) thick. Drag the papers onto sheet pans (see Figure 16-15, page 842).

5. Bake immediately at 425°F (219°C) for approximately 8 minutes or until just baked through.

White Chocolate Bavarian Cream

6 cups (1 l, 440 ml)

1¹/₂ cups (360 ml) heavy cream
4 teaspoons (12 g) unflavored gelatin
  powder
¹/₃ cup (80 ml) cold water
5 ounces (140 g) granulated sugar
6 egg whites (³/₄ cup/180 ml)
grated rind of one lemon
grated rind of two oranges
¹/₂ cup (120 ml) lemon juice (see note
  from previous recipe)
5 ounces (140 g) white chocolate,
  melted

*D*o not make this filling until you are ready to use it.

1. Whip the cream to soft peaks. Reserve in the refrigerator.

2. Sprinkle the gelatin over the cold water and set aside to soften.

3. Combine the sugar and egg whites in a mixer bowl. Heat over simmering water, stirring constantly to prevent the egg whites from cooking, until the mixture reaches 140°F (60°C). Remove from the heat while continuing to stir. Whip at high speed until the mixture is cold and has formed soft peaks. Reserve the meringue.

4. Add both grated citrus rinds and the lemon juice to the softened gelatin. Place the mixture over a bain-marie and heat until the gelatin is dissolved. Do not overheat. Quickly stir in the white chocolate.

5. Combine the reserved whipped cream with the meringue. Gradually, to avoid lumps, add the white chocolate mixture.

Wild Strawberries Romanoff in Caramel Boxes

16 servings

one-third recipe Chiffon Sponge Cake batter (page 272)

or

one-quarter recipe Sponge Cake batter (page 268)

dark coating chocolate, melted

sixteen Caramel Boxes and Squares (page 444)

1/2 cup (120 ml) curaçao liqueur

1/4 cup (60 ml) Plain Cake Syrup (page 10)

3 cups (720 ml) heavy cream

1 tablespoon (15 g) granulated sugar

1 teaspoon (5 ml) vanilla extract

one-quarter recipe Strawberry Sauce (page 1081)

1 pound, 8 ounces (680 g) wild strawberries (red or a mixture of red and white), stems and hulls removed

sixteen Caramel Corkscrews (page 960)

sixteen mint sprigs

This contemporary adaptation of the classic Strawberries Romanoff is served in an elegant Caramel Box garnished with golden sugar corkscrews. This presentation was served recently at a graduation celebration that included over 300 friends, family members, and faculty. The desserts were produced by the junior pastry class with only one month of experience in hands-on production. The point I am trying to make here is that while the large number of steps (when you include making the boxes) and the elegant presentation may suggest this is a time-consuming and/or difficult dessert, it is not. We replaced the wild strawberries with a mixture of fresh raspberries and blueberries, which made the plates, with the whipped cream on top, look very patriotic and colorful. For another version of Strawberries Romanoff see page 499.

1. Bake the cake batter in a greased and floured 9-inch (22.5-cm) cake pan. Let the sponge cool.

2. Place a small amount of melted coating chocolate in a piping bag. Cut a very small opening and pipe two parallel lines about 3/4 inch (2 cm) apart across the center of a dessert plate. Turn the plate 90° and repeat. Decorate sixteen plates (or as many as you plan to serve) and set them aside to cool and harden.

3. Dip the top edge of the same number of Caramel Boxes 1/4 inch (6 mm) into the chocolate. Set aside to harden.

4. Combine the curaçao liqueur and the Cake Syrup. Brush the syrup mixture generously over both sides of the sponge. Cut the sponge into 1 3/4-inch (4.5-cm) squares. Cover and reserve.

5. Whip the heavy cream with the granulated sugar and vanilla until stiff peaks form. Place in a pastry bag with a no. 5 (10-mm) star tip. Reserve in the refrigerator until time of service. Place the Strawberry Sauce in a piping bottle and reserve.

6. Presentation: Place a square of sponge cake in the bottom of a Caramel Box (insert the tip of a paring knife into the top of the sponge square and guide it into the box). Pipe a 1/2-inch (1.2-cm) layer of whipped cream on top of the sponge. Fill the box with wild strawberries. Pipe a dot of whipped cream slightly off-center on one of the decorated plates just behind the spot where the chocolate lines intersect. Pipe a rosette of cream on top of the berries in the box. Pipe a second rosette of cream on the plate, to the right side, between two of the parallel lines, and near the edge. Gently push a Caramel Corkscrew into the rosette (use the tip of a paring knife to push the bottom of the decoration into the cream). Place a mint sprig next to the corkscrew and arrange a few berries around the rosette. Place the box on the dot of whipped cream near the center of the plate. Stand a Caramel Square up in the rosette on the plate. Pipe Strawberry Sauce around the plate in small teardrop shapes. Serve immediately.

Wine Foam and Blackberry Bavarian Greystone

16 servings

one Ribbon Sponge Sheet (page 276)

1¼ cups (300 ml) Riesling wine

8 ounces (225 g) blackberries

5 teaspoons (15 g) unflavored gelatin powder

4 egg yolks (⅓ cup/80 ml)

¾ cup (180 ml) heavy cream, whipped

one-quarter recipe Swiss Meringue (page 592)

4 ounces (115 g) Short Dough (page 54)

1 teaspoon (2.5 g) unsweetened cocoa powder

one-third recipe Vanilla Tulip Paste (page 1047)

1 pound, 12 ounces (795 g) Cape gooseberries (see note 2)

honeydew melon cut into 200 tiny melon balls

Simple Syrup (page 11)

Marzipan (page 1022), tinted brown

Raspberry Sauce (page 1080)

NOTE 1: Draw a grape leaf about 5½ inches (13.7 cm) in diameter on 1/16-inch (2-mm) thick cardboard. Draw a frame and handle around it and then cut out the template.

NOTE 2: Select the sixteen best-looking gooseberries. Cut between the ridges of the husks with pointed scissors and open them up to reveal the berries. Reserve these for the presentation. To make the sauce, remove the husks from the remainder, add ⅓ cup (80 ml) Simple Syrup (page 11), purée, strain, and discard the solids. Add the seeds of one vanilla bean, thicken with cornstarch, and let cool. Place in a piping bottle.

NOTE 3: Instead of cake rings, you can use strips of polyurethane or acetate formed into rings or, even better, pieces of PVC pipe cut to size. These can be used again for any recipe that does not require baking.

This was one of the sweets offered at the grand opening of Greystone, the Culinary Institute of America's Napa Valley campus. The theme was "a harvest of the valley," so this seemed like a natural, with the melon, blackberries, and cape gooseberries grown right there. I got the idea for the presentation from CIA's Hyde Park Master Pastry Chef Joe McKenna. To make my template for the cookie grape leaf, I simply walked over to the school's vineyard across the street and selected a leaf to use as a guide (see note 1).

1. Cut 1-inch- (2.5-cm-) wide strips, crosswise, from the Ribbon Sponge Sheet, making them long enough to line the inside of cake rings 2 inches in diameter by 2 inches high (5 × 5 cm) (see note 3). Place the sponge strips with the striped side against the rings and set the rings on a sheet pan. Use a 1½-inch (3.7-cm) plain cookie cutter to cut out rounds from the scraps; place these in the bottom of the rings. Freeze the remaining sponge for another use.

2. Add ¼ cup (60 ml) of the wine to the blackberries. Purée, strain through a fine mesh strainer, and reserve. Sprinkle the gelatin over half of the remaining wine. Set aside to soften.

3. Add the remainder of the wine to the egg yolks. Place over a bain-marie and whip to a sabayon-like consistency. Remove from the heat and continue whipping until cold. Combine the whipped cream with the cold meringue. Fold in the sabayon and the blackberry juice mixture. Heat the softened gelatin to dissolve. Quickly stir this into about one-fourth of the mixture and then rapidly mix into the remainder. Divide the filling between the prepared forms. Refrigerate for at least 2 hours to set.

4. Roll out the Short Dough to ⅛ inch (3 mm) thickness. Cut out 18 cookies using a 1¾-inch (4.5-cm) fluted cutter. Place the cookies in plain tartlet forms of about the same diameter. Use a plain 1-inch (5-cm) cutter to cut the center out of each one. Bake the cookie rings at 375°F (190°C) for about 10 minutes.

5. Grease and flour the back of even sheet pans or use silicone mats. Stir the cocoa powder into 2 tablespoons (30 ml) of the Tulip Paste. Place a portion in a piping bag. Spread the plain paste on the pans or mats within the template (see Figures 19-55 and 19-56, pages 1046 and 1047). Make 18 to allow for breakage. Pipe veins on each leaf using the cocoa-colored paste. Bake at 425°F (219°C). Immediately form the soft cookies over a rolling pin.

6. Toss the melon balls in Simple Syrup (or orange liqueur).

7. Presentation: Place a tulip leaf and a Bavarian (unmolded) in the upper half of a dessert plate. Place a cookie ring on the Bavarian. Pipe gooseberry sauce inside the ring and top with one of the reserved gooseberries. Pipe an oval pool of gooseberry sauce on the right side of the plate and arrange 12 melon balls to look like grapes. Attach a grape stem made from brown Marzipan. Pipe a zigzag of Raspberry Sauce to the left.

11

Charlottes and Bavarois, Custards, Mousses, and Soufflés

Charlottes and Bavarois

    Apple Rum Charlotte
    Apricot Bavarois
    Charlotte Charente
    Citrus Cream with Pink
        Grapefruit and Orange
    Pear Charlotte with Golden
        Caramel Sauce
    White Chocolate Bavarois
        with Macadamia and
        Pistachio Nuts

Custards

    Apple Crème Brûlée
    Blancmange with
        Florentina Halos, Dried
        Kumquats, and Kumquat
        and Pear Sauces
    Chocolate Rum Pudding
        with Chocolate Beetles
    Crème Brûlée
    Crème Caramel Nouveau
    Fruit and Coconut Tapioca
        Pudding Maui
    Lingonberry Cheese
        Pudding

    Riz à la Malta
    Trifle with Fresh Fruit
    Vanilla Pots de Crème

Mousses

    Cappuccino Mousse with
        Sambuca Cream in a
        Chocolate Coffee Cup
    Chocolate Mousse in
        Ribbon Teardrops
    Cupid's Treasure Chest
    Raspberry-White Chocolate
        Mousse
    Triple Chocolate Terrine
    White Chocolate and
        Pistachio Mousse with
        Chocolate Lace
    White Chocolate
        Bavarian-Style Tri-Color
        Mousse

Soufflés

    Blueberry Soufflé
    Crepe Soufflé
    Liqueur Soufflé
    Pecan-Raisin Soufflé
    Soufflé Rothschild

The chief similarity of the desserts in this chapter is that they all contain eggs (with the one exception of the Apple Charlotte). However, the eggs are used for totally different reasons in each of the various selections. In custards eggs are used in combination with heat and protein to coagulate, or thicken, the liquid. Beating air into whole eggs, egg yolks, and/or egg whites makes them usable to produce a light texture in mousses. Eggs contribute flavor and a smooth texture in Bavarian creams and charlottes (without the eggs a Bavarian cream filling would basically become a blancmange). In soufflés the beaten egg whites, in conjunction with the hot oven, are what makes this creation rise high above its baking mold.

Charlottes

In addition to being an excellent dessert in and of themselves, Bavarian creams are the foundation for cold charlottes. Charlottes are molded desserts typically made in pail-shaped, straight-sided molds. These may be individual serving sizes or forms which will serve up to ten. The molds are first lined before the filling is added. In the case of the well-known versions Charlotte Royal and Charlotte Russe, the molds are lined with jelly rolls and ladyfingers, respectively. In other recipes the molds are lined with different sponge or meringue products, or sliced fruit can be used as in the recipes for the Pear and Persimmon Charlottes in this chapter and the Holiday chapter.

The classic hot charlotte is made with a fruit filling, typically apple, which is baked in a shell made of buttered bread slices. Hot charlottes came first and were the inspiration for the cold versions, but the only things these desserts have in common is that they are made in the same molds and the molds are always lined. Hot charlottes do not contain gelatin. Instead, the filling is cooked until the proper thickness is achieved. Occasionally pectin is added as a further thickening agent.

Bavarian Creams

These are also known as Bavarians, or by the French term *Bavarois*. A classic Bavarian cream is made by adding gelatin and whipped cream to a custard sauce made with whole eggs (see Figure 20–1, page 1082). The mixture is then flavored with fruit purée, liqueur, chocolate, or nuts and is poured into molds or used as a filling for cakes or pastries. Many modified versions are created by using egg yolks alone in the custard base, or by adding whipped egg whites instead of, or in addition to, the whipped cream. A Bavarian is always unmolded before it is served. Because Bavarian creams are set up by chilling the gelatin-strengthened mixture, the chef does not have the same control as when making a cooked product where the cooking time can be adjusted to achieve a desired texture. Therefore, precise measurement and proper incorporation of the gelatin are a must (see page 291 to review working with gelatin). If too little gelatin is used, or if the gelatin is added improperly so that part of it starts to set up (forms lumps) before it can be fully incorporated, the dessert will not hold its shape and will be impossible to unmold. On the other hand, if too much gelatin is used, the Bavarian cream will be tough and rubbery. It is also important to remember that many tropical fruits will inhibit the gelatinization process if you are using a protein- (animal-) based gelatin unless they are first poached or puréed and brought to a boil to destroy the meat-tenderizing enzyme (see page 1110).

Like other gelatin-based desserts, Bavarian creams can be made up and used over two to three days if they are kept properly covered and refrigerated in their original molds. To unmold, dip the outside of the form into hot water for a few seconds, wipe the bottom, and invert onto a serving plate or paper-lined sheet pan. Repeat the procedure if the dessert does not unmold easily. With experience you will learn how long to hold the form in the water. Take care not to immerse the form too long or you will melt the filling. A Bavarian can also be helped out of its mold by using the back of a spoon to gently push the filling away from the side of the mold, thereby breaking the suction.

Custards

Simply stated, custards are liquids that have been set using a combination of egg and heat—the coagulation of the egg protein. They are easy to prepare, can be made one to two days in advance, and need little or no finishing touches. The consistency of the finished custard is determined by the type of liquid used and the ratio of eggs to liquid. When the custard is to be unmolded, a ratio of two eggs per cup of liquid is required; an example of this is Crème Caramel. Custards presented in their baking cups, such as Pots de Crème and Crème Brûlée, use less eggs or yolks and a thicker liquid, heavy cream. This results in a softer and richer product. A custard may be cooked and thickened by stirring it on top of the stove, as in vanilla custard sauce, or by baking it in a bain-marie. In either case heating the custard above 185°F (85°C) will cause it to become curdled and watery as a result of the moisture having separated from the toughened protein. An exception to this rule is pastry cream, which, due to the addition of a starch thickener with its inherent stabilizing properties, can and should be brought to the boiling point. Custards are generally baked in individual earthenware cups but can be made in larger ovenproof dishes to serve on a buffet.

Mousses

Mousses are not cooked. They are made up of whipped cream, beaten eggs, beaten egg whites and/or yolks, and the desired flavoring. The word *mousse* means "foam" or "froth" in French. Like custards, mousses are simple to produce and can be made well in advance. A chocolate mousse, which seems to be synonymous with the word mousse, should not require any thickener other than the chocolate itself. A fruit or liqueur mousse must usually be fortified with pectin or gelatin. When using either thickener take care not to get it too hot or you may melt and deflate the cream. In some recipes the egg whites are incorporated ahead of the cream to prevent overmixing the cream as the egg whites are added, which can result in a loss of volume. By whipping the cream to soft peaks only, it can be added prior to the egg whites with no ill effect. Mousses are extremely versatile, and the introductions to some of the individual recipes in this chapter suggest variations on the main recipe or presentation.

Soufflés

Soufflés have a reputation for being complicated and troublesome, and when compared to the other desserts described here, this certainly is true. A soufflé requires quick and precise steps as soon as the dessert is ordered; if something goes wrong you usually do not have the opportunity to start over. Timing is essential and requires good cooperation with the dining room: The server must know when to "fire" the order and must be there to pick it up at the prescribed time. It is said that "a soufflé is just a sauce that takes a deep breath, and holds it," so you must be sure that the server takes the soufflé directly to the customer before it starts to fall. As long as these rules are followed, making and presenting a soufflé correctly is no more difficult than any other dessert; it simply requires teamwork.

The most common soufflé variety, the liqueur soufflé, is basically a pastry cream which has whipped egg whites and liqueur folded in before baking. The air whipped into the egg whites expands in the oven and makes the soufflé rise. To make a fruit soufflé, fruit pulp is first reduced and then added to the pastry cream, before the egg whites are folded in. The third soufflé variety, crêpe soufflé, consists of a thin pancake with a small amount of soufflé batter baked inside. A crêpe soufflé is served directly on a dessert plate rather than in a ramekin. The sauce is served on the plate, unlike the liqueur and fruit soufflés, in which the sauce is served in a small dish on the side.

Charlottes and Bavarois

 ## Apple Rum Charlotte
12 servings

two Brioche Loaves (page 148)
12 ounces (340 g) melted unsalted butter
Apple Rum Filling (recipe follows)
one recipe Mousseline Sauce (page 1076)
¼ cup (60 ml) dark rum
½ cup (120 ml) heavy cream
½ teaspoon (2.5 g) granulated sugar
Chocolate Sauce for Piping (page 1072)
twelve lady apples with stems attached, or other sweet crab apples (see note 1)
twelve small mint leaves
edible fresh flower petals

NOTE 1: Cut each apple in half from the top, leaving the stem attached to one half. Rub lemon juice on the cut sides of the apples with stems and reserve these for decoration. Use the stemless apple halves in the filling.

NOTE 2: The melted butter must be thin, and therefore hot, when you apply it to the Brioche slices. If the butter is cold and thick, too much will stick to the bread. The excess butter accu-

*T*his is an old classic that will never lose its popularity. An Apple Charlotte *is a hot pudding that can be made in individual forms, or in larger sizes which serve eight to ten people. They are assembled and baked in characteristically deep, rounded molds. The dish originated in England around the beginning of the eighteenth century. History speculates that Apple Charlotte was named for Queen Charlotte (wife of George III), who had a particular liking for apples..*

Mrs. Betton suggests in the Apple Charlotte recipe in her Guide to Household Management, *1861, that "if a pretty dish is desired" one can line the molds with overlapping disks of bread dipped into "oiled" butter. She cautions, however, that "this method occupies considerable time."*

I suggest that you make the full recipe of Brioche Loaves. The leftover can be reserved (frozen if necessary) for use in bread pudding, together with the scrap pieces left from lining the forms. I prefer to use Brioche for this purpose whenever possible, not just for the taste but also because this somewhat sweet dough gives the baked charlottes a beautiful rich color. The fine texture of the bread is also helpful when lining the molds. An egg bread such as Challah or Braided White Bread baked in a loaf pan (see page 70) can also be used with great results. Avoid the temptation to use store-bought bread for toasting; it tends to fall apart when buttered.

1. Trim the crust from the Brioche (or other bread) and slice ⅛ inch (3 mm) thick (do not cut it any thinner; a little thicker is okay if it happens). Cut twenty-four 3-inch (7.5-cm) circles from the sliced bread. Brush both sides of twelve circles with melted butter (or dip them in butter; see note 2) and place in the bottom of 3-inch (7.5-cm) round forms or cake rings (I use coffee cups with straight sides) (see note 3). Cut 1½-inch (3.7-cm) strips from the remaining bread slices, brush butter on both sides, and use to line the sides of the forms. You will need

mulates on the bottom of the forms, soaking the bread slices instead of toasting them. You will not have this problem if you use cake rings since the excess butter will simply run out onto the sheet pan. In this case you must be careful not to over toast the bread on the bottom.

NOTE 3: If you use cups with a different diameter cut the bread circles accordingly. With 5-ounce (150-ml) ramekins, which are a little wider and lower than most coffee cups, cut the bread slices a little narrower. For a more elegant, but also slightly more time-consuming, presentation, cut the bread strips across into 1-inch (2.5-cm) pieces and use these pieces to line the sides (you will need seven pieces for each 3-inch/7.5-cm diameter mold). The small pieces are easy to attach to the sides once they are dipped in butter. This version is shown in the color insert.

to miter the ends to go all the way around the inside. Reserve the scraps for bread pudding or bread crumbs.

2. Fill the forms with the Apple Rum Filling up to the top of the Brioche on the sides. Mound the filling slightly so it will not become concave as it bakes. Brush the remaining bread circles with butter on both sides and put in place over the filling to enclose it completely.

3. Bake the charlottes at 400°F (205°C) for approximately 30 minutes or until the Brioche is golden brown (invert one to check). Let the charlottes cool to room temperature before attempting to unmold them. If you wait until they are completely cold you will have to reheat them slightly or the butter will cause them to stick to the forms. (This dessert should be served at warm or at room temperature, never chilled.)

4. Stir the rum into the Mousseline Sauce. Reserve in the refrigerator until time of service.

5. Whip the heavy cream and the granulated sugar until stiff peaks form. Place in a pastry bag with a no. 7 (14-mm) star tip. Reserve in the refrigerator.

6. Presentation: Pour enough Mousseline Sauce on a dessert plate to cover the base in a thin layer. Hold the plate with one hand and lightly tap the edge with the palm of your other hand to make the surface of the sauce smooth. Place the Chocolate Sauce for Piping in a piping bag and cut a very small opening. Pipe two concentric circles, 1/2 inch (1.2 cm) apart, next to the edge of the sauce. Drag a small wooden skewer through the lines in a series of small circles (see Figure 19–26, page 1002). Place an inverted Apple Charlotte in the center of the plate. Pipe a rosette of whipped cream on top and decorate with half of a lady apple and a mint leaf. Place petals of edible flowers on top of the sauce around the dessert.

 Apple Rum Filling

approximately 4 cups (960 ml)

3 ounces (85 g) dark raisins

1/4 cup (60 ml) dark rum

3 pounds, 8 ounces (1 kg, 590 g) cooking apples, such as Granny Smith or Golden Delicious

5 cups (1 l, 200 ml) or one recipe Plain Poaching Syrup (page 13)

4 ounces (115 g) light brown sugar

1/2 cup (120 ml) reserved poaching liquid

3 tablespoons (45 ml) lemon juice

1 tablespoon (9 g) pectin powder (see note)

1 teaspoon (1.5 g) ground cinnamon

*T*his is my Mom's favorite apple tart and pie filling, to which I have added rum and raisins. This amount of filling will make two 9-inch (22.5-cm) pies. You may also use this filling instead of Chunky Apple Filling in turnovers or other Puff Pastry treats.

1. Combine the raisins and rum. Set aside to macerate for at least 30 minutes.

2. Peel, core, and cut the apples in quarters. Cook in the Poaching Syrup until soft. Drain, reserving 1/2 cup (120 ml) of the liquid. Use the remainder for cake syrup. Chop the apples into small pieces.

3. Combine the apples, half of the sugar, the reserved poaching liquid, and the lemon juice in a saucepan. Cook over medium heat until the apples start to fall apart. Mix the pectin powder and cinnamon with the remaining sugar and add this to the apple mixture. Continue cooking over low heat until the mixture is reduced to a pastelike consistency

NOTE: Use regular fruit pectin for canning; 100 percent pure pectin is too strong.

(don't over-reduce however; there should still be a few chunks of apple left). Remove from the heat and stir in the raisin and rum mixture.

Apricot Bavarois

sixteen 5-ounce (150-ml) servings

2 pounds (910 g) fresh apricots, pitted
   or
1 pound, 8 ounces (680 g) strained canned apricots
one recipe Plain Poaching Syrup (page 13)
5 teaspoons (15 g) unflavored gelatin powder
⅓ cup (80 ml) cold water
⅓ cup (80 ml) or 4 ounces (115 g) honey
4 eggs, separated
4 ounces (115 g) granulated sugar
3 cups (720 ml) heavy cream
one recipe Apricot Sauce (page 1068)
Raspberry or Strawberry Sauce (pages 1080 and 1081)
eight small apricots

*I*t is not known how the simple, quickly-prepared Bavarian cream desserts, also known as bavarois, got their name, but one would assume that they were originally connected to Bavaria in the south of Germany. These versatile fillings are used in a wide variety of desserts, cakes, and pastries and in scores of hybrids and variations, such as this one with its slightly tangy apricot flavor. This particular dessert differs a great deal from the classical Bavarian cream in its preparation. It does not contain milk, and the eggs are separated, heated, and whipped independently to produce a lighter texture. Be sure to check that the apricot purée has cooled sufficiently before incorporating the other ingredients or the bavarois will have a grainy texture. This can also occur if the gelatin is overheated. In addition to adversely affecting the texture, if either of these ingredients are too hot, the whipped cream will melt, creating less volume but leaving the same amount of gelatin to stabilize the bavarois. This results in an overly firm, dense product. (Approximately 1 tablespoon of gelatin is generally sufficient for every pound of filling, however the air whipped into the filling is also taken into consideration and it, of course, does not weigh anything.)*

1. Lightly poach the fresh apricots in Poaching Syrup (if you substitute canned apricots, do not poach them). Purée the apricots and strain the purée. Cook the purée over low heat, stirring from time to time, until it has been reduced by one-third. You should have about 1 cup (240 ml) of reduced purée.

2. Sprinkle the gelatin over the cold water and set aside to soften.

3. Place the honey in a small saucepan and bring to a boil. At the same time start whipping the egg yolks. Gradually pour the honey into the yolks while whipping. Continue whipping until the mixture has cooled and has a light and fluffy consistency. Reserve.

4. Place the egg whites and sugar in a bowl set over simmering water and heat, stirring constantly, until the mixture reaches 140°F (60°C). Remove from the heat and whip until stiff peaks form and the mixture is cold.

5. Heat the gelatin mixture to dissolve. Working quickly, add the gelatin and the yolk mixture to the apricot purée. Cool to about 110°F (43°C) (a little warmer than body temperature).

6. Whip the heavy cream to soft peaks and fold into the meringue (be certain the meringue is cold). Gradually fold the cooled apricot mixture into the cream mixture.

7. Divide the filling between sixteen 5-ounce (150-ml) capacity molds and refrigerate until set, about 2 hours.

8. Unmold the number of bavarois you anticipate serving by briefly dipping the forms into hot water and inverting on a sheet pan lined with baking paper. Be careful not to heat the forms too much or you will melt the filling. Reserve in the refrigerator.

9. Presentation: Place a bavarois in the center of a dessert plate. Pour an oval pool of Apricot Sauce in front of the dessert. Use a piping bag to decorate the sauce with either Raspberry or Strawberry Sauce (see pages 998 to 1006). Cut a small apricot in half and slice thinly. Place the slices in a half-circle behind the bavarois.

Charlotte Charente

16 servings

one and one-half recipes Chocolate
 Ladyfingers batter (page 276)
Charente Bavarois (recipe follows)
3 cups (720 ml) heavy cream
2 tablespoons (30 g) granulated sugar
one recipe Mousseline Sauce
 (page 1076)
2 tablespoons (30 ml) cognac or
 brandy
Chocolate Sauce for Piping
 (page 1072)
dark chocolate shavings
sixteen small strawberry wedges

*C*harlotte Charente hails from the wonderful, gastronomically rich Bordeaux region in the northwest of France, which includes the provinces of Charente, Dordogne, and Gironde and is famous for its red wine, cognac, and the highly touted species of truffle the Périgord. This is my version of a local speciality called Plessis Charente. I discovered this dessert in a small restaurant in Sainte, which is located just a few miles from the more well-known town of Cognac. If time does not permit you to make the Ladyfingers, don't let that stop you from enjoying the unusual and "pleasant" (plessis means pleasant in French) flavor combination of cognac, port wine, and currant raisins. Simply pipe the Charente Bavarois into small individual molds, unmold when set, decorate with a whipped cream rosette, and serve with fresh fruit. Although it is convenient to use ramekins when assembling the desserts with the Ladyfingers, small (3-inch/7.5-cm) diameter cake rings work as well placed on a lined sheet pan. You can also make your own rings from polyurethane or acetate: cut strips 9¹/₂ inches (23.7 cm) long and 1¹/₂ inches (3.7 cm) wide, overlap the ends ¹/₂ inch (1.2 cm), and tape together.

1. Draw six 1³/₄-inch (4.5-cm) wide strips, the length of a full sheet pan, spaced ¹/₂ inch (1.2 cm) apart. Invert the paper on a sheet pan. Place the Ladyfingers batter in a pastry bag with a no. 3 (6-mm) plain tip. Pipe the batter onto the pan, crosswise between the lines, the full length of the pan. Pipe left to right and right to left, continuing within the 1³/₄-inch (4.5-cm) width, so that once the Ladyfingers are baked, they will form a solid, wavy strip.

2. Bake at 425°F (219°C) for about 10 minutes. Immediately transfer the strips (attached to the paper) to cold sheet pans, or the tabletop, to prevent them from drying out as they cool.

3. Line the sides of sixteen 3-inch (7.5-cm) diameter soufflé ramekins with strips of polyurethane or acetate to prevent the Ladyfingers from sticking.

4. Trim enough from one long side of each Ladyfinger strip to make them even. Cut each strip into three pieces; they will be a little less than 8 inches (20 cm) long. Fit one strip inside of each of the prepared ramekins, arranging the strip so that the trimmed, even edge is in the bottom of the mold, and the flat (bottom) side faces the inside of the mold (Figure 11–1). If you have trouble bending the strips, follow the directions on softening a roulade sheet in the note on page 270.

5. Divide the bavarois between the lined forms. Refrigerate until set, at least 2 hours.

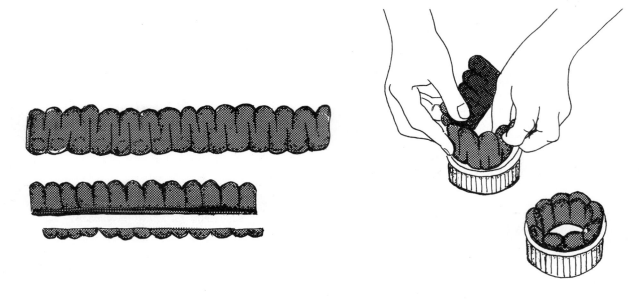

FIGURE 11–1 *The baked Ladyfinger strip with the bottom edge trimmed; using the trimmed piece to line the inside of a ramekin*

6. Whip the heavy cream with sugar to stiff peaks. Place in a pastry bag with a no. 4 (8-mm) plain tip. Reserve in the refrigerator.

7. Make the Mousseline Sauce and stir in the cognac or brandy. Reserve.

8. Presentation: Unmold a charlotte from the soufflé ramekin by dipping the bottom very briefly into hot water and invert into the palm of your hand. (If you are using rings, simply remove them.) Place the charlotte flat-side down in the center of a dessert plate. Use a piping bottle to cover the base of the plate around the dessert with Mousseline Sauce. Use a piping bag to decorate the Mousseline Sauce with the Chocolate Sauce for Piping (see pages 998 to 1006). Pipe dots of whipped cream, the size of hazelnuts, on top of the charlotte, covering the entire surface. Decorate the whipped cream with shaved chocolate and a small strawberry wedge.

VARIATION
Charlotte Russe

Charente Bavarois
6 cups (1 l, 440 ml)

2½ ounces (70 g) dried currants

½ cup (120 ml) port wine

¼ cup (60 ml) cognac

1 tablespoon (9 g) unflavored gelatin powder

*F*ollow the instructions for lining the forms with Ladyfingers as described. Fill the molds with Classic Chocolate Bavarian Cream (see page 1085). Follow the same presentation instructions given with Charlotte Charente.

1. Macerate the currants in half of the port wine, preferably the day before, but at least several hours before proceeding with the recipe.

2. Add the cognac to the remaining port. Sprinkle the gelatin over the mixture and set aside to soften.

3. Whip the egg yolks for 1 minute. Bring the Simple Syrup to a boil and gradually incorporate into the yolks while whipping rapidly. Continue whipping until the mixture has a light and fluffy consistency. Reserve.

6 egg yolks (¹/₂ cup/120 ml)

¹/₄ cup (60 ml) Simple Syrup
　(page 11)

1 pint (480 ml) heavy cream

3 egg whites

4 ounces (115 g) granulated sugar

NOTE: Do not make this filling until you are ready to use it. Allow it to thicken slightly before filling the prepared forms to prevent the currants from sinking to the bottom.

 **VARIATION**

Citrus Cream with Pink Grapefruit and Orange

sixteen 4-ounce (120-ml) servings

one-third recipe High Ratio or Chiffon
　Sponge batter (pages 274 and 272)

¹/₂ cup (120 ml) Plain Cake Syrup
　(page 10)

Citrus Cream (recipe follows)

Piping Chocolate (page 904), melted

grapefruit segments from
　approximately eight grapefruits

one-half recipe Raspberry Sauce
　(page 1080)

Sour Cream Mixture for Piping
　(page 1081)

orange segments from approximately
　five oranges

small mint leaves

NOTE 1: If you have a silicone mat available, spread the batter onto that instead and bake as directed. When the sponge is removed from the oven invert onto a sheet of baking paper that has been dusted lightly with flour. Peel the silicone mat from the back of the sponge.

4. Whip the cream to soft peaks. Set aside in the refrigerator.

5. Combine the egg whites and sugar in a bowl. Set over simmering water and heat to 140°F (60°C) while whipping constantly. Remove from the heat while continuing to whip, and then whip until the meringue is cold and holds soft peaks.

6. Combine the yolk mixture and whipped cream. Fold in the meringue. Heat the gelatin and wine mixture to dissolve the gelatin. Quickly add all of the gelatin to about one-fourth of the cream mixture to temper. Still working quickly, add this to the remaining cream. Fold in the macerated currants, including the port.

Charente Bavarois can be served as a dessert by itself. Omit the Ladyfingers and pipe the mixture into small individual molds. Unmold when set and decorate with a small rosette of whipped cream.

This dessert evolved from one of the most popular cakes that I make— Lemon Chiffon Cake. Although the filling contains cream, Citrus Cream with Pink Grapefruit and Orange uses fresh fruit for decoration rather than all of the whipped cream used in icing the chiffon cake. And while that is not quite enough to qualify it for the Light Dessert chapter, it's at least a step in the right direction in keeping with the public's growing health consciousness. The downside of this dessert is that it requires quite a few steps to complete. If necessary, some alterations can be made to speed things up without taking too much away from the appearance. For example, I have made the Citrus Cream omitting the sponge in the bottom, and you can simply pour a pool of sauce in front of, or all around, the dessert instead of piping a chocolate teardrop to hold the sauce.

1. Spread the sponge batter into a 15-by-22-inch (37.5-×-55-cm) rectangle on a sheet of baking paper. Drag the paper onto a sheet pan (see Figure 16–15, page 842). Bake at 425°F (219°C) until the sponge is baked through and begins to color, about 6 minutes. Remove from the oven and transfer the sponge to a second (cool) sheet pan (see note 1).

2. Place sixteen 3¹/₂-by-1-inch (8.7-×-2.5-cm) cake rings on a sheet pan lined with baking paper (see note 2). Cut sixteen circles from the sponge sheet, using a 3¹/₂-inch (8.7-cm) plain cookie cutter. Brush (or spray) the Cake Syrup over the sponge circles. Place a sponge circle in the bottom of each cake ring.

3. Divide the Citrus Cream between the rings, filling them to the top. Spread the surface smooth and even. Cover with baking paper, pressing the paper gently so it adheres to the filling. Refrigerate for at least 2 hours or, preferably, overnight.

4. Remove the rings by running a warm paring knife between the rings and the filling (or simply cut the tape and peel away the polyurethane or acetate).

NOTE 2: You can easily make the cake rings from polyurethane or acetate. Use the same cookie cutter used to cut the sponge as a guide, and see note 2, page 478 for instructions.

5. Cut baking paper strips to the exact circumference and height of the unmolded Citrus Creams. Place two strips at a time on a full sheet of baking paper. Place Piping Chocolate in a piping bag and cut a small opening. Pipe the chocolate in parallel lines at a 45° angle to the paper strips across and outside (onto the paper) the strips, first in one direction and then in the other (see Figure 11–14, page 572). Pick up the first strip and wrap it chocolate-side-in around one of the Citrus Creams (leaving the cream in place on the work surface) so that the chocolate sticks to the filling. You will achieve a better finish if you wait until the chocolate is just beginning to set up before you wrap it. If done immediately the chocolate lines will flatten to some degree when pressed against the side. Continue making chocolate strips and wrapping them around until all of the creams are covered. Refrigerate for 5 minutes, then carefully pull the paper strips away leaving the chocolate on the Citrus Cream.

6. Cover the tops of the desserts with grapefruit segments in a circular pattern. Refrigerate.

7. Presentation: Place a small amount of Piping Chocolate in a piping bag and cut a small opening. Pipe a curved teardrop of chocolate on one side of a dessert plate. Wait for the chocolate to set up, then fill the teardrop with Raspberry Sauce. Pipe a line of Sour Cream Mixture in the center of the sauce the length of the teardrop. Swirl it into the sauce using a wooden skewer. Carefully transfer a Citrus Cream to the center of the plate. Place 3 orange segments and a mint leaf to the right of the dessert.

Citrus Cream

8 cups (1 l, 920 ml)

2 tablespoons (18 g) unflavored
    gelatin powder
$^{1}/_{3}$ cup (80 ml) light rum
10 eggs, separated
12 ounces (340 g) granulated sugar
$^{3}/_{4}$ cup (180 ml) lemon juice (see note)
3 cups (720 ml) heavy cream

NOTE: You can substitute orange juice for the lemon juice if desired. If you do, add one table-spoon (45 ml) of orange flower water to the juice.

1. Sprinkle the gelatin over the rum to soften.

2. Beat the egg yolks with approximately one-quarter of the sugar to the ribbon stage. Add the lemon juice, and whip over a bain-marie until the mixture has reached 140°F (60°C) and is light and foamy. Remove from the heat. Place the gelatin mixture over the bain-marie and heat until dissolved. Do not overheat. Add the gelatin mixture to the egg yolk mixture and let cool to 100°F (38°C).

3. Combine the egg whites with the remaining sugar. Set the bowl over the bain-marie and heat to 140°F (60°C), whipping constantly. Remove from the heat and whip until the mixture has cooled completely and stiff peaks form.

4. Whip the heavy cream to soft peaks. Fold the lemon mixture into the egg whites. Fold in the whipped cream.

Pear Charlotte with Golden Caramel Sauce

16 servings

five medium-sized pears

one recipe Plain Poaching Syrup (page 13)

1 pound, 4 ounces (570 g) granulated sugar

4 drops lemon juice

2½ cups (600 ml) water, approximately

Pear Bavarois (recipe follows)

¾ cup (180 ml) heavy cream

1 teaspoon (5 g) granulated sugar

one recipe Caramel Sauce I (page 1070)

sixteen Marzipan Pears (page 1031)

NOTE 1: Place the sugar in a small thick-bottomed saucepan. Add the lemon juice. Stir the sugar constantly over medium heat until it melts and caramelizes.

NOTE 2: Unmold only as many charlottes as you are planning to serve. If kept in the forms, covered and refrigerated, they will stay fresh for up to three days.

FIGURE 11–2 The form for a Pear Charlotte lined with slices of pear

The term charlotte *is used to describe two significantly different desserts: hot charlottes, which are baked with a fruit filling, and cold charlottes, which have a bavarois or custard filling. The two characteristics these desserts share is that the charlotte molds are lined before the filling is added (with buttered bread, sponge cake, or thinly sliced fruit), and after the filling has set up the desserts are unmolded before they are served. The first well-known chilled charlotte was Charlotte Russe, which was invented by Antonin Carême at the beginning of the nineteenth century and was derived from the original classic Apple Charlotte.*

I first tasted the inspiration for the following Pear Charlotte in a small elegant restaurant located on I'le St. Lous (an island in the River Seine, just a stone's throw away from Notre Dame). I was immediately impressed by the light texture and flavor of the filling. After I ordered and carefully tasted a second Charlotte aux Poires Sauce Caramel Blond *it become quite evident that part of the whipped cream in the filling had been replaced with meringue (a sure way of cutting fat and calories in many desserts). Although I'm sure my version does not quite measure up to the original, I think I have come very close. I have occasionally prepared this dessert substituting peaches or nectarines for the pears. When substituting, use firm but ripe fruit. Poach and remove the skin, but do not macerate the fruit in caramel. Replace the pear brandy in the filling with amaretto liqueur (and, of course, change the name).*

1. Peel the pears. Poach in Poaching Syrup until they are soft (see page 13). Set aside to cool.

2. Caramelize the first measurement of granulated sugar to a dark brown color (see note 1). Immediately add the water and cook out any lumps that form. Remove from the heat and let cool. Thin the caramel, if necessary, by adding additional water; it should be the consistency of Simple Syrup.

3. Remove the pears from the poaching liquid, core, and cut in half lengthwise. (If you do not have a corer handy, slice the pears in half first and then use a melon-ball cutter to remove the core from each half.) Slice the pear halves into thin slices crosswise, using just the wider part of the pears. Save the leftover pieces for fruit salad or pear sauce. Put the pear slices in the thinned caramel, cover, and set aside to macerate at room temperature. Start macerating the pears at least 4 hours before you assemble the desserts, or preferably the day before, to ensure that the pear slices absorb the color and flavor of the caramel.

4. Remove the pear slices from the liquid and pat dry with paper towels.

5. Line the sides of sixteen 5-ounce (150-ml) charlotte cups, using four or five pear slices for each one, evenly spaced, in a tulip pattern (Figure 11–2). If charlotte cups are not available, any form that has a similar shape and is smooth inside, such as pots de crème cups, or even coffee cups, can be used.

6. Divide the Pear Bavarois between the cups. Refrigerate for at least 2 hours.

7. Whip the heavy cream with the remaining sugar until stiff peaks form. Place in a pastry bag with a no. 7 (14-mm) star tip. Reserve in the refrigerator.

8. To unmold the charlottes, dip them in hot water just long enough so that they can be removed from the forms (not too long or you will melt the bavarois) and invert onto a paper-lined sheet pan (see note 2). Place a portion of the Caramel Sauce in a piping bottle and reserve.

9. Presentation: Place a charlotte in the center of a dessert plate. Pipe just enough Caramel Sauce around the sides to cover the base of the plate. Pipe a rosette of whipped cream on top of the dessert, and decorate the cream with a Marzipan Pear.

Pear Bavarois

2¹/₂ quarts (2 l, 400 ml) bavarois or sixteen 5-ounce (150-ml) servings

3 tablespoons (27 g) unflavored gelatin powder
³/₄ cup (180 ml) cold water
8 egg yolks (²/₃ cup/160 ml)
2 ounces (55 g) granulated sugar
3 cups (720 ml) milk
one vanilla bean, split
   or
1 teaspoon (5 ml) vanilla extract
¹/₂ cup (120 ml) pear brandy
3 cups (720 ml) heavy cream
one-quarter recipe Italian Meringue (page 591)

NOTE: Do not make the bavarois until you are ready to use it.

1. Sprinkle the gelatin over the cold water and set aside to soften.

2. Beat the egg yolks and sugar just enough to combine. Heat the milk with the vanilla bean (if used) to the scalding point. Remove the bean and reserve for another use. Gradually pour the milk into the egg mixture, beating constantly.

3. Heat the gelatin mixture to dissolve. Stir into the milk mixture. Add the vanilla extract (if used) and the pear brandy. Set aside to cool, stirring occasionally. If you want to speed up the cooling process, place the mixture over ice water and stir until it is slightly warmer than body temperature. (Should it get too firm, or lumpy, reheat the mixture and start again.)

4. Whip the cream until soft peaks form. Gradually fold the milk mixture into the cream. Fold that combination into the Italian Meringue. Do not incorporate the bavarois into the Italian Meringue until the bavarois has started to thicken or the mixture may separate.

VARIATION

*P*ear Bavarois makes an excellent quick dessert by itself. Instead of lining forms with the macerated pear slices, just pour the bavarois directly into small, fluted forms. Unmold when set and serve with Caramel Sauce I (see page 1070).

White Chocolate Bavarois with Macadamia and Pistachio Nuts

sixteen 4-ounce (120-ml) servings

4 ounces (115 g) macadamia nuts

1¼ cups (300 ml) milk

one vanilla bean, split

  or

1 teaspoon (5 ml) vanilla extract

2 ounces (55 g) pistachio nuts

2½ tablespoons (23 g) unflavored gelatin powder

½ cup (120 ml) cold water

6 eggs, separated

6 ounces (170 g) granulated sugar

10 ounces (285 g) white chocolate, finely chopped

2½ cups (600 ml) heavy cream

¼ cup (60 ml) macadamia nut liqueur

½ cup (120 ml) heavy cream

½ teaspoon (2.5 g) granulated sugar

one recipe Kiwi Sauce (page 1074)

mango or papaya slices

*W*hite chocolate is not, as the name may suggest, made from some rare albino cocoa bean. Instead, this misnomer is simply a form of flavored cocoa butter—a "chocolate" which does not contain any chocolate (chocolate liquor) and therefore has very little chocolate flavor. The white chocolate fad in this country started in the late 1970s with white chocolate mousse, and it quickly become popular as a confectionery ingredient in many dessert preparations.

This dessert is a converted blancmange recipe in which the macadamia nuts and white chocolate replace the almonds. It came about after a trip to the Hawaiian islands in the mid-1980s, hence the tropical garnish. The bavarois is just as good, however, served with a seasonal fruit salad and presented with the sauce surrounding the dessert as in Crème Caramel Nouveau. Do not be afraid to experiment with a different sauce. Pineapple Sauce, for example, provides an excellent contrast to the sweet bavarois and makes a good canvas for the fruit.

1. Toast the macadamia nuts. Grind the nuts to a paste with ¼ cup (60 ml) of the milk. Mix into the remaining milk and add the vanilla bean (if used). Bring the mixture to a boil, then remove from heat and set aside to steep for 15 minutes.

2. Blanch the pistachio nuts and remove the skins (a pinch of salt added to the blanching water helps to bring out the green color). Reserve sixteen of the best-looking nuts for the garnish. Chop the remaining nuts coarsely: large pieces make the dessert look more attractive and also prevent a grainy texture.

3. Sprinkle the gelatin over the cold water and set aside to soften.

4. Mix the egg yolks with half of the sugar until well combined. Reheat the milk mixture to boiling, remove the vanilla bean if used, and gradually pour the milk into the egg yolk mixture, while stirring rapidly. Strain through a fine mesh strainer. Stir in the white chocolate and continue to stir until all of the chocolate has melted.

5. Heat the gelatin and water mixture to dissolve the gelatin. Add to the warm white chocolate mixture. Add the vanilla extract if using. Let cool to about 100°F (38°C).

6. Whip the 2½ cups (600 ml) of heavy cream to soft peaks and reserve in the refrigerator.

7. Place the egg whites and the remaining 3 ounces (85 g) of sugar in a bowl and set over a bain-marie. Heat to 140°F (60°C) while stirring constantly. Remove from the heat and whip until the mixture holds soft peaks. Gradually add the white chocolate-custard mixture to the whipped cream, then fold this into the whipped egg whites. Fold in the chopped pistachios and the liqueur. Divide the mixture between sixteen ramekins 3½ inches (8.7 cm) in diameter (or if not available, other forms or even coffee cups of the appropriate shape and size). Refrigerate to set, at least 2 hours.

8. Whip the remaining ½ cup (120 ml) of heavy cream and ½ teaspoon (2.5 g) of sugar to stiff peaks. Place in a pastry bag with a no. 4 (8-mm) tip; reserve in the refrigerator. Place a portion of the Kiwi Sauce in a piping bottle and reserve.

9. Presentation: Unmold a bavarois (see Apricot Bavarois, page 534) and place in the center of a dessert plate. Pipe an oval pool of Kiwi Sauce in front of the dessert. Place three thin slices of mango or papaya fanned in the space behind the bavarois. Pipe a rosette of whipped cream on top of the bavarois and place one of the reserved pistachio nuts on the rosette.

Custards

 ## Apple Crème Brûlée

12 servings

one recipe Crème Brûlée, custard
(page 546)

twelve medium-sized green apples
such as Pippin, Macintosh, or
Granny Smith

acidulated water

two recipes Spiced Poaching Syrup
(page 13)

3 ounces (85 g) unsalted macadamia
nuts, lightly toasted

one recipe Caramel Sauce I
(page 1070) (see note)

granulated sugar

ground cinnamon

twelve raspberries or other fruit for
decoration

twelve small mint leaves

twelve Caramel-Dipped Apple
Wedges (page 965)

NOTE: Make the Caramel Sauce thick enough so that it will not run on the plate (hold back some of the water at the end). If you do not have a piping bottle handy, pour ⅓ cup (80 ml) of the sauce in the center of the plate and use the back of a small spoon to spread and shape the sauce into a circle.

*T*his unusual adaptation of the classic (and delicious, but let's face it, boring) Crème Brûlée not only provides an opportunity for a little more creativity in the pastry department but the combination of custard and fruit is always welcome. As with many of the recipes in this text, the presentation can be simplified without losing the whole effect. Here, by omitting the Caramelized Apple Wedge you can cut the preparation time and reduce the skill level needed to complete the dessert. Another option is to bake the custard directly in the hollowed-out apples. In this case do not poach the apples first. The only disadvantage is that when the fruit and custard are baked together, the skin on the apples becomes much more wrinkled and discolored, and this takes away from the appearance of the finished dish. If you need a substitution for the macadamia nuts, hazelnuts are a good choice (blanch the nuts to remove the skin and then toast; see note on pages 965 and 966). Although they are only part of the decoration, the crunchy nuts provide a nice contrast to the soft custard and apple shell.

1. Follow the directions for Crème Brûlée in step one, pages 546 and 547. Pour the custard into an earthenware baking form. It can be any shape but should be close to the size of a 10-inch (25-cm) cake pan. Place inside a larger pan and add hot water to come approximately to the same level as the custard on the sides of the pan.

2. Bake at 350°F (175°C) for 25 to 30 minutes or until the custard is set. Set aside to cool.

3. Slice the top and bottom off of each apple, cutting the bottom even so the apples will stand straight. Use a melon-ball cutter to scoop out the insides, leaving a ³⁄₈-inch (9-mm) shell all around including the bottom. Place the apples in acidulated water as you work to prevent oxidation.

4. Bring the Poaching Syrup to a simmer, add the apple shells, and cook for about 5 minutes, making sure that all of the shells are submerged in the liquid. They are done when they just start to become soft. (Overcooking the apples causes the peel to become wrinkled, which detracts from the appearance.) Remove the apples from the Poaching Syrup and let them cool upside-down to drain.

5. Using two spoons, portion the baked custard into the apple shells, keeping the skin on the top of the custard upright as much as possible so it becomes the top of the filling. Depending on the size of the apples, you may have a little custard left over. Wipe off any custard that gets on the sides of the apples. Place the apples in the refrigerator until needed. Chop (do not crush) the macadamia nuts into raisin-sized pieces. Reserve. Place a portion of the Caramel Sauce in a piping bottle and reserve.

6. Presentation: Sprinkle just enough granulated sugar over the custard on one filled apple to cover. Caramelize the sugar by placing the apple under a broiler or salamander or by using a torch. Pipe a 5-inch (12.5-cm) circle of Caramel Sauce in the center of a dessert plate (see note). Lightly sift ground cinnamon over the rim of the plate, using a fine mesh strainer. Place the apple in the center of the sauce. Sprinkle some of the reserved macadamia nuts around the apple in the sauce. Decorate the top of the apple with a raspberry and a mint leaf. Lean a Caramelized Apple Wedge against the side of the Apple Crème Brûlée. Serve immediately.

Blancmange with Florentina Halos, Dried Kumquats, and Kumquat and Pear Sauces

12 servings

2 tablespoons plus 2 teaspoons (24 g) unflavored gelatin powder

1 cup (240 ml) cold water

1 pound, 8 ounces (680 g) blanched almonds (see note 1)

twenty blanched bitter almonds

1 pound, 8 ounces (680 g) granulated sugar

3 cups (720 ml) milk

2 cups (480 ml) heavy cream

2 cups (480 ml) Acidophilus Yogurt (page 2)

1 cup (240 ml) kirschwasser

one-half recipe Chantilly Cream (page 1083)

one-half recipe Kumquat Sauce (page 1075)

one-quarter recipe Pear and Dried Cranberry Sauce (page 760) (see note 2)

Oven-Dried Kumquat Slices (recipe follows)

twelve Florentina Halos (page 1009)

twelve whole kumquats

*B*lancmange dates all the way back to the Middle Ages. It was, and still is, made from colorless ingredients, as its name implies. At first the name was used for a savory dish made of chicken (usually capon) or less often veal, pounded into a paste and thickened with grated stag's horn. Later, beef and mutton juice were used as thickening agents before gelatin eventually took their place. (Some recipes call for thickening with cornstarch instead of gelatin.) Blancmange gradually transformed into the sweet molded custard we know today. The earlier spelling, blancmanger, translates to "eat white," blanc being French for "white" and manger meaning "to eat." The "r" at the end did not disappear until the 1800s.

In earlier years this dessert required a great deal of manual labor, because not only did the almonds have to be blanched and the skins removed by hand but, moreover, the grinding was done using a mortar. It was regarded as a difficult dish and only was judged perfect if it was snow-white and smooth as silk. The following recipe produces a pure white custard, with a slight tang from the bitter almonds and the yogurt, that is balanced nicely by the sweeter pear sauce and very colorful Kumquat Sauce. When kumquats are out of season or unavailable, use Pear Sauce alone or substitute Orange Sauce. Save the cutouts from making the Florentina Halos and use these instead of whole kumquats in the presentation, placing the cutout either on the rosette behind the Halo or standing it inside turned so its edges are perpendicular to the Halo.

1. Sprinkle the gelatin over the cold water and set aside to soften.

2. Place both types of almonds in a food processor with the sugar and grind to the consistency of AA confectioners' sugar. Do not grind too fine.

3. Place the almond mixture in a saucepan with the milk. Heat to scalding. Set aside to infuse until cool to the touch. Strain (squeeze) through a cheesecloth. You should have 3 cups (720 ml) of almond-

NOTE 1: Use any type of purchased blanched almonds (sliced, slivered, or whole). If you blanch them yourself, soak in cold water for one hour after blanching and removing the skins to whiten them. Then allow to dry thoroughly at room temperature, preferably overnight, before grinding. If you must speed this up by drying the almonds in a low oven be very careful not to let them color at all.

NOTE 2: Make the sauce as instructed but strain out the cranberries before using.

flavored milk. If not, add milk to reach this measurement. Save the almonds for another use such as Bear Claw filling, or discard. Reserve the almond-flavored milk.

4. Whip the heavy cream to soft peaks. Mix the whipped cream into the yogurt. Add the reserved almond milk and the kirsch liqueur.

5. Place the gelatin mixture over a bain-marie and heat until dissolved. Take care not to overheat. Quickly whisk the gelatin into a small amount of the milk and cream mixture to temper, then, still working quickly, add this to the remaining mixture.

6. Pour into 3½-inch (8.7-cm) diameter, 5-ounce (150-ml) capacity soufflé ramekins or other suitable molds of approximately the same size. Refrigerate for at least 2 hours or, preferably, overnight.

7. Unmold by dipping each form briefly into hot water, then invert onto a tray or sheet pan lined with baking paper. Cover and place in the refrigerator until time of service.

8. Place the Chantilly Cream in a pastry bag with a no. 8 (16-mm) star tip. Reserve in the refrigerator. Place the Kumquat Sauce and the Pear Sauce into separate piping bottles.

9. Presentation: Place a Blancmange (inverted) in the center of a dessert plate. Pipe an irregularly shaped ring of Kumquat Sauce centered between the dessert and the edge of the base of the plate. Pipe dots of Pear Sauce on the base of the plate on either side of the Kumquat Sauce. Place approximately eight dried kumquat slices randomly on top of the sauces. Pipe a rosette of Chantilly Cream on top of the Blancmange. Stand a Florentina Halo in the rosette, pushing it partially into the Blancmange. Place a whole kumquat on top of the cream rosette centered in the opening of the Halo. Serve immediately.

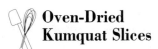

Oven-Dried Kumquat Slices

approximately 100 slices

twenty kumquats

NOTE: Because the fruit has not been treated with sulphur, as is done with commercially prepared dried fruit, it will darken from oxidation. This is a small price to pay, however, for a healthier and more economical product.

The method used here to dry the kumquat slices may be applied to a variety of other fruits as well. The time required for drying will vary with different varieties. Prepare the fruit as necessary, removing hulls, peel, pits, or cores as appropriate. Cut into ¹⁄₁₆-inch (2-mm) thick slices (cut cherries in halves). When using bananas, rub the cut sides with a little lemon juice.

1. Remove the stems if present and wash the kumquats. Slice across into ¹⁄₁₆-inch (2-mm) round slices. Place the slices on nonstick pans or silicone mats. Do not use the end pieces.

2. Bake at 180–200°F (82–94°C) for approximately one and one-half hours or until dried all the way through, turning the slices over halfway through the process.

Chocolate Rum Pudding with Chocolate Beetles

16 servings

sixteen Chocolate Rum Puddings
(recipe follows)
one recipe Chocolate Glaze
(page 1016)
one recipe Mousseline Sauce
(page 1076)
¼ cup (60 ml) dark rum
cocoa powder
Chocolate Sauce for Piping
(page 1072)
sixteen Chocolate Leaves (page 897)
candied violets
sixteen Chocolate Beetles (page 885)

*T*he word pudding *is used for a wide variety of dishes both savory and sweet. The term is derived from the old French word* boudin, *meaning "sausage," and was originally used to describe a dish of encased meat or innards. Later, the name evolved to mean a pastry-lined form filled with chopped meat, such as the popular kidney pie, for example. Yorkshire pudding, which is an indispensable component of a traditional English roast beef dinner, appeared in the eighteenth century together with the type of dessert puddings we know today. Some of their quickly thrown together forerunners included corn-meal mush, a type of Indian pudding also known as hasty pudding. The well-known holiday favorite plum pudding is another somewhat confusing example since it does not contain any plums. "Plum" in the early 1800s referred to raisins and various other fruits. Many of these first interpretations of puddings, both savory and sweet, were cooked in a bag or cloth by boiling or steaming. Gradually the recipes were adapted so that they could be cooked by direct heat, which opened the way for today's rice puddings, bread and butter variations such as the chocolate and rum flavored pudding that follows, and the widespread American favorite, cornstarch-thickened puddings (which the average consumer thinks can only be made using a familiar, small, rectangular box).*

To simplify the presentation of this recipe you can replace the Chocolate Beetle and the Chocolate Leaf with a whipped cream rosette topped with a Chocolate Figurine. The flavor of course will not change, but the originality rating will suffer a bit. When I last featured this recipe on the menu my students told me that these small cakes looked just like Ding-Dongs (before they were decorated), a nickname which did not sit well with me. During one lunch service, after hearing "ordering, one Ding-Dong" and "ordering, two Ding-Dongs" dozens of times, I firmly stated that from now on I did not want that name used in my kitchen and that the dessert was to be fired using its proper name. When I later discussed the matter with my wife (born and raised in the United States) and told her that I wanted to change the shape of the dessert so it would not look like a mass-produced, grocery-store snack cake, I was told that yes, they do look very much like Ding-Dongs, but that I was simply overreacting!

1. Unmold the Chocolate Rum Puddings and place them crust-side down on an aspic rack or cake cooling rack. Allow plenty of room between them. Set the rack on a sheet pan and pour or pipe the Chocolate Glaze over the puddings (see Figures 19–36 and 19–37, pages 1014 and 1015). The glaze should run down over the sides and cover them completely. Adjust the consistency as needed to ensure proper coverage.

2. Once the glaze has formed a skin, carefully remove the puddings from the rack using a palette knife. Reserve in the refrigerator until serving time or for a short period at room temperature.

3. Combine the Mousseline Sauce with the rum. Place a portion of the sauce in a piping bottle. Reserve it and the remainder of the sauce in the refrigerator.

4. Presentation: Sift cocoa powder lightly over the rim of a dessert plate. Cover the base of the plate with Mousseline Sauce. Pipe a ring of Chocolate Sauce just inside the perimeter of the Mousseline

Sauce. Drag a wooden skewer through the ring of sauce, toward the center of the plate, at 1-inch (2.5-cm) intervals. Place a pudding in the center of the sauce and decorate with a Chocolate Leaf, a small piece of candied violet, and a Chocolate Beetle.

Chocolate Rum Pudding

sixteen 5-ounce (150-ml) servings

6 ounces (170 g) white bread crumbs, toasted
3 cups (720 ml) heavy cream
2 teaspoons (10 ml) vanilla extract
melted unsalted butter
granulated sugar to coat forms
8 ounces (225 g) sweet dark chocolate
8 ounces (225 g) soft unsalted butter
8 ounces (225 g) granulated sugar
8 eggs, separated
6 ounces (170 g) almonds, ground fine
¼ cup (60 ml) dark rum

1. Combine the bread crumbs, cream, and vanilla. Set aside for 15 minutes.

2. Brush the inside of sixteen 3½-inch (8.7-cm) diameter ramekins, coffee cups, or other ovenproof molds with approximately the same diameter and straight sides, with melted butter. Coat with granulated sugar.

3. Melt the dark chocolate; set aside but keep warm.

4. Beat the butter with half of the sugar to a light and creamy consistency. Add the egg yolks a few at a time, then quickly incorporate the melted chocolate. Add the ground almonds, rum, and the bread crumb mixture.

5. Whip the egg whites and remaining sugar to soft peaks. Gradually fold the chocolate mixture into the egg whites.

6. Fill the prepared molds with the batter. Set the forms in a larger pan and add hot water around the forms to come halfway up the sides.

7. Bake at 350°F (175°C) for about 35 minutes; the puddings should spring back when pressed lightly. Set aside to cool.

Crème Brûlée

sixteen 5-ounce (150-ml) servings

10 egg yolks (⅞ cup/210 ml)
6 eggs
8 ounces (225 g) light brown sugar
5 cups (1 l, 200 ml) heavy cream
1 teaspoon (5 g) salt
2 teaspoons (10 ml) vanilla extract
6 ounces (170 g) light brown sugar
sixteen Pirouettes (page 222)

NOTE 1: Traditional Crème Brûlée dishes are made of ceramic and are 4½ inches (11.2 cm) in diameter and ¾ inch (2 cm) deep.

NOTE 2: If you are not certain your oven temperature is accurate, test it with an oven thermometer. If you do not have a removable thermometer, start cooking the custards at 325°F (163°C). If after 30 minutes the custard is still

*O*ne could easily argue that, even though they have many similarities, Crème Brûlée is in several ways the opposite of Crème Caramel. These small cholesterol bombs use all heavy cream and additional egg yolks (as opposed to milk and whole eggs in the other); the sugar goes on the top instead of the bottom; and the sugar is caramelized after the custards are baked, unlike Crème Caramel, where the sugar is caramelized first and then poured on the bottom of the molds before the custard is added and the desserts are baked. Finally, Crème Brûlée is served in its baking dish, while Crème Caramel is inverted onto a serving plate.

This rich, smooth-textured dessert is known as "Burnt Cream" in England where it has been popular since the seventeenth century. It was not, however, until late in the nineteenth century that the French term crème brûlée (which means precisely the same thing) became popular and the dessert became standard fare in many American restaurants.

The richness of the custard lends itself extremely well to being paired with fresh fruit, either as part of the presentation, as a flavoring for the custard itself, or as a container for the custard (see Apple Crème Brûlée, page 542). In some variations the custard is cooked on the stove top instead of being thickened the traditional way by baking in a water bath. This method is particularly useful when the custard is presented in a hollowed-out fruit shell.

1. Mix, do not whip, the egg yolks, eggs, and 8 ounces (225 g) brown sugar until combined. Heat the cream to the scalding point, then

as liquid as when you started, your thermostat is incorrect and you should increase the temperature. Wasting a half hour is better than overcooking the custard due to a poorly calibrated oven.

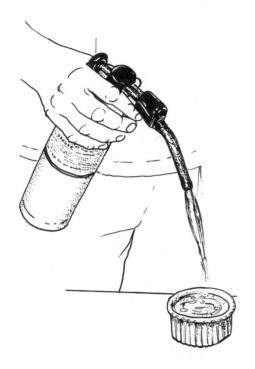

gradually pour into the egg mixture while stirring constantly. Add the salt and the vanilla.

2. Divide the custard between sixteen Creme Brûlée forms (see note 1) or ovenproof forms such as 3½-inch (8.7-cm) diameter soufflé ramekins. If using the latter you should add a few minutes to the baking time. Place the forms in hotel pans or other suitable pans and fill them close to the top with custard. Add hot water around the forms to reach about three-fourths of the way up the sides. Move the pan to the oven and then "top off" each form with the remaining custard. Be sure to fill the forms all the way to the top because Crème Brûlée—like any custard—will settle slightly while it is cooking.

3. Bake at 350°F (175°C) for about 25 minutes or until the custards are set. Do not overcook or the custard may break and have an unpleasant texture (see note 2). Remove the custards from the water bath and let them cool slightly at room temperature, then refrigerate until thoroughly chilled. The custards may be stored in the refrigerator for four to five days at this point, left in their baking forms and covered tightly.

4. Place the second measurement of brown sugar on a sheet pan lined with baking paper and spread into a thin even layer. Dry in the oven for a few minutes at 300°F (149°C). Let cool. Use a rolling pin or dowel to crush the sugar and separate the grains. Reserve.

5. Presentation: Sift or sprinkle just enough of the dry brown sugar on top of a custard to cover the surface. Wipe away any sugar on the edge of the form. Caramelize the sugar in a salamander, under a broiler, or with a blowtorch. Place the form on a dessert plate lined with a doily. Serve immediately with a Pirouette on the plate.

Crème Caramel Nouveau

16 servings

one-quarter recipe Vanilla Tulip Paste (page 1047)

1½ teaspoons (4 g) unsweetened cocoa powder

sixteen Gingered Caramel Custards (recipe follows)

one recipe Caramel Sauce I (page 1070)

2 pounds (910 g) assorted fresh seasonal fruit (preparation instructions follow)

sixteen Caramel Spirals (page 962)

In its basic form, Crème Caramel is simply a custard baked in a mold that has been coated with caramelized sugar on the bottom. This dessert is known as Crème Renversée in France (literally translated: cream turned upside down) and as flan in Spanish. The caramel coating colors and flavors the bottom of the custard (which becomes the top after it is inverted) during baking. When the cold custard is inverted onto a serving plate, a portion of the caramel which has become liquified (it takes about 48 hours in the refrigerator for all of the caramel to melt) runs over and around the dessert, doubling as a sauce.

It is of the utmost importance that the temperature on the sides of the molds never exceeds 212°F (100°C) since this custard, as opposed to Pastry Cream, for example, does not contain any starch. Crème Caramel is therefore always baked in a water bath to help keep the temperature in check. Overheating will cause the custard to separate or curdle. The first sign of this is the appearance of small brown dots on the sides of the custard. If you are unfamiliar with the oven you are using, it is a good idea to start out with a slightly lower temperature than called for. The water in the bain-marie should be barely bubbling, a rolling boil indicates that the oven heat (to which the top of the custard is exposed) is too high (see note 2 following Crème Brûlée, preceding recipe). I have heard and read about various tricks to prevent curdling from starting with cold water in the

NOTE: Unmold the custards on a separate unmolding plate, and then transfer to the serving plate (or reserve them temporarily on a sheet pan lined with baking paper) with a small spatula or palette knife. To unmold, run a thin knife around the inside of the form without cutting down into the custard. You only need to loosen the top skin from the sides of the form. Invert the form on top of the plate and, holding the form and plate together, shake vigorously up and down a few times until the custard falls out onto the plate. Another option is to use a spoon to gently press the skin away from the sides and then, holding the custard about 1 inch (2.5 cm) above the plate, use the back of the spoon to lightly push part of the custard away from the side of the form to release the suction; the custard should drop right out.

bain-marie to placing newspaper in the bottom of the same. I suppose that if your oven tends to be hotter on the bottom the paper will help to insulate the custards, but so would double-panning (placing a sheet pan underneath), which would be less messy.

There is not much of the old classic left in this dressed-up interpretation. The original dessert, although very good if made correctly and served cold, is a little plain looking; we used to call this "general custard" as a pun on General Custer, referring to the dessert's "general" and plain look. This nouvelle presentation goes to show that it is easy to make a ho-hum dessert exciting with a little attention and imagination.

For the best visual effect, the Caramel Spirals should be suspended high enough to make five or six loops before the bottom loop comes to rest on top of the fruit. The spiral will then bounce gently as the dessert is presented to the guest. To be certain of this, pipe the sugar thin and keep the loops of the spiral fairly close together.

1. Place 3 tablespoons (45 ml) of the Tulip Paste in a small cup. Add the cocoa powder and stir until smooth. Set aside. Spread the remaining Tulip Paste into twenty rectangles, following the instructions and using the template for Blueberry Pirouettes on page 442 (you only need sixteen, but some will inevitably break as you form them).

2. Place a portion of the cocoa-colored Tulip Paste in a piping bag and cut a very small opening. Pipe three diagonal lines in the center of each rectangle. Bake and form the cookies following the directions in the Blueberry Pirouettes recipe. Reserve.

3. Unmold as many custards as you plan to serve (see note) and place them in the refrigerator until serving time. The remainder can be stored, refrigerated in their baking forms, for several days. Store any extra cookies in an airtight container. Place a portion of the Caramel Sauce in a piping bottle and reserve.

4. Presentation: Place a custard in the center of one of the decorated plates. Pipe just enough Caramel Sauce around the custard to cover the plate. Arrange some of the prepared fruit on top of the sauce, using three or four pieces of each variety. Gently push one of the baked cookie tubes halfway into the center of the custard; make sure it is standing straight. Place a Caramel Spiral on top of the tube. Serve immediately.

To prepare the fresh fruit

Although you are limited, of course, to whatever fresh fruit is in season in your area, try to use at least four different kinds with contrasting colors. As close to serving time as possible, cut the fruit into pieces about the size of a raspberry. Keep each variety separate. Fruits such as peaches, nectarines, apricots, and plums, which tend to look dry a short time after they are cut, should be refreshed with a little orange liqueur before being placed on the serving plate.

Gingered Caramel Custards

16 servings

2 tablespoons (30 ml) finely chopped
    fresh ginger root
2 quarts (1 l, 920 ml) milk
1 pound, 8 ounces (680 g) granulated
    sugar
1/4 teaspoon (1.25 ml) lemon juice
1 pound (455 g) granulated sugar
3 1/2 cups (840 ml) eggs
    (approximately fourteen)

*NOTE: An alternative method to placing the
bottom of the pan into cold water, to prevent the
sugar from becoming any darker, is to add a
small amount of water, 1/4 cup (60 ml) for this
amount of caramel, when the sugar has reached
the desired color. Stand back as you add the
water as the mixture may splatter. This method
works particularly well if the caramel is cooked
to a dark color.*

1. Combine the ginger root and milk in a saucepan. Bring to the scalding point, then remove from the heat and set aside to infuse while preparing the caramel.

2. Place the first measurement of sugar and the lemon juice on a baking paper and rub the lemon juice well into the sugar. Put the mixture in a thick-bottomed saucepan. Place over medium heat and stir constantly with a wooden spoon until the sugar melts and caramelizes to a rich brown color. Immediately plunge the bottom of the pan into cold water to stop the caramelization (see note).

3. Pour a 1/8-inch (3-mm) layer of caramel on the bottom of sixteen 3-inch (7.5-cm) diameter soufflé ramekins or coffee cups with straight sides. Set the forms aside.

4. Reheat the milk to the scalding point. Whisk together the remaining sugar and eggs. Gradually add the hot milk to the sugar mixture while whisking constantly. Strain the custard and discard the ginger.

5. Place the forms in a hotel pan or in another suitable pan. Fill the forms almost to the top with custard. Add hot water to the larger pan to reach about three-fourths of the way up the sides of the forms. Move the pan to the oven. Fill each form to the top with custard.

6. Bake at 350°F (175°C) for approximately 35 minutes or until the custard is set. Let cool completely, then refrigerate.

VARIATION
Cardamom Custard

16 servings

sixteen Gingered Caramel Custards
    (see step one)
1 cup (240 ml) heavy cream
1 tablespoon (15 g) granulated sugar
Piping Chocolate (page 904), melted
one recipe Caramel Sauce I
    (page 1070)
sixteen Chocolate Figurines
    (page 906)
fresh fruit

1. Follow the recipe and instructions for Gingered Caramel Custards, substituting an equal amount of ground cardamom for the ginger root. Do not strain in step four.

2. Whip the heavy cream and sugar until stiff peaks form. Place in a pastry bag with a no. 4 (8-mm) star tip. Reserve in the refrigerator.

3. Unmold as many custards as you anticipate serving (see note on page 548) and reserve in the refrigerator. Any remaining can be refrigerated in their molds for up to three days.

4. Decorate as many dessert plates as you will need using the Piping Chocolate.

5. Presentation: Place a custard in the center of one of the prepared dessert plates. Use a piping bottle to pipe just enough Caramel Sauce around the custard to cover the base of the plate. Pipe a rosette of whipped cream on top of the custard. Decorate with a Chocolate Figurine and a small piece of fresh fruit.

🥄 Fruit and Coconut Tapioca Pudding Maui

16 servings

one recipe Vanilla Tulip Paste
(page 1047)
¹/₂ teaspoon (1.25 g) cocoa powder
green food coloring
Piping Chocolate (page 904), melted
Tapioca Pudding (recipe follows)
tropical fruit (preparation instructions
follow)
fresh coconut shavings
4 ounces (115 g) lightly toasted
macadamia nut halves
seeds from one-half pomegranate

NOTE: If you are using finger bananas, it is not necessary to bend the base of the trunk back to make it stand up. Instead, leave the trunks flat and make a cut halfway through the finger bananas. Stand the palm tree upright by sliding the trunk into the cut.

I am sure I must have eaten tapioca pudding while growing up. I honestly can't recall; but if not, I am certainly making up for it now by eating a big bowl with fresh fruit almost every day for lunch during the time that this dessert has been on the menu! Since it is both good and good for you, I can handle the associated ridicule from my colleagues. What I do distinctively remember from childhood is my Mom's standby—sago and dried fruit soup. For some reason the sago pearls were always pink. This dessert was, it seemed, always available, and we kids loved it, especially when served cold. Sago, which is very similar to tapioca and is used in much the same way, could easily be substituted in this recipe. Sago is obtained from the pith of the sago palm; tapioca is extracted from the root of the tropical cassava plant.

Tapioca pearls must first be soaked before cooking. It is best to follow the instructions on the individual packages if you buy them at your local grocer. If you have access to an Asian market, tapioca can be usually be obtained in bulk for less than one-tenth the cost (although the label will usually be in a foreign language).

As a variation, try substituting unsweetened coconut milk for the half-and-half, and large tapioca pearls for the smaller size. Large pearls require longer soaking. Cover the tapioca with water by about 2 inches and leave to soak overnight. Drain, place in a saucepan, and cover with fresh water to the same level. Bring to a boil and let simmer for 15 to 20 minutes or until the pearls have turned soft and translucent. Drain the water and add the coconut milk. To prepare the fresh coconut shavings for the garnish, refer to page 1099 for instructions on cracking a fresh coconut, then use a vegetable peeler to shave the meat. Do not prepare the shavings too far ahead of service and keep them covered and refrigerated to prevent their drying out.

1. Make the templates for the palm trees (Figure 11–3). The templates as shown are the correct size for this recipe. Trace the drawings, creating a frame and handle around each of them (see page 660), and then cut them out of ¹/₁₆-inch (2-mm) cardboard. Combine the cocoa powder with 1 tablespoon (15 ml) of the Tulip Paste and stir until smooth. Place in a piping bag and reserve. Color one-half of the remaining paste pale green. Reserve.

2. Lightly grease the back of clean, even, sheet pans. Coat with flour, then shake off as much flour as possible. (Alternatively, use silicone mats, which do not need to be greased and floured.) Spread the green Tulip Paste flat and even within the template for the palm tree crowns (see Figures 19–55 and 19–56, pages 1046 and 1047). Bake the crowns at 400°F (205°C) for approximately 6 minutes or until light brown in a few spots. Before they cool completely, transfer the crowns to a sheet pan lined with baking paper and reserve.

3. Spread the plain Tulip Paste within the template for the trunk using the same procedure as for the crowns. Do not place more than five or six per sheet pan or you will not have enough time to form them. Place the cocoa-colored Tulip Paste in a piping bag. Pipe three large X shapes along the length of each trunk beginning 1 inch (2.5 cm) from the top. Bake the trunks as directed for the crowns.

FIGURE 11–3 The template used to make the palm trees for Fruit and Coconut Tapioca Pudding Maui

4. Leave the pan in the oven and remove the trunks one at a time. Bend the pointed wide base of the trunk back lengthwise, 90° or more, to allow it to stand upright. Using the support box for Chocolate Chalet will work well, but any V- or L-shaped object will do. Use a small, square piece of wood to push against the trunk to aid in forming. Set the trunks aside with the crowns (see note).

5. To assemble the palm trees invert the crowns and place in a line. Pipe a small dot of melted Piping Chocolate in the center toward the bottom of one crown. Place an inverted trunk on top and press down lightly to secure. Repeat with the remaining trees. Place the palm trees in the refrigerator for a few minutes to set the chocolate. Do not refrigerate too long or they will become soft.

6. Carefully turn the assembled palm trees right-side up. Pipe two groups of three "coconuts" each in the center of each crown using Piping Chocolate.

7. **Presentation:** Spoon Tapioca Pudding across the center of a dessert plate. Stand a palm tree up in center of the pudding. Arrange tropical fruit around and partially on top of the pudding. Sprinkle fresh coconut shavings, macadamia nuts, and pomegranate seeds on top. Serve immediately.

To prepare the tropical fruit

two medium-sized papaya (Hawaiian rather than Mexican)

or

two medium-sized mangoes

one pineapple (about 4 pounds/ 1 kg, 820 g)

sixteen finger bananas

or

four red bananas

four starfruit

or

four kiwifruit

Although dependent on seasonal availability, price, and perhaps personal taste, there is now an immense variety of new tropical and subtropical fruits on the market from which to choose. That is not to say that these fruits are newly discovered, but that they are now receiving wide retail distribution. It was not long ago that both papaya and kiwi were unavailable or unknown in many markets. Today they are available almost year round, together with pineapple and mangoes. We do not even think of the yellow bananas as a tropical fruit any longer, and there are always plenty of citrus varieties to be had. Both finger and red bananas are offered not only in ethnic food stores but in the produce section of the local supermarket as well. The combination of fruit suggested for this dessert both looks and tastes good together, but when available, try using carambola, also called starfruit. This fruit can be turned into an instant decoration by first trimming away the very edge of its ribs and then slicing crosswise to form stars. I use pomegranate seeds to add color and a crunchy texture in the fall. When they are not available, small strawberry halves may be used instead. While strawberries are not a true tropical fruit, they do grow on the Hawaiian Islands. Feijoas are a small aromatic fruit with the appearance of a shaved kiwi. The whole fruit is edible, including the dark green skin, and would make a good addition or substitution if desired.

1. Peel the papaya and cut in half. Remove the seeds and slice lengthwise. If using mango, peel and cut all around down to the stone on the pointed side of the fruit (so you are cutting down to the pointed edge of the flat stone). Insert a small knife into the cut and cut around the stone to remove the half in one piece. Repeat with the other half. Slice the halves crosswise.

2. Peel the pineapple, core, and cut into half-circles (see page 1104 for more information).

3. Peel the finger bananas. Slice in half lengthwise or leave whole. If using red bananas, peel and slice diagonally.

4. Use a vegetable peeler to remove the skin from the five ridges of the starfruit. Slice the fruit across. Remove the skin from the kiwis using a spoon (see Figures 6–2, 6–3, and 6–4, page 251). Slice crosswise.

1. Place the tapioca in a bowl and pour the cold water on top. Set aside to soak for 1 to 2 hours.

2. Strain the tapioca and combine with the half-and-half. Place the mixture over simmering water. Whisk the sugar and eggs together in a separate bowl, just enough to blend. Add this to the tapioca mixture along with the vanilla. Heat, stirring constantly, until the custard thickens, approximately 20 minutes. Remove from the heat, cover, and set aside to cool. Store in the refrigerator.

Tapioca Pudding

twelve 4-ounce (120-ml) servings

³/₄ cup (180 ml) small or medium pearl tapioca

2 cups (480 ml) cold water

6 cups (1 l, 440 ml) half-and-half

8 ounces (225 g) granulated sugar

4 eggs

1 teaspoon (5 ml) vanilla extract

NOTE: If you are filling individual forms, pour or spoon into the molds while the pudding is hot.

Lingonberry Cheese Pudding

sixteen 5-ounce (150-ml) servings

4 ounces (115 g) melted unsalted butter, approximately

8 ounces (225 g) Graham Cracker Crumbs (page 8)

2 pounds (910 g) cream cheese, at room temperature

4 eggs

10 ounces (285 g) granulated sugar

1 pound, 14 ounces (855 g) sour cream

4 ounces (115 g) granulated sugar

1 cup (240 ml) lingonberries, puréed and strained (see note 1)

water

Sour Cream Mixture for Piping (page 1081)

NOTE 1: It is assumed that you are using canned and sweetened lingonberries for the purée. If you are fortunate enough to find fresh lingonberries, cook and sweeten them before puréeing. You will need approximately 1 pound, 8 ounces (680 g) of fresh berries to make the amount called for in the recipe.

*W*hile you will probably find that these pretty, individual-size cheesecakes take a bit longer to make than a traditional ten-inch cake, due to their small size they bake, cool, and are ready to serve much earlier, so this is definitely the way to go if you need to prepare cheesecake on short notice. They can easily be completed from "homemade" Graham Cracker Crumbs through plating in less than three hours.

For good reason, lingonberries are known in my native country as "the red gold of the forest." Although they are cultivated to some extent, the majority are a product of nature growing wild all over Sweden, especially in the north. By the time they reach the United States lingonberries demand a fairly steep price, so if they are too expensive, or are not available, try this variation: Bake the sour cream topping plain, let cool, and then top with five thin strawberry slices, cut lengthwise, arranged in a fan shape with the points toward the center. You will need one medium-size attractive strawberry per pudding. Glaze the fruit with Pectin or Apricot Glaze and serve with Strawberry Sauce. This alternative to the real thing is sure to be judged equally delicious by anyone other than those born in Sweden!

1. Cut out pieces of baking paper to line the forms, using Figure 11–4 as a guide (see note 2). The drawing as shown is the correct size for typical soufflé ramekins that are 3¹/₂ inches (8.7 cm) in diameter. If this size form is not available, coffee cups close to the same size work well. Adjust the size of the cutout accordingly. Trace the drawing, then cut sixteen of the shapes out of baking paper. The flaps should extend about ³/₄ inch (2 cm) above the form on either side so you can hold on to them to remove the dessert. Make a test before cutting all of the papers to be sure the flaps are long enough and adjust as needed.

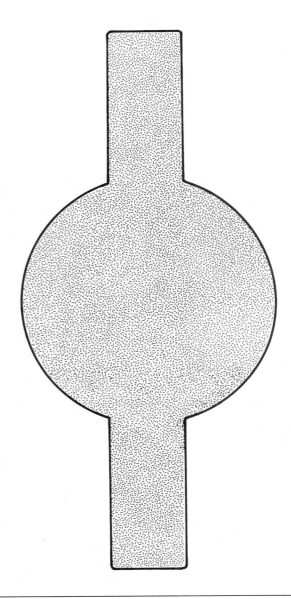

FIGURE 11–4 The template used to cut baking paper strips to line the forms for Lingonberry Cheese Pudding

NOTE 2: There are two grades of baking paper (silicone paper) available in this country. The thicker grade is preferable for this recipe because the thinner (regular) paper tends to break if the puddings are left in the cups overnight, which is usually the case.

2. Grease the inside of sixteen 3¹/₂-inch (8.7-cm) diameter ramekins with melted butter. Line the forms with the papers pressing the flaps against the sides.

3. Mix the Graham Cracker Crumbs with the remaining melted butter. If the crumbs are very dry you may need additional butter to ensure that they bind together. Divide among the forms and press the crumbs evenly over the bottoms.

4. Soften the cream cheese in a mixer on low speed, taking care not to incorporate too much air. Add the eggs to the 10 ounces (285 g) of sugar and stir until well combined. Gradually add the mixture to the cream cheese, scraping the sides and bottom of the bowl frequently to avoid lumps.

5. Place the batter in a pastry bag with a no. 6 (12-mm) plain tip. Pipe the batter into the forms, dividing it equally between them. Be very careful not to get any batter on the sides at the top of the forms, as this will detract from the final presentation.

6. Bake the puddings at 375°F (190°C) for approximately 20 minutes or until just done. Take into consideration that they will set further as they cool.

7. Mix the sour cream with the remaining 4 ounces (115 g) of sugar. Place the mixture in a pastry bag with a no. 6 (12-mm) plain tip. Pipe the sour cream on top of the puddings. Flatten the top of the sour cream with the back of a spoon by moving it up and down a few times on top of the sour cream layer, or by tapping the forms against the table.

8. Place part of the lingonberry purée in a paper pastry bag (see page 23) and cut a small opening. Pipe a small amount of the purée in a spiral pattern on top of the sour cream layer in each of the forms, starting in the center. Reserve the remaining purée for the sauce. Pull a small wooden skewer from the center of the spiral to the outside to create a spiderweb pattern (see Figure 19–24, page 1001).

9. Bake the puddings for 4 minutes at 375°F (190°C) to set the sour cream. Let cool completely.

10. Thin the remaining lingonberry purée with water to a sauce-like consistency. Reserve.

11. Unmold the puddings by running the blade of a small knife around the inside of the ramekin; do not cut the flaps. Carefully lift the pudding out by the paper flaps. If the puddings have been refrigerated, dip them in hot water first.

12. Presentation: Place a pudding off-center on a dessert plate. Pour a small, round pool of sauce in front of the pudding. Decorate the sauce with the Sour Cream Mixture for Piping, making the same spiderweb design used on the pudding.

Riz à la Malta

sixteen 4-ounce (120-ml) servings

1¼ teaspoons (4 g) unflavored gelatin powder

4 teaspoons (20 ml) cold water

one recipe Cherry Sauce (page 1071)

2½ cups (600 ml) milk

one vanilla bean, split

or

1 teaspoon (5 ml) vanilla extract

5 ounces (140 g) long grain rice, blanched (see note)

2 tablespoons (30 ml) Grand Marnier liqueur

grated zest of one orange

¼ cup (60 ml) cold water

4 teaspoons (12 g) unflavored gelatin powder

2 cups (480 ml) heavy cream

6 ounces (170 g) granulated sugar

Sour Cream Mixture for Piping (page 1081)

NOTE: *Before adding the rice to the milk, wash it in cold water, drain, and cover with fresh water, using approximately three times the amount of the rice. Bring to a boil and cook over low heat for 5 minutes. Drain the rice and proceed with the recipe. Blanching the rice before cooking it in milk will speed up the cooking process and reduce your chances of burning the rice. As an alternative to cooking the rice on the stove, you can cook it covered in a shallow pan in a 400°F (205°C) oven, stirring from time to time. With either method, avoid stirring the rice with a whip and be careful not to break or smash the grains as the rice becomes tender. Remove from the heat when the grains flatten easily when pressed gently between your fingers. Converted rice should not be used in this recipe.*

*T*he pretty island of Malta (actually part of a group of three islands, including the much smaller Gozo and Comino) is located about sixty miles south of Sicily and is an independent member of the British commonwealth. In French culinary parlance, the name Maltaise almost always signifies orange flavoring of some kind. Typically "Rice Maltaise Style" refers to a sweet rice pudding served with blood orange sauce and blood orange segments.

A simple, lightly sweetened rice pudding is traditionally served for dessert after Christmas Eve dinner in Sweden, and it is also customary to serve Riz à la Malta on Christmas Day. Usually enough rice pudding had been prepared for the first batch so that the busy cook on Christmas had only to fold in sweetened whipped cream and make some type of red sauce to accompany the pudding, usually cherry.

Typically, the soft pudding is simply spooned onto serving plates. I have added a little gelatin and molded the rice in this version to make the presentation a bit more stylish. If you prefer, omit the gelatin and the cherry aspic and serve the pudding the old-fashioned way.

1. Sprinkle 1¼ teaspoons (4 g) gelatin over 4 teaspoons (20 ml) of cold water to soften. Stir into ¾ cup (180 ml) of the Cherry Sauce (reserve the remaining sauce). Place the mixture over a bain-marie and heat to dissolve the gelatin. Do not overheat. Pour on the bottom of sixteen 4-ounce (120-ml) capacity Brioche forms and place in the refrigerator to set.

2. Bring the milk to scalding point with the vanilla bean, if used. Add the rice and cook over medium heat, stirring from time to time, until the rice is tender and the mixture has started to thicken (see note). Remove from the heat and add the vanilla, if used, or remove the vanilla bean.

3. Add the Grand Marnier liqueur and the grated orange zest to the remaining ¼ cup (60 ml) of cold water. Sprinkle the remaining 4 teaspoons (12 g) of gelatin on top to soften. Place the mixture over a bain-marie and heat until the gelatin is dissolved. Stir into the rice mixture and set aside to cool to room temperature. Do not refrigerate.

4. Whip the heavy cream and sugar to soft peaks. Gently fold the cream into the rice. Fill the prepared forms and return to the refrigerator until the pudding has set up, about 2 hours.

5. Dip the bottom and sides of the forms into hot water very briefly and unmold on a paper-lined sheet pan. Reserve in the refrigerator until needed. Place a portion of the Cherry Sauce in a piping bottle and reserve.

6. Presentation: Place a rice pudding in the center of a dessert plate. Pipe Cherry Sauce around the dessert, using just enough to cover the base of the plate. Place the Sour Cream Mixture in a piping bag and pipe a ring around the pudding halfway between it and the edge of the sauce. Use a wooden skewer to swirl the Sour Cream Mixture into the sauce (see Figure 19–21, page 1000).

VARIATION
Riz l'Impératrice

16 servings

1¼ teaspoons (4 g) unflavored gelatin powder

4 teaspoons (20 ml) cold water

one recipe Melba Sauce (page 1076)

2½ cups (600 ml) milk

one vanilla bean, split

    or

1 teaspoon (5 ml) vanilla extract

5 ounces (140 g) long grain rice, blanched (see note from preceding recipe)

2 tablespoons (30 ml) Grand Marnier liqueur

grated zest of one orange

¼ cup (60 ml) cold water

4 teaspoons (12 g) unflavored gelatin powder

⅓ cup (80 ml) light corn syrup

6 egg yolks (½ cup/120 ml)

1½ cups (360 ml) heavy cream

6 ounces (170 g) chopped mixed candied fruit

Sour Cream Mixture for Piping (page 1081)

In keeping with its royal name, this is probably the finest and most elegant of all rice puddings. "Rice in the style of the Empress" is said to have been inspired by Empress Eugénie, the Spanish wife of Napoleon III. You don't see this one-time champion much anymore; I suppose it has had to yield to the modern "high-tech" elaborately garnished desserts popular in most restaurants today. But, if you're looking for a classical rice dessert, think of this old aristocrat.

1. Sprinkle 1¼ teaspoons (4 g) gelatin over 4 teaspoons (20 ml) of the cold water to soften. Stir into ¾ cup (180 ml) of the Melba Sauce (reserve the remaining sauce). Place the mixture over a bain-marie and heat to dissolve the gelatin. Do not overheat. Pour on the bottom of sixteen 4-ounce (120-ml) capacity Brioche forms and place in the refrigerator to set.

2. Bring the milk to scalding point with the vanilla bean, if used. Add the rice and cook over medium heat, stirring from time to time, until rice is tender and the mixture has started to thicken (see note with main recipe). Remove from the heat and add the vanilla, if used, or remove the vanilla bean.

3. Add the Grand Marnier liqueur and the grated orange zest to the remaining ¼ cup (60 ml) of cold water. Sprinkle the remaining 4 teaspoons (12 g) of gelatin on top to soften. Place the mixture over a bain-marie and heat until the gelatin is dissolved. Stir into the rice mixture and set aside to cool to room temperature. Do not refrigerate.

4. Bring the corn syrup to a boil. At the same time start whipping the egg yolks. Gradually, while continuing to whip, pour the hot syrup into the yolks and continue to whip until the mixture is cold and is light and fluffy in consistency. Whip the heavy cream to soft peaks separately. Add the whipped yolk mixture to the rice together with the cream. Stir in the candied fruit.

5. Fill the prepared forms and return to the refrigerator until the pudding has set up, about 2 hours.

6. Dip the bottom and sides of the forms into hot water very briefly and unmold on a paper-lined sheet pan. Reserve in the refrigerator until needed. Place a portion of the Melba Sauce in a piping bottle and reserve.

7. Presentation: Place a dessert in the center of a dessert plate. Pipe Melba Sauce around the dessert, using just enough to cover the base of the plate. Place the Sour Cream Mixture in a piping bag and pipe a ring around the dessert halfway between it and the edge of the sauce. Use a wooden skewer to swirl the Sour Cream Mixture into the sauce (see Figure 19–21, page 1000).

Trifle with Fresh Fruit

12 servings

4 cups (960 ml) or about 1½ pounds (680 g) prepared fresh fruit (see step one)

1 teaspoon (3 g) unflavored gelatin powder

2 tablespoons (30 ml) cold water

one 10-inch (25-cm) Sponge Cake (page 268)

or

about the same amount of leftover sponge pieces

¾ cup (180 ml) orange liqueur, approximately

one-half recipe Pastry Cream (page 1088), freshly made

1½ cups (360 ml) heavy cream

1 teaspoon (5 ml) vanilla extract

2 teaspoons (10 g) granulated sugar

dark chocolate shavings

NOTE 1: If you would prefer not to use alcohol, substitute fruit juice for the liqueur.

NOTE 2: Although in a pinch you can use a chilled custard that is already made (providing it is smooth and soft), the Trifle will look much nicer if warm custard is draped over the sponge, filling all the crevices and holding the sponge chunks together when set.

During Elizabethan times a trifle was a simple "syllabub," that is to say, a dessert consisting of whipped cream flavored with sugar, cherry or madeira wine, lemon, and cinnamon. Gradually, macaroons soaked in wine, ratafias (macaroons with the addition of butter), and biscuits were added. This variation became extremely popular in eighteenth-century England. Eventually custard was used between the layers of macaroons and biscuits, and the dessert was then topped with the syllabub. This evolved into the trifle we know today. The Italian version of this dessert is called "Zuppa Inglese" (English Soup), created by an Italian chef who was inspired by the spirit-laden English speciality.

Trifle should be assembled in, and served from, a large glass bowl so that all of the layers can be seen. It is therefore better suited to buffet service, or use on a pastry cart, than as a dessert served directly from the kitchen. Trifle is an excellent way of using dry or leftover sponge pieces. Instead of the traditional raspberry jam, I prefer to use seasonal fresh fruit. However, the variations of this dessert are endless. Here are two of my favorites.

1. Prepare the fruit. Although you are of course limited to the available fresh fruit in season, a good combination is peaches, oranges, kiwis, and strawberries (the flavor of peaches and strawberries goes very nicely with the orange liqueur). To prepare 1 cup (240 ml) of each variety, you will need one medium-size peach, pitted; 2 oranges, peeled and sectioned (see Figures 12–4 and 12–5, page 596); one-half basket of strawberries (6 ounces/170 g), stems removed. Cut the fruit into pieces about the size of a raspberry. If you use small berries such as raspberries or blueberries, leave them whole. Set aside approximately ½ cup (120 ml) of the fruit to use in decorating.

2. Sprinkle the gelatin over the water and set aside to soften.

3. Cut the skin from the top of the Sponge Cake and slice the cake into two layers. Use bite-sized chunks from half of the cake to cover the bottom of a glass serving bowl approximately 10 inches (25 cm) in diameter. Sprinkle 6 tablespoons (90 ml) of the orange liqueur generously over the sponge pieces. You may need to use more liqueur, depending on how dry the sponge is. The pieces should be well saturated—after all, Trifle is not known as "tipsy pudding" for nothing!

4. Place the gelatin mixture over a bain-marie and heat to dissolve. Do not overheat. Whisk the gelatin into the warm Pastry Cream. Spoon half of the custard over the sponge and spread it out to the edge of the bowl.

5. Sprinkle half of the fruit on top of the custard. Layer the reserved sponge (in chunks), remaining orange liqueur, custard, and fruit in the same manner. Place the Trifle in the refrigerator to chill.

6. Whip the heavy cream to stiff peaks with the sugar and vanilla. Spread enough cream on top of the Trifle to cover the fruit. Place the remaining whipped cream in a pastry bag with a no. 6 (12-mm) star tip. Pipe a border around the edge. Sprinkle shaved chocolate in the center and decorate around the chocolate with the reserved fruit.

VARIATION
Amaretto-Chocolate Trifle

Replace the Sponge Cake with Cocoa Almond Sponge (see page 271), and use amaretto rather than orange liqueur. If they are in season, try using cherries instead of mixed fresh fruit.

Vanilla Pots de Crème

sixteen 5-ounce (150-ml) servings

8 egg yolks (²/₃ cup/160 ml)
6 eggs
10 ounces (285 g) granulated sugar
2 quarts (1 l, 920 ml) half-and-half
one vanilla bean, split
   or
1 teaspoon (5 ml) vanilla extract
whipped cream (optional)
candied violets (optional)

NOTE: To prevent spilling the custard as you transfer the pan to the oven, fill the forms about three-fourths of the way and then "top off" with the remaining custard after placing the pan in the oven.

The formula for Pots de Crème is comparable to both Crème Caramel and Crème Brûlée in that it can be prepared using either light cream or, as in this recipe, half-and-half, and it uses both whole eggs and egg yolks. What sets this dessert apart from the other two is that it does not include caramelized sugar, which is placed on the bottom of the custard before baking in Crème Caramel and on top as part of the presentation in Crème Brûlée (although the Pots de Crème could very well be flavored with caramel rather than the traditional vanilla or chocolate if desired). And, of course, Pots de Crème are baked in specific covered forms known as Pots de Crème cups.

The surface of the baked custard should have an even, glossy appearance. It is therefore important to skim off any foam that accumulates on top before placing the forms in the oven, and, if you do not have the proper covered cups, you must cover the forms you are using with a lid or sheet of foil, leaving only a tiny hole to allow steam to escape.

Chocolate mousse served in Pots de Crème cups is often erroneously labeled as Chocolate Pots de Crème. All French dessert crèmes—Crème Brûlée, Crème Caramel, Pots de Crème, as well as the variations of all three, are custards, which by definition means they are thickened by heat rather than chilled until set.

1. Whisk the egg yolks, eggs, and sugar just until combined. Heat the half-and-half to the scalding point with the vanilla bean, if used. Remove the bean and reserve for another use. Gradually stir the half-and-half into the egg mixture. Add the vanilla if used.

2. Strain the mixture and pour into Pots de Crème cups, filling them all the way to the top (see note). If these forms are not available, use individual ovenproof pudding cups or other small dessert dishes with an approximate capacity of 5 ounces (150 ml). Skim off any foam that forms on the top of the custards. Place the forms in a larger pan and add hot water around the forms to come about 1 inch (2.5 cm) up the sides. Place the lids on the Pots de Crème cups.

3. Bake at 350°F (175°C) for about 30 minutes or until the custard is set. Be careful not to overcook (see note 2 following Crème Brûlée, page 546). Transfer the custards to a sheet pan. Let cool slightly at room temperature, then refrigerate, covered, until needed.

4. Presentation: Traditionally Pots de Crème are served just as they are. If you are not using Pots de Crème forms, however, you may want to dress them up a bit. Pipe a rosette of whipped cream on the top using a no. 4 (8-mm) star tip in your pastry bag. Place a small piece of candied violet in the cream.

VARIATION
Chocolate Pots de Crème

Cut 6 ounces (170 g) of unsweetened chocolate and 6 ounces (170 g) of dark sweet chocolate into very small pieces. Stir into the hot half-and-half (off the heat) and keep stirring until all of the chocolate is melted before stirring into the egg mixture.

Mousses

Cappuccino Mousse with Sambuca Cream in a Chocolate Coffee Cup

16 servings

Cappuccino Mousse (recipe follows)
sixteen Chocolate Coffee Cups
    (directions follow)
one recipe Mousseline Sauce
    (page 1076)
¹/₂ cup (120 ml) sambuca liqueur
1 cup (240 ml) heavy cream
finely ground coffee
sixteen Tulip Cookie Spoons
    (page 1048)
edible fresh flowers

NOTE: *If you are preparing several of these desserts and must start the assembly ahead of time, always add the spoon at the very last moment or it may become soft and fall over.*

Of the many ways to present a mousse, this is probably about as fancy as it gets (or as fancy as you would want to get). There is, of course, a price to pay in the many steps it takes to complete this dessert. But if you compare this presentation to the typical mousse—piped in a champagne glass with a rosette of whipped cream on top—the effort is worthwhile and, besides the aesthetic difference, the whole presentation is edible. Luckily, all of the components can be prepared ahead of time.

I mention in the procedure not to fill any more Chocolate Coffee Cups than you will be serving right away. This is to prevent wasting any of the labor-intensive cups because, while the mousse must be kept cold, the cups should not be refrigerated for more than a short period of time or they will discolor from condensation when they are removed. The mousse can be made ahead and refrigerated. It is easy to soften it to a pipeable consistency as required.

By omitting the chocolate handle, you can create chocolate shells to hold a variety of other mousses or desserts. Also, you can alter the shape and size of the finished cups by using different sizes and shapes of balloons and by varying the height to which you dip them. The cups can be made four or five days ahead of time, provided they are stored in a cool place. One last thought, if you want to give the dessert more color, use Raspberry Sauce as a border for the Mousseline Sauce, or for a different presentation, leave the sauce out, use the shade template instead (see Strawberries Romanoff, page 499), and place the Cookie Spoon on the plate.

1. If necessary, soften the Cappuccino Mousse to a pipeable consistency by stirring it briefly over hot water. Place the mousse in a pastry bag with a no. 7 (14-mm) plain tip. Pipe the mousse into the Chocolate Cups, forming smooth mounds on the tops. Do not fill more Chocolate Cups than you plan to serve within an hour. Reserve in the refrigerator. (The filled cups can be refrigerated for that length of time without being damaged.)

2. Flavor the Mousseline Sauce with half of the sambuca liqueur. Place a portion of the sauce in a piping bottle and reserve in the refrigerator with the remaining sauce.

3. Add the remaining liqueur to the cream and whip to soft peaks. Reserve in the refrigerator.

4. Presentation: Cover the base of a dessert plate with Mousseline Sauce. Hold the plate in one hand and tap the rim with the palm of your other hand to even the surface of the sauce. Sift coffee lightly over the sauce. Use a spoon to place a large dollop of sambuca cream on top of the mousse in one of the prepared cups. Hold a Cookie Spoon by the handle and gently push the tip partway into the cream. Do not hide the entire bowl of the spoon or the effect will be wasted. Place an edible flower next to the spoon. Place the cup in the center of the plate, giving it a careful twist to ensure it will not slide in the sauce. (It is a good idea to wear latex gloves when handling the Chocolate Cups to avoid leaving fingerprints.)

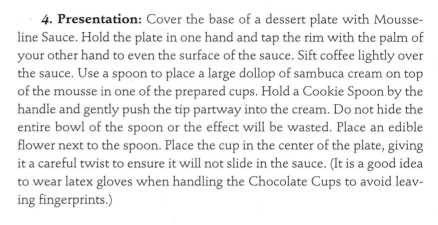

Cappuccino Mousse

8 cups (1 l, 920 ml)

3 cups (720 ml) heavy cream
6 egg yolks (¹/₂ cup/120 ml)
¹/₃ cup (80 ml) or 4 ounces (115 g) honey
¹/₄ cup (60 ml) coffee liqueur
10 ounces (285 g) sweet dark chocolate
4 ounces (115 g) unsweetened chocolate

1. Whip the heavy cream to soft peaks. Set aside.

2. Whip the egg yolks to the ribbon stage.

3. Heat the honey just until it starts to boil, then immediately whip the honey into the egg yolks (since it is just a small amount, be sure to throughly scrape all of the honey out of the pot). Continue whipping until cold. Stir in the liqueur.

4. Melt the dark chocolate and unsweetened chocolate together. Rapidly incorporate the melted chocolates into the egg mixture. Fold in the whipped cream.

Chocolate Coffee Cups

tempered sweet dark chocolate
    or
dark coating chocolate (does not need to be tempered)
sixteen small balloons (see note)
vegetable oil
Simple Syrup (page 11)

NOTE: Use the smallest round or tear-shaped balloons you are able to find. You may need to buy a package of assorted sizes and pick out the small ones.

1. Melt the chocolate to the appropriate temperature for the variety you are using (see pages 883 to 885).

2. Blow up the balloons to the size which will make the finished Chocolate Cups 3¹/₂ inches (8.7 cm) wide when measured across the top. Make a few test cups if you are unsure of the size.

3. After tying the balloons, wash your hands and use them to squeeze the middle section of the balloon to force air into the bottom (round) end to make sure the rubber is evenly stretched. This is necessary because the balloons are not fully inflated, which leaves a small area of thicker rubber at the round end. If not properly stretched, this area absorbs part of the oil and sticks to the chocolate. Lightly coat the portion of the balloons that will be dipped into the chocolate with the vegetable oil by rubbing it on with your hand. Do not use too much oil; this can prevent the chocolate from adhering and can also ruin the remaining chocolate supply if the oil becomes incorporated.

4. One at a time, push the round end of a balloon into the chocolate, holding it straight, and covering the bottom 2 inches (5 cm) with chocolate. Let the excess chocolate drip back into the bowl (Figure 11–5). Scrape the bottom of the balloon against the side of the bowl to remove more excess chocolate (Figure 11–6). Blot the bottom on baking paper (Figure 11–7) and then carefully set the dipped balloon on a sheet pan lined with baking paper.

FIGURES 11–5 and 11–6 *Dipping the round end of a balloon into melted chocolate, letting the excess chocolate drip back into the bowl. Removing more excess chocolate by scraping the bottom of the balloon against the side of the bowl.*

FIGURE 11–7 *Blotting the bottom of the balloon on baking paper before setting the balloon aside*

FIGURE 11–8 *Removing the balloon from the hardened Chocolate Cup, wearing a glove on the hand that touches the chocolate to avoid leaving fingerprints.*

5. Place the cups in the refrigerator for 2 minutes to set the chocolate. Wearing gloves to prevent fingerprints on the chocolate, gently twist and pull the balloons away from the chocolate cups (Figure 11–8). This method makes it possible to reuse the balloons. If you find you are breaking the cups, or if you do not need to reuse the balloons, a much easier and foolproof method is to simply puncture the balloons. Puncture the balloons with a toothpick at the very top next to where they are tied closed, and set them aside to release the air slowly.

6. If necessary, warm a metal spatula and use it to smooth the top edge of the cups (Figure 11–9).

7. Trace the template shown in Figure 11–10. Secure a piece of baking paper over your drawing. Make Piping Chocolate by adding a few drops of Simple Syrup to a small amount (approximately ¹/₃ cup/80 ml) of the melted chocolate. Place in a piping bag, cut a small opening, and pipe out handles, using the drawing as a guide (Figures 11–11 and 11–12). Make about twenty handles to allow for breakage. Place the handles in the refrigerator for one minute to harden. Remove them from the paper, quickly dip the ends in chocolate, and attach the handles to the cups (Figure 11–13).

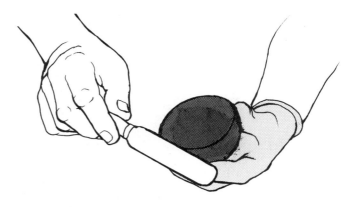

FIGURE 11–9 Using a heated metal spatula to smooth the top of the Chocolate Cup

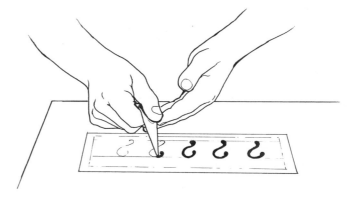

FIGURE 11–10 The template used as a guide to pipe out the handles for the Chocolate Cups

FIGURE 11–11 Piping the chocolate handles on a sheet of baking paper with the template drawing under the paper

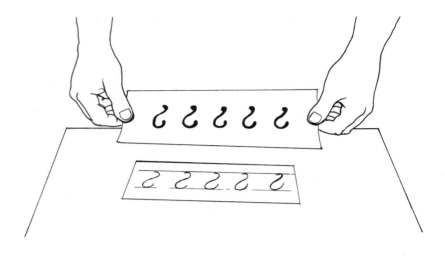

FIGURE 11–12 *Lifting up the sheet of baking paper with the finished chocolate handles*

FIGURE 11–13 *Attaching a hardened handle to the side of a Chocolate Coffee Cup while wearing gloves on both hands to prevent fingerprints on the chocolate*

Chocolate Mousse in Ribbon Teardrops

sixteen 4-ounce (115-g) servings

Dark Chocolate Mousse Filling
    (recipe follows)
White Chocolate Mousse Filling for
    Teardrops (recipe follows)
tempered dark chocolate, melted
tempered white chocolate, melted

*A*s in the preceding recipe, while this presentation is quite elegant, it is admittedly much more time-consuming then the traditional one where the mousse is piped into a glass or goblet. This is not to say that there is anything wrong with a simple presentation. In many instances the amount of time devoted to the presentation must be justified with the bottom line of a particular banquet and, unfortunately, at times it simply depends on how rushed you are. Although it is not going to win any prizes for originality, a mousse served in a champagne glass can be made quite acceptable by topping it with whipped cream and a tall Chocolate Figurine or Chocolate Fan.

unsweetened cocoa powder
forty-eight Chocolate Figurines
   (page 906)
sixteen physalis (Cape gooseberry)
White Chocolate Noodles (page 917)
Dark Chocolate Noodles (page 917)

NOTE: When Cape gooseberries are unavailable, use another seasonal berry accompanied by a mint sprig.

The teardrop shells can be made up well in advance during a slow time and will keep for weeks if stored properly. If the shells are made ahead it is best to leave the plastic strips attached until serving time. Even the mousse fillings can be prepared up to three days ahead of serving and kept well covered in the refrigerator. Other ways to save time are to make only one flavor of mousse and use it to fill all three shells, and/or skip the Chocolate Noodles and replace with a rosette of whipped cream with the fruit garnish on top.

The procedure for making the Chocolate Teardrops can be used to make many different shapes and can be used with a variety of fillings. If desired, you can also make a bottom on the shells by following the instructions given in the note with the recipe for Cupid's Treasure Chest (page 567).

1. Make the Dark Chocolate Mousse Filling and the White Chocolate Mousse Filling for Teardrops. Cover and refrigerate both fillings while making the Chocolate Ribbon Teardrops.

2. Cut out forty-eight 9-by-1¼-inch (22.5-×-3.1-cm) polyurethane or acetate strips. Spread the melted dark and white chocolate on the strips following the instructions on pages 918 and 919 for making Chocolate Ribbons. To shape the ribbons into teardrops, bend the plastic strips (with the chocolate on the inside) to make the two short ends meet. Attach a paper clip to hold the ends together. Stand the teardrops on a sheet pan lined with baking paper. They can be stored this way until needed but should always be placed in the refrigerator briefly prior to removing the plastic to ensure a glossy surface.

3. Wearing latex gloves to avoid leaving fingerprints on the chocolate, remove the paper clips and gently pull the plastic strips away from the hardened chocolate.

4. Presentation: Sift cocoa powder lightly over the base of a dessert plate (see page 1040 for instructions on using a pie tin template for this). If not using the pie tin method, wipe the rim of the plate clean if necessary. Stir the fillings to make them smooth and then place the White Chocolate Mousse Filling for Teardrops and the Dark Chocolate Mousse Filling in two pastry bags, both with no. 6 (12-mm) plain tips. Place three Chocolate Ribbon Teardrops as far off-center on the plate as possible with the points angled toward each other (again, at this point you should be wearing latex gloves to prevent fingerprints). Pipe White Chocolate Mousse Filling into the center shell. Pipe Dark Chocolate Mousse into the two other shells. Place a Chocolate Figurine on top of each teardrop. Place a Cape gooseberry where the tips of the teardrops meet. Arrange Dark and White Chocolate Noodles on the plate in front of the teardrops.

Dark Chocolate Mousse Filling

8 cups (1 l, 920 ml)

one-quarter recipe Swiss Meringue
 (page 592)
2½ cups (600 ml) heavy cream
4 ounces (115 g) unsweetened cocoa
 powder
¾ cup (180 ml) warm water
¼ cup (60 ml) dark rum
8 ounces (225 g) sweet dark chocolate
6 egg yolks (½ cup/120 ml)
¼ cup (60 ml) or 3 ounces (85 g)
 light corn syrup

1. Make the Swiss Meringue and set it aside.

2. Whip the heavy cream to stiff peaks and set aside in the refrigerator.

3. Mix the cocoa powder into the warm water. Add the rum. Melt the sweet dark chocolate and add it to the cocoa powder mixture. Set aside and keep warm.

4. Whip the egg yolks for a few moments until just broken up. Bring the corn syrup to a boil and then gradually pour the hot syrup into the yolks while continuing to whip constantly. Whip until the mixture is thick and fluffy. Fold the warm chocolate mixture into the egg yolks. Fold into the reserved whipped cream, then gradually add this mixture to the reserved Swiss Meringue. Cover and place in the refrigerator.

White Chocolate Mousse Filling for Teardrops

4½ cups (1 l, 80 ml)

1½ cups (360 ml) heavy cream
2 teaspoons (6 g) unflavored gelatin
 powder
¼ cup (60 ml) cold water
1 tablespoon (9 g) pectin powder
 (see note)
3 ounces (85 g) granulated sugar
4 egg whites (½ cup/120 ml)
8 ounces (225 g) white chocolate,
 melted

NOTE: Use regular canning pectin. If pectin is not available, increase the gelatin by 1 teaspoon (3 g) for a total of 1 tablespoon (9 g).

1. Whip the heavy cream to soft peaks; do not overwhip. Reserve in the refrigerator.

2. Sprinkle the gelatin over the cold water and set aside to soften.

3. Combine the pectin powder and the granulated sugar in a mixing bowl. Stir in the egg whites. Place the bowl over simmering water and heat, stirring constantly with a whisk, until the mixture reaches 140°F (60°C). Remove from the heat and immediately whip until the mixture has cooled completely and has formed stiff peaks.

4. Place the gelatin mixture over simmering water and heat to dissolve. Working quickly, first stir the gelatin into the melted white chocolate. Then stir the chocolate mixture into one-third of the meringue to temper it. Add this to the remaining meringue. Stir in the reserved whipped cream.

Cupid's Treasure Chest

16 servings

dark coating chocolate, melted
Piping Chocolate (page 904), melted
one 10-inch (25-cm) Sponge Cake
 (page 268)
orange liqueur
one-half recipe Raspberry-White
 Chocolate Mousse (page 568)
dark chocolate shavings

*T*his dessert was originally created for a Valentine's dinner a few years back (the magical allure and history of that day are discussed in the introduction to Valentine's Day Hearts on page 519). Cupid's Treasure Chest also makes a beautiful presentation on many other occasions when a special dessert is called for, such as a romantic anniversary dinner or an engagement celebration. The treasure chest lid alone can be used to garnish a slice of cake, a serving of mousse, or an individual pastry anytime you want to create a romantic look. If you do not have a free form heart template from making these desserts previously, just trace around a heart-shaped cookie cutter of the appropriate size.

As in the preceding recipe, the chocolate cases, and here the lids as well, can be made in advance ready to fill and serve. For a look that is even more elegant, try piping white chocolate onto the acetate strips before spreading the dark

sixteen Marzipan Rosebuds
    (page 1034)
sixteen Marzipan Leaves (page 1038)
one recipe Raspberry Sauce
    (page 1080)
Sour Cream Mixture for Piping
    (page 1081)

NOTE: If you wish to make a chocolate bottom for the treasure chests instead of, or in addition to, the Sponge Cake, place a sheet of baking paper on a cardboard or inverted sheet pan and spread a thin layer of melted dark coating chocolate over the paper. Set the chocolate hearts on top, moving them back and forth just a little to make sure they adhere (wear latex gloves to avoid leaving fingerprints on the chocolate). Pipe a border of dark chocolate all around the inside of the base. Let the chocolate set at room temperature (do not refrigerate or the chocolate will become too hard and brittle), then cut around the outside of each heart and carefully break off the excess chocolate. At this stage the hearts can be reserved covered in a cool dry place for up to two weeks.

chocolate on top (see Miniature Marco Polo, page 468). For an engagement dinner you can place two interlocking rings made of marzipan on top of the chocolate shavings under the lid (if the party consists of more than two be certain you are not giving the rings to the wrong guests or who knows what you might start!).

1. Cut sixteen thin polyurethane or acetate strips 1¼ inches (3.1 cm) wide and exactly as long as the inside circumference of a heart-shaped cookie cutter that is approximately 4 inches (10 cm) across at the widest point; the length of the strips will be approximately 12¾ inches (32 cm). (The strips will not follow the heart shape precisely, but don't worry; if anything, the free form shape just adds to the appearance.)

2. Place the strips, one at a time, on a sheet of baking paper in front of you. Spread a thin layer of melted coating chocolate over the strip, covering it completely. To cover the strip completely it will be necessary to spread a little chocolate onto the baking paper all around. Carefully lift up the plastic at one end by sliding the tip of a knife underneath. Hold the plastic at one short end and run your thumb and index finger along the edges on both sides for a cleaner look. Position the strip inside the heart cutter with the plastic side against the cutter and the two ends meeting at the point of the heart. Press lightly to make sure that the bottom edge lines up evenly. Refrigerate for a few minutes to set. (It will obviously go faster if you have more than one cutter, but if not, you can be working on the lids as you wait.)

3. When the chocolate has set, brush some additional chocolate at the tip where the ends join (this chocolate will set immediately since the heart is cold). Carefully remove the heart from the mold (run a thin knife around the inside perimeter if it is stuck), leaving the plastic strip attached. Place on a sheet pan. Repeat to make sixteen hearts. Place the hearts in the refrigerator for 1 minute to ensure a glossy finish. Do not leave them for too long or they could become brittle and break. Remove from the refrigerator and carefully peel off the plastic strips. Reserve.

4. To make the lids for the heart boxes, place one chocolate heart on top of a piece of thick paper such as a cake box. Trace around, and cut out the shape. Use this template to draw twenty hearts on a sheet of baking paper (you need to make a few extra lids to allow for breakage). Invert the baking paper.

5. Place Piping Chocolate in a piping bag and cut a small opening. Pipe the chocolate, tracing the outline of the heart first, then fill in by piping back and forth at a diagonal, in both directions, spacing the lines about ½ inch (1.2 cm) apart. Make sure you connect with the outline on each side. Set aside to harden.

6. Cut the skin from the top of the Sponge Cake, cutting it even at the same time. Slice the sponge into three thin layers. Cut out sixteen hearts, using the same template used to trace the lids, or use a smaller heart-shaped cutter if you have one (the template is best because cake cut with a cutter will not fit exactly and the filling may run out at the bottom). Brush the cake pieces with orange liqueur. Cover and reserve in the refrigerator.

7. Place the Raspberry-White Chocolate Mousse in a pastry bag with a no. 7 (14-mm) plain tip. Reserve in the refrigerator until time of service. Place a portion of the Raspberry Sauce in a piping bottle.

8. Presentation: Place a heart-shaped sponge in the bottom of a chocolate heart. Place centered in the top half of a dessert plate. Pipe raspberry mousse into the shell, filling it to the top. Use a spoon to carefully sprinkle chocolate shavings over the mousse without getting any on the plate. Place a Marzipan Rosebud and Leaf in the upper right side of the heart, sticking the bud lightly into the filling. Run a thin knife under one of the piped lids to loosen it. Place the lid on top of the heart, sticking it partially into the filling on the left side to hold it in a half-open position. Pipe a large pool of Raspberry Sauce in front of the dessert and decorate the sauce with the Sour Cream Mixture, making a series of hearts (see Figure 19–25, page 1002). Serve immediately.

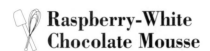

Raspberry-White Chocolate Mousse

sixteen 4-ounce (120-ml) servings

2 cups (480 ml) heavy cream
3 tablespoons (27 g) powdered pectin (see note 1)
6 ounces (170 g) granulated sugar
1 cup (240 ml) egg whites
1 tablespoon (9 g) unflavored gelatin powder
1/3 cup (80 ml) cold water
8 ounces (225 g) white chocolate, melted
2 1/2 cups (600 ml) strained raspberry purée at room temperature (see note 2)
1/3 cup (80 ml) lemon juice
1/2 cup (120 ml) heavy cream
1/2 teaspoon (2.5 g) granulated sugar
dark chocolate shavings
fresh raspberries
sixteen Almond Macaroon Cookies (page 202)

NOTE 1: Use regular pectin for canning fruit. Pure pectin powder is too strong for this recipe.

*T*his easy-to-make and versatile mousse filling is used as a base for several recipes in this text. White chocolate complements any slightly acidic berry or other fruit, and these may be used in place of the raspberries. By using either blueberries or blackberries you will not only create a delicious flavor but both varieties produce a very vivid color when mixed with the white chocolate and cream. If it is necessary for the filling to set up enough to be sliced, double the amount of gelatin and increase the water to 1/2 cup (120 ml). For a plain white chocolate filling in a cake or pastry, where the filling must set up to a greater degree than an individual serving of mousse in a goblet, for instance, use the White Chocolate Mousse Filling on page 574, omitting the nuts at the end.

The serving presentation is just as quick and simple as making the mousse filling; it is an ideal dessert when you don't want to have (or don't have time for) any last-minute details. The mousse can be prepared up to two days in advance if it is kept covered in the refrigerator.

1. Whip the 2 cups (480 ml) of heavy cream to soft peaks. Reserve in the refrigerator.

2. Combine the pectin powder with 6 ounces (170 g) granulated sugar. Add the egg whites. Heat the mixture over simmering water until it reaches 140F (60°C), stirring constantly to make sure that the egg whites on the bottom do not get too hot and cook. Remove from the heat and whip until the mixture is cold and has formed stiff peaks. Reserve the meringue.

3. Sprinkle the gelatin over the cold water and set aside to soften.

4. Stir the melted white chocolate into the raspberry purée (make sure that the raspberry purée is not colder than room temperature). Add the lemon juice.

5. Place the gelatin mixture over a bain-marie and heat until dissolved. Do not overheat. Quickly add the gelatin to the raspberry mixture. Gradually (to avoid lumps) fold this mixture into the reserved

NOTE 2: You will need approximately 2 pounds (910 g) fresh or frozen raspberries to make the purée. If fresh raspberries are out of season, or are too expensive, substitute frozen berries and omit them from the decoration. If the berries are frozen in sugar or sugar syrup, use only half the amount of sugar called for in the recipe.

meringue. Fold into the reserved whipped cream. Pipe into dessert glasses or cups. Refrigerate for about 2 hours to set.

6. Whip the remaining ¹/₂ cup (120 ml) of heavy cream with ¹/₂ teaspoon (2.5 g) granulated sugar to stiff peaks. Place in a pastry bag with a no. 7 (14-mm) star tip. Reserve in the refrigerator.

7. Presentation: Pipe a rosette of whipped cream in the center of a mousse. Decorate the cream with a small amount of the shaved dark chocolate. Arrange a ring of raspberries circling the rosette. Place the glass on a dessert plate lined with a doily and serve with an Almond Macaroon Cookie on the plate.

Triple Chocolate Terrine

16 servings

Baked Chocolate Sheet
(recipe follows)
Triple Chocolate Fillings
(recipes follows)
one recipe Raspberry Sauce
(page 1080)
Sour Cream Mixture for Piping
(page 1081)
fresh raspberries
sixteen small mint sprigs

NOTE 1: If the baker is using all of his bread forms, and the garde manger will not part with his pâté molds, you can make a form out of corrugated cardboard by following the directions given in White Chocolate and Pistachio Pâte, pages 830 and 831.

NOTE 2: The terrine should be sliced while it is frozen, but the slices must be allowed to thaw before serving. If you know you will use all sixteen servings within a short period of time, place the frozen slices directly onto dessert plates instead of the sheet pan to avoid moving them twice.

*B*ecause this dessert is fairly time-consuming and a bit complicated to produce, it makes a lot of sense to prepare more than you need while you are at it. The time required certainly does not expand relative to the yield, and if properly wrapped, the terrines will keep in the freezer for up to one month with no loss in quality. In other words, if you don't need sixteen servings it is silly to scale the recipe down; most of the time I double it. The base is very rich—a chocoholic's dream—and the presentation quite appealing, so I guarantee you won't be taking up space in the freezer too long!

While the initial steps take some time, plating and finishing the servings are just the opposite, which makes this dessert a favorite of mine when I need an elegant offering that can be served by someone with limited experience. All that is really required is to simply remove the terrines from the freezer, slice the pieces, and set on them on the plates. While the slices are softening there is plenty of time to add the sauce and garnish.

1. Line the bottom and the two long sides of a terrine mold that is approximately 3¹/₂ inches tall, 3¹/₂ inches wide, and 12 inches long (8.7 × 8.7 × 30 cm) with baking paper (see Figures 1–8 and 1–9, page 25). Cut the Chocolate Sheet into four pieces the size of the bottom of the mold. Place one piece in the bottom of the mold.

2. Add the Milk Chocolate Filling. Place a second sheet of cake on top. Add the White Chocolate Filling and place another cake layer on top. Add the Dark Chocolate Filling and top with the remaining cake sheet. Cover and place in the freezer for a least 3 hours or, preferably, overnight, to harden.

3. Remove the terrine from the freezer. Remove the form and peel away the baking paper. Position the terrine so that the layers run vertically. Cut into sixteen ³/₄-inch (2-cm) slices, using a thin knife dipped in hot water. Place the slices onto a sheet pan lined with baking paper as you cut them and place in the refrigerator until serving time (see note 2). Make sure each slice has thawed before serving.

4. Presentation: Carefully place a thawed slice of terrine, centered in the back half, on a dessert plate. Pour a pool of Raspberry Sauce in front of the slice and decorate the sauce with the Sour Cream Mixture (see pages 998 to 1006). Place three raspberries and a mint spring behind the dessert. Serve immediately.

Baked Chocolate Sheet

6 eggs, separated
4 ounces (115 g) granulated sugar
6 ounces (170 g) sweet dark
　chocolate, melted

Triple Chocolate Filling Base

3 ounces (85 g) granulated sugar
6 egg yolks (1/2 cup/120 ml)
2 eggs
1 cup (240 ml) heavy cream
individual filling ingredients
　(recipes follow)

Milk Chocolate Filling

1/2 teaspoon (1.5 g) unflavored gelatin
　powder
1 tablespoon (15 ml) cold water
6 ounces (170 g) sweet light
　chocolate, melted
one-third Triple Chocolate Filling Base

NOTE: Because such a small amount of gelatin
is used, it is impractical to soften and heat it in
a separate container and then add it to the
chocolate. By softening and dissolving the
gelatin in the mixing bowl you will not lose any
of the gelatin.

White Chocolate Filling

1/2 teaspoon (1.5 g) unflavored gelatin
　powder
1 tablespoon (15 ml) cold water
6 ounces (170 g) white chocolate,
　melted
one-third Triple Chocolate Filling
　Base

1. Beat the egg yolks with half of the sugar until light and fluffy. Set aside.

2. Whip the egg whites to a foam. Gradually add the remaining sugar and whip to soft peaks.

3. Combine the melted chocolate with the egg yolk mixture. Carefully fold in the egg whites. Spread the batter out to a 12-by-14-inch (30-×-35-cm) rectangle on a sheet of baking paper. Drag the paper onto a sheet pan (see Figure 16–15, page 842).

4. Bake immediately at 375°F (190°C) for about 15 minutes.

1. Prep the base and the other ingredients for all three fillings simultaneously, but assemble and add them to the terrine one at a time as you are ready to use them.

2. Combine the sugar, egg yolks, and whole eggs in a mixing bowl. Set the bowl over simmering water and heat the mixture, stirring constantly, to 140°F (60°C). Remove from the heat and whip at high speed until the mixture is cold.

3. Whip the heavy cream to soft peaks, then carefully fold the egg mixture into the cream. Divide into three equal portions (approximately 1 1/4 cups/300 ml each) and proceed as follows.

1. In an oversized mixing bowl, sprinkle the gelatin over the cold water and set aside to soften.

2. Make sure the melted chocolate is warm but not hot. Quickly stir the chocolate into a small portion of the filling base to temper it and prevent lumps. Then, still working quickly, add this mixture to the remainder of the filling base.

3. Place the gelatin mixture (still in the mixing bowl) over a bain-marie and heat to dissolve the gelatin. Do not overheat. Quickly add a small part of the chocolate mixture to the gelatin in the bowl, then stir in the remaining chocolate mixture.

Follow the directions for Milk Chocolate Filling. Take care not to overheat the white chocolate or it will become grainy.

Dark Chocolate Filling

¹/₂ teaspoon (1.5 g) unflavored gelatin powder

1 tablespoon (15 ml) cold water

5 ounces (140 g) sweet dark chocolate, melted

one-third Triple Chocolate Filling Base

Follow the directions for Milk Chocolate Filling.

White Chocolate and Pistachio Mousse with Chocolate Lace

16 servings

White Chocolate Mousse Filling (recipe follows)

Piping Chocolate, melted (page 904)

one-half recipe White Chocolate Sauce (page 1083)

Bitter Chocolate Sauce (page 1072)

small raspberries

reserved pistachios from the filling

edible flower petals

NOTE 1: I use 1³/₄-inch (4.5-cm) diameter plastic tubing cut into 3-inch (7.5-cm) lengths. The tubing can be purchased at a plastic or hobby supply store. Alternatively, you can make your own tubes by cutting 3-by-6¹/₄-inch (7.5-×-15.6-cm) pieces of polyurethane or acetate, overlapping the short ends, and taping together. This will give you a finished tube that is 1³/₄ inches (4.5 cm) in diameter. Be certain that the tubes stand up straight, and if not, adjust as necessary before lining them with baking paper.

It is not as important that tubes measure 1³/₄ inches (4.5 cm) in diameter as it is that the width of the paper used to pipe the chocolate lace is cut to the same size as the inside circumference of the tubes. The long edges can either miter together precisely or be slightly apart but must not overlap even the slightest bit or the lace will break when the paper is removed.

*T*his elegant towering dessert is one of the selections featured on the show "Spectacular Desserts" in the PBS program Cooking at the Academy. Although some of the steps are rather delicate, the final assembly (wrapping the chilled mousse in the chocolate lace) is actually much easier than it appears, providing you are properly organized, have a light touch, and have some experience in piping chocolate. My original intention was for this to be used as an à la carte dessert only, but I have made them for banquet service as well, including a recent graduation party for three hundred and fifty guests. That proved to be quite a challenge as the temperature was normal when we started to prep at the beginning of the week, but ended up hovering around 100°F outside some four days later; in fact it broke all records in San Francisco for June. The desserts turned out fine with some special attention, but I think I would put in a call to the weather forecaster before I tried that number again!

Heat wave or not, it is important that you pipe the chocolate lines for the lace as close together as specified and that the tubes of mousse are well chilled, or even still partially frozen, when you attach the lace. The chocolate lace is not only decorative but it helps to support the mousse after it thaws and softens. (One could, of course, add extra gelatin for support but the texture would suffer.) If it is not possible, or practical, for you to assemble the plates to order, you can decorate the plates with the sauces up to 30 minutes ahead of time and keep the desserts in the refrigerator, filled with raspberries, ready to be set on the plates as needed. Wear latex gloves when handling the desserts. Use the thicker grade of baking paper both for lining the tubes and piping the chocolate lace if it is available. The thinner grade of paper will wrinkle slightly from the moisture in the filling and this pattern will be visible on the side of the mousse.

1. Line the inside of sixteen tubes that are 1³/₄ inches in diameter and 3 inches tall (4.5 × 7.5 cm) with rectangles of baking paper cut 3 by 6 inches (7.5 × 15 cm). The paper will overlap inside the tubes about ¹/₂ inch (1.2 cm) (see note 1). Stand the tubes on end on a sheet pan.

2. Cut twenty additional rectangles of baking paper 4 inches wide and 5¹/₂ inches long (10 × 13.7 cm). You actually need only sixteen, but this will give you a few extra.

3. Place the White Chocolate Mousse Filling in a pastry bag with a no. 6 (12-mm) plain tip. Pipe the filling into the tubes. Place the tubes

NOTE 2: The frozen mousse will take about 3 hours to thaw in the refrigerator. If you need to serve the desserts sooner than that, leave them at room temperature for 30 minutes before applying the chocolate or, better yet, do not freeze them after filling the tubes, and let the mousse set up in the refrigerator instead. If you use this method you will have to be very careful when you attach the chocolate lace because the mousse will not be as firm. In any case, do not remove the paper from the desserts until you are ready to serve. The paper will protect the chocolate, and the desserts can be refrigerated overnight this way with no ill effects.

(still on the sheet pan) in the refrigerator overnight, or in the freezer for at least 2 hours, to set.

4. Place two of the reserved baking paper rectangles on a full sheet of baking paper. Place Piping Chocolate in a larger than normal piping bag (use a large enough bag and enough chocolate so that you can complete two desserts without refilling.) Cut a small opening in the bag. Pipe a straight line along the top long edge of one sheet. Then pipe a zigzag pattern diagonally over the paper first in one direction and then the opposite way, spacing the lines about ¼ inch (6 mm) apart (Figure 11–14). Be sure the diagonal lines extend out onto the larger sheet of paper on all sides. Repeat on the second sheet of paper.

5. As soon as you finish piping the second sheet of paper, pick up the first one, without disturbing the chocolate, and place it in front of you (Figure 11–15). Place one of the frozen servings of mousse at the

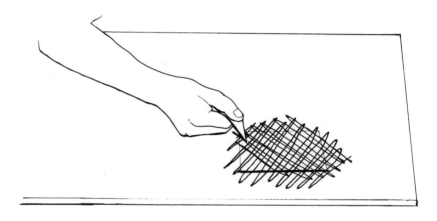

FIGURE 11–14 *Piping diagonal lines of chocolate in both directions after first piping a solid chocolate line along the top long edge of the baking paper rectangle*

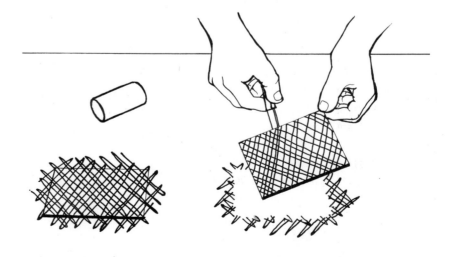

FIGURE 11–15 *Carefully lifting the paper with the chocolate piping by sliding a knife underneath and touching only the very edge, after completing the piping on a second baking paper rectangle*

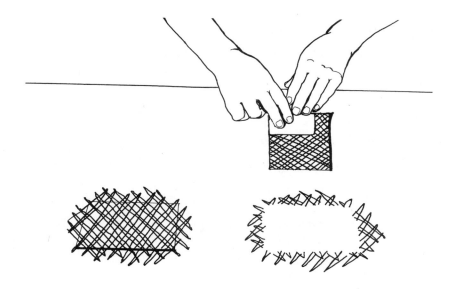

FIGURE 11–16 *Wrapping the chocolate lace around a frozen serving of mousse with the bottom edge of the mousse even with the edge of the baking paper, so that a portion of the chocolate lace and the solid chocolate line extend above the mousse at the opposite end*

edge of the paper, even with the bottom, so that there is 1 inch (2.5 cm) of piping above the mousse including the straight chocolate line. Roll the paper around the mousse so that the piped chocolate and the paper stick to the mousse (Figure 11–16). Do not overlap the ends; they should line up evenly. Stand the mousse on end. Repeat with the second sheet of paper. Cover the remaining servings with chocolate lace in the same way. Reserve in the refrigerator with the papers attached. (see note 2).

6. Adjust the consistency of the White Chocolate Sauce if necessary so that it is thick enough to hold its shape. Place a portion of the sauce in a piping bottle and reserve.

7. **Presentation:** Stand a serving of mousse on end, centered in the top half, on the base of a dessert plate. Carefully peel the paper away. Pipe quarter coin-sized dots of White Chocolate Sauce, very slightly apart, in a half circle in front of the dessert at the very edge of the base of the plate. Pipe a much smaller dot of Bitter Chocolate Sauce in the center of each white dot, using a piping bag. Drag a wooden skewer through the chocolate dots in a wavy pattern to create a series of hearts (see Figure 19–29, page 1004). Place approximately one dozen small raspberries on top of the dessert inside the chocolate "basket." Sprinkle the same amount of raspberries between the dessert and the sauce. Sprinkle some of the reserved pistachio nuts around the raspberries. Place a few edible flower petals among the berries and nuts.

White Chocolate Mousse Filling

6 cups (1 l, 440 ml)

6 ounces (170 g) pistachio nuts

2 cups (480 ml) heavy cream

4 teaspoons (12 g) unflavored gelatin powder

½ cup (120 ml) cold water

2 tablespoons (18 g) pectin powder (see note)

4 ounces (115 g) granulated sugar

4 egg whites (½ cup/120 ml)

12 ounces (340 g) white chocolate, melted

NOTE: Use regular canning pectin. If pectin is not available, increase the gelatin by 1 teaspoon (3 g) for a total of 5 teaspoons (15 g).

*B*e sure not to whip the cream any further than soft peaks and also be careful not to overheat the white chocolate. Not paying attention here will cause the filling to separate and become grainy. If this happens there is nothing that can be done but to start over. Don't make the filling until you are ready to use it because it will start to set fairly quickly.

1. Blanch the pistachio nuts. Remove the skins and chop the nuts coarsely. Reserve half of the nuts for decoration, choosing the better-looking pieces. Set the others aside to use in the filling.

2. Whip the heavy cream to soft peaks; do not overwhip. Reserve in the refrigerator.

3. Sprinkle the gelatin over the cold water and set aside to soften.

4. Combine the pectin powder and the granulated sugar in a mixing bowl. Stir in the egg whites. Place the bowl over simmering water and heat, stirring constantly with a whisk, until the mixture reaches 140°F (60°C). Remove from the heat and immediately whip until the mixture has cooled completely and has formed stiff peaks.

5. Place the gelatin mixture over simmering water and heat to dissolve. Working quickly, first stir the gelatin into the melted white chocolate. Then, stir the chocolate mixture into one-third of the meringue to temper it. Add this to the remaining meringue. Stir in the reserved whipped cream and the nuts set aside for the filling.

White Chocolate Bavarian-Style Tri-Color Mousse

16 servings

½ cup (120 ml) strained raspberry juice

1 teaspoon (5 ml) Beet Juice (page 3)

⅓ cup (80 ml) orange juice

grated zest of one orange

6½ teaspoons (20 g) gelatin powder

⅓ cup (80 ml) rum

6 ounces (170 g) granulated sugar

6 egg whites (¾ cup/180 ml)

2½ cups (600 ml) heavy cream

6 ounces (170 g) white chocolate, melted

3 ounces (85 g) sweet dark chocolate, melted

1 ounce (30 g) unsweetened chocolate, melted

unsweetened cocoa powder

*T*his is a rather exotic presentation for a mousse, requiring a few extra, but worthwhile, steps. If you don't mind just one more, try serving the mousse with fresh fruit sprinkled on the base of the plate around, but not on top of, the cocoa-powder decoration. This dessert looks best if served the same day it is made. While the dessert would be acceptable, the raspberry juice layer tends to bleed and stain the orange filling layer if it is kept for more than one day.

You will need a triangular form to make this recipe—ideally, one made from stainless-steel approximately 16 inches long, 3¾ inches deep, and 3¾ inches wide at the top (40 × 9.3 × 9.3 cm). If you do not have a stainless-steel form, you can use either the form from the Strawberry Pyramids recipe (see page 502) sectioned off at 16 inches (40 cm), or the Chalet Support Box (see page 835). Line either of these with baking paper, using a heavier grade since the thinner standard-grade paper will wrinkle slightly from moisture as the filling sets. If you are making a cardboard form specifically for this recipe, use the measurements above and follow the instructions for the Chalet Support Box.

1. Boil the raspberry juice until reduced to ⅓ cup (80 ml). Stir in the Beet Juice and then set aside to cool.

2. Combine the orange juice and orange zest. Sprinkle 2 teaspoons (6 g) of the gelatin on top.

3. Sprinkle 2 teaspoons (6 g) of gelatin on top of the cooled raspberry juice.

one-quarter recipe Chocolate Sauce
(page 1072) (see note)

one-quarter recipe Romanoff Sauce
(page 1081)

*NOTE: Prepare the Chocolate Sauce using ¹/₂
cup (120 ml) less water than specified in the
recipe. If you are using sauce that has already
been prepared, add melted chocolate to thicken
it to the proper (not too runny) consistency.*

4. Sprinkle the remaining 2¹/₂ teaspoons (8 g) of gelatin on top of the rum.

5. Combine the sugar and egg whites in a mixer bowl. Place the bowl over simmering water (bain-marie) and heat, whipping constantly to prevent the egg whites from cooking, to 140°F (60°C). Remove from the heat while continuing to stir. Place the bowl on the mixer and whip at high speed until soft peaks form. Reserve the meringue.

6. Whip the heavy cream to soft peaks. Reserve in the refrigerator.

7. Quickly add the melted white chocolate to about one-third of the reserved meringue to temper it. (The chocolate can be warm but not hot.) Add this, still stirring rapidly, to the remaining meringue. Divide the mixture (bavarian base) into three equal portions.

8. Heat the orange juice mixture to dissolve the gelatin. Quickly incorporate the juice into one portion of the bavarian base. Fold in one-third of the reserved whipped cream. Spoon into the bottom of a triangular form (see introduction). Spread out level, taking great care not to get any filling on the long sides of the form above the orange layer. Place the form in the refrigerator.

9. Heat the raspberry juice to dissolve the gelatin. Rapidly add this to one portion of the bavarian base. Fold in half of the remaining whipped cream. Spoon this filling on top of the orange filling and spread level in the same manner. Replace the form in the refrigerator.

10. Heat the rum to dissolve the gelatin. Stir into the melted dark and unsweetened chocolates. Quickly mix in about one-quarter of the remaining bavarian base to temper the mixture. Still working quickly, add this combination to the remainder of the base. Fold in the remaining whipped cream. Spread the chocolate filling on top of the raspberry filling in the form.

11. Place the finished dessert in the refrigerator for at least 2 hours to set the filling.

12. To remove the mousse from a stainless-steel form, quickly dip the bottom 1-inch (2.5-cm) into a hot-water bath, then run a knife dipped in hot water around all four sides, at the same time gently pushing the mousse away from the sides to let in air and release the suction. Invert onto a sheet of cardboard covered with plastic wrap. Use a palette knife to smooth the long edges as necessary to remove any melted mousse for a clean look. If you are using a form lined with baking paper as directed in the introduction, cut the mousse free from the form at the short ends, invert, and then peel away the baking paper. Refrigerate until time of service.

13. Presentation: Copy the template in Figure 11–17 and cut it out of ¹/₁₆-inch (3-mm) thick cardboard. The template as shown is the correct size to use in this recipe. Attach the template to a pie tin frame (see page 1040). Place the template on a dessert plate with the point of the triangle toward you. Lightly sift cocoa powder over the template and then remove it carefully. Repeat on as many dessert plates as you expect to need. Check the consistency of the Chocolate Sauce and the

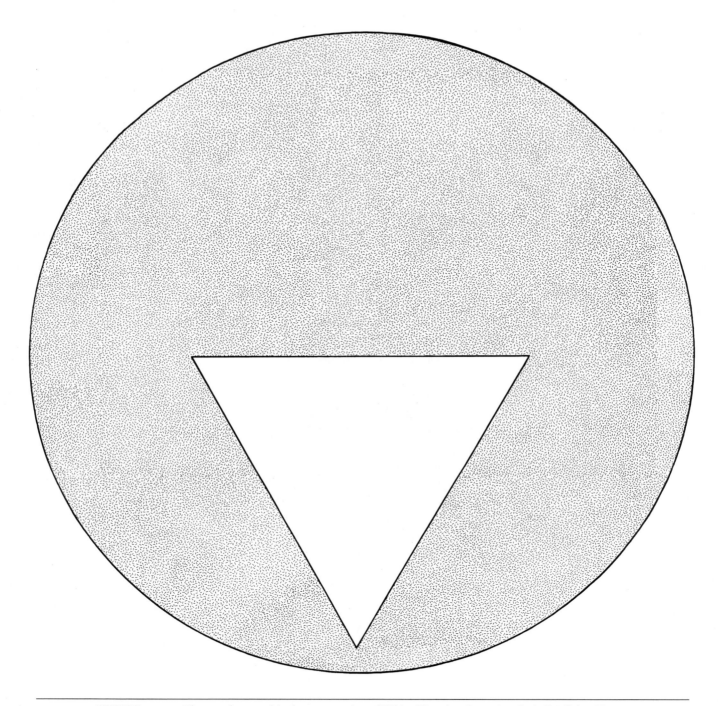

FIGURE 11–17 The template used in the presentation of White Chocolate Bavarian-Style Tri-Color Mousse

Romanoff Sauce. They must be fairly thick so that they will not run on the plate, and both must have the same consistency. Adjust if necessary. Place each sauce in a piping bottle and reserve.

14. Using a thin, sharp knife dipped into hot water, trim one short end of the mousse, if needed, to make a clean edge, and then cut a slice just slightly less than 1 inch (2.5 cm) wide. (Be sure to dip the knife into hot water and wipe it clean between each cut when slicing the remaining servings, as well.) Stand the slice on end just behind the cocoa-powder triangle on one of the prepared dessert plates, so that the cocoa powder appears as a shadow. Pipe dime-sized dots of Chocolate Sauce, evenly spaced approximately ³/₄ inch (2 cm) apart, around the perimeter of the base of the plate. Pipe a dot of Romanoff Sauce the same size between each of the Chocolate Sauce dots. Run a skewer through the center of the dots in one long sweeping motion around the plate. Serve immediately.

Soufflés

The French word *soufflé* literally means "to puff" or "to blow" up. Unfortunately, soufflés have a somewhat undeserved reputation as not only being delicate and airy but also a rather frustrating test of the chef's skill, since they may fail to rise at all or, having done so, collapse at the wrong time! The phrase "timing is everything" certainly applies here.

There is probably no dessert that causes more fear and insecurity in the average cook than the soufflé. They have intimidated most of us at some point, at least until one realizes how easy they actually are, and apparently we are not alone. Mrs. Beeton proclaimed in her book of 1861 that "Soufflés demand, for their successful manufacture, an experienced cook." She also advised that "The most essential thing to insure success of these, the prettiest but most difficult of all entremets, is to secure the best ingredients from an honest tradesman." Louis Eustache Ude's *The French Cook,* 1813, had this to say about soufflés, "If sent up in proper time they are very good eating, if not, they are no better than other puddings." And the soufflé even took its toll on Augustus Escoffier who, at one very important dinner party, was so worried about the timing that he fired batches every three minutes to ensure that some would be ready at exactly the right moment. (I must confess this is a trick I have taken advantage of myself at times, although no one ever told me about it. I guess if you are thrown in the water you learn to swim.)

I have a vivid memory from the time I was just starting out of being told by the head chef "Bo, starting tomorrow you are in charge of the soufflés." I knew he expected only the best. His standard joke, which he played on every unsuspecting new cook, was to peek into the oven about the time the soufflés he had made himself were finished and say "Quick, hand me a knife. I need to cut my soufflé away from the top of the oven!" This was his way of letting us know he was very proud of the height of his soufflés.

I think what really has people worried when it comes to making soufflés is that should they make a mistake there is no quick recovery since it takes a minimum of 15 minutes to produce a replacement. However, there is no reason for this to happen. Once the daunting characteristics of the soufflé myths have been overcome, and your self-confidence has returned, making soufflés is just another part of the day's work. This is exactly what I tell my students when I do my soufflé lecture and demonstration. And to dispel the tales that caution you to whisper and tiptoe around the kitchen while the soufflés are in the oven, or the only one that really has any foundation—not to open the oven door during baking, I do just that about halfway through (but just for a second, and I close it very gently). When I remove the soufflés from the oven, puffed twice as high as the ramekins to the amazement of my students, I tell them I think I just proved my point.

Soufflés fall into two categories: dessert or savory. Cheese soufflé is probably the best known of the savory variety, but these are also made with spinach, other vegetables, and seafood. Among dessert soufflés, the classic liqueur soufflé cannot be beat; this category includes the famous and tremendously popular Soufflé Grand Marnier and the Harlequin Soufflé, which, with its two types of batter baked together, offers the ultimate proof that the chef has mastered the soufflé technique when prepared successfully. A liqueur soufflé will always rise higher than a fruit soufflé, such as blueberry or apricot for example, since the evaporating alcohol fumes contribute to the process which makes the souffle rise: Essentially, the air that is trapped in the whipped egg whites becomes lighter and expands as it is heated. Soon after the soufflé is removed from the oven the trapped air begins to escape and the soufflé deflates like a punctured balloon. While you don't want this to happen before the guest has seen the dessert, it is actually desirable and is a good test of a perfectly made soufflé. If a soufflé just sits there high and mighty and never deflates, it is either overbaked and dried out from below so you are looking at an empty shell, or the soufflé is much too heavy and probably tastes more like pudding than a soufflé. Soufflés cooked a shorter time in a hotter oven will rise slightly higher, but will fall faster when removed than those which are cooked longer at a lower heat.

To aid the soufflé batter in rising straight up from the form, it should always be baked in a traditional round, soufflé ramekin with straight sides. The two most common sizes for individual servings are 3½ inches in diameter with a capacity of approximately 5 ounces and 4½ inches in diameter, which holds about 1 cup. The largest size used has a two-quart capacity and will serve eight to ten.

Fruit soufflés can get a little bit tricky, and depending on the variety, you may have to use trial and error when reducing the fruit pulp. Enough moisture must be removed to concentrate the flavor and keep the mixture from becoming too thin, but if the pulp becomes too dense the egg whites will not support it. Fruit soufflés are sometimes baked in a fruit shell, the most prevalent being an orange. These soufflés are really more show than substance, however, since the batter must be little more than flavored whipped egg whites in order for it to be able to puff up and out of the fruit.

Crepe soufflés, as indicated by their name, are made by baking soufflé batter inside a crepe. This is generally done by spreading the batter on a cooked crepe, folding it in half, and baking à la minute as with any other soufflé. My complaint with this method is that the deskserts turn out very flat, and one of the main characteristics of a soufflé is its height. Therefore, I place the crepe inside a ramekin, fill with soufflé batter, bake, and then carefully remove the crepe from the ramekin and transfer to a serving plate. Even with the ramekin for support, this type of soufflé will not rise as high as a conventional soufflé since the batter will stick to the crepe on the sides.

Other desserts influenced by soufflés are the Soufflé Omelette (page 709) and Soufflé Pancakes (page 675). Both use whipped egg whites folded into a batter, causing it to expand rapidly in a hot oven.

 ## Blueberry Soufflé
12 servings

one recipe Liqueur Soufflé batter (page 581)
1 pound, 6 ounces (625 g) fresh or thawed frozen blueberries
3 ounces (85 g) granulated sugar
powdered sugar
one recipe Raspberry Sauce (page 1080)

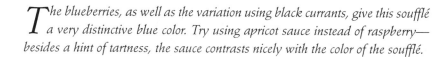
The blueberries, as well as the variation using black currants, give this soufflé a very distinctive blue color. Try using apricot sauce instead of raspberry—besides a hint of tartness, the sauce contrasts nicely with the color of the soufflé.

1. Prepare the full recipe of soufflé batter through step four, omitting the liqueur and using 8 egg whites rather than 10.

2. Purée the blueberries with the sugar. Place in a heavy saucepan and reduce by half over low heat, forming a thick pulp. Stir frequently, especially when the blueberries start to thicken, to prevent the mixture from burning. Remove from the heat and reserve.

3. Prepare twelve 3½-inch (8.7-cm) diameter, 5-ounce (150-ml) capacity, soufflé ramekins as directed in the recipe for Liqueur Soufflé.

4. Add the blueberry pulp to the soufflé batter base.

5. About 30 minutes before the soufflés are to be served, whip the egg whites and sugar to stiff peaks and fold the soufflé base into the egg whites. For à la carte service, follow the directions in Liqueur Soufflé, but use 1½ parts base to 2 parts egg white. Pipe the batter into the prepared ramekins, filling them to the top.

6. Bake immediately at 400°F (205°C) for approximately 20 minutes or until done. The sides should be light brown.

7. Sift powdered sugar lightly over the tops. Serve immediately with Raspberry Sauce.

 ## VARIATIONS

The recipe for Blueberry Soufflé can be used with other fruits and berries as well. Depending on the natural sweetness of the fruit you choose, you might need to adjust the amount of sugar added when you purée it. Fruits such as apricots or plums are excellent choices when in season. Use the same amount of fruit as in the Blueberry Soufflé (weigh the fruit after you have removed the stones). Leave the skin on if using plums; it will add a nice color to the pulp. Purée and reduce as directed in Blueberry Soufflé. Another variation that looks and tastes very distinctive uses black currants. Follow the directions for Blueberry Soufflé substituting black currants for the blueberries. Serve with Apricot Sauce. If using canned black currants in heavy syrup, drain and discard the syrup before weighing the fruit (or use it for sorbet after adjusting the Baumé), and omit the sugar in the recipe.

Crepe Soufflé

16 servings

4 ounces (115 g) granulated sugar

1½ ounces (40 g) cornstarch

1½ ounces (40 g) bread flour

1½ ounces (40 g) soft unsalted butter

1½ cups (360 ml) milk

6 egg yolks (½ cup/120 ml)

½ teaspoon (2.5 ml) vanilla extract

⅓ cup (80 ml) liqueur

sixteen Crepes (page 5) (see note)

6 egg whites (¾ cup/180 ml)

one and one-half recipes Strawberry
    Sauce (page 1081)

Sour Cream Mixture for Piping
    (page 1081)

powdered sugar

NOTE: *Use the typical 6-inch (15-cm) Crepe
or a slightly smaller size. The outer edge of a
larger Crepe will not be supported by the
ramekin and will fall over during baking.*

*T*he traditional crepe soufflé is actually closer to a soufflé pancake than a
soufflé, (crepe, of course, is the French word for pancake) and as discussed
in the introduction to soufflés, presents itself rather flat. This version also differs
from the norm in that the sauce is served on the plate rather than on the side in a
sauce boat.

1. Combine about one-third of the sugar with the cornstarch.
Reserve.

2. Mix the flour and butter to form a paste. Heat the milk to the
scalding point in a heavy saucepan. Add the butter and flour mixture
and stir with a whisk; it will melt into the milk. Quickly mix in one-
third of the egg yolks. Bring to a boil over low heat, stirring constantly.
Cook the mixture until it thickens, about 1 minute. Remove from the
heat but continue to stir for 10 to 15 seconds.

3. Add the remaining egg yolks, vanilla, liqueur, and the sugar and
cornstarch mixture. Cover the custard mixture and reserve. It will keep
for up to two days if refrigerated.

4. Thirty minutes before the Crepe Soufflés are to be served, place
one Crepe for each serving you are firing, browned-side down, on top
of a 5-ounce (150-ml) soufflé ramekin that is 3½ inches (8.7 cm) wide.
Push the Crepes halfway into the forms.

5. Whip the egg whites until they have quadrupled in volume and
have a thick and foamy consistency. Gradually whip in the reserved
two-thirds of the sugar, then whip a few seconds longer until the egg
whites are stiff but not dry. Fold the egg whites into the reserved custard mixture.

6. Pipe the soufflé batter into the ramekins on top of the Crepes so
that the Crepes are pushed to the bottom and line the sides and bottom
of the ramekins. Fill the forms even with the rim of the ramekins.

7. Bake immediately at 400°F (205°C) for approximately 20 minutes. These do not puff up as high as a regular soufflé but will stick to
the Crepe and crack on the top.

8. Presentation: Cover the base of as many dessert plates as you
have soufflés in the oven with Strawberry Sauce. A few minutes before
the soufflés are finished baking, pipe five evenly spaced dots of Sour
Cream Mixture, about the size of a quarter coin, in the Strawberry
Sauce on each plate close to the perimeter of the Strawberry Sauce. Use
the tip of a small wooden skewer to shape the Sour Cream Mixture
into hearts with tails (see Figure 19–30, page 1005). Remove the soufflés from the oven. Quickly, but gently, remove them from the
ramekins by inverting each one into your hand. Place the soufflés right-
side up in the center of the prepared plates. Sift powdered sugar lightly
over the tops. Serve immediately.

Liqueur Soufflé

twelve 3¹/₂-inch (8.7-cm) diameter soufflés or eight 4¹/₂-inch (11.2-cm) diameter soufflés

melted unsalted butter
granulated sugar to coat forms
5 ounces (140 g) granulated sugar
1¹/₂ ounces (40 g) cornstarch
2 ounces (55 g) bread flour
2 ounces (55 g) soft unsalted butter
2 cups (480 ml) milk
10 egg yolks (⁷/₈ cup/210 ml)
1 teaspoon (5 ml) vanilla extract
¹/₂ cup (120 ml) liqueur
10 egg whites (1¹/₄ cups/300 ml), at
    room temperature
one recipe Sabayon (page 718)
    (see note)
powdered sugar

four 3¹/₂-inch (8.7-cm) diameter soufflés or two 4¹/₂-inch (11.2-cm) diameter soufflés

melted unsalted butter
granulated sugar to coat forms
2 ounces (55 g) granulated sugar
2 tablespoons (16 g) cornstarch
1 ounce or 4 tablespoons (30 g) bread
    flour
1 ounce or 2 tablespoons (30 g) soft
    unsalted butter
³/₄ cup or 12 tablespoons (180 ml)
    milk
3 egg yolks (¹/₄ cup/60 ml)
¹/₄ teaspoon (1.25 ml) vanilla extract
3 tablespoons (45 ml) liqueur
3 egg whites, at room temperature
one-third recipe Sabayon
    (page 718)
powdered sugar

NOTE: Traditionally, a Liqueur Soufflé is always served with Sabayon. However, you may want to substitute Vanilla Custard Sauce (page 1082), which is much more convenient as it can be made ahead of time and therefore

*T*his *recipe can be used to make any type of Liqueur Soufflé. Just use the desired flavor in the soufflé base and use the same liqueur to flavor the sauce. If the amount of liqueur called for in the recipe does not give the soufflé enough flavor when using a particular variety, intensify it by soaking Ladyfingers (see page 275) in the same liqueur and placing two in the middle of the soufflé batter as you fill the forms.*

1. Use the melted butter to thoroughly grease the insides of the appropriate number of soufflé ramekins depending on the size used. Fill one of the forms halfway with granulated sugar. Twist the form so that the sugar coats the entire inside, then pour the sugar into the next form. Repeat until all the forms are coated, adding more sugar as necessary. Set the forms aside.

2. Combine about one-third of the measured sugar with the cornstarch. Reserve this mixture and the remaining sugar separately.

3. Mix the flour and butter to form a paste. Heat the milk to the scalding point in a heavy saucepan. Add the butter and flour mixture and stir with a whisk; it will melt into the milk. Quickly mix in one-third of the egg yolks. Bring to a boil over low heat, stirring constantly. Cook the mixture until it thickens, about 1 minute. Remove from the heat but continue to stir for 10 to 15 seconds to ensure a smooth cream.

4. Add the remaining egg yolks, vanilla, liqueur, and the sugar and cornstarch mixture. Cover the mixture and reserve. It will keep for up to two days if refrigerated.

For banquet service

1. About 35 minutes before serving, whip the egg whites until they have quadrupled in volume and have a thick and foamy consistency. Gradually whip in the reserved two-thirds of the sugar, then whip a few seconds longer until the egg whites are stiff but not dry. Gradually fold the reserved custard mixture into the egg whites.

2. Immediately place the soufflé batter in a pastry bag with a no. 8 (16-mm) plain tip. Pipe into the prepared soufflé ramekins, making a smooth mound slightly above the rim of the ramekin. Be sure the batter does not actually stick to the rim itself.

3. Bake at once at 400°F (205°C) for about 25 minutes or until done. The sides and top should be light brown. While the soufflés are baking make the Sabayon and pour into sauce pitchers.

4. Presentation: Quickly remove the soufflés from the oven and sift powdered sugar lightly over the tops. Place the ramekins on dessert plates lined with doilies. Serve immediately with the accompanying sauce.

For à la carte service

1. Whip your egg whites and sugar as needed for each order as it comes in. Until you have enough experience to divide those ingredients into single portions by eye, whip extra whites to ensure that you will

allows the chef to concentrate on the soufflé at the last moment. If you wish, flavor the custard sauce with a little of the same liqueur used in the soufflé.

have enough (in which case you will also need more sugar than what was set aside).

2. Combine approximately two parts whipped egg whites with one part custard base and spoon into the form. Unless you have another order immediately, do not use any leftover whipped egg whites. Instead, try to adjust the amount you use for the next order. If you suspect that you will need all of the soufflés, but not all at the same time, you can assemble the soufflés all together and hold them (unbaked) in a hot bain-marie (about 160°F/71°C). You can keep them for up to 30 minutes before baking without compromising the quality. When you are ready to proceed, remove them from the bain-marie and bake as directed, reducing the baking time by a few minutes. This method is also helpful when you have a misunderstanding with the dining room about when the order was fired.

VARIATIONS
Chocolate Soufflé

12 small or 8 large servings

*P*repare the full recipe for Liqueur Soufflé as directed with the following changes:

1. Substitute an equal amount of crème de cacao for the liqueur in the batter.

2. Mix 1¹/₂ ounces (40 g) unsweetened cocoa powder with the cornstarch.

3. Add 1 ounce (30 g) melted sweet dark chocolate to the warm custard.

4. Add 2 additional egg whites. Bake and serve as directed for either banquet or à la carte service.

5. Substitute Vanilla Custard Sauce flavored with crème de cacao for the Sabayon.

For the small recipe, add 5 teaspoons (12.5 g) unsweetened cocoa powder, ¹/₂ ounce (15 g) melted sweet dark chocolate, and 1 extra egg white.

Harlequin Souffle

12 servings

*A*fter coating the soufflé ramekins with butter and sugar, stand a piece of cardboard in the center of each form (Figure 11–18). Reserve. Prepare the full Liqueur Soufflé recipe as directed, making the following changes:

1. Divide the custard, reserved sugar, and egg whites in half, separately.

2. Add 1 ounce (30 g) of unsweetened cocoa powder and 1 tablespoon (15 ml) melted sweet dark chocolate to one portion of the custard.

3. Add 1 additional egg white to one portion of the egg whites. Set next to the chocolate-flavored custard to distinguish it.

4. Combine the custard with sugar and egg whites as directed, making two separate batters and using the larger group of egg whites in the chocolate batter to compensate for the addition of the chocolate.

5. Fill one side of each of the prepared forms with the plain and chocolate batters. Pull the cardboard *straight* up and out. Bake and serve as directed for either banquet or à la carte service.

FIGURE 11–18 Using a small piece of cardboard to divide a soufflé ramekin in half for Harlequin Souffle

Pecan-Raisin Soufflé

12 servings

melted unsalted butter

granulated sugar to coat the ramekins

one recipe Liqueur Soufflé batter
(page 581)

¹/₂ cup (120 ml) whiskey

one-half recipe Vanilla Custard Sauce
(page 1082) (see note following
Liqueur Soufflé)

one-quarter recipe Caramelized
Pecans (page 965)

1 tablespoon (12 g) Hazelnut Paste
(page 9)

2 ounces (55 g) dark raisins

powdered sugar

*I*t is certainly recommended that the soufflé be baked immediately after the whipped egg whites have been folded into the batter. However, if they are beaten perfectly stiff, the filled unbaked soufflé ramekins can be refrigerated for up to two hours.

1. Prepare twelve 3¹/₂-inch (8.7-cm) diameter, 5-ounce (150-ml) capacity soufflé ramekins as directed in the recipe for Liqueur Soufflé. Reserve.

2. Prepare the full recipe of Liqueur Soufflé batter through step four, substituting ¹/₄ cup (60 ml) of the whiskey for the liqueur.

3. Add the remaining ¹/₄ cup (60 ml) of whiskey to the Custard Sauce and reserve. If refrigerated, bring to room temperature before serving.

4. Coarsely crush the Caramelized Pecans. Mix the pecans, Hazelnut Paste, and raisins into the soufflé batter before combining with the whipped egg whites. Fill the prepared soufflé ramekins and bake as directed in Liqueur Soufflé for either banquet or à la carte service.

5. Sift powdered sugar over the tops and serve immediately with the whiskey-flavored sauce.

Soufflé Rothschild

12 servings

melted unsalted butter

granulated sugar to coat the forms

6 ounces (170 g) mixed candied fruit
including candied cherries

³/₄ cup (180 ml) Danzinger
Goldwasser liqueur

one-half recipe Mousseline Sauce
(page 1076)

one recipe Liqueur Soufflé batter
(page 581)

powdered sugar

fresh cherries

or

strawberries dipped halfway in dark
coating chocolate

*R*othschild, the famous banking family, has lent its name to a number of desserts, created by equally famous (if not as wealthy) chefs who worked for them. The most celebrated being Carême, who invented Soufflé Rothschild, distinguished by candied fruit mascerated in Goldwasser liqueur. If candied cherries are not available, use maraschino cherries. Rinse the cherries and dry thoroughly before chopping them.

1. Prepare twelve 3¹/₂-inch (8.7-cm) diameter, 5-ounce (150-ml) capacity soufflé ramekins as directed in the recipe for Liqueur Soufflé. Reserve.

2. Chop the candied fruit into small pieces, approximately the size of dried currants. Add a little more than ¹/₂ cup (120 ml) Danzinger Goldwasser liqueur (save the remainder to flavor the sauce). Set the fruit aside to macerate for at least one hour.

3. Flavor the Mousseline Sauce with the remaining liqueur and reserve. If refrigerated, bring the sauce to room temperature before serving.

4. Prepare the full recipe of Liqueur Soufflé batter, substituting the fruit-liqueur mixture for the liqueur.

5. Fill the prepared soufflé forms and bake as directed in Liqueur Soufflé for either banquet or à la carte service.

6. Sift powdered sugar lightly over the tops. Place a few fresh cherries or a chocolate-dipped strawberry on the plate and serve immediately with the Mousseline Sauce in a separate container.

12

Meringues

Basic Meringues

    French Meringue

    Italian Meringue

    Japonaise Meringue Batter

    Meringue Noisette

    Swiss Meringue

Meringue Desserts

    Baked Alaska

    Blackberry Meringue
      Tartlets

    Budapest Swirls

    Cassata Parfait
      with Meringue

    Frozen Raspberry Mousse
      with Meringues

Gâteau Arabe

Ice Cream Cake Jamaica

Individual Baked Alaska
    Bee Hives

Japonaise

Marjolaine

Meringue Black Forest
    Cake

Meringue Glacé Leda

Meringue Landeck

Mocha Meringues

Snowbird in a Chocolate
    Cage

Vacherin with Plum Ice
    Cream

Meringue can be loosely defined as a mixture of beaten egg whites and granulated sugar. While the name is French, the origin is not documented, although history tells us that meringue may have been named for either the Swiss town of *Meringen* or the German city of *Mehrinyghen.* We do know that meringue has been around since the early sixteenth century.

Composition

Meringue is made of egg whites and sugar whipped together to incorporate air and form soft or stiff peaks. Egg whites whipped without sugar are not meringue; they are simply egg whites whipped to a dry consistency.

In the recipes that follow, egg whites are measured by volume rather than by number. This measurement is not only more precise, but it is also easier in professional kitchens where a supply of egg whites is usually on hand. There are 7 to 8 egg whites in 1 cup (240 ml). Using the even number (8) makes it easier to divide when measuring fractions of a cup and is simple

to remember along with 4 whole eggs and 12 egg yolks per cup. See page 1130 for further equivalency information on both egg whites and egg yolks.

How Egg Whites Expand

Eggs have excellent foaming ability. When egg yolks, which contain a fatty substance that destroys the albumen's ability to foam, are removed, egg whites alone can increase in volume by up to eight times. This is possible through close teamwork by the two proteins albumen and ovalbumin. When the egg whites are beaten, the albumen protein forms a very stable mass of tiny air bubbles while part of the protein molecules bond together and form a fragile network that holds the moisture in place (an egg white contains about 85 percent water). This alone would suffice if the beaten egg whites were not to be cooked, but because air expands when it is heated, the network of denatured proteins on the surface would be destroyed and immediately collapse if it were not for the ovalbumin protein. While the ovalbumin does not play such an important role when the egg whites are beaten, it coagulates when heated, forming its own network in the meringue and making it resistant to collapse as the water evaporates. In other words, the ovalbumin protein is what makes it possible to change a liquid foam into a solid dry mass with heat.

The Effects of Sugar

Meringue would be very bland without the addition of sugar, and sugar also helps to stabilize the foam, especially in the oven. Its addition, however, is something of a mixed blessing since sugar also delays the foaming process and decreases the volume and lightness of the meringue. This is especially noticeable when meringue is whipped by hand, but even when using an electric mixer the granulated sugar must be introduced gradually, and in most cases never before the whipped egg whites have increased approximately four times in volume, so that the sugar will not prevent the albumen from working to stiffen the foam. As an example of what it means to add the sugar gradually, when making the recipe for French Meringue, which uses 2 pounds of sugar, it should take approximately 3 minutes to add this amount of sugar to the egg whites (a little longer if the egg whites are cold).

The amount of sugar used in a meringue will vary in accordance with the desired texture and intended use of the finished product. Soft meringues, which are typically used for toppings on tarts and pies, can be made with equal quantities of sugar and egg white by weight. Hard meringues, which are baked dry, usually have a sugar to egg white ratio of two to one.

Salt

Just like sugar, salt has a mixed effect. While it acts as a flavor enhancer, it increases the amount of time needed to whip the whites and also decreases the foam's stability, although both of these occur only to a very small degree.

The Addition of Acid

Citric acid (lemon juice), Tartaric Acid Solution, and cream of tartar (which is the solid salt of the tartaric acid mixed with cornstarch) have no effect on the volume of the meringue, but they help to stabilize the foam by decreasing the pH level in the albumen, making the foam less apt to collapse. Only a small amount of any of these acids should be used, as too much, in addition to adversely changing the taste of the meringue, will impede coagulation during baking. It has been commonly accepted that a copper mixing bowl produces a superior and more rapidly whipped egg white foam. However, current research indicates that the degree to which a copper mixing bowl is preferable to a stainless bowl is questionable. While you should certainly avoid plastic or wood, because both are very hard to clean of fat, aluminium, which is corrosive and tends to impart a grayish color, and glass, which is not really suited for use in the kitchen, the benefit of copper and its alleged ability to impart an acidity to the whites as it comes in contact with the albumen is a phenomenon which is now disputed. Although there is certainly no proof of any disadvantage to using a copper bowl, the addition of any of the acids previously mentioned will generate the same result.

Whipping

Meringue whipped to a soft peak will not hold its shape; it will slowly settle, or fall, instead. Meringue properly whipped to a stiff peak will not change shape as you pipe it from a pastry bag or work with it; you should actually be able to turn the bowl of meringue upside down after it is finished whipping with no problem (or mess). Be observant: There is a fine line between stiff peaks and overwhipped, dry, peaks. Meringue that is overwhipped and dry is hard to pipe out into precise shapes and is impossible to fold into a batter without getting small lumps of meringue throughout. Meringue whipped to stiff peaks should still appear shiny, not dry or broken.

Precautions

For perfect meringue, follow these guidelines:

1. Although it is not critical, if at all possible use egg whites at room temperature.

2. Be sure the egg whites are not so old that they have started to deteriorate. The substance becomes thinner and clearer as the protein starts to diminish.

3. Because fat prevents the albumen in egg whites from expanding, make certain they are clean and free of any egg yolk particles. The mixing bowl and whip or whisk must also be perfectly clean.

4. Make sure there are no foreign particles (such as flour) in the sugar.

5. Using a copper bowl and/or a balloon whisk can be helpful when making meringue, but they are not absolutely necessary.

Uses

Meringue is a key ingredient in the pastry kitchen. Baked layers of meringue are used in cakes and pastries, such as the famous Marjolaine; it is piped into ornate shapes for Vacherin and Dacquoise; it is made into cookies, added to buttercream, and used to top desserts such as Baked Alaska and Lemon Meringue Pie. In Europe today, many pastry shops do not make their own meringue, but to save time and money they buy it from companies that specialize in baked meringue products. This makes sense, since the meringue formulas are basically generic, and it is what you create with them that makes the difference.

Varieties

There are three basic types of meringue: French, Swiss, and Italian. The ingredients for each of the three types are essentially the same, but the methods of preparation and the end results are different. A fourth type, Japonaise, is a hybrid of French meringue with the addition of almond meal and a small amount of cornstarch.

French Meringue

French Meringue is best for baking *au naturel,* for mixing with nuts, and for use as a cake base. If it is made and baked correctly, French Meringue is very tender, light, and fragile. It should be piped or spread out immediately after whipping, or the egg whites may start to separate from the sugar. This type of meringue should not be added to fillings that will not be baked, or otherwise eaten raw, unless the meringue is made with pasteurized egg whites to guard against salmonella.

Italian Meringue

Italian Meringue is a better choice if the meringue must stand for some time. It is denser because the egg whites are partially cooked, and therefore it holds up longer before starting to deflate. Italian Meringue is also preferable to use in a dessert when the meringue is eaten raw, or with only partial further cooking as, for example, when it is added to a filling or when only the outside is browned as in Baked Alaska. When Italian Meringue is baked all the way through it is harder than French Meringue and not very pleasant to eat.

Swiss Meringue

Swiss Meringue could be described as a mixture between the French and Italian Meringues. It can be eaten raw since the egg whites have been pasteurized by being heated to 140°F (60°C) with the sugar. Swiss Meringue is quicker and easier to produce than its Italian counterpart, but it is not as stable and should be used fairly soon once it has been prepared. It is typically used in buttercream and fillings, but it can also be piped out into cookies or made into other shapes, then baked or dried in the same way as French Meringue. However, for this use, Swiss Meringue should be made with less sugar to ensure a better volume and a stiff peak.

Flavoring and Coloring

Nuts, cocoa powder, and other flavorings, as well as coloring, can be added to meringue. These are added just before the meringue is finished being whipped to the proper stiffness. Use regular water-soluble food coloring for this, adding just a small amount at a time.

Baking

Meringue should be baked at a low temperature. For most types of meringue this is between 210 and 220°F (99–104°C). In the case of a meringue containing ground nuts, such as Japonaise, the nuts will absorb some of the moisture in the egg whites and allow the meringue to dry more quickly.

You do not bake meringue so much as you dry it out. Meringue should not color as it is baked but should remain white. However, a slight hint of color (off-white) is acceptable.

Storage

While meringue batter is never prepared in advance as a *mise en place* item, generally speaking, the more sugar that has been whipped into the whites, the longer the batter will maintain its volume and stiffness without deflating as it is shaped. French and Japonaise Meringues should be piped out or spread into the desired shape immediately after whipping, even if the batter cannot be baked right away as it should be. The meringue will have less stability and will deflate to a greater degree as it is agitated (through spreading and/or being placed in a piping bag) after sitting for even as short a time as 10 minutes. Italian and (to a lesser degree) Swiss Meringues will hold their shapes for a much longer time. The Italian variety has greater stability because it is partially cooked during preparation. If made properly, it will keep for several hours. However, if too much sugar ends up sticking to the side of the bowl or the whip, the keeping time will decrease accordingly.

All cooked (dried) meringue is susceptible to becoming soft from absorbing moisture in the air and should always be stored airtight in a warm, dry place. Plain baked meringue will keep fresh this way for many weeks. Japonaise, or other meringues which contain nuts, can become rancid if stored too long.

The following table, Figure 12–1, contrasts the formulas and characterizes some of the differences in the basic varieties of meringue.

Comparison of Meringue Formulas Relative to One Pint (approximately 16) Egg Whites					
	FRENCH	**ITALIAN**	**SWISS**	**JAPONAISE**	**NOISETTE**
Egg White	1 pint (480 ml)	1 pint (480 ml)	1 pint (480 ml)	1 pint (480 ml)	1 pint (480 ml)
Granulated Sugar	2 pounds (910 g)	1 pound, 8 ounces (680 g)	1 pound, 8 ounces to 2 pounds (680 to 910 g)	1 pound, 6 ounces (625 g)	2 pounds (910 g)
Cornstarch	0	0	0	2 ounces (55 g)	2 ounces (55 g)
Corn Syrup	0	1 cup (240 ml)	0	0	0
Water	0	1 cup (240 ml)	0	0	0
Nuts	0	0	0	1 pound (455 g)	8 ounces (225 g)
Other	lemon juice	0	0	0	vanilla extract
Preparation Method	The lemon juice is added to egg whites at room temperature. The whites are whipped until they have quadrupled in volume. The sugar is added gradually as the mixture is whipped to stiff peaks.	The sugar, corn syrup, and water are boiled to 240°F (115°C). The hot syrup is added to partially whipped whites at medium speed. The mixture is whipped at high speed until it has cooled and formed stiff peaks.	The sugar and egg whites are placed in a bain-marie and heated to 140°F (60°C) while being whipped constantly. The mixture is then whipped off the heat until it has cooled and formed soft or stiff peaks, depending on the amount of sugar used and the application.	Finely ground blanched almonds and cornstarch are combined. The sugar is gradually added to partially whipped whites as they are whipped to stiff peaks. The nut mixture is then folded in by hand.	Ground hazelnuts and cornstarch are combined. The sugar is gradually added to partially whipped whites as they are whipped to stiff peaks. The vanilla is added, and the nut mixture is then folded in by hand.
Uses					
Cake Layers	Yes	No	Occasionally	Yes	Yes
Dessert Topping	No	Yes	Yes	No	No
Fillings	No	Yes	Yes	No	No
Meringue Glace	Yes	No	Occasionally	No	Yes
Cookies and Pastries	Yes	No	Occasionally	Yes	Yes
Buttercream	No	Yes	Yes	No	No
Sherbet	No	Yes	Yes	No	No

FIGURE 12–1 A comparison of meringue formulas relative to one pint of egg whites

Basic Meringues

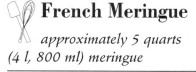 **French Meringue**

approximately 5 quarts (4 l, 800 ml) meringue

1 pint (480 ml) egg whites, at room temperature

3 drops lemon juice or Tartaric Acid Solution (page 1115)

2 pounds (910 g) granulated sugar

NOTE: Ideally, French Meringue should not only be piped or shaped right away after it is prepared, it should also be baked immediately after forming.

1. In a copper or stainless-steel bowl, whip the egg whites with the lemon juice or tartaric acid until the mixture has quadrupled in volume and has the consistency of a thick foam, 1 to 2 minutes.

2. Still whipping at high speed, gradually add the sugar; this should take about 3 minutes. Continue to whip the meringue at high speed until stiff peaks form. Do not overwhip.

3. Immediately pipe or spread the meringue into the desired shape (see note).

4. Bake at 210–220°F (99–104°C) until dry or follow the instructions given in the individual recipes.

Italian Meringue

approximately 5 quarts (4 l, 800 ml) meringue

1 pint (480 ml) egg whites
1 pound, 8 ounces (680 g) granulated sugar
12 ounces (340 g) or 1 cup (240 ml) light corn syrup
1 cup (240 ml) water

NOTE: *If you do not have a sugar thermometer, boil the sugar to the soft ball stage, following the directions on page 1133 for determining this level without a thermometer.*

1. Place the egg whites in a mixing bowl so you will be ready to start whipping them when the sugar syrup is ready.

2. Boil the sugar, corn syrup, and water. When the syrup reaches 230°F (110°C), begin whipping the egg whites on high speed. Continue boiling the syrup until it reaches 240°F (115°C).

3. Remove the syrup from the heat and lower the mixer speed to medium. Pour the syrup into the egg whites in a thin, steady stream between the whip and the side of the bowl (if the syrup hits the whip it will splatter and cause lumps). Turn the mixer back to high speed and continue to whip the meringue until it has cooled completely and has formed stiff peaks.

Japonaise Meringue Batter

four 10-inch (25-cm) or ninety 2¹/₄-inch (5.6-cm) shells

8 ounces (225 g) finely ground blanched almonds (see note)
1 ounce (30 g) cornstarch
1 cup (240 ml) egg whites
11 ounces (310 g) granulated sugar

NOTE: *If you do not have blanched almonds already ground (almond meal), substitute whole or sliced blanched almonds, combine with one-third of the sugar, and grind together in a food processor to a fine consistency. Process by pulsing on and off to prevent the mixture from heating up and sticking together.*

1. Prepare your sheet pans, pastry bag, and a template if you are using one.

2. Combine the ground almonds and cornstarch. Reserve.

3. Whip the egg whites to a foam; they should quadruple in volume. Gradually add the sugar and whip to stiff peaks.

4. Gently fold the almond mixture into the egg whites by hand. Pipe or spread into the desired shape immediately.

5. Bake as directed in the individual recipes.

Meringue Noisette

four 10-inch (25-cm) or about sixty 3-inch (7.5-cm) shells

4 ounces (115 g) hazelnuts, toasted
1 ounce (30 g) cornstarch
1 cup (240 ml) egg whites
1 pound (455 g) granulated sugar
1 teaspoon (5 ml) vanilla extract

1. Draw four 10-inch (25-cm) circles on two sheets of baking paper. Place the papers upside down on sheet pans and set aside.

2. Remove as much of the skins from the toasted hazelnuts as comes off easily, then grind the nuts to a fine consistency. Combine with the cornstarch.

3. Whip the egg whites to a thick foam; they should quadruple in volume. Still whipping, gradually add the sugar, taking 3 to 4 minutes to add all of it. Continue to whip the meringue until it forms stiff peaks.

FIGURE 12–2 Piping Meringue Noisette batter into a spiral within the circle drawn on a sheet of baking paper

Add the vanilla. Carefully fold the nut and cornstarch mixture into the meringue by hand.

4. Place the Meringue Noisette batter in a pastry bag with a no. 4 (8-mm) plain tip (use a no. 3/6-mm tip if making the smaller size). Pipe the batter in a spiral within the four circles drawn on the papers, starting in the center and working to the outside (Figure 12–2).

5. Bake immediately at 250°F (122°C) for approximately 1 hour or until dry.

 Swiss Meringue

2 to 3 quarts
(1 l, 920 ml to 2 l, 880 ml)
meringue

1 pint (480 ml) egg whites
1 pound, 8 ounces to 2 pounds (680 to
   910 g) granulated sugar (see note)

NOTE: If the meringue is to be dried in the oven, or piped or spread on top of a dessert, less sugar should be used to ensure a stiffer and lighter meringue.

1. Combine the egg whites and sugar in a mixing bowl. Place the bowl over simmering water and heat to 140°F (60°C), whipping constantly to avoid cooking the egg whites.

2. Remove from the heat and whip the mixture at high speed until it has cooled completely.

Meringue Desserts

 Baked Alaska

12 servings

2½ cups (600 ml) Vanilla Ice Cream
   (page 640)
2½ cups (600 ml) Strawberry Ice
   Cream (page 639)
2½ cups (600 ml) Coffee-Scented
   Chocolate Ice Cream (page 629)

*T*he forerunner of this dish is said to have originated in China. The idea was introduced to France in 1866 when a master cook from a visiting Chinese delegation taught the French chef Balzaac of the Grand Hotel in Paris how to prepare a dessert of vanilla and ginger ice creams baked in a pastry crust. The French took hold of the concept, naming their dish Surprise Omelette. (The first recorded note of a dish that was simultaneously hot and cold was made by Thomas Jefferson in 1802, however.) The American-born physicist Benjamin Thompson, who later earned the title Count Rumford, is credited with the invention, or realization, that whipped egg whites are both an excellent insulator and

one 14-by-24-inch (35-×-60-cm)
   Almond Sponge (page 270)
¼ cup (60 ml) Plain Cake Syrup
   (page 10)
¼ cup (60 ml) orange liqueur
one-quarter recipe Italian Meringue
   (page 591) (see note 1)
powdered sugar
glacéed red cherries
one recipe Strawberry Sauce
   (page 1081)
151-proof rum (see note 2)

NOTE 1: Clean and save two nice-looking eggshell halves to use in the presentation.

NOTE 2: Any liqueur or spirit with an alcohol level of 80 percent can be used to flambé, although 151-proof rum is convenient and foolproof, since it will ignite cold. If you use alcohol with a lower proof, you must warm it before igniting. Before using 151-proof rum for all flambé work, however, take into consideration that the flavor of the rum may interfere with the flavor of some desserts if it is spooned over the top or used as part of the sauce (as in Persimmon Pudding, for example).

a poor conductor of heat and thus could prevent the ice cream from melting as the meringue was browned in the oven. Using this information at the turn of the century, the pastry chef at the Hotel de Paris in Monte Carlo, Jean Giroix, popularized the modern form of the dessert, calling it Omelette Norwégienne, presumably because of its resemblance to arctic ice and its frozen interior. Soon afterward, the creation made its way to Delmonico's restaurant in New York City, where it became known as "Alaska and the Florida," representing the temperature differences of these two geographic areas and the two components of the dish. It is said that Fannie Farmer was one of those involved in changing the name to Baked Alaska in celebration of America's purchase of Alaska in 1868, although by this time it was admittedly a bit after the fact. The first recorded use of the term Baked Alaska is in the 1909 edition of the Fannie Merritt Farmer cookbook.

1. Layer the three ice creams in a chilled paper-lined bread pan (see Figures 1–8 and 1–9, page 25), or other rectangular pan approximately 11 inches long, 4 inches wide, and 4 inches deep (27.5 × 10 × 10 cm). You will need to soften the ice cream a bit first to create smooth, even layers. Let each layer harden in the freezer before adding the next. Reserve in the freezer until firm.

2. Cut a strip from the sponge sheet that is as wide as the pan is long, and long enough to wrap all the way around the ice cream block.

3. Unmold the ice cream, remove the paper, and place on the sponge sheet. Roll to completely cover all four long sides. Use some scrap pieces of sponge to cover the ends. Place on a chilled ovenproof serving tray.

4. Combine the Cake Syrup and the orange liqueur and brush the mixture lightly over the top and sides of the rectangle.

5. Spread a ½-inch (1.2-cm) thick layer of meringue over the top and all four sides, using a metal spatula to achieve a smooth and even finish. Place the remaining meringue in a pastry bag with a no. 4 (8-mm) star tip. Pipe the meringue onto the iced rectangle, decorating after your own taste. Incorporate into your design a place on top near each end for an eggshell half. Return the assembled Baked Alaska to the freezer until serving time.

6. Lightly sift powdered sugar over the meringue. Decorate with cherries, and place the two eggshell halves in the meringue to hold the rum. Push the eggshells into the meringue far enough to make them as inconspicuous as possible.

7. Place the tray in a hot oven or salamander to brown the meringue.

8. Pour Strawberry Sauce on the base of the tray around the dessert.

9. Turn down the lights in the dining room, pour a little rum into the eggshells, ignite, and present immediately. As you or the server slice the servings, remove and discard the eggshell halves.

Blackberry Meringue Tartlets

16 servings

one-half recipe French Meringue
  (page 590)
one-half recipe Blackberry Sauce (see
  Raspberry Sauce, page 1080)
2¹⁄₂ cups (600 ml) or one-half recipe
  Lemon Curd (page 1087)
1 pound (455 g) fresh blackberries,
  approximately
Sour Cream Mixture for Piping
  (page 1081)

*M*ake this quick and delightfully refreshing dessert when blackberries are *perfectly ripe and sweet so their flavor will offset the slightly tangy Lemon Curd. Any of the blackberry hybrids, such as boysenberries, loganberries, or "olallie" blackberries, may be substituted, but I prefer blackberries since they are smaller and make a more attractive arrangement on top of the meringue shell. The other components of this dessert can be made in advance: The meringue shells can be stored airtight in a warm place ready to be filled as needed, and Lemon Curd is always handy to have around. It can be kept well covered in the refrigerator for up to a month.*

Blackberry Meringue Tartlets could very well be classified as a light dessert, but when no one is counting the calories, try serving them with a scoop of Vanilla Ice Cream. It's a delicious combination, though it does upset the presentation.

1. Draw sixteen 4-inch (10-cm) circles, properly spaced, on sheets of baking paper. Invert the papers and place on sheet pans.

2. Place the meringue in a pastry bag with a no. 4 (8-mm) plain tip. Pipe a ring of pointed dots ("kisses") next to each other all around the insides of the circles. For a perfectly clean look, use your finger or a small spoon to straighten up the points. To make the bottom of the cases, pipe rings of meringue inside the dots, using the same technique used for Meringue Noisette (see Figure 12–2, page 592), but holding the tip closer to the sheet pan to make the bottom thinner and allow enough space for the filling later.

3. Bake immediately at 210–220°F (99–104°C) for approximately 2 hours or until the meringue has dried all the way through.

4. Place the Blackberry Sauce in a piping bottle. Reserve.

5. Presentation: Fill a meringue shell with just over 2 tablespoons (30 ml) of Lemon Curd. Place the shell off-center on a dessert plate (put a dab of curd underneath to prevent it from sliding). Arrange whole fresh blackberries on top of the filling. Pipe a half-circle of Blackberry Sauce in front of the dessert, and decorate with the Sour Cream Mixture for Piping (see pages 998 to 1006).

Budapest Swirls

16 servings

Butter and Flour Mixture (page 4)
one and one-half recipes Japonaise
  Meringue Batter (page 591)
2 teaspoons (6 g) unflavored gelatin
  powder
¹⁄₄ cup (60 ml) cold water

*B*udapest Swirls are a good example of a pastry transformed into a plated *dessert by the addition of a sauce and garnish. In a European pastry shop they would more typically be offered the way you would one of the selections in the Individual Pastries chapter—eaten as is with your fingers, or served on a plate to enjoy with coffee.*

Although the filled roulade is not a good keeper, the baked sheet before it is filled can be kept, well wrapped in a cool place, for several days. If the sheet becomes too hard to roll without cracking, try placing it (with the baking paper still attached) on a hot sheet pan lined with a damp towel. To simplify the pre-

three-quarter recipe Quick Bavarian Cream (page 1089)

orange segments from six medium-sized oranges (directions follow)

Bitter Orange Sauce (page 1078)

Chocolate Sauce (page 1072), at room temperature

powdered sugar

strips of orange zest

edible fresh flowers

NOTE: Ideally, the Japonaise sheet should be baked the day before assembly and placed in the refrigerator overnight to ensure that it will be soft enough to roll. If necessary, follow the directions for softening sponge sheets given in the note on page 270. While it is preferable to bake the sheet one day ahead of time, the Budapest Swirls should be assembled the day they are to be served; if left too long, the meringue will absorb moisture from the filling and become soggy.

sentation, serve a Budapest Swirl with a pool of Bitter Orange Sauce placed in front of the dessert, and decorate the plate with orange segments.

1. Line a full sheet pan (16 by 24 inches/40 × 60 cm) with baking paper. Lightly grease the paper with the Butter and Flour Mixture. (If you have a silicone baking mat, use it instead; it does not need to be coated with the Butter and Flour Mixture.) Place the Japonaise Meringue Batter in a pastry bag with a no. 5 (10-mm) plain tip. Pipe the batter into 15-inch (37.5-cm) strings, side by side and touching, across the width of the pan (the strings will end 1 inch/2.5 cm away from the edge of the pan on one side); continue piping down the full length of the pan.

2. Bake the sheet at 300°F (149°C) for about 15 to 20 minutes. It should begin to color and have a crust on top, but it should not be dry all the way through. (To put it in another way, remove the sheet from the oven when it is only half baked as compared to regular Japonaise sheets.) Slide onto a cold sheet pan and let cool completely (see note).

3. Sprinkle the gelatin over the cold water and set aside to soften.

4. Invert the cold Japonaise sheet onto a baking paper and peel the other paper (or the silicone mat) off the back.

5. Place the softened gelatin mixture over a bain-marie and heat to dissolve. Do not overheat. Working quickly, add the gelatin to a small portion of the Bavarian Cream to temper it. Still working quickly, add this to the remaining Bavarian Cream. Spread the Bavarian Cream out evenly over the Japonaise sheet.

6. Reserve forty-eight good-looking orange segments to use for decorating. Arrange the remaining orange segments in a straight line, lengthwise, approximately 1 inch (2.5 cm) from the top long edge of the sheet. Refrigerate for about 15 minutes to partially set the cream.

7. Roll up the sheet as for a roulade by lifting the back of the paper and letting the pastry roll toward you (Figure 12–3). Refrigerate again until the cream is completely set, approximately 1 hour.

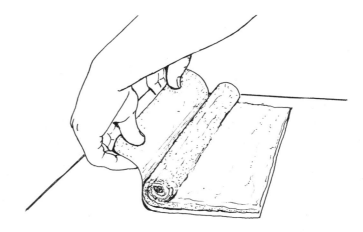

FIGURE 12–3 Using the baking paper underneath to facilitate rolling the Japonaise sheet into a roulade for Budapest Swirls

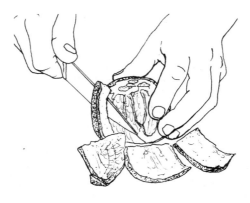

FIGURE 12–4 *Cutting the peel and all of the white pith away from the orange flesh, making slightly rounded cuts to keep the natural shape of the orange*

FIGURE 12–5 *Cutting between the membranes to release the orange segments, with the orange held over a bowl to catch the juice*

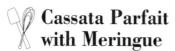 **Cassata Parfait with Meringue**

16 servings

one recipe French Meringue
 (page 590)
dark coating chocolate, melted
$^1/_2$ cup (120 ml) heavy cream
Cassata Parfait (recipe follows)
one-half recipe Chocolate Sauce
 (page 1072)
sixteen Chocolate Figurines (page 906)
seventy-five fresh cherries,
 approximately
candied violets

8. Cut the roll into 1$^1/_2$-inch (3.7-cm) slices at a slight angle, holding the knife straight up and down so that the width of the slices is even. Place the Orange Sauce and the Chocolate Sauce into separate piping bottles.

9. Presentation: Sift powdered sugar lightly over the rim of a dessert plate and on top of a Budapest Swirl. Decorate the rim of the plate with small curls of orange zest. Pipe a large backward S design (like a question mark without the dot) of Chocolate Sauce in the center of the dessert plate, covering the base. Place the pastry in the center of the design. Pipe quarter-sized dots of Orange Sauce on each side. Arrange three orange segments in front and then decorate with edible flowers.

To cut orange segments

1. Cut the top and bottom off the orange and set the orange on a cutting board.

2. Cut away the skin on the sides, cutting from top to bottom, removing all of the white pith and keeping the natural shape of the orange (Figure 12–4).

3. Hold the orange in your hand over a bowl to catch the juice. With a small, sharp paring knife, cut between the inside membranes to remove the segments (Figure 12–5).

T his variation of the traditional Italian dessert Cassata Neapolitan is a good choice for a make-ahead dessert. All of the components can be prepared and held in their proper place for quick assembly at the last minute. Though the same is true of most frozen desserts, the Cassata Parfait, while fairly simple, has quite an elegant appearance. The shape and size can be altered to suit your particular taste. This dessert also pairs well with Cherry Sauce instead of Chocolate Sauce, omitting the candied violets.

1. Cut a 3$^1/_2$-by-2$^1/_2$-inch (8.7-×-6.2-cm) rectangle from cardboard. Using the cardboard as a guide, trace twenty rectangles, evenly spaced, on a sheet of baking paper with a heavy marking pen. Place a second sheet of baking paper on top.

2. Place the meringue in a pastry bag with a no. 3 (6-mm) plain tip. Pipe out rows of meringue within each rectangle in a back-and-forth pattern as shown in Figure 11–1, page 536. Drag the paper with the

NOTE: Since the whole cherries used for garnish are unpitted, I always cut one in half just before putting it on the plate, to expose the pit. I think it looks good and it also alerts the customer to the pits.

meringue onto a sheet pan (see Figure 16–15, page 842). Place a new sheet of paper over your template and pipe twenty additional rectangles in the same manner. (You only need thirty-two for this recipe, but some will inevitably break.) Drag the second sheet of meringue rectangles to a second sheet pan.

3. Bake the meringue rectangles at 210–220°F (99–104°C) until dry, approximately 2 hours. Let cool completely. Dip the short ends of the rectangles into melted coating chocolate, covering ¹⁄₂ inch (1.2 cm). Set aside. If you do not plan to serve all of the meringue the same day, only dip as many as you expect to need (two per serving). Before they are dipped in chocolate, the meringue rectangles can be kept for several weeks stored in a warm dry place. If they should become soft they can be dried again in a low oven.

4. Whip the heavy cream to stiff peaks. Place in a pastry bag with a no. 4 (8-mm) plain tip. Reserve in the refrigerator.

5. Unmold the frozen Cassata and cut it into ³⁄₄-inch (2 cm) slices, using a knife dipped in hot water. Do not cut more slices than you will need. Sandwich the slices between two meringue rectangles, inverting the bottom piece. Reserve the assembled Cassatas (and any uncut Cassata) in the freezer.

6. Presentation: Pour or pipe a pool of Chocolate Sauce, off-center toward the front, on the base of a dessert plate. Pipe a small dot of whipped cream on the other half of the plate, and at the same time pipe a mound of cream in the center on top of one of the prepared Cassatas. Place the Cassata on the plate, on top of the cream to keep it from sliding, arranging it so that one corner is in the sauce. Carefully place a Chocolate Figurine on top of the cream mound. Place four or five cherries next to the sauce (see note). Sprinkle a few broken pieces of candied violet over the sauce. Serve immediately.

1. Make a form out of corrugated cardboard that is 13 inches long, 3¹⁄₂ inches wide, and 2¹⁄₂ inches high (32.5 × 8.7 × 6.2 cm), following the instructions given in the recipe for White Chocolate Pâte, pages 830 and 831. Line the inside of the form with baking paper and set aside (see note 2).

2. Whip the heavy cream to stiff peaks. Reserve in the refrigerator.

3. Whip the whole eggs and egg yolks at high speed for 3 minutes. While the eggs are whipping, combine the sugar, honey, and water in a saucepan. Bring to a boil, lower the speed on the mixer, and add the hot syrup to the whipped eggs. Whip at high speed until the mixture is light and fluffy and has cooled completely.

4. Cut the candied fruit into raisin-sized pieces. Cut the Macaroon Cookies into ¹⁄₂-inch (1.2-cm) pieces. Put the cookie pieces in a bowl. Add the maraschino liqueur and toss to coat the cookies with the liqueur. Add the chopped fruit and combine.

Cassata Parfait
8 cups (1 l, 920 ml)

2 cups (480 ml) heavy cream

2 eggs

4 egg yolks (¹⁄₃ cup/80 ml)

2 ounces (55 g) granulated sugar

3 tablespoons (45 ml) honey

2 tablespoons (30 ml) water

4 ounces (115 g) mixed candied fruit (see note 1)

4 ounces (115 g) Almond Macaroon Cookies (page 202)

¹⁄₄ cup (60 ml) maraschino liqueur

NOTE 1: The candied fruit should include cherries as well as orange or other citrus peel. If you are unable to find candied cherries, you may substitute maraschino cherries. Cut them in half, stem, pit, rinse, and dry throughly. The green color of angelica (see page 1106) adds a nice contrast if you can find it. Please do not substitute green cherries.

NOTE 2: You can use any form that is close to the specified size. Adjust accordingly when you make the meringue rectangles.

Frozen Raspberry Mousse with Meringues

sixteen 5-ounce (150-ml) servings

Raspberry Mousse Filling
    (recipe follows)
one-half recipe Meringue Noisette
    batter (page 591) (see note 1)
1 cup (240 ml) heavy cream
1 teaspoon (5 g) granulated sugar
one recipe Mousseline Sauce
    (page 1076)
1/4 cup (60 ml) Riesling wine
fresh raspberries
Chocolate Sauce for Piping
    (page 1072)

NOTE 1: Use 1 additional egg white, 5 rather than 4, for the half recipe.

NOTE 2: If you do not have the correct size of cake rings available, you can easily make your own: Cut sixteen strips of polyurethane or acetate 9¹/2 inches long by 1¹/2 inches wide (23.7 × 3.7 cm). Tape the ends together, overlapping them ¹/2 inch (1.2 cm) to create 3-inch (7.5-cm) diameter rings. As a second alternative, use 3-inch (7.5-cm) diameter, 5-ounce (150-ml) capacity soufflé ramekins.

5. Fold the reserved whipped cream into the whipped egg mixture. Fold in the fruit and cookie mixture. Spoon into the prepared form and spread the filling smooth on top. Place in the freezer for at least 4 hours or, preferably, overnight.

M ousse *is a hard-to-define French word for a dish that is made in so many different ways it becomes impossible to generalize. However, in the pastry kitchen, the term mousse typically refers to a sweet dessert, flavored with fruit or liqueur, that is served either cold or frozen. There are also, of course, the classic chocolate and coffee mousses and their innumerable variations. Savory mousses can be made from seafood, poultry, meat, vegetables, or liver, and they are offered as an appetizer or main course. These may be served hot or cold but are never frozen. Frozen dessert mousses, sometimes called ice mousses, are very similar in composition to parfaits except that a parfait never contains whipped egg whites but instead uses beaten egg yolks. A dessert mousse sometimes has both. Frozen mousses do not need to be fortified with gelatin as do most cold mousses (chocolate mousse being the exception, as chocolate is, itself, a thickening agent). In the recipe for Raspberry Mousse that follows, a small amount of pectin is used to help prevent the filling from losing its shape when the desserts begin to thaw as they are prepared for service.*

1. Place sixteen cake rings that are 3 inches (7.5 cm) in diameter and 1¹/2 inches (3.7 cm) tall on a sheet pan lined with baking paper (see note 2). Line the inside of the rings with strips of baking paper. Divide the Raspberry Mousse Filling evenly between the rings. Even the tops with a palette knife or plastic scraper. Cover and place in the freezer for at least 4 hours or, preferably, overnight.

2. Place the Meringue Noisette batter in a pastry bag with a no. 3 (6-mm) plain tip. Pipe out 3-inch (7.5-cm) circles following the instructions given in the recipe for Meringue Noisette (see Figure 12–2, page 592). You need thirty-two for this recipe, but you should get about thirty-five. Bake at 250°F (122°C) for about 40 minutes or until dry. Set aside the sixteen best-looking shells to use for the tops.

3. Remove the cake rings from as many servings of frozen mousse as you are planning to serve and peel away the strips of baking paper. (If you used plastic strips instead of cake rings, simply cut the strips. Unmold each frozen mousse from ramekins by dipping the bottom and sides of the molds briefly into hot water, just long enough to loosen the mousse, and use a fork to gently help you remove them. Take care not to get any water on the mousse itself.) Place an unmolded mousse onto each of the bottom meringues and set the reserved meringues on top. Press lightly to be sure they adhere. Return the servings to the freezer.

4. Whip the cream and sugar to stiff peaks. Place in a pastry bag with a no. 3 (6-mm) star tip. Reserve in the refrigerator until time of service. Flavor the Mousseline Sauce with the Riesling wine and place a portion of the sauce in a piping bottle.

5. Presentation: Pipe Mousseline Sauce in a circle on the base of a dessert plate, leaving a small area exposed in the center of the plate. Pipe a dot of whipped cream on the uncovered spot and place a frozen Raspberry Mousse on top. Pipe a border of small dots, or "kisses," of whipped cream on the top meringue. Place five raspberries, standing on end, within the cream border. Decorate the Mousseline Sauce with the Chocolate Sauce for Piping (see pages 998 to 1005). Serve immediately.

 **Raspberry Mousse Filling**
about 2³/₄ quarts (2 l, 640 ml)

3 cups (720 ml) heavy cream
2 tablespoons (18 g) pectin powder (see note 1)
8 ounces (225 g) granulated sugar
5 egg whites (⁵/₈ cup/150 ml)
1 pound (455 g) fresh raspberries, puréed and strained (see note 2)
3 ounces (90 ml) Chambord liqueur

NOTE 1: Use regular pectin for canning fruit. Pure pectin is too strong for this purpose.

NOTE 2: If fresh raspberries are not available, and you substitute frozen or canned, do not use raspberries packed in sugar syrup. The mousse will be overly sweet and will not freeze well.

1. Whip the cream to stiff peaks and reserve in the refrigerator.

2. Combine the pectin powder and the sugar. Add the egg whites. Heat the mixture over simmering water, whipping constantly, until it reaches 140°F (60°C). Be careful not to let the egg whites get too hot and cook. Remove from the heat and whip until the mixture is cold and has formed stiff peaks.

3. Add the liqueur to the raspberry purée. Gradually (to prevent lumps) fold the purée into the reserved whipped cream. Fold this mixture into the whipped egg whites.

Gâteau Arabe

two 10-inch (25-cm) cakes

Butter and Flour Mixture (page 4)

one-half recipe High Ratio Sponge
    Cake batter (page 274)

2 pounds, 10 ounces (1 kg, 195 g)
    Vanilla Buttercream (page 978)

1 teaspoon (4 g) mocha paste
    or

¼ cup (60 ml) Coffee Reduction
    (page 5)

¾ cup (180 ml) Plain Cake Syrup
    (page 10)

4 ounces (115 g) smooth red currant
    jelly

four 10-inch (25-cm) Meringue
    Noisette (page 591)

sliced almonds, toasted and lightly
    crushed

Light Piping Chocolate (page 904),
    melted

Chocolate Rounds (page 890)

*NOTE : For a different look, reserve only a few
tablespoons of buttercream and use the remainder to ice the cakes. After removing the cutters
in step 5, fill the center portion of the cakes
with shaved chocolate. Attach the Chocolate
Rounds with small dots of the reserved buttercream (omit piping the buttercream lines).*

*I*t probably goes without saying that the title of this cake comes from the
*coffee-flavored buttercream used for the filling and icing. It was the Arabs,
after all, who, after discovering how to boil water in approximately A.D. 1000,
first made an infusion using green coffee beans. Subsequently they discovered
that roasting the beans would intensify the flavor of the drink, and then that
grinding the roasted beans before boiling them in water was even more of an
improvement, thereby inventing what was to become a fashionable drink in
most of the modern world for the coming centuries. Coffee (the name derives
from an Arabic word* gahwah, *which refers to wine, coffee, or other beverages
made from plants) quickly became favored throughout the entire Islamic
world—as well as in the Arab-controlled territories, occupied from wars, such as
Turkey, North Africa, and the Balklands—and as far east as Spain. Its popularity was no doubt due in some part to the fact that alcoholic beverages are prohibited by the Koran. Coffee bars, known in Arabic as* gahneh khaneh, *soon
sprang up in increasing numbers providing men (women were not allowed) with
a place to enjoy the stimulating effect of the drink, listen to music, play games,
and in general discuss important matters. Coffee played an important role in
family life as well once women, who at first were looked upon with suspicion,
began to enjoy the brew. Coffee was in fact regarded with such high esteem that
a husband's failure to provide coffee for his wife was legal grounds (no pun
intended) for divorce.*

1. Brush the Butter and Flour Mixture over two 10-inch (25-cm)
cakes pans or line the bottom of the pans with circles of baking paper
(see Figures 1–10, 1–11, and 1–12, page 26). Divide the sponge batter
evenly between them. Bake at 400°F (205°C) for approximately 15
minutes or until the sponge springs back when pressed lightly in the
middle (the sponges will only be about 1 inch/2.5 cm high). Let the
sponges cool completely.

2. Flavor the Vanilla Buttercream with the mocha paste or Coffee
Reduction, working it smooth at the same time. Measure 6 ounces
(170 g) or 1 cup (240 ml) of buttercream to use in decorating. Reserve
both portions (see note).

3. Cut the skin from the top of the sponges and even off the tops,
if necessary. Cut each sponge into two layers. Set the top layers aside
and brush the bottom layers with half of the Cake Syrup. Divide the
red currant jelly between the two sponge layers and spread it out
evenly. Place a Meringue Noisette on top of each one.

4. Spread some of the larger portion of buttercream in a ⅛-inch
(3-mm) layer on the Meringue Noisettes that are on the sponges. Place
the remaining two Meringue Noisettes on top of the buttercream layer.
Spread a ⅛-inch (3-mm) layer of buttercream over the meringues. Top
with the remaining sponge layers. Brush with the remaining Cake
Syrup. Trim any meringue that protrudes outside the sponge so that
the sides of the cakes are even (see Figure 8–11, page 325). Ice the tops
and sides of the cakes using all of the buttercream (other than the portion reserved for decorating).

5. Place 6-inch (15-cm) round cookie cutters on top of the cakes in the centers. Cover the sides of the cakes, and the outside top around the cutters, with the crushed almonds (see Figure 8–5, page 296). Remove the cutters and refrigerate the cakes until the buttercream is firm.

6. Place the Piping Chocolate in a piping bag and cut a very small opening. Pipe a letter A on each Chocolate Round. Cut or mark the cakes into the desired number of serving pieces. Place the reserved 6 ounces (170 g) of buttercream in a pastry bag with a no. 2 (4-mm) plain tip. Pipe two straight lines of buttercream in the center of each slice, covering the length of the slice. Place a Chocolate Round on top of the buttercream lines at the wide end of each piece.

Ice Cream Cake Jamaica

two 10-inch (25-cm) cakes

1 ounce (30 g) unsweetened cocoa powder
2 ounces (55 g) granulated sugar
one-half recipe French Meringue (page 590) (see step two)
dark coating chocolate, melted
Rum Parfait (recipe follows)
2¹/₂ cups (600 ml) Vanilla Ice Cream (page 640)
1 quart (960 ml) heavy cream
2 tablespoons (30 g) granulated sugar
dark chocolate shavings
2 tablespoons (30 ml) dark rum
one-half recipe Mousseline Sauce (page 1076)
strawberry wedges
Chocolate Sauce for Piping (page 1072)

*J*amaica is a nation in the West Indies occupying the third largest island in the Caribbean Sea. Agriculture and the mining of bauxite and alumina (both of which are used in the production of aluminum) are the island's main industries. Spices, coffee, cocoa, and many species of tropical fruits are cultivated and are exported through the ports of Montego Bay and Jamaica's capitol, Kingston. The production and processing of sugar and the distillation of rum both play a major role in Jamaica's economy as well.

Rum was made in the Caribbean as early as the beginning of the seventeenth century, many years after Christopher Columbus brought sugarcane to the area from the Azores. The rum industry developed in step with the growth of sugar plantations on the islands. This alcoholic beverage is distilled from by-products of the sugar-making process; molasses is typically used as the basis. The darker and heavier rums, known as "Jamaican-style," are produced mostly in (not surprisingly) Jamaica, Barbados, and Guyana on Central America's east coast along the Demrara River. These are made from a combination of molasses and the skimmings from sugar boiling vats, which is allowed to ferment to improve the rum's aroma and flavor. After distilling, the rum is darkened with the addition of caramel and is then aged for up to seven years.

Ice cream cakes, just like any other cake, are a faster and more efficient way of preparing a number of servings instead of making individual portions. They are also a bit unusual today and can remind us of those great ice cream sandwiches we enjoyed as children, which consisted of a rectangular slab of ice cream between two cake-like chocolate cookies, a variety that has been around since the turn of the century. More recently a variation made with chocolate chip cookies has become well-known.

1. Draw four 10-inch (25-cm) circles on baking papers. Invert the papers, place them on sheet pans, and set aside.

2. Combine the cocoa powder and 2 ounces (55 g) granulated sugar and add to the French Meringue on low speed as it is finished whipping.

3. Place the meringue in a pastry bag with a no. 3 (6-mm) plain tip. Pipe the meringue inside the circles on the reserved papers, starting

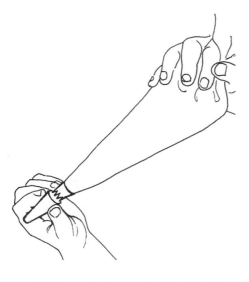

FIGURE 12–6 Placing a pastry tip on the outside of the bag over an existing tip that is already in place

FIGURE 12–7 Holding the new tip in place as the content is piped out

in the center and making a spiral to the outside (see Figure 12–2, page 592).

4. Bake at 210–220°F (99–104°C) for approximately 1 hour or until dry. Let the meringues cool completely, then brush a thin layer of melted coating chocolate on the top side of all four meringue circles.

5. Place two of the meringues, chocolate-side up, on 12-inch (30-cm) cake cardboards for support. Place 10-inch (25-cm) cake rings on top of the meringues and trim the meringues to fit. If the rings are not made of stainless-steel, line the insides with polyurethane or acetate strips to prevent the metal from staining the filling. (If you do not have cake rings, using the plastic strips alone works fine. Wrap them around the trimmed meringues and tape the ends together). Place in the freezer until chilled.

6. Gradually add the Rum Parfait to the Vanilla Ice Cream (the ice cream must be reasonably soft). Divide the mixture between the two prepared forms. Place the remaining meringue shells, chocolate-side down, on top of the filling. Trim the meringues if necessary to help them fit inside the rings. Cover and place in the freezer for at least 4 hours or, preferably, overnight.

7. Whip the heavy cream with the remaining sugar until stiff peaks form. Remove the cake rings and plastic strips from the cakes. Return one cake to the freezer. Spread just enough whipped cream on the top and sides of the other cake to cover.

8. Cut the cake into serving pieces. Sprinkle dark chocolate shavings over the center 6 inches (15 cm) of the cake. Return the cake to the freezer. Repeat with the second cake.

9. Place the remaining whipped cream in a pastry bag with a no. 7 (14-mm) star tip. Reserve in the refrigerator until time of service. Mix the rum into the Mousseline Sauce. Place a portion of the sauce in a piping bottle. Reserve it and the remainder of the sauce in the refrigerator.

10. Presentation: Pipe a small dot of whipped cream, slightly off-center, on a chilled dessert plate. Place a slice of cake on top. Place a no. 4 (8-mm) plain tip on the outside of the pastry bag with the whipped cream and hold it in place as you pipe (Figures 12–6 and 12–7). Pipe whipped cream onto the iced side of the slice in a vertical zigzag pattern. Remove the plain tip and pipe a rosette on top of the slice near the end. Place a strawberry wedge on the rosette. Pipe a pool of Mousseline Sauce on the plate in front of the cake and decorate the sauce with the Chocolate Sauce for Piping (see pages 998 to 1006).

Rum Parfait

8 cups (1 l, 920 ml)

5 ounces (140 g) golden raisins

³/₄ cup (180 ml) dark rum

¹/₃ cup (80 ml) or 4 ounces (115 g) light corn syrup

8 egg yolks (²/₃ cup/160 ml)

1 tablespoon (9 g) unflavored gelatin powder

¹/₄ cup (60 ml) cold water

4¹/₂ cups (1 l, 80 ml) heavy cream

NOTE: If you do not have time to macerate the raisins overnight it is better to omit them. If the raisins have not absorbed enough rum, they will be hard and unpleasant to eat when frozen.

1. Combine the raisins and rum in a saucepan and heat to about 175°F (80°C). Remove from the heat and let the raisins macerate in the rum overnight.

2. Place the corn syrup in a small saucepan and bring to a boil. Whip the egg yolks for 1 minute. Gradually pour the hot corn syrup into the egg yolks while whipping constantly and continue to whip until the mixture is cold and fluffy. Reserve.

3. Sprinkle the gelatin over the cold water to soften.

4. Whip the heavy cream to soft peaks.

5. Place the gelatin mixture over a bain-marie and heat until dissolved. Do not overheat. Rapidly mix the gelatin into a small part of the whipped cream, then stir into the remaining cream. Gradually fold the rum, raisins, and the egg mixture into the cream. Although the filling must be used soon after it is made, it should start to thicken slightly before it is used to fill the cakes to prevent it from leaking out.

 Individual Baked Alaska Bee Hives

16 servings

one-half recipe Dobos Sponge batter (page 273)

orange liqueur

one recipe Rhubarb or Strawberry Ice Cream (pages 638 and 639)

one-half recipe Italian Meringue (page 591)

one recipe Rhubarb Sauce (page 1080)

powdered sugar

sixteen edible fresh flowers

sixteen Marzipan Bumble Bees (page 1025)

NOTE 1: If you are expecting to serve a lot of these, you know you have a large order coming up, or you just want to prep ahead, you can place the sponge circles with ice cream 3 inches (7.5 cm) apart on sheet pans lined with baking paper. Make sure that the ice-cream scoops are small enough that you have room to pipe the first row of meringue on the sponge and not on the sheet pan. Pipe the meringue as directed. Reserve in the freezer until needed.

*T*his is another of my desserts that appeared in the original PBS television series Cooking at the Academy, *and for the program we had planned a flambéed presentation. When the show was filmed the bee hives were the last item I was to prepare in the day's shoot, and it was to be very simple, or so I thought until I discovered that there wasn't any 151-proof rum available, convenient because it can be ignited cold. (It seems that the person who was supposed to get the rum had forgotten, and since he was the one who signed my paycheck at that time, I gracefully accepted the blame.) At this point we had to change the format to use the more conventional method of heating the spirit or liqueur first before burning. Easy enough, however, when poured on a frozen dessert like this one, the alcohol cools down and stops burning very rapidly. I piped meringue bee hives and poured hot brandy on top a half-dozen times, but when I got to the flambé part, it always ended with a resounding "cut!" from the director, who could not see enough of the flames before the brandy had cooled and stopped burning. I then decided to apply some Hollywood-type special effects and use pure alcohol (since no one was actually going to eat the dessert; it was just for the film), which resulted in a spectacular fire show and, unfortunately, a bee hive resembling the charred black remains of a forest fire! Finally, after trial and error (on a plate instead of a bee hive), we came up with the right combination of pure alcohol and brandy so that the flames showed up on film but didn't burn so long that the dessert was ruined. By the time we finished filming this "simple" dessert it was 4 o'clock in the morning!*

Having said all of this, you may have trouble believing that the bee hives are really very easy to execute, but it's true. They can be prepped long in advance and held in the freezer ready to brown and serve. The bees can even be left out if time does not allow you to make them (after all, they could just as well be inside their hives instead of sitting on top.)

(They can be left this way for up to 24 hours.) Sift powdered sugar on top just before browning.

NOTE 2: For a dramatic dining room presentation, pour 151-proof rum on the dessert, ignite, and quickly present to the guest. This technique is really more practical for the larger classic version of Baked Alaska (page 592), since you don't want to flambé the Marzipan Bee, and you must either place it in the sauce (which is not as appealing), add it after the flames go out (which is a little awkward), or risk being reported to the Society for the Prevention of Cruelty to Animals!

1. Spread the Dobos batter into a 16-by-14-inch (40-×-35-cm) rectangle on a sheet of baking paper. Drag the paper onto a sheet pan (see Figure 16–15, page 842). Bake as directed in the sponge recipe. Let cool.

2. Cut sixteen 2³/₄- to 3-inch (6.8- to 7.5-cm) circles from the sponge sheet. Brush orange liqueur over the circles. Place a 2¹/₂- to 3-ounce (75- to 90-ml) scoop of ice cream on each circle. Cover and reserve in the freezer.

3. Presentation: Place the meringue in a pastry bag with a no. 4 (8-mm) plain tip. Place a frozen sponge circle with ice cream in the center of an ovenproof dessert plate. Working quickly, completely cover the sponge and ice cream with meringue by piping circles of meringue on top of each other starting on the plate around the dessert (see Figure 14–1, page 692). Pour just enough Rhubarb Sauce around the bee hive to cover the base of the plate. Lightly sift powdered sugar over the meringue and the rim of the plate. Brown the meringue by placing the dessert under a broiler or salamander, or by very carefully using a blowtorch. Place a flower and a Marzipan Bumble Bee on top of the bee hive, and a second flower next to the hive in the sauce. Serve immediately.

 # Japonaise

40 pastries

one recipe Japonaise Meringue Batter (page 591)

2 pounds (910 g) Vanilla Buttercream (page 978)

6 ounces (170 g) Hazelnut Paste (page 9)

or

3 ounces (85 g) commercial hazelnut paste

Fondant (page 1011), tinted pink

NOTE : You can make templates for Japonaise from ¹/₈-inch (3-mm) thick food-grade rubber by cutting out the desired size circles with a utility knife.

J *aponaise can be found in virtually every pastry shop in central Europe. These familiar, classical pastries never seem to go out of style, and for good reason, since they are both practical and delicious. In addition, the Japonaise bases can be used to make a number of variations by changing the filling and/or the decoration. Try filling them with coffee-flavored buttercream instead of hazelnut and replacing the Fondant dot on top with a candy coffee bean or one made out of Marzipan (page 1029). Zuger Kirsch Pastries are another popular variation and are made as follows:*

- *Prepare Japonaise through step four.*
- *Make one recipe Almond Sponge batter (page 270), spread over the entire surface of a paper-lined full sheet pan, and bake.*
- *Flavor the buttercream with ¹/₃ cup (80 ml) kirsch liqueur.*
- *Cut forty 2¹/₄-inch (5.6-cm) rounds from the sponge sheet. Brush the sponge circles with a mixture of ³/₄ cup (180 ml) kirsch liqueur and ¹/₄ cup (60 ml) water.*
- *To assemble each pastry, spread cherry-flavored buttercream on the top sides of two Japonaise circles and sandwich them together with a soaked sponge circle inside. Refrigerate until firm.*
- *Follow steps six and seven as directed, except do not decorate the tops with crumbs or Fondant. Instead, sift powdered sugar on top, then use the wire of a hard-boiled egg slicer to mark the sugar first in one direction and then at a 45° angle, to create a diamond pattern. If the powdered sugar dissolves in the buttercream, sprinkle fine granulated sugar (castor sugar) on the surface before sifting the powdered sugar on top.*

- Place a candied cherry half or a small amount of chopped blanched pistachio nuts in the center of each pastry.

1. The fastest and most efficient way of making Japonaise shells is to spread the batter over rubber templates made expressly for this purpose (see note). If these are not available, you can make a pattern by drawing 2¼-inch (5.6-cm) circles, spaced 1 inch (2.5 cm) apart, on baking paper, using a heavy pen. (Draw the circles before you make the Japonaise Meringue Batter.) Fasten the pattern to the table with a dab of butter in each corner. Place a second sheet of baking paper on top.

2. Place the meringue batter in a pastry bag with a no. 2 (4-mm) plain tip. Pipe the batter following the pattern under the paper, starting in the center of the circles and working to the outside, to fill in the circles completely as in Meringue Noisette (see Figure 12–2, page 592). Drag the filled paper onto a sheet pan (see Figure 16–15, page 842). Repeat to make the remaining shells. If you are making just a few shells, invert the paper with the pattern, and pipe the shells directly on the back of the paper. After you have had some practice you can eliminate using the guide completely, and just pipe the batter into circles, keeping the shells the same size by piping an equal number of rings for each one.

3. Bake immediately at 300°F (149°C) until the meringues are completely dry, about 30 minutes. Make sure that the oven is not too hot; too high a temperature will cause the shells to puff up, become brittle, and be very hard to work with.

4. Set aside about ten of the least attractive shells. Trim any of the remaining shells as needed so that they are round and all about 2¼ inches (5.6 cm) in diameter. Reserve the trimmings.

5. Flavor the Vanilla Buttercream with the Hazelnut Paste. Place it in a pastry bag with a no. 3 (6-mm) plain tip. Pipe a layer of buttercream on half of the shells, using the same piping technique that you used to make the shells. Invert the remaining shells on top and press down lightly making sure the sides are lined up evenly. Refrigerate until the buttercream is firm.

6. Crush the ten reserved shells, as well as any trimmings from the others, to very fine crumbs. Pass the crumbs through a sifter.

7. Spread a very thin layer of buttercream on the sides and top of the chilled pastries. (You can do this faster by holding two pastries together while you ice the sides.) Roll the sides in the reserved crumbs and sprinkle crumbs over the tops to completely cover the buttercream. Pipe a small dot of melted pink Fondant, about ½ inch (1.2 cm) in diameter, in the center of each Japonaise. Store, covered, at room temperature up to four days.

Marjolaine

12 servings

one-quarter recipe Chocolate Chiffon
   Sponge Cake batter (page 272)

Nut Meringue (recipe follows)

Praline Buttercream (recipe follows)

one-half recipe Crème Parisienne
   (page 1086)

12 ounces (340 g) Ganache
   (page 1086)

1½ teaspoons (4.5 g) unflavored
   gelatin powder

3 tablespoons (45 ml) cold water

one recipe Chantilly Cream
   (page 1083) (see step three)

unsweetened cocoa powder

one recipe Raspberry Sauce
   (page 1080)

Sour Cream Mixture for Piping
   (page 1081)

thirty-six raspberries

twelve small mint leaves

This fabulous dessert is definitely worth all of the steps involved, especially if you take into consideration that the uncut layered sheet will keep fresh in the refrigerator for up to one week, or up to one month in the freezer, if well wrapped. (It is best to wait and ice the top after the sheet has thawed if it is to be frozen). With this in mind, you may want to consider doubling the recipe to make a half sheet rather than a quarter so you can freeze part of it for later use.

You must plan ahead when making this dessert: After the Marjolaine is assembled it must be refrigerated for at least eight hours or, better yet, overnight to ensure that the meringue has softened sufficiently to enable you to cut through it cleanly. Because this is a fairly rich cake, you can stretch the yield to 15 servings instead of 12 by cutting the pieces slightly smaller if needed.

Marjolaine is the best-known dish invented by the late French chef Fernand Point, owner of the three-star La Pyramide. Exactly why he picked this name I do not know, but it could have something to do with a special lady who liked chocolate (Marjolaine is a girl's name in France). The original recipe has been changed (possibly improved) over the years to suit each chef's taste. Here is my version—enjoy!

1. Line the bottom of a half-sheet pan (16 by 12 inches/40 × 30 cm) with baking paper. Spread the sponge batter evenly over the pan. Bake immediately at 400°F (205°C) for about 15 minutes or until the sponge springs back when pressed lightly in the middle. Set aside to cool.

2. Make the Nut Meringue and the Praline Buttercream.

3. Whip the Crème Parisienne to stiff peaks and reserve in the refrigerator. (Do not whip the Chantilly Cream until you are ready to use it.)

4. Cut the meringue sheets in half crosswise to make four meringue layers, 8 by 12 inches (20 × 30 cm) each. Do not separate the meringue from the baking paper at this time.

5. Cut around the edge of the sponge sheet and remove it from the pan. Cut in half crosswise and reserve one half for another use. Cut the skin from the top of the remaining piece, remove the baking paper from the back, and place on a sheet pan or sheet of cake cardboard lined with baking paper.

6. To assemble: Reserve one-third of the Ganache. Soften the remainder, and spread it evenly on top of the sponge sheet. Pick up one of the meringue layers, holding it by the baking paper, invert on top of the Ganache, and peel off the paper.

7. Spread the Crème Parisienne on top of the meringue. Add a second meringue sheet using the same method as before; top this one with the Praline Buttercream. Add the third meringue sheet.

8. Sprinkle the gelatin over the cold water to soften. Whip the Chantilly Cream to soft peaks. Place the gelatin mixture over a bain-marie and heat to dissolve. Do not overheat. Rapidly mix the gelatin into a small portion of the cream to temper. Still working quickly, add this to the remaining cream. If the Chantilly Cream is too soft to hold its shape, give it a few more turns with the whip. Spread the cream evenly on top of the third meringue sheet. Place the last meringue sheet on top of the cream. If necessary, press the top of the pastry lightly with the bottom of a sheet pan to level the top.

9. Warm the reserved Ganache until it is liquid. Spread a thin layer over the top of the Marjolaine. Once the Ganache has started to set, but before it sets up completely, use the back of a chef's knife to mark diagonal lines, $^1/_2$ inch (1.2 cm) apart in both directions, making a diamond pattern in the Ganache. Drag the knife across without putting much pressure on it. Refrigerate until firm.

10. Dust cocoa powder lightly over the top. Using a thin sharp knife dipped in hot water, trim about $^1/_2$ inch (1.2 cm) from one of the long sides to make a clean edge. Starting from that edge, mark or cut the sheet into three equal strips lengthwise, each approximately $2^1/_4$ inches (5.6 cm) wide. Trim one short end on each, and then cut each strip into four square pieces (the same length as the width of the strip). Be sure to hold the knife at a 90° angle so that the sides of the pastries are straight. This cake will keep for several days in the refrigerator if left whole, so it is best not to cut more servings than you expect to need.

11. Place a portion of the Raspberry Sauce in a piping bottle. Reserve.

12. Presentation: Pipe a 3-inch (7.5-inch) circle of Raspberry Sauce centered on the lower half of the base of a dessert plate. Use the tip of the piping bottle or a wooden skewer to form the circle into a heart shape approximately $4^1/_2$ inches long and $4^1/_2$ inches wide at the top (11.2 × 11.2 cm) by first elongating the bottom of the circle into a point and then widening the top. It is not necessary to make two rounded edges on top of the heart. Instead, place a Marjolaine square diagonally on the plate so that the bottom corner of the pastry rests in the top of the sauce and creates the heart shape. Use a piping bag to pipe two thin lines of Sour Cream Mixture along the inside perimeter of the heart. Swirl the lines into the sauce with a wooden skewer (see Figure 19–26, page 1002). Place three raspberries and a small mint leaf on the plate.

Nut Meringue

two 12-by-16-inch (30-×-40-cm) sheets

6 ounces (170 g) almonds
4 ounces (115 g) hazelnuts
1 ounce (30 g) bread flour
8 egg whites (1 cup/240 ml)
8 ounces (225 g) granulated sugar

NOTE: If you keep finely ground nuts on hand, purchased from a bakery supplier, use those instead, using all almonds (almond meal) or all hazelnuts depending on availability.

1. Grind the almonds and hazelnuts to a fine consistency (see note). Mix in the flour.

2. Whip the egg whites until they are foamy and have doubled in volume. Gradually add the sugar and whip to stiff peaks. Carefully fold in the ground nut mixture by hand.

3. Divide the batter equally between two half sheets of baking paper (12 by 16 inches/30 × 40 cm). Using a spatula, spread the batter in an even layer over the papers to cover them completely. Drag the papers onto half sheet pans (see Figure 16–15, page 842).

4. Bake immediately at 350°F (175°C) for about 15 minutes or until golden brown and dry.

Praline Buttercream

8 ounces (225 g) Vanilla Buttercream
  (page 978)
1 tablespoon (15 ml) Hazelnut Paste
  (page 9)
¼ teaspoon (1 g) mocha paste
  or
2 teaspoons (10 ml) Coffee Reduction
  (page 5)

*B*uttercream tends to break when liquid is added, especially if the buttercream is cold.
Should this happen, stir the mixture over warm water until it is smooth.

1. Mix a small amount of Vanilla Buttercream into the Hazelnut Paste to soften it.

2. Mix back into the remaining buttercream together with the coffee flavoring. Continue to mix until smooth.

Meringue Black Forest Cake

two 10-inch (25-cm) cakes

two-thirds recipe or 3 pounds (1 kg, 365 g) Crème Parisienne
  (page 1086) (see note)
⅓ cup (80 ml) kirschwasser
dark coating chocolate, melted
four 10-inch (25-cm) Meringue Noisette (page 591)
one 10-inch (25-cm) Chocolate Chiffon Sponge Cake (page 272)
⅓ cup (80 ml) Simple Syrup
  (page 11)
⅓ cup (80 ml) kirschwasser
Dark Chocolate Triangles (page 890)
  (see step four)
1½ cups (360 ml) heavy cream
2 teaspoons (10 g) granulated sugar
Dark Chocolate Squares (page 890)
unsweetened cocoa powder

NOTE: Crème Parisienne must be refrigerated for a minimum of 8 hours or, preferably, overnight before it can be whipped to stiff peaks. If this is not practical, substitute the full recipe of Chocolate Cream (see page 1084).

*T*his cake is a variation combining the chocolate-flavored whipped cream
and Sponge Cake of the traditional German Black Forest Cake with the
meringue layers and kirsch flavoring of the Swiss specialty, Sugar Kirsch Cake.
    *The Chocolate Triangles make a spectacular decorative finish, but they can
be a bit time consuming to make. A much quicker, and perfectly acceptable,
method is to simply break the chocolate sheet into small pieces after it has hardened. Place the pieces on the whipped cream as directed for the triangles. This
rustic version was born of necessity at the school when a young future chef
decided to challenge nature and attempted (and would not give up) to cut the triangles out of a thin sheet of chocolate after first placing the sheet in the refrigerator for quite some time! A second option, which is very showy when the cake is
to be presented whole, is to decorate the slices with Chocolate Fans (see page
892). Place the fans in concentric circles starting at the perimeter of the cake.*

1. Combine the Crème Parisienne and ⅓ cup (80 ml) of kirschwasser and whip to stiff peaks. Reserve.

2. Brush a thin layer of melted coating chocolate on the top sides of the Meringue Noisettes. Place two of the meringues, chocolate-side up, on cardboard cake circles for support. Place one-quarter of the Crème Parisienne on each and spread out flat.

3. Cut the skin from the top of the chocolate sponge, cutting it even at the same time. Cut the sponge into two layers and place them on top of the Crème Parisienne, pressing down lightly. Combine the Simple Syrup and the remaining ⅓ cup (80 ml) kirschwasser. Brush the mixture over the sponges, using all of it. Divide the remaining Crème Parisienne on top of the sponges and spread out evenly. Place the remaining meringue bottoms chocolate-side down on top of the cream and press down lightly. Do not worry if the meringues stick out beyond the sponge; you will trim them later. If you plan to present the cakes in serving pieces rather than whole, place the cakes in the freezer at this point until they are hard before finishing them. This will make them easier to cut.

4. Make the Chocolate Triangles 1¹/₂ inches (3.7 cm) tall and ³/₄ inch (2 cm) wide at the bottom. Reserve.

5. Trim any meringue that protrudes outside the sponge so that the sides of the cakes are even (see Figure 8–11, page 325). Whip the heavy cream and sugar to stiff peaks. Divide the cream between the cakes and ice the tops and sides, spreading just a thin layer on the sides and the remainder on the tops.

6. Cut or mark the cakes into the desired number of serving pieces, making sure the cakes are still half-frozen when you cut them to avoid smashing the layers.

7. Decorate the length of each slice with the Dark Chocolate Triangles. Start by placing one triangle at the tip of the slice, then two behind it, and three behind those, continuing as the piece becomes wider. Stick the pointed ends into the cream so that the triangles stand up at a very slight angle. Fasten a Chocolate Square on the side of each slice. Sift cocoa powder lightly over the top.

Meringue Glacé Leda

16 servings

one-quarter recipe French Meringue (page 590)

three-quarter recipe Hippen Decorating Paste (page 1018)

¹/₂ teaspoon (1.25 g) unsweetened cocoa powder

Spun Sugar (page 972), colored light pink

1 cup (240 ml) heavy cream

2 teaspoons (10 g) granulated sugar

one recipe Vanilla Ice Cream (page 640)

NOTE: If the weather is humid or rainy, it will be very difficult to produce attractive Spun Sugar. You may want to substitute Chocolate Sauce (page 1072) decorated with Sour Cream Mixture for Piping (page 1081). The decoration shown in Figure 19–23, page 1001, would be appropriate to suggest waves.

*I*t is impossible to discuss Leda without simultaneously speaking of Helen of Troy (see Pears Belle Hélène, page 479), since according to Greek mythology, Helen was hatched from an egg that was either laid by, or entrusted to, Leda for safekeeping. It all depends on which of several conflicting stories one chooses to "believe." In one version, the beautiful Leda attracted the attention of Zeus who, disguised as a swan, flew down from Mount Olympus and ravished her. However, according to this legend, at the time of her rape Leda had recently been impregnated by Tyndareus, who was the king of Sparta and Leda's husband. At the term of her pregnancy, Leda laid two eggs. Helen and Clytemnestra emerged from one egg and Pollux and Castor from the other. Helen and Pollux were thought to be the children of Zeus, whereas Clytemnestra and Castor were supposed to have been fathered by Tyndareus. Another version has it that Zeus and the goddess Nemesis made love in the form of swans, and that Nemesis laid the egg. There are further twists and turns in this story with the egg either abandoned by Nemesis and then found by or given to Leda by a third party, or entrusted to Leda by Nemesis herself. After receiving the egg Leda either waited for the egg to hatch or swallowed it and then delivered the egg herself. When Helen was hatched from the egg she was so beautiful that Leda claimed her as her own daughter.

1. Place the meringue in a pastry bag with no. 8 (16-mm) star tip. Pipe into sixteen 3-inch (7.5-cm) long, cone-shaped shells on a sheet pan lined with baking paper (see Figures 9–25 and 9–26, pages 423 and 424). Bake at 210–220°F (99–104°C) for approximately 3 hours or until dry.

2. Color 1 tablespoon (15 ml) of the Hippen Paste with cocoa powder. Reserve.

3. Make the templates for the wings and neck (Figure 12–8). The templates as shown are the correct size for this recipe. Trace the draw-

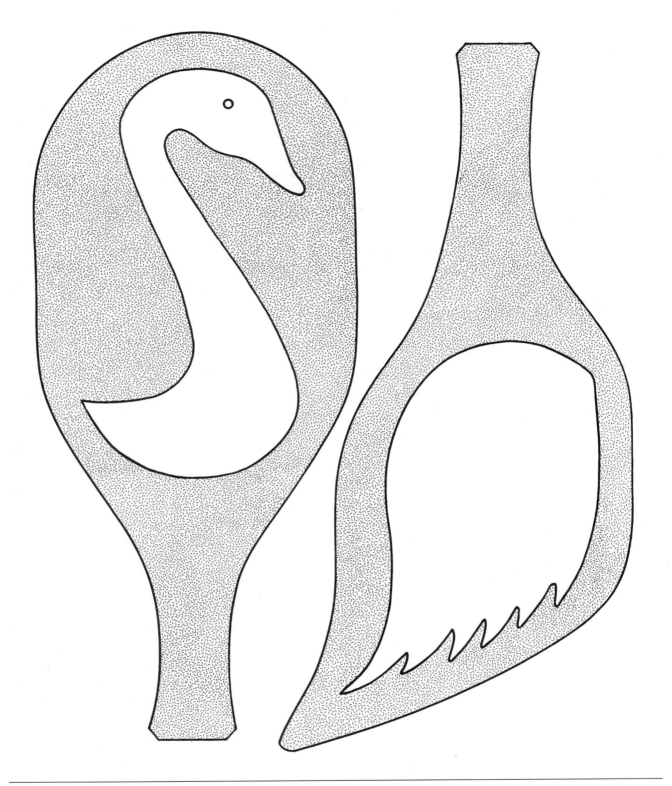

FIGURE 12–8 *The templates used to shape the Hippen Paste for Meringue Glacé Leda*

ings and then cut them out from 1/16-inch (2-mm) thick cardboard (cake boxes work fine for this).

4. Lightly grease the back of even sheet pans, coat with flour, and shake off as much flour as possible. (Or better yet, use silicone mats, which do not need to be greased and floured.) Adjust the Hippen Paste if necessary, until is easily spreadable but not runny (see recipe). Spread the paste flat and even within the templates on the prepared pans (see Figures 19–55 and 19–56, pages 1046 and 1047). Make a few extra head-neck pieces to allow for breakage. Make sixteen wings, then turn the template over and make sixteen more so you will have a left and right wing for each swan.

5. Place the reserved cocoa-colored paste in a piping bag and pipe one small dot on each head for an eye.

6. Bake at 375°F (190°C) until they start to color slightly, about 10 minutes. Let cool completely before removing from the sheet pans. Reserve in an airtight container. The baked pieces can be stored for up to one week at this point.

7. Make the Spun Sugar as close to serving time as possible. Reserve in an airtight container. It is a good idea to place a small amount of a dehumidifying agent in the container to protect the sugar against moisture, even if it is only a few minutes before serving time, and it is essential if the sugar will be kept longer.

8. Whip the heavy cream and sugar to stiff peaks. Place in a pastry bag with a no. 8 (16-mm) star tip. Reserve in the refrigerator.

9. Presentation: Pipe a small dot of whipped cream in the center of a chilled dessert plate. Place a meringue shell on the cream. Use an ice-cream scoop to portion a scoop of Vanilla Ice Cream on top of the meringue. The scoop must be large enough to slightly protrude beyond the sides of the meringue. Fasten one left and one right wing, top side facing out and flat side against the ice cream, on the sides. Place a head and neck piece between the meringue and ice cream, angled back over the body. Pipe a small amount of whipped cream at the back for a tail. Arrange Spun Sugar on the plate around the swan. Serve immediately.

Meringue Landeck

24 pastries

one quarter recipe French Meringue
    (page 590)
one-half recipe Ladyfingers batter
    (page 275)
Sambuca Cream (recipe follows)
dark coating chocolate, melted
powdered sugar

*L*andeck is a quaint little town high up in the Austrian alps that I highly recommend you visit if you are traveling in that area. It is a comfortable day trip from Garmisch Partenkirchen in Germany by heading southwest, or from Innsbruck, Austria, by driving west along the River See. There is now also the option of taking the autobahn, making your return back to base quick and easy. But better yet, make Landeck an overnight stop on your journey while you choose between continuing to follow the River See south toward Italy, or heading west across the Swiss border into Zurich, for there is no practical route across the Alps in between.

    I borrowed the idea for this pastry some twenty-five years ago during my first visit to Landeck. Since then the recipe has been altered somewhat to lighten *the flavor and texture. Although the pastries can be kept overnight if covered and refrigerated, ideally they should be assembled and served the same day.*

1. Draw six 2½-inch (6.2-cm) wide strips, evenly spaced, across the width of a sheet of baking paper. Invert the paper on a sheet pan. Place the French Meringue in a pastry bag with a no. 8 (16-mm) plain tip. Pipe a rope of meringue lengthwise along both marked edges of four of the strips. Pipe the ropes a little flatter than they come out of the tip of the bag, leaving just enough room between the meringue ropes for a rope of Ladyfingers batter. Pipe a single rope of meringue down the center of the remaining two strips (Figure 12–9). You will have a small amount of meringue left over. Pipe out a few cookies on another pan or discard the meringue.

2. Place the Ladyfingers batter in the pastry bag. Pipe a single rope of Ladyfingers batter between the meringue ropes on the first four strips and one Ladyfinger rope on either side of the meringue ropes on the last two strips.

3. Bake at 210–220°F (99–104°C) until the strips are dry and the Ladyfingers batter has turned golden brown, approximately 2 hours. Set aside to cool.

4. Trim the strips as needed so they are all the same width. Reserve the two best-looking of the four strips with two meringue ropes. Place the other two on cardboard strips for support. Spread a little less than half of the Sambuca Cream over the strips on the cardboards. Place the two strips composed in the opposite pattern (two Ladyfinger, one meringue) on top of the cream. Ice the tops and the long sides of the strips using all of the remaining Sambuca Cream (Figure 12–10). Top with the reserved strips. Brush melted chocolate lightly over the two meringue ropes on each assembled strip. Refrigerate for a minimum of 2 hours to set the cream.

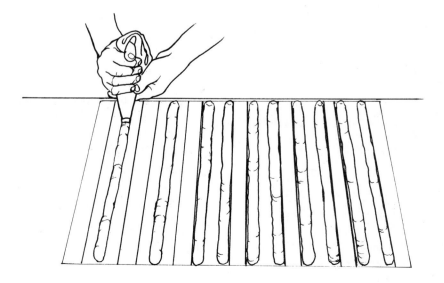

FIGURE 12–9 Piping ropes of meringue within the marked lines on a sheet of baking paper for Meringue Landeck

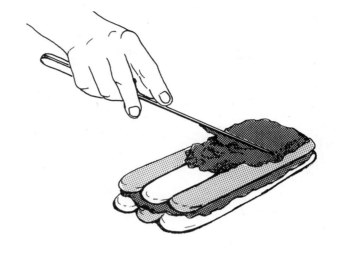

FIGURE 12–10 Adding the second layer of filling in assembling Meringue Landeck, using Crème Parisienne to make the recipe variation

5. Cut each strip into twelve slices using a serrated knife dipped in hot water. Sift powdered sugar over the tops of the pastries.

 VARIATION
Chocolate Meringue Landeck

*F*ollow the directions as given, replacing the Sambuca Cream with one-half recipe or 2 pounds, 4 ounces (1 kg, 25 g) Crème Parisienne (page 1086).

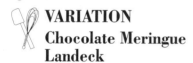 **Sambuca Cream**

approximately 3 cups (720 ml)

2 teaspoons (6 g) unflavored gelatin powder
¼ cup (60 ml) cold water
1½ cups (360 ml) heavy cream
¼ cup (60 ml) sambuca liqueur
one-quarter recipe Italian Meringue (page 591)

1. Sprinkle the gelatin over the water to soften.
2. Whip the heavy cream to soft peaks. Add the liqueur and combine with the Italian Meringue.
3. Heat the gelatin mixture over a bain-marie to dissolve. Do not overheat. Working quickly, add the gelatin to a small part of the cream mixture to temper, then quickly mix this into the remaining cream. Do not make this cream until you are ready to use it.

Mocha Meringues

about 50 pastries

one-half recipe French Meringue
(page 590)

1 pound, 8 ounces (680 g) Vanilla
Buttercream (page 978)

$^1/_2$ teaspoon (2 g) mocha paste

or

2 tablespoons (30 ml) Coffee
Reduction (page 5)

sliced almonds, toasted and lightly
crushed

one hundred $1^1/_2$-inch (3.7-cm)
Chocolate Curls (page 887)

powdered sugar

NOTE: If you do not have time to make the
Chocolate Curls, substitute small Chocolate
Rectangles (page 890).

You might say the name Mocha Meringues is little misleading, since the mocha flavoring is not in the meringue component but is instead in the buttercream filling. However, this is part of the charm of these little pastries, as it allows you to change the flavor as needed to suit a special occasion or request, or provide a greater variety if you are already offering several selections with coffee flavoring. If stored properly, and under ideal conditions, the meringue shells can be made up to several weeks in advance, allowing you to fill and finish the pastries as required. One of my favorite alterations is to flavor the buttercream with either orange or kirsch liqueur (use $^1/_3$ to $^1/_2$ cup/80 to 120 ml, depending on the strength). You can decorate the fruit-flavored meringues with Chocolate Curls as described in the original recipe, or garnish the orange liqueur version with a Marzipan Orange (see page 1030) and the kirsch-flavored pastries with a Marzipan and chocolate decoration as shown in Figure 8–21, page 362. Pipe the chocolate stems directly on the buttercream lines on top of each pastry, with the lines for the stems perpendicular to the buttercream lines. Regardless of which option you choose, these pastries easily enhance a typical assortment. They are a breath of fresh air compared to the usual rectangular, square, or piped selections.

1. Place the meringue in a pastry bag with a no. 8 (16-mm) plain tip. Pipe it onto sheet pans lined with baking paper, in $1^1/_2$-inch (3.7-cm) wide domes. Leave the tops as flat as possible as you pipe, without "tails" sticking up (in other words, the mounds should *not* be shaped like chocolate kisses).

2. Bake at 210–220°F (99–104°C) until completely dry, 3 to 4 hours.

3. Flavor the buttercream with the mocha paste or Coffee Reduction, mixing until soft and smooth. Place in a pastry bag with a no. 2 (4-mm) plain tip. Pipe a mound of buttercream the size of a cherry on top of half of the meringues. Invert the remaining meringues on top of the buttercream, and press down lightly to level the tops.

4. Spread enough buttercream on the sides of the stacked meringues to completely fill in the gap between them and make the sides straight. Then roll the sides in the crushed almonds to coat. Using the same tip as before, cover the tops of the meringues with parallel lines of buttercream, piping back and forth in a zigzag pattern with the lines touching.

5. Set two Chocolate Curls on top of each pastry, arranging them diagonally across the buttercream lines.

6. Place six to eight pastries next to each other. Place a $^3/_4$-inch-wide (2-cm) strip of cardboard on top, perpendicular to the curls. Sift powdered sugar over the pastries. Remove the cardboard and repeat with the remaining pastries. Mocha Meringues can be stored at room temperature for one or two days under normal conditions. Refrigerate if the weather is very warm.

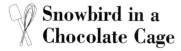

Snowbird in a Chocolate Cage

16 servings

2 cups (480 ml) heavy cream
2 teaspoons (10 g) granulated sugar
sixteen Chocolate Cages (page 904)
one recipe Kiwi Sauce (page 1074)
sixteen Snowbirds (recipe follows)
Spun Sugar (page 972) (see note)

NOTE: Make the Spun Sugar as close to serving time as possible, and reserve in an airtight container. Place a dehumidifying agent in the container to protect the sugar against moisture. This is a good idea even if you make the Spun Sugar just before serving, and it is essential if it will be stored longer.

Snowbirds

20 birds

4 ounces (115 g) Short Dough
   (page 54)
one-quarter recipe French Meringue
   (page 590)
finely ground almonds or hazelnuts
1/2 ounce (15 g) Marzipan (page 1022),
   tinted red
dark coating chocolate, melted

NOTE: Although the unfilled birds can be stored in a dry place for several days, it is best

While an intricate dessert such as this one is not really suitable for a large banquet or mass production (although it certainly could be done if the labor cost could be justified), as is true of many desserts that are complicated or labor-intensive, it can be scaled down with good results and without losing its attraction. The following presentation can be greatly simplified by eliminating the cage and serving the snowbirds "free-range," resting in their nests of Spun Sugar. Not only will you save yourself some work but you will save your guests some calories as well. Moreover, if the uncaged birds are filled with the lighter Italian Cream (see page 1087) instead of whipped cream, the result is a dessert very low in fat. These appealing little birds can also be used alone (without the cage or sugar) to enhance a simple dessert such as a Bavarian cream or a serving of ice cream. Another alternative is to turn them into spectacular individual French pastries by filling the birds with flavored buttercream instead of whipped cream.

1. Whip the heavy cream and the granulated sugar to stiff peaks. Place in a pastry bag with a no. 5 (10-mm) plain tip. Reserve in the refrigerator.

2. No more than 30 minutes prior to serving, place one Chocolate Cage for every serving you anticipate needing in the refrigerator. Place a portion of the Kiwi Sauce in a piping bottle; reserve.

3. Presentation: Pipe a pearl pattern (see Figure 19–6, page 983) of whipped cream in a ring the same size as the bottom of a Chocolate Cage, centered on the base of a dessert plate. Pipe whipped cream between the two halves of the body on one of the assembled birds, completely filling the open space and mounding the filling slightly above the sides. Attach the neck and head to the front. Arrange a little Spun Sugar inside the whipped cream ring on the plate, then a set a Snowbird on top of the nest. Carefully place a Chocolate Cage on top of the whipped cream ring. Pipe Kiwi Sauce around the dessert to cover the base of the plate. Serve immediately.

1. Roll the Short Dough out to 1/8 inch (3 mm) thick, using flour to prevent it from sticking. Cut out twenty 1 1/2-inch (3.7-cm) cookies, using a plain cookie cutter. Reserve the dough scraps for another use. Bake at 375°F (190°C) until golden brown. Set aside to cool.

2. Place the meringue in a pastry bag with a no. 6 (12-mm) plain tip. Pipe out approximately fifty teardrop shapes, 2 1/2 inches (6.2 cm) long, for the bodies of the birds (each body requires two pieces) on a sheet pan lined with baking paper. Hold a no. 4 (8-mm) plain tip in place over the other tip (see Figures 12–6 and 12–7, page 602), and pipe out approximately fifty 1 1/2-inch (3.7-cm) teardrops on a second pan lined with baking paper for the wings. Sprinkle ground nuts over the wings. Replace the no. 4 tip with a no. 3 (6-mm) tip. Pipe out twenty-five 1 1/2-inch (3.7-cm) neck and head shapes, as shown in Figure 12–11 on the pan with the wings.

not to assemble more birds than you can use right away, since the individual meringue pieces (before assembly) can easily be dried in the oven should they become soft during storage.

3. Bake all of the meringue shapes at 210°F (99°C) for 1 to 2 hours or until dried all the way through. The necks will be done quite a bit sooner than the bodies.

4. To assemble the birds, select the twenty best head and neck pieces. Trim just a little from the front of the head to create a flat edge. Roll the red Marzipan into a 6-inch (15-cm) string. Cut the string into twenty equal pieces. Roll the pieces into tiny cones, pressing the bottom of each cone against the table so it becomes flat. Place the cones and the head/neck pieces of meringue together on a plate or cardboard and refrigerate for a few minutes until cold.

5. Place melted chocolate in a piping bag. Cut a small opening and pipe a tiny drop of chocolate on the flat side of a Marzipan cone and then press it gently against the flat side of a Snowbird head. Hold in place for a just a few seconds; the chilled surfaces will cause the chocolate to set quickly. Repeat with the remaining pieces. Pipe an eye on each head (Figure 12–11).

6. Arrange the bodies, wings, and Short Dough bases as shown in Figure 12–12. Refrigerate just long enough to chill the pieces. It is best to do this in small groups so that none of the pieces lose their chill as

FIGURE 12–11 *The Marzipan beak and the meringue head and neck piece for the Snowbird; after attaching the Marzipan beak and piping the chocolate eye on the head*

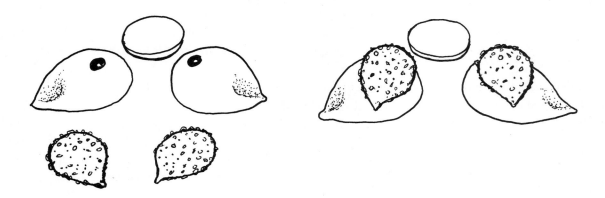

FIGURE 12–12 *The grouped pieces ready to assemble one Snowbird, with chocolate piped on the body pieces to attach the wings*

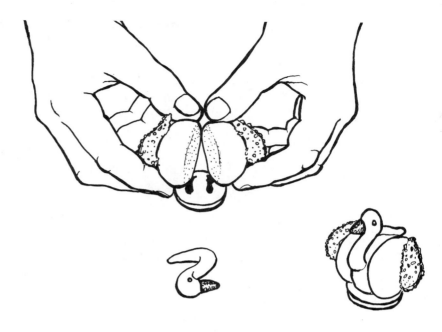

FIGURE 12–13 *Attaching the body pieces to the Short Dough base with lines of chocolate after attaching the wings to the bodies; the assembled Snowbird*

you work on the others. Working with one group of parts at a time, pipe chocolate on the body pieces as illustrated and attach the wings. When the wings are set, pipe two lines of chocolate on the Short Dough base and quickly attach the two body/wing pieces straight up, perpendicular to the base, angling the pieces so that the tails touch in back and there is an opening about ³/₄ inch (2 cm) wide in front (Figure 12–13). Hold a few seconds until set. Pipe a little chocolate inside the tail to hold the side pieces more securely until the birds are filled. Assemble the remaining birds in the same manner.

 Vacherin with Plum Ice Cream

16 servings

one-half recipe French Meringue (page 590)
dark coating chocolate, melted
one-half recipe Plum Ice Cream (page 636)
1 cup (240 ml) heavy cream
1¹/₂ teaspoons (8 g) granulated sugar
four small plums
one recipe Plum Sauce (page 1079)

*M*arie Antoinette is said to have occasionally amused herself with cooking, and this decorative meringue bowl was one of her favorite and most successful efforts. The name Vacherin *is borrowed from a variety of French and Swiss cheeses that are made from cow's milk. Vacherin is derived from the French word* vace, *meaning cow. Vacherin cheeses are circular and flat, traditionally bordered with a strip of spruce bark.*

Like many popular creations, there are many versions of the dessert Vacherin, all of which combine meringue with either ice cream, whipped cream, or both. One simple but delicious example is Meringue Glacé Chantilly (recipe follows). The classic rendition of Vacherin consists of two or three crisp meringue rings (or rings made from Almond Macaroon Paste) stacked on top of one another and placed on a meringue base. The shell is then filled with fruit and/or Chantilly Cream. A glacé or frozen Vacherin is filled with ice cream, decorated with whipped cream, and then garnished with fresh or crystallized fruit.

Vacherin may be made in sizes for multiple servings or in individual portions as I do in this recipe.

1. Draw thirty-two 3-inch (7.5-cm) circles on sheets of baking paper. Invert the papers on sheet pans. Place the meringue in a pastry bag with a no. 4 (8-mm) plain tip. Pipe the meringue onto the prepared baking papers, using the circles as a guide (see Figure 12–2, page 592). As you come to the outside of each circle, pipe two additional rows of meringue on top of the outside ring to form the sides of the case. Make sixteen cases; the remaining sixteen circles are used as a guide to pipe out the lids: Using a no. 2 (4-mm) plain tip held in place over the bag as you pipe (see Figures 12–6 and 12–7, page 602), pipe five equally spaced, parallel lines of meringue across one circle, then pipe five additional lines at a 45° angle to the first set to make a diamond pattern. Repeat to make the remaining sixteen lids.

2. Bake immediately at 210–220°F (99–104°C) until dry. The cases will take approximately 4 hours and lids about 2 hours. Made up to this point, the meringue shells will keep for several weeks if kept in a warm, dry place. Therefore, finish only the amount you expect to serve right away.

3. Holding the cases upside down, dip the rims in melted dark coating chocolate. Carefully shake off the excess chocolate before setting them right-side up to prevent any chocolate from dripping down the sides.

4. Fill each Vacherin with Plum Ice Cream. Place the filled meringue shells in the freezer.

5. Whip the cream and sugar to stiff peaks. Place in a pastry bag with a no. 3 (6-mm) plain tip. Reserve in the refrigerator. Cut the plums into quarters. Fan the pieces and reserve in the refrigerator. Place a portion of the Plum Sauce in a piping bottle and reserve.

6. Presentation: Pipe the whipped cream in a spiral on top of a vacherin, starting in the center and continuing to the chocolate-covered rim, in the same way that you piped the base of the shells. Place a lid on top. Top with a fanned plum garnish. Pipe a small dot of whipped cream off-center on a dessert plate and place the finished vacherin on top to prevent it from sliding. Pipe a small pool of Plum Sauce in front of the Vacherin. Serve immediately.

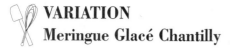

VARIATION
Meringue Glacé Chantilly

16 servings

*V*acherin Glacé is actually Meringue Glacé Chantilly in a fancy shape. You can make this classic by using the same ingredients with the addition of chocolate shavings and the following procedure.

1. Place the meringue in a pastry bag with a no. 6 (12-mm) star tip. Pipe the meringue into sixteen 2$\frac{1}{2}$-inch (6.2-cm) corkscrews (like a telephone cord) or other pretty shapes.

2. Bake, cool, and dip the pieces halfway into melted dark coating chocolate.

3. Place the whipped cream in a pastry bag with a no. 9 (18-mm) star tip. Pipe a large rosette of cream on the serving plate; sprinkle some chocolate shavings on top.

4. Arrange the ice cream, meringue, Plum Sauce, and a fanned plum in a nice presentation around the rosette. Do not forget to put a little whipped cream under the ice cream to prevent it from sliding.

13

Ice Cream and Frozen Desserts

Ice Creams

    Banana Poppy Seed Ice
      Cream
    Caramel Ice Cream
    Cashew Nut Ice Cream
    Cinnamon Ice Cream
    Coffee-Scented Chocolate
      Ice Cream
    Fresh-Coconut Ice Cream
    Gooseberry Ice Cream
    Macadamia Nut Ice Cream
    Mango Ice Cream
    Maple-Pecan Ice Cream
    Mint and Parsley Ice Cream
    Papaya Ice Cream
    Peach Ice Cream
    Pistachio Ice Cream
    Plum Ice Cream
    Pomegranate Ice Cream
    Rhubarb Ice Cream
    Rum-Raisin Ice Cream
    Strawberry Ice Cream
    Sun-Brewed Jasmine Tea
      Ice Cream
    Vanilla Ice Cream
    White Chocolate Ice Cream
      with Ginger

Philadelphia-Style Ice Creams

    Low-Fat Philadelphia-Style
      Ice Cream
    Philadelphia-Style
      Chocolate Ice Cream
    Traditional Philadelphia-
      Style Ice Cream

Frozen Yogurts

    Banana-Tofu Frozen Yogurt

    Calvados-Tofu Frozen
      Yogurt
    Gingered Pineapple Frozen
      Yogurt
    Honey-Scented Pear Frozen
      Yogurt
    Honey-Vanilla Frozen
      Yogurt
    Strawberry-Rhubarb Frozen
      Yogurt with Ginger

Sorbets and Sherbets

    Bing and Royal Anne
      Cherry Sorbet
    Blood Orange Sorbet
    Blueberry Sorbet
    Champagne Sorbet
    Feijoa Sorbet
    Gooseberry Sorbet
    Honey Mandarin Sorbet
    Honeydew Melon Sorbet
    Kiwi Sorbet
    Lemon-Lime Sherbet
    Lemon-Thyme
      and Mascarpone Sherbet
    Mango Sorbet
    Prickly Pear Sorbet
    Raspberry Sorbet
    Red Currant Sorbet
    White Nectarine Sorbet

Bombes

    Basic Bombe Mixture
    Bombe Aboukir
    Bombe Bourdaloue
    Bombe Ceylon
    Bombe Monarch

Coupes

    Coupe Bavaria
    Coupe Belle Hélène
    Coupe Hawaii
    Coupe Niçoise
    Coupe Sweden

Frozen Desserts

    Benedictine Soufflé Glacé
    Caramel Ice Cream
      in a Caramel Cage
    Cherries Jubilee
    Feijoa Sorbet with Kiwi,
      Pineapple, and
      Strawberry Sauces
    Frozen Hazelnut Coffee
      Mousse
    Lingonberry Parfait
    Macadamia Nut Ice Cream
      in a Chocolate Tulip
      with Mango Coulis
    Mango Ice Cream
      with Chiffonade
      of Lemon-Mint
      and a Chocolate Twirl
    Oven-Braised Black Mission
      Figs with Honey-Vanilla
      Frozen Yogurt
    Passion Fruit Ice Cream
      Parfait
    Peach Ice Cream
      in Florentina Baskets
    Poached Pears with Ginger
      Ice Cream and Two
      Sauces
    Soufflé Pancakes with
      Gooseberry Ice Cream
    Wild Strawberry Parfait

Ice creams and other frozen desserts in different shapes and combinations have always been favorites of guests and chefs alike. Ice cream seems to bring out the child in us, making it almost impossible to resist. The taste is refreshing, which is especially appreciated in the summer, and the light consistency makes it easy to digest. Ice cream and many ice cream desserts are also very practical for the chef because they can be made days in advance. Today, the home cook can make wonderful ice creams as effortlessly as the professionals with the small electric ice cream freezers available at a reasonable cost. Churning ice cream by hand has become almost obsolete. Many of the ice creams that follow are used as part of another recipe or in a plate presentation elsewhere in this book. In some cases a particular accompaniment such as a sauce, a type of fresh fruit, or a tulip is suggested with the ice cream recipe, when it goes particularly well with a certain flavor.

Custard-Based Ice Cream

The term *ice cream* generally refers to the custard-based variety, which is a confection made from cream or milk (usually a mixture of the two), sugar, and egg yolks. These ingredients are cooked over a bain-marie until the cus-

NOTE: *Italian gelatos differ from the so-called French ice creams in that they have more powerful flavors and denser textures, thanks to the inclusion of more solids and less air. Although gelatos are usually made with milk instead of cream, their higher percentage of eggs gives them an equally rich, if not richer, taste than the French variation. (Technically speaking, gelato is any kind of frozen concoction served in an Italian ice cream shop or gelateria.)*

tard has thickened sufficiently to coat a spoon—when you pull a wooden spoon out of the mixture you will not be able to see the wood—which is also referred to as the ribbon or nappe stage. It is important not to overheat and coagulate the eggs while cooking. The custard base is first chilled, then placed in an ice-cream freezer together with the desired flavorings, and the mixture is frozen to a temperature below 32°F (0°C) while being churned to incorporate air and produce the desired texture and overrun. The result should be smooth, airy, and creamy. Vanilla ice cream is the forerunner of this type and the most common flavor produced. Its taste mixes and blends well with a wide range of other desserts, and the custard itself (unfrozen) also serves as the base for many other flavors of ice cream, as you will see in the recipes that follow. There are many hybrids and variations of custard-based ice creams, two examples being Philadelphia-style ice creams, which do not contain egg products (although sometimes a relatively small amount is added to improve "mouth feel"), and gelato, which is typically made using whole milk and is churned incorporating a minimal amount of air, which produces little or no overrun (see note).

Composition

Ice cream is composed of milk products, sweeteners, eggs, flavorings, and stabilizers or emulsifiers. The U.S. Food and Drug Administration requires that commercial products labeled ice cream must contain no less than 10 percent milkfat (butterfat) and must have at least 20 percent MSNF (milk solids no fat). A good quality ice cream should have a minimum of 40 percent total solids (fat, sweetener, and MSNF). Milk solids contribute to the whipping capability of the custard; however, if the custard contains too large a percentage of milk solids, the lactose (milk sugar) can crystallize, making the custard feel gritty; this is known as sanding.

Ice creams are judged and rated on the following points:

• *Texture and Smoothness.* This is determined primarily by the size of the ice crystals and the emulsifying or whipping ability of the custard combined with the amount of milk sugar (lactose) that is added.

• *Mouth Feel or Body.* This is established by the total solids in the custard in conjunction with the overrun, which is the name for the amount of air incorporated while freezing.

• *Richness and Flavor.* These factors are produced from the composition of the custard. The fat and MSNF contained in premium ice cream should come from a mixture of whole milk and cream. Evaporated, condensed, or dried milk should not be used, since these products adversely affect the fresh taste of the finished ice cream.

Fat Content

The fat content of the cream and milk blend, and the proportions of cream and milk required to achieve the desired percentage in the fin-

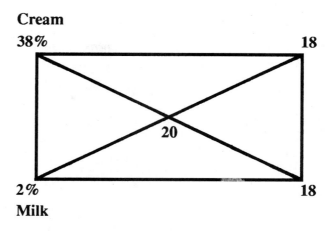

FIGURE 13–1 *The formula used to calculate the proportions of milk and cream required to achieve the desired fat content in the finished ice cream*

ished product, can be calculated using the following method: Draw a rectangle with two lines crossing diagonally. In the upper left corner write the fat percentage of the cream you are using. Write the fat percentage of the milk you are using in the lower left corner. In the center, write the desired fat content for the finished ice cream. Subtract the desired fat percentage from the cream fat percentage and write the result in the opposite diagonal corner. Subtract the milk fat percentage from the desired fat percentage and write this figure in the remaining corner. The resulting figures are the proportions of milk and cream you should use in order to achieve the desired fat content. The example (Figure 13–1) shows the fat content in an ice cream using half-and-half. In other words, since both figures are 18, you would use equal parts of milk and cream; if the cream figure was 10 and the milk figure was 30, you would use one part cream to three parts milk.

While it is true that milk fat (this term is used to describe the fat from either the milk or the cream, since cream comes from milk) is responsible for the most part for the rich and creamy flavor we associate with superior ice cream, too much milk fat (using too much heavy cream) will not only effect the whipping ability, it will cause the finished product to be more compact and the overrun (yield) will also be impaired. Another problem that can occur is that the milk fat can be churned into tiny lumps of butter, causing a grainy finished ice cream. This often happens with custards composed of whole cream, or when using mascarpone or white chocolate as part of the base.

Sweeteners

Sucrose (cane or beet sugar) is the typical sweetener used in ice cream, but maple syrup, molasses, and honey are also common. When substituting honey for granulated sugar in an ice cream custard, the amount should be reduced about 20 percent. Keep in mind also that once it has been frozen the ice cream will not taste as sweet as the custard, since freezing dulls the intensity of the sweet flavor. And even though the sugar content of the total solids in a custard is typically close to 15 percent, particular flavors will require a sweeter custard than others. While a relatively high proportion of sugar can be beneficial in keeping an ice cream smooth and pliable after freezing, too much sugar can prevent the ice cream from becoming firm enough to use.

Eggs

Egg yolks enhance both the smoothness and color of the custard. They also greatly improve the body of the ice cream due to their emulsifying properties, although they have almost no effect on the freezing ability of the ice cream in the way that sugar does. Egg yolks and whole eggs must be pasteurized by heating the custard to a temperature above 180°F (82°C). Uncooked ice creams, such as Philadelphia-style, which do not contain any egg products, benefit from the use of mono- and diglycerides as emulsifiers, and gelatin or gums as stabilizers.

Churning

A warm ice cream custard should never be poured directly into the ice-cream freezer. It should cool slowly and then be refrigerated for several hours or overnight. The extra cooling time will result in a smoother finished product. When the ice cream has churned to the desired consistency, turn off the freezer unit of the ice cream maker, but keep the churner on for a few minutes longer if your machine has this option, before removing the finished ice cream. This will cause a minimum amount of ice cream to stick to the sides of the container.

The amount of air churned into the ice cream during freezing determines the volume and lightness of the finished product. As a rule, higher quality ice cream is lower in volume, when compared by weight. Because an ice cream made with heavy cream is more compact in its composition, it yields less than an ice cream made with milk or half-and-half and is richer and smoother.

Overrun

Overrun is the term used for the amount, or volume, of ice cream obtained after churning that is in excess of the volume of the base. It is actually the amount of air incorporated into the mix during the freezing and churning process. Overrun is discussed as the percentage of overrun. A 100 percent overrun would describe a custard that has doubled in volume during freezing. This is the maximum overrun allowed by the FDA. While some overrun is necessary for a smooth and light texture, too much will give the ice cream an airiness and a less intense flavor. High quality ice cream such as gelato has a lower percentage of overrun (sometimes none) than the average ice cream. Overrun is determined by:

- the freezing equipment;
- the length of time the ice cream spends in the ice-cream freezer (it should be removed as soon as it is frozen);
- the amount of custard in relation to the freezer size—for maximum overrun the freezer should only be filled halfway;
- the ingredients in the mixture which effect its ability to increase, for example, eggs; and
- the total solid content of the base. A custard which has a total solid content of 40 percent (fat, sweetener, and MSNF combined) can produce an overrun of up to 100 percent without diminishing in quality.

Additions to Ice Cream

Many of the recipes in this chapter can be enhanced and varied with the addition of a flavoring such as chunks of white, milk, or dark chocolate, toasted nuts, candy (for the holidays try adding crushed peppermint candy to vanilla ice cream), dried or candied fruit, crushed cookies, chopped brownies, caramel sauce, and/or chocolate sauce mixed into the finished product. Some classic combinations are vanilla ice cream with candied pecans and swirls of caramel, chocolate ice cream with chips or chunks of dark chocolate, and vanilla ice cream marbleized with fruit preserves. Do not use fresh puréed fruit for this; it must first be sweetened and reduced by cooking or it will not produce the desired marble look and will also adversely effect the texture, freezing hard and icy.

Most additions should be incorporated after the ice cream has been churned, in order to avoid breaking or mashing the pieces. Stir the flavoring in while the ice cream is still soft before placing it in the freezer, taking care to distribute the pieces evenly. When adding fresh or dried fruit, it should first be macerated in a spirit or liqueur, a sugar syrup, or a combination of the two, so that the fruit will not freeze so hard that it becomes unpleasant to eat. To crate a marbleized or swirled pattern using sauces or fruit preserves, alternate layers of freshly churned soft ice cream with much thinner layers of the desired flavor as you place the ice cream in the storage container. With ice-cream machines that extrude the finished product through a spigot, add the sauce layers as the ice cream flows into the container. Insert a wooden spoon or spatula straight down through the center of the layered mixture after the container is full. Pull from side to side—left to right and back to front— once in each direction, then pull straight out. It is important not to mix the layers too much, or instead of ripples you will simply incorporate the flavoring into the base; the swirled pattern will be accentuated as you scoop the frozen ice cream.

Storage and Serving

It is possible to store ice cream for three to four weeks without any loss of volume or quality, provided it is stored in airtight containers. Ice cream should be frozen at 6°F (–15°C) so it will harden quickly. It should then be stored at a temperature between 6 and 14°F (–15 to –9°C). However, ice cream should be served at a higher temperature so that it is pleasant to eat, and easy to scoop and work with. The ideal temperature for serving varies with different flavors and types. Ice cream and other frozen desserts can be unmolded or scooped into serving glasses 1 to 2 hours in advance and held in the freezer, but final touches and garnishes must be applied at the last moment. Sorbets taste best when freshly made and still soft. Sorbets and parfaits should not be kept longer than one or two weeks at the most.

Sanitation

To achieve a finished product of the highest quality, it is immensely important that ice cream is made using only fresh and pure, first-rate raw materials that have been properly pasteurized to kill bacteria. The equipment and utensils which come in contact with ice cream must not only be made of stainless steel or another noncorrosive material, they must also be properly cleaned and sterilized after each use. The importance of this can not be overstated. Absolute cleanliness is so essential because the ice cream mixture provides a perfect breeding ground for bacteria. Bacteria is defined as unicellular microscopic organisms belonging to the plant kingdom—either cocci, which are spherical in shape; the rod-shaped bacilli; or spirilla, which are formed in a spiral. All reproduce by division and fusion. The factors which accelerate or eliminate their growth are temperature, oxygen, moisture, food particles, chemicals, and light.

Sanitizing Agents

Soap is not a good cleaning agent for ice-cream equipment because it leaves a film that can be difficult to rinse away. Heat is the most common and reliable source for sanitizing food equipment, and it can also have the added advantage of speeding up the drying time, provided the temperature is high enough. For proper water sanitizing, however, the equipment must be submerged in water with a temperature between 180 and 212°F (82–100°C) for at least 10 minutes. Obviously this is not practical for the ice-cream maker itself, so a chemical agent must be applied to that piece of equipment. For the chemical to be completely effective, the item must be thoroughly clean so that its surface comes in direct contact with the chemical. It is also critical that the solution has the proper concentration of the active chemical and, most importantly, that the sanitizing agent is in contact with the equipment for a sufficient time to kill the bacteria. The time will vary with the type of chemical used. A quick, inexpensive, and effective solution can be made from regular laundry bleach. Use 1–2 tablespoons (15–30 ml) bleach per gallon of warm water. The water should not exceed 110°F (43°C). This solution must be in contact with the surface for a minimum of 1 minute.

Ice Creams

 ## Banana Poppy Seed Ice Cream

approximately 6 cups (1 l, 440 ml)

8 ounces (225 g) granulated sugar
10 egg yolks (⁷/₈ cup/210 ml)
3 cups (720 ml) milk
2 cups (480 ml) heavy cream
2 pounds (910 g) ripe bananas
   (four medium-sized)
juice from one-quarter lime
2 ounces (55 g) poppy seeds
¹/₃ cup (80 ml) Frangelico liqueur

NOTE: As with any custard-based ice cream, Banana Poppy Seed Ice Cream will have a smoother texture if you rest the custard in the refrigerator for about 8 hours before freezing. Do not prepare, or stir in, the banana purée until you are ready to process the ice cream in the freezer.

I am surprised that this flavor combination has not made its way into the commercial marketplace. This recipe was given to me by a friend many years ago. It had been in his family for quite some time. This ice cream goes with just about any dessert, but I particularly like it served with fresh strawberries or strawberry sauce. Like mangoes and papayas, ripe bananas have a creamy full-bodied texture when puréed, which gives the ice cream a silky-smooth consistency. The crunchy poppy seeds contrast wonderfully. Any nut-flavored liqueur may be substituted for the Frangelico if you want to experiment. Macadamia nut liqueur is especially nice if you can find it.

1. Beat the sugar and egg yolks together lightly to combine. Heat the milk and cream to the scalding point. Stirring constantly, gradually pour the hot liquid into the egg mixture. Place over simmering water and, continuing to stir with a whisk or wooden spoon, heat until the custard thickens enough to coat the spoon. Be careful not to overcook and break the custard. Set aside to cool at room temperature, then cover and refrigerate until thoroughly chilled.

2. Peel the bananas and purée with the lime juice. (If you use fruit that is not fully ripe, it may not purée smoothly, making it necessary to pass the pulp through a fine mesh strainer before proceeding.) Stir the banana purée into the custard together with the poppy seeds and liqueur.

3. Process immediately in an ice-cream freezer according to the manufacturer's directions. Place a bowl in the freezer at the same time so it will be chilled to hold the finished product. Store the ice cream covered in the freezer.

Caramel Ice Cream

*approximately 5 cups
(1 l, 200 ml)*

one-half recipe Caramel Sauce I
    (page 1070)
1 quart (960 ml) half-and-half
10 egg yolks (⁷/₈ cup/210 ml)
3 ounces (85 g) granulated sugar
2 cups (480 ml) heavy cream
one-quarter recipe Nougatine Crunch
    (page 969)

*B*ecause of the addition of Caramel Sauce, this ice cream remains creamy and malleable, without softening or smoothing, even after days in the freezer. Be careful, nonetheless, not to add more caramel than specified in the recipe, because too much sugar will keep the ice cream from freezing, leaving you with a product which is pliable to the point of being unmanageable. Caramel Ice Cream, like Vanilla, has a neutral flavor that goes well with many desserts.

1. Place the Caramel Sauce and half-and-half in a saucepan and heat to the scalding point.

2. Whip the egg yolks and sugar until fluffy. Gradually add the scalded milk mixture to the egg yolks while whipping rapidly. Heat the mixture over simmering water, stirring constantly with a whisk or wooden spoon, until it is thick enough to coat the spoon. Remove from the heat and stir in the heavy cream. Let the custard cool slightly at room temperature, then cover and refrigerate until thoroughly chilled.

3. Process in an ice-cream freezer according to the manufacturer's directions. Stir in the Nougatine Crunch and store the finished ice cream covered in the freezer.

Cashew Nut Ice Cream

approximately 5 cups (1 l, 200 ml)

1 pound (455 g) unsalted cashew nuts
3 cups (720 ml) milk
one vanilla bean, split lengthwise
    or
1 teaspoon (5 ml) vanilla extract
12 egg yolks (1 cup/240 ml)
10 ounces (280 g) granulated sugar
2 cups (480 ml) heavy cream

NOTE: Rather than discarding these expensive nuts, try to find a use for them in cookies, a torte, or even Bear Claw filling. Rinse to remove the milk, then spread out on a sheet pan to dry. Use within a few days.

*R*aw unsalted cashew nuts (whole or in pieces) are not only quite expensive, they can be difficult to find in the retail market. Often a health or natural foods store is a good place to look. If you must settle for roasted and salted nuts, blanch and dry them to rid them of the salt, and omit toasting the nuts in step one. The distinctive buttery rich flavor of cashews is delightful in combination with fresh ripe fruits such as peaches, nectarines, and especially mangoes.

1. Toast the cashew nuts, cool, and then crush coarsely. Reserve 2 ounces (55 g) or about ¹/₂ cup (120 ml) of the nuts.

2. Place the remaining nuts in a food processor with ¹/₂ cup (120 ml) of the milk and process to a paste-like consistency.

3. Place the remaining milk in a heavy saucepan and add the vanilla bean if used. Bring to a boil, then remove from the heat and stir in the nut paste. Cover the pan and set the mixture aside to steep for a minimum of 30 minutes.

4. Whip the egg yolks and sugar together until light in color. Bring the milk mixture back to boiling, then strain through a fine mesh strainer or a cheesecloth (see note). Remove the vanilla bean and save for another use. Gradually stir the hot milk into the yolk mixture.

5. Set the bowl over simmering water and, stirring constantly with a whisk or wooden spoon, heat the custard until it is thick enough to coat the spoon. Remove from the heat. Stir in the heavy cream, the vanilla extract if used, and the reserved crushed nuts. Let cool at room temperature, then cover and refrigerate the custard until it is completely cold.

6. Process in an ice-cream freezer according to the manufacturer's instructions. Transfer the finished ice cream to a chilled container. Cover, and store in the freezer.

Cinnamon Ice Cream

approximately 5 cups
(1 l, 200 ml)

---

one recipe Vanilla Ice Cream custard
   (page 640)
two cinnamon sticks
2 teaspoons (3 g) ground cinnamon

*C*innamon is the inner bark of a young tree. It was once a commodity of great value and together with two other important spices—nutmeg and clove—has been the reason for much human bloodshed over time. The Arabs kept their source of cinnamon a highly guarded secret for many centuries and tried to discourage anyone from finding an alternate source by telling stories of monsters inhabiting countries they suspected of containing the spice. The fact that cinnamon grows wild throughout Ceylon did not come to be known before the fourteenth century.

   Cinnamon Ice Cream makes a wonderful accompaniment to many types of fruit desserts and, because of the natural affinity of the two flavors, especially any containing apple. Warm apple desserts such as apple pie, turnovers, crisp, or apples en croûte *are particularly pleasing as the cold, creamy ice cream provides a delicious contrast to the crisp crust and tart apple filling and melts into a cinnamon-flavored custard sauce.*

Follow the directions for Vanilla Ice Cream with these changes:

   • Add the cinnamon sticks to the half-and-half and vanilla bean in step one.
   • After bringing the mixture to the scalding point, remove from the heat and set aside to infuse for 30 minutes.
   • Mix the ground cinnamon into the granulated sugar before combining it with the egg yolks.
   • After chilling the custard (preferably overnight), remove the cinnamon sticks before processing in an ice-cream freezer.

Coffee-Scented Chocolate Ice Cream

approximately 6 cups (1 l, 440 ml)

---

1 quart (960 ml) half-and-half
4 ounces (115 g) unsweetened cocoa
   powder
1/2 cup (120 ml) espresso coffee
one vanilla bean, split lengthwise
   or
1 teaspoon (5 ml) vanilla extract
4 ounces (115 g) sweet dark chocolate
8 egg yolks (2/3 cup/160 ml)
6 ounces (170 g) granulated sugar

*I*f you are a chocolate lover, you will not be able to stop eating this rich chocolate ice cream. It has just a hint of coffee flavor, which, if you prefer, can easily be left out. I recommend you do so rather than use instant coffee if espresso is not available. Try serving this ice cream with a splash of Grand Marnier or Cointreau on top and one or two Florentina cookies on the side—it is heaven.

   1. Gradually mix enough half-and-half into the cocoa powder to dissolve it and make a smooth paste. Stir in the remaining half-and-half and the espresso. Bring to the scalding point with the vanilla bean if used.
   2. Chop the chocolate into small pieces. Remove the cream mixture from the heat, add the chopped chocolate, and stir until completely melted.
   3. Whip the egg yolks with the sugar until light and fluffy. Remove the vanilla bean from the half-and-half and reserve for another use, or

add the vanilla extract if used. Gradually pour the hot half-and-half into the yolk mixture while stirring rapidly. Place over simmering water and heat, stirring constantly with a whisk or wooden spoon until the mixture is thick enough to coat the spoon. Set aside to cool. Then cover and refrigerate until thoroughly chilled, preferably overnight.

4. Process in an ice-cream freezer according to the manufacturer's directions. Store covered in the freezer.

Fresh-Coconut Ice Cream

approximately 6 cups (1 l, 440 ml)

two medium-sized fresh coconuts, about 2 pounds (910 g) each

3 cups (720 ml) coconut milk from fresh coconuts

milk (as needed)

one vanilla bean, split lengthwise
  or

1 teaspoon (5 ml) vanilla extract

2 cups (480 ml) heavy cream, approximately

10 egg yolks (⅞ cup/210 ml)

3 ounces (85 g) granulated sugar

The value of the coconut palm to the native inhabitants wherever it flourishes cannot be described better than in the old native proverb, "He who plants a coconut tree plants vessel and clothing, food and drink, a habitat for himself and a heritage for his children." I am using only a small portion of the "tree of life" in this recipe—the coconut milk and meat. Coconut Ice Cream is ideal paired with fresh tropical fruit and a Macadamia Nut Cookie.

1. When selecting the coconuts, test the freshness by shaking them; there should be plenty of milk inside. Puncture the three eyes and drain the coconut milk, reserving 3 cups (720 ml). If the coconuts do not contain that much liquid, add enough regular milk to make the amount needed.

2. Tap the coconuts all around with a hammer or heavy cleaver to help loosen the meat from the shell. Crack the coconuts open using the same tool. Remove the meat from the shell, then use a vegetable peeler to remove the brown skin from the meat. (If some pieces did not separate from the shell, place them on a sheet pan and bake at 350°F (175°C) for about 30 minutes to loosen.) Chop the coconut meat finely in a food processor.

3. Combine the coconut meat, coconut milk, and vanilla bean (if used), in a saucepan. Heat to scalding, remove from the heat, cover, and let infuse for at least 30 minutes.

4. Strain the mixture, pressing with a spoon to remove as much liquid as possible from the coconut meat. Remove the vanilla bean and save it for another use. Discard the coconut meat. Add enough heavy cream to the strained coconut milk to make 5 cups (1 l, 200 ml) of liquid. Return to the saucepan and heat to scalding.

5. Beat the egg yolks and sugar together for a few minutes. Gradually pour the hot liquid into the yolk mixture, whisking continuously. Heat the mixture over simmering water, stirring constantly with a whisk or wooden spoon until it thickens enough to coat the back of the spoon. Remove from the heat and continue to stir for a minute to prevent overcooking on the bottom or sides. Add the vanilla extract if used. Let cool at room temperature, then cover and refrigerate until completely cold.

6. Process in an ice-cream freezer according to the manufacturer's directions. Store covered in the freezer.

Quick Coconut Ice Cream

*I*f you just can't live with yourself if you use anything but fresh coconut to make your Coconut Ice Cream (and I agree there is a difference), use the preceding recipe. However, if you are short on time this is a very good quick compromise: Use the recipe for Vanilla Ice Cream (page 640), replacing 2 cups (480 ml) of the half-and-half with unsweetened, canned coconut milk, and use only 4 ounces (115 g) sugar. This makes approximately 5 cups (1 l, 200 ml).

Gooseberry Ice Cream

approximately 2 quarts (1 l, 920 ml)

1 pound, 8 ounces (680 g) green or
    yellow gooseberries (see note)
¹/₄ cup (60 ml) water
6 ounces (170 g) granulated sugar
one recipe Vanilla Ice Cream custard
    (page 640)

NOTE: Green and yellow gooseberries turn amber or white when they are fully ripe, and they also lose most of their tartness at this point, becoming rather bland. You may want to leave out part or even all of the sugar when cooking the fruit, depending on the stage of ripeness. It is necessary to trim the berries since the fruit is not strained after cooking. The easiest way to remove both the blossom portion and the stem from the berries is to use small pointed scissors. A nail clipper (designated as a kitchen tool or properly sterilized in boiling water first) also works well.

*G*ooseberries are so popular and common in Sweden that not having gooseberry bushes growing in your yard is practically considered unpatriotic! This is a wonderful, tart ice cream with a very distinctive flavor. It is great teamed with any of the pear desserts in the Country Desserts chapter, or enjoy it topped with caramel sauce alongside a slice of gugelhupf.

1. Rinse the gooseberries and then trim both the flower and stem ends. Place in a saucepan with the water and sugar. Bring to a boil and cook over medium heat until the berries pop open and fall apart. Lower the heat and continue cooking until the mixture has been reduced by half. Watch carefully during this time, and stir as needed, to prevent the mixture from burning.

2. Stir the fruit into the ice cream custard, cover, and place in the refrigerator to chill, preferably overnight.

3. Process in an ice-cream freezer following the manufacturer's directions. Store covered in the freezer.

Macadamia Nut Ice Cream

*approximately 2 quarts
(1 l, 920 ml)*

1 pound (455 g) unsalted macadamia
    nuts
1 quart (960 ml) milk
one vanilla bean, split lengthwise
    or
1 teaspoon (5 ml) vanilla extract
12 egg yolks (1 cup/240 ml)
14 ounces (400 g) granulated sugar
2 cups (480 ml) heavy cream

*NOTE: Do not discard these costly nuts. Dry
the fine pieces and use them in cookies or in a
nut torte. The nuts will not keep very long,
however, after being soaked in milk.*

*I f you think it is a shame to grind up these expensive nuts and put them to
soak in some milk, please wait and pass judgment after you have tasted the
finished product! I first had Macadamia Nut Ice Cream on a trip to Maui a few
years back and set about right away to try to duplicate the rich and creamy yet
delicate flavor. If you have macadamia nut liqueur, try pouring a little over the
top just before serving and accompany with a sweet tropical fruit.*

1. Toast the macadamia nuts and set aside until cool. Grind or
crush the nuts coarsely, combine with ½ cup (120 ml) of the milk, and
grind to a paste in a food processor.

2. Add the vanilla bean (if used) to the remaining milk (3½
cups/840 ml) and bring it to a boil. Mix in the nut paste. Remove the
pan from the heat, cover, and set aside to steep for at least 30 minutes.

3. Whip the egg yolks and sugar until light and fluffy (ribbon
stage). Reheat the milk mixture to boiling, then strain through a fine
mesh strainer or cheesecloth (see note). Remove the vanilla bean and
scrape the seeds back into the strained mixture, using the back of a paring knife. Discard the vanilla bean. Gradually add the hot milk to the
beaten yolks while stirring constantly.

4. Cook the custard over hot water, stirring with a whisk or
wooden spoon, until it thickens enough to coat the spoon. Stir in the
heavy cream and the vanilla extract if used. Let cool at room temperature, then cover and chill the mixture until it is completely cold.

5. Process in an ice-cream freezer according to the manufacturer's
directions. Transfer to a chilled container and store covered in the
freezer.

Mango Ice Cream

*approximately 6 cups
(1 l, 440 ml)*

3 cups (720 ml) milk
1 cup (240 ml) heavy cream
2 eggs
10 ounces (285 g) granulated sugar
2 pounds (910 g) fresh whole ripe
    mangoes (two medium-sized)
⅓ cup (80 ml) lime juice

*NOTE: If you use fruit that is not fully ripe, it
is better to first peel the mangoes and then cut
the flesh away from the stones.*

*T he mango has been described as the world's most delicious fruit. In the
tropical part of the globe it is the fruit most commonly eaten out of hand (the
way you might think of an apple in this country), and it ranks fifth in worldwide
consumption. Mangoes are also one of the most difficult fruits when it comes to
removing the peel and stone, if you're hoping to keep the flesh intact for decoration. To serve mango with the peel on, simply cut the two halves free of the stone
lengthwise and use a small sharp knife to cut through the flesh down to the peel
in both directions on each cut half. Then turn the halves inside-out to raise the
scored flesh in a hedgehog pattern (Figure 13–2).*

1. Combine the milk and cream in a saucepan and heat to scalding.
Whip the eggs and sugar in a mixing bowl until well combined. Gradu-
ally add the hot milk mixture to the eggs while whisking constantly.
Place the bowl over a bain-marie and cook, stirring with a whisk or a
wooden spoon until the custard has thickened slightly (nappe stage).
Set aside to cool.

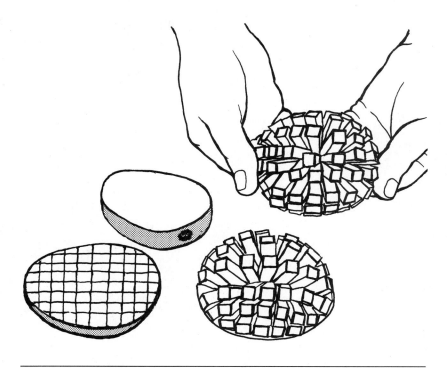

FIGURE 13–2 Making a mango "hedgehog." The two halves cut away from the center stone and surrounding flesh leaving the peel on the fruit, with the flat cut sides of each half then scored in both directions down to, but not through, the skin; turning the halves inside-out to raise the cut flesh.

2. Slice each mango into two halves by cutting through on both sides of the large flat stone. Use a spoon to scrape the flesh away from the skin and the stones. Purée, strain, and discard the solids. Stir the purée into the cooled custard together with the lime juice (see note). Cover, and place in the refrigerator until completely cold, preferably overnight.

3. Transfer the custard to an ice-cream freezer and process following the manufacturer's directions. Store covered in the freezer.

Maple-Pecan Ice Cream

approximately 8 cups (1 l, 920 ml)

1¹/₂ cups (360 ml) pure maple syrup
   (the real thing, no cheating)

1 quart (960 ml) half-and-half

10 egg yolks (⁷/₈ cup/10 ml)

3 ounces (85 g) granulated sugar

1 cup (240 ml) heavy cream

8 ounces (225 g) pecans, lightly
   toasted and crushed

There is no reason to make Maple-Pecan Ice Cream (or anything else that calls for maple syrup for that matter) unless you use the real thing—pure maple syrup. While there are some blends of maple and corn syrups that come a little closer, artificially-flavored pancake syrups and other maple-flavored substitutes are absolutely unacceptable and simply will not produce that distinctive, deep, unmistakable taste. Real maple syrup is actually not all that expensive if you consider that it takes about three gallons of boiled sap to produce the amount of syrup used in this recipe. Maple syrup is collected mainly in Vermont and the surrounding states. The "sugarers" wait until the end of winter for the first thaw when the sap begins to flow through the sugar maple trees, also known as Rock Maple or Hard Maple. A small tap hole is bored about 2 inches deep into the trunk. The spout is driven in, and then a sap bucket is hung under the spout. Slashing the trunk is another method used to collect the syrup.

1. Place the maple syrup and the half-and-half in a saucepan and heat to the scalding point.

2. Whip the egg yolks with the sugar until the mixture is starting to foam, about 2 minutes. Gradually add the scalded cream mixture while whipping rapidly.

3. Place over simmering water and heat, stirring constantly with a whisk or wooden spoon, until the mixture is thick enough to coat the spoon (ribbon stage).

4. Remove from the heat and immediately stir in the heavy cream. Let the custard cool to room temperature. Cover and refrigerate until thoroughly chilled.

5. Process in an ice-cream freezer following the manufacturer's directions. Stir in the crushed pecans. Store covered in the freezer.

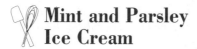

Mint and Parsley Ice Cream

approximately 6 cups (1 l, 440 ml)

4 ounces (115 g) fresh mint leaves
twelve (1/2 ounce/15 g) Italian parsley stems
2 cups (480 ml) milk
2 cups (480 ml) heavy cream
8 ounces (225 g) granulated sugar
12 egg yolks (1 cup/240 ml)
1 cup (240 ml) Crème Fraîche (page 1073)
1/3 cup (80 ml) crème de menthe

You will find that numerous recipes in this book use mint in the presentation (generally peppermint, although spearmint or lemon mint can be used as well). Since I use only the smaller top leaves or sprigs for garnish, I am naturally left with a steady and abundant supply of usable large leaves, which are perfect for making mint ice cream or sorbet. It makes sense even if you have no immediate use for the ice cream, since once it is frozen it will keep for several weeks provided it is stored properly, and the same certainly does not hold true for the picked-over fresh leaves, which don't keep very long and cannot be frozen without turning black. Although mint leaves are a very pretty dark green color, they do not produce much color when mixed with other ingredients. For this reason I use parsley to tint the ice cream light green. It is only a little extra work, and I feel it is worthwhile instead of using the commercial shortcut of green dye.

1. Finely chop the mint leaves and parsley stems.

2. Place the milk in a saucepan, add the mint and the parsley, and bring the mixture to a boil. Remove from the heat and set aside to steep for 1 hour.

3. Add the heavy cream to the milk mixture. Place back on the stove and bring to the scalding point.

4. While the milk is heating, beat the sugar and egg yolks together just to combine. Strain the milk and cream mixture into the egg and sugar mixture while whisking rapidly. Discard the contents of the strainer.

5. Place the custard over a hot water bath and heat, stirring constantly with a whisk or wooden spoon, until it thickens to the ribbon stage; do not overheat. Let cool to room temperature, then cover and refrigerate until completely cold, preferably overnight.

6. Stir the Crème Fraîche and crème de menthe into the custard.

7. Process in an ice-cream freezer following the manufacturer's instructions. Store covered in the freezer.

Papaya Ice Cream

approximately 7 cups
(1 l, 680 ml)

4 pounds (1 kg, 820 g) papaya
   (four small)
one recipe Vanilla Ice Cream custard
   (page 640)
³/4 cup (180 ml) lime juice (about five
   limes)

For a special and festive presentation, serve Papaya Ice Cream in a Chocolate Tulip with Kiwi Sauce and fresh tropical fruit, as directed in the recipe for Macadamia Nut Ice Cream in a Chocolate Tulip with Mango Coulis (page 670). Both presentations are as colorful as the Hawaiian Islands themselves, which is what inevitably comes to mind when either of these ice creams are mentioned.

1. Peel the papayas, cut in half, and remove the seeds. Purée the fruit and measure. You should have approximately 3 cups (720 ml) of purée. (If you use fruit that is not fully ripe, it may not purée smoothly, making it necessary to pass the pulp through a fine mesh strainer before proceeding.) Combine the Vanilla Ice Cream custard, papaya purée, and lime juice. Cool to room temperature, then refrigerate, covered, until completely cold, preferably overnight.

2. Process in an ice-cream freezer following the manufacturer's instructions. Chill a container to hold the finished product. Store the ice cream covered in the freezer.

Peach Ice Cream

approximately 6 cups
(1 l, 440 ml)

2 pounds (910 g) fresh peaches,
   ripe but firm
¹/3 cup (80 ml) amaretto liqueur
5 ounces (140 g) granulated sugar
10 egg yolks (⁷/8 cup/210 ml)
1 quart (960 ml) half-and-half
2¹/2 cups (600 ml) Plain Poaching
   Syrup (page 13)

NOTE: For the best results with this ice cream, prepare the macerated peaches and the custard (separately) one day before freezing the ice cream. The custard will have a smoother texture if allowed to mature, and the fruit should absorb as much sugar as possible or it will freeze rock-hard in the ice cream.

If this ice cream will be eaten the same day it is made—and it will be if it is made as Peach Ice Cream so often is, as part of a backyard barbeque party in the summertime—skip the macerating step. And, if the peaches are tree-ripened or perfectly ripe, you can omit puréeing them as well. But do include the amaretto if you have some. Peaches and almonds are just made for each other. Peach Ice Cream is great for topping many pies and tarts à la mode, *especially those that contain nuts.*

1. Pick out one-third of the firmest peaches, wash, cut in half, and discard the pits. Cut into pea-sized chunks and macerate the peach chunks in the amaretto for 4 to 5 hours or, preferably, overnight.

2. Whip the sugar and egg yolks to the ribbon stage. Scald the half-and-half and gradually combine with the egg mixture, while stirring rapidly. Set over simmering water, stirring constantly with a whisk or wooden spoon, and thicken the custard until it coats the spoon. Be careful not to overheat or you will coagulate the yolks. Remove the custard from the heat and let it cool to room temperature. Cover and refrigerate until completely cold, preferably overnight.

3. Wash the remaining peaches, cut in half, discard the pits, and remove the skin. If you lose too much pulp as you do this, add an additional peach. Place the peaches in a saucepan with the Poaching Syrup. Simmer until the fruit starts to fall apart. Remove the fruit from the syrup. Purée the fruit and set the mixture aside to cool. (If you use fruit that is not fully ripe, it may not purée smoothly, making it necessary to pass the pulp through a fine mesh strainer before proceeding.) Discard the Poaching Syrup.

4. Add the macerated peach chunks and peach purée to the custard. Process the mixture in an ice-cream freezer. Place in a chilled container and store covered in the freezer.

Pistachio Ice Cream

approximately 2 quarts
(1 l, 920 ml)

10 ounces (285 g) pistachio nuts
3 cups (720 ml) milk
one recipe Vanilla Ice Cream custard
    (page 640) (see step three)

*C*ontrary to the impression you might get from some of the commercial pistachio ice creams on the market, pistachio nuts have a very mild flavor and are not nearly green enough to color the ice cream to the bright shade often found. This recipe makes an ice cream with a delicious, subtle taste and just the hint of green color, which comes naturally from the nuts.

1. Boil the pistachios in water for 1 minute. Drain, cool, and remove the skin with your fingers. Toast the nuts at 325°F (163°C) until they start to color lightly. Reserve 2 ounces (55 g) of the nuts and grind the remainder finely.

2. Combine the ground pistachios with the milk in a saucepan. Heat to scalding, then remove from the heat, cover, and allow to steep for 30 minutes. Strain through a fine mesh strainer or cheesecloth, forcing all of the liquid from the nuts. (Since they are fairly expensive, try to use the nuts for another project, such as a torte or Bear Claw filling, instead of discarding them at this point.)

3. Prepare the Vanilla Ice Cream custard, using only half the amount of sugar called for in the recipe. Stir the strained pistachio liquid into the custard. Crush the reserved pistachios coarsely and add. Let cool to room temperature, then cover and refrigerate until completely cold.

4. Process in an ice-cream freezer following the manufacturer's directions. Store covered in the freezer.

Plum Ice Cream

approximately 6 cups
(1 l, 440 ml)

2 pounds (910 g) tart plums (see note)
1/4 cup (60 ml) Simple Syrup
    (page 11)
1/4 cup (60 ml) plum brandy or liqueur
one recipe Spiced Poaching Syrup
    (page 13)
5 ounces (140 g) granulated sugar
10 egg yolks (7/8 cup/210 ml)
1 quart (960 ml) half-and-half

*W*hile I generally try to get the Laroda or Casselman variety of plum for cooking, the tart skin of the Santa Rosa plum gives this ice cream a wonderful color and a tart, puckery taste. It is a wonderful companion to many sweet desserts, particularly any based on meringue, such as the Vacherin with Plum Ice Cream on page 617.

1. Wash the plums, cut in half, and discard the pits. Cut one-third of the fruit into pea-sized chunks. Combine the chunks with the Simple Syrup and brandy or liqueur. Set aside to macerate for a few hours or, preferably, overnight.

NOTE: *When the short season for fresh plums is over, canned tart plums may be substituted. Drain, and use the liquid as part of the poaching syrup, adjusting the sweetness and amount as needed. Canned plums only require about 5 minutes of poaching.*

2. Place the remaining plums in a saucepan with the Poaching Syrup. Cook until the plums are soft and begin to fall apart. Remove from the heat and strain off the poaching liquid, reserving 1 quart (960 ml) to use as a sauce for the ice cream if desired, or discard. (To use the poaching liquid as a sauce, reduce it by approximately half or until it has thickened slightly.)

3. Whip the sugar and egg yolks to the ribbon stage. Heat the half-and-half to scalding. Gradually pour the hot cream into the egg yolk and sugar mixture while whisking rapidly. Place over simmering water and heat, stirring constantly with a whisk or wooden spoon, until the custard is thick enough to coat the spoon. Remove from the heat and stir in the reserved poached plums and the macerated plum chunks. Let cool at room temperature, then cover and refrigerate until completely cold.

4. Process in an ice-cream freezer following the manufacturer's directions. Place the finished ice cream in a chilled container and store covered in the freezer.

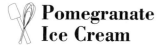 **Pomegranate Ice Cream**

approximately 2 quarts (1 l, 920 ml)

2 pounds (910 g) pomegranate seeds (about seven medium pomegranates)

1¹/₂ cups (360 ml) water

8 ounces (225 g) granulated sugar

2 teaspoons (10 ml) Beet Juice (page 3)

one recipe Vanilla Ice Cream custard (page 640) (see step two)

*T*he season for pomegranates lasts only from September to December, peaking in October. This is much too short a time to be able to take advantage of this decorative, juicy fruit. Luckily, whole pomegranates can be kept in the refrigerator for up to three months, and the seeds can be frozen indefinitely. To simplify the tedious task of separating the edible seeds from the spongy, bitter membrane that surrounds them, freeze and thaw the fruit, then slice in half. This will dislodge the kernels, allowing you to pull them apart quite easily. If you have extras seeds, try making a pomegranate drink: Add 3 cups water and one-quarter of a lemon to every 6 ounces of pomegranate seeds (one large fruit). Boil about 15 minutes to release the color and flavor from the seeds. Add 4 ounces of granulated sugar and bring the liquid back to boiling. Strain through a cheesecloth and chill. Makes 4 servings.*

1. Place the pomegranate seeds, water, and granulated sugar in a saucepan. Bring to a boil and cook over medium heat until reduced by half. Stir in the Beet Juice.

2. Make the Vanilla Ice Cream custard, using only half the amount of sugar specified. Stir the pomegranate mixture into the vanilla custard. Cool to room temperature, then cover and refrigerate until completely cold, preferably several hours or overnight.

3. Process in an ice-cream freezer following the manufacturer's directions and store covered in the freezer.

Rhubarb Ice Cream

approximately 5 cups
(1 l, 200 ml)

2 pounds, 8 ounces (1 kg, 135 g) fresh
    rhubarb stalks

⅓ cup (80 ml) water

5 ounces (140 g) granulated sugar

one-half recipe Vanilla Ice Cream
    custard (page 640)

½ teaspoon (2.5 ml) Tartaric Acid
    Solution (page 1115)

2 teaspoons (10 ml) Beet Juice
    (page 3) (see note)

*NOTE: Because rhubarb does not produce
enough color on its own, and I do not want to
use artificial coloring, I add Beet Juice to
enhance the appearance of the ice cream. Due
to its intense color, Beet Juice makes a great
natural food coloring. Raspberry juice also
works well, but it is not as strong.*

Rum-Raisin
Ice Cream

approximately 5 cups (1 l, 200 ml)

1 cup (240 ml) light rum

8 ounces (225 g) dark raisins

one recipe Vanilla Ice Cream custard
    (page 640) (see step two)

*I*n botanical terms, rhubarb is a vegetable, but we tend to use this "pink-hued
celery" more as you would a fruit. It is great in tarts and pies that are topped
with meringue and is, in fact, actually referred to as "pie plant." It is also pleasing as a cool, refreshing ice cream. Rhubarb leaves are potentially poisonous (in
excessive amounts), because their oxalic acid content is high enough that it can
interfere with calcium and iron absorption.

1. Wash the rhubarb and trim both ends of each stalk. Chop the
rhubarb stalks into small pieces. Place in a saucepan with the water and
granulated sugar and mix to combine. Cook over medium heat until
the rhubarb falls apart and the mixture has thickened to a jamlike consistency, approximately 20 minutes. Remove from the heat and set
aside to cool.

2. Stir the rhubarb mixture into the Vanilla Ice Cream custard
together with the Tartaric Acid Solution and the Beet Juice. Cover and
refrigerate until completely cold, preferably several hours or overnight.

3. Process in an ice-cream freezer following the manufacturer's
instructions. Store covered in the freezer.

*U*sing dark rum in this ice cream would generate a more pronounced rum
flavor, but I don't care for the muddled color it produces. Don't skip macerating the raisins in rum. It is a necessary step, not only to prevent them from
freezing into little rocks, but also because it gives the raisins a wonderful rum
flavor that comes across the instant you bite into one. The alcohol also keeps the
ice cream itself soft and pliable, even when stored overnight.

1. Heat the rum to around 150°F (65°C), then add the raisins.
Cover, and let macerate at room temperature overnight.

2. Make the Vanilla Ice Cream custard, using only half the amount
of sugar specified in the recipe. Let cool a bit, then cover and refrigerate
overnight.

3. Pour the custard into an ice-cream freezer and process following
the manufacturer's directions until the ice cream begins to thicken. Add
the raisins and any rum that has not been absorbed. Finish churning.
Transfer the ice cream to a chilled container. If necessary, stir gently to
distribute the raisins. Cover and store in the freezer.

Strawberry Ice Cream

approximately 7 cups (1 l, 680 ml)

one recipe Vanilla Ice Cream custard (page 640) (see step one)

1 pound (455 g) fresh, ripe strawberries

4 ounces (115 g) granulated sugar, approximately

½ cup (120 ml) strained raspberry purée, approximately

NOTE: Because this recipe does not use any artificial ingredients, the color may not be as bright as you are used to seeing in commercial strawberry ice creams. The raspberry juice is added to intensify the hue. Adjust the amounts of sugar and raspberry juice according to how ripe (and sweet) the strawberries are.

*L*ike peach, this is another ice cream that is traditionally made at home in the summertime. And, as mentioned in the Peach Ice Cream recipe, the fruit must be prepared with sugar before it is added, unless the ice cream is to be eaten the same day it is made. This is necessary because both peaches and strawberries contain a large amount of juice, which is not always as sweet as needed to create a soft, rather than icy, texture. Try serving Strawberry Ice Cream with Rhubarb Meringue Tart (page 252).

1. Make the ice cream custard, using only half the amount of sugar specified in the recipe.

2. Clean and stem the strawberries. Chop into small pieces. Place in a saucepan with the sugar and cook over medium heat, stirring from time to time, until the mixture starts to thicken, about 10 minutes.

3. Add to the ice cream custard, together with the raspberry purée. Cool at room temperature, then cover and refrigerate until completely cold.

4. Process in an ice-cream freezer according to the manufacturer's instructions.

Sun-Brewed Jasmine Tea Ice Cream

approximately 5 cups (1 l, 200 ml)

1 ounce (30 g) jasmine tea leaves

½ cup (120 ml) cold water

one recipe Vanilla Ice Cream custard (page 640) (see step two)

*F*or a less calorie-charged alternative, add the strained tea to the base for Honey-Vanilla Frozen Yogurt (page 645), omitting the lemon juice and vanilla extract from that recipe. If you wish, customize the tea infusion according to your own taste, using either a green tea, as suggested here, or a black tea. Possible black tea choices are darjeeling or assam, a blend such as orange spice, or a scented tea such as Earl Grey, for example.

1. Combine the tea leaves and water in a glass jar. Leave to brew in the sun or in a warm place in the kitchen for 2 to 3 hours.

2. Make the ice cream custard, substituting heavy cream for the half-and-half.

3. Strain the tea mixture and add it to the custard. Cover, and place the mixture in the refrigerator overnight or for at least 8 hours, to mature.

4. Process in an ice-cream freezer following the manufacturer's directions. Transfer to a chilled container and store covered in the freezer.

Vanilla Ice Cream

*approximately 5 cups
(1 l, 200 ml)*

1 quart (960 ml) half-and-half
one vanilla bean, split lengthwise
   or
2 teaspoons (10 ml) vanilla extract
10 egg yolks (⁷/₈ cup/210 ml)
10 ounces (285 g) granulated sugar

NOTE: Vanilla Ice Cream will improve in texture if the custard is made the day before churning and left to rest in the refrigerator.

*T*his is the "old granddad" of custard ice creams. The base is used to make numerous variations; it is simple to prepare; and Vanilla Ice Cream makes an excellent companion to just about any dessert you can think of. In the other recipes in this chapter that call for Vanilla Ice Cream custard, use this recipe proceeding through step three. In an emergency frozen Vanilla Ice Cream can be melted back down to a liquid and used as Sauce Anglaise, which is basically what it starts out as. Any leftover melted ice cream should not be saved, however. This fabulous ice cream can be kept in the freezer for several days and still remain soft, creamy and easy to serve.

1. Heat the half-and-half with the vanilla bean (if used) to scalding.

2. Beat the egg yolks and sugar until light and fluffy. Remove the vanilla bean and use the back of a paring knife to scrape the seeds back into the half-and-half. Discard the rest of the bean. Gradually pour the half-and-half into the whipped egg yolk mixture while whisking rapidly (place a towel under the bowl to keep it from turning with your whisk).

3. Heat the mixture over simmering water, stirring constantly with a whisk or wooden spoon, until it thickens enough to coat the spoon. Take care not to overheat and break (coagulate) the custard. Remove from the heat and continue to stir for a few seconds to keep the mixture from overcooking where it touches the hot bowl. Stir in the vanilla extract if used. Let cool to room temperature, then refrigerate, covered, until completely cold, several hours or, preferably, overnight.

4. Process the mixture in an ice-cream freezer following the manufacturer's instructions. Transfer to a chilled container and store covered in the freezer.

White Chocolate Ice Cream with Ginger

approximately 5 cups (1 l, 200 ml)

1 ounce (30 g) fresh ginger root, sliced
3 cups (720 ml) half-and-half
2 cups (480 ml) heavy cream
8 egg yolks (²/₃ cup/160 ml)
3 ounces (85 g) granulated sugar
8 ounces (225 g) white chocolate, cut in small chunks
¹/₂ ounce (15 g) Crystallized Ginger (page 6), chopped fine

*T*o make plain (although it is hardly that) White Chocolate Ice Cream, simply omit the ginger root and candied ginger and increase the white chocolate by 2 ounces (55 g) for a total of 10 ounces (285 g). This ice cream is incredibly rich and luxurious, but you do have to baby it a little. By adding the white chocolate to the hot custard and stirring until it is melted, you do not risk overheating this sensitive ingredient as you can so easily do when melting it over heat. Also be careful not to overchurn the ice cream. The added fat from the cocoa butter in the chocolate can make the ice cream gritty very readily.

1. Combine the fresh ginger root, half-and-half, and cream in a saucepan. Heat to scalding. Set aside to steep for 30 minutes. (If you leave out the ginger it is not necessary to set the mixture aside at this point.)

2. Beat the egg yolks with the sugar until light and fluffy. Strain the ginger root from the cream mixture, and reheat to the scalding point. Gradually whisk the hot cream into the egg yolk mixture.

NOTE: You will get a richer tasting ice cream if you make the custard the day before, or at least several hours before, freezing. You must, of course, keep the custard base in the refrigerator.

3. Place over simmering water and heat, stirring constantly with a whisk or wooden spoon (do not whip), until the custard is thick enough to coat the spoon.

4. Remove from the heat and add the white chocolate, continuing to stir until all of the chunks are melted. Stir in the Crystallized Ginger. Cool to room temperature and then refrigerate until completely cold.

5. Process in an ice-cream freezer according to the manufacturer's directions. Transfer the finished ice cream to a chilled container and store covered in the freezer.

Philadelphia-Style Ice Creams

Philadelphia-style ice creams are uncooked and, though they are frozen in the same way as a custard-based ice cream, they do not contain eggs (or only a very small amount), making them fairly close to sherbet in their composition. Because they lack the emulsifying properties of eggs—which act to keep the water molecules separate during freezing—this type of ice cream, although quicker to make and a healthier choice than the classic custard-based version, tends to have a slightly grainy consistency. The texture is significantly improved by using a thick fruit pulp such as mango, papaya, or banana, which provides its own emulsifying action. Chocolate also acts as a smoothing agent, improving the appeal of the finished product to the largest degree.

Low-Fat Philadelphia-Style Ice Cream

approximately 7 cups (1 l, 680 ml)

1¹/₂ cups (360 ml) part skim ricotta cheese

4¹/₂ cups (1 l, 80 ml) Acidophilus Yogurt (page 2), made with low fat milk

2 cups (480 ml) pure maple syrup (do not use imitation)

seeds from one vanilla bean (see note)

or

1 teaspoon (5 ml) vanilla extract

10 ounces (285 g) mango or papaya purée, strained

NOTE: Split the vanilla bean lengthwise and use the back of a paring knife to scrape out the seeds. Save the bean for another use.

This recipe is a low-fat variation, which uses yogurt and ricotta cheese in place of cream and fruit pulp to improve the texture. In the more conventional Philadelphia-style recipe that follows, fruit pulp is listed as an option. The bona fide version of this old favorite consisted simply of sweetened cream flavored with vanilla.

1. Process the ricotta cheese in a food processor until smooth. Transfer to a bowl and stir in the yogurt, maple syrup, vanilla, and fruit purée.

2. Process the mixture in an ice-cream freezer. Store covered in the freezer.

Philadelphia-Style Chocolate Ice Cream

approximately 7 cups (1 l, 680 ml)

12 ounces (340 g) sweet dark
   chocolate
5 cups (1 l, 200 ml) half-and-half
8 ounces (225 g) granulated sugar,
   approximately
seeds from one vanilla bean (see note
   from preceding recipe)
   or
1 teaspoon (5 ml) vanilla extract

*NOTE: You may want to adjust the amount of
sugar, depending on the sweetness of the particular brand of chocolate you are using.*

1. Melt the chocolate in an oversize bowl set over simmering water. Remove from the heat and quickly stir in the half-and-half. Add the sugar and vanilla, stirring until the sugar is completely dissolved. Cool to room temperature.

2. Process in an ice-cream freezer following the manufacturer's directions. Store covered in the freezer.

 ## Traditional Philadelphia-Style Ice Cream

approximately 7 cups (1 l, 680 ml)

2 cups (480 ml) heavy cream
3 cups (720 ml) half-and-half
12 ounces (340 g) granulated sugar
seeds from one vanilla bean
   (see note with Low-Fat
   Philadelphia-Style Ice Cream)
   or
1 teaspoon (5 ml) vanilla extract
12 ounces (340 g) thick fruit pulp,
   optional

1. Combine the heavy cream, half-and-half, and sugar and stir until the sugar is dissolved. Add the vanilla bean seeds or vanilla extract and the fruit pulp if used.

2. Process in an ice-cream freezer following the manufacturer's instructions. Store covered in the freezer.

Frozen Yogurts

Frozen yogurts are a type of ice cream that is churned and frozen in an ice-cream maker. They contain cultured milk with varying percentages of fat (typically low fat), flavorings, sweeteners (usually honey or sucrose), emulsifiers such as vegetable oil, or pasteurized eggs or egg yolks (in a much lesser amount than a custard-based ice cream), and they can be made with or without a stabilizer. The final product has a tangy, refreshing flavor and, due to the typically low percentages of milkfat and egg yolks, frozen yogurt is often very low in calories and cholesterol. This ancient food did not catch on in the United States until relatively recently when eating less fatty and healthier foods became a concern.

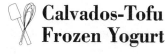

Banana-Tofu Frozen Yogurt

approximately 6 cups (1 l, 440 ml)

12 ounces (340 g) tofu

2 pounds (910 g) ripe bananas (about four medium-sized)

4 teaspoons (20 ml) lime juice (one-half lime)

1/2 cup (120 ml) vegetable oil

1 1/2 cups (360 ml) Acidophilus Yogurt (page 2)

3/4 cup (180 ml) or 9 ounces (255 g) honey

2 teaspoons (10 ml) vanilla extract

1. Blend the tofu, peeled bananas, and lime juice in a food processor until smooth. Transfer to a bowl, and stir in the oil, yogurt, honey, and vanilla.

2. Process in an ice-cream freezer following the manufacturer's instructions. Transfer to a chilled bowl and store covered in the freezer.

Calvados-Tofu Frozen Yogurt

approximately 2 quarts (1 l, 920 ml)

1 pound, 8 ounces (680 g) cooking apples such as Pippin or Granny Smith

or

1 pound (455 g) unsweetened apple purée

1 pound, 8 ounces (680 g) tofu

3/4 cup (180 ml) vegetable oil

1 pound (455 g) Acidophilus Yogurt (page 2)

1/4 cup (60 ml) Calvados

1 tablespoon (15 ml) vanilla extract

1 cup (240 ml) or 12 ounces (340 g) honey

The first reaction my students always seem to have to this recipe title is a frown, but that changes when they taste the finished product. The flavor is great, slightly tart and very refreshing, and it has a smooth texture that would normally require a quantity of cream and eggs to achieve. Try serving it with an apple tart.

1. If you are using fresh apples, peel them, core, and cut each one in half. Poach the apples in Plain Poaching Syrup (page 13) until soft.

2. In a food processor, blend the poached apples or apple purée, the tofu, and the vegetable oil until smooth.

3. Transfer the apple mixture to a mixing bowl and stir in the yogurt, Calvados, vanilla, and honey.

4. Process the mixture in an ice-cream freezer according to the manufacturer's directions. Transfer to a chilled container and store covered in the freezer.

Gingered Pineapple Frozen Yogurt

approximately 2 quarts
(1 l, 920 ml)

1 pound (455 g) granulated sugar
  (see note 1)
1 cup (240 ml) pineapple juice
1 ounce (30 g) thinly sliced fresh
  ginger root
3 eggs, separated
1 tablespoon (15 ml) vanilla extract
5 cups (1 l, 200 ml) Acidophilus
  Yogurt (page 2)
6 ounces (170 g) puréed fresh
  pineapple (see note 2)

NOTE 1: You may need to adjust the amount of sugar depending on the ripeness (sweetness) of the pineapple.

NOTE 2: If you are making this recipe to accompany Pineapple Fritters, the end slices from the pineapple, which are often too small to cut into proper-sized pieces for fritters, are ideal to use here.

1. Place half of the sugar, the pineapple juice, and the sliced ginger root in a saucepan. Bring to a boil over low heat and boil for 1 minute. Remove from the heat and let steep in the saucepan for at least 30 minutes.

2. Reheat the syrup to about 150°F (65°C). Beat the egg yolks for a few seconds to combine, then gradually strain the hot syrup into the yolks while whipping rapidly. Discard the ginger root. Add the vanilla to the yolk mixture and set aside to cool to room temperature.

3. Whip the egg whites until foamy. Gradually add the remaining sugar and continue whipping until stiff peaks form.

4. Place the yogurt in a bowl and stir with a whisk until smooth. Stir in the cooled yolk mixture and the pineapple purée. Fold in the whipped egg whites.

5. Process in an ice-cream freezer following the manufacturer's directions. Store covered in the freezer.

Honey-Scented Pear Frozen Yogurt

approximately 6 cups (1 l, 440 ml)

2 pounds (910 g) Bosc pears (about
  five medium-sized)
one recipe Plain Poaching Syrup
  (page 13)
¼ cup (60 ml) or 3 ounces (85 g)
  honey
2 eggs
4 ounces (115 g) granulated sugar
4 cups (960 ml) Acidophilus Yogurt
  (page 2)

NOTE: If you are making this yogurt to serve with the Asian Pear Tart on page 685, save the pear stems to use in the tart presentation.

1. Peel, core, and cut the pears in half, placing them in acidulated water as you work to prevent oxidation (see note). Remove from the water and place the pear halves in a saucepan with the Poaching Syrup. Poach until soft. Drain, purée until smooth, and set aside to cool. Discard the syrup or save for another use.

2. Bring the honey to a boil in a small saucepan. At the same time whip the eggs and sugar together until frothy, about 1 minute. Add the honey to the egg and sugar mixture while whipping constantly, and continue to whip until the mixture is cold.

3. Stir the egg mixture into the yogurt together with the cool pear purée.

4. Process in an ice-cream freezer following the manufacturer's directions. Store covered in the freezer.

Honey-Vanilla Frozen Yogurt

approximately 5 cups (1 l, 200 ml)

6 ounces (170 g) granulated sugar

1/3 cup (80 ml) or 4 ounces (115 g) honey

1 tablespoon (15 ml) lemon juice

1 tablespoon (15 ml) vanilla extract

2 eggs, separated

4 cups (960 ml) Acidophilus Yogurt (page 2)

1. Place half of the sugar, the honey, and the lemon juice in a saucepan. Bring to a boil over low heat. Boil for 1 minute, then remove from the heat and add the vanilla.

2. Beat the egg yolks, stir in some of the sugar syrup to temper, then add remaining syrup. Cool to room temperature.

3. Whip the egg whites until they are foamy. Gradually add the remaining sugar and whip to stiff peaks.

4. Place the yogurt in a bowl and stir smooth with a whisk. Fold in the syrup and egg yolk mixture, then the whipped egg whites.

5. Process in an ice-cream freezer according to the manufacturer's directions. Store covered in the freezer.

Strawberry-Rhubarb Frozen Yogurt with Ginger

approximately 2 quarts (1 l, 920 ml)

8 ounces (225 g) rhubarb stalks

five quarter-coin size slices fresh ginger

1 cup (240 ml) water

1 pound (455 g) fresh, ripe strawberries

8 ounces (225 g) granulated sugar (see note)

1/3 cup (80 ml) or 4 ounces (115 g) light corn syrup

2 eggs

4 cups (960 ml) Acidophilus Yogurt (page 2)

NOTE: This amount of sugar will produce a tangy refreshing flavor. Adjust the amount of sugar as needed, depending on the sweetness of the strawberries and your own taste.

1. Wash the rhubarb and trim the top and bottom of each stalk. Cut the stalks into small pieces and place in a saucepan with the ginger and the water. Cook over medium heat until the rhubarb is soft and begins to fall apart. Remove the ginger slices. Strain the remaining mixture, then return the pulp to the saucepan. Discard the liquid.

2. Clean and stem the strawberries. Chop them into small pieces and add to the rhubarb pulp in the saucepan together with the sugar. Cook over medium heat, stirring from time to time, until the strawberries fall apart and the mixture begins to thicken. Remove from the heat and set aside.

3. In a separate small saucepan, bring the corn syrup to a boil. At the same time whip the eggs until they are foamy. Whisk the corn syrup into the eggs and continue to whip until the mixture is cold. Stir the egg mixture into the yogurt together with the reserved fruit mixture. Cover, and refrigerate until cold.

4. Process in an ice-cream freezer following the manufacturer's instructions. Store covered in the freezer.

Sorbets and Sherbets

There is often confusion between sorbets (which are also called fruit or water ices) and sherbets. And for good reason—in some books they are considered to be the same thing, distinguished only by *sorbet* being the French word for sherbet. Actually, it is the other way around—*sherbet* is an American word derived from the French name *sorbet,* which came first (although in recent years it seems the term *sorbet* has become more fashionable here). There is a difference between the two products, albeit a rather confusing one: In America, a small portion of dairy product (milk or cream and sometimes egg) is typically added to the basic mixture, and this is called a sherbet. A classic sorbet never contains any milk or cream but can contain a very small amount of lightly beaten egg whites (they should be pasteurized) or Italian Meringue. This is added during churning to lighten the texture and improve overrun (yield). Although meringue does contribute to a smooth mouth feel, at the same time it dulls the flavor and color. So as you can see, a sorbet can always become a sherbet, but a sherbet can not be made into a sorbet.

As compared to ice creams, sorbets and sherbets have a lower percentage of solids, generally contain no emulsifiers, and therefore have a less creamy texture and a lower melting point. This is also due to the fact that they have a higher water and sugar content then the richer ice cream. Stabilizers are sometimes added to ensure that the finished product holds together, especially in the case of sorbets. It is also critical that the sugar content is adjusted properly to control overrun and to prevent the finished product from bleeding (separating).

Sorbets

Sorbets are made from a wide variety of fruit juices or purées. Recently the addition of spices and herbs, such as thyme, rosemary, and basil, have been popularized by some adventurous chefs, along with savory sorbet variations. These are served as refreshing first courses, or *intermezzos,* to cleanse the palate.

The flavor of the sorbet base is adjusted to the proper level of sweetness by the addition of either water or sugar syrup. This is most easily done using a saccharometer, also known as a syrup-density meter, hydrometer, or Baumé hydrometer, which measures the sugar content in a liquid. A saccharometer is a hollow glass tube weighted at the bottom, which will read 0° in tepid water. The mixture therefore must be at room temperature for the reading to be accurate. The calibration on the scale, usually from 0 to 50°, refers to degrees of Baumé, named for the Frenchman Antoine Baumé. The reading for sorbet and ices is generally between 12 and 20°, depending on their use (by comparison, icy granitás typically have a Baumé reading around 8–12°). In some instances, the mixture may be too thick for the saccharometer to float freely, which is also necessary in order to give an accurate reading. In this case a small amount of the mixture can be diluted with an equal amount of water, measured, and the "diluted" reading on the saccharometer is then doubled to determine the Baumé level for the remaining mixture.

If you do not have a saccharometer, use trial and error to determine the proper sugar level: Use the amounts of water and/or Simple Syrup specified in the recipes that follow and freeze the sorbet as directed. If necessary, thaw, adjust the mixture by adding Simple Syrup or water, and refreeze. Unlike ice creams and sherbets, which contain dairy, sorbets are not adversely affected by thawing and refreezing. When sorbets are based on a spirit, wine, or liqueur, it is not necessary to check and adjust their Baumé level because with these ingredients, unlike fresh fruits, the sugar and alcohol content are predetermined.

The level of sweetness for a sorbet depends on its use. If it is served as a dessert or as a component thereof, it is made a bit sweeter, usually between 16 and 20° Baumé. If it is served between courses as a palate cleanser, it should be crisp and refreshing with a reading around 12° Baumé. The majority of the sorbets in this section are suitable and can be used for an *intermezzo* ("in between the work") or at the end of a large meal before dessert, by lowering the sugar content appropriately—although granitás are the classical choice for this purpose.

Sorbet Stabilizers

There is generally some liquid such as sugar and/or alcohol in both sorbets and sherbets, which does freeze solid. This liquid can "bleed" (separate from the ice crystals) in the finished product, especially in the case of sorbets. A stabilizer or thickening agent is used to prevent this and to improve the texture. The stabilizer also allows the finished product to be stored in the freezer for a longer period of time. Gelatin, agar-agar, pectin, and gum tragacanth are commonly used as stabilizers. The amount required per quart of sorbet mixture is approximately 2 teaspoons (6 g) powdered gelatin or a combination of 1 teaspoon (3 g) pectin powder and 1 teaspoon (3 g) gum tragacanth. The gelatin must first be softened in water (1/3 cup/80 ml for this amount), and then heated to dissolve. It is then quickly whisked into the sorbet mixture while it is still warm or is at room temperature. If pectin and gum are used, they should be mixed with a small amount of granulated sugar (3 ounces/85 g in this case), stirred into part of the mixture, and heated to dissolve.

When a sorbet is based on an ingredient that is rich in fiber and pulp such as mango, papaya, peach, or nectarine, it does not require a stabilizer, or it requires a much smaller amount of stabilizer relative to other varieties. The same is true for sorbets based on ingredients which are naturally high in pectin—citrus fruits, apples, and blueberries are examples of these—so ideally you should not strain these mixtures apart from removing skin and seeds. However, when using fruit that is not fully ripe, it can be difficult to achieve a smooth purée. It may be necessary to pass the pulp through a fine mesh strainer in that instance.

Sherbets

Sherbets, although close to sorbets in character, are always served as a dessert. They contain milk or cream and sometimes a small amount of egg, giving them a smoother and richer texture than sorbets. When made without eggs they compare very closely to Philadelphia-style ice creams; however, sherbets lack the richness associated with a traditional custard-based ice cream.

Spooms

When a greater amount of Italian Meringue is added to a sorbet (approximately 25 percent), the product becomes known as a spoom. Spooms should placed in the freezer for several hours to set further after churning.

Granitá and Granité

Granitá and granité are the Italian and French names, respectively, for a type of dessert ice. They use basically the same ingredients as sorbets; however, they have a lower sugar content and are still frozen without churning. The name granitá is taken from the Italian word *grana,* meaning grainy, which refers both to the coarse texture of the ice crystals in the finished product and its resemblance to the grainy pattern of the Italian rock slabs known as granite. Granitás are said to have become popular in Paris in the late nineteenth century and were mentioned by Mark Twain in his book *The Innocents Abroad* (1869), in which he described "people at small tables in Venice smoking and taking granitá." Granitás quickly become favored in the United States, where they are usually known by the French name granité.

Granitás or granités are made by combing simple syrup or water with various fruit purées, liqueurs, wines, or brewed coffee or tea. In general, a granité or granitá has less sugar than a sorbet; the ratio is typically four parts liquid to one part sugar, resulting in a Baumé level of 8–12°. The mixture is frozen in a shallow pan, preferably stainless-steel, without churning. Sometimes the base is stirred with a fork from time to time as it hardens, but it is commonly simply placed in the freezer to still freeze. The mixture is then scraped into flakes and granules at serving time. Granités and granitás may be served for dessert accompanied by fresh fruit or other garnishes, or plain as a palate cleanser between courses. In either case, they benefit from being presented in a well-chilled glass, because even though they should be served slightly thawed and slushy, they melt and return to liquid very quickly due to their delicate structure.

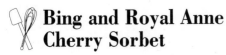

Bing and Royal Anne Cherry Sorbet

approximately 6 cups (1 l, 440 ml)

2 pounds (910 g) fresh Bing cherries
2 pounds (910 g) fresh Royal Anne cherries

1. Rinse, stem, and pit the cherries. Place in a saucepan with the sugar and the water. Stir to combine and bring to a boil. Cook over medium heat, stirring from time to time, until the cherries start to soften, about 10 minutes. Purée the mixture in a food processor. Force through a fine mesh strainer and discard the solids.

2. Combine the cherry juice with most of the Simple Syrup. Test the Baumé level (sugar content) using a saccharometer and, if needed,

4 ounces (115 g) granulated sugar

1 cup (240 ml) water

1½ cups (360 ml) Simple Syrup (page 11), at room temperature, approximately

a few drops Tartaric Acid Solution (page 1115), or lemon juice

add Simple Syrup to bring the mixture to between 16 and 20° Baumé. Add the Tartaric Acid or lemon juice.

3. Process in an ice-cream freezer following the manufacturer's instructions. Transfer to a chilled container and store covered in the freezer.

Blood Orange Sorbet

approximately 6 cups
(1 l, 440 ml)

2 pounds, 12 ounces (1 kg, 250 g) blood oranges (approximately ten)

2 cups (480 ml) Simple Syrup (page 11), at room temperature

1 cup (240 ml) water, approximately

a few drops Tartaric Acid Solution (page 1115), or lemon juice

1. Juice the oranges. Strain the juice and discard the seeds and solids. You should have approximately 2 cups (480 ml) of juice. Proceed as long as it is reasonably close to this amount.

2. Combine the orange juice and Simple Syrup. Add enough water to bring the mixture to between 16 and 20° Baumé (see page 646). Add the Tartaric Acid or lemon juice.

3. Process in an ice-cream freezer following the manufacturer's directions. Transfer to a chilled container and store covered in the freezer.

Blueberry Sorbet

approximately 5 cups
(1 l, 200 ml)

2 pounds, 8 ounces (1 kg, 135 g) fresh blueberries

1 cup (240 ml) water

2 cups (480 ml) Simple Syrup (page 11), at room temperature, approximately

a few drops Tartaric Acid Solution (page 1115), or lemon juice

1. Place the blueberries and water in a saucepan and cook over medium heat for about 10 minutes or until the blueberries pop open and begin to fall apart. Strain, pressing firmly on the contents of the strainer, and discard the pulp. Add enough Simple Syrup to the blueberry juice to bring the mixture to between 16 and 20° Baumé (see page 646). Add the Tartaric Acid or lemon juice.

2. Process in an ice-cream freezer following the manufacturer's instructions. Transfer to a chilled bowl and store covered in the freezer.

Champagne Sorbet

approximately 2 quarts
(1 l, 920 ml)

3½ cups (840 ml) dry champagne

2½ cups (600 ml) Simple Syrup (page 11), at room temperature

1½ cups (360 ml) water

⅓ cup (80 ml) lemon juice

NOTE: When making ice from wine, spirits, or liqueur, it is not necessary test the Baumé level prior to freezing because, as compared to fruits and berries, the sugar content of the alcoholic

1. Combine the champagne, Simple Syrup, water, and lemon juice.

2. Process in an ice-cream freezer following the manufacturer's instructions. Place in a chilled container and store covered in the freezer.

*beverages does not vary to the same degree.
When serving Champagne Sorbet as an inter-
mezzo between courses, reduce the Simple
Syrup by half.*

 ## Feijoa Sorbet

*approximately 5 cups
(1 l, 200 ml)*

3 pounds (1 kg, 365 g) feijoas
¹/₂ cup (120 ml) lime juice
1¹/₂ cups (360 ml) unsweetened
  pineapple juice
2 cups (480 ml) Simple Syrup
  (page 11), at room temperature
¹/₂ cup (120 ml) water, approximately

*NOTE: It is important that the strainer and the
other utensils are made of a noncorrosive material or the acid will discolor the fruit.*

1. Use a vegetable peeler to remove the skin from the feijoas. You
should have approximately 2 pounds (910 g) of fruit left. Cut the fruit
into small pieces.

2. Place the fruit pieces in a food processor with the lime juice.
Process to a smooth purée. Force the mixture through a fine mesh
strainer, then discard the seeds and solids.

3. Add the pineapple juice and Simple Syrup to the purée. Add
enough of the water (or additional Simple Syrup, depending on the
ripeness of the fruit) to bring the mixture to between 16 and 20° Baumé
(see page 646).

4. Process in an ice-cream freezer according to the manufacturer's
instructions. Transfer the finished sorbet to a chilled container and
store covered in the freezer.

 ## Gooseberry Sorbet

*approximately 6 cups
(1 l, 440 ml)*

3 pounds, 8 ounces (1 kg, 590 g) fresh
  gooseberries (see note)
12 ounces (340 g) granulated sugar
¹/₂ cup (120 ml) water
1¹/₂ cups (360 ml) Simple Syrup
  (page 11), at room temperature,
  approximately

*NOTE: This sorbet can be prepared with
canned gooseberries if you cannot obtain fresh
or it is during the off-season. Canned gooseberries require only about 5 minutes of cooking.
Because they are usually sold in sugar syrup,
adjust the amount of granulated sugar accordingly, or leave it out altogether. Since the flavor
of canned gooseberries is usually a bit bland, it
is a good idea to add a few drops of Tartaric
Acid Solution (page 1115) or lemon juice.*

1. Rinse the gooseberries. Place in a saucepan with the sugar and
water and stir to combine. Cook over medium heat, stirring from time
to time, until the gooseberries burst, about 10 minutes. Force the mixture through a fine mesh strainer and discard the seeds and solids.

2. Add most of the Simple Syrup to the gooseberry juice. Test the
sugar content with a saccharometer (Baumé thermometer) and add
additional Simple Syrup as needed to bring the mixture to between 16
and 20° Baumé.

3. Process in an ice-cream freezer following the manufacturer's
directions. Transfer to a chilled container and store covered in the
freezer.

Honey Mandarin Sorbet

approximately 6 cups (1 l, 440 ml)

3 pounds, 8 ounces (1 kg, 590 g) honey mandarins (approximately eight medium-sized)
2 cups (480 ml) Simple Syrup (page 11), at room temperature
2¹/2 cups (600 ml) water, approximately
a few drops Tartaric Acid Solution (page 1115), or lemon juice

NOTE: To make other citrus sorbets, such as orange, tangerine, or tangelo, simply substitute the desired juice for the mandarin juice in the recipe.

1. Juice the mandarins. Strain the juice and discard the seeds and solids. You should have approximately 2 cups (480 ml) of juice. Proceed as long as it is reasonably close to this amount; the measurement need not be exact.

2. Combine the mandarin juice and Simple Syrup. Add enough water to bring the mixture to between 16 and 20° Baumé (see page 646). Add the Tartaric Acid or lemon juice.

3. Process in an ice-cream freezer following the manufacturer's instructions. Transfer to a chilled bowl, cover, and store in the freezer.

 Honeydew Melon Sorbet

approximately 6 cups (1 l, 440 ml)

4 pounds (1 kg, 820 g) honeydew melon (one medium-sized or two small)
3 cups (720 ml) Simple Syrup (page 11), at room temperature
¹/2 teaspoon (1.5 g) gum tragacanth powder
¹/2 teaspoon (1.5 g) powdered pectin
1¹/2 cups (360 ml) water, approximately
a few drops Tartaric Acid Solution (page 1115), or lemon juice

NOTE: The amount of water required in this recipe can vary quite a bit depending on the sugar content of the melon, which fluctuates with the time of year.

1. It is important that the melons are fully ripe, not just for the flavor, but so you will get enough juice out of the pulp when you purée them. Cut the melons into sections, scoop out the seeds, and cut the meat away from the rind. Purée to a smooth pulp. You should have approximately 3 cups (720 ml). Proceed as long as it is reasonably close to this amount; the measurement need not be exact. Stir in the Simple Syrup.

2. Combine the gum tragacanth and pectin powder with a small amount of the water. Heat to dissolve and then stir into the fruit juice mixture. Add enough of the remaining water to bring the mixture to between 16 and 20° Baumé (see page 646). Add the Tartaric Acid or lemon juice.

3. Process in an ice-cream freezer following the manufacturer's directions. Transfer the finished sorbet to a chilled bowl and store covered in the freezer.

Kiwi Sorbet

approximately 6 cups
(1 l, 440 ml)

4 pounds (1 kg, 820 g) kiwifruit
(about ten medium-sized)
½ cup (120 ml) lime juice
2 cups (480 ml) Simple Syrup
(page 11), at room temperature
2 cups (480 ml) water, approximately

1. Peel the kiwis (see Figures 6–2, 6–3, and 6–4, page 251). Cut in half lengthwise and remove the small hard section at the bottom. Place the fruit in a food processor, add the lime juice, and purée just until the mixture is smooth. Be careful not to overprocess the fruit; too many broken seeds will turn the mixture a grayish color. The seeds are what give this sorbet its distinctive look, so the pulp should not be strained.

2. Stir in the Simple Syrup and enough of the water to bring the mixture to between 16 and 20° Baumé.

3. Process in an ice-cream freezer following the manufacturer's instructions. Transfer to a chilled container and store covered in the freezer.

 ## Lemon-Lime Sherbet

approximately 2 quarts
(1 l, 920 ml)

1 cup (240 ml) strained lemon juice
1 cup (240 ml) strained lime juice
finely grated zest from eight lemons
finely grated zest from six limes
2 cups (480 ml) Acidophilus Yogurt
(page 2)
4 cups (960 ml) Simple Syrup
(page 11), at room temperature,
approximately

1. Combine the juices and grated zests. Stir into the yogurt. Add enough of the Simple Syrup to bring the mixture to between 16 and 20° Baumé.

2. Process in a ice-cream freezer according to the manufacturer's directions. Transfer to a chilled bowl and store covered in the freezer.

 ## Lemon-Thyme and Mascarpone Sherbet

approximately 7 cups (1 l, 680 ml)

3 cups (720 ml) water
twelve sprigs lemon-thyme, chopped
½ cup (120 ml) or 6 ounces (170 g)
honey
8 ounces (225 g) granulated sugar
⅓ cup (80 ml) lemon juice
12 ounces (340 g) Mascarpone Cheese
(page 9)
1½ cups (360 ml) Crème Fraîche
(page 1073)

1. Place the water, lemon-thyme, honey, sugar, and lemon juice in a saucepan. Bring to a boil. Remove from the heat and set aside to steep for 1 hour.

2. Beat the Mascarpone Cheese for 1 or 2 minutes or until smooth. Add the Crème Fraîche and mix to combine. Strain the reserved infusion to remove the lemon-thyme. Gradually incorporate the liquid into the cheese mixture.

3. Process in an ice-cream freezer following the manufacturer's directions. Store covered in the freezer.

Mango Sorbet

approximately 6 cups (1 l, 440 ml)

4 pounds (1 kg, 820 g) ripe mangoes
  (about four medium-sized)
½ cup (120 ml) lime juice
2 cups (480 ml) Simple Syrup (page 11)
2 cups (480 ml) water, approximately

NOTE: If the mangoes are not fully ripe, they will contain more stringy fibers, reducing the yield. Mangoes that are somewhat unripe are easier to work with if you peel them first and then cut the flesh from the stones.

1. Slice each mango in half by making a cut on either side of the large flat stone. Use a spoon to scrape the flesh away from the skin and the stones. Place the flesh in a food processor. Add the lime juice and purée the fruit until smooth. Strain through a china cap and discard the solids (see note).

2. Stir in the Simple Syrup and enough of the water to bring the mixture to between 16 and 20° Baumé.

3. Process in an ice-cream freezer according to the manufacturer's directions. Transfer the sorbet to a chilled container, cover, and store in the freezer.

 # Prickly Pear Sorbet

approximately 3 cups (720 ml)

2 pounds, 8 ounces (1 kg, 135 g)
  prickly pears (about eight)
½ cup (120 ml) Simple Syrup
  (page 11), at room temperature,
  approximately
⅓ cup (80 ml) water, approximately
¼ cup (60 ml) kirschwasser
juice from one lime

1. Cut the prickly pears in half crosswise and scoop out the pulp using a small spoon. Save the shells to use in serving or discard them. Place the fruit pulp, Simple Syrup, and water in a saucepan. Heat, stirring, until the fruit falls apart. Do not boil.

2. Strain the mixture and discard the solids. Add the kirschwasser and lime juice to the fruit juice. Cool.

3. Adjust the Baumé level of the liquid to between 16 and 20° by adding water if it is too high or Simple Syrup if it is too low.

4. Process in an ice-cream freezer following the manufacturer's instructions. Transfer to a chilled container, cover, and store in the freezer.

 # Raspberry Sorbet

approximately 6 cups (1 l, 440 ml)

1 pound, 4 ounces (570 g) fresh
  raspberries (approximately 5 cups,
  loosely packed)
2 cups (480 ml) Simple Syrup
  (page 11), at room temperature
2 cups (480 ml) water, approximately
a few drops Tartaric Acid Solution
  (page 1115), or lemon juice

NOTE: It is important to use a chilled container for storage or the sorbet will start to liquify immediately. The amount of water needed in the recipe can vary quite a bit depending on the time of year or the sweetness of the particular variety of raspberry.

1. Purée the raspberries in a food processor. Strain. You should have about 2 cups (480 ml) of juice. Proceed as long as it is reasonably close to this amount; the measurement need not be exact.

2. Combine the raspberry juice and Simple Syrup. Add enough water to bring the mixture to between 16 and 20° Baumé (see page 646). Add the Tartaric Acid or lemon juice.

3. Process in an ice-cream freezer according to the manufacturer's directions. When finished, transfer to a chilled bowl, cover, and store in the freezer.

Red Currant Sorbet

approximately 4 cups (960 ml)

2 pounds (910 g) fresh red currants
1 cup (240 ml) water
1¼ cups (300 ml) port wine
5 ounces (140 g) granulated sugar
a few drops Tartaric Acid Solution
    (page 1115), or lemon juice
water or Simple Syrup (page 11), at
    room temperature, as needed

1. Wash the currants and remove the berries from the stems. Place the currants in a saucepan with the water, port wine, and granulated sugar. Stir to combine and bring the mixture to a boil.

2. Purée the mixture and strain through a fine mesh strainer. Discard the solids. Add the Tartaric Acid or lemon juice to the liquid. Let cool to room temperature.

3. Add additional water or Simple Syrup as needed so that the sugar content measures between 16 and 20° Baumé (add water if it is too high; add syrup if it is too low).

4. Process in an ice-cream freezer following the manufacturer's instructions. Place the finished sorbet in a chilled container, cover, and store in the freezer.

 ## White Nectarine Sorbet

approximately 6 cups (1 l, 440 ml)

2 pounds, 8 ounces (1 kg, 135 g) ripe
    white nectarines (see variation)
2 cups (480 ml) water
2 cups (480 ml) Simple Syrup
    (page 11), at room temperature,
    approximately
a few drops Tartaric Acid Solution
    (page 1115), or lemon juice

1. Wash, stone, and cut the nectarines into small pieces. Place in a saucepan with the water and half of the Simple Syrup. Bring to a boil and cook, stirring occasionally, until the fruit falls apart, about 10 minutes. Remove from the heat and force through a fine mesh strainer.

2. Let cool to room temperature. Add enough of the remaining Simple Syrup to bring the mixture to between 16 and 20° Baumé. Add the Tartaric Acid or lemon juice.

3. Process in an ice-cream freezer according to the manufacturer's directions. Transfer the finished sorbet to a chilled container, cover, and store in the freezer.

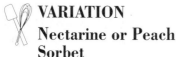 ## VARIATION
Nectarine or Peach Sorbet

*I*f you can not obtain white nectarines, you can easily substitute regular nectarines or peaches. The color of the sorbet will be golden rather than ivory (unless, of course, you use white peaches).

Bombes

A bombe is a type of frozen dessert made by lining a chilled mold, typically a half-sphere, with ice cream, sorbet, or sherbet. In some recipes you may use multiple layers of ice cream in different flavors and/or with contrasting colors. The mold is filled with a Bombe Mixture which is made from egg yolks, sugar, and cream in the style of a parfait. The Bombe Mixture is flavored according to the individual recipe, of which there are dozens upon dozens of classic variations. When fruit (other than candied fruit) is added to the Bombe Mixture it must first be macerated in liqueur and/or sugar syrup to prevent it from freezing too hard. Once filled, the mold is covered with a lid, which clamps in place, and the bombe is frozen. After it is unmolded, the bombe remains inverted to reveal the dome shape. The original bombe dessert was nearly round, and the name, which is of French origin—correctly translated *Bombe Glacé*—comes from the shape of cannonball-type bombs.

Bombes lend themselves to opulent decorations, so the pastry chef can really express his or her style and fantasy. If the bombe is presented to the guests before being sliced and served, the accompanying sauce should be served separately in a sauceboat. The most common size bombe mold has a capacity of approximately 5 cups (1 l, 200 ml) and serves six to ten people, making this a great time-saver for the chef, especially since the bombe can be prepared well in advance, then unmolded and decorated just before it is needed.

In creating the different variations, follow these basic steps in each bombe recipe:

NOTE: Bombes can also be unmolded, wrapped well, and stored in the freezer for several days should you need to reuse the molds, for example.

1. Lightly oil the inside of the molds and place in the freezer until thoroughly frozen.

2. Line the chilled molds with a ³/₄-inch (2-cm) layer of softened ice cream, using a spoon dipped in hot water. If the ice cream becomes too soft, refreeze until you can work with it again. Freeze the ice cream layer in the molds.

3. Pour the Bombe Mixture into the ice cream shell, cover, and freeze until hard, at least 4 hours.

4. To unmold the bombe, remove the clamped lid and place a thin (¹/₈-inch/3-mm) sheet of sponge cake (the same size as the base of the mold) on the surface of the filling to prevent the bombe from sliding on the serving platter. Dip the sides of the mold into hot water just long enough to loosen the frozen bombe. Place one hand flat on the base and your other hand on the round side. In one motion, push the base down and to one side and place the inverted bombe on a chilled silver tray or other serving platter. The bombe can be decorated at this point or returned to the freezer for a short period of time (see note). Once decorated, the bombe is traditionally presented to the guests before it is sliced. A bombe should not be held in the freezer after it is decorated.

Basic Bombe Mixture

enough for two 5-cup (1-l, 200-ml) bombes

8 ounces (225 g) granulated sugar
¹/₂ cup (120 ml) water
10 egg yolks (⁷/₈ cup/210 ml)
3 cups (720 ml) heavy cream

1. Dissolve two-thirds of the sugar in the water in a heavy saucepan and cook the mixture until it reaches 240°F (115°C) (see pages 936 and 937 for information on how to boil sugar).

2. While the syrup is cooking, whip the egg yolks with the remaining sugar until light and fluffy. With the mixer running at slow speed, gradually add the hot syrup to the egg yolks, pouring it in a thin steady stream between the whip and the side of the bowl, then whip at medium speed until cool.

3. Cover the mixture and place in the refrigerator until needed; it can be kept for up to one week at this point.

4. When you are ready to fill a bombe, whip the heavy cream to soft peaks, then carefully fold the yolk mixture and the desired flavoring into the cream. Pour the filling into the prepared bombe mold, cover, and place in the freezer.

Bombe Aboukir

two 5-cup (1-l, 200-ml) bombes

1 quart (960 ml) Pistachio Ice Cream (page 636)

one recipe Basic Bombe Mixture (page 655)

one-half recipe Hazelnut Paste (page 9)

or

1½ ounces (40 g) commercial hazelnut paste

1 ounce (30 g) pistachios, blanched, skins removed

two ⅛-inch (3-mm) rounds of Sponge Cake (page 268), the same diameter as the base of your molds

whipped cream

Chocolate Figurines (page 906)

hazelnuts, toasted, skins removed

fresh fruit

Chocolate Sauce (page 1072)

This dessert shares its name with Aboukir Bay, the delta in the northern part of Egypt where the Nile River empties into the Mediterranean. Although pistachios are indigenous to that region and are an important element in this recipe, history seems to suggest that Bombe Aboukir was named not for that muddy bay, but for the battle of Aboukir, which took place in 1798. The battle ended with the English navy, led by Admiral Nelson, defeating the French fleet, isolating Napoleon and his army in Egypt, and restoring British power in the Mediterranean. There is also a cake with the name Aboukir; it consists of sponge cake baked in a charlotte mold, layered with chestnut cream, and iced with coffee-flavored fondant.

1. Line the chilled bombe molds with Pistachio Ice Cream. Reserve in the freezer.

2. Add a little of the Bombe Mixture to the Hazelnut Paste to soften it, then mix this into the remaining mixture.

3. Chop the pistachio nuts and add to the filling. Pour the filling into the reserved shells. Freeze and unmold as described on page 655.

4. Decorate the bombes with whipped cream rosettes, Chocolate Figurines, hazelnuts, and fruit. Serve with Chocolate Sauce.

Bombe Bourdaloue

two 5-cup (1-l, 200-ml) bombes

5 cups (1 l, 200 ml) Vanilla Ice Cream (page 640)

one recipe Basic Bombe Mixture (page 655)

3 tablespoons (45 ml) anisette liqueur

two ⅛-inch (3-mm) rounds of Sponge Cake (page 268), the same diameter as the base of your molds

whipped cream

candied violets

Strawberry Sauce (page 1081)

This is another classical bombe creation. While very pretty, the components of Bombe Bourdaloue were chosen for their distinct and complimentary flavors rather than to create a visual showpiece, as is done in some of the other varieties. This bombe is named for a street in Paris, Rue Bourdaloue, where the shop of the pastry chef who invented the recipe, during the Belle Époque in France, was located.

1. Line the chilled bombe molds with the Vanilla Ice Cream. Reserve in the freezer.

2. Flavor the Bombe Mixture with anisette. Pour into the reserved shells. Freeze and unmold as described on page 655.

3. Decorate the bombes with whipped cream rosettes and candied violets. Serve with Strawberry Sauce.

Bombe Ceylon

*two 5-cup (1-l, 200-ml)
bombes*

5 cups (1 l, 200 ml) Sun-Brewed
Jasmine Tea Ice Cream (page 639)

one recipe Basic Bombe Mixture
(page 655)

¼ cup (60 ml) Cointreau liqueur

two ⅛-inch (3-mm) rounds of
Chocolate Sponge Cake (page 270),
the same diameter as the base of
your molds

¼ cup (60 ml) Cointreau liqueur

Mousseline Sauce (page 1076)

whipped cream

orange segments

Chocolate Figurines (page 1072)

*C*eylon *is a small island located in the Indian Ocean at the southern tip of India and is inhabited by some 18 million people. Despite its relatively small size, the island has a large climatic and geographic diversity. Half of the population relies on agriculture for its livelihood, with rice being the largest crop, but coconuts, rubber, and pineapple are also cultivated on the flatlands. A much wider variety of produce is grown in the mountain regions, including tea, oranges, and many vegetables. The island was given its independence from British rule in 1948 and changed its name to Sri Lanka (beautiful island) in 1972.*

1. Line the chilled bombe molds with the Jasmine Tea Ice Cream. Reserve in the freezer.

2. Flavor the Bombe Mixture with the first measurement of Cointreau. Pour into the reserved shells. Freeze and unmold as described on page 655. Add the remaining cointreau to the Mousseline Sauce.

3. Decorate the bombes with whipped cream, orange segments, and Chocolate Figurines. Serve with Mousseline Sauce.

Bombe Monarch

*two 5-cup (1-l, 200-ml)
bombes*

3½ cups (840 ml) Peach or
Strawberry Ice Cream
(pages 635 and 639)

one recipe Basic Bombe Mixture
(page 655)

3 tablespoons (45 ml) benedictine
liqueur

two thin rounds of Sponge Cake
(page 268), the same diameter as
the base of your molds

whipped cream

Chocolate Monarch Butterfly
Ornaments (page 910)

fresh fruit

Cherry Sauce (page 1071)

NOTE: If you are in a hurry, replace the Chocolate Butterfly Ornaments with Cookie Butterflies (see page 1052).

*B*utterflies *(and moths) develop through a four-stage complete metamorphosis; perhaps the ultimate story of an ugly duckling turning into a swan. The small egg laid by the female produces the caterpillar, which eats its way out of the shell. The caterpillar feeds and grows for about one month on the average, but sometimes for much longer. Eventually, after having periodically molted its old skin several times, the fully grown larva produces a mummy-like pupa. It is within this shelter that the last and most incredible transformation takes place: the creation of a beautiful, brightly colored butterfly, sometimes in as little as a few days.*

The monarch butterfly of North America is well known for its mass migration, which is similar to that of birds. These butterflies have only one food source, milkweed, which grows throughout North America. In the summer, the monarchs can be found all over California, the Great Basin, the Western plains, and in the east, in New England and into Canada. As temperatures cool in autumn, they migrate to specific groves of trees to spend the winter. One famous spot in California is Pacific Grove between Carmel and Monterey. During migration monarchs may travel up to 80 miles in one day.

Ornamental butterflies made from cookies, chocolate, and sugar make impressive and elegant decorations on pastries and desserts.

1. Line the chilled bombe molds with the Peach or Strawberry Ice Cream. Reserve in the freezer.

2. Flavor the Bombe Mixture with benedictine liqueur. Pour into the reserved shells. Freeze and unmold as described on page 655.

3. Decorate the bombes with whipped cream rosettes, Chocolate Monarch Butterflies, and fresh fruit. Serve with Cherry Sauce.

Coupes

These popular and practical individual ice cream servings can look very elegant if served in suitable dishes and decorated attractively. In the United States the all-American hot fudge sundae and banana split have been teenage favorites for years, and some people may think of this type of dessert—a combination of ice cream or sorbet decorated with liqueur, sauces, fruits, nuts, and/or whipped cream—as an American invention, but they are extremely popular in Europe. In ice cream parlors and every *konditorei,* or pastry shop, all over Europe, you will find a separate menu (usually illustrated) describing the coupes served. They are typically named for a particular country, or historical person or place, according to their composition. Many of these are based on recipes and formulas established many years ago by masters such as Carême and Escoffier. Some coupes are elaborately decorated with cookies and marzipan or chocolate figures, while others are plain and simple. Coupes must always be assembled and decorated to order. Following are some of the most popular of the hundreds of classic variations, along with a few of my own creations.

Coupe Bavaria

variable yield

Coffee-Scented Chocolate Ice Cream (page 629)

fresh sweet dark cherries, stemmed and pitted

maraschino liqueur

whipped cream

strawberry wedges

Chocolate Curls (page 887)

Strawberry Hearts (page 412)

Presentation: Place one or more scoops, depending on size, of Chocolate Ice Cream in a goblet, coupe glass, or dessert bowl. Top with cherries. Lightly sprinkle maraschino liqueur over the cherries and ice cream. Decorate with whipped cream rosettes, strawberry wedges, and two Chocolate Curls. Place the serving dish on a plate lined with a doily or napkin, and serve immediately with a Strawberry Heart on the plate.

Coupe Belle Hélène

variable yield

poached pear halves (see page 13)

Vanilla Ice Cream (page 640)

Hot Fudge Sauce (page 1074)

pistachio nuts, blanched, skins removed, and coarsely chopped

Pirouettes (page 222)

1. Fan one pear half per serving and reserve.

2. **Presentation:** Place one or more scoops, depending on size, of Vanilla Ice Cream in a goblet, coupe glass, or dessert bowl. Fan one of the reserved pear halves and place on top of the ice cream. Pour Hot Fudge Sauce over the bottom part of the pear. Sprinkle pistachio nuts on the sauce. Set the serving dish on a dessert plate lined with a doily or napkin, and serve immediately with a Pirouette on the plate.

Coupe Hawaii

variable yield

Fresh or Quick Coconut Ice Cream
    (pages 630 and 631)

whipped cream

fresh pineapple

palm trees made following the
    instructions in steps one through
    six in the recipe for Fruit and
    Coconut Tapioca Pudding Maui
    (page 550) (see note)

Chocolate-Filled Macadamia Morsels
    (page 408)

*NOTE: Use the palm tree template (Figure
13–3) or the template shown with the recipe for
the Tapioca Pudding. Because the trees are supported by the ice cream, it is not necessary to
bend the trunk back as described in step four of
the Tapioca Pudding recipe.*

Presentation: Place one or more scoops, depending on size, of Coconut Ice Cream in a goblet, coupe glass, or dessert bowl. Decorate the ice cream with whipped cream rosettes and fresh pineapple. Stand one of the palm trees in the center, pushing the tree down far enough into the ice cream so that it stands up straight. Place the serving dish on a plate lined with a doily or napkin, and serve immediately with a Macadamia Morsel on the plate.

Coupe Niçoise

variable yield

mixed fresh fruit salad
    (see note on page 469 for
    suggestions)

Honey Mandarin or Orange Sorbet
    (page 651)

curaçao liqueur

whipped cream

raspberries or strawberries

Orange Macaroons (page 220)

Presentation: Place a portion of fruit salad in the bottom of a goblet, coupe glass, or dessert bowl. Place one or more scoops, depending on size, of Honey Mandarin or Orange Sorbet on top. Sprinkle curaçao liqueur on the sorbet. Decorate with whipped cream rosettes and raspberries (or use strawberry wedges if raspberries are not available). Place the serving dish on a plate lined with a doily or napkin, and serve immediately with an Orange Macaroon on the plate.

Coupe Sweden

variable yield

Chunky Apple Filling (page 1085)

White Chocolate Ice Cream (see
    introduction to White Chocolate Ice
    Cream with Ginger, page 640)

Calvados

whipped cream

dark chocolate shavings

Florentina Halos (page 1009)

Presentation: Cover the bottom of a goblet, coupe glass, or dessert bowl with Chunky Apple Filling. Place one or more scoops, depending on size, of White Chocolate Ice Cream on top. Sprinkle Calvados on the ice cream. Decorate with whipped cream rosettes, chocolate shavings, and a Florentina Halo. Place the serving dish on a dessert plate lined with a doily or napkin, and serve immediately with the cutout from the Florentina Halo on the plate.

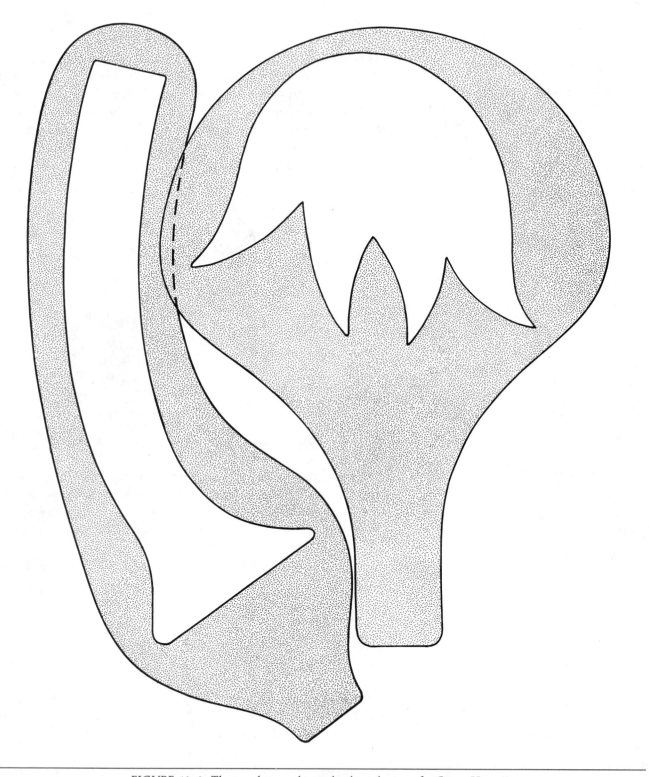

FIGURE 13–3 The template used to make the palm trees for Coupe Hawaii

Frozen Desserts

The title for this section may seem a bit redundant, given the fact that everything in this chapter is, in fact, a frozen dessert. What differentiates the following is that each of these recipes includes a specific plate presentation. These selections include classical parfaits, frozen soufflés (soufflé glacé) and frozen mousses. Some of these desserts are not actually frozen, per se, but include ice cream or frozen ice as an accompaniment. All of the recipes in this section have one other thing in common: They must be served immediately once they are plated. Unfortunately this is not always practical, especially when serving a large number at once, but on the positive side, in most cases all of the prep work can be done far in advance.

Many of the frozen desserts that were created years ago are now classics, such as Cherries Jubilee, Pears Belle Hélène, Baked Alaska, and Peach Melba, but there is still plenty of room for your particular taste and imagination.

Parfaits

Parfaits have a different meaning in Europe than in America. In the "New World" we use the word *parfait* to describe a dessert of alternating layers of ice cream, fruit, and liqueur in a tall glass topped with whipped cream. This actually constitutes a coupe by classical definition. The American parfait version most likely got its name because the tall serving glasses are similar in shape to the original parfait molds. Parfaits are a delicate frozen dessert, usually lighter and less sweet than ice cream, made from a mixture of egg yolks and sugar syrup whipped to the ribbon stage, with the addition of whipped cream and flavoring. To achieve the distinctive, light texture it is important to combine the ingredients very carefully, preserving the air that has been whipped in. The parfait mixture is then poured into tall slender molds and still frozen (without churning). Parfaits are unmolded before they are served.

A parfait mixture, which is essentially the same thing as a bombe mixture, can also be used together with ice cream to create elegant ice bombes, or it can be used as, or as part of, a filling in frozen cakes.

Soufflé Glacé

Soufflé glacé, or frozen soufflés, are a type of smooth and light-textured dessert in which Italian meringue is added to a parfait or bombe mixture to give the dish a hint of the lightness found in a hot soufflé. The base is flavored with liquor, liqueur, or a fruit mixture, in the same way as a parfait. The filling is then piled high above the rim of a soufflé mold (typically an individual mold for a single serving), which has been lined with a collar to support the filling. The desserts are still frozen and are served in the form.

Frozen Mousses

Frozen mousses are yet another variety of frozen dessert and are closely related to both parfaits and soufflé glacé. Although each of these three desserts is classically made using a different formula, in actual practice the base is very well interchangeable from one to the other. All of them achieve lightness and volume from the air that is whipped into either cream, eggs, or meringue. All are still frozen, and because the freezing process serves to solidify and stabilize the content, they require little or no stabilizers such as gelatin or pectin. What distinguishes a frozen mousse from a parfait is the inclusion of whipped egg whites, which are never used in a true classical parfait mixture.

Benedictine Soufflé Glacé

12 servings

4 cups (960 ml) heavy cream
1/4 cup (60 ml) benedictine liqueur
2 teaspoons (10 ml) vanilla extract
8 egg yolks (2/3 cup/160 ml)
2 teaspoons (6 g) unflavored gelatin powder
2 teaspoons (6 g) pectin powder
1/3 cup (80 ml) cold water
one-half recipe Italian Meringue (page 591)
unsweetened cocoa powder
twelve Pirouettes (page 222)

NOTE: You can make any type of liqueur soufflé glacé by substituting other flavors of liqueur for the benedictine. Depending on the strength of the liqueur you choose, you may wish to increase or decrease the amount. Keep in mind, however, that too much alcohol (like too much sugar) will prevent the filling from freezing properly.

Ice soufflés, the English translation of soufflé glacé, are much less capricious than their better-known "big brother," the hot soufflé, which has a somewhat undeserved reputation for being unpredictable or overly difficult. The mousse-like filling in a soufflé glacé should extend about 2 inches (5 cm) above the rim of the ramekin to resemble a hot soufflé rising from its baking dish. This is achieved by using a collar for support while the dessert freezes. Soufflé glacé are guaranteed not to fall if served within 5 minutes after removing from the freezer. As is true of many frozen desserts, soufflé glacé is an excellent choice when there is no time for numerous last-minute steps. Although the soufflés are very light, and this portion size is sure to be finished, using the standard 3¹/₂-inch (8.7-cm) soufflé ramekins as directed yields a fairly generous serving, especially if you wrap the collars around the outside of the forms. Using smaller forms, 2¹/₂ to 3 inches (6.2 to 7.5 cm) in diameter with a 3¹/₂-ounce (105-ml) capacity will not only make the soufflés higher and more attractive, it will produce sixteen servings instead of twelve.

If you are only serving a few desserts at a time à la minute, you may omit the gelatin, pectin, and water if you wish (steps four and six).

1. Prepare twelve 3¹/₂-inch (8.7-cm) soufflé ramekins (instructions follow). Reserve in the freezer.

2. Whip the heavy cream to soft peaks. Refrigerate.

3. Add the liqueur and vanilla to the egg yolks. Place over simmering water and heat, whisking constantly, until the mixture has thickened to the consistency of a sabayon. Remove from the heat and whip until cold.

4. Sprinkle the gelatin and pectin powders over the cold water to soften.

5. Combine the whipped cream and the egg yolk mixture. Gradually stir this into the Italian Meringue.

6. Place the gelatin mixture over simmering water and heat to dissolve. Do not overheat. Quickly stir the gelatin into a small portion of the filling. Then, still working fast, stir this into the remaining filling.

7. Promptly place the filling in a pastry bag with a no. 7 (14-mm) plain tip and pipe into the prepared molds. It should extend about 2

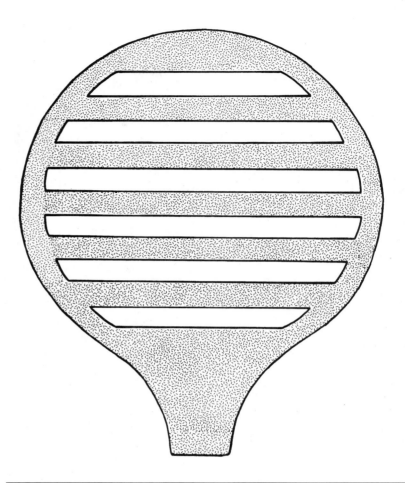

FIGURE 13–4 *The template used in the presentation of Benedictine Soufflé Glacé*

inches (5 cm) above the rim of the molds for an authentic soufflé look. Place the soufflés in the freezer for at least 4 hours or, preferably, overnight.

8. Trace the drawing in Figure 13–4, then cut the template out of thin cardboard. Cake boxes 1/16 inch (2 mm) thick work fine.

9. Presentation: Remove the collar from a soufflé. Place the template on top and sift cocoa powder lightly over the template, taking great care not to get any on the rim of the form. Remove the template carefully without disturbing the pattern. Place the soufflé glacé on a plate lined with a doily or napkin, and serve immediately with a Pirouette on the plate.

VARIATION
Ginger Soufflé Glacé

*F*ollow the recipe and directions with the following changes:

• Replace the benedictine with an equal amount of muscat or other sweet wine.

• Julienne 1½ ounces (40 g) of Crystallized Ginger (page 6). Set aside the twenty-four best-looking pieces to use for decoration and finely chop the remainder. Add the chopped ginger to the wine (be sure the small pieces are not stuck together) as you add it to the filling.

• Place two pieces of julienned Crystallized Ginger on top of the soufflé when serving.

To prepare the ramekins

1. Cut twelve polyurethane or acetate strips 1¹/₂ inches (3.7 cm) wide and slightly longer than the inside circumference of the ramekins measured under the recessed lip; this will be approximately 10 inches (25 cm) for 3¹/₂-inch (8.7-cm) ramekins. Make a collar of each strip by taping the ends together, adjusting so it will fit snugly around the inside lip of the ramekin. Brush soft butter in a fairly thick layer on the inside edge of a ramekin.

2. Place the collar in the butter to make it adhere and adjust to make the top level. Repeat with the remaining ramekins.

You can alternatively use strips that are approximately 3 inches (7.5 cm) wide. Adjust them to fit tight against the inside and simply stand them on the bottom of the mold. This eliminates the need to butter the sides and level the tops but makes the strips a bit more difficult to remove later on.

Gluing the collars to the recessed rim of the ramekins will give you the most authentic soufflé "rising from the mold" look. This is only practical, however, if time is no object. A much more commonly used technique is to use a rubber band to fasten the collar around the outside of the molds so that they extend 2 inches (5 cm) above the rim. This will yield only eight servings, since the soufflés will be slightly wider on top.

 Caramel Ice Cream in a Caramel Cage

16 servings

one 10-inch (25-cm) layer light
    sponge cake (any variety),
    approximately ¹/₈ inch (3 mm) thick
one recipe Chocolate Sauce
    (page 1072)
one recipe Chantilly Cream
    (page 1083)
one recipe Caramel Ice Cream
    (page 628)
chocolate shavings
sixteen Caramel Cages (page 957)
Sour Cream Mixture for Piping
    (page 1081)

If you do not have time to prepare Caramel Cages, you can certainly enjoy the Caramel Ice Cream without them. Top the ice cream with the Chocolate Sauce (or Hot Fudge Sauce, page 1074) and Chantilly Cream, sprinkle with chopped nuts, and serve the dessert with a cookie, and you have just created a delightful coupe or sundae. In the following presentation, the elegant Caramel Cage, resting on top of whipped cream and encircled by a band of decorated Chocolate Sauce, is all it takes to transform these same delicious flavors into a spectacular dessert for a more formal occasion. Keep in mind when you make the cages that the sugar lines should be very thin, not just for the sake of appearance, but more importantly so that your guests can actually consume them without risk of cutting their gums on thick, sharp caramel. For this recipe the Caramel Cages should be made 4 inches in diameter and 2 inches high (10 × 5 cm).

1. Use a 2-inch (5-cm) plain, round cookie cutter to cut sixteen rounds from the sponge layer. Cover and reserve.

2. Place a portion of the Chocolate Sauce in a piping bottle.

3. Place the Chantilly Cream in a pastry bag with a no. 6 (12-mm) plain tip. Reserve in the refrigerator.

4. Presentation: Using a no. 10 (4-ounce/120-ml) scoop, place a scoop of Caramel Ice Cream on top of one of the sponge rounds. Place the sponge and ice cream in the center of a dessert plate. Pipe small, tall mounds of Chantilly Cream on the plate, forming a ring around the base of the ice cream scoop. The whipped cream ring should be the same size as the bottom of the Caramel Cages. Place chocolate shavings on top of the ice cream. Set a Caramel Cage over the ice cream, resting it on top of the whipped cream mounds. Pipe just enough Chocolate Sauce on the plate around the dessert to cover the base of the plate. Decorate the sauce with the Sour Cream Mixture (see pages 998 to 1006). Serve immediately.

Cherries Jubilee

8 servings

1 pound, 6 ounces (625 g) pitted fresh cherries (preferably Bing or Rainier)

or

1 pound, 8 ounces (680 g) canned cherries

1½ cups (360 ml) Plain Poaching Syrup (page 13)

or

¾ cup (180 ml) liquid from canned cherries

1 cup (240 ml) kirschwasser

2½ cups (600 ml) White Chocolate Ice Cream (see introduction to White Chocolate Ice Cream with Ginger, page 640)

1 tablespoon (8 g) cornstarch

There was a time when Cherries Jubilee was considered "the" dessert to end an elegant dinner. There is not too much you can do to change or improve this classic flambéed dessert, except possibly when it comes to the flamboyance of the presentation. Although it is traditional to serve vanilla ice cream with Cherries Jubilee in America, I suggest White Chocolate Ice Cream instead because its rich texture is a perfect complement to the cherries. It is always a good idea to keep macerated cherries on hand in the refrigerator should you want to pamper an unexpected guest or friend. This dessert is very simple to prepare and people always seem to enjoy the theatrics of any flambéed dish.

1. Poach fresh cherries as directed for Cherry Sauce (page 1071). Reserve ¾ cup (180 ml) of the poaching liquid (or the same measurement of liquid from canned cherries if using). Discard the remainder or save for another use. Add the cherries and ¾ cup (180 ml) of the kirschwasser to the Poaching Syrup or juice. Macerate the cherries in the liquid for at least 1 hour.

2. Scoop ice cream into individual servings, place on a serving platter, and reserve in the freezer.

3. Fifteen minutes before serving, dissolve the cornstarch in a small portion of the macerating liquid, then stir back into the remaining liquid and cherries. Transfer to a chafing dish or copper sauté pan. Bring to a boil over medium heat, stirring constantly. Reduce the heat and let simmer for about 1 minute to eliminate the cornstarch flavor.

4. Presentation: Transfer the chafing dish or sauté pan filled with the cherries to the stand of the *guéridon* in the dining room. Put the prepared ice cream and appropriate serving dishes or dessert plates nearby. Continue simmering the cherries, stirring from time to time, for a few minutes. Spoon the ice cream onto the serving dishes. Pour the remaining ¼ cup (60 ml) kirschwasser over the cherries in the pan, turn up the flame, and let the liqueur heat up a few seconds. Do not stir the liqueur into the sauce. Tilt the pan to ignite the liqueur (this looks a little more "showy" than using a match or lighter) and spoon the flaming cherries over the ice cream. Serve immediately.

Feijoa Sorbet with Kiwi, Pineapple, and Strawberry Sauces

12 servings

three limes
one-half recipe Kiwi Sauce
(page 1074)
one-half recipe Pineapple Sauce
(page 1078)
one-half recipe Strawberry Sauce
(page 1081)
twelve Chocolate Tulips, (see note 1,
page 1046)
one recipe Feijoa Sorbet (page 650)
powdered sugar

It has been a long time since a dessert has been so enthusiastically received by my students as was the Feijoa Sorbet. We experimented with several batches in order to achieve the correct balance between the lime and pineapple juices, and the word quickly spread around the campus that something brand new and rather unusual was being created. I introduced this recipe in mid-January when the domestic feijoa crop is available and relatively inexpensive. The imported fruit, from Chile and down under, can be enjoyed later in the year, but the price is a bit higher.

Feijoas, or pineapple guavas as they are commonly known, have a very distinctive flavor—roundly complex and unquestionably tropical. Just picking up the fruit and smelling its perfume-like fragrance tells you this is something out of the ordinary. The petals of the feijoa flower measure up to 1½ inches (3.7 cm) across. They are pinkish white on the outside and deep pink within. These somewhat fleshy petals have an incredibly sweet tropical flavor all their own. They can be used as a garnish or can be added to the sorbet. To use the petals in the sorbet, heat the pineapple juice to scalding in a noncorrosive saucepan. Stir in ¼ cup (60 ml) of flower petals and set aside to cool to room temperature. Combine with the remaining ingredients in step three of the sorbet recipe.

Feijoa Sorbet can be stored in the freezer for several weeks if properly covered; however, based on my experience it is unlikely that you will have to be concerned about long-term storage!

1. Use a zester to remove the zest from the limes in long curling threads. Place the zest in water until needed to prevent it from drying out. (Use the limes to make the sorbet.)

2. Place each of the three sauces in a separate piping bottle.

3. Presentation: Pipe the sauces on the base of a dessert plate in three evenly sized, wedge-shaped sections. Use two kitchen spoons to portion a large football-shaped scoop of sorbet into a Chocolate Tulip. Carefully place the Tulip in the center of the sauce. Sprinkle lime zest over the sorbet. Sift powdered sugar over the entire plate.

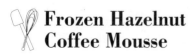

Frozen Hazelnut Coffee Mousse

(Palais Schwarzenberg)

16 servings

Hazelnut Coffee Mousse Filling
(recipe follows)
¾ cup (180 ml) heavy cream
1 teaspoon (5 g) granulated sugar
Piping Chocolate (page 904)
thirty-two medium-sized strawberries

Austria's capital, Vienna, is deeply imbedded in the history of baking and pastry making. Some of the many famous creations said to have originated or been inspired by this noble town are croissants, pretzels, Gugelhupf, and the Sacher Torte. But Vienna is also well known for its numerous special blends of coffee, the leading one being "viennese roast." While the city is full of konditoreis displaying tempting pastries to accompany a cup of coffee, there are also smaller shops, all over town and throughout Austria for that matter, which sell nothing but coffee in any imaginable combination of roast, flavor, and strength. There are generally no chairs, instead everyone stands up around a long counter sipping and savoring that perfect cup of fresh coffee.

Frozen Hazelnut Coffee Mousse is an adopted version of a dessert I had many years ago at the Palais Schwarzenberg restaurant in Vienna. Although

sixteen Black Tie Strawberries
   (procedure follows)
mint springs (as needed; see note)

NOTE: If the leaves and hulls on the Black Tie Strawberries look fresh and appealing, leave them on. Otherwise, remove the tops and use mint sprigs in their place.

the combination of coffee and hazelnuts is nothing really new or unusual, I think you will find they come together particularly well in this dessert. With a good cup of coffee the meal will certainly end on a happy note.

1. Divide the Hazelnut Coffee Mousse Filling equally between sixteen 3¹/₂-inch (8.7-cm) diameter, 5-ounce (150-ml) capacity ramekins. Alternatively, you can use any round molds that are close to the same size and capacity such as, appropriately enough, coffee cups with straight sides, or for a special occasion such as Valentine's Day, individual coeur à la crème molds as shown in the color insert. Smooth the tops to make them level and then place the molds in the freezer for at least 4 hours or, preferably, overnight.

2. Unmold as many mousses as you plan to serve by dipping each mold into hot water for about 10 seconds or just long enough to loosen the filling. Insert a small fork into the mousse, invert, and twist the fork to unmold the mousse onto a sheet pan lined with baking paper. Return the mousses to the freezer.

3. Whip the heavy cream and sugar to stiff peaks. Place in a pastry bag with a no. 8 (16-mm) star tip. Reserve in the refrigerator.

4. Pipe a zigzag design, using Piping Chocolate, on the upper half of the base of as many dessert plates as you are planning to use. Set the plates aside.

5. Wash and hull two strawberries per serving. Cut the strawberries into thin slices lengthwise, keeping the slices from each berry together. Reserve in the refrigerator.

6. Presentation: Pipe a small dot of whipped cream in the center of the decorated portion of one of the prepared dessert plates. Place a frozen mousse on the cream to prevent the mousse from sliding on the plate. Pipe a rosette of cream on top of the mousse. Arrange a half circle of strawberry slices on the lower portion of the plate, with the tips of the strawberries pointing away from the dessert (do not use the smaller end pieces of strawberry). Place a Black Tie Strawberry on the whipped cream rosette. Place a mint sprig standing up behind the strawberry if needed to replace the strawberry hull and leaves.

Hazelnut Coffee Mousse Filling

3 ounces (85 g) lightly toasted
   hazelnuts
2 ounces (55 g) granulated sugar
3 cups (720 ml) heavy cream
1 teaspoon (3 g) unflavored gelatin
   powder
2 teaspoons (6 g) pectin powder
¹/₄ cup (60 ml) cold water
¹/₄ cup (60 ml) coffee liqueur
7 eggs, separated
8 ounces (225 g) granulated sugar

1. Remove as much skin as possible from the toasted hazelnuts by rubbing them between your palms. Grind the nuts with the first measurement of sugar in a food processor to a very fine consistency. Reserve.

2. Whip the heavy cream to soft peaks. Reserve in the refrigerator.

3. Sprinkle the gelatin and pectin powders over the cold water to soften.

4. Add the coffee liqueur to the egg yolks. Heat, whipping constantly, over simmering water until the mixture reaches 140°F (60°C). Remove from the heat and whip to a light and fluffy consistency.

5. Add the remaining sugar to the egg whites. Heat over simmering water, stirring constantly, until the mixture reaches 140°F (60°C). Remove from the heat and continue whipping until stiff peaks form and the meringue is cold. Fold the yolk mixture into the reserved whipped cream together with the ground hazelnuts. Mix this into the meringue.

6. Heat the gelatin and pectin mixture over a bain-marie until dissolved. Do not overheat. Quickly stir the gelatin mixture into a small portion of the filling to temper. Still working rapidly, add this to the remaining filling.

Black Tie Strawberries

variable yield

fresh, well-shaped, medium- or large-sized strawberries
white coating chocolate, melted
dark coating chocolate, melted

NOTE: If the hulls of the strawberries look wilted, they should be removed after the strawberries are decorated and the chocolate has hardened (not before since you need them to hold onto to dip the berries). Use the tip of a paring knife or a melon-ball cutter to remove the hulls and then fill in the empty hole with a little melted white chocolate, using your fingertip.

These cute dressed-up berries should not be restricted to plated dessert decorations. They make a great addition to a buffet or a cookie or pastry tray, and they can be made one day ahead if kept well covered in the refrigerator. Try to use large berries or, even better, use long-stemmed strawberries to make them even more elegant. To make the Black Tie Strawberries easier to handle, and more pastrylike, place them on top of a small chocolate-dipped cookie made from Short Dough. Roll out Short Dough to ⅛ inch (3 mm) thick. Cut out cookies 1½ inches (3.7 cm) in diameter, using a plain or fluted cutter. Bake, let cool, and then, using a dipping fork, dip the cookies into melted dark coating chocolate, covering them completely. Place a Black Tie Strawberry on top of each cookie before the chocolate on the cookie has set up.

When making the Black Tie Strawberries, be sure that there is enough melted white chocolate in the bowl so that the berries can be dipped straight down without touching the bottom. It is also a good idea not to dip the berries straight from the refrigerator but to allow them to come to room temperature first.

1. Wash and thoroughly dry the strawberries.

2. Hold onto the hull and dip one berry at a time into melted white chocolate, being careful not to get any chocolate on the hull. Move the berry up and down over the bowl of chocolate a few times to allow excess chocolate to drip off, and then scrape the bottom against the side of the bowl to remove more chocolate. Set the strawberry on a sheet pan lined with baking paper. Repeat with the remaining berries. If the chocolate spreads out around the berry on the pan forming a "foot," drag the berry to a clean spot on the baking paper before the chocolate hardens.

3. To put the tuxedo jackets on the strawberries, pick up a white chocolate coated berry by the hull and dip the lower two-thirds into melted dark chocolate, first at a 45° angle to the left side, and then at the same angle to the right (see the photograph of Frozen Hazelnut Coffee Mousse in the color insert). Return to the sheet pan lined with baking paper, setting it on a clean section of the pan. Repeat with the remaining berries, moving them on the paper as you did before if they begin to form feet.

4. Place a small amount of melted dark chocolate in a piping bag and cut a very small opening. Pipe three small buttons and a bow tie on the white "shirt" portion of each strawberry.

Lingonberry Parfait

16 servings

one-half recipe Baked Chocolate
   Sheet batter (page 570)
   (see step one)
1 ounce (30 g) bread flour, sifted
Parfait Filling (recipe follows)
³/₄ cup (180 ml) heavy cream
1 teaspoon (5 g) granulated sugar
one recipe Cranberry Coulis
   (page 1073)
Sour Cream Mixture for Piping
   (page 1081)
sixteen Chocolate Figurines
   (page 906)

*L*ingonberry Parfait is a simple and spectacular choice to cool and refresh your guests on a hot day. The pretty, pale pink, slightly tart parfait is a perfect companion to the sweeter, vibrant red Cranberry Coulis. The recipe assumes you are using lingonberries from a can or jar, which have sugar added. Depending on the sweetness of a particular brand you may need to adjust the amount of sugar in the recipe. Not only should the flavor of the parfait be on the tart side, but in addition, too much sugar will inhibit freezing. In the event that you are lucky enough to find fresh or frozen berries to work with, you must first cook them to a jamlike consistency, adding sugar to taste (reserve a few fresh berries to use for decorating). Cranberries, fresh, frozen, or canned, may be substituted for the lingonberries with excellent results, although the parfait will not have quite the same exotic taste or appeal as when using the "red gold" of the Scandinavian forest. This dessert provides an excellent opportunity to use up small leftover pieces of Ribbon Sponge, should you have them on hand, by substituting these for the Baked Chocolate Sheet. Although the ribbon stripes will be underneath the dessert, they can contrast elegantly if the parfait is placed strategically on the plate. The sponge circles may also be left out completely, in which case you may have to freeze the batter to thicken it slightly before filling the rings (so it does not leak out) and also pipe a dot of whipped cream in the center of the dessert plates before putting the parfaits on top.

1. Add the 1 ounce (30 g) bread flour to the Chocolate Sheet batter when you fold in the egg whites. Spread the batter into a square slightly larger than 12 inches (30 cm) on a sheet of baking paper. Bake as directed in the recipe. Set aside to cool.

2. Place sixteen cake rings 3 inches in diameter by 1³/₄ to 2 inches tall (7.5 cm × 4.5–5 cm) on a sheet pan lined with baking paper. Line the rings with strips of baking paper. If you do not have cake rings this size, or slightly smaller, you can make them easily from polyurethane or acetate. Cut sixteen strips 9¹/₂ inches long by 1¹/₂ inches wide (23.7 × 3.7 cm). Bend the strips around the outside of a plain 3-inch (7.5-cm) cookie cutter to form them, tape the ends together, and remove from the cutter (these do not need to be lined with baking paper).

3. Remove the baking paper from the Chocolate Sheet. Use a 3-inch (7.5-cm) plain cookie cutter to cut out sixteen rounds. If you are using cake rings of a different size, adjust the size of the rounds accordingly. Place the rounds inside the rings. Divide the Parfait Filling equally between the rings. Cover and place in the freezer for at least 4 hours or, preferably, overnight.

4. Whip the heavy cream and sugar to stiff peaks. Place in a pastry bag with a no. 8 (16-mm) star tip. Reserve in the refrigerator.

5. Remove the rings and peel the paper from the side of as many parfaits as you plan to serve (parfaits left in the rings can be stored in the freezer for up to two weeks if kept well covered). Return the parfaits to the freezer. Place a portion of the Cranberry Coulis in a piping bottle (if necessary, first adjust the consistency of the coulis so that it will just level out when piped).

6. Presentation: Pipe just enough Cranberry Coulis over the base of a dessert plate to cover. Using a piping bag, pipe two concentric circles of Sour Cream Mixture, about ¹/₂ inch (1.2 cm) apart, close to the perimeter of the coulis. Drag a wooden skewer through the lines toward the outside of the plate, every 1 inch (2.5 cm) or so all around the sauce. Place a parfait in the center of the plate. Pipe a rosette of whipped cream on top. Decorate the cream with a Chocolate Figurine and serve at once.

1. Purée the lingonberries. (Do not over-purée or you will add too much air and the mixture will lose color.) Add the lime juice and set aside.

2. Whip the heavy cream to soft peaks and reserve in the refrigerator.

3. Whip the eggs, egg yolks, and sugar over simmering water until the mixture reaches 140°F (60°C). Remove from the heat and continue whipping until completely cooled. The mixture should be light and fluffy. Gently fold the reserved whipped cream into the egg mixture, being careful not to deflate the mixture. Fold in the lingonberry purée.

Parfait Filling

approximately 9 cups (2 l, 160 ml)

14 ounces (400 g) lingonberries
¹/₃ cup (80 ml) lime juice (two limes)
3 cups (720 ml) heavy cream
5 eggs
6 egg yolks (¹/₂ cup/120 ml)
4 ounces (115 g) granulated sugar

Macadamia Nut Ice Cream in a Chocolate Tulip with Mango Coulis

16 servings

two kiwifruit
one papaya
one recipe Mango Coulis (page 1075)
¹/₂ cup (120 ml) Chocolate Sauce (page 1072)
one recipe Macadamia Nut Ice Cream (page 632)
sixteen Chocolate Tulips (see note 1, page 1046)
2 ounces (55 g) unsalted macadamia nuts, toasted and crushed
powdered sugar

Macadamias, the king of all nuts, are indigenous to Australia and were named for a chemist from that country, John Macadam. The nuts were brought to Hawaii at the end of the seventeenth century and planted at Kukui-haele on the big island. It was not long before the macadamia industry was in full bloom. Today it is the island's third most important agricultural commodity, exceeded only by sugar and pineapple. Pairing the ice cream with vibrant Mango Coulis and the starkly contrasting Chocolate Tulip makes for a beautiful tropical presentation. Papayas, another of Hawaii's tropical treasures, were part of the island long before macadamia nuts were introduced. The Hawaiian chocolate industry, however, is just getting started, currently marketing a good quality chocolate made from cocoa beans grown at plantations in Kona and Keaau on the big island of Hawaii.

1. Remove the skin from the kiwis (see Figures 6–2, 6–3, and 6–4, on page 251). Cut in half lengthwise and then slice thinly. Remove the skin from the papaya, cut in half, and scrape out the seeds. Cut the flesh into sixteen pieces. Cover the fruit and reserve.

2. Place a portion of the Mango Coulis in a piping bottle.

3. Presentation: Pipe a large round pool of Mango Coulis in the center of a dessert plate. Decorate the perimeter of the sauce with the Chocolate Sauce, using a piping bag (see pages 998 to 1006). Use two kitchen spoons to portion a large oval (quenelle-shaped) scoop of ice cream into a Chocolate Tulip. Set the Tulip in the center of the coulis. Garnish the ice cream with the prepared fruit and a sprinkling of macadamia nuts. Sift powdered sugar lightly over the top and serve immediately.

Mango Ice Cream with Chiffonade of Lemon-Mint and a Chocolate Twirl

16 servings

one-half recipe Cherry Sauce (page 1071)

powdered sugar

sixteen Magnolia Cookie Shells (see note 1)

one recipe Mango Ice Cream (page 632)

lemon-mint cut in chiffonade

sixteen Chocolate Twirls (page 916) (see note 2)

NOTE 1: To make the Magnolia Shells, follow the instructions in steps one through five on pages 715 to 718 in the recipe for Red Currant Sorbet in Magnolia Cookie Shells, making only the smaller size shell, using template 14–9B. You will only need one-half recipe of Vanilla Tulip Paste. Before spreading the paste within the template, remove 2 tablespoons (30 ml) of paste and color it with 1 teaspoon (2.5 g) of sifted cocoa powder, mixing the cocoa powder in thoroughly. Before baking the cookie shells, pipe a vertical line of cocoa-colored paste on each flower petal.

NOTE 2: To stabilize the Chocolate Twirls for this presentation (and keep them from bending on top of the round ice cream scoop), pipe a thin line of melted coating chocolate, the same length of a finished Twirl, on a sheet of baking paper. Set a Twirl on top before the chocolate line hardens and hold in place a few seconds until set. The chocolate will set up faster if you chill the Twirls briefly first.

*T*he spectacular Chocolate Twirls featured in the presentation can be utilized to decorate many desserts. They are especially appropriate with chocolate offerings, and I use them frequently to top a slice of Chocolate Decadence or Chocolate Ganache Cake (leaving out the Cookie Butterfly on the latter). Although the Twirls are a bit time-consuming to prepare, they can be made up many days in advance (as can the Tulips and the Mango Ice Cream) if stored in their protective glasses or in plastic tubes in a cool, dry place. When preparing the Twirls it is inevitable that some will break. The broken pieces can be used as you would Chocolate Noodles (see page 917), either to decorate another dessert or placed on top of the Mango Ice Cream here for a different and almost as impressive finish.

1. Place the Cherry Sauce in a piping bottle and reserve in the refrigerator.

2. Presentation: Sift powdered sugar lightly over the base of a dessert plate. Place a Magnolia Cookie Shell in the center of the plate and fill with a large scoop of Mango Ice Cream. Pipe quarter-coin sized dots of Cherry Sauce on the base of the plate, evenly spaced around the dessert. Sprinkle mint over the sauce dots. Carefully set a Chocolate Twirl on top of the ice cream by inserting the handle of a wooden spoon inside the Twirl and using this to lift and position it. Serve immediately.

Oven-Braised Black Mission Figs with Honey-Vanilla Frozen Yogurt

12 servings

thirty-six medium-sized fresh Black
   Mission figs
1/2 cup (120 ml) water
8 ounces (225 g) granulated sugar
8 ounces (225 g) toasted pine nuts
2 tablespoons (30 ml) honey
1/3 cup (80 ml) Armagnac
3 ounces (85 g) unsalted butter
thirty-six Sponge Cake rounds
   (see note)
one-half recipe Honey-Vanilla Frozen
   Yogurt (page 645)
edible fresh flower petals

NOTE: Use any type of light sponge cake you have on hand. Slice it thinly, then cut out thirty-six rounds, using a 1/2-to-3/4-inch (1.2-to-2-cm) plain cookie cutter. Cover until needed.

*T*he fig tree, like the grape vine, was held in high regard by the ancient Greeks and Romans. The Greeks, believing the tree was a gift to Athens from Ceres (the goddess of grain and agriculture), planted a grove of fig trees in the public square. The Romans also honored the fig, recalling that their founding princes, Romulus and Remus, were born under its sheltering branches. They offered a sacrifice each year in the fig grove planted in the forum. Since these ancient beginnings figs have been one of the predominant fruits along the Mediterranean seaboard.

Although there are a tremendous number of fig varieties (especially in the aforementioned region), the most popular and versatile is the Black Mission fig, brought to California by the Spaniards who came there to establish missions (hence the name). Since the fig season is rather short (approximately June to September), and fresh figs are not good keepers, you may want to consider trying canned figs, which work fairly well in this recipe. The greenish-yellow skinned Kadota fig is readily available as such, typically packed in heavy syrup. When using canned figs, reduce the braising time by half and omit both the water and granulated sugar, replacing them with 2 cups (480 ml) of the syrup from the can, poured over the figs while braising.

1. Place the whole figs, standing on end, in a buttered ovenproof dish just large enough to hold them in one layer.

2. Heat the water and sugar in a saucepan until the mixture is simmering and the sugar has dissolved. Pour the syrup over the figs. Bake at 375°F (190°C) for 15 minutes, basting the figs with the cooking liquid from time to time. Add the pine nuts and continue cooking for approximately 10 minutes longer, or until the figs are soft.

3. Transfer the figs to another dish (leaving the pinenuts in the liquid) and let them cool at room temperature.

4. Pour the cooking liquid and the nuts into a skillet and boil until the mixture is syrupy. Add the honey and Armagnac and cook the sauce, stirring constantly, until the ingredients are completely incorporated. Swirl in the butter. Let the sauce cool to room temperature.

5. Presentation: Place three figs close together, in the center of a dessert plate. Spoon a portion of the sauce over the figs and also in three uneven pools, evenly spaced on the base of the plate, around the figs; make sure you include some of the pine nuts in the sauce. Place a sponge round between each of the sauce pools. Top each sponge with a small oval scoop of yogurt (use an oval ice-cream scoop or make "quenelles" using two soup spoons). Decorate with edible flowers and serve immediately.

Passion Fruit Ice Cream Parfait

2 quarts (1 l, 920 ml)

10 eggs, separated
¹⁄₃ cup (80 ml) or 4 ounces (115 g) light corn syrup
4 ounces (115 g) granulated sugar
2 cups (480 ml) heavy cream
1 cup (240 ml) passion fruit pulp (about twelve passion fruit)
¹⁄₄ cup (60 ml) curaçao liqueur

NOTE: As this is a mix between an ice cream and a parfait, it is not necessary to churn the base as it is freezing.

Passion fruit pulp gives this fluffy ice cream parfait a refreshing pungent taste and enticing aroma that are indisputably tropical. Fortunately neither the scent nor the flavor dissipates through storage or freezing. The small black seeds of the passion fruit are fully edible, although the crunchiness may not be pleasing to some. I prefer to leave them in to add texture and character. An easy way to remove the seeds, if desired, is to warm the pulp (do not boil) until the seeds loosen. Pass through a strainer and discard the seeds.

1. Beat the egg yolks until they are light and fluffy, about 5 minutes. Bring the corn syrup to a boil. Add the corn syrup to the egg yolks while whipping at medium speed. Increase to maximum speed, and whip until the mixture has cooled completely. Reserve.

2. Combine the egg whites and granulated sugar in a mixing bowl. Set the bowl over simmering water and heat, whipping constantly, to 140°F (60°C). Remove from the heat and whip until the mixture has cooled and formed stiff peaks. Reserve.

3. Whip the heavy cream until soft peaks form. Fold the cream into the yolk mixture together with the passion fruit pulp and the liqueur. Gently incorporate the meringue. Pour the mixture into a suitable container and place in the freezer until firm, at least 4 hours or, preferably, overnight. To serve as a plated dessert, follow the presentation instructions in Wild Strawberry Parfait, page 677.

Peach Ice Cream in Florentina Baskets

12 servings

one-half recipe Florentina Batter (page 214)
one recipe Caramel Sauce II (page 1071)
1 tablespoon (15 ml) amaretto liqueur
2 tablespoons (30 ml) unsalted butter or whipped cream (for presentation)
6 cups (1 l, 480 ml) Peach Ice Cream (page 635)
two peaches thinly sliced with the skin on
twelve small fanned strawberries

Peach Ice Cream is one of the most popular flavors to make in the summertime at the height of the season, especially if you are lucky enough to have a peach tree in your backyard. Many times on the spur of the moment, out comes the ice cream maker, and I can remember many times when I had to take my turn on the old hand-cranked machine. Next to eating a fresh ripe peach plucked right off the tree, I can think of no better way to enjoy them than in ice cream. Because of the creamy texture of the fruit itself, the ice cream comes out silky smooth, and the amaretto-infused chunks of peach, which due to the alcohol do not freeze too hard, combine wonderfully with the nut flavor of the crunchy Florentina cookie shell. Add the rich Caramel Sauce and the humble picnic dessert is transformed into an elegant restaurant offering!

1. Draw twelve 4³⁄₄-inch (11.8-cm) circles on baking paper. Invert the papers onto sheet pans. Divide the Florentina Batter between the circles. Spread the batter, bake, and trim the cookies following the instructions in the recipe for Florentinas.

2. Reheat the cookies until they are soft enough to bend. Immediately bend ¹⁄₂ inch (1.2 cm) of the edge of each cookie up 45° to form a shallow hexagon-shaped basket (with the top of the cookie facing out). Alternatively, fold the cookies over the back of a small bowl or jar, or use two brioche molds to make the baskets by placing a smaller

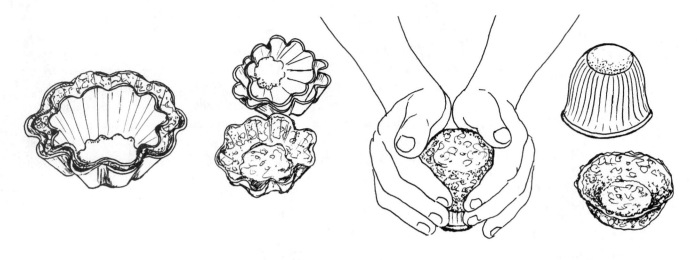

FIGURE 13–5 *Forming Florentina baskets by pressing the soft cookies between a smaller and larger mold with the same shape; folding the soft cookie over the back of a small inverted mold and shaping it by hand*

mold inside a larger mold, with the cookie pressed between them (Figure 13–5).

3. Flavor the Caramel Sauce with the amaretto. Chill dessert plates in the freezer.

4. Presentation: Place a small dot of butter or whipped cream in the center of a dessert plate. Set a Florentina basket on top and fill with a scoop of Peach Ice Cream. Arrange the peach slices fanned on top of the ice cream. Pour a pool of Caramel Sauce in front of the basket. Place a fanned strawberry on the sauce. Serve immediately.

Poached Pears with Ginger Ice Cream and Two Sauces

16 servings

eight Bartlett pears
7¹/₂ cups (1 l, 800 ml) Spiced Poaching Syrup (page 13)
four small slices of fresh ginger root, about the size of a quarter coin
2 ounces (55 g) pistachio nuts
sixteen Sponge Cake rounds (see note)
5 cups (1 l, 200 ml) White Chocolate Ice Cream with Ginger (page 640)

Because of the pear's distinctive form—spherical on the bottom with a tapered top—pear-shaped has become an adjective as widely used and readily understood as describing an object as shaped like a doughnut. Pears are grown in the temperate regions all across the globe in thousands of varieties. Their name stems from the Latin pirum *(pears are called* poire *in French,* birne *in German, and* päron *in Swedish).*

By large account the most popular pear in this country is the Bartlett, used in this recipe. Known as William's in Europe, it was developed in eighteenth-century England and brought across the Atlantic to the Colonies by the early settlers. Here it was named after Enoch Bartlett, a Massachusetts resident who promoted and popularized the variety. Bartlett pears turn from dark green to light golden yellow when they are perfectly ripe, which is actually not preferable for this particular recipe. A pretty red-skinned strain of Bartlett has also been developed. These are great for use in a fruit display or fruit basket, or served fresh with cheeses. Red Bartletts are of no significance for peeling and cooking since the flavor is no different from the original. Pears not only rival the apple in popularity, but the two are actually closely related. Both are members

one recipe Romanoff Sauce
(page 1081)
one recipe Raspberry Sauce
(page 1080)
Marzipan Leaves (page 1038)

NOTE: Use any type of light sponge cake you have on hand. Slice thin, then cut out sixteen rounds, using a 1¹/₂-inch (3.7-cm) plain cookie cutter. Cover and reserve.

of the rose family and are classified as pome fruits, meaning they have a distinct seeded core.

1. Peel the pears and cut in half lengthwise. Place them directly into the Poaching Syrup as you are working, to prevent oxidation. Add the fresh ginger and poach the pears until they are tender. Remove from the heat and let cool in the syrup.

2. Blanch the pistachios using a pinch of salt in the blanching water to amplify the green color of the nuts. Remove the skins and dry the nuts. Crush to a fine consistency. (If you dry the nuts in an oven, do not toast them or you will lose the color.)

3. Remove the pear halves from the poaching liquid, core, and pat dry with towels. Chill dessert plates in the refrigerator.

4. Presentation: Place a sponge round in the center of a dessert plate. Put a small scoop of ice cream on top and lightly flatten the ice cream with the back of the scoop. Arrange a pear half on top of the ice cream (flat side down), pressing it down to secure. Cover the stem half of the pear with Romanoff Sauce, spooning it straight across the center and letting it run out to cover the plate next to the pear. Spoon Raspberry Sauce over the bottom half of the pear in the same manner. Make sure that the sauces are thick enough to cover the pear but at the same time run out onto the plate. Sprinkle a thin line of pistachios across the center where the two sauces meet. Place a Marzipan Leaf next to the stem of the pear and serve immediately.

Soufflé Pancakes with Gooseberry Ice Cream

12 servings

Soufflé Pancake Batter
(recipe follows)
melted unsalted butter to grease the iron
one-third recipe Gooseberry Ice Cream (page 631)
twelve Sponge Cake rounds (see note 1)
edible fresh flowers
powdered sugar
gooseberry preserves (see note 2)

NOTE 1: Use any type of sponge or pound cake you have on hand. Either light or chocolate would be fine; leftover pieces of Ribbon Sponge

This is a variation of a recipe I have had in my files for many years called Pancakes Johann Strauss. In the original the Soufflé Pancakes are cooked on both sides, then sandwiched together with orange segments and served with orange sauce. I did not include that recipe in this text because it is fairly similar to the recipe for Crepes Vienna.

If you do not have a small Swedish pancakes pan, plättiron, it is best to use a 6-inch crepe pan instead and portion only one pancake per serving (two sandwiched together). In this case, cut the pancake into four wedges before putting it into the hot oven to "soufflé." The pancakes will spread out too far if you attempt to make the small size in a standard skillet, reducing their height when souffléd during the final baking. Either way, whole or sliced into quarters, the pancakes should be served just like a bona fide soufflé—immediately after they are removed from the oven. The precooked, sandwiched pancakes, however, can be stored in the refrigerator, well wrapped, for up to two days before the final baking, with excellent results. Please do not serve these cold; though fairly acceptable, your guests will unfortunately never know what they are missing.

1. Heat a *plättiron* (see Small Swedish Pancakes Pan, page 1124), large skillet, or other suitable cooking vessel until medium hot. Grease lightly with melted butter and pour approximately 2 tablespoons (30 ml) of batter into each depression in the pan (or about ¹/₃ cup/80 ml for

are ideal. Slice the cake thin, and cut out twelve rounds, using a 1¹/₂-inch (3.7-cm) plain cookie cutter. Cover and reserve.

NOTE 2: Use commercial gooseberry preserves or make one-third of the gooseberry mixture in the Gooseberry Ice Cream recipe (see page 631), but reduce and thicken it further.

NOTE 3: Soufflé Pancakes are wonderful as a brunch offering. Try sandwiching sliced peaches or bananas between the pancakes in step one. The banana version is fabulous served with maple syrup and toasted pecans, and the peach-stuffed pancakes are great with cinnamon butter.

Soufflé Pancake Batter

approximately eighty-five 3-inch (7.5-cm) pancakes

6 ounces (170 g) bread flour
4 ounces (115 g) cake flour
2 cups (480 ml) water
1 teaspoon (5 g) salt
5 ounces (140 g) unsalted butter
10 eggs, separated
grated zest of three medium-sized lemons
1¹/₄ cups (300 ml) heavy cream
6 ounces (170 g) granulated sugar

each pancake if using a 6-inch skillet). Cook the pancakes for about 3 minutes, adjusting the heat as necessary. They should be light brown on the bottom but still liquid on top. Remove the pan from the stove and let the pancakes finish cooking for 1 minute off the heat. The top will thicken to a sticky consistency. Use a narrow palette knife to remove the pancakes, being very careful not to damage the sides. Place them brown-side down on a sheet pan lined with baking paper. Make a second batch and invert these on top of the first set so that the raw sides are sandwiched together. Before they cool completely, transfer the pancakes to another area of the pan to keep them from sticking. Repeat with the remaining batter. You need seventy-two pancakes for this recipe (thirty-six after sandwiching). The batter will make about a dozen extra single pancakes. Cover the pancakes and reserve in the refrigerator until serving time.

2. Arrange the pancakes in groups of three (or four quarters if making the larger size) on small pieces of baking paper. Preheat two sheet pans stacked together (double-panned), in a 400°F (205°C) oven.

3. Use a no. 20 (1³/₄-ounce/50-ml) ice-cream scoop to portion a scoop of Gooseberry Ice Cream on top of each sponge circle. Reserve in the freezer.

4. Remove the petals from flowers of two or three different colors and reserve on a damp paper towel.

5. **Presentation:** Place a set of three pancakes on the hot sheet pans in the oven. Bake until they are puffed, about 4 minutes. Sift powdered sugar over the base of a dessert plate. Place a sponge round with ice cream in the center of the plate. Use the bottom of a false-bottom tart pan (or something similar) to remove the puffed pancakes from the oven. Place them around the ice cream. Quickly, sift powdered sugar on top, place a small dollop of gooseberry preserves on each pancake, decorate with flower petals between each pancake, and serve at once.

1. Sift the flours together and set aside.

2. Combine the water, salt, and butter in a saucepan and bring to a boil. Stir in two-thirds of the flour mixture (1³/₄ cups/420 ml), reserving the remainder. Continue to cook, stirring constantly, until the paste is smooth and comes away from the sides of the pan, approximately 2 minutes. Remove from the heat.

3. Mix in the egg yolks one or two at a time together with the lemon zest. Cover and set aside to cool.

4. Whip the heavy cream to soft peaks. Reserve in the refrigerator.

5. When the batter is cold, whip the egg whites and granulated sugar to stiff peaks. Set aside briefly. Gradually fold the reserved whipped cream into the batter. Add the reserved flour to a small portion of the batter, then mix this into the remaining batter, followed by the egg whites. Use immediately.

🥄 Wild Strawberry Parfait

12 servings

3 pounds, 8 ounces (1 kg, 590 g) fresh wild strawberries (see note 1)

3 eggs

2 egg yolks

2 ounces (55 g) granulated sugar

1/2 cup (120 ml) or 6 ounces (170 g) honey

2 1/2 cups (600 ml) heavy cream

3 ounces (85 g) white coating chocolate

fat-soluble food colorings

1 cup (240 ml) heavy cream

twelve Miniature Tulip Crowns (page 1058)

twenty-four Florentina Twists (page 1010)

NOTE 1: It is best to use a mix of red and white berries, or all red. Using exclusively white wild strawberries will not produce as appetizing a color; however, the flavor will be just as good. If you have to use all white berries, add a few tablespoons of raspberry purée or Beet Juice (page 3) to improve the color.

NOTE 2: This amount of white chocolate is actually more than you need, but it is not practical to melt and tint a smaller portion. The leftover may be stored and melted to use again later. Keep the ramekins in a shallow pan of hot water as you decorate the plates so the chocolate does not set up as you are working.

*W*ild strawberries are also known as Alpine Strawberries and as fraise des bois *(strawberries of the wild). These names may suggest that they are native only to the mountain regions of France, but in fact, wild strawberries grow in the open patches and meadows of the woodlands all over Europe, from Italy in the south to Lapland in the north. These small intensely sweet strawberries are, for good reason, considered the queen of all strawberries. They produce a bounty of fruit from early July until the first frost appears. I used to pick wild strawberries as a kid, and we would thread them into strands on tall thin stalks from a sort of weed to make beautiful, edible necklaces (that is any that did not go straight into our mouths!). Commercially, wild strawberries are fairly expensive, mainly because they are time-consuming to pick and the fruit is quite susceptible to hot spells in the weather. There are both red and white (actually a pale yellow) varieties. Unlike their larger counterparts, red wild strawberries are still pale white inside even when they are fully ripe.*

When I was starting out as an apprentice in Sweden, Wild Strawberry Parfait was considered the dessert to order when money was no object and only the best would do. If you have not been exposed to wild strawberries previously, you are in for a real treat.

1. Line the inside of a 4-by-3 1/2-by-8-inch (10-×-8.7-×-20-cm) bread pan (or any size close to this) with baking paper. Set the form aside.

2. Select approximately eighty of the nicest-looking strawberries and set aside (leaving the stems attached) to use in serving. Remove the stems from the remaining berries. Reserve about one-fourth of the stemless berries and then purée the remainder. Set the purée and the two groups of berries aside separately.

3. Whip the eggs, egg yolks, and sugar until light and fluffy, about 3 minutes. Bring the honey to a boil and gradually pour it into the egg mixture while whipping constantly. Continue to whip until the mixture is cold.

4. Whip the first measurement of heavy cream until soft peaks form. Gently incorporate the whipped egg mixture into the cream. Fold in the reserved strawberry purée and then the whole stemless strawberries. Pour the mixture into the prepared form and place in the freezer for at least 4 hours or, preferably, overnight.

5. Chop the white chocolate into small pieces, place in a bowl set over hot water, and stir constantly until melted. Do not walk away and do not overheat the chocolate or it will likely turn into a thick gritty paste. Divide the melted chocolate into four equal portions and place each in a small cup or ramekin (see note 2). Using the tip of a paring knife, add a very small amount of fat-soluble color to each portion, tinting them red, yellow, blue, and green (use equal parts blue and yellow to make green). Keep the colors to pale shades and remember that powdered coloring is very concentrated; use a little at the beginning as you can always add more. Using a small artist's brush, brush dabs of the different colors over the bases of twelve dessert plates. This can be done well in advance, even the day before. Set the plates aside until ready to serve.

6. Whip the remaining heavy cream until stiff peaks form. Place in a pastry bag with a no. 5 (10-mm) star tip and reserve in the refrigerator.

7. Remove the frozen parfait from the form. Cut into twelve slices slightly less than ³/₄ inch (2 cm) thick, using a sharp thin knife dipped in hot water. Place the slices on a chilled sheet pan lined with baking paper as you work. Cover and reserve in the freezer.

8. Presentation: Place five of the reserved wild strawberries with stems attached in one of the Tulip Crowns. Pipe a small dot of whipped cream in the center of one of the prepared dessert plates. Working quickly, place a slice of parfait on top of the cream. Pipe a rosette of cream on one side of the slice and set a reserved strawberry on the rosette. Lean a Florentina Twist against one side of the parfait slice and set the filled cookie basket on the plate on the other side of the slice. Serve immediately.

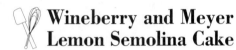

Wineberry and Meyer Lemon Semolina Cake

two 10-inch (25-cm) cakes

1 pound, 6 ounces (625 g) soft butter

1 pound, 10 ounces (740 g) granulated sugar

8 eggs, at room temperature

14 ounces (400 g) cake flour

6 ounces (170 g) fine semolina flour

6 ounces (170 g) medium yellow corn meal

4 teaspoons (16 g) baking powder

1 pound (455 g) sour cream, at room temperature

2 tablespoons (30 ml) vanilla extract

one recipe Meyer Lemon Syrup (recipe follows)

Honey-Vanilla Frozen Yogurt (page 645)

wineberries (see note)

Seaweed Wafers (recipe follows)

NOTE: If Japanese wineberries are not in season or are unavailable, use one of the many similar berries on the market such as red, black, or yellow raspberries, blackberries, or

*T*his is a quick, easy to make cake that can be served plain with just the berries, or can dressed up accompanied by frozen yogurt and wafers as is suggested in the following presentation. One of the most decorative and unusual food plants, Japanese wineberries are small and golden in color ripening to a light red shade. These raspberry look-alikes are juicy and refreshing with a flavor similar to grapes. For an even prettier plate presentation, make individual servings by piping the batter into cake rings instead. You will need sixteen cake rings that are 3 × 2 inch (7.5 × 5 cm). These, of course, will require a much shorter baking time.

1. Line the bottom of two 10-inch (25-cm) cake pans that are 2 inches (5 cm) tall with baking paper (see page 26). Set aside.

2. Using the paddle attachment, cream the butter and sugar together until light and fluffy in consistency. Gradually incorporate the eggs, scraping down the bowl once or twice, and continue to mix at medium speed for 5 to 10 minutes.

3. Meanwhile, sift together the dry ingredients. Mix the dry ingredients into the egg mixture in two portions alternating with the sour cream. Add the vanilla extract.

4. Divide the batter between the prepared caked pans.

5. Bake in a 325°F (163°C) oven for approximately 60 minutes or until the center springs back when pressed lightly. Let cool. Run a paring knife around the inside circumference of the cake pans. Unmold, peel the paper from the bottom of the cakes, and place them right-side up on a cake rack set over a sheet pan.

one of the numerous hybrids that have been developed as a result of crossing various "rubus" species. Loganberries, boysenberries, and dewberries are examples of these.

Meyer Lemon Syrup

approximately 2¹/₂ cups (600 ml) syrup

1¹/₂ cups (360 ml) meyer lemon juice
12 ounces (340 g) granulated sugar
¹/₂ cup (120 ml) water

Seaweed Wafers

approximately thirty 6 × 4-inch (15×10-cm) wafers

8 ounces (225 g) powdered sugar, sifted
3 ounces (85 g) unsalted butter, softened
2 egg whites, at room temperature
2 to 3 ounces (55–85 g) bread flour, sifted
³/₄ cup (180 ml) strained orange juice, at room temperature

6. Brush or spray the Meyer Lemon Syrup heavily over the cakes including the sides. Store covered in the refrigerator.

7. Presentation: Cut each cake into 12 pieces. Serve with frozen yogurt and wineberries, decorate with Seaweed Wafers.

1. Combine all of the ingredients in a saucepan and bring to a boil.
2. Let cool and then store covered in the refrigerator.

These thin, crisp, unusual looking decorations will add a futuristic appearance to any presentation, as well as a palatable contrast to a soft dessert like this cake and frozen yogurt combination. The thin lacy nature of the wafers also makes them very fragile, however, you will find that the broken pieces can be used as well. The wafers are a little easier to handle when they are made with the larger amount of flour specified, but they are also less lacy.

1. Stir the powdered sugar into the soft butter and beat for a few minutes until light and fluffy.

2. Stir in the egg whites one at a time, and then the flour. The paste should be smooth. Stir in the orange juice, continuing to stir until well combined. Do not be concerned about the mixture appearing loose and broken at this point; this is expected and is part of the character of the batter.

3. Spread the batter into thin irregular shapes approximately 5 × 3 inches (12.5 × 7.5 cm) on silicone mats; they will expand just a little in the oven.

4. Bake in a 400°F (205°C) oven until the pieces begin to show some color, approximately 15 minutes. Remove from the silicone mat with the help of a pallete knife or small spatula as soon as the pieces can be handled, and place them on a sheet pan lined with baking paper or drape over a round object if you wish to curl them. Seaweed decorations can be made ahead and stored in an airtight container.

14

Light Desserts

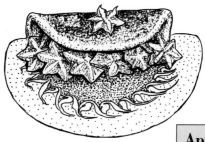

Apricot Gratin with Sabayon
of Muscat Wine

Asian Pear Tart with Honey-
Scented Pear Frozen Yogurt

Baked Bananas with Banana-
Tofu Frozen Yogurt

Blood Orange Gratin

Caramelized Pineapple Barbados

Crepes Vienna

Dacquoise Baskets with
Raspberries and Two Sauces

Fresh Strawberries with
Champagne Sabayon Sauce

Fruit Salad

Fruit Valentines

Kardinals with Sambuca-
Scented Italian Cream
and Fresh Fruit

Lemon Chiffon Pouches

Low-Cholesterol Sponge Cake

Lychee Charlotte Royal

Marbled Cheesecake
with Quark

Minola Tangelo Givré
with Toasted Meringue
and Cookie Citrus Rind

Oeufs à la Neige with a
Caramelized Sugar Sphere

Omelette Pancake with
Sautéed Starfruit,
Pomegranate Sauce,
and Mango Coulis

"Out-of-Season" Fresh Fruit
Baskets with Feijoa Sorbet

Pears California
with Cointreau-Flavored
Almond Filling

Rainbow of Summer Sorbets
in a Cookie Flower

Red Currant Sorbet
in Magnolia Cookie Shells

Sabayon

Salzburger Soufflé

Strawberry-Peach Yogurt
Creams

Vineyard Barrels

Winter Fruit Compote in Late
Harvest Wine Syrup

Zinfandel Poached Pears
with Honey-Scented Pear
Frozen Yogurt

We live in an era of heightened health awareness and food consciousness, combined with a national obsession regarding weight loss. Thin is definitely "in," and people are realizing that they cannot eat whatever and whenever they want and still remain healthy. Everyone seems to be trying to lower his intake of fat and sodium, lower his blood pressure and blood cholesterol level, and increase his consumption of low-fat foods. Exercise, too, plays a big role in the current fitness frenzy. By the thousands people are vacationing at extravagant health spas and taking "spa" cruises, the old and young alike are signing up for aerobic classes and diet programs, the supermarket shelves are bursting with "low-fat" and fat-free products, and more and more magazines and cookbooks are offering low-fat and heart-healthy recipes. I have always felt fortunate that my love of exercise has offset any weight gain from my love of food. (Of course there are those who say you should never trust a skinny chef!)

The desserts in this chapter should not be confused with dietetic desserts, which in my experience usually taste as if something is missing. Instead, these lower-calorie and/or lower-fat desserts taste terrific and can be enjoyed by nondieters as well as those who are keeping track of their calories and fat grams. In fact, many are recipes I have been preparing for years, long before there was so much emphasis on lighter food. In addition to the recipes in this section, there are others throughout the text that can be served as light desserts, in some cases with only small modifications, which are noted when applicable. Also, any of the sorbets and most of the frozen yogurts in the Ice Cream and Frozen Desserts chapter make an excellent choice in this regard. A selection of sorbets or fresh fruit ices, attractively presented, are always good to have on your menu to provide an alternative for those guests looking for a low-fat, non-chocolate, and/or nondairy option.

One important factor that has become accepted relatively recently is that the fat content of food is just as important, if not more so, as the calorie content for those who want to lose weight or prevent weight gain. Guidelines established by the National Academy of Sciences, the National Institutes of Health, and the American Heart Association state that your total fat intake should account for 30 percent or less of your total calories. Another way to look at this is that no more than 30 percent of the calories in any food serving should come from fat, including saturated fats. Based on those guidelines, a serving of dessert with 300 calories should not contain more than 90 calories from fat. Since each fat gram contains 9 calories, 10 grams of fat (90 fat calories) would be the maximum amount acceptable in this portion size. There are numerous differing opinions, and new research is being conducted on the subject of diet and weight loss all the time, and while this text does not in any way attempt to deliver the final word on this subject, current information indicates that a reduction in calories must be combined with a reduction in fat intake *and* regular exercise, consistently, for any of the three to be effective over the long term. The recommendations set forth by the U.S. Department of Agriculture and the U.S. Department of Health and Human Services are no more than 65 grams of fat in a 2,000-calorie per day diet, and no more than 80 grams of fat in a 2,500-calorie per day diet. These recommendations are also endorsed by the National Cholesterol Education Program and the Food and Nutrition Board of the National Research Council. Quantities of fat, cholesterol, sodium, carbohydrate, and protein per serving, as well as the percentage of Daily Values for such, are now required by the Food and Drug Administration on all packaged foods sold in this country and are listed as Nutrition Facts.

Many restaurants today offer reduced-calorie and reduced-fat alternatives to their regular menu selections. But a tasty and attractive dessert is not always as easy to produce as, for example, grilling fish instead of frying it, or sautéing chicken breasts in reduced stock instead of butter. The principal ingredients in many desserts are virtually bursting with calories. Butter has an amazing 1,600 calories (184 grams of fat) per cup, granulated sugar 770 calories (0 grams of fat), whole eggs 360 calories (25 grams of fat), egg yolks 870 calories (75 grams of fat), all-purpose flour 455 calories (1.5 grams of fat), and heavy cream 820 calories (88 grams of fat). As you can see, this limits the classical dessert possibilities quite a bit if one wants to stay within the guidelines discussed above.

It is feasible, in some cases, to achieve fairly good results by replacing a high-fat or calorie-rich ingredient in a recipe with a low-calorie or low-fat one, such as substituting meringue for whipped cream, using nonfat sour cream instead of regular sour cream, replacing whole milk with skim milk, using egg whites instead of whole eggs, or using yogurt or tofu as a base for ice cream instead of egg yolks and heavy cream. Unfortunately these changes can make for a less satisfying dessert, because without further modifications, the alternate ingredients usually change the texture, moisture content, cooking time, and/or appearance of the final product. While ingredient substitutions are an option that may be appropriate for the home chef, a professional does not usually have time for trial and error and will find it more reliable to use a recipe that starts out lower in calories or fat or has been created as a light dessert and thoroughly tested (like these).

Pastry chefs are often blamed for tempting the hapless consumer to devour excess calories and fat. And yes, you can certainly gain weight, and plenty of it, by overindulging in some of the recipes in this book if you do not have the willpower to limit yourself to occasional, or small, portions. However, I do feel dessert—in moderation—can be part of a balanced diet and a healthy lifestyle. I like good flavorful food, and I believe in the old saying, "If I can't have what I want, I'm not going to settle for whatever I can get." I would much rather have a serving of perfectly ripe, fresh fruit than a watered-down dessert that has no taste or uses artificial sweeteners and flavorings, as do many so-called diet desserts. The recipes in this chapter are all sweet and satisfying, yet none contain more than 400 calories per serving (and more than half contain less than 300), none uses artificial ingredients, and only five of the twenty-eight recipes exceed the recommendation of no more than 30 percent of the total calories generated by fat. These recipes simply use ingredients naturally low in fat and calories, and sometimes a smaller portion. The following are desserts that can be enjoyed not only for what they are not but also for what they are: delicious.

NOTE: The calorie and fat counts given with each recipe were calculated based on making Acidophilus Yogurt with skim milk when yogurt is used as an ingredient in the recipe or in a sub-recipe such as a frozen yogurt.

Apricot Gratin with Sabayon of Muscat Wine

8 servings; each serving contains approximately 365 calories and 6.5 grams of fat

twenty large, fresh, ripe apricots (approximately 3 pounds/1 kg, 365 g)
10 ounces (285 g) granulated sugar
4 cups (960 ml) muscat wine
10 egg yolks (⅞ cup/210 ml)
small edible whole fresh flowers such as borage, or edible flower petals

NOTE: I do not remove the apricot skins in this dish, but if you wish to do so, blanch the whole apricots in boiling water for just a few seconds, transfer to cold water, and peel off the skins. Be very careful, since ripe apricots can fall apart quickly. Conversely, if you are unable to find perfectly ripe apricots, you can soften them easily by heating the muscat wine to the boiling point and leaving the apricots in the wine (off the heat) until they are soft. Watch them closely, because the apricots will soften fairly quickly. Lastly, if the apricots are overripe, they can still be used, but omit placing them in the wine altogether.

This simple and refreshing dessert can easily be prepared in less than one hour, and that amount of time can even be cut in half if your apricots are nice and ripe and you skip the macerating step. On the other hand, if there is no hurry and you want to dress up the plate a little, make Miniature Tulip Crowns (page 1058) and fill them with a small scoop of Honey-Vanilla Frozen Yogurt (page 645). Place the filled crown on top of the sauce in the center of the plate just before serving. The crisp cookie shell and cold yogurt each add another dimension and pleasant contrast to the dessert.

1. Cut the apricots in half. Remove the pits and discard them.

2. Add approximately one-third of the granulated sugar to the wine. Heat the mixture to about 150°F (65°C). Stir to make certain that the sugar is completely dissolved. Remove from the heat and add the apricot halves. Set aside to infuse until they have cooled completely.

3. Once the wine and apricots have cooled, remove the apricots carefully with a slotted spoon. Measure and reserve 2½ cups (600 ml) of the muscat wine mixture. Save the remainder for cake syrup or another use.

4. Cut thirty-two of the best-looking apricot halves in half again to make sixty-four quarters. Place these and the eight remaining apricot halves on a sheet pan lined with baking paper. Cover, and set aside.

5. Place the remaining sugar in a bowl with the egg yolks. Set the bowl over simmering water and whisk for 1 minute to thoroughly combine. Add the reserved muscat wine and heat, whisking constantly, until the mixture is thick and fluffy. Remove from the heat. The sauce should be used within 30 minutes. If you are unable to use the sabayon within that time, whisk the sauce over an ice bath until it is completely cold as soon as you remove it from the heat.

6. Presentation: Place one of the apricot halves, flat-side down, in the center of an ovenproof dessert plate. Arrange eight apricot quarters in a spoke pattern around the apricot half. Spoon or pipe approximately 1 cup (240 ml) of the sabayon sauce over the fruit. The sauce should coat the apricots, but the outline of the fruit should still be visible. If the sauce is too thick, thin it with a little of the leftover muscat wine mixture. Place the plate under a broiler or salamander to *gratinée*. Sprinkle edible flowers or flower petals over the top and serve immediately.

Asian Pear Tart with Honey-Scented Pear Frozen Yogurt

12 servings; each serving contains approximately 390 calories and 10 grams of fat

4 pounds (1 kg, 820 g) Asian pears (approximately 10; see note 1)

one recipe Spiced Poaching Syrup (page 13)

twenty-four sheets phyllo dough (one package)

1/2 cup (120 ml) clarified unsalted butter, melted

1 pound (455 g) Pastry Cream (page 1088) (see note 2)

Cinnamon Sugar (page 5)

powdered sugar

one-half recipe Honey-Scented Pear Frozen Yogurt (page 644) (see note, page 683)

NOTE 1: Since you will only have about 10 pears to stem (and assuming all of those have their stems intact, which is not always the case), it does not take much figuring to realize you will be short a few stems. The solution is to transplant from other pears. In addition to using Asian pears as donors, save the stems from the Bosc pears when you make the frozen yogurt. Bosc pears have long, elegant stems, quite similar to those of Asian pears.

Asian pears vary tremendously in size. Try to get small or medium-sized fruit for this recipe because it is difficult to arrange wedges from larger pears attractively.

NOTE 2: Prepare the Pastry Cream as directed, substituting skim milk for the whole milk in the recipe.

This tart features poached Asian pears surrounded by layer upon layer of crisp phyllo dough. Unfortunately, Asian pears are not available throughout the year as so many other pear varieties are. If you can't obtain Asian pears, try using Bosc pears instead, they have the same attractive long stems (and like Asian pears they also require a longer poaching time than most other varieties). Peel the Bosc pears and poach them whole with the stems attached. After poaching, cut off the stem including 1 inch (2.5 cm) of the top of the pear to use in the presentation.

I like to feature this tart on the menu around November and December served with Pomegranate Sauce (see page 1079). Both pears and pomegranates have a holiday feel to them, and both are at their prime during that time. As a variation, try this festive presentation: Pipe a 1 1/2-inch (3.7-cm) wide ring of Pomegranate Sauce around the perimeter of the base of a dessert plate. Place the tart in the center. Sprinkle a few pomegranate seeds on top of both the tart and the sauce. Place one of the reserved pear stems in the center of the tart. Sift powdered sugar lightly over the pomegranate seeds.

1. Remove the stems from the pears and reserve the stems. Peel the pears and cut in half lengthwise. Poach in the Poaching Syrup until the pears are soft to the touch. Asian pears take longer to poach than European varieties—up to 45 minutes, even if they are ripe. Allow the pears to cool in the liquid.

2. Use a melon-ball cutter to remove the cores. Slice the pear halves lengthwise into 1/2-inch (1.2-cm) wedges approximately the size of an orange section. Place the pear wedges on a sheet pan lined with baking paper. Reserve.

3. Cut a 6-inch (15-cm) template from cardboard or have a lid or plate of about the same size handy.

4. Carefully unroll the stacked phyllo sheets. Cut into four sections, making each section large enough to be able to cut circles from it using the template (place the template on top to determine where to make the cuts. Depending on the size of the phyllo dough sheets, you will probably have to stagger the cuts to fit). Do not cut around the template at this point. Place the cut pieces in two stacks. Cover one stack loosely with plastic wrap and then with a lightly dampened towel.

5. Place a sheet from the remaining stack on the table in front of you. Brush butter very lightly on top. Place a second sheet of dough on top and brush butter lightly over this piece. Continue until you have eight sheets stacked with butter between them. Do not brush butter on the top sheet. Cover the remaining phyllo sheets.

6. Working quickly, place the round template on top of the stacked sheets and cut around with a paring knife. Remove the scrap pieces and discard or save for another use. Brush butter over the top layer of the round stack. Immediately and carefully, press the dough into a 4 1/2-inch (11.2-cm) individual tart pan or crème brûlée mold (see Figure 10–9, page 447).

7. Pipe approximately one-twelfth of the Pastry Cream into the form on top of the dough. Place eight pear wedges on top of the Pastry Cream in a spoke pattern. Fold the sides of the phyllo dough in toward the center all around, using gentle pressure, but enough so that the dough will stay in place. Brush butter lightly over the exposed phyllo dough edges.

8. Repeat steps five, six, and seven to make a total of twelve tarts. Place the forms on a sheet pan. Sprinkle Cinnamon Sugar over the tops of the tarts.

9. Bake at 400°F (205°C) for approximately 20 minutes or until the phyllo dough is golden brown. Let cool before removing the desserts from the forms.

10. Presentation: Sift powdered sugar lightly over a tart and a dessert plate. Heat the tart under a broiler or salamander (or use a propane torch) until the sugar begins to caramelize. Watch carefully and move the tart as needed so that it browns evenly. Place the tart in the center of the prepared plate. Arrange three small quenelle-shaped scoops of frozen yogurt on the plate around the dessert. Place a reserved pear stem in the center of the tart and serve at once.

Baked Bananas with Banana-Tofu Frozen Yogurt

16 servings; each serving contains approximately 250 calories and 11 grams of fat

three oranges
¹/₄ cup (60 ml) or 3 ounces (85 g) honey
1 tablespoon (15 ml) vanilla extract
eight medium-sized ripe bananas
lemon juice
2 ounces (55 g) soft unsalted butter
6 cups (1 l, 440 ml) Banana-Tofu Frozen Yogurt (page 643) (see note, page 683)
mint sprigs

NOTE: If you wish to cook the bananas à la carte, or if you are making only a few servings, cut pieces of aluminum foil to the appropriate size, place a banana half on one side of each piece of foil, and top with butter as above. Fold the foil over and crimp the edge to seal. Place the individual packets on a sheet pan to bake.

Only about 5 percent of the bananas sold in the United States are cooked before they are eaten, which is really a shame because a cooked banana has a very rich and exotic flavor. On the other hand (no pun intended), one can easily understand why so many bananas never make it into the kitchen but are instead eaten fresh, when you consider their contents: A medium-sized (6-to-7-inch) ripe banana is not only a delicious and sweet snack, it has only about 80 calories (and like all fruits and vegetables, no cholesterol), is almost fat-free, and is both high in carbohydrates and an excellent source of potassium. Bananas are composed of about 75 percent water and 20 percent sugar; the remaining 5 percent is a combination of starch, fiber, protein, and ash.

While the bananas for this recipe should be ripe, if overripe they will turn to mush when they bake. The bananas in a retail produce market are typically sold in one of the last three stages of ripeness, either yellow with green tips (in this stage they are firmest to the touch), completely yellow, or yellow with brown spots. In the third stage all of the starch has dissolved and become sugar and while the bananas are at their sweetest, they should not be used for cooking (unless they are puréed, as in banana bread, for example) because they will most likely become a sweet, syrupy pulp. Bananas at the second (all yellow) stage are perfect for cooking. To keep them from ripening any further, place the bananas in the refrigerator; the flavor will not suffer although the skin will eventually turn brown and then black. Bananas taste best if brought to room temperature if they are to be eaten raw. As a variation try grilling the bananas instead of baking them. Sprinkle evenly with granulated sugar and cook the banana halves on a hot grill, turning once, until they are heated through and have distinctive grill stripes or markings. Present as directed in the main recipe.

1. Remove the zest from the oranges in long threads using a zester. Extract the juice from the oranges and combine with the zest, honey, and vanilla. Set aside.

2. Peel the bananas and cut in half lengthwise. Rub a little lemon juice on the bananas to keep them from getting brown. Place cut-side up in a hotel pan or other ovenproof dish (see note). Place a piece of butter on top of each one, dividing it evenly. Cover the dish with aluminum foil, crimping the foil against the edge of the dish to seal it tightly.

3. Bake the bananas at 375°F (190°C) for approximately 6 minutes or until they are soft (the time will vary depending on the ripeness of the fruit).

4. **Presentation:** Cut one of the banana halves in five or six places along the outside (longer) edge, cutting at a 45° angle and going almost to the opposite side. Place it flat-side up on a dessert plate and bend into a half-circle to fan out the cut pieces. Spoon some of the orange juice mixture over the banana without using any of the zest. Place a scoop of Banana-Tofu Frozen Yogurt inside the circle and place some of the orange zest on the yogurt. Garnish with a mint sprig and serve immediately.

Blood Orange Gratin

16 servings; each serving contains approximately 300 calories and 12 grams of fat

sixteen large blood oranges
1 ounce (30 g) fresh ginger root
1/3 cup (80 ml) or 4 ounces (115 g) honey
3/4 cup (180 ml) water
2 tablespoons (30 ml) orange liqueur
1/2 cup (120 ml) grenadine
1/2 teaspoon (1 g) ground allspice
5 egg yolks
3/4 cup (180 ml) Acidophilus Yogurt (page 2) (see note, page 683)
1 1/4 cups (300 ml) heavy cream
2 1/2 cups (600 ml) Honey-Vanilla Frozen Yogurt (page 645) (see note, page 683)
dark coating chocolate, melted
sixteen Miniature Tulips (page 1058)

*G*ratin *is the name applied to a dish that is quickly placed under a broiler or salamander to form a golden brown crust or skin on the surface. By classic definition the top of the food should first be coated with grated cheese and/or bread crumbs, sometimes combined with eggs or melted butter. The word* gratin *is French derived from the word* gratté, *which translates to "grate" in English. This expression did not come about as one might assume from the grating of cheese or other food on top of the dish, but rather was originally the name given to the crust that would inevitably stick to the side of the pan and had to be scraped (or* gratté *in French) free. The term* gratin *is commonly used to describe the method of cooking, or finishing, pasta, vegetables, fish, meat, and nowadays even dessert preparations.*

Even though the Orange Gratin is not baked per se, be certain that the dessert plates or dishes are heatproof, since it will take quite a bit longer to brown the surface of the sabayon than it does, for example, to brown a meringue-topped dessert.

1. Peel the oranges and cut out the segments (see Figures 12–4 and 12–5, page 596), holding the oranges over a bowl to catch the juice. Place the segments in rows in a hotel pan as you remove them. Squeeze all of the juice out of the orange membranes and into the juice bowl after removing the segments. Reserve the segments and juice separately. Peel the ginger root and cut it into two or three slices. Reserve.

2. Place the honey and water in a saucepan. Heat to simmering, then add the ginger root. Reduce the syrup by half. Add the reserved orange juice and the orange liqueur. Mix in the grenadine and the allspice.

3. Cool the mixture slightly, then pour over the reserved orange segments (avoid mixing to prevent breaking the segments). Remove and discard the slices of ginger root. Cover the orange segments and refrigerate for at least 4 hours or, preferably, overnight to develop the flavors.

4. Beat the egg yolks for a few seconds just to combine, then mix in the yogurt. Whip the cream to soft peaks, and fold the yogurt mixture into the cream.

5. Tilt the pan and pour off the liquid from the orange segments. Measure ³/₄ cup (180 ml) and stir into the cream mixture. Discard the remainder or save for another use.

6. Line the orange segments up on paper towels and pat somewhat dry to ensure that the sauce will adhere properly. Reserve.

7. Scoop sixteen small scoops of Honey-Vanilla Frozen Yogurt, taking care to keep them neat and uniform. Place them on a chilled sheet pan lined with baking paper. Place the chocolate in a piping bag. Streak the chocolate across the frozen yogurt scoops, in two directions, as shown in Figure 6–1, page 246. Reserve in the freezer.

8. Presentation: Arrange ten to twelve orange segments in a spoke pattern on the base of an ovenproof serving plate. Check the consistency of the cream and yogurt mixture: if it is too thin it will run off the segments without coating them. Whip the mixture to thicken it if necessary and then place in a piping bottle with a large opening. Pipe just enough of the mixture on top of the orange segments to coat them and the base of the plate. Avoid piping any more than necessary on the plate surface. Place under a hot broiler or salamander until light brown. Place a Tulip in the center of the dessert. Place one of the reserved yogurt scoops in the Tulip, using two spoons to transfer it. Serve immediately or the yogurt will melt on the warm plate.

Caramelized Pineapple Barbados

12 servings; each serving contains approximately 260 calories and 2 grams of fat

two medium-sized fresh pineapples, about 4 pounds (1 kg, 820 g) each

4 ounces (115 g) granulated sugar

2 cups (480 ml) Orange Sauce (page 1077)

¹/₄ cup (60 ml) or 3 ounces (85 g) honey

*B*arbados, the colorful and most eastern island in the West Indies, has given its name to this dessert not so much for the pineapple, although they are certainly grown there, as for the rum-flavored sauce. The production of sugarcane and refined sugar, together with their by-products—molasses and rum—comprised the core of the island's commerce for many years, and Barbados rum has long been considered one of the finest dark rums in the world. Only recently has tourism edged out agriculture as the leading industry. Barbados gained independence from being a British colony in 1966. The name Barbados is also given to the Barbados cherry, a small tree native to, and growing all across, the West Indies. The fruit, which is similar to a red cherry, is used primarily to make drinks and preserves. Another Barbados fruit is the Barbados gooseberry, sometimes called blad apple. The gooseberry-looking yellow berry is actually the fruit of a cactus. It has an excellent flavor and is eaten raw.

$^1/_2$ cup (120 ml) dark rum

2 tablespoons (30 ml) green
    peppercorns, chopped

2$^1/_2$ cups (600 ml) Honey-Vanilla
    Frozen Yogurt (page 645)
    (see note page 683)

fresh pineapple leaves for decoration

*NOTE: While it would be ideal to cook the
pineapple slices to order, this is often not practical. However, the slices should not be cooked
more than one hour in advance, and they should
be held at room temperature. If you do not have
a salamander, cook the pineapple in a very hot
skillet to caramelize the topping.*

*A simple way of trimming the pineapple slices into octagonal shapes is to
use a template as a guide. The inside (cutout) from the Raspberry Wafer template (Figure 10–24A, page 486) works fine if you increase the size $^1/_4$ inch (6
mm) to make the solid piece 3$^3/_8$ inches (8.4 cm). By placing this template on top
as you cut, you not only get precise shapes but all the servings are the same size.
Save your pineapple trimmings, as well as the core, to make the pineapple
drink on page 481.*

1. Rinse the pineapples, twist off the crowns, and reserve the
crowns to use in the presentation. Cut the top and bottom off each
pineapple, stand the fruit upright, and cut away the rind. It is not necessary to cut deep enough to remove all of the "eyes," since the edges
will be trimmed. Cut the pineapples into slices approximately $^3/_4$ inch
(2 cm) thick. Cut the core out of each slice using a plain $^3/_4$-inch (2-cm)
cookie cutter, then trim the sides to make the slices octagonal. Make
twelve slices.

2. Place the pineapple slices on sheet pans lined with baking paper.
Sprinkle half of the granulated sugar evenly over the top. Turn the slices
over and sprinkle the remaining sugar on the other side. Rub some of
the sugar that collects on the pan over the cut sides. Reserve.

3. Combine the Orange Sauce, honey, and rum in a saucepan.
Bring to a boil over high heat and reduce to a sauce-like consistency.
Pour into a container and reserve at room temperature.

4. Place the pineapple slices under a hot salamander and cook until
the sugar is caramelized. Quickly turn the slices and caramelize the
other side (see note).

5. Presentation: Pour a round pool of sauce in the center of a
dessert plate. Place a slice of caramelized pineapple on top. Sprinkle
some of the chopped peppercorns on the pineapple. Place a small scoop
of Honey-Vanilla Frozen Yogurt in the center of the slice and decorate
with a few small, fresh-looking pineapple leaves from the reserved
crowns. Serve immediately.

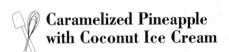 **Caramelized Pineapple
with Coconut Ice Cream**

*C*aramelized pineapple is wonderful served with Coconut Ice Cream (see
page 630) if you do not need to watch the calories. Spoon Caramel Sauce
II (see page 1071) on the base of the plate and set the pineapple slice on top.
Decorate the edge of the Caramel Sauce with Chocolate Sauce for Piping (see
page 1072). Place a scoop of Coconut Ice Cream on the pineapple, then sprinkle a few Candied Lime Peels (see page 978) or toasted macadamia nuts on the
ice cream. Garnish with fresh pineapple leaves.

Crepes Vienna

16 servings; each serving contains approximately 250 calories and 8 grams of fat

2 tablespoons (30 ml) orange liqueur
1 ounce (30 g) dark raisins
1 ounce (30 g) golden raisins
one-half recipe Crepes batter
    (page 5)
four oranges
1 dry pint (480 ml) raspberries
⅓ cup (80 ml) heavy cream
½ teaspoon (3 g) granulated sugar
4 cups (960 ml) Orange Sauce
    (page 1077)
fresh raspberries

NOTE 1: The Crepe batter can be stored for up to three days in the refrigerator. While leftover crepes (cooked the previous day) are suitable for many dishes that are served hot (crepe soufflé for example), one-day old Crepes should not be used in this recipe as they tend to be a bit rubbery when eaten cold.

NOTE 2: If you are serving this as part of your regular menu and the calorie count is not crucial, use two Crepes per serving.

The humble pancake, called pfannkuchen *in Germany and* crêpe *in France, is made from ingredients so basic they can be found on any rural farm that has chickens for eggs, cows for milk and butter, and wheat growing in the fields. However, this once unassuming breakfast food has come to play a part in elegant dessert offerings on restaurant menus all over the world, generally using the French title. These dressed-up versions are often drenched in fruit syrups or liqueurs, filled with creams, wrapped around or folded over fruit fillings, or flambéed at the table. A number of these desserts have become classics, such as Crepes Suzette, Crepes Empire, Crepes Jacques, and Crepe Soufflé.*

The recipe for Crepes Vienna that follows could be varied to use any fruit filling of your choice. For a perfect accompaniment, serve with a scoop of frozen yogurt on the side.

1. Warm the liqueur just a little and add the dark and golden raisins. Set the raisins aside to plump.

2. Make sixteen Crepes following the directions with the recipe. (If you will not be serving all sixteen portions the same day, do not cook any more Crepes than you expect to use; see note 1).

3. Cut the peel from the oranges and cut out the segments (see Figures 12–4 and 12–5, page 596). Hold the oranges over a bowl as you cut the segments to catch the juice for the orange sauce. Cut the orange segments in half crosswise.

4. Place the Crepes in front of you with the golden brown side down. Place four or five pieces of orange, and an equal amount of raspberries, in a line down the center of each crepe. Roll the Crepes up tightly around the fruit and place them, seam-side down, next to each other on paper-lined sheet pans.

5. Whip the heavy cream and sugar until soft peaks form. Reserve in the refrigerator.

6. Gently stir the plumped raisins and the orange liqueur into the Orange Sauce.

7. Presentation: Place a Crepe, seam-side down, in the center of a dessert plate. Spoon Orange Sauce, including some of the raisins, across the Crepe in the center so that there is a small pool of sauce on either side. Place a small dollop of softly whipped cream on top of the Crepe in the center. Place a raspberry on the cream.

VARIATIONS
Crepes Empire

Fill the Crepes with diced pineapple that has been macerated in kirsch. Serve with Cherry Compote (see page 452).

 **Crepes Jacques**

 **Dacquoise Baskets with Raspberries and Two Sauces**

16 servings; each serving contains approximately 375 calories and 12 grams of fat

sixteen to twenty paper cones such as the type used for shaved ice

one-half recipe French Meringue (page 590) (see note 2)

4 ounces (115 g) finely ground blanched almonds (almond meal)

dark coating chocolate, melted

Simple Syrup (page 11)

$1/3$ cup (80 ml) raspberry juice or Raspberry Sauce (page 1080)

one-half recipe Italian Cream (page 1087) (see note 4)

1 pound (455 g) fresh raspberries

Raspberry Sauce (page 1080)

Mango Coulis (page 1075)

NOTE 1: Since the Dacquoise should be served crisp, it is best to fill them to order, but if necessary they can be filled and then refrigerated for up to two hours.

NOTE 2: Follow the recipe and instructions for French Meringue, making this change: Stir a small handful of the granulated sugar into 4 ounces (115 g) of finely ground blanched almonds (almond meal). Fold this into the finished meringue.

NOTE 3: If necessary, the meringue baskets and handles can be stored in an airtight container for a few days at room temperature. If at all possible, however, it is best to store the baskets with the paper cones removed and without any chocolate, so that they can be returned to the oven to dry should it become necessary.

*F*ill Crepes with sliced bananas that have been sautéed in a small amount of butter. Serve with Apricot Sauce and orange liqueur.

*T*he people who live in the town of Dax, located in the southwestern part of France, are known as Dacquoise, just as the inhabitants of Boston are known as Bostonians. The Dacquoise cake is traditional in that region, especially so in that town, and came to share the name. The classic Dacquoise contains layers of Japonaise Meringue sandwiched together with flavored whipped cream or buttercream, fresh fruit, and/or nuts. In my version the meringue is formed into pretty individual baskets instead of cake layers. I use fewer ground nuts in the meringue than is typical to keep the color of the meringue light (too many nuts would cause the meringue to turn golden brown once it is baked). The Dacquoise Baskets may be prepared several hours ahead of service and refrigerated if you are using them as part of a buffet display. In that case, fill them with buttercream flavored with orange liqueur instead of the Italian Cream and raspberry filling to prevent the meringue from becoming soft. The buttercream filling complements not only raspberries but many other types of fruit as well. Fill the baskets about two-thirds full of flavored buttercream, then place a scrap piece of meringue on top (you may want to pipe out some thin disks of meringue, using any meringue that is left after piping the baskets, to use for this purpose). Pipe a small amount of additional buttercream on top of the meringue before mounding the raspberries on top. (Of course, with buttercream filling the pastries are no longer a "light" dessert.)

1. Trim the open end of the paper cones to make cones that are $2^{1}/_{2}$ inches (6.2 cm) tall. Take great care to make straight cuts so the baskets will not lean later. You only need sixteen cones for this recipe, but it is a good idea to make a few extra to allow for breakage. Wrap the outside of the cones with plastic wrap. Use only as much plastic as is needed to cover the paper, pull it tight, then secure the end inside the cones at the bottom. Place the wrapped cones, spaced well apart, on a sheet pan lined with baking paper.

2. Place the French Meringue in a pastry bag with a no. 4 (8-mm) plain tip. Pipe the meringue around the cones in concentric circles, one on top of the other, starting the first circle on the baking paper at the base of the cone (Figure 14–1).

3. Bake the cones at 200°F (94°C) for about 3 hours or until they are completely dry.

4. Carefully remove the paper cones from the inside of the meringue baskets by pulling the plastic wrap away from the meringue all around the bottom and then pulling it out. Use a small, thin knife to trim the narrow end of the cones so that they are flat and the cones will stand straight once they are inverted to become baskets.

5. Brush melted coating chocolate on the inside of the cones to cover the bottom 1 inch (2.5 cm) of the narrow ends. This will reinforce the bottom so that the cones will be sturdier when filled. Dip the top rim of the cones into melted coating chocolate, moving them up and

NOTE 4: One-half of a recipe of Italian Cream requires one-eighth of a recipe of Italian Meringue; this is such a small quantity of meringue that it is not practical to make. Therefore, it makes sense to prepare a quarter-recipe of meringue and either discard half, use half for another project, or use the meringue to make a full recipe of Italian Cream and use the other half of the filling somewhere else.

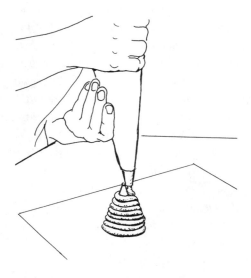

FIGURE 14–1   *Piping meringue around an inverted paper cone for Dacquoise Baskets*

down a few times over the bowl to remove all the excess, so the chocolate will not drip on the sides as the baskets are placed right-side up. Stand the cones on their narrow ends, and let the chocolate set up.

6. Pipe sixteen 1½-inch (3.7-cm) rounds of chocolate on a sheet of baking paper. Stand the cones in the center of the circles before the chocolate sets up.

7. Thicken ¾ cup (180 ml) of the melted coating chocolate by adding about 5 drops of Simple Syrup or enough to make the chocolate thick enough to hold its shape when piped. Place the thickened chocolate in a small pastry bag with a no. 0 (1-mm) plain tip. Pipe out twenty handles (allows extra for breakage) using the template (Figure 14–2) as a guide. (The template as shown is the correct size for use in this recipe. Trace the shape onto a piece of paper using a heavy pen. Place a sheet of baking paper on top of your drawing.) Pipe out a solid line following the curved edge of the template, followed by an intersecting wavy line on top, as shown in the color insert. Slide the baking paper to the side so an unused portion of baking paper is over the template and continue in the same manner until you have made twenty handles.

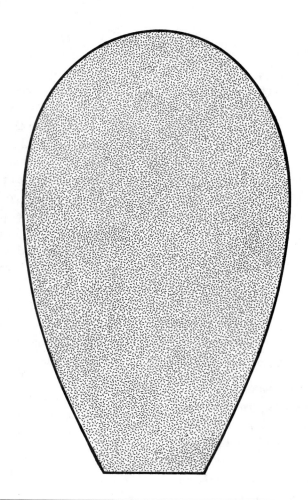

FIGURE 14–2   *The template used as a guide to pipe the chocolate handles for the baskets*

8. Refrigerate the handles and the baskets for a few minutes before removing them from the paper (see note 3).

9. Stir the raspberry juice or ¹/₃ cup (80 ml) Raspberry Sauce into the Italian Cream. Place in a pastry bag with a no. 6 (12-mm) plain tip and reserve in the refrigerator. Adjust the consistency of the Raspberry Sauce and Mango Coulis if needed so that each has the correct thickness and both are the same. Place the sauces in piping bottles.

10. Presentation: Pipe the cream filling into one of the baskets filling it to about ¹/₂ inch (1.2 cm) from the top (see note 1). Carefully push a handle into the cream. Top with raspberries. Pipe a 2-inch (5-cm) wide ring of Mango Coulis around the perimeter of a dessert plate. Fill the center with Raspberry Sauce, keeping the border where the two sauces meet circular. Use the blunt side of a wooden skewer to feather the sauces together (see Figure 19–31, page 1005). Place a filled basket in the center of the plate. Serve immediately.

Fresh Strawberries with Champagne Sabayon Sauce

16 servings; each serving contains approximately 200 calories and 4 grams of fat

3 pounds, 12 ounces (1 kg, 705 g) strawberries, perfectly ripe

2 tablespoons (30 ml) curaçao liqueur

two recipes Sabayon, made with champagne (page 718)

Candied Lime Peels (page 978)

It is hard to imagine not having access to fresh strawberries in the pastry kitchen, yet it hasn't been all that long (relatively speaking) since they were strictly a summer fruit. Today, and especially so in California, strawberries are not only available but affordable throughout the year, in large part to due to the lower cost of air freight. Among the dozen or so recipes in this text that feature strawberries in the spotlight are the old favorites Strawberries Romanoff, Strawberry Shortcake, Strawberry Ice Cream, and Strawberry-Rhubarb Tart, but aside from eating them right out of your hand, this recipe is definitely the one to choose when you have access to perfect, fully ripe, red, sweet berries. This classical and refreshing dessert is both simple and fast; it can be made from start to finish in less than 30 minutes. Although strawberries are the most traditional choice for topping with hot Sabayon (many of us have seen the dish prepared in a few minutes sitting at the counter of an exhibition-style kitchen), most other soft fresh fruits can also be paired successfully—berries, figs, or apricots, for example. Another variation on this dessert that has become popular is to arrange the fruit on a plate, top with Sabayon, and then place the dish under a salamander to gratinée the top (see Apricot Gratin with Sabayon of Muscat Wine, page 684 and Blood Orange Gratin, page 687).

1. Clean the strawberries and reserve sixteen of the largest and most attractive berries. Cut the remaining strawberries into ¹/₂-inch (1.2-cm) chunks. Macerate the cut strawberries in the curaçao liqueur for at least 1 hour, tossing gently from time to time. Cut the reserved berries into thin slices lengthwise.

2. Presentation: Line the sides of sixteen 6-ounce (180-ml) saucer-type champagne glasses with the sliced strawberries, placing the cut sides against the glass. Divide the macerated berries evenly between the glasses. Pour hot Sabayon on top. Decorate with the Candied Lime Peels and serve immediately.

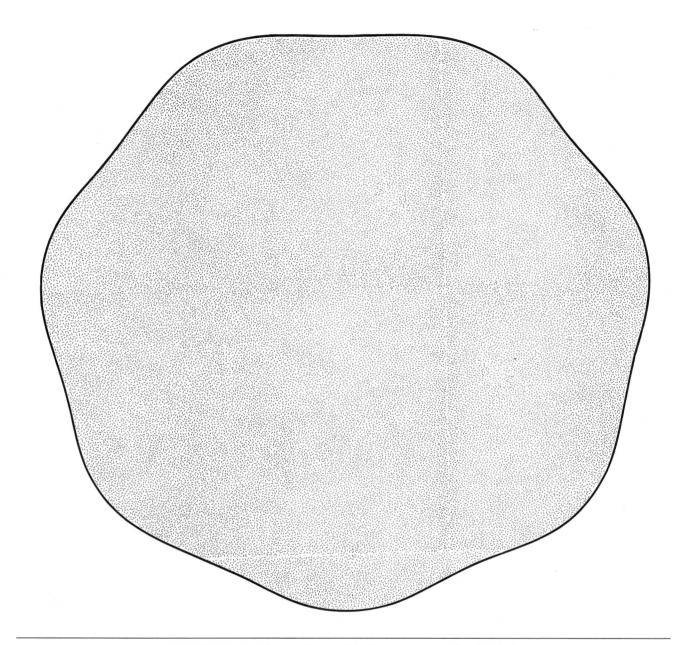

FIGURE 14–3   *The template used in the presentation of Fruit Salad*

Fruit Salad

16 servings; each serving contains approximately 200 calories and 0 grams of fat

12 cups (21, 880 ml) prepared fresh fruit, approximately (see step one)

*S*erving a fruit salad at the end of a meal is one of the least time-consuming options for dessert, surpassed only by simply serving assorted pieces of whole fresh fruit in a basket. In addition to using fresh fruit in dessert salads, it is incorporated into appetizer salad course offerings now more than ever in the form of greens with citrus segments, pears, or fresh cherries, for example, or fruit and vegetable slaws. These combinations are especially welcome on today's lighter menus. The old-fashioned fruit cocktail and that erstwhile favorite—the canned peach half with a scoop of cottage cheese(!)—have thankfully disap-

one-half recipe Orange Sauce
(page 1077), freshly made
and still warm

$1/4$ cup (60 ml) orange liqueur

6 ounces (170 g) strawberry preserves

powdered sugar

sixteen mint sprigs

peared from the restaurant scene. I can certainly recall when it was common-place in both the pastry and garde manger kitchens to use canned mixed fruit in numerous presentations, and although there are times when canned fruit can be perfectly acceptable, in that case the color of the fruit was invariably faded and the individual flavors of the various components barely recognizable. As simple as it is, a fresh fruit salad made with top-quality, ripe, seasonal ingredients can be visually appealing, delicious, and a very healthy alternative.

1. Choose seasonal ripe fruit for the filling, such as apricots, peaches, orange and grapefruit segments, bananas, kiwis, and melons. Cut the fruit into chunks approximately $3/4$ inch (2 cm) in size. Do not cut thin slices or roughly chop the fruit, but try instead to make the pieces uniform and attractive. Use a melon-ball cutter for the melons. If using bananas, coat the pieces lightly with lime or lemon juice to prevent oxidation. Use blueberries, raspberries, or cut strawberries in the presentation, but do not include them in the mixture because they will stain the other pieces.

2. Prepare the Orange Sauce and then add the orange liqueur. Gently fold the prepared fruit into the sauce while the sauce is still warm. Place in the refrigerator and allow the fruit to chill in the sauce. Do not leave it any longer than 2 to 3 hours or the fruit will begin to fall apart.

3. Force the strawberry preserves through a fine sieve. Cover and set aside.

4. Make the template shown in Figure 14–3. The template is the correct size for this recipe, but it can be altered to better fit a particular plate. It should lie flat on the base of your dessert plate, and there should be some room between the template and the perimeter of the base (not the rim). Trace the drawing, then cut the template out of $1/16$-inch (2-mm) cardboard (cake boxes work fine). Attach a small loop of tape in the center to aid in lifting the template off the plate.

5. Place some of the reserved jam in a piping bag and cut a small opening.

6. Presentation: Place the template in the center of a dessert plate. Lightly sift powdered sugar over the exposed part of the plate, including the rim. Carefully remove the template. Pipe a thin string of strawberry jam next to the powdered sugar following the outline left by the template. Arrange approximately $3/4$ cup (180 ml) of the well-chilled fruit and sauce mixture attractively within the border of jam, letting the sauce flow out to the edge of the jam but not over it. Decorate the top of the fruit salad with a few fresh raspberries, blueberries, or cut strawberries and a mint sprig. Be careful not to get fingerprints on the powdered sugar border when serving.

Fruit Valentines

16 servings; each serving contains approximately 300 calories and 2 grams of fat

one-half recipe French Meringue
(page 590)

dark coating chocolate, melted

2 tablespoons (30 ml) orange liqueur

1/4 cup (60 ml) Simple Syrup
(page 11)

3 pounds (1 kg, 365 g) well-chilled
fresh fruit prepared as described in
the introduction

Sour Cream Mixture for Piping
(page 1081)

Raspberry Sauce (page 1080)

This tempting light dessert should not be limited only to Valentine's Day or Mother's Day but is appropriate anytime you need a simple yet elegant presentation for low-calorie fresh fruit. Use a colorful mixture featuring at least three different types of fruits and/or berries. A nice combination is blueberries or blackberries, raspberries, strawberries, and kiwis or honeydew melons. Cut the fruit into small pieces, making them about the same size as the berries (leave berries, other than strawberries, whole). Keep each variety covered separately in the refrigerator until you are ready to assemble a dessert to prevent the fruits from staining one another, which detracts from the presentation. If you can afford a few more calories, try filling the shells with frozen yogurt before adding the fruit mixture. The frozen yogurt may be placed in the shells ahead of time and the filled shells can be reserved in the freezer to top with fruit to order.

1. Make the Fruit Valentine Template (Figure 14–4). The template as shown is the correct size for use in this recipe. Trace the drawing, then cut the template out of 1/4-inch (6-mm) thick cardboard, such as corrugated cardboard used for cake rounds. Draw sixteen hearts on two sheets of baking paper (eight on each), tracing around the inside of the template. Reserve.

2. Invert two sheet pans and cover the back of the pans with additional baking paper (not the paper with the tracing). Fasten the papers to the pans with a little meringue to keep them from slipping. Form eight meringue hearts on each pan, spreading the meringue flat and even within the template (see Figures 19–55 and 19–56, pages 1046 and 1047).

3. Place the remaining meringue in a pastry bag with a no. 3 (6-mm) plain tip. Pipe two ropes of meringue, one on top of the other, around the edge of the hearts.

4. Invert two more sheet pans and attach the reserved baking papers as before, inverting the papers so the tracing is on the bottom. Place a no 2. (4-mm) plain tip on the outside of the pastry bag, and hold it in place as you pipe (see Figures 12–6 and 12–7, pages 1046 and 1047). Pipe a border of meringue around the traced hearts, then pipe four diagonal lines across the inside of each one, attaching the lines to the frame on either end.

5. Bake all of the meringue at 200°F (94°C) for approximately 2 hours or until dried through. Remove the thinner hearts (the lids) sooner if they begin to show color. Let the meringues cool completely.

6. Place a small amount of melted coating chocolate in a piping bag and cut a small opening. Streak the chocolate in diagonal lines at right angles to the lines of meringue, on the thinner hearts (Figure 14–5).

7. Combine the orange liqueur and the Simple Syrup.

FIGURE 14–4 *The template used to form the base of the meringue shells for Fruit Valentines*

8. Presentation: Place ¾ cup (180 ml) of mixed prepared fruit in a small bowl. Add a little of the orange syrup and toss gently to coat. Pipe a small dot of Sour Cream Mixture in the center of the upper half of a dessert plate. Place a meringue case on top. Fill the case with the fruit filling, mounding it on top and letting it spill out onto the plate on one side. Place a lid leaning against the other side of the filled heart. Pour a small pool of Raspberry Sauce in front of the dessert, and decorate the sauce with the Sour Cream Mixture for piping (see pages 998 to 1006). Serve immediately.

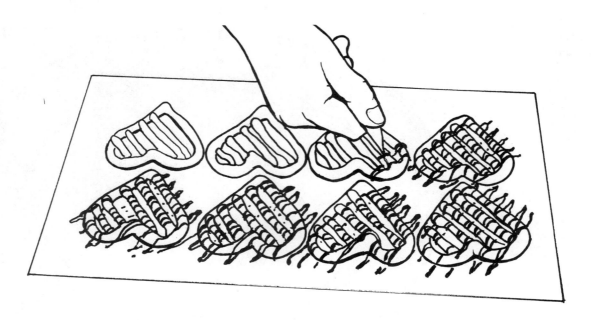

FIGURE 14–5   *Streaking chocolate over the baked meringue lids*

Kardinals with Sambuca-Scented Italian Cream and Fresh Fruit

16 servings; each serving contains approximately 350 calories and 10 grams of fat

one-quarter recipe French Meringue (page 590)

one-half recipe Ladyfingers batter (page 275)

2 teaspoons (6 g) unflavored gelatin powder

¹/₄ cup (60 ml) cold water

one recipe Italian Cream (page 1087) (see note 1)

¹/₄ cup (60 ml) sambuca liqueur

unsweetened cocoa powder

2 pounds (910 g) prepared fresh fruit, approximately (see note 2)

In this recipe meringue and sponge batter are piped out together, baked until featherlight, dry, and crumbly, and then filled with sambuca cream. Italian meringue in the filling makes it light, palatable, and merciful on your waistline, while the anise-flavored liqueur creates a nice bridge between the cream and the slightly acidic fresh fruit. I like this dessert just as well when it is one day old, after the sponge and meringue sheets have absorbed moisture from the filling and become a bit chewy. If you wish, try serving Kardinals with Honey-Vanilla Frozen Yogurt (page 645).

1. Draw four 3³/₄-inch (9.3-cm) wide strips, evenly spaced across the width, on a sheet of baking paper. Invert the paper on a sheet pan. Place the meringue in a pastry bag with a no. 8 (16-mm) plain tip. Pipe three ropes of meringue lengthwise within each of the marked strips, piping two along the outside edges and the third down the center so there is equal space on either side of the center strip (Figure 14–6).

2. Squeeze any remaining meringue out of the bag and discard. Place the Ladyfingers batter in the same pastry bag. Pipe two ropes of batter per strip, piping them between the meringue ropes.

3. Bake at 210–220°F (99–104°C) until both batters are dry and the Ladyfingers have turned golden brown, approximately 2 hours. Let the strips cool.

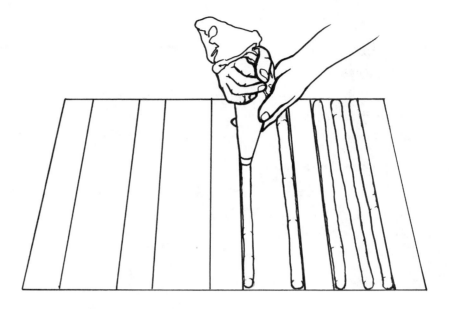

FIGURE 14–6   Piping three evenly-spaced ropes of meringue in each section between the lines drawn as a guide on a sheet of baking paper

NOTE 1: Make the Italian Cream as directed, adding ¼ cup (60 ml) sambuca liqueur to the whipping cream.

NOTE 2: Use four or five varieties of fruit cut into distinct pieces (not chopped or sliced thinly). Reserve each type of fruit separately in a covered bowl until serving time.

4. Sprinkle the gelatin over the cold water and set aside to soften.

5. When the meringue and Ladyfinger strips are cold, invert and peel the paper from the back. Turn the strips right-side up and place on a sheet of cardboard or on an inverted sheet pan.

6. Heat the gelatin mixture to dissolve. Quickly mix the gelatin into one-fourth of the Italian Cream. Then, still working quickly, mix this into the remaining cream. Select the two best-looking meringue and Ladyfinger strips to use for the tops. Place the Italian Cream mixture in a pastry bag with a no. 8 (16-mm) plain tip and pipe it over the other two strips, using all of it. Set the top strips on the cream and press down lightly to be sure they adhere. Cover and refrigerate for at least 2 hours or, preferably, overnight.

7. Make a 6-inch (15-cm) round stencil. Attach the stencil to an appropriately sized bottomless pie tin (see page 1040 for more information). Reserve.

8. Cut the chilled dessert strips into eight pieces each. The servings will be approximately 1³/₄ inches (4.5 cm) wide.

9. Presentation: Place the stencil against the base of a dessert plate. Sift cocoa powder lightly over the top and at the same time over a dessert slice (not on the plate). Carefully remove the template and place the slice in the center of the cocoa round. Arrange pieces of fresh fruit around the cocoa on the base of the plate.

Lemon Chiffon Pouches

16 servings; each serving contains approximately 225 calories and 11 grams of fat

one-half recipe Crepes batter
    (page 5)
oranges
Lemon Chiffon Filling (recipe follows)
one recipe Strawberry Sauce
    (page 1081)

NOTE: Should the calorie count not be an issue, use two pouches per serving.

FIGURE 14–7 Tying Lemon Chiffon Pouches closed with strips of orange rind

*T*he technique of filling Crepes and shaping them into appealing little pouches can be used to create other desserts and is also popular in the hot kitchen, where in addition to Crepes, round sheets of pasta are also used as holders. When made with a savory filling the pouches are usually secured with a strip of blanched scallion or chive. Phyllo dough can be used for the wrappers as well and is obviously paired with fillings that can be baked. To make pouches using phyllo dough, follow the instructions in the recipe for Asian Pear Tart (page 685) steps three through six, using only four sheets of dough in each stack. Gather the edges of the dough together after placing the filling in the center, then twist and pinch closed above the filling but below the edges of the dough. Be certain they are securely closed, especially if you use a filling which will expand in the oven; you may need to use a little Egg Wash on the inside or tie the pouches closed. Brush butter over the outside of the dough before baking. A nice stuffing for the phyllo dough pouches is Chunky Apple Filling (page 1085). Serve these hot placed in a pool of Vanilla Custard Sauce (page 1082) and topped with a sprinkling of cinnamon and powdered sugar. As a variation on the following recipe try filling the Crepe pouches with berries instead of, or in addition to, the Lemon Chiffon Filling. Insert one or two small berries in the center of the filling before tying the pouches closed, or use all berries for a dessert even lower in calories.*

1. Make sixteen 7-inch (17.5-cm) Crepes, following the directions with the recipe. Make sure the Crepes are thin, as well as uniform in size and shape. If they are not round, place a plate or other round object of the correct size on top and trim the edges. Cover and reserve.

2. Using a citrus stripper, cut sixteen 8-inch (20-cm) strips of orange rind to use as strings to tie the pouches closed. Reserve.

3. Center the Crepes on top of 3-inch (7.5-cm) diameter soufflé ramekins (or other forms of approximately equal size) with the nicest side on the bottom. Push the center of the Crepes into the forms.

4. When the Lemon Filling has started to set slightly, place it in a pastry bag with a no. 6 (12-mm) plain tip. Pipe the filling on top of the Crepes, dividing it equally between the forms. Working with one at a time, bring up the sides of the Crepes, lift them out of the forms, and tie them closed with the orange rind (Figure 14–7). Place on a sheet pan lined with baking paper, cover, and refrigerate until serving time, but no longer than a few hours.

5. Place a portion of the Strawberry Sauce in a piping bottle.

6. **Presentation:** Pipe a 5-inch (12.5-cm) circle of Strawberry Sauce in the center of a dessert plate. Do not cover the entire base of the plate. Place a pouch in the center of the sauce. Serve immediately.

Lemon Chiffon Filling

approximately 4 cups (960 ml)

1/2 cup (120 ml) lemon juice

2 teaspoons (12 g) finely grated lemon zest

3 eggs

1/3 cup (80 ml) water

3 1/2 ounces (100 g) granulated sugar

1 tablespoon (9 g) unflavored gelatin powder

1/4 cup (60 ml) cold water

3/4 cup (180 ml) heavy cream

1. Combine the lemon juice and grated lemon zest. Set aside.

2. Whip the eggs until they are thick and light in color. Combine the first measurement of water with the sugar and boil until the syrup reaches 230°F (110°C). Pour the hot syrup into the whipped eggs in a steady stream. Continue whipping until the mixture is cold.

3. Sprinkle the gelatin over the cold water and set aside to soften.

4. Whip the heavy cream to soft peaks. Combine the egg mixture, whipped cream, and lemon juice with zest.

5. Place the gelatin mixture over a bain-marie and heat until dissolved. Do not overheat. Place about one-fourth of the cream mixture in a separate bowl and rapidly mix in the dissolved gelatin; quickly mix this into the remaining cream.

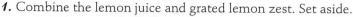

Low-Cholesterol Sponge Cake

one 10-inch (25-cm) sponge cake or 12 servings; each serving contains approximately 195 calories and 3.5 grams of fat

5 ounces (140 g) cake flour

1 1/2 ounces (40 g) arrowroot

16 egg whites (2 cups/480 ml)

a few drops of lemon juice

10 ounces (285 g) granulated sugar

1 teaspoon (5 ml) vanilla extract

2 ounces (55 g) melted unsalted butter

NOTE: To make a Chocolate Low-Cholesterol Sponge Cake, replace 1 1/2 ounces of the cake flour with unsweetened cocoa powder.

This cake bears a close resemblance to Angel Food Cake. Although not quite as featherlight, it is much easier to make. Using this cake as a base, you can create many light variations of desserts in this book. To make a lower-fat version of Lemon Chiffon Cake, for example, use this sponge and the less rich Lemon Chiffon Filling from the preceding recipe, following the directions for assembly on page 342 with the Lemon Chiffon Cake recipe. Do not ice the cake with whipped cream and omit the chocolate decorations on the side. Instead, spread the Pectin or Lemon Glaze directly on top of the Lemon Filling and pipe a small rosette of whipped cream at the edge of each slice. For a second variation of that cake, substitute the Lychee Bavarois (see page 704) for the Lemon Filling and replace the glaze with Red Currant Glaze (see page 1017). Or create a delightful cream cake by filling and icing this sponge with Italian Cream (see page 1087) and decorating the top with seasonal fruit.

1. Line the bottom of a 10-inch (25-cm) round cake pan with baking paper. Set aside.

2. Sift the cake flour and the arrowroot together twice. Reserve.

3. Whip the egg whites until they have tripled in volume. While continuing to whip at high speed, add the lemon juice and then gradually incorporate the sugar. Whip until the meringue holds stiff peaks. Carefully fold in the flour mixture, and then gently incorporate the vanilla and the melted butter. Pour the batter into the prepared pan.

4. Bake at 350°F (175°C) for approximately 20 minutes or until the center of the cake springs back when pressed lightly. Dust flour over the top and invert onto a paper-lined sheet pan to cool.

Lychee Charlotte Royal

16 servings; each serving contains approximately 350 calories and 10 grams of fat

one-half recipe Almond Sponge batter (page 270)
8 ounces (225 g) smooth raspberry jam
Lychee Bavarois (recipe follows)
Red Currant Glaze (page 1017)
one-half recipe Raspberry Sauce (page 1080)

Lychees are not only the most famous but I would guess also the most popular of all Chinese fruits. Around ten years ago when I traveled to China with two other chefs, Jacques Pepin and Cindy Pawlcyn, to teach Western-style cooking, it seems like lychees and either mandarins or oranges were (unfortunately) just about the extent of what we were served for dessert, although after some of the incredible banquets that included twenty and even thirty courses, that was plenty!

The wide spreading lychee tree has dense green foliage and loose clusters of fruit growing on long stems. Fresh lychees have a scarlet-colored knobby shell enclosing a firm, translucent, white or pinkish juicy pulp, which in turn surrounds a large brown inedible seed. Lychees are at their peak in June and July; to enjoy one fresh, peel from the stem down to keep the fruit in one piece. Lychees are also known as litchis and in their dried form are called lychee nuts. Fresh lychees can be difficult to find, but the fruit is commonly available canned in syrup.

This recipe was obviously inspired by an old classic—Charlotte Royal. To make the original version, follow the instructions for lining the forms as directed here and then fill with Classic Bavarian Cream (page 1085). For the presentation pipe a rosette of whipped cream on top of the charlotte and decorate the cream with a raspberry or slice of strawberry. This presentation can also be used for the Lychee Charlotte if you are not offering it as a light dessert.

1. Spread the sponge batter out evenly to ¼ inch (6 mm) from the edge on all sides of a 16-by-24-inch (40-×-60-cm) sheet of baking paper. Drag the paper onto a sheet pan (see Figure 16–15, page 842). Bake immediately at 425°F (219°C) for about 8 minutes or until just done. To prevent the thin sponge from drying out, slide it onto a second (cool) sheet pan or onto the table. Let cool.

2. Invert the sponge sheet onto a second sheet of baking paper, then peel the paper off the back. (If the sponge has been made ahead and refrigerated, the skin will become loose and must be removed from the top before the sponge is inverted.) Trim ½ inch (1.2 cm) from each long side of the sponge. Spread the raspberry jam on top; there should be just enough to cover the sponge and make it sticky. Roll the sheet lengthwise into a tight rope following the directions for Yule Logs (see step 7, page 810). Place the sponge roll in the freezer to firm up and make it easier to slice while you are making the Lychee Bavarois.

3. Cut the firm sponge roll into slices ⅛ inch (3 mm) thick. Use the slices to line the bottom and sides of deep, round bavarois molds, or other suitable molds (appropriately shaped coffee cups work great) with an approximate capacity of ½ cup (120 ml), placing one slice in the bottom of each mold and four slices around the sides. Fill the molds with Lychee Bavarois as soon as it shows signs of thickening. Refrigerate for at least 2 hours to set.

4. Unmold as many charlottes as you anticipate serving the same day by gently pressing the back of a spoon around the edge on top of each one to loosen the filling, and then invert onto a sheet pan lined with baking paper (you may need to dip the forms in hot water briefly, but be careful not to melt the bavarois). Brush Red Currant Glaze over the jelly roll slices. Reserve in the refrigerator until needed.

5. Place a portion of the Raspberry Sauce in a piping bottle.

6. Presentation: Place a Lychee Charlotte Royal in the center of a dessert plate. Pipe Raspberry Sauce around the dessert.

 **VARIATION**

This method creates horizontal stripes of sponge and jam on the sides of the charlottes.

1. Make a full recipe of Almond Sponge batter and make a second sponge sheet the same size as the first. Make one sheet into a jelly roll as directed above. Weigh out an additional 8 ounces (225 g) of jam. Use souffle ramekins that are 3¹/₂ inches (8.7 cm) in diameter and have a 5-ounce (150-ml) capacity instead of the bavarois molds.

2. Invert and remove the paper from the second sponge sheet. Cut a rectangle approximately 8¹/₂ inches (21.2 cm) wide and the length of the sheet. Adjust the width, if necessary, so that it matches the circumference of the inside of the ramekins you are using. Reserve the remaining piece of sponge.

3. Cut the rectangle across into four equal pieces, each approximately 8¹/₂ by 5³/₄ inches (21.2 × 14.5 cm). Cut two more pieces the same size from the reserved piece of sponge. Save the remainder for another use.

4. Stack the pieces, layering raspberry jam between them. Place in the freezer to make the sponge firm and easier to slice.

5. Use thin, ¹/₈-inch (3-mm), slices of the roulade (the rolled sponge sheet) to line the bottom of the ramekins. (You will have some of the roulade left; wrap and reserve in the freezer for another use.) Cut ¹/₈-inch (3-mm) slices lengthwise from the layered sponge strip and use these pieces to line the sides of the ramekins. (A serrated knife dipped in hot water works best for slicing.)

6. Fill the lined ramekins and follow the instructions in the main recipe.

Lychee Bavarois

7 cups (1 l, 680 ml)

8 egg yolks (²/₃ cup/160 ml)

2 ounces (55 g) granulated sugar

2 tablespoons (18 g) unflavored gelatin powder

¹/₂ cup (120 ml) cold water

2 cups (480 ml) strained lychee juice (see instructions in note)

one vanilla bean, split lengthwise

or

1 teaspoon (5 ml) vanilla extract

1 cup (240 ml) heavy cream

one-quarter recipe Swiss Meringue (page 592)

NOTE: Your chances of finding fresh lychees are limited by where you live and the time of year. And if you are lucky enough to find them fresh, it would be a shame to purée this exceptional and fragrant fruit, especially since the canned variety works just fine in this recipe. You will need approximately 3 pounds (1 kg, 365 g) of canned lychees to get 2 cups (480 ml) of strained juice. Strain the canned lychees and reserve the liquid. Purée the fruit and pass it through a fine sieve. Add the reserved liquid if needed to make 2 cups (480 ml) of juice. The recipe presumes you are using lychees canned in sugar syrup.

1. Whip the egg yolks and sugar until light and fluffy. Reserve.

2. Sprinkle the gelatin over the cold water and set aside to soften.

3. Bring the lychee purée to the scalding point with the vanilla bean, if used. Gradually pour the hot liquid into the yolk mixture while whipping rapidly. Return the mixture to the heat and bring back to the scalding point, stirring constantly. Do not boil. Remove from the heat, stir in the reserved gelatin, and set aside to cool, stirring from time to time.

4. Whip the cream to soft peaks. Remove the vanilla bean from the custard and save for another use, or add the vanilla extract if used. Gradually stir the whipped cream into the Swiss Meringue. When the custard has cooled, slowly stir it into the cream and meringue mixture.

Marbled Cheesecake with Quark

one 10-inch (25-cm) cake or 16 servings; each serving contains approximately 350 calories and 11 grams of fat

¹/₄ cup (60 ml) vegetable oil

8 ounces (225 g) Graham Cracker Crumbs (page 8)

1 pound, 5 ounces (595 g) quark cheese

*Q*uark is a continental-style fresh cheese that is similar to the cottage cheese found in the United States. This curd cheese is slightly more acidic than cottage cheese but just as low in fat and calories, typically containing about 1 gram of fat and 85 calories per 3¹/₂-ounce (100-g) serving. Quark is immensely popular in Germany, accounting for almost half of the cheese consumption there, with the majority of it being used in cooking. In addition to the obvious application of cheesecake, quark is used in a number of different German cakes, including the delicious quarksahnetorte (quark and cream cake), and is also an ingredient in dishes such as quark apfelkuchen (quark apple pie) or quark pfannkuchen (quark pancakes). When some of the fat that is skimmed off during the processing of the cheese is added back to the lean curd at the end, the cheese is called speisequark. This enriched type of quark is sold plain or mixed

12 ounces (340 g) low-fat cream
  cheese, at room temperature
14 ounces (400 g) granulated sugar
1 tablespoon (15 ml) vanilla extract
6 eggs
1½ ounces (40 g) unsweetened cocoa
  powder, sifted
1 ounce (30 g) powdered sugar, sifted
¼ cup (60 ml) water

NOTE: If the cake is not baked long enough for the plain filling to turn golden on top, the top of the cake will stick to the plastic when the cheesecake is inverted.

with fruit and fruit pulp, very much like the way we are used to seeing yogurt packaged in this country. Quark is often available in ethnic markets, but if you are unable to find it, low-fat cottage cheese can be substituted in this recipe with good results. You can replace up to half of the cream cheese in this recipe with drained nonfat yogurt (see note 2, page 2) to bring the calorie and fat counts down even lower.

1. Combine the vegetable oil and Graham Cracker Crumbs and pat the mixture evenly over the bottom of a 10-inch (25-cm) cake pan with 2-inch (5-cm) sides.

2. Place the quark in a food processor and process until it is completely smooth, scraping down the sides and bottom of the processor bowl once or twice. Beat the cream cheese for a few seconds using the paddle attachment in an electric mixer, just until the cream cheese is smooth. Add the quark cheese to the cream cheese and mix until the two are combined. Add the sugar and vanilla, then gradually incorporate the eggs on medium speed, scraping down the bowl several times to ensure there are no lumps in the batter. Be careful not to overmix.

3. Combine the cocoa powder and powdered sugar in a small bowl. Add the water and stir to make a smooth paste. Incorporate the paste into 2 cups (480 ml) of the cheesecake batter and reserve.

4. Set aside 1 cup (240 ml) of the plain batter. Pour the remaining plain batter into the prepared pan. Pour the chocolate batter in the center, making a 6-inch (15-cm) circle on top of the plain batter. Pour the remaining plain batter in the center on top of the chocolate batter; you should see three rings of batter. Use a spoon to swirl the batters together into a marble pattern, using your imagination; do not mix too much. Place the pan into a hotel pan or other suitable baking dish and add hot water to come halfway up the sides.

5. Bake at 350°F (175°C) for about 45 minutes or until the cake is set and golden on the top (see note). Carefully remove the cake pan from the bain-marie and set it aside to cool at room temperature. Once the cake has cooled, cover it and place in the refrigerator for at least 4 hours or, preferably, overnight. The cake can be kept refrigerated for up to three days at this point.

6. To unmold the cake, stretch a sheet of plastic film over the top of the cake pan, place a cardboard cake circle on top of the plastic, and then invert the cake. Remove the pan. Place a second cake cardboard on top of the inverted cake (on the bottom) and invert again to place the cake right-side up on the cardboard. Carefully peel away the plastic film without damaging the top of the cake. Cut the cake into sixteen servings, using a thin, sharp knife dipped into hot water and wiped clean between each cut.

Minola Tangelo Givré with Toasted Meringue and Cookie Citrus Rind

12 servings; each serving contains approximately 290 calories and 5 grams of fat

twelve Minola tangelos
Simple Syrup (page 11)
water
one-half recipe Italian Meringue
   (page 591)
twelve Cookie Figurines (page 1054)
twelve Cookie Citrus Rinds
   (page 1054) (see note)
powdered sugar
1 pint (480 ml) fresh raspberries

NOTE: Make the Cookie Citrus Rinds slightly smaller in diameter than specified in the recipe.

The terms "givré" or "frosted" are used to describe a frozen fruit shell that has been filled with a sorbet or ice made from the removed fruit pulp, for example "lemon givré" or "frosted tangerines." The most commonly used fruits for these presentations are those in the citrus family, including lemons, grapefruits, oranges, mandarins, and, as in this recipe, tangelos, but melon is also a good choice. Because the whole fruit is used in the presentation, it is important to select it carefully (avoid bruises or other imperfections in the shell) and to choose fruit that is evenly shaped.

To make the givré, the top is sliced off the whole fruit and is reserved to use later as a lid. The shell is then hollowed out using a spoon or a melon-ball cutter. Again, be careful at this point not to damage the skin or rind of the fruit shell and also take care not to scrape any of the bitter white pith into the flesh that will be used for the filling. The hollow shells are frozen while the filling is prepared; in the classic version the filling is always a sorbet, but ice cream can also be used. The frozen shells are then filled with the mixture either by scooping it into the shells and flattening the surface, if it is to be topped with meringue as in this version, or by piping the filling into the shells decoratively using a plain or star tip in the pastry bag, finishing with a design on top. If meringue is used it is piped or spread over the filling and then quickly browned using a salamander or propane torch. The reserved lids are set on the tops at an angle to reveal the filling.

If you are able to obtain tangelos (or mandarins) with the stems on and a few leaves attached, try this pretty variation: Fill the fruit shells with sorbet to within 1/8 inch (3 mm) of the top and return to the freezer along with the lids. Remove the rind from one or two additional tangelos or mandarins and cut 1/8-inch (3-mm) round slices that are about the same diameter as the top of the filled givrés. To serve, place one of the slices of fruit on top of the filled givré (the idea is that it gives the appearance of the natural fruit the way it would look if you just cut the top off), pipe a small rosette of whipped cream to one side on the fruit slice, and set the lid on the cream at an angle to reveal the top. Serve immediately.

1. Wash the tangelos. Cut off approximately one-quarter from the top end. Cut just enough from the opposite end, if necessary, so that each tangelo will stand straight and level. Working over a bowl, use a melon-ball cutter to carefully remove the flesh from the inside of the shells and from the pieces removed from the tops. As you are removing the flesh, keep the shells intact and attractive to use in the presentation. Discard the tops. Cover the shells and place in the freezer.

2. Squeeze as much juice as possible from the tangelo flesh. Strain through a fine mesh strainer. Discard the seeds and the pulp. Measure the juice. Add an equal amount of Simple Syrup. Add enough water to bring the mixture to between 16 and 20° Baumé (see page 646).

3. Process in an ice-cream freezer following the manufacturer's directions. Transfer to a chilled container.

4. Fill the reserved tangelo shells with the tangelo sorbet, spreading it even on the top. Cover, then place the filled shells in the freezer for at least 1 hour.

5. Place the Italian Meringue in a pastry bag with a no. 8 (16-mm) plain tip. Pipe a large mound of meringue on top of the sorbet in each tangelo shell. Use a small spoon to create a rough surface with peaks and swirls and, at the same time, be certain that all of the sorbet is covered by meringue. Return the shells to the freezer until time of service.

6. **Presentation:** Remove a Tangelo *Givré* from the freezer. Sift powdered sugar lightly over the meringue. Brown the meringue by placing the tangelo shell under a salamander or broiler, or by using a propane torch in a sweeping motion. Place the tangelo shell in the center of a dessert plate. Push a Cookie Figurine into the meringue on top of the dessert. Push the tail end of a Cookie Citrus Rind into the meringue next to the figurine, then arrange the rest of the rind carefully so it sits on top of the meringue and trails down to the plate. Sift powdered sugar over the dessert and the plate. Sprinkle six to eight raspberries around the base of the plate and serve immediately.

Oeufs à la Neige with a Caramelized Sugar Sphere

12 servings; each serving contains approximately 380 calories and 3 grams of fat

6 cups (1 l, 440 ml) lowfat (1%) milk
14 egg whites (1³/₄ cups/420 ml)
1 pound (455 g) granulated sugar
2 teaspoons (10 ml) vanilla extract
Light Vanilla Custard Sauce (recipe follows)
twelve Caramelized Sugar Spheres (directions follow)
fresh edible flower petals

Oeufs à la Neige, *which translates to "snow eggs" in English, is very close to, and more times than not confused with, Floating Islands (*île flottante*). One can easily see why: In both desserts fluffy, soft meringue floats on top of a light custard sauce. The main difference is that floating islands consists of one large round "island" which is baked before it is set forth upon the sea of custard; this can be an individual portion or a meringue large enough to serve four guests. In oeufs à la neige, the beaten egg whites are formed into small, egg-shaped pieces, three or four per serving, and are poached rather than baked. The old-fashioned French version of floating islands did not use meringue at all, but instead, rounds of sponge cake, moistened with liqueur or spread with jam and then topped with a layer of whipped cream, were served in a pool of custard sauce.*

Do not be too generous when shaping the snow eggs; they will increase in size considerably as they poach. Snow eggs can be poached in advance and reserved in one layer, preferably on top of the custard or in about one inch of milk, in a shallow pan in the refrigerator. Be certain to place the Caramel Sphere so that it rests on the meringue. If the thin strings of Spun Sugar are placed in the sauce, or come into contact with the sauce, the caramel will melt into the custard within a few minutes.

1. Follow the usual procedures for making meringue and whip the egg whites until they have tripled in volume. Gradually add the sugar and then the vanilla and continue whipping until the meringue holds stiff peaks, but be careful not to overwhip.

2. Pour the milk into a 10-inch (25-cm) sauté pan and bring to a simmer.

3. Using two soup spoons dipped in cold water to prevent the meringue from sticking, shape 2-inch (5-cm) ovals of meringue (the same shape as a quenelle) and drop each one carefully into the milk as it is formed. Do not crowd the pan; poach only as many at one time as will fit without touching. Poach the meringue ovals for 3 to 4 minutes, turn carefully, and cook the other side for approximately the same length of time. Remove using a slotted spoon and drain on a towel. Remove any skin that forms on the surface of the milk. Continue shaping and poaching the remaining meringue in the same manner. Measure 4½ cups (1 l, 80 ml) of the poaching milk to use in making the sauce. Discard the remainder. Set the meringues aside until serving time. Refrigerate if longer than 1 hour (see introduction).

4. Presentation: Pour ⅓ cup (80 ml) of Light Vanilla Custard Sauce on the base of a deep dessert plate. Arrange three meringue ovals on top of the sauce evenly spaced, forming a circle in the center of the plate. Place a Sugar Sphere on the meringues in the center of the plate. Sprinkle flower petals over the meringue.

Light Vanilla Custard Sauce

5½ cups (1 l, 320 ml)

4½ cups (1 l, 80 ml) low fat (1%) milk, reserved from preceding recipe
one vanilla bean, split lengthwise
   or
2 teaspoons (10 ml) vanilla extract
4 eggs
4 ounces (115 g) granulated sugar

1. Place the milk and the vanilla bean (if used) in a heavy-bottomed saucepan. Bring to scalding. Remove from the heat and let steep for 30 minutes. Remove the vanilla bean and set aside. (If you are not using the vanilla bean you may skip step one.)

2. Place the saucepan back on the stove and reheat the milk to simmering.

3. In an oversized bowl, whisk the eggs and sugar together until well combined. Gradually whisk in about one-third of the hot milk to temper the eggs. Then, still whisking constantly, add the remaining milk. Place the bowl over a bain-marie and heat, continuing to stir until the sauce has thickened enough to coat the back of a spoon. Do not heat to simmering or the eggs may curdle.

4. Immediately strain the sauce into a bowl. Scrape the seeds from the reserved vanilla bean into the sauce using the back of a paring knife and then discard the vanilla bean, or stir in the vanilla extract if using. Let cool, then store in the refrigerator.

Caramelized Sugar Spheres

12 decorations

one recipe Caramelized Spun Sugar (page 973)

When the humidity is close to 100 percent outside, it becomes virtually impossible to make Spun Sugar. If you have no choice, increase the glucose or corn syrup a little and prepare the sugar just before it will be served. Under good conditions, Spun Sugar can be prepared well in advance, provided it is placed in an airtight container and stored in a warm place with a dehumidifying agent.

1. Form the Caramelized Spun Sugar into loose balls about the size of an orange as you spin the sugar.

2. Place in an airtight container and set aside until needed.

Omelette Pancake with Sautéed Starfruit, Pomegranate Sauce, and Mango Coulis

16 servings; each serving contains approximately 320 calories and 12.5 grams of fat

2 pounds (910 g) starfruit (carambola) (about eight medium-sized) (see note 1)

1 cup (240 ml) water

8 ounces (225 g) granulated sugar

vegetable oil

Omelette Pancake Batter (recipe follows)

one recipe Mango Coulis (page 1075)

one recipe Pomegranate Sauce (page 1079)

Sour Cream Mixture for Piping (page 1081)

powdered sugar

NOTE 1: Starfruit vary considerably in size, and many times you do not have much of a choice. If you can not obtain medium-sized fruit (about 4 inches/10 cm long), smaller fruit will work fine. For aesthetic reasons, you should definitely avoid the large mango-sized starfruit for use in this recipe.

NOTE 2: This dessert should be made to order since the soufflé-type pancake will fall rather quickly. Although the taste is the same, they look so much more attractive when a bit puffy.

I created this version of a dessert omelette for a special event where the host requested a dessert that was unusual, light, seasonal, and did not contain chocolate. Since this was in the late fall when both starfruit and pomegranate (which are considered unusual to most people) are available, I used those. If these two are not in season when you want to make this dessert you can substitute any fruit that looks attractive when sliced, such as strawberries, kiwis, mangoes, or papaya. None of these need to be sautéed or poached as is done with the starfruit, and they should not be. (Actually, poaching is not really necessary with the starfruit either, but it adds some flavor since they tend to be rather bland without it; this is probably why starfruit are used primarily as a garnish.) Use either Raspberry or Strawberry Sauce instead of the Pomegranate Sauce when using these other fillings. Since Pomegranate Sauce is time-consuming to produce, you may want to make the substitution to save time even when pomegranates are available. If it is not possible to cook both the starfruit and the pancakes to order, you can precook all of the starfruit at once in the following manner: Bring the sugar and water to a boil (or use 1¹/₃ cups/320 ml Simple Syrup). Reduce to a simmer, add the starfruit slices, and poach for 2 minutes. Remove the slices, place in a shallow pan, and pour the cooking syrup on top. Set aside until needed. Do not do this too far ahead as the fruit starts to lose its juice once combined with the sugar, and the slices begin to look a little ragged.

1. Using a vegetable peeler, remove the hard (and often bruised) skin from the top of the five ridges on each starfruit. Slice the fruit across ¹/₄ inch (6 mm) thick. Reform the fruit, placing the cut sides of the slices together and including the end pieces, to keep the slices from drying out. Cover and reserve.

2. Combine the water and granulated sugar in a saucepan. Bring to a boil and boil for 2 minutes. Remove from the heat and set aside.

3. Brush a thin film of vegetable oil over a standard crepe pan. Heat the pan and then pour just over 1 cup (240 ml) of batter into the center. The batter is rather thick, so you will need to tilt the pan so that the batter covers the entire surface. Cook over medium heat for about 2 minutes. Turn the pancake over and cook the other side 1 minute longer. Slide the pancake out of the pan.

4. Just before you are ready to turn the pancake, place five to seven slices of starfruit (depending on size), including one end piece, in a separate skillet with 2 tablespoons (30 ml) of the sugar syrup. Bring to a boil while sautéing the fruit and cook for 1 minute. Remove from the heat. Place a portion of the Mango Coulis and a portion of the Pomegranate Sauce into separate piping bottles.

5. Presentation (see note 2): Pipe the Mango Coulis in a 1¹/₂ inch (3.7 cm) wide band on the bottom half of a dessert plate following the perimeter of the base. Pipe Pomegranate Sauce on the lower half of the base of the plate, leaving room for the pancake above. Pipe a line of Sour Cream Mixture for Piping along the border where the two sauces meet. Using a wooden skewer, feather the sauces together using a circular motion (see Figure 19–31, page 1005).

Arrange the cooked starfruit slices (reserving the end piece) along the lower edge of the pancake. Fold the top of the pancake over, covering the top half of the starfruit slices and leaving the bottom half of each slice visible. Dust powdered sugar over the top of the dessert and then carefully set it on the plate, partially on top of the Pomegranate Sauce, so that the fruit is in the sauce and a band of both Pomegranate Sauce and Mango Coulis is showing. Decorate the top of the omelette with the reserved end piece of starfruit. Serve immediately.

1. In a thick-bottomed saucepan, melt the butter and then mix in the flour, cornstarch, and salt to form a paste. Cook the roux, without browning, for 1 minute. Stir in the milk and bring the mixture to a boil while stirring constantly. Remove from the heat and stir until smooth.

2. Stir in the egg yolks a few at a time. Stir in the lemon zest.

3. Whip the egg whites and granulated sugar to soft peaks. Fold the egg whites into the milk mixture. Use immediately.

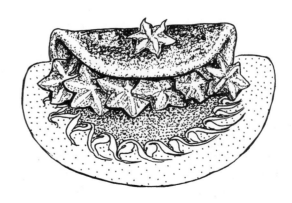

Omelette Pancake Batter

about sixteen 6-inch (15-cm) pancakes

4 ounces (115 g) unsalted butter
2 ounces (55 g) bread flour
2 ounces (55 g) cornstarch
1/2 teaspoon (2.5 g) salt
1 1/4 cups (300 ml) milk, at room
   temperature
8 eggs, separated
grated zest of three lemons
6 ounces (170 g) granulated sugar

NOTE: Do not whip and fold in the egg whites until you are ready to cook the pancakes. Prior to whipping the whites, the batter can be held for several hours or even overnight (refrigerated), if necessary.

"Out-of-Season" Fresh Fruit Baskets with Feijoa Sorbet

8 servings; each serving contains approximately 400 calories and 10 grams of fat

one-half recipe Vanilla Tulip Paste
   (page 1047)
1 1/2 teaspoons (4 g) cocoa powder,
   sifted
2 pounds (910 g) assorted fresh fruit
   as described in the introduction
Piping Chocolate (page 904), melted
1/4 cup (60 ml) orange liqueur

*T*his is a very interesting and attractive dish with a highly confusing title. The inspiration for this dessert comes from the fact that the seasonal availability of certain fresh fruits has literally been turned upside down in the last few years. All of the wonderful varieties of fruit and berries that reach their peak season around July and August in California are now available from the "down under" producers such as New Zealand and Australia, and South American countries such as Chile (among others), during our winter months, so we now have the opportunity to enjoy "summer" fruits twice a year. This increase in availability is due mainly to the jet age making air freight more affordable. Compared with the local product, the quality of the imported fruit suffers little or not at all from its long journey, since most commercially grown stone fruits, such as peaches, nectarines, apricots, and in some cases even plums, are picked and shipped before they are fully ripe anyway to avoid bruising. On the other hand, subtropical fruits such as feijoas, carambolas (starfruit), and the annonas, which include cherimoyas and their close relative the sweetsop or sugar apple, which previously were not found until late summer when they came from down under

¼ cup (60 ml) orange juice
one-half recipe Feijoa Sorbet
    (page 650)

(during their winter season), are now grown commercially in California and Florida and are not only readily available during our early winter months but are also very affordable. So, the idea here is that you can not only put together an unusual mix of fruit that previously would have been impossible, because they were not all available simultaneously, but you can also offer this dessert at two different times of the year, either combining our fresh local summer fruit with imported winter varieties, or our fresh local winter fruits with imported summer varieties. In any case, use a mixture of both berries and soft fruit and include four to six types with contrasting colors for the best effect. Do not chop the fruit; cut each variety according to its own particular shape, but keep all of the pieces roughly the same size.

You may find it difficult to handle and form the large cookie bowls at first, but with practice you will soon get the hang of it. If they harden too quickly, or if you form them off-center, just reheat to soften, and then start over. Keep in mind that if the cookies are not baked long enough (they should be brown on the edges and have random brown spots all over) they will not harden into delicious crisp shells.

1. Make a 9-inch (22.5-cm) round stencil using ¹/₁₆-inch (2-mm) thick cardboard (a cake box works great).

2. Butter and flour the back of four perfectly even sheet pans (if you have silicone baking mats use these instead; they do not need to be greased and floured).

3. Work the Tulip Paste to make it smooth if necessary. Remove 3 tablespoons (45 ml) of the paste and stir the cocoa powder into it. Reserve this portion. Spread the plain paste out flat and even within the stencil, making two circles on each prepared sheet pan (see Figures 19–55 and 19–56, pages 1046 and 1047).

4. Place a portion of the cocoa-colored paste in a piping bag. Cut a small opening and pipe a repeating design of horizontal "S" shapes around the edge of each circle.

5. Have four shallow soup plates or bowls, approximately the same size as the circles, ready to form the cookies as they come out of the oven. Ideally, two of them should be slightly smaller so they will fit inside the others. Bake the cookies one sheet at a time at 400°F (205°C) for approximately 8 minutes or until light brown spots appear in a few places.

6. Keep the sheet pan in the oven and leave the oven door open. Turn the two smaller bowls upside down. Pick up one of the baked circles using a small palette knife and quickly invert it on top of an upside-down bowl. Still working quickly, adjust the circle so that it is centered over the bowl, then place one of the larger bowls on top. Press down firmly to mold the cookie into a bowl shape. Form the second cookie in the same manner. Allow the cookies to remain in the molds for 30 seconds or so to ensure they will hold their shape. Repeat baking and forming the cookies until you have made eight shells.

7. Prepare the fruit by cutting it into pieces approximately ½ inch (1.2 cm) in size. Cut cubes or wedges rather than slices, with the exception of carambolas. Keep each fruit separate from the others. Cover and reserve in the refrigerator until time of service.

8. Place a small amount of Piping Chocolate in a piping bag and cut a small opening. Pipe out eight chocolate figurines on baking paper, making horizontal "S" shapes to match the design on the cookie shells. Reserve.

9. **Presentation:** Mix the orange liqueur and orange juice. In a separate bowl combine 1 cup (240 ml) of assorted prepared fruit. Place the mixed fruit in the center of a cookie bowl and place the bowl on a dessert plate. Pour 1 tablespoon (15 ml) of the orange juice mixture on top. Place a medium-sized scoop of Feijoa Sorbet in the center. Place a chocolate figurine on the sorbet. Serve immediately.

Pears California with Cointreau-Flavored Almond Filling

16 servings; each serving contains approximately 320 calories and 7.5 grams of fat

sixteen medium-sized Bosc pears, with stems
Spiced Poaching Syrup (page 13)
¼ cup (60 ml) Cointreau liqueur, approximately
10 ounces (285 g) Almond Paste (page 3)
one recipe Apricot Sauce (page 1068)
Sour Cream Mixture for Piping (page 1081)
Chocolate Sauce for Piping (page 1072)
sixteen Chocolate Leaves (page 897)

This dessert got its name from the combination of pears, apricots, and almonds, each of which play a large part in California's agricultural industry. The majority of the state's pear crop is made up of Bartlett or "Bartlett-style" fruit such as Comice or Anjou, but I actually prefer to use the Bosc variety here. They stand tall and majestic, and the long, thin Bosc stems seem to stay on better than the stems from some of the other types. For this dessert, try to find nicely shaped, medium-sized pears that all have the same degree of ripeness. A pear that is too large will look clumsy, although they can be trimmed down to some extent as you remove the peel. Peel the pears using a vegetable peeler, working from top to bottom and removing the skin in long strips to retain the natural pear shape. Keep the fruit as smooth as possible (it should not look like a peeled potato when you have finished), since any imperfection on the surface will show in the presentation.

1. Peel the pears, leaving the stems attached. Place them in acidulated water as you work to prevent browning. Poach the pears in Poaching Syrup until soft and tender. This can take anywhere from 5 to 45 minutes depending on the type of pear and the stage of ripeness (see page 13). Let the pears cool in the syrup to fully absorb the flavor of the spices.

2. Mix just enough Cointreau into the Almond Paste to make it pipeable. Place in a pastry bag with a no. 6 (12-mm) plain tip and reserve.

3. Remove the pears from the Poaching Syrup and pat them dry with a napkin. Make a horizontal cut ½ inch (1.2 cm) below the stem on each pear, going only three-quarters of the way through to keep the stem attached. Push a corer through the bottom of the pears up to the cut and remove the cores. Pipe the Almond Paste mixture into the cavities. Reserve the pears in the refrigerator until ready to serve.

4. **Presentation:** Pour just enough Apricot Sauce on a dessert plate to cover the surface. Decorate a 2-inch-wide (5-cm) band at the outer edge of the sauce with Sour Cream Mixture for Piping and Chocolate Sauce for Piping (see pages 998 to 1006). On a separate plate, pour

Apricot Sauce over one of the filled pears so it is completely covered. Carefully, without disturbing the sauce coating, transfer the pear to the center of the decorated sauce on the plate. Cut a small slit 1/4 inch (6 mm) below the stem at a downward angle and fasten a Chocolate Leaf inside. Serve immediately.

Rainbow of Summer Sorbets in a Cookie Flower

16 servings; each serving contains approximately 360 calories and 11 grams of fat

one recipe Vanilla Tulip Paste (page 1047)

1 1/2 teaspoons (4 g) cocoa powder, sifted

powdered sugar

one recipe Gooseberry Sorbet (page 650)

one recipe Bing and Royal Anne Cherry Sorbet (page 648)

one recipe White Nectarine Sorbet (page 654)

approximately 2 pounds (910 g) fresh fruit for decorating, prepared as described in note

NOTE: Ideally, use the same type of fruit for decorating as was used to make the sorbets, reserving a portion as you prepare the sorbet mixture. Cut gooseberries in half; cut cherries in half and remove the pits; and cut the white nectarines into uniform pieces about the same size as the cherries; do not chop the fruit. Reserve each type of fruit separately so that the colors do not bleed together.

*I*f you have traveled in the eastern part of the Mediterranean you are certainly familiar with street vendors peddling snow-like cracked or shaved ice in paper cones. These frozen refreshments are offered with a choice of syrup toppings that are made from colorful fruits and other flavorings. This custom is also widespread in the Caribbean where the ices are known as frio frio and in South America. Flavored shaved ice is most likely popular in most of the third world since it is the oldest and simplest method of preparing frozen treats. In Persia, fruit ice is known as sharbat, which explains our name for it—sherbet. In France it is known as sorbet or granité, and in Italy it is called granitá. These titles become a little more complicated, however, since sorbets are distinguished from sherbets not by language but by the fact that sorbets never contain any dairy product (see chapter introduction to Ice Cream and Frozen Desserts).

The sorbets used in this recipe give the presentation a bright and colorful appearance; keep color contrast in mind if you decide to substitute other flavors. Unless you are using overripe or very soft fruit, save some of the better-looking pieces to use for decorating. Garnishing the plate with the same variety of fresh fruit used in the preparation helps the guest identify the flavor of the ice. The sorbet can be scooped onto the flower petals and reserved in the freezer for up to 30 minutes before serving. Avoid the temptation to chill the dessert plates, even if you eliminate the powdered sugar on the plates. The chilled plates will fog up and look unattractive when they are exposed to the warmer room temperature.

1. Make the template shown in Figure 14–8. The template as shown is the correct size to use in this recipe. Trace the drawing and then cut the template out of 1/16-inch (2-mm) cardboard (cake boxes are a good choice for this). Grease and flour the back of flat, even sheet pans, or use silicone mats if you have them. The silicone mats do not need to be greased and floured.

2. Color 3 tablespoons (45 ml) of the Tulip Paste with the cocoa powder, mixing to form a smooth paste. Reserve. Spread the plain Tulip Paste on top of the prepared sheet pans or silicone mats, spreading it flat and even within the template (see Figures 19–55 and 19–56, pages 1046 and 1047). Make eight to ten cookie petals per pan or mat.

3. Place some of the reserved cocoa-colored Tulip Paste in a piping bag. Pipe three thin lines the length of each petal, starting evenly spaced at the wide end and ending together at the tip. Bake the cookies, one pan at a time, at 400°F (205°C) until they begin to turn light brown in a few places. Leave the pan in the oven with the door open. Quickly pick up the petals one at a time and drape them (striped-side up) across a rolling pin that is approximately 4 inches (10 cm) in diam-

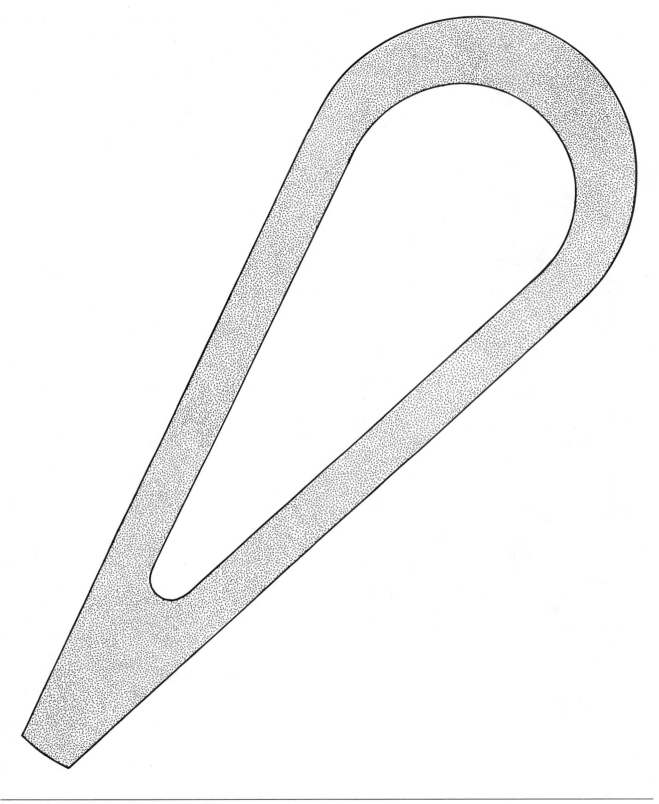

FIGURE 14–8   *The template used to form the Tulip Paste for the Cookie Flower Petals*

eter. Gently press both ends of the cookie against the pin so that the cookie follows the curved shape. Repeat spreading the paste and baking and forming the cookies until you have made fifty-five to sixty cookie petals. You need a total of forty-eight for this recipe, three per serving, but it is a good idea to make a few extra to allow for breakage.

4. Presentation: Sift powdered sugar over the base of a dessert plate. Using a 1^1/$_2$-ounce (45-ml) ice-cream scoop, place a scoop of sorbet on the wide section of three cookie petals, using a different flavor of sorbet on each; be very careful not to break the curved tips of the petals in the process. Quickly, and carefully, use a palette knife to lift the filled cookie petals and place them, evenly spaced, in the center of the plate, arranging them so that the tips point toward the center. Decorate the plate with some of the fresh fruit. Serve immediately.

Red Currant Sorbet in Magnolia Cookie Shells

16 servings; each serving contains approximately 320 calories and 11 grams of fat

one recipe Vanilla Tulip Paste (page 1047)
one recipe Kiwi Sauce (page 1074)
one recipe Red Currant Sorbet (page 654)
sixteen clusters of fresh red currants

NOTE: Any sorbet stored in the pastry bag will become too hard to pipe, so it is not practical to fill the shells to order. However, the filled shells should not be stored in the freezer for more than a few hours, and the unfilled shells will stay fresh for up to one week covered in a dry place, so it is important to try and fill only as many as you can use during one service.

Although the magnolia tree is treated as something of a sacred cow by many southerners, it is more like a mixed blessing to anyone who has the responsibility for its upkeep when the big, hard, fallen leaves, flowers, and seed heads cover the ground from the late spring through the fall. The necessary cleanup is tolerated for the tree's handsome foliage and glorious flower displays (that is, when they are still on the tree), which are found in a remarkable variety of colors and sizes, some up to 12 inches across. The western part of the United States is mostly familiar with the evergreen magnolia, Grandiflora, which produces bright white flowers throughout the summer, but the deciduous magnolia, Soulangina, often nicknamed the tulip tree because of its cup-shaped, brightly colored flowers, is one that inspired the name of this dessert.

The dramatic cookie shells make an impressive holder for any type of sorbet (or ice cream) which, or course, could also be scooped into the shells instead of piped. If red currants are not available, try using another red sorbet such as blood orange or raspberry; either would go well with the Kiwi Sauce.

1. Make the Magnolia Templates shown in Figure 14–9 A and B (template 14–10 is used elsewhere in the text). The templates as shown are the correct size for use in this recipe, however because of the size it is only possible to show half of each one on the page. Trace the drawings and then match the dotted lines in the center to draw the other half so they look like the small example shown. Cut the templates out of ^{1}/$_{16}$-inch (2-mm) thick cardboard. Grease and flour the backs of clean, even sheet pans, or if you have them, use silicone mats, which do not need to be greased and floured.

2. Spread the Tulip Paste flat and even within the templates on the prepared sheet pans or silicone mats (see Figures 19–55 and 19–56, pages 1046 and 1047). Place four large flowers or eight of the smaller size per pan or mat and make sure you have enough bowls and cups available to form them.

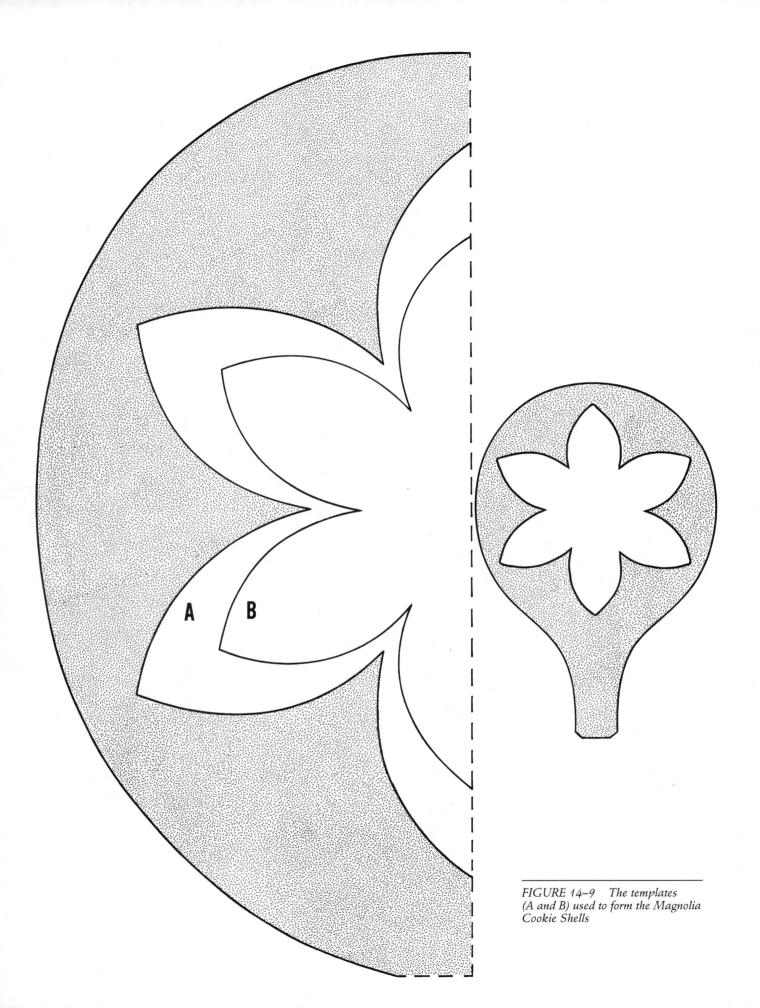

A B

FIGURE 14–9   The templates
(A and B) used to form the Magnolia
Cookie Shells

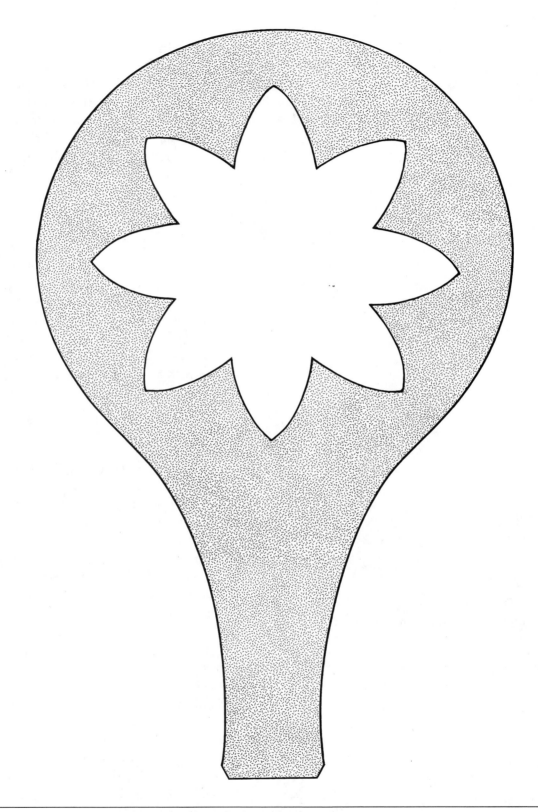

FIGURE 14–10   *The template for Miniature Tulip Crowns; instructions are in the Decorations chapter*

3. Bake one pan at a time at 400°F (205°C) for approximately 8 minutes or until there are a few light brown spots on the cookies. Leave the sheet pan in the oven with the door open.

4. Quickly, place each cookie, top-side up, in a cup or bowl of the appropriate size and shape, and gently press the cookie against the sides of the form. Let each cookie sit in the form until it is crisp, about 30 seconds (less for the smaller size). Repeat baking and forming the cookies until you have at least sixteen each of the small and large size (it doesn't hurt to have a few spares).

5. Place a portion of the Kiwi Sauce in a piping bottle and reserve. As close as possible to serving time, place a portion of the sorbet in a pastry bag with a no. 8 (16-mm) star tip. Pipe a large, pointed rosette of sorbet inside as many of the small cookie shells as you anticipate serving (see note). Return the filled shells and the remaining sorbet to the freezer.

6. Presentation: Cover the base of a dessert plate with a thin layer of Kiwi Sauce. Place one of the large cookie shells in the center of the sauce. Carefully set a filled small cookie shell inside the larger one (using two spoons, one on each side, to transfer or lower the filled shell works well). Decorate with a cluster of fresh red currants and serve immediately.

Sabayon

about 4 cups (9 dl, 6 cl) or eight servings; each serving contains approximately 155 calories and 4 grams of fat

6 egg yolks (½ cup/120 ml)
6 ounces (170 g) granulated sugar
1½ cups (360 ml) dry white wine or champagne

NOTE: To make the original Sabayon, the Italian zabaglione, substitute sweet marsala for the wine and use only 4 ounces (115 g) of sugar.

Sabayon *is the French name for the great Italian dessert* zabaglione. *Though marsala is traditionally used in the preparation, any kind of wine will do. Sabayon is included in the category of stirred custards, meaning custards that are thickened on top of the stove rather than in the oven (see Figure 20–1, page 1082). This dessert, or sauce, is cooked over simmering water or in a saucepan over direct heat, while being stirred constantly (actually whipped to also incorporate air) to prevent it from curdling. The addition of alcohol also aids in this by lowering the boiling point of the mixture. Other stirred custards used in the pastry kitchen include Vanilla Custard Sauce, Lemon Curd, and the most common of all—Pastry Cream. In the cases of Lemon Curd and Pastry Cream, they are stirred not so much to prevent curdling—since Pastry Cream contains a starch and Lemon Curd doesn't have any milk or cream—but to keep them from burning.*

Used as a sauce, Sabayon is the classic companion to many hot soufflés, especially liqueur-flavored soufflés. Sabayon is also poured over fresh strawberries or other fruits and served as is, or gratinéed. *It can be a light dessert by itself without the fruit, served plain or garnished with a light sprinkling of nutmeg. Try to make the Sabayon as close to serving time as possible; it tends to lose some of its fluffiness and will separate if it stands too long. Should this happen, place it back on the stove and repeat the thickening process.*

1. Beat the egg yolks and sugar in a stainless-steel bowl until light and fluffy. Add the wine or champagne.

2. Place over simmering water and continue to whip constantly until the mixture is hot and thick enough to coat a spoon. Serve hot as soon as possible.

Cold Sabayon

1. Soften ¹/₂ teaspoon (1.5 g) unflavored gelatin powder in 1 tablespoon (15 ml) of the wine or champagne. Stir into the remaining liquid.

2. Continue as for hot Sabayon.

3. Once the mixture has thickened, remove from the heat and place over ice water, then whip slowly until cold. Stir in additional wine or champagne as needed, depending on how you are serving the Sabayon.

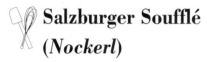

Salzburger Soufflé (*Nockerl*)

4 servings; each serving contains approximately 250 calories and 8 grams of fat

6 egg whites (³/₄ cup/180 ml)
4 ounces (115 g) powdered sugar, sifted
3 egg yolks (¹/₄ cup/60 ml)
1 tablespoon (15 g) Vanilla Sugar (page 14)
grated zest from one-quarter lemon
3¹/₂ tablespoons (20 g) bread flour
2 tablespoons (30 g) unsalted butter
2 tablespoons (30 ml) half-and-half
1 teaspoon (5 ml) vanilla extract
powdered sugar

NOTE 1: You will need an oval dish approximately 12 inches (30 cm) long if, as is traditional, you are baking and presenting the dessert in the same dish.

NOTE 2: Nockerl is nice accompanied by Chocolate Sauce (page 1072) or with Vanilla Custard Sauce (page 1082) and fresh raspberries or strawberries.

*A*nyone who has traveled in Austria and dined in Salzburg has certainly been exposed to this wonderful dessert specialty in one form or another (and in addition to dessert, Salzburger Soufflé is also eaten as a light meal in Austria). Salzburger Soufflé is basically a meringue, lightly baked and browned in the oven. It requires a delicate touch when folding in the egg yolks, and the dish must be presented immediately after baking before the meringue begins to collapse. Just as with a hot soufflé, the Nockerl (which means little mountain; the word is also used for dumplings) is always made to order for two or more persons.*

1. Take the usual precautions for whipping meringue and whip the egg whites at full speed until they have increased to about three times their original volume. Lower the speed and gradually add the sifted powdered sugar. Continue whipping at high speed until stiff peaks form, but do not overwhip.

2. Beat the egg yolks with the Vanilla Sugar for a few seconds, just to combine. Stir in the lemon zest and flour. Carefully fold the egg yolk mixture into the egg whites, mixing them only halfway: you should still be able to see swirls of yolk in the whites.

3. Place the butter in a shallow, ovenproof, oval dish. Warm the dish in the oven until the butter is melted. Add the half-and-half and vanilla to the melted butter in the pan. Using a rubber spatula, place the egg mixture in the baking dish, forming three large, triangular ridges (*nockerln*) (Figure 14–11).

4. Bake at 450°F (230°C) for about 8 minutes, or until the top is dark brown. The inside should remain creamy. Sift powdered sugar lightly over the top and serve immediately.

FIGURE 14–11   Placing the meringue mixture in the baking pan in triangular ridges for Salzburger Soufflé

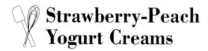 **Strawberry-Peach Yogurt Creams**

16 servings; each serving contains approximately 240 calories and 9.5 grams of fat

Citrus Aspic (recipe follows)
fourteen medium-sized round-shaped
    strawberries, approximately
Peach Cream Filling (recipe follows)
one recipe Strawberry Sauce
    (page 1081)
Sour Cream Mixture for Piping
    (page 1081)

NOTE: *The baba molds must be made of aluminum or stainless-steel. If these are not available, use 5- to 6-ounce (150- to 180-ml) custard cups instead. If the bottoms are much larger than those of baba molds, make a double recipe of aspic to be sure you will have enough.*

*D*on't miss out on serving Strawberry-Peach Yogurt Creams at least once during the summer season when local peaches and strawberries are ripe, plentiful, and inexpensive. The desserts are simple to put together, they can be finished in less than four hours, and the majority of that time is devoted to waiting for them to set up in the refrigerator while you can be working on other projects. Because they are fast to make, there is really no reason to prep them a day ahead, and it's not a good idea anyway because the decorative strawberries on top may bleed slightly. If you must leave them overnight this problem can be nearly eliminated by using strawberries which are firm and ripe, but not overripe, for the decoration. If you have no choice but to use peaches which are not fully ripe, be sure to poach them properly or the filling will oxidize and turn light brown. The accompanying Strawberry Sauce balances the slightly tangy yogurt-based cream perfectly.*

1. Cover the bottom of sixteen baba molds, or other molds of about the same shape and size, with the Citrus Aspic, dividing it evenly. Place the molds in the refrigerator to set the aspic.

2. Cut three strawberries across to make sixteen thin, round slices (do not use the pointed ends). Place one strawberry slice on the firm aspic in each form.

3. Divide the Peach Cream Filling between the molds. Place the molds back in the refrigerator and chill for about 3 hours to set.

4. Unmold as many servings as you anticipate needing by dipping the forms briefly into hot water (don't place them in the water too long or the filling will melt and the presentation will look sloppy) and inverting onto a sheet pan lined with baking paper. Reserve the unmolded servings in the refrigerator.

5. Rinse the remaining strawberries and remove the hulls. Place a portion of the Strawberry Sauce and the Sour Cream Mixture into piping bottles.

6. Presentation: Place a Yogurt Cream in the center of a dessert plate. Pipe Strawberry Sauce around the dessert to cover the base of the plate. Pipe five dime-sized dots of Sour Cream Mixture in the Strawberry Sauce around the dessert. Pull a wooden skewer through the dots to make large hearts that have a small curved tail at each end (see Figure 19–30, page 1005). Cut a strawberry into eight wedges and, using five of the wedges, place them cut-side up between the sour cream hearts with the pointed ends toward the edge of the plate.

Citrus Aspic

approximately ¼ cup (60 ml)

1 teaspoon (3 g) unflavored gelatin powder
2 tablespoons (30 ml) cold water
1 teaspoon (5 ml) lime juice
2 tablespoons (30 ml) orange liqueur

1. Sprinkle the gelatin over the cold water, lime juice, and orange liqueur to soften.

2. Place the mixture over a bain-marie and heat to dissolve. Remove from the heat and use immediately.

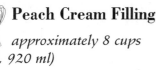

Peach Cream Filling

approximately 8 cups (1 l, 920 ml)

3 pounds (1 kg, 365 g) ripe peaches (approximately six medium-sized)
one recipe Plain Poaching Syrup (page 13)
¹/₂ cup (120 ml) lime juice
¹/₂ cup (120 ml) orange juice
2 tablespoons plus 1 teaspoon (21 g) unflavored gelatin powder
1¹/₂ cups (360 ml) heavy cream
3 ounces (85 g) granulated sugar
1 pound (455 g) Acidophilus Yogurt (page 2) (see note, page 683)

NOTE: The filling can be prepped ahead of time up to the point of adding the gelatin. Do not add the gelatin until you are ready to use the filling.

1. Poach the peaches in the Poaching Syrup until they are soft but not falling apart. If they are fully ripe, 5 minutes is probably enough. Plunge into ice water, then remove the skin. Cut the peaches in half, remove the pits, and place the flesh in a food processor. Add half of the lime juice and purée until smooth. Force through a fine mesh strainer and place in the refrigerator to chill.

2. Combine the remaining lime juice and the orange juice. Sprinkle the gelatin on top and set aside to soften.

3. Whip the cream and sugar until soft peaks form. Stir in the yogurt and the reserved peach purée. Place the gelatin mixture over a bain-marie and heat until dissolved. Be careful not to overheat. Rapidly stir the gelatin into a small portion of the cream. Still working quickly, add this to the remaining cream.

Vineyard Barrels

16 servings; each serving contains approximately 280 calories and 10.5 grams of fat

one-half recipe Vanilla Tulip Paste
    (page 1047)
1 teaspoon (2.5 g) unsweetened cocoa
    powder, sifted
one-half recipe Angel Food Cake
    (page 271)
one-half recipe Italian Cream
    (page 1087)
2 pounds (910 g) Champagne grapes
    or other small seedless grapes (see
    note)

NOTE: Champagne grapes are very small grapes also called Zante Currants or Black Corinth. If you are not able to find these or another petite variety, other types of fresh fruit can be substituted; berries work especially well. Cut larger fruits into pieces about the size of a raspberry; leave raspberries, blackberries, or blueberries whole.

This simplified version of the Cherry Basket dessert on page 449 is a better choice if you are making quite a few servings, or to offer as a pastry rather than a plated dessert, since in addition to the time saved in not having to make and connect the fragile separate handles (these built-in handles are virtually unbreakable), the barrels are easier to move and work with because they have an attached bottom.

The barrel shells can be made several days in advance if they are stored covered in a warm place. Fill the barrels and top with grapes as close as possible to when they will be served. They will become a bit soft, but are still acceptable 30 minutes after filling; however, they should not be held any longer than that. Vineyard Barrels make an impressive addition to a pastry display or buffet table for not only are they eye-catching, but it is easily recognizable that the barrels are formed from a single cookie piece. Placing the barrels on fresh grape leaves makes a particularly nice display.

1. Make the Vineyard Barrels Template (Figure 14–12). The template as shown is the correct size for use in this recipe, however, due to the size of this particular template, it is only possible to show half of it on the page. Trace the drawing as shown, invert your paper and match the dotted line in the center, then trace the other half so the template looks like the small example shown. To form the barrels you will need two or more cake rings approximately 2¹/₂ inches (6.2 cm) in diameter or you can purchase a few pieces of PVC or plastic tubing with that diameter (if using plastic tubes, cut them to about 4 inches/10 cm long).

2. If you do not have silicone mats (which do not need to be greased and floured), lightly grease the backs of four even sheet pans, coat with flour, and shake off as much flour as possible.

3. Remove 2 tablespoons (30 ml) of the Tulip Paste and stir the cocoa powder into this amount. Place a portion of the cocoa-colored paste in a piping bag and reserve.

4. Spread the Tulip Paste flat and even within the template on one of the prepared pans (see Figures 19–55 and 19–56, pages 1046 and 1047). Make four barrel shapes on each pan. Pipe two lines of cocoa-colored Tulip Paste the length of each barrel, evenly spaced across the width. Pipe one small dot in the center of each handle.

5. Bake one pan at a time at 425°F (219°C) for approximately 6 minutes or until any of the cookies begin to show a few brown spots. Leave the pan in the oven with the door open.

6. Working quickly, pick up the cookie that has the most brown spots and place it flat on the table, upside-down, with the large circle (the part that will become the bottom of the barrel) closest to you. Place a cake ring or piece of pipe on top of the circle and quickly pull the remainder of the strip up and around the ring. Lay the barrel on its side with the seam underneath to prevent it from unfolding. Remove the next most done cookie and form it in the same way. Continue baking and forming the cookies until you have made sixteen barrels.

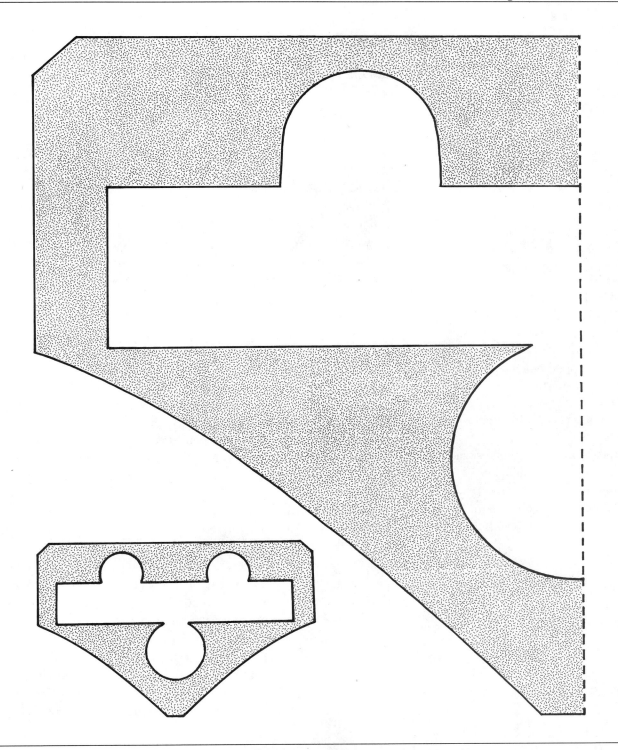

FIGURE 14–12 *The template used to make Vineyard Barrels*

7. Use a cookie cutter to cut round pieces of Angel Food Cake that will fit inside the barrels. Cover and reserve.

8. Place the Italian Cream in a pastry bag with a no. 6 (12-mm) plain tip. Reserve in the refrigerator.

9. To assemble, place a cake round in the bottom of a cookie barrel. Pipe Italian Cream inside the barrel filling it to within ¼ inch (6 mm) of the rim. Arrange grapes on top of the cream in a mound so that the barrel appears to be full of grapes. If the barrels are used as a plated dessert, serve them with a fruit or sabayon sauce.

Winter Fruit Compote in Late Harvest Wine Syrup

12 servings; each serving contains approximately 215 calories and 3.5 grams of fat

twelve whole dried prunes, pitted

twenty-four dried apricot halves

twenty-four dried peach halves

one orange

3 cups (720 ml) late harvest Riesling wine

one cinnamon stick

one vanilla bean, split lengthwise

one bay leaf

2 ounces (55 g) granulated sugar

1 teaspoon (5 ml) whole cloves

eight whole green peppercorns

four whole black peppercorns

three medium-sized firm Bartlett or Anjou pears

6 tablespoons (90 ml) Crème Fraîche (page 1073)

twelve Caramelized Walnut Halves (page 965)

mint sprigs

Compote is a Latin word which literally means "to bring together" or "to unite." The term is usually applied to a mixture of fresh and dried fruit that has cooked slowly in a sugar syrup with various spices or flavorings. Compotes are most often served chilled but can also be offered warm or at room temperature. These simple dishes are found all over the world, influenced by a particular cuisine and the availability of ingredients. This compote with its slightly spicy syrup tastes great paired with a slice of either Basil and Tarragon Pound Cake or White Spice Buttermilk Cake (pages 770 and 773). Be sure to cook the fruit gently to ensure that the pieces retain their natural shape. You can substitute Gewürztraminer or muscat for the Riesling or, in a real pinch, use a dry wine and add extra sugar.

1. Soak the prunes, apricots, and peaches in hot water for 10 minutes.

2. Slice the orange into quarters and put the pieces in a saucepan together with the wine, cinnamon stick, vanilla bean, bay leaf, and sugar. Tie the cloves and peppercorns in a piece of cheesecloth and add to the wine mixture. Bring to a boil and let simmer for 10 minutes.

3. Peel, core, and cut the pears into quarters. Add to the wine mixture.

4. Drain the dried fruits, pat dry, and add to the wine mixture. Simmer until the pears are lightly poached but not falling apart (see page 13). Remove from the heat and let the fruit cool in the liquid.

5. Remove the vanilla bean and save for another use. Remove and discard the cinnamon stick, bay leaf, orange pieces, and the spices in the cheesecloth bag. Reserve the poached fruit, in the poaching liquid, at room temperature until ready to serve.

6. **Presentation:** Spoon one prune, two apricot halves, two peach halves, and one pear quarter into a glass serving bowl or onto a dessert plate. Top with some of the poaching liquid. Spoon approximately ¹/₂ tablespoon (8 ml) of Crème Fraîche on top of the fruit. Place a Caramelized Walnut on the Crème Fraîche, and garnish with a sprig of mint.

Zinfandel Poached Pears with Honey-Scented Pear Frozen Yogurt

12 servings; each serving contains approximately 355 calories and 5.5 grams of fat

twelve medium-sized Bosc pears

Whenever possible in any pear dish, I prefer to serve the fruit standing on end. Pears have such a graceful contour, and it's an easy enough way to give the presentation some height. One exception is the fanned variation of this dessert, which allows you to show off the pretty two-tone color of the wine-poached pears. If zinfandel wine is not available, merlot will work just fine; however, if you must use a lighter red wine, the pears should be left in the poaching liquid a bit longer to allow the color to penetrate. The time (and color)

7 cups (1 l, 680 ml) zinfandel

1 cup (240 ml) grenadine

1 pound, 4 ounces (570 g) granulated
    sugar

four or five whole cloves

one cinnamon stick

one-half recipe Cointreau Pear Sauce
    (page 1073)

Piping Chocolate (page 904), melted

twelve Miniature Tulip Crowns
    (page 1058)

one-half recipe Honey-Scented Pear
    Frozen Yogurt (page 644)
    (see note, page 683)

twelve Tulip Leaves (page 1049)
    (see note)

edible fresh flowers or flower petals

*NOTE: To create a natural-looking color varia-
tion on the Cookie Leaves, pipe the cocoa-colored paste in a straight line down the center as
directed in the recipe, but do this with the template still in place around the paste. Then make
one pass over the top with your palette knife to
blend the paste gently; do not make more than
one pass. Wipe the knife clean before proceeding with the next cookie.*

*can be adjusted to suit your taste, but the pears look best if they are left in the
syrup long enough for the wine to color the pears about ¹/₂ inch (1.2 cm) deep,
giving the fruit just the right color contrast. In addition to showing off the color
contrast a bit more, the fanned presentation offers a lower calorie alternative and
a smaller portion size. Cut a wedge out of each pear and remove the core and
seeds, as directed for the upright version. Save the cutout wedges for another
use. Place the pear on its cut side and push down carefully to flatten it. Starting
¹/₂ inch (1.2 cm) from the stem, cut the pear into thin slices vertically, leaving the
top intact. Pipe a zigzag pattern of melted dark chocolate over the left side of the
base of a dessert plate. Allow the chocolate to harden. Place the sliced pear half
flat-side down on the right side of the plate so that part of the pear rests on the
chocolate lines. Fan the pear slices out decoratively. Serve with either Honey-
Scented Pear Frozen Yogurt or Cointreau Pear Sauce, but not both as in the
main recipe.*

1. Peel the pears, keeping the stems intact. Place the pears into
acidulated water as you work to keep them from oxidizing.

2. Combine the zinfandel, grenadine, sugar, cloves, and cinnamon
stick in a large saucepan. Add the pears and poach over medium heat
until the pears are soft to the touch. Keep the pears submerged in the
poaching liquid at all times, to avoid light spots on the cooked pears, by
placing one or two plates on top of the pears to weight them down.
Place a layer of paper towels between the pears and the plates. Light
spots and uneven coloring can also occur if the pears are too crowded
in the pan. Remove the pan from the heat and set the pears aside to
macerate in the liquid (still covered and submerged) for at least
24 hours.

3. Remove the pears from the poaching syrup. Carefully cut a vertical wedge out of each pear, removing approximately one-sixth of the
pear, cutting into and removing the core but keeping the stems intact.
Remove the core from the cutout wedges and any remaining seeds or
core from the inside of the pears, using a melon-ball cutter. Do not
overdo it; there should not be a large hole. Cut the wedges into thin
slices lengthwise, keeping them attached at the top. Reserve.

4. Place a portion of the Cointreau Pear Sauce into a piping bottle
and reserve. Place some melted Piping Chocolate in a piping bag. Pipe a
zigzag pattern of chocolate on the left side of the base of as many
dessert plates as you anticipate using.

5. Presentation: Stand a poached pear on end in the upper right
side of the base of one of the prepared dessert plates with the open
cutout portion visible. Place one of the fanned wedges to the left of the
pear on top of the chocolate lines. Fill a Tulip Crown with a small scoop
of frozen yogurt and place on the plate below the fanned wedge. Carefully slide a Cookie Leaf underneath so that it points toward the fanned
wedge. Pipe a small pool of Cointreau Pear Sauce in front of the pear
and decorate with edible flowers or flower petals. Serve immediately.

15

Country Desserts

Recently there has been quite an increase in the use of terms like "country-style," "farm-fresh," "back to basics," and so on. It seems the pendulum has swung from the newer-is-better theory to remembering the good old days. These adjectives have become popular not only as they relate to food and the restaurant industry but also in periodicals pertaining to home design and decor and in a great deal of advertising. In each case much of this attention no doubt stems from the fact that so many people are frustrated with the rapid pace of modern society and are looking for a way to recapture a less complex, more innocent time. Having grown up on a farm in a small town, and during a more conservative era, I can certainly relate (although, as is true of most things involving the media, the idyllic image of life in the country that is portrayed in advertisements is a far cry from normal day-to-day existence for any of us, regardless of where we make our home). The other factor that has influenced this so-called return to hearth and home in the food world is the general public's increased awareness about what they eat and the difference that fresh, quality ingredients make in both taste and nutritional value. Many of the big supermarket chains now feature organic produce sections, and farmer's markets—a return to the grower selling his or her own freshly harvested goods—have become commonplace in the area where I live. For some unfortunate people (and I'm afraid there are quite a few) who grew up eating mostly canned and frozen fruits and vegetables, their first taste of vine-ripened tomatoes or freshly picked, juicy, tree-ripened peaches or apricots is no doubt a real eye-opener, and who would want to settle for less?

Country-style desserts are often the ones we remember having been prepared at home, whether home was on the farm, out in the country, or in the suburbs. Many of the following recipes feature fruit as the main component, and I'm sure these were originally developed to use up whatever ingredients were at hand, especially in times of harvest or surplus. If one had a big crop of apples, what could be easier than preparing whole baked apples or apple jam to turn into Mom's Apple Cake later in the year? When berries were abundant they were simply put into a casserole with a little sugar and some biscuit dough on top and placed in the oven to bake along with dinner. And just because the saying goes "If life gives you lemons, make lemonade," it doesn't mean you can't just as easily create a Lemon Pudding Cake or Lemon Meringue Pie.

As is true of many of the recipes in this book, the recipes in the Country Desserts chapter could very well appear in other chapters instead: Date Bars are really cookies; pound cakes are basically the same as tea cakes, crisps and cobblers can be plated desserts, and so on. And by the same token there are plenty of recipes in other chapters that could be included here: Almost all of the muffins and tarts, simple cakes like the Carrot Cake (provided you leave out the Marzipan Carrots), the less complex Danish pastries, certainly ice cream, poached fruit, custards, the less fancy cookies, the list could go on and on. I suppose what qualifies the following desserts for this chapter as opposed to one of the others is that for the most part these are easy to make (requiring just a few steps and in most cases little or no special equipment) and, perhaps more importantly, they have also been around a long time and are classics of the homespun category. These desserts are meant to be served simply, many with nothing more than a little powdered sugar on top, a pitcher of heavy cream on the side, or a scoop of ice cream. But depending on the situation, these straightforward preparations can present something of a paradox for the professional pastry chef, who is used to dressing everything up, especially so in these days of very elaborate plate designs and sky-high presentations (but that is a different trend—and a different chapter—entirely). In some cases I have taken the original concept and made it a little fancier for restaurant service. The Queen's Apple takes the age-old idea of baked stuffed apples wrapped in pie dough and gives it a new spin by using a template to create an eye-catching design in the Puff Pastry shell. In the presentation for Strawberry Shortcake I have combined the traditional idea with a gratinéed sabayon sauce for a beautiful finish that still retains the homey feel of the original. The plate presentation for Peach and Berry Crisp calls for serving the baked fruit and crisp topping in a charming Florentina basket since this dessert tends to run on the plate and often looks a bit messy. Chocolate Bread Pudding with Cookie Citrus Rind features a rich, intensely chocolate-flavored traditional bread pudding baked in individual round molds to create precise servings, then each one is topped with a very modern-looking cookie spiral you would definitely never find on the farm.

Many of the names for old-fashioned early American desserts are quite intriguing but rather puzzling. Following are definitions for some of the better known, yet most often confused, titles and some of the more unusual names. I think it is interesting to note that, as discussed earlier, these are almost exclusively based on fruit.

Apple Pandowdy

Apples seem to be the only fruit specified for this dessert. It consists of sliced apples that are flavored with sugar and spices and baked under a biscuit topping, making it a cross between an apple crisp and an apple cobbler. The dish originated in America, and it is also called apple grunt.

Betty

A betty is a dessert in which fruit (apples are typical but other types are used) is combined with small cubes of bread or bread crumbs, sugar, and spices and is then baked beneath a layer of additional buttered bread cubes or crumbs. This dessert is also called Brown Betty.

Buckle

The best known of these is blueberry buckle, but buckles can be prepared with other berries. The fruit is mixed with a cake batter, spread in a baking pan, and topped with additional batter before baking.

Cobbler

Cobblers are deep-dish baked desserts consisting of a fruit filling, usually sweetened, and a biscuit-like topping. The name originated in America in the mid-nineteenth century. Cobblers are usually made from soft fruits such as peaches and berries and are served warm.

Crisp

Sometimes called fruit crisps, these contain a layer of fruit baked under a crumbly topping of flour, brown sugar, butter, sometimes oat flakes, and spices. The topping is very much like streusel. Crisps are made primarily with firmer fruits like apples and pears. They are best served warm but can be served cold. The British name for these desserts is "crumble" (which probably makes sense since they use the name "crisp" for what we call potato chips).

Crumble

(see Crisp, above)

Crunch

Almost the same as a crisp, except that the fruit is mixed with tapioca, and the topping mixture is placed under as well as over the fruit layer.

Flummery

A flummery is very old term going back as far as the 1600s when it was used in England to describe a type of oatmeal porridge. By the end of the seventeenth century the name was used for a dish of jellied cream served topped with wine, which later became a firm egg custard flavored with sherry or Madeira. The modern version of this dessert would be a bavarois. Flummeries can also be fruit puddings made with cornstarch.

Fool

This is another very old dessert dating back to the Victorian era. It is a mixture of puréed cooked fruit mixed with whipped cream. The most well known is gooseberry fool. The name is thought to have come about (like trifle) as a reference to something light and flighty.

Grunt

A Colonial dessert of cooked berries topped with a leavened dough, making it similar to cobbler, but in this case the dessert is steamed in a covered kettle rather than baked. Grunts are served hot with cream. This dessert is about the same as a slump.

Hasty Pudding

Also called Indian pudding in reference to the ingredient cornmeal, which the colonists dubbed "Indian" as they did anything made from corn. Hasty pudding is dish of soft cornmeal mush that is sweetened with molasses or maple syrup and sometimes flavored with spices. Interestingly, rather than being "hasty," it is cooked by baking very slowly, in some recipes for several hours. Hasty pudding is served warm with cream and was enjoyed by the early settlers both for breakfast and as an after-dinner dessert.

Hermit

Hermits are spice cookies with raisins. The name was used in the late 1800s. The origin of the title is unknown, but it may have to do with the keeping properties of the cookies, although one reference book suggests the bumpy brown cookies may resemble a hermit's tattered robes.

Jumble

One of the first American cookies, jumbles can be rolled out but are generally formed as drop cookies. The name comes from the addition of nuts and/or raisins "jumbled" together. The first cookbook to give a recipe for jumbles was *The Kentucky Housewife,* 1839. More recent recipes call for shredded coconut rather than, or in addition to, nuts and raisins.

Plum Pudding

Plum pudding may sound like a rather straightforward name for inclusion with some of these other more mysterious words; that is, until you realize that it does not contain plums and it is much closer to what we now think of as a cake than a pudding. This dessert is made like a steamed fruit cake with the typical candied and dried fruits (raisins were known as "plums" in the seventeenth century).

Shoo-Fly Pie

Created by the Pennsylvania Dutch, there are many varieties of this pie, some are more cake-like and others have a more liquid filling. A pie pan is lined with a standard crust and baked with a filling based on molasses and a crumb mixture made from flour, butter, and spices like streusel. More of the crumb mixture is placed on top of the filling before baking. Most sources agree that the name comes from the idea that flies are attracted to sweets and have to be "shooed away" from this dessert; however, one source says that this pie may have been created for use as a decoy to attract flies away from other foods. (This seems highly unlikely to me, because why in the world would anyone go to the trouble and waste of baking a pie instead of simply putting out a saucer of molasses?) This type of pie belongs to the category of transparent pies, which are made with fillings composed of eggs and sugar. Another example of this type is the more familiar pecan pie.

Slump

Another antique (eighteenth-century) fruit dessert. Slumps contain cooked fruit, stewed on the stove, with a raised dough dropped on top and cooked with the fruit mixture as you would dumplings on a meat stew.

Snickerdoodle

This silly-sounding name belongs to a sugar cookie from New England, originating in the 1800s when it was customary to make up funny names for cookies. Others in this vein are Brambles, Kinkawoodles, and Tangle Breeches.

Apple Strudel, Austrian Style

about 16 servings

4 ounces (115 g) white-bread croutons, 1/4 inch (6 mm) or smaller

6 ounces (170 g) melted unsalted butter, approximately

1 pound, 14 ounces (855 g) peeled, cored and thinly sliced Granny Smith, pippin, or other cooking apples

3 ounces (85 g) granulated sugar

6 ounces (170 g) dark raisins

6 ounces (170 g) coarsely crushed nuts

1 teaspoon (1.5 g) ground cinnamon

4 ounces (115 g) firm unsalted butter

12 ounces (340 g) bread flour

1 egg

2 ounces (55 g) soft unsalted butter

1/2 teaspoon (2.5 g) salt

3/4 cup (180 ml) cold water, approximately

vegetable oil

bread flour

Vanilla Custard Sauce (page 1082) or

Chantilly Cream (page 1083)

To many people Apple Strudel is the most famous of all Austrian pastries; it has always been closely associated with Vienna in particular. However, it is generally accepted that the dessert did not originate in Austria at all. The Hungarians, who call their strudel retes, *first adopted the incredibly thin strudel dough from the Turkish pastry* baklava. *The Hungarians filled the dough with apples, nuts, raisins, and whatever cake or bread crumbs were at hand. History differs on exactly how this Hungarian strudel arrived in Vienna, but the general theory is this: With the departure of the Ottoman invaders (the Ottoman Empire at its height included Vienna), the now unemployed Turkish and Hungarian cooks took their skills and specialities (and certainly strudel was among them) to the kitchens of the Viennese aristocrats in the new Austro-Hungarian empire. On another note the Turks (although they lost) certainly deserve additional recognition for the coffee addiction they left behind in Vienna, which in turn gave birth to the many great coffeehouses that are so renowned in Austria today.*

Strudel is a German word that literally translates to whirlpool, eddy, or vortex—in this case a swirling mass of pastry dough and filling. Although apple is by far the most well known variety, the number of different strudel fillings is almost limitless and includes both sweet and savory. The savory varieties are especially popular among eastern Europeans and in fact are a staple food for the majority.

The paper-thin strudel dough is stretched rather than rolled to achieve its almost transparent composition. Strudel dough has been described as being "so thin that you must look twice to see it," or as a German colleague of mine says, "You should be able to read a newspaper through the dough!"

Successfully producing a properly stretched strudel dough requires time, patience, and a large work space. For these reasons many people purchase the dough already prepared. If strudel dough is not available, phyllo dough makes a fine substitute. To use phyllo dough in this recipe, overlap the edges of the sheets and glue them together with melted butter on top of a tablecloth to create a large rectangle, the same size specified for the strudel dough. Use two layers of phyllo with melted butter brushed between them, and also brush butter on top of the second layer. You will not be able to lift the rolled strudel onto a sheet pan as directed if it is made with phyllo dough. Instead, cut the rope into two pieces and roll them, one at a time, onto a sheet of baking paper, then lift the paper onto the sheet pan.

1. Sauté the croutons in a portion of the melted butter until they are golden brown and crisp. Reserve the croutons and the remaining melted butter separately.

2. Combine the sliced apples, granulated sugar, raisins, nuts, ground cinnamon, and about half of the croutons. Cut the firm butter into small chunks and gently toss together with the apple mixture. Set aside.

3. Place the flour, egg, soft butter, and salt in a mixer bowl. Mixing with the dough hook on low speed, add enough of the cold water to make a soft dough. Knead the dough at medium speed until it is smooth and elastic, about 5 minutes. Form the dough into a ball and coat it with oil. Cover and let rest at room temperature for about 1 hour.

4. Cover a work surface approximately 3 by 4 feet (90 cm × 1 m, 20 cm) with a clean tablecloth. The cloth is used to facilitate stretching and rolling the dough. To prevent the cloth from sliding, fasten it under the table with thumbtacks. Sprinkle bread flour lightly and evenly over the cloth. Place the relaxed dough in the center of the cloth. Using a rolling pin, roll the dough out to make a small rectangle. Then, using first your fingertips and second the top part of your hands, gradually and evenly lift and pull the dough into a thin membrane approximately 40 inches long by 30 inches wide (1 m × 75 cm) (Figure 15–1). Let the dough relax and dry on the table for 2 to 3 minutes.

5. Trim away the thick edge all around as well as any dough that hangs over the edge of the table. Distribute the apple filling next to the long edge of the dough closest to you. Form the filling into a thick rope with your hands. Brush some of the reserved melted butter (heat if necessary) generously over the remainder of the dough. Sprinkle the remaining croutons over the dough.

6. Remove the thumbtacks to free the cloth. Using the cloth to help lift the dough, roll the strudel, starting from the filling side, into a fairly loose spiral (Figure 15–2). Place the strudel seam-side down in a horseshoe shape on a sheet pan lined with baking paper (Figure 15–3).

7. Bake at 375°F (190°C) about 35 minutes, brushing several times with the remaining melted butter (and/or using the juices that run out of the pastry).

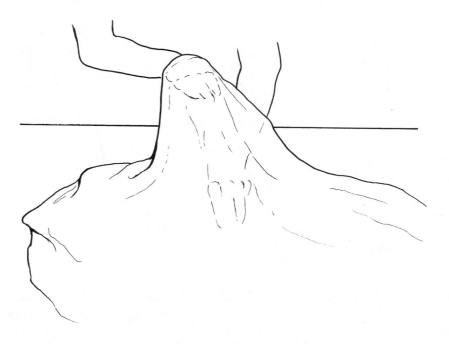

FIGURE 15–1 Using the top part of the hands to pull and stretch strudel dough into a thin membrane

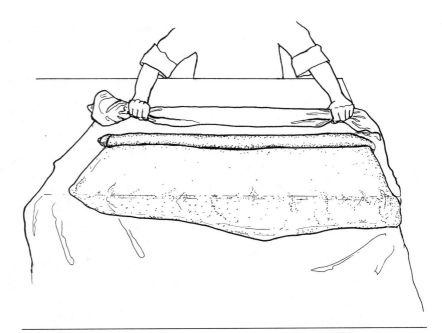

FIGURE 15–2 Using the tablecloth under the dough to help guide the filled strudel as it is rolled into a spiral

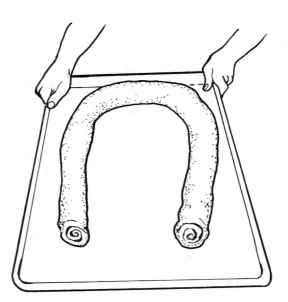

FIGURE 15–3 The assembled Austrian Style Apple Strudel arranged in a horseshoe shape on the baking pan

8. Let the strudel cool slightly, then slice into the desired number of servings. Sift powdered sugar over the slices. Serve hot or cold with Vanilla Custard Sauce or with Chantilly Cream.

Banana Layer Cake with Maple-Cream Cheese Frosting and Pecans

one 10-inch (25-cm) cake

one-half recipe Banana Bread batter (page 281)

three medium-sized ripe bananas

1/2 cup (120 ml) Plain Cake Syrup (page 10)

or

orange juice

Maple-Cream Cheese Frosting (recipe follows)

4 ounces (115 g) lightly toasted pecan halves

This cake is a variation that starts with the Banana Bread tea cake recipe and dresses it up with crisp oven-dried banana chips, tangy rich cream cheese frosting infused with maple syrup, and crunchy toasted pecans. While the addition of fruits and vegetables to a cake batter generally help to retain moisture and make the cakes suitable for longer storage, Banana Layer Cake must be served the same day it is assembled or the sliced bananas between the layers will oxidize and turn dark.

1. Line the bottom of a 10-inch (25-cm) cake pan with baking paper. Pour the Banana Bread batter in the pan and spread it level on top. Bake at 375°F (190°C) for approximately 35 minutes or until baked through. Unmold by inverting on a cake rack and remove the pan.

2. Reduce the oven temperature to 175°F (80°C). Peel one of the bananas and cut it diagonally into thin slices. Arrange the pieces on a sheet pan lined with lightly oiled baking paper, or on a silicone baking mat. Place in the oven and dry until crisp, turning the pieces from time to time. Reserve the dried pieces at room temperature.

3. Cut the crust from the top of the banana cake, slicing it level at the same time. Slice the cake horizontally into two layers. Brush Cake Syrup or orange juice over the bottom layer. Spread one-quarter of the Cream Cheese Frosting on top.

4. Remove the skin from the remaining two bananas and cut each into four pieces lengthwise. Arrange the banana quarters on top of the filling, covering the entire surface in a even layer. Spread one-third of the remaining frosting over the bananas. Top with the remaining cake layer. Brush Cake Syrup or orange juice over the top layer. Use the remaining Cream Cheese Frosting to ice the top and sides of the cake.

5. Reserve one pecan half for each serving of cake. Coarsely chop the remaining nuts. Cover the sides of the cake with the chopped nuts (see Figure 8–5, page 296). Use a palette knife to press the nuts against the side of the cake for an even finish. Cut or mark the cake into the desired number of servings and decorate the top of each piece with a pecan half and some of the dried banana chips.

Maple-Cream Cheese Frosting

1 pound (455 g)

3/4 cup (180 ml) heavy cream

6 ounces (170 g) cream cheese, at room temperature

2 ounces (55 g) soft unsalted butter

1/4 cup (60 ml) pure maple syrup

1. Whip the heavy cream until stiff peaks form. Reserve.

2. Soften the cream cheese by stirring with the paddle attachment on low speed; do not incorporate air. Mix in the butter and then gradually incorporate the maple syrup, continuing to mix until smooth and spreadable.

3. Fold in the whipped cream. Store covered in the refrigerator no longer than one day. Bring to room temperature and mix until soft before using.

Bread Puddings

Bread puddings have been popular in England since the thirteenth century, at which time you could find in virtually every kitchen a deep bowl called the pudding basin that was used to gradually collect stale bread. This dessert was first known as "poor man's pudding," because instead of being moistened with the rich milk or cream custard we are used to, stale bread was first soaked in hot water and then squeezed dry before it was mixed with sugar, spices, and other ingredients. The early settlers brought the pudding to America, but because wheat was not readily available in the Colonies they at first made their "hasty puddings," as they were known, with cornmeal. From such modest beginnings delicious bread puddings have become popular throughout the industrialized world, certainly so in the United States and especially in New Orleans, where you can find some type of bread pudding on virtually every restaurant menu.

Bread puddings in today's restaurants are often made with "trendy" breads such as panettone, brioche, croissant, and yes, even biscotti. This, of course, invalidates the original intention of the dish—to use up plain stale bread—but at least these use bread, unlike some recipes I have seen which call for sponge cake or worse yet cake crumbs! These "desserts" in my opinion have nothing to do with bread pudding.

Some of the old-fashioned recipes specify removing the bread crust, in others it is left on; there are recipes that use sliced bread and some where the bread is cubed, but all stipulate that the bread should be stale or day-old. When the bread is buttered and toasted before the pudding is assembled, the dish is called bread and butter pudding. Bread puddings are best served hot or warm, but some can be acceptable cold. They are always accompanied by a sauce or ice cream.

Brandy Bread and Butter Pudding

one pan 11 by 9 inches (27.5 × 22.5 cm) or 12 servings

3 ounces (85 g) melted unsalted butter

1 pound, 8 ounces (680 g) white or egg bread, approximately two loaves (see note)

6 ounces (170 g) soft unsalted butter

5 ounces (140 g) granulated sugar

8 eggs, at room temperature

1¼ cups (300 ml) warm milk

⅓ cup (80 ml) brandy

1 teaspoon (5 ml) vanilla extract

½ teaspoon (.75 g) ground cinnamon

6 ounces (170 g) golden raisins

2 cups (480 ml) heavy cream

8 ounces (225 g) Streusel Topping (page 14)

Brandied Whipped Cream (page 846), made without nutmeg

Cinnamon Sugar (page 5)

fruit for decoration

NOTE: Any type of leftover plain white bread can be used. Although in a way it defeats the purpose of bread puddings, there may be times when you have no choice but to bake a batch of bread especially for this use. I prefer either Brioche or Challah, formed into loaves. You might as well make the full recipe of either, even though you only need half. Any leftover makes great toast (or more bread pudding).

*B*randy Bread and Butter Pudding is very rich; it must be left to soak long enough before baking for the cream mixture to thoroughly penetrate the bread. If you are in a hurry, or want a less rich pudding, replace the cream with half-and-half or milk, adding it all at once, and omit the soaking step. This express method will result in a slightly less rich pudding, so be sure to serve it with plenty of brandy-flavored whipped cream.

1. Use some of the melted butter to butter a hotel pan or other baking dish approximately 11 by 9 by 2 inches (27.5 × 22.5 × 5 cm). Set aside.

2. Trim the crust from the bread and cut the bread into ½-inch (1.2-cm) thick slices. Place on a sheet pan. Brush the slices with the remainder of the melted butter. Toast in a 400°F (205°C) oven for approximately 10 minutes or until golden brown.

3. Beat the softened butter and sugar together. Beat in the eggs. Add the warm milk, brandy, vanilla, and cinnamon.

4. Place a level single layer of bread in the buttered baking pan. The sides of the bread should touch so that the pan is completely covered. Sprinkle the raisins evenly on top of the bread. Pour half of the custard slowly and evenly over the bread. Cover with a second bread layer, and press down with your hands to make the top level. Pour the remaining custard evenly over the second layer; press down again. Pour 1 cup (240 ml) of the cream over the top. Cover with baking paper and place another pan, just slightly smaller, over the paper, then weight down the top with cans. Let sit at room temperature for 2 hours or, preferably, refrigerate overnight.

5. Remove the weights, pan, and baking paper. Pour the remaining 1 cup (240 ml) of cream evenly over the pudding. Sprinkle the Streusel over the top.

6. Bake covered at 350°F (175°C) for 30 minutes. Uncover and bake approximately 30 minutes longer or until the pudding is set and the top is golden brown. Let cool to room temperature. Cut into 12 servings.

7. Presentation: Set a piece of bread pudding in the center of a dessert plate. Spoon Brandied Whipped Cream in front of the pudding. Sprinkle Cinnamon Sugar lightly over the cream. Decorate the opposite side of the plate with fresh seasonal fruit for color. Serve warm or at room temperature, do not serve chilled.

Chocolate Bread and Butter Pudding *Kungsholm*

one pan 11 by 9 inches
(27.5 × 22.5 cm) or 12 servings

3 ounces (85 g) melted unsalted butter
one loaf Chocolate Apricot or Black
    Forest Bread (pages 89 and 75)
    (see note 1)
      or
1 pound, 8 ounces (680 g) black or
    dark bread
2 ounces (55 g) unsweetened cocoa
    powder
6 ounces (170 g) granulated sugar
6 ounces (170 g) soft unsalted butter
8 eggs, at room temperature
1½ cups (360 ml) warm milk
⅓ cup (80 ml) brandy
1 teaspoon (5 ml) vanilla extract
1 tablespoon (5 g) ground cinnamon
2¾ cups (660 ml) heavy cream
one-half recipe Bourbon Sauce
    (page 1069)
dark coating chocolate, melted
powdered sugar
one-half dry pint fresh raspberries

NOTE 1: If you are going to the extra step of making Chocolate Apricot Bread or Black Forest Bread for the pudding, make the full recipe of either. They are both great tasting breads that keep well and can be frozen for several weeks.

NOTE 2: This looks great provided you are using plates that have little or no pattern on the rim. If your plates have a pattern, either omit the piping or pipe only over the base to avoid a look that is too busy.

*B*ack in the sixties and the early part of the seventies, there were dozens of passenger ships that sailed back and forth across the Atlantic between the east coast of the United States (mainly New York City) and Europe. These ships plowed the transatlantic route from June until early September and then would switch to cruising in warmer climates and less hostile waters as the winter approached. Cruising, or making the crossing as the typically nine-day Atlantic journey was known, was at that time reserved only for the rich, and it seemed to a budding young pastry chef like myself that all of the passengers were of a rather advanced age (what we actually used to say was that they were somewhere between sixty and dead!). This of course has changed, and cruises can now be enjoyed by almost anyone, but unfortunately the transatlantic crossing has changed as well and just one ship continues to sail the Atlantic in the summer (and she now makes the trip in a speedy five days).

Back when passengers still had a choice of ships, travel books not only gave recommendations for hotels and sightseeing once in Europe but also on how to get there, reviewing and rating the various ships from five stars on down. I was proud to see in the 1967 Fodors Guide that both of the ships I had worked on had received five-star ratings, but more than that, of all the adjectives that could have been used to describe the ship I was working on before coming to live in the United States—the brand new (splashing into the water for the first time in 1966) gorgeous MS Kungsholm—the reviewer wrote "she is 660 feet and 26½ thousand tons of delightful Swedish pastry!" The writer obviously had a sweet tooth, but money being no object (or so it seemed) we did put together some very impressive desserts and baked goods.

Chocolate Bread and Butter Pudding Kungsholm was mainly served during the transatlantic crossing when we had around 1,100 passengers rather than the 450 that was the ship's cruising capacity (for cruising there was no such thing as tourist class, only first). This dessert was quick and easy for mass production and we always had plenty of dark bread on hand since it was part of the bread basket on the dining tables. Because this type of bread is not always readily available in this country you may need to bake your own, or you can try the other chocolate bread pudding which follows this one in the text. This recipe can easily be stretched to serve sixteen rather than twelve; you will need to increase the amount of raspberries to decorate sixteen servings.

1. Use some of the melted butter to butter an 11-by-9-inch (27.5-×-22.5-cm) baking pan. Set aside.

2. Trim the crust from the bread, cut into ¼-inch (6-mm) slices, and place on a sheet pan. Brush with the remainder of the melted butter and toast in a 400°F (205°C) oven for approximately 10 minutes or until lightly crisp on top.

3. Sift the cocoa powder on top of the sugar. Combine the two well. Beat the softened butter and sugar mixture together. Beat in the eggs, then add the warm milk, brandy, vanilla, and cinnamon. If the mixture appears separated at this point, it means the milk was not warm enough and the butter has solidified. Warm the custard over a bain-marie, stirring constantly, until the butter melts and the mixture is smooth. Do not allow it to become hot enough to cook the eggs.

Chocolate Ganache Cake

Chocolate Ganache Cake

Dessert Sampling Platter

Assorted Petits Fours Sec

Crème Caramel Nouveau

White Chocolate and Pistachio Mousse with Chocolate Lace

Chocolate Mousse in Ribbon Teardrops

Valentine's Day Hearts

Assorted Individual Pastries

Assorted Individual Pastries

Strawberries Romanoff

Chèvre-Scented Coeur à la Crème with Pistachio Crust

Swedish Pancakes Filled with Apples

Vacherin with Plum Ice Cream

Plum Kuchen

Mango Ice Cream with Chiffonade of Lemon-Mint and a Chocolate Twirl

Rainbow of Summer Sorbets in a Cookie Flower

"Out-of-Season" Fresh Fruit Baskets with Feijoa Sorbet

Strawberry Shortcake

Red Banana Truffles in Phyllo Dough

Apple Rum Charlotte

Caramelized Pineapple Barbados

Kardinals with Sambuca-Scented Italian Cream and Fresh Fruit

Crepe Soufflé

White Chocolate Bavarois with Macadamia and Pistachio Nuts

Sour Apple and Cheese Turnovers

Trio of Cannolis

Almond Wafers

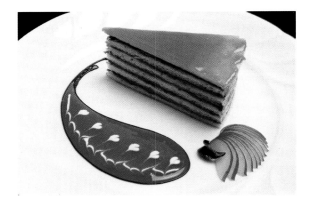

Dobos Torte

4. Make a level single layer of bread in the buttered baking pan. The sides of the bread should touch so that the bread completely covers the bottom of the pan. Pour half of the custard slowly and evenly over the bread. Cover with a second bread layer, and press down with your hands to make the top level. Pour the remaining custard evenly over the second layer; press down again. Pour 2 cups (480 ml) of the cream over the top. Cover with baking paper and place another pan, just slightly smaller, over the paper to weight down the top. Let sit at room temperature for 1 hour.

5. Remove the pan and the baking paper. Pour the remaining ³/₄ cup (180 ml) of cream evenly over the pudding.

6. Bake at 350°F (175°C) for approximately 40 minutes. Let cool to room temperature, then cut into twelve servings.

7. Place a portion of the Bourbon Sauce in a piping bottle and reserve in the refrigerator with the remainder of the sauce. Place melted coating chocolate in a piping bag and cut a small opening. Decorate dessert plates, including the rims, by piping the chocolate over the plates in a series of large figure-eights (see note 2). Reserve the plates.

8. Presentation: Sift powdered sugar lightly over one serving of bread pudding. Place the pudding in the center of a prepared plate. Pipe Bourbon Sauce in large dots and teardrops randomly around the dessert. Sprinkle a few raspberries on top.

Chocolate Bread Pudding with Cookie Citrus Rind

12 servings

1 pound, 8 ounces (680 g) French bread or other noncrumbly white bread, at least one day old

6 cups (1 l, 440 ml) milk

8 ounces (225 g) sweet dark chocolate

6 ounces (170 g) unsweetened chocolate

twelve blood oranges

10 eggs

8 ounces (225 g) granulated sugar

2 tablespoons (30 ml) vanilla extract

4 ounces (115 g) Streusel Topping (page 14)

2 tablespoons (30 ml) orange liqueur

one recipe Mousseline Sauce (page 1076)

one recipe Cookie Citrus Rinds and Cookie Figurines (page 1054)

powdered sugar

*T*he only old-fashioned part of this bread pudding is the taste which, although lighter and less sweet than the more traditional renditions, has a wonderful rich chocolate flavor that is amplified by the use of bitter chocolate. Instead of the more familiar method where sliced bread is soaked in the custard mixture in the same dish it is baked in, and one pan provides multiple servings, here the bread is cut into small cubes instead, and after soaking the mixture is divided among individual cake rings. If the rings are not convenient, bake the pudding in an 11-by-9-by-2-inch (27.5-×-22.5-×-5-cm) hotel pan instead and slice into twelve pieces. The art deco Cookie Citrus Rind used in the presentation is sure to raise a few eyebrows in pleasant surprise. The beautiful, and to many people uncommon, blood oranges are paired with the Mousseline Sauce not only for color but to add a distinctive flavor. When blood oranges are unavailable (which is unfortunately the majority of the time), use perfectly ripe ruby red grapefruit instead. And, of course, if you do not feel like going a little bit wild with your presentation, you may replace the cookie rind with strips of real orange rind, sprinkled on top of the powdered sugar.

1. Cut twelve 6¹/₂-inch (16.2-cm) squares of aluminum foil (if you are using a thin grade of foil, use a double thickness). Set a cake ring that is 3 inches in diameter by 2 inches tall (7.5 × 5 cm) in the center of each square. Fold and pleat the edges of the foil up against the rings to form a tight seal. Be sure the foil reaches at least three-quarters of the way up the sides of the rings, because the puddings will be placed in a water bath. Place the rings in a hotel pan and set aside.

2. Remove the crust from the bread. If you are using baguette loaves, do not remove all of the crust or you will not have enough bread left. Cut the bread into $^1/_2$-inch (1.2-cm) cubes. Place in a bowl and reserve.

3. Heat the milk to scalding. Chop both chocolates into small pieces and add to the milk. Remove from the heat and stir until the chocolate is completely melted. Finely grate the zest of half of the blood oranges into the chocolate mixture. Reserve the zested oranges with the others.

4. Whisk together the eggs, sugar, and vanilla until well combined, then whisk this mixture into the chocolate mixture. Pour the custard over the bread cubes and stir gently to ensure all of the bread is moistened. Set aside to soak for 30 minutes.

5. Divide the bread filling evenly between the prepared rings. Press down gently to compact the filling and even off the tops. Sprinkle the Streusel over the tops.

6. Place the hotel pan in a 350°F (175°C) oven. Add enough hot water to the pan to reach about $^1/_2$ inch (1.2 cm) up the sides of the rings. Bake for approximately 40 minutes or until the custard is set. Remove the puddings from the water bath and let them cool to room temperature.

7. Remove the rind and all of the white pith from the oranges and then cut out the segments (see Figures 12–4 and 12–5, page 596). Place the segments in a single layer on a sheet pan lined with baking paper. Cover and refrigerate.

8. Stir the orange liqueur into the Mousseline Sauce. Place a portion of the sauce in a piping bottle. Cover the remaining sauce and reserve all of the sauce in the refrigerator until needed.

9. Presentation: Peel the foil from the sides and bottom of a bread pudding. Slide off the cake ring. Place the pudding in the center of a dessert plate. Pipe Mousseline Sauce on the base of the plate all around the pudding. Arrange ten to twelve orange segments in a spoke pattern around the dessert on top of the sauce. Use the tip of a paring knife to make three small cuts, spaced evenly apart, on top of the pudding. Gently insert Cookie Figurines into two of the cuts. Push the tip of a Cookie Citrus Rind into the other and arrange the spiraling end of the cookie around the dessert, supporting it on top of the figurines. Sift powdered sugar over the top.

Butterless, Eggless, Milkless Spice Cake

one 10-inch (25-cm) tube pan

Butter and Flour Mixture (page 4)
1 cup (240 ml) strong brewed coffee
   (leftover is fine)

This spice cake is based on a recipe from my wife's family, where it was known as Mrs. Ruby's Cake (it was very typical in this country at one time for food dishes to be named for the person the recipe came from, as in "Mrs. Smith's Casserole," etc.). The recipe is unusual in that (as evidenced by the title) it contains no dairy products. This type of dessert was popularized in World War I in part due to food shortages and also because it was very economical. Like many of the simple desserts in this chapter, this cake is composed of ingre-

1 cup (240 ml) vegetable oil
8 ounces (225 g) granulated sugar
5 ounces (140 g) dark raisins
1/2 teaspoon (1 g) ground nutmeg
2 teaspoons (3 g) ground cinnamon
1 teaspoon (2 g) ground cloves
1 teaspoon (4 g) baking soda
1 tablespoon (15 ml) water
1 teaspoon (4 g) baking powder
6 ounces (170 g) bread flour
2 ounces (55 g) walnuts, coarsely
    chopped

dients almost always in stock in the pantry, and at the same time it finds a use for leftovers, coffee in this case. The batter can be put together in just a few minutes; the cake has a nice deep spice flavor, a moist texture, and it keeps well; like many tea cakes it actually improves after one or two days. This is a good choice for an afternoon snack with tea or coffee.

1. Brush Butter and Flour Mixture over the inside of a 10-inch (25-cm) tube pan. Reserve.

2. Pour the coffee and vegetable oil into a saucepan. Add the sugar, raisins, and the spices. Bring the mixture to a boil and boil 3 minutes. Remove from the heat and set aside to cool for about 10 minutes.

3. Stir the baking soda into the water. Stir this combination into the mixture in the saucepan; it will foam up.

4. Sift together the baking powder and flour. Stir into the batter. Stir in the walnuts. Spoon the batter into the prepared pan.

5. Bake at 350°F (175°C) for approximately 35 minutes or until baked through. Cool to room temperature, unmold, and store tightly wrapped.

Cobblers

Cobblers are a very simple and quick way of using fresh seasonal fruit to create a delicious ending to a meal. Peach cobbler is an American favorite and is probably the best-known version; topped with home-made vanilla ice cream, it is almost synonymous with Fourth of July celebrations for some people. The only thing I do not like about cobblers made in the traditional form is that they really do not present very well and can often end up looking something like a pie gone wrong! But then, a cobbler that does not look a little disheveled is not the genuine article. If the cobbler is not to be plated in the kitchen, use any presentable baking dish, such as an earthenware casserole, with a 2-quart (1-l, 920-ml) capacity. Cobblers are part of the "clump cake" category of desserts, which includes slumps, grunts, buckles, and betties. The French call them *poupeton,* which translates to "mess in the pan." Though none of these names may sound particularly appetizing, the continued popularity of these unaffected desserts after literally hundreds of years is ample proof of how good they are.

Cobbler with Apples and Ginger

two 10-inch (25-cm) cobblers or 16 servings

1½ ounces (40 g) Crystallized Ginger (page 6)
6 pounds, 8 ounces (2 kg, 955 g) tart cooking apples such as pippin or Granny Smith (approximately fifteen medium-sized)
¼ cup (60 ml) lemon juice
8 ounces (225 g) granulated sugar
4 ounces (115 g) unsalted butter
Cobbler Topping (recipe follows)
Cinnamon Sugar (page 5)
one recipe Bitter Orange Sauce (page 1078)
mint sprigs

NOTE: Try serving with Calvados Whipped Cream (page 747); it is much quicker to prepare than making the Bitter Orange Sauce, and it tastes great with the apples. Whipped cream flavored with bourbon is also good.

1. Finely chop the Crystallized Ginger and reserve.

2. Peel the apples, core, and cut into ½-inch (1.2-cm) wedges. Place the wedges in a bowl with the lemon juice as you cut them, tossing them in the juice to coat.

3. Transfer the apples to a skillet or saucepan and add the sugar and butter. Cook over medium heat, stirring, until the apples are soft but not mushy. Mix in the ginger.

4. Divide the apples, including all of the liquid, between two 10-inch (25-cm) cake pans with 2-inch (5-cm) high sides. Press the apples into the pans firmly.

5. Use your hands or two spoons to place the Cobbler Topping on the apples in random piles, leaving 1 inch (2.5 cm) of apples uncovered around the outside of the pans to allow the batter to bake out. Do not smooth the batter over the top; it will not be an authentic cobbler if you do so. Sprinkle Cinnamon Sugar lightly over the top.

6. Bake at 425°F (219°C) for approximately 40 minutes or until the topping is golden brown and baked through. Set the cobblers aside for at least 30 minutes before serving, to allow the crust to absorb part of the liquid in the pan. Warm before serving if necessary; cobbler should be served warm or hot, never chilled. Divide each pan into eight portions.

7. Presentation: Place a portion of cobbler on a dessert plate. Pour a pool of Bitter Orange Sauce on the side, and decorate with a sprig of mint.

 ## Cobbler Topping

3 pounds, 6 ounces (1 kg, 535 g)

1 pound, 6 ounces (625 g) bread flour
1 teaspoon (5 g) salt
3 tablespoons (36 g) baking powder
4 ounces (115 g) cold unsalted butter
3¼ cups (780 ml) heavy cream

NOTE: Do not make the Cobbler Topping until you are ready to use it.

1. Sift together the flour, salt, and baking powder. Cut the butter into small chunks, add, and cut into the flour mixture to the size of peas.

2. Pour in the cream all at once and stir rapidly with your hand to form a soft dough.

3. Place on a floured work surface and pat out to a rectangle 1½ inches (3.7 cm) thick. Make two rough single turns (see page 160), shaping the dough with your hands and not a rolling pin.

Cobbler with Blueberries, Strawberries, or Raspberries

*one 10-inch (25-cm) cobbler or
8 servings*

8 ounces (225 g) granulated sugar
3 tablespoons (24 g) cornstarch
¼ teaspoon (.4 g) ground cinnamon
¼ teaspoon (.5 g) ground nutmeg
1 cup (240 ml) water
1 quart (960 ml) blueberries,
    strawberries, or raspberries
    (see note)
one-half recipe Cobbler Topping
    (page 742)
Crème Fraîche (page 1073), sweetened
    whipped cream, or ice cream

NOTE: If you are using strawberries, remove the hulls and cut the berries in half before measuring.

1. In a saucepan, combine the sugar, cornstarch, and spices. Gradually stir in the water. Bring the mixture to a full boil, stirring constantly. Remove from the heat.

2. Place the berries in a 10-inch (25-cm) cake pan. Pour the hot liquid over the fruit.

3. Bake at 400°F (205°C) for 10 minutes; do not cover the pan.

4. Remove from the oven and place the Cobbler Topping on top of the fruit in random piles.

5. Continue baking until the topping is golden brown and baked through, about 15 minutes longer. Serve warm with Crème Fraîche, whipped cream, or ice cream.

Cobbler with Peaches and Cinnamon

*two 10-inch (25-cm) cobblers or
16 servings*

5 pounds (2 kg, 275 g) ripe peaches
    (about eighteen medium-sized)
3 ounces (85 g) Cinnamon Sugar
    (page 5)
one recipe Cobbler Topping
    (page 742)
one recipe Mascarpone Sauce
    (page 1075)
ground cinnamon

1. Wash the peaches, remove the pits, and cut each one into about eight wedges, leaving the skin on. Place in a bowl and toss with the Cinnamon Sugar. Divide between two 10-inch (25-cm) cake pans, lightly pressing the fruit into the forms with your hands.

2. Follow the instructions in Cobbler with Apples and Ginger, page 742, for adding the Cobbler Topping and baking.

3. **Presentation:** Place a portion of cobbler on a dessert plate. Spoon Mascarpone Sauce over one side of the cobbler, letting the sauce run onto the plate. Sprinkle cinnamon lightly on the sauce.

Cobbler with Rhubarb and Honey

two 10-inch (25-cm) cobblers or 16 servings

5 pounds (2 kg, 275 g) rhubarb stalks

2 ounces (55 g) cornstarch

12 ounces (340 g) granulated sugar

3/4 cup (180 ml) or 9 ounces (225 g) honey

2 ounces (55 g) Crystallized Ginger (page 6)

one recipe Cobbler Topping (page 742) (see step three)

one recipe Romanoff Sauce (page 1081)

mint sprigs

NOTE: Rhubarb cobbler is excellent served with Honey-Vanilla Frozen Yogurt (see page 645) rather than Romanoff Sauce.

1. Wash and dry the rhubarb. Trim the top and bottom off each stalk and discard. If any stalks are wider than 1 inch (2.5 cm), cut them in half lengthwise. Cut the stalks into 1/2-inch (1.2-cm) slices.

2. Place a stainless-steel bowl in the oven until it is hot. Stir the cornstarch and sugar together in the bowl, add the rhubarb pieces, and toss to coat them thoroughly. Mix in the honey and set aside at room temperature for about 30 minutes.

3. Chop the ginger and add it to the Cobbler Topping mixed with the dry ingredients.

4. Transfer the rhubarb, with all of the liquid, to a saucepan. Cook over low heat, stirring constantly, until the rhubarb starts to turn a little soft. Do not overcook; the rhubarb will fall apart very quickly at this point.

5. Divide the rhubarb mixture between two 10-inch (25-cm) cake pans, lightly pressing the fruit into the pans with your hands. Use two spoons or your hands to drop the Cobbler Topping over the rhubarb in random piles, leaving 1 inch (2.5 cm) of rhubarb uncovered around the outside of the pans to allow the topping to bake out. Do not smooth the batter over the top.

6. Bake at 425°F (219°C) for about 30 minutes or until the topping is golden brown and baked through. Set the cobblers aside for at least 30 minutes before serving to allow the crust to absorb part of the liquid in the pan. Warm before serving if necessary. Cobbler should be served warm or hot, never chilled. Divide into sixteen portions.

7. Presentation: Place a portion of cobbler on a dessert plate. Pour a pool of Romanoff Sauce on the side, and decorate with a sprig of mint.

Chèvre-Scented Coeur à la Crème with Pistachio Crust

12 individual or two 3-cup (720-ml) heart molds

1 1/2 cups (360 ml) heavy cream

7 ounces (200 g) granulated sugar

8 ounces (225 g) soft cream cheese

3 1/2 ounces (100 g) soft mild chèvre such as Montrachet

1 pound, 8 ounces (680 g) farmer's cheese or cottage cheese

one-half recipe Strawberry Sauce (page 1081)

Coeur à la crème, *literally "heart with cream" in English, can be made from any combination of fresh cheeses such as farmer's cheese, cottage cheese, or cream cheese. It is a very simple dish with only a few ingredients— the cheese, sugar, cream (or meringue to make a lighter version), and fruit. The flavor varies according to the proportion of whipped cream and/or meringue added. This recipe is not too sweet and has a little bite, which comes from the addition of chèvre (goat's milk cheese). Coeur à la crème is traditionally served with sweetened fresh strawberries and strawberry sauce. Although the cheese dessert is the classic interpretation, the name* coeur *is sometimes used to describe a heart-shaped frozen mousse.*

Heart-shaped wicker baskets and heart-shaped porcelain molds with small holes in the bottom are made especially for this dessert in sizes that make individual servings and larger ones that can hold up to eight servings. Before the forms are filled they are lined with slightly dampened cheesecloth. The cheese filling is placed in the forms, and they are left overnight in the refrigerator to allow the whey to drain off, leaving a smooth creamy mixture. I prefer the porce-

5 ounces (140 g) pistachio nuts,
    blanched, skins removed, and
    coarsely crushed
twelve medium-sized fresh
    strawberries
twelve large mint leaves cut into
    julienne (see note)
twelve Curly Cues (page 1055)

NOTE: To cut the mint leaves, stack three or
four together and use a chef's knife to slice
across the width into ⅛-inch (3-mm) pieces.
Discard the pieces from the tip and stem ends.

lain molds, since the little drainage holes can be taped over allowing you to use the molds for other purposes (see Frozen Hazelnut Coffee Mousse, page 666).

If you do not have coeur à la crème molds (or you do not have enough molds for the number of servings you are making), leave the cheese mixture to drain in a fine mesh strainer or a colander lined with cheesecloth. The next day you can pack the mixture into a heart-shaped metal form lined with cheesecloth, or for individual servings, a heart-shaped cookie cutter (or a coeur à la crème mold provided you have at least one—it does create a much more attractive shape). Press the cheese in tightly, using a palette knife. Place in the freezer for 10 minutes, remove, unmold, and repeat until you have made the desired number of servings.

1. Line twelve individual or two 3-cup (720-ml) coeur à la crème molds with damp cheesecloth, using enough for an overhang around the edges. Set the molds aside.

2. Whip the heavy cream and granulated sugar until soft peaks form. Reserve in the refrigerator.

3. Place the cream cheese and chèvre in a mixer bowl. Using the paddle attachment, beat until the mixture is smooth, scraping down the sides of the bowl a few times to make sure there are no lumps.

4. Place the farmer's or cottage cheese in a food processor and blend until completely smooth. Blend this into the cream cheese mixture. Fold the reserved whipped cream in by hand.

5. Pipe or pour the mixture into the lined molds, dividing it equally. Fold the cheesecloth over the top to cover. Place the molds in the refrigerator overnight, setting them on a sheet pan or tray to catch the whey as it drains off.

6. Place a portion of the Strawberry Sauce in a piping bottle. Reserve in the refrigerator together with the remaining sauce.

7. Spread the crushed pistachios out in a flat layer in a shallow dish.

8. Presentation: Lift a Coeur à la Crème out of the mold. Peel away the cheesecloth and place the heart flat-side down on top of the pistachio nuts so that the nuts adhere to the bottom of the dessert (the side that was exposed when it was in the mold). Press some of the nuts into the side of the heart around the bottom edge as well. Place the heart, nut-side down, slightly above the center of a dessert plate. Slice the stem end off one strawberry, cutting the end flat and removing the hull. Cut one thin round slice from this end, then cut the remainder of the strawberry into thin slices lengthwise. Arrange three of the larger lengthwise slices on the base of the plate around the top half of the heart, with the points toward the rim of the plate. Place the round slice on top of the sliced strawberries next to the heart. Pipe teardrops of Strawberry Sauce on the base of the plate on both sides and around the bottom of the Coeur à la Crème. Sprinkle julienned mint leaves over the sauce. Place a Curly Cue leaning against the point of the heart with the tip angled toward the strawberries.

Crisp Waffles

about 16 servings

1 pound, 8 ounces (680 g) bread flour

10 ounces (285 g) cornstarch

2 ounces (55 g) granulated sugar

1 teaspoon (5 g) salt

1 quart (960 ml) warm water

6 eggs, at room temperature

6 ounces (170 g) melted unsalted
    butter

finely grated zest of one-half lemon
    (optional)

2 teaspoons (10 ml) vanilla extract

1 quart (960 ml) heavy cream

powdered sugar

Apple Jam with Calvados
    (instructions follow)

Calvados Whipped Cream
    (recipe follows)

*NOTE: The amount of batter needed for each
waffle will vary, depending on the type of iron
used. Belgian waffle irons use more batter
because of the deep grooves.*

*T*o many people waffles are synonymous with breakfast, but I think you will
find that this crisp light waffle makes a tempting dessert when paired with
cream and apple jam. That is unless you have to face the combination every day
for two weeks in a row, as my colleagues at the lunch table did when I first starting making this waffle recipe again. It is one I have had since my days as an
apprentice, and when I dug it up a few years ago it was clear right away that
something was amiss. Back then it was a common practice to write down your
special recipes using a protective code of some sort to sabotage anyone who
copied your recipes without permission. For example, you might add 100 grams
to all of the dry ingredient weights and/or delete a set percentage of all liquid
quantities. Well, you guessed it, I had forgotten my code, and I had to start from
scratch using my colleagues as guinea pigs!

The waffles should be served as soon as they are made, while still warm,
to taste their best. If it is necessary to make them ahead of time, reserve them
placed on a cake rack in a single layer in a low oven (220°F/104°C). This will
keep the waffles crisp; however, they must not be kept this way longer than
about 15 minutes or they will start to dry all the way through. Any leftover waffle batter can be kept in the refrigerator for three or four days.

1. Sift the flour and cornstarch into a mixing bowl. Stir in the sugar
and salt.

2. Gradually incorporate the water, mixing with a whisk. Whisk in
the eggs, and then the butter and lemon zest, if used. Mix until you
have a smooth paste, about 3 minutes longer. Stir in the vanilla.

3. Cover the batter and let it rest for 30 minutes.

4. Whip the heavy cream to stiff peaks. Fold the cream into the
waffle batter.

5. Heat a waffle iron (grease if not using a nonstick iron). Portion 1
to 2 cups (240 to 480 ml) of batter onto the iron and quickly spread it
out a little (see note). Close the lid and bake approximately 3 minutes
per side if using a stove-top iron, or about 5 minutes total if using an
electric iron. Warm the Apple Jam.

6. Presentation: Place two or three waffles (depending on size)
off-center on a dessert plate, placing one of the waffles leaning against
the other(s). Sift powdered sugar lightly over the tops of the waffles
and over the plate. Spoon a large dollop of warm Apple Jam on the
plate next to the waffles. Pour a pool of Calvados Whipped Cream in
front of the dessert and over a corner of the waffles. Serve immediately.

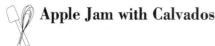

Apple Jam with Calvados

*M*ake one-half of the Apple Rum Filling recipe (page 533), substituting
Calvados for the rum and omitting the pectin powder.

Calvados Whipped Cream

2¹/₄ cups (540 ml)

1 pint (480 ml) heavy cream
1 tablespoon (15 g) granulated sugar
¹/₄ cup (60 ml) Calvados
1 teaspoon (5 ml) vanilla extract

VARIATION

Strawberry-Lime Sauce

2¹/₂ cups (600 ml)

2 pounds (910 g) fresh strawberries
6 ounces (170 g) granulated sugar
3 tablespoons (45 ml) or 2 ounces
   (55 g) honey
¹/₂ cup (120 ml) lime juice
2 tablespoons (16 g) cornstarch
2 tablespoons (30 ml) strained
   raspberry purée (optional)

NOTE: If the sauce is pale from using straw-
berries that were not perfectly ripe, adding the
raspberry purée will give the sauce a more
attractive color.

1. Whip the cream and sugar until the mixture is fairly thick yet still pourable. Stir in the Calvados and vanilla.

2. Reserve covered in the refrigerator. If necessary, adjust the consistency of the sauce at serving time by adding additional cream to thin it, or by whipping it a little longer to thicken. The sauce should be thick enough not to run on the plate.

*T*ry serving these waffles for brunch with the following Strawberry-Lime *Sauce and whipped cream flavored with vanilla. You will need 1 cup (240 ml) of heavy cream whipped with ¹/₂ teaspoon (2.5 ml) vanilla extract.*

1. Remove the hulls from the strawberries (a small melon-ball cutter works well for this). Wash, purée, and strain the berries.

2. Add the sugar, honey, and lime juice. Stir the cornstarch into a small part of the liquid, then mix into the remainder.

3. Bring the sauce to a boil and cook for 2 minutes over low heat to eliminate any aftertaste from the cornstarch.

Crisps

You could easily argue that a crisp is nothing but a cobbler with a different topping, and you would be absolutely right. Fruit crisps and cobblers are as traditional as the all-American fruit pie. Like a pie, they have a thick fruit filling, are easy and quick to make, and they're wonderful served warm with ice cream. But unlike a pie, neither has a bottom crust. Do not feel bound to use the exact type and proportions of fruit specified in these recipes. These happen to be two of my favorites, but a fruit crisp (like a pie or a cobbler) is a great way to improvise and celebrate the abundant harvest of fresh ripe fruit.

Cobbler, crisp, crunch, or crumble—what is the difference, you ask? Basically, not much except for the topping. The biscuit-style topping of the cobbler is thick and soft. A crisp has a thin and crunchy topping, a crunch has almost the same topping except it is put on the bottom as well as the top, and a crumble is the name used more typically by the British for the same thing as a crisp. Does this make sense to you? It doesn't to me, but then I did not grow up with these wonderful fruit treats. For a more detailed explanation see the chapter introduction.

Fall Fruit Crisp with Cranberries

one 10-inch (25-cm) crisp

Filling

2 pounds (910 g) cooking apples such as Granny Smith or pippin (approximately five medium-sized)

2 pounds (910 g) Bartlett or Anjou pears (approximately four medium-sized)

4 ounces (115 g) dried cranberries

2 tablespoons (16 g) bread flour

3 tablespoons (45 ml) lemon juice

1/4 cup (80 ml) or 3 ounces (85 g) honey

Topping

5 ounces (140 g) bread flour

3 ounces (85 g) rolled oats

5 ounces (140 g) light brown sugar

1 teaspoon (1.5 g) ground cinnamon

6 ounces (170 g) firm unsalted butter

This crisp makes a refreshing alternative to the pies that are traditionally served for Thanksgiving, and it is most appropriate since cranberries (like blueberries) are native to this country. I use dried cranberries here to prevent the cranberry juice from staining the fruit filling, but if this is not a concern replacing the dried cranberries with fresh will work fine. Use 8 ounces (225 g) of fresh cranberries and add 4 ounces (115 g) of granulated sugar. Place in a saucepan over medium heat and cook stirring constantly until the cranberries have popped open and the sugar is melted. Let cool a bit before combining with the apple and pear mixture.

For a delicious and unusual combination, try substituting domestic feijoas—which are inexpensive and available from late fall through the winter—for about 8 ounces (225 g) of the fruit mixture (one pear or apple). Use 8 ounces (225 g) or two medium-sized feijoas. Remove the skin from the feijoas with a vegetable peeler. Cut the flesh into 1/2-inch (1.2-cm) cubes and combine with the apple and pear chunks.

1. Peel, core, and cut the apples and pears in half. (Or cut them in half after peeling and use a melon-ball cutter to cut out the core.) Cut each half into 3/4-inch (2-cm) chunks. Place the apples, pears, and dried cranberries in a bowl and toss to combine.

2. Combine the 2 tablespoons (16 g) of flour and the lemon juice. Add the honey and then combine with the fruit cubes and cranberries, tossing to combine well. The lemon juice will help to keep the fruit from turning brown and add a nice accent to the flavor as well.

3. Press the fruit pieces into a 10-inch (25-cm) cake pan, including any liquid.

4. Prepare the topping by combining the remaining flour, rolled oats, brown sugar, and cinnamon. Cut the butter into small pieces and add to the flour mixture, mixing just until the topping starts to come together; it should still be lumpy. Sprinkle the topping evenly over the fruit mixture.

5. Bake at 375°F (190°C) for approximately 50 minutes. The apple and pear chunks should be soft and the liquid released by the fruit during the initial cooking stage should be reduced to a small quantity of syrup. To check on the fruit and the amount of liquid, carefully lift off a small piece of the topping (it should be crisp and brown) and look inside. If the fruit needs to cook further and/or there is too much liquid, continue baking and check again. If the topping is already brown, cover the pan to protect the topping from becoming too dark. Serve the crisp warm, accompanied by Bourbon Sauce (see page 1069) if desired.

🥄 Peach and Berry Crisp

16 servings

Crisp Filling (recipe follows)
one and one-quarter recipes
    Florentina Batter (page 214)
1 cup (240 ml) heavy cream
1 teaspoon (2 g) ground ginger
one recipe Raspberry Sauce
    (page 1080)
Sour Cream Mixture for Piping
    (page 1081)
Crisp Topping (recipe follows)
powdered sugar
berries and sliced peaches for
    decoration

NOTE: For a simple, traditional presentation omit the Florentina cookie shells and bake the topping on the fruit filling, using one or two pans as described in the recipe or individual earthenware forms. Do not cover with foil when baking. Individual forms will bake in a shorter time.

*T*his unconventional way of serving a simple and humble fruit crisp transforms country-style fare into an elegant dessert. You can use the same treatment for fruit cobblers as well. If you do not want to be bothered with making handles for the Florentina baskets (I leave them out all the time for larger banquets), make a single recipe of Florentina Batter. In this case you can achieve some height in your presentation by piping the whipped cream rosette on the cookie that tops the dessert rather than on the plate in front. Place the sliced fruit on the rosette as directed.

1. Divide the Crisp Filling evenly between two 10-inch (25-cm) cake pans or place it in one small hotel pan (see note). Cover the pans with aluminum foil and puncture a few holes in the foil to allow steam to escape. Bake the filling at 375°F (190°C) until the fruit is soft and cooked through, approximately 1 hour. Set aside to cool to room temperature.

2. If you are making handles for the baskets, reserve a little less than one-fourth of the Florentina Batter. Draw sixteen 5-inch (12.5-cm) circles on a sheet of baking paper. Invert the paper on top of a sheet pan. Divide the remaining Florentina Batter between the circles. Spread out, bake, and trim the cookies following the instructions on page 213, using a 5-inch (12.5-cm) plain, round cookie cutter to trim them.

3. A few at a time, reheat the trimmed cookies to soften them. Using a shallow, round form approximately 4 inches (10 cm) in diameter with straight sides, shape the cookies into shallow bowls (see Figure 13–5, page 674). Reserve.

4. To make the handles shape the reserved Florentina Batter into an 8-by-16-inch (20-×-40-cm) rectangle on a sheet pan lined with baking paper, patting it out with your hands. Bake as for the cookies; the rectangle will take a little longer. Cut across into twenty ³/₄-inch (2-cm) strips (you only need sixteen, but chances are a few will break). The strips should be 7 to 8 inches (17.5–20 cm) long. Reheat the strips and form them into curved handles by draping them over a rolling pin when they come out of the oven.

5. Whip the heavy cream with the ground ginger until stiff peaks form. Place the whipped cream in a pastry bag with a no. 6 (12-mm) star tip. Reserve the cream in the refrigerator.

6. Presentation: Cover the base of a dessert plate with Raspberry Sauce. Place some of the Sour Cream Mixture in a piping bag and cut a small opening. Pipe the mixture on top of the sauce in a spoke pattern, as if you were cutting a cake into twelve pieces. Drag a small wooden skewer through the lines in a spiral (see Figure 19–28, page 1004). Using two soup spoons, lift up about ¹/₃ cup (80 ml) of the fruit filling and place it in one of the prepared Florentina baskets. Place one of the Crisp Topping cookies in the center of the filling; the filling should be exposed around the sides. Sift powdered sugar lightly over the top. Place the dessert in the center of the plate on top of the sauce. Pipe a rosette of whipped cream in front of the dessert and decorate the cream with a slice of peach and a berry (use the same type of berry you used in the filling). If you are using handles, set a handle in place, pushing it gently into the filling to secure. Serve immediately.

Crisp Filling

About 5 cups (1 l, 200 ml) or 16 servings

3 pounds (1 kg, 365 g) firm, ripe peaches
1 pound, 6 ounces (625 g) fresh berries (blueberries and blackberries are best, but raspberries or strawberries work as well)
2 tablespoons (16 g) cornstarch
1¹/₂ ounces (40 g) cake flour
4 ounces (115 g) granulated sugar

1. Wash, stone, and cut the peaches into ¹/₄-inch (6-mm) slices. Place the sliced peaches in a mixing bowl and add the berries.

2. Sift together the cornstarch, cake flour, and sugar. Sprinkle on top of the fruit and combine gently, using your hands.

Crisp Topping

1 pound, 12 ounces (795 g) or 16 portions

8 ounces (225 g) light brown sugar
7 ounces (200 g) soft unsalted butter
7 ounces (200 g) cake flour
¹/₂ teaspoon (2 g) baking powder
¹/₂ teaspoon (2 g) baking soda
4 ounces (115 g) sliced almonds, lightly crushed
¹/₂ teaspoon (2.5 g) salt

1. Mix the brown sugar and the butter together until just combined. Sift the flour with the baking powder and baking soda. Stir the flour mixture into the butter and sugar mixture together with the sliced almonds and salt. The mixture should be the consistency of streusel.

2. Divide the topping into sixteen equal portions and form them into mounds 1¹/₂ inches (3.7 cm) in diameter on a sheet pan lined with baking paper.

3. Bake at 375°F (190°C) until lightly browned, about 12 minutes. The cookies should be crisp throughout, rather than soft and chewy.

Date Bars

one half-sheet pan 16 by 12 inches (40 × 30 cm)

1 pound, 10 ounces (740 g) dates, pitted
    or
1 pound, 8 ounces (680 g) pitted dates
1¹/₂ cups (360 ml) water
10 ounces (285 g) granulated sugar
³/₄ cup (180 ml) lemon juice

*B*ars, *as the name suggests, are pastries or cookies cut into shapes, usually squares, rectangles, or diamonds, after baking. They can be the crumbly type or moist and chewy like brownies, lebkuchen, and the Date Bars that follow. Both Trier Squares and Tosca in the Individual Pastries chapter belong to this group as well; however, both of those are dressed up a bit.*

Try replacing the dates with other dried fruits such as pears, prunes, or apricots, which are particularly refreshing. Reconstitute first in water as needed. Date Bars make a homey dessert served warm topped with a scoop of ice cream; they are great to take along on picnics or outings and can be made into ice cream sandwiches as follows: Cut the baked sheet in half crosswise to make two 8-by-12-inch (20-×-30-cm) rectangles. Spread slightly softened ice cream over one half in a layer about ¹/₂ inch (1.2 cm) thick. Place the remaining date bar sheet

12 ounces (340 g) rolled oats

14 ounces (400 g) bread flour

1 pound, 4 ounces (570 g) light brown
sugar

1 teaspoon (4 g) baking soda

1 teaspoon (5 g) salt

1 pound, 4 ounces (570 g) melted
unsalted butter

on top and press down firmly. Freeze until hard. Use a serrated knife to cut the
sheet into sandwiches of the desired size.

1. Combine the pitted dates and water in a saucepan. Cook over medium heat, stirring frequently, for approximately 5 minutes. The mixture should form a thick paste. Remove from the heat and stir in the granulated sugar and the lemon juice. Set aside.

2. Thoroughly combine the rolled oats, bread flour, brown sugar, baking soda, and salt. Stir in the melted butter.

3. Press half of the oat mixture in an even layer over the bottom of a half sheet pan 16 by 12 inches (40 × 30 cm). Spread the date filling evenly on top. Crumble the remaining oat mixture evenly over the date filling and then press it flat with your hands.

4. Bake at 350°F (175°C) for about 40 minutes. Let cool slightly, then cut into the desired size pieces.

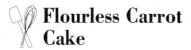

Flourless Carrot Cake

two 10-inch (25-cm) cakes

12 egg yolks (1 cup/240 ml)

$^1/_3$ cup (80 ml) or 4 ounces (115 g)
honey

12 ounces (340 g) carrots, peeled and
finely grated (see note)

2 tablespoons (30 ml) dark rum

1 teaspoon (5 ml) vanilla extract

1 pound (455 g) blanched almonds,
ground to a fine powder or almond
meal

3 ounces (85 g) dry white cake crumbs

12 egg whites (1$^1/_2$ cups/360 ml)

10 ounces (285 g) granulated sugar

powdered sugar

NOTE: It is important that the carrots are
grated very finely. The texture should be similar
to macaroon coconut, for example. If necessary,
chop the grated carrots with a knife to achieve a
finer consistency. For a slightly more dense, less
crumbly cake, measure and remove 1 cup (240
ml) of the carrot juice that will collect in the bot-
tom of the bowl after grating the carrots. Dis-
card the liquid or drink it (carrot juice is very
good for you).

*C*arrot cakes are probably the best-known survivor of the large group of *cakes made with root vegetables such as parsnips, potatoes, turnips, and to a lesser extent beets, that were popular throughout the eighteenth and nineteenth centuries. This recipe has a lighter composition than the more traditional Carrot Cake in the recipe on page 304. Here, finely ground almonds are used as a binding agent instead of flour (eggs are also a binding ingredient). If you do not have ready-made almond flour (almond meal) and are grinding the blanched almonds in a food processor, add* $^1/_4$ *cup (60 ml) of the sugar to the almonds as you grind them to help absorb the oil released by the nuts and prevent the mixture from caking. The almonds should ideally be as fine as granulated sugar after processing. This cake is a great keeper; it may be stored in the refrigerator, well wrapped, for up to a week and in the freezer for much longer.*

1. Line the bottom of two 10-inch (25-cm) cake pans with baking paper (see Figures 1–10 to 1–12, page 26). Reserve

2. Whip the egg yolks and honey to the ribbon stage. Fold in the carrots (including the juice), rum, and vanilla. Fold in the almond flour and cake crumbs.

3. Whip the egg whites to soft peaks while gradually adding the granulated sugar. Carefully fold this mixture into the carrot mixture. Divide the batter between the prepared pans.

4. Bake at 375°F (190°C) for 10 minutes. Lower the heat to 350°F (175°C) and continue baking approximately 30 minutes longer. Let the cakes cool for 10 to 15 minutes.

5. Run a knife around the inside perimeter of the cake pans and remove the cakes by inverting them onto cardboard; immediately turn them right-side up again. When the cakes are completely cool, or better yet the next day (wrap and refrigerate if leaving overnight), place a lattice design template on top and sift powdered sugar over the cakes. Cut into the desired number of slices.

Fresh Peaches in Puff Pastry

12 servings

2 pounds, 8 ounces (1 kg, 135 g) Puff Pastry (page 44)

Amaretto Filling (recipe follows)

Egg Wash (page 7)

Cinnamon Sugar (page 5)

twelve medium-sized ripe freestone peaches

one recipe Caramel Sauce II (page 1071)

Sour Cream Mixture for Piping (page 1081)

Strawberry Sauce (page 1081)

powdered sugar

Cinnamon Ice Cream (page 629)

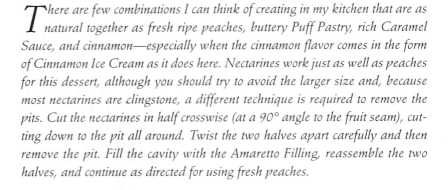

*T*here are few combinations I can think of creating in my kitchen that are as natural together as fresh ripe peaches, buttery Puff Pastry, rich Caramel Sauce, and cinnamon—especially when the cinnamon flavor comes in the form of Cinnamon Ice Cream as it does here. Nectarines work just as well as peaches for this dessert, although you should try to avoid the larger size and, because most nectarines are clingstone, a different technique is required to remove the pits. Cut the nectarines in half crosswise (at a 90° angle to the fruit seam), cutting down to the pit all around. Twist the two halves apart carefully and then remove the pit. Fill the cavity with the Amaretto Filling, reassemble the two halves, and continue as directed for using fresh peaches.

1. Follow steps two through seven (and also read the notes and introduction) in the recipe for Queen's Apple, page 778, making the following changes:

- Substitute peaches for the apples (do not poach them). Remove the peach pits by using a ³⁄₄-inch (2-cm) plain cookie cutter to cut a hole down from the stem end of each peach to the pit, then use a paring knife to remove the pits.
- Pipe Amaretto Filling into the peaches instead of Calvados Filling.
- When cutting the twelve round cookies from the scrap Puff Pastry dough, use a ³⁄₄-inch (2-cm) fluted cutter and, in addition, cut out twelve leaves, using a leaf cutter or cutting freehand with the tip of a paring knife. Attach the leaves next to the cookies on top of the peaches.

2. **Presentation:** Cover the base of a dessert plate with Caramel Sauce. Pipe a ring of Sour Cream Mixture close to the perimeter of the sauce. Pipe a ring of Strawberry Sauce ¹⁄₂ inch (1.2 cm) away from the Sour Cream Mixture toward the center of the plate. Blend the two sauces together using a small wooden skewer (see Figure 19–26, page 1002). Sift powdered sugar lightly over the top of a baked peach. Place in the center of the plate, securing it to prevent it from sliding by gently pressing it down to the plate. Serve immediately with Cinnamon Ice Cream in a separate bowl.

Amaretto Filling

12 ounces (340 g)

1 ounce (30 g) dry currants

¹⁄₂ cup (120 ml) amaretto liqueur

4 ounces (115 g) Almond Paste (page 3)

3 ounces (85 g) blanched almonds, finely ground

¹⁄₂ teaspoon (.75 g) ground cinnamon

2 tablespoons (30 g) granulated sugar

1. Combine the currants and amaretto liqueur in a saucepan. Heat to approximately 120°F (49°C). Remove from the heat and set aside to macerate for at least 30 minutes.

2. Gradually add the currant mixture to the Almond Paste. Add the ground almonds. Mix the cinnamon and granulated sugar together and then stir into the filling.

Italian Cheese and Cranberry Strudel

12 servings

4 ounces (115 g) granulated sugar

4 ounces (115 g) soft unsalted butter

8 ounces (225 g) Mascarpone Cheese (page 9)

4 egg yolks (1/3 cup 80 ml), at room temperature

6 ounces (170 g) Ricotta Cheese (page 11)

1 1/2 teaspoons (7.5 ml) vanilla extract

2 ounces (55 g) dried cranberries

grated zest from one orange

grated zest from one lemon

4 egg whites (1/2 cup/120 ml), at room temperature

3 ounces (85 g) cake flour, sifted

4 ounces (115 g) finely ground almonds (almond meal)

twelve sheets phyllo dough, about one-half of a package (see note)

4 ounces (115 g) melted unsalted butter

one-half recipe Caramel Sauce II (page 1071)

one-half recipe Cranberry Coulis (page 1073)

1 pound, 4 ounces (570 g) Candied Chestnuts (page 4), about twenty-four halves

powdered sugar

NOTE: *Phyllo sheets vary in size from 12 by 14 inches (30 × 35 cm) to 16 by 18 inches (40 × 45 cm), depending on the brand used. Each one-pound (455-g) package typically contains about twenty-four sheets. Frozen phyllo dough must be allowed to defrost slowly in the refrigerator overnight before it is used. If it is thawed too quickly the thin sheets tend to break.*

*P*hyllo dough, or fillo (which appropriately enough is the Greek word for leaf), has been used in the Mediterranean since ancient times. It is an interesting concept: The multiple leaves provide a layer structure very similar to Puff Pastry, but phyllo dough sheets are virtually fat-free, making the dough suitable for the preparation of low-fat or low-cholesterol desserts. Naturally, you must take into consideration the butter that is brushed onto the leaves of dough, but this can be cut down if desired, and vegetable oil can be used if cholesterol is a concern. One option is to spray the melted butter or oil onto the dough instead of using a brush, or some people spray the sheets with a pan coating instead of butter to reduce the fat. This recipe is not in the low-fat category, but the phyllo crust may allow you to feel a bit more virtuous as you enjoy the creamy, rich filling.*

Italian Cheese and Cranberry Strudel should be served warm or, at the least, room temperature; it should not be served cold. If you really want to splurge, omit the Caramel Sauce and Cranberry Coulis and serve the strudel country-style with a scoop of Vanilla Ice Cream or with a ladle of Sauce Anglaise (actually, assuming you serve the strudel warm, the ice cream will melt and you will end up with a little of each anyway!).

1. Combine one-third of the granulated sugar with the soft butter and Mascarpone. Beat until light and fluffy, about 5 minutes. Beat in the egg yolks one at a time. Stir in the Ricotta Cheese. Add the vanilla, dried cranberries, and grated citrus zests. Set aside.

2. Whip the egg whites at high speed until foamy. Gradually add the remaining sugar and whip to stiff peaks. Fold the reserved cheese mixture into the meringue. Combine the flour and ground almonds and then carefully fold into the filling. Reserve.

3. Unwrap and unroll the phyllo dough. Keep the stack of dough from drying out by covering it with a piece of plastic wrap and then a slightly damp (not wet) towel as much as possible while you are working. Cut three sheets of baking paper to approximately the same size as the sheets of phyllo dough.

4. Place one of the baking paper sheets on the table in front of you with a short side closest to you. Place a sheet of phyllo dough on top. Brush the sheet lightly with melted butter. Top with a second phyllo sheet, brush butter on top, and continue until you have a stack of four sheets, with butter between each layer. Lightly brush the top of the stack with butter.

5. Place one-third of the filling horizontally starting about 1 1/2 inches (3.7 cm) from the bottom (short) end of the stack and leaving about the same amount of dough uncovered on both sides. Fold the sides in toward the center (Figure 15–4). Roll the stack into a strudel shape by picking up the short end of the baking paper next to the filling and, using

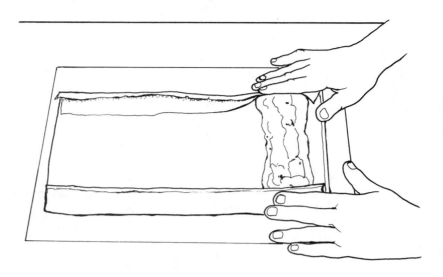

FIGURE 15–4 *Folding the long sides of the phyllo dough in toward the center before enclosing the filling in the dough*

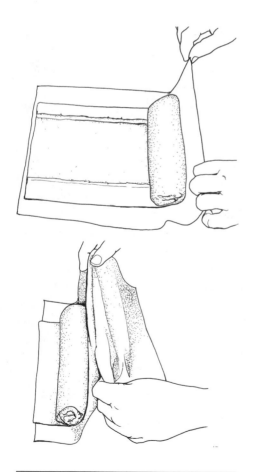

your hands to guide the dough, gently fold it over four times (Figure 15–5). If necessary, turn the strudel so that the seam is underneath. Leaving the strudel in place on the baking paper, pick up the paper and place the strudel on a sheet pan. Brush butter over the top and sides.

6. Repeat steps four and five two times to form two more strudels with the remaining dough, filling, and butter.

7. Use a serrated knife to score the dough on top of each strudel diagonally, marking four servings. This will make it possible to cut cleanly through the dough after baking.

8. Bake at 375°F (190°C) for approximately 25 minutes or until golden brown. Let cool for 10 to 15 minutes. Cut into serving pieces at the scored lines, using a serrated knife with a sawing motion until you cut through to the filling all around, then cut straight down. Reserve at room temperature for up to 1 hour or refrigerate until needed.

9. Place the Caramel Sauce and Cranberry Coulis in separate piping bottles. The sauces should be thick enough to allow you to pipe them out without running or changing shape more than slightly.

10. Slice the Candied Chestnuts into small chunks, four from each half.

11. Presentation: Warm a serving of strudel if necessary. Sift powdered sugar over the slice. Pipe a small dot of Caramel Sauce in the center of the plate to keep the strudel from sliding and set the slice on top. Pipe six small pools of Caramel Sauce around the dessert on the base of the plate. Pipe a dot of Cranberry Coulis in the center of each Caramel Sauce pool. Use a small wooden skewer to swirl the two sauces together (see photo in color insert). Arrange approximately six to eight chestnut pieces evenly around the plate between the sauce pools.

Lemon Pudding Cake

12 servings

melted unsalted butter

5 ounces (140 g) unsalted butter, at room temperature

14 ounces (400 g) granulated sugar

10 eggs, separated and at room temperature

grated zest from two medium lemons (2 tablespoons/36 g)

3¹/₂ ounces (100 g) bread flour

2¹/₂ cups (600 ml) milk, at room temperature

1¹/₄ cups (300 ml) lemon juice

dark coating chocolate, melted

one-half recipe Strawberry or Raspberry Sauce
    (see pages 1081 and 1080)

sliced fresh fruit (see note 1)

powdered sugar

twelve mint sprigs

NOTE 1: Use four or five different varieties of fruit or berries. Slice the fruit into precise pieces; leave berries whole. Try to cut the fruit as close to serving time as possible so the pieces do not become dry.

NOTE 2: If cake rings are not available, you can use sixteen 5-ounce (150-ml) souffle ramekins that are 3¹/₂ inches (8.7 cm) in diameter. This will make slightly smaller portions, which can be served in the forms or unmolded to display the pudding on top.

*P*udding cakes date all the way back to Colonial times, originating from what were called "flour" or "plain" puddings; today, they are also known as "sponge custards." Pudding cakes are basically egg custards with the addition of a small amount of flour and a large amount of air—the air whipped into the separated egg whites. During baking the air rises, causing the top portion of the dessert to develop a sponge cake-like texture while at the same time the remaining custard settles on the bottom and becomes a moist pudding. Lemon and orange pudding cakes are the most common and seem to work best due to the acidity of the citrus juice, which both aids in setting the cake layer and keeps the bottom layer from becoming too compact. Just like other custards, pudding cakes must be protected from extreme heat that would cause them to curdle, by baking in a bain-marie (because water can never reach a higher temperature than the boiling point—212°F/100°C—the surrounding water equalizes the temperature and acts as an insulator to protect from overcooking). The puddings should be left in the bain-marie for 10 minutes after they are removed from the oven to allow them to stabilize.

In this recipe I use individual cake rings to create a presentation more suited to restaurant service; however, pudding cakes are meant to be served very simply and are great with just about any fresh fruit or fruit sauce, and/or a dollop of whipped cream or a scoop of ice cream. For the more traditional method of baking and presenting the pudding cake in a single large casserole dish, bake the batter in a buttered 10-inch pan (at least 2 inches deep) lined with a buttered round of baking paper in the bottom, and increase the baking time by about 10 minutes. Use two large spoons to remove the portions, being careful to include some of each layer. If you plan to unmold the larger size pudding cake, let it cool at room temperature first then refrigerate for at least 4 hours or, preferably, overnight. Before unmolding, place the cake in the oven for a few minutes to warm it slightly or the custard will stick.

1. Cut twelve 6¹/₂-inch (16.2-cm) squares of aluminum foil (if you are using a thin grade of foil, double the thickness). Set metal cake rings 3 inches (7.5 cm) in diameter and 2 inches high (5 cm) in the center of the squares. Pleat and fold the edges of the foil up tightly against the rings all around to form a tight seal. (Be sure the seal reaches at least three-quarters of the way up the sides of the rings because the puddings are to be baked in a water bath.) Brush melted butter over the inside and "bottoms" of the rings. Place the rings in a hotel pan and set aside (see note 2).

2. Cream the soft butter with one-third of the sugar. Beat in the egg yolks a few at a time. Stir in the lemon zest, flour, milk, and lemon juice. Continue stirring until all of the ingredients are completely incorporated. If the eggs—and, even more so, the milk—were cooler than specified (they should be around 70°F/21°C) the emulsion will break. This can be corrected by warming the mixture slightly, but the finished puddings will be dense and not as high.

3. Whip the egg whites until they have tripled in volume. Gradually add the remaining sugar and whip until soft peaks form. Carefully stir the whipped whites into the lemon mixture. Pour or spoon the batter into the prepared cake rings, dividing it equally. Add ¹/₂ inch (1.2 cm) of hot water to the hotel pan.

4. Bake at 350°F (175°C) for approximately 40 minutes or until set. The sponge on top of the desserts will develop a light brown color. Set aside still in the water bath for 10 minutes. Remove the puddings from the water bath, allow them to cool to room temperature, then refrigerate for a minimum of 3 hours to allow the custard to set. The puddings may be stored in the baking rings, covered in the refrigerator, for up to three days.

5. Place some melted coating chocolate in a piping bag. Pipe a design of four intersecting lines over the base and rim of twelve dessert plates, forming an open diamond-shaped box in the center of the lines, and placing the lines so that the diamond is positioned slightly off-center toward the lower part of the plate. Set the plates aside.

6. Place the Strawberry or Raspberry Sauce in a piping bottle. Reserve.

7. Presentation: Peel the aluminum foil away from the sides of one dessert. Place one hand underneath the foil on the bottom and hold onto the cake ring with the other hand. Tilt the dessert (so it doesn't slide out) and peel the foil away from the bottom. Carefully set the pudding (with the cake ring still attached) on the upper part of the base on one of the prepared dessert plates, next to the diamond-shaped box. Remove the cake ring. Pipe Strawberry or Raspberry Sauce inside the chocolate lines of the center diamond. Arrange fresh fruit around the pudding. Sift powdered sugar over the pudding and the plate. Garnish with a mint sprig and serve immediately.

 Meyer Lemon Bars

24 bars

10 ounces (285 g) soft unsalted butter
8 ounces (225 g) light brown sugar
1 egg
13 ounces (370 g) bread flour
Meyer Lemon Filling (recipe follows)
powdered sugar

There are two types of lemons: sweet and acid. The latter are the most popular of commercially grown lemons, the bulk of which are either Eureka (recognizable by a short neck at the stem end) or Lisbon (on which the blossom end appears as a pointed nipple). Lisbons are just about seedless as well, which is also true of the sweet, roundish (no neck or nipple) thin-skinned Meyer lemon. Biologically not a true lemon, this hybrid was discovered near Peking, China (now Beijing), by Frank Meyer. It was introduced to this country in the beginning of the twentieth century, and since then the compact size and shape of the tree has made this citrus variety the most popular among homegrown lemons.

If you prefer your Lemon Bars a bit more tangy, either reduce the amount of sugar in the recipe by a few ounces or use an acid type of lemon and possibly increase the sugar a little.

1. Place the butter, brown sugar, and egg in a mixing bowl. Mix at low speed, using the dough hook attachment, until the ingredients are just combined. Add the flour and continue to mix until the dough is smooth, scraping down the sides of the mixing bowl once or twice; do not mix any longer than necessary. Refrigerate the dough until it is firm enough to work with.

2. Line the bottom of a half-sheet pan (12 by 16 inches/30 × 40 cm) with baking paper. Roll the chilled dough out to a rectangle slightly larger than the pan and line the bottom and sides of the pan with the dough; you should use up all of the dough. Prick the dough well over the bottom of the pan. Cut a sheet of baking paper to cover the bottom and long sides of the dough in the pan. Place the paper on top of the dough and fill with dried beans or pie weights.

3. Bake at 375°F (190°C) until the crust is golden brown around the top edges, approximately 15 minutes. Remove the beans or pie weights (be certain to get any that stick to the dough on the short ends) and the baking paper, then return the shell to the oven to finish baking the crust on the bottom, about 5 minutes longer.

4. Make the filling while the crust is baking. Pour the filling over the hot crust as soon as it is removed from the oven. Return to the oven and lower the oven temperature to 350°F (175°C). Bake for about 25 minutes longer or until the filling has thickened and a very light brown skin has formed on top.

5. Let cool completely and then cut into twenty-four bars, four strips lengthwise by six across. Sift powdered sugar lightly over the bars.

 Meyer Lemon Filling

about 6 cups (1 l, 440 ml)

4 tablespoons (32 g) cornstarch
1 pound, 8 ounces (680 g) granulated
   sugar
12 eggs
4 egg yolks (¹/₃ cup/80 ml)
finely grated zest from four lemons
2¹/₂ cups (600 ml) Meyer lemon juice

1. Stir the cornstarch into the sugar. Mix in the eggs, egg yolks, lemon zest, and lemon juice, stirring until the ingredients are well combined; do not whip or beat the mixture.

2. Place the mixture over a bain-marie and heat, stirring constantly, until the filling has thickened; do not overheat.

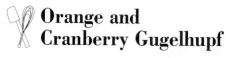

Mom's Applecake (Mor's Äppelkaka)

one 10-inch (25-cm) cake

3 pounds (1 kg, 365 g) cooking apples such as Golden Delicious or Granny Smith (approximately seven medium-sized)

12 ounces (340 g) granulated sugar, approximately

1¼ cups (300 ml) water

juice of one-half lemon

3 ounces (85 g) melted unsalted butter

10 ounces (285 g) finely ground white bread crumbs, toasted

1 teaspoon (5 ml) vanilla extract

8 ounces (225 g) Streusel Topping (page 14)

powdered sugar

one-half recipe Vanilla Custard Sauce (page 1082)

ground cinnamon (optional)

This traditional Swedish country-style variation of an apple pie was standard at home and was one of my favorites as a child. It was always served with a thick and rich vanilla sauce and sometimes, if we were really lucky, some whipped cream on the side. This dessert was quick and simple to prepare since there was no pie tin to line, and there was always a supply of stale bread either dried (to prevent mildew) or already made into bread crumbs. Homemade apple jam was plentiful in the cellar after the harvest, so it was really just a question of layering the two ingredients together. I have added the Streusel Topping for a little more finished look, but it can very well be left out. And if you then (as I often do) replace the vanilla sauce with ice cream—which can be purchased along with the apple jam and bread crumbs—you have just run out of excuses for not trying this recipe. A word of caution: do not leave the Applecake in the oven too long; although the jam will seem very loose when the cake first comes out of the oven, the natural pectin will set it as it cools.

1. Peel and core the apples. Chop into large chunks. Place in a saucepan with the sugar, water, and lemon juice. If the apples are very sweet, decrease the sugar a bit; the filling should be tart and refreshing. Stir to combine and cook over medium heat, stirring from time to time, until the apple pieces are soft. Remove from the heat and process in a food processor until smooth.

2. Use some of the butter to coat the inside of a 10-inch (25-cm) cake pan or other ovenproof dish of approximately the same size. Add the remaining butter to the bread crumbs along with the vanilla. Mix to combine thoroughly. Sprinkle half of the bread crumb mixture evenly over the bottom of the pan. Press down to compact. Spread half of the apple filling over the top. Repeat with the remaining crumb mixture and remaining filling to make a total of four layers.

3. Sprinkle the Streusel Topping evenly over the second apple filling layer.

4. Bake at 400°F (205°C) for approximately 12 minutes or until the Streusel begins to color. Let cool to room temperature.

5. Run a knife around the inside perimeter of the pan, invert onto a cake cardboard or platter and then invert again to turn right-side up. Sift powdered sugar lightly over the top. Cut into the desired number of servings. Serve with Vanilla Custard Sauce and sprinkle cinnamon lightly over the sauce if you like.

Orange and Cranberry Gugelhupf

two 5-cup (1 l-, 200-ml) capacity gugelhupf pans

Butter and Flour Mixture (page 4)

1½ cups (360 ml) orange juice

These turban-shaped cakes are extremely popular in the German-speaking countries of Europe. The configuration is said to have been modeled after the headdress of a sultan. Gugelhupf cakes were introduced by an inventive Viennese pastry chef in the seventeenth century. For more information see the traditional version on page 163, which is leavened with yeast, unlike this quick-bread style, which uses chemical leaveners. If you do not have a gugelhupf pan,

4 tablespoons (72 g) grated orange zest

¹/₂ cup (120 ml) or 3 ounces (85 g) dried cranberries

3 ounces (85 g) unsalted butter

8 ounces (225 g) cake flour

¹/₂ teaspoon (2.5 g) salt

1¹/₂ teaspoons (6 g) baking powder

¹/₂ teaspoon (2 g) baking soda

3 eggs

8 ounces (225 g) granulated sugar

1 cup (240 ml) buttermilk

12 ounces (340 g) walnuts, chopped to raisin-sized pieces

using a bundt pan will work just fine; however, if you must resort to using a loaf pan, you will need to increase the baking time slightly. The gugelhupf pan is designed not only to produce an attractive presentation that makes it look as if there is more there than meets the eye but like any tube pan, the hole in the center allows the heat to penetrate and bake the cake from all sides.

1. Brush the Butter and Flour Mixture over the inside of two 5-cup (1-l, 200-ml) capacity gugelhupf pans or other suitable tube pans.

2. Combine the orange juice, orange zest, cranberries, and butter in a saucepan. Bring to a boil. Remove from the heat and let stand for 30 minutes.

3. Sift together the flour, salt, baking powder, and baking soda. Reserve.

4. Beat the eggs with the granulated sugar at high speed until frothy, about 1 minute. Incorporate the orange mixture. Add the flour mixture in two additions, alternating with the buttermilk. Stir in the walnuts.

5. Divide the batter between the prepared pans.

6. Bake at 350°F (175°C) for approximately 35 minutes or until a cake tester inserted into the cakes comes out dry. Unmold onto a cake rack and let cool.

Pear Brown Betty with Pear and Dried Cranberry Sauce

16 servings

Pear and Dried Cranberry Sauce (recipe follows)

melted unsalted butter

6 pounds, 8 ounces (2 kg, 955 g) Anjou or Comice pears (approximately twelve medium-sized)

10 ounces (285 g) unsalted butter

5 ounces (140 g) light brown sugar

5 ounces (140 g) granulated sugar

1 tablespoon (5 g) ground cinnamon

1¹/₂ cups (360 ml) orange juice, at room temperature

1 pound, 4 ounces (570 g) bread, cut into ¹/₂-inch (1.2-cm) cubes (see note 2)

cranberries reserved from preparing the sauce

1 cup (240 ml) heavy cream

1 teaspoon (5 g) granulated sugar

orange or mandarin segments

sixteen mint sprigs

*T*he elusive Brown Betty has a long and interesting history. Most likely it was brought to the United States from Europe in early Colonial times. This type of dessert was most popular in the northeast, where it was made with apples and was known originally as Apple Pan Dowdy. (Today, the name pan dowdy is used for a dessert consisting of a layer of fruit baked with cake batter on top.) The name Brown Betty is said to have originated in Virginia. At Christmas it was customary for each plantation to put on a minstrel show with the characters portrayed by African slaves. The two main roles were that of Father Christmas and Mother Christmas, who was also known as Old Beth. At the conclusion of the play Father Christmas would distribute presents while Old Beth served a dessert which was very similar to the old-fashioned version of Apple Pan Dowdy. By the mid-1800s Old Beth's treat had become known as Apple Brown Betty in many cookbooks.

One of the reasons that this dessert and others like it were so popular at that time is that not only were they simple to prepare but they could be cooked in a slow oven alongside other dishes for a long period of time without attention (one old recipe actually directs that the dish be cooked overnight). Since we do not have the luxury of this much time (or perhaps patience) today, the fruit—either the traditional apples, or pears as in this version—should be precooked before baking, either by poaching, or sautéing with butter and sugar to a light caramel as is done here. This precooking step is even more critical if you prepare the dessert in the conventional form using a single large casserole or gratin dish. Brown Betty should always be served hot or warm accompanied by cream or ice cream.

NOTE 1: This dessert is best served warm. It may be served at room temperature but should never be served chilled.

NOTE 2: Use any plain white bread; slightly stale is best. Avoid using commercial-type sandwich bread, which tends to fall apart when it becomes moist. Leftover Brioche is an ideal choice.

1. Prepare the Pear and Dried Cranberry Sauce. Reserve.

2. Brush melted butter over the inside of sixteen ovenproof coffee cups or ramekins approximately 3 inches (7.5 cm) in diameter with straight sides. Reserve.

3. Peel and core the pears. Cut the pears into ³/₄-inch (2-cm) cubes.

4. Place half of the butter in a large skillet and place it over medium heat. Sprinkle the brown sugar and the first measurement of granulated sugar on top. Add the pear cubes and stir to combine, making sure all of the sugar has been moistened. Cook the mixture, stirring from time to time at the beginning and constantly at the end (the pears will release a great deal of moisture at the start), until the liquid has been reduced to approximately 1 cup (240 ml) of thick syrup; it will be a light caramel color.

5. Add the cinnamon and the orange juice. Bring to a boil, cook for 1 minute, then remove from the heat. Melt the remaining butter and stir it into the pear mixture. Let the filling cool for a few minutes.

6. Add the bread cubes and two-thirds of the cranberries to the pear mixture, tossing with your hands until thoroughly combined. Reserve the remaining cranberries to use in the presentation. Divide the filling among the prepared coffee cups and press it down lightly.

7. Bake at 375°F (190°C) for 15 minutes. Place a cover over the desserts and continue baking about 30 minutes longer. The desserts should be light brown on the sides. Allow to cool slightly, then unmold onto a sheet pan lined with baking paper.

8. Whip the heavy cream and 1 teaspoon (5 g) sugar to stiff peaks. Place in a pastry bag with a no. 7 (14-mm) star tip. Reserve in the refrigerator until needed.

9. Presentation: Place an inverted Brown Betty centered in the upper half of a dessert plate (warm the dessert first if necessary). Pour Pear and Dried Cranberry Sauce over part of the dessert and onto the plate, forming a pool in front. Sprinkle five or six of the reserved dried cranberries on top of the sauce. Arrange three or four orange or mandarin segments around the sauce. Pipe large rosettes of whipped cream on the plate on either side of the Brown Betty. Place a mint sprig on top of the dessert and serve immediately.

 Pear and Dried Cranberry Sauce

4 cups (960 ml)

¹/₄ cup (60 ml) lime juice
   (approximately two limes)
¹/₂ cup (120 ml) cranberry juice
4 ounces (115 g) granulated sugar
6 ounces (170 g) dried cranberries
3 pounds (1 kg, 365 g) ripe pears
   (approximately six medium-sized)
one recipe Plain Poaching Syrup
   (page 13)

1. Combine the lime juice, cranberry juice, granulated sugar, and dried cranberries in a saucepan. Bring to a boil over medium heat and cook for 1 minute. Remove from the heat and set aside to steep.

2. Peel, core, and cut the pears in half, placing them in the Poaching Syrup as you work to prevent oxidation. Poach the pears in the syrup until they are soft and tender.

3. Place the drained poached pear halves in a blender with ¹/₃ cup (80 ml) of the poaching liquid. Reserve the remaining poaching liquid for another use. Process the pears to a smooth paste.

4. Strain the cranberries from the juice mixture and set aside to use for the Brown Betty (see note). Add enough of the juice mixture to the cornstarch to dissolve. Stir back into the remaining juice along with the

1 tablespoon (8 g) cornstarch

4 ounces (115 g) melted unsalted butter

1/4 cup (60 ml) pear brandy

NOTE: If you are preparing this sauce to accompany a dessert other than the Brown Betty, you may choose to leave the cranberries in the sauce, or they may be refrigerated or frozen to use in other recipes such as Italian Pear, Almond, and Cranberry Tart or muffins.

 # Pear Upside-Down Cake

two 10-inch (25-cm) cakes

12 ounces (340 g) unsalted butter

10 ounces (285 g) light brown sugar

6 pounds, 12 ounces (3 kg, 70 g) Bartlett or Anjou pears (approximately twelve medium-sized)

two recipes Plain Poaching Syrup (page 13)

7 ounces (200 g) soft unsalted butter

14 ounces (400 g) granulated sugar

3 eggs, at room temperature

1 tablespoon (15 ml) vanilla extract

1 pound (455 g) cake flour

2 tablespoons (24 g) baking powder

1 3/4 cups (420 ml) milk, at room temperature

Maple-Pecan Ice Cream (page 633)

pear purée. Bring the sauce to a boil. Remove from the heat and stir in the melted butter and the pear brandy. Let the sauce cool to room temperature before using. Thin with additional cranberry juice or poaching liquid as needed, depending on the level of sweetness desired. Do not serve chilled.

*T*his type of cake gained popularity in the 1930s and is still going strong today. Upside-down cakes are also known as skillet cakes because they were originally baked in cast iron skillets, something that was more useful to have in the old days than a cake pan, plus it was simple enough to melt the butter and sugar in the skillet and then simply pour the batter on top instead of transferring the sugar mixture to another pan. The best-known version is the traditional pineapple upside-down cake, although just about any type of fruit can be used in this application. During the baking process the sugar, butter, and fruit juices cook together into a light caramel underneath the cake batter. When the cake is inverted the caramel glazes the fruit on top of the cake in much the same way as in a caramelized apple tart like Tart Tatin. It is important that the cake itself is dense enough to be able to absorb the juices and caramel without falling apart. For this reason the batter is closer to the formula for a pound or tea cake than that of a sponge cake. Upside-down cakes should be served warm. As a dessert serve with ice cream or whipped cream or offer as is for brunch or a coffee break.*

To make the pineapple version you will need a fresh pineapple weighing about 2 pounds (910 g). Rinse the fruit, cut off the crown, and cut away the skin, cutting deep enough to remove all of the eyes. Cut the pineapple into 1/4-inch (6-mm) slices. Cut out the core using a plain cookie cutter. Place two of the largest pineapple slices on top of the sugar mixture in the center of the pans. Cut the remaining slices across to make half-rings. Arrange the cut pieces side by side with the round edge against the pan, beginning at the edge and forming concentric circles around the center ring. Proceed as directed for the Pear Upside-Down Cake except that pineapple upside-down cake should be inverted as soon as it is removed from the oven and should be left this way for a few minutes before removing the baking pan.

1. Melt the first measurement of butter. Stir in the brown sugar. Spread the mixture evenly over the bottom of two 10-inch (25-cm) cake pans. Set aside.

2. Peel, core, and cut the pears in half, placing them into acidulated water as you work. Transfer the pear halves to the Poaching Syrup and poach just until they begin to soften. Let cool in the liquid.

3. Remove the pears from the liquid. Cut each half into three wedges. Arrange the pear wedges round-side down in a spoke pattern on top of the sugar mixture in the cake pans. Reserve.

4. Cream the soft butter with the granulated sugar until light and fluffy. Beat in the eggs and vanilla and continue beating for 1 minute. Sift the flour and baking powder together and add to the batter in two additions, alternating with the milk.

5. Divide the cake batter between the two prepared pans, spreading it out evenly on top of the pears.

6. Bake at 375°F (190°C) for approximately 45 minutes. Remove from the oven and let the cakes cool for 10 minutes. Run a knife around the sides of the pans to loosen the cakes. Invert the cakes onto serving platters or cake cardboards. Serve warm with Maple-Pecan Ice Cream.

Pies

Caramelized Apple Pie with Lattice Crust

one 10-inch (25-cm) pie

5 pounds (2 kg, 275 g) cooking apples
    such as pippin, Granny Smith, or
    Golden Delicious (approximately
    eleven medium-sized)
10 ounces (285 g) unsalted butter
2 teaspoons (3 g) ground cinnamon
1 pound (455 g) granulated sugar
one-third recipe Pie Dough (page 36)
1 cup (240 ml) bourbon whiskey
1/2 cup (120 ml) orange liqueur
1 cup (240 ml) heavy cream
2 ounces (55 g) melted unsalted butter

*A*lthough there is no question that apples were formed into tarts and baked between layers of dough dating back as far as the Middle Ages, the first recorded use of the particular name "apple pie" was in late sixteenth-century England with the spelling of pie as "pye."

America is now the country considered to epitomize pies, and apple in particular, evidenced by the popular phrase "as American as apple pie." My grandparents emigrated from Sweden to America (separately) at the end of the 1800s. They met here, married, worked hard and saved their money, and returned to southern Sweden where they bought a small farm and, as was the norm, started a large family. As a kid I loved spending part of each summer at my grandparents' house, where my two favorite activities were sitting on my Farfar's lap listening to stories about the big country of America and, second, eating Farmor's apple pies. The pies had a thick double crust (a trick she had no doubt picked up while in America), and to a hungry kid they were just as delicious a few days after they were baked as they were right out of the oven.

In this recipe the apples are cooked in a rich caramel syrup flavored with whiskey and orange liqueur before they are enclosed in the pie crust. Some of this liquid is drained off and becomes an instant apple-flavored caramel sauce, the perfect accompaniment to the pie. If you do not have time to fuss with making a lattice top, there is ample Pie Dough for a solid top crust. Regardless of the style of crust, if at all possible serve this pie with a scoop of ice cream, either Vanilla, Cinnamon, or Maple-Pecan (see pages 640, 629, and 633).

1. Peel, core, and cut the apples in half. Cut the halves into 1/4-inch (6-mm) slices. Melt the first measurement of butter in a large skillet or sauté pan. Add the apples and cook over medium heat, stirring frequently, for 5 minutes. Mix the ground cinnamon into the sugar. Add this to the apples, stirring until thoroughly combined. The juice released from the apples in combination with the melted sugar will cause a large amount of liquid to collect in the pan. Continue cooking the apples, still stirring frequently, until they are caramelized and translucent but still firm to the touch. Depending on the apples used and their stage of ripeness, it may be necessary to remove some of the liquid to expedite the caramelizing process and avoid overcooking the apples. If so, boil the liquid in a separate pan until it is reduced to a thick syrup and then add it back to the apples.

2. While the apples are cooking, roll the Pie Dough out to a rectangle 11 inches (27.5 cm) wide and $^1/_8$ inch (3 mm) thick, using flour to prevent the dough from sticking. Cut the dough in half across. Cover one piece and place in the refrigerator. Use the remaining piece to line a 10-inch (25-cm) pie pan. Reserve in the refrigerator.

3. Once the apples are caramelized add the bourbon, orange liqueur, and the cream. Continue cooking until the mixture has reduced and thickened again. Remove from the heat and strain the apples in a colander, reserving the liquid. Let the apples cool before proceeding.

4. Brush some of the melted butter over the bottom of the lined pie pan. Fill the crust with the apples, shaping them into an even mound on the top. Cut the reserved Pie Dough into $^3/_8$-inch (9-mm) strips and arrange on top of the apples in a lattice pattern (instructions follow). Pinch the ends of the strips against the edge of the bottom crust. Cover the dough scraps and save for another use. Brush the remainder of the melted butter (reheat if necessary) over the lattice strips.

5. Bake at 375°F (190°C) for approximately 1 hour. Let cool a bit and then serve with the reserved apple cooking liquid as a sauce. If the liquid has cooled substantially, it may have to be warmed to a pourable consistency.

To make a lattice pattern crust

1. Arrange vertical strips of dough evenly spaced across the pie letting the ends hang over on either side.

2. Starting with the strip on the left, lift up and fold back every other strip halfway.

3. Place a strip of dough horizontally across the center of the pie. Return the folded strips to their original position so they cross over the horizontal strip (Figure 15–6).

4. Starting with the second strip on the left this time, fold back every other strip. Place a second horizontal strip evenly spaced below the first. Return the folded strips to their original position.

5. Repeat this pattern until you have covered the bottom half of the pie, then turn the pie around and repeat with the other half (Figure 15–7).

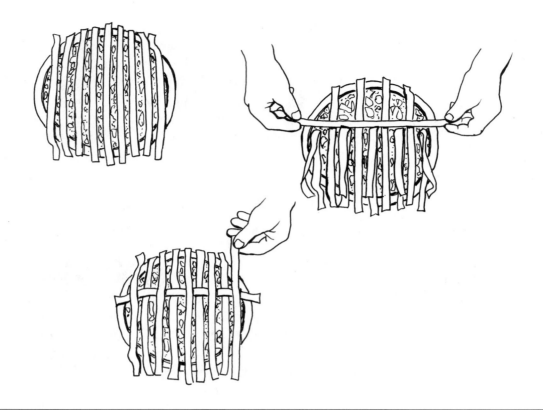

FIGURE 15–6 *Strips of pie dough arranged vertically over the top of the filling; placing a strip of dough horizontally over the filling after folding back every other vertical strip halfway; unfolding the vertical strips to return them to their original position, now over and under the horizontal strip*

FIGURE 15–7 *Adding a second horizontal strip after folding back every other vertical strip again, but beginning with the second strip from the left this time; unfolding the vertical strips to return them to their original position, now over and under the second horizontal strip; unfolding the last vertical strip to return it to its original position after repeating the pattern on both sides to cover the top of the pie*

Lemon Meringue Pie

two 10-inch (25-cm) pies

one-half recipe Pie Dough (page 36)

3 ounces (85 g) cornstarch

1 pound, 8 ounces (680 g) granulated
   sugar

1 teaspoon (5 g) salt

3 cups (720 ml) water

5 ounces (140 g) unsalted butter

10 egg yolks (⅞ cup/200 ml)

¾ cup (180 ml) lemon juice

1 tablespoon (18 g) finely grated
   lemon zest

Meringue Pie Topping (recipe follows)

Like the apple pie, Lemon Meringue Pie is an American favorite and has been since the nineteenth century. The sweet billowy meringue topping perfectly offsets the slightly tart lemon base, which seems by far to be the preferred portion of the pie, judging by the meringue often left on the dessert plate. The meringue topping is definitely the trouble spot in this dessert. I am constantly asked by my students (often prompted by the boss at their after-school jobs) how to prevent the meringue from weeping and separating from (sliding off) the filling. First of all, this really cannot be avoided in a pie that is more than 24 hours old, and this is a well-known and easy gauge used by the consumer to judge if they are being served a pie that is not too fresh.

In making meringue the baker must consider Mother Nature. Just as spun sugar is much more susceptible to breaking down or weeping in rainy weather or if the humidity is high, the sugar in the meringue will absorb moisture from the air and melt, releasing a liquid, under these same conditions. There are some chefs who emphasize that the lemon filling should be cold when the meringue is placed on lemon pie filling, and yet others specify just the opposite. Even though it does make sense to spread the meringue on a hot filling, since it has a better chance of adhering to a soft surface rather than a slick, firm filling which has been refrigerated, this is not always practical. In my experience it is usually sufficient if the filling is no cooler than room temperature, as long as it has been covered to prevent a skin from forming. A more important factor is the meringue itself. Proper procedure must be followed for whipping the meringue, placing it on the pie, and baking. Overwhipped egg whites or meringues prepared without enough sugar tend to break down and release moisture (weep) much faster after baking. Baking the topping at too high a temperature (which generally results in not baking long enough) makes the meringue brown too quickly before the structure of the egg whites has had time to fully gelatinize, which again will cause the meringue to release moisture after it has cooled. To keep the meringue from shrinking away from the pie shell, it is important to make certain that the meringue is touching the crust all around the edge with no gaps. The Meringue Topping used here includes a small amount of cooked cornstarch, which helps to stabilize the topping just as it does in the lemon filling. If it happens that your meringue still does not behave after following all of these rules, you can take some consolation in the fact that you are by no means alone.

1. Roll out the Pie Dough to ⅛ inch (3 mm) thick, line two 10-inch (25-cm) pie pans, and flute the edges (see Figures 2–2 and 2–3, page 37). Cover the dough scraps and save for another use. Place the shells in the refrigerator until firm.

2. Prick the bottom of the pie shells. Cover the dough with rounds of baking paper and fill with dried beans or pie weights. Bake at 375°F (190°C) until the dough begins to color around the edges, about 15 minutes. Remove the weights and the baking papers and continue baking until the shells are light brown and baked through, approximately 10 minutes longer. Set aside to cool.

3. Place the cornstarch, granulated sugar, and salt in a saucepan and mix until thoroughly combined. Incorporate the water, stirring with a whisk. Cook over low heat, stirring constantly with the whisk, until the mixture comes to a boil. Boil gently for several minutes. Add the butter and stir until it is melted and incorporated. Remove from the heat.

4. Add a portion of the cornstarch mixture to the egg yolks to temper, then add this back to the remaining cornstarch mixture and stir until combined. Add the lemon juice and grated lemon zest. Place the saucepan back on the stove over low heat and cook the filling, stirring constantly, until it has boiled for about 2 minutes.

5. Immediately divide the hot filling between the two prepared pie shells. Cover to prevent a skin from forming while you make the Meringue Pie Topping. Evenly distribute the Meringue Pie Topping over the filling, spreading it into peaks and swirls, and making sure it is attached to the pie crust all around the edges.

6. Place the pies on double sheet pans and bake at 375°F (190°C) for about 10 minutes or until the meringue is nicely browned. The pies must be refrigerated for several hours before serving to allow the filling to set.

Meringue Pie Topping

2¹/₂ tablespoons (20 g) cornstarch
³/₄ cup (180 ml) water
1¹/₄ cups (300 ml) egg whites
2 or 3 drops of lemon juice
10 ounces (285 g) granulated sugar
2 teaspoons (10 ml) vanilla extract

1. Combine the cornstarch and water in a small saucepan. Bring to a simmer while stirring constantly. Cook for about 1 minute until the mixture is translucent. Remove from the heat and set aside.

2. Whip the egg whites with the lemon juice until tripled in volume. Gradually add the sugar and continue whipping until soft peaks form.

3. Still whipping, add the vanilla and then the cornstarch mixture, a little at a time. Whip the meringue to stiff peaks but be careful not to overwhip. Use immediately.

Sweet Potato Pie

two 10-inch (25-cm) pies

one-half recipe Pie Dough (page 36)
5 eggs
3 cups (720 ml) cooked sweet potato purée (directions follow)
12 ounces (340 g) granulated sugar
1 teaspoon (5 g) salt
2 teaspoons (3 g) ground cinnamon
1 teaspoon (2 g) ground ginger
¹/₂ teaspoon (1 g) ground cloves
3¹/₂ cups (840 ml) half-and-half
1 pint (480 ml) heavy cream
1 tablespoon (15 g) granulated sugar

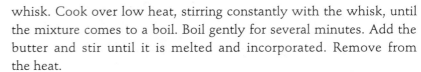

*S*weet potatoes and sweet potato pie have deep ties to the American South and southern regional cooking. Sweet potatoes are also an important agricultural crop in the southern states, though they are grown elsewhere in the country (New Jersey and California being the other top producers) as well. The flesh is naturally sweet due to an enzyme in the potato that converts the majority of its starches to sugar as the potato matures. Still, most traditional American recipes call for generous quantities of additional sweeteners such as maple syrup, brown sugar, molasses, and, of course, marshmallows for the odd, but apparently essential, candied sweet potatoes served for Thanksgiving dinner (this strange combination was popularized in the 1920s, and though it is doubtful that anyone other than young children actually like it, is so ingrained in the holiday menu we will probably never be rid of it).

The sweet potato is not related to the common white potato but is part of the morning glory family. Native to America, it was brought back to Europe by Columbus in the late 1400s. By the middle of the sixteenth century, the sweet *potato was cultivated in Spain and had been introduced to England, and sweet potato pie had became popular enough in England by the turn of the century to be mentioned by Shakespeare in* The Merry Wives of Windsor. *Sweet potatoes were so widely cultivated by the American colonists that this high-energy tuber was actually the main food source for some of the early settlers and soldiers in the Revolutionary War. (Sweet potatoes are, in fact, one of the most nutritious of all vegetables, containing only trace amounts of fat and approximately five times the RDA of vitamin A in a single small potato, as well as substantial amounts of the vitamins B₆ and C.) The term* sweet potato *was not used in America until the mid-1700s, at which time it came about as a means to distinguish sweet potatoes from the white potatoes that had come to the New World with the Irish immigrants.*

There are two different varieties of sweet potato: The moist orange-fleshed type has a darker skin and is longer and more narrow in shape. The dry-fleshed variety has a slightly lighter skin, closer to the color of a russet potato, and is rounder, shaped something like a football. Darker moist-fleshed sweet potatoes are often erroneously called "yams." Genuine yams are from a different botanical family and are much larger—growing up to seven feet in length and up to 100 pounds—and are found in Asia and Africa; they are seldom available in this country. Because of its widespread usage, this misnomer has become generally accepted.

1. Roll the Pie Dough out to ¹/₈ inch (3 mm) thick. Line two 10-inch (25-cm) pie pans and flute the edges (see Figures 2–2 and 2–3, page 37). Cover the dough scraps and save for another use. Cover the dough in the pans with rounds of baking paper and fill the shells with dried beans or pie weights. Bake the shells at 375°F (190°C) until the dough is set but has not yet started to color, about 12 minutes. Let the shells cool completely, then remove the paper and beans or pie weights. Reserve.

2. Beat the eggs lightly to mix. Stir in the sweet potato purée. Mix together the first measure of granulated sugar, the salt, cinnamon, ginger, and cloves. Add this to the egg mixture. Stir in the half-and-half. Divide the filling evenly between the two pie shells.

3. Bake at 375°F (190°C) for approximately 50 minutes or until the filling has puffed slightly and is firm around the edges. Let the pies cool.

4. Whip the heavy cream with the second measure of granulated sugar until stiff peaks form. Slice the pies into the desired sized pieces. Serve at room temperature with a large dollop of whipped cream.

To make the sweet potato purée

Start with about 2 pounds (910 g) of raw potatoes (preferably the darker, moist-fleshed variety) with the skin on. Boil them gently until soft, peel, and purée or force through a fine sieve.

Plum Kuchen

12 servings

Butter and Flour Mixture (page 4)
10 ounces (285 g) cake flour
2 teaspoons (8 g) baking powder
1 teaspoon (4 g) baking soda
1 teaspoon (5 g) salt
$^{1}/_{2}$ teaspoon (.75 g) ground cinnamon
4 ounces (115 g) firm unsalted butter
6 ounces (170 g) light brown sugar
3 eggs
2 teaspoons (10 ml) vanilla extract
$^{1}/_{2}$ cup (120 ml) buttermilk
4 ounces (115 g) dried currants
Cinnamon Sugar (page 5)
2 pounds (910 g) plums such as
     Queen Ann or Nubiana (about ten
     medium or eight large)
Simple Syrup (page 11)
one-half recipe Plum Sauce
     (page 1079)
powdered sugar
Vanilla Ice Cream (page 640)

Kuchen *is a German word for pastry or cake (it can also mean tart but is used less often in that capacity). Using a German name in a plum dessert seems especially appropriate to me since plums are used so frequently in pastry kitchens all over Europe. Plums are also used to make wine, liqueur, and jam. I like them best (other than eaten fresh from my trees) baked into a custard or other filling in a tart shell. In the photograph of the following presentation I use three very different looking plums: The bluish Italian prune plum is the only European variety among the three, and oddly enough it originated in Germany, not Italy. Prune plums are too sweet to have a real plum taste when baked but are great to eat fresh; they are used for garnish and, of course, they are dried to make prunes. Their flesh has a slight green tint before the plums are fully ripe. The yellow Wickson plum originated in California. Like the Italian prune plum, this one is better to eat fresh or use as a garnish than to use for cooking. The reddish Japanese Kelsey plum can either be cooked or eaten fresh.*

This country-style dessert is effortless to make. I use rectangular tart pans, but you can also use two 8- or 9-inch (20- or 22.5-cm) round pans. As a variation, try serving Plum Kuchen with Chantilly Cream (page 1083) instead of the Vanilla Ice Cream and Plum Sauce.

1. Brush Butter and Flour Mixture over the inside of two 14-by-4-inch (35-×-10-cm) fluted, false-bottom tart pans. Reserve.

2. Sift together the flour, baking powder, baking soda, salt, and ground cinnamon. Place in a mixing bowl. Cut in the firm butter, continuing until the mixture is the consistency of streusel and the pieces of butter are about the size of small peas.

3. In a separate bowl, mix together the brown sugar, eggs, and vanilla. Stir in the buttermilk and the currants. Add this to the flour mixture, stirring just until combined. Divide the batter evenly between the two prepared pans; they should be filled halfway. Spread the batter level. Sprinkle the Cinnamon Sugar over the batter.

4. Cut the plums in half and remove the stones. Place each plum half skin-side down and make three cuts, lengthwise, without cutting all the way through. Place the plum halves on top of the batter, skin-side down and evenly spaced, in two rows at a 45° angle to the long sides of the pan. Press the plums halfway into the batter.

5. Bake the cakes at 400°F (205°C) for approximately 35 minutes or until dark golden brown. The cake between the plums should spring back when pressed lightly. Let the cakes cool, then remove them from the pans.

6. Brush Simple Syrup over the plums. Cut each cake strip into six wedges (this will leave you with a small piece from each end to sample). Place the Plum Sauce in a piping bottle and reserve.

7. Presentation: Place a wedge of Plum Kuchen slightly off-center on a dessert plate. Sift powdered sugar lightly over the cake and the entire plate. Pipe a pool of Plum Sauce in front of the dessert on the left side of the plate. Place a scoop of Vanilla Ice Cream to the right of the sauce and serve immediately.

Pound Cakes

Pound cakes—cakes prepared with one pound each of butter, sugar, eggs, and flour—were made in England beginning in the mid-1600s. At first these cakes also contained dried and candied fruits, nuts, and spices, as was popular in most of the desserts of that era. These original pound cakes (although they were not known as such) were the first deviation from the yeast-leavened, or bread-style cakes (similar to stollen or panettone) that had been made up to that point and were, in fact, the forerunners of the butter cakes and sponge cakes we know today. It was not until about a century later that the batter was baked plain without the extra flavorings, and the term *pound cake* came into fashion. And it was approximately one hundred years after that (mid-1800s), that pound cake really hit its stride with recipes included in most of the cookbooks of the day. These often varied slightly from the one-pound-each formula, using a little more flour or sugar to suit a particular cook's taste. These recipes generally included some liquid as well, such as brandy, sherry, or rose water, calling for about eight ounces to the one pound each of the other ingredients. In *Mrs. Beeton's Book of Household Management,* 1861, she states that "A glass of wine can sometimes be added to the mixture, but this is scarcely necessary as the cake will be found quite rich enough without it." In the twentieth century bakers began to add leaveners to the basic mixture along with some additional flour and sugar to maintain the density associated with the original.

An authentic pound cake contains only butter, sugar, eggs, and flour, in equal proportions. Salt and flavorings such as vanilla or almond extract, citrus rind, or spices are optional. Because these classic pound cakes do not contain any baking powder or baking soda, there is no residual flavor from a chemical leavener to mask the flavor of the ingredients, and as the name of the Vanilla-Butter Pound Cake suggests, the taste of these ingredients really comes through. But as good as they are plain, pound cakes lend themselves quite well to flavorful additions and hybrids as shown in the recipes for Almond Pound Cake, Basil and Tarragon Pound Cake, Lemon Buttermilk Pound Cake, Mustard Gingerbread, and White Spice Buttermilk Cake with Gingered-Dried Fruit Compote.

Almond Pound Cake

two 5-cup (1-l, 200-ml) capacity tube pans

melted unsalted butter
finely ground almonds
8 ounces (225 g) Almond Paste
    (page 3)
6 ounces (170 g) granulated sugar
11 ounces (310 g) soft unsalted butter
6 eggs, at room temperature
7 ounces (200 g) bread flour
7 ounces (200 g) cake flour
1 tablespoon (12 g) baking powder
1 teaspoon (5 g) salt
grated zest of one lemon
1 teaspoon (5 ml) vanilla extract
³/₄ cup (180 ml) milk
4 egg whites (¹/₂ cup/120 ml)
6 ounces (170 g) granulated sugar

*S*econd to the Vanilla-Butter Pound Cake, this recipe is closest of the group to the classic version. It may not look as if the ingredients are in line with the one-pound-each formula at first glance, but when you consider that the Almond Paste is basically half fat and half sugar, this brings the combined fat measurement to 15 ounces and the combined sugar weight to 16 ounces. With the flour at 14 ounces and the combined whole eggs (six at 2 ounces) and egg whites (four at 1 ounce each) weighing 16 ounces, this cake actually comes quite close to the original except for the addition of a leavener and milk, which are not used in the classical formula but work well in this recipe to give the cake a rich almond flavor from the Almond Paste without becoming too heavy. And since almonds are hygroscopic (they absorb moisture from the air) this cake is a great keeper.

1. Brush melted butter over the inside of two 5-cup (1-l, 200-ml) capacity tube pans or other suitable pans. Coat the inside of the pans with the ground almonds. Set the pans aside.

2. Combine the Almond Paste, the first measurement of granulated sugar, and the soft butter (add the butter gradually to avoid lumps). Cream until light and fluffy. Beat in the eggs a few at a time.

3. Sift together both flours, the baking powder, and the salt. Add this to the Almond Paste mixture along with the lemon zest, vanilla, and milk.

4. Whip the egg whites until foamy. Gradually add the remaining sugar while whipping to stiff peaks. Fold the egg whites into the cake batter one-third at a time. Divide the batter between the prepared cake pans.

5. Bake at 375°F (190°C) for approximately 35 minutes or until the cakes are baked through; they should spring back when pressed lightly on top. Unmold onto a cake rack and let cool.

Basil and Tarragon Pound Cake

two 8-by-4-inch (20-×-10-cm) cakes

Butter and Flour Mixture (page 4)
1 pound (455 g) soft unsalted butter
1 pound (455 g) granulated sugar
8 eggs, at room temperature
8 ounces (225 g) bread flour
8 ounces (225 g) cake flour
¹/₂ teaspoon (2.5 g) salt
2 teaspoons (10 ml) very finely
    chopped fresh basil leaves
¹/₄ teaspoon (1.25 ml) very finely
    chopped fresh tarragon

1. Coat the inside of two 8-by-4-inch (20-×-10-cm) loaf pans with Butter and Flour Mixture.

2. Cream the butter and sugar until light and fluffy. Beat in the eggs one at a time.

3. Sift together the bread flour, cake flour, and salt. Add the basil and tarragon and combine well so there are no clumps of herbs. Add the flour mixture to the butter mixture and beat until thoroughly blended. Divide between the prepared pans.

4. Bake at 325°F (163°C) for approximately 1 hour or until baked through.

 Lemon Buttermilk Pound Cake

two 5-cup (1-l, 200-ml) capacity tube pans

Butter and Flour Mixture (page 4)
6 ounces (170 g) soft unsalted butter
12 ounces (340 g) granulated sugar
5 eggs, at room temperature
12 ounces (340 g) cake flour
1 tablespoon (12 g) baking powder
¹/₄ teaspoon (1 g) baking soda
1 teaspoon (5 g) salt
³/₄ cup (180 ml) buttermilk
finely grated zest of four lemons
juice of two medium-sized lemons

1. Coat the inside of two 5-cup (1-l, 200-ml) capacity tube pans with Butter and Flour Mixture. Reserve.

2. Cream the butter and sugar together until the mixture is light and fluffy. Beat in the eggs one at a time. Continue beating for 1 minute.

3. Sift together the flour, baking powder, baking soda, and salt. Combine the buttermilk, lemon zest, and lemon juice. Add the dry ingredients to the egg mixture in two parts, alternating with the buttermilk.

4. Divide the batter evenly between the two prepared pans. They should not be more than three-fourths full.

5. Bake at 375° (190°C) for approximately 35 minutes or until baked through. A wooden skewer inserted into the cake should come out clean. Let the cakes cool for a few minutes, then unmold and finish cooling on a rack. If left to cool in the pans, they will become wet from trapped steam.

 Mustard Gingerbread

two 8-by-4-inch (20-×-10-cm) cakes

melted unsalted butter
8 ounces (225 g) soft unsalted butter
1 pound (455 g) granulated sugar
8 eggs
1 pound (455 g) bread flour
2 teaspoons (8 g) baking soda
2 teaspoons (8 g) baking powder
2 teaspoons (10 g) salt
1 tablespoon (6 g) ground ginger
4 teaspoons (8 g) dry mustard
1 teaspoon (1.5 g) ground cinnamon
¹/₂ teaspoon (1 g) ground cloves
1¹/₂ cups (360 ml) pumpkin purée
4 ounces (115 g) chopped pecans

1. Coat the inside of two loaf pans approximately 8 by 4 inches (20 × 10 cm) with melted butter. Set aside.

2. Cream the soft butter and granulated sugar together until light and fluffy. Add the eggs and mix to combine.

3. Sift together the flour, baking soda, baking powder, salt, and spices. Add half of the dry ingredients to the creamed butter mixture. Mix in the pumpkin purée. Mix in the remaining dry ingredients and lastly the pecans. Pour the batter into the prepared pans.

4. Bake at 350°F (175°C) for about 60 minutes or until baked through. Cool in the pans for 10 minutes, then remove and finish cooling on a cake rack.

Vanilla-Butter Pound Cake

two 8-by-4-inch (20-×-10-cm) cakes

melted unsalted butter

6 eggs, at room temperature

6 egg yolks (1/2 cup/120 ml), at room temperature

1 tablespoon (15 ml) vanilla extract

1 tablespoon (15 ml) water

1 pound (455 g) soft unsalted butter

1 pound, 2 ounces (510 g) Vanilla Sugar (page 14) or granulated sugar

1 teaspoon (5 g) salt

14 ounces (400 g) cake flour, sifted

As is true of many things that are very simple and are comprised of only a few components, if not prepared correctly the desired outcome of this classic pound cake will be lost. Properly made pound cakes walk a fine line between rich and moist but not too heavy or compact. Because authentic pound cakes, like classic sponge cakes, rely solely on the air that is incorporated into the batter for leavening, the mixing technique is critical. It is different from the technique used with sponge cake, however, because pound cakes contain such a large percentage of butter, which, though it contributes to their rich flavor, can make them too dense and heavy if they are not prepared correctly. A common mixing method is to cream the butter, sugar, and egg yolks together, incorporate the flour, whip the egg whites to stiff peaks separately, and then fold the whites into the batter. This makes a light pound cake but one that is not as moist and rich as a classic pound cake should be (although this technique is used successfully with the some of the pound cake hybrids in this section, which achieve the necessary body from the addition of other ingredients). The method used in the following recipe incorporates the eggs (plus extra egg yolks) without separating and so does not benefit from the added air whipped into the whites, but because the eggs are incorporated very slowly, and because extra yolks are used, which are an excellent emulsifier, an emulsion is created that is able to support the trapped air and moisture in the correct balance, producing a cake that is rich, moist, and buttery without being too airy and fluffy on one end or rubbery and heavy on the other. To create and maintain the emulsion, it is critical not only to add the eggs very gradually but also that all of the ingredients are at about 70°F (21°C). If the mixture is too cold it will curdle and the trapped air will escape. Because of the dense batter, pound cakes are baked at a relatively low temperature.

This cake is wonderful with Crème Fraîche and fresh fruit; the acidity of both offsets the rich, sweet cake nicely. Slices of Vanilla-Butter Pound Cake are also very good toasted; watch closely, however, as they brown quickly due to the high sugar content.

1. Brush melted butter over the inside of two 8-by-4-inch (20-×-10-cm) loaf pans and then line the pans with baking paper as shown in Figures 1–8 and 1–9, page 25). Set aside.

2. Place the eggs, egg yolks, vanilla, and water in a small bowl. Mix to break up the eggs and combine the ingredients without beating in any air. If the mixture is cooler than approximately 70°F (21°C), place the bowl in a bain-marie and stir for a moment or two to warm it. Do not heat to the point of cooking the eggs. Set aside off the heat.

3. Place the soft butter in a mixer bowl and beat using the paddle attachment for about 2 minutes. Add the sugar gradually and continue beating for 4 to 5 minutes until the mixture is light in color (almost white) and fluffy. With the mixer running, pour the egg mixture in very gradually, taking about 5 minutes to add all of it. Beat in the salt. Fold in the sifted cake flour one-fourth at a time. Divide the batter between the two prepared pans.

4. Bake at 350°F (175°C) for about 1 hour. A wooden skewer inserted in the top of the cakes should come out clean. Unmold from the baking pans and cool to room temperature. Wrap and store at room temperature for up to one week.

White Spice Buttermilk Cake with Gingered-Dried Fruit Compote

16 servings

White Spice Buttermilk Cake
   (recipe follows)
Gingered-Dried Fruit Compote
   (recipe follows)
Honey-Yogurt Sauce (recipe follows)
powdered sugar

Presentation: Trim one end of a Buttermilk Cake. Cut a ³/₄-inch (2-cm) slice and set it in the center of a dessert plate. Spoon approximately ¹/₂ cup (120 ml) of the compote, including some of the syrup, over one side of the slice and onto the plate. Place a dollop of the Honey-Yogurt Sauce on top of the cake. Sift powdered sugar over the dessert and plate, including the rim.

White Spice Buttermilk Cake

two 8-by-4-by-3¹/₂-inch (20-✕-10-✕-8.7-cm) cakes

Butter and Flour Mixture (page 4)
10 ounces (285 g) bread flour
4 ounces (115 g) cake flour
1¹/₂ teaspoons (6 g) baking powder
1 teaspoon (4 g) baking soda
4 teaspoons (8 g) ground cardamom
1 teaspoon (2 g) ground ginger
¹/₂ teaspoon (1 g) ground white pepper
10 ounces (285 g) soft unsalted butter
10 ounces (285 g) granulated sugar
4 eggs, at room temperature
1 tablespoon (15 ml) vanilla extract
2 teaspoons (10 ml) finely grated
   lemon zest
1¹/₂ cups (360 ml) buttermilk

1. Brush Butter and Flour Mixture over the inside of two 8-by-4-by-3¹/₂-inch (20-✕-10-✕-8.7-cm) loaf pans.

2. Combine the bread flour, cake flour, baking powder, baking soda, cardamom, ginger, and white pepper. Reserve.

3. Beat the soft butter with the sugar until the mixture is light and fluffy. Mix in the eggs two at a time. Add the vanilla and the lemon zest. Stir in the dry ingredients in two additions, alternating with the buttermilk. Divide the batter between the prepared pans.

4. Bake the cakes at 350°F (175°C) for approximately 50 minutes or until they are golden brown and baked through. Let the cakes cool in the pans for 10 minutes. Unmold onto a rack and let cool completely. Wrap the cakes in plastic and store in the refrigerator.

Gingered-Dried Fruit Compote

2 quarts (1 l, 920 ml)

3 cups (720 ml) dry white wine
3 cups (720 ml) water
one vanilla bean, split lengthwise
one 3-inch (7.5-cm) piece fresh ginger
   root, peeled and thinly sliced
zest of two lemons removed in long
   strips
ten cardamom pods, crushed
ten whole black peppercorns
10 ounces (285 g) dried pears,
   quartered
8 ounces (225 g) dried apricots
6 ounces (170 g) dried cherries

NOTE: To substitute fresh pears, start with 1
pound, 8 ounces (680 g) or three medium-sized
pears. Peel, core, and cut the pears in half.
Slice each half into six pieces lengthwise. Keep
the slices in acidulated water until you are
ready to use them.

1. Combine the wine, water, vanilla bean, sliced ginger, lemon zest, cardamom, and peppercorns in a heavy-bottomed saucepan. Bring the mixture to a boil, then reduce the heat and simmer for 30 minutes.

2. Remove from the heat, cover, and set aside at room temperature to steep for 3 hours.

3. Strain the liquid and return it to the saucepan. Scrape the seeds out of the vanilla bean and add to the liquid. Discard the remaining bean and the solids in the strainer. Add the pears and simmer for 10 minutes. Add the apricots and continue simmering for 5 minutes. Add the cherries and simmer 2 or 3 minutes longer.

4. Remove from the heat and let cool to room temperature. Cover and place in the refrigerator overnight.

Honey-Yogurt Sauce

approximately 1¼ cups (300 ml)

1 cup (240 ml) Acidophilus Yogurt
   (page 2)
3 tablespoons (45 ml) honey
1 teaspoon (5 ml) vanilla extract

1. Combine the yogurt, honey, and vanilla.
2. Cover and refrigerate until needed.

Pretzel Pastries

36 pastries

1 pound (455 g) Puff Pastry
   (page 44)
1 pound (455 g) Short Dough
   (page 54)
Egg Wash (page 7)
sanding sugar
sliced almonds, crushed
Simple Syrup (page 11)

*T*he combination of two completely different doughs twisted into an interesting pretzel shape brings a smile of pleasant surprise to everyone who bites into one of these pastries; the flaky, unsweetened Puff Pastry and sweet, crumbly Short Dough compliment each other perfectly. I teach this recipe in a class on basic doughs, and I have yet to come across a student who had either heard of, or tasted, these simple pastries previously.

Perhaps instead of pastries I should call these time-consuming cookies, since they really straddle the fence between the two. Pretzel Pastries can be made up very quickly anytime you have Puff Pastry and Short Dough handy; they are a good way to utilize scraps of either. The step that seems to present problems more times than not is the baking. Since Short Dough will normally bake faster than Puff Pastry, it is important to heed the instruction to bake double-panned and at the specified temperature, since these are not too forgiving.

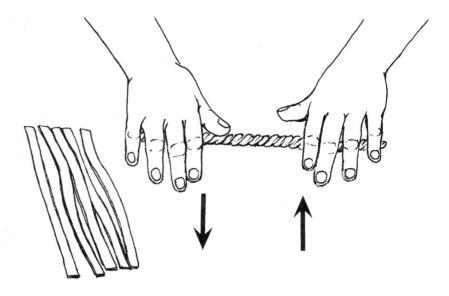

FIGURE 15–8 Twisting the layered strip of Puff Pastry and Short Dough into a corkscrew shape by rolling it against the table, moving the hands in opposite directions

NOTE: Anything made with Puff Pastry is best the day it is baked, so bake only as many Pretzel Pastries as you will use the same day. The formed Pretzels can be frozen and baked as needed.

1. Roll the Puff Pastry into a rectangle 9 by 14 inches (22.5 × 35 cm) using the smallest possible amount of flour to prevent the dough from sticking. The dough should be about ⅛ inch (3 mm) thick. Place the dough on a sheet of cardboard or on an inverted sheet pan.

2. Roll the Short Dough to the same size as the Puff Pastry, again using as little flour as possible to prevent the dough from sticking. It will be slightly thicker.

3. Brush Egg Wash on the Puff Pastry. Carefully, so you do not alter the shape, roll the Short Dough up on a dowel and unroll it on top of the Puff Pastry. Press the two pieces together by rolling the dowel over them. Refrigerate until firm.

4. Mix equal amounts (by volume) of sanding sugar and crushed almonds. Place the mixture on a sheet pan and reserve.

5. With a dowel or ruler as a guide, use a sharp knife or pastry wheel to cut the sheet lengthwise into ¼-inch (6-mm) strips.

6. Twist each strip into a corkscrew by rolling the ends in opposite directions against the table (Figure 15–8), then form the corkscrew into a pretzel shape (Figure 15–9). (Do not use any flour while forming the Pretzels.) Set the Pretzel on the sugar and almond mixture and press gently to make sure the mixture adheres. Continue forming Pretzels in the same way.

7. When the pan of sugar mixture is full, transfer the Pretzels, sugar-side up, to a sheet pan lined with baking paper. Repeat with the remaining strips. If the strips get soft or sticky and hard to work with, refrigerate for a short time.

8. Bake the pastries double-panned at 375°F (190°C) for about 15 minutes or until golden brown. As soon as the Pretzels are removed from the oven, brush Simple Syrup lightly over the tops.

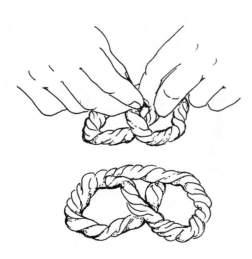

FIGURE 15–9 Forming the twisted strip into a pretzel shape

Puddings

Double Chocolate Pudding

8 servings

4¹/₂ cups (1 l, 80 ml) milk
8 ounces (225 g) granulated sugar
¹/₄ teaspoon (1.25 g) salt
4 tablespoons (32 g) cornstarch
2 ounces (55 g) unsweetened cocoa
   powder
2 eggs
4 egg yolks (¹/₃ cup/80 ml)
8 ounces (225 g) sweet dark chocolate
2 ounces (55 g) unsweetened
   chocolate
2 ounces (55 g) unsalted butter
2 teaspoons (10 ml) vanilla extract
Chantilly Cream (page 1083)
Chocolate Figurines (page 906)
   or
dark chocolate shavings

*T*he term pudding *can be rather confusing since puddings can be baked, steamed, or cooked over direct heat, they may be either sweet or savory, and at one time pudding was simply a generic term for any type of dessert! Pudding now refers most often to a cooked, milk-based dessert mixture that is thickened. See also the introduction to Chocolate Rum Pudding with Chocolate Beetles (page 545) for additional information.*

This recipe is an example of a classic cornstarch-thickened pudding, the type many people grew up eating in America. Puddings sort of fell by the wayside when mousses become the rage, but they seem to be making a comeback with the current interest in home-style cooking. Cornstarch puddings or custards are the same as blancmange and, although of course not as thick, they really differ not at all from pastry cream. In Double Chocolate Pudding melted dark chocolate is included in addition to cocoa powder to give the dessert a deep chocolate taste and a rich texture.

1. Combine 4 cups (960 ml) of the milk, 4 ounces (115 g) of the sugar, and the salt in a saucepan. Heat to boiling.

2. While the milk mixture is heating, combine the remaining 4 ounces (115 g) of sugar with the cornstarch and cocoa powder in an oversized bowl. Gradually (to avoid lumps) stir in the remaining ¹/₂ cup (120 ml) of milk and mix until thoroughly combined.

3. Gradually whisk the hot milk mixture into the cocoa powder mixture. Transfer back to the saucepan and bring to a boil, stirring constantly with the whisk. Boil for 2 minutes.

4. Beat the eggs and egg yolks together until broken up. Slowly whisk in a small amount of the milk mixture to temper, then add this back to the remaining milk mixture. Cook, continuing to stir constantly with the whisk, for about 2 minutes or until thickened; do not boil. Pour into a bowl and cover with a piece of baking paper set directly on the top of the pudding to prevent a skin from forming. Set aside at room temperature.

5. Chop both chocolates into small pieces and melt together with the butter over simmering water. Stir the melted chocolate into the cocoa custard together with the vanilla.

6. Spoon into individual serving dishes and cover without touching the pudding to prevent disturbing the shiny surface. Refrigerate until cold.

7. Pipe a rosette of Chantilly Cream on top of each serving and decorate with a Chocolate Figurine or shaved chocolate.

Jasmine Rice Pudding with Coconut Milk and Toasted Baby Coconuts

12 servings

8 ounces (225 g) Jasmine rice

3 cups (720 ml) milk

peel from one orange, removed in a long strip

10 ounces (285 g) granulated sugar

2¹/₂ cups (600 ml) heavy cream, at room temperature

3 cups (720 ml) canned unsweetened coconut milk, at room temperature

1 tablespoon (15 ml) vanilla extract

one recipe Cherry Compote (page 452), made without black pepper

fresh coconut shavings (see note 1)

eighteen baby coconuts (coquitos), halved and lightly toasted

twelve small mint springs

Florentina Twists (page 1010) (see note 2)

NOTE 1: To prepare the coconut shavings, follow the directions on page 1099 for cracking a fresh coconut. Remove the brown skin from the meat and then use a vegetable peeler to shave off long, thin strips of coconut meat. Do not prepare too far in advance, and keep the shavings wrapped to prevent them from drying out.

NOTE 2: Follow the recipe and procedure for making Florentina Twists through step two. Cut twenty-four ³/₄-inch (2 cm) strips across the width. Let cool until firm and then separate the pieces. (Do not twist the strips.)

*R*ice is the grain grown most extensively throughout the world, and it is a principal food for more than one-third of the world's population. More than two dozen types of rice are available in the marketplace. Short- or medium-grain varieties are generally used for puddings because their starch breaks down and aids in the thickening process. Long-grain types (such as the Jasmine rice used here) will work as well, provided they are cooked long enough.

It is easy to draw a parallel between rice puddings and bread puddings, for throughout many countries both are typically made from rice or bread that is leftover from a previous meal with the addition of sugar, honey, eggs, and milk or cream. In this recipe the pudding is molded into individual servings to give the dessert a better dining room appearance. For a more country-style presentation, it can also be spooned directly into serving dishes with the sauce drizzled over the top. The mini coconuts (coquitos) used as garnish can easily be left out. Although the Cherry Compote is really delicious with this dessert, either Cherry Sauce or Caramel Sauce II (see page 1071) go almost as well. Any of the three can be made well in advance and will keep for weeks stored covered in the refrigerator. Another example of rice pudding is Riz à la Malta (see page 556).

1. Rinse the rice in a colander and then parboil in water for 5 minutes. Drain and reserve.

2. In a heavy-bottomed saucepan, bring the milk to scalding. Add the orange peel, sugar, and the drained rice. Cook over very low heat, stirring frequently, until the rice is tender. Remove from the heat and discard the orange peel.

3. Mix the cream and coconut milk into the cooked rice.

4. Transfer the mixture to a hotel pan or other ovenproof dish. Cover and continue cooking in a 375°F (190°C) oven, stirring from time to time to prevent overcooking on the sides and bottom, for approximately 1 hour and 15 minutes or until the rice is very soft and the mixture has thickened. (If you are in a hurry, this process can be accelerated by leaving the rice mixture in the saucepan and cooking over low heat for about 30 minutes while stirring constantly. You will need to increase the milk by 1 cup/240 ml to compensate for the evaporation when the mixture is cooked on the stove.) Remove from the heat and stir in the vanilla.

5. Divide the rice pudding between 12 soufflé ramekins 3¹/₂ inches (8.7 cm) in diameter with a 5-ounce (150-ml) capacity, or other suitable molds. Cover and refrigerate until the puddings are firm enough to unmold.

6. Presentation: Unmold one serving and place inverted in the center of a dessert plate. Spoon Cherry Compote on the base of the plate around the dessert. Sprinkle fresh coconut shavings over the compote. Arrange three baby coconut halves in a cluster on top of the pudding. Decorate with a sprig of mint. Lean two Florentina strips against the pudding, placing them on opposite sides.

Maple Indian Pudding

8 servings

melted unsalted butter

2 cups (480 ml) milk

3 ounces (85 g) yellow cornmeal

2 ounces (55 g) granulated sugar

3 ounces (85 g) light brown sugar

1/2 cup (120 ml) pure maple syrup

1 teaspoon (5 g) salt

2 ounces (55 g) unsalted butter

1/2 teaspoon (1 g) ground ginger

1 teaspoon (2 g) ground cloves

2 teaspoons (10 ml) finely grated fresh ginger root

finely grated zest of one lemon

3 cups (720 ml) half-and-half

6 ounces (170 g) dark raisins

heavy cream

　or

Vanilla or Cinnamon Ice Cream (pages 640 and 629)

ground cinnamon

NOTE: If you are using this for à la carte service, you can keep the pudding hot, covered in the bain-marie, for several hours in a low oven. While it is not traditional, Maple Indian Pudding has a nice flavor and texture served cold (mold or slice the servings) with Vanilla Custard Sauce (see page 1082).

This is also known as hasty pudding, although I'm not quite sure why since many recipes direct baking it for more than two hours! The pudding has a very nice subtle maple and spice flavor, and a smoother texture than you might expect with cornmeal, due to the long cooking process. Indian Pudding originated in New England and is one of the most well-known American Colonial desserts; the colonists also enjoyed it for breakfast. Traditional recipes call for molasses rather than maple syrup; you may substitute an equal amount if you would like to try a more authentic version. While this is not going to compete with the selections in the Desserts for Plated Presentation chapter when it comes to appearance, this type of simple, modest dessert can be a nice change of pace. If your raisins are very soft, add them part way through cooking to prevent them from breaking down.

1. Brush melted butter over the inside of a 6-cup (1-l, 440-ml) glass or ceramic baking dish.

2. Combine the milk and cornmeal in a saucepan. Bring to a boil stirring constantly and cook for about 3 minutes.

3. Reduce the heat to very low and stir in both sugars, the maple syrup, salt, butter, ground spices, grated ginger, and the grated lemon zest, mixing until smooth. Incorporate the half-and-half gradually to avoid lumps.

4. Increase the heat and bring the mixture back to boiling while stirring constantly. Stir in the raisins and pour into the prepared pan.

5. Set the casserole in a larger pan and add water to the larger pan to reach to the level of the pudding. Bake at 350°F (175°C) for approximately 1 hour and 15 minutes, stirring every 30 minutes or so.

6. Spoon the pudding into individual dishes and serve hot with heavy cream or Vanilla or Cinnamon Ice Cream and a sprinkling of ground cinnamon.

Queen's Apple

12 servings

twelve medium-sized cooking apples such as pippin or Granny Smith

Plain Poaching Syrup (page 13)

2 pounds, 8 ounces (1 kg, 135 g) Puff Pastry (page 44)

Calvados Apple Filling (recipe follows)

Egg Wash (page 7)

True to its name, this is a "majestic" version of the good, old-fashioned, unpretentious baked apple. At home when I was growing up baked apples were not typically filled and wrapped in pastry or pie dough, they were simply baked whole—skin, core, and all—until they were soft and gooey; they would wrinkle up like raisins a few minutes after they were removed from the oven. The baked apples were served warm with a custard sauce or ice cream. It was still something special that we kids were willing to behave for a whole day to have. Queen's Apple is so named because the baked Puff Pastry-wrapped apple becomes round on the top with a fairly flat bottom, and when the slits on the sides bake open, it resembles a crown. It is a much more elegant presentation than the more conventional method of encasing the apples, commonly called apple

Cinnamon Sugar (page 5)

one-half recipe Strawberry Sauce
    (page 1081)

one recipe Mousseline Sauce
    (page 1076)

ground cinnamon

powdered sugar

Vanilla or Cinnamon Ice Cream
    (pages 640 and 629) (optional)

*NOTE: The wrapped apples should be refriger-
ated for a minimum of 30 minutes before they
are baked. If they are wrapped more than 2
hours in advance of baking, use Egg Wash only
on the inside and to attach the Puff Pastry cookies; do not brush Egg Wash over the outside of
the dough. Cover the apples with plastic wrap
in the refrigerator. Brush Egg Wash over the
outside of the apples just before baking.*

*dumplings, but a bit more time-consuming. You can of course skip using the tem-
plate, cut the rounds of Puff Pastry using any round guide of the appropriate size,
such as a plate, and then cut out the wedges freehand, but you will still have to
deal with some leftover scrap dough. The "dumpling" method leaves virtually no
scrap pieces and is much easier to make. For this technique, prepare the apples
as instructed but use only 2 pounds (910 g) of Puff Pastry. Roll the dough out to
a 18-by-24-inch (45-×-60-cm) rectangle; it should be approximately ⅛ inch (3
mm) thick. Place the dough on a full sheet of cardboard, or fold in half and place
on a large sheet pan, and refrigerate to relax and firm the dough.*

*Remove from the refrigerator and adjust as needed to make the dough even
and the same size as before. Cut the dough into twelve 6-inch (15-cm) squares.
Follow the instructions in the main recipe for assembling, baking, and serving
the apples (except you will not have any cookies to decorate the tops with).*

1. Peel, core, and poach the apples in the Poaching Syrup until they
give when pressed lightly. Do not overcook the apples at this stage or
they will fall apart when they are baked later. Remove the apples from
the syrup and set aside to cool.

2. Cut the Puff Pastry dough in half. Roll each piece into a 14-by-
20-inch (35-×-50-cm) rectangle, in two or three phases, alternating the
pieces and letting one piece rest in the refrigerator as you work on the
other. Refrigerate both finished pieces for 30 minutes to allow the
dough to relax and become firm.

3. Make the template shown in Figure 15–10. The template as
shown is the correct size to use in this recipe, but it can be sized up or
down if the apples you are using are particularly large or small. Trace
the drawing and then cut out two templates from thick or corrugated
cardboard, making one a solid round and cutting the wedges indicated
by the dotted lines out of the other.

4. Place the Calvados Apple Filling in a pastry bag with a no. 6
(12-mm) plain tip. Set aside.

5. Using the tip of a paring knife and the solid template as a guide,
cut out six circles from each of the chilled Puff Pastry sheets, twelve
total. Place the circles back into the refrigerator. Use a fluted cookie cutter about 1¼ inches (3.1 cm) in diameter to cut twelve cookies from the
scrap pieces (refrigerate the scrap piece before cutting the cookies if the
dough seems soft). Place the cookies in the refrigerator. Cover the
remaining scrap pieces and reserve for another use.

6. Remove two circles at a time from the refrigerator. Place the
template with the cutouts on the circles one at a time and cut out the
four wedges. Cover the dough scraps and reserve for another use.
Brush Egg Wash over the cross-shaped pieces of dough. Sprinkle Cinnamon Sugar lightly over the entire surface of two apples, then place an
apple in the center of each cross. Pipe Calvados filling into the cavity
where the core was removed in each apple. Bring two opposite flaps of
the Puff Pastry dough together and press to secure; you will have to
stretch the dough slightly as you do this. Bring the remaining two flaps
together in the same way. Place the apples inverted on a sheet pan lined

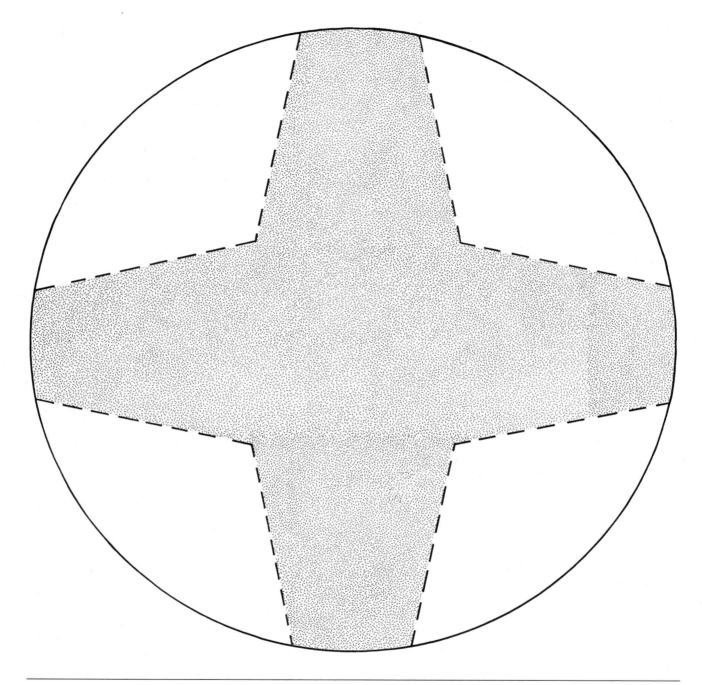

FIGURE 15–10 The template used as a guide to cut the Puff Pastry for Queen's Apple

with baking paper. Repeat to fill and wrap the remaining apples in the same way. Brush Egg Wash over the top and sides of each apple and then set a Puff Pastry cookie on top of each one. Brush Egg Wash over the cookies. Refrigerate the apples (see note).

7. Approximately 1 hour before the desserts are to be served, bake the apples at 375°F (190°C) for about 40 minutes or until both the Puff

Pastry and the apples are baked through. Remove from the oven and reserve in a warm spot. Fill a piping bottle with Strawberry Sauce and a second bottle with Mousseline Sauce.

8. Presentation: Pipe a 5-inch (12.5-cm) circle of Strawberry Sauce in the center of the base of a dessert plate. Pipe a ring of Mousseline Sauce, filling in the space between the Strawberry Sauce and the perimeter of the base of the plate. Using a small, fine mesh strainer, lightly sift ground cinnamon over the Mousseline Sauce. Sift powdered sugar over a baked apple and set in the center of the Strawberry Sauce, securing it so it will not slide by gently pressing down to the plate. Serve immediately. When serving Queen's Apple with Vanilla or Cinnamon Ice Cream, omit the Mousseline Sauce. Place a baked apple in the center of the plate and pipe three irregularly shaped pools of Strawberry Sauce around the apple. Place a small scoop of ice cream between each of the sauce pools.

Calvados Apple Filling

14 ounces (400 g)

1 ounce (30 g) dry currants
½ cup (120 ml) Calvados
6 ounces (170 g) Almond Paste
    (page 3)
2 ounces (55 g) finely ground
    hazelnuts
½ teaspoon (.75 g) ground cinnamon
2 tablespoons (30 g) granulated sugar

1. Combine the currants and Calvados in a saucepan and heat to approximately 120°F (49°C). Remove from the heat and set aside to macerate for a minimum of 30 minutes.

2. Gradually, to avoid lumps, combine the currant mixture with the Almond Paste. Add the ground hazelnuts. Mix the cinnamon and sugar together and stir into the filling.

Sour Apple and Cheese Turnovers

16 servings

2 pounds (910 g) Puff Pastry (page 44)
5 ounces (140 g) sharp Cheddar
    cheese, finely chopped
3 ounces (85 g) Parmesan cheese,
    ground
Egg Wash (page 7)
Chunky Sour Apple Filling (see note 1)
one-half recipe Caramel Sauce II
    (page 1071)
ground cinnamon
Cinnamon Custard Sauce (see note 2)
apricots or other seasonal fruit for
    decoration
sixteen mint sprigs

I came upon the idea for this dessert as a result of having a leftover sheet of Puff Pastry dough that had been prepared for cheese straws. I made it into apple turnovers on a whim and thought the combination was great. After a few adjustments to the cheese and the apple filling, this recipe, which has a nice tangy bite, was born. You may want to vary the amount of Cheddar, use a different aged cheese, and/or decrease the amount of Parmesan if it is particularly strong or salty. The Apple Rum Filling (page 533) used for the Apple Rum Charlotte can be used here as well. You will need one-half recipe made without brown sugar or pectin powder and with Calvados or another brandy instead of rum.

1. Roll the Puff Pastry dough into a 20-inch (50-cm) square. The dough should be about ⅛ inch (3 mm) thick. Let the dough rest in the refrigerator for 30 minutes to firm up and relax the dough and help minimize shrinking.

2. Cut the sheet into four rows lengthwise and four rows across to make sixteen 5-inch (12.5-cm) squares. Leave the squares in place.

NOTE 1: To make Chunky Sour Apple Filling, make one-half recipe or 1 pound, 4 ounces (570 g) Chunky Apple Filling (page 1085), omitting the sugar.

NOTE 2: To make the Cinnamon Custard Sauce, follow the recipe and instructions for one recipe Vanilla Custard Sauce (page 1082), adding 1 teaspoon (1.5 g) of ground cinnamon at the end of the recipe.

3. Combine the Cheddar and Parmesan cheeses. Brush Egg Wash over the Puff Pastry squares. Place 1 tablespoon (15 ml) of the cheese mixture in the center of each square. Spread the cheese out a little and press it into the dough. Pipe or spoon a mound of Sour Apple Filling in the center of each square on top of the cheese, dividing it evenly. Fold the top of each square over diagonally to form a triangle. Press the edges together firmly with your fingers.

4. Brush Egg Wash on top of the turnovers, and invert them into the remaining cheese mixture. Place cheese-side up on a sheet pan lined with baking paper. Make a small cut in the center of each turnover.

5. Bake the turnovers at 375°F (190°C) until completely baked through, about 45 minutes. Cover the turnovers with baking paper or aluminum foil as needed to keep the cheese from getting too dark. You may need a second pan underneath as well to prevent overbrowning on the bottom. Place the Caramel Sauce in a piping bottle with a small opening and reserve.

6. Presentation: Sift ground cinnamon lightly over the rim and base of a dessert plate. Place a warm turnover in the center of the plate. Pour a round pool of Cinnamon Custard Sauce in front of the turnover. Pipe Caramel Sauce in a ring near the perimeter of the sauce pool. Use a small wooden skewer to swirl the sauces together (see Figure 19–21, page 1000). Decorate with fresh apricot slices or other seasonal fruit. Place a mint sprig in the center of the sauce. Serve immediately.

Strawberry Shortcake

16 servings

Biscuit Dough for Strawberry
    Shortcake (recipe follows)
Egg Wash (page 7)
granulated sugar
1 pound, 8 ounces (680 g)
    strawberries (approximately two dry
    pint baskets)
3 cups (720 ml) heavy cream
4 teaspoons (20 g) granulated sugar
1 teaspoon (5 ml) vanilla extract
powdered sugar
two recipes Sabayon (page 718),
    made with white wine
sixteen mint sprigs

NOTE: For a simplified presentation, replace the Sabayon with Strawberry Sauce (page 1081) (do not gratinée the Strawberry Sauce).

*S**hortcakes are an American classic. They are made from a quick bread dough that is baked, split, filled with fruit (most commonly strawberries), and topped with whipped cream or ice cream. The application of shortcake differs from place to place although the name derives—just as with the short dough—from the use of shortening, butter, or other fat in the dough for a crisp and crumbly texture. Having never made or even heard of this dish before I came to this country (and I certainly did not want to ask any of the customers who requested it what it was), for many years I made strawberry shortcake using a sponge cake base. Little did I know that this was probably not what most of the guests had in mind, since no one complained.*

For a purist, shortcake should be made from biscuit dough. It can be prepared using one large, round, cake-like biscuit for several servings or with individual biscuits. The dish most likely began as a way to create a dessert using leftover biscuits or rolls from the dinner table. Strawberry shortcake is mentioned in writings from England as far back as the 1500s. It was not before the 1830s, however, that it became so loved and well-known in America as the popularity of strawberries increased, in fact to such a level that by 1850 there was talk of "strawberry fever."

The biscuit dough recipe can be used to makes great biscuits in and of themselves, with or without the poppy seeds and/or orange rind. I got the idea of adding poppy seeds to the dough from my Strawberry Poppy Seed Cake recipe, where the flavors complement each other nicely, and they add a pleasant bite and crunch here as well. To make the more traditional round biscuits instead of the triangular shape used in the recipe, roll the dough as directed and cut out biscuits using a 3¼-inch (8.1-cm) plain or fluted cookie cutter. Gather the scrap dough, pat it out gently, and cut the remainder. You will only get twelve round biscuits rather than sixteen of the triangles. Instead of forming the remaining scraps again, just bake them alongside the biscuits for a snack.

1. Roll the Biscuit Dough out to a 12-inch (30-cm) square and give the dough a second single turn. Roll the dough into a 7-by-18-inch (17.5-✕-45-cm) rectangle, about ¾ inch (2 cm) thick. Cut the strip in half lengthwise. Cut each half into eight triangles. (You can reshape the end pieces and cut two more triangles if necessary, to make sixteen pieces.)

2. Brush the tops of the triangles with Egg Wash, then invert them in granulated sugar. Place sugar-side up on a sheet pan lined with baking paper. Score the top of each piece with three parallel lines, then repeat at a 45° angle to form a diamond pattern.

3. Bake the biscuits at 400°F (205°C) for about 15 minutes. Set aside to cool.

4. Rinse the strawberries and remove the hulls. Cut the strawberries into thin slices lengthwise (from the point). Cover and reserve.

5. Whip the heavy cream, 4 teaspoons (20 g) sugar, and vanilla until stiff peaks form. Place in a pastry bag with a no. 4 (8-mm) plain tip.

6. Presentation: Cut a biscuit in half horizontally. Pipe whipped cream onto the bottom half of the biscuit, covering it in a zigzag pattern. Cover the cream with sliced strawberries, reserving the best-looking slices for garnish. Pipe a second layer of cream on top of the berries in the same way. Make a second layer of strawberries. Place the top of the biscuit on the strawberries at an angle. Sift powdered sugar lightly over the top. Cover the base of a serving plate with Sabayon. Brown (gratinée) the sauce under a salamander or broiler. Using the reserved (best-looking) strawberry slices, line them up next to each other, points toward the outside, next to the rim of the serving plate on top of the sauce. Place the assembled shortcake on top of the sauce in the center of the plate. Decorate with a mint sprig and serve immediately.

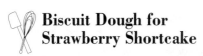

Biscuit Dough for Strawberry Shortcake

sixteen 3½-inch (8.7-cm) triangles

1 pound, 6 ounces (625 g) bread flour
1 teaspoon (5 g) salt
3 tablespoons (36 g) baking powder
2 ounces (55 g) poppy seeds
4 ounces (115 g) cold unsalted butter
grated zest from one orange
3¼ cups (780 ml) heavy cream

1. Sift together the flour, salt, and baking powder. Mix in the poppy seeds. Cut the butter into small chunks and add it to the flour mixture. Cut the butter into the flour mixture until it is the size of peas.

2. Stir the orange zest into the cream. Pour the cream into the flour mixture all at once and stir rapidly with your hand to form a soft dough. Take care not to overmix.

3. Place on a floured work surface and pat out to a rectangle 1½ inches (3.7 cm) thick. Make one rough single turn (see Figures 4–15 and 4–16, page 160), shaping the dough with your hands and not a rolling pin. The Biscuit Dough can be covered and refrigerated for a day at this point, if desired.

Toasted Panettone with Mascarpone Sauce

16 servings

one-half recipe Panettone dough
   (page 795)
Egg Wash (page 7)
sixteen Brown Turkey or Mission figs
one recipe Plain Poaching Syrup
   (page 13)
two recipes Mascarpone Sauce
   (page 1075)
2 ounces (55 g) Candied Orange Peel
   (page 978), cut in julienne

*D*on't miss out on making this humble, yet elegant, dessert when figs are in season. Be sure they are ripe but still on the firm side and free from blemishes. If you use Mission figs, choose the larger size. Although the direct method Panettone is just as easy to make as Brioche, you may substitute Brioche in this recipe if desired; it is a good choice when you do not have Candied Orange Peel for the decoration. Sprinkle edible fresh flower petals such as bright yellow calendula on top of the sauce for garnish instead.

1. Follow steps one, two, three, and four for Panettone.

2. Divide the dough into two pieces. Pound and roll each piece into an even, sausage-shaped, 9-inch (22.5-cm) loaf. Place the loaves on a sheet pan lined with baking paper. Let rise in a warm place until the loaves have slightly less than doubled in volume.

3. Brush Egg Wash over the loaves. Bake at 375°F (190°C) for approximately 30 minutes or until baked through.

4. Poach the figs in Poaching Syrup until soft, approximately 5 minutes. Leave them to cool in the liquid. (If the figs are really ripe you may not need to poach them.)

5. When the Panettone loaves have cooled, trim off the ends, then cut each loaf into sixteen ³/₄-inch (2-cm) slices. Place on a sheet pan and toast the slices lightly in a 450°F (230°C) oven. The toast should be crisp on the outside but still soft in the center.

6. Adjust the consistency of the Mascarpone Sauce if necessary. Place a portion of the sauce in a piping bottle and reserve in the refrigerator along with the remaining sauce.

7. Presentation: Place two slices of toast in the center of a dessert plate. Pipe Mascarpone Sauce over one-third of the slices, letting it run out into an even pool on the plate in front of the dessert. Arrange four or five strips of Candied Orange Peel in a crisscross pattern on top of the sauce. Cut a fig in half and place the pieces, with the cut sides up, next to each other beside the sauce.

Torta Ricotta

two 11-inch (27.5-cm) tarts

one-half recipe Cornmeal Crust
   (page 33)
2 pounds, 4 ounces (1 kg, 25 g)
   Ricotta Cheese (page 11)
12 ounces (340 g) soft cream cheese
3 egg yolks (¹/₄ cup/60 ml)
6 ounces (170 g) granulated sugar
grated zest of two lemons

*R*icotta is a curd cheese traditionally prepared from the residual whey left after making other cheeses. It is quite easy to make your own ricotta using the recipe on page 11. If you follow the recipe carefully it will be well worth your time, since ricotta cheese purchased in the store often has a grainy feel in the mouth and can be lacking in flavor. Making the Pastry Cream called for in this recipe will only set you back slightly, and it gives the filling a lighter and more pleasant taste. But if you do not have any on hand and don't have time or want to make it, leave it out, increase the ricotta by one pound, double the amount of sugar, and use whole eggs rather than egg yolks.

The cornmeal-based short dough provides a wonderful, crisp crust. But if you are not making your own ricotta cheese, see the note that accompanies the Chestnut Torta Ricotta Variation on page 785.

2 teaspoons (10 ml) vanilla extract

one-third recipe or 2 pounds (910 g) Pastry Cream (page 1088)

1¹/₂ cups (360 ml) heavy cream

1 tablespoon (15 g) granulated sugar

fresh fruit

NOTE: To ensure that the crust will bake properly, place the tarts directly on the oven racks; do not set them on a sheet pan.

1. Line two 11-inch (27.5-cm) tart pans with Cornmeal Crust rolled ¹/₈ inch (3 mm) thick (see Figure 2–14, page 56). Set aside. Cover the scrap dough and reserve for the top.

2. Gradually mix the Ricotta Cheese into the soft cream cheese. Add the egg yolks, 6 ounces (170 g) granulated sugar, lemon zest, and vanilla. Avoid mixing air into the filling. Fold in the Pastry Cream.

3. Divide the filling evenly between the two prepared tart pans.

4. Roll out the reserved dough to a rectangle about 11 inches (27.5 cm) wide and ¹/₈-inch (3-mm) thick. Cut into ³/₈-inch (9-mm) wide strips, using a plain pastry wheel (refrigerate the dough first if necessary).

5. Arrange the dough strips ¹/₂ inch (1.2 cm) apart over the filling. Place additional strips on top of these at a 45° angle to form a diamond pattern (see Figure 9-32 on page 429). Press the strips with your thumbs to pinch them off the edge of the pans all around.

6. Bake at 350°F (175°C) for approximately 30 minutes or until the filling is set.

7. Whip the heavy cream with the remaining sugar until soft peaks form. Cut the tarts into the desired number of servings. Serve with a large spoonful of whipped cream and sliced fresh fruit.

VARIATION
Chestnut Torta Ricotta

NOTE: Since commercial ricotta is homogenized, when it is baked, the liquid separates from the cheese, leaks into the pastry shell, and makes it soggy. The solution is to first cook the ricotta in a skillet over medium heat for about 20 minutes, stirring frequently, forcing the liquid out and partially evaporating it. Then wrap the ricotta in a cheese cloth and allow it to hang and drain for 20 minutes. This produces an almost dry cheese.

*F*ollow the directions in the main recipe with these changes:

• increase the Ricotta Cheese to 3 pounds, 4 ounces (1 kg, 480 g)
• omit the Pastry Cream
• add:
— 1 pound (455 g) fresh chestnuts in the shell
    or
— 12 ounces (340 g) whole roasted shelled chestnuts (these are usually packaged in glass bottles)
• 4 ounces (115 g) granulated sugar
• ¹/₂ cup (120 ml) dark rum
• ¹/₂ cup (120 ml) water
• 1 ounce (30 g) unsalted butter
• 2 tablespoons (30 ml) vanilla extract

1. If you are using fresh chestnuts, prepare them as directed for Chestnut Purée (see page 802) but leave whole after cooking.

2. Chop the prepared or bottled chestnuts to about one-quarter of their original size. Combine with the granulated sugar, dark rum, water, and butter in a small saucepan. Cook over high heat, stirring frequently, until the liquid has thickened, about 5 minutes. Remove from the heat and stir in the vanilla.

3. Stir the chestnut mixture into the completed ricotta filling so it is marbled throughout. Do not overmix. Divide the filling between the shells.

16

Holiday Classics and Favorites

Breads
- Braided Stollen
- Chestnut Bread
- Dresdener Stollen
- Lucia Buns
- Panettone
- Sweet Pig's Head
- Swedish Spice Bread
- Triestine Bread

Cakes, Tarts, Tortes, and Pies
- Brandied Gingerbread Cake
- Chestnut Rum Torte
- Florentine Torte
- Fruitcake
- Persimmon Tarts
- Pumpkin Pie
- Yule Logs

Cookies and Pastries
- Chocolate-Orange Pillows
- Chocolate Snow Hearts
- Christmas Cookie Ornaments

- Christmas Tree Pastries
- Cinnamon Stars
- Gingerbread Cookies
- Holiday Candle Pastries
- Lebkuchen
    - Lebkuchen Bars
    - Lebkuchen Hearts
- Springerle
- Yule Log Pastries

Plated Desserts
- *Bûche de Noël* Slices with Pomegranate Sauce and Starfruit
- Chocolate Chalet with White Chocolate and Pistachio Pâte and Bitter Chocolate Sauce
- Mont Blanc with Pomegranate Seeds and Vanilla Curly Cues
- Persimmon Charlotte
- Persimmon Cream Slices with Cookie Christmas Trees and Cranberry Coulis

- Persimmon Pudding
- Pumpkin Bread
- Pudding with Dried Cranberries and Maple Whipped Cream

Gingerbread Houses
- Traditional Gingerbread House
- Santa's Gingerbread Chalet

Marzipan Holiday Decorations
- Marzipan Angel
- Marzipan Children for the Traditional Gingerbread House
- Marzipan Pig with Two Santas
- Marzipan Santa for the Traditional Gingerbread House

The Christmas season is a hectic time for many people, and especially so for those of us involved in the food service industry. Like me, you probably find yourself wishing there were a few more hours in the day to enable you to take advantage of all the business (as we all know if you are not busy at this time of the year, you are simply not doing too well) and still leave a little time left to celebrate your own traditions. Although it is a lot of fun getting into the Christmas spirit and preparing all of those special treats that we haven't seen since last year, come Christmas Eve we are usually glad it's over. Unfortunately, most retailers simply start too early: Christmas decorations go up in the stores before Thanksgiving, and Santa often arrives in the malls before December first. I am afraid the day will be here soon when parents will only have to make one trip to the lot with their children, and they will be able to choose the Halloween pumpkin and the Christmas tree at the same time!

Having grown up on a farm in Sweden, with all of the traditional customs, I am saddened to see Christmas so commercialized today. At home the holiday season started early, but in a much more subtle way. Four weeks before Christmas, Advent began with the lighting of the first of four candles; one more would be lit each week until Christmas, when all four would be burning. We children had our Advent calendar with a window to open on each day of December, each showing a different picture and ending with a picture of *Jultomten* (Santa Claus) on Christmas Eve. My Dad saved a few wheat husks from the harvest, which we would attach to a broomstick and put out for the birds as soon as the first snow covered the ground.

Every year my Dad and a neighbor would slaughter a pig in early December. The two families shared it, and my Mom made delicious dishes from the pig for our Christmas table. There was also baking to be done, from the *Vörtbröd* to the gingerbread figures that my sister and I helped decorate for the Christmas tree. And there could not be Christmas without marzipan candies, one of which was always a pig in some shape or form. In addition we would arrange an abundance of nuts, bunches of large, dried raisins on the stem, dates, and citrus fruits from California. In the midst of all of these preparations Lucia Day, the darkest day of the year, was celebrated with its own special ceremony and traditional breakfast pastries including Lucia Buns.

The week before Christmas my Dad and I walked out into the snow-covered forest to cut down the preselected tree. We put it in a special stand with water to keep it from getting dry. This was especially important since we used real candles to decorate the branches. After the other ornaments were placed on the tree it remained in place until the thirteenth of January, twenty days after Christmas.

On Christmas Eve, the culmination of all of this preparation and anticipation, we shared the most lavish meal of the year with all of our friends and relatives. It was customary to save the broth from cooking the ham, and the feast officially started with the ceremony known as *doppa i grytan,* or "dip in the pot," where everyone would dip a piece of *Vörtbröd* into the broth. The traditional rice pudding was served for dessert, with one bitter almond hidden inside; the story was that whoever found the almond would marry the next year.

The Christmas Eve buffet was always eaten early so there would be time for my Dad to "go to the neighbor's house to lend a helping hand," and every year, by coincidence, this was when Santa would arrive at our house dressed in his red suit and carrying our presents! After Santa left, we moved the furniture (Dad was always back by then to help) and brought the Christmas tree to the center of the room. Everyone then joined hands around the tree and sang Christmas songs.

On Christmas Day we ate (the inevitable) *"lutfisk"* (sun-dried and lime-cured ling cod; not too popular with children) for dinner, accom-

panied by a white sauce and homemade mustard. And for dessert the custom called for *Riz à la Malta* served with cherry sauce, a light fluffy rice dessert made from the leftover rice pudding served on Christmas Eve, with the addition of whipped cream and chopped almonds.

In the pastry shops, preparations of all the candies, chocolates, and marzipan items started in late November. The first Sunday of Advent was also the big "window display Sunday" all over Sweden. The shops would try to out do each other, as well as their own displays from the previous year, and people would crowd outside the windows to view the fantasy worlds inside. At the end of my five-year apprenticeship I was very excited and proud to be given the responsibility of decorating the shop window, and I made a landscape of gingerbread houses and marzipan figures. Though I have certainly created more elaborate work since then, this project remains special to me as one of my first accomplishments. Unfortunately the photographs I took of it have been lost over the years.

Today, a large part of all of these traditional food preparations are just a memory. Only the most dedicated continue to slaughter their own pigs and make all of the sweets at home. Instead, most Christmas food is purchased ready-made.

Although many items are made only at Christmas time—either because of the availability of the ingredients or just simply for tradition—many of the recipes in this chapter can be made anytime, and many are suited to other holidays as well: Snow Hearts for Valentine's Day, Cinnamon Stars for the Fourth of July, and Pumpkin Pie or Pumpkin Bread Pudding for Halloween or Thanksgiving. Gingerbread cookies and cakes can be adapted to serve year-round, and in the recipes that use persimmon, try substituting another fruit with approximately the same texture (apricots or peaches, for example).

Conversely, you can dress up many standard pastries and desserts for the holidays by placing a Christmas decoration on top. For example, Rum Balls can be made in a log shape, lightly dusted with powdered sugar, and topped with a tiny gingerbread heart with a red dot piped in the center. The Princess Cake with its green marzipan cover lends itself very well to a Christmas presentation: Pipe a Christmas tree outline on each slice, dot here and there with red piping gel for ornaments, and sift powdered sugar lightly over the top for snow.

Breads

 ## Braided Stollen

four 1-pound, 2-ounce (510-g) loaves

2 ounces (55 g) fresh compressed yeast

1½ cups (360 ml) warm water (105–115°F, 40–46°C)

1 ounce (30 g) malt sugar
   or
3 tablespoons (45 ml) or 2 ounces (55 g) honey

3 ounces (85 g) granulated sugar

1 tablespoon (15 g) salt

grated zest of one orange

½ teaspoon (2.5 ml) orange flower water

½ teaspoon (2.5 ml) vanilla extract

2 eggs

3 ounces (85 g) blanched almonds, finely ground

4 ounces (115 g) soft unsalted butter

7 ounces (200 g) golden raisins

2 pounds (910 g) bread flour, approximately

Egg Wash (page 7)

Cinnamon Sugar (page 5)

*T*his is a simplified version of the richer stollen that is studded with the familiar candied and dried fruits. Although it lacks most of those goodies, Braided Stollen has a delightful flavor of its own supplied by the orange zest, orange flower water, and golden raisins (known in Europe as sultana raisins). While the Dresdener and Weihnacht varieties of stollen are made only for the Christmas holiday, many other types of stollen are enjoyed throughout the year in Germany and Switzerland. Some of these, with almond, cheese (quark or cottage), or poppy seed filling, resemble a Danish-style coffee cake more than anything else and are made to be enjoyed with a cup of coffee or tea.

Braided Stollen can be baked directly on paper-lined sheet pans if suitable loaf pans are not available. It is delicious toasted and topped with sweet butter as soon as the hot slices pop out of the toaster, so that the butter melts into the bread.

1. Dissolve the yeast in the warm water. Add the malt sugar or honey, granulated sugar, and salt. Combine the orange zest, orange flower water, vanilla, and eggs. Add this to the yeast mixture, together with the almonds, butter, and raisins.

2. Reserve a handful of the bread flour and incorporate the remaining flour into the mixture, kneading for a few minutes. Adjust the consistency of the dough by adding the reserved flour, if necessary, to make a soft and elastic dough. Cover the dough and let it rise in a warm place until it has doubled in volume.

3. Punch down the dough and divide it into four equal pieces, approximately 1 pound, 2 ounces (510 g) each. Divide each of these pieces into four pieces again. Pound and roll each of the sixteen small pieces into a rope 12 inches (30 cm) long (see Figures 3–3 to 3–5, pages 77 and 78). Braid each group of four ropes following the instructions for the Four-String Braid II on page 80.

4. Place the braided loaves in greased 8-by-4-inch (20-×-10-cm) bread pans. Brush with Egg Wash, then sprinkle Cinnamon Sugar over the tops. Let the loaves rise until one-and-one-half times the original size.

5. Bake at 400°F (205°C) for approximately 30 minutes or until baked through. Remove from the pans immediately and transfer to racks to cool.

Chestnut Bread

four 1-pound, 8-ounce (680-g) loaves

Sponge

1 ounce (30 g) fresh compressed yeast

1 cup (240 ml) warm water (105–115°F, 40–46°C)

1/4 cup (60 ml) or 3 ounces (85 g) honey

8 ounces (225 g) high-gluten bread flour

Dough

1 pound, 12 ounces (795 g) chestnuts in the shell

or

1 pound, 8 ounces (680 g) shelled chestnuts

2 ounces (55 g) unsalted butter

1 1/2 ounces (40 g) fresh compressed yeast

2 cups (480 ml) warm milk (105–115°F, 40–46°C)

12 ounces (340 g) unsweetened chestnut purée

4 1/2 teaspoons (23 g) salt

8 ounces (225 g) whole wheat flour

1 pound, 10 ounces (740 g) high-gluten bread flour, approximately

I nearly gave up on this recipe in the beginning because while the flavor was great, it seemed that no matter what I did, or how carefully I treated the dough, I simply could not get a healthy, attractive, oven-spring in the baked bread. I singled out the chestnuts as the culprit, but it took few tries before I realized exactly how they were adversely affecting the loaves: Because of their high starch content, the chestnuts reduced the gluten strength of the bread flour I was using to approximately that of ordinary cake flour. Switching to high-gluten flour made all the difference.

You can enjoy Chestnut Bread any time of the year by making it with canned chestnut purée and packaged whole roasted chestnuts. (The best quality whole chestnuts seem to be the French imports packed in glass jars.) This bread also makes an excellent poultry stuffing for Thanksgiving—the chestnuts are already included! If you do not have bannetons *to form the bread as it bakes, follow the instructions given with Onion-Walnut Bread (see page 102), or make regular round or oval free-form loaves; these will be just as good with the same rich chestnut flavor.*

1. To make the sponge, dissolve the yeast in the warm water, then add the honey and the bread flour and stir until the mixture is smooth. Cover and let the sponge proof in a warm place until it has doubled in volume and starts to fall.

2. If using chestnuts in the shell, follow the instructions on page 802 to shell them and then proceed. Chop the shelled chestnuts into 1/2-inch (1.2-cm) pieces. Place in a skillet with the butter and sauté gently over medium heat until they feel soft to the touch. Reserve.

3. To start the dough, dissolve the yeast in the warm milk in a mixer bowl. Add the chestnut purée, salt, the sponge, and the whole wheat flour, mixing until combined.

4. Reserve a handful of the bread flour and incorporate the remainder into the dough. Knead for 8 to 10 minutes on low speed using the dough hook. Adjust the consistency by adding the reserved flour (or more) if necessary to make a smooth and elastic dough. Add the prepared chestnuts and mix only until they are incorporated.

5. Cover and allow the dough to rest in a warm place until it has doubled in volume.

6. Divide the dough into four equal pieces approximately 1 pound, 8 ounces (680 g) each. Dust four round *bannetons* (see page 1119) with bread flour. Form each piece of dough into a round loaf (see Figures 3–1 and 3–2, page 70) and place seam-side up in the prepared forms. Let proof until one-and-one-half times their original size.

7. Gently invert the loaves onto sheet pans lined with baking paper. Bake at 400°F (205°C) for approximately 35 minutes or until the loaves feel light when handled and sound hollow when tapped sharply on the bottom.

Dresdener Stollen

*three 1-pound, 5-ounce
(595-g) loaves*

2 ounces (55 g) glacéed red cherries

4 ounces (115 g) Candied Orange Peel
(page 978)

4 ounces (115 g) pecans

4 ounces (115 g) golden raisins

4 ounces (115 g) dark raisins

3 tablespoons (45 ml) dark rum

1½ ounces (40 g) fresh compressed
yeast

¾ cup (180 ml) warm milk
(105–115°F, 40–46°C)

1½ teaspoons (8 g) salt

1½ teaspoons (5 g) malt sugar
or

1 tablespoon (15 ml) honey

1½ ounces (40 g) granulated sugar

2 eggs

¼ teaspoon (.5 g) ground cloves

1½ teaspoons (3 g) ground cardamom

1 teaspoon (1.5 g) ground cinnamon

½ teaspoon (1 g) ground allspice

1 pound, 6 ounces (625 g) bread flour,
approximately

10 ounces (285 g) soft unsalted butter

melted unsalted butter

Quick Vanilla Sugar (recipe follows)

Dresdener Stollen is a rich German bread laden with fruit and nuts. The shape of the loaves resembles a giant, curved Parkerhouse roll but was originally intended to symbolize Jesus Christ as he was found wrapped in swaddling clothes (the German word stollen *means "support"). The most popular versions of stollen are the Christmas or* Weihnacht *stollen and the better known* Dresdener *stollen, named for the German city of Dresden. Although they look very much the same, their taste differs in that* Dresdener *stollen has nearly three times more butter than the Christmas stollen and it does not contain eggs. The Christmas stollen also, confusingly enough, generally lacks the spices we associate with Christmas treats, such as cloves, cardamom, and cinnamon.*

This recipe is a combination of the two: I reduced the amount of butter in the classic Dresdener style and added a few eggs instead, which makes the yeast easier to manage and the dough is still plenty rich. A nice variation is to replace about two ounces of the raisins with candied angelica chopped to the same size. The angelica adds an attractive contrasting color, but if you can't get it, please do not substitute glacéed green cherries.

A properly baked stollen will keep fresh for many weeks, well wrapped and stored in the refrigerator, or for months in the freezer. This Christmas treat is a must for anyone of German heritage and for some Swedes as well. I often bring it to a friend's home at the holidays, and there seems to be someone every time who is unsure and will ask "Is this stollen?" And I can never resist the joke "Of course not, I baked it myself."

1. Chop the cherries, Candied Orange Peel, and pecans into raisin-sized pieces. Add the golden and dark raisins and the rum. Let macerate for at least 24 hours, stirring from time to time if possible.

2. Dissolve the yeast in the warm milk. Add the salt, malt sugar or honey, granulated sugar, eggs, and spices. Mix in about half of the flour. Add the softened butter and remaining flour.

3. Knead until an elastic (glutenous) dough has formed, about 10 minutes. Cover the dough and let proof in a warm place until doubled in volume.

4. Knead in the fruit mixture by hand. Cover the dough and let it rise until doubled a second time.

5. Punch the dough down and divide it into three equal pieces, approximately 1 pound, 5 ounces (595 g) each. Knead the pieces into round loaves (see Figures 3–1 and 3–2, page 70), picking up any nuts or fruit that fall off and pushing them back into the dough. Shape the pieces into oval loaves with the palm of your hands. Roll the loaves against the table to make them slightly tapered at the ends and then leave them seam-side down on the table.

6. Using a dowel, roll the loaves flat, keeping the same general shape. Fold the flattened pieces almost in half lengthwise, making the bottom part about ½ inch (1.2 cm) wider than the top half. Bend the loaves into a slightly curved shape, with the fold on the inside of the curve (Figure 16–1). Place on sheet pans lined with baking paper. Let rise until the loaves are one-and-one-half times their original size.

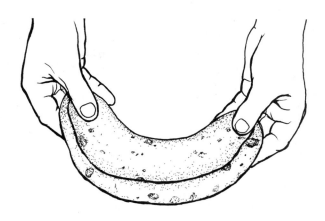

FIGURE 16–1 Bending a folded Dresdener Stollen loaf into a slightly curved shape with the folded side on the inside of the curve

7. Bake double-panned at 375°F (190°C) for about 1 hour or until baked through. Brush the loaves with melted butter immediately after removing them from the oven. As soon as they are cool enough to handle invert the loaves into the Quick Vanilla Sugar.

Quick Vanilla Sugar

12 ounces (340 g)

1¹/₂ teaspoons (7.5 ml) vanilla extract
8 ounces (225 g) granulated sugar
4 ounces (115 g) powdered sugar

1. Rub the vanilla into the granulated sugar, using your hands.
2. Mix in the powdered sugar.

Lucia Buns

30 rolls, approximately
2 ounces (55 g) each

one recipe Cinnamon Snails dough
   (page 154)
saffron
dark raisins
Egg Wash (page 7)
sanding sugar (optional)
sliced almonds (optional)

NOTE: You can also form the dough into
braided loaves and wreaths (see Braided White

*L*ucia Buns (also called Lucia Cats because some of the shapes resemble a cat) are traditionally made in Sweden for Lucia Day, the thirteenth of December. This is the darkest, shortest day of the year, and we celebrate the fact that the days start to get lighter and longer from that point.

Every city or village has crowned a Lucia or Ljusets Drottning, which means the "Queen of Light." Bearing on her head a wreath made of pine boughs studded with candles, and wearing a long, plain white dress, she would bring light to the darkest day. Lucia appears in the morning singing the song "Saint Lucia" and offering coffee, Lucia Buns, and gingerbread hearts.

The Lucia Buns are made from cardamom dough flavored with saffron, but it is a good idea to make some plain, as not everyone likes saffron. Saffron wreaths and breads are also traditionally made for the Christmas holidays in Sweden. They are always left undecorated except for the raisins, either in the dough or on top, and the sugar and almonds sprinkled over them.

Bread, pages 76 to 82, and Mayor's Wreath, page 184). Sprinkle these with a combination of equal parts sanding sugar and sliced almonds. Bake at a slightly lower temperature for a little longer time.

1. Reserve whatever portion of the Cinnamon Snails dough (if any) you do not want to flavor with saffron. Add a few grams of saffron to the remainder of the dough; the amount will vary depending on how much dough you are flavoring, your taste, and your pocketbook, since saffron is very expensive. Soak the saffron in hot water before adding it to the dough, using 1 tablespoon (15 ml) hot water for every 1 to 5 grams of saffron. Knead the saffron into the dough until it is thoroughly incorporated and no streaks of yellow are visible. Cover the dough and let it rest for 10 minutes. At this stage, the dough can be placed in the freezer, well covered, for later use.

2. Divide the dough into three equal pieces, approximately 1 pound, 4 ounces (570 g) each. Roll each piece into a rope, and cut each rope into ten equal pieces, about 2 ounces (55 g) each. Keep the pieces well covered.

3. Divide each piece in half when you are ready to form the buns. Roll the 1-ounce (30-g) pieces into ropes about 5 inches (12.5 cm) long and taper the ends. Use two ropes per roll, and form the desired shape or shapes (Figure 16–2). Alternatively, you may leave some or all of the pieces 2 ounces (55 g) and use a single rope for each bun, as shown in the bottom row of the illustration. You will probably need to roll these pieces a bit longer than 5 inches (12.5 cm), depending on the shape(s) you create.

4. Place the formed buns on sheet pans and decorate with raisins as shown. Be sure to press the raisins in firmly, all the way to the bottom of the dough, or they will fall off. Let the buns rise until one-and-one-half times their original size.

5. Brush the buns with Egg Wash. Sprinkle sanding sugar and sliced almonds over the tops if desired. Bake at 400°F (205°C) for about 15 minutes or until golden in color and baked through.

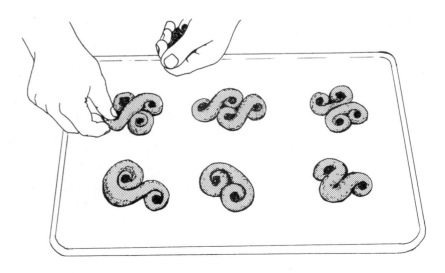

FIGURE 16–2 Decorating Lucia Buns with raisins before baking

Panettone

four 1-pound, 6-ounce (625-g) loaves

2 ounces (55 g) fresh compressed yeast

2 cups (480 ml) warm water (105–115°F, 40–46°C)

6 ounces (170 g) powdered sugar

6 egg yolks (1/2 cup/120 ml)

1 tablespoon (15 g) salt

grated zest of two lemons

1 tablespoon (15 ml) orange flower water

2 pounds, 11 ounces (1 kg, 220 g) bread flour, approximately

8 ounces (225 g) soft unsalted butter

6 ounces (170 g) golden raisins

4 ounces (115 g) Candied Orange Peel (page 978), diced

Egg Wash (page 7)

The towering round Italian bread Panettone *is a specialty of the city of Milan. It is made from a dough that is rich in egg yolks and butter—similar to Brioche—giving the bread its distinctive golden color. Just like the other holiday breads such as the German* stollen *and the Swiss* Triestine, Panettone *contains a mass of raisins and candied fruits (plus nuts on occasion, although nuts are not part of the classic rendition). While Panettone is traditionally served at Christmas time—both as is, to accompany a cup of coffee, or embellished and offered as a dessert—in Italy it is also made from time to time throughout the year for weddings and for christening celebrations. The word* panettone *derives from* panetto, *a form of* pane *(bread). According to history, Panettone was invented by a baker from Milan whose name was* Tonio, *hence* Pane de Tonio, *which became* Panettone.

Panettone molds can be the reusable type made of metal, or paper molds that stay around the bread when it is sold. If Panettone molds are not available to you, use any round mold that has sides at least two inches high. Empty cans of the appropriate size lined with baking paper, small six-inch cheesecake forms, and even trimmed paper bags may be used. (If you use cans, do not remove the bottoms to form rings; the dough will proof and bake out from both ends!)

This recipe uses the straight dough method (meaning it does not start with a sponge) and contains a slightly smaller quantity of butter and egg yolks than the very rich old-fashioned doughs that call for proofing and punching the dough down many times as the egg yolks and fat are added very gradually, to protect the yeast. Some of these recipes took most of the day to complete.

1. Dissolve the yeast in the warm water.

2. In a separate bowl, combine the powdered sugar with the egg yolks and beat for a few seconds. Add to the yeast mixture. Incorporate the salt, the lemon zest, orange flower water, and all but a handful of the flour. Add the soft butter and knead for 5 minutes, using the dough hook. Adjust by adding the remaining flour if necessary to make a smooth, elastic dough.

3. Cover and let rise in a warm place until the dough has doubled in volume.

4. Knead the raisins and Candied Orange Peel into the dough by hand.

5. Line the inside of Panettone molds with baking paper (if Panettone molds are not available, use four metal cans 4 1/2 inches deep and 4 inches in diameter (11.2 × 10 cm). Scale the dough into four equal pieces, approximately 1 pound, 6 ounces (625 g) each. Form each piece into a round ball, then roll the balls against the table to make cylinders that will fit inside the forms or cans. Place the loaves in the forms with the seams hidden, taking care not to wrinkle the baking paper. Let rise in a warm place until the dough just crests above the rim of the forms. Brush Egg Wash over the tops.

6. Bake at 375°F (190°C) for approximately 35 minutes or until baked through. To be certain they are done, check one loaf by removing it from the form or can—it should have a light brown crust. As soon as you take the breads out of the oven, unmold them and let cool on a rack lying on their sides. If they are left in the baking forms the loaves will become soggy from condensation.

Sweet Pig's Head

9 breakfast pastries

one recipe Cinnamon Snails dough (page 154)
Egg Wash (page 7)
1 pound, 8 ounces (680 g) Pastry Cream (page 1088)
whole wheat flour
Royal Icing (page 1019)
dark coating chocolate

As discussed at length elsewhere in this text, the domestic pig earns celebrity status at Christmas time in both Scandinavia and the German-speaking countries of Europe for various reasons. In Sweden many of the items on the Christmas smörgåsbord are made from pork, edible pigs are created out of marzipan, chocolate, cookie dough, and many different yeast doughs, and there are pig decorations formed from weaver's and salt doughs as well.

Adorable Sweet Pig's Head pastries never fail to bring a smile, and they are very quick and easy to produce. The only equipment necessary is a saucer or bread and butter plate, a few cookie cutters, and a plain piping tip. A fun variation (in addition to the individual dinner rolls which follow) is to make a whole pig pastry instead of just the pig's head (they are admittedly a little abstract, but clearly well-fed; see the illustration with the dinner roll variation).

To make two large pigs, omit the Pastry Cream filling and make only one-half recipe of Cinnamon Snails dough. Roll the dough out to an 11-by-25-inch (27.5-×-62.5-cm) rectangle ¼ inch (6 mm) thick. Chill the dough briefly so it is relaxed and firm. Cut out two 10-inch (25-cm) rounds for the bodies of the pigs, two 5-inch (12.5-cm) rounds for the heads, and two 2-inch (5-cm) rounds for the snouts. Cut two holes across the center of the snouts using a no. 4 (8-mm) plain pastry tip. Roll some of the remaining dough to ⅛ inch (3 mm) thick and cut out two 2½-inch (6.2-cm) circles. Cut two oval ears out of each one using the same cutter. Pound and roll two small pieces of the leftover dough into thin, 7-inch (17.5-cm) strings that are tapered at the ends, for the tails.

To assemble the pigs, brush Egg Wash on the bodies and place the heads at the bottom of the circles. Brush Egg Wash over the heads and place the snouts at the base of the heads. Attach the ears to the top of the heads, then attach the tails in a curled position at the top of the bodies. Brush Egg Wash on the snouts, ears, and tails. Sift whole wheat flour over the pigs, covering them completely. Do not let the pigs proof much, if at all. Bake, cool, and form the eyes as in Sweet Pig's Head.

1. Divide the dough into two equal pieces and form each one into a ball. Cover the dough rounds and refrigerate for 30 minutes.

2. Cut an X on top of each ball of dough, cutting down to the center of the ball. Push the corners out on each round to form two squares (see Figure 2–6, page 45). Roll each piece of dough out to 16 by 24 inches (40 × 60 cm); it should be about ⅛ inch (3 mm) thick. Return the dough sheets to the refrigerator (or place briefly in the freezer) to relax and firm the dough.

3. Cut out eighteen 6-inch (15-cm) circles, using the tip of a knife and a plate of that size as a guide. Cut out nine 2½-inch (6.2-cm) circles, using a plain cookie cutter. With a no. 4 (8-mm) plain pastry tip, cut two holes across the middle of the small circles to form snouts.

4. Roll some of the larger dough scraps to ¹/₁₆ inch (2 mm) thick. Cut out nine circles with a plain 3-inch (7.5-cm) cookie cutter. Cut two ears out of each circle using the same cutter, by making two cuts that meet in the center, to create two pointed ovals. Place the ears in the refrigerator together with the remaining dough, which should be covered and saved for another use.

To assemble the pig's heads

5. Brush Egg Wash over nine of the larger circles.

6. Put the same pastry tip used to cut the holes in the snouts in a pastry bag and add the Pastry Cream. Pipe the cream, dividing it evenly, over the nine egg-washed rounds, staring at the center and making concentric circles toward the outside. Stop to leave a ¹/₂-inch (1.2-cm) border around the edge.

7. Place the nine remaining large circles on top of the filling and press down firmly from the outside of the circles all around to make sure the edges stick or the filling will ooze out as it bakes. Brush the top of the filled "heads" with Egg Wash. Place the small circles with the holes (the snout) on the lower half of the heads. Attach the ears to the top of the heads, curving them forward. Brush Egg Wash over the snouts and ears.

8. Using a medium mesh sifter, sift whole wheat flour over the heads, covering them completely. These pastries do not require much proofing and will most likely be ready to bake after assembling.

9. Bake at 375°F (190°C) until golden brown and baked through, about 25 minutes. Let cool.

10. When the pastries have cooled, scrape away the whole wheat flour at two spots fairly close together between the ears and the snout where the eyes should be. Pipe pea-sized dots of Royal Icing on these marks. Pipe a small dot of melted coating chocolate on the Royal Icing to mark the pupils (you can have some fun here by making the pig look left, right, or cross-eyed).

VARIATION
Dinner Rolls

18 rolls

one-half recipe Braided White Bread
    dough (page 76)
Egg Wash (page 7)
whole wheat flour
Royal Icing (page 1019)
dark coating chocolate

*T*he Pig's Head can also be made into a whimsical dinner roll, any time you want to show someone what you think of their appetite! For a fun loaf bread make whole pigs using this dough and following the instructions for the whole pig pastry described in the introduction.

1. Roll the dough out to a 23-by-16-inch (57.5-×-40-cm) rectangle about ¹/₄ inch (6 mm) thick. Cut out eighteen 4-inch (10-cm) circles and eighteen 1¹/₂-inch (3.7-cm) circles. Use a no. 2 (4-mm) plain tip to cut the snouts from the smaller circles. Press the scrap dough together (do not knead it) and refrigerate.

FIGURE 16–3 *Piping the eyes on Pig's Head Dinner Rolls; a whole pig loaf before and after baking (whole wheat flour was sifted over the rolls and the loaf before baking)*

NOTE: *For a different look, assemble and egg wash the pig's heads first, then sift whole wheat flour over the entire head as is done with the filled version.*

2. Brush Egg Wash over the larger circles and the snouts. Sift whole wheat flour over the snouts, then attach them close to the lower edge on each head.

3. Roll the scrap dough ¹⁄₈ inch (3 mm) thick. Cut the ears as in step 4 of the main recipe, using a 2-inch (5-cm) cutter. Attach the ears at the top of the heads and curve them forward. Brush Egg Wash over the ears.

4. Let the rolls rise until one-and-one half times the original size.

5. Bake at 400°F (205°C) for about 15 minutes. Decorate as directed in the main recipe (Figure 16–3).

 Swedish Spice Bread (*Vörtbröd*)

four 1-pound, 2-ounce (510-g) loaves

1 cup (240 g) or 12 ounces (340 g) molasses

2 cups (480 ml) porter, heated to 120°F (49°C)

1¹⁄₂ ounces (40 g) fresh compressed yeast

1 pound, 2 ounces (510 g) bread flour

9 ounces (255 g) medium rye flour

2 teaspoons (4 g) ground cloves

2 tablespoons (12 g) ground ginger

2 tablespoons (12 g) ground anise seed

Vört *is the Swedish word for wort, which is the sweet brown liquid that is created after the first three basic steps in beer making: The barley is first soaked to facilitate germination. The partially germinated kernels are dried to stop the enzymes in the process of digesting the starch, and to develop the proper color and flavor. The barley is then mashed in warm water, reconstituting the enzymes and producing the wort or* vört. *In the old days this liquid could be purchased from breweries and through bakery suppliers during the months of November and December. The* vört *was boiled until it had been reduced by two-thirds to give it the strong flavor necessary for a good* Vörtbröd. *Porter or drought beers can also be used, but in addition to being inferior to* vört *in flavor, they are relatively expensive for large commercial operations (these do not need to be reduced, however). In the baking industry today,* vört *extract is primarily used rather than* vört. *Not being able to find* vört *when I first came to this country, I substituted molasses and porter and added a few spices not usually found in this type of rye bread. After a few adjustments and some tinkering back and forth, I was pleasantly surprised at how close this "no-vört-Vörtbröd" comes to the real thing.*

2 tablespoons (12 g) ground fennel
 seed

1 tablespoon (15 g) salt

8 ounces (225 g) Candied Orange Peel
 (page 978), finely chopped

2 ounces (55 g) soft unsalted butter

4 ounces (115 g) bread flour,
 approximately

4 ounces (115 g) dark raisins

medium rye flour

vegetable oil

Due to the large amount of sugar in the dough, in conjunction with rye flour, which itself is sweet and contains little or no useable gluten, it is extremely important not to allow the dough temperature to fall below 80°F (26°C). For this reason, be sure to start the sponge with the slightly higher-than-normal temperature of liquid (porter in this case) to counter the cooling-off effect when it is mixed with the molasses.

In addition to being used for the traditional Swedish Christmas Eve celebration known as doppa i grytan, Vörtbröd *tastes great with Christmas ham and mild cheeses.*

1. Combine the molasses and porter. Add the yeast and mix to dissolve. Incorporate the first measurement of bread flour and mix to form a smooth sponge. Place the sponge in an oiled bowl, cover, and let rise in a warm place until it has doubled in volume.

2. Combine the rye flour with the spices and salt. Mix into the sponge, together with the Candied Orange Peel and the butter. Add the remaining bread flour, adjusting the amount if necessary to form a very soft dough. Knead with the dough hook until smooth and elastic, about 5 minutes.

3. Add the raisins and mix just long enough to incorporate them. Place the dough in an oiled bowl, turn to coat both sides with oil, cover, and let rise in a warm place until doubled in volume.

4. Punch the dough down and divide it into four equal pieces, approximately 1 pound, 2 ounces (510 g) each. Shape the pieces into oval loaves, slightly tapered on the ends (see Figure 3–24, page 120). Place the loaves on sheet pans dusted with rye flour. Let rise until one-and-one half times the original size.

5. Bake at 375°F (190°C) for approximately 40 minutes, using a second pan underneath to protect the bottom of the loaves from becoming too brown. Brush the baked loaves with vegetable oil and transfer to a rack to cool.

Triestine Bread

*four 1-pound, 4-ounce
(570-g) loaves*

Sponge

1 cup (240 ml) warm milk
 (105–115°F, 40–46°C)

1/2 ounce (15 g) or 1 tablespoon
 (15 ml) fresh compressed yeast

8 ounces (225 g) bread flour

I first came across Triestine Bread in the early seventies while I was spending a few days around Lago Maggiore *in the southern part of Switzerland (although the majority of this beautiful lake is actually in Italy). My trip was not planned—I was attempting to escape horrible weather in central Europe by crossing through the Alps—and I actually ended up spending the first night sleeping in my car since I arrived on a weekend that happened to be the New Year's holiday, and there was not a hotel room to be found at any price. But at least I discovered this wonderful bread.*

Triestine is basically a Panettone made in a different shape. Instead of being baked in a tall, cylindrical form, this variation is made as a freestanding round loaf. The top and sides of the loaves are coated with a ground almond mixture and then covered with sliced, blanched almonds. After proofing, the loaves are heavily dusted with enough powdered sugar to completely cover the almonds.

Dough

1 cup (240 ml) warm milk (105–115°F, 40–46°C)

1½ ounces (40 g) fresh compressed yeast

5 teaspoons (15 g) malt sugar

or

2 tablespoons (30 ml) honey

3 ounces (85 g) granulated sugar

2 teaspoons (10 g) salt

2 eggs

grated zest of one lemon

1 teaspoon (5 ml) orange flower water

4 ounces (115 g) soft unsalted butter

1 pound, 8 ounces (680 g) bread flour, approximately

4 ounces (115 g) Candied Orange Peel (page 978), finely chopped

4 ounces (115 g) glacéed or candied red cherries, finely chopped

4 ounces (115 g) sliced almonds

Topping

4 ounces (115 g) finely ground blanched almonds, approximately

2 ounces (55 g) granulated sugar

2 egg whites (¼ cup/60 ml)

1 ounce (30 g) sliced almonds

powdered sugar

During the oven-spring this coating breaks apart, leaving a beautiful contrast with a very seasonal look resembling snow-covered stones in moving water.

Like the other sweet breads in this chapter, Triestine must be "babied" through the dough stage to ensure that it is neither too hot nor too cold, since a great fluctuation in temperature will adversely effect the bread's ability to rise.

1. Make the sponge by dissolving the yeast in the warm milk and then mixing in the flour. Let rise, covered, until doubled in volume.

2. Using the ingredients listed for the dough, dissolve the yeast in the warm milk. Stir this into the sponge, then add the remaining ingredients in the order listed, but hold back a little of the flour in case you do not need it all. The dough should be fairly firm. Let rest, covered, for 10 minutes.

3. Divide the dough into four equal pieces approximately 1 pound, 4 ounces (570 g) each. Form the pieces into round loaves (see Figures 3–1 and 3–2, page 70). Do not overknead; the loaves should be just firm enough to spring back when pressed lightly. Flatten the loaves slightly with your hands to make a surface for the topping.

4. Make the topping by combining all but small portion of the ground almonds with the granulated sugar and egg whites. Add more ground almond if necessary; the mixture should be spreadable but not runny. Spread the topping over the tops and halfway down the sides of the loaves. Top with sliced almonds, pressing them on with your hands so they stick. Let the loaves rise until they have doubled in volume.

5. Sift enough powdered sugar over the top of the loaves to cover the almonds. Bake at 375°F (190°C) until golden brown, about 35 minutes. Cool on racks. You may need to protect the loaves from over-browning by placing a second pan underneath or by covering the tops with baking paper.

Cakes, Tarts, Tortes, and Pies

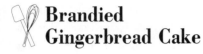

Brandied Gingerbread Cake

two 11-inch (27.5-cm) cakes

Butter and Flour Mixture (page 4)

one recipe Soft Gingerbread Cake batter (page 284)

ten small kumquats

*O*ne of my very favorite Christmas sweets is the simple Soft Gingerbread Cake from the Tea Cakes chapter. This rendition, which is a bit more "dressed up," is still very easy to prepare.

The pomegranates and kumquats give the cake a festive air, but if they are not available, decorate after your own taste or simply use the Ganache alone, which gives an elegant, rich look. If you are serving the cake as a plated dessert, decorate by dusting ground cinnamon over the base or the rim of the plates and serve with Brandied Whipped Cream (see page 846). The cakes can be prepared several days in advance without any negative side effect but do not ice them more than one or two days ahead of serving and do

⅓ cup (80 ml) Simple Syrup
   (page 11)
⅓ cup (80 ml) brandy
¼ cup (60 ml) orange juice
6 ounces (170 g) Ganache (page 1086)
seeds from one-quarter pomegranate
powdered sugar

not prepare the kumquat decorations more than a few hours ahead; they start to dry out quickly.

1. Follow the recipe for the Soft Gingerbread Cakes through step four, brushing the Butter and Flour Mixture on the inside of two 11-inch (27.5-cm) fluted tart pans. Divide the batter between the pans.

2. Bake at 350°F (175°C) for approximately 35 minutes or until the cakes spring back when pressed lightly. Let cool and then invert to remove them from the baking pans.

3. Prepare the kumquats by slicing in half at a sharp angle and then use a small melon-ball cutter to scoop out the flesh. Discard the flesh. Place the Simple Syrup in a small saucepan. Bring to a boil and reduce for 1 minute. Remove from the heat (if the syrup has reduced too far and it is very thick, add a little water). Add the kumquat shells and carefully stir them to ensure they are completely covered with syrup. Immediately remove them from the syrup and place the kumquat shells upside down (open end down) on a sheet pan lined with baking paper to drain.

4. Combine the brandy and the orange juice. Brush over the top and sides of the inverted cakes.

5. Warm the Ganache until it has an easily spreadable consistency. Divide the Ganache between the cakes and spread it out over the tops, leaving a border of approximately ¼ inch (6 mm) around the top edges. Move the tip of the palette knife back and forth across the tops in long even stokes to create a wavy pattern in the Ganache. Refrigerate just long enough to set the Ganache.

6. Cut or mark the cakes into ten servings each. Place a kumquat shell on its longer side at the edge of each slice with the open end toward the edge of the cake. Place three or four pomegranate seeds inside each shell. Sift powdered sugar lightly over the center of the cakes.

Chestnut Rum Torte

one 10-inch (25-cm) torte

Butter and Flour Mixture (page 4)
8 ounces (225 g) soft unsalted butter
9 ounces (255 g) granulated sugar
5 eggs, separated
3 tablespoons (45 ml) dark rum
2½ cups (600 ml) Chestnut Purée
   (recipe follows)
2 cups (480 ml) heavy cream
2 teaspoons (10 g) granulated sugar
½ teaspoon (2.5 ml) vanilla extract
finely chopped pecans
shaved dark chocolate

*B*ecause fresh chestnuts, persimmons, and pomegranates are primarily available only during the few months from late fall to Christmas time, it makes the seasonal treats prepared with them all the more special. This dessert has a distinctive light texture, which can only be produced by using fresh chestnuts. Unfortunately, most professional kitchens find it is too time-consuming to make their own chestnut purée, and although the difference will be noticeable, canned unsweetened chestnut purée may be substituted with good results, or try the variation of this recipe which follows.

This recipe can be prepared without flour due to the large amount of starch in the chestnuts (chestnuts, in fact, contain more starch than any other nut and are actually considered closer to a fruit than a nut). Not only do the chestnuts act as a binding agent instead of flour, but because starch does not contain any gluten, the texture is much lighter and more delicate than it would be if made with flour. The Chestnut Cake variation includes a sponge cake that is very similar to the torte, except that flour replaces some of the chestnut purée and *baking powder is added. A more substantial difference is found in the filling, which contains chunks of sponge cake and is fortified with gelatin. For another dessert featuring the unbeatable combination of chestnuts and rum, try Chestnut Torta Ricotta on page 785.*

1. Brush the Butter and Flour Mixture over the inside of two 10-inch (25-cm) cake pans. Set aside.

2. Cream the soft butter with half of the first measurement of sugar (4½ ounces/130 g) until the mixture is light and fluffy. Beat the egg yolks lightly, then stir into the butter mixture together with the rum and Chestnut Purée, mixing the ingredients together thoroughly.

3. Whip the egg whites to stiff peaks, gradually adding the remainder of the sugar (4½ ounces/130 g). Carefully fold about one-third of the egg whites into the batter, then fold in the remainder. Take care not to overmix and deflate the egg whites. Divide the batter between the reserved cake pans.

4. Bake immediately at 350°F (175°C) for approximately 45 minutes or until baked through. Let the tortes cool for at least several hours or, preferably, refrigerate until the next day.

5. Whip the heavy cream, 2 teaspoons (10 g) of sugar, and vanilla to stiff peaks.

6. Remove the tortes from the cake pans. Carefully cut the skin from the top of the tortes, cutting them level at the same time if necessary. Place one layer on a cardboard cake round. Spread a ¼-inch (6-mm) layer of cream on top. Place the second layer on the cream. Ice the torte with the remaining cream. Cover the side of the torte with the chopped pecans and sprinkle shaved chocolate on the top. Cut into the desired number of servings.

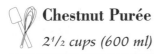

Chestnut Purée

2½ cups (600 ml)

2 pounds, 8 ounces (1 kg, 135 g) fresh chestnuts in the shell

1. Cut a small X in the flat side of each nut using the point of a paring knife.

2. Place the chestnuts in a saucepan with enough water to cover. Bring to a boil, reduce the heat, and simmer for 15 to 30 minutes. Be careful not to overcook the chestnuts. Peel one and check the inside: It should be dry and have a mealy texture something like a baked potato.

3. Drain the chestnuts and let them cool until they can be handled comfortably, but don't let them cool completely or they will be much more difficult to peel. Remove the shells and skin, and purée in a food processor just until smooth. Do not overprocess or the chestnuts will become gummy.

VARIATION
Chestnut Cake

two 10-inch (25-cm) cakes

1 pound (455 g) soft unsalted butter

1 pound, 2 ounces (510 g) granulated sugar

10 eggs, separated and at room temperature

1/3 cup (80 ml) dark rum

4 ounces (115 g) bread flour

2 teaspoons (8 g) baking powder

2 1/2 cups (600 ml) canned unsweetened chestnut purée, at room temperature

Chestnut Rum Filling (recipe follows)

1 quart (960 ml) heavy cream

2 tablespoons (30 g) granulated sugar

2 teaspoons (10 ml) vanilla extract

shaved dark chocolate

*M*aking the Chestnut Rum Torte in a large quantity is, unfortunately, quite time-consuming for a busy kitchen. The variation using canned chestnut purée is a very nice substitute.

For a different look you can create a striking nouvelle finish by covering the sides of the cakes with Ribbon Sponge Sheets. Follow the recipe making the following changes:

• Make one Ribbon Sponge Sheet (see page 276), forming the ribbons in any direction you wish. One sheet is actually enough to cover the sides of up to six cakes, but it is not practical to make a partial sheet, and the leftover may be frozen for another use.

• In step four, use adjustable cake rings or plastic strips around the layers so that they fit loosely. Cut 1 3/4-inch (4.5-cm) wide strips from the Ribbon Sponge and place them with the striped side against the cake rings or plastic strips. Tighten the cake rings or plastic strips so that they fit snugly.

• Use only half the amounts of heavy cream, sugar, and vanilla in step five and ice only the tops of the cakes with whipped cream, not the sides.

• Do not pipe cream on the sides of the cakes in step six.

1. Cream the butter with half of the first measurement of sugar (9 ounces/255 g) until the mixture is light and fluffy. Beat the egg yolks lightly, then stir into the butter mixture, together with the rum. Sift the flour and baking powder together and add to the batter with the chestnut purée, mixing the ingredients together thoroughly.

2. Whip the egg whites to stiff peaks, gradually adding the remainder of the sugar (9 ounces/255 g). Carefully fold about one-third of the egg whites into the batter, then fold in the remainder. Take care not to overmix and deflate the egg whites. Divide the batter between two full sheet pans (16 by 24 inches/40 × 60 cm) lined with baking paper. Spread the batter out to the full length of the pans but only 14 inches (35 cm) wide.

3. Bake at 375°F (190°C) for about 20 minutes or until baked through. Let cool and then cut two 10-inch (25-cm) circles from each sheet. Tear the scrap pieces into small chunks and reserve for the filling.

4. Place two of the layers on cardboard cake rounds for support. Place 10-inch (25-cm) stainless-steel cake rings snugly around each layer. If cake rings are not available, secure strips of polyurethane or acetate around the sponge layers instead. Divide the Chestnut Rum Filling evenly between the cakes. Place the remaining sponge layers on top. Refrigerate, covered, until set.

5. Whip the heavy cream, sugar, and vanilla to stiff peaks. Remove the rings (or plastic strips) from the cakes and ice the tops and sides with just enough whipped cream to cover the sponge.

6. Place the remaining cream in a pastry bag with a no. 4 (8-mm) plain tip. Decorate the sides of the cakes by piping the cream up and down in one continuous line all around (see Figure 11–1, page 536).

Smooth the top of the cakes with a spatula, removing any whipped cream from above the edge. Pipe a pearl-pattern border (see Figure 19–6, page 983) around the top edge of the cakes. Sprinkle the shaved chocolate over the entire surface within the border.

1. Sprinkle ¹/₂ cup (120 ml) of the rum over the cake scraps.

2. Sprinkle the gelatin over the remaining rum and let sit until softened.

3. Whip the heavy cream and sugar until soft peaks form.

4. Place the gelatin mixture over a bain-marie and heat until dissolved. Do not overheat. Rapidly mix the gelatin into a small part of the cream, then add to the rest. Carefully fold in the sponge chunks without breaking them apart.

Chestnut Rum Filling

6¹/₂ pints (3 l, 120 ml)

1¹/₂ cups (360 ml) dark rum

reserved cake chunks from the chestnut sponge

2 tablespoons (18 g) unflavored powdered gelatin

6 cups (1 l, 440 ml) heavy cream

2 ounces (55 g) granulated sugar

NOTE: Do not make the filling until you are ready to use it.

Florentine Torte

two 10-inch (25-cm) tortes

melted unsalted butter

finely ground hazelnuts

1 pound, 4 ounces (570 g) hazelnuts, almonds, walnuts, and/or pecans

14 ounces (400 g) granulated sugar

14 ounces (400 g) sweet dark chocolate, grated

3 ounces (85 g) Candied Citron or Orange Peel (page 978), finely chopped

16 eggs, separated

2 teaspoons (10 ml) vanilla extract

powdered sugar

rum

soft Ganache (page 1086)

pecan halves

*Y*ou can make this dessert using any combination of the nuts specified. Try to make Florentine Torte a few days in advance and store it in the refrigerator. The nuts will absorb moisture during this time improving both the flavor and texture.

The star template can be used to give a holiday appearance to desserts other than the Florentine Torte. The template can also be used in several different ways. You may cut out the center star (leaving the circular frame), place the template on a dessert, and sift powdered sugar over the top to create a star pattern made of sugar. Or, you can do the opposite and place the cutout star on top of the cake, then sift powdered over the exposed part to create a star silhouette. The second method looks especially nice on a cake or torte iced with chocolate, such as Gâteau Malakoff or Caramel Walnut Tart. You can also mark the places where the ovals are shown in the template, then pipe small teardrops of Ganache, pointed in toward the center of the dessert on the ovals. Place a pecan half on each. Lastly, the template can be traced using either of the two methods described for tracing a design on Marzipan (see page 1022). Start at the outline and pipe following every other oval as a loop in one unbroken line. Then pipe over the remainder of the outline and loops in the same way.

1. Line the bottoms of two 10-inch (25-cm) cake pans with circles of baking paper (see Figures 1–10 to 1–12, page 26). Brush melted butter over the papers and the sides of the pans. Coat with ground hazelnuts.

2. Grind the assorted nuts with 7 ounces (200 g) of the sugar to the consistency of whole wheat flour (the sugar will absorb some of the fat in the nuts and prevent them from turning into a paste). Mix the chocolate, Citron or Orange Peel, egg yolks, and vanilla with the ground nuts.

3. Whip the egg whites to a foam. Gradually add the remaining 7 ounces (200 g) of sugar and whip to stiff peaks. Add a small amount of the whipped egg whites to the nut mixture to loosen it, then carefully fold the nut mixture into the remaining whites. Pour the batter into the prepared cake pans.

4. Bake at 350°F (175°C) for about 30 minutes. Let the tortes cool completely.

5. Make the star template shown in Figure 16–4. This template is the correct size for a 10-inch (25-cm) cake. Trace the drawing and then

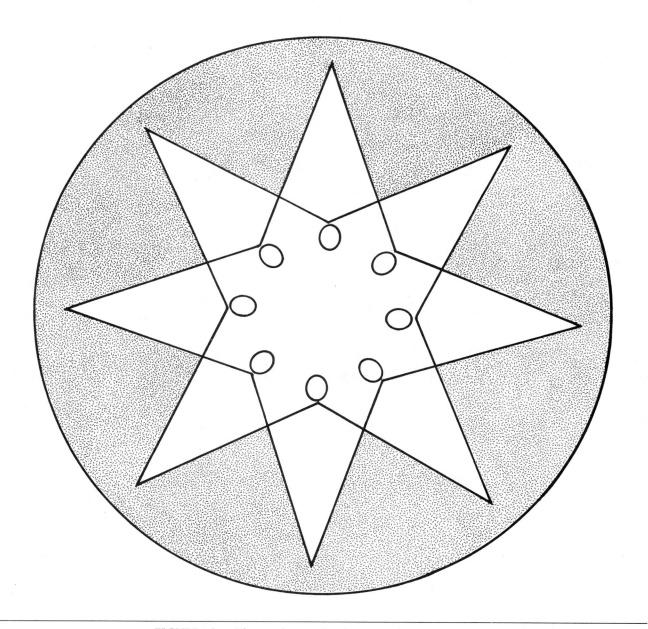

FIGURE 16–4 The template used in decorating the Florentine Torte

cut the template from ¹/₁₆-inch (2-mm) cardboard (a cake box works fine), making the shaded area a solid piece. The lines and ovals shown in the center are explained in the introduction.

6. Unmold the tortes and immediately turn right-side up again to prevent damage to the skin on top.

7. Center the template on top of one torte. Sift powdered sugar lightly over the top. Carefully remove the template and repeat with the second torte.

8. Using a small brush, "paint" rum in a ¹/₂-inch (1.2-cm) band next to the edge of the tortes to melt the powdered sugar so the Ganache will stick to the tortes.

9. Place the Ganache in a pastry bag with a no. 4 (8-mm) plain tip. Pipe a pearl-pattern border of Ganache at the edge of the tortes (see Figure 19–6, page 983). Place pecan halves around the edge, sticking them into the Ganache and spacing them evenly to place one on each serving.

Fruitcake

two 2-pound (910-g) loaves

Fruit Mixture

¹/₂ cup (120 ml) brandy
8 ounces (225 g) golden raisins
8 ounces (225 g) currants
8 ounces (225 g) pecan quarters
6 ounces (170 g) candied citron peel, chopped to raisin-sized pieces
6 ounces (170 g) dried apricots, coarsely chopped
6 ounces (170 g) dried sweet cherries, coarsely chopped

Batter

melted unsalted butter
10 ounces (285 g) soft unsalted butter
10 ounces (285 g) granulated sugar
5 eggs, at room temperature
2 tablespoons (30 ml) golden syrup
2 tablespoons (30 ml) brandy
grated zest of one orange
grated zest of one lemon
6 ounces (170 g) bread flour
6 ounces (170 g) cake flour
¹/₂ cup (120 ml) brandy
additional brandy to brush on the cakes

The typical old family fruitcake—heavy as a brick—is the butt of many jokes around Christmas time. To a lot of people a fruitcake is something special to make and give away as a gift; the problem seems to be that there are too many makers and not enough consumers. In my opinion many of the old classics are too sweet, too dense, and have too much fruit without enough cake. Some recipes proudly proclaim that the cakes can be made in early summer and kept alive with liquor for months until they are given to some unsuspecting soul during the holidays. Others declare (frighteningly enough) that, if moistened from time to time, they can even last for years! These amazing powers of preservation will be of no concern to you if you give this recipe a try (it differs a bit from the norm in that it is actually meant to be eaten). Although there is plenty of fruit and brandy, there is also a fair share of cake in between it all. But what really distinguishes this cake from the aforementioned style is the generous use of raisins, nuts, and dried fruit, such as apricots, rather than the garish artificially colored candied fruit mix sold for fruitcakes. If you prefer a fruitcake with less alcohol flavor, skip the seven-day period of brushing with brandy and add one-half cup of orange juice to the brandy brushed on the cakes once they have cooled. Not only can you then enjoy the fruitcakes sooner, but the fruit flavor will not be overpowered by brandy.

1. Combine all of the ingredients in the fruit mixture and let macerate for 24 hours.

2. Brush the melted butter on the inside of two 8-by-4-inch (20-×-10-cm) loaf pans. Line the pans with baking paper (see Figures 1–8 and 1–9, page 25). Brush the paper with melted butter. Set the pans aside.

3. Cream the soft butter with the sugar until light and fluffy. Incorporate the eggs one at a time. Combine the syrup, first measure of brandy, and citrus zests. Add to the sugar mixture.

4. Sift the flours together. Remove a handful of flour and toss with the fruit mixture. Mix the remaining flour into the batter. Fold in the fruit mixture. Divide the batter between the reserved pans.

5. Bake at 300°F (149°C) for 1 hour. Lower the heat to 275°F (135°C) and continue to bake approximately 30 minutes longer (a wooden skewer inserted in the middle of the cake should come out dry). Unmold onto a cake-cooling rack and allow to cool.

6. Pierce the bottom of the cakes all over with a skewer. Brush the second measure of brandy over the bottom and sides of the cakes. Wrap the cakes tightly. Uncover and brush with additional brandy every day for seven days, keeping the cakes tightly covered in between. Don't be a miser here: you should be using ¹/₃ to ¹/₂ cup (80–120 ml) of brandy every time you brush the cakes!

 Persimmon Tarts

two 11-inch (27.5-cm) tarts

2 pounds (910 g) Short Dough
  (page 54)
6 ounces (170 g) smooth apricot jam
one-half recipe Persimmon Pudding
  batter (page 844)
powdered sugar

Just like the Brandied Gingerbread Cake (see page 800), this is a variation that uses the batter from another recipe baked in a different shape. Because persimmons can be enjoyed for a comparatively short time each year, I like to utilize them as much as possible, besides that they are inexpensive, good, and good for you. The Short Dough crust gives the Persimmon Pudding batter a whole different flavor in addition to adding another textural dimension. Persimmon Tarts are equally appropriate presented as is for a buffet selection or served as a plated dessert accompanied by either Persimmon Sauce (see page 1078) or Brandied Whipped Cream (see page 846).

1. Roll the Short Dough out ¹/₈ inch (3 mm) thick. Line two 11-inch (27.5-cm) tart pans (see Figure 2–14, page 56). Roll the Short Dough scraps to the same thickness as before and into a rectangle 12 inches (30 cm) long. Refrigerate the sheet of dough.

2. Divide the apricot jam between the two tart shells and spread over the bottom. Divide the persimmon batter equally between the pans. Smooth the tops to make them level.

3. Cut the reserved Short Dough into ¹/₄-inch (6-mm) strips, using a fluted pastry wheel. Place the strips over the tarts in parallel lines ¹/₂ inch (1.2 cm) apart. Then arrange a second set of strips on top at a 45° angle to form a diamond pattern. Cover any leftover dough and reserve for another use.

4. Bake the tarts at 375°F (190°C) for approximately 40 minutes or until baked through. Let cool to room temperature.

5. Sift powdered sugar lightly over the tops of the tarts. Present whole or cut into the desired number of servings.

Pumpkin Pie

two 10-inch (25-cm) pies

one-half recipe Pie Dough (page 36)
5 eggs
3 cups (720 ml) cooked sugar
     pumpkin purée (directions follow)
12 ounces (340 g) granulated sugar
1 teaspoon (5 g) salt
2 teaspoons (3 g) ground cinnamon
1 teaspoon (2 g) ground ginger
1/2 teaspoon (1 g) ground cloves
3 1/2 cups (840 ml) half-and-half
1 pint (480 ml) heavy cream
1 tablespoon (15 g) granulated sugar

*P*umpkins are one of several squashes that were eaten as a staple food by the American Indians at the time the colonists landed in America. The European settlers quickly learned to appreciate for themselves the numerous favorable attributes of this large, round, yellow to orange vegetable. One important consideration was that due to their protective shells, pumpkins kept fresh for several months in the cool climate of Northeastern America. The colonists made beer and soup from the pumpkin flesh and toasted the seeds to enjoy as a snack. Even the shell made a convenient bowl—if only temporarily. Pumpkin pies were originally served at the settler's second Thanksgiving feast and continue to be the traditional Thanksgiving dessert hundreds of years later. Pies are by far the most widely known and widely consumed sweet made from pumpkin. As with so many foods in this relatively young country, pumpkin pie has an origin elsewhere as well. It is known to have existed in the early 1600s when it was called pompion or pompion pudding in England. Pumpkin pies and other open-faced pies with soft fillings were referred to as pumpkin puddings early on in America. Even though it is easy enough to make your own pumpkin purée, the time involved makes it prohibitive for most people, who prefer to use canned, and in fact it really tastes just about as good.

My first exposure to pumpkin was indeed making pumpkin pies, and it was certainly a memorable experience, if not a very funny one at the time. I was working on the cruise ship MS Kungsholm, and we were experiencing very rough weather in the Atlantic on our way from New York to the West Indies. Not only did neither I nor my two German colleagues know anything about pumpkin pies, but the tossing ship would have made it hard to prepare just about anything. The word from our executive chef was "It is Thanksgiving and we must have pumpkin pies for the Americans, storm or no storm." He also cautioned us not to fill the pie shells more than halfway. Once we made the very liquid filling we knew right away why that was and also that we were in for big trouble. The filling spilled out all over the ovens causing smoke to pour out, the smell was horrible, and the portholes were all bolted shut due to the storm! I do not think we ever got the ovens completely clean again. The only consolation in this mess was that instead of needing dessert for 400 passengers, the storm caused a much smaller number to venture out of their cabins or, for that matter, to have dinner at all.

1. Roll the Pie Dough out to 1/8 inch (3 mm) thick. Line two 10-inch (25-cm) pie pans and flute the edges (see Figures 2–2 and 2–3, page 37). Cover the dough scraps and save for another use. Cover the dough in the pans with pieces of baking paper and fill the shells with dried beans or pie weights. Bake the shells at 375°F (190°C) until the dough is set but has not yet started to color, about 12 minutes. Let the shells cool completely, then remove the paper and beans or pie weights. Reserve.

2. Beat the eggs lightly to mix. Stir in the pumpkin purée. Mix together the first measure of granulated sugar, the salt, cinnamon, ginger, and cloves. Add this to the egg mixture. Stir in the half-and-half. Divide the filling evenly between the two pie shells.

3. Bake at 375°F (190°C) for approximately 50 minutes or until the filling has puffed slightly and is firm around the edges. Let the pies cool.

4. Whip the heavy cream with the second measure of granulated sugar until stiff peaks form. Place the cream in a pastry bag with a no. 7 (14-mm) star tip. Pipe a shell border of cream around the edge of the pies (see Figure 19–6, page 983). Slice the pies into the desired sized pieces. Serve at room temperature.

To make the Pumpkin Purée

You will need a 3-pound (1-kg, 365-g) sugar pumpkin. Bake the pumpkin at 375°F (190°C) until it feels soft when you press it with your thumb, about 1½ hours. Cool, peel or cut away the skin, cut in half, and remove the seeds (save the seeds and toast them for snacks). Purée or mash the pumpkin flesh and pass it through a sieve.

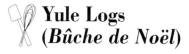

Yule Logs (Bûche de Noël)

two 11-inch (27.5-cm) logs

one recipe Cocoa Almond Sponge batter (page 271)

3 ounces (85 g) Marzipan (page 1022), colored green

½ ounce (15 g) Marzipan (page 1022), colored red

1 pound, 12 ounces (795 g) Chocolate Buttercream (page 977)

8 ounces (225 g) Rum Ball Filling (page 419) (see step eight)

14 ounces (400 g) Marzipan (page 1022), untinted

dark coating chocolate, melted

Meringue Mushrooms (recipe follows)

Piping Chocolate (page 904), melted

powdered sugar

NOTE: If the sponge sheet is refrigerated overnight, the skin on the top tends to separate from the sponge and should be scraped free from the top before peeling the paper from the back in step 5.

*T*he tradition of the yule log has been passed down in Northern European countries dating back to ancient times. During the pre-Christian era, large bonfires brightened the night sky during the Scandinavian Jul (Yule) festivities, which honored the God Thor and celebrated the winter solstice. When Christmas celebrations later took the place of the winter Yule festivities, the yule log lost most of its religious significance, but the traditions and superstitions surrounding the log prevailed. In France the custom of the yule log dictated that the tree or log be cut down by the male members of the family, with the entire family going together to select the tree in some cases (the log was not to be cut or provided by someone outside the family). The tree was brought ceremoniously into the house and the family members circled the tree three times. After it was placed in the fireplace, a glass of wine was poured over the log, and it was honored with songs as it burned. Affluent families hired minstrels to do the singing, while village family members each took a turn. The heat from the log was used to prepare Reveillon, the traditional Christmas Eve midnight supper. Ashes from the log were believed to contain magical and medicinal powers and were strewn over the fields to fertilize crops, mixed with animal feed to promote breeding, and kept in the house throughout the year to ward off evil spirts. In some cases a piece of charred wood from the log was saved to light the next year's log. When the time came that fireplaces and logs were scarce in some French cities, the custom of making log-shaped cakes began as a way for those without a fireplace to participate in the celebration.

It seems as if every pastry chef has his or her own version of Bûche de Noël (the French translation of yule, or Christmas, log). It is customary to cover the logs with a rough coat of Chocolate Buttercream to simulate tree bark. My rendition is not only iced with Chocolate Buttercream, it is then covered with layers of Marzipan and dark chocolate. This combination looks and tastes good and also serves to prevent the sponge cake from drying out. Use your imagination in decorating the logs. It might not make sense to make up a batch of meringue just to produce four or five mushrooms unless you have a use for the remainder, but if you have small gingerbread cookies such as deer, stars, or *hearts, for example, from another project, these could be used to attractively decorate the logs instead. A stunning showpiece can be created by placing a seated Marzipan Santa on top of the log (see instructions with the Marzipan Pig on page 866), guiding a gingerbread sleigh filled with Marzipan packages and led by gingerbread deer (I always put a tiny drop of red Royal Icing or red piping gel on the nose of the lead deer).*

1. Spread the sponge batter evenly over a sheet of baking paper 24 by 16 inches (60 × 40 cm). Drag the paper onto a sheet pan (see Figure 16–15, page 842). Bake at 425°F (219°C) for about 10 minutes or until just done.

2. Dust a sheet of baking paper with flour and invert the sponge on top to prevent it from becoming dry from sitting on the hot pan. Let cool. If the sponge is needed immediately but seems too dry to roll into a log, follow the procedure in the note on page 270 to soften it. If made for later use, store the sponge sheet covered in the refrigerator (see note).

3. Roll out the green Marzipan (using powdered sugar to prevent it from sticking) to $^1/_{16}$ inch (2 mm) thick. Cut out circles using a $2^1/_2$-inch (6.2-cm) plain cookie cutter. Using the same cutter, make two cuts that meet in the center, to create two pointed ovals. Make about twelve leaves for the two logs. Mark veins on the leaves using the back of a small knife. Use a no. 3 (6-mm) plain piping tip to cut out scalloped edges all around the leaves. Set the leaves on a dowel and leave them to dry in a curved shape. Roll the scraps to the same thickness as before and cut out two strips 5 inches (10 cm) long and 1 inch (2.5 cm) wide. Reserve.

4. Roll the red Marzipan into pea-sized balls (holly berries). Make three balls for every two leaves. Reserve.

5. Peel the paper off the back of the inverted sponge sheet (leave the other paper underneath) and trim the sponge to 22 by 15 inches (55 × 37.5 cm). Reserve the scraps.

6. Spread approximately four-fifths of the Chocolate Buttercream evenly over the sponge sheet (use less buttercream on the bottom 1 inch/2.5 cm of the long edge or it will ooze out as the log is rolled).

7. Roll up the cake starting from the top long edge and rolling toward you (see Figure 12–3, page 595). Pull the paper toward you as you roll to help make a tight log. Leaving the paper around the log, hold the bottom of the paper in place with your left hand and push a dowel or ruler against the log on top of the paper; the paper will wrap around the log and make it tight (Figure 16–5). Refrigerate the roulade, covered, seam-side down, until the buttercream is firm.

8. Roll the Rum Ball Filling into a rope 5 inches (12.5 cm) long and approximately $1^1/_2$ inches (3.7 cm) in diameter. (If you do not have Rum Ball Filling, use the reserved sponge scraps mixed with enough buttercream to make a doughlike consistency.) Roll out 2 ounces (55 g) of the untinted Marzipan $^1/_{16}$ inch (2 mm) thick. Spread a thin film of buttercream on the Marzipan and use to cover the rum-ball rope (see Rum Chocolate Spools, Figure 9–23, page 420). Refrigerate until cold.

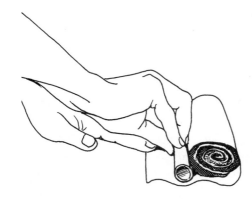

FIGURE 16–5 Pushing a dowel against a Yule Log roulade with baking paper between the log and the dowel, while pulling the opposite end of the baking paper at the same time to tighten the paper around the log

9. Cut the rum ball rope in half and then cut each piece in half again at a 45° angle to make the pieces straight on one end and slanted on the other. Dip these "branch stumps" into melted dark coating chocolate to cover completely. Let set until the chocolate hardens, then reserve.

10. Place the chilled roulade on an inverted sheet pan covered with baking paper. Spread a thin layer of the reserved buttercream over the log, spreading it to where the log meets the sheet pan. Do not try to spread it underneath. Even the surface of the buttercream by pulling a paper around the log (Figure 16–6). Add the buttercream that was scraped off back to the remainder.

11. Roll out the remaining 12 ounces (340 g) of untinted Marzipan (using powdered sugar to prevent it from sticking) to $1/16$ inch (2 mm) thick, rolling it wide and long enough to cover the log to where it meets the pan (like the buttercream, the Marzipan does not go underneath or on the ends). Cover the log with the Marzipan, smoothing it to fit with your hands. Trim any excess Marzipan to make the ends even. Remove the buttercream from the trimmings and save the Marzipan for another use.

12. Spread melted dark coating chocolate over the Marzipan, spreading it back and forth rapidly until the chocolate starts to set up. It should not look completely smooth but rather show long marks from the palette knife.

13. Trim both ends of the log and then cut the log into two equal pieces approximately 11 inches (27.5 cm) each, using a knife dipped in hot water. Cover the exposed ends of each log with part of the remaining Chocolate Buttercream.

14. Dip the slanted ends of the reserved branches into melted dark coating chocolate and fasten them to the top of the logs, one on each side, close to the ends. This is much easier to do if you chill either the

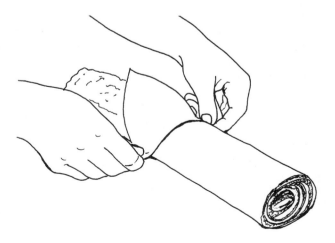

FIGURE 16–6 Pulling a piece of baking paper with a straight edge along the length of the Yule Log to make the buttercream smooth and even

logs or the stumps, so that the chocolate will harden immediately. Decorate the logs with Meringue Mushrooms and the Marzipan holly leaves and berries, placing two leaves and three berries next to the branch stumps; attach all of the decorations with Piping Chocolate.

15. Make a larger-than-normal piping bag and cut a larger-than-normal opening. Place Piping Chocolate in the bag and pipe a spiral on the ends of the branch stumps and on the ends of the logs. Sift powdered sugar over the logs for a snow effect.

16. Write "Merry Christmas" or "Happy Holidays" on each of the reserved strips of green Marzipan, using Piping Chocolate in a piping bag with a small opening. Fasten one strip in the center of each log using Piping Chocolate to secure.

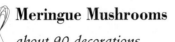

Meringue Mushrooms
about 90 decorations

one-quarter recipe French Meringue (page 590)
unsweetened cocoa powder
Piping Chocolate (page 904) (see note)

NOTE: If you have Ganache on hand, use that instead of chocolate to attach the stems. It works better but it really doesn't make sense to prepare it just for this use.

1. Place the meringue in a pastry bag with a no. 5 (10-mm) plain tip. Pipe out mounds approximately 1 inch (2.5 cm) in diameter on a sheet pan lined with baking paper, using approximately two-thirds of the meringue to make the mushroom caps.

2. To make the stems, hold a no. 3 (6-mm) plain tip in place on the outside of the other tip (see Figures 12–6 and 12–7, page 602) and pipe 1-inch (2.5-cm) lengths, using the remaining meringue.

3. Bake at 215°F (102°C) until dry, approximately two hours.

4. When the meringue has cooled, sift cocoa powder lightly over the caps, using a medium mesh strainer to create large dots of cocoa powder.

5. Place some melted Piping Chocolate in a piping bag. One at a time, pick up a mushroom cap, holding it by the edges so as not to disturb the cocoa powder, and drill a small hole in the back with a paring knife. Pipe chocolate into the hole and then push a meringue stem into the chocolate.

VARIATION
Chocolate Roulade
approximately 20 servings

1. Follow the recipe through step twelve, omitting steps three, four, eight, and nine and using only one-half recipe of Cocoa Almond Sponge batter, spread into a 14-by-24-inch (35-×-60-cm) rectangle in step one.

2. Cut the roulade into 1-inch (2.5-cm) pieces, using a serrated knife.

3. Place the slices in paper cups, pressing the bottom of the cups flat on both sides to create a stable base so that the pastries will not fall over.

4. Decorate each slice by piping an S shape of Chocolate Buttercream, using a no. 1 (2-mm) plain tip in your pastry bag. Place a small candied violet in the center of the S.

Cookies and Pastries

 ## Chocolate-Orange Pillows

72 cookies

1 pound, 4 ounces (570 g) sweet dark
   chocolate
4 ounces (115 g) unsweetened
   chocolate
4 ounces (115 g) unsalted butter
7 ounces (200 g) bread flour
1¹/₂ teaspoons (6 g) baking powder
8 ounces (225 g) finely ground
   blanched almonds (almond meal)
6 eggs
7 ounces (200 g) granulated sugar
¹/₃ cup (80 ml) orange liqueur
finely chopped zest of four oranges
granulated sugar
powdered sugar

*NOTE: The soft dough tends to stick to the
knife. Dipping the knife in flour and scraping
the blade clean will help. You can also use a
small ice cream scoop, no. 40 (1¹/₂-table-
spoon/22.5-ml) capacity, to portion the dough.
Dip the scoop into hot water from time to time.*

*T*hese *delightful cookies look like a winter wonderland and will brighten up
any Christmas cookie tray. The spotted powdered sugar effect, created by
the crust breaking open as the leavening goes into action in the oven, reminds me
of new-fallen snow on top of rocks in a mountain river. Because these cookies do
not have the traditional holiday spices they are suitable for offering all year long.*

*Rolling the cookies in two kinds of sugar is a bit unusual, but do not skip
the granulated sugar step—it is there for a reason, and be sure that the dough
is sticky so it will adhere. Without the granulated sugar coating, most of the
powdered sugar would be absorbed into the dough during baking, and the finished appearance would be closer to snow that has fallen on a wet surface!*

*These cookies should be stored in airtight containers, in a single layer. If
you must stack them, place a sheet of baking paper between the layers to help
protect the coating.*

1. Chop the chocolates into small pieces. Place in a bowl and add
the butter. Melt together over simmering water. Set the mixture aside
but keep it warm.

2. Sift the bread flour and baking powder together. Stir in the
ground almond meal and reserve.

3. Whip the eggs and sugar to the ribbon stage. Stir in the orange
liqueur and orange zest. Mixing with a spoon or with the paddle
attachment, pour the melted chocolate mixture into the eggs and combine. Stir in the reserved dry ingredients. The dough will be quite soft,
even runny.

4. Place the dough in the refrigerator for about 4 hours to become
firm.

5. Divide the dough into six equal pieces. Using flour to prevent
the dough from sticking, roll the pieces into 12-inch (30-cm) ropes. Cut
each rope into twelve equal pieces (see note).

6. Roll the small pieces into balls and then roll the balls first in granulated sugar and then twice in powdered sugar. The cookies must be
thoroughly coated with powdered sugar in order to remain white after
baking. Place the balls on sheet pans lined with baking paper. Press
down lightly, just enough to keep them from rolling.

7. Bake at 375°F (190°C) for approximately 20 minutes or until
baked through. The cookies will puff up, leaving a cracked white crust
on the outside.

Chocolate Snow Hearts

120 cookies

1 pound, 6 ounces (625 g) finely
    ground blanched almonds
    (almond meal)
1 pound (455 g) powdered sugar
4 egg whites (¹/₂ cup/120 ml)
14 ounces (400 g) sweet dark
    chocolate, melted
granulated sugar

NOTE: You can simplify things if you have almond paste on hand by using 2 pounds, 6 ounces (1 kg, 80 g) of almond paste instead of the ground almonds and powdered sugar (omit the processing step as well). Begin by gradually mixing the egg whites into the almond paste in the mixing bowl, then stir in the chocolate.

T his is another delightful, chewy holiday cookie that is made in Switzerland and Germany. They are actually made all through the year but in different shapes (the Swiss make them in the shape of a flower and call them Brunsli*). Although they do not become hard or unpleasant if slightly overbaked (just crunchy), I like them best when they are moist and chewy. You can soften dry cookies by placing them in airtight containers with a few slices of apple or, better yet, pineapple quince if you have it. You will notice a difference in texture after just a few hours, but leaving them overnight will soften the cookies all the way through. Like the Cinnamon Stars on page 817, Chocolate Snow Hearts are a variety of macaroon cookie.*

1. Process the ground almonds, half of the powdered sugar, and the egg whites in a food processor to make a fine paste (see note). Transfer to a mixing bowl and stir in the remaining powdered sugar and the chocolate. Cover and refrigerate until firm.

2. Work the dough smooth and then roll it out, using granulated sugar to keep it from sticking, to ¹/₄ inch (6 mm) thick. Cut out cookies using a 2-inch (5-cm) heart cutter. Place the cuts so there will be a minimum of scrap dough. Place the cookies on sheet pans lined with baking paper. Knead the scrap dough together, then roll out and cut the remainder of the cookies in the same manner.

3. Bake the cookies at 425°F (219°C) for about 8 minutes or until slightly puffed. Be careful: They are very easy to overbake because of their color. Do not try to remove the cookies from the paper before they are completely cold. If they stick, follow the instructions for removing the cookies from the paper in Almond Macaroon Cookies (see Figure 5–2, page 202). Store in airtight containers.

Christmas Cookie Ornaments

approximately 65 cookies

8 ounces (225 g) Gingerbread Cookies
    dough (page 818)
Lemon-Butter Cookie Dough
    (recipe follows)
Egg Yolk Wash (page 7)
whole blanched almonds
Piping Chocolate (page 904)
Royal Icing (page 1019)
powdered sugar
dark coating chocolate

I t is traditional in Sweden to decorate the Christmas tree in part with edible ornaments, such as chocolate figures, Marzipan Santas, and a variety of decorated gingerbread cookies. The cookies were not to be touched be any eager little children's hands when I was growing up, only looked at with wide eyes. We each had our favorites picked out and spoken for long before Christmas day, when we were finally allowed to taste them. These are simple enough that they can be made into regular Christmas cookies instead of ornaments; just omit the hole for the string.

1. Make the Gingerbread Cookies dough the day before you plan to use it and reserve in the refrigerator.

2. Roll out the Lemon-Butter Cookie Dough to ³/₈ inch (9 mm) thick. Mark the top with a tread type rolling pin (see page 1125) or, if you do not have that tool, drag a fork across the dough to mark it. Transfer the dough to a sheet pan or sheet of cardboard. Brush Egg Yolk

NOTE: You can also reverse the decorations and place the lemon dough on top of the gingerbread dough. In that case, of course, you will need more gingerbread dough. Roll both doughs to ⅛ inch (3 mm) thick. Mark the lemon dough with the tread roller in the same way, but do not try to mark the gingerbread dough.

Wash over the dough and place it in the refrigerator or freezer for a few minutes to dry the Egg Wash a little.

3. While the lemon dough is in the refrigerator, roll out the gingerbread dough to ¹/₁₆ inch (2 mm) thick. Transfer to a sheet pan or sheet of cardboard and reserve in the refrigerator.

4. Remove the lemon dough from the refrigerator and cut out stars, hearts, and round shapes about 2 inches (5 cm) in diameter. Place on sheet pans lined with baking paper. Knead the scrap dough together well, roll it out, and cut more cookies. Repeat until all of the dough has been used. Set the cookies aside.

5. Remove the gingerbread dough from the refrigerator. Cut out small shapes that will fit on top of the lemon cookies, using your imagination to contrast with the lighter cookie dough. Smaller heart and star shapes look good placed in the center of a lemon cookie of the same shape, as does a small gingerbread heart in the center of a round lemon cookie, surrounded by four or five blanched almonds. If you have holiday cutters that are small enough, use these.

6. Decorate the lemon cookies with the gingerbread shapes and blanched almonds. Use a no. 3 (6-mm) plain piping tip to cut a hole in each cookie for a string or ribbon if you plan to hang them on the tree.

7. Bake at 375°F (190°C) for about 15 minutes or until golden brown. When the cookies have cooled, decorate with Piping Chocolate, Royal Icing, or sifted powdered sugar. Or dip whole cookies without contrasting dough on top in thinned coating chocolate (see Noisette Rings, page 399, in the introduction and step five) and decorate with Royal Icing or Piping Chocolate, writing "Merry Christmas" or a person's name. When the chocolate and icing are dry, tie ribbons or gold thread through the holes.

Lemon-Butter Cookie Dough

14 ounces (400 g) powdered sugar
14 ounces (400 g) soft unsalted butter
3 eggs
grated zest of one lemon
1 teaspoon (5 ml) vanilla extract
1 pound, 12 ounces (795 g) bread
   flour

1. Mix the powdered sugar and butter well, but do not cream. Add the eggs, lemon zest, and vanilla.

2. Incorporate the flour and mix just until combined. It is important not to overmix this dough, because the additional air will make the cookies "bake out" and change shape.

3. Refrigerate the dough, if necessary, to make it easier to handle.

Christmas Tree Pastries

52 pastries

1 pound, 5 ounces (595 g) Short Dough (page 54)

5 ounces (140 g) smooth strawberry jam

4 pounds, 10 ounces (2 kg, 105 g) Mazarin Filling (page 1088)

2 ounces (55 g) Vanilla Buttercream (page 978)

1 pound (455 g) Marzipan (page 1022), tinted light green

dark coating chocolate, melted

Piping Chocolate (page 904)

strained strawberry jam (see note)

powdered sugar

NOTE: You only need about 3 tablespoons (45 ml) of jam. If you have red piping gel on hand or another smooth red jam or jelly you can use this instead, as long as it is thick enough to hold its shape and not run when piped.

*T*hese are year-round pastries that are decorated at Christmas time, just as we do with real Christmas trees. They are a derivative of Angelica Points, cut into a more elongated triangle and covered with green Marzipan instead of untinted. The decoration used here can be applied to other pastries and to larger cakes as well to give them an instant holiday air. And just as the triangular shape of these pastries lends itself to simulating a tree, the ring shape of Paris-Brest or Spritz Rings, for example, makes them easy to turn into wreaths by adding a bow at the top made from Marzipan or piped chocolate (however, I strongly recommend against tinting either dough green). A Brioche can become a plump (and squat) Santa by decorating the smaller ball as his head, piping the features with royal icing or piping chocolate, and adding a red hat on top and a white beard below, both fashioned from Marzipan. A triangle shape such as this pastry or a slice of cake can also be made into a Santa: The very top of the point makes a natural hat, and the wider bottom is easy to decorate as his coat.

1. Line the bottom of a half-sheet pan (16 by 12 inches/40 × 30 cm) with baking paper. Roll the Short Dough out to ¹/₈ inch (3 mm) thick and line the bottom of the pan. Cover the dough scraps and reserve for another use.

2. Spread the 5-ounce (140-g) measurement of strawberry jam over the dough. Top with the Mazarin Filling and spread it out evenly.

3. Bake the sheet at 375°F (190°C) until baked through, about 40 minutes. Let cool to room temperature, then refrigerate.

4. When the mazarin sheet is cold (preferably the day after baking), cut off the skin and even the top of the sheet. To do this, leave the mazarin sheet in the pan and cut with a serrated knife held parallel to the top of the cake, using the edge of the pan as a guide for your knife. Run the tip of the knife around the inside edge of the pan and then invert the sheet to unmold. If the bottom of the sheet sticks to the pan, do not force it. Instead, place a hot sheet pan on the outside for a few seconds to soften the fat in the Short Dough, and then try again. Remove the sheet pan and the baking paper and turn the the sheet right-side up. Spread a thin film of buttercream on top of the Mazarin Filling.

5. Roll the Marzipan out to ¹/₁₆ inch (2 mm) thick; it should be slightly larger than the mazarin sheet. Roll the Marzipan up on a dowel and unroll on top of the buttercream. Place a clean cardboard on top and invert. With the pastry upside down, trim away the excess Marzipan. Remove any crumbs or buttercream and save the Marzipan trimmings for another use. Refrigerate until the buttercream is firm, but no longer than a few hours or the Marzipan will become wet on top.

6. Still working with the pastry upside down, trim both long sides and then cut the sheet lengthwise into four strips, holding the knife at a 90° angle so that the edges are straight; a serrated knife or the very tip of a sharp chef's knife works best.

7. Cut each strip into thirteen triangles with two longer sides and a narrower base. Place the pieces, Marzipan-side up, on a sheet pan lined with baking paper.

8. Dip each triangle into melted dark coating chocolate, coating the bottom and sides up to the Marzipan (as shown for Tosca, Figures 9–27 through 9–31, page 428).

9. Place the Piping Chocolate in a piping bag and cut a small opening. Pipe an abstract tree outline on each pastry, starting at the top and using the design shown in the recipe for Poppy Seed Cake (see Figure 8–16, page 348). End the design about ³/₈ inch (9 mm) from the bottom, then pipe two vertical lines in the center at the base of the pastry to mark the tree trunk.

10. Place the strained strawberry jam in a piping bag and cut a small opening. Pipe one dot of jam at the top point on each pastry plus six or seven among the branches below. Sift powdered sugar lightly over the pastries.

Cinnamon Stars

90 cookies

1 pound (455 g) granulated sugar

2 tablespoons (30 ml) light corn syrup

4 egg whites (¹/₂ cup/120 ml)

3 tablespoons (15 g) ground cinnamon

1 pound, 5 ounces (595 g) finely ground blanched almonds, approximately

1 cup (240 ml) Royal Icing (page 1019) (see note 1)

NOTE 1: Do not use any lemon juice when making the Royal Icing. Instead, add a small amount of cornstarch. This will prevent the icing from becoming too brown in the oven.

NOTE 2: If you have difficulty removing the cookies from the cutter without damaging the icing, either the icing is too thick (too much powdered sugar) or it was not chilled long enough.

C innamon Stars are a typical Swiss-German holiday cookie. They are not only easy to make, but their cinnamon flavor, chewy texture, and crisp topping make them an unusual addition and a welcome alternative to the traditional assortment of chocolate and butter cookies. They will keep for many weeks provided the dough is not made too dry by incorporating more ground almond than is necessary. When you make the dough, take into consideration that the ground almonds will continue to absorb moisture as the dough rests, making it firmer (the finer the almonds are ground, the more moisture they absorb). Do not make the dough too loose, however, just to play it safe; if the dough is too soft the cookies will not hold their shape during baking, which detracts greatly from their appearance.

1. Combine the sugar, corn syrup, egg whites, and cinnamon. Hold back a small amount of the ground almonds and incorporate the remainder, using the paddle attachment in a mixer or by hand with a spoon. Adjust the consistency if necessary by adding more almond to form a smooth, workable paste. Place on a sheet pan lined with baking paper, cover, and refrigerate for at least 1 hour or, preferably, until the next day.

2. Roll the dough out to ¹/₄ inch (6 mm) thick, using flour to prevent it from sticking. Place on a cardboard or inverted sheet pan.

3. Adjust the Royal Icing to a spreadable but not runny consistency by adding additional powdered sugar or egg whites as needed. Spread just enough on top of the dough to cover the surface. Refrigerate for about 30 minutes or place in the freezer for a few minutes to firm the dough and icing.

4. Cut out cookies using a 2¹/₄-inch (5.6-cm) star cutter, placing the cuts so you have a minimum of scrap dough (see note 2). Place the cookies on sheet pans lined with baking paper (icing-side up). Work the scrap dough to completely incorporate the Royal Icing, then roll out and spread with more icing as you did the first time. Continue to cut the cookies and reroll the dough until all the dough has been used.

5. Bake at 425°F (219°C) for about 6 minutes or until the icing just starts to turn light brown at the edges. Let the cookies cool completely before removing them from the paper. Store in airtight containers.

Gingerbread Cookies

about ninety 3-inch (7.5-cm) cookies

15 ounces (430 g) unsalted butter
15 ounces (430 g) granulated sugar
1½ cups (360 ml) or 1 pound, 2 ounces (510 g) corn syrup
¾ cup (180 ml) milk
2 pounds, 10 ounces (1 kg, 195 g) bread flour
1 tablespoon (12 g) baking soda
4 tablespoons (20 g) ground cinnamon
2 tablespoons (12 g) ground cloves
2 tablespoons (12 g) ground ginger

A detailed history of gingerbread (which can be traced back in time farther than any other baked good except bread) is covered in some of the other gingerbread recipes in this book. It is interesting to note here, however, that the Swedish name for gingerbread cookies, pepparkakor, *would suggest that pepper is one of the ingredients, just as the name of another popular cookie,* pepparnötter, *better known by its German name* pfeffernüsse, *might lead you to the same conclusion. But this is not so. Although ground black pepper was used in lebkuchen when it was first made many centuries ago, in gingerbread cookies the word* peppar *is simply a reference to the overall spicy flavor.*

It is important to plan ahead, since this gingerbread dough must be refrigerated overnight before the consistency becomes workable. Because the dough will keep fresh stored covered in the refrigerator for several months, and even longer in the freezer, there is really no reason to make just the amount required for one project or to try to make the dough just before it is needed. Having a supply ready to go will come in very handy during the holidays, not only for freshly baked cookies for the cookie tray, but also for gingerbread figures and ornaments and small decorations on yule logs, gingerbread houses, and plated desserts.

These cookies are very brittle and crisp, which is part of their charm, but the proper texture will only be achieved if the dough is rolled out extremely thin as instructed. Failing to do so will result in cookies that are hard and unpleasant. Because the dough becomes soft rather quickly when it is rolled out so thinly, it is important to work with only a small portion at a time as specified, keeping the remaining dough chilled.

This type of gingerbread cookie is made throughout the year in Sweden using round or fluted cutters. Heart-shaped gingerbread cookies are generally reserved for Christmas. If this dough is used to make larger cookies, such as the traditional gingerbread figures made for Christmas, it should be rolled a bit thicker (⅛ inch/3 mm). For gingerbread houses, replace the butter with margarine and increase the flour by 6 ounces (170 g) to make a firmer dough. You do not necessarily need the butter flavor in a gingerbread house, since by the time it is eaten (if at all) it will most likely be stale, and butter can also cause the dough to shrink when it is used in combination with the additional flour, which means longer kneading. Although baked Gingerbread Cookies cannot be kept as long as the dough, they will remain fresh for many weeks if stored—or perhaps I should say hidden—in airtight containers in a dry place.

1. Place the butter, sugar, corn syrup, and milk in a saucepan. Heat to about 110°F (43°C), stirring the mixture into a smooth paste at the same time.

2. Sift the flour, baking soda, and spices together. Incorporate into the butter mixture.

3. Line the bottom of a sheet pan with baking paper. Dust the paper with flour and place the dough on top. Flatten the dough, then refrigerate, covered, overnight.

4. Roll out a small portion of dough at a time to $^1/_{16}$ inch (2 mm) thick. Keep the dough you are not working with in the refrigerator. The dough will feel sticky, but do not be tempted to mix in additional flour. The flour used in rolling the dough will be enough, and too much flour will make the baked cookies too hard and not as pleasant tasting.

5. Cut out cookies using a 3-inch (7.5-cm) heart or star-shaped cookie cutter. Place the cookies, staggered, on sheet pans lined with baking paper. Add the dough scraps to the fresh dough as you roll out the next batch.

6. Bake the cookies at 400°F (205°C) for about 10 minutes or until they have a rich brown color.

Holiday Candle Pastries

40 pastries

---

1 pound (455 g) Short Dough (page 54)

4 ounces (115 g) smooth raspberry jam

1 pound, 6 ounces (625 g) Mazarin Filling (page 1088)

bread flour

12 ounces (340 g) Marzipan (page 1022), untinted

4 ounces (115 g) Gingerbread Cookies dough (preceding recipe) or Short Dough (page 54)

dark coating chocolate

Marzipan Candles (directions follow)

NOTE: The quantities of Short Dough and Mazarin Filling specified are based on using a small mazarin form, which measures 2¹/₄ inches in diameter across the top, 1³/₄ inches across the bottom, and ³/₄ inch high (5.6 × 4.5 × 2 cm). Any type of form, fluted or plain, that

*T*hese are really cute and quite easy to produce—they are nothing more than a Mazarin pastry dressed up for the holidays. When combined with Christmas Tree Pastries (another variation on the same theme) and the petite Yule Log Pastries, they give a very seasonal, elegant appearance to your pastry selection. If you need to simplify things, make plain Mazarins (omitting the Marzipan rings and dipping the top of the pastries in chocolate), push the Marzipan Candles gently into the glaze on top of the pastries, and place the small cookies around the edges before the glaze starts to dry. The quicker version will not have quite as long a shelf life as the chocolate-dipped holiday pastries, which stay fresh up to one week.

1. Roll the Short Dough out to ¹/₈ inch (3 mm) thick, using just enough flour to prevent the dough from sticking. Line forty small mazarin forms with the dough (see Figures 2–15 to 2–18, pages 57 and 58) (see note). Place the forms, staggered, on a sheet pan. Cover the scrap dough and reserve for another use.

2. Place the jam in a piping bag and pipe a small dot of jam, about ¹/₄ teaspoon (1.25 ml), on the bottom of each form. Place the Mazarin Filling in a pastry bag with a no. 5 (10-mm) plain tip. Pipe the filling into the forms, filling them to just below the rim.

3. Bake at 400°F (205°C) for approximately 12 minutes or until light brown around the edges. Remove from the oven, dust bread flour lightly over the tops, and invert. Set aside to cool upside down. Remove the forms before the pastries have cooled completely.

is close to this size can be substituted, but the amounts of filling and dough may need to be increased or decreased. The size of the Marzipan rings should be adjusted as well if a different size form is used.

4. Roll the Marzipan out to slightly thicker than $^1/_8$ inch (3 mm), using powdered sugar sparingly so it will not stain the Marzipan. Texture the surface with a waffle roller. Cut out forty circles, using a $2^1/_4$-inch (5.6-cm) plain cookie cutter. Use a $^3/_4$-inch (2-cm) plain cutter to cut out the centers, leaving rings. (If you are working with the precise amount of Marzipan called for, you will have to roll out and cut about half of the circles, cut out the centers, and reroll the centers to make the second half.) Reserve the Marzipan rings.

5. Roll out the Gingerbread Cookies dough or Short Dough to $^1/_{16}$ inch (2 mm) thick. Cut out 120 small hearts or stars about $^3/_4$ inch (2 cm) in diameter. Bake at 400°F (205°C) until brown (light brown for Short Dough) about 4 minutes. Set the cookies aside.

6. Hold the pastries upside-down and dip the top surface into melted coating chocolate. Set right-side up on a sheet pan lined with baking paper. Place a Marzipan ring on top and insert a Marzipan Candle in the center of each ring before the chocolate hardens. After a while you will be able to determine how many pastries you can dip before stopping to place the Marzipan pieces on top. Be careful not to get any chocolate on the Marzipan or on the sides of the pastries as you work.

7. Place a small amount of melted chocolate in a piping bag. Pipe three very small, evenly spaced dots around the candle on the Marzipan ring. Set one of the small cookies on top of each dot.

Marzipan Candles

40 decorations

10 ounces (285 g) Marzipan (page 1022), untinted
red food coloring
a few drops of egg white

NOTE: *To give the candles an authentic "burning" look, roll a tiny piece of the leftover untinted Marzipan into a teardrop shape to simulate a drop of melted wax and attach with egg white to the front of each candle, hanging from the lower, rounded edge.*

1. Divide the Marzipan into two equal pieces and roll each one into a 20-inch (50-cm) rope. Place the ropes side by side and cut them into 1-inch (2.5-cm) pieces. If the Marzipan has become very soft from rolling the ropes, refrigerate the ropes for a short time before cutting to produce clean cuts without flattening the ends.

2. Use a small melon-ball cutter to scoop out a half-sphere at an angle on one end of each piece. Work the cutout pieces together and reserve. Smooth and shape the cut end of each candle, using your thumb and forefinger, placing them in straight rows on a sheet pan or sheet of cardboard lined with baking paper as you finish each one.

3. Color about $^3/_4$ ounce (22 g) of the reserved Marzipan (a piece about the size of quail's egg) with red food coloring. Reserve the remaining Marzipan for another use. Roll the red Marzipan into a 15-inch (37.5-cm) rope. Cut the rope into forty pieces. Roll the pieces into round balls and then into $^1/_2$-inch (1.2-cm) ovals pointed on both ends.

4. Use a pointed marzipan tool or a no. 1 (2-mm) plain pastry tip to make a small hole on top of each candle (in the scooped-out end), and use a little egg white to glue the candle wicks in place.

Lebkuchen

Gingerbread dates back thousands of years. A look through the history books shows it was invented by either the Romans or the Greeks as early as 2800 B.C. Since bread baking was well established at this time in both civilizations, and both areas were part of the spice route from the Far East to Europe, either seems equally likely to have been responsible for gingerbread's creation. Gingerbread cakes, cookies, and ornaments are part of the Christmas tradition in many countries, with almost as many different variations as there are countries that make it. In Scandinavia, gingerbread cookies are known as *pepparkakor* and are made to be very thin, hard, and crisp. German lebkuchen, although quite similar in taste, is soft, chewy, and much thicker, due to the addition of honey and the use of different leavening agents. There are lebkuchen variations such as *honig kuchen, pfefferkuchen,* and the Swiss *Basler Leckerli.*

Lebkuchen was introduced to Germany around A.D. 800. It became a fashionable item enjoyed by the affluent citizens, and various cities and areas became well-known for producing their unique style of lebkuchen (just as San Francisco is known for producing a distinct type of sourdough bread). These included the northern capitol of the Romans, Augusta Treverorum (today the town of Trier in the Mosel region of Germany), Aachen, Basel, and the best known, Nuremberg, where the style of lebkuchen we know today is said to have originated. In those days honey, a significant ingredient in lebkuchen, was typically gathered from beehives kept at monasteries. (Interestingly, candlemakers used to make lebkuchen because they had a surplus of honey available as a by-product of making beeswax candles.) The word *leb* refers to both life and healing. The monks of Nuremberg distributed lebkuchen to the villagers for its supposed medicinal properties.

Lebkuchen was originally made using yeast as a leavening agent, but yeast was found to be too strong as it causes the dough to expand in all directions. Experiments with ammonium carbonate and potash eventually proved that using them together was the best solution. Further trial and error developed the technique of preparing a "starter" lebkuchen dough without leavening and leaving it to rest for two or three days before incorporating the leavening with the remaining ingredients and forming the cookies. In some old-fashioned recipes the initial dough was left to rest for months, since it was determined that the resting period favorably changed the taste and lightened the texture of the finished product. The use of two leavening agents, combined with the resting period, resulted in a more even rise to the dough, allowing more precise work, and the art of making lebkuchen became more refined as molds carved from wood, made from ceramic, and cut from metal, came to be used.

Decoration has always been an important factor in making lebkuchen. Tinted icings were piped on the cookies in artistic designs that reflected the style of the times. During the Romantic period, small colored pictures depicting angels, Santas, and other seasonal motifs were glued to the top of the shiny dark brown cookies. Lebkuchen cookies are also made with fillings of almond paste, nuts, and candied fruit.

Following are two recipes for lebkuchen. The first, Lebkuchen Bars, is a simplified filled version in which the filling is actually mixed with the dough, and the dough is spread into a baking pan and cut into bars after baking. The second, Lebkuchen Hearts, makes a more traditional-style cookie.

Lebkuchen Bars

one 16-by-12-inch (40-×-30-cm) pan or 24 pieces

¹/₂ teaspoon (2 g) baking soda

¹/₂ teaspoon (2 g) baking powder

1 teaspoon (5 g) salt

1 teaspoon (2 g) ground nutmeg

1 teaspoon (1.5 g) ground cinnamon

1 teaspoon (2 g) ground cloves

10 ounces (285 g) bread flour

2 ounces (55 g) Candied Orange Peel (page 978), finely chopped

2 ounces (55 g) mixed Candied Citrus Peels (page 978), finely chopped

2 ounces (55 g) candied angelica or candied red cherries, finely chopped

3 ounces (85 g) blanched almonds, finely chopped

3 eggs

4 ounces (115 g) brown sugar

grated zest and juice from one-half lemon

1 cup (240 ml) or 12 ounces (340 g) honey

¹/₂ cup (120 ml) Fondant (page 1011)

Simple Syrup (page 11), as needed

NOTE: Lebkuchen Bars will keep fresh for up to five days if refrigerated and covered. It is best, however, to slice the pieces as needed if the cookies are to be stored for that length of time.

1. Add the baking soda, baking powder, salt, and spices to the flour. Sift together and reserve.

2. Combine the Candied Orange Peel, Candied Citrus Peel, candied angelica or cherries, and the almonds. Reserve.

3. Whip the eggs and brown sugar together until the mixture is light and fluffy. Add the lemon zest and juice, the honey, and half of the flour mixture. Blend until smooth. Incorporate the remaining flour mixture. Stir in the fruit and almond mixture.

4. Line a half-sheet pan (12 by 16 inches/30 × 40 cm) with baking paper. Spread the batter evenly over the pan. Bake at 375°F (190°C) for approximately 25 minutes or until baked through. Let the sheet cool just long enough so that you can handle it comfortably.

5. Adjust the consistency of the Fondant by adding Simple Syrup or water as needed so that it is easy to spread. Spread the glaze evenly over the warm Lebkuchen. Set aside until completely cool.

6. Run a knife around the perimeter of the pan, invert, peel the paper from the back, and then turn right-side up. Use a sharp knife to cut the sheet into twenty-four bars. Store well wrapped in the refrigerator.

Lebkuchen Hearts

about 80 cookies

1 pound, 8 ounces (680 g) or 2 cups (480 ml) honey

4 ounces (115 g) or ⅓ cup (80 ml) molasses

6 ounces (170 g) granulated sugar

⅓ cup (80 ml) water

1 pound, 4 ounces (570 g) rye flour

7 ounces (200 g) bread flour

3 tablespoons (15 g) ground cinnamon

2 teaspoons (4 g) ground cloves

2 teaspoons (4 g) ground cardamom

2 teaspoons (4 g) ground nutmeg

1 teaspoon (5 g) salt

4 egg yolks (⅓ cup/80 ml)

4 teaspoons (14 g) ammonium carbonate

3 tablespoons (45 ml) milk

2 teaspoons (7 g) potash

2 tablespoons (30 ml) milk

11 ounces (310 g) bread flour

egg white

NOTE: If ammonium carbonate is not available, substitute a mixture of baking powder and baking soda (in equal amounts).

These cookies require advance planning since the "starter dough" must rest for a minimum of two days in the refrigerator. Gingerbread makers discovered many hundreds of years ago that potash is a leavener. In the past it was obtained by leaching the ash from plants, which is where the name comes from. Potash (also known as potassium carbonate) can be obtained from a chemical laboratory.

1. Heat the honey and molasses to about 120°F (49°C).

2. Place the sugar in a saucepan with the water, bring to a boil, and then stir into the honey and molasses mixture. Set aside to cool to approximately 85°F (29°C).

3. Incorporate the rye flour and the first measurement of bread flour, mixing just until a smooth dough has formed. Cover tightly and allow to rest in the refrigerator for a minimum of two days or, preferably, one week.

4. Remove the dough from the refrigerator and allow to sit at room temperature until somewhat softened. Add the spices and salt to the egg yolks and stir into a smooth paste.

5. Dissolve the ammonium carbonate in the first measurement of milk and the potash in the second measurement of milk. Add the yolk and spice mixture, both leavening mixtures, and the remaining bread flour to the dough, mixing until the dough is smooth.

6. Place the dough on a sheet pan that has been lined with baking paper and dusted with flour. Cover and refrigerate until the dough is firm enough to work with, preferably overnight.

7. Roll out a portion of dough at a time to ¼ inch (6 mm) thick, using the minimum amount of flour necessary to prevent the dough from sticking. Cut out cookies using a 3-inch (7.5-cm) diameter heart-shaped cookie cutter or another shape of approximately the same size. Place on sheet pans lined with baking paper and brush egg white lightly over the tops of the cookies.

8. Bake, double-panned, at 425°F (219°C) for approximately 12 minutes or until dark brown. As soon as the cookies are removed from the oven, lightly brush egg white over the tops again. If you are unable to do this immediately (or if you forget), don't brush the cookies later, just skip this step.

Springerle

variable yield

¹/₂ teaspoon (1.75 g) ammonium carbonate (see note on page 823)

¹/₄ cup (60 ml) milk, at room temperature

6 eggs, at room temperature

1 pound, 9 ounces (710 g) powdered sugar, sifted

4 ounces (115 g) soft unsalted butter

1 teaspoon (5 g) salt

1 teaspoon (5 ml) anise oil (or another flavoring, see introduction)

2 pounds, 4 ounces (1 kg, 25 g) cake flour

powdered sugar, sifted

Springerle, which in the Swabian German dialect means "little horse," are traditional German Christmas cookies possibly so named because they were originally shaped in the form of animals. In the pre-Christian era it was customary for the German tribes to celebrate the winter solstice (Jul Fest) by sacrificing live animals or token animals shaped from dough. These beautifully molded, anise-flavored cookies have been closely associated with Christmas festivities for centuries. The German village bakers inspired the early intricately carved molds (many of which are now hundreds of years old and can be seen in museums) by holding annual competitions in time for Christmas baking with each shop hoping their carver would produce the most elaborate molds, since the baker with the prettiest cookies would no doubt reap the largest share of the holiday business. Not surprisingly, the horse was a popular ancient theme, but other classical motifs included hunting scenes, baskets of fruit or flowers, which were symbols of prosperity, and many that portrayed biblical images. European immigrants gave up precious room in their baggage to bring their heirloom springerle molds to this country, and many of these original molds are still passed down from generation to generation in German families. Those of us not lucky enough to have these treasures in our possession are fortunate that high-quality exact replicas of historical molds can be found in some cookware stores along with contemporary molds.

If you do not share the old country love of anise flavoring, substitute lemon oil or finely grated lemon zest. The baked cookies can be left plain to enjoy with coffee or tea (sometimes they get so hard they need a little dunking first), or they can be painted and used as ornaments. For ornaments, make a hole using a small plain pastry tip before baking the cookies, and thread a ribbon through the hole after decorating.

Like most things it takes some experience to get a feel for working with springerle dough and molds: Keep the following points in mind:

• It is important to have enough flour in the dough to make it firm enough to keep it from sticking to the mold and also so that the dough will retain the imprint from the mold precisely. However, too much will give the cookies a floury taste and can make the dough too firm to pick up very intricate or small designs. The dough becomes firmer as it chills, and you should work with it cold and firm from the refrigerator.

• Work in an area that is well lit so you can see if the print is clear. If it is not, gather the dough, reroll, and try again. A light source directed from the side will help you see very complex patterns best.

• Be sure that the mold is clean, using a brush to remove excess flour, powdered sugar, or tiny bits of dough stuck in the design, before each impression is made. Do not use a sharp object such as a knife tip to remove bits of dough or you may damage the mold.

• When using very deep molds it is sometimes easier to get a clear impression by pressing the dough into the mold rather than the other way around as is typical. To use this method place the mold on the table design-side up and lay a piece of dough that is just slightly larger

than the mold on top. Use your fingertips to gently press the dough into the mold, being careful not to move the dough from side to side and paying special attention to areas of the mold that are very deep. Roll a rolling pin over the top of the dough, then place a sheet of cardboard on top and carefully invert (this is where you must be extremely careful not to move the mold or the dough, even a fraction, or you can blur the image). Remove the mold and then slide the cookie off of the cardboard and onto the sheet pan.

• If you have cutters that are the same dimension as your molds (cutters that match the molds exactly can sometimes be ordered with the molds), use these to cut the images out of the dough. The cutters must match exactly unless you want to have a frame of dough around the image, which sometimes looks nice. Or cut the cookies apart with a pastry wheel in the case of molds with multiple images. If the edges look ragged, trim again after the cookies have dried overnight.

• Be sure to brush any excess powdered sugar from the cookies before baking, using a very gentle hand and a soft brush. If there is only a light dusting it is best to remove it after the cookies have dried overnight, as you are less likely to disturb the image, but if there are large specks they should be brushed away prior to drying or they can create a tiny dent in the surface. So much sugar on the cookies probably means you are using too much or the dough is too soft, either from a lack of flour or from not being cold, or a combination of both.

• Before you risk ruining a large intricate design, bake as many small test cookies (one at a time) as needed until you have the oven temperature adjusted correctly. If it is too hot the cookies will puff and the carefully created image will disappear. Double or even triple panning may be necessary. Watch them very closely as they bake; the cookies should become light golden brown on the bottom but should not really change color on top and should not change shape at all except for puffing up slightly.

Springerle molds can be used to press designs into rolled Marzipan in much the same way as they are used to shape the cookies (of course the Marzipan is not baked as the cookies are). The Marzipan pieces may be used as ornaments or can be placed on top of a cake or pastry, left plain, painted, or coated with a thin film of melted cocoa butter. Use Marzipan that is quite firm so that it will hold the image from the mold.

1. Stir the ammonium carbonate into the milk to dissolve. Set aside.

2. Using the paddle attachment, beat the eggs with a handful of the powdered sugar until light and fluffy, about 5 minutes. Slowly add the remaining sugar and continue beating several minutes longer until creamy and smooth. Beat in the soft butter followed by the ammonium carbonate mixture, the salt, and the anise oil.

3. Gradually incorporate the flour. Place the dough on a sheet pan lined with baking paper, cover, and place in the refrigerator until well chilled.

4. Remove a portion of the dough from the refrigerator and work it smooth. Keep the dough you are not working with covered and chilled to prevent it from drying on the surface. Roll the dough to ¼ inch (6 mm) thick (very deep molds will require thicker dough), using just enough powdered sugar to keep the dough from sticking. Rub the surface of the dough with powdered sugar; it should not show. Press the springerle mold very firmly straight down into the dough without moving it from side to side. Remove the mold and cut the image out of the dough, leaving a frame of dough around the design or not as desired. Transfer the cookies to sheet pans lined with baking paper.

5. After forming all of the cookies, set them aside to dry at room temperature overnight, lightly covered with a cloth or towel.

6. Bake the cookies at 250°F (122°C) for approximately 20 minutes (see introduction); very large cookies will take up to twice as long. Store in airtight containers at room temperature. The flavor and texture of the cookies will improve after several days of storage, and they can be kept for many weeks. Decorated cookie ornaments that will not be eaten should be left in the open to dry thoroughly and can be also sprayed with lacquer.

Yule Log Pastries

40 pastries

one-half recipe or 2 pounds,
    12 ounces (1 kg, 250 g) Rum Ball
    Filling (page 419)
1 pound, 2 ounces (510 g) Marzipan
    (page 1022), untinted
2 ounces (55 g) Vanilla Buttercream
    (page 978)
3 ounces (85 g) Gingerbread Cookies
    dough (page 818)
    or
Short Dough (page 54)
dark coating chocolate, melted
strained strawberry jam or preserves
powdered sugar

Just as there are some classical and ethnic holiday specialties that are almost never made except at Christmas—springerle, lebkuchen, fruitcake, gingerbread figures, and dozens of others that tradition demands be part of our celebrations—there are many other year-round pastries that can simply be modified slightly to create a seasonal facade. Like the Angelica Points that become Christmas Tree Pastries and the Mazarins that are transformed into Holiday Candle Pastries, Rum Chocolate Spools were a natural for this alteration into miniature yule logs. Chocolate and Marzipan are a delicious combination to start with, and the addition of the small tree branches, which at first glance appears tedious and time-consuming, is actually pretty easy if you plan appropriately. If the chilled Rum-Ball ropes have gotten close to room temperature, chill the branch stumps quickly in the freezer (or simply put them in the refrigerator before you begin to cut the ropes). Before attaching the branches to the logs, one or the other must be cold so that the chocolate sets up immediately. Besides the opportunity to use dry or leftover scrap pieces in the Rum Ball Filling, here is also a chance to use leftover cocoa-colored Marzipan or Marzipan that may have gotten crumbs mixed into it. Leftover Marzipan that was tinted red and green for other projects can be combined to produce a light brown tint and used here as well.

1. Divide the Rum Ball Filling into five equal pieces, approximately 9 ounces (255 g) each. Reserve.

2. Roll the Marzipan into a rectangle 16 inches wide and 20 inches long (40 × 50 cm). It should be very thin, about $1/16$ inch (2 mm).

3. Roll each piece of Rum Ball dough into a rope the same length as the width of the Marzipan (16 inches/40 cm), using powdered sugar to prevent it from sticking to the table.

4. Trim the short side of the Marzipan that is closest to you to make it straight and even. Spread a thin film of Vanilla Buttercream on top of the Marzipan. Place a Rum Ball rope on top of the Marzipan next to the straight edge. Roll the Marzipan around the rope to enclose, then cut the rope away (see Figure 9–23, page 420). The edges of the Marzipan should line up evenly, not overlap. Cover the remaining ropes in the same way. (If you should need to reroll the Marzipan sheet during the covering process, scrape the buttercream off the top, knead the Marzipan back together, and roll out again.)

5. Roll each rope against the table to stretch it to 18 inches (45 cm). Transfer the ropes to a sheet pan (if they do not fit, cut them in half first) and place in the refrigerator until firm, about 1 hour.

6. While the ropes are chilling, scrape all of the buttercream off of the leftover Marzipan scraps, weigh out a 2-ounce (55-g) piece of Marzipan, and roll it into a thin rope 20 inches long (50 cm) and about $3/8$ inch (9 mm) in diameter. Cover the remaining scraps and use for another project. Cut the rope into forty $1/2$-inch (1.2-cm) pieces. Cut these pieces in half at a 45° angle to make two branch stump decorations for each log. Reserve these decorations.

7. Roll out Gingerbread Cookies dough or Short Dough to $1/16$ inch (2 mm) thick. Cut out forty cookies using a $1/2$-inch (1.2-cm) heart-shaped cutter. Bake the cookies at 375°F (190°C) for approximately 6 minutes or until baked through.

8. Cut each chilled Rum Ball rope into eight $2^1/4$-inch (5.6-cm) pieces. Immediately, while the logs are still cold, attach two branch stumps to each log by dipping the angled cut side of the stumps into the melted chocolate and attaching them to the top of each log, slightly off-center at opposite ends, pointing ("growing") in the same direction.

9. Set the logs, one at a time, on a dipping fork and dip into the coating chocolate. As you remove each log, move it up and down over the bowl to remove as much chocolate as possible. Finish this process by scraping the bottom of the pastry against the rim of the bowl. Place the dipped logs on a sheet pan lined with baking paper (see Figures 9–27 to 9–31, page 428; do not insert the fork into the pastries as shown in the illustration). Place one of the cookie hearts flat on top of each log, centered between the branch stumps, before the chocolate hardens. Pipe a small drop of strawberry jam or preserves in the center of each cookie. Sift powdered sugar lightly over the pastries.

Plated Desserts

Bûche de Noël Slices with Pomegranate Sauce and Starfruit

16 servings

one recipe Yule Logs (page 809)
   (see step one)
eight to ten medium-sized carambola
   (starfruit)
dark coating chocolate, melted
one recipe Pomegranate Sauce
   (page 1079)
seeds from one pomegranate
powdered sugar

Bûche de Noël *are always featured on holiday menus in my kitchen. Certainly not for their practicality, for they can be quite time-consuming at such a busy time of the year, but because tradition (and the public) demands it. However, the complexity of the logs can be offset by the relative simplicity of some of the other desserts offered. For example, a nicely balanced selection of plated holiday desserts is Persimmon Pudding, Minola Tangelo Givré, Princess Cake (with a Christmas decoration), and* Bûche de Noël *Slices with Pomegranate Sauce and Starfruit; all but this one being rather easy.*

Because the yule log slices should be presented standing upright, and since this includes their journey to the dining room carried by the waitstaff, it is very important that the sponge batter is not spread out too thick to begin with, and, although the slices are cut at an angle to the log, they must be cut straight down so they do not lean over. Both slices with thick sponge (which makes them taller) and slices that lean are prone to falling over in the sauce. If your slices seem to be so "inclined," it is better to arrange the plate presentation with the slice flat on the plate. If you suspect there may be a problem before the log is sliced, cut it into wedges instead (as if you were cutting croissants from a single strip). By creating a wider end you will prevent any accidents and you will still achieve the desired height.

1. Follow the recipe for Yule Logs through step twelve, making sixteen holly leaves and forty-eight holly berries (you will need approximately 1 ounce/30 g red and 4 ounces/115 g green Marzipan). Omit the Rum Ball Filling and steps eight and nine as well. Place the iced log in the refrigerator until the buttercream is set, 30 to 60 minutes. Place the holly leaves and berries in the refrigerator as well, but do not leave them for more than one hour or they will start to get sticky from the moist air.

2. Peel the skin from the ridges of the starfruit, using a vegetable peeler. Slice the fruit thinly, reshape with the cut sides together, cover, and reserve in the refrigerator.

3. Using a knife dipped in very hot water, slice the log into sixteen pieces, cutting the slices on a bias.

4. Attach one chilled holly leaf decoration and three berries to the top of each slice, using melted coating chocolate to secure them.

5. Presentation: Place a decorated yule log slice, standing up, centered at the rear of a dessert plate. Arrange five to six starfruit slices in front of the dessert on the left side of the plate. Pour a pool of Pomegranate Sauce to the right of the fruit slices. Sprinkle a few pomegranate seeds on top of the sauce and over the base of the plate. Sift powdered sugar lightly over the yule log slice and the plate; powdered sugar should be visible on the pomegranate seeds in the sauce.

Chocolate Chalet with White Chocolate and Pistachio Pâte and Bitter Chocolate Sauce

16 servings

White Chocolate and Pistachio Pâte
   (recipe follows)
2 ounces (55 g) Gingerbread Cookies
   dough (page 818)
Royal Icing (page 1019)
dark coating chocolate, melted
powdered sugar
Bitter Chocolate Sauce (page 1072)
seeds from one medium pomegranate
Chocolate Chalets (directions follow)
Chocolate Fences (directions follow)

"Here he goes again," you are probably saying, "with one of these labor-intensive, complicated desserts that no one could realistically produce outside of a cooking school." Wrong. First of all there are times when more is not necessarily better, and as I'm sure you can imagine, this is definitely the case when it comes to working with students who have hundreds of questions even if they usually are for good reasons. For mass producing this type of showy, multistep dessert, I would rather have two trained workers than twelve trainees. But that aside, this dessert is much easier than it appears. Last year the sixth and final graduation ceremony of the year was scheduled a few days before the Christmas holiday break, and because it is customary for myself and the junior class to put together something really special for the graduating seniors, this dessert was my choice. Due to all of the other work connected with the holidays we had only one full day to prepare all of the components for 320 guests. The desserts came out beautifully, although we did cut corners by using gingerbread hearts instead of hearts made from Marbleized Chocolate. You can speed things up even further by eliminating the chimney on the chalet if necessary. If you are still thinking that this presentation is too complex, consider that both the Chocolate Chalets (assembled or in pieces) and the White Chocolate Pâte can be prepared weeks in advance. And I can guarantee that your efforts will pay off when you serve this creation (it not only looks spectacular but the flavors marry wonderfully); it generates such an ecstatic response that you will be thankful that you did not simply place a slice of pâte on a plate with a boring rosette of whipped cream on top!

1. Line a pâte mold or other suitable form approximately 3½ by 3½ by 12 inches long (8.7 × 8.7 × 30 cm) with baking paper as shown in Figures 1–8 and 1–9, page 25, (or if making a cardboard form—directions follow—line this as well). Pour the White Chocolate Pâte into the form. Cover and place in the freezer until firm, at least 4 hours or, preferably, overnight.

2. Roll out the gingerbread dough to ¹⁄₁₆ inch (2 mm) thick. Cut out sixteen (or a few extra in case of breakage) small deer, using a deer-shaped cookie cutter. Place them on a sheet pan lined with baking paper and bake at 400°F (205°C) for about 5 minutes or until baked through. Set aside to cool.

3. Work the Royal Icing smooth and adjust by adding more egg white if necessary for a soft, but not runny, consistency. Place a small amount of icing in a piping bag and pipe tiny dots on the deer cookies to mark the eyes. Place a small amount of melted coating chocolate in a piping bag and pipe an even tinier dot on the icing dots to mark the pupil of the eyes. Lightly sift powdered sugar over the deer. Do not shake the sifter; instead, hit it with the back of a knife so that you create clearly defined spots on the deer. Set the deer aside.

4. Remove the frozen pâte from the form. Cut it across into sixteen ³⁄₄-inch (2-cm) slices, using a thin chef's knife dipped into hot water between each slice. To be able to cut cleanly through the pistachio nuts in the filling, the pâte must be sliced while it is still firm; however, it should not be served for at least 30 minutes so it has time to thaw. Try not to cut and thaw more slices than you will be serving right away. Store the thawed slices covered in the refrigerator until needed.

5. Place a portion of the Bitter Chocolate Sauce in a piping bottle, adjusting the consistency first as needed.

6. Presentation: Pipe large irregular teardrop shapes of Chocolate Sauce over the base of a dessert plate. Set a slice of pâte in the center of the plate. Sprinkle pomegranate seeds around the pâte on the base of the plate. Wearing vinyl food-handling gloves so that you do not leave fingerprints on the chocolate, place a Chocolate Chalet in one corner on the pâte slice, pushing it all the way down to the plate. If you hit a pistachio in the pâte, do not force the chalet or it will break, instead lift it up and shift the position a little. Place a Chocolate Fence in front of the chalet and to the left, positioning it so that the fence is parallel to the left edge of the pâte slice. Place a deer between the fence and the chalet toward the right side of the pâte slice. Sift powdered sugar lightly over the chalet and the plate.

White Chocolate and Pistachio Pâte

8 cups (1 l, 920 ml)

4 ounces (115 g) pistachio nuts

2¹/₂ cups (600 ml) heavy cream

4 teaspoons (12 g) unflavored gelatin powder

¹/₂ cup (120 ml) cold water

10 ounces (285 g) white chocolate

3 tablespoons (27 g) pectin powder (see note)

8 ounces (225 g) granulated sugar

1 cup (240 ml) egg whites

NOTE: Use regular fruit-canning pectin; pure pectin would be too strong here. If pectin is not available, increase the gelatin to a total of 2 tablespoons (18 g).

NOTE: Keep in mind that the side of the cardboard that you draw on and cut will become the outside of the box.

1. Add a pinch of salt to a pint of boiling water, blanch the pistachio nuts, drain, and remove the skins. Set aside.

2. Whip the heavy cream to soft peaks; do not overwhip. Reserve in the refrigerator.

3. Sprinkle the gelatin over the cold water and set aside to soften.

4. Chop the white chocolate into small pieces and melt over a bain-marie, using low heat and stirring frequently to prevent overheating, which would cause the chocolate to become lumpy. Set aside and keep warm.

5. Combine the pectin powder and granulated sugar in a mixing bowl. Stir in the egg whites. Place over a bain-marie and heat, stirring constantly with a whisk, until the mixture reaches 140°F (60°C). Remove from the heat and immediately whip to stiff peaks.

6. Quickly stir the melted white chocolate into one-third of the meringue to temper. Then, still working quickly, add this to the remaining meringue.

7. Heat the gelatin mixture to dissolve. Rapidly mix the gelatin into the meringue mixture. Fold in the pistachio nuts and then the reserved whipped cream.

To make a cardboard form for the White Chocolate and Pistachio Pâte

Necessity is the mother of invention, and this handy and easy-to-make box came about in the same way as many of the other forms in this book: It seems to be impossible ever to have enough molds and forms

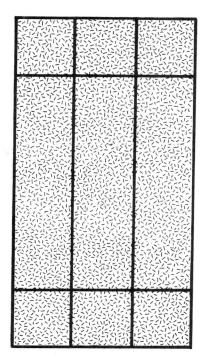

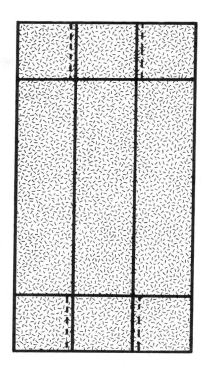

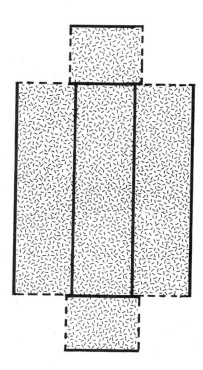

FIGURE 16-7 The lines drawn on the cardboard rectangle after measuring

FIGURE 16-8 The dotted lines drawn as instructed

FIGURE 16-9 The dotted lines showing where to cut to remove the corners

Block-style cream cheese is often packaged in sturdy, rectangular cardboard boxes, and I have used these not only to hold this pâte but to mold Ganache and parfaits until set as well. The size that I use are 9¼ inches long, 3¼ inches wide, and 3 inches high (23.1 × 8.1 × 7.5 cm). One and one-half boxes of this size (place a divider in the center of one box and set a weight against it) are needed to mold the pâte recipe.

to go around in a busy school with many different kitchens, and sometimes one just gives up and makes his or her own. If you measure and cut precisely you will create a straight and uniform mold, which, if completely lined, can be used over and over. However, if the filling should leak out and stain the cardboard, the box should be discarded.

1. Use a utility knife with a sharp blade to cut a flat sheet of corrugated cardboard into an 18½-by-9-inch (46.2-×-22.5-cm) rectangle (I start with a full sheet pan-sized cardboard that is lined on both sides).

2. Measure and draw two lines, 3 inches (7.5 cm) apart, lengthwise. Measure and draw a line 3 inches (7.5 cm) in from each short end (Figure 16–7). You now have three equal squares at each short end. Draw dotted lines just outside the square that is in the center of each end as indicated by the dotted lines in Figure 16–8. Cut on the dotted lines and also across the line of the corner squares that borders the left and right long rectangles and remove the corners (Figure 16–9).

3. Cut halfway through the remaining solid lines. Invert the cardboard. Bend all four sides up to make a rectangular box. Use a glue gun to glue the short ends onto the center or just tape the box together around the outside at the corners.

Chocolate Chalets

16 chalets

one full sheet Marbleized Chocolate
   (page 900)
Chalet Support Box (directions follow)
Dark Piping Chocolate (page 904)

*T*he technique of spreading chocolate into a thin sheet, letting it set, and then using a warm knife to cut the sheet into precise pieces (with or without a template) is quite common and is most often used to create small elegant chocolate boxes to hold truffles and other pralines. When made from plain chocolate, the lid of the box (and sometimes the sides) is usually decorated by piping intricate chocolate designs on top. When making boxes from Marbleized Chocolate this is not necessary, and actually if it is to be done at all it should be kept to a minimum or the combination will look busy. Using the method described for the chalets, you can build this type of elegant bonbon box, as they are commonly referred to in the industry, or practically anything else.

If you need to simplify the chalet construction, replace the chocolate heart with a gingerbread heart, or use hearts made out of plain or cocoa Short Dough. If you are making this dessert around the holidays (as intended), gingerbread makes a very appropriate substitute, and it also makes sense if you are using gingerbread deer as part of the presentation. If you substitute gingerbread you will need about one-third less chocolate and about 6 ounces (170 g) of Gingerbread Cookies dough (see page 818).

1. Trace the chalet templates A and B in Figure 16–10 and cut out of sturdy cardboard such as the type used for matting pictures. Have ready a heart-shaped cookie cutter approximately 3 inches wide and 3 inches tall (7.5 × 7.5 cm). If you do not have a cutter, cut template C out of cardboard as well.

2. Set up your workstation next to the stove with the Marbleized Chocolate (attached to the baking paper) on a wooden surface. Place a pan on the stove with 1/2 inch (1.2 cm) of water and keep it at the scalding point.

3. Place the heart cutter in the water for a few seconds to heat the metal (if you are making a large number of chalets it is best to work with two cutters). Shake the water off the cutter against a towel and then cut a heart (which will become a roof support) out of the Marbleized Chocolate sheet by letting the hot cutter melt through the chocolate. Reheat the cutter as needed and repeat to cut a total of sixteen hearts, alternating cutting up and down to minimize scrap pieces. Cut the hearts starting from a long edge so the other long edge is left intact to cut the roof strips. If the chocolate breaks, you are either pushing too hard or the cutter is not hot enough. As you cut the hearts, slide a palette knife underneath and transfer them to a sheet pan lined with baking paper before the chocolate hardens and causes them to stick together. If you are using template C as a guide instead of a metal cutter, place it on top of the chocolate and cut around the outside using the tip of a hot knife.

4. Heat a thin chef's knife over a gas stove, Bunsen burner, or even chafing dish fuel (sterno). Use the roof template (template A) to

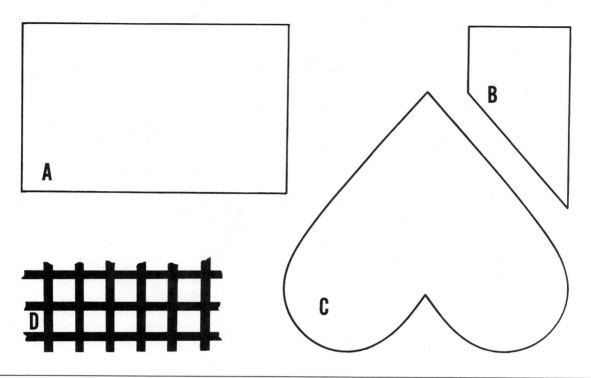

FIGURE 16–10 *The templates used for cutting the Marbleized Chocolate sheet for Chocolate Chalet and the template used as a guide to pipe out the Chocolate Fences*

gauge and measure the width and then cut out three strips the full length of the chocolate sheet, wiping the knife clean and reheating it as needed. Slide a palette knife under each strip as it is cut (do not use the warm chef's knife) and transfer it to a sheet of cardboard or an inverted sheet pan. Using the roof template as a guide and wearing food-handling gloves to protect the chocolate from fingerprints, cut across the strips to make thirty-two roof pieces.

5. Using the same technique of heating the knife, cut sixteen chimney pieces from the strips and from any large enough scrap pieces from the sheet using template B. Be sure that you are cutting each chimney with the template right-side up or you will have to attach them on different sides of the roofs later. Save the remaining scraps (see note 2 following the Marbleized Chocolate recipe).

6. Place the hearts and chimneys in the refrigerator.

7. Wearing gloves, arrange eight pairs of roof pieces in the support box, marbleized side down, with their short ends touching as shown in the illustration. Place melted Piping Chocolate in a piping bag and cut a small opening. Weld the roof pieces together by piping chocolate where they meet, covering about 1/2 inch (1.2 cm) of the seam on each end, but without covering the center of the seam.

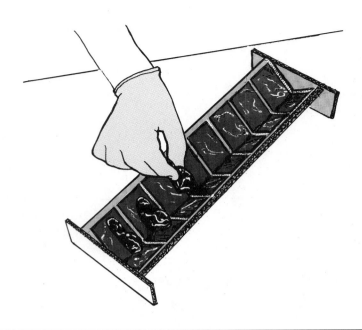

FIGURE 16–11 Attaching Marbleized Chocolate hearts between pairs of Marbleized Chocolate roof pieces set in the support box

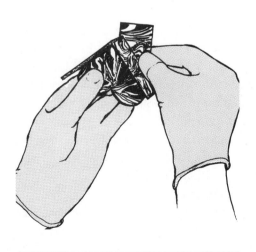

FIGURE 16–12 Attaching a chimney to the roof of a Chocolate Chalet

8. Use the tip of a pairing knife to lightly mark the center of the roof pieces vertically. Remove eight hearts from the refrigerator (you should still be wearing gloves to protect the chocolate). Holding a heart upside down by the rounded edge, pipe chocolate along the straight edges up to the curve. Immediately position the heart between two roof pieces, using your marks to find the center (Figure 16–11). Be certain the heart is standing straight. Repeat with the remaining seven hearts.

9. Remove the chalets from the support box and place them on a sheet pan lined with baking paper with the marbleized side of the hearts facing up.

10. Repeat steps seven, eight, and nine to form the remaining eight chalets.

11. Remove eight chimney pieces from the refrigerator. Attach the chimneys to the right sides of the roofs by piping chocolate on the bottom edge of a chimney and holding it place on the roof a few seconds until set (be sure the chimney is straight and that the left short side extends fully above the crest of the roof) (Figure 16–12). Repeat until all sixteen chimneys have been attached.

12. Cover the chalets and reserve in a cool, dry area until needed; do not refrigerate.

Chalet Support Box

NOTE: Although this box will last through many uses if properly handled, making a support box from wood is the ideal long-term solution. In that case it makes sense to create a box that is as long as a full sheet pan.

This box is also useful for shaping both the Cookie Butterflies on page 1052, and the Chocolate Monarch Butterfly Ornaments on page 910.

1. Use a sharp utility knife to cut a 6-by-21-inch (15-×-52.5-cm) rectangle from corrugated cardboard, such as a cardboard sheet for cake support. Measure and cut two pieces 2³/₈ inches (5.9 cm) wide from one end of the strip as shown in the illustration.

2. Measure and cut a line lengthwise in the center of the large piece, cutting only halfway through. Invert the piece and bend the sides up into a V shape. Place the heart cookie cutter (or template) used to cut the Chocolate Chalet hearts in the V, adjust the sides so they are snug against the cutter, and tape across the top of the box to hold the sides at this angle (Figure 16–13).

3. Hold one of the small cardboard pieces centered against one short side of the V, making sure it is level. Trace the V onto the end piece where it touches, marking on the top side of the V. Repeat with the other end piece on the opposite side.

4. Using a hot glue gun, apply lines of glue just below your marks on the end pieces and secure them to each end of the support box. Remove the tape across the top. Apply a little additional glue around the inside edge as needed (Figure 16–14).

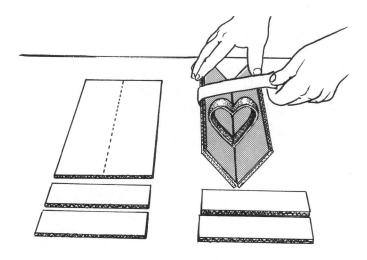

FIGURE 16–13 Taping across the top of the support box with the cutter in place to hold the sides of the box at the proper angle

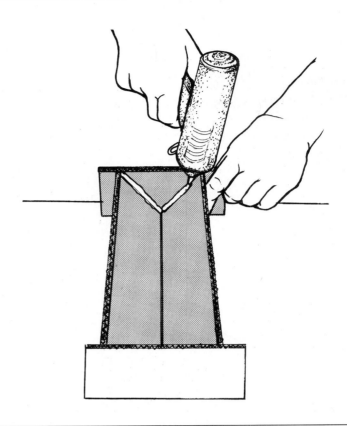

FIGURE 16–14 *Applying glue to the inside of the box after gluing the end pieces in place and removing the tape*

Chocolate Fences

Piping Chocolate (page 904)

Unless you are making a large number of fences, it is not necessary to copy multiple rows of the template. The following procedure works fine if producing enough fences for one Chocolate Chalet recipe.

1. Trace the pattern shown in template D of Figure 16–10 (page 833) onto a small piece of baking paper, using a heavy black pen. Place a sheet of baking paper over the tracing with the tracing positioned under the top left edge of the larger paper.

2. Place Piping Chocolate in a piping bag and cut a larger-than-normal opening. Pipe out one fence following the lines of the tracing, piping the vertical lines (the fence posts) first. Slide the drawing to the right underneath the larger paper and pipe out the second fence in the same way. Continue around the perimeter of the paper until you have made about twenty fences. You only need sixteen but some are likely to break.

3. Store the Chocolate Fences attached to the baking paper in a cool, dry place until needed. Refrigerate the fences briefly if necessary to make them easier to handle before removing them from the paper.

Mont Blanc with Pomegranate Seeds and Vanilla Curly Cues

12 servings

one-quarter recipe French Meringue
    (page 590)

one recipe Chestnut Purée (page 802)
    (see step three)

2 cups (480 ml) milk

one vanilla bean, split lengthwise

one-quarter recipe Vanilla Tulip Paste
    (page 1047)

one-half recipe Chantilly Cream
    (page 1083)

$1/2$ cup (120 ml) pomegranate seeds

powdered sugar

NOTE: Since removing the shell and skin from fresh chestnuts is very time-consuming, cooked or dried chestnuts can really be a blessing. These are available vacuum packed, frozen, or packed in water. The chestnuts in water tend to be soggy and lacking in flavor and are not recommended for this recipe. The outrageously expensive canned "marrons glaces," candied whole chestnuts in heavy syrup imported from France, are a luxury well worth trying if you love chestnuts. The much more affordable canned, unsweetened chestnut purée, also usually imported from France, can be used in this recipe and will just about cut the preparation time in half, unfortunately at the expense of the flavor. If you substitute canned chestnut purée, sweeten it with Simple Syrup and flavor with vanilla extract as needed.

*M*ont Blanc is a picturesque mountain located in the French part of the Alps bordering Italy. Because of its high elevation, the top of the mountain is always capped with snow. Mont Blanc has lent its name to this speciality consisting of vermicelli-like strands of vanilla-scented Chestnut Purée formed into a fragile mountain that is topped with Chantilly Cream. According to an old-world tradition, Mont Blanc should be eaten slowly using a small, silver spoon.

Chestnut trees grow wild in many parts of Europe where their name, from the Greek word kastanéa, changes, depending on location, to kastanjer in Sweden and castagne in Italy. Chestnuts ripen in October when the spiked green outer skin turns light brown, opens, and reveals the shiny, sweet, edible nuts inside; usually there are two per pod. The hard mahogany-colored shells and bitter interior skin must be removed before the chestnuts are eaten. Most of the fresh chestnuts available in the United States are imported, and the majority of these come from Italy. Fresh chestnuts are available as early as October, and they play a big role in holiday creations both savory and sweet. The most simple of all chestnut preparations are the whole nuts roasted over an open fire made famous by a popular Christmas carol and sold by street vendors in some cities in the winter. These are prepared using a special skillet-type of roasting pan that has a long handle and a perforated bottom. For all other uses there is no way to avoid the tedious task of removing the shell and skin.

Mont Blanc is one of the classic and most elaborate of the dessert interpretations made from chestnuts. Piping the Chestnut Purée into shapely little mountains as is done here is a bit time-consuming if you are making a fair number. Many chefs recommend forcing the purée through a ricer or even a colander, but I find that a small hand-cranked meat grinder, clamped onto the edge of the table, which gives you one free hand to turn the plate as the Chestnut Purée is extruded, works much better although you do not have the precise control that comes with piping by hand.

1. Draw twelve 3-inch (7.5-cm) circles, evenly spaced, on a sheet of baking paper. Invert the paper and place on a sheet pan. Place the French Meringue in a pastry bag with a no. 0 (1-mm) plain tip. Pipe the meringue into spirals within the circles, starting in the center (see Figure 12–2, page 592).

2. Bake immediately at 210°F (99°C) for approximately one hour or until the meringue is dry. Let cool.

3. Follow the recipe and procedure for the Chestnut Purée but do not purée the chestnuts after peeling. Instead, chop the peeled chestnuts coarsely and place in a saucepan with the milk and the vanilla bean. Cover and simmer over low heat, stirring from time to time, for 20 minutes. Drain, reserving the milk and the vanilla bean.

4. Add $1/4$ cup (60 ml) of the reserved milk to the chestnuts. Purée the mixture until completely smooth, adding more of the reserved milk if necessary. The purée should have the consistency of firm mashed potatoes. Do not overprocess or it will become gummy. Discard any leftover milk. Place the purée in a bowl and reserve at room temperature if serving within an hour, or cover and refrigerate if it will not be used within that time.

5. Scrape the seeds from the vanilla bean into the Tulip Paste. Use the paste to make at least twelve Curly Cues, following the directions on page 1055, but omit the Chocolate Tulip Paste line in the center.

6. Place the Chestnut Purée, a portion at a time, in a pastry bag with a no. 0 (1-mm) plain tip. (If the purée has been refrigerated you may need to stir it smooth first). Pipe the purée on top of the meringue disks in a somewhat random pattern (like a series of figure eights at different angles), letting the purée fall in such a way that it forms 2-inch (5-cm) pointed mounds.

7. Presentation: Place a small dollop of Chantilly Cream in the center of a dessert plate. Place a Mont Blanc on the cream and place a second dollop of cream on top of the pointed tip, giving the cream a rough and uneven surface with the back of the spoon. Sprinkle pomegranate seeds around the dessert on the base of the plate. Lean a Curly Cue against the right side of the dessert. Dust powdered sugar lightly over the top.

Persimmon Charlotte

twelve 5-ounce (150-ml) servings

three medium-sized Fuyu persimmons
Persimmon Bavarois (recipe follows)
1½ cups (360 ml) or one-half recipe Cranberry Coulis (page 1073)
Simple Syrup (page 11) or orange liqueur, as needed
mint leaves cut into julienne (see note on page 745)
powdered sugar

This dessert just barely earns the title "charlotte" since the forms aren't actually lined with persimmon slices; the fruit circles are really just a decoration. Slicing the Fuyu persimmons across the width reveals a decorative spoke pattern produced by the eight soft, flat, seeds inside. Although persimmons are most bountiful around Christmas, don't limit them to holiday desserts only; they can usually be obtained from November through the end of February. Many times persimmons actually hit the market in October, but these early arrivals often don't belong there, in some cases being so unripe that the fruit has not even turned orange yet. The persimmons available in January and February on the other hand (which for the most part are the Fuyu), are ripe, sweet, and juicy. Persimmon purée can also be purchased and is usually packaged with sugar added. If prepared, sweetened purée is used in this recipe, the amount of sugar in the bavarois filling should be reduced. Since this is a good recipe to use several months out of the year, a rather neutral presentation is specified here. When presenting Persimmon Charlotte around the holidays, you might want to add a few seasonal touches such as the Cookie Christmas Trees and/or the persimmon stars used for Persimmon Cream Slices (see page 840).

1. The Fuyu persimmons should be firm to the touch so they can be sliced easily. Place the persimmons on their sides and slice them ⅛ inch (3 mm) thick across the width, using a sharp knife. Use a 2-inch (5-cm) plain cookie cutter to cut rounds from the slices. Place one slice in the bottom of each of twelve 5-ounce (150-ml) soufflé ramekins, or other forms of approximately the same size with smooth sides (with other forms use an appropriate cutter to produce slices that are slightly smaller than the bottom of the forms). Save the leftover persimmon pieces to use in the bavarois.

2. Divide the Persimmon Bavarois equally among the twelve prepared forms. Refrigerate until set, about 2 hours.

3. Place the Cranberry Coulis in a piping bottle.

4. Presentation: Unmold a charlotte by dipping the bottom of the mold very briefly into hot water, invert, and unmold in the center of a dessert plate. Brush Simple Syrup or orange liqueur over the persimmon slice if it appears dry on top. Pipe Cranberry Coulis around the dessert on the base of the plate in an uneven circular pattern without covering the plate entirely. Sprinkle julienned mint leaves over the coulis. Sift powdered sugar lightly over the whole plate. Serve immediately.

Persimmon Bavarois

approximately 9 cups (2 l, 160 ml)

1 pound, 8 ounces (680 g) perfectly ripe Fuyu or Hachiya persimmons

1 tablespoon (15 ml) lime juice

3 cups (720 ml) heavy cream

4½ teaspoons (14 g) unflavored gelatin powder

⅓ cup (80 ml) cold water

⅓ cup (80 ml) or 4 ounces (115 g) light corn syrup

4 eggs, separated

4 ounces (115 g) granulated sugar

1. Cut the persimmons in half. Scoop out the flesh, using a melon-ball cutter or a small spoon, scraping the inside of the skin well to remove all of the pulp. Purée the pulp and force through a fine mesh strainer. You should have approximately 2 cups (480 ml) of purée. Stir in the lime juice and reserve.

2. Whip the heavy cream to soft peaks and reserve in the refrigerator.

3. Sprinkle the gelatin powder over the cold water and set aside to soften.

4. Place the corn syrup in a small saucepan and bring to a boil. At the same time, start whipping the egg yolks. Gradually beat the corn syrup into the yolks. Continue whipping until the mixture is light and fluffy. Reserve.

5. Place the egg whites and sugar in a bowl set over simmering water and heat, stirring constantly, until the mixture reaches 140°F (60°C). Remove from the heat and whip until stiff peaks have formed and the mixture is cold.

6. Fold the whipped cream into the meringue together with the yolk mixture and the persimmon pulp. Heat the gelatin to dissolve. Working quickly, add the gelatin to a small portion of the bavarois to temper then, still working fast, stir this into the remainder. The bavarois should not be made until you are ready to use it.

Persimmon Cream Slices with Cookie Christmas Tree and Cranberry Coulis

16 servings

Gingerbread Sponge (recipe follows)

Persimmon Filling (recipe follows)

2 tablespoons (30 ml) cold water

2 tablespoons (30 ml) brandy

1 teaspoon (3 g) unflavored gelatin powder

one recipe Chantilly Cream (page 1083) (see step three)

three firm Fuyu persimmons

one-half recipe Cranberry Coulis (page 1073)

Simple Syrup (page 11) or orange liqueur

sixteen Cookie Christmas Trees (directions follow)

powdered sugar

sixteen whole cranberries

This is a great, versatile recipe, which should not be categorized as a "holiday only" dessert. The small triangular pieces can be offered as part of a buffet assortment anytime, in which case the only decoration needed is a little powdered sugar sifted over the top. When persimmons are not in season, I make this recipe using mangoes or papayas instead. With either of those fruits you must bring the strained purée to a quick boil to neutralize the enzyme they contain, since the raw fruit will inhibit the gelatin from setting. Also omit the ginger and nutmeg from the sponge, replacing it with one teaspoon (1.5 g) of ground cinnamon, and use honey in place of the molasses. For a different plate presentation, keep the pieces square instead of cutting each one diagonally to form triangles and follow the presentation instructions for Marjolaine (see page 606) using Bijou Coulis (see page 1068) instead of Raspberry Sauce as specified. Or, roll out Marzipan, cut out tiny ribbons, and place them on top of the squares to transform the cream slices into "wrapped" packages. Present these as directed for Tropical Surprise Packages (see page 516), including the kiwi slice garnish and sauce. Regardless of the filling or presentation you use, try not to cut more pieces than you will use within a few hours. The uncut sheet will keep fresh for several days, covered in the refrigerator.

1. To make this recipe you need a 10-inch (25-cm) square pan approximately 2 inches (5 cm) high. If you do not have one, make a frame by cutting two strips of corrugated cardboard 2 inches wide by 20 inches long (5 × 50 cm). Cut halfway through the cardboard across the width of both strips. Bend the strips from the uncut side at a 90° angle and tape the corners together to form a 10-inch (25-cm) square. Set the frame on an inverted sheet pan lined with baking paper.

2. Peel the paper from the back of the Gingerbread Sponge sheet. Invert and scrape the skin from the top of the sponge, removing it entirely if it is loose or just the pieces that come off easily if not. Cut two 10-inch (25-cm) squares from the sponge sheet. Place one sponge, skin-side up, in the pan or prepared frame. Pour the Persimmon Filling on top of the sponge and spread it out evenly. Place in the refrigerator until partially set (or place in the freezer to accelerate the process).

3. Combine the cold water and brandy. Sprinkle the gelatin powder over the top and set aside to soften. Whip the Chantilly Cream to soft peaks. Heat the gelatin to dissolve. Quickly add the gelatin to a small potion of the cream to temper, then quickly add this to the remaining cream. Immediately spread the Chantilly Cream on top of the Persimmon Filling.

4. Place the remaining sponge sheet on top with the skin side against the cream. Press the sponge lightly so it adheres. Place in the refrigerator for at least 2 hours to set completely or, preferably, chill overnight.

5. Stand the persimmons on their sides, trim away the ends, and cut four ⅛-inch (3-mm) slices from each one. Use a 2¼-inch (5.6-cm) star-shaped cookie cutter to cut a star out of each slice (use a smaller cutter if needed to stay within the persimmon slice). Place the stars on a sheet pan lined with baking paper. Cover and reserve.

6. Remove the assembled cake from the refrigerator. If the cake was assembled in a pan, cut around the inside perimeter, invert the cake onto a cardboard, then invert again to turn right-side up. If you used a cardboard frame, simply remove it. Using a thin sharp knife dipped in hot water, trim the sides if necessary and then cut the cake into four strips approximately 2¼ inches (5.6 cm) wide. Then cut each of these strips into four squares. Be sure to hold the knife at a 90° angle so that the sides of the cake will be straight.

7. Place the Cranberry Coulis in a piping bottle. Reserve. Brush Simple Syrup or orange liqueur over the persimmon star garnishes.

8. Presentation: Pipe Cranberry Coulis in a zigzag pattern across the base of a dessert plate. Cut a persimmon square in half diagonally to make two triangles. Arrange the pieces, one on its sponge side and one on a shorter filling side, slightly off-center on top of the coulis. Decorate with a Cookie Christmas Tree, placing it next to the taller triangle. Sift powdered sugar over the dessert and the plate. Place a cranberry or a small piece of persimmon on top of the sponge of the triangle resting on its sponge side. Lean a persimmon star against the cranberry. Serve immediately.

Gingerbread Sponge

one 12-by-22-inch (30-×-55-cm) sponge sheet

4 ounces (115 g) soft unsalted butter
1 ounce (30 g) light brown sugar
8 ounces (225 g) cake flour
1 tablespoon (6 g) ground ginger
½ teaspoon (1 g) ground nutmeg
1 teaspoon (4 g) baking soda
3 eggs, separated, and at room temperature
½ cup (120 ml) warm water
¼ cup (60 ml) or 3 ounces (85 g) molasses
2 ounces (55 g) granulated sugar
bread flour

NOTE: Before using the sponge to assemble the cream slices, the skin on top must be removed at least partially. Failing to do so will result in the filling pulling away from the sponge when the cake is sliced later. Use the edge of a chef's knife to scrape the skin off.

1. Beat the butter and brown sugar together until light and fluffy.

2. Sift together the flour, ginger, nutmeg, and baking soda.

3. Beat the egg yolks for a few seconds just to combine. Slowly mix in the water and molasses.

4. Add the dry ingredients to the butter and brown sugar mixture in two portions, alternating with the egg yolk mixture. Reserve.

5. Whip the egg whites to a thick foam. Gradually add the granulated sugar and continue to whip to stiff peaks. Slowly mix the reserved batter into the whipped egg whites.

6. Spread the batter out evenly to 12 by 22 inches (30 × 55 cm) on a sheet of baking paper. Drag the paper onto a sheet pan (Figure 16–15).

7. Bake immediately at 375°F (190°C) for about 12 minutes or until just baked through.

8. Dust bread flour lightly on top of a sheet of baking paper. As soon as possible after the sponge has come out of the oven, pick it up by the two corners on one long side of the baking paper and invert it onto the floured baking paper. Let cool completely. If the sponge is not to be used within a short time, cover and refrigerate.

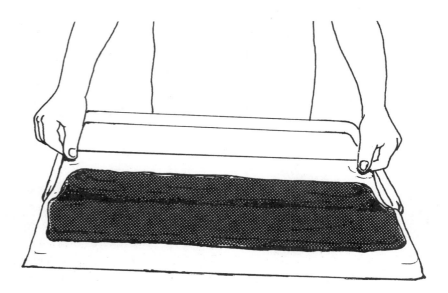

FIGURE 16–15 *Dragging a sheet of baking paper onto a sheet pan after spreading the sponge cake batter over the paper. This technique is used instead of spreading the batter over the paper while it is in place on the pan, to prevent the sides of the pan from getting in the way as the batter is spread out.*

Persimmon Filling

5 cups (1 l, 200 ml)

1 pound, 4 ounces (570 g) perfectly
   ripe persimmons
2 teaspoons (10 ml) lemon juice
1/3 cup (80 ml) orange liqueur
2 tablespoons (18 g) unflavored
   gelatin powder
1/2 cup (120 ml) cold water
1 1/2 cups (360 ml) heavy cream

*I*t is important that you use perfectly ripe persimmons, either Hachiya or Fuyu, *for the pulp. Do not make the filling until you are ready to assemble the dessert. If it sets prematurely, softening the filling will ruin its texture.*

1. Cut the persimmons in half. Scoop out the flesh using a melon-ball cutter or a small spoon, scraping the inside of the skin thoroughly. Discard the skin.

2. Purée the persimmon pulp, strain through a very fine sieve, and measure. You should have approximately 1 1/2 cups (360 ml) of pulp; proceed as long as the quantity is reasonably close. Stir in the lemon juice and orange liqueur. Set aside.

3. Sprinkle the gelatin over the cold water and set aside to soften.

4. Whip the heavy cream to soft peaks. Reserve.

5. Place the gelatin mixture over a bain-marie and heat to dissolve. Do not overheat.

6. Gradually fold the persimmon mixture into the whipped cream. Quickly mix the dissolved gelatin into a small portion of the mixture, then, still working fast, mix this back into the remainder of the filling.

Cookie Christmas Trees

30 tree decorations

one quarter recipe Vanilla Tulip Paste
   (page 1047)
1 teaspoon (2.5 g) cocoa powder
green food coloring
dark coating chocolate, melted

1. Make the Christmas Tree template shown in Figure 16–16. The tree as shown is the correct size to use in this recipe. Trace the drawing and then cut the stencil out of 1/16-inch (3-mm) cardboard.

2. Butter and flour the back of even sheet pans, or better yet use silicone mats if you have them; they do not need to be greased and floured.

FIGURE 16–16 The template used to form Cookie Christmas Trees

NOTE: *If you do not have time to curve the trees, simply remove the sheet pan from the oven and let the trees cool on the pan. Flat trees are not quite as interesting but will do just fine.*

3. Place 2 tablespoons (30 ml) of Tulip Paste in a cup or small bowl and mix in the cocoa powder, stirring until completely smooth. Cover and set aside. Color the remaining paste pale green.

4. Spread the green Tulip Paste onto the silicone mats or prepared pans, spreading it flat and even within the template (see Figures 19–55 and 19–56, pages 1046 and 1047).

5. Place a portion of the cocoa-colored paste in a piping bag and cut a small opening. Pipe a few lines to indicate branches and a tree trunk on each tree without overdoing it; the trees should be mostly green.

6. Bake at 400°F (205°C) for approximately 5 minutes or until the trees begin to turn light brown around the edges. Leave the pan in the oven with the door open. Quickly remove the cookies one at a time and drape them, upside-down, lengthwise, over a rolling pin, so that the trees are slightly curved left to right (not top to bottom) and are concave rather than convex. Once the trees have firmed up, place them in the refrigerator just long enough to make them cold; do not leave them too long or they will become soft.

7. Pipe out one dot of melted chocolate per tree on a sheet of baking paper, making them the size of a quarter coin. Space the dots far enough apart that the trees can stand up in them without touching. Watch closely and as soon as the first dot of chocolate shows signs of setting up, stand a tree straight upright in the center. Repeat with the remainder. Store the trees in an airtight container in a cool, dry area.

Persimmon Pudding

two 2-quart (1-l, 920-ml) puddings; 12 servings each

1 pound (455 g) dark and golden raisins

1½ cups (360 ml) brandy

Butter and Flour Mixture (page 4)

2 pounds, 4 ounces (1 kg, 25 g) ripe Hachiya or Fuyu persimmons (see note)

1 pound, 12 ounces (795 g) granulated sugar

2 tablespoons (30 ml) vegetable oil

1 tablespoon (15 ml) vanilla extract

12 ounces (340 g) bread flour

1 tablespoon (12 g) baking soda

2 teaspoons (10 g) salt

1 teaspoon (2 g) ground cloves

1 teaspoon (2 g) ground nutmeg

10 ounces (285 g) coarsely chopped walnuts

Early settlers in the mid and southeastern portion of what was to become the United States found they were in for quite a culinary experience upon encountering native persimmons for the first time. For as delicious, creamy, and sweet as the perfectly ripe fruit can be (they should be so ripe in fact that they are just about falling apart), taking a bite of an unripe persimmon will surely make you pucker and reach desperately for a glass of water to wash away the unpleasant sour and bitter taste and the peculiar dry feeling the unripe fruit leaves in your mouth. But through trial and error, and from seeing that the Native Americans used persimmons extensively (to make puddings and breads among other things), the settlers were soon supplementing their diets with the bountiful wild persimmons. Wild persimmons have a different flavor and are also much smaller than the Asian variety, usually known as Japanese persimmons, which are found in the markets in the fall.

I first made this recipe approximately fifteen years ago for a lavish banquet where each of the fifty states was represented by their regional specialty; this pudding was the pride of Indiana. If you have never tried persimmons, or you have had a bad experience from eating a raw one that was not ripe, or think you do not like persimmon pudding, my guess is you will be pleasantly surprised by this pudding. Many people have told me that they never liked persimmon pud-

1½ cups (360 ml) milk
Brandied Whipped Cream (recipe
  follows)
ground nutmeg
cranberries
mint sprigs

NOTE: Hachiya persimmons are the type most commonly found in stores. They have a slightly oblong shape and are pointed at the bottom end. The Hachiya are very high in tannin and can be eaten raw only when fully ripe (the fruit should be almost jelly-like throughout). Otherwise the fruits have an unpleasant dry, almost rough taste. The smaller Fuyu persimmon is shaped like a tomato. It has very little tannin and can therefore be eaten raw before it is completely ripe and soft. This persimmon is easy to peel using a vegetable peeler.

The unpleasant dry taste associated with an unripe Hachiya will disappear when the fruit is cooked, so it is acceptable to use unripe fruit in the Persimmon Pudding if necessary. Unripe Hachiyas must first be frozen solid and then thawed to make them soft enough to purée. (After freezing and thawing, the fruit will be as soft as when perfectly ripe, but they will still have the dry taste.) If you are planning far enough in advance, place the fruit in a plastic bag with a ripe apple for a few days; this will speed up the ripening process and eliminate the dry taste.

When either variety is very ripe and soft to the point of falling apart, just remove the stems, purée with the skin on, and then force the purée through a fine strainer. Prepared persimmon purée freezes well. Add 1 tablespoon (15 ml) lemon juice for every 2 cups (480 ml) purée. Since persimmons are not available year-round, it is a good idea to prepare some persimmon pulp to store in the freezer. Pack in freezer containers, cover, and freeze. (If you are using the purée in a recipe that calls for lemon or lime juice leave it out since it is already in the persimmon pulp.)

ding until they tried this one. Still, sometimes people are just too polite for their own good. Up until just a couple of years ago, for about twelve years in a row I celebrated Christmas dinner with two of my closest friends, a German couple who recently retired and moved out of state. Naturally enough, I always brought dessert, which with only a few exceptions was this persimmon pudding. They always had a big group for dinner, everyone seemed to love the dessert, and the holiday table presentation seemed fitting and special. Well, prior to the very last Christmas we shared together before they moved, I inquired as usual as to how many guests were expected and then for some reason, I asked my friend and hostess if she had any particular request for dessert (up to this point I had always decided myself). Imagine my surprise when she almost whispered "I'm sure anything you bring will be lovely, Bo, but, please, not persimmon pudding. Neither one of us is all that crazy about persimmons."

1. Combine the raisins and brandy and set aside to macerate.

2. Cut two rings of baking paper to fit the bottom of two 2-quart (1-l, 920-ml) angel food cake pans, or other tube pans of the same size with a flat bottom. Place the paper in the pans, then brush the entire inside of the pans, including the paper, with Butter and Flour Mixture.

3. Slice the persimmons in half and then use a melon-ball cutter or small spoon to scoop out the flesh, scraping the skin thoroughly. Discard the skin. Purée the pulp, strain, and measure: you should have very close to 3 cups (720 ml). Mix the persimmon purée with the sugar, oil, and vanilla.

4. Sift together the flour, baking soda, salt, cloves, and 1 teaspoon (2 g) ground nutmeg. Mix the dry ingredients into the purée mixture. Stir in the walnuts, milk, and the raisin mixture including all of the brandy. Divide the batter equally between the reserved pans.

5. Bake at 325°F (163°C) for about 1 hour and 15 minutes or until baked through. Let the puddings cool in the pans completely before unmolding. Unmold, remove the baking paper rings, and cut the puddings into twelve slices each.

6. Presentation: Place a slice of Persimmon Pudding, on its side, in the center of a dessert plate. Spoon Brandied Whipped Cream over the narrow end of the slice, letting some fall onto the plate in front of the dessert. Sprinkle nutmeg lightly over the cream. Place three cranberries (in a triangle to look like holly berries) in the cream on the plate. Set a mint sprig next to the berries.

7. Holiday Table Presentation: Place a whole pudding on a serving platter. Heat ⅓ cup (80 ml) of brandy to the scalding point, but do not boil. Pour the brandy into a small flameproof cup and place in the middle of the pudding ring. Turn down the room lights, ignite the hot brandy, and spoon it, flaming, on top of the pudding. Serve Brandied Whipped Cream on the side.

Brandied Whipped Cream

6 cups (1 l, 440 ml)

3 cups (720 ml) heavy cream
2 tablespoons (30 g) granulated sugar
$^1/_3$ cup (80 ml) brandy
1 teaspoon (2 g) grated nutmeg
1 teaspoon (5 ml) vanilla extract

1. Whip the cream and sugar until the mixture is quite thick but still pourable. Stir in the brandy, nutmeg, and vanilla.

2. Cover and reserve in the refrigerator. Adjust the consistency of the sauce at serving time; it should be thick enough so that it will not run on the plate.

Pumpkin Bread Pudding with Dried Cranberries and Maple Whipped Cream

one 11-by-9-inch (27.5-×-22.5-cm) pan or 12 servings

melted unsalted butter
1 pound, 8 ounces to 2 pounds (680 to 910 g) white or egg bread, preferably Brioche
6 ounces (170 g) soft unsalted butter
6 ounces (170 g) granulated sugar
8 eggs
2 teaspoons (3 g) ground cinnamon
2 teaspoons (4 g) ground ginger
1 teaspoon (2 g) ground cloves
1 teaspoon (5 g) salt
1$^1/_2$ cups (360 ml) cooked pumpkin purée (purchased or see page 809)
3 cups (720 ml) half-and-half, scalded
6 ounces (170 g) dried cranberries
1 cup (240 ml) heavy cream
4 ounces (115 g) Streusel Topping (page 14)
one recipe Cranberry Coulis (page 1073)
powdered sugar
Maple Whipped Cream (recipe follows)

NOTE: The mixture may appear broken at this point if the eggs were very cold or if the half-and-half was not warm enough. Do not be concerned; this will not adversely effect the outcome of the dessert in any way.

*A*s discussed elsewhere in this book, the term pudding *covers a wide range of both sweet and savory dishes. Although many of these hail from England, the British by no means have a monopoly on puddings; there are several famous French and American interpretations as well. The old-fashioned steamed or boiled puddings that were made in England and Colonial America were typical of the rustic homespun desserts of that era. Unfortunately, many of these were known to play havoc with one's digestive system due to the abundance of suet or suet made into mincemeat that they contained. The more common of the holiday fare included suet pudding, pumpkin pudding, mincemeat pudding, and, of course, the well-known plum pudding. These did not contain plums but were given this title since raisins were known as plums (spelled ploms) in old English. This pudding also became known as "plum duff" (still without plums, however), and it later evolved into the celebrated flaming Christmas pudding now synonymous with English Christmas celebrations.*

The only thing the following Pumpkin Bread Pudding has in common with any of these ancient steaming cannonballs of suet, raisins, bread, and spices is that it too is made for the holidays (although this recipe is actually equally appropriate for Thanksgiving as well as Christmas). If egg bread is not available, any white bread will do but avoid using a dense or underproofed bread, since the custard may not penetrate all the way through.

1. Brush melted butter over the inside of a baking pan or hotel pan measuring approximately 11 by 9 inches (27.5 × 22.5 cm). The sides of the pan should be at least 2 inches (5 cm) high. Set the pan aside.

2. Trim the crust from the bread and then cut it into $^1/_2$-inch (1.2-cm) thick slices.

3. Beat the softened butter and granulated sugar together. Beat in the eggs.

4. Mix the spices and salt into the pumpkin purée. Stir in the half-and-half. Add this to the butter mixture (see note).

5. Place a single, even layer of bread in the prepared pan. Trim the bread slices as needed so that each piece fits tight against the others and the entire pan is covered. Reserve $^1/_2$ cup (120 ml) of the best-looking dried cranberries to use for the presentation. Sprinkle half of the remaining cranberries over the bread. Slowly pour half of the custard evenly over the bread. Do not pour it all in one spot but instead work your way from one side to the other, back to front, so that all of the bread will absorb the mixture.

6. Add a second layer of bread slices covering the entire pan in the same manner as before. Pour the remaining custard mixture over the bread using the same method as before.

7. Place a sheet of baking paper on top of the pudding. Place a pan on top (just slightly smaller than the baking pan so it will fit against the top of the pudding) and weigh down the top with cans. Let sit at room temperature for 2 hours or, better yet, refrigerate overnight.

8. Remove the weights, pan, and baking paper. Pour the heavy cream evenly over the pudding. Sprinkle the remaining cranberries over the top (still reserving $1/2$ cup [120 ml] to use in serving). Distribute the Streusel Topping evenly over the pudding.

9. Bake covered at 350°F (175°C) for 30 minutes. Uncover and continue baking approximately 30 minutes longer or until the custard is set and the pudding is a pleasant golden brown on top. Let cool to room temperature. Cut into twelve servings. Place a portion of the Cranberry Coulis in a piping bottle, adjusting the consistency first if necessary. Reserve.

10. Presentation: Place a serving of Pumpkin Bread Pudding in the center of a dessert plate. Pipe Cranberry Coulis on the base of the plate around the dessert. Sprinkle some of the reserved dried cranberries in the sauce. Sift powdered sugar lightly over the cranberries and the pudding. Place a dollop of Maple Whipped Cream on top of the pudding.

Maple Whipped Cream

approximately 2 cups (480 ml)

2 tablespoons (30 ml) pure
   maple syrup
$1^{1}/_{4}$ cups (300 ml) heavy cream

This also makes a nice topping for pumpkin pie.

1. Add the syrup to the heavy cream and whip until very soft peaks form.

2. Refrigerate until needed.

Gingerbread Houses

Exactly when the custom of building gingerbread houses at Christmastime began is not clear, but we do know that it started after the Grimm brothers retold the tale of Hansel and Gretel in the nineteenth century. Building and displaying a small gingerbread house is a traditional part of Christmas for many families in Sweden. It can be a project for the whole family; the children not only love to help assemble the house but also to tear it apart after Christmas. A gingerbread house is also a typical part of the seasonal decor in the pastry shop. These are usually large, very elaborate creations that light up at night and are displayed in the shop windows. Smaller simple houses are made for sale such as the Santa's Gingerbread Chalet or a smaller version of the Traditional Gingerbread House. If the houses are made in an assembly-line fashion, they can be very profitable for your business, and they give the shop a feeling of old-fashioned Christmas spirit.

Traditional Gingerbread House

one recipe Gingerbread Cookies
   dough (page 818) (see step one)
red cellophane
two recipes Royal Icing (page 1019)
$^{1}/_{4}$ cup (60 ml) egg whites
one-half recipe Boiled Sugar Basic
   Recipe (page 936)
Marzipan Santa (page 869)
Marzipan Children (page 865)
powdered sugar

NOTE 1: The gingerbread house can be fully assembled using Royal Icing (keep the icing fairly stiff) rather than Boiled Sugar to attach the pieces, but you must do so in stages, supporting the sides at the beginning and letting them set for several hours before adding the roof, chimney, and balcony, which must also be supported until dry. At that point the house must be allowed to dry overnight before decorating. It is much more practical to use sugar, which makes it possible for you to decorate and finish the house immediately after assembling it.

NOTE 2: It is not necessary to have a light inside a smaller house, as it is a purely decorative option, but a house made the size of the larger version specified in the platform instructions should always be equipped with a light. It is not only decorative but it also keeps the house warm and prevents the gingerbread from getting soft and eventually collapsing as it absorbs moisture from the air. The light should therefore be turned on at least once every day for a few hours or longer during the evening and night.

I realize that this thirty-three-step-plus project may appear overwhelming to a novice at gingerbread house construction, but I can assure you that every year dozens of nonprofessional students have constructed this same house during the one-day gingerbread house workshops I conduct each Christmas. After two hours of lecture and demonstration covering assembly and decorating, each student is given the baked pieces for one house, as well as icing, candies, other decorating materials, and a Marzipan Santa. After three hours of fun (and help when needed), each student takes his or her beautiful creation home. If you don't feel you are up to this model without that kind of head start, try Santa's Gingerbread Chalet. It can be finished in about two hours (even without a teacher in the room).

The decorating instructions in this recipe are for making a fairly ornate house (which could be changed and simplified according to your own imagination) measuring approximately 8 inches wide, 10 inches long, and 11 inches high (20 × 25 × 27.5 cm) without counting the chimney. You can enlarge the templates accordingly to make this size, or reduce or enlarge them to any size you like to create a smaller or larger house (if you are making a larger house, see the information following this recipe, page 858). Of course, you must enlarge or reduce all of the templates equally so they will fit together. The roof pieces should always be large enough for a one-inch overhang on all four sides. Smaller houses limit the decorating possibilities quite a bit, which makes them suitable for decorating in an identical layout.

1. Make the Gingerbread Cookies dough, replacing the butter with margarine and increasing the flour by 6 ounces (170 g). Cover and place in the refrigerator overnight.

2. Make a platform base measuring 12 by 16 inches (30 × 40 cm) from two $^{1}/_{4}$-inch (6-mm) sheets of corrugated cardboard glued together. Or make a reusable base from plywood (directions follow the recipe).

3. Enlarge the gingerbread house templates in Figures 16–17 through 16–22 to the size specified in the introduction (or as desired) then trace and copy onto sturdy cardboard (the type used to mat framed artwork is an excellent choice). Cut the templates out using a utility knife.

4. Work the Gingerbread dough smooth with your hands. Roll out a portion at a time to $^{1}/_{4}$ inch (6 mm) thick (or slightly thinner for a small house), using as little flour as possible. Place the pieces on sheet pans lined with baking paper and reserve in the refrigerator.

5. When the dough is firm, place the templates on top and cut out the pieces, using a paring knife or utility knife to cut the widows and door:

• Cut two identical pieces for the front and back except cut one with two windows and the other with one window and a door (Figure 16–17). When you cut out the piece for the door, save it to attach later.

• Cut two identical long pieces for the sides (Figure 16–18).

• Cut out the center support piece (Figure 16–19) if making a large house (see page 858).

• Make a balcony (Figure 16–20) to attach later to the front of the house. Cut two of each piece; the two long pieces will be the front side panel and the floor, and the short pieces will be the sides. Decorate the balcony pieces by pressing horizontal lines into the dough with the back of a knife, then cut small hearts out of the pieces.

• Choose one of the chimney designs (or use one of each as shown in the photograph in the color insert). The one attached to the point of the roof (Figure 16–21) makes a small house look bigger. The other design (Figure 16–22) goes on the slope of the roof. Cut out two sets of either design (four pieces total per chimney). If you would like to make a brick design in the dough for the chimney, do it before you cut the pieces. Roll out a piece of scrap dough left from cutting the sides large enough for all four pieces and $1/8$ inch (3 mm) thick. Use a straight piece of the cardboard used to make the templates, or a ruler with an edge $1/16$ (2 mm) thick, and press parallel lines into the dough every $1/4$ inch (6 mm). Cut a strip of cardboard $1/4$ inch (6 mm) wide and use the end to press lines at a 90° angle to the parallel lines, staggering the rows to simulate bricks. Place the dough in the refrigerator if it has become soft while you were "laying the bricks," then cut out your chimney pieces.

• Make a template that measures 8 inches on each side, 13 inches across the top and $11^{1}/2$ inches across the bottom ($20 \times 32.5 \times 28.7$ cm) if using the other templates at the size specified in the introduction. Increase or decrease the size of the template appropriately if using another size. Make one of the sides straight (at a 90° angle to the top and bottom) and the other side slanted. Use the template to cut out two pieces for the roof; remember to invert the template when you cut the second piece so that the point of the overhang will match up later. Save all of the scrap dough.

• Choose one of the two fence designs: either the ranch-style shown in the drawing on page 787 or the picket fence as seen in the color insert. For the ranch-style fence use scrap pieces and/or reroll scrap dough and cut out fence posts and planks. Make the plank pieces slightly bent and uneven for a rustic look. For the picket fence make two 12-inch (30-cm) and two 18-inch (45-cm) fence sections following the directions in steps six and seven on page 859 in Santa's Chalet.

• Use your imagination to cut the other scrap pieces to create your own personalized house. For example, you can make shutters and windowsills for the windows, and extra fence posts can be turned into a stack of fireplace logs.

• To decorate the roof, roll out a piece of gingerbread dough to $^1/_8$ inch (3 mm) thick and cut out twelve $^1/_2$-inch (1.2-cm) wide strips the length of the roof; you actually only need eight to ten (four or five on each side, depending on the size of the house), but it is always a good idea to make a few extra. Like the ranch-style fence planks, the strips for the roof should be bent so they are slightly uneven and resemble pieces cut from a tree that was not perfectly straight.

• Cut out four pieces to trim the edges of the roof overhang making them 7 inches long and 1 inch wide (17.5 × 2.5 cm). Place them on a sheet pan and use a small heart cutter to cut out hearts along the length of each piece (they are too hard to move to the sheet pan after cutting the hearts). Make two left-sided and two right-sided. (You may want to make extras of these because they can break easily).

• Roll out more dough slightly thinner, $^1/_{16}$ inch (2 mm), and cut out hearts using a 1- and/or $1^3/_4$-inch (2.5–4.5-cm) heart cutter. The amount needed will depend on how you plan to decorate the roof. As an alternative you can omit the roof planks and use the smaller size hearts as shingles covering the whole roof (do not forget to start at the bottom edge of the roof).

• You can either create a tree by tying small pieces of pine to a dowel, and then drilling a hole in the cardboard or plywood (after the platform has been iced) to secure the tree trunk, or you can cut out large and small trees from scrap dough using the templates from either Santa's Gingerbread Chalet (Figure 16–23C, page 862) or the template for the Cookie Christmas Trees (Figure 16–16, page 843), enlarging either of them as desired.

6. Bake the pieces at 375°F (190°C) until they are dark brown and done. Make sure that the larger pieces are baked all the way through, and avoid placing large and small pieces on the same pan so you will not have to move them before they are cool. Set the pieces aside to cool completely.

7. When the gingerbread has cooled, trim the edges of the side and roof pieces so they fit together as well as possible. Treat the edges of the chimney and balcony pieces in the same way. Woodworking files and no. 50 to no. 80 grade sandpaper work well for this, but a serrated paring knife or utility knife can also be used. Be careful as you trim the pieces not to press too hard or they can break. Turn the pieces upside-down.

8. Cut pieces of red cellophane slightly larger than each of the windows. Reserve.

9. Soften 2 cups (480 ml) of Royal Icing by adding the extra $^1/_4$ cup (60 ml) of egg whites. Spread a thin film of icing over the back of the trimmed pieces to protect them from moisture, using the side of a paring knife to force the icing into the pores of the gingerbread. (This is absolutely necessary if you are not using a light inside the house, and still a good idea even if you do. If you are using any gingerbread figures or trees standing out in the "garden," they should be given the same treatment to prevent them from collapsing.) Ice the back of the side house pieces one at a time and immediately press the cellophane squares over the windows while the icing is wet. Once all of the windows are installed, place some of the icing in a piping bag and pipe additional icing at the edge of the cellophane squares. Use your fingertip to smooth that icing out to the icing on the gingerbread so the cellophane pieces are secure. Leave all of the pieces upside-down until they are dry to the touch.

10. Turn the front, side, and back pieces right-side up. Pipe Royal Icing (not the thinned portion) on the pieces making any design you wish around the outline of the door and windows and around the edges, using a piping bag with a small opening. Set aside with the roof pieces.

11. To assemble the chimney, pipe a thin line of Royal Icing next to the edge of the long sides on the two wider chimney pieces. Fit the other two pieces between them, adjusting so the edges line up properly. Set aside to dry.

12. To assemble the balcony, pipe a thin line of Royal Icing at the front top edge of the bottom balcony piece (without hearts) and glue the long front piece to the bottom. Repeat to attach the two short sides. Set the balcony aside to dry with the other pieces for at least 2 hours or, preferably, overnight before continuing.

To assemble the house

13. Draw lines on the platform to show exactly where the house will be attached.

14. Boil the sugar to the hard crack stage, 310°F (155°C).

15. Use a knife to spread a little of the sugar on the edges of one side piece and the front piece. Quickly attach these to the platform and to each other (you can use the help of two extra hands at this point). Attach the remaining side and the back of the house in the same way. Be careful as you complete these steps not to get any boiled sugar on the windows or on the front of the pieces. Place a portion of the Royal Icing in a pastry bag with a no. 3 (6-mm) plain tip. Pipe a string of icing along all four inside seams, "floor to ceiling," for extra support.

16. Test the roof pieces to make certain they fit. If not, trim the edges of the frame on the platform as needed. Carefully, but quickly, spread sugar on the underside of the roof pieces in a 1-inch (2.5-cm) band where the roof will connect with the sides of the house. Attach the pieces one at a time, holding each one until secure.

17. Check that the angle of the chimney will fit with the angle of the roof so the chimney stands straight. Attach the chimney to the roof, using sugar to secure it. Take a good look at the chimney from all sides to be certain it is standing straight.

18. Attach the balcony with boiled sugar. Pipe strings of Royal Icing over the three seams where the balcony meets the house.

19. Adjust the consistency of the remaining Royal Icing if necessary until it is spreadable but not runny.

20. Spread enough icing on the roof to completely cover the gingerbread, including the sides of the chimney if you have not made "bricks." Smooth over and fill in any cracks where the chimney is attached to the roof but do not make the icing completely smooth; it should look a little rustic. (Or you can leave the plain chimney without icing on the sides, and then decorate it with some piped icing later as you would with the brick-style chimney.) Try to make the icing "hang over" the bottom edge of the roof, then make icicles by immediately pulling the icing down randomly across the sides. If the icing falls off in chunks instead, it is too soft. Using a little less will help compensate.

21. Attach the roof planks on each side, pressing them lightly into the icing.

22. Using the Royal Icing in the pastry bag, fasten rows of the gingerbread hearts between the roof planks with small dots of icing.

23. Use your imagination to decorate the platform: Using some baked scrap pieces, make one or two small hills on the platform by gluing the pieces together with Royal Icing. Spread a covering of icing over the hills. Spread a thick covering of icing over the entire platform around the house. Stack your firewood pieces in a pile. Use a palette knife to clear a path through the snow leading up to front door.

24. To build the ranch-style fence, use a melon-ball cutter to scrape away small spots of Royal Icing $1/2$ inch (1.2 cm) away from the edge of the platform and approximately 4 inches (10 cm) apart all around the perimeter of the platform. Do not forget to make an opening for a gate. Dip the bottom of the fence posts in the boiled sugar (warm the sugar first if necessary) and attach them to the platform at the markings made in the icing. Make sure the posts are standing straight. Glue the fence planks to the posts with Royal Icing attaching one at the top of the posts and another halfway down.

25. If you are using the picket fence, use a fine saw or a serrated knife to carefully trim the pieces to the proper length for your design. Place them $1/2$ inch (1.2 cm) away from the edge of the platform, pushing them into the soft icing. Using the icing in the pastry bag, pipe icing to connect the fence pieces at the corners.

26. Apply icing trim by piping from top to bottom at each corner of the house. Pipe icing on the short sides of the roof covering the exposed gingerbread. Attach a heart (or pretzel as shown in the photograph) at the very top of the house on each side. Carefully push the four roof trim pieces with the heart cutouts in place in the icing.

27. Pipe a line of icing along the bottom of the balcony and use the tip of the pastry bag to pull the icing down into icicles as you did on the long sides of the roof.

28. If you are using trees made of pine, drill holes in the platform where you want the trees, making the holes the same size as the dowels, then secure the trees using Royal Icing. Or place gingerbread trees here and there, and maybe a few gingerbread deer among them.

29. Attach the door in an open position. If you have made a marzipan figure to stand in the doorway, put him or her in place first.

30. Pipe around the fence posts to cover any exposed sugar if necessary. Apply snow by piping icing on top of the fence posts and planks (be sure the planks of the ranch-style fence are dry or the weight of the snow will make them fall off), around the top of the chimney, around the top edge of the balcony, on top of the firewood, and on the gingerbread trees. Dot icing here and there on top of the branches of the pine tree if you are using one, and on any other exposed part of the landscape.

31. Fasten some cotton inside the chimney to simulate smoke. Place the Marzipan Santa in the garden and the Marzipan Children on the balcony.

32. Dust the whole house and garden with powdered sugar, blowing at the same time to make some windblown "snow" adhere to the sides of the house.

33. Stand back and enjoy your masterpiece! (If your house is equipped with electricity, plug in the light inside first.) A time-consuming and elaborate house like this one does not have to be thrown away after the holidays, but can be covered with a plastic bag, stored in a dry area, and used again next year (perhaps with some renovation or repair).

Building a plywood platform and connecting a light inside the house

These instructions are for making a platform for a larger house measuring 11 inches wide, 15 inches long, and 15 inches high without the chimney (27.5 × 27.5 × 37.5). If you are making the regular size house from the main recipe but want to make a plywood platform, make it 12 by 16 inches (30 × 40 cm) instead.

1. Cut a rectangle measuring 16 by 24 inches (40 × 60 cm) out of ¹/₂-inch (1.2-cm) plywood. Cut out a square opening approximately 3 by 3 inches (7.5 × 7.5 cm), large enough to insert a small light bulb (and your fingers), should you need to replace the light. To use the space on the platform in the most efficient way, I recommend that you place the house in one corner, with the long sides of the house parallel to the long sides of the platform, and with the front door facing the open, garden area. For the best effect with the light, the opening should be cut so that the bulb is just about in the center of the house once it is assembled. Keep the location of the house in mind when cutting the opening.

2. Cut out four small pieces of plywood from your scraps and glue or nail one under each corner to raise the platform and allow space for the electrical cord.

3. Screw a light bulb holder to the plywood next to the opening and attach a cord that will just reach to one side of the platform. Attach a male plug to the end of the cord. (It is more practical to use a short cord like this attached to the house itself and then combine it with

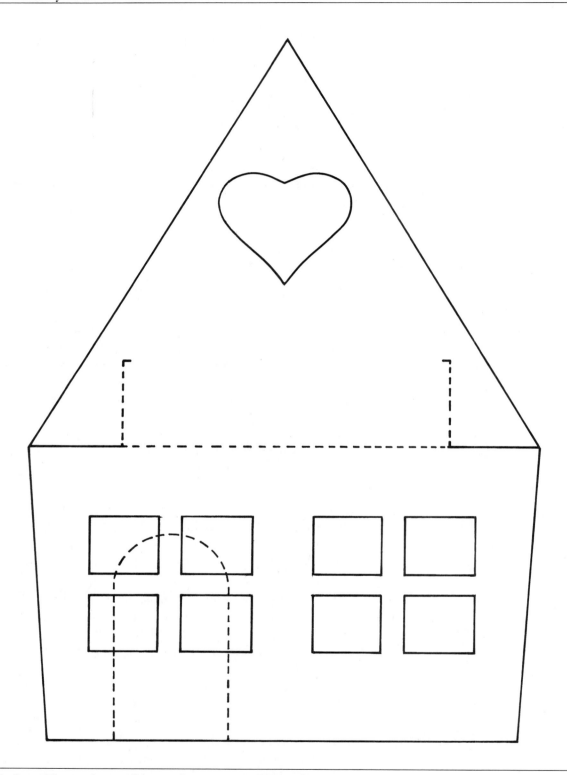

FIGURE 16–17 *The template used as a guide to cut out the front and back of the Gingerbread House; make one piece with two windows and the other with one window and a door (indicated by the curved dotted line). The dotted lines on the second story indicate the placement of the balcony later.*

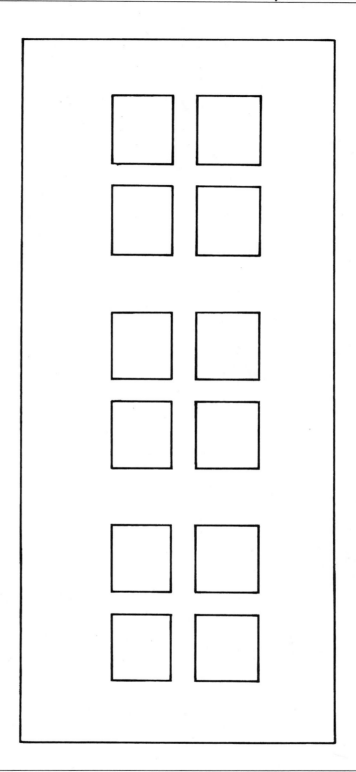

FIGURE 16–18 *The template used as a guide to cut the sides of the Gingerbread House; cut two identical pieces*

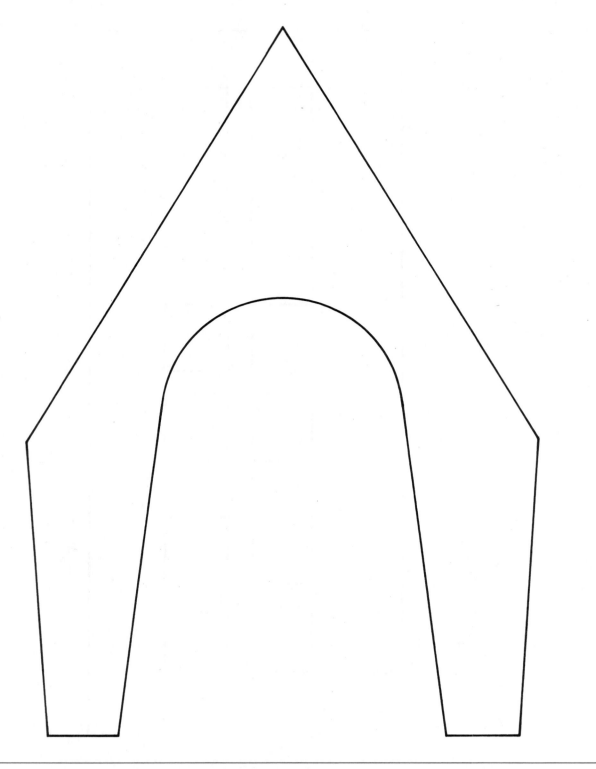

FIGURE 16–19 The template used as a guide in cutting a center support piece for large houses

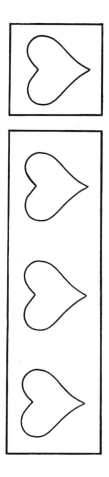

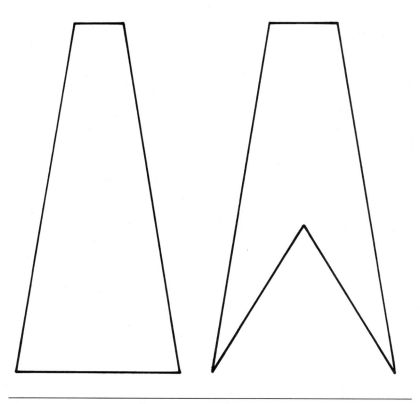

FIGURE 16–21 *The templates used for cutting the chimney pieces for a chimney that attaches to the point of the roof; cut two of each piece*

FIGURE 16–20 *The templates used as a guide when cutting the balcony pieces; cut two of each, cutting hearts out of only one of the longer pieces*

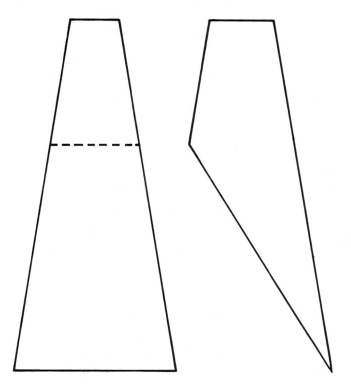

FIGURE 16–22 *The templates used for cutting the chimney pieces for a chimney that attaches to the slope of the roof; cut two of each piece, making one of the pieces shown on the left side of the drawing only as large as the top part of the drawing above the dotted line*

whatever length extension cord is necessary so you will not have a long cord in your way, and you can use the same platform many times in different locations by changing only the extension cord.)

4. Draw lines on the platform exactly where you want to attach the house (remember that, ideally, the light attachment should be in the center). Screw a 15–25-watt bulb into the holder; plug it in, and test to make sure it works before you build the house. Place a piece of foil over the bulb while you are working.

Special instructions for larger houses

If you are making a larger house, such as the dimensions given in the platform instructions, cut out a piece to make a center supporting wall (to fit across the width of the house) when you cut the other gingerbread pieces (Figure 16–19, page 856). For this size house you will need two recipes of Gingerbread Cookies dough and three recipes of Royal Icing. Increase the size of the fence, trees, and other decorations appropriately.

Santa's Gingerbread Chalet

1 ounce (30 g) bread flour

1 pound, 2 ounces (510 g) or one-quarter recipe Gingerbread Cookies dough (page 818)

one-half recipe Royal Icing (page 1019)

1 teaspoon (5 ml) egg white

one-quarter recipe Boiled Sugar Basic Recipe (page 936)

one Marzipan Santa's head (see note 1)

melted coating chocolate

gingerbread deer (optional)

powdered sugar

NOTE 1: To make the Marzipan Santa's head you will need:

  • *one ¹/₂-ounce (15-g) piece of untinted Marzipan for the head and beard*
  • *one ¹/₄-ounce (7-g) piece of light pink Marzipan for the face*
  • *one ¹/₃-ounce (10-g) piece of red Marzipan for the hat*

*O*ut of all of the numerous holiday pastries and other goodies, gingerbread, and especially gingerbread figures, are probably the most loved. They are certainly one of the sweets most closely associated with the holiday season—a gingerbread man or woman immediately makes you think of Christmas—and a large part of their popularity hinges on the fact that they are inexpensive, easy to make, and something the whole family can get involved in, from Grandma on down to the little ones. Even if you are not a great artist, gingerbread figures are pretty hard to ruin; it simply takes a sensitive nose to tell when the dough is done. Next to making gingerbread men and women, gingerbread houses are the most popular.

This cute little chalet was originally made using a thicker Germanic lebkuchen type of gingerbread dough. It also had, as do most houses, four sides. But after a few Scandinavian remodeling touches it became the slightly whimsical (and rather drafty) version that follows. The chalet is perfect if you do not have time to make a larger more traditional house; it will take only a few hours to complete once you have made the dough and cut out the templates. The only time-consuming step here is making Santa's head from Marzipan, and this really should not be left out, since Santa is lending his name to this creation.

1. Work the extra bread flour into the gingerbread dough, continuing to work the dough until it is smooth and then roll it out to a 10-by-18-inch (25-×-45-cm) rectangle approximately ¹/₄ inch (6 mm) thick. Place the dough on an inverted sheet pan lined with baking paper and refrigerate until firm.

2. Trace the chalet templates (Figure 16–23, A, B, C, D, and E, pages 861 and 862) and copy onto sturdy cardboard such as the type used to mat artwork. (If you have a heart-shaped and/or a tree-shaped cookie cutter that is approximately the same size as the templates,

- *egg white*
- *Royal Icing (page 1019)*
- *dark coating chocolate, melted*

Follow the procedure in steps five through sixteen on pages 871 and 872. To create the Santa shown in the chalet in the color insert, use the beard variation described in the introduction on page 870.

NOTE 2: Instead of cutting the base from gingerbread dough, you can use two 9-inch (22.5-cm) corrugated cardboard cake circles glued together. Spread the icing directly on the cardboard and do not forget to ice the edge so the cardboard will not show. You will not need quite as much gingerbread dough, and you can cut all of the thicker pieces from the first roll out of dough.

use these instead.) Cut the templates out of the cardboard using a utility knife.

3. Place a 9-inch (22.5-cm) cardboard cake round on top of the firm gingerbread dough (leaving it in place on the inverted pan) and cut out the base for the chalet (see note 2). Using the tip of a paring knife, cut out two heart-shaped pieces (template A). Using a 2-inch (5-cm) plain round cookie cutter, cut a hole two-thirds of the way from the point of one heart.

4. From the scrap pieces, cut out the chimney (template B) plus six fence posts. Make the fence posts 1³/₄ inches tall by ¹/₄ inch wide (4.5 cm × 6 mm). Also cut out one tree (template C) and one tree support (template D). Leave all the cut pieces in place on the inverted pan.

5. Work the remaining scraps pieces together and roll out to a rectangle just slightly larger than 7 by 8 inches (17.5 × 20 cm); the dough should be the same thickness as before, ¹/₄ inch (6 mm). Cut out two identical pieces for the roof (template E).

6. Combine and roll the scrap pieces again, rolling the dough ¹/₈ inch thick and at least 6 inches in length (3 mm × 15 cm). Cut two strips 6 inches long by ¹/₄ inch wide (15 cm × 6 mm) to be used for the fence planks. Cut deer from the leftover dough if desired. Place all of the pieces cut from the scrap dough on a second sheet pan lined with baking paper.

7. To make the fence, line up the first and last fence post pieces so there is 5 inches (12.5 cm) between them. Arrange the remaining four posts evenly spaced between them. Use a chef's knife or ruler to align the tops of the posts so they are all at the same height. Place the two fence planks horizontally on top of the posts approximately ³/₈ inch (9 mm) from both the top and the bottom so they are ³/₄ inch (2 cm) apart; they will overlap the posts on both sides.

8. Bake all of the pieces at 400°F (205°C) until dark brown, approximately 12 minutes. It may be necessary to remove some of the smaller pieces a little earlier. Let the pieces cool completely.

9. Place the two heart pieces back to back and use a file or no. 50 grade sandpaper to trim the straight sides so that they are even (if not, the roof will not fit flat against them). Trim the side of the chimney that attaches to the roof so that it is flat. Trim the tree support piece to the proper angle so that the tree will stand straight.

10. Combine ¹/₂ cup (120 ml) of the Royal Icing with the egg white. Place some of the mixture in a piping bag and cut a larger-than-normal opening. Holding the bag close to the pieces, pipe flat lines of icing on the back side of the fence, tree, and the deers, if used. Use a small spatula to spread a thin film of icing on the back side of each of the remaining pieces. Leave the iced pieces icing-side up until dry to the touch, about 30 minutes. It is important not to skip this step: The icing will protect the gingerbread from moisture and the subsequent collapse of your chalet.

11. Work the remaining Royal Icing smooth and adjust the consistency with egg white or powdered sugar as needed to make it easily spreadable but not runny. Spread a generous amount of icing in a uneven pattern on top of the circular base. The icing should have small peaks to resemble snow drifts. Hold one of the hearts upside down and stand it 1½ inches (3.7 cm) toward the center, measuring from the edge of the circle farthest away from you, and centered within the width of the circle. Lift it up and move the heart 2 inches (5 cm) straight toward you and then set it down to make a second set of marks. Set the heart aside. Scrape away the icing on the base at the four marks made by the heart, using a melon-ball cutter.

12. Follow the procedure with the recipe and boil the sugar to the hard crack stage (310°F/155°C). Let the sugar cool until it has thickened considerably and can be spread.

13. Spread a little sugar on the rounded edges of the solid heart. Quickly stand the heart at the first set of marks (closest to the edge of the base) with the iced side facing the center. Hold the heart straight for 30 seconds or so until set. Attach the heart with the hole in the same manner at the second set of marks, placing it so that the icing side on this piece faces the other heart. The two hearts must line up perfectly even or the roof will be crooked.

14. Spread a small amount of sugar on the underside (iced) edge of the roof pieces where they attach to the sides. Put them in place and hold a few seconds until secure. Use sugar to attach the chimney to the roof, placing the chimney so that the icing side faces the back of the chalet.

15. Working on one side at a time, spread enough icing on the roof to completely cover the gingerbread. Then, before the icing forms a skin, create icicles by pulling the icing down randomly across the sides and front with a paring knife.

16. Chill the Marzipan Santa's head in the freezer for one minute. Place a small amount of Royal Icing in a piping bag. Place a small amount of melted coating chocolate in a second piping bag. Pipe a dot of chocolate on the bottom of the "door" (the hole in the heart). Immediately position Santa's head on the chocolate and pipe a second dot to attach his hat to the top of the door. Hold until secure. Pipe Royal Icing around the spots where the head is attached, piping the icing so that it shows as little as possible. The icing will hold the head more securely than the chocolate in the event that the chocolate becomes warm.

17. Pipe Royal Icing on the front of the tree to decorate it and use icing to attach the tree support to the back. Reserve the tree.

18. Place Royal Icing in a pastry bag with a no. 2 (4-mm) plain tip. Pipe a string of icing along each side where the roof connects with the sides.

19. Attach the fence to the left side of the base in front of the chalet, pushing it into the icing on the base. Attach the tree to the right side of the base, using a small amount of icing. Put the deer in place if using. Pipe icing on top of the chimney, fence, and tree to simulate a heavy snow fall. Dust powdered sugar over the entire house.

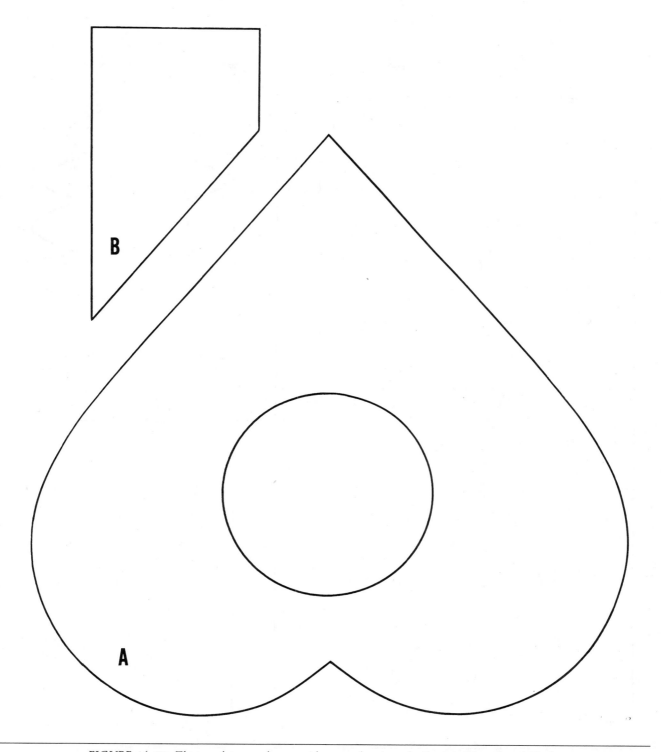

FIGURE 16–23 The templates used as a guide to cut the pieces for Santa's Gingerbread Chalet

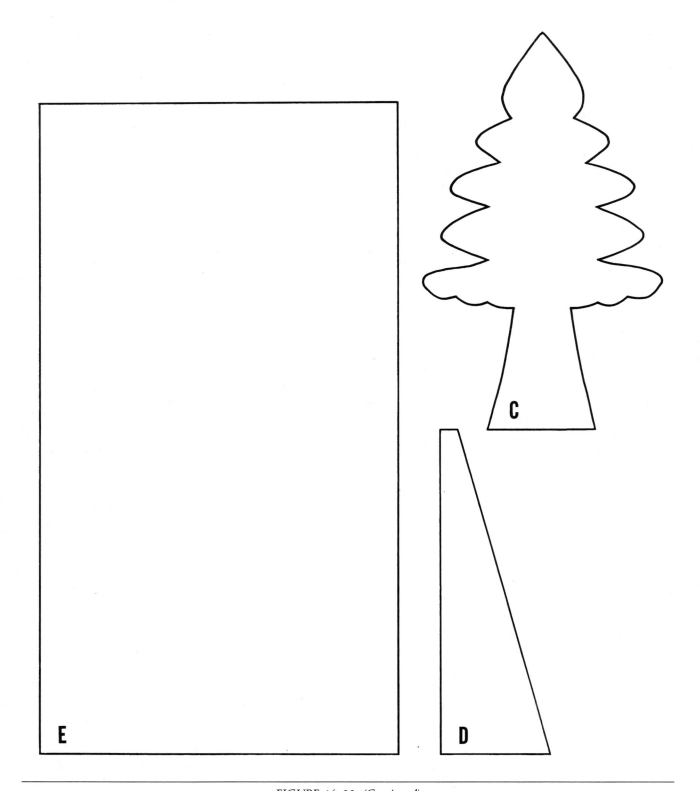

FIGURE 16–23 (Continued)

Marzipan Holiday Decorations

Marzipan Angel

one 3¹/₂-ounce (100-g) figure

4¹/₂ ounces (130 g) Marzipan
(page 1022), untinted
yellow food coloring
powdered sugar
red food coloring
egg white
Royal Icing (page 1019)
dark coating chocolate, melted
one small candle (such as a birthday
cake candle)

NOTE: If you wish to decorate the body with Royal Icing (buttons above the arms or a pattern to mark the skirt), do this while the figure is lying down. If you are planning to keep the figure for any length of time, brush a thin film of hot cocoa butter over the figure before piping.

*B*iblically, angels are said to be messengers of God, belonging to the lowest class in the celestial hierarchy (in culinary jargon this would probably be the equivalent of an apprentice). The label is used to signify something or someone good or good for you, a person with a high standard of morality or virtue, or someone who watches over you, such as a guardian angel. The word angel and its divine association have several references in the food world such as angel hair pasta, angels on horseback, angel food cake, and angel or angelica parfait.

Next to using a mold to press out Marzipan figures (which is becoming increasingly more common every year due to the time it takes to create molded Marzipan by hand), this angel is among the easiest handmade figures to produce. It does require a bit of advance planning since the body, most particularly the wings, must dry overnight after forming before the figure can be stood on end.

1. Refer to Figure 16–24 as a guide in constructing the angel. As always when working with Marzipan, be sure your hands and working area are spotlessly clean. Divide the Marzipan into four pieces: two ¹/₃-ounce (10-g) pieces, one 2¹/₂-ounce (70-g) piece, with 40 g (a bit more than 1 ounce) left.

FIGURE 16–24 The Marzipan shapes used for the Marzipan Angel; the finished angel

2. Color this remaining piece pale yellow. Roll it out a little thinner than $1/8$ inch (3 mm), using powdered sugar to prevent it from sticking.

3. Cut out a heart using a heart-shaped cutter $2^1/2$ inches (6.2 cm) wide. Place the heart on a sheet of cardboard. Make a cut in the wings (heart), starting at the pointed tip and going three-quarters of the way toward the top. Spread the cut apart at the tip so it is open $1/2$ inch (1.2 cm). Set the wings aside.

4. To make the hair you can color a piece of the scraps left from the wings with cocoa powder to a dark brown, or leave it yellow. Roll it out even thinner and cut out a fluted circle using a $1/2$-inch (1.2-cm) cutter. Reserve this piece (which will be the hair) covered. (You will have some yellow Marzipan leftover, since it would be impossible to roll out the exact amount needed to cut the heart; cover and save for another use.)

5. Use a very small amount of red food coloring to color one of the small ($1/3$-ounce/10-g) pieces pale pink (see note on page 865). Pinch off a tiny piece the size of a pinhead and color this piece red to use for the mouth. Reserve. Roll the rest of the piece (the head) into a perfectly round ball. Holding it carefully in one of your palms (so that it will remain perfectly round), mark two small indentations for the eyes using a marzipan tool or other small blunt object.

6. Roll the small red piece for the mouth round between your thumb and index finger of your free hand, and then fasten to the head using egg white to make it stick. Using a pointed marzipan tool or an instant-read thermometer, press in the center of the mouth to make a small round hole; the mouth should look as if the angel is singing.

7. Fasten the reserved round fluted piece (the hair) to the top of the head using egg white. Set the head aside.

8. Take out the large, reserved piece and roll between your hands until it is soft and pliable, then roll it into a ball. Place the ball on the table and roll into a 3-inch (7.5-cm) long cone with a blunt tip at the narrow end. Pick up the cone and firmly tap the wide end against the table a few times to flatten it so the angel will stand upright.

9. Brush some egg white down the center of the reserved wings above the cut. Lay the cone on top of the wings, placing the narrow end level with the top in the center.

10. Roll the final reserved piece of Marzipan into a 4-inch (10-cm) rope that is very tapered at each end. Fasten the rope (arms) to the body with egg white, draping them from the shoulders to the waist. Leave the body laying flat for 24 hours to allow the wings to dry sufficiently.

11. Stand the angel up (cut the bottom flat if necessary) and attach the head to the body with egg white.

12. Pipe dots of Royal Icing in the indentations for the eyes, using a piping bag with a small opening. Place melted chocolate in a second piping bag and pipe two very small dots of chocolate on the icing for pupils. Pipe a very fine line above each eye for eyebrows. Gently place the candle in the arms.

Marzipan Children for the Traditional Gingerbread House

4 partial figures

3¹/₂ ounces (100 g) Marzipan (page 1022), untinted
red food coloring
yellow food coloring
unsweetened cocoa powder
egg white
Royal Icing (page 1019)
dark coating chocolate, melted

NOTE: When coloring such small pieces of Marzipan, it is impossible not to add too much color if you add it directly. Instead put a drop of color on a piece of baking paper or on a saucer and use the very tip of a paring knife to add just a speck of color to the Marzipan.

*A*nyone who works with Marzipan very often probably already has a supply in various colors, in which case the instructions for tinting the small pieces can be ignored. If this is not the case and you still have decided to go through the trouble of making these little children, my recommendation is to tint a base supply making red, yellow, and green with food coloring and brown using cocoa powder, and keep these on hand for future projects, adjusting and mixing the colors as needed. Although red and green can be combined to make brown, cocoa powder gives the Marzipan a nice chocolate flavor so I prefer to use that instead. Any leftover pieces of Marzipan can be stored for a year or more if they are kept tightly wrapped in an airtight container, so it is impractical to go through the process of tinting small pieces for each new venture. However, if I have failed to convince you and you prefer to tint only enough Marzipan for this particular project, use the directions that follow. Be sure to clean your hands thoroughly after tinting and working with the different colors so that small specks of color are not transferred from one piece to another. Refer to the photograph of the gingerbread house in the color insert pages when making the children. If you want to put ears and noses on the faces as shown in the photograph, start with a bit more Marzipan and reserve slightly larger pieces of pink and brown in steps three and five.*

1. As always when working with Marzipan, be sure your hands and work area are spotlessly clean before you start. Weigh out 2 ounces (55 g) of Marzipan and roll this into a 4-inch (10-cm) rope. Cut the rope into four pieces; they do not need to be exactly equal, but they should all be roughly as long as the balcony is high since the heads of the figures will be placed on these for support (if they are much shorter, the head will not be visible; if much taller, the base itself will show). Stand these "bodies" on end and reserve.

2. Roll the remaining Marzipan out to the same length as before and mark the rope into five equal sections. Cut off one section (one-fifth), wrap this piece in plastic, and reserve.

3. Cut the remaining four-fifths in half and tint one piece pale pink. Pinch off a tiny piece of pink the size of a pea and reserve with the first smaller untinted piece (one-fifth of the rope).

4. Divide the remaining pink piece in half and roll both halves into round balls; set aside.

5. Divide the remaining larger untinted piece in half and tint one piece pale yellow and the other light brown. Pinch off a pea-size piece of each, set the small pieces aside, roll the larger pieces into round balls, and place them with the pink balls.

6. Use a marzipan tool or other suitable tool to make indentations in all four heads to mark the eyes. Make four mouths using tiny balls of pink Marzipan (do not use it all) and attach to the faces using a pointed tool to push them in place and at the same time create round, open mouths.

7. Use the reserved piece of yellow to make hair and attach to one of the pink heads using egg white as glue. Divide the reserved brown

Marzipan in half and use half for hair on the remaining pink head and the remainder, tinted slightly darker with cocoa powder, to make hair on the brown head. Attach both using egg white.

8. Make and attach ears and noses if desired (see introduction).

9. Use a small piece of the untinted Marzipan, rolled into a flattened string to create a hood, on the yellow face by wrapping it around the top of the head and securing it with egg white.

10. Pipe a small dot of Royal Icing in the indentations made for the eyes. Pipe a smaller dot of melted chocolate on top to mark the pupils.

11. Place the bodies (step 1) on the gingerbread house balcony, securing them with a little Royal Icing.

12. Roll the remaining untinted Marzipan into four small balls, and place them on top of the bodies, using egg white to glue them and pressing to flatten them slightly.

13. Brush a little egg white on top of the "necks" and carefully set the heads in place.

Marzipan Pig with Two Santas

one 10-pound (4 kg, 550 g) showpiece

Marzipan (page 1022) divided and tinted as follows:

For the Pig

body 9 pounds, 6 ounces (4 kg, 265 g) untinted Marzipan

tongue $1/10$ ounce (3 g) light pink Marzipan

eyebrows $1/6$ ounce (5 g) untinted Marzipan

ears 3 ounces (85 g) untinted Marzipan

tail $2/3$ ounce (20 g) untinted Marzipan

For the Santas

legs two $5/6$-ounce (25-g) pieces green Marzipan

bodies two $5/6$-ounce (25-g) pieces red Marzipan

arms two $2/3$-ounce (20-g) pieces red Marzipan

sack $5/6$ ounce (25 g) brown Marzipan

mittens $1/3$ ounce (10 g) yellow Marzipan

*I*n general, the domestic pig has gotten a bad rap, for contrary to its questionable reputation regarding cleanliness and behavior (and although the Jewish and Islamic religions forbid the consumption of pork on the grounds that the pig is unclean), pigs are actually clean creatures who roll and poke in the mud as protection from heat and to rid themselves of parasites (as, in fact, do many other mammals), and pigs are among the most intelligent of all domestic animals. They are easily trained, and some species are kept as household pets, the most famous being the small Vietnamese potbellied pig. Pigs also have a highly developed sense of smell, making them greatly regarded by the French for sniffing out the renowned and extremely expensive truffles found in the Périgord region. Unfortunately, we humans have a bad habit of using the word pig to describe someone who is greedy, dirty, selfish, chauvinistic, or otherwise undesirable, to say nothing of someone with bad table manners or a generous appetite.

The domesticated pig was introduced to North America by Columbus in 1493, and pig farming has been an important agricultural industry in this country since the late 1800s. Pigs have always been a popular farm animal, one reason certainly being the pig's ability to eat and grow fat from just about any food source, thus converting scraps into meat quickly and efficiently with a minimum of expense for feed. Just about every part of the pig carcass is used and marketed, from the flesh, which is turned into roasts, chops, sausage, bacon, headcheese, and is cured for ham, to the stomach, which is eaten as tripe, and the pig's feet, which are considered a true delicacy in many countries in Europe and elsewhere. The pig's fat is also sold as lard, the hides are tanned to make leather, and the list goes on and on.

As mentioned in the introduction to this chapter, the fact that so many holiday recipes are created from pork (the Christmas ham being the most traditional) is the reason for the celebration of the pig in various decorations and ornaments at this time of the year. This Marzipan Pig, transporting not one but

boots and cuffs ½ ounce (15 g) brown Marzipan

presents and decorations for jackets two ⅓-ounce (10-g) pieces any color scrap Marzipan

For the Santas' Heads

heads and beards two ½-ounce (15-g) pieces untinted Marzipan

faces two ¼-ounce (7-g) pieces light pink Marzipan

hats two ⅓-ounce (10-g) pieces red Marzipan

egg white

hot cocoa butter

Royal Icing (page 1019)

dark coating chocolate, melted

NOTE: Because the Marzipan used for the pig's body is a fairly large piece, it can take some time to work it smooth and soft enough to form. If the Marzipan is very firm, either because of the quality or due to a cold room temperature, you can speed up the softening process by placing it in a microwave oven for five-second intervals. This is preferable to using an electric mixer to soften the Marzipan, as that can cause some of the oil to separate.

two Santas, makes a whimsical showpiece that is sure to delight and bring a festive old world touch to your display. All of the components are edible, but if you do not have the heart to cut into your artistry, wrap it carefully and store it in a cool dry place until next year. The Marzipan will be very hard and no longer fit for consumption, but the pig and Santas can be used again for display with just a few small cosmetic repairs to restore them to their original glory. It will be helpful to refer to the photograph in the color insert when making the pig and the Santas.

1. Make sure your work surface and your hands are impeccably clean. Weigh and color the individual Marzipan pieces for the pig and the two Santas as specified above. Cover the pieces for the Santas and set aside.

To form the pig

2. To form the pig's body, work that piece of Marzipan smooth and soft with your hands (see note). Roll it into a cylinder 15 inches (37.5 cm) long, well rounded on one end and tapered on the other. Bend the body to make it slightly curved. Flatten the tapered end by pressing against the Marzipan with the blade of a chef's knife, moving the knife straight up at the same time until you have a 1½-inch (3.7-cm) slightly oval flat area in the front for the pig's snout.

3. Make a cut on the inside curve at a 45° angle starting at about the center of the pig. Pull this piece out and form the rear leg. Make a second cut at the same angle starting about 3 inches (7.5 cm) from the snout, pull out, and form the front leg. Form and shape the body and legs while the Marzipan is still soft and pliable.

4. Make a small vertical indentation on the front at the base of each leg to form the pig's feet.

5. Carefully bend the front 4 inches (10 cm) of the pig upward. Support the head with a piece of scrap Marzipan until the head stays at the desired angle. Make a small cut in the lower part of the pig's snout for the mouth and open it slightly. Use a pointed tool to make two holes in the front of the snout.

6. Form the pink Marzipan into a small flat tongue (really just the tip) and attach it in the pig's mouth.

7. Use a round Marzipan tool (or other suitable tool) to mark fat folds in the bend behind the snout.

8. Mark the spots for the eyes. Roll the Marzipan reserved for the "eyebrows" into round pieces and attach using a little egg white for glue, pushing the pieces in place with a rounded tool to create a curved crescent above each eye.

9. Roll the ear pieces between your hands one at a time to make them smooth, and then form each one into a 3–3½-inch-long triangular piece that is 2 inches wide across the base (7.5–8.7 × 5 cm). Use egg white to attach the ears to the head placing them 1 inch (2.5 cm) behind the eyebrows. Shape the ears so they first curve backward and then fold over in front. Support the ears with scrap pieces of Marzipan until they hold their shape.

10. Roll the piece reserved for the tail round and smooth between your hands, then roll it into a 4-inch (10-cm) tapered rope. Use a marzipan tool or the back of a chef's knife to mark a vertical line at the back of the pig where the rear leg meets the body. Attach the tail at the top in a curled shape, using egg white. Let the Marzipan harden sufficiently for the ears and head to support themselves.

Making the Santas

11. Roll the green Marzipan for the legs, one piece at a time, until smooth, and then roll it round between the palms of your hands. Place on the table and roll into a 5-inch (12.5-cm) rope, slightly tapered at the ends. Bend the piece in half to make two legs. Place the legs straddling the pig's back, attaching them with egg white, and arranging them slightly behind the pig's ears so that the feet end up right next to the eyes. Form the second pair of legs in the same way and attach these sitting on top of the pig at the back by the rear leg, with both legs hanging over the "front" side of the pig (the side of the pig with legs).

12. Roll one of the red body pieces to make it smooth and round. Place the ball between the lower part of your palms and shape it into a slightly pear-shaped oval 1½ inches (3.7 cm) tall. Use your thumb to make a smooth indentation in the center at the top of the front pair of legs, and then attach the oval body on top using egg white, placing the wider end on the legs. Repeat to form and attach the body on the back Santa.

13. Roll one of the red Marzipan pieces reserved for the arms out in the same way as for the legs, making this piece 4 inches (10 cm) long. Make a cut ½ inch (1.2 cm) deep across the top of the body of the front Santa, cutting from shoulder to shoulder. Open the edges of the cut, flatten the Marzipan in the center of the arms, and push the arms in the opening, attaching with egg white. Use your forefinger and thumb to press the edges of the cut together at the same forming a flat surface, sharply angled down toward the front of the body, on which to place the head. Form and attach the arms on the back Santa in the same way.

14. Roll the brown Marzipan for the sack, shaping it into an oval as for the bodies. Open the top (narrow end) of the sack by carefully pushing a rounded marzipan tool into the top, rotating it gently (or use another small rounded object). Make a window pane design on the sides of the sack using a marzipan tool or the back of a knife. Attach the sack with egg white to the rear Santa's left side.

15. Cut the yellow Marzipan for the mittens into four equal pieces. One at a time roll the pieces into ¾-inch (2-cm) cones. Bend the pointed third of the cone against the remainder to form a thumb. Bend the mitten into a slightly curved position (as if starting to close the hand), taking into account which side the thumb should be on. Repeat with the remaining three pieces so you have two left and two right hands. Attach all four mittens to the ends of the arms using egg white, placing the front Santa's mittens so he is holding on to the ears of the pig and the rear Santa is holding on to his sack.

16. Divide the brown Marzipan for the boots into six equal pieces. Roll four of the pieces into balls and press a "boot" onto the bottom of each leg using a little egg white to secure. Divide the two remaining brown pieces in half to form four small pieces. Roll these one at a time between your fingers into very thin ropes and then flatten. Wrap one piece around the end of each Santa's arm above the mitten to hide the seam where the arm and mitten meet. Attach with egg white, trimming any excess, and decorate the cuffs with a pointed marzipan tool.

17. Use the two scrap Marzipan pieces to decorate the Santas' jackets as shown in the photograph and to form two or three presents for the sack. Secure these pieces with egg white.

18. Using the Marzipan specified for the heads, follow the instructions on pages 871 and 872, steps five through fourteen, to form the two heads. Attach the heads to the bodies, using just enough egg white to make the surface sticky; too much will cause the heads to slide off.

19. To protect the Marzipan, carefully apply hot melted cocoa butter to the Santas and the pig using a brush or spray bottle.

20. Place a small amount of Royal Icing in a piping bag and cut a very small opening. Pipe eyes on the Santas and the pig.

21. Place a small amount of melted chocolate in a piping bag and cut a very small opening. Pipe the pupils on the eyes of the Santas (and above each eye for an eyebrow) and on the pig (the pig and the front Santa can look at one another) and also pipe a thin line of chocolate on the top of the pig's "eyebrows" and in the indentations made on the pig's feet.

Marzipan Santa for the Traditional Gingerbread House

one 3¹/₂-ounce (100-g) figure

3¹/₂ ounces (100 g) Marzipan (page 1022), untinted
green food coloring
red food coloring
cornstarch
egg white
melted cocoa butter (optional)
Royal Icing (page 1019)
dark coating chocolate, melted

Many hundreds of years ago (mid-fifth century) in what is now Turkey, a Christian bishop named Saint Nicholas became famous for his great compassion and generosity. One story tells how he saved the daughters of a poor family from a life of prostitution by tossing bags of gold coins through their window, thus providing dowries that allowed them to find honorable marriages. This story was the origin for the custom of giving gifts on the saint's traditional feast day, December sixth. The legend of Saint Nicholas became so loved by Christians that his popularity eventually spread all over the globe, and he was honored in hundreds of churches. The Dutch name for Saint Nicholas was Sinter Klass, and it was the Dutch settlers in New Amsterdam who introduced his story to America, where Sinter Klass eventually became the legendary American figure Santa Claus, associated with the celebration of Christmas.

Many of Santa's distinctive characteristics, such as his trek down the chimney and his red suit trimmed in fur, are of Dutch origin; the suit derives from the Bishop's cape worn by Saint Nicholas. The stories regarding Santa's fleet of reindeer and his home at the icy North Pole, however, come from Scandinavia. Much of the modern concept of Santa, which depicts him as a laughing, jolly, rotund, bearded fellow (sometimes smoking a pipe), was popularized in the late

NOTE: *If the Santa is to be kept for a period of time, brush a thin film of hot melted butter over the surface of the Marzipan before dipping it in chocolate and applying the Royal Icing and piped chocolate. In addition to protecting the Marzipan from drying out, the cocoa butter gives it an attractive satin shine.*

nineteenth century media by cartoonist Thomas Nast, whose work appeared in Harpers Weekly, *and in the 1822 poem written by Clement Moore, "A Visit from Saint Nicholas." Santa Claus, Saint Nicholas, or Old St. Nick is known as Father Christmas in England,* Kris Kringle *in Germany,* Grandfather Frost *in Russia,* Père Noël *in France, and* Jultomten *in Sweden.*

This standing Santa is certainly the most complex of the Marzipan figures featured in this text, and although it can be made without any special tools, a set of marzipan modeling tools will make the project much easier. It is not necessary to own the bona fide set imported from Europe. The simple sets of wooden tools intended for sculpture that are sold at art supply stores make a good substitute and are generally available for about one-tenth the cost of a twelve-piece marzipan set.

The following directions are for a fully equipped Santa, but you may simplify without offending him too much, I'm sure. By deleting the sack you can also omit the mittens and the present. Add the 15 g of Marzipan for the sack (without tinting it green) to the weight for the body instead. For a different look (which is shown in the color photograph of Santa's Chalet), form the beard by rolling a small piece of Marzipan to ¹/₈ inch (3 mm) thick and then use a ruffled rolling pin, a marzipan tool, or the back of a knife to press vertical lines on top. Cut out a round using a 1¹/₄-inch (3.1-cm) fluted cutter. Cut away about one-quarter of the top using just the bottom half of a ³/₄-inch (2-cm) fluted cutter, creating a crescent-shaped beard with a scalloped edge. Attach the beard to the head just under the face (before adding the mustache), using egg white to secure.

1. Before you begin to work, make absolutely certain that your hands and your work area are both perfectly clean. Refer to Figure 16–25 in forming the Santa. Divide the Marzipan as follows:

- 50 g for the body
- 10 g for the head
- 15 g for the sack; color this piece green
- color the remainder (25 g) red. Divide into one 10-g piece for the boots and mittens and one 15-g piece for the cape.

To make the body

2. Cover and reserve all of the pieces other than the cape piece. Roll this piece out, using cornstarch to prevent it from sticking, to a circular shape ¹/₁₆ inch (2 mm) thick. Use a plain round cookie cutter approximately 2⁵/₈ inches (6.5 cm) in diameter to cut out the cape. Cover and reserve the cape and the scrap pieces separately. The scrap pieces are used to make the hat and to tint the face.

3. Roll the large piece of untinted Marzipan for the body between your palms for a few seconds to make it soft and pliable. Roll it into a smooth round ball, and then position the ball between the lower part of your palms and roll the lower half of the ball into a thick rope (Figure 16–26) to form the rounded stomach and upper torso of the Santa; the piece should be 2¹/₂ inches (6.2 cm) long overall. Lay the body down and flatten the side that is against the table slightly. Cut off a

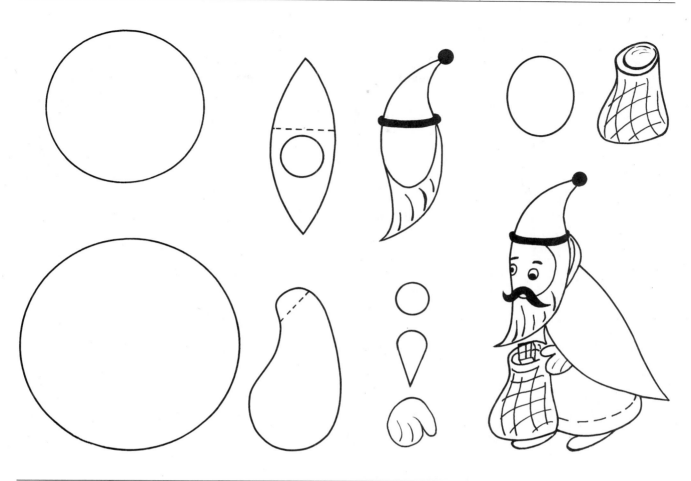

FIGURE 16–25 The Marzipan shapes used for the Marzipan Santa; the assembled Santa

small piece at the narrow end cutting at a 45° angle to create a flat, slanted surface for the neck. Reserve the body piece but do not cover it.

To make the head

4. Add just enough of the red scrap piece left from the cape to the untinted piece cut off the neck to color this piece pale pink. Work the pieces together well and reserve for the face.

5. Roll the untinted Marzipan for the head smooth and then into a round ball. Position your hands as you did to form the body and roll the ball between the lower part of your palms so it is 1 inch (2.5 cm) long and tapered at each end. Using a round marzipan tool or, if you do not have one, the back of a $1/2$-inch (1.2-cm) or smaller melon-ball cutter, press a shallow hole, about the diameter of a dime, in the center (Figure 16–27).

6. Cover and set aside two tiny pieces of pink Marzipan about the size of peppercorns to be used for the ears and one piece slightly smaller to use for a nose. Roll the remainder into a smooth, round ball.

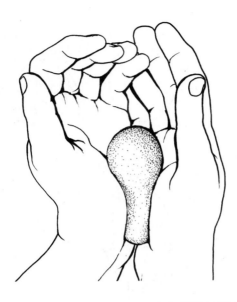

FIGURE 16–26 Forming the body for the Marzipan Santa

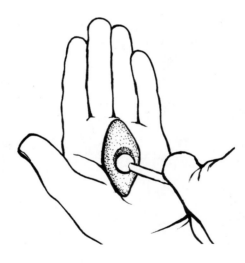

FIGURE 16–27 Using a round marzipan tool to press a shallow indentation in the marzipan for the Santa's face

Apply a little egg white in the indentation in the head and attach the round piece for the face.

7. Position the head piece between your palms as before, and finish shaping the head by rolling it to 1½ inches (3.7 cm) in length, and pointed at both ends (Figure 16–28).

8. Use a marzipan modeling tool, or any tool with a smooth round end about ¼ inch (6 mm) in diameter, to mark two indentations for the eyes.

9. Lightly flatten the untinted Marzipan on one side of the face using a spade-shaped tool, and then make vertical indentations using the same tool to create the beard. If you do not have a spade-shaped marzipan tool, a paring knife is a good substitute; use the back of the knife to make the vertical marks. Cut off the pointed portion of untinted Marzipan on the other end of the head. Cover and reserve this piece.

10. Roll the remaining scraps of red Marzipan smooth and round and then tapered as you did with the head, but only taper one end to form the hat. Cut a small slice off the wide end to make it flat. Bend the opposite end into a gentle curve. Attach the hat to the top of the head using egg white to secure (Figure 16–29).

11. Roll a very small piece of the reserved untinted Marzipan into a 2-inch (5-cm) rope and flatten it. Using egg white to make it stick, wrap the band around the bottom of the hat hiding the seam where the hat meets the head.

12. Roll the tiny reserved ear pieces into round balls between your thumb and forefinger. Attach to the head with egg white. Roll the nose piece round and then flatten it slightly and attach in the same way.

13. Roll a tiny piece of the reserved untinted Marzipan (about the same size used for the ears) between your fingers to make it ¾ inch (2 cm) long and pointed on both ends. Attach as a mustache at the point on the head slightly above where the white beard begins. Bend the edge of the beard so it curves gently toward Santa's face.

14. Roll another untinted piece about the same size into a round ball and attach at the top of the hat.

15. Place a small amount of Royal Icing in a piping bag and cut a small opening (see note). Pipe icing into the indentations made for the eyes.

16. Place melted coating chocolate in a piping bag and cut a very small opening. Pipe small dots of chocolate on top of the Royal Icing to mark the pupils in the eyes. Pipe a tiny line of chocolate above each eye for an eyebrow. Set the head aside.

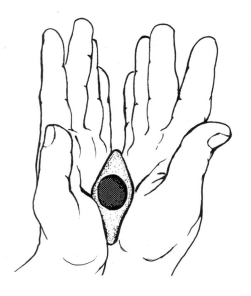

FIGURE 16–28 Tapering the ends of the Marzipan piece, using the lower part of the palms of the hands

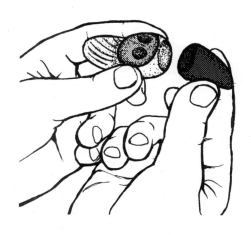

FIGURE 16–29 Attaching the hat to the top of the Santa's head

To finish the body

17. Divide the 10-g piece of red Marzipan for the boots and mittens into four equal pieces. Roll two of the pieces between your palms to make round balls and then make these slightly oval. Press to flatten one-half of each piece across the width. Stand Santa's body up and place on these two pieces so that the rounded edge of the pieces protrude in front of the body as boots (it is not necessary to use egg white here). Press the body forward so it stands securely; at the same time the boot pieces will flatten against the table.

18. Make the mittens by rolling the two other pieces into round balls as before, and then taper one end on each to make 1-inch (2.5-cm) cones. Bend one-third of the narrow end around against the wider end to make the thumb portion of the mitten. (Bend the thumb on one mitten to the left and the other to the right so you have both a left and a right hand for the Santa.) Bend the mittens slightly as if the hands are grabbing onto something. Reserve.

19. Roll the green Marzipan for the sack into a smooth, round ball and then taper one end (as in Figure 16–26 for the body) to make a 1¼-inch (3.1-cm) sack. Use the same round tool used to create the indentation for the face to make an "opening" in the top of the sack. Press vertical and horizontal lines into the sides of the sack using the same tool used to make the beard. Reserve.

To assemble the Santa

20. Use your finger to spread just enough egg white on the cut part of the Santa on top of the body to make the surface sticky (too much will cause the head to slide off). Carefully, using light pressure, attach the head. Spread a little egg white on the back side of the round cape piece and drape around the "shoulders," forming a collar and at the same time forming a support for the head. Using a little egg white and the round tool used to make the indentation in the top, press the sack into place under the beard. Attach one mitten so it is protruding from under the coat and the other holding onto the sack, using a little egg white and a light touch; a marzipan tool will be of help here.

21. Use some scraps to create a small rectangular package and attach on the sack opening. Pipe thin lines of Royal Icing on the package for the strings.

17

Chocolate Decorations and Chocolate Candies

Many describe chocolate as the world's most perfect food, some even consider it to have mystical properties, and with the exception of Asia, it is probably the best-loved flavor worldwide. Certainly no one can argue that life would be very different for anyone in our profession without this most wondrous ingredient. The transformation of the bitter cocoa bean into a delicious piece of smooth creamy chocolate candy, or an elegant chocolate dessert, is not only a lengthy and complex process, the evolution of the production technique itself covers hundreds of years and much of the globe.

History; Chocolate as a Beverage

Chocolate is derived from the fruit of the cocoa tree, which the Swedish botanist Carolus Linnaeus designated *Theobroma* (Greek for "food of the gods") *Cacao* in 1728. But long before that time, chocolate was a enjoyed as a beverage by ancient civilizations including the Mayas, Aztecs, and Toltecs. The cocoa tree originated in South America and was brought north to Mexico by the Mayas prior to the seventh century A.D. The Aztecs, too, subscribed to the theory that chocolate was heaven-sent, believing it to be a gift from their god *Quetzalcóatl*.

The word *chocolate* comes by way of the Spanish from the Aztec Indian word *xocolatl,* meaning "bitter water" or "cocoa water," referring to the beverage made by the Aztecs using ground cocoa beans. The Aztecs, who placed such a high value on cocoa beans that they were used as a form of currency, flavored their chocolate drink with spices (even chilies) but did not add any sweetener (I'm sure any of us who have tasted unsweetened baking chocolate can relate to the "bitter" designation). Columbus brought cocoa beans to Spain following his fourth and final voyage (1502–1504), but it is the explorer Hernán Cortés who is given credit for popularizing and making the importance of cocoa understood, by introducing the drink known as "chocolate" to Spain after returning from his Mexican expedition in 1519. Cortés first tasted chocolate at a ceremony with the Aztec emperor Montezuma. One of Cortés' lieutenants, Bernal Díaz del Castillo, in writing about their journey said that Montezuma believed the chocolate to have powers as an aphrodisiac and though "he ate very little," Montezuma would drink from more than fifty golden cups a day that were "filled with foaming chocolate."

The Spanish added sugar to the beverage, resulting in something vaguely similar to today's hot chocolate (although it was prepared with water rather then milk), and the popularity of the drink spread from Spain through Europe and then to England. Chocolate became a fashionable drink, and chocolate houses, like coffeehouses, became important social meeting places in the seventeenth and eighteenth centuries. The Dutch sent cocoa beans to New Amsterdam and by the early 1700s the chocolate beverage was being offered by pharmacists in Boston who touted it as the latest cure-all. America's oldest chocolate company was founded in 1765 by Dr. James Baker.

Chocolate Candy

At that time there was still no "hard" form of chocolate comparable to the candy we know today. That development did not occur until 1828 when the Dutchman Conrad J. Van Houten, whose family had a chocolate business in Amsterdam, produced chocolate powder with the invention of a screw press that removed the majority of the cocoa butter from the finely ground cocoa beans. His intention was to use the chocolate powder to make the chocolate drink less rich and oily. However, the extracted pure cocoa butter proved to be the key ingredient that led to hardened eating chocolate: By adding extra cocoa butter to the chocolate powder, a paste was developed that was smoother, more malleable, and more easily combined with sugar. Though it was still a far less refined product than we are familiar with, this forerunner of modern chocolate candy caught on in a big way. (Cocoa butter, because it melts at a temperature just under body temperature, is the ingredient that gives chocolate candy its melt-in-mouth consistency.)

Dutch-Process Cocoa

In another attempt to improve the chocolate beverage, Van Houten also invented the process known as "Dutching," which means treating either the chocolate nibs (the crushed cocoa beans) or the chocolate liquor (the paste produced during the initial step in chocolate production) with an alkaline solution to raise its pH level. This produces cocoa powder that is darker in color, sometimes reddish, and more mild in taste. The terms "Dutch-process" and "Dutch" cocoa are both used today for unsweetened cocoa powder that has been treated with an alkali, usually potassium carbonate.

Refinements in Candy Production

With the process of making chocolate candy using additional cocoa butter established, two English companies, the Cadbury Company and Fry and Sons, were selling the product by the mid-1800s. The next significant development occurred in 1875 when the Swiss manufacturer Daniel Peter added the newly discovered product condensed milk, producing the first milk chocolate. The person responsible for the invention of condensed milk was none other than Henri Nestlé of Switzerland, who was at that time manufacturing baby foods. (Nestlé Brands to this day is one of the largest producers of food products in the world and was the creater of the first "chocolate chip" made for cookies in 1939.) Closely following the milk chocolate breakthrough, Rodolphe Lindt invented the technique known as conching in 1879. This process, named for the shell-shaped trough which Lindt used to hold the mixture, consists of slowly kneading the chocolate to develop a smooth texture and incorporate still a greater ratio of cocoa butter; conching elevated chocolate standards considerably. The first molded and filled chocolate shells were made by Jules Suchard in 1913.

American Manufacturers

None of these European companies set up shop to mass-produce milk chocolate in the United States, however. That distinction belongs to American-born Milton Snaveley Hershey (1857–1945), who started his candy career just over a century ago in 1894. In 1903, after a few years of attempting to manufacturer several different candies, Hershey made the decision to specialize in chocolate and started a factory in a town known at that time as Derry Church. What began as housing for the Hershey factory employees ultimately became the city of Hershey, Pennsylvania. The Hershey Bar was a phenomenal success, and the Hershey factory eventually became the world's largest chocolate manufacturing plant. The Hershey Resort, which is located at the site of the original factory, draws almost two million visitors per year and includes a twenty-three-acre rose garden, amusement park rides, the

Hotel Hershey (which features a circular dining room because Mr. Hershey is said to have disliked restaurants where "they put you in a corner"), the more informal Hershey Lodge with three restaurants of its own, numerous other fast-food dining options, a sports arena where the Hershey Bears hockey team can be found, the Hershey Theatre featuring Broadway plays and musical performances, and the Milton Hershey School, which, when established in 1909, was originally a home for orphans and is now a home for low-income students. Hershey was the first manufacturer of a powdered "hot chocolate" or "hot cocoa" mix and, of course, invented the ever-popular Hershey's Kiss.

Two other chocolate companies, Ghirardelli and Guittard, were started in California after the gold rush, and both are still major U.S. producers. Italian immigrant Domingo Ghirardelli founded Ghirardelli Chocolate in 1852. The site of the original Ghirardelli chocolate plant in San Francisco is now a popular tourist spot called Ghirardelli Square and features restaurants, art galleries, and specialty shops. The Guittard Chocolate Company is located just south of San Francisco.

Continuing Popularity

During World War II chocolate bars were included in the rations issued to American soldiers, resulting in a shortage of chocolate in the stores back home. The Nestlé company capitalized on this in their marketing efforts, proclaiming that "chocolate is a fighting food, it supplies the greatest amount of nourishment in the smallest possible bulk." Scientist Alexander von Humbolt (1769–1859) had previously expressed an almost identical sentiment when he stated "Nature has nowhere else concentrated such an abundance of the most valuable foods in such a limited space as in the cocoa bean." Although nutritionists today probably would not endorse this assessment, the popularity of chocolate is more widespread than ever, and besides being a pleasure for the palate, chocolate is still a favorite source of quick energy, used by some athletes to prevent fatigue and gain stamina during sporting events.

In the last two decades the public's devotion to chocolate has generated hundreds of books as well as monthly magazines devoted to the subject; it has inspired chefs to try to surpass each other at creating the richest, most-intensely-chocolate, and "decadent" desserts; and there are growing numbers of people who go so far as to say they are "addicted" to chocolate, referring to themselves as "chocoholics" and advertising their devotion on everything from T-shirts to bumper stickers to coffee mugs.

Research has been conducted to study the possibility of medicinal properties in chocolate, which has long had a place in folk medicine, and many people strongly believe in chocolate's mood-lifting ability. There is some scientific basis for this theory: Chocolate is rich in phenylethylamine, a naturally occurring substance that acts similarly to amphetamines. Two American psychiatrists have introduced a hypothesis that people who go on "chocolate-eating binges" as a result of depression are actually trying (perhaps unknowingly) to stabilize their body chemistry by ingesting phenylethylamine. Chocolate also contains caffeine, although a significant amount is not consumed unless one were to eat a large quantity of straight chocolate liquor or unsweetened baking chocolate. Commercial chocolate products contain about 0.1 percent caffeine, and an average serving of chocolate candy contains far less caffeine than a cup of coffee.

The United States consumes the largest share of the world's chocolate production, almost 2.5 billion pounds per year, but ranks tenth in annual chocolate consumption per capita, with a rate of approximately 10 pounds. The Swiss are in first place, eating an average of 21 pounds per person annually, closely followed by England, Germany, and Belgium.

Cultivation

The cocoa or cacao tree is an evergreen that can be found all through the equatorial belt (within 20° north or south) where the average temperature is 80°F (26°C) and humidity is high, in areas including Costa Rica, Guatemala, Nicaragua, Nigeria, Panama, Trinidad, and the Ivory Coast. The trees can grow higher, but in most plantations are kept to about 25 feet tall. Like the citrus family, cocoa trees bear buds, blossoms, and fruit all at the same time. Each tree produces about 30 oblong fruits, or pods, which, unlike other types of fruit, grow directly on the trunk and branches. Each pod is 6–10 inches long, 3–4 inches in diameter, and contains anywhere from 20 to 50 one-inch-long beans imbedded in the fleshy interior. The majority of the world crop of cocoa beans (which averages 1.5 million tons annually) comes from Africa. The largest African producer is Ghana, where the "Forastero" bean is cultivated.

The cocoa fruits are harvested year-round, although the first few months are generally a slower time, with the main harvesting taking place twice per year following the rainy seasons. The seeds, along with the white flesh, or pulp, are scraped out of the pods by hand and placed in heaps covered with banana leaves, or left in boxes with slatted bottoms to allow the liquid to drain. The beans are then left to ferment, a process which is crucial to developing the flavor and takes from as little as a few days to three weeks, depending on the climate. During the fermentation process the pulp breaks down and the temperature rises, biochemical changes take place, the cell walls in the beans are broken down, and some of the bitterness is eliminated.

The fermented beans are spread out on mats and dried in the sun to remove most of the water content. After drying, the beans develop a more pronounced cocoa aroma. At this stage the beans are ready to be packed into jute sacks and shipped.

Production

When the beans arrive at the chocolate factories they are thoroughly cleaned. Generally several types of beans are blended at this point to create the desired flavor and to ensure a consistent finished product. The beans are then roasted at a fairly low temperature (250°F/122°C) to develop a richer flavor and aroma. After cooling, the whole beans are crushed, then the shells or husks are separated, using an air current to blow the lighter husk away; this process is known as winnowing. The husks are used for both fertilizer and animal feed. The roasted, crushed kernels of cocoa bean are called nibs.

The nibs are milled very fine, producing a thick liquid known as cocoa paste, cocoa mass, or chocolate liquor, which contains 53–55 percent cocoa butter (the term *chocolate liquor* has no reference to alcohol and should not be confused with spirits known as chocolate liqueurs). This is the main ingredient for a variety of chocolate products (see Figure 17–1), and all processing after this point is based on additional refining to create the individual products. Part of the cocoa mass is placed under high hydraulic pressure to extract the cocoa butter, a valuable aromatic fat that is an essential part of every chocolate recipe, and the ingredient that gives chocolate a fine texture and attractive glaze. The cocoa cakes that are left after the fat has been removed are crushed, ground into a fine powder, and sifted to produce pure unsweetened cocoa powder.

Cocoa butter, sugar, and milk powder, in the case of milk chocolate, are added to the cocoa mass to make chocolate. The combination is kneaded together in large mixers with S-shaped blades until a smooth homogeneous mixture has developed. This can now be called chocolate, but it is not yet the smooth confection we think of when we use that name.

Refining or Milling

To remove the gritty taste still present at this stage, the chocolate is conveyed to large refiners, heavy machines with rollers 40–60 inches long and 12–16 inches in diameter. The mixture is passed through the rollers, each set of rollers becoming progressively more narrow (like rolling out pasta dough using a manual machine), until the particles are so fine as to be undetectable on the palate.

Conching

The chocolate is now ready for the final refining process called conching. Chemical changes take place during conching that further develop chocolate's characteristic flavor. To conch the chocolate it is placed in machines that knead and roll it on rotary bases continuously for two to three days; the microscopic sugar and fat particles do not become any smaller, but the sharp edges become rounded. During this process the

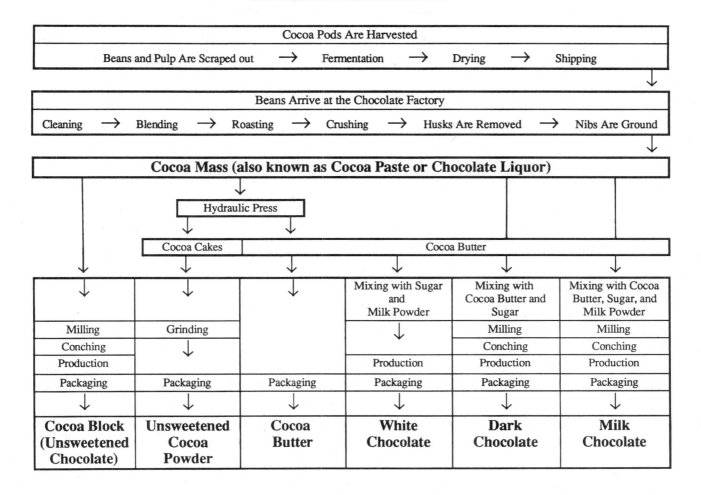

FIGURE 17–1 The process for chocolate production

mixture is typically warmed to between 70 and 160°F (21–71°C), although the temperature can be as high as 200°F (90°C) for some dark chocolate varieties; to evaporate excess moisture, at the same time, the chocolate is exposed to blasts of fresh air. For the highest quality chocolate, additional cocoa butter is added, and if liquid flavorings such as vanilla, or emulsifiers such as lecithin are used, they are added at this time as well. Lecithin (derived from soybeans), besides being less expensive than cocoa butter, brings out the chocolate flavor (which might otherwise be overpowered by excess cocoa butter) and is used to establish the appropriate viscosity necessary for smooth flow in coating and molding. The end result is a velvety-smooth chocolate product. The chocolate is poured and formed into blocks, wrapped, and stored in a cool, well-ventilated room. Dark chocolate will keep this way (if unopened) for up to one year, milk and white chocolates for slightly less time.

Identifying Finished Chocolate

It can be a bit confusing seeing the term *chocolate* or *chocolate coating* on one manufacturer's label and the word *couverture* on another. The French word *couverture,* roughly translated, means "to cover" or "to coat." However, couverture is not the same as coating chocolate; it is simply a term used by some European manufacturers for their product. To further the confusion, chocolate (or couverture as the case may be) is available in several different grades. Generally, the better-quality (more expensive) grades of chocolate are used for candy fillings and for dipping candies, or for any other application where superior taste and texture are critical. Premium grades of chocolate are determined by a higher ratio of cocoa butter and a longer conching time.

Coating Chocolate

True chocolate should not be confused with coating chocolate, a much used chocolate-flavored product also known as chocolate icing or confectionery coating and often nicknamed non-temp chocolate. Coating chocolate does not need to be tempered because the cocoa butter has been replaced with other fats (such as hydrogenated palm kernel oil and lecithin). Coating chocolate is easier to use than the real thing, and, although it falls short of genuine chocolate in both taste and texture, a high-quality coating chocolate can be used for most of the decorating techniques in this chapter (with the exception of modeling chocolate) with a good result. Coating chocolate is not appropriate for candy fillings or use in any recipe where chocolate is used as an ingredient rather than as a glaze or decoration. Candies or other products made entirely with coating chocolate can not legally be sold labeled as chocolate.

White Chocolate

The term *white chocolate* is a misnomer. This product is not a true chocolate as it contains no cocoa paste. Instead, it is a mixture that must contain a minimum of 20 percent cocoa butter and a maximum of 55 percent sugar. The remaining ingredients, other than flavorings and stabilizers, are milk solids and milk fats. The milk solids and fats make white chocolate very sensitive to heat. It is essential to use a low temperature in the bain-marie when melting it, watching closely and stirring frequently to prevent the white chocolate from overheating, which can cause it to thicken and develop a gritty texture.

Rating Finished Chocolate

Taste or flavor is the most subjective element and can be a matter of individual opinion. In judging the chocolate you should look for:

Temper: The temper of the chocolate refers to its structure and is largely based on the crystallization of the cocoa butter particles. The grain structure should be tight and even throughout. The chocolate should break sharply rather than bend or crumble (naturally the chocolate must be at the appropriate temperature to judge this accurately).

Texture: The texture of the chocolate when it is eaten should always be smooth with no gritty or sandy feel. Chocolate should melt readily as soon as it is in your mouth.

Color: The chocolate should have an even color throughout with no greyish streaking.

Aroma: Chocolate can easily pick up foreign odors. It should smell only of chocolate or any added flavorings such as nut paste.

Tempering Chocolate

To achieve the desired high gloss and hard, brittle texture, and to make the chocolate more resistant to warm temperatures, it is necessary to temper it. The cocoa butter is an unstable fat, consisting of different fat groups which have various heating points. The fats that melt at the higher temperature are also the first ones to solidify as the melted chocolate cools. These fats must be distributed all around and coaxed through tempering into a particular crystalline state since they are what gives the chocolate its gloss and solidity (a properly tempered chocolate should break with a crisp snap). One might say that these high-melting-point fats act as a starting point around which the remaining chocolate solidifies.

There are various methods used to temper chocolate by hand. They all consist of three basic steps: melting, cooling, and rewarming. The more commonly used methods are called *tabliering* and *seeding*. Many busy chefs today prefer to speed up the process by cooling the chocolate over ice water, referred to in the following instructions as the *cold water method* (see note 1).

Tabliering

NOTE 1: Under difficult circumstances, the tempering process can be helped by the addition of melted coating chocolate at the beginning of the cooling down process, a ratio of three parts chocolate and one part coating is usually enough.

1. Cut the chocolate into small pieces (a serrated knife works great for this) and place it in a bowl over hot water to melt (see note 2). Stir it constantly to avoid overheating or burning; this is especially important if you are working with milk chocolate, which tends to get lumpy if overheated. Stirring is essential when melting white chocolate, which can become grainy and useless very quickly. To completely melt all of the fats, heat the chocolate to approximately 115–120°F (46–49°C). Ideally, the chocolate should then be held at this temperature for at least 30 minutes before proceeding with the tempering process.

2. Cool (temper) the melted chocolate by removing it from the heat and pouring about two-thirds of it onto a marble slab. Using a metal spatula in combination with a metal scraper, spread the chocolate out and scrape it back together until it cools to just under 80°F

NOTE 2: Make sure that the water is nowhere near boiling to avoid steam. An ideal temperature is 140°F (60°C). Also, the bowl should fit the pan perfectly and not float on the water.

(26°C) and shows signs of thickening (the high-melting-point fats are starting to crystallize). Before the chocolate sets completely, stir it back into the remaining two-thirds of the chocolate, continuing to stir until it forms a homogeneous mass.

3. The chocolate is now too thick to use and must be warmed slowly over hot water to 85–90°F (29–32°C), which is the correct working temperature depending on the type of chocolate and the manufacturer. If the chocolate is still too thick to use for a particular purpose at this temperature, thin it by adding a small amount of cocoa butter. Great care must be taken in this final (third) step. If you should let the chocolate get just a few degrees above the recommended temperature, too much fat will melt and the chocolate will require a longer time to set. It also will not be as attractive since part of the fat will separate and show on the surface in the whitish pattern known as "bloom."

Seeding

NOTE: A variation of this method, appropriate for small batches, is known as the Block Method. Here, one solid piece of chocolate is added to the melted chocolate and stirred until it reaches the working temperature. The unmelted portion of the piece is removed. The chocolate is then ready to use after testing. Adding a solid piece rather than additional grated chocolate, when it only needs to be cooled a little more ensures that there will not be any unmelted pieces (lumps) in the finished chocolate.

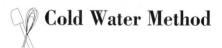

Cold Water Method

1. Cut the chocolate into pieces and melt over a water bath as described in tabliering. Remove it from the heat source and stir in grated chocolate at a ratio of one part grated chocolate to three parts melted, stirring the grated chocolate in gradually and waiting until each addition is completely incorporated before adding the next one.

2. When the chocolate is perfectly smooth and the temperature has dropped to about 80°F (26°C), hold the chocolate at this temperature while stirring for at least 2 minutes, then slowly warm it to 85–90°F (29–32°C) for dark chocolate or 85–86°F (29–30°C) for white or milk chocolate. When using this method it is important that the grated chocolate was itself tempered before setting.

Cooling the chocolate by simply placing the bowl of melted chocolate over ice water is the quickest and most efficient method for tempering. You will find, however, that very few chocolate manufacturers recommend it since the quality of the temper is not as high and water can get in the chocolate. Still, this method comes in handy when you needed tempered chocolate "five minutes ago."

1. Chop the chocolate into pieces and melt over a water bath as directed in tabliering, using an oversize bowl.

2. Place the bowl over ice water and stir from time to time during the first few minutes. When the chocolate begins to set up on the sides and the bottom of the bowl, scrape down the sides and stir constantly until the chocolate is thick and pasty, around 80°F (26°C).

3. Return the bowl to the bain-marie and warm the chocolate to 85–90°F (29–32°C).

Using Pre-Tempered Chocolate

If you have a special thermostatically controlled bain-marie, and you have no need to use the chocolate in a hurry (this process can take up to 12 hours), it is also possible to warm pre-tempered chocolate very slowly and omit the cooling process, provided that the temperature never exceeds 85–90°F (29–32°C) at any time.

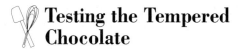

Testing the Tempered Chocolate

Before starting to work with the product, it is always a good idea to check whether the chocolate has been tempered correctly, regardless of the method used. Do this by dipping the corner of a small piece of baking paper into the chocolate (triangles of paper made up for piping bags are ideal, and these are generally on hand in a kitchen where chocolate is used frequently). Fold the dipped part of the paper back onto the clean area and let the chocolate cool at a room temperature of 64–68°F (18–20°C). Within 5 minutes the chocolate should have set enough so that it is not sticky when you pull the folded paper apart and if scraped with a knife it should roll up like a Chocolate Curl. You can expedite the test by placing the paper with chocolate into the refrigerator; the chocolate should break in half with a clean snap after 1 or 2 minutes.

Chocolate Decorations

Chocolate Beetles

16 beetles

5 ounces (140 g) Dark Modeling Chocolate (page 902) (see note 1)
sixteen whole almonds with skin
Piping Chocolate (page 904), melted

NOTE 1: If you do not have Modeling Chocolate on hand and do not have time for it to set up overnight, substitute Marzipan colored and flavored with cocoa powder.

NOTE 2: Unless you are making a large amount of bugs, it is not worth the time it takes to copy multiple rows of the template onto baking paper. To produce one recipe's worth, trace the template from the book onto a small piece of

*A*nimals and insects have long been a source of inspiration and a favorite form of creative expression for bakers and pastry chefs in Europe: Butterflies are made into elegant chocolate and sugar decorations, the well-respected gardner's helper the lady bug and the cute, shy porcupine are both reproduced in cakes, breads, and pastries, and what could be more appropriate on a small child's birthday cake than an edible teddy bear? Holiday seasons are marked by rabbits and chickens at Easter, cats at Halloween, and at Christmas time, the domestic pig is everywhere—in some European countries it is as popular as the famous reindeer. Spring, which is always so highly celebrated after the harsh winters in central and northern Europe, brings this friendly little bug. Known appropriately enough as Mai Käfer (May Beetle) in the German-speaking countries, they are called ollon borre in Sweden and Cockchafer or May Beetle in the United States. Not active during the day, these insects can be seen on warm spring evenings flying between trees. They feed on the leaves of the trees, preferring those of the chestnut and oak. Although not as popular as the lady bug (and not as well known in this country), the Cockchafer beetle has its time of glory in the European pastry shops during the spring where they are consumed in large quantities as a candy or as a decoration on cakes and pastries (certainly a better fate than in real life where they are eaten by large birds). For

baking paper, using a heavy black pen. Place the copy under a sheet of baking paper, setting it at the edge. Pipe one set of legs, slide the drawing underneath to one side, and pipe the next, continuing around the perimeter of the paper.

A more realistic beetle can be produced by placing the legs on top of a thick dowel or other cylindrical object such as a piece of PVC pipe, about 2 inches (5 cm) in diameter, after piping them out so that the legs set up in a "walking" position rather than flat on the paper as if the bug had been stepped on. Cut a few more 2-by-2¹/₂-inch (5-×-6.2-cm) rectangles from baking paper than you need bug legs (remember, bugs break their legs too). Center a rectangle over the template and pipe out the legs. Drape the paper lengthwise over the dowel or pipe. Attach the bodies as soon as the legs begin to set up, or remove and store the legs attached to the papers to assemble later. When you are ready to assemble the beetles, place the legs back over the dowel, pipe a little chocolate on top, and attach the bodies. This is obviously more complicated than the squashed-flat-as-a-bug version, but the effect of the walking bug is adorable.

large-scale production, the beetle legs are available ready-made, which makes it practical to produce and sell the candies competitively. These decorations are shown in the photograph of Chocolate Rum Pudding in the color insert pages.

1. Work the Modeling Chocolate smooth with your hands and then roll it against the table to make a 16-inch (40-cm) rope.

2. Cut the rope into sixteen equal pieces. Leaving the pieces lined up, make a cut through each one to divide it into a ¹/₄-inch (6-mm) piece and a ³/₄-inch (2-cm) piece.

3. One at a time roll each of the larger pieces into a round ball and then into a pointed teardrop shape as shown in Figure 17–2. (The teardrops must be the same length as shown in the drawing to ensure that the assembled bodies will fit properly on top of the legs later.) Set the pieces on a sheet of cardboard lined with baking paper. Using a paring knife, carefully and without deforming the shape, press the wide end of each body vertically to create a flattened spot where you will attach the head later.

4. Roll each of the small pieces of chocolate into a round ball; these will be the heads of the beetles. Place the pieces in front of the pointed bodies but do not attach them yet. Set aside in the refrigerator.

5. Stand the almonds on their narrow sides and use a serrated knife with a back and forth motion to separate each nut into two halves for the wings. Line them up, cut-side down, on a sheet of cardboard, keeping the halves from each nut together. Refrigerate the almond halves.

6. Attach the heads to the bodies by dipping the flat spot on each head (the bottom of the ball where it was sitting on the paper) into Piping Chocolate and quickly pressing it against the flat spot on the body. Set the beetles aside.

7. Place a small amount of Piping Chocolate in a piping bag and cut a larger than normal opening. Pipe out about twenty sets of beetle legs on a sheet of paper using the template (Figure 17–3) as a guide (see note 2). (You only need sixteen, but some are likely to break later.) Before

FIGURE 17–2 The shapes for the beetle heads and bodies

 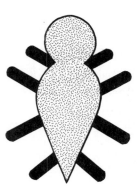

FIGURE 17–3 The template used to pipe out the beetle legs; the Chocolate Beetle head and body positioned over the legs

the chocolate sets up, position the beetles on top of the legs. For the best result this should not be done immediately as the weight of the bodies will displace the chocolate piping. If you wait too long, however, and the legs have set up completely, pipe a thin line of chocolate down the center to make the body adhere.

8. To finish the beetles, pipe a tiny dot of Piping Chocolate on both sides of each body in back of the head, and then attach an almond half to each side, placing them cut-side down with the rounded part of the almond next to the head of the beetle. The cold almonds will set the chocolate quickly, but you will need to hold them in position for a few seconds. Depending on conditions, you may need to keep the beetles in the refrigerator during service. The legs have a tendency to break if the chocolate becomes soft. For longer storage, keep them as you would anything made from chocolate, in a cool, dry place. To remove the beetles from the baking paper, carefully slide a thin knife underneath.

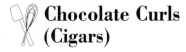

Chocolate Curls (Cigars)

NOTE: Working in a kitchen without temperature control during hot weather, it is just about impossible to produce Chocolate Curls without the use of a marble slab or table. Conversely, when the room temperature is cold, working on marble may be too much of a good thing, and a wooden surface can be preferable. Do not use a wooden cutting board, wooden workbench, or table, or bits of wood will be scraped up into the curls. The wooden surface must be made of hardwood and must be smooth with few or no cuts on it.

*D*o not be discouraged if you are not successful in your first attempts at making Chocolate Curls. They take a bit of practice to master. One thing that is helpful to remember is that the ideal room temperature for chocolate work is approximately 68°F (20°C). The more the temperature varies from this figure, in either direction, the harder it will be to work with the chocolate. Getting the chocolate just the right consistency to curl is the key. If it is too soft it will just smear and stick to the knife instead of curling. If this happens, wait a few seconds until it has set further. If that does not help (if the room and/or the surface is too warm), place a chilled sheet pan on top. If it has set too hard, the chocolate will break when you try to curl it. Use a hair dryer to soften it or, providing you have spread the chocolate thin enough, you can warm it by rubbing your hand over the top as you work your way down the strip.*

Chocolate Curls using coating chocolate

1. Pour a strip of melted coating chocolate on a marble or perfectly smooth hardwood surface (see note). Using a palette knife, spread it as close to the edge as possible, in a strip about $1/16$ inch (2 mm) thick, or as thin as possible without being able to see the surface through the chocolate. Make the strip a bit wider than the length you want the finished curls (Figure 17–4).

2. As soon as the chocolate has set up, make a cut lengthwise next to each edge to even the sides and make the strip as wide as the desired length of the finished curls (Figure 17–5).

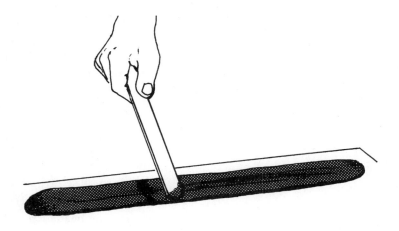

FIGURE 17-4 *Spreading out a thin strip of chocolate for Chocolate Curls, making the strip a bit wider than the desired length of the finished curls*

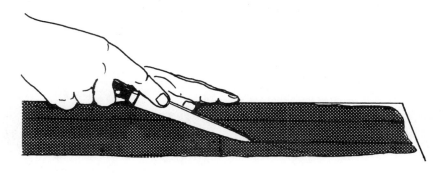

FIGURE 17-5 *Cutting lengthwise next to each edge to make the center section of the chocolate strip as wide as the desired length of the finished curls*

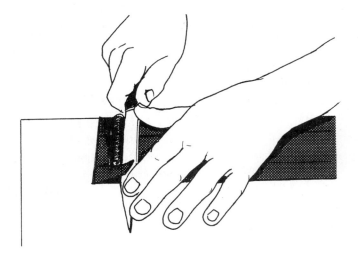

FIGURE 17-6 *Making a Chocolate Curl using a chef's knife*

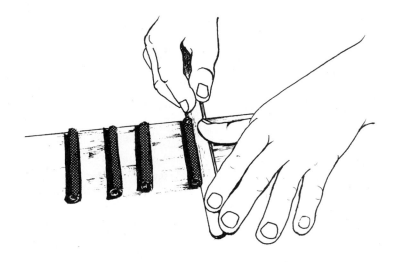

FIGURE 17–7 Making a Chocolate Curl using a palette knife

3. Hold a chef's knife (or palette knife) at a 45° angle to the surface and push the knife away from you to cut off and curl about 1 inch (2.5 cm) of the strip (Figures 17–6 and 17–7).

Chocolate Curls using tempered chocolate

NOTE: If you need Chocolate Curls that are all precisely the same length, use coating chocolate and the method described prior to this one, since you cannot make the lengthwise cuts to even the edges when using a sheet pan.

1. Cut chocolate into small pieces. Melt over a bain-marie and temper using the cold water method described on page 884. Have one or two clean and perfectly even sheet pans ready.

2. Place the sheet pan in the oven for just a few seconds so it is just slightly warmer than body temperature (you should be able to remove the pan comfortably with your bare hands, but it should not feel cool to the touch). Invert the sheet pan.

3. Spread the tempered chocolate out in a strip approximately $1/16$ inch (2 mm) thick, or as thin as possible without being able to see the pan underneath. Let the chocolate set up. To speed up the process you can place the pan in the refrigerator but only for the amount of time it takes for the chocolate to become firm.

4. When the chocolate has set, immediately brace the pan between your body and the back of the table so it is held steady. Push the blade of a knife, dough scraper, or caulking spatula against the chocolate to make the desired shape and size curl. By manipulating the angle and pressure of the blade, together with the length of the strip curled, it is possible to make either loose curls or tight and compact (cigarette-type) curls. Transfer the curls to a sheet pan lined with baking paper, taking care not to leave fingerprints.

Chocolate Cutouts

Squares, rectangles, rounds, hearts, and triangles

This is a quick method for creating decorations that can be made up in advance. The assorted chocolate shapes can be used to decorate the sides of a cake or placed at an angle on top. They are used this way in Swedish Chocolate Cake, Meringue Black Forest Cake, and Gâteau Arabe, to name a few. Finished Chocolate Cutouts can be enhanced with the streaking technique described on page 912, applying the same or a different color chocolate for contrast. Although cutouts are usually made from dark chocolate, they can also be made from Marbleized Chocolate sheets (see page 900) or sheets of two-tone chocolate created using the technique in Chocolate Ribbons (see page 918). Chocolate Cutouts are good to have on hand to use as a finishing touch; they can be placed on top of virtually any dessert to give it a special finesse.

1. Place a sheet of baking paper on the table and pour coating or tempered chocolate on top. Spread it out very thin (1/16 inch/2 mm) and evenly, using a palette knife (Figure 17–8). Make sure the table around the paper is clean so you do not have to worry about spreading the chocolate beyond the paper onto the table.

2. Immediately pick up the paper by two diagonal corners (Figure 17–9) and place it on a cardboard or inverted sheet pan. Allow the chocolate to set partially. Do not refrigerate.

3. Cut squares or rectangles using a sharp knife (Figure 17–10) or a multiple pastry wheel (Figure 17–11). Avoid cutting through the paper. Cut out circles, hearts, or other shapes using an appropriate size and shape cookie cutter. If necessary, heat the cutter by dipping it in hot water; quickly shake off the water and dry the cutter on a towel before using. You can probably cut four or five pieces before reheating the cutter. Chocolate triangles can be cut using the same technique and pattern described in cutting Croissants (see Figure 4–13, page 158) if you

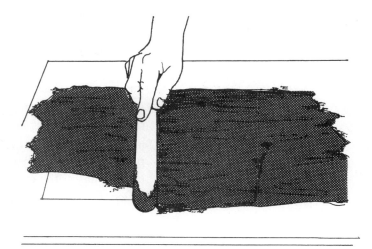

FIGURE 17–8 Spreading a thin coating of melted chocolate over a sheet of baking paper

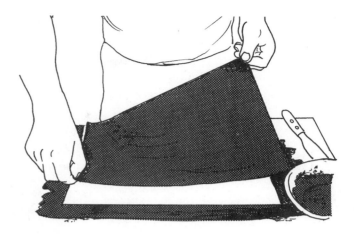

FIGURE 17–9 Lifting the chocolate-covered paper by two diagonal corners

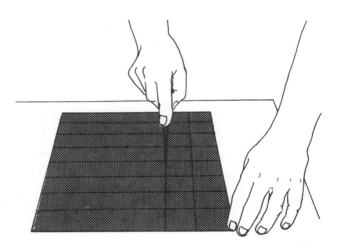

FIGURE 17–10 Cutting square Chocolate Cutouts using a chef's knife

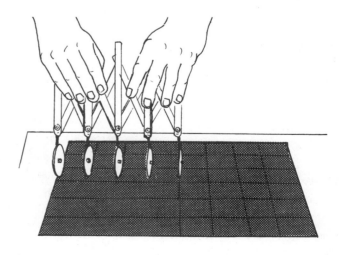

FIGURE 17–11 Cutting squares using a multiple pastry wheel

FIGURE 17–12 *Pressing gently underneath the paper to facilitate removing the hardened Chocolate Cutouts*

are making a full sheet. When only a few triangles are needed (to decorate one Meringue Black Forest Cake, for example), simply cut them out from strips using a knife.

4. Store the Chocolate Cutouts (still attached to the paper) in a dark cool place. Do not store them in the refrigerator. To remove them, place one hand underneath and push up gently to separate the decorations from the paper as you lift them off with your other hand (Figure 17–12). This technique is especially helpful when working with large, extra thin, or unusual shapes.

Chocolate Fans

two full sheet pans or four half-sheets of chocolate, producing a variable yield depending on the size of the fans

10 ounces (285) sweet dark chocolate
6 ounces (170 g) unsweetened
     chocolate

NOTE: *If you prefer, you can also form the fans using a dough scraper or a caulking spatula. Use the same technique described in step six but move the tool counterclockwise, from the 3:00 o'clock position to the 9:00 o'clock position, instead.*

*U*nless *you are a chocolatier by profession, producing perfect and consistent Chocolate Fans, or ruffles as they are also called, requires practice and patience and, for all of us, the right weather. The latter of course is not a concern if you have a temperature-controlled work area (keep it around 68°F/20°C), but if not, try to choose a cool day. Working with chocolate when the temperature gets close to three digits, and/or the humidity is high, is not only time-consuming, it is very frustrating. If you have no choice but to try to produce these decorations under adverse temperature conditions, add 2 tablespoons (30 ml) of vegetable shortening (do not substitute butter or another fat) to every 1 pound (455 g) of chocolate as it is melting. This will make the chocolate a bit more malleable. It is also helpful to keep a few new sheet pans reserved for this use only since once they have been used for baking, they not only become stained and scratched, they are also susceptible to warping. Make the fans using fresh (new) chocolate that has not been previously melted. To create longer ruffles, for covering the top of a cake in four or five concentric rings, for example, use the same technique as described for fans, making the half-circles much longer and wider* *(using a greater area on the pan) to create the size needed. Place directly on the cake, shaping to fit as necessary. Instead of combining sweet and unsweetened chocolates you may substitute 1 pound (455 g) bittersweet chocolate.*

1. Cut the chocolates into small pieces and melt over simmering water, stirring frequently and taking care not to overheat. Have ready two perfectly even, clean, full-size sheet pans (16 by 24 inches/40 × 60 cm) or four half-sheet pans.

2. Place one sheet pan in the oven for a few seconds to warm it: you should still be able to remove the pan comfortably using your bare hands. If it becomes too hot, wait until it has cooled down a bit before starting to spread the chocolate.

3. Place the warm pan inverted on the table. Immediately spread one-half (or one-quarter if using the smaller pans) of the melted chocolate evenly over the back of the pan.

4. Place the pan in the freezer for about 10 minutes, or into the refrigerator for at least 30 minutes, to set the chocolate.

5. Repeat warming the pan(s), spreading and chilling the remaining chocolate.

6. Remove the first pan from the freezer or refrigerator and let it stand at room temperature until the consistency is just right. To determine this, try to curl some chocolate on one edge of the pan: if the chocolate is too hard it will shatter as you try to curl it, if too soft it will cake up on the tool. When the texture is right, brace the sheet pan between your body and the back of the table (or other suitable object) to hold it steady. Hold onto the blade of an offset palette knife next to the handle with your right hand and hold the end of the blade with your left hand (switch this if you are left-handed). Position the blade at a 10° angle to the chocolate and move the blade in a sweeping motion making a half-circle clockwise (from the 9:00 o'clock position to the 3:00 o'clock position) with your right hand, keeping the end of the blade almost still with your left hand (Figure 17–13). The left hand acts

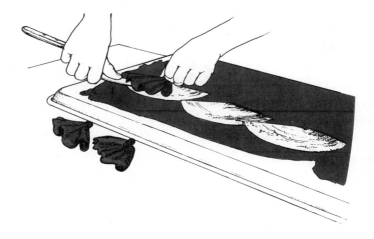

FIGURE 17–13 Making Chocolate Fans

as a pivot as the chocolate is gathered tight at the base of the fan (see note). Work from left to right and top to bottom on the pan.

7. After forming the first fan, check the bottom side: if the chocolate has picked up metal shards from the sheet pan, you are pressing too hard (or your palette knife may have a rough or nicked edge); discard the fan if this should happen. As each fan is formed, transfer it to a sheet pan lined with baking paper. Adjust the angle of the ruffle as needed and/or trim the fans while they are still slightly soft and flexible. Be careful not to leave fingerprints on the chocolate when adjusting or transferring the fans. Continue until the desired number of fans have been made, removing the remaining sheets of chocolate from the refrigerator or freezer one at a time.

8. Store the finished Chocolate Fans in a cool, dry place. If you are unable to do so because of the weather (or if the chocolate is particularly soft), store them in the refrigerator. While this is not generally recommended for chocolate or chocolate decorations, because the change in temperature will cause moisture to collect on the surface once they are removed, in this case it is preferable to losing the fans. And if they are placed on the dessert at the last possible moment before serving, the condensation will not have time to form.

Chocolate Goblets

small balloons (see note)
vegetable oil
tempered bittersweet chocolate or
    melted dark coating chocolate

NOTE: *Different brands of balloons vary considerably in their performance for this project. Experiment until you find a brand or type that will not explode suddenly (sometimes this happens while the balloons are still covered with wet melted chocolate!) and/or stick to the chocolate. In some cases even balloons that are made by the same company but produced in different manufacturing plants perform differently. I found that balloons made in Mexico were preferable to those made in Canada by the same company, so keep trying other products should you have problems with the balloons you are using.*

Dipping inflated balloons into dark or white chocolate to produce tulip-shaped goblets is not that much more difficult than creating the chocolate containers used for Cappuccino Mousse with Sambuca Cream in a Chocolate Coffee Cup (see page 560). The goblets just require a little practice in order to create the rounded sides in an even height all around. However, the striped dark and white goblets, and the multicolored goblets, so beautifully made by professional chocolatiers, are a completely different story. Without the proper equipment it is not possible to duplicate their artistry, combining different shades of chocolate in perfect, precise, transparent patterns that are visible from both sides (in other words, the pattern is not piped on top but rather is part of the chocolate shell itself). Though you can only come so close using the method that follows, it should still leave your guests plenty impressed. When the streaked chocolate pattern goes all the way through the shell so it appears on both sides, it creates the same rich effect as the natural pattern found in granite or marble. The more conventional methods—piping a chocolate design on the inflated balloon, letting it set up and then dipping the balloon in a contrasting color chocolate, or dipping the balloon and then piping the contrasting pattern on the outside—while pretty, both produce a design that is visible on one side only. This will unfortunately be the case when using this technique as well, should you push the balloons too deep into the base chocolate instead of just picking up the lines piped on the surface.

1. Blow up as many balloons as you are making goblets to the size of large oranges, tying knots at the ends. After tying the balloons, wash your hands and then use them to squeeze the rubber of the middle section of the balloons to force air into the round ends to make sure the rubber is evenly stretched. This is necessary because the balloons are not fully inflated, which leaves a small area of thick rubber at the round ends. If not properly stretched, this area will absorb oil and stick to the chocolate.

2. Lightly coat the portion of each balloon that you will be dipping in chocolate with oil, by rubbing it on with the palm of your hand. Avoid using too much oil as this will prevent the chocolate from adhering in a thin even edge at the top and can also ruin the remaining chocolate supply should too much oil become incorporated into the bowl of chocolate. Set the balloons side.

3. Warm or melt the chocolate to the appropriate temperature for the variety you are using. Use the correct size bowl based on the amount of chocolate so there is ample room to move the balloon around inside the bowl, and the melted chocolate is deep enough to allow you to create the desired design.

4. One at a time, push the round end of a balloon into the chocolate, and then tilt it slightly from side to side to create a roundish leaf shape on two opposite sides. Turn the balloon 90° and repeat, so that the base of the balloon is coated with chocolate and there are four even round edges at the top of the coating, creating a scalloped pattern (refer to the photograph of Strawberries Romanoff in the color insert pages). Let the excess chocolate drip back into the bowl. Scrape the bottom of the balloon against the side of the bowl to remove more chocolate, blot the bottom of the balloon on a piece of baking paper, and then set it on a sheet pan lined with baking paper (see Figures 11–5 to 11–7, page 562; in this case the top edge of the chocolate coating will not be straight and level as shown in the illustrations).

5. After dipping as many balloons as desired, place the goblets in the refrigerator for 2 minutes to harden the chocolate.

6. Puncture the balloons with a small wooden skewer at the very top where they are tied closed and set aside for the air to release slowly, instead of having the balloons explode. You can speed up the process by moving the skewer within the hole to widen the opening while carefully holding onto the balloon with your other hand.

7. Wearing latex gloves to prevent leaving fingerprints on the chocolate, pull the deflated balloons out of the goblets. As mentioned, the balloons have a tendency to stick at the very bottom. If you have no choice but to pull the balloon out with a bit of chocolate attached creating a hole, the hole can be repaired provided it is small and does not show on the sides. To repair any holes, place the goblet(s) back on the sheet pan and fill in the holes by piping chocolate inside using a piping bag.

8. Store the goblets covered in a cool, dry location.

To make striped or multicolored goblets

tempered bittersweet chocolate or melted dark coating chocolate

tempered white chocolate or melted white coating chocolate

fat soluble food coloring

Although the principles for making striped or multicolored goblets are the same as for dark goblets, these take a little more experience and a lot more chocolate. Striped and multicolored goblets can be made using either dark or white chocolate as the base, although multicolored goblets usually look best if the base is made of white chocolate or white coating chocolate. Since you will probably have more use for the leftover chocolate if you start with a dark base, however, this may be a more practical alternative.

1. Blow up and oil the balloons as directed for dark chocolate goblets.

To make dark chocolate goblets with white chocolate stripes or white chocolate goblets with dark chocolate stripes

2. Warm or melt both chocolates to the appropriate temperature. Pour a 2-inch (5-cm) layer of the base chocolate (dark or white) in a wide shallow pan such as a hotel pan.

3. Place some of the contrasting color chocolate for the stripes (dark or white) in a piping bag and cut a small opening. Pipe or streak this chocolate over the base chocolate in the pan, creating the desired design. Whatever design you make on the surface of the base chocolate is what will appear on both sides of the goblets.

4. Place a balloon on top of the chocolate in a position that allows you to tilt the balloon in all four directions to complete the goblet without using more of the piped chocolate design than necessary. Do not push the balloon into the chocolate as is done when making the solid color goblets, and avoid dragging it. Instead, gently rock it back and forth clockwise, creating five or six roundish leaves of equal height, skimming the surface only to pick up the piped chocolate lines. If you dip the balloon too deep and pick up the base chocolate underneath the lines, the design will be visible only on the inside of the goblets. Let the excess chocolate drip back into the pan, blot the bottom against a sheet of baking paper, and set the balloon on a sheet pan lined with baking paper. Repeat with additional balloons until all the lines on the surface have been picked up.

5. Skim the surface of the base chocolate to one side in the pan. Pipe more contrasting chocolate lines on the cleaned base chocolate surface, and continue until you have made the desired number of goblets, or until the chocolate in the pan becomes too marbled to use. If you use dark chocolate as the base, the leftover "marbled" chocolate can be used as part of the chocolate in recipes such as Brownies, Decadence Cake, or other chocolate-rich baked goods.

To make multicolored goblets

Proceed as above, using white or dark chocolate as the base layer in the pan and coloring white chocolate with fat soluble coloring to create the desired shade or shades for piping the lines on top.

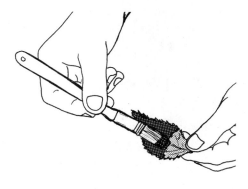

Chocolate Leaves

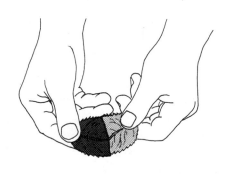

FIGURE 17–14 Brushing melted chocolate over the back of a real leaf to create a Chocolate Leaf

FIGURE 17–15 Peeling the real leaf away from the Chocolate Leaf after the chocolate has hardened

Chocolate Shavings and Small Curled Shavings

Method I

1. Spread tempered chocolate or melted coating chocolate over a sheet of baking paper as described in the directions for Chocolate Cutouts (see page 890).

2. When the chocolate has set partially, use the tip of a small knife to cut out leaves of the appropriate size and shape (short and wide for rose leaves, longer and narrower for a pear leaf).

3. Carefully, without cutting all the way through, score the top to show the veins of the leaf (see Figure 19–49, page 1038). Let set, store, and remove as directed in Chocolate Cutouts.

Method II

1. A more eye-catching (but also more time-consuming) way to make Chocolate Leaves is to paint a thin layer of tempered chocolate or melted coating chocolate on the back of a real leaf (typically a rose leaf) (Figure 17–14).

2. Let the chocolate set, then carefully peel the real leaf away from the chocolate leaf (Figure 17–15). You should be able to use the same leaf three or four times before the chocolate begins to stick.

3. Any type of leaf can be produced in this manner as long as it is thin enough to be bent and peeled from the chocolate leaf without the chocolate breaking. Naturally you want to make sure any leaves you use are nontoxic; citrus trees are safe, and small citrus leaves produce a good result.

Chocolate Shavings are made by holding a small knife at a 90° angle to a piece of chocolate and scraping away from you, letting the shavings fall onto a paper-lined sheet pan (Figure 17–16). Small, elegant 180° curls can be created using a melon-ball cutter with a sharp edge in the same way. Move the melon-ball cutter away from you, in short strokes. As described in some of the other decorations, the chocolate must have the correct consistency to produce a good result: if it is too warm, chocolate will cake up on the tool; if too cold, it will break into small unattractive specks and pieces. Using milk or light chocolate, which by nature is softer than dark chocolate, will make it much easier to create thin shavings or pretty Curled Shavings. Store the shavings or curls covered in a cool dry place to use as needed. Do not store in the refrigerator. You can refrigerate the shavings for just a few minutes right before using them, if it is necessary, to keep them from melting and sticking to your hand (if you are placing them on the side of a cake for example). In most instances, where the shavings are to be sprinkled on top of the dessert, it is best to use a spoon to avoid contact with the heat of your hands.

FIGURE 17–16 *Making Chocolate Shavings by scraping the surface of the chocolate with a small sharp knife*

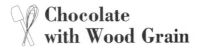

Chocolate with Wood Grain

dark coating chocolate
white coating chocolate
sweet dark chocolate
white chocolate

NOTE 1: Warming the graining tool and the chocolate as you work is only necessary, and should only be done, when using coating chocolate. This chocolate, by nature, sets up much quicker if used at its proper working temperature.

Making this unusual wood-grain design in chocolate takes time to master fully. You will need one or two wood-graining tools. These are small, inexpensive plastic tools that are available at well-stocked hardware or paint stores. They are made for texturing paint on furniture, but they can be used to do the same thing to chocolate as well (a similar tool, made especially for the pastry chef, is also available). It is helpful to work with two tools so you can switch quickly and continue working before the chocolate sets up should one become clogged. You will also need a hair dryer, sheets or strips of acetate or polyurethane, depending on what size decoration you are making (the sheets must be of a thick enough grade of plastic that they will lay flat), a sheet pan or corrugated cardboard, and, of course, the melted chocolate. Chocolate decorated with a wood-grain pattern can be used to form bonbon boxes or other containers, for larger Chocolate Cutouts, and to wrap around the side of a cake. Because the design will not really be distinct on small pieces, this technique is not suited for use in wrapping around a pastry or making small forms using strips.

As with any chocolate work, the room temperature should be close to 68°F (20°C) for the best result. Working in hot or humid weather (unless you have a temperature-controlled work area) makes it much harder and, after a point, impossible, to achieve the desired effect.

1. Cut the chocolates into small pieces and melt separately over hot water, stirring frequently and taking care not to overheat. This is particularly important concerning the white coating, because not only

NOTE 2: To use this method to make Ribbon Sponge Sheets (page 276), replace the acetate sheet with a silicone mat, the dark chocolate with Chocolate Tulip Paste (page 1047), and the white chocolate with Ribbon Sponge Base I or II. For the best effect, spread a very thin layer of tulip paste on top of the silicone pad. (You do not need to use a hair dryer.) Follow steps 4 and 5 on this page, then continue as directed for ribbon sponge sheets, steps 2 through 5.

is it sensitive to overheating (becoming gritty) but if it is too hot it will melt and smudge the pattern created with dark chocolate when it is spread on top.

2. Check that both of your graining tools are clean. Warm them slightly using the hair dryer just before starting.

To make sheets

3. Place the acetate or polyurethane sheet on top of an inverted sheet pan or sheet of corrugated cardboard, positioning it so that a short side is closest to you. Secure the plastic so that it will not move as you work. Spread a very thin layer of melted dark chocolate over the plastic sheet. Use the hair dryer, as needed, in smooth sweeping motions to prevent the chocolate from starting to set up as you cover the sheet.

4. Starting at the top left (long) side of the sheet, working in a straight line back toward yourself, press the graining tool hard against the chocolate, lightly pivoting the surface of the tool up and down in smooth motions covering 1/2 inch (1.2 cm) of chocolate each time, and, at the same time, drag the tool in a straight line to the bottom of the sheet (if longer wood grains are desired, drag the tool a little farther between each rocking motion). Use the hair dryer in your other hand as needed throughout the process to keep the chocolate from starting to set. If it does, it will clog the grooves of the tool and the tool will not leave an impression in the chocolate. If this happens switch to the other tool.

5. When you come to the bottom of the sheet after making the first row, start again at the top to make the design in a parallel row, spacing the rows slightly apart, and warming the chocolate as needed. Continue until the whole sheet is covered by the wood-grain design, continuing to warm the chocolate if necessary. However, do not direct the hair dryer toward areas of sheet where the design has already been formed.

6. Place the sheet in the refrigerator for a few minutes to set the chocolate.

7. Check the temperature of the white chocolate to be sure it is not too warm, then spread white chocolate over the entire sheet, just thick enough to cover the dark chocolate if the sheet is to be used to decorate desserts and pastries, or to 1/8 inch (3 mm) thick if the wood-grain chocolate will be used for constructing bonbon boxes or other containers.

8. Place the sheet in the refrigerator until the chocolate is set. Avoid leaving it too long when making the thinner sheets, as they tend to curl.

9. Invert the hardened sheet, peel off the plastic, and use as desired. If possible, leave the chocolate attached to the plastic during storage.

To make strips to cover the sides of a cake

1. Cut polyurethane or acetate strips to the exact width and length needed to cover the side the cake (convenient 2-inch/5-cm wide acetate strips are available both precut into 24-inch/60-cm lengths or in one continuous long roll).

2. Place one strip on the upper part of an inverted sheet pan or sheet of corrugated cardboard lined with baking paper. Secure the strip so it will not move as you work.

3. Spread the dark chocolate as directed for the sheet (you will have to spread the chocolate out onto the baking paper around the strip in order to cover it completely). Make one pass lengthwise with the graining tool, keeping the distance between pivoting and dragging the tool short for the best effect, and following the same instructions for warming the chocolate as needed to keep it from setting up as you create the design.

4. Use a paring knife to pick up the strip at two corners and move it to a clean area on the paper. Refrigerate briefly to set the dark chocolate; the strips will curl if left longer than a few seconds.

5. Spread white chocolate over the strip just thick enough to cover it completely. Immediately pick up the strip and wrap it around the cake; the ends must not overlap or you will not be able to remove the plastic without breaking part of the chocolate band. Chill briefly to set the chocolate and then peel away the plastic.

 Marbleized Chocolate

one full sheet

1 pound (455 g) dark coating chocolate or melted and tempered dark chocolate
6 ounces (170 g) white coating chocolate or melted and tempered white chocolate

NOTE 1: Because coating chocolate used at the proper temperature sets rather quickly (compared to real tempered chocolate), you may need to warm the sheet pan by placing it in the oven briefly or warm the chocolate using a hair dryer, in order to have time to properly marbleize the chocolate before it sets up, especially if you are working in a room that is too cold. If you are using tempered chocolate, it is not very likely you will have this problem. Another technique is to warm the back of the sheet pan by holding it about 8 inches (20 cm) above a gas burner, moving it back and forth until it is evenly warm all over.

*M*arbleized Chocolate can be used for Chocolate Cutouts following the instructions on page 890, and for constructing containers or forms using the method in Chocolate Chalet (see page 832). You can also form a marbleized pattern on strips of polyurethane or acetate as described in Molding Chocolate Strips and use the strips to wrap around a cake or pastry or to form containers as described in Chocolate Mousse in Ribbon Teardrops (see page 564) or Cupid's Treasure Chest (see page 566). Because you will be using the back side of the chocolate in that case (the side that is against the plastic), reverse the order in the instructions, piping the white chocolate lines first and spacing them well apart so they do not blend together completely later on. Spread the dark chocolate on top, using an offset palette knife or the even side of a plastic scraper to gently flatten and swirl the piped lines into irregular shapes. You will also need to use a thinner layer of chocolate for strips that will be bent.*

1. If you are using dark and white coating chocolates, melt them separately over bain-maries. Be very careful not to overheat the white coating chocolate. Use low heat and stir frequently or it will become lumpy. Keep the chocolates warm (about 110°F/43°C for the coating chocolate) over their bain-maries in your workstation.

2. Invert a full-size, clean, perfectly even sheet pan and place a full sheet of baking paper (the thicker reusable grade is best since it does not curl as easily after the chocolate hardens) on the back of the pan. If even sheet pans are scarce or unavailable, place the paper on a full sheet of corrugated cardboard. Have ready a wooden skewer and a disposable paper pastry bag (see page 23).

NOTE 2: Leftover scrap pieces of Marbleized Chocolate may be melted and used to partially replace the chocolate in Rum Balls, Brownies, or Chocolate Decadence. I do not recommend using all Marbleized Chocolate in these recipes, but around 25 percent will not impair the texture or flavor.

3. Quickly spread the dark chocolate over the paper into a 15-by-23-inch (37.5-×-57.5-cm) rectangle (11 by 15 inches/27.5 × 37.5 cm for a half recipe); it will be approximately $1/16$ inch (2 mm) thick.

4. Immediately place the white chocolate in the prepared pastry bag and cut a small opening. Pipe one continuous line of white chocolate, moving back and forth lengthwise over the entire sheet of dark chocolate and then repeating crosswise, using all of the white chocolate (Figure 17–17).

5. Still working quickly, use the tip of the wooden skewer to feather the chocolates together, moving it in a circular pattern lengthwise over the sheet, left to right and then right to left without picking up the skewer, making four passes over the sheet (Figure 17–18). Do not push the skewer all the way through to the paper, as this can create small holes in the finished sheet, which will cause the chocolate to break at those points. Let the chocolate sheet harden.

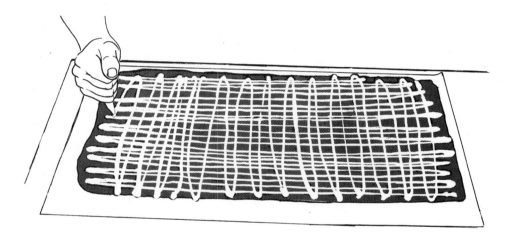

FIGURE 17–17 *Piping lines of melted white chocolate lengthwise and crosswise over the dark chocolate for Marbleized Chocolate*

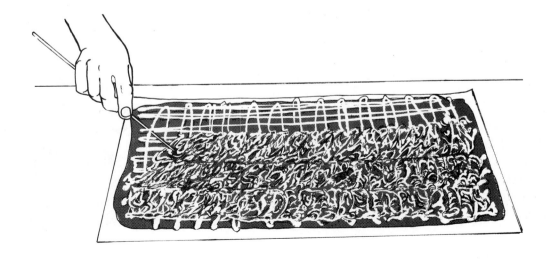

FIGURE 17–18 *Using the tip of a wooden skewer to swirl the dark and white chocolate together creating the marbleized design*

Modeling Chocolate

Dark Modeling Chocolate

1 pound, 8 ounces (680 g)

14 ounces (400 g) sweet dark chocolate
2 ounces (55 g) unsweetened chocolate
²/₃ cup (160 ml) or 8 ounces (225 g) light corn syrup

NOTE: You may have to adjust the recipe to the brand of chocolate you are working with, increasing or decreasing the amount of corn syrup accordingly.

Also known as plastic chocolate, this very pliable and certainly edible paste can be used to create figurines and flowers, or to drape around a cake, much as you would Marzipan. It should be said, however, that it is a bit more difficult to work with than Marzipan since Modeling Chocolate sets up rather quickly (as does any chocolate) when left alone. Therefore you must shape your design in a quick and precise manner to achieve a satisfactory result. Do not substitute coating chocolate for the real chocolate in this recipe, since it is the large amount of cocoa butter in conjunction with the cocoa mass in real chocolate that gives the Modeling Chocolate the pliability necessary for shaping it and also provides stability after the particular shape is formed. These qualities will vary to some degree, depending on the chocolate used and its ratio of cocoa butter to cocoa mass.

1. Chop both chocolates into small pieces. Place in a bowl and melt over simmering water while stirring constantly. Do not heat higher than about 110°F (43°C). Remove from the heat.

2. Heat the corn syrup to the same temperature. Pour into the melted chocolate and stir until thoroughly combined. Allow the Modeling Chocolate to cool completely. Cover and let sit at room temperature for at least 24 hours.

3. Work the mixture into a smooth paste by forcing it against the table with the back of a knife and/or by using the warmth of your hands. If you are working with a substantial amount, this tedious and sometimes difficult step can be accelerated by using a manual pasta machine.

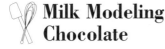 Milk Modeling Chocolate

1 pound, 8 ounces (680 g)

NOTE: If you are making all three, Dark, Milk, and White Modeling Chocolates, or if you already have White and Dark Modeling Chocolate on hand, simply combine those two to create the desired milk chocolate shade.

Follow the recipe for Dark Modeling Chocolate, substituting milk chocolate for both the sweet dark and unsweetened chocolates in the recipe.

White Modeling Chocolate

1 pound, 14 ounces (855 g)

1½ ounces (40 g) cocoa butter

1 pound, 2 ounces (510 g) white chocolate (see note and introduction)

5 ounces (140 g) glucose or 44% light corn syrup

½ cup (120 ml) Simple Syrup (page 11)

NOTE: *You may need to adjust the recipe to the brand of chocolate you are using. If the paste is too hard, increase the glucose. If too soft, increase the amount of chocolate.*

This white chocolate paste is very versatile and can be used for many applications: It can replace Marzipan or rolled fondant for covering cakes or pastries or for making ribbons, or it can be formed, much like Marzipan, into fruit, flower, or animal decorations. To make thin sheets, roll it out with a rolling pin or use a sheeter. Use powdered sugar to keep the chocolate paste from sticking. White Modeling Chocolate doesn't color very well since "white" chocolate is actually an ivory or pale yellow color from the cocoa butter. The chocolate paste will soften as you work with it but will firm up rather quickly after it is shaped and set aside. As with any chocolate product, Modeling Chocolate should not be stored in the refrigerator, but it can be chilled for short periods if necessary with no ill effects. Ideally, make the Modeling Chocolate two or three days prior to when you will need it in case it requires more time to set. With some brands of chocolate the cocoa butter may separate from the paste (the mixture looks broken). Ignore this, set it aside as directed, then work the cocoa butter back into the mixture, using the back of a knife after the paste has been left to set.

1. Cut the cocoa butter and white chocolate into small pieces. Place in a bowl and set over simmering water. Heat, stirring constantly, just until melted. Do not overheat.

2. Remove the bowl from the heat and stir in the glucose (or corn syrup) and Simple Syrup. Continue mixing until smooth.

3. Cover and let the mixture rest overnight to set up.

4. Work the mixture into a smooth paste by forcing it against the table with the back of a knife and/or using the warmth of your hands. If you are working with a substantial amount, using a small, manual pasta machine works great. If the chocolate is too soft to work with after resting overnight, leave it to set further (dry) until the next day. This is usually all it takes. If you cannot wait and must use the chocolate right away, add more melted chocolate to correct the consistency.

5. Store the chocolate paste tightly covered in a cool place. It will keep for several weeks, but as it becomes older it will become harder and will require a little extra effort to soften.

 **Chocolate Roses**

about 10 medium-sized production roses

one-half recipe Dark, Milk, or White Modeling Chocolate (preceding recipes)

Successful Chocolate Roses can only be created from a properly made, firm, Modeling Chocolate—one that may require a few extra minutes to work into a malleable paste. Very warm working conditions make it hard, if not impossible, to create Chocolate Roses.

Work the chocolate soft and then form it following the directions for Marzipan Roses (Figures 19–42 to 19–48, pages 1035 to 1038).

Piped Chocolate Decorations

 ## Piping Chocolate

1 cup (240 ml)
piping chocolate

12 ounces (340 g) dark coating
    chocolate
1/4 to 1/2 teaspoon (1.25–2.5 ml)
    Simple Syrup (page 11) or orange
    liqueur, approximately

Piping Chocolate can be purchased from chocolate manufacturers, but the quality of the product is not commensurate with the price, considering that you can make the same thing for about one-eighth of the cost. For practical reasons, I prefer to use coating chocolate for Piping Chocolate decorations that will be moved after they have hardened, since I can be certain the coating chocolate will set up firm. If you do not have, or do not want to use, coating chocolate, real chocolate must be perfectly tempered to be utilized the same way. In cases where the decoration is not moved, when it is piped directly on to a pastry or is used for decorating a dessert plate, for example, real chocolate can be used without tempering, since the addition of a liquid will aid in setting the chocolate sufficiently. The consistency of Piping Chocolate made from real chocolate should be kept a bit thicker than is necessary when using coating chocolate.

1. Chop the chocolate into small pieces, place in a small bowl, and set over simmering water, stirring until melted. Do not overheat.

2. Using a drop bottle, add the Simple Syrup or orange liqueur gradually. The amount needed will vary depending on the brand of chocolate. Add enough for the chocolate to form soft peaks.

3. Piping Chocolate will keep as long as any dark chocolate stored covered in a cool place. Melt over hot water to use.

 ## Chocolate Cages

small balloons
vegetable oil
Piping Chocolate (preceding recipe)

Making Chocolate Cages is a very delicate procedure and should not be attempted on a hot day without the proper facility for working with chocolate. Because the piped chocolate mesh must be open enough (the lines spaced far enough apart) to display whatever item the cages are placed over, their structure is very fragile.

The cages are formed by piping chocolate lines over inflated balloons. There are several different methods of securing the balloons after they are inflated, the obvious one being simply tying a knot, but this means that the balloons must be punctured to deflate them and remove the cages, and therefore they cannot be reused. This is of little consequence if you are only making a few cages but could make a difference if you need to produce a large number (not so much because of the cost of the balloons, but it can be difficult at times to find a large quantity of balloons that work well; see note on page 894). By twisting the end of the balloon shut and then clamping a binder clip on top, you can deflate the balloon without puncturing it and then blow it up and use it again. Another method is to use short straws with the same diameter as the necks of the balloons. Coat the outside end of the straws with silicone caulking to form a tight seal between the straw and the balloon and insert the silicone-coated end into the neck of the balloon. Once the silicone has dried, blow up the balloons through the straws. Fold the end of the straw in half and secure it with a binder clip or paper clip. (Be careful to apply silicone only to the outside of the straw; if the silicone gets inside it will plug the hole and you will be very red in the face trying to inflate the balloon.) With this method the balloons can be reused many times; it is especially efficient for making a fair amount of cages. If your cages shatter when you deflate the balloons (this is usually caused by not greasing the top of the balloon sufficiently or letting the air out too fast), use the knot method so the air leaks out naturally and very slowly.

1. Have ready small, wide, glasses such as "on the rocks" glasses or other suitable containers, on which to rest the balloon after piping the chocolate (you might have to shorten the straw so it fits inside the container when folded); you will need one for each cage you are making. Have an equal number of binder clips or paper clips available. Blow up as many balloons as desired to the size of a grapefruit. Secure the ends either by tying a knot and then attaching a binder clip to the knot (the weight of the clip helps to keep the balloon steady on top of the glass) or by twisting the end and then attaching the clip. If using the straw method described in the introduction, fold the end of the straw in half and then secure with a clip.

2. Using the palm of your hand, generously oil as much of each balloon as you plan to pipe on, and then set each on top of a glass. If the top of any of the balloons seems dry when you are ready to pipe the chocolate, re-oil that portion.

3. Place some Piping Chocolate in a piping bag and cut a small opening. Pick up a balloon, hold it steady with your free hand, and pipe the chocolate over the top in smooth overlapping circles (see Figure 18–10, page 959). Turn the balloon to the side and continue the same pattern down to the widest point, creating an even base all around at the same time. Carefully return the piped cage to the top of the glass. Prepare the remaining cages in the same way. Place the cages in the refrigerator for a few minutes to set the chocolate.

4. Remove the set cages from the balloons in one of the following ways: If you tied a knot, use the tip of a wooden skewer to make a hole as close to the knot as possible on each balloon. Return the balloons to their resting place and place back in the refrigerator. The air will slowly leak out and the balloon will fall to the bottom of the container, leaving the cage perched on top. If you used one of the binder clip methods, remove the clips and ever so slowly untwist or unfold to release the air gradually, depositing the cage in the palm of your hand. Be patient in doing this: If the air escapes too fast, the delicate structure is likely to break.

5. Handling them carefully, place the cages on a pan and store in a cool, dry place. Refrigerate the cages for a few minutes before attempting to pick them up in order to strengthen the chocolate.

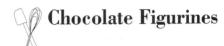 ## Chocolate Figurines

*I*n *addition to being used to coat and dip pastries, cookies, or cakes, coating chocolate (dark, milk, or white) is very practical for piping various decorative ornaments, either directly onto a cake or petit four freehand, or onto baking paper (sometimes with the help of a template) to place on the item after the decoration has hardened (tempered chocolate may also be used). The latter method is an efficient way of making fancy decorations when you are not too busy, because they can be made up far in advance and stored in a dark cool place (but not in the refrigerator). If you want the chocolate to float out slightly, use it as is, but if it is important to the design that the chocolate stay in precise lines, use Piping Chocolate.*

FIGURE 17–19 Designs that can be made using Piping Chocolate. Most of these are intended for piping directly onto a cake or pastry, but the smaller figures may be lifted off the paper after they have hardened, provided the outlines are partially or totally filled in with additional chocolate

1. Trace any of the small individual designs you would like to make from the examples shown in Figures 17–19 to 17–21 onto a sheet of paper, drawing as many as you need of each design. (Figures 17–22 and 17–23 show border and lettering designs, which are piped directly onto a cake, pastry, or rolled sheet of Marzipan.)

2. Attach the paper securely to a sheet of cardboard. Place a piece of baking or waxed paper on top, and attach it securely so it will not shift as you pipe the designs.

3. Make a piping bag (see page 27) and fill it with a small amount of melted coating chocolate, tempered chocolate, or Piping Chocolate. Cut a small opening in the bag. Pipe the chocolate over the design, tracing it in one unbroken line as much as possible.

FIGURE 17–20 The designs in the top row can be used in the same way as those in Figure 17–19; the designs shown in the bottom three rows are additionally appropriate for piping on top of petits fours or French pastries

4. Let the chocolate harden, then store the figures attached to the paper. To remove them, place one hand under the paper and push up very gently to separate the chocolate from the paper, as you lift the design off with the other hand. If they are very fragile, slide the blade of a thin knife underneath instead.

Some of the figurines look especially nice with a combination of dark, milk, and light chocolate in the same design. To create these, make the frame using Piping Chocolate and let it harden. Fill in the design with coating or tempered chocolate in the desired shade or shades. When the chocolate has set, place these two-tone designs on the cake or pastry flat-side up. Different shades and colors can also be obtained by blending the dark, milk, and white chocolates, or tinting white chocolate using fat-soluble coloring.

FIGURE 17–21 *These designs are used for piping directly onto petits fours or may be piped onto baking paper to remove and place on top of a cake or pastry, either flat or standing upright*

Because the tip and the opening of the piping bag are so small, the chocolate will set up very quickly in that spot. When you pause while piping out the designs, hold the tip between your pinched fingers to keep it warm. If you forget, and only the chocolate at the very tip of the bag has set up, hold the tip of the piping bag against the side of a warm pot on the stove, or on the oven door, to melt it quickly.

Although it may seem like only a small amount of chocolate is involved, piping bags with chocolate left inside (partially used bags or bags with chocolate that set up before it could be used) should not be discarded. Put the used bag in the refrigerator to harden, then open it up and the chocolate will fall right out and can be put back into the bowl to melt again.

FIGURE 17–22 Border designs that can be piped out using Piping Chocolate or Fondant

FIGURE 17–23 Examples of lettering and numeral designs

Chocolate Monarch Butterfly Ornaments

Piping Chocolate (page 904)
melted light coating chocolate or
    tempered light chocolate
melted white coating chocolate or
    tempered white chocolate
fat-soluble orange food coloring

The simplified smaller and sturdier of the two butterfly designs that follow can be assembled by simply placing the wings between two metal bars or wooden dowels to hold them at the proper angle as you attach them to the bodies. To save time the antenna may be left off of this version without their losing too much appeal. The larger more elegant butterfly design requires a V-shaped assembly box. If you do not have one, you can make one following the instructions on page 835 for the Chalet Support Box, or make a scaled down form: Score a cut lengthwise down the center of a 6-inch (15-cm) strip of corrugated cardboard, bend the strip into a V and tape across both ends to hold the V at the proper angle. To secure the form as you are working, place it between the rows of an inverted muffin tin. The larger butterfly design is shown in the photograph of Chocolate Ganache Towers in the color insert pages.

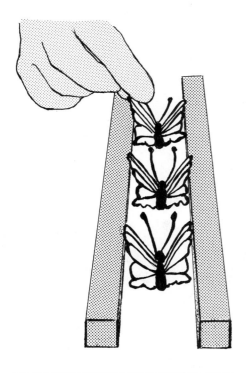

FIGURE 17–24 Attaching the antennae to the small version of Chocolate Monarch Butterflies

Small butterflies

1. Trace the butterfly template in Figure 17–20 onto a sheet of paper, tracing only the wings; the antenna and the body are piped free-hand. Attach the traced template to a sheet of cardboard.

2. Cut baking paper into squares slightly larger than the butterfly, cutting one square of paper for each butterfly you plan to make. Place one of the squares on top of the template and secure it with paper clips or a small piece of tape so it will not move as you pipe.

3. Place a small amount of Piping Chocolate in a piping bag. Cut a small opening and pipe the chocolate out following the outline and patterns of the wings (do not connect the wings to each other). Remove the square of paper with the wings and set it aside on a sheet pan. Secure another square of paper over the template, pipe the next set of wings, set it aside, and continue until you have piped all of the wings.

4. After the chocolate is set, fill in the interior sections of the wings with milk, white, and orange coating chocolate or tempered chocolate (use the fat-soluble coloring to tint white chocolate orange). Let the chocolate set and reserve the wings.

5. Using dark Piping Chocolate, pipe out two antennae for each butterfly on a sheet of baking paper. This is done by piping a small dot about the size of the head of a pin, then attaching a slightly curved line approximately 1 inch (2.5 cm) long. Set the antennas aside.

6. Place two metal bars (or use dowels secured with a piece of dough) about 1¹/₂ inches (3.7 cm) apart on a sheet pan covered with baking paper. Place Piping Chocolate in a piping bag and cut a large opening. Pipe a small dot with a 1-inch (2.5-cm) tapered body behind it (try to approximate the one in the drawing) between the bars.

7. Wearing latex gloves to avoid leaving fingerprints on the chocolate, place two wings, flat-side up, into the chocolate, leaning them against the bars to get the proper angle. Repeat until all of the wings are attached. Once you can gauge how fast the chocolate is setting up, you can pipe out several bodies at once.

8. Place the antennas in the refrigerator for a few minutes. Wearing gloves, dip the plain ends (not the ends with the dots) in dark chocolate and fasten to the front of each butterfly in a V shape (Figure 17–24) (they will stick immediately since they have been chilled, which is essential since holding on to them very long would cause them to melt between your fingers). Once the chocolate is firmly set, you can remove the bars and store the butterflies in a cool dark place. Do not store them in the refrigerator.

Large butterflies

1. Follow the instructions for small butterflies through step three, tracing the butterfly design in Figure 17–25 instead.

2. Let the frames harden and then partially fill in the interior sections with white and orange coating or tempered chocolate, leaving part of each wing unfilled. Set the wings aside to harden.

FIGURE 17–25 *The template used as a guide in piping the wings for the larger version of Chocolate Monarch Butterflies. The shaded area indicates where to fill in with white- and orange-colored chocolate.*

3. Line the inside of a V-shaped form (see introduction) with baking paper. Wearing gloves, carefully remove the wings from their papers and line up as many pairs in the box as will fit, placing them inverted (flat-side up)

4. Place Piping Chocolate in a piping bag and cut a large opening. Pipe a body between each set of wings tapering it toward the end. Let the chocolate harden, then remove the butterflies carefully. Repeat steps three and four until all of the butterflies are assembled.

 **Streaking**

A very simple and elegant way to decorate petits fours, pastries, candies, and serving plates is to pipe a series of very thin lines across them. The lines can be piped in just one direction as in Strawberry Hearts, or in opposite directions as shown in Pecan Whiskey Tart (see Figure 6–1, page 246). Examples of this technique can be seen in the color photographs of Nectarine Meringue Tart and Assorted Petits Fours Sec. It is important to use a small opening in the piping bag to keep the lines thin. Fill the bag with a small amount of tempered chocolate or melted coating chocolate. Pipe the chocolate, moving the bag very quickly over the item alternating left to right and right to left. You need to extend the lines out just beyond the edge of the item and let them fall on a paper to get the desired effect (with the exception of some designs piping onto serving plates, where this may not be the case).

Chocolate Casting or Painting

In addition to making individual decorations such as the butterfly ornaments, you can apply the same basic technique to create stunning showpieces with chocolate. The only prerequisites are a steady hand and a good eye for composing the various shades of chocolate in the design.

NOTE: If the Piping Chocolate sets up too hard, the thin lines will pull away from the surface (this will also happen if the room you are working in is too cold) and can cause the background chocolate to seep under later, when the background is poured. You can remedy this by thinning the Piping Chocolate slightly with soybean oil (or a commercial thinning agent).

1. Draw or trace your picture on a sheet of paper. Try to use uncomplicated designs with clean lines. Attach the paper to a solid base such as an inverted even sheet pan or a sheet of corrugated cardboard. Remember that the design will be reversed (mirror image) in the finished piece. If that matters (for example, with lettering) follow the directions in the note with Method II on page 1022 to reverse the image.

2. Fasten a piece of Plexiglas or a sheet of acetate or polyurethane (use a thicker grade than you would use for lining cake rings) on top of the drawing. Or, as a last resort, stretch a sheet of plastic wrap around it tightly. The plastic must be absolutely wrinkle-free because any imperfection here will show and be very disappointing when you turn over the finished piece.

3. Trace the drawing using Piping Chocolate (see page 904) in a piping bag with a small opening (see note). There is no reason to use real chocolate here, since the finished piece is not meant to be eaten. Fill in the interior areas with different shades made by blending dark, light, and white coating chocolate, as desired. You can color white coating chocolate using fat-soluble coloring to make soft pastel shades. Think of the plastic or Plexiglas as your canvas, the chocolate as your paint, the piping bag as your brush, and yourself as the artist.

4. When you have finished your artwork, move the painting to a corner or other safe place with the proper temperature, where it can remain for at least a few hours once the background chocolate is poured.

5. Place metal bars around the edges, or use any other straight object that will keep the poured chocolate from leaking out. Corrugated cardboard cut into strips will work if oiled on the side that will be next to the chocolate. Seal the base of the frame all around the outside with clay or even Short Dough. Apply the background by pouring coating chocolate of the desired shade over the design within the frame. Make absolutely sure the temperature is not above 105°F (40°C) or it can partially melt and destroy your piping underneath. On the other hand, if it is too cold (and therefore too thick), it will not flow out and cover properly, leaving an uneven and rough finish. The chocolate for the background should be poured very close to the painting to avoid bubbles. Gauge the thickness of the background in proportion to the size of the painting. For example: if the painting is 12 by 16 inches (30 × 40 cm), the background should be ¹/₂ inch (1.2 cm) thick for the proper strength. Leave your artwork to set for at least several hours.

6. In the meantime make a base and stand. For the size painting above, pour coating chocolate into a circle about 10 inches (25 cm) in diameter and $1/2$ inch (1.2 cm) thick. For the rear support pour a piece in the shape of a triangle with one long side at right angles to the short side, about 8 inches (20 cm) across the bottom, 14 inches (35 cm) tall, and the same thickness as the base.

7. Place the painting in the refrigerator for 10 minutes to ensure a glossy finish. Carefully remove the metal bars or cardboard frame from around the painting (cut them free with a thin knife if they do not separate easily). Place an inverted sheet pan or sheet of heavy cardboard on top, hold on securely with both hands, and turn the painting right-side up. Remove the other sheet pan or cardboard, as well as the plastic or Plexiglas, to reveal the painting. You may wish to add a border of piped chocolate or molded Marzipan before placing it on the stand.

8. Chill the base of the stand and the rear support. Dip the bottom of the support in coating chocolate and quickly fasten it to the base. Hold it straight until it has set. Pipe some chocolate down the front of the support and carefully attach the painting. Hold until set. Pipe additional chocolate at the bottom behind the painting.

Cocoa Painting

NOTE 1: Carbon paper must be used to stencil onto the Pastillage. First, cut the paper to the same size as your motive and tape the two together. Then tape them to the Pastillage. Use a fine-point pen to trace and transfer the motive to the Pastillage.

NOTE 2: Another media that can be used is a mixture of cocoa butter and vegetable oil at the ratio of two parts melted cocoa butter to one part oil. Add cocoa powder as needed depending upon the desired shade. For the best results, keep the mixture warm while working.

Although cocoa painting is quite an advanced decorating technique, with some practice and "help from a friend" (a stencil in this case), even a beginner can create simple designs with attractive results. Naturally it is helpful if you have some prior experience in drawing or in painting.

The canvas for a cocoa painting is made of Marzipan or Pastillage rolled out in cornstarch. I prefer the off-white color of Marzipan, which blends in a more subtle way with the various cocoa tones, rather than the stark white of Pastillage. Powdered sugar is not used to roll out the Marzipan in this case, as it leaves small grains of sugar on the surface that absorb the cocoa paint and leave unsightly dots on the finished piece. The sheet of Marzipan or Pastillage must also be completely smooth for the same reason. Pastillage must be allowed to dry and then sanded before you can begin to paint, while the Marzipan only needs to dry slightly after it is rolled out.

If you do not have a natural talent for drawing freehand, the stenciling technique described in Method II on page 1022 can help frame an outline for your design. The stenciling should be done before the Marzipan is left to dry (see note 1).

The cocoa paint is made from unsweetened cocoa powder diluted in water, a clear spirit, such as vodka, or clear lemon extract (the acid here, just as the alcohol in the vodka, speeds up the drying process) to produce an extensive number of varying shades (see note 2). Food color should be used sparingly (or your finished work will look like something you can buy at a garage sale).

Using artist's brushes, start by applying the lighter shades first, then finish with the darker tones. Practice blending the shades together so that no clear line is visible where the lighter tone ends and the darker one starts. When completed, the painting can be used to decorate the top of a cake, or it can be framed in Marzipan and used as a showpiece.

Hollow Chocolate Figures Using Molds

Only metal or plastic chocolate molds in perfect condition should be used to make hollow figures, because the smallest scratch can cause the chocolate to stick.

1. Clean the molds, using soap and hot water, rinse, and dry thoroughly. Polish the inside of the molds with cotton balls (if using metal molds, dip the cotton balls in a little powdered chalk, then remove any trace of the chalk with a clean cotton ball). The molds as well as the work area must be around 68°F (20°C).

2. Before filling, coat the inside of the mold with a thin layer of tempered chocolate, using a good brush, to eliminate any small bubbles on the surface.

3. Immediately clip the two halves of the mold together and fill with chocolate. If the thin layer of chocolate is left to set up completely before filling, it can separate from the rest of the mold later.

4. Lightly tap the side of the mold with a dowel to release bubbles.

5. Wait a few minutes until a thick enough layer of chocolate has formed to be sure the mold will not break when handled (a larger mold will need a thicker layer), then invert the mold over the bowl of chocolate and allow the chocolate to run back out. Tap the mold lightly with a dowel to help remove the chocolate.

6. Place the molds (standing upright) on a sheet pan lined with baking paper. When they start to set, remove the clips and refrigerate for a few minutes until the chocolate has started to shrink away from the molds (this is easy to see with a plastic mold; you will just have to take an educated guess with a metal mold). Carefully remove the molds. Wear latex gloves whenever you handle the figures from this point to avoid leaving fingerprints.

7. To make the bottom, spread a thin layer of chocolate on a sheet of baking paper, place the hollow chocolate figure on top, and let it set. Cut away any excess chocolate around the figure. If a seam protrudes where the two halves were joined together, it should be removed after a few hours with a sharp, thin knife.

When making molds with two or more different chocolates (a white beard on a Santa, for example, or milk chocolate in spots on dark chocolate for a rabbit), brush or pipe on the contrasting color first, and allow it to set slightly before continuing. Milk, white, and dark chocolates can be mixed to create different shades or white chocolate may be tinted using fat-soluble coloring. The finished figures may be decorated by spraying with chocolate as described on page 919.

Molded Chocolate Strips

With this method it is possible to make containers of almost any shape to hold mousses, bavarois, or other dessert items; see Chocolate Mousse in Ribbon Teardrops, page 564, and Cupid's Treasure Chest, page 566. In addition to using plain chocolate as described here, the same technique can be used with Chocolate Ribbon Strips, page 918.

1. Cut strips of polyurethane or acetate as wide as you would like the height of the container, and to the precise length of the circumference of the finished container. Place one plastic strip on a sheet of baking paper and spread a thin layer of tempered chocolate (or coating chocolate) on top.

2. Pick up the strip carefully before the chocolate has set and bend it into the desired shape.

3. Once the chocolate has hardened, peel away the plastic (in some cases you may need to refrigerate the item briefly before removing the plastic).

4. If you would like to put a base on the container, spread tempered chocolate or coating chocolate out thinly on a sheet of baking paper and set the container on top. Pipe a string of chocolate around the inside bottom perimeter. Let the chocolate set partially. Cut around the outside with a thin knife and let it set completely.

A chocolate strip can also be wrapped around the side of a cake as described in Chocolate Truffle Cake with Raspberries on page 324.

Chocolate Twirls

NOTE: *Although it is not practical to make the Twirls any larger than the size made here, smaller sizes can be very showy as well. Adjust the size of both the plastic strips and the glasses or pipe accordingly.*

Your guests will be amazed when they see these elaborate decorations delicately balanced on top of their desserts. Chocolate Twirls are specified in the presentation instructions for the plated version of Mango Ice Cream but can be used to crown many other items in this book as well. If you will be making a large number of Twirls, it is a good idea to buy PVC pipe from the hardware store or clear plastic pipe from a plastic supply store (the clear pipe is more expensive but is easier to use since you can see the decoration inside). The pipe should have an inside diameter of $2^{1}/_{4}$–$2^{1}/_{2}$ inches (5.6–6.2 cm) and should be cut into lengths of 6 inches (15 cm). Purchasing the pipe will probably benefit your working relationship with the bar since you will no longer have to borrow their highball glasses, and glass is not very practical for use in the kitchen anyway.

1. Cut strips of acetate or polyurethane 2–3 inches (5–7.5 cm) wide and 9–10 inches (22.5–25 cm) long.

2. Make a piping bag, fill it with a small amount of melted chocolate, cut a small opening in the bag, and reserve it in a warm spot where the chocolate will not set up and the bag will be at hand when you need it. (I heat a cake pan in the oven and then set the bag on the hot inverted pan next to where I am working.)

3. Place one of the plastic strips on a sheet of baking paper positioning it horizontally near the top of the paper. Spread a thin layer of melted dark coating chocolate or tempered dark chocolate over the plastic. To completely cover the plastic quickly, you will have to spread chocolate out onto the paper around the edges as well.

4. Use the tip of a paring knife to pick up the strip and move it to the lower (clean) area of the paper keeping it in the same position. Place a metal bar used for candy making, or a small ruler, next to one long edge and on top of about ⅛ inch (3 mm) of the chocolate-covered plastic strip (cover the smallest portion of chocolate required to still be able to use the metal bar or ruler to hold the plastic steady).

5. Quickly, before the chocolate sets up, drag a small trowel with ⅛- or ¼-inch (3- or 6-mm) notches that are ¹⁄₁₆ inch (2 mm) deep along the strip to remove half of the chocolate in a ribbon pattern (see Figures 7–4 and 7–5, page 277), using the metal bar or ruler as a guide. It may also be necessary to hold the end of the strip steady with your thumb. Be sure to press down firmly as you drag the trowel to avoid moving the plastic. Remove the metal bar or ruler.

6. Using the prepared piping bag, pipe a line of chocolate across each short end to join the strips of chocolate together when the plastic is removed.

7. Still working quickly before the chocolate sets up, lift up the plastic strip and curl it diagonally, with the chocolate on the inside of the plastic, by pushing the strip into a highball glass or piece of pipe at an angle. The strip should curl loosely, and the plastic should not overlap at any point or the curls will be impossible to remove without breaking. If the plastic starts to overlap as you push the strip into the glass (in other words the front end does not slide into the glass at the same rate as you push the opposite end), help the front end along with the tip of a paring knife. Store the finished Chocolate Twirls in a cool dry place until needed.

8. Before unwrapping, place the glass or tube in the refrigerator for 1 or 2 minutes. Carefully pull the plastic strip out of the mold and set it on the table. Carefully peel away the plastic from both short ends. To move the Twirl insert the handle of a wooden spoon or a small wooden dowel and use that to lift it; do not touch the decoration with your hands.

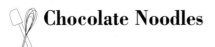 **Chocolate Noodles**

C hocolate Noodles are an eye-catching garnish that looks very much like curled, dried fettucini. They can be placed on top of cakes or formed into a little pile on the base of a plate next to a serving of dessert (see the photograph of Chocolate Mousse in Ribbon Teardrops in the color insert). Mixing dark, light,

and white Chocolate Noodles produces a good effect. Store them in a cool, dry place. (Broken Twirls—previous recipe—make excellent Chocolate Noodles.)

1. Place a strip of acetate or polyurethane, 3 inches wide by 12 inches long (7.5 × 30 cm), horizontally, on top of a sheet of baking paper. Spread a thin layer of tempered dark, light, or white chocolate on top.

2. Use the tip of a paring knife to pick up the strip and place it in front of you keeping it in the same position. Place a metal bar used for candy making, or a small ruler, next to one long edge and on top of about ⅛ inch (3 mm) of the chocolate-covered plastic strip (cover the smallest portion of chocolate required to still be able to use the metal bar or ruler as a guide and to hold the plastic steady). Quickly, before the chocolate sets up, drag a trowel with ⅛- or ¼-inch (3- or 6-mm) notches that are 1/16 inch (2 mm) deep along the strip to remove half of the chocolate in a ribbonlike pattern (see Figures 7–4 and 7–5, page 277). Be sure to press down firmly as you drag the trowel to avoid moving the plastic.

3. Wait until the chocolate is just starting to set up and then with the chocolate on the inside, roll the plastic into a loose spiral diagonally and place it in a tall glass or 6- to 8-inch (15- to 20-cm) length of pipe (see introduction to Chocolate Twirls on page 916). Repeat until you have made as many Chocolate Noodles as desired.

4. Refrigerate for a few minutes to set the chocolate.

5. Hold each plastic strip close over a small bowl or a sheet pan and carefully unroll it. The noodles will fall off the plastic into the container. Some noodles will break and this is to be expected, but they are still usable for most applications. Store covered in a cool, dry location until needed.

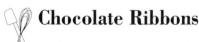 ## Chocolate Ribbons

NOTE: If you use coating chocolate (which produces a very good result) rather than tempered, it will set up faster and, of course, especially so if you are working in a cold climate, making the plastic curl after the chocolate lines are formed. It is therefore best to only coat four to five strips with lines of dark chocolate before finishing with the white chocolate coating and the shaping process. When working with either type of chocolate (particularly if your work surface is marble or granite), it is very helpful to place a full sheet of corrugated cardboard on top of the table to work on. The cardboard provides insulation to prevent the chocolate from setting as quickly, and it is also handy should you need to

Chocolate Ribbons are formed utilizing the same technique as for Ribbon Sponge Sheets, with chocolate instead of Tulip Paste and sponge cake. When the chocolate pattern is formed on narrow plastic strips as directed, they can be used to produce containers of any shape as described on page 916. The striped chocolate strips may also be used to wrap around the outside of a cake as in Chocolate Truffle Cake, page 324. Whole sheets of ribbon chocolate may also be created using this method, starting with polyurethane or acetate sheets approximately the size of a full sheet pan (these may need to be secured in the corners with straight pins). Pieces can be cut out of the sheet using a warm knife for constructed forms like the Chocolate Chalets, page 832, and the boxes in Trio of Chocolates with Marzipan Parfait, page 510, or they can be used for Chocolate Cutout decorations, as described on page 890.

1. Cut the number of polyurethane or acetate strips you need into the desired length and width for the containers you are creating. Place one strip at a time in front of you, horizontally, in the top left corner (if you are right handed) on top of a sheet of baking paper. Spread a thin layer of tempered dark chocolate over the strip, covering it completely.

secure the corners of the plastic with straight pins to prevent it from moving.

To do this you will have to spread a little chocolate onto the baking paper all around it. Use the tip of a paring knife to find the edge of the plastic strip at two corners. Pick up the plastic and move it to the lower area of the paper.

2. Working quickly, place a metal bar for candy making, or a small ruler, along the lower, long side of the strip for a guide. Drag a trowel with 1/16-inch (2-mm) deep square notches over the chocolate, using the metal bar as a guide to keep the lines straight (see Figures 7–4 and 7–5, page 277). Press down hard as you drag the trowel to make sure that the lines are completely free of chocolate, and that the plastic strip does not move (when you are using a very small piece of plastic, as in making the teardrop design, for example, you may need to secure the ends with a straight pin). Set the strip aside and repeat until you have prepared the desired number of strips.

3. One at a time place a chocolate-coated strip in front of you on a clean sheet of baking paper. Quickly spread a thin layer of tempered white chocolate on top, filling in the empty lines left by the trowel. Be sure that the white chocolate is not so warm that it will melt the dark chocolate lines. Pick up the strip in the same way as before and, holding the plastic by the edges at one short end, run your thumb and index finger down both long edges to smooth them. Before the chocolate sets up, bend the strip into the desired shape, inside a mold such as cookie cutter or by securing the short ends with a paper clip for a free-form design—in either case with the chocolate side facing the interior (not against the mold). Once you have a sense of how fast the chocolate sets up, you can speed up the production process by coating several strips with chocolate before picking one up to shape it. To ensure that the chocolate will have a glossy surface, always place the shaped strips in the refrigerator for a few minutes before removing the plastic.

Spraying with Chocolate

NOTE: Having one or more extra containers for the sprayer comes in handy if you are using solutions with varying percentages of cocoa butter. The leftovers can be stored in the container and melted in a bain-marie as needed. It is an absolute must to disassemble and clean the spray gun immediately after using paint. However, since the cocoa butter rich chocolate melts quickly, it is not necessary when spraying with chocolate. Place the spray gun on a tray in a low temperature oven for one or two minutes and it will be ready to use again.

Most people associate power sprayers with house paint, wood stain, or plant insecticides. However, they have been used in our industry for quite some time, even as far back as when I was attending culinary school in Sweden. At that time we were shown how to use power sprayers for applying egg wash to proofed doughs such as croissant, braided bread, and other delicate items. Using a power sprayer for egg wash has three advantages: speed, production of a perfectly even coating, and no risk of deflating the item by using a heavy hand with a brush. Back then it was only practical to use a technique like this in a high-volume shop, since besides being bulky, the sprayers were also expensive. Today one can buy a small electric power sprayer for less than the cost of a set of good-quality pastry cutters, although you should get a sprayer that has an adjustable nozzle and the capability of controlling the air pressure.

Sprayed chocolate can be utilized in many different ways. Plates used for dessert presentations can be enhanced by spraying chocolate lightly and evenly over the whole surface (especially appropriate if the plates are solid white), or a portion of the plate can be highlighted by fanning the chocolate over one side. To decorate plates with chocolate using a template, place the template on the base of the plate and hold it steady by placing a small heavy object (such as a metal nut or bolt) on top. Spray the solution over the plate, using low air pressure. Remove the template (it is helpful to attach a loop of tape to the top to act as a handle) and let the chocolate set. Fill in the exposed area with a sauce as shown in the photograph of Hot Chocolate Truffle Cake, or leave the exposed area plain. For the reverse effect, place a stencil on the plate and spray the chocolate over it to create a chocolate silhouette of the shape. This is nice for a seasonal motif such as a tree or star on one side of the base of a plate. Another option is to use a stencil with a design that will appear over the entire base of the plate, either protecting the rim of the plate to leave it without decoration, or covering the rim with chocolate at the same time as shown in the photograph of Chocolate Decadence Cake. If possible set the spray gun on low whenever you are using a template or stencil to avoid disturbing the pattern as you spray. For a different look with any of these techniques, place the plates in the freezer for a few minutes before spraying: the chocolate will set up immediately, creating a velvet finish.

Molded Chocolate Figures can also be sprayed to give them a different and unusual look. Just like the plates, they can be placed in the freezer beforehand to alter the finish. Chocolate designs may also be sprayed onto Chocolate Cutouts and Chocolate Candies.

It may seem obvious, but it is worth stating that under no circumstance should you use the same equipment on food as for spraying paint or other nonfood items. At the minimum one should have a complete set consisting of piston, housing pump, spray tip assembly, filter assembly, and, of course, the container, reserved for kitchen use only. The main portion, the gun assembly, can be used for any purpose since liquid does not pass through it. However, the ideal solution is to have a sprayer that is dedicated to the pastry kitchen alone as well as one or more extra containers for the solution (see note). (If you do not want to invest in a power sprayer, see Cocoa Solution for Manual Spray Bottle, page 475).

Spraying the chocolate solution is really no different than spraying a thick viscosity paint, so read the instructions from the manufacturer before starting. Be sure to protect the immediate surrounding areas wherever you are spraying with sheets of baking paper.

Chocolate Solution for Spraying

1 pound (455 g) sweet dark chocolate
1 pound (455 g) cocoa butter

NOTE: The neutral 50–50 proportion of this mixture will produce a very fine texture. For a coarser and darker finish a ratio of up to two parts chocolate to one part cocoa butter may be used. However, when using that much chocolate it should be tempered first.

1. Chop the chocolate and cocoa butter into small pieces, place together in a bowl, and melt over simmering water. Continue to heat the mixture to 130°F (54°C) and hold as close to this temperature as possible while spraying for the best result.

2. Have your plates ready and also the template or stencil if you are using one. Warm the spray gun to ensure that the chocolate does not set up inside. Place the warm solution in the sprayer and spray the desired design over the serving plates with or without a template or stencil as desired. Let the plates dry. This should not take more than 10 minutes unless your work area is adversely warm; if so, place the plates in the refrigerator to expedite the process or use the velvet-finish method discussed in the introduction. The plates can be decorated many hours ahead of service and reserved in a cool, dry area.

3. The sprayer should be disassembled and cleaned immediately after you finish spraying to prevent the spray assembly from becoming clogged (if this happens, warm the pieces in a very low oven to melt the chocolate). If the spray-gun container is made of plastic (which I highly recommend), the solution can be stored there until next time and then melted in a microwave oven or over a bain-marie. Regardless of the storage container, the leftover solution should be covered; it will keep for up to six months.

Chocolate Candies

Chocolate Candies, known in Europe as pralines, have a liquid or solid filling (referred to as the interior) and are coated with a thin layer of chocolate using dipping tools. They are decorated in a simple elegant manner after coating. As when working with any tempered chocolate, make sure the room temperature is approximately 68°F (20°C) when you dip the candies. The candy interiors should be the same, or a slightly higher, temperature for a satisfactory result. If the interiors are too cold, the chocolate will harden too quickly from the inside, resulting in a thicker coating than is desirable. Also, rather than a proper satin finish, the surface can become dull and whitish-gray (you will see the same thing happen to a box of candies left in a warm location after the chocolate hardens again). Once the candies have been covered, they can be left to harden at a slightly lower temperature to speed up the process. A slow-moving fan can also be used. Candies should be stored in the same way as any chocolate: covered in a well-ventilated room with a temperature of 60–65°F (16–19°C).

Fig Logs

80 candies

4 ounces (115 g) dried figs

8 ounces (225 g) blanched almonds, lightly toasted

12 ounces (340 g) powdered sugar

1 tablespoon (15 ml) light rum, approximately

1 teaspoon (5 ml) vanilla extract

sweet dark chocolate, tempered

1. Remove the stems from the figs. Place the figs in a saucepan with enough water to cover. Bring to a boil and cook for 10 minutes. Drain the water and purée the figs in a food processor. Set aside.

2. Process the almonds with half of the sugar in a food processor until the mixture is the consistency of granulated sugar. Transfer to a bowl and stir in the remaining sugar, rum, vanilla, and fig purée. Adjust with additional rum as needed to make a firm paste.

3. Divide the filling into four equal pieces. Roll each piece into a 30-inch (75-cm) rope, using powdered sugar to prevent it from sticking. Place the ropes next to each other and cut across, slicing each one into twenty 1½-inch (3.7-cm) pieces. Place the pieces slightly apart on a sheet pan lined with baking paper and allow them to dry overnight on a covered rack.

4. Dip the candies into tempered dark chocolate, using a two-pronged dipping fork. Slide off onto sheet pans lined with baking paper. Before the chocolate sets, mark the top of the candies with the dipping fork, making two lines in the center of the logs, perpendicular to the long sides.

 **Gianduja**

3 pounds, 12 ounces (1 kg, 705 g) Gianduja

10 ounces (285 g) hazelnuts

10 ounces (285 g) blanched almonds, lightly toasted

1 pound (455 g) powdered sugar

4 ounces (115 g) cocoa butter, melted

1 pound, 4 ounces (570 g) sweet dark chocolate, melted

Gianduja is a creamy chocolate confection flavored with toasted nut paste. While actually a candy, Gianduja is also used a great deal in the pastry shop as a flavoring and in fillings. It is quite easy to make, but most professionals today purchase it from a supplier.

1. Lightly toast the hazelnuts and rub them between your hands or against a large-mesh drum sieve to remove the skins. Process the hazelnuts, almonds, and sugar in a high-speed food processor, continuing to grind the mixture until the oil begins to separate from the nuts and a thick paste is formed. If the mixture turns into a powder rather than a paste, just proceed with the recipe; the Gianduja will not be as smooth, but it will still be quite usable.

2. Combine the cocoa butter and chocolate. Add the nut mixture and stir until you have obtained a smooth mass. Place in a covered container. Store and reheat as you would chocolate. Gianduja will keep fresh for up to six months.

 Gianduja Bites

approximately 100 candies

1 pound (455 g) Gianduja (preceding recipe), melted

12 ounces (340 g) sweet light chocolate, melted

1. Combine the Gianduja, melted light chocolate, and sliced almonds. Pour into a 9-inch (22.5-cm) ring placed on a sheet pan or cardboard lined with baking paper. Allow to set.

2. Cut out rounds using a 1-inch (2.5-cm) plain candy or cookie cutter. Knead the scraps together, form, cut, and repeat until you have cut all of the filling. Fasten a whole almond to the top of each candy, using a small drop of melted chocolate.

6 ounces (170 g) sliced almonds,
lighted toasted
100 whole blanched almonds,
lightly toasted
sweet light chocolate, tempered

3. Dip the candies in the tempered chocolate, using a three-pronged dipping fork.

 ## Mimosa

approximately 60 candies

6 ounces (170 g) granulated sugar
a few drops of lemon juice
³/₄ cup (180 ml) heavy cream, hot
1 pound, 4 ounces (570 g) sweet light
chocolate, melted
sweet light chocolate, tempered
sweet dark chocolate, tempered
candied violets

NOTE: Tempered chocolate is thick enough that the marks left by the dipping fork will remain when the candy is inverted onto the baking paper. If coating chocolate is used, slide the candy off the fork instead and wait until the chocolate starts to thicken (about 30 seconds if the chocolate is at the proper temperature). Then mark two lines crosswise in the center by placing the dipping fork into the chocolate and pulling straight up.

1. Place the sugar and lemon juice in a small, heavy-bottomed saucepan. Cook over medium heat, stirring constantly with a wooden spoon, until all of the sugar has melted and turned light golden brown. Quickly, and carefully, to avoid being splattered, add the hot cream. Stir over the heat until any lumps have been cooked out.

2. When smooth, remove from the heat and stir in the melted light chocolate. If you overcaramelize the sugar, the mixture will separate. To bring it back together, add 1 tablespoon (15 ml) heavy cream. Return to the heat and stir until the cream is mixed in and the mixture is smooth.

3. Pour the mixture into a 9-inch (22.5-cm) ring placed on a sheet pan lined with baking paper. Let set. Cut out ovals using a 1¹/₄-inch (3.1-cm) oval cookie cutter. Knead the scraps of filling together, form, cut, and repeat until all of the filling is used.

4. Brush the top of the candies with a thin layer of tempered light chocolate (to prevent them from sticking to the dipping fork).

5. Place the candies, chocolate-side down, on a two-pronged dipping fork and dip into tempered dark chocolate. Place them on sheet pans lined with baking paper, turning the candies over as you remove them from the fork to mark the tops (see note). Place a small piece of candied violet (about the size of a grain of rice) in the center before the chocolate hardens.

 ## Nougat Montélimar

approximately 80 candies

powdered sugar
5 ounces (140 g) whole blanched
almonds, lightly toasted
5 ounces (140 g) whole toasted
hazelnuts, skins removed
3 ounces (85 g) pistachios, skins
removed, lightly dried
5 ounces (140 g) candied red cherries,
coarsely chopped
4 egg whites (¹/₂ cup/120 ml)
³/₄ cup (180 ml) or 9 ounces (255 g)
honey
12 ounces (340 g) granulated sugar

1. Dust a small area of a marble slab or table with powdered sugar.

2. Combine the nuts and cherries. Reserve in a warm place such as covered in a very low oven.

3. Whip the egg whites for a few seconds just until foamy. Bring the honey to a boil and then gradually pour it into the egg whites in a steady stream, with the mixer on low speed. Increase to high speed and continue whipping until the mixture has cooled and formed stiff peaks. Reserve.

4. Take the usual precautions for sugar boiling (see Boiled Sugar Basic Recipe page 936) and boil the sugar, glucose or corn syrup, and water to 295°F (146°C). Immediately pour the hot syrup into the egg white mixture in a slow steady stream, while stirring constantly with a whisk. Return the mixture to the saucepan and continue to cook for about 10 minutes longer, stirring rapidly, over medium heat. Test to see if it is done by dropping a small piece into cold water: It should be quite firm.

12 ounces (340 g) glucose or corn
   syrup
½ cup (120 ml) water
cocoa butter, melted
sweet dark chocolate, tempered

5. Stir in the reserved (warm) nuts and cherries. Pour the nougat mixture on top of the prepared marble surface. Roll and form into a ³/₄-inch (2-cm) thick rectangle using a rolling pin dusted lightly with powdered sugar. Let cool partially.

6. Brush away the excess powdered sugar from the top and bottom of the nougat. Cut into strips 1¹/₄ inches (3.1 cm) wide, then cut each strip into slices ³/₈ inch (9 mm) thick (use a serrated knife with a sawing motion if the nougat tends to stick to the chef's knife).

7. Brush one cut side of each piece with a thin film of hot cocoa butter. Use a three-pronged dipping fork to dip the bottom and sides into melted dark chocolate, leaving the cocoa butter side exposed.

 Orange Moons

approximately 65 candies

grated zest of two small oranges
6 ounces (170 g) soft unsalted butter
6 ounces (170 g) smooth Fondant
   (page 1011)
2 tablespoons (30 ml) orange liqueur
1 pound (455 g) sweet dark chocolate,
   tempered
sweet light chocolate, tempered
sweet dark chocolate, tempered

NOTE: *Generally chocolate does not need to be tempered when it is added to a filling. In this recipe it helps harden the interior, but it is not absolutely necessary.*

1. Mix the orange zest into the butter and Fondant and cream together well. Stir in the orange liqueur. Gradually mix in 1 pound (455 g) tempered dark chocolate (see note). Wait until the filling starts to thicken, then pour into a 9-inch (22.5-cm) ring set on a sheet pan or cardboard lined with baking paper. Allow the filling to set up.

2. Cut out 1¹/₂-inch (3.7-cm) rounds, using a plain cookie cutter. Roll the scraps between sheets of baking paper and continue to cut rounds until all the filling is used. Cut the rounds in half.

3. Dip each candy into tempered light chocolate, using a three-pronged dipping fork. Place on sheet pans lined with baking paper, turning the candies over as you remove them from the fork to mark the tops. When the coating is set, decorate the rounded part of the top edge by piping a design with dark chocolate.

 Pistachio Slices

80 candies

10 ounces (285 g) Praline Paste
   (page 10)
4 ounces (115 g) melted cocoa butter
4 ounces (115 g) sweet light
   chocolate, melted
4 ounces (115 g) sweet dark
   chocolate, melted
4 ounces (115 g) blanched pistachios,
   skins removed and chopped fine
sweet light chocolate, tempered
sweet dark chocolate, tempered

1. Adjust ¹/₂-inch (1.2-cm) thick metal bars to make an 8-by-7¹/₂-inch (20-×-18.7-cm) rectangle, or cut and tape heavy cardboard to size. Place the form on a paper-lined sheet pan or cardboard.

2. Combine the Praline Paste, cocoa butter, melted light and dark chocolates, and pistachios. Pour the mixture into the frame and allow it to set. You may want to help it along by placing it in the refrigerator briefly. Cut crosswise into five 1¹/₂-by-8-inch (3.7-×-20-cm) strips.

3. Brush a thin layer of tempered light chocolate over the strips and allow it to set. Place the strips, chocolate side down, on a wire rack, positioning them so that the wires run at a 90° angle to the strips so it will be easier to remove them later. Spread a thin layer of tempered light chocolate on the top and sides with a spatula. Immediately transfer them to a sheet pan or cardboard lined with baking paper. Streak thin lines of tempered dark chocolate (the short way) across the strips. Cut each strip crosswise into sixteen ¹/₂-inch (1.2-cm) wide slices.

Dark Truffles

approximately 60 candies

1 cup (240 ml) heavy cream
1/2 teaspoon (2.5 ml) vanilla extract
1 pound, 2 ounces (510 g) sweet dark
    chocolate, chopped
3 ounces (85 g) soft unsalted butter
powdered sugar
sweet dark chocolate, tempered

 ## Light Truffles

approximately 65 candies

1 cup (240 ml) heavy cream
1/2 teaspoon (2.5 ml) vanilla extract
1 pound, 5 ounces (595 g) sweet light
    chocolate, chopped
3 ounces (85 g) soft unsalted butter
powdered sugar
sweet light chocolate, tempered

 ## White Truffles

approximately 75 candies

1 cup (240 ml) heavy cream
1 pound, 2 ounces (510 g) white
    chocolate, chopped
3 ounces (85 g) Praline Paste
    (page 10)
3 ounces (85 g) soft unsalted butter
3 ounces (85 g) cocoa butter, melted
powdered sugar
white chocolate, tempered

*NOTE: If time does not permit making all three
fillings for the truffles, make one kind and
divide the filling into three parts. Roll and coat
each with the various types of chocolate, and
you will still have a nice assortment of truffles,
in only half the time.*

1. Heat the cream and vanilla to the boiling point. Remove from heat and add the chopped chocolate, stirring until it is completely melted. Cool the mixture to approximately 86°F (30°C) and then stir in the butter.

2. Wait until the filling starts to thicken, then transfer it to a pastry bag with a no. 6 (12-mm) plain tip. Pipe out in small mounds the size of cherries, or a little less than 1/2 ounce (15 g) each, on sheet pans lined with baking paper. Refrigerate for a few minutes to set.

3. Roll the centers into round balls between your hands, using powdered sugar to keep them from sticking. Let them firm up again, then precoat by rolling on a thin coat of tempered chocolate with your hands. When the coating has hardened and the interiors have reached the proper temperature, dip them into tempered chocolate, using a round dipping fork. As they are dipped, transfer to a fine wire rack and roll to produce the typical uneven (spiked) surface.

*F*ollow the instructions for Dark Truffles (preceding recipe).

1. Heat the cream to boiling point. Remove from the heat and stir in the chopped chocolate. Keep stirring until the chocolate is completely melted. Set aside to cool to approximately room temperature.

2. Combine the Praline Paste and butter and beat to a creamy consistency. Stir into the chocolate mixture. Mix in the cocoa butter. Continue with steps two and three as directed for Dark Truffles, precoating and covering the candies with tempered white chocolate.

18

Sugar Work

Sugar is a truly amazing commodity and is one that is indispensable to the baker. The term *sugar* can be applied to more than one hundred different naturally occurring organic compounds that by definition will form white or clear crystals when purified, are sweet in flavor, and are water soluble. All forms of sugars are part of the carbohydrate food group. Sugar as we know it in the kitchen—granulated, powdered, confectioners', or brown—is sucrose and is the product of an extensive refining process that begins with sugarcane or sugar beets. Although these two plants are totally different in their botanical composition and are often cultivated on opposite sides of the globe, you cannot identify by taste alone whether the sugar you use to sweeten your coffee came from sugarcane or sugar beets; their chemical composition and their flavor are identical after refining. While sugar in different forms has been commercially important since ancient times—the sugar trade, in fact, having affected the world as much as any other single commodity during a period that lasted several hundred years—only in the last 150 years have its chemistry and biochemical distinctions been studied. Nobel prizes for studies in sugar chemistry were awarded in 1902, 1937, and 1970.

Nutritional Value

Sugar consumption as it relates to nutrition has been the topic of much debate, and there are those who feel that eating sugar can produce negative side effects running the gamut from depression to hyperactivity, especially in children. While it is accepted that consuming sugar can lead to dental problems, no other physical or emotional detriments have been substantiated by research. The FDA has stated that "... there is no conclusive evidence on sugars that demonstrates a hazard to the general public when sugars are consumed at the levels that are current and are now practiced." In other words, like everything else, moderation is the key. Of course, there are individuals with specific health concerns that require them to monitor their intake of sugar or abstain from it altogether. All sugars are converted to glucose in the body in the same way, whether the source is refined sugar or naturally occurring sugar—in fruit, for example. Sugar, like all carbohydrates, provides 4 calories per gram, the same as protein, and is obviously fat-free. With today's focus on reducing fat consumption, sugar can play an important role in providing flavor and appeal without fat. However, while carbohydrates are the body's primary source of energy, sugar calories are basically "empty calories," containing only trace amounts of vitamins and minerals.

Types of Sugar

The word *sugar* is most commonly used to refer to granulated table sugar. However, many other types of sugar, with different chemical structures, are used in the pastry shop. The specifics and distinctions between various sugar products, such as granulated sugar, brown sugar, confectioners' sugar, maple sugar, invert sugar, turbinado sugar, and so on, are discussed on pages 1114 and 1115.

Sugars are divided into two basic groups: double-sugars, called disaccharides, which consist of two simple sugars linked together—these include sucrose (beet and cane sugar), maltose (known as malt sugar), and lactose (the sugar found in milk)—and single-sugars, or simple sugars, which are called monosaccharides. Simple sugars include glucose (also called dextrose) and fructose (also called levulose). In sugarcane and sugar beets, glucose and fructose, both monosaccharides or simple sugars, combine chemically to form the disaccharide or double-sugar, sucrose. Glucose is used as a sweetener in wine and drug production and is added to boiled sugar for many of the techniques in this chapter (see page 1114). Glucose is also the form of sugar into which digested carbohydrates are metabolized in the body. Fructose is used as a food preservative as well as a sweetener. These different types of sugar vary a great deal in their sweetness. Lactose is less sweet than sucrose, and fructose is sweeter than both lactose and sucrose.

History

The production of sugar has a long and interesting history and has been responsible for changing the course of many nations, and indeed world history, through sugar's commercial exchange and consumption.

Though sugar has brought pleasure and riches to many, scores of people were sacrificed during the evolution of its production since nearly all of the early mass sugar trade was supported by slavery.

Europeans first tasted sugar at the time of the Crusades. Until then honey had been the only sweetener known in that part of the world, but sugar (although not in the form we know it) had already existed in the tropical parts of the world for many hundreds of years. Presumably, sugarcane and therefore its early refinement originated in New Guinea and then spread through the islands of the South Pacific to Southeast Asia and India. From there it went to China and the ancient Arab world, all long before eventually reaching Europe, and much longer still before it came to what would later be known as America. Over time, the taste of "red honey," as sugar was once called, improved with better refining techniques, although the process used all the way from the Middle Ages up to the 1800s (when machinery changed the manufacture) was fundamentally the same—extracting the sugarcane juice, boiling the juice, clarifying (this was done at one time using egg white or animal blood), and crystallizing—the methods used to accomplish these tasks have simply become more modern over time. The partially purified sugar that was originally introduced to Europe from the East had a bitter aftertaste and was very expensive compared with honey, which had a better flavor. Sugar, therefore, was definitely a luxury item at first, more common as a status symbol and as a medicinal agent than as a sweetener. It was to be some time before the confectioners', or "sugarbaker" (as it was appropriately called at one time), craft came into being.

In the 1400s European explorers, including Columbus, brought sugarcane cuttings to the Caribbean and South America, and the plants flourished in the moist warm climate. When the explorers returned with news of these desirable and unprotected lands, perfect for growing sugarcane, the possibilities for production and the end to dependence on the Eastern sugar sources were immediately evident. By the middle of the 1500s and early 1600s, sugar had become a major trade commodity and a form of currency. Europe was importing several tons annually, and a person with a large chunk of sugar (a sugarloaf) in his kitchen was considered very well-to-do. Sugar production in South America and the Caribbean islands had become the largest, most lucrative industry in the world at the start of the 1600s, supported for the most part by slave trade. Much of the Caribbean islands, as well as the coasts of western Africa, Brazil, and Mexico, had been colonized first by Portugal and Spain, and then by the English, Dutch, and French. Hundreds of sugar factories were in production, and native island populations were virtually exterminated through forced labor on the plantations. Soon African slaves were abducted and brought to the islands, resulting in a trade network between the islands, the North American Colonies, and Europe, and paving the way for the future slave era in the southern United States. Sugar trade continued to affect the world for the next century: Numerous land exchanges and political decisions were based on its production, and the wealth it brought shifted the balance of power. When France lost the Sugar Islands in the West Indies to England in the late 1700s, it severely affected France's economic standing and was one of the reasons that France supported the American Colonists in the Revolutionary War, and the huge fortunes made by English plantation owners contributed in large part to the financing of the Industrial Revolution. Abolitionists, meanwhile, most especially in Britain, were fighting for a ban on sugar products because of the slave labor used in its production, and sugar manufacturers in East India, who made their product without slaves, as well as the retailers offering East Indian sugar, made it a point to let that be known. Eventually, as the European countries gradually outlawed slavery in the West Indian Colonies, sugarcane production in the areas declined. This era of sugar virtually controlling the world had lasted approximately two hundred years during which millions of human beings lost their lives to its cause. In *A History of Food* by Maguelonne Toussaint-Samat, 1987, Werner Sombart is quoted on this subject as saying, "We grew rich because whole races died for us. For us, continents were depopulated." The same source quotes Bernardin de Saint-Pierre expressing a similar sentiment, "I do not know whether coffee and sugar are necessary to the happiness of Europe, but I know very well that those two plants have brought misfortune on both parts of the world."

Because the majority of the sugarcane was grown far away, required transportation, and its availability and price in Europe continued to be dependent on world conditions, Europeans were attempting to cultivate sugarcane at home, although without success. A breakthrough occurred in the mid-1700s when a German pharmacist, Andreas Marggraf, discovered that the sucrose in beets was identical in chemical composition to the sucrose in sugarcane. In 1787 he perfected a way to boil the sap from a particular variety of beet that rendered a coarse grain with the look and taste of cane sugar. With this, the sugar beet industry was born, and the trend then spread to France, Russia, Sweden, and Austria-Hungary. The first sugar-beet factory was opened in Germany in 1803. Today, the sugar-beet industry is responsible for more than one-third of the world's sugar production.

Sugarcane Production in North America

Sugarcane production in North America began during the 1600s; the first sugar refinery was located in New York City and was started in 1689. Sugar production did not become a major industry in the United States, however, until the 1830s. In 1868 Claus Spreckels of San Francisco invented a new, faster method for refining sugar and opened a major refinery in California. Finally, by the late 1800s, sugar had become the affordable, much used product in America as we know it today. Since 1979 the world has made more sugar than can be sold. Consumption in the United States now stands at about 9 million pounds per year.

The ratio of sugar used in the food industry to that used by consumers has changed drastically in the last several decades. In the early to middle part of the century, when most food was prepared at home, consumer use accounted for about two-thirds of total sugar consumption, and food manufacture was responsible for about one-third. Now, with much less of the food production requiring large amounts of sugar being done at home—baking, fruit canning, curing of meats, and the preparation of jams and preserves—those numbers have almost exactly reversed, with the food industry currently using a bit more than two-thirds of the total production in the manufacture of processed products.

Sugar Production

Sugarcane and sugar beets are the primary sources for commercial sugar production, which consists of the harvesting of these sucrose-rich plants and converting the sucrose into crystallized sugar. Other sources that yield sucrose are maple sap, sorghum cane, some date and palm trees, watermelons, and grapes, but their cultivation for the purpose of sugar production is negligible in comparison. The world's largest producers of cane sugar are Brazil, India, Cuba, Mexico, the United States, and Pakistan. Producers of beet sugar include the Ukraine, Russia, Germany, France, and the United States.

All green plants manufacture glucose in their leaves through a process called photosynthesis, by which plants transform the sun's energy into food. In the leaves, the glucose is converted to sucrose, before being transported to the roots and stems. Most plants convert the sucrose a step further, making it into starch, for storage. Sugarcane and sugar beets manufacture sucrose in great quantities, but unlike most other plants, they store it unchanged. Figure 18–1 illustrates the process for refining sugarcane and sugar beets.

Refining and Processing Sugarcane

Sugarcane is a tropical grass that is cultivated in warm, moist climates. The canes grow from a little less than a year to close to three years before harvest, each cane growing to between 10 and 20 feet high. Raw cane sugar contains 12–14 percent sucrose. Sugarcane is produced in the United States in Florida, Louisiana, Hawaii, and Texas. The production process occurs in two locations: at sugar mills and sugar refineries. The plants are harvested by cutting the cane off close to the ground with machines, or in some areas by hand using a machete. The leaves are stripped off the stalks, and the cane stalks are transported to a sugar mill. The refining process begins by crushing and shredding the stalks. The resulting material is passed through and pressed under a series of heavy rollers to extract the cane juice. The waste product left from this process is called bagasse and is most often used as fuel to run the mills but is also processed into paper. The cane juice is clarified by adding milk of lime (made from limestone) and carbon dioxide. As the carbon dioxide creates bubbles, the lime forms calcium carbonate, and

Sugar Production and Refinement

Processing Sugarcane

Sugarcane Is Harvested → Transported to Sugar Mill

At the Sugar Mill

Stalks Are Crushed and Shredded → Juice Is Extracted →

Cane Juice Is Clarified Using Milk of Lime and Carbon Dioxide →

Juice Is Concentrated by Boiling under Vacuum →
Syrup Is Now Called Massecuite

Massecuite Is Crystallized by Evaporating Remaining Water →

Crystals Are Spun in a Centrifuge →

Product Becomes Golden Raw Sugar →
(By-product of Boiling and Spinning Is Molasses)

Shipped to Refinery

At the Sugar Refinery

Raw Sugar Is Washed in a Sugar Syrup →

Crystals Are Spun in a Centrifuge to Separate the Molasses Film →

Crystals Are Dissolved into a Syrup →

Syrup Is Filtered in Stages to Remove Color and Impurities →

Syrup Is Concentrated →

Syrup Is "Seeded" with Sugar Crystals →

After the Formation of Larger Crystals, Spun in a Centrifuge and Washed →

Crystals Are Dried → Crystals Are Sifted →

Sugar Is Packaged for Consumer and Food Industry Use

Processing Sugar Beets

Sugar Beets Are Harvested → Transported to Sugar Beet Factory

At the Sugar Beet Factory

Beets Are Washed and Sliced →

Slices Are Placed in Diffuser with Hot Water →

Sugar-Laden Water Is Drawn Off →

Mixture Is Clarified Using Milk of Lime and Carbon Dioxide →

Liquid Is Filtered →

Moisture Is Evaporated under Vacuum to Produce Syrup →

Syrup Is Filtered →

Syrup Is Boiled → Crystals Form →
Syrup Is Now Called Massecuite

Massecuite Is Spun in Centrifuge →

Mixture Is Washed → White Sugar Crystals Form →

Crystals Are Dried → Crystals Are Sifted →

Sugar Is Packaged for Consumer and Food Industry Use

FIGURE 18–1 The production and refinement of sugarcane and sugar beets

these chalklike crystals bubble through the mixture attracting the non-sugar matter such as wax, fats, and gums away from the juice. The calcium carbonate and other materials then settle to the bottom, leaving the clarified sugarcane juice. The juice is next concentrated by boiling in several stages under a vacuum, which allows the syrup to boil at a lower temperature to protect it from caramelizing. At this stage it becomes a thick brown syrup called massecuite. The syrup is crystallized by evaporating the last amount of water and is then passed into a centrifuge with a perforated basket at the center. After spinning and drying, the result is golden raw sugar. (A by-product of the boiling and spinning stages is molasses.)

The raw sugar is approximately 96–98 percent sucrose. The crystals are light brown because they are covered by a thin film of molasses. The molasses film contains sugar, water, and impurities such as plant materials. At this stage the raw sugar is transported from the sugar mill to a sugar refinery, almost always by ship, which is the reason that major refineries are located at seaports.

At the refinery the raw sugar is transformed into granulated sugar, brown sugar, and other products for both consumers and the food industry. The raw sugar is first mixed with a warm syrup made of water and sugar, which essentially washes the raw sugar to loosen the molasses coating. The mixture is spun in large centrifuges again, separating the molasses film from the crystals. The crystals are washed and dissolved into a syrup that is filtered to remove any remaining molasses and impurities. The sugar is now a clear golden liquid. Further filtering removes the remaining color, leaving a transparent white syrup (whiteners or bleaches are not used to remove color). Some of the water content is removed and the concentrated syrup is conveyed to a vacuum where fine sugar crystals are added. As evaporation occurs larger sugar crystals form around the fine crystal "seeds," producing the proper size. The sugar goes to a centrifuge again where any non-crystallized syrup is spun off and the crystals are washed. The damp crystals then go to dryers, and after drying, the sugar granules are sifted through screens to separate the various sized crystals for packaging.

Refining and Processing Sugar Beets

Sugar beets grow in temperate climates and store sugar in their roots underground. Sugar beets are raised in many states throughout the country including California, Colorado, Idaho, Michigan, Ohio, Oregon, Washington, and many of the Great Plains states. The U.S. sugar beet crop provides slightly less than half of the total U.S. sugar crop. Sugar beets weigh about two pounds each and contain 16–18 percent sucrose in their raw form. Their growing season is about five months long. Unlike sugarcane, the process for refining sugar beets takes place all at one location, generally near the growing area since they do not travel well. Sugar beet factories operate seasonally in response to the harvest, and during the time of operation the facilities may be in production continuously day and night every day of the week. The refining process is basically the same as for sugarcane, although not as many procedures are involved. The first step at the factory is to wash and slice the beets. The sliced beets then go into a tank known as a diffuser, where they are agitated as hot water washes over the slices. The sugar-laden water is drawn off, and the remaining beet pulp is processed separately, usually for livestock feed. The watery beet juice is treated with milk of lime and carbon dioxide in carbonation tanks, as is done with the sugarcane juice. After the juice is filtered it is thin and light brown. This is evaporated under vacuums where it becomes a syrup. The syrup is filtered again, boiled again, and crystals now begin to form. The crystal and syrup combination, as in cane sugar production, is called massecuite. The massecuite is sent to a centrifuge, and after spinning it is washed to produce pure white crystals of sugar. These are dried and sifted to separate the various sizes of crystals before being packaged.

Effects of Sugar in Baking

By looking at the ingredients listed in most pastry recipes, you can clearly see that a pastry chef would find it almost impossible to produce the majority of the traditional bakery products (keeping the desired flavor and appearance) without using some type of sugar. In addition to providing a sweet flavor that seems to be universally popular, sugar acts as an emulsifying (creaming) agent when mixed with fat by incorporating air; becomes a foaming agent when mixed with eggs; weakens the gluten structure of flour, contributing to a tender and fine-textured product; provides food for the developing yeast; enhances the smoothness and mouth feel of frozen ice cream; caramelizes when heated to give an appetizing color and crust to just about all baked items; delays coagulation of egg proteins in custards; helps to prevent jams and preserves from spoiling; and last, by retaining moisture, increases the shelf life of baked goods.

Decorative Sugar Work

Sugar is the single ingredient used in the largest number of recipes (nearly all) throughout this text. This chapter explains the artistic side of its use. Sugar can be boiled into a thick syrup and turned into a variety of shapes by casting, blowing, or pulling, or it can be spun into delicate threads to be used as a decoration. With the addition of gum tragacanth or gelatin, sugar can be made into a paste to be rolled, formed, or molded in almost any way imaginable. Caramelized sugar is used to coat fruit and nuts for dessert garnishes; it can be made into fragile cages to showcase a simple dessert like ice cream and make it special; or it can be piped out into ornaments, figurines, and even flexible spirals. When nuts are added to caramelized sugar, it becomes nougatine, which has many decorative uses. Royal icing is made by mixing powdered sugar and egg whites, and it too can be used to create decorative ornaments to garnish cakes and pastries, or it can be used for showpieces.

To master all or even a few of the many techniques for using sugar decoratively takes many years of experience, but the good news is that time is really the only investment you will need to make, as many projects can be completed with very little equipment, and sugar itself is very inexpensive.

Equipment Required to Work with Sugar

The single most expensive item you need in order to get started is a professional sugar thermometer. You can buy a regular home-use candy thermometer for about one-tenth of the price, but these are easily broken and should also be checked for accuracy before use (the thermometer must read exactly 212°F/100°C when placed in boiling water at sea level). The first thing required for sugar boiling is obviously a heat source; this does not have to be a stove, a portable electric burner works fine for this purpose—since the sugar syrup should boil gently—and often makes more sense if you set up an area for sugar work that is out of the way of other production. The basic equipment you should have in addition is as follows:

- a copper or stainless-steel pan with a 2 quart (1 l, 920 ml) capacity,
- a bain-marie; the bowl should be large enough to hold the pan,
- a small bowl with a brush dedicated for use in sugar boiling,
- a sugar thermometer as described above,
- a metal scraper,
- a sieve or perforated spoon for skimming,
- a small drop bottle,
- a pint or quart measuring cup,
- a fixative syringe or air brush for spraying the finished pieces with color or lacquer, and,
- if you are not working on a marble or granite worktable, a small slab of either one or a silicone mat.

The basic ingredients needed are:

- clean water measured into the pan according to the individual recipes, in the small bowl with the brush, and in the bain-marie;
- sanding or granulated sugar, preferably a newly opened bag to ensure there has not been any contamination;
- tartaric acid solution in the drop bottle prepared 1:1 (tartaric acid powder dissolved in an equal amount of hot water by weight);
- food coloring in liquid, paste, or powdered form (powders and pastes are many times more concentrated; before using powders in sugar work they must be dissolved in water);
- edible lacquer and a dehumidifying agent to protect the finished pieces (discussed in more detail in the following section); and
- glucose, 44° Baumé or, if not obtainable, light corn syrup (substitute an equal amount).

Storing and Protecting Finished Sugar Pieces

Because sugar is hygroscopic (it attracts and absorbs moisture), it must be protected both from contact with moisture and against absorption of moisture in the air. This is especially important for finished pieces that are stored, whether it is a simple pulled sugar rose or ribbon or an elaborate showpiece, but it also applies to leftover sugar scraps and pulled sugar prepared ahead and ready to reheat and use. Showpieces can be both displayed and preserved in glass or Plexiglas boxes or domes with silica gel or quicklime hidden inside the holder. For storage only, a plastic bag works great; you still need the dehumidifying agent inside. Portioned slabs or pieces of prepared sugar will keep for many months stored in an airtight container with silica gel or quicklime.

Silica gel blue and quicklime are the most common dehumidifying agents used to protect the sugar from moisture. Silica gel is a polymer of silicic acid separated from the whole by water and formed from two hydroxide groups. It changes color depending on its water content: when dry the crystals are blue; when it has absorbed the maximum amount of moisture possible, the color changes to pink. When this happens the crystals can be dried out in a 300°F (149°C) oven for a few minutes until they return to the original blue color; silica gel crystals are reusable indefinitely. Quicklime is a type of sedimentary rock that forms over million of years and solidifies over the course of time. It is quarried, crushed into smaller pieces, and then burned for many hours at an extremely high temperature, during which time, through chemical reaction, it becomes CaO, calcium oxide. Three areas in Europe where quicklime is found are the White Cliffs of Dover in Great Britain, White Stone of Ulm in Germany, and Champagne in France. Quicklime is also known as burnt lime and simply "lime." Many industrial chemicals require its use, and quicklime is used in the processing of cane and sugar beet juices. When cold water comes in contact with quicklime it produces an impressive reaction of steam and heat—up to 212°F (100°C). It is strongly caustic and can severely irritate skin and should therefore never be touched, especially with wet hands. As the quicklime absorbs humidity it will turn to powder and must then be replaced. This can take from a few days to one year, depending on the percentage of humidity and the amount of quicklime used. In most cases only a few small chunks are needed. The quicklime should be kept apart from the sugar it is protecting in a small container with air holes to prevent any mess as it disintegrates. Both silica gel and quicklime are available as dehumidifying agents under various brand names.

Boiled Sugar

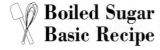

Boiled Sugar Basic Recipe

3 cups (720 ml) or 1 pound, 8 ounces (680 g)

1 cup (240 ml) water

2 pounds, 8 ounces (1 kg, 135 g) sanding or granulated sugar

8 ounces (225 g) glucose or light corn syrup

food color, optional for some uses

*T*his recipe is used for Spun Sugar, Cast Sugar, and Pulled or Blown Sugar. Make sure that your sugar and tools are absolutely clean. Scoop the top layer of sugar to one side in the bin before taking out what you need. Try to use sanding sugar if possible. And never use the flour scoop when measuring the sugar!

There are two important reasons for using glucose when boiling sugar: it helps prevent recrystallization, and it gives the finished sugar mass some elasticity (see note 2 on page 955). Tartaric acid is also of utmost importance in cooking sugar for its low pH value and because it too delays or prevents recrystallizing as in the presence of acid and heat inverts (or splits) part of the sugar into fructose and glucose. Tartaric acid also acts to give the sugar flexibility. It must be added at the proper time using a drop bottle.

12 drops Tartaric Acid Solution
(page 1115), optional for some uses
(see note 2)

NOTE 1: It is a good idea, especially if you are boiling a large amount of sugar, to remove the pan from the heat a few degrees before it reaches the specified temperature, watch the mercury rise to the required temperature off the heat, then plunge the pan into cold water.

NOTE 2: Be precise when measuring the acid. Using too much will make the finished sugar too soft and difficult to work with.

NOTE 3: If you work with sugar frequently, make a larger batch of this recipe. Cook the sugar through step three, then store and finish cooking in smaller portions as needed.

1. Fill a bowl that is large enough to hold the pan used to cook the sugar with enough cold water to reach halfway up the sides of the pan. Set the bowl of water aside.

2. Place the water and sugar in a sugar pan (see page 1125) or a heavy saucepan. Stir the mixture gently over low heat until all of the sugar has dissolved and the syrup has started to boil. If any scum accumulates on top from impurities in the sugar, remove it with a skimmer or small sieve so that it does not cause the sugar to recrystallize later. Add the glucose or corn syrup, stirring until it is thoroughly mixed in. Do not stir any further after this point.

3. Turn the heat to medium, place a lid on the pan, and let the sugar boil hard for a few minutes. The steam trapped inside the pan will wash down the sugar crystals that form on the sides of the pan at this stage. Or you can wash down the sides using a clean brush dipped in water instead (the brush should be dedicated to use in sugar boiling). (See note 3).

4. Place a sugar thermometer in the pan. When the temperature reaches 265°F (130°C), add the coloring if it is being used. Stop brushing and boil the sugar to 280°F (138°C), then add the Tartaric Acid Solution, if used. Continue to boil, watching the temperature constantly, until the desired temperature is reached according to the specific recipe and use.

5. Remove the pan from the heat and dip the bottom of the pan into the bowl of cold water to stop the temperature from going any higher.

Boiled Sugar Method I

NOTE: Pour the extra sugar into a rectangular shape on the oiled marble or onto a silicone mat. When a skin has formed on the top, use a metal scraper to mark the sugar into appropriate sized pieces. Let it solidify and cool completely. Break the sugar into sections at the markings, then store the pieces in an airtight container with a dehumidifying agent to absorb any moisture. The sugar can be stored this way for many weeks.

To reheat the stored sugar, place it on the working frame under heat lamps. Depending on the amount of sugar and the number of heat lamps, it can take from 5 to 25 minutes for the sugar to become soft enough to work with. Keep turning the sugar every few minutes to assure even heat distribution and prevent recrystallization from overheating.

These instructions are used for Pulled and Blown Sugar. It seems that, depending upon the philosophy of a particular chef, the desired temperature to which the syrup should be boiled, and the amount of tartaric acid to use, will vary. This is simply a matter of personal preference. Sugar boiled to a higher temperature in combination with less acid will produce a more stable finished product, but with the expense of having to work with a hotter sugar.

1. Following the recipe and directions in the Boiled Sugar Basic Recipe, boil the syrup to 297°F (148°C). Quickly plunge the bottom of the pan into cold water to stop the cooking process. Let stand for about 10 seconds, then remove the pan from the water and wipe off the bottom with a cloth. Set the sugar aside a few seconds longer to allow most of the bubbles to subside. Remove the sugar thermometer and pour the syrup in a steady steam onto a lightly oiled marble slab or table, or a silicone mat (which does not need to be oiled), pouring it into a round puddle (if you do not plan to use all of the sugar right away, see note).

2. As soon as the sugar has formed a skin, slide an oiled metal spatula under the edge of the sugar puddle and fold it in toward the center. Repeat, moving evenly around the circle until the sugar no longer runs and has cooled to the point that it can be pulled in your hands. Start to aerate the sugar as described in the recipe for Pulled and Blown Sugar, pages 940 and 941.

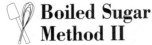

Boiled Sugar Method II

6 cups (1 l, 440 ml) or 3 pounds (1 kg, 365 g) boiled sugar

2 pounds (910 g) sanding or granulated sugar

3¹/₂ cups (840 ml) or 2 pounds, 10 ounces (1 kg, 195 g) light corn syrup

10 ounces (285 g) glucose or additional light corn syrup

food coloring, optional for some uses

12 drops Tartaric Acid Solution (page 1115) (see note 2)

NOTE 1: If any sugar crystals form on the sides of the pan during the boiling period, they must be washed down as described in Boiled Sugar Basic Recipe.

NOTE 2: Be precise when measuring the acid: Using too much will make the finished sugar too soft and difficult to work with.

NOTE 3: When making multiple batches or stock syrup for later use, bring the syrup to a second boil at this point. Remove from the heat and skim the surface to remove any impurities. Pour the syrup into a storage container, cover tightly with plastic wrap, and store at room temperature. When needed, continue to boil the required amount of syrup as directed in Step 2.

This recipe is also used for Pulled and Blown Sugar. It is especially suitable for preparing ahead to warm and soften the precooked sugar in a microwave.

1. Fill a bowl that is large enough to hold the pan used for cooking the sugar with enough cold water to reach halfway up the sides of the pan. Set the bowl aside.

2. Combine the sugar and corn syrup in a sugar pan (see page 1125) or heavy saucepan. Stir constantly over low heat until the mixture comes to a boil. Brush down the sides of the pan, add the glucose (see note 3), and continue boiling over medium heat. When the temperature reaches 265°F (130°C), add color if using. It is important to add the color at this temperature to ensure that the color has sufficient time to blend with the sugar syrup without stirring, and to provide ample time for additional color to be added if needed. Boil the sugar to 280°F (138°C) and then add the Tartaric Acid Solution. Boil to 305°F (152°C). Immediately plunge the bottom of the pan into cold water for about 10 seconds to stop the cooking process. Remove the pan from the water and wipe off the bottom with a towel, wait a few seconds longer, then pour the sugar in a puddle on a lightly oiled marble slab or table, or on a silicone mat (which does not need to be oiled).

3. As soon as the sugar has formed a skin, slide an oiled metal spatula under the edge of the sugar puddle and fold it in toward the center. Repeat, moving evenly around the circle until the sugar no longer runs and has cooled to the point that it can be pulled in your hands. Start to aerate the sugar as described in the recipe for Pulled and Blown Sugar, see pages 940 and 941.

If the sugar is to be stored, pour it directly into three or four separate microwavable plastic containers at the end of step two (if you are not sure they can stand up to the heat of the sugar, test the containers first). When the sugar is completely cold, cover and store until needed. To use the sugar, reheat it in a microwave just long enough so that the sugar can be removed from the container. It does not have to be totally liquid; do not boil it. Pour the sugar out onto the oiled marble slab or table. To ensure that the sugar cools evenly, use a lightly oiled metal scraper and fold the outside of the puddle in toward the middle continuously until the sugar has cooled to the point where it no longer runs. Start to aerate the sugar as described in the recipe for Pulled and Blown Sugar (see pages 940 and 941) as soon as you can pick it up.

Using Colors in Sugar Work

If the entire batch of sugar is to be colored (this applies to Spun, Cast, Pulled, or Blown Sugar), add regular water-soluble food coloring (or powdered coloring dissolved in water first) when the sugar reaches 265°F (130°C), blending the three primary colors of red, yellow, and blue as desired to make various shades. If black food color is not available, make black by mixing equal amounts of the primary colors. Milk-white is obtained by adding a liquid whitener (a food-coloring containing glycerin and titanium dioxide) at the rate of $1/2$ teaspoon (2.5 ml) for the basic sugar recipe or 1 teaspoon (5 ml) for Boiled Sugar Method II. The whitener is added at the same temperature as any other color (265°F/130°C), but for the best milk-white effect, stop boiling the sugar at 295°F (146°C); a drawback, however, is that the sugar will not be as ridged. If you are unable to find liquid whitener, you can make your own by using calcium carbonate (also known as precipitated chalk), which can be ordered from a laboratory. It is made from natural limestone or chalk that contains nearly 100 percent calcium carbonate. Stir 8 ounces (225 g) of the chalk into $2/3$ cup (160 ml) of water and mix into a smooth paste. Store in a sealed glass jar and use as needed. This paste is not as strong as the commercial whitener; you will need to add three times as much solution to obtain a proper milk-white color. The liquid whitener or precipitated chalk can also be added to any other color to turn it opaque; this is especially desirable with cast sugar pieces. Keep in mind when designing your project that adding a whitener will make the shade lighter. If the sugar is to be pulled, it is not necessary to color it white. As the sugar is pulled, the air that is worked into it produces a pleasant, opaque white color.

Spraying Colors

NOTE: Marzipan lacquer is quick drying which is important here, however since this is an expensive lacquer and a majority of these sugar pieces are decorative, clear lacquer from the hardware store works just as well.

A different method is used when casting small figures, because it is not practical to split the sugar into different boils and color them separately. Besides being time-consuming, it is hard to boil a very small amount to a precise temperature. You have to remove the sugar thermometer from its protective casing and hold on to it while you tilt the pan to make the solution deep enough to get a reading. It is easy to overheat the sugar, which can caramelize in an instant at temperatures above 310°F (155°C). Therefore, it makes sense to cast the whole figure in one base color (preferably white), then spray on the desired shades. The color can be sprayed (blown) on using a clever little tool called a fixative syringe. You submerge one end in the color and put the other in your mouth, then spray by blowing air into the syringe. A more modern and convenient method is to use an airbrush. You can obtain different shades by spraying at an angle to the flat surface, because more color will adhere to the area closest to the sprayer. You can also cover part of the surface with paper to achieve a contrasting effect.

Make your own colors for spraying by dissolving a small amount of powdered food coloring in Marzipan lacquer in a small stainless-steel cup. Try to make up only the amount you need at that time. Spray the color onto a paper first to check the effect and strength of the color before applying it to the cast sugar. Naturally, the closer you hold the sprayer to the sugar, and the more forcefully you blow in the case of the syringe or the higher the setting if using an airbrush, the more concentrated the color will be. When you are finished, clean the container and the syringe or airbrush with denatured alcohol. You can also use this technique to apply color to blown sugar pieces.

Pulled and Blown Sugar

This type of sugar work requires you to have an artist's hand and many years of practice before you can produce anything close to what you see in some of the specialty sugar books. Unfortunately, pulling and blowing sugar are becoming more and more obsolete today for these reasons. It is one thing to learn and practice the techniques in school, and another to try and incorporate them into the workplace without going broke at the same time. The problem, of course, is that learning to blow and pull sugar takes a large amount of time away from your other chores and regular production work. You therefore must be interested enough in these types of sugar work to make it a hobby. The weather also plays an important role: If you live in a damp climate you will find it very difficult to work with sugar because the humidity accelerates recrystallization. If you are a beginner, making a rose from pulled sugar, or blowing a small piece of fruit or even a vase, would be a realistic starting point once you have a basic knowledge of sugar work.

Both pulled and blown sugar can be made using the instructions for Boiled Sugar Method I (see page 937) or Boiled Sugar Method II (see page 938). The procedure for cooking, aerating, and forming (pulling and blowing) the sugar is the same for both. Using Method II may give you an edge because the sugar is less likely to recrystallize, plus you can use the microwave to soften the sugar as often as needed while you are working.

After the sugar is cooked, aerate it by drawing it out evenly using your hands, folding it up, and pulling it out again as many times as necessary until enough air has been mixed in to give the sugar a silky sheen (Figure 18–2). Wearing surgical-type gloves will help somewhat to protect your hands from the heat if they are not calloused enough; however, a better alternative is to use cleaning-type rubber gloves. These gloves are thick and clumsy, which does not matter at this point, and will protect and "save" your hands for later steps in the process. You should wear the thin gloves at all times to protect the sugar from sweat on your hands as you work with it. The sugar is now ready to use for either pulling or blowing, or it can also be stored in an airtight container at this stage for later use. Place a dehumidifying agent in the container to absorb moisture. Be careful not too work the sugar too long; if overpulled it will recrystallize and take on a dull matte finish. This will also happen if the sugar is allowed to become too hard or cold while it is being pulled.

Once the sugar has been aerated, keep the part you are not working with warm under the heat lamp at all times to keep it soft while you are forming your design. Check the sugar and turn it frequently to

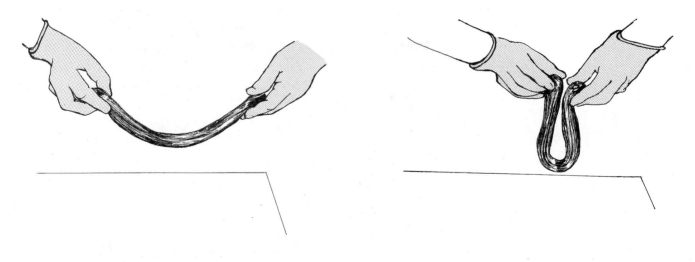

FIGURE 18–2 *Aerating boiled sugar by repeatedly drawing it out, folding it in half, and drawing it out again*

make sure it is not getting overheated. If a thin part of the surface of the sugar should harden, do not attempt to mix it back into the remaining sugar without softening it first; the hardened part will not melt but break into small pieces, ruining the appearance.

Before you begin the following two projects you will need:

- a heat lamp or lamps,
- a Sugar Workbox with screen (see page 944),
- a pair of scissors,
- a Bunsen burner,
- a leaf mold to form the larger rose leaves or a ³/₄-inch (2-cm) oiled dowel when making the sugar bow, and
- a hand-sprayer (called a fixative syringe) or an airbrush to spray the finished pieces.

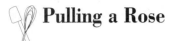

Pulling a Rose

NOTE: Instead of attaching each petal to the center as you make it, you can make up all of the petals individually, then assemble the rose by heating the base of each hardened petal as you attach it. The drawback to this method is that you can no longer mold or alter the shape of the rose as you can when the petals are attached while they are still soft.

1. Prepare pink and green pulled sugar as described above. Once the sugar has the proper consistency and shine, form each piece into a tight ball. Draw out a thin strip from the pink ball about 1 inch (2.5 cm) wide and 4 inches (10 cm) long. Cut this piece off with scissors.

2. Coil the strip into a small conical shape about 1 inch (2.5 cm) long to make the center of the rose. If the strip sets and is too firm to bend, warm it under the heat lamp until it is pliable. (You can also form the rose center using the same technique as for Marzipan Roses; see Figure 19–45, page 1036).

3. Using the thumbs and forefingers of both hands, pull the top part of the pink sugar ball up into a thin ridge (Figure 18–3). Grasp the center of the ridge and draw the edge away to make a slightly elon-

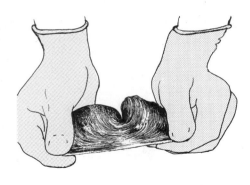

FIGURE 18–3 Pulling the edge of a soft ball of sugar into a thin ridge for the first step in making a sugar rose petal

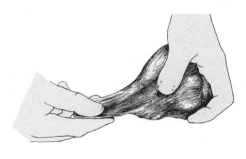

FIGURE 18–4 Pulling an elongated petal out of the thin ridge

gated petal (Figure 18–4). Separate the petal from the sugar ball by pinching it off with your other hand. Quickly curl the top of the petal back as you would for Marzipan Roses (see Figure 19–48, page 1038), then attach it to the center of the rose immediately. Pull and shape two additional elongated petals of the same size and attach them evenly around the center.

4. Make the remaining petals slightly larger and rounded, folding the tops back a little more and forming them into a rather hollow shape like a cupped hand. Attach them as you form them (see note).

5. To make a rosebud, use just the three elongated petals and the center. Fasten the petals together in a close triangular shape around the base, one inside the other.

6. Pull small, pointed green leaves to the desired length from the green sugar ball using the same technique as for the elongated petals. Bend the points back and attach the ends to the roses or buds. Make slightly larger and wider leaves to go on the stems of the roses. Quickly and firmly press them into the leaf mold to transfer the leaf pattern to the sugar. Bend into a nicely curved shape (warm the sugar if necessary) and reserve to place around your rose display.

7. To make a rose stem, use a ridged wire (a coat hanger works fine) cut to the desired size. Push the wire through the soft, green sugar ball. The faster you push it through, the thinner the coating of sugar will be. If you move too fast the sugar will simply break; it may take a few tries to get just the right speed. Heat the tip of the wire over the Bunsen burner and push it into the base of the rose. If you prefer not to have the wire inside (if you are laying the rose on cake or using it to garnish an individual dessert serving), just pull out a thin rope of green sugar for the stem. However, if you want to display the rose standing up, in a basket for example, you must use the wire.

8. Curls or tendrils are easy to make and are a very nice complement to your rose display. To make them, lightly oil a round handle of a small wooden spoon, or you can use a pen that is about the same shape and diameter. Pull a thin rope out of the green sugar ball and quickly wind it around the spoon or pen like a telephone cord; slide it off once it has hardened (see Figures 18–12 and 18–13, page 960).

9. Display your rose, or roses, with a few buds, leaves, and tendrils on a small base cast in sugar, or within a frame made by curling a thick rope of green sugar into a round disk.

10. To prevent the finished sugar pieces from deteriorating due to moisture, keep them in an airtight container with a dehumidifying agent. The pieces can also be sprayed with marzipan lacquer or, if they are to be used for display purposes only, with a thin film of a fast-drying, clear shellac.

Sugar Bow with Ribbons

one bow about 4 inches (10 cm) across with 6-inch (15-cm) long ribbons

NOTE: *Keep in mind that the faster the pulled sugar cools down at this piont, the better it will retain its shape.*

Making a beautiful sugar bow to decorate a petits fours or candy tray, for example, or to use as part of a showpiece, can be done fairly quickly—especially if you have some pieces of colored sugar left from previous sugar work. If so, follow the instructions for softening the sugar on page 940. If the sugar has already been aerated, you will only need to pull it back and forth a few times to bring back its sheen. To make one bow with ribbons you need three or four pieces of colored sugar (one should be white) weighing about 12 ounces (340 g) each.

If you do not have any scrap sugar, make one recipe of Boiled Sugar Method II (page 938). After you add the tartaric acid, continue boiling the sugar approximately 1 minute longer. Divide the syrup into three or four batches, depending on the number of colors you want to use. Then, boil, color, and aerate each batch individually, following the instructions. You should make at least three colors, one of them white.

1. Keep the colored sugar soft under a heat lamp. Pull out a rope of sugar about 4 inches (10 cm) long from each different color. Each rope should be approximately 1/4–1/2 inch (6 mm–1.2 cm) thick, depending on how much of that particular color you want to use in your bow and ribbons. You can, of course, use the same color twice. Place the ropes next to one another (not stacked) in the desired pattern. The ropes should be warm enough to stick together. If necessary, leave them this way under the heat lamp until they are soft enough to stick, turning the ropes from time to time. Do not get any oil on the sugar ropes, as this can prevent them from sticking together.

2. Once the ropes are attached side-by-side, take the whole strip out from under the lamp and let it cool for approximately 30 seconds, turning it over a few times; do not place it directly on a marble slab or marble table or it will cool too much (a silicone mat is useful here).

3. Slowly pull the whole strip of sugar out lengthwise until it has about doubled in length.

4. Using an oiled pair of scissors, cut the strip in half crosswise. Lay the two halves side-by-side under the heat lamp and leave them until they stick together. Pull the strip out lengthwise a second time until doubled in length. You can stop here or repeat the cutting and pulling procedure one more time for a very elaborate ribbon, depending on how thin the sugar is at this point. If the strip is thinner and narrower than you would like, you are probably pulling too fast or working with sugar that is too soft (warm), or both (see note).

5. To make the ribbons, start by pulling one end of the striped sugar out to make a thin strip approximately 1 inch (2.5 cm) wide and 12 inches (30 cm) long. (Don't just hold onto one end and pull it out to the final length all at once. To make the strip uniform in width and thickness you need to pull a few inches, then move your fingers back to where you started, pull a few inches further, start at the base again, and so on.)

6. Using oiled scissors, trim away the very end of the strip, which will be too thick and unattractive. Then cut off two 6-inch (15-cm) pieces, cutting them at an angle crosswise. Pleat the pieces slightly. Attach two narrow ends together to make an upside-down V. Set this piece aside.

7. To make the loops of the sugar bow you need thirteen pieces 4 inches (10 cm) long (it is a good idea to make a few extra to allow for breakage). Pull out one piece at a time from the thick piece of sugar, making them the same width and thickness as the ribbons. Continue to warm the sugar as needed to keep the correct consistency. Cut off each piece as you pull it out and quickly form it into a smooth, curved loop by bending it in half over an oiled wooden dowel or other round object approximately ³/₄ inch (2 cm) thick; then pinch the flat ends together. Immediately pinch the attached flat edges in the opposite direction so that the bottom of the loop comes together in a point and the sides of the loop pleat slightly; this will make it easier to fit the loops together when assembling the bow later. Warm the loops under the heat lamp while you are working so that they are soft enough to shape easily, but be sure that the sugar has cooled sufficiently to hold its shape before removing each loop from the dowel and setting it aside.

8. To assemble the bow, start by flattening a small disk of sugar to approximately the size of a nickel. Attach seven evenly spaced loops around the edge of the disk with the tips pointing in, first softening the tip of each loop until sticky by holding it over a Bunsen burner. You can also make the tip sticky by holding it right next to the heat lamp, but you risk deforming the thin loops. Attach a second layer of five loops in the same way, placing these overlapping the first set slightly and attaching them closer to the center of the disk. Finish by attaching a single loop covering the center of the disk.

9. Attach the finished bow to the reserved ribbons by softening the sugar at the tip where the ribbons meet, then carefully setting the bow on top.

10. Spray the bow and ribbons with marzipan lacquer, using a fixative syringe or airbrush (do not forget to spray the bottom). Store in an airtight container with a dehumidifying agent if desired for extra protection against moisture. If the sugar is completely sealed you should be able to use this mini-showpiece many times.

Sugar Workbox

NOTE: *If you do not have time to build a frame, a silicone mat makes an excellent substitute on which to place the sugar under the heat lamps. However, using one half-size mat on top of the box and another (half or full size) next to*

1. Make a rectangle with the outside dimensions of 11¹/₂ by 15¹/₂ inches (28.7 × 38.7 cm), using 2¹/₂–3-by-¹/₂-inch (6.2–7.5-×-1.2-cm) strips of plywood or cut wood trim. (This size box will fit on a half sheet pan, which is convenient.)

2. Glue and screw the sides together, then sand the edges smooth. (It is bad enough you are going to get blisters on your fingers from the hot sugar; you don't need splinters too!)

the workbox, allowing you to move the sugar between the two areas to regulate the heat as needed, would be the ideal setup.

3. Stretch a piece of nylon window screen tight across the top and staple it in place. The sugar should not actually be worked on the frame: it is just used to support the sugar while it is being softened and/or kept warm under the heat lamps.

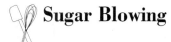

Sugar Blowing

*I*n addition to the tools needed for sugar pulling, you need a cooling fan (a hair dryer with a cool air setting placed on a stand can be used), a small brush, and a one-way, hand-operated air pump with a wooden mouthpiece. If you do not have an air pump, you can blow the sugar by mouth, in much the same way that glassblowers produce their magic, using blow pipes with various openings. Sugar blowing was always done this way in the past before the hand-pump was developed some sixty years ago. Since sugar takes longer to cool than glass, and the blow pipes do not have a one-way valve to prevent the air from escaping, it is much easier to use the hand-pump. The cooling time becomes a real issue when you blow larger pieces; using a more powerful fan can help.

1. Prepare the sugar as directed on pages 940 and 941. Once it has been aerated and has developed the proper shine and temperature, form the sugar into a tight ball and then cut off the amount you need with scissors, cutting from all sides to keep the ball round.

2. Make an indentation in the cut surface with your thumb. Attach a separate small piece of sugar around the wooden mouthpiece or blow pipe, heat both this and the indented surface, and join the two together leaving a small, natural air chamber from the indentation.

3. Pump the air in with one hand to expand the air chamber (see note), while shaping the sugar with the other hand. If the ball of sugar has an uneven thickness, or is warmer on one side than the other, the thinner and/or warmer side will expand faster. To control this, even out the temperature, either cooling the warmer areas by holding them next to the fan or by covering them with your hand while you warm the cooler areas under the lamp.

4. Begin by making a sphere of the appropriate size. Gradually work the sphere away from the wooden tube to produce a small neck, which you will use later to separate the finished piece from the tube. For example, to make a Bosc pear, elongate the shape of the sphere, then warm the area close to the mouthpiece while stretching and bending it slightly, to produce the curved neck typical of the pear. Start a vase the same way, but keep the elongated sphere straight; then warm the opposite end while pumping in air until it has expanded to the size you want. Flatten the bottom so the vase will stand straight.

5. Once the pieces are formed, cool them with a fan so they do not change shape. Reheat the neck later over a Bunsen burner and cut the mouthpiece away with scissors while the sugar is warm (smooth the cut edge). Cut the top of the vase even using a red-hot knife or wire.

NOTE: If the chamber does not expand, the blow pipe has probably been pushed all the way up against the sugar. To remedy this quickly, remove the airhose from the blow pipe and push the blunt end of a wooden skewer through it and into the sugar.

6. Follow the directions for Spraying Colors (see page 939) to decorate the pieces. (To make the tiny spots that are so typical on a pear, dip the top of the bristles of a fairly stiff brush in color, then bend them back to make the color fly off.)

7. Protect the finished pieces using the same methods described for pulled sugar. Blown pieces that are not too fragile can simply be painted rather than sprayed.

Casting with Sugar

NOTE 1: Since a cast sugar figure must be solid enough to be able to support itself to some degree, and since tartaric acid (in addition to acting to inhibit recrystallization) gives the sugar flexibility, leave it out when cooking sugar for casting to ensure maximum rigidity of the cast pieces.

NOTE 2: It is inevitable that that you will break a piece of cast sugar, assembled or unassembled, now and then. The most precarious time is, of course, when attaching the base or raising the figure, but it also can happen when you leave the piece too long on the table before loosening it. You can repair it quite easily by heating the two edges together over a Bunsen burner until the sugar is liquid and then pressing them together again. Hold the pieces until set or, if you can, lay them flat. Put a little vegetable oil on your finger and smooth the cut while the sugar is still slightly soft. If it will not show from the front, fasten a piece of cast sugar on the back to act as a splint for the fracture and to give added support.

NOTE 3: In some instances when casting clear sugar, it may be desirable to have the back wrinkled to reflect the light in an interesting way. In this case crumple the foil and then smooth it out again before using. (Do not overdo this—you want the wrinkles to show.)

F or the average person, casting is probably the easiest way of making spectacular showpieces with sugar, since it does not demand the years of practice and experience that pulled and blown sugar do. Casting sugar can be a relatively inexpensive occasional recreation, but you do need to have the basics down on how to boil and handle sugar. As in most artwork, you need a good eye for color and proportions, you should be neat and precise, and yes, it does take a steady hand to pour the sugar, especially for the small and narrow shapes. If you do not have much experience, start by casting small simple figures such as the rooster, baker, or peasant girl (Figures 18–5, 18–6, and 18–7). These templates can be enlarged to make the figures any size you like. The baker is designed to hold a tray in his hand as part of the display. You might want to make him 12 inches (30 cm) tall to hold a small tray with a few candies on it as a buffet showpiece, or as large as 3 feet (90 cm) tall to place in the shop window holding a large serving platter. When you cast the baker, cast a small thin oval or circle of sugar making the diameter in proportion to the size you make the figure; then attach it later as directed, placing it flat on his hand. This can be the actual tray for the small figure, or a real serving tray can be placed on top if you make the circle large enough to support it.

Since you will need so much sugar and must boil it in so many different batches (especially for large, complicated castings), it is a good idea to make a large quantity of basic sugar solution once you have made a reasonable calculation of how much you will need. It is better to make too much than not enough; leftover syrup can be stored in a sealed jar for many weeks.

1. Follow the recipe and instructions for Boiled Sugar Basic Recipe (page 936) but omit the Tartaric Acid Solution (see note 1). Let the sugar boil gently for a few seconds before adding the glucose or corn syrup to make certain all of the sugar crystals have dissolved. Add the glucose or corn syrup. After the syrup comes back to a boil, boil 1 minute, brushing down the sides of the pan. Remove from the heat.

2. As you are ready to cast each section, in various colors, measure off the amount of sugar needed, and continue boiling the smaller amount to the proper temperature. (When casting a small figure it is best to pour the various parts or sections in one color only, plain or

FIGURE 18–5 The template used to make a cast sugar rooster

FIGURE 18–6 *The template used to make a cast sugar baker; the outstretched arm is designed to hold a tray*

FIGURE 18–7 The template used to make a cast sugar peasant girl

white, and then apply the color with a brush or sprayer, since it is difficult to boil a small amount of sugar accurately.)

You can make your own forms for casting using either metal strips (the kind that are used to secure crates and boxes) or plastilina, which is a variant of plasteline, a nonhardening modeling clay made from clay mixed with oil or wax, or you can use both in combination. Molds made from metal strips can be used over and over, but the metal strips are difficult and time-consuming to bend into small or intricate shapes, while plastilina can be rolled out to a sheet of the required thickness and cut into any shape with a thin sharp knife. To use plastilina, begin by making a copy of the drawing (enlarging it as desired), then glue it to a piece of sturdy paper (a cake box works great) and cut out the shape with a utility knife. Transfer the rolled plastilina sheet to a cardboard, place the drawing on top, and cut out tracing around the shape. Then slide the cut piece back onto an oiled marble slab or table or onto a silicone mat (which does not need to be oiled). (Just like the marble surface, any side of the plastilina that comes in contact with the sugar must be lightly greased with vegetable oil.) The one drawback with this method is that you can only use the mold once. A third option is to take the plastilina cutout instead of the frame that is left and use the cutout to make a silicone rubber casting template (directions follow on page 952) (see note 4).

When making the mold using metal strips, place a piece of baking paper or other transparent paper on top of the drawing to keep it clean. Fasten the drawing to a sheet of cardboard. Form and solder the metal strips according to the directions on page 952. In making forms from either plastilina or metal strips, be sure you make them deep enough.

3. Lightly grease a marble slab or table with vegetable oil (make sure the table is level). Treat the inside of your individual forms or molds in the same way, and wipe off any excess with a cloth. Arrange the forms on the oiled marble (or use a silicone mat if it is large enough). If any of the forms do not lay flush, weigh them down or the sugar will leak out. You can also place aluminum foil on top of any flat surface and arrange the forms, metal or plastilina, on this. Tape the corners down to secure the foil. The obvious advantage to using foil or a silicone mat is that you do not need a marble surface, and the cast pieces can be easily moved when finished. The back of the cast sugar will also be free from oil as it is not necessary to grease the foil or mat. However, when using foil the back of the sugar will also have an uneven surface, so foil should not be used when casting clear sugar (as opposed to opaque shades). The foil is easily peeled off once the sugar has hardened (see note 3, page 946).

4. Boil the measured amount of sugar to 265°F (130°C) and add color and/or whitening if using. Continue boiling until the sugar reaches 305°F (152°C). Immediately remove from the heat and plunge the pan into cold water for a few seconds. Wipe the bottom of the pan dry.

5. As soon as bubbles stop appearing on the top, pour the sugar into the molds in a thin steady stream (Figure 18–8); use a metal scraper to catch any drops as you move from one mold to the next. Vary the thickness of the sugar in proportion to the size of the piece. For a

NOTE 4: *Another method of containing the sugar is the use of food grade rubber mats, available in thicknesses from* 1/64 *inch (1/2 mm) to* 1/2 *inch (1.2 cm). These can be used for chocolate and batters as well. The thin mats are useful as stenciling plates (neoprene works also, but is not approved for use with food). Rubber mats can be purchased in whole sheets or in precut patterns. Neoprene is available at most hardware stores.*

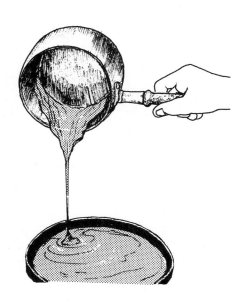

FIGURE 18–8 *Pouring boiled sugar into a metal mold*

12-inch (30-cm) figure the sugar should be poured $^1/_4$ inch (6 mm) thick; for a 3-foot (90-cm) figure, cast the sugar $^3/_4$ inch (2 cm) thick.

6. If you are making a mirror image (such as the chickens in Figure 18–7), and using forms made of metal strips, wait a few seconds after the sugar is poured to allow the sugar closest to the form to harden a little. Tap the metal strip lightly with the back of a knife and remove the form. Invert the form and place it in another area on the marble. Then cast a second chicken (this time facing in the opposite direction). If the sugar in the pan starts to cool and thicken before you are finished, place it back over medium heat, stirring constantly to heat the sugar evenly. If any of the pieces are to be marked or outlined, for example putting some lines in the baker's hat in Figure 18–6, this should be done as soon as a skin has formed on the top.

7. Loosen the cast pieces from the marble by carefully sliding the blade of a metal spatula underneath before they harden completely. Remember that disturbing them too soon will leave unsightly wrinkles.

8. When joining pieces by casting one next to the other, as in the neck and tail of the rooster, first burn off the connecting edges with a red-hot knife to remove any oil which would prevent the pieces from adhering. Heat an old knife over a Bunsen burner until it gets red-hot. Quickly wipe the knife on a wet towel to cool it slightly, then move the knife back and forth over the adhesion points. The larger that you make the figures the more important this procedure is. (Make sure the knife is hot enough to melt the sugar, but not so hot that the sugar caramelizes, or it will leave ugly stains.)

9. When casting a small shape inside a large piece, cast the larger piece first so the heat will not soften and disturb the shape of the smaller one.

10. Before assembling the figures, first spray any pieces that are to be colored (see Spraying Colors, page 939). If individual pieces are to be assembled on top of each other, burn off any oil from the back of the pieces that will be "glued" as needed. This can give the baker, for example, a more three-dimensional look: The baker's head, shoes and sleeve (but not his hand) can be cast separately and pasted on top of the existing figure (you would still cast the entire figure first) to make it look as if his hand is coming out of his jacket.

11. To paste the pieces together, reheat some of the sugar left over from casting. Let it start to thicken slightly before using, do not use too much, and do not use the sugar too hot or you can soften the pieces you are gluing. Always assemble the pieces lying flat on the table to ensure that the parts stay in the position you want until the sugar is cold.

12. Cast a wedge-shaped back support, as well as a base, for any figure that is to be displayed vertically. Make these pieces in proportion to the size of the figure and in the same thickness. Shape the back support so that one long side of the wedge (the one attached to the figure) and the bottom are at right angles to ensure that the figure stands straight. Once the base and back support have been cast and allowed to harden, carefully move the figure to the edge of the table and burn the bottom edge, where the base will go.

13. Carefully raise the figure (you now need an assistant to finish the assembly) and burn the back where the back support will attach. Attach the base with the "sugar-glue," being sure that the figure is standing straight, then glue on the back support using slightly thicker sugar; hold the figure until the back support is set. Coat the whole figure with marzipan lacquer or spray it with a fast-drying clear lacquer as a protection against moisture and fingerprints.

Depending on the shape of the figure, you may need to attach a second support horizontally or vertically. The baker's outstretched arm and hand, for example, would slowly collapse if not supported. The second support should angle down to the main vertical support. This is especially necessary since the arm and torso are usually cast in white (the color of a chef's jacket), and white sugar is softer.

If you are not using white or another opaque color (see Using Colors in Sugar Work, page 939), and you are not spraying on the colors after casting, the colored sugar will be transparent. This does not look good, especially if you are supporting the figure from the back, or if the figure can be seen from all sides. To remedy this, first cast a thin layer of the whole figure in milk white. Then, using that as the base, section off and cast the various colors on top of the white. The back of the figure will be clean, look good, and be well supported (although it will look a little too thick from the side).

Soldering the metal forms

Working with metal strips, also known as band iron, takes a little extra effort since they have to be soldered after they are shaped. But they can be used indefinitely, and one form can be used in either direction to make a mirror image. If you are making a butterfly, for example, you would only have to make one wing form. Metal strips may be a little hard to find since plastic strips are used more often today to secure boxes for shipping. If the local hardware store does not have any, you may find used strips at the lumber yard. If you have a choice, 1/2-inch-wide (1.2-cm) strips are the easiest to work with. You also need soldering wire, flux, cold water, a blowtorch (or Bunsen burner), flat- and round-nosed pliers, a metal cutter, and a metal file.

1. Form the strip, using your hands and the pliers, until it matches the drawing. Overlap the ends by 1/2 inch (1.2 cm).

2. Smear flux at the solder points or dip them into solder fluid.

3. Cut off a small piece of soldering wire, fold in half, and place in between the two ends to be joined, holding them in place with the pliers. The pieces must line up exactly so the form will lay flat.

4. Heat the ends from both sides with the blowtorch until the solder melts. Dip into cold water and file off any excess solder to even the joint.

To make silicone casting templates

Instead of making a plastilina frame, the plastilina can be used in reverse (using the cutout) to cast figures in series or to make customized motifs for special occasions, by making a silicone template or mold. Although the process requires a bit more time and expense, the templates can be used over and over.

1. Roll out plastilina to the desired thickness (as deep as you want the molds). Place the cardboard cutout of your drawing (or a cutter if using one) on top, and cut out the design.

2. Stretch plastic wrap over a sheet of corrugated cardboard (or place a sheet of plastic directly on the work surface if it can be left there undisturbed for 24 hours). Arrange the cutouts on top, leaving at least 1 inch (2.5 cm) of space between them. Frame the cutouts with metal bars such as those used for making candy (or use strips of corrugated cardboard wrapped in plastic) and secure them with weights on the outside.

3. Carefully brush vegetable oil over the top and sides of the cutouts and over the inside edges of the frame.

4. Mix the gelling agent into the silicone rubber according to the manufacturer's instructions. Avoid stirring in any air bubbles. Pour the silicone rubber mixture around your cutouts inside the frame, up to the top edge of the cutouts; do not cover them. You usually have a few minutes before the mixture turns viscous, so pour slowly and precisely. Leave the silicone rubber to harden; this usually takes about 24 hours.

5. Remove the frame from around the edges. Pull out the plastilina cutouts, placing one hand underneath to aid in removing them.

6. Use the tip of a sharp utility knife to cut away threads of rubber around the bottom of the rubber molds.

7. Place the template on a sheet of foil, a marble surface, or a silicone mat as directed in the casting instructions and proceed.

Caramelized Sugar

Sugar starts to turn from golden to light brown in color and starts to caramelize when the temperature reaches 320°F (160°C). There are two ways of bringing the sugar to this temperature: the dry method or a water method. Caramelizing sugar dry takes about half the time, and you do not have to worry about recrystallization, but it requires more attention since the sugar must be stirred constantly to prevent it from caramelizing too fast (before all of the sugar granules have melted) or, worse, from burning. If you use the dry method, do not use a skillet or pan that is any larger than necessary, or you will have a larger area to cover when stirring, and you may not be able to keep the sugar from getting too dark. In the second method, by adding a small amount of water to the sugar, the caramel does not need to be stirred during the entire cooking process, but it takes longer to caramelize because you must wait for the water to evaporate. Either way is much faster and easier if you use a sugar pan: an unlined copper pan made especially for cooking sugar. The acidity of the copper reacts with the sugar in such a way that some of the sugar breaks down into invert sugar, which is more resistant to recrystallization. Invert sugar is a mixture of equal parts glucose and fructose. Be careful though: Since the copper is almost the same color as the caramelized sugar, it becomes harder to tell the exact moment the pan should be pulled off the heat and placed in cold water to stop the cooking process. It is helpful to pour a few small test puddles on a silicone mat or a sheet of baking paper to determine the color more accurately. If the sugar is heated much above 320°F (160°C) and you are not using it immediately, you cannot stop it right there; the sugar will continue to darken even as it sits in the water off the stove, from its own residual heat. This problem is intensified by using a copper pan. With caramelized sugar you do not have to use a sugar thermometer since the color of the sugar will tell you when it is done.

Caramelized Sugar, Dry Method

2¹/₄ cups (540 ml) syrup

2 pounds (910 g) granulated sugar
1 teaspoon (5 ml) lemon juice
   or
12 drops Tartaric Acid Solution
   (page 1115)

NOTE: If you are caramelizing more than 2 pounds (910 g) of sugar at one time, it is easier if you do not add all of it at the beginning. Instead, start with about one-quarter of the total amount. Once it has melted but not changed color, add one-quarter more and repeat, adding the remaining sugar in the same way. This way you do not have to stir the entire amount from the start.

If you have lumps of unmelted sugar when the rest of the sugar has caramelized, the temperature was too high and/or the sugar was not stirred properly, which is especially important once it begins to liquefy. The lumps cannot be melted without darkening the rest of the sugar, and it is not practical to strain them out unless the caramel is to be used for a sauce (in that case strain after adding the water). Therefore, the best thing to do is pick them out of the syrup instead.

The addition of lemon juice or tartaric acid not only makes the sugar softer, it also delays the caramelization process allowing more time to properly melt all of the sugar.

1. Fill a bowl that is large enough to hold the pan used for cooking the sugar with enough cold water to reach halfway up the sides of the pan. Set the bowl aside.

2. Place the sugar, lemon juice, and tartaric acid on a baking paper and rub together well (this will help prevent lumps later). Place the mixture in a copper or stainless-steel pan. Cook, stirring constantly over low heat, until the sugar is completely melted.

3. Cook until the sugar has caramelized to just a shade lighter than the desired color.

4. Remove from the heat and immediately place the bottom of the pan in the bowl of cold water to stop the cooking process. Use the caramel as directed in the individual recipes. If you need to reheat the caramel, stir the sugar constantly over low heat to prevent the sugar from getting any darker than necessary.

Caramelized Sugar with Water

2¹/₄ cups (540 ml) syrup

1 cup (240 ml) water
2 pounds (910 g) granulated sugar
3 ounces (85 g) glucose or
    light corn syrup

1. Fill a bowl that is large enough to hold the pan used for cooking the sugar with enough cold water to reach halfway up the sides of the pan. Set the bowl aside.

2. Place the water and sugar in a copper or stainless-steel pan. Stir to combine and dissolve the sugar in the water over low heat. Wash down the sides of the pan with water, using a brush dedicated to sugar boiling.

3. Bring the mixture to a rolling boil, add the glucose or corn syrup, then lower the heat to medium to ensure that the liquid will not boil too hard. Do not stir once the sugar starts boiling. Instead, brush down the sides of the pan with water as needed until the sugar reaches 280°F (138°C), the crack stage. Keep boiling until the sugar has caramelized to the desired color.

4. Quickly remove the pan from the heat and place the bottom of the pan in cold water to stop the cooking process. Use as directed in the individual recipes.

Caramelized Sugar for Decorations

2³/₄ cups (660 ml) syrup

1 cup (240 ml) cold water
    (see note 1)
2 pounds (910 g) granulated sugar
7 ounces (200 g) glucose or light corn
    syrup (see note 2)

NOTE 1: If you experience the problem of the sugar recrystallizing despite taking all of the suggested precautions, it may be the fault of the tap water in your area. To eliminate this occurrence, use bottled water or distill your water first, including the water used for washing down the sides of the pan.

NOTE 2: If glucose is not available, use light corn syrup instead. Glucose can be produced from a variety of starches while corn syrup is, of course, made from corn. Try to get the thicker 44° Baumé corn syrup if possible. If you must work with sugar in high humidity, the amount of glucose or corn syrup should be drastically reduced, or left out altogether. This ensures that the finished pieces will harden properly.

The old-fashioned dry method for caramelizing sugar is still the fastest and easiest way when only a small amount of caramel is needed, for a few ornaments or a batch of Crème Caramel for example. If necessary, you can speed up the process in the following recipe in a similar way, by reducing the amount of both the water and glucose or corn syrup, provided you are very careful. If you use the full amount of water and glucose or corn syrup called for, there will be plenty of liquid to help the sugar dissolve properly.

The most convenient method for caramelizing sugar for decorations is to keep a stock of sugar syrup on hand (as described in step three following). You then simply pour off whatever amount is needed at the time and continue cooking it to the desired stage.

1. Fill a bowl that is large enough to hold the cooking pan with enough cold water to reach halfway up the sides of the pan. Set the bowl aside.

2. Place the water and sugar in a copper or stainless-steel pan. Dissolve the sugar in the water over low heat. Bring to a boil, stirring constantly, and remove any scum that accumulates on the surface.

3. Add the glucose or corn syrup. Bring the syrup back to boiling. Wash down the sides of the pan with a clean brush that is dedicated to sugar boiling, dipped in water. Remove any additional scum from the surface if necessary. If you are making sugar syrup for general mise en place, pour it into a clean container at this point (or just pour off the excess) and store until needed.

4. Continue cooking the sugar, washing down the sides of the pan as long as sugar crystals are accumulating; do not stir from this point on. When the sugar begins to change from clear to light amber, watch it very closely, it will turn to golden brown very quickly since most of the water has evaporated at this point, and the temperature is now around 315°F (157°C).

5. When the syrup just starts to show a hint of golden brown, remove the pan from the stove and set it in the bowl of cold water. Hold it there until all of the bubbles have subsided. Remove the pan from the water, wipe the bottom of the pan, and let the sugar cool at room temperature as necessary, depending on the intended use.

Caramelized Decorations

A few words of caution are definitely called for at this point, as working with cooked sugar is potentially very dangerous. Unfortunately, most of us have experienced accidentally splashing boiling water on bare skin and know how painful that is. Consider this: boiling water is only 212°F (100°C). I say "only" because when you heat sugar, boiling more and more moisture out of it to the point of caramelization, it is between 320 and 330°F (160–166°C). Getting this hot syrup on your skin can literally scar you for life! It is not my intention to discourage anyone doing this for the first time by saying this, but I want to stress the importance of taking precautions and using plain old-fashioned common sense.

First of all, especially if this is new to you, wear medical-type latex gloves to protect your hands (although they will help only to a point; you must still, of course, use a pot holder when taking hold of the pan). Do not move around a crowded kitchen with a pan of hot sugar. If you absolutely must do so, let your colleagues know in no uncertain terms that you are walking past them by saying clearly and firmly "Hot pan coming through." Be sure to walk slowly, holding the sugar pan in one hand and holding your other hand out in front of you as a bumper— this is especially important when going around corners. A much more sensible way is to work with the sugar next to where it was cooked.

Making Spun Sugar or Corkscrews, for example, is by no means as dangerous, nor does it take as much skill and tolerance of the heat, as piped sugar decorations. Since using a strong and secure pastry bag (even one made of vinyl) is, unfortunately, out of the question for piping hot sugar, I make bags out of baking paper in the usual way, but I use a double thickness to ensure the bag will not break under pressure, which could spray the hot sugar all over my hands.

You can make a bag of a good workable size by simply starting with a full sheet of baking paper (24 by 16 inches/60 × 40 cm) folded in half crosswise. Form the doubled sheet into a disposable bag as described on page 23. Be certain that the tip has been pulled tight so it will not leak. You cannot put the sugar syrup into the bag with a spoon or scraper as you would with other fillings, so again, take caution when filling the bag with the hot syrup. Look around to be sure there is no one who might bump you, then hold the paper pastry bag securely in one hand, carefully pick up the sugar pan with your other hand, and pour the sugar into the bag in a steady steam, filling it with no more than 1½ cups (360 ml) or half of the Caramelized Sugar for Decorations recipe. Close the top securely, wrap a towel around the bag to protect your hands from the heat, and cut a small opening in the tip using scissors. Pipe out the sugar as directed in the individual instructions that follow.

As the sugar cools down, it will clog the tip of the bag. It is therefore very important that you work quickly, so you will not have to stop in the middle of your design. Once the tip is clogged the only thing you can do is cut a larger opening and squeeze the lump through. If this leaves an opening that is too large to use, squeeze all of the sugar out of the bag back into the saucepan and start over. But if the opening is not too large, you should still be able to create thin elegant strands by holding the bag a little higher and moving it a little faster as you pipe.

Reheat the sugar in the pan as needed, stirring the sugar constantly over low heat to protect it from getting any darker than necessary in the process.

You can make clear or colored decorations by following the instructions given for cooking and coloring the sugar in Spun Sugar, page 972.

All sugar decorations are very susceptible to moisture and should be made as close to the time of serving as possible. You can increase their resistance, and store them for up to one week under optimal conditions, if you coat the finished shapes on both sides with edible lacquer. This should be done immediately after they have cooled and not as a means of trying to save pieces that are already starting to get sticky.

Caramel Cages

variable yield

one recipe Caramelized Sugar for
   Decorations (page 955)
vegetable oil

NOTE: To remove the hardened sugar from the spoon (and most other tools used to manipulate sugar, such as the whip for spun sugar), place it in a small plastic bag and strike it hard against the edge of a table.

This amount of caramel can make about 25 cages if you are experienced and don't break too many. It is virtually impossible not to break any, so do not be discouraged if your first attempts are not successful. With a little practice you will find it is not difficult to make thin elegant cages. If you are making a large quantity of cages (for a beginner a large quantity might be anything more than one), you may want to start by trying the Simplified Caramel Cages (instructions follow).

1. Use a ladle or any dome-shaped object (such as a bowl) that is approximately 2½ inches high and 6 inches in diameter (6.2 × 15 cm). If you are working with two ladles, have ready a small tub filled with granulated sugar to place the handle of the first ladle in as you make the next cage. Hold the ladle or bowl upside down and use the palm of your hand to coat it lightly with a thin film of oil. Too much oil will cause the caramel to slide off as you apply it (this can also happen if the caramel has become too cool and has therefore become too thick). You should be able to make two or three cages before regreasing.

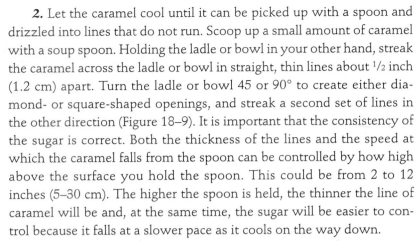

2. Let the caramel cool until it can be picked up with a spoon and drizzled into lines that do not run. Scoop up a small amount of caramel with a soup spoon. Holding the ladle or bowl in your other hand, streak the caramel across the ladle or bowl in straight, thin lines about 1/2 inch (1.2 cm) apart. Turn the ladle or bowl 45 or 90° to create either diamond- or square-shaped openings, and streak a second set of lines in the other direction (Figure 18–9). It is important that the consistency of the sugar is correct. Both the thickness of the lines and the speed at which the caramel falls from the spoon can be controlled by how high above the surface you hold the spoon. This could be from 2 to 12 inches (5–30 cm). The higher the spoon is held, the thinner the line of caramel will be and, at the same time, the sugar will be easier to control because it falls at a slower pace as it cools on the way down.

3. As an option you can finish the base of the cage by forming a thin line of caramel all around. It gives a more neat appearance and helps to make the cage sturdier, but I must admit I often leave out this step myself.

4. If you are working with two ladles or bowls, set the first one aside to harden at this point and make the next cage in the same manner. If you are using just one ladle or bowl wait briefly until the cage is hard (this can take 10 seconds to 1 minute; placing it in the refrigerator will speed it up greatly) and then cup your hand around the cage and gently lift it off the ladle or bowl. If the cage does not cool and set up right away it probably means that the lines of sugar are too thick. Thick lines not only take longer to cool but they make for an unattractive clumsy-looking cage. Thick lines are often the result of the sugar in the pan having cooled down too much. Aesthetics aside, caramel that is too cool also tends to slide right off the ladle even when applied in thin lines. To reheat the caramel, place the pan over low heat and stir constantly to make sure the caramel at the bottom does not become too dark. I also find it helpful to chill the ladle or bowl in the refrigerator while I am warming the sugar.

FIGURE 18–9 Streaking lines of caramel across a ladle in both directions for a Caramel Cage

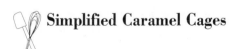 **Simplified Caramel Cages**

The simplified cages are made using the same technique as regular cages, but they are easier, making them a good choice when a large number are needed or for a beginner. Just as when piping with chocolate, it is easier to make curved lines than it is to make lines that are perfectly straight.

1. Hold the oiled ladle or bowl over a silicone mat or sheet of baking paper to catch any stray caramel.

2. Instead of making straight lines, drizzle and swirl the sugar over the ladle or bowl, creating intersecting curved lines (Figure 18–10). Each line must connect to the others, following the principles of basic building so that the cage will hold together. Create your own individual design but don't overdo it: you should be able to see through the cage.

3. Remove the cage from the bowl following the instructions in the main recipe (Figure 18–11).

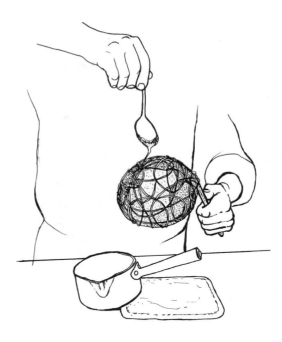

FIGURE 18–10 *Creating intersecting curved lines of sugar over a ladle for a Simplified Caramel Cage*

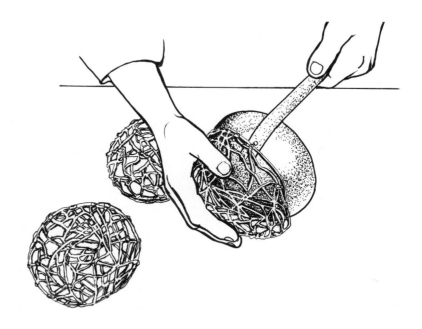

FIGURE 18–11 *Removing the finished Caramel Cage by cupping the hand around it gently as it is lifted off*

Caramel Corkscrews

variable yield

one recipe Caramelized Sugar for
    Decorations (page 955)
vegetable oil

This is definitely the easiest of the caramel decorations discussed in this section, and also the safest one to produce, yet the Corkscrews look incredibly showy spiraling high into the air. An added advantage is that they can be made from leftover caramel (for instance after you piped out decorations or dipped fruit or nuts), since the caramel must be very thick (but still sticky). Forming the Corkscrews on a knife-sharpening steel works well since steels are the right diameter, the fine grooves and the way the tools are made make them nonstick so it is unnecessary to oil the surface, and the tapered ends allow you to push each Corkscrew off easily. In addition, the handle helps, since it gives you something to hold on to. You can, however, use any smooth, glossy object of the appropriate thickness (I use a ballpoint pen for very narrow Corkscrews or tendrils, for example). I think you will find the technique for Corkscrews easy to learn with just a little practice. The key, besides having the syrup at the correct consistency, is a smooth rhythm when rotating the sugar around the steel.

1. Let the caramelized sugar cool until it is very thick. You will find out rather quickly if the sugar is too thin, because the strands created by moving the spoon around the steel will not be strong enough to wind and will simply fall to the table.

2. Oil a sheet of baking paper to hold the finished corkscrews (they are extremely fragile and will definitely break if they stick to the surface).

3. Dip a soup spoon into the caramel and swirl it around until a small amount of caramel sticks to the spoon. Pull a thread of sugar out of the mass as you pull the spoon out of the pan. (If the caramel just runs off the spoon, it is still too warm.) Hold the steel in your other hand and rotate the thread of caramel around the steel starting about 6 inches (15 cm) from the tip (Figure 18–12). When you get to the tip of the steel, push the finished Corkscrew off and place it on the oiled baking paper (Figure 18–13). If the sugar was cooked to a golden brown

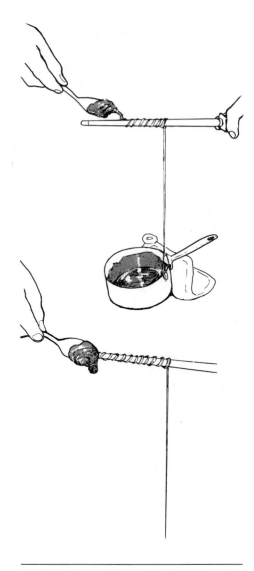

FIGURE 18–12 Winding a thin strand of caramel around a knife-sharpening steel to make a Caramel Corkscrew

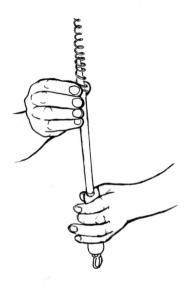

FIGURE 18–13 Pushing the finished Corkscrew off the steel

caramel and the Corkscrews are as thin as they should be, they will set up immediately.

4. Repeat to make as many as desired, plus a few extra to break. Reheat the caramel as needed, stirring constantly.

Caramel Fences

variable yield

one recipe Caramelized Sugar for Decorations (page 955)
vegetable oil

1. Read the instructions and precautions for Caramel Decorations (page 956) and make a disposable pastry bag from a double thickness of baking paper as described. It is important to use a double thickness to ensure that the bag will not break as it is squeezed, which would cause serious burns. The extra paper also helps to protect your hands from the heat as you are working.

2. Oil a marble slab or have a silicone mat ready. (You can alternatively use a sheet of silicone-coated baking paper, but unless it is the thicker reusable type it tends to buckle.)

3. Let the sugar cool until it is the consistency of a thick syrup. Ideally the sugar should be thick enough (having cooled sufficiently) that it will start to set immediately as it touches the surface. If the sugar is too thin (too hot) it will bleed together and subsequently break where the lines cross.

4. Carefully pour about 1 cup (240 ml) into the paper bag. Do not attempt to work with more than this at one time and be sure the bag is sealed on the other end. Wrap a towel around the bag and cut a small opening.

5. Pipe the sugar out in the fence shape (Figure 18–14). This should be done in one continuous motion. Pipe five zigzag lines, 4 inches (10 cm) long and about $3/8$ inch (9 mm) apart, with smooth, round, corners, then pipe another set of three lines on top of the first at a 90° angle.

FIGURE 18–14 Piping out Caramel Fences

Caramel Spirals

variable yield

one recipe Caramelized Sugar for
Decorations (page 955)

*It seems that all of the caramel decorations make a big impression on people,
but this simple space-age spiral has got to be counted at the top of the list. It
never ceases to amaze the guests that sugar can actually be so flexible as they
watch it bounce up and down above the plate when it is presented (most of the
time they cannot resist trying this for themselves, pulling on the bottom with their
fingers or a spoon). I featured Caramel Spirals on my television program "Spectacular Desserts" in the presentation of Crème Caramel Nouveau. Of all of the
techniques I demonstrated, the spirals were by far the item that attracted the
most interest from the viewers.*

*The only real skill required to make the spirals successfully (if you can call
it a skill) is a fairly high tolerance to the heat as you pipe, since it is necessary
to put even pressure on the hot pastry bag much longer than it takes to make the
Caramel Fences, for example.*

1. Read the instructions and precautions for Caramel Decorations
(page 956) and make a few disposable pastry bags, using a double
thickness of baking paper as described. It is important to use a double
thickness to ensure that the bags will not break as you pipe, which
would cause serious burns. The extra paper also helps to protect your
hands from the heat as you are working. To keep the bags from unfolding, fold the bottom 2 inches (5 cm) of the tip back and make a sharp
crease down one side with your fingers.

2. Have one or two silicone mats ready. (You can alternatively use
a sheet of silicone-coated baking paper, but unless it is the thicker
reusable type it tends to buckle.)

3. Let the sugar cool until it is the consistency of a thick syrup. If
your hands are up to it you can actually start piping the spirals much
sooner than with the other decorations since the lines do not touch
each other, still, if the sugar is too hot, it will shrink into little droplets
instead of forming a line when it hits the cooler surface.

4. Unfold the bottom of a paper pastry bag and carefully pour
about 1½ cups (360 ml) or half of the recipe into the bag. Do not
attempt to work with more than this at one time. Close the top of the
bag securely. Wrap a towel around the bag and cut a small opening.

5. Pipe out spirals about 7 inches (17.5 cm) in diameter, starting in
the center with a small teardrop (Figure 18–15). The teardrop will facilitate balancing the spiral on top of a dessert later. Close the spiral by
piping the very last inch or so on top of the previous circle. If you plan
ahead and position them correctly you can fit six spirals on each silicone mat or sheet of paper. The thinner the lines and the more concentric circles you have in each spiral, the more elegant the finished decorations will look. Making them very thin, however, is pointless, as they
will break when you lift them off the mat (Figure 18–16). Piping the
caramel too thick, on the other hand, not only looks clumsy and odd
but if the sugar is very thick it will not flex, and the spiral will just sit on

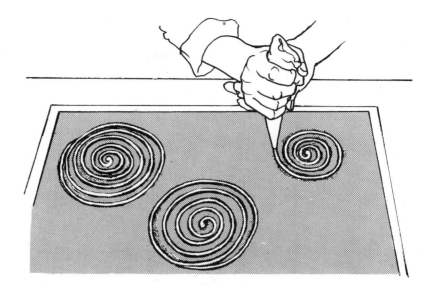

FIGURE 18–15 Piping out Caramel Spirals

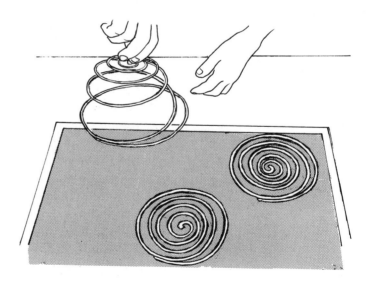

FIGURE 18–16 Lifting a finished Caramel Spiral off the silicone mat

top of the dessert instead of falling down around it. This can also happen even if the sugar is thin if you do not pipe the circumference of the spiral wide enough so that the larger outer rings pull the spiral down with their weight.

Caramel-Dipped Fruit and Nuts

variable yield

one recipe Caramelized Sugar for
Decorations (page 955)

This technique is similar to the one used for Glazed Fruit (page 966) except that here the caramel is cooked further—to 320°F (160°C)—to produce a golden brown color. Also, the tartaric acid is left out, which makes the sugar set up hard and hold its shape after it cools. If desired, you can make these decorations with clear or colored sugar instead by using the Glazed Fruit recipe. Although I am limiting my instructions for fruit to the Caramel-Dipped Figs and Apple Wedges that are featured in the recipes in this book, the same technique can be applied to other fruits, either whole or sliced.

Caramel-Dipped Figs

NOTE: *As mentioned in other recipes, it is crucial that the fruit be dipped in caramel as close to the serving time as possible. The hot caramel will start to cook the surface of the fruit, softening it and causing the juice to leak out. By leaving the skewer inserted in the fruit until the last moment, it will hold up a little better.*

Be very careful as you move the figs while holding them by the skewers that you do not tilt the skewers down or the figs can slip off.

1. Let the sugar cool until it is very thick but still liquid.

2. Prepare your work area by placing sheets of baking paper on the floor in front of your worktable. Place a ruler or thin strip of wood at the edge of the table and set a heavy can on top at each end to hold it in place (setting a couple of weights from your baking scale at either end also works well). Have ready as many wooden skewers as you will need (one for each fig).

3. Insert the pointed end of a skewer horizontally through the base of a fig about ⅓ inch (8 mm) from the bottom, without pushing the skewer all the way through. Dip the whole fig into the caramel syrup, lift it out holding it so that the stem end is pointing down, and secure the blunt end of the skewer under the ruler. The fig should extend out from the table over the floor above the baking papers in order to catch any excess caramel, with the stem end of the fig pointing straight down. Dip the remaining figs in the same manner working from left to right if the sugar pot is on your right or right to left if the sugar pot is on your left, so that you will not drip across any figs after they are dipped.

4. When the caramel on the figs has hardened, heat the blade of a knife and use it to melt through the caramel tail at the desired length, anywhere from 4 to 8 inches (10–20 cm) from the fig (Figure 18–17).

5. Transfer the figs to a sheet pan, holding them up by the wooden skewer or, if it is possible, leave them in place until needed (see note). Touching the caramel with your hands will leave fingerprints. When you are ready to remove the skewers, wear a latex surgical-type glove on the hand that touches the caramel, hold the fruit securely, and twist out the skewer with the other hand.

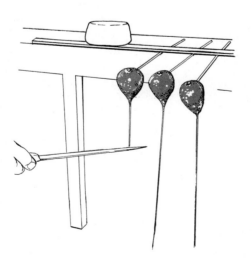

FIGURE 18–17 *Using a hot knife to cut the tail of a Caramel-Dipped Fig to the desired length*

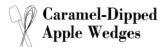 **Caramel-Dipped Apple Wedges**

1. Coat the apple wedges with lemon juice to prevent oxidation. Poach for 1 or 2 minutes in the liquid leftover from poaching the hollowed-out apples in the Apple Crème Brûlée recipe, or in a small amount of Plain Poaching Syrup if using them for another presentation. If the apples are not poached prior to being dipped in caramel, the juice on the cut sides will cause the hot caramel to bubble instead of leaving a smooth surface. Blot the wedges dry.

2. Proceed as for Caramel-Dipped Figs above, inserting the skewers from the side at either end of the wedges, and positioning skewers after dipping so that the caramel tails form in a smooth line from the apples wedges as shown in the photograph of Apple Crème Brûlée in the color insert pages.

Caramel-Dipped Macadamia Nuts or Hazelnuts

1. Follow the instructions for Caramel-Dipped Figs. Dipping nuts is actually a much easier undertaking, and you will need much less caramel. The only trick to master here is inserting the skewers into the sides of the nuts: If you push them in too far and/or from the wrong side you will divide the nut into two halves; if you do not push them in far enough, the nuts will fall off the skewers into the caramel.

2. Arrange the dipped nuts so that the tiny point on the nut faces straight down, creating a tail in a straight line from that point (refer to the photograph of Caramel Boxes with Caramel-Macadamia Nut Mousse in the color insert pages). Be extra careful when you remove the skewers.

Caramelized Almonds, Hazelnuts, Walnuts, and Pecans

14 ounces (400 g) nuts

7 ounces (200 g) nuts
vegetable oil
6 ounces (170 g) granulated sugar
$^{1}/_{2}$ teaspoon (2.5 ml) lemon juice
2 tablespoons (30 ml) water
$^{1}/_{2}$ ounce (15 g) unsalted butter

NOTE: To remove the skin from almonds, pour boiling water over them, cover, and let them

1. Remove the skin from the almonds or hazelnuts (see note). If using almonds, toast them to a golden brown color at 350°F (175°C) after removing the skin. Keep the nuts warm.

2. If you do not have a silicone mat, lightly oil a marble slab or a sheet pan.

3. Place the sugar, lemon juice, and water in a copper or heavy-bottomed saucepan. Cook over medium heat until the temperature reaches 240°F (115°C) on a sugar thermometer; brush down the sides of the pan with water a few times during the cooking process.

4. Remove the pan from the heat and immediately add the warm nuts. Stir gently with a wooden spoon or spatula.

5. Return the mixture to medium heat and reheat, continuing to stir gently. The mixture will appear crystallized at this point but will start to melt as it is heated. Keep stirring until the sugar starts to caramelize and turn golden brown, at 320°F (160°C).

soak for 5 minutes. Drain the water and immediately pinch the nuts between your fingers to remove skin.

The skin on hazelnuts is easiest to remove by placing the nuts in a 400°F (205°C) oven for about 10 minutes or until they start to turn golden, provided they are to be toasted anyway (as in this recipe). Let cool, then rub the nuts between your hands or in a towel to remove the skin. This method will not remove all of the skin on all of the nuts. For recipes where that is necessary, one option is to toast more nuts than you will need, allowing you to pick out the better-looking ones and use the others where a little remaining skin does not matter. Or, to remove all of the skin, pour boiling water with a little baking soda added (1 teaspoon/4 g to 1 quart/960 ml) over the nuts, let stand 5 minutes, and then remove the skins. For this recipe the nuts would then need to be toasted.

Walnuts and pecans are always caramelized (and otherwise used) with the skin on.

Glazed Fruit

vegetable oil
fresh or dried fruit
lemon juice
Plain Poaching Syrup (page 13)
walnut halves
Marzipan (page 1022), untinted
rum
Simple Syrup (page 11)
food coloring
pistachio extract
Boiled Sugar Basic Recipe (page 936)

6. Remove the pan from the heat, add the butter, and stir until the butter is completely incorporated.

7. Pour the mixture onto the silicone mat or oiled marble slab or sheet pan. Using two forks, turn the nuts over, making sure the sugar coats all of the nuts, and separate the nuts so that none of the sides touch. As the caramel starts to cool down you can do this more effectively with your fingertips. Store the caramelized nuts in airtight containers.

If the nuts are to be crushed after they are caramelized, there is no need to separate them individually. Instead, let the mixture cool completely on the mat, marble, or sheet pan, then crush it to the desired coarseness. For a denser caramelization, crush the nuts before adding them to the hot syrup.

*S*mall, fresh, stemmed strawberries, glazed with sugar boiled to the hard crack stage, can be used as a garnish for a strawberry soufflé, as part of a petits fours tray served after a meal, or on top of a Valentine dessert. They are quite elegant and look magnificent. Orange, apple, and pear wedges can be glazed and used to enhance the presentation of desserts made with those fruits such as a pear or apple charlotte, or a Grand Marnier soufflé.

Because the juices that are released when fresh fruits are dipped into hot caramel will eventually penetrate and melt the sugar shell, Glazed Fruits should be prepared as close as possible to serving time. Glazed dried fruits, on the other hand, hold up much better and can be kept in an airtight container for a few days if needed. They are generally used as a colorful addition to a candy or petits fours tray, rather than to garnish a dessert.

Nuts sandwiched together with flavored Marzipan can be glazed with sugar in the same way, and they make a nice addition to a selection of Glazed Fruit.

1. If you do not have a silicone mat on which to place the dipped pieces, lightly oil a baking sheet to hold the glazed fruits.

2. Prepare the fruits or candies to be dipped in the following ways:

• Small strawberries: Leave whole, stem on if possible.

• Oranges: Pull the skin off the oranges by hand; do not peel with a knife. Pull the segments apart. Remove as much of the white pith as possible.

• Apples or pears: Leave the skin on for color, cut into thin wedges, and coat with lemon juice to prevent oxidation. Poach the wedges for 1 or 2 minutes in a small amount of Plain Poaching Syrup. Blot dry.

• Filled walnuts: Flavor a small amount of Marzipan with rum; roll into olive-shaped pieces; fasten a walnut half on each side using Simple Syrup.

• Filled dates, dried figs or prunes: Cut open and remove the pits from medium-sized dates or prunes. Color a small amount of Marzipan light pink and fill the fruit so that some of the Marzipan can be seen along the cut. Form the fruit so the pieces are uniform in shape.

• Filled apricots: Flavor a small amount of Marzipan with pistachio extract. If desired, add a touch of green food coloring to tint the Marzipan pale green. Sandwich the Marzipan between two apricot halves; shape them like the dates.

3. Insert a wooden skewer into each of the fruit pieces or candies (dip stemmed strawberries by holding onto the stem).

4. To glaze about twenty-five pieces, make half of the Boiled Sugar Basic Recipe (you will have some sugar left over, but it cannot be avoided in order to dip the fruit properly into the syrup) and boil the syrup to 310°F (155°C). Immediately place the bottom of the saucepan into cold water for about 10 seconds to stop the cooking process. Remove the pan from the water and wait until most of the bubbles have disappeared before dipping the fruit.

5. Quickly dip each fruit or candy into the syrup, holding it by the skewer, then gently move it up and down over the syrup to remove excess sugar. Lightly scrape the bottom against the side of the pan to remove the last drips and place onto the silicone mat or oiled sheet pan. Reheat the syrup as it starts to cool and thicken. It is essential that the fruits have only a very thin shell of caramel, or they will be unattractive and impossible to eat. Let cool completely, then remove the skewers by holding the candy in place with a fork as you pull them out; avoid touching the glazed candies with your fingers.

 Gum Paste with Gum Tragacanth

3 pounds (1 kg, 365 g) gum paste

2 pounds, 10 ounces (1 kg, 195 g) powdered sugar, approximately

2 tablespoons (18 g) gum tragacanth powder

¹/₂ cup (120 ml) water

2 tablespoons (30 ml) glucose or light corn syrup

1 tablespoon (15 ml) lemon juice

1 ounce (30 g) white vegetable shortening, approximately

food coloring (optional)

*U*sing gum tragacanth in gum paste, rather than gelatin, produces a paste that is more pliable and more convenient to work with since it does not dry out as quickly. This is also due in part to the addition of shortening, which acts as a moistening agent. Gum Paste with Gum Tragacanth is ideal for small, time-consuming projects—for example, sculpting the head or arms of a figure, or when rolling the paste and marking an intricate design such as the bricks in a castle wall—as the paste allows you more working time. The working time can be extended even further, up to 2 hours, by rubbing a thin film of vegetable shortening over the surface as soon as the paste has been rolled out, cut, or formed. This will delay the formation of a crust while you finish your design, and the shortening will slowly be absorbed by the paste and will not be visible in the finished piece. The drawback with using shortening in the paste and/or rubbed on the surface is that not only does the paste dry out more slowly while you are working but your finished showpiece will take up to a week longer to dry completely than if you use a gelatin-based paste. Gum Paste with Gum Tragacanth is not practical for use when a large quantity of paste is called for, as gum tragacanth is not readily available and costs about ten times more than powdered gelatin.

1. Sift the powdered sugar and reserve a few handfuls.

2. Thoroughly mix the gum tragacanth into the remaining sugar. Set aside in a mixer bowl.

3. Combine the water, glucose or corn syrup, and the lemon juice. Warm the mixture slightly, stirring until well blended.

4. Using the dough hook, gradually incorporate the liquid into the powdered sugar mixture, adding some of the reserved powdered sugar if needed to make a fairly stiff paste. The consistency of the paste should be firm enough that it could easily be rolled out.

5. Mix in the shortening and continue kneading with the dough hook until you have an easily moldable paste. It takes some experience to get the consistency just right. You may need to add some additional shortening, depending on the amount of powdered sugar used. If so, or if you are adding extra shortening to extend the working time, just rub it onto the top of the paste and knead it in by hand.

6. If any portion of the paste is to be tinted, use water-soluble food coloring and mix it in at this point. Cover with plastic wrap and store in an airtight container. Gum Paste with Gum Tragacanth can be kept at normal room temperature for several weeks. It will harden a little, but it can be reworked with a small amount of additional shortening.

Nougat

about 1 pound, 10 ounces (740 g) nougat

10 ounces (285 g) finely chopped or thinly sliced blanched almonds
1 pound (455 g) granulated sugar
1 teaspoon (5 ml) lemon juice
2 ounces (55 g) unsalted butter (optional)
Royal Icing (page 1019)

NOTE: Nougat can be made without butter, but using butter will give the finished product an extra shine.

*N*ougat, also known as nougatine, is made of caramelized sugar and sliced or chopped almonds. It was invented as late as the 1800s, and it has many uses in the pastry shop: It can be served as a candy cut into small bars and left plain or dipped in chocolate, it is crushed and added to ice creams or fillings, it can be made into shells for individual dessert presentations, or it is molded and cut into various shapes to create tall, elaborate, spectacular showpieces known as pièces montées. These are used to hold candies or fruit, as cake pedestals for a towering Croquembouche, or alone simply for ornamentation. Unlike other decorative materials, such as Pastillage, for example, Nougat not only looks great but it is also very tasty. Although the recipe itself is quite simple, working with Nougat takes a lot of practice, proper planning, and fast precise steps to make a showpiece or even a dessert mold. No special equipment is needed (with the exception of molds if used for forming). Nougat is relatively expensive compared with other sugar formulas used in similar ways because of the almonds.

Before you begin, assemble the tools and equipment you will need to form the Nougat. Cut your pattern out from heavy paper, such as a cake box. Lightly *oil the mold, or object you are planning to form the Nougat in (or over), with vegetable oil. Clean and oil a heavy rolling pin (preferably one made of metal), a metal spatula, and a chef's knife. Clean, dry, and lightly oil a marble slab and one or two inverted sheet pans.*

1. Sift the almonds using a large flour sifter to remove any small broken pieces or powder that could cause the sugar to recrystallize. Warm the almonds in a low oven, set them aside, and keep them warm.

2. Place the sugar and lemon juice in a heavy saucepan, preferably copper. Cook over low heat, stirring constantly until all of the sugar has melted and is light golden in color.

3. Stir in the almonds and continue stirring until the mixture turns a little darker, about 1 or 2 minutes. Stir in the butter if used and continue to stir until all of the butter is incorporated.

4. Quickly pour the Nougat onto the prepared marble slab. Let it cool for a few seconds, then flip it over with the spatula so it will cool evenly and not become any darker. As soon as you can, roll the Nougat to about 1/8 inch (3 mm) thick; it should never be more than 1/4 inch (6 mm) thick for the best appearance and flexibility.

5. Transfer the Nougat to the sheet pan(s) and place in front of a 250°F (122°C) oven with the door open, to keep it warm and malleable. The work area should be as close to the oven as possible.

6. Place your pattern on top and quickly cut out shapes with the oiled chef's knife. Form the pieces, if required. Let cool, then glue the pieces together with Royal Icing or sugar cooked to the hard crack stage, 310°F (155°C).

If the Nougat becomes too hard to work with at any time during rolling, cutting, or shaping, place it (on the sheet pan) inside the oven until soft and workable again. Be careful that you do not overheat the Nougat and darken it, or you might have several different shades in your finished showpiece, which does not look good.

To reuse scrap pieces, place them on top of each other, soften in the oven, then roll them out again. Or store scraps in airtight containers and use as candy or for Nougatine Crunch.

Nougatine Crunch

Crush cooled Nougat into currant-sized pieces, using a heavy dowel or rolling pin. Store in airtight containers. Should the stored Nougatine Crunch become wet and sticky, dry it in the oven for a few minutes, then re-crush it to separate the pieces.

Pastillage

5 pounds, 8 ounces
(2 kg, 500 g) paste

1 ounce (30 g) unflavored gelatin
     powder
1¼ cups (300 ml) cold water
4 pounds, 3 ounces (1 kg, 905 g)
     powdered sugar
10 ounces (285 g) cornstarch
1 teaspoon (2 g) cream of tartar

NOTE: *Ideally, do not make any more Pastillage than you will be able to use within an
hour, and do not make it until you are ready to
begin working with the paste. If the Pastillage
should become too firm, you can soften it to
some degree by kneading it a little longer in the
mixer (the friction will warm the paste and at
the same time the gelatin). If it becomes necessary to store the Pastillage until the following
day, it must first be wrapped in plastic, then
covered with a wet towel and refrigerated.*

Pastillage is also known as gum paste, from the time when a vegetable gum such as gum tragacanth (see page 967) was used in place of gelatin. It is a sugar paste perfectly suited for making show and display pieces, or other deco-rative items. Pastillage is also preferred over Marzipan as a canvas for cocoa paintings by some artists. It can be molded around almost any object and cut or pressed into many different shapes. It is also very inexpensive to produce.

Theoretically Pastillage is edible, but it is rarely intended to be (nor should it be) eaten when it is dry. It is as hard and brittle as glass, and I really do not recommend that you try it even if you have a ravenous appetite, strong teeth, and good insurance!

Pastillage is most typically left pure white, but it can be colored before it is rolled out and formed, or painted or sprayed when dry. As always when using color on or in food, take care to keep the colors to soft pastel shades. The same precautions that must be taken when making Marzipan apply to working with Pastillage as well, to preserve its white color. Use a stainless-steel bowl for mix-ing, never a corrosive bowl such as aluminum, which will turn the paste gray. Always wash and dry the work surface and rolling pin thoroughly (try to use marble, if possible, as this will give the rolled paste a smooth and even surface, which is essential for cocoa painting).

Pastillage dries and forms a crust almost immediately if left exposed, so assemble everything you will require ahead of time and keep the unused portion of the paste covered with a wet towel while you work. Have your templates cut out and ready, and be sure to use paper that is thick enough to allow you to quickly and precisely cut around the patterns with a thin, pointed, sharp knife. If the Pastillage is to be molded, dust the forms (or object you are shaping it around) with cornstarch to keep it from sticking. Plan how you will cut the sheet of Pastillage before you roll it out: remember you will not have time to stop and think once it is rolled. Try to use as much of each rolled sheet as possible, since in most cases the scrap pieces can not be softened and reused.

Use a very small amount of cornstarch to keep the Pastillage from sticking. Too much will cause the surface to dry rapidly and form a crust as the cornstarch draws moisture out of the paste, which will cause the paste to crack when it is shaped. Roll it out to ⅛ inch (3 mm) thick for the most attractive and elegant pieces. If rolled too thick, Pastillage looks clumsy and amateurish. Cut out the desired shapes, then carefully transfer the cutouts to an even surface or to the mold, if you are using one. As soon as the pieces are partially dry and can be handled, turn them over or remove them from the molds to allow the bottom to dry. Continue to turn them from time to time so that they dry evenly (the mois-ture tends to sink to the bottom). This is especially important in large, flat pieces, which have a tendency to curl if not turned properly. Once dry, the pieces can be filed and sanded to help them fit together better and to smooth any sharp edges.

Pastillage is assembled using Royal Icing as cement. Take care not to use too much, since none will be absorbed, and the excess will squeeze out when the pieces are pressed together, spoiling the final appearance. Because Royal Icing does not set up quickly after it is applied (as chocolate and boiled sugar do), the pieces must be supported for several hours. Use any object that fits to hold a particular shape or angle. It can take several days to assemble a larger design.

Once completely dry, the finished showpiece will keep forever if it is stored covered in a dry place.

This is intentionally a fairly small recipe, but since the paste is so quick and easy to make, and it does not stay workable very long, you might even consider measuring several half-batches and making each up as you use the previous one.

1. Sprinkle the gelatin over the cold water and set aside to soften.

2. Sift together the sugar, cornstarch, and cream of tartar and place in a stainless-steel mixer bowl. Place the gelatin mixture over a bain-marie and heat until dissolved. Do not overheat. Gradually add the gelatin mixture to the sugar mixture while mixing on low speed with the dough hook.

3. Continue mixing, scraping down the sides occasionally, until you have a smooth, elastic paste (it will still stick to the bottom of the bowl). Cover the paste with a wet towel immediately.

Rock Sugar

variable yield

1 cup (240 ml) water
2 pounds (910 g) granulated sugar
2 tablespoons (30 ml) firm Royal Icing
    (page 1019)
food coloring

NOTE 1: Rather than adding the coloring to the Rock Sugar as it is cooking, you can spray colors on with a syringe or airbrush to achieve special effects. This is best done once the pieces are placed on the showpiece.

NOTE 2: For a lighter and slightly more crumbly Rock Sugar, add a touch more Royal Icing.

*R*ock Sugar is named for its porous, rough, rocklike appearance. It adds an unusual decorative touch to showpieces. Once it has hardened, it can be broken into irregular "rocks" or cut into precise shapes using a serrated knife. It is quite amazing to see how the white mass of sugar rises up in the pan—resembling milk about to boil over—once the Royal Icing has been incorporated. The eruption (swelling) and recrystallization occur as a reaction to quickly beating in the egg white and sugar in the icing. Rock Sugar, unlike other types of sugar, holds up very well to moisture. It is quite easy to make once you get the timing down.

1. Preheat the oven to 250°F (122°C). Line the inside of a bowl about 8 inches (20 cm) in diameter with aluminum foil. Have an absolutely clean wooden spoon available.

2. Combine the water and sugar in a large copper or heavy saucepan (the sugar mixture will swell to double in size, so the pan must be large enough to accommodate it). Stir over low heat until all of the sugar has dissolved and the mixture starts to boil. Take the usual precautions for boiling sugar: Remove any scum that accumulates on the surface, brush the sides of the pan clean from any sugar crystals, and partially cover the pan, then turn the heat to medium and boil for a few minutes.

3. Uncover and place a sugar thermometer in the syrup. Add the coloring when the sugar reaches 255°F (124°C).

4. Continue boiling to 285°F (141°C). Remove the pan from the heat and quickly stir in the Royal Icing, mixing it in well. Do not overwork the mixture; you may have to try a few times to get the right feel here so don't be discouraged if it does not work the first time.

5. Stop stirring. The sugar will rise to almost double its original volume, fall slowly, and then start to rise again. If it fails to rise again you can help it along by stirring rapidly for a second or two.

6. After the second rising, quickly pour the sugar into the prepared bowl. The sugar will continue to increase in size. Immediately place the bowl in the oven for 10 minutes to harden the sugar and prevent it from falling again.

7. Set the sugar aside in a dry place, still in the bowl, for about 8 hours.

8. Remove the rock sugar from the bowl. Break or cut it with a serrated knife into pieces suitable for your decoration.

Spun Sugar

variable yield

Boiled Sugar Basic Recipe (page 936)
food coloring (optional)

NOTE 1: It is impossible to predict a precise yield when spinning sugar. On a rainy or humid day, you will get a much smaller volume. Also, depending on how many times you have to reheat the sugar, you may not be able to use all of the syrup.

NOTE 2: If you spin the sugar in a dry place, you can store it for up to two days by lining the bottom of an airtight container with a dehumidifying agent covered with a sheet of foil.

Spun Sugar is traditionally used to decorate ice cream desserts, but it can be used to dress up many others as well. It looks very showy but is actually easy to make. The mass of thin, hair-like, sugar threads is also used to decorate pièces montées such as Croquembouche. Gâteau Saint-Honoré is also decorated with Spun Sugar on some occasions.

Unless the weather is dry, it is best to make Spun Sugar immediately before serving. Moisture is gradually absorbed by the thin threads, which become sticky and eventually dissolve. When Spun Sugar is used as part of a plate presentation it should not come in contact with a sauce or it will melt.

As with any sugar work, you should prepare everything you will need before you begin to boil the sugar. Clean, dry, and lightly oil two wooden or metal dowels. Place them, parallel, about 18 inches (45 cm) apart, extending over the edge of the table. Place a heavy cutting board on top at the back to hold them in place. Place a couple of sheet pans on the floor beneath the dowels to catch any drips. Cut the end off a metal whisk and spread the wires apart slightly (Figure 18–18). Have an airtight container handy to put the sugar in as it is ready. If you are adding color, keep in mind that the color will appear much lighter after the sugar is spun into thin threads, so a darker shade than is normally used is called for here.

1. Following the recipe and directions in Boiled Sugar Basic Recipe, but omitting the tartaric acid or cream of tartar, boil the syrup to 310°F (155°C), the hard crack stage, adding the coloring at 265°F (130°C), if used. Immediately remove from the heat and plunge the bottom of the pan into cold water for a few seconds to stop the cooking process and cool the sugar a little. Take the pan out of the water and let the syrup stand until slightly thickened before you start to spin to prevent too many drops falling off the whisk during the spinning process. Do not stir the sugar.

2. Dip the cut whisk about ¹/₂ inch (1.2 cm) into the sugar. Gently shake off excess by moving the whisk in an up and down motion just above the surface of the sugar syrup. Do not hold the whisk up too high when you do this or the sugar drops will cool down too much as they fall back into the pan, and this can cause the sugar to recrystallize.

Sugar Work 973

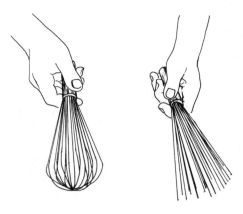

FIGURE 18–18 *A metal whisk before and after removing the rounded end and spreading the wires apart slightly to use for Spun Sugar*

FIGURE 18–19 *Making Spun Sugar by flicking the hot sugar syrup back and forth between two dowels extended over the edge of a table*

3. Spin the sugar by flicking the whisk back and forth in a rapid motion between the two dowels (Figure 18–19). Continue dipping and spinning the sugar until a reasonable amount has accumulated on the dowels.

4. Gather the sugar off the dowels and place in the airtight container. Continue spinning the remaining sugar. Sugar will start to accumulate on the whisk and glue the wires together. Remove it by placing the whisk inside a small plastic bag. Tighten the bag around the handle and strike the whisk sharply against the edge of the table. If the syrup cools down too much, warm it over low heat, stirring constantly to prevent the sugar from becoming any darker than necessary.

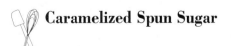 **Caramelized Spun Sugar**

Follow the preceding directions, cooking the sugar to 320°F (160°C) or until it is golden brown. Remember that the color will appear lighter after the sugar is spun. Do not add coloring.

19

Decorations

Buttercream
  Chocolate Buttercream
  French or Italian
    Buttercream
  Vanilla Buttercream
Candied Citrus Peels
Decorating with a Pastry
  Bag
  Basketweave Pattern
  Buttercream Roses
  Buttercream Leaves
  Rosettes
  Pearl and Shell Patterns
Decorating with a Piping Bag
  Piping Designs for
    Special-Occasion
    Cakes
  Piping Gel
Decorating with Sauces
  Corkscrew Pattern
  String of Hearts Pattern
  Weave Patterns
  Spiderweb Pattern
  Curved String of Hearts
    Pattern
  Ripple Pattern
  Hearts with Weave
    Pattern
  Spiral Spiderweb Pattern
  Two-Tone String

  of Hearts Pattern
  Hearts with Stems
    Pattern
  Feathered Two-Tone
    Pool Pattern
  Swirled Zigzag Pattern
Edible Flowers
Florentina Decorations
  Florentina Cookies
    for Marco Polo
  Florentina Halos
  Florentina Twists
Fondant
Decorating with Fondant
Glazes
  Apricot Glaze
  Chocolate Glaze
  Orange Glaze
  Pectin Glaze
  Red Currant Glaze
Gold Leaf
Hippen Decorating Paste
Icings
  Royal Icing
  Simple Icing
Marzipan
  Marzipan Apples
  Marzipan Bear

Marzipan Bumble Bees
Marzipan Carrots
Marzipan Easter Bunny
Marzipan Easter
  Chicken
Marzipan Coffee Beans
Marzipan Forget-Me-
  Not Flowers
Marzipan Oranges
Marzipan Pears
Marzipan Piglet
Marzipan Roses
Pâte à Choux for
  Decoration
Pie Tin Templates and
  Template Holders
Tulip Paste Decorations
  and Containers
  Tulips
  Vanilla Tulip Paste
  Chocolate Tulip Paste
  Tulip Cookie Spoons
  Tulip Leaves and
    Cookie Wedges
  Cookie Butterflies
  Cookie Citrus Rinds
    and Cookie Figurines
  Curly Cues
  Miniature Tulips
Wedding Cake Assembly
  and Decoration

Borage

Wild Roses

Honeysuckle

Marigolds

Pansies

Handmade decorative ornaments and elaborate design work are labor-intensive arts that are becoming lost due to today's high labor costs and greater emphasis on production. Unfortunately, more and more shops now use decorations made in factories. While in some instances it makes good sense to use prefabricated designs (marzipan and chocolate ornaments, for example), I believe that everything placed on a cake or pastry should be edible. Plastic cars and animals on a child's birthday cake, especially when combined with too many bright artificial colors, can be frightful. One exception to using only edible ornaments is the use of fresh flowers. While one or two edible fresh flowers are a lovely addition to individual dessert servings (this is discussed in greater detail within this chapter), cascades of flowers that are not meant to be consumed can be artistically arranged on a wedding cake for a popular, easy, and refreshing alternative to traditional white buttercream alone. These are removed by the person slicing the cake before the cake is served. If the cut stems are inserted into the top of the cake layers, the stems should be covered in plastic wrap unless the flowers are edible. Naturally, even though the flowers are not served, you should use a variety that is nontoxic.

The key to decorating (besides having a steady hand and an awareness of neatness and symmetry) is to make the finished product look tasteful and elegant, rather than busy or cluttered. This chapter offers methods and techniques, as well as a few tricks of the trade, for using basic materials to create decorations quickly and economically.

Buttercream

Buttercream is indispensable in the pastry kitchen. It is mostly used to fill, ice, and decorate cakes and pastries, but it is also used to make buttercream roses and leaves. Buttercream should be light and smooth and should always be made from a high-quality sweet butter. Icings made with margarine or shortening can be very unpleasant to eat (because of their higher melting point they tend to leave a film of fat in your mouth), but a small amount of margarine or shortening added to the buttercream stabilizes it without detracting from the taste. On very hot days, or in hot climates, you can increase the ratio of butter to margarine to equal amounts, but only if absolutely necessary to prevent the buttercream from melting. Since many weddings take place in the summertime, it often becomes necessary to display a buttercream-iced cake for several hours in a warm room during the reception. Another trick in this situation is to freeze the cake layers (fully or partially) after icing and decorating with buttercream so that the cake will stay cold and prevent the buttercream from melting. It is important to be certain that there will be enough time for the cake to have thawed all the way through before it is served if you use this method, and it should not be used with a filling that will suffer from freezing and thawing.

Buttercream can be stored at normal room temperature for three or four days and in the refrigerator for up to two weeks. It can also be frozen for longer storage. Buttercream that is kept in the refrigerator should be taken out in plenty of time to soften before using. If you need to soften it quickly, warm it slightly over simmering water, stirring vigorously, until smooth. Be careful not to overheat and melt the buttercream; you should continue to stir after you take it off of the heat, because the bowl will stay hot a little longer and can melt the buttercream on the sides. Use the same warming technique to repair buttercream that has broken. When buttercream breaks it is generally because the butter was too cold when it was added to the meringue, but this can also occur when a cold flavoring, such as Lemon Curd from the refrigerator, is added. Softening buttercream on a low setting in the microwave is a technique you might want to try if it is more convenient for you.

Meringue-based buttercream (soft butter beaten into whipped egg whites and sugar) is probably the most widely used. It is quick and easy to make and has a very light and fluffy texture. French or Italian Buttercream is made by whipping whole eggs or egg yolks to a thick foam with hot sugar syrup, and then whipping in soft butter. This is a very rich, yet light, buttercream.

In an emergency, you can make a quick buttercream by creaming together equal amounts of soft unsalted butter and Pastry Cream. Adjust the sweetness with powdered sugar. If you do not have Pastry Cream, cream together two parts soft unsalted butter and one part Fondant. Both of these methods will result in a rather heavy product, not nearly as palatable as real buttercream, and should only be used as a last resort.

The following buttercream recipes can easily be multiplied, or scaled down, with no loss of flavor or texture.

Chocolate Buttercream

4 pounds, 6 ounces (1 kg, 990 g)

2 pounds (910 g) soft unsalted butter
14 ounces (400 g) granulated sugar
1/3 cup (80 ml) water
1 tablespoon (15 ml) light corn syrup
4 eggs
2 egg whites (1/4 cup/60 ml)
1 teaspoon (5 g) salt
1 teaspoon (5 ml) vanilla extract
1 pound, 8 ounces (680 g) sweet dark chocolate, melted and at 110°F (43°C)

NOTE: Another, more convenient, reverse tempering method, is to make a well in the center of the buttercream mixture in the mixer bowl (after taking it off of the machine) and pour the chocolate into the well. Gradually, but still working quickly, mix a little of the buttercream from the sides into the chocolate, before mixing this into the remaining buttercream.

French or Italian Buttercream

4 pounds, 8 ounces (2 kg, 45 g)

1 pound, 8 ounces (680 g) granulated sugar
1/2 cup (120 ml) water
12 egg yolks (1 cup/240 ml)
2 pounds (910 g) soft unsalted butter
2 teaspoons (10 ml) vanilla extract

To make White Chocolate Buttercream substitute melted white chocolate for the sweet dark chocolate in equal amounts. Both white or dark Chocolate Buttercream can be flavored with Hazelnut Paste or Praline Paste, and dark Chocolate Buttercream is also nice with the addition of Coffee Reduction to create a mocha flavor.

1. Cream the butter until light and fluffy (warm it first if necessary). Reserve.

2. Combine the sugar, water, and corn syrup in a saucepan. Boil to 240°F (115°C), brushing down the sides of the pan. Do not stir.

3. While the syrup is boiling, whip the eggs, egg whites, salt, and vanilla, using a whip on low speed, just to combine. Remove the syrup from the heat, wait about 10 seconds, then gradually pour the hot syrup into the egg mixture, adding it in a steady stream between the whip and the side of the bowl, with the mixer at medium speed. Increase to high speed and whip until cold.

4. Reduce to low speed and gradually mix in the reserved butter. Remove the mixing bowl from the machine. Place one-third of the butter mixture in a separate bowl and quickly mix in the melted chocolate to temper. Still working quickly, add this to the remaining buttercream.

---

1. Place the sugar and water in a saucepan. Bring to a boil, stirring to dissolve the sugar. Reduce the heat and boil until the sugar syrup reaches 240°F (115°C).

2. While the syrup is boiling, whip the egg yolks until light and fluffy. Lower the speed on the mixer, and then carefully pour the hot syrup into the egg yolks, pouring it in a steady stream between the whip and the side of the bowl. Whip at high speed until the mixture is cool and light in texture.

3. Turn to low speed and gradually add the softened butter, adding it only as fast as it can be absorbed. Mix in the vanilla.

Vanilla Buttercream

*5 pounds, 4 ounces
(2 kg, 390 g)*

2 pounds (910 g) soft unsalted butter
10 ounces (285 g) soft vegetable
    margarine
one recipe Swiss Meringue (page 592)
2 teaspoons (10 ml) vanilla extract

*NOTE: If you replace the margarine with
unsalted butter, add 1 teaspoon (5 g) of salt to
the recipe, whipped with the egg whites.*

This recipe can be used as a starting point to create numerous other flavors: Vanilla Buttercream can be flavored with Lemon Curd, Coffee Reduction, Chestnut Purée, Hazelnut Paste, Praline Paste, or various liqueurs to use as both a filling or icing. When used as a filling only, you can also add chopped toasted nuts or candied fruit. When using fresh fruit with a buttercream filling, it is best to arrange thin slices of fruit on top of a layer of buttercream and then cover with additional buttercream rather than to mix the two together, both to make uniform level layers and because the added moisture can cause the buttercream to break.

1. Thoroughly combine the butter with the margarine. Reserve at room temperature.

2. When the meringue has been whipped to stiff peaks and is almost cold, lower the speed on the mixer, add the vanilla, and then gradually whip in the butter mixture. The butter mixture must not be too cold when it is added, or the buttercream may break.

Candied Citrus Peels (Orange, Lemon, Lime, or Grapefruit)

2 pounds (910 g) candied peels, approximately

1 pound, 10 ounces (740 g) citrus fruit
    shells, prepared as described in
    step one
1 tablespoon (15 g) salt
20° Baumé Sugar Syrup
    (recipe follows)
3 ounces (85 g) glucose
    or
¼ cup (60 ml) or 3 ounces (85 g) light
    corn syrup

NOTE: Because the syrup must be at or close to 60°F (16°C) to get an accurate reading, you must remove the pan from the heat when you think it has reduced enough, pour off a little syrup to cool and test, and then return the pan to the heat to continue boiling if it has not reduced sufficiently. Since this can be inconvenient, an alternative is to measure the syrup hot (not boiling or you can break the Baumé thermometer); however, hot syrup will read 3° lower so the reading should be 21° in that case.

This recipe should really be referred to as sugar preservation of citrus peels rather than candied, as, accurately speaking, the peel must be preserved in syrup before it can be candied. The true procedure for making candied fruit involves covering the exterior surface of sugar-preserved fruit with a thin, crystallized layer of sugar, which prevents it from drying out too rapidly. These days most people do not have the time to go through the rather lengthily process used here and instead either purchase candied fruit already prepared or use the quick-method variation that follows this recipe.

1. Cut oranges, lemons, limes, or grapefruits in half, juice them (reserve the juice for another use), and scrape the remaining flesh from the shells. Cut the shells in half again to make quarters.

2. Blanch the shells in boiling water for a few minutes. Pour off the water, add fresh water, and blanch for a few minutes longer. Repeat this step once more to remove the bitter taste from the peels.

3. Add fresh water again (just enough to cover), together with the salt, and simmer until the peels are soft, about 30 minutes. Plunge into cold water to cool. Remove and pat dry.

4. The white part of the peel, the pith, is usually left on but can be removed at this point with a small spoon or a melon-ball cutter if desired.

5. Stack the peels inside each other in a flat, noncorrosive pan such as a hotel pan. Weigh them down with a lid (also noncorrosive) or plates to prevent them from floating to the surface when you add the syrup.

6. Pour the hot sugar syrup over the peels to cover. Let sit for 24 hours.

7. Pour the syrup off into a saucepan. Boil it until it is reaches 24° on the Baumé thermometer (see note) (this can be accelerated by adding more sugar to the syrup). When the syrup reads 24°, pour it back over the peels and let stand another 24 hours.

8. Repeat step seven, bringing the syrup to 4° higher each day until the syrup reaches 34° Baumé. This will take five days from the day you started. Heat the peels in the syrup to scalding every other day. When the syrup is boiled for the last time, add the glucose or corn syrup to prevent recrystallization. During the entire process the peels should be kept covered at room temperature. Store the peels in the syrup (it will be very thick at this point), covered, at room temperature. The candied peels will keep for months.

1. Combine the water, sugar, and glucose or corn syrup in a saucepan. Heat to boiling and boil for 1 minute.

2. Remove the pan from the heat and skim off any scum that has developed on the surface of the syrup. Use hot.

20° Baumé Sugar Syrup

10 cups (2 l, 400 ml) syrup

6 cups (1 l, 440 ml) water

1 pound, 8 ounces (680 g) granulated sugar

1½ cups (360 ml) glucose or light corn syrup

NOTE: This quantity of syrup will probably appear to be a great deal more than you need for the amount of citrus peel you are preparing. It is necessary to begin with a large amount as the peels absorb part of the syrup, and the syrup is reduced several times during the preparation process.

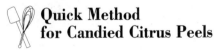

Quick Method for Candied Citrus Peels

4 ounces (115 g) candied peels

8 ounces (225 g) orange, lemon, lime, or grapefruit peel, removed using a vegetable peeler, without any white pith

2 ounces (55 g) powdered sugar

1. Cut the peels into very thin julienne.

2. Blanch the strips in water for a few minutes to remove the bitter taste. Strain and pat dry with a towel. Spread the peels in a single layer (but not too far apart) on a sheet pan lined with baking paper. Sift the powdered sugar over the top.

3. Dry the peels at 100°F (38°C) for approximately 30 minutes. Move the peels around to make sure all sides are coated with the sugar and they are not sticking together.

4. Continue drying the peels about 30 minutes longer. Be careful not to overcook them. When cold, store the candied peels in an airtight container to use as needed.

Decorating with a Pastry Bag

Refer to pages 21 to 23 for information on filling, using, and caring for pastry bags.

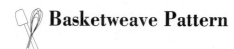 **Basketweave Pattern**

*T*his design can be done with any type of tip, but it looks best made with a flat tip (plain or star). If you do not have one, you can flatten the end of a regular tip yourself.

1. Start by piping a vertical line close to one edge of the item you are decorating. (In the case of a round cake you can start anywhere on the sides.)

2. Pipe horizontal lines on top of the vertical line leaving a space between them the same size as the width of the lines. The length of the horizontal lines should be three times the width, and the ends must line up evenly.

3. Pipe a second vertical line, one line-width from the first one, just slightly overlapping the ends of the horizontal lines.

4. Pipe more horizontal lines between the first rows, going over the second vertical line. Repeat alternating vertical and horizontal lines until finished (Figure 19–1).

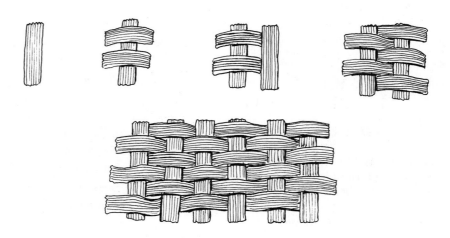

FIGURE 19–1 The consecutive steps in piping a Basketweave Pattern in butter-cream

Buttercream Roses

NOTE: *If you are making up Buttercream Roses in advance, cut squares of baking paper just slightly larger than the head of the decorating nail, attach a paper to the nail with a little buttercream, and form a rose on the paper square. Lift the paper off the nail and set the paper on a sheet pan in the refrigerator. To use, peel the rose off the paper with the tip of a knife and place on the cake or other item.*

*I*t is easier than it looks to make a Buttercream Rose, but it does require prac-tice. You also need a very smooth buttercream that is not too soft, a decorating nail (it looks like a nail with a very large head) about 1½ inches (3.7 cm) in diameter, and a special rose-petal tip for the pastry bag (no. 124 for a medium-sized rose). If you tint the buttercream for roses, keep the colors to pale shades.

1. Place the buttercream in the pastry bag with the rose-petal tip. Hold the stem of the decorating nail between the thumb and forefinger of your left hand (if you are right-handed). Hold the pastry bag so that the opening in the tip is perpendicular to the nail, with the wider end of the opening at the bottom.

2. Start by making the base of the rose: Place the bottom of the tip directly on the nail just outside the center. Angle the top of the tip just a little toward the center and pipe while turning the nail one complete turn. You should now have a small cone in the center of the nail. Make a second cone on top of the first one, slightly smaller and coming to a point at the top (Figure 19–2).

3. To form the petals, pipe the buttercream in a clockwise direction while turning the nail counterclockwise. Hold the bag in the same way you did to make the cone: wide end at the bottom. For the first row of petals, place the bottom of the tip slightly above the base of the cone and the top of the tip angled out just a little (Figure 19–3). The first row of petals should look fairly closed. Pipe three petals, evenly spaced, around the cone, lifting the tip up and then down in an arc to make the rounded shape (Figure 19–4).

4. Make a second row of three petals in the same way, starting the bottom of these petals just below the first row, angling the top out a lit-tle further so the second row of petals has opened a bit more than the first, and placing the second row so the petals are staggered, not directly on top of other three (Figure 19–5).

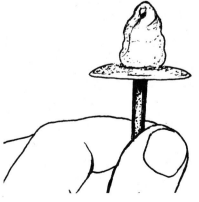

FIGURE 19–2 The center cone for a Buttercream Rose

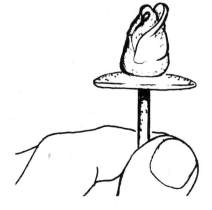

FIGURE 19–3 After piping the first petal

FIGURE 19–4 After piping three petals evenly spaced around the center cone

FIGURE 19–5 After piping the second row of petals staggered between those in the first row

5. The third row should contain four or five petals. Using the same turning and piping method, start this row a little below the row before, angle the top out a bit more, and again stagger the petals so they fall between those in the second row. You can stop at this point, with three rows, or continue to add more rows to reach the desired size.

6. To remove the rose from the nail, cut it off with a thin knife and set it on the cake or other item. The roses are easier to cut off if you chill them first.

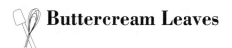

Buttercream Leaves

*P*ipe Buttercream Leaves directly on the cake or pastry after you have set the rose in place, using buttercream tinted to a pale green shade if desired.

1. Use a leaf tip in the pastry bag. Hold the bag at a 45° angle with the base of the tip against the cake. Squeeze the bag with the palm of your hand while holding the tip in place for a split second to make the base of the leaf flow out. Gradually decrease the pressure as you pull the tip along, making the leaf narrower and bringing it to the length you want.

2. Stop pressing on the bag and pull the tip away to bring the end of the leaf to a point. If you have difficulty forming a point at the end, the buttercream is not soft enough.

Rosettes

*T*his technique applies to forming rosettes using other fillings—whipped cream, Ganache, etc.—as well as buttercream.

1. Place a star tip in the pastry bag. Add the filling. Hold the bag almost straight up and down above the place you want the rosette.

2. As you apply pressure, simultaneously move the bag in a tight 360° circle.

3. Stop the pressure, then lift the bag to finish the rosette.

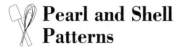 **Pearl and Shell Patterns**

*T*he technique used to make these two patterns is the same. You simply use a plain tip to make the pearls (also known as a bead pattern) and a star tip for the shells. As with the Rosettes, the same method is applied for any soft filling.

1. Hold the bag at approximately a 45° angle. The tip should just barely touch the surface you plan to pipe on.

2. Squeeze the bag with the palm of your hand, applying enough pressure to make the filling flow out to a wide base for the shell or pearl, then gradually relax the pressure as you slowly move the tip along to form the narrow point of the shell or pearl.

3. Stop squeezing and pull the bag away to finish the design. This design is used individually or as part of a border design. For a border, start the next shell or bead just slightly overlapping the narrow tip of the last one (Figure 19–6).

FIGURE 19–6 The finished Pearl Pattern; piping a Shell Pattern

Decorating with a Piping Bag

See Figures 1–13 to 1–17, page 27, for instructions to make a piping bag from baking paper. Also see pages 906 to 910 for instructions and templates for piped chocolate decorations.

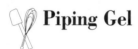

Piping Designs for Special-Occasion Cakes

The following templates or illustrations in Figures 19–7 to 19–20 suggest particular motifs such as Christmas, Valentine's Day, Easter, a child's birthday, and so on. They can serve merely as inspiration for you to create your own designs, or they can be used as a pattern to press into Marzipan as described in Decorating with Fondant Method II (page 1012). Once made in this fashion, the "stamps" can be kept virtually forever to use as needed. You may also want to use these templates to create designs on Marzipan by following the instructions for tracing onto Marzipan, on page 1022.

Enlarge the templates to the appropriate size for the cake you are decorating.

Piping Gel

Piping gel is purchased ready to use. It is made from sugar, corn syrup solids, and vegetable gum, such as gum arabic. It is very sweet and not very pleasant to eat by itself (as you can probably imagine from the ingredient list), but it is one of the most practical decorating materials in today's pastry shop. Although it looks artificial next to a chocolate decoration (for special petits fours or showpieces you should use Piping Chocolate), nevertheless, the fact that piping gel is so inexpensive and easy to work with makes it a useful tool for everyday decorating or to add just a small touch of color. For example, you can use it to fill in some of the small loops in a design piped in chocolate. Piping gel is available in a clear colorless form as well as in various colors. Because many of the colors are a bit bright, I recommend buying the clear gel and coloring it yourself to pastel shades.

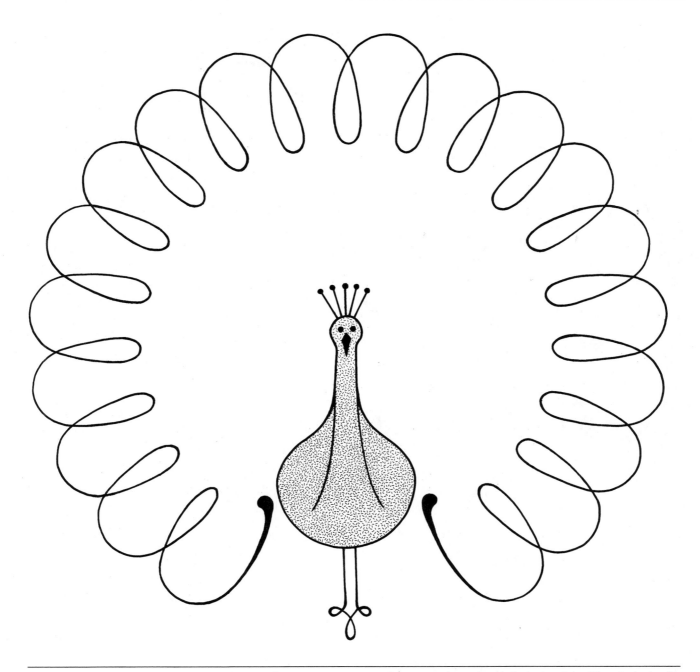

FIGURE 19-7 A piping design that can be used for various occasions. After tracing the outline in dark chocolate, fill in the body of the peacock with light chocolate, or use the design shown in the color insert

FIGURE 19–8 *A piping design for an engagement party or bridal shower cake*

FIGURE 19–9 A piping design for a boy's birthday cake

FIGURE 19–10 A piping design for a child's birthday cake

FIGURE 19–11 A piping design for a Valentine cake

FIGURE 19–12 A piping design for a Mother's Day cake

FIGURE 19–13 A piping design for a Christmas cake

FIGURE 19–14 A piping design for a Father's Day cake

FIGURE 19–15 A piping design for a New Year's cake

FIGURE 19–16 A piping design for a springtime cake

Tropical Surprise Packages

Zinfandel Poached Pears with Honey-Scented Pear Frozen Yogurt

Assorted Holiday Pastries

Christmas Cookies

Traditional Gingerbread House

Marzipan Pig with Two Santas

Traditional Gingerbread House

Traditional Gingerbread House

Santa's Gingerbread Chalet

Marzipan Pig with Santa

Yule Log and Bûche de Noël Slices with Pomegranate Sauce and Starfruit

Pig's Head Loaf Bread and Rolls

Brandied Gingerbread Cake

Persimmon Cream Slices with Cookie Christmas Tree and Cranberry Coulis

Chocolate Chalet with White Chocolate and Pistachio Pâte and Bitter Chocolate Sauce

Marzipan Bear Birthday Cake

Wild Strawberries Romanoff in Caramel Boxes

Chocolate Ganache Towers

Baklava with Mascarpone Bavarian and Cherry Sauce

Apple Crème Brûlée

Nectarine Meringue Tart with Rhubarb

Citrus Cream with Pink Grapefruit and Orange

Strawberry Pyramids

Budapest Swirls

Tropical Mousse Cake

Meringue Glacé Leda

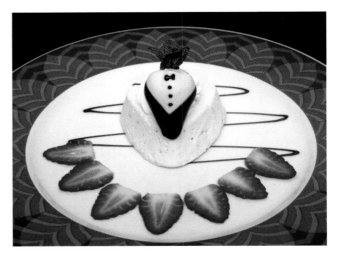

Frozen Hazelnut Coffee Mousse with Black Tie Strawberrie

FIGURE 19–17 A piping design for a girl's birthday cake

FIGURE 19–18 A piping design for an Easter cake

FIGURE 19–19 A piping design for an Easter cake

FIGURE 19–20 A piping design for a baby shower cake

Decorating with Sauces

Decorating desserts, and also savory dishes, with sauces has become very fashionable in restaurants. It is an excellent and easy way to dress up the presentation, personalize the dessert, and make it stand out as something memorable. Although to be able to "paint" you need to use enough sauce to cover the base of the plate, or cover one portion of it, be careful not to overdo it. Too much sauce can be overwhelming, as well as messy, and can take away from the flavor of the dessert.

The instructions for making the various designs described here assume that the dessert plates are large enough to give you some space around the dessert to use as a "canvas." These designs are for plates that are 11–12 inches (27.5–30 cm) across with a base that is 7–8 inches (17.5–20 cm) in diameter. All white or fairly plain china patterns are more suitable for elaborate presentations, just as plates with a very ornate decorated rim (especially if several colors are used) require a more understated sauce design so the effect does not become busy. This is even more important if a decorating material such as cocoa powder, streaked chocolate, or sprayed chocolate is used on the rim of the plate, where it looks completely out of place if the rim is already decorated. These instructions also assume you have prepared the dessert item the same size as called for in the recipes, or in the case of a slice of cake, that a 10-inch (25-cm) cake has been cut into 12 to 14 pieces.

These are general decorating ideas for sauces. They can, of course, be combined or changed to suit a particular taste or occasion. The designs shown in a small pool of sauce can be made on the entire surface of the plate as well, and vice versa. Keep in mind that the more complicated the design, the less suitable it is for serving a large number. Even though in some cases the sauce can be poured on the plates in advance, piping on the decoration must be done just before the desserts are served or it will start to deteriorate.

As specified in the recipes for Sour Cream Mixture for Piping (see page 1081) and Chocolate Sauce for Piping (see page 1072), it is essential that the piping mixture or contrasting sauce and the sauce on the plate are the same consistency. You will not get a good result if they are not. In most cases the base sauce should be applied using a piping bottle with a fairly large opening, the exception being when the base sauce is piped as a frame (such as a hollow teardrop design) to be filled in with the contrasting sauce. The piping mixture or contrasting sauce should be applied using a piping bottle with a small opening or with a piping bag. The exception to this is when the contrasting sauce is piped directly on the plate next to the other sauce, as in the Feathered Two-Tone Pool Pattern. I use small, plastic squeeze bottles with approximately a 2-cup (480-ml) capacity. If you store leftover sauce in the bottles, be sure to check the consistency before using again and shake, strain, thin, thicken, etc., as necessary, since the consistency often changes during storage.

Corkscrew Pattern

*T*his decoration is quick and looks especially good with a round dessert such as a charlotte or bavarois, or whenever the sauce is served encircling the dessert.

1. Place the dessert in the center of the plate and pipe sauce all around to cover the base of the plate in a thin layer.

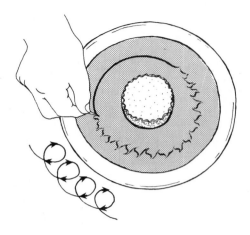

FIGURE 19–21 *Making a Corkscrew Pattern*

2. Pipe a ring of the contrasting sauce between the dessert and the edge of the plate.

3. Use a small wooden skewer to draw a "corkscrew" pattern through the two sauces (Figure 19–21).

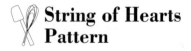 **String of Hearts Pattern**

*T*his design takes a little longer to complete. It is especially elegant when you do not have too much space between the dessert and the edge of the plate.

1. Place the dessert in the center of the plate and pipe sauce all around to cover the base of the plate in a thin layer.

2. Pipe a series of small dots, about 1 inch (2.5 cm) apart, forming a ring between the dessert and the edge of the plate.

3. Drag a small wooden skewer through the center of the circles in one continuous motion to create a string of hearts (Figure 19–22). You can also pick the skewer up and wipe it off between each heart to get a different effect.

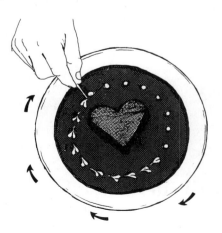

FIGURE 19–22 *Making a String of Hearts Pattern*

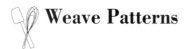

Weave Patterns

1. Place the dessert in the center of the upper half of the plate. Using a piping bottle, pipe a small oval pool of sauce in front (the side that will be facing the customer).

2. Pipe three or four horizontal lines of the contrasting sauce across the pool.

3. Drag a small wooden skewer through the lines toward the edge of the plate. You can also alternate directions to make a herringbone pattern (Figure 19–23), or drag the lines through on the diagonal.

Spiderweb Pattern

1. Place the dessert in the center of the upper half of the plate. Using a piping bottle, pipe a small oval or round pool of sauce in front (the side that will be facing the customer).

2. Pipe a thin spiral of the contrasting sauce on top, making it oval or round to correspond with the pool.

3. Drag a small wooden skewer from the center to the outside in evenly spaced lines (Figure 19–24) or from the outside toward the center, or alternate directions.

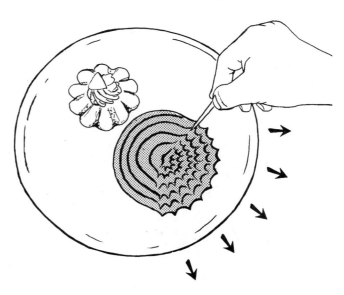

FIGURE 19–23 Making a Herringbone-Style Weave Pattern

FIGURE 19–24 Making a Spiderweb Pattern

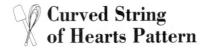 ## Curved String
of Hearts Pattern

This is a variation of the String of Hearts Pattern.

1. Place the dessert in the center of the upper half of the plate. Using a piping bottle, pipe a small oval or round pool of sauce in front (the side that will be facing the customer).

2. Pipe the contrasting sauce on top in a random series of dots.

3. Drag a small wooden skewer through the dots, making a succession of smooth turns, to create curved hearts (Figure 19–25).

 ## Ripple Pattern

This design is very fast to make and is especially useful when there is a limited amount of space on the plate.

1. Place a slice of cake in the center of the dessert plate. Using a piping bottle, pipe a small oval pool of sauce at the tip of the slice (letting the sauce float out on both sides of the slice).

2. Pipe two lines of the contrasting sauce, close to each other, at the edge of the pool.

3. Drag a small wooden skewer through the two lines, making connected circles as for the Corkscrew Pattern (Figure 19–26).

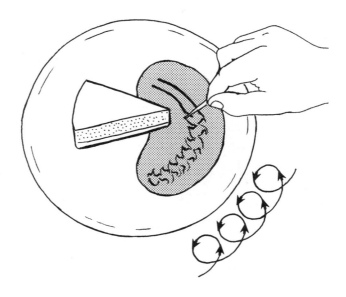

FIGURE 19–25 Making a Curved String of Hearts Pattern

FIGURE 19–26 Making a Ripple Pattern

FIGURE 19–27 Making a Hearts with Weave Pattern

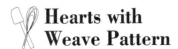 **Hearts with Weave Pattern**

*T*his design creates both hearts and a herringbone pattern.

1. Place the dessert in the center of the upper half of the plate. Using a piping bottle, pipe a teardrop-shaped pool of sauce on the plate so that the narrow end of the pool wraps halfway around the dessert.

2. Using the contrasting sauce, pipe a line of small dots, spaced about ¹/₂ inch (1.2 cm) apart, and then two parallel solid lines under the dots, centered across the width of the pool.

3. Drag a small wooden skewer up and down through the pattern without picking it up, dragging through both the dots and the solid lines when moving toward the edge of the plate and through the solid lines between each dot when moving toward the dessert (Figure 19–27).

Spiral Spiderweb Pattern

This pattern creates a spiderweb pattern using the reverse of the technique for the plain Spiderweb Pattern: Instead of piping the sauce in a spiral and dragging the skewer in radiating lines, the sauce is piped in a spoke pattern and then the skewer is dragged through in a spiral. Place the dessert in the center of the sauce after the pattern is completed.

1. Cover the base of the plate with a thin layer of sauce. Pipe the contrasting sauce on top in a spoke pattern.

2. Starting at the edge of the sauce pool, drag a small wooden skewer through the sauces in a spiral, ending in the center of the plate (Figure 19–28).

Two-Tone String of Hearts Pattern

This is another variation of the String of Hearts Pattern. You can use just two sauces or use a third type (and color) for the center dots (hearts).

1. Cover the base of a plate with a thin layer of sauce. Pipe dots of the contrasting sauce fairly close together around the perimeter of the sauce, making them about the size of a quarter coin. Pipe smaller dots of the first sauce in the center of each quarter-size dot.

2. Drag a small wooden skewer in a curved side-to-side pattern through the center of the small dots, moving all the way around the plate in one continuous line (Figure 19–29). Place the dessert in the center of the plate.

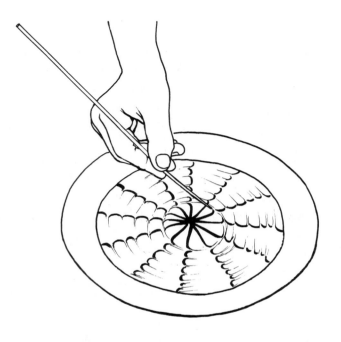

FIGURE 19–28 Making a Spiral Spiderweb Pattern   *FIGURE 19–29 Making a Two-Tone String of Hearts Pattern*

Hearts with Stems Pattern

*T*his design makes a more elaborate heart shape.

1. Cover the base of the plate with a thin layer of sauce. Pipe five quarter-sized dots of the contrasting sauce, evenly spaced, centered in the area that will be left between the dessert serving and the edge of the base sauce.

2. Dip the tip of a small wooden skewer into one of the dots of contrasting sauce to pick up a little sauce on the skewer. Place the tip of the skewer into the sauce on the plate about ¹/₂ inch (1.2 cm) away from the dot, and then drag it through the dot and out the other side in a slightly curved motion, creating a heart with a stem (Figure 19–30). Repeat with the remaining dots. Place the dessert in the center of the plate.

Feathered Two-Tone Pool Pattern

NOTE: Depending on the sauces used and/or the amount of contrast desired, use either the pointed or the blunt end of the skewer. This pattern can also be used by piping the sauces in two half-circles that cover the base of the plate side-by-side, meeting in the center.

1. Using a piping bottle, pipe a pool of sauce in the center of the plate that is large enough to accommodate the dessert serving and leave a border of sauce visible. Using a second piping bottle, cover the base of the plate around the pool with a layer of the contrasting sauce.

2. Drag a wooden skewer in a series of connecting circles through both sauces where they meet (Figure 19–31). Place the dessert in the center of the plate.

FIGURE 19–31 Making a Feathered Two-Tone Pool Pattern

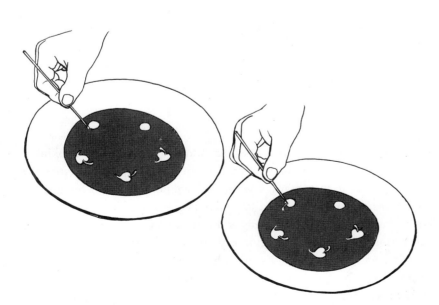

FIGURE 19–30 Making a Hearts with Stems Pattern

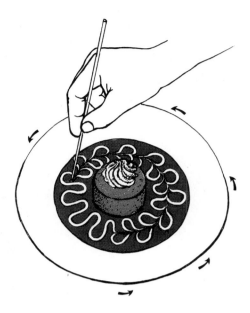

FIGURE 19–32 *Making a Swirled Zigzag Pattern*

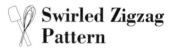

Swirled Zigzag Pattern

*T*his looks best with a round dessert.

1. Place the dessert in the center of the plate and use a piping bottle to pipe sauce all around to cover the base of the plate. Pipe a continuous, curved zigzagging line of the contrasting sauce between the dessert and the edge of the sauce on the plate.

2. Drag a small wooden skewer through the center of the line all the way around the plate in one continuous motion (Figure 19–32).

Edible Flowers

Decorating with edible fresh flowers and/or using them in cooking is nothing new. Flowers have been used in food preparation since the Middle Ages; in fact, many flowers that we now grow for ornamental purposes, such as roses and lavender, were originally cultivated for their flavor. The interest in using edible flowers in savory dishes as well as desserts has grown tremendously over the last few years.

It is safe to say that most of us have probably eaten flowers without realizing it: Artichokes and broccoli are basically the bud or immature flower of the plant; dried daylily petals are used in Chinese hot and sour soup; and herbal teas often include chamomile flowers or hibiscus, rose, or jasmine petals. When I was a kid I used to enjoy sucking the sweet moisture out of clover flowers, which grew wild in the meadows, without regarding it as anything unusual.

When using edible flowers in food or as a decoration (unless you grow them yourself) it is crucial to be sure of how they have been cared for. Most flowers that are purchased at a nursery or florist shop have been sprayed with pesticide and should not be eaten. Produce companies and farmer's markets that offer organically grown edible flowers are a better choice for a supplier.

In many countries, including my native country, Sweden, and our close neighbor, Canada, it is against the law to put anything on a plate of food or use any decoration on food intended for consumption, unless it is edible. And yet here, and I have been guilty of this myself, we think nothing of decorating a wedding cake with any type of beautiful fresh flowers since we know they will be removed before the cake is served. (When using nonedible flowers on a cake, make sure they are nontoxic, even though they will not be consumed, and cover the stems with plastic wrap if they are inserted into the cake.)

In some flowers both the stamen and styles can be bitter and unpleasant to eat, even though they are not poisonous. In addition, the pollen of some edible flowers can cause an allergic reaction in certain individuals. Therefore the sepals should be removed in all flowers except Johnny-jump-ups, lavender sprigs, violas, and pansies. With others, only the petals are edible; this applies to tulips, roses, chrysanthemums, and calendula. The petals should be separated from the remainder of the flower just before they are used. Additionally, roses, chrysanthemums, and marigolds have a white portion at the end of the petal that is bitter and should be broken off before they are used. You can use the entire flower with the varieties borage, violet, Johnny-jump-up, marigold, and honeysuckle. Two tropical varieties that are edible, and are also grown in parts of the United States, are the flowers from passion fruit and feijoa. Both have a perfumed scent, are very pretty, and are something of a rarity.

Unfortunately, some of nature's prettiest creations are not edible, either because they have an unpleasant flavor or because they contain toxins in varying degrees that can make you sick and can even be fatal: lily of the valley, clematis, sweet pea, and foxglove fall into this category. So, please remember: just because you may have seen a flower served with food does not mean that it is safe to eat. Just as when gathering wild mushrooms, if you can not positively identify the flower as edible and be certain of its source, do not eat it and, moreover, do not place it on your customer's plate.

Edible flowers are used in many culinary creations in addition to desserts, as a garnish for beverages or mixed with salad greens, and some larger varieties such as zucchini and squash blossoms are stuffed and deep fried. Flowers from rosemary, oregano, chives, and some other herbs have a scent which makes them unsuitable for the pastry kitchen. The table in Figure 19–33 provides a partial list of the flowers that are both edible and appropriate for use with sweets.

EDIBLE FLOWERS				
Name	Appearance	Usable Portion	Flavor	Notes
BORAGE	Small, star-shaped, sky blue flowers tinged with light pink.	The whole flower can be eaten.	Bittersweet	Wilts quickly once removed from the stem. Can have a diuretic effect and should not be consumed in large quantities.
CALENDULA (Pot Marigold)	Yellow or orange fluffy round flowers.	Use the petals only.	Bitter	No fragrance. The petals used more for color than for flavor.
ELDERBERRY	White or off-white. Dramatic clusters of small flowers are called elderblow.	Flowers only. They must be cooked. The leaves, branches, tree bark, and even the stems are poisonous.	Exceptionally sweet fragrance and flavor.	The berries are used to make wine, jam, and tea. Like the flowers, they must never be eaten raw.
HONEYSUCKLE	Small trumpet-shaped flowers are first white and then turn pale yellow.	Petals only. Only the Lonicera japonica variety is edible.	Perfumed flavor; wonderful sweet scent.	The flowers contain a drop of sweet nectar, which is the source of their flavor.
JASMINE (Arabian Jasmine)	Small, tubular, star-shaped white flowers.	Whole flower. Do not use Carolina jasmine or Jessamine, which are poisonous.	Sweet perfumed flavor.	Part of the olive family. Jasmine flowers are widely used to flavor tea.
JOHNNY-JUMP-UP	Small, multicolor, purple, white, and yellow flowers.	The whole flower can be eaten.	Petals have almost no flavor. If the whole flower is eaten, including the sepal, it has a mint flavor.	A member of the viola family; related to pansies. Contains saponins and can be toxic in large amounts.
LAVENDER	Clusters of very small light to dark purple flowers grow at the end of a thin stalk.	Use only the sprig.	Perfumed flavor with a faint lemon taste.	From the mint family. Used extensively in perfumes, soaps, and sachets.
PANSY	Purple, blue, yellow, maroon, and pink. Both single and multicolors.	The whole flower can be eaten.	Grassy, vegetable flavor.	Same shape as Johnny-jump-up, but about twice as large.
ROSE	Grows in virtually all colors and in many sizes.	The petals only are used.	Perfumed flavor.	Roses are used to scent soaps, perfumes and are included in potpourri.
TUBEROUS BEGONIA	White, red, yellow, and combinations.	Use the petals only. Do not eat other begonias. Only hybrid tuberous begonias are edible.	Citrus flavor.	Should be eaten sparingly since they contain oxalic acid.
TULIP	All colors; large oval-shaped flowers.	Use the petals only.	Flavor similar to a green bean.	Part of the lily family. Some people have an allergic reaction in the form of a rash from eating tulips.
VIOLET	Colors range from deep violet to white and rose. Very small flowers.	The whole flower can be eaten.	Perfumed flavor.	Leaves are also edible and can be used in salads.

FIGURE 19–33 Descriptions and usage of edible flowers suitable for the pastry kitchen

Florentina Decorations

Florentina Cookies for Marco Polo

sixteen 9-by-1¹/₂-inch (22.5-×-3.7-cm) cookies and sixteen 4¹/₂-by-1¹/₂-inch (11.2-×-3.7-cm) cookies

one-half recipe or 12 ounces (340 g) Florentina Batter (page 214)

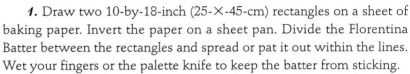

1. Draw two 10-by-18-inch (25-×-45-cm) rectangles on a sheet of baking paper. Invert the paper on a sheet pan. Divide the Florentina Batter between the rectangles and spread or pat it out within the lines. Wet your fingers or the palette knife to keep the batter from sticking.

2. Bake at 375°F (190°C) for about 12 minutes or until light brown. Carefully slide the baking paper onto a sheet of corrugated cardboard or onto your worktable. Using a sharp knife, trim the rectangles to make them 9 inches (22.5 cm) wide. Cut across the width every 1¹/₂ inches (3.7 cm) to make twelve 1¹/₂-by-9-inch (3.7×-22.5-cm) strips from each rectangle. Cut eight of the twenty-four strips in half crosswise to make sixteen large and sixteen small cookies. Reheat the Florentina as needed during this process to keep it from breaking.

3. Place the cookies in the oven just long enough to soften. Drape the pieces, top-side up, over a can or other round object 6 inches (15 cm) in diameter and let sit until firm.

Florentina Halos

twenty 4-inch (10-cm) decorations

one-half recipe or 12 ounces (340 g) Florentina Batter (page 214)

*T*his amount of Florentina Batter will make a few more than twenty Halos, but some will inevitably break (or be eaten).

1. Draw twenty 4-inch (10-cm) circles on a sheet of baking paper, using a plain cookie cutter as a guide. Invert the paper on a sheet pan. Divide the Florentina Batter evenly between the circles using two spoons, then flatten it and spread it out within the circles. Wet your fingers or the spoons to keep the batter from sticking.

2. Bake at 375°F (190°C) until golden brown, approximately 10 minutes. Let the cookies cool just a little, then use the same cutter used to draw the circles to cut the cookies round. Let the cookies cool completely, then break off the uneven edges (techniques for trimming the edges even are described in more detail in the recipe for Florentinas, see pages 212 and 213).

3. Warm the trimmed cookies slightly, and then, using a 1³/₄-inch (4.5-cm) plain round cookie cutter, cut the centers out of the cookies to create Halos. Save the centers if desired to use in the presentation for Blancmange as described in the introduction to that recipe (page 543).

Florentina Twists

approximately 20 decorations

one-quarter recipe or 6 ounces (170 g)
Florentina Batter (page 214)

1. Draw a 7-by-16-inch (17.5-×-40-cm) rectangle on a piece of baking paper. Invert the paper, place the Florentina Batter on top, and pat or spread it out to form a rectangle within the lines. Wet your fingers or the palette knife to keep the batter from sticking.

2. Place the paper on a sheet pan and bake at 375°F (190°C) for approximately 10 minutes or until it is a light caramel color. Slide the paper off the pan onto the table. Trim just enough from each long side to make it even.

3. Cut the strip crosswise into wedges that measure approximately ³/₄ inch (2 cm) at the wide end and ¹/₄ inch (6 mm) at the narrow end, as shown in the illustration. Let the sheet cool and harden, then separate the wedges and place them on a paper-lined sheet pan. A few at a time, place the wedges back in the oven just long enough to soften them.

4. One at a time, twist each wedge into a spiral (Figure 19–34). If you are making a large quantity, you can wind the wedges around a small dowel or other suitable tool; I use the handle of a brush that is slightly tapered. This will produce the version shown in the photograph of Wild Strawberry Parfait. Store the Florentina Twists in an airtight container until needed.

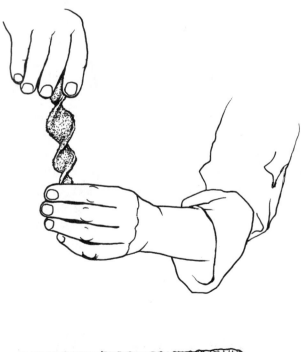

FIGURE 19–34 Twisting a softened wedge-shaped Florentina cookie to make a Florentina Twist

Fondant

2 quarts (1 l, 920 ml)

2 cups (480 ml) water

4 pounds (1 kg, 820 g) granulated
   sugar

$^2/_3$ cup (160 ml) glucose or corn syrup,
   warmed

$^1/_2$ teaspoon (1 g) cream of tartar

1 cup (240 ml) cold water

NOTE: If you are making a large batch of Fondant, you can work the sugar in a mixer instead of doing it by hand. Place the cooled syrup in the mixing bowl carefully. Do not get any on the sides of the bowl (hold the bowl next to the table and scrape the mixture in with the bench scraper). Use the paddle and mix on low speed until the Fondant is smooth and creamy. You may need to scrape down the sides of the bowl to ensure that all of the Fondant is mixed evenly. Scoop the Fondant into a container and cover with the cold water as above.

F ondant is widely used in the pastry shop for glazing and decorating. If properly applied, it dries to a silky-smooth icing that not only enhances the appearance of a pastry but preserves it as well, by sealing it from the air. Fondant is a sugar syrup that is recrystallized to a creamy white paste. Glucose and cream of tartar are used to invert part of the sugar to achieve the proper amount of recrystallization. Without these ingredients the cooked sugar would harden and be impossible to work with. Conversely, if too much glucose or cream of tartar is used, there will not be enough recrystallization, and the Fondant will be soft and runny.

Although Fondant is inexpensive and relatively easy to make (once you get the hang of it), it is almost always purchased in a professional kitchen either ready-to-use or as a powder to which you add water. To make your own Fondant you will need a precise sugar thermometer (test in boiling water to determine accuracy), a sugar pan (see page 1125) or a heavy saucepan, a wide spatula or bench scraper, a marble slab (2 by 2 feet/60 × 60 cm for this recipe), four steel or aluminum bars, and, as in all sugar work, quick reaction time when the sugar has reached the proper temperature.

1. Clean, dry, and lightly oil the marble slab and metal bars with vegetable oil. Place the bars at the edge of the marble to make a frame to hold the hot syrup when it is poured on the slab. Oil a stainless-steel scraper, and place the cold water close by.

2. Combine the 2 cups (480 ml) water and the granulated sugar in a saucepan. Bring to a boil, stirring to dissolve the sugar. Reduce the heat to medium, stop stirring, and brush the sides of the pan with water. Be sure to brush down all of the crystals. It takes only a few particles of sugar left on the sides to make the mixture recrystallize (before you want it to) when the sugar becomes hotter.

3. When the temperature reaches 225°F (108°C) add the warm glucose or corn syrup and the cream of tartar dissolved in a little hot water. Continue boiling until the syrup reaches 238–240°F (114–115°C). Pay close attention; the syrup will reach this temperature quicker than you might think.

4. Immediately pour the syrup onto the prepared surface and sprinkle about 2 tablespoons (30 ml) of the cold water on top. It is critical that the temperature does not exceed 240°F (115°C), so if your marble is not right next to the stove, place the saucepan in a bowl of cold water for a few seconds first to prevent overcooking. Insert the sugar thermometer into the thickest part of the puddle and let the sugar cool to 110°F (43°C).

5. Remove the bars and start to incorporate air: Using the oiled, stainless-steel scraper, work the sugar by sliding the scraper under the edge, lifting it, and folding in toward the center. After awhile the sugar will start to turn white and become firmer. Continue to work the Fondant slowly either by hand or in a mixing bowl (see note) until it has a smooth and creamy consistency.

6. Pack the Fondant against the bottom of a plastic container and pour the remaining cold water on top to prevent a crust from forming. Store at room temperature.

The Fondant must rest about 24 hours before it will be soft enough to use. Fondant will keep for months if covered properly. Pour off the water before using and keep the bowl covered with plastic wrap while you are working. Add a new layer of water and then cover to store until the next use.

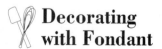
Decorating with Fondant

Method I

Fondant is an excellent decorating material for making designs using a piping bag. It needs to be fairly cold for piping the outline (85–95°F/29–34°C) and quite firm. If needed, add only enough Simple Syrup so you can pipe it—the Fondant used for the outline should still hold its shape once it is piped out. For filling in the piped designs you need to warm the Fondant just a little (not over 100°F/38°C), and then thin it, as needed, with Simple Syrup so it will flow out slightly within the outline. Be sure to keep the Fondant covered at all times to prevent a skin from forming.

1. To make small, individual ornaments, place a perfectly flat sheet of acetate or polyurethane about 1/16 inch (2 mm) thick on top of your drawing (you may want to use the designs shown in Figures 17–20 and 17–21, pages 907 and 908, or your own creations) and secure the plastic so it will not shift as you pipe. Depending on the type of plastic used, you may need to rub a thin film of vegetable oil over the top to keep the ornaments from sticking.

2. Put a small amount of Fondant in a piping bag and pipe a thin frame of Fondant around the figures. (Unlike chocolate ornaments made using a similar method, Fondant ornaments are placed on the cake or pastry right-side up. Small detail lines within the figure are piped on top after filling the frame with warm Fondant. They are not piped out at the same time as the outline.)

3. Fill in with the warmer Fondant, moving the piping bag back and forth to get a smooth surface and to build up your design and create height. Be careful not to disturb the frame. The Fondant can be tinted with water-soluble food coloring or chocolate if desired; see Glazing or Icing with Fondant, pages 1014 and 1015, steps four and five, for information on mixing colors.

4. Let the design dry overnight, then loosen it by moving the plastic over a sharp edge, bending it down lightly. Place the finished decoration on top of your cake or pastry. If you are not using the decoration right away, leave it attached to the plastic until you need it.

Method II

Fondant can also be piped directly on top of a cake or pastry in the same way as Method I if you have the skill to pipe the design freehand. Even if you are not a great artist (and most of us are not), you can use the following tracing method to make almost any design you like on a sheet of Marzipan, which can then be placed on top of a cake.

1. Draw or copy the design onto a paper. To make the figure appear facing the same direction as the drawing after stamping it on the Marzipan, rub vegetable oil onto the paper to make it transparent and then invert the paper so the design appears backwards. If it is not a problem that the design will be reversed (mirror image) on the cake then you do not need to do this step. (In other words, in the illustration it does not matter which direction the bear is walking—except maybe to the bear—but with lettering, you would end up using a different language without this step.)

2. Tape the drawing to a sheet of cardboard. Place a small piece of ¼-inch (6-mm) thick plastic (or at least thick enough that it will not bend) on top of the drawing.

3. Make a small amount of Royal Icing (see page 1019). Put the icing in a piping bag, cut a small opening, and trace over your design. Let the Royal Icing harden overnight.

4. Roll out Marzipan to ⅛ inch (3 mm) thick. Cut out a round or oval shape slightly larger than the design. Hold the glass upside down and press the design into the Marzipan. Remove the glass and trace over the design with Fondant (or Royal Icing or chocolate), using a piping bag with an opening just large enough to cover the lines (Figure 19–35). The design can be left as is with just the outline, or filled in partially or totally with additional Fondant, as in Method I. Let set until the Fondant is firm and then place on the cake.

This is a good way to make up a supply of cake decorations on a slow day to have ready at a busy time like Easter, Mother's Day, or Christmas. You can keep the Marzipan from looking old and dry by coating it with a thin layer of cocoa butter before you stamp out the pattern. To use this method on a cake that is entirely covered with Marzipan (Princess Cake, for example), press the design into the Marzi-

NOTE: Instead of plastic, you can have a glass shop make rectangles 8 by 9 inches (20 × 22.5 cm) from regular window glass. Make sure they round the corners and sand the edges smooth. It is important that the glass or plastic is clean and free of fingerprints before you pipe on it, and also that the Royal Icing is not too dry or hard. Both of these things can keep the icing from sticking to the glass, and it can then come off in the Marzipan.

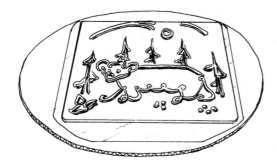
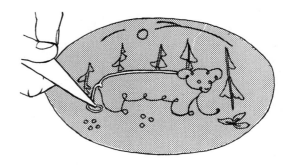

FIGURE 19–35 *A design piped in Royal Icing on a small piece of glass, following the lines of a drawing set under the glass. Filling in the design with piped Royal Icing after pressing the hardened Royal Icing lines into a thin sheet of rolled Marzipan (the finished design appears as a mirror image of the original drawing)*

pan just before you place it on the cake and then pipe over it once it is in place. A decoration made this way is certainly handmade, and no one will know you had a little help from a friend.

Glazing or icing with fondant

NOTE: Some chefs use egg white or heavy cream alone (without Simple Syrup) to thin Fondant to ensure a good shine. If you use egg whites, make sure they have been pasteurized.

1. Warm the Fondant over simmering water, stirring constantly, until it reaches approximately body temperature, 98°F (37°C). When Fondant is heated over 100°F (38°C), it begins to lose its shine and at the extreme it becomes hard and unpleasant to eat as well. Should you overheat the Fondant, wait until it has cooled to the correct temperature before you apply it (unless it has melted into a syrup, in which case you should discard it). On the other hand, if you try to play it safe and the Fondant is not hot enough when you apply it, it will take too long to form a skin, and you will not have a nice satin shine; further, the pastries will be sticky and hard to work with and can collect dust while they are drying.

2. Thin the warm Fondant to the proper consistency with Simple Syrup (adding egg white along with the Simple Syrup will add an extra shine to the Fondant; see note). Test the thickness by coating a few pastries. The contours and separate layers of a petit four should be clearly visible through the icing.

3. Either pipe or pour Fondant on top of Petits Fours or Othellos. Never coat them by dipping the pastry into the Fondant, as you will get crumbs in the Fondant. If you are only coating a few dozen pastries, the most practical method is to pipe it on (Figure 19–36). When covering a

FIGURE 19–36 Using a pastry bag to apply Fondant to Petits Fours

large number, a much faster way is to pour the Fondant from a saucer. Line up your pastries or Petits Fours to be covered on an aspic or cooling rack as you would if you were piping the Fondant. Hold the bowl of Fondant in one hand and the saucer in the other. Scoop up Fondant in the saucer and pour it slowly and evenly over the pastries holding it just above them (Figure 19–37). Always start with the pastry farthest away from you so that you will not drip on the pastries once they are coated. Have enough Fondant on the saucer so you can cover each row in one stroke. The drawback with this method is that you need to work with a large amount of Fondant; however, the Fondant that drips onto the pan can be reused or saved for later use.

4. If you plan to tint a portion of the Fondant, start by coating as many Petits Fours as desired in white, then tint part of the white Fondant yellow. Use the leftover yellow to make green, and reserve any leftover green. Next make and apply pink Fondant, made by tinting the remaining white Fondant. If any of that is left, you can combine it with the green to make a mocha color.

5. To make chocolate Fondant, quickly add melted unsweetened chocolate to the warm Fondant. The chocolate will thicken the Fondant, so you will need to add more Simple Syrup.

FIGURE 19–37 Using a saucer to apply Fondant to Petits Fours

Glazes

Apricot Glaze

2 cups (480 ml) glaze

1 pound (455 g) apricot jam
3 ounces (85 g) granulated sugar
¹/₃ cup (80 ml) water

NOTE: If you cook the glaze too long it will become too thick to use properly. Unless it has started to caramelize, just add a small amount of water and cook to the thread test again.

1. Place the jam, sugar, and water in a heavy-bottomed saucepan. Bring to a boil over medium heat, stirring constantly.

2. Lower the heat and continue cooking until the mixture can be pulled into a ¹/₄-inch (6-mm) thread between your thumb and index finger.

3. Quickly remove the pan from the heat, strain (discard the solids), and use immediately. Store the leftover glaze at room temperature. Reheat the glaze to use again, and if it is too thick, add a small amount of water.

Chocolate Glaze

4¹/₂ cups (1 l, 80 ml) glaze

1 pound (455 g) sweet dark chocolate
5 ounces (140 g) soft unsalted butter
5 tablespoons (1¹/₂ ounces/40 g)
   unsweetened cocoa powder, sifted
¹/₄ cup (60 ml) dark rum
³/₄ cup (180 ml) or 9 ounces (255 g)
   light corn syrup

NOTE: If a fatty film develops on the top of the glaze once it has cooled, the chocolate you are using contains too much cocoa butter; it is probably semisweet or bittersweet instead of sweet. Decrease the amount of butter in the recipe to compensate. If you desire a firmer glaze, increase the amount of sweet chocolate in the recipe.

1. Cut the chocolate into small chunks and melt over hot water. Remove from the heat, add the butter, and stir until the butter is fully incorporated.

2. Stir the cocoa powder into the rum, mixing until smooth. Add the corn syrup and then stir into the chocolate mixture.

3. Let cool and then store in a covered container. The glaze does not need to be refrigerated. To use, heat the glaze to the consistency suitable for the recipe in which you are using it. If a skin forms on the surface during storage, pour a little hot water on top, wait a few seconds, and then pour the water off.

Orange Glaze

approximately 1 cup (240 ml) glaze

1 cup (240 ml) orange preserves or
   marmalade
3 ounces (85 g) granulated sugar
¹/₃ cup (80 ml) water

1. Place the preserves or marmalade, sugar, and water in a heavy-bottomed saucepan. Bring to a boil over medium heat, stirring constantly.

2. Lower the heat and continue cooking, stirring from time to time, until the mixture has reduced sufficiently to hold a thread ¹/₄ inch (6 mm) long when pulled between your thumb and index finger.

3. Quickly remove the pan from the heat and strain the glaze. Discard the solids in the strainer. Use the glaze immediately. Store leftover glaze at room temperature. To reuse, add a small amount of water and heat to boiling.

Pectin Glaze

approximately 3 cups (720 ml) glaze

3 cups (720 ml) water
1 tablespoon (9 g) pure pectin powder (grade usp-nf)
1 pound, 6 ounces (625 g) granulated sugar
Tartaric Acid Solution (page 1115)

NOTE: If the glaze does not set properly, bring the solution back to a boil and cook for a minute or two. If the glaze sets up too fast or too thick, add a small amount of water. Always make a small test portion of glaze first before applying it to the food.

*P*ectin Glaze is used in combination with Tartaric Acid Solution, which acts as a catalyst to make the glaze gel and also gives it a slightly tart flavor that is especially complementary to fruit. The ability to gel quickly prevents the glaze from soaking into the fruit; instead it leaves a thin shiny coat on the top.*

1. Heat the water to the scalding point in a saucepan.

2. In the meantime mix the pectin powder with 3 ounces (85 g) of the sugar. Whisk into the water when the water is ready, making sure it is thoroughly combined. Bring the mixture to a boil, then stir in the remaining sugar. Bring back to a boil again, but this time check to see exactly when the mixture begins to boil, then reduce the heat and boil for 5 minutes. Remove from the heat and let cool.

3. Skim off any foam or scum that appears on the surface. The Pectin Glaze will keep for months at this stage if stored covered in the refrigerator.

4. To set (gel) the glaze, use approximately 4 drops of Tartaric Acid Solution for every 1 ounce (30 ml) of Pectin Glaze; stir in the tartaric acid quickly and use the glaze immediately. The amount required will vary depending on the consistency of the glaze. The flavor should definitely be tart but not to the point where it is unpleasant (also, adding too much liquid can prevent the glaze from setting). Add tartaric acid only to the amount of glaze you are ready to use at the moment because it will not work as well if it has to be softened again once it has set. You can keep the glaze from setting up while you are working by stirring it every few seconds.

Red Currant Glaze

2 cups (480 ml) glaze

1 pound (455 g) red currant jelly
4 ounces (115 g) granulated sugar

1. Place the jelly and sugar in a saucepan. Stirring constantly, bring to a boil over low heat. Keep stirring until all of the lumps have dissolved.

2. Lower the heat and simmer for a few minutes until the mixture has a glossy shine. Strain, then use immediately. Store leftover glaze covered. Reheat to a liquid consistency to use again.

Gold Leaf

For a spectacular and elegant effect for a special occasion, gold leaf can be applied to many different desserts, but it is shown off to its best advantage against a background of rich, dark chocolate. Wrapping the gold leaf around a whole strawberry or other suitably-sized fruit can also produce a stunning decoration.

The thin (this is a major understatement) 22 karat gold leaf, also known as patent gold, is sold in sheets separated by tissue paper. The gold leaf I use comes in sheets that are 3¼ inches (8.1 cm) square;

smaller sizes such as this are the easiest to work with. The sheets can be purchased through some bakery suppliers, and gold leaf is often sold in Indian grocery stores, where it is known as *Vark*. In India, gold leaf and gold dust are widely used to decorate desserts and other foods, including soup where the thin leaves are floated on the surface. In Germany, Danziger Goldwasser liqueur is made with small flecks of glimmering gold. While completely edible (although I wouldn't make it a habit since the craving can be rather expensive), gold is not absorbed by the body.

Working with gold leaf can be very frustrating—all the more so considering the expense—because the sheets turn to powder or clump into an unusable mass if the following rules are not observed:

• Be sure there is absolutely no draft whatsoever, including someone working or walking near by. The slightest shift in the air is enough to make the thin sheets fly up somewhere other than where you are trying to place them.

• To transfer a whole sheet of gold leaf to any object, slide it off of the nonstick tissue paper it comes on, onto the desired food or area. *Never touch the gold leaf with your fingers or try to pick up the sheet with your hands.* It will stick immediately, and you will have lovely gold-covered fingertips—but no more gold leaf to use for decoration.

• To transfer a small piece of gold leaf, use a dry artist's brush. Simply touch the tip of the brush to the gold leaf (a small piece will stick to the brush) and then touch the brush to the pastry. Some people use tweezers, but I find the brush to be easier and work better.

Hippen Decorating Paste

3 cups (720 ml) or 1 pound, 8 ounces (680 g) paste

6 egg whites (³/₄ cup/180 ml)
1 pound, 8 ounces (680 g) Almond Paste (page 3)
1¹/₂ ounces (40 g) bread flour
¹/₂ teaspoon (3 g) salt
¹/₄ teaspoon (.5 g) ground cinnamon
3 drops lemon juice
milk, as needed

This paste is used for making decorations and containers to hold assorted desserts. It is always spread directly onto greased and floured sheet pans or onto a silicone baking mat following the shape of a template. Hippen paste is quite versatile; it can be tinted in various colors and bent 360° if needed.

1. Add approximately five of the egg whites to the Almond Paste, mixing them in one at a time to avoid lumps. Mix in the flour, salt, cinnamon, and lemon juice. Mix in the remaining egg white. Let the mixture rest covered for 30 minutes.

2. Adjust the consistency with milk if necessary. The paste should be thin enough to spread out easily but should hold the shape made by your template without floating out.

Icings

Royal Icing

6 cups (1 l, 440 ml) or 3 pounds, 7 ounces (1 kg, 565 g) icing

1 cup (240 ml) egg whites (see note)
2 pounds, 8 ounces (1 kg, 135 g) sifted powdered sugar, approximately
$1/2$ teaspoon (1 g) cream of tartar

NOTE: *As mentioned in the introduction, Royal Icing is used mostly for decorating showpieces and as such is rarely intended for consumption. If it is used as a major component of an item that will be eaten (more than just piping the eyes on a Porcupine pastry, for example), you should use pasteurized egg whites.*

This type of icing is also called decorating icing, because that is its principal use. Royal Icing is one of the best materials with which to practice piping. It is inexpensive and easy to make, and it can be piped and formed into almost any shape. Royal Icing is used a great deal around Christmastime to decorate gingerbread and Christmas cookies, and it is essential for making gingerbread houses. Because Royal Icing becomes hard and brittle when dry, it is used mostly for decorations rather than for eating. However, it is traditional in some countries to use it on special-occasion cakes such as wedding cakes. Personally, I limit its use to showpieces, or for piping a small amount on a cake or pastries.

This recipe makes a large amount of Royal Icing. If you only need a small amount simply add powdered sugar to one egg white until you reach the proper consistency, stir rapidly until the mixture is light and fluffy, then add a small pinch of cream of tartar to prevent the icing from yellowing. This will make approximately $3/4$ cup (180 ml) of icing.

Be very careful to keep Royal Icing covered at all times, and clean off any icing on the side of your cup or bowl. The icing dries very quickly, and the small lumps will interfere with your piping. A wet towel on top functions well while you are working, but use plastic wrap and pour a layer of water on the icing for longer storage.

1. Pour the egg whites into a mixer bowl. Using the paddle attachment with the machine set at low speed, gradually add all but a few handfuls of the powdered sugar and the cream of tartar. Mix until it forms a smooth paste, adding the remaining powdered sugar if necessary.

2. Beat at high speed for a just a few seconds if you are using the Royal Icing for piping. If you will be spreading the icing—on the top of a gingerbread house, for example—beat the icing a bit longer to make it light and fluffy.

3. Immediately transfer to a clean, covered container to prevent a skin from forming. Or, if you are going to use it within a few minutes, place a damp towel on top. Stored covered in the refrigerator, Royal Icing will keep for up to a week.

Royal icing ornaments and showpieces

Fancy Royal Icing ornaments or showpieces, typically composed in elaborate lace patterns, are easy to make in the following manner.

1. Place a thin sheet of acetate or polyurethane on top of your "blueprint." Fasten them together with paper clips so that they will not move as you pipe. (For small ornaments you may want to use some of the designs shown in Figures 17–20 and 17–21, pages 907 and 908.)

2. Trace over your design with Royal Icing using a piping bag. Before the icing hardens you can bend the sheet into any shape you like, either draping it over an object to act as a mold or joining the edges and securing with paper clips.

3. Let the design dry overnight, then carefully peel away the plastic. Join the shapes together with additional Royal Icing as needed. Frequently, part of a showpiece is made from Pastillage rather than using Royal Icing for all of the elements, to make the showpiece more durable.

Royal Icing can also be used to pipe on plastic or glass templates for decorations on Marzipan, as described in Decorating with Fondant, Method II (page 1012).

Simple Icing

3 cups (720 ml) icing

2 pounds (910 g) powdered sugar
3 tablespoons (45 ml) corn syrup (see note)
³/₄ cup (180 ml) hot water, approximately

NOTE: The corn syrup prevents the icing from crystallizing when stored for several weeks. If the icing will be used within a few days the corn syrup may be omitted.

This icing is also known as flat icing, or water icing. If you are using Simple Icing as part of your daily routine, here is a simple way to make it: Fill your storage container with powdered sugar and add as much hot water as the sugar will absorb; do not stir, but let it settle for a few minutes. Pour enough additional water on top to cover the surface in a 1-inch (2.5-cm) layer. Let the icing sit overnight. The next day not only do you have perfectly fine Simple Icing, but the water on the top of the icing (now a syrup) can be poured off and used instead of Simple Syrup on Danish pastries or puff pastry items.

1. Place the powdered sugar in a mixing bowl. Pour the corn syrup into the hot water and stir until melted. Add the liquid to the powdered sugar and mix until smooth.

2. Adjust the thickness with additional water as needed. The icing should be the consistency of sour cream.

3. Cover the surface with a thin layer of water to prevent a crust from forming (pour off before using). Store covered at room temperature.

Marzipan

Marzipan is used extensively in European pastry shops, particularly in Germany, Austria, Switzerland, and Scandinavia. It is made of Almond Paste and powdered sugar with the addition of a moistening agent such as glucose or corn syrup. Some recipes substitute egg whites or even Fondant, but the purpose is the same.

There was a time when every pastry chef had to make his own Almond Paste by grinding the blanched almonds with an equal weight of sugar until it became a fine paste. Today Almond Paste is readily available, making it much more convenient, in turn, to make your own Marzipan. Of course, Marzipan can be purchased from bakery supply houses as well, but it is quite easy to make it yourself. Marzipan must be made in a stainless-steel bowl to prevent discoloration.

Due to its large sugar content (60–70 percent), Marzipan dries very quickly when exposed to air and should be kept covered at all times. If the Marzipan becomes dry (but it has not dried all the way through), you can reconstitute it by kneading in a small amount of water, although this will shorten its shelf life considerably. Keep your tools and workplace scrupulously clean, and always wash your hands immediately prior to rolling or molding Marzipan with your hands. The almond oil, which is brought to the surface as you work the Marzipan, will pick up and absorb even a small trace of dirt on your hands, which not only ruins the off-white color of the Marzipan but can lead to spoilage.

Marzipan is rolled out in the same manner as a pastry dough (but powdered sugar is used instead of flour to prevent the paste from sticking). It can be left smooth or may be textured in various patterns before being used to cover cakes, petits fours, and pastries. It is an ideal surface to decorate and pipe on, either freehand, using the technique described in Decorating with Fondant, Method II, or using the tracing method that follows. It is also used on petits fours and pastries that are to be coated with Fondant or chocolate to keep the coating from soaking into the sponge and to achieve an even surface. A thin layer of Marzipan on a *Bûche de Noël* or chocolate cake prevents the thin layer of chocolate coating from mixing with the buttercream on top of the cake. Not only does the Marzipan make a smooth finish possible, but the combination of chocolate and Marzipan also gives the pastry a very special and distinctive flavor. With very few exceptions, Marzipan should never be rolled out thicker than 1/8 of an inch (3 mm) or it can look clumsy and unattractive, and when used on top of cake or pastry the flavor can be overwhelming.

Coloring Marzipan

You can use water-soluble food coloring to tint the Marzipan, but keep the colors to soft pastel shades as much as possible. A green color (such as for the Princess Cake) should usually be toned down with the addition of a tiny bit of yellow. When adding color to a small amount of Marzipan, or when you need only a hint of color, put a drop of color on a piece of baking paper and add some of it to the Marzipan using the tip of a knife. Knead the Marzipan until the color is completely worked in. Use unsweetened cocoa powder to produce brown in various shades unless for some reason you do not want, or need, the chocolate flavor (it is obviously a lot less expensive to use food color). Work the desired amount of cocoa powder into the Marzipan, and keep kneading it until all of the marbled effect is gone and you have a smooth, evenly colored, Marzipan. If you are adding a large amount of cocoa powder, you may have to compensate by working in some Simple Syrup or water to prevent the Marzipan from getting too dry. To color

Marzipan bright white, use 4 to 6 drops of titanium dioxide for every 1 ounce (30 g) of untinted Marzipan. This should only be used for figurines or showpieces that will not be eaten.

Marzipan will keep almost indefinitely if you take proper care in the mixing and handling. It should be placed in airtight containers and stored in a very cool place or the refrigerator. It can also be stored in the freezer should you need to keep it for a long time. If the oil separates from the Marzipan after it has thawed, making it crumbly and hard to work with, add a small amount of water and some powdered sugar. Continue to knead the Marzipan until it is smooth and elastic.

Marzipan

approximately 4 pounds, 6 ounces (1 kg, 990 g)

2 pounds (910 g) Almond Paste (page 3)

1/2 cup (120 ml) glucose or light corn syrup

2 pounds (910 g) sifted powdered sugar, approximately

NOTE: The amount of powdered sugar needed will depend on the consistency of the Almond Paste. Always mix at low speed and take care not to overmix. The friction will make the Marzipan warm, thereby softening it, and you will end up adding too much powdered sugar.

1. In a stainless-steel mixing bowl, use the hook to mix the Almond Paste with the glucose or corn syrup, at low speed, until combined.

2. Start adding the sugar, scraping the sides of the bowl down as necessary. Add enough of the powdered sugar to make a fairly firm, yet workable, dough.

3. Store the Marzipan wrapped in plastic, inside an airtight container in a cold place.

Tracing onto marzipan

The templates and illustrations in this book (or any other drawings) can be traced quite easily on top of a sheet of Marzipan using one of the following methods.

Method I

1. Roll out high-quality Marzipan a little thinner than 1/16 inch (2 mm), using the smallest possible amount of powdered sugar. This will make the Marzipan transparent.

2. Place the Marzipan on top of the drawing and cut the edges to the proper size and shape.

3. Trace over the design using either Piping Chocolate or piping gel. Transfer the finished piece to the top of a cake or save it to use later.

Method II

If you are using tinted Marzipan, it may not be transparent when rolled thin. This method allows you to transfer the image to the Marzipan, but because you will be pressing the lead from the pencil onto the Marzipan, this technique is not recommended for anything other than show or display cakes. A second option is to use the technique described in Decorating with Fondant, Method II (see page 1012).

NOTE: Remember that this will be a mirror image. To avoid this, rub a small amount of vegetable oil on the back side of the paper to make the paper transparent, invert the drawing, and place another piece of paper on top. Then retrace the picture so the image appears as the reverse of the way you want it to appear on the Marzipan.

1. Trace the drawing on top of a sheet of baking paper using a soft pencil.

2. Roll out the Marzipan 1/8 inch (3 mm) thick, using no powdered sugar at all on the top so that this side will stay fairly sticky.

3. Invert your drawing on top of the Marzipan and roll a rolling pin gently over the drawing, pressing the image onto the Marzipan (see note).

4. Remove the drawing and pipe over the pencil marks as directed above.

Marzipan Apples

24 decorations

4 ounces (115 g) Marzipan (page 1022), tinted pale green
powdered sugar
twenty-four whole cloves
Beet Juice (page 3)
   or
red food coloring

*T*hese simple little apples can be used to decorate many cakes and pastries in this book. In addition to their appealing diminutive size, they are completely free from seeds! When placed on a dessert with an apple filling, this garnish gives the customer a clear indication of the flavor inside.

If you make the apples more than a few days ahead of when they will be eaten, you can keep the outside of the Marzipan from drying out by coating the apples lightly with hot, melted cocoa butter, using just the tip of a brush. This should be done after applying the red color. The cocoa butter also gives the Marzipan a nice satin shine so it always a good idea to apply it to Marzipan decorations.

1. Take the usual precautions for working with Marzipan by making certain that your hands and your work space are clean. Work the Marzipan soft and pliable in your hands. Roll it into a 12-inch (30-cm) rope, using powdered sugar if necessary to prevent it from sticking to your work surface. Cut the rope into twenty-four $\frac{1}{2}$-inch (1.2-cm) pieces.

2. Roll each piece between your palms first into a round ball and then very slightly oblong. Use a Marzipan tool to make a small dimple in each end.

3. Make a hole on top of each apple and carefully, without altering the shape, insert the clove end of a whole clove so only the stem is protruding.

4. Put a tiny amount of Beet Juice or red food coloring (less than a drop) on a piece of paper and apply the color to the very tip of a coarse, flat brush. Holding each apple by the stem, streak the color from top to bottom.

Marzipan Bear

one 3¹/₂-ounce (100-g) figure

3¹/₂ ounces (100 g) Marzipan (page 1022), untinted
egg white
Royal Icing (page 1019)
dark coating chocolate, melted

1. See Figure 19–38 as a guide in constructing the bear. Be certain that your hands and work area are absolutely clean. Divide the Marzipan as follows: One ²/₃-ounce (20-g) piece for the rear legs; one ¹/₂-ounce (15-g) piece for the front legs; one ¹/₂-ounce (15-g) piece for the head; one ¹/₆-ounce (5-g) piece for the tail. Cover these pieces with plastic to prevent them from drying out.

2. Use the remaining Marzipan for the body. Roll this large piece between the palms of your hands for a few seconds to make it soft and pliable. Roll it into a smooth, round ball. Position the ball between the lower part of your palms and taper one-half of the ball almost to a

FIGURE 19–38 *The Marzipan shapes used for the Marzipan Bear; the assembled bear*

NOTE: *If the figure is to be kept for some time, brush a thin film of hot cocoa butter over the Marzipan before piping on the Royal Icing or the chocolate.*

point. Form the opposite end to narrow it slightly, leaving the center of the ball in a rounded shape which will be the stomach of the bear. Roll and shape the body to make it 2 inches (5 cm) long. Slightly flatten the narrow end on top (the neck). Set the body aside.

3. Divide the piece of Marzipan reserved for the rear legs (²/₃ ounce/20 g) into two equal pieces. Roll the pieces (separately) to make them soft, then roll them into smooth, round balls. Place them, one at a time, between the lower part of your palms and roll to 2 inches (5 cm) in length, tapering one end slightly. Bend the front part of the narrow end on each leg to form the bear's paws. Apply a small amount of egg white to the inside of the legs where they will touch the body. Attach the legs to the wide end of the body (placing the bear so it is seated), pressing to flatten and widen the rear part of the legs at the same time. Position the body in the way that you want the bear to be posing: leaning forward or sitting back.

4. Repeat step three, using the piece reserved for the front legs (¹/₂ ounce/15 g), but roll the front leg pieces to only 1³/₄ inches (4.5 cm) long. Fasten them to the upper part of the body. Depending on how you arrange the front legs, you may need to use some type of support until the pieces are firm.

5. Pinch off a raisin-sized piece from the piece reserved for the head (¹/₂ ounce/15 g); this small piece will be used to make the ears. Roll the remainder of the Marzipan for the head to make it soft, then roll it into a smooth, round ball. Place the ball between the lower part of your palms and taper one side to a small, delicate point; leave the opposite side of the head round, not oblong. Hold the head in the palm of one hand. Use the tip of a small knife to make a ¹/₄-inch (6-mm) cut for the mouth just below the tip of the nose. Twist the knife to open up the mouth slightly. Use a Marzipan tool or other object with a small rounded end to make two shallow indentations for the eyes. Carefully (so you do not deform the head in the process) fasten the head to the body using egg white. To be able to attach the head in the exact position desired, apply a thin film of egg white to both the neck and the bottom of the head. Wait until the egg white is almost dry but is still sticky. Very carefully place the head on the neck, giving it a slight twist at the same time to seal the pieces together. Part of a toothpick, pressed into the body first so that just the tip is sticking out from the neck, can be very helpful to support the head. However, a toothpick should be used only if the figure is exclusively for display.

6. Roll the small piece for the ears between your thumb and forefinger to make it soft. Divide in half and roll the pieces one at a time into smooth, round balls. You may need to adjust the size of the pieces if they look too large; remember, bears have very small ears. Use the same rounded tool that you used to make the indentations for the eyes and press the ears into the top of the head, using egg white as glue.

7. Roll the remaining piece of Marzipan soft and round. Roll it into an oblong shape and fasten it to the back of the bear as the tail.

8. Make three small grooves in the end of each paw to make the bear's claws, using a Marzipan tool or a blunt pointed object such as an instant-read thermometer.

9. Set the figure aside for a few hours or until the next day to allow the surface to dry slightly.

10. Place a little Royal Icing in a piping bag and cut a small opening. Pipe icing into the indentations made for the eyes.

11. Place melted coating chocolate in a second piping bag and cut an even smaller opening. Pipe a small dot of chocolate in each of the marks made for the claws. Pipe a larger dot of chocolate on the tip of the bear's nose. Wake the bear up by piping a small dot of chocolate on top of the icing in the eyes to mark the pupils. Last, pipe a thin eyebrow above each eye.

 Marzipan Bumble Bees

16 bee decorations

¹/₂ ounce (15 g) Marzipan (page 1022), untinted
unsweetened cocoa powder
3¹/₂ ounces (100 g) Marzipan (page 1022), untinted
yellow food coloring
egg white
sliced almonds

Though it can be a bit more difficult to work with very small pieces of Marzipan as is done here, do not be tempted to plump up the Bumble Bees; they can easily begin to take the shape of a small hummingbird, and while the two may share the same interest in flowers, the larger creatures look quite out of place when placed on a beehive. Following these instructions produces life-size bees, admittedly rather simplified.

1. Be certain that your work area and your hands are both absolutely clean. Color the ¹/₂-ounce (15-g) piece of Marzipan dark brown by mixing cocoa powder into it. Roll it out to a rope 6 inches (15 cm) long and then cut the rope into sixteen equal pieces. Cover the pieces and set them aside.

2. Color the remaining piece of Marzipan pale yellow. Roll this piece out to make a 16-inch (40-cm) rope and cut it into sixteen equal pieces. Roll one of the yellow pieces between the palms of your hands to make it soft and pliable and then into a round ball. Roll the ball against the work surface to make it oblong, about 1 inch (2.5 cm) in length, and slightly tapered at both ends. Repeat with the remaining yellow pieces of Marzipan to form the bodies of the bees.

3. Roll one of the reserved cocoa-colored pieces of Marzipan between your thumb and forefinger to make it soft and pliable. Divide the piece in half. Roll each of these two small pieces into a smooth round ball.

4. Slightly flatten one end of a bee body and attach a cocoa-colored ball, using egg white as glue. This will be the bee's head. It should be slightly larger than the end of the bee where it is attached. Cut the body of the bee in half across the width, flatten the second cocoa-colored ball, and attach it between the two body halves using egg white. Place the bee on top of a 2-inch (5-cm) diameter dowel set on a sheet pan lined with baking paper (secure the dowel with a little Marzipan so it will not roll) so the bee will dry in a slightly curved position. Assemble the remaining Marzipan Bumble Bees in the same way.

5. For the wings, select thirty-two unbroken almond slices. Pair them so that the wings on each bee will be the same size. Use a paring knife to make a small insertion point on both sides of each bee just behind the head and then carefully push the narrow end of an almond slice into the cuts. If necessary, allow the bees to remain on the dowel until they will hold their shape.

 ## Marzipan Carrots

24 carrot decorations

5 ounces (140 g) Marzipan (page 1022), untinted
red, yellow, and green food coloring

1. Color 1 ounce (30 g) of the Marzipan green. Cover and reserve. Use red and yellow food coloring to tint the remainder orange.

2. Roll the orange Marzipan out to an 18-inch (45-cm) rope. Cut the rope into twenty-four ³/₄-inch (2-cm) pieces, one piece for each carrot. Keep the pieces covered with plastic to prevent them from drying out.

3. Roll the pieces one at a time (two at a time after some practice) into round balls between your palms. Roll the balls into cone shapes, about 1 inch (2.5 cm) long, by rolling them back and forth against the table.

4. Mark the cones crosswise with the back of a knife to make them look ringed like a carrot: Starting at the wide end, turn them slowly and make random marks, crosswise, all around. Make a small round hole in the wide end of each carrot, using a Marzipan modeling tool or the end of an instant-read thermometer.

5. Roll the green Marzipan into a thin rope. Cut into twenty-four pea-sized pieces. Roll each one into a ¹/₂-inch (1.2-cm) string, tapered on both ends. Insert one end of the green stem into the hole in each carrot. Cut and fan the other end of each one to resemble a carrot top.

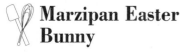

Marzipan Easter Bunny

one 3-ounce (85-g) figure

3 ounces (85 g) Marzipan (page 1022), untinted
egg white
Royal Icing (page 1019)
dark coating chocolate, melted

NOTE 1: If you wish to keep the figure fresh for some time, brush a thin film of hot cocoa butter on the Marzipan before dipping it in chocolate and applying the Royal Icing and piped chocolate.

NOTE 2: For a different look to the bunny, cut the thick end of the cone instead of the narrow end in step six. Bend the cut halves so that the flat sides face the table, and spread them out and forward alongside the body on both ends like a rabbit about to jump. Flatten the uncut

1. See Figure 19–39 as a guide in constructing the bunny. Weigh out 2¹/₃ ounces (65 g) of Marzipan to use for the body. Cover and reserve the remaining ²/₃ ounce (20 g) to use for the head. Be sure that the work area and your hands are impeccably clean.

2. Roll the larger piece of Marzipan between your hands for a few seconds until soft, then form into a completely smooth, round ball.

3. Place the Marzipan on the table in front of you and roll the ball into a 4-inch (10-cm) long cone-shaped body with a blunt tip at the tapered end.

4. Use a thin, sharp knife to cut a very small slice off the thick end to flatten it enough that it will stand straight when turned upright. Reserve the piece you cut off to use later for the tail.

5. Stand the cone so the wide cut end is flat on the table and carefully bend the Marzipan so that the front one-third is also on the table, and the middle is up about 1¹/₂ inches (3.7 cm) in the air (like the silhouette of a cat about to pounce).

6. Make a cut in the front end, lengthwise, and twist the pieces toward the center so that the cut sides are against the table. Spread the two pieces apart slightly to form the front legs of the bunny. (Keep in mind that these steps must be completed rather quickly to prevent the softened Marzipan from hardening again, and cracking or wrinkling as you mold it.)

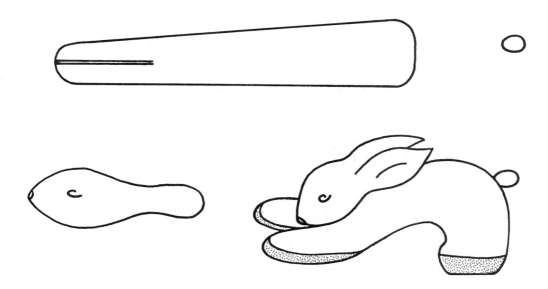

FIGURE 19–39 The Marzipan shapes used to make the Marzipan Easter Bunny; the assembled bunny with the base dipped in chocolate

narrow end slightly and place the head on top. Or, for a third alternative, taper both ends of the body when rolling it out, cut both ends, position one front leg over the other, and arrange the rear legs in the same way to resemble a resting rabbit (laying on its side).

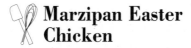

Marzipan Easter Chicken

one 2-ounce (55-g) figure

$^1/_3$ ounce (10 g) Marzipan (page 1022), untinted

slightly more than 1$^1/_2$ ounces (45 g) Marzipan (page 1022), tinted pale yellow

egg white

one blanched almond or sliver of almond

dark coating chocolate, melted

Royal Icing (page 1019)

7. Set the body aside, placing it over a dowel of suitable thickness to hold the curved shape, if necessary.

8. Roll the piece of Marzipan reserved for the head to make it soft, then roll into a round ball. Form the ball between the lower part of your palms to make it into a shape resembling a bowling pin but tapered at the wide end. The piece should be 2$^1/_4$ inches (5.6 cm) in length.

9. Place the head on the table and make a 1-inch (2.5-cm) cut lengthwise starting at the narrow end. Spread the two pieces apart and flatten the ends with your fingers a little to form the ears. Make two small indentations for the eyes.

10. Using egg white as glue, attach the head to the body, placing the nose between the front legs. Roll the small remaining piece into a ball and glue in place as the tail. Set the figure aside for a few hours or overnight to allow the surface to dry somewhat.

11. Dip the bottom $^1/_4$ inch (6 mm) of the bunny in melted chocolate. Pipe a small dot of Royal Icing in each of the indentations made for the eyes. Lastly, make the bunny come alive by piping a smaller dot of melted chocolate on the tip of the nose and on top of the Royal Icing to make pupils in the eyes.

---

1. See Figure 19–40 as a guide in constructing the chick. Make sure that your work area and hands are very clean. Roll the untinted Marzipan in your hands until soft, then roll into a ball. Place on the table and make a shallow depression on the top with your thumb, pressing hard enough to make the ball slightly flat on the bottom so that it will not roll (it should be the size of a quarter). Set this piece (the nest) aside.

2. Cover and reserve a little less than $^1/_3$ ounce (9 g) of the yellow Marzipan. Roll the remainder between your palms to soften, then roll into a smooth, round ball. Roll the ball between the lower part of your palms to form a 2$^1/_2$-inch (6.2-cm) long cone, rounded on both ends.

3. Bend the narrow end up slightly and press to flatten it a bit. Mark two lines on top of the flattened part using a modeling pin, or the back of a paring knife, to form a tail.

4. With a small pair of scissors make a thin cut from the rear about midway on either side of the wide end to form the wings. Bend the cut parts down slightly and mark each wing in two places, as for the tail. Use a little egg white as glue and attach the chicken to the reserved nest.

5. Cut a pointed piece out of the almond to use for the chicken's beak.

6. Roll the reserved piece of yellow Marzipan soft, then into a perfectly round ball. Make a small depression in the chicken's body where the head should go, and attach the head using egg white.

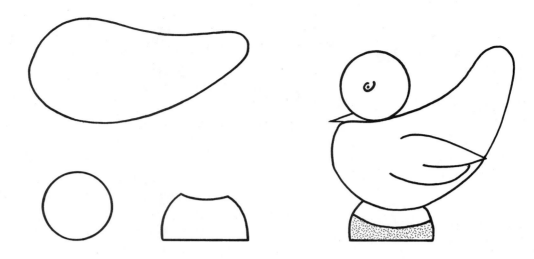

FIGURE 19–40 *The Marzipan shapes used to make the Marzipan Easter Chicken; the assembled chick with the base dipped in chocolate*

7. Push the blunt end of the beak between the head and the body. Mark two small points with a Marzipan tool (or other small pointed object) on either side of the head (not in the front) where the eyes will be. Allow the figure to dry for a few hours or overnight.

8. Dip the bottom ¼ inch (6 mm) of the nest in melted coating chocolate. Place a small amount of Royal Icing in a piping bag and pipe a small dot of icing in the impressions made for the eyes. Pipe an even smaller dot of chocolate on top of the icing for pupils. If you plan to keep the figure for some time, follow the instructions in note 1 for the Easter Bunny (page 1027).

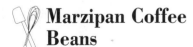

Marzipan Coffee Beans

24 decorations

2 ounces (55 g) Marzipan (page 1022), untinted
unsweetened cocoa powder

1. Color the Marzipan dark brown by kneading in a small amount of cocoa powder.

2. Roll the Marzipan into a 12-inch (30-cm) rope. Cut the rope into twenty-four equal pieces.

3. Roll one piece at a time between your palms to make it soft, then roll into a ball. Roll the ball into an oval. Place the oval in the palm of your hand and use a Marzipan tool or the back of a chef's knife to make a mark lengthwise in the center, pushing the tool halfway into the "bean." Make the remaining decorations in the same way.

Marzipan Forget-Me-Not Flowers

twenty 1-inch (2.5-cm) flowers

sanding sugar

granulated sugar

3 ounces (85 g) Marzipan (page 1022), tinted light pink

powdered sugar

$^1/_2$ ounce (15 g) Marzipan (page 1022), tinted yellow

Piping Chocolate (page 904), melted

1. Fill a 10-inch (25-cm) cake pan (or something similar) with a 1-inch (2.5-cm) layer of sanding sugar. Smooth the top even. Reserve.

2. Put a small amount of granulated sugar in a saucer or any small form. Set aside.

3. Roll the pink Marzipan out to slightly thinner than $^1/_8$ inch (3 mm), using powdered sugar to prevent it from sticking. Cut out circles using a 1-inch (2.5-cm) fluted cookie cutter. Place the circles on top of the confectioners' sugar in the baking pan.

4. Using your thumb, press down in the center of each one, pushing the circles into the sugar to make them concave.

5. Gather the scrap pieces of Marzipan, roll the Marzipan out again to the same thickness, and continue cutting circles and placing them in the sugar in the same manner until you have made twenty.

6. Roll the yellow Marzipan into a $^1/_4$-inch (6-mm) diameter rope. Cut the rope into twenty equal pea-sized pieces. Two at a time, roll the pieces into round balls between your thumbs and index fingers, using both hands, and then drop them into the granulated sugar on the saucer. Roll the balls in the sugar so the sugar sticks to the Marzipan. Reserve.

7. Place the Piping Chocolate in a piping bag and cut a small opening. Pipe a small dot of chocolate in the center of each of the pink Marzipan circles. Place one of the yellow Marzipan balls on top of the chocolate before the chocolate sets up.

8. Let the flowers dry for one day in a warm place. Do not cover them.

9. Brush off any confectioners' sugar that sticks to the back of the Marzipan as you remove the flowers from the sugar. Store covered in a dry place.

Marzipan Oranges

60 decorations

5 ounces (140 g) Marzipan (page 1022), tinted orange

melted cocoa butter (optional)

1. Divide the Marzipan into two equal pieces and roll the pieces into ropes. Cut the ropes into thirty pieces each.

2. Roll the small pieces into balls, keeping them covered until you form them to prevent them from drying out.

3. Roll the balls lightly over a fine grater to give them an orange-peel texture. Use a small wooden skewer to make a small indentation in one end where the stem would be.

4. The finished oranges can be stored for weeks. To keep them looking fresh, coat them with a thin film of cocoa butter. Place a small amount of cocoa butter in the palm of one hand and gently, without altering the shape or texture on the outside, roll a few Marzipan Oranges at a time between your palms.

Marzipan Pears

16 decorations

4 ounces (115 g) Marzipan (page 1022), tinted pale green
powdered sugar
sixteen whole cloves
red food color
    or
Beet Juice (page 3)
cocoa butter, melted (optional)

*D*o not limit the use of these decorations to pear-flavored desserts only, although they certainly are a smart way of indicating the flavor inside when this is the case. Marzipan Pears can also be served as a candy, included in a selection for a bonbon box or on a tray. They are completely edible except for the cloves used as stems. If the pears are made more than a few days ahead of time, keep the outside from drying by coating the pears lightly with cocoa butter, applying it with a brush or simply using your fingers as you roll them in the palm of your other hand. This should be done after applying the red color. In addition to protecting the Marzipan, the cocoa butter adds a nice satin shine.*

1. Take the usual precautions for working with Marzipan by making sure that your hands and work area are very clean. Work the Marzipan soft and pliable in your hands and then roll it against the work surface to make a rope 12 inches (30 cm) long, using powdered sugar if necessary to prevent it from sticking. Cut the rope into sixteen equal pieces.

2. Roll the pieces one at a time first into a round ball and then taper one end to form a pear-shaped neck (see Figure 16–26, page 872).

3. Use a Marzipan tool to make a small dimple in both ends on each pear. Make a hole in the top of the stem end and carefully, without altering the shape, insert the clove end of a whole clove so that only the stem is showing.

4. Put a tiny amount of Beet Juice, less than a drop, on a piece of paper. Apply some color to the very tip of a coarse, flat brush. One at a time, hold a pear by the stem and using a light touch of the brush, streak a few lines of color from top to bottom. (If you happen to overdo it you can always call them red Bartlett pears!)

Marzipan Piglet

one 3¹/₂-ounce (100-g) figure

3¹/₂ ounces (100 g) Marzipan (page 1022), tinted light pink
red food coloring
egg white
Royal Icing (page 1019)
dark coating chocolate, melted
cocoa butter, melted (optional)

NOTE: If you plan to keep the figure more than a week or so, brush a thin film of cocoa butter on it before piping the eyes or dipping in chocolate, to keep it from drying.

1. See the top half of Figure 19–41 as a guide in constructing the piglet. Starting with clean hands and a clean working surface, work a small piece of the Marzipan soft in your hands, then roll it out, or flatten it, to ¹/₁₆ inch (2 mm) thick. Cut out two triangles (these will be the pig's ears) with 1-inch (2.5-cm) sides. Cover and reserve.

2. Color a small piece of the scraps, the size of a pea, with red food coloring. Roll it round and reserve.

3. Combine the scraps with the remaining Marzipan. Pinch off a piece about the same size used to make both ears, cover it, and reserve for the tail.

4. Roll the remaining Marzipan soft in your hands and roll it into a round ball. Place the ball on the table and roll out to a 4-inch (10-cm) cone, keeping the wide end nicely rounded.

5. Place your thumb and index finger on either side of the narrow end, press lightly, and at the same time use the flat edge of the blade of a small knife to flatten the narrow end of the cone, moving the knife

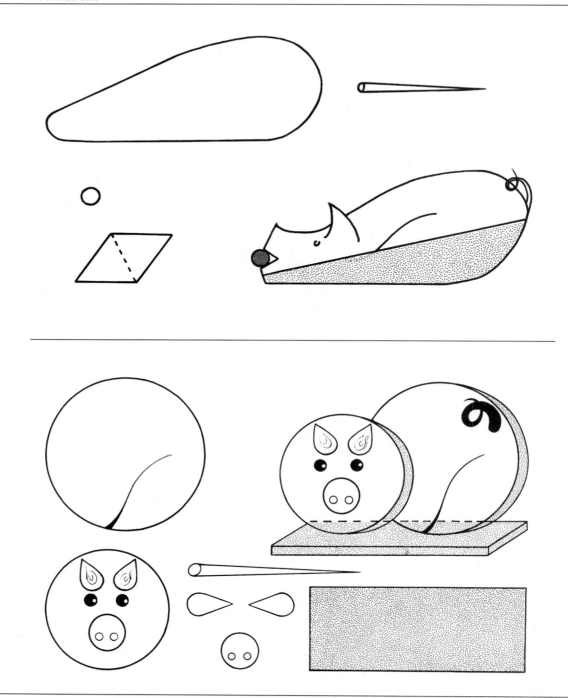

FIGURE 19–41 *The top drawing shows the Marzipan shapes used to make the Marzipan Piglet and the assembled piglet with the base dipped in chocolate. The bottom drawing shows the Marzipan shapes used to make the Whimsical Pig variation and the finished Whimsical Pig set on its chocolate stand*

from the bottom to the top to form the snout of the pig. Make a small cut for the mouth about two-thirds of the way from the top. Open the cut and place the reserved red ball (the apple) in the mouth.

6. Use a cone-shaped Marzipan tool (or the tip of an instant-read thermometer) to make two deep holes for the ears to sit in, placing them about 1 inch (2.5 cm) from the snout. One at a time form the reserved triangles around the tip of the cone tool, put a little egg white on first, then push into the holes. Arrange the ears so that they point slightly forward.

7. Make two small indentations close together between and below the ears for the pig's eyes, using the same tool. Make two identical marks in the upper part of the snout.

8. Place both index fingers on the sides of the pig about ¼ inch (6 mm) behind the head. Angle them 45° toward the back and press hard, making two deep indentations to form the pig's body. Use a Marzipan tool or a paring knife to make a vertical line in the center of the back end of the pig.

9. Roll the small piece of Marzipan reserved for the tail smooth, then roll it into a 2-inch (5-cm) long thin rope, tapered to a point at one end. Use a little egg white to fasten the tail to the body, curling the pointed end. Let the pig dry for a few hours or, preferably, overnight.

10. Using a piping bag, pipe two small dots of Royal Icing in the indentations made for the eyes, but remember: pigs have small eyes set very close together. Using a piping bag with a small opening, pipe two smaller dots of chocolate on the Royal Icing to indicate the pupils. Dip the bottom of the pig into the melted chocolate holding it at an angle to coat the pig about ¼ inch (6 mm) in the front and halfway up the sides in the back.

Whimsical Marzipan Pig

10 decorations

14 ounces (400 g) Marzipan (page 1022), tinted pale pink
powdered sugar
dark coating chocolate, melted
egg white
Royal Icing (page 1019)
cocoa butter, melted (optional) (see note on page 1031)

*T*his is any easy-to-make alternative using Marzipan rolled out into a sheet instead of molded in your hands, which allows you to create several decorations at the same time in a quick assembly-line fashion.

1. Refer to the bottom half of Figure 19–41 as a guide in constructing the whimsical pigs. Roll out the Marzipan to ³⁄₈ inch (9 mm) thick, using powdered sugar to prevent it from sticking. Cut out ten circles using a 2¼-inch (5.6-cm) plain cookie cutter and ten more using a 1³⁄₄-inch (4.5-cm) cutter. Cover the scrap pieces and reserve them.

2. Mark the large circles with a slightly curved line, using the back of a paring knife or a Marzipan tool to suggest the rear leg on each pig as shown in the drawing.

3. One at a time set each of the Marzipan circles (both sizes) on a dipping fork and dip the bottom flat edge and the sides into melted coating chocolate. Scrape the bottom against the side of the bowl, and then blot on a sheet of baking paper to remove the excess chocolate (see Figures 9–27 to 9–31, page 428, but do not insert the dipping fork as shown in the drawings). Set the circles aside.

4. Spread some melted chocolate on a sheet of baking paper to make a 6½-inch (16.2-cm) square, slightly more than ⅛ inch (3 mm) thick. Let the chocolate harden, then cut out ten rectangles 3 inches long by 1¼ inch wide (7.5 × 3.1 cm), using a warm knife. Line the rectangles up on a paper-lined pan or sheet of cardboard and place in the refrigerator.

5. Roll out a small piece from the reserved scraps of Marzipan to ⅛ inch (3 mm) thick. Cut out ten circles for the pigs' snouts, using a no. 7 (14-mm) plain pastry tip. Mark two small holes across the center of each snout with a pointed Marzipan tool.

6. Attach the snouts to the lower half (on the undipped side) of the 1¾-inch (4.5-cm) Marzipan circles, using egg white as glue. Using a blunt Marzipan tool or other suitable instrument, make two indentations above the noses to mark the pig's eyes. Make two more indentations at the top of each head on both sides where the ears will be attached.

7. Roll the remaining Marzipan scraps into a ¼-inch (6-mm) rope. Cut the rope into thirty pieces—twenty for the ears and ten for the tails. One at a time roll ten pieces against the table into 1-inch (2.5-cm) tapered strings and then curl them for the tails. Reserve the tails in the refrigerator.

8. Roll the remaining small pieces into ½-inch (1.2-cm) cones for the ears and attach to the heads, using a blunt Marzipan tool to create a round indentation at the base of each ear and and at the same time bending the ears so they point forward, using egg white as glue.

9. Remove the chocolate rectangles and pigs' tails from the refrigerator. Attach the pig heads and bodies to the rectangles by piping dots of chocolate on the base before setting the circles on top standing upright. Fasten the tails to the bodies using chocolate.

10. Place a small amount of Royal Icing in a piping bag and pipe dots of icing in the indentations made for the eyes. Decorate the bodies with dots of icing if desired. Pipe a small dot of chocolate on top of the icing in the eyes to mark the pupils.

Marzipan Roses

8 medium-sized roses

A Marzipan Rose may not be as elegant as the famed pulled-sugar rose, but it certainly is more practical, since it can be made in minutes, and in addition, it can be eaten. Although a Marzipan Rose made for a special occasion should have twelve or more petals (depending on the shape and size of the rose), a nice-looking "production rose" can be made using only three petals attached to the center. The three-petal rose is naturally quicker and easier to make, and it actually looks very much like a rosebud that is just about to bloom out.

Use either a marble table or slab, or a hardwood board or table, to work on. The wooden surface should not be one that has been cut on a great deal, because the uneven surface will make it difficult to produce an optimum result. Take the usual precautions for working with Marzipan by making sure that your hands and work surface are clean and dry. Also make sure the Marzipan has a firm, smooth, consistency. If it is too dry or hard the Marzipan will crack when you shape the petals. If too soft it can not be worked thin enough without it sticking to the knife and falling apart. Adjust with a small amount of water or powdered sugar as needed.

To make eight medium-sized ²/₃-ounce (20-g) roses you need to start with 10 ounces (285 g) of Marzipan (you will have quite a bit left when you finish and cut off the bottoms). You may tint the Marzipan if desired (see page 1021), but for the best effect you should use very pale pink or yellow tones.

1. Start by working one-fourth of the Marzipan smooth and pliable (keep the remainder covered with plastic). Roll it out to a 16-inch (40-cm) rope.

2. Place the rope approximately 1 inch (2.5 cm) away from the edge of the table in front of you. Use your palm to flatten the rope into a wedge shape, with the narrow side toward the edge of the table (Figure 19–42). Keep the rope in a straight line and make sure it sticks to the table (use powdered sugar to prevent the Marzipan from sticking to your hand).

3. Lightly coat a palette knife or chef's knife with vegetable oil. Holding the palette knife at an angle to keep the wedge shape, work the knife over the rope, making long even strokes and using enough pressure to flatten the rope to a 1-inch (2.5-cm) wide strip (Figure 19–43). The strip should be paper-thin in the front.

4. Cut the flattened strip away from the table by sliding a thin knife underneath, moving under the length of the strip in one smooth motion. Cut the strip diagonally into eight 2-inch (5-cm) pieces (Figure 19–44).

5. Roll each piece around itself so that it forms a cone with the narrow part of the piece at the top. Then fold one end back slightly so that it looks like a bud about to open.

6. Squeeze the bottom of the bud to secure the shape, and set the bud on the table in front of you (Figure 19–45). Repeat with the remain-

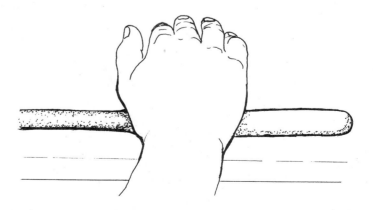

FIGURE 19–42 Using the palm of the hand to flatten the Marzipan strip into a wedge shape with the narrow side closest to the edge of the table

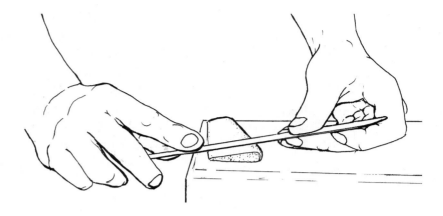

FIGURE 19–43 *Using a palette knife with long even strokes to flatten the edge further, making it paper-thin in front*

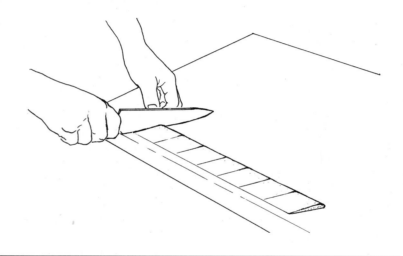

FIGURE 19–44 *Cutting the flattened strip diagonally into 2-inch (5-cm) pieces*

FIGURE 19–45 *The center cone for a Marzipan Rose as it is formed from one of the cut pieces into the shape of a bud*

ing seven pieces. When you have finished making the centers, clean the work surface by scraping off any Marzipan left from making them.

7. Work the remaining Marzipan soft. Roll it into a 16-inch (40-cm) rope. Cut the rope into twenty-four equal pieces. Roll the pieces into round balls. Place three to six balls (depending on how much work space you have) 8 inches (20 cm) apart, in a row in front of you at the edge of the table or marble slab. (Keep the remaining pieces covered with plastic.)

8. Flatten one side of each ball, as you did with the rope, to make them wedge shaped; the flattened part should be on the left or right, rather than the back or front. Make sure the pieces are stuck to the table.

9. Use an oiled chef's knife or palette knife held parallel to the table to enlarge the pieces, keeping the round shape, and working them out paper-thin on the flat side (Figure 19–46). This can also be done using the top of a light bulb or a plastic scraper.

10. Cut the petals free from the table by sliding a knife underneath, but leave them in place. Use the tip of your index finger to make an indentation on the thicker side of each petal (Figure 19–47). This will make it easier to bend the petals into the proper shape.

11. Pick up the pieces one at a time, and curl the thin edge back slightly to form a petal (Figure 19–48).

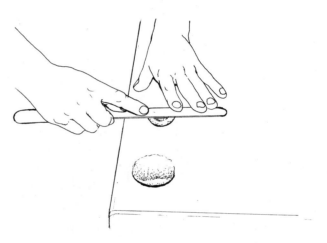

FIGURE 19–46 Using a palette knife to extend and flatten a Marzipan circle for a rose petal making it paper-thin on one side

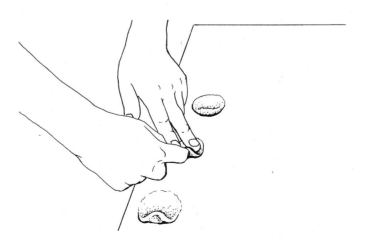

FIGURE 19–47 Using the index finger to create an indentation on the thicker side of each petal

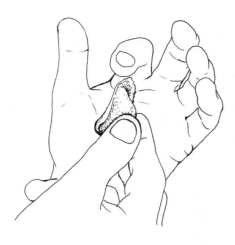

FIGURE 19–48 *Curling the edge of the petal back slightly*

12. Fasten three petals around the center of the rose made earlier. Squeeze just above the base of the rose to secure the petals and make them open out slightly.

13. Cut away the excess Marzipan from the bottom (save and use again). Repeat to make the remaining roses. Take care not to flatten too many petals at one time, or they will dry quickly and become difficult to form. The completed roses, however, can be made up days in advance without looking wilted. The thin edges will dry and become lighter in color, but that makes them look more realistic.

14. For a rose stem, roll light green Marzipan into a thin string. Make the thorns by making small angled cuts in the stems here and there with scissors. As on a real rose stem, the thorns should point upward.

Marzipan rose leaves

15. Make rose leaves (Figure 19–49) by rolling out light green Marzipan 1/16 inch (2 mm) thick. Using a sharp paring knife, cut out leaves of the appropriate size. Keep the tip of the knife clean and free from any pieces of Marzipan or the cuts will have a ragged and unattractive appearance. Mark veins on the leaves using the back side of the knife. Place a dowel on a sheet pan and prevent it from rolling (and throwing the leaves off) by fastening a small piece of Marzipan under each end. Put the leaves on the dowel so they will dry with a slightly bent, elegant curve. Let the leaves dry in a warm place for a few hours or, preferably, overnight.

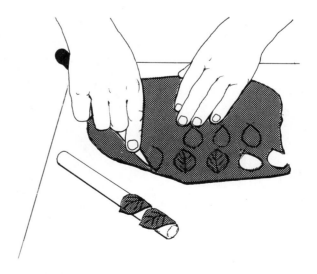

FIGURE 19–49 *Cutting Marzipan leaves and leaving them to dry over a dowel to make them curved*

Pâte à Choux for Decoration

4 ounces (115 g) paste

¹⁄₄ cup (60 ml) milk
¹⁄₂ ounce (15 g) unsalted butter
3 tablespoons (36 g) bread flour
small pinch of salt
2 egg yolks
milk, as needed

*P*iping out small, individual decorations with Pâte à Choux is done in much the same way as with chocolate; the main difference is that Pâte à Choux must then be baked before it is transferred to the pastry or cake, and it is therefore never piped directly on top of the item, as chocolate is in many cases. (Also, these decorations are used right-side up, while chocolate ornaments are displayed using the side that was against the paper.) This method is comparatively very easy to use (the Pâte à Choux will not set up if you work slowly as chocolate does), and since it is not very widely used today, it makes the finished pastries that the decorations are used on unusual and personalized. If possible, reserve a small amount of Pâte à Choux in the freezer when you make éclairs or cream puffs to use later in making decorations. If you do not have any leftover to use, you probably will only need to use the proportions given here, since a little goes a long way.

1. Follow the directions for making the paste on page 36. Pass the Pâte à Choux through a fine sieve before piping it out. If the Pâte à Choux seems too stiff to pipe, stir in a small amount of milk, one drop at a time.

2. Make a piping bag and cut a small opening. Pipe the figures onto baking papers following the same designs and techniques used for chocolate decorations (see Figures 17–19 to 17–21, pages 906 to 908). If the figures are complicated, or you want them to be identical, you can draw or trace the patterns onto the baking paper with a heavy pencil, invert the papers, and pipe on the other side so that the Pâte à Choux does not come in contact with the lead. If it matters that the figures will be reversed (with lettering, for example), or if you are making several of the same shape, place a second paper on top of the one with the tracings and secure the corners so that the papers will not slide as you pipe (a little Pâte à Choux makes an excellent glue).

3. Leave just the outline or fill in the designs, partially or fully, using a slightly modified version of Hippen Decorating Paste (recipe follows). The paste can be left plain or tinted to light pastel colors to contrast with the golden Pâte à Choux: for example, a New Year's bell filled with light brown hippen paste, or an oak leaf filled in with a pale green tint. Use a thicker grade of baking paper if you are filling in with the hippen paste as the thinner paper tends to curl from the moisture.

4. Bake the decorations at 375°F (190°C) until they start to turn light brown in a few spots (watch them like a hawk; it does not take very long, and this is not something you want to burn). After the decorations are cool place them on the cake or pastries, or they may be stored well covered in a dry place for a week or two.

Modified Hippen Decorating Paste for Pâte à Choux Ornaments

¹/₂ cup (120 ml) or 4¹/₂ ounces (130 g) paste

1 egg white
2¹/₂ ounces (70 g) Almond Paste (page 3)
3 tablespoons (27 g) powdered sugar, sifted
2 teaspoons (5 g) bread flour
milk, as needed
unsweetened cocoa powder (optional)

1. Incorporate the egg white into the Almond Paste and mix until smooth.

2. Mix in the powdered sugar, flour, and, if necessary, enough milk so that the paste will just barely flow out to the edges of the frame when piped inside the patterns.

3. For a brown color add unsweetened cocoa powder until you reach the shade you want. If necessary add a few extra drops of milk.

Pie Tin Templates and Template Holders

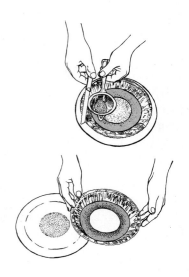

Several of desserts in this text, Tiramisu with Fresh Fruit, Trio of Chocolates with Marzipan Parfait, Strawberries Romanoff, and Chocolate Ganache Towers, to name a few, require sifting cocoa powder or powdered sugar over the base of the dessert plate in a precise pattern as part of the plate presentation. This technique often presents a challenge in the case of large designs where the rim of the plate may prevent you from laying the template flat against the base of the plate making it difficult to create well-defined shapes. With smaller templates this is not a problem since they will lay flat, but with these it is hard to avoid getting the cocoa powder or powdered sugar on the rim of the serving plate. These same problems can occur when streaking chocolate over the base of the plate as well. Using a modified disposable pie tin, as a template itself or as a frame in conjunction with a cardboard template, is an easy and inexpensive solution.

Select a disposable aluminum pie tin with a base that will sit flat against the base of the serving plates you are using. You can either cut the desired design out of the base of the pie tin, or you may cut away part or all of the bottom of the pie tin (depending on the size and shape of template to be used), leaving a side frame which can be used to hold various templates, attaching them as needed. (Figure 19–50). Cutting the design out of the base of the pie tin can be difficult because the sides of the pan get in the way and, because you must apply much more pressure on the utility knife to cut through the aluminum as opposed to cardboard, and since the blade will dull quickly, it is much more difficult to make smooth, rounded edges. The advantage, however, is that a template cut directly from the pie tin is much more durable, so it can be used for a long period of time.

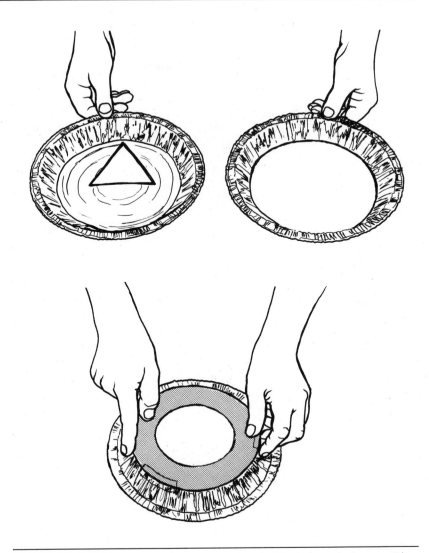

FIGURE 19–50 *The top row shows a template cut directly from the bottom of a pie tin and the entire base of the pie tin removed to hold a cardboard template. The bottom shows a cardboard template being attached to the bottomless pie tin holder.*

You may need to extend the protection of the rim of the plate by taping baking paper to the sides of the pie tin when streaking chocolate, since this technique sometimes extends beyond the edge of the plate.

A paper plate with a sloping edge can be used instead of a pie tin. They are easier to cut but are not, of course, as sturdy.

To use a pie tin template

1. Cut the desired template from the base of the pie tin.

2. Place the pie tin on the base of the dessert plate and sift powdered sugar or cocoa powder on top. Remove the pie tin carefully.

3. To make an overlapping design follow the instructions in steps four, five, and six in the following instructions.

To use the pie tin holder with a cardboard template

1. Trace the desired template and cut it out of cardboard from a cake box. Tape the template to the bottom of the pie tin frame as shown in the illustration on the previous page.

2. Place the pie tin on the dessert plate and sift cocoa powder or powdered sugar on top.

3. Carefully remove the frame (Figure 19–51).

4. To make an overlapping design, such as a powdered sugar shape over a cocoa powder design, tape toothpicks around the edge of the frame of the second template (Figure 19–52). This will hold the second template just slightly above the plate and prevent it from smearing the first design.

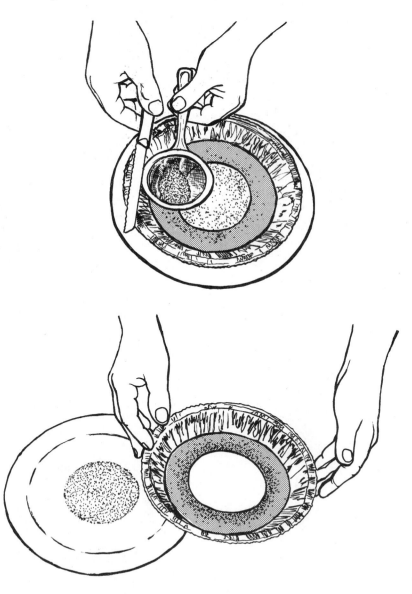

FIGURE 19–51 *Sifting cocoa powder over a dessert plate with the pie tin holder and template set on the plate; removing the template and holder*

FIGURE 19–52 Attaching toothpicks to the base of a second template to hold it just slightly above the cocoa powder design when it is placed on the plate

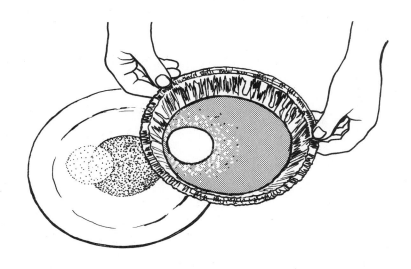

FIGURE 19–53 Lifting the template and holder off of the plate after sifting powdered sugar over the second template

5. Carefully set the frame on the plate and sift powdered sugar (or cocoa powder) over the top.

6. Remove the frame (Figure 19–53).

Tulip Paste Decorations and Containers

This versatile decorating paste can be formed or made into almost any shape you like. Its French name, *pâte à cigarette,* stems from its use in making the familiar thin, tube-shaped "cigarette" cookies (also known as pirouettes), which are usually decorated by dipping the ends in chocolate. The name *tulip* no doubt comes from its original application where the paste is spread into 7-to-8-inch (17.5-to-20-cm) circles on greased and floured sheet pans, and the flexible, warm cookies are then sandwiched between two bowls to form a tulip-shaped cup after baking. These are typically used as containers for sorbet or ice cream. The use of greased and floured sheet pans is yielding rapidly to the more convenient nonstick silicone mats, and the classic tulip shape is giving way to new, intricate modern designs. There are numerous recipes in this book that utilize Tulip Paste to make containers in various shapes and sizes including: Red Currant Sorbet in Magnolia Cookie Shells, where a smaller cookie is nestled inside a larger one to form a flower; Blueberry Pirouettes, where Tulip Paste is rolled into a tube to hold the filling; Tulip Paste is decorated to look like a wrapped present and wrapped around a frozen filling in Tropical Surprise Packages; and it is made into fruit baskets and wine barrels in the recipes for Cherry Baskets and Vineyard Barrels, respectively. In addition to containers, Tulip Paste is often used to form edible decorations: In Tapioca Pudding Maui it is used to create a standing palm tree complete with coconuts; Tulip Paste forms the Cookie Spoon used in the presentation for Cappuccino Mousse with Sambuca Cream; the Cookie Butterflies perched atop Chocolate Ganache Cake are made from this paste, as are Curly Cues, which are used to decorate several recipes.

Tulip Paste also plays an important role in making the elegant and decorative Ribbon Sponge Sheets, where it is used rather than a second sponge batter to form the contrasting stripes. Tulip Paste is perfect for this function because, unlike sponge batter, it can be spread into very precise shapes and then frozen briefly before baking (to prevent it from smearing when the sponge batter is spread over the top) with no ill effect.

In the recipes in this book that use Tulip Paste you first need to trace and cut out a template from cardboard or plastic to use in creating the desired shape. Some of the templates are specifically designed to coordinate with the presentation for a particular recipe, but many generic shapes may be purchased from suppliers. These templates are available in stainless-steel, aluminum, or plastic, and while obviously more durable than a template made from cardboard (the metal templates will last forever), they are relatively expensive since they are almost always imported from Europe.

This simple recipe consists of only four ingredients, used in equal weights. Due to the gluten in the flour the shapes will shrink just a little during baking, but they will do so evenly all around and as long as this is taken into consideration, in cases where it will matter, the shrinkage does not cause a problem. The apparent solution to avoiding or reducing shrinkage would be to reduce the gluten strength of the flour, but this is not a viable option because by doing so the baked pieces would become too fragile. Take care not to overmix the batter once the flour has been incorporated to avoid developing the gluten any more than necessary. Tulip Paste was a main focus of my show

FIGURE 19–54 The templates used to form Tulips and Miniature Tulips

"Spectacular Desserts" on PBS, where I demonstrated its use in several applications and showed that while it is true that some shapes take a bit more experience than others, most can be mastered rather quickly.

 Tulips

about 25 large cookie shells

one-half recipe Vanilla Tulip Paste (recipe follows)

NOTE 1: To make Chocolate Tulips, substitute Chocolate Tulip Paste. Plain Tulips also may be decorated by piping Chocolate Tulip Paste on top before baking. If you do not have Chocolate Tulip Paste on hand, use 1 teaspoon (2.5 g) of sifted unsweetened cocoa powder for every 2 tablespoons (30 ml) of Vanilla Tulip Paste and mix the two together until thoroughly combined and smooth.

NOTE 2: Tulips made using the large template in Figure 19–54 look best if made in a shallow bowl shape as instructed. To make a taller, more narrow holder, use the smaller template in Figure 14–9 (see page 716) instead.

NOTE 3: I have found this arrangement to work well when making any tulip-shaped container: hang three or four round-bottomed ladles of the desired size on the lip of a round bain-marie-type container. The bain-marie and the ladles should be of approximately the same height, so the bases of the ladles are horizontal. If the fruit is smaller than the ladle, simply roll it around inside to shape the cookie. This way you can begin forming the next tulip without having to wait for each one to become firm.

1. Make the larger version of the Tulip Template (Figure 19–54) (see note 2). The template as shown is the correct size for use in this recipe (the small template shown in the center is used in other recipes). Trace the drawing, then cut the template out of ¹/₁₆-inch (2-mm) cardboard (cake boxes are ideal).

2. Use silicone mats if you have them or grease the backs of even sheet pans very lightly, coat the pans with flour, then shake off as much flour as possible.

3. Spread the Tulip Paste onto the silicone mats or prepared pans, spreading it flat and even within the template (Figure 19–55). Be careful when you pick up the template from the pan after spreading each one. Hold down the opposite end with your spatula as you lift off the template to avoid disturbing the paste (Figure 19–56).

4. Bake at 425°F (219°C) for approximately 8 minutes or until there are a few light brown spots on the cookies. Leave the sheet pan in the oven and remove the Tulips one at a time.

5. Working quickly, form the Tulips (with the brown side out) by pressing each cookie gently over a shallow inverted bowl. Use one that will give you a 4-inch (10-cm) opening at the top of your finished Tulip. If you are making quite a few at once, it is faster to form them by placing each cookie, brown-side down, inside a bowl or ladle of about the same size and then press an orange on top of the Tulip. (See Figure 13–5, page 674.)

FIGURE 19–55 Spreading Tulip Paste flat and even within the template

FIGURE 19–56 *Holding down the opposite side of the template as it is removed to prevent distorting the shape*

Vanilla Tulip Paste

1 pound, 14 ounces (855 g) or 3¹/₄ cups (780 ml) paste

8 ounces (225 g) soft unsalted butter

8 ounces (225 g) powdered sugar, sifted

1 cup (240 ml) egg whites, at room temperature

1 teaspoon (5 ml) vanilla extract

8 ounces (225 g) cake flour, sifted

1. Cream the butter and powdered sugar together. Incorporate the egg whites a few at a time. Add the vanilla. Add the flour and mix just until incorporated; do not overmix.

2. Store covered in the refrigerator. Tulip Paste will keep for several weeks. Allow the paste to soften slightly after removing it from the refrigerator, then stir it smooth and into a spreadable consistency before using. If the paste is too soft, the edges of the Tulips will be ragged and unprofessional looking. If this happens, chill the paste briefly.

Chocolate Tulip Paste

1 pound, 14 ounces (855 g) or 3¹/₄ cups (780 ml) paste

8 ounces (225 g) soft unsalted butter

8 ounces (225 g) powdered sugar, sifted

1 cup (240 ml) egg whites, at room temperature

1 teaspoon (5 ml) vanilla extract

6 ounces (170 g) bread flour, sifted

2¹/₂ ounces (70 g) unsweetened cocoa powder, sifted

1. Cream the butter and powdered sugar together. Gradually incorporate the egg whites and vanilla.

2. Sift the flour with the cocoa powder. Add to the paste and mix just until incorporated; do not overmix.

3. Store covered in the refrigerator. Tulip Paste will keep for several weeks. Use as directed in step two of Vanilla Tulip Paste.

Tulip Cookie Spoons

about 60 spoon decorations

Butter and Flour Mixture (page 4)

one-quarter recipe Vanilla Tulip Paste
   (page 1047)

$1/2$ teaspoon (1.25 g) unsweetened
   cocoa powder, sifted

1. Make the Cookie Spoon template (Figure 19–57). The template as shown is the correct size required for this recipe. Trace the drawing,

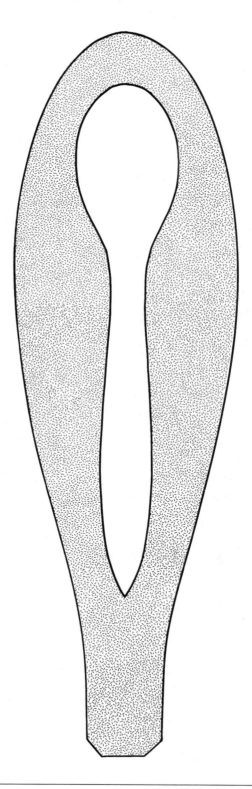

FIGURE 19–57 The template used to form Cookie Spoons

then cut the template out of ¹/₁₆-inch (2-mm) thick cardboard (cake boxes work fine for this).

2. Brush the Butter and Flour Mixture on the backs of clean, even sheet pans (or if you have silicone mats, use them instead; they do not need to be greased and floured). Have ready at least two or, better yet, four identical small metal spoons approximately the same size as the template.

3. Color 1 tablespoon (15 ml) of the Tulip Paste with the cocoa powder, mixing until completely smooth. Place the cocoa-colored paste in a piping bag.

4. Spread the plain Tulip Paste onto the prepared sheet pans (or silicone mats), spreading it flat and even within the template (see Figures 19–55, and 19–56, pages 1046 and 1047). Do not spread more than eight to ten spoons on each pan or mat or you will not have time to form them before the small cookies get too dark.

5. Pipe three small dots of the cocoa-colored paste in the handle of each spoon.

6. Bake at 425°F (219°C) for approximately 4 minutes or until there are a few light brown spots on the cookies.

7. Leave the pan in the oven and remove the Cookie Spoons one at a time. Working quickly, form them by pressing each cookie gently between two metal spoons: Center the cookie over one spoon, place a second spoon on top, and press together to shape the bowl of the spoon. Repeat to bake and form the remaining spoons. Reserve until time of service. The Cookie Spoons can be kept for several days at this point if stored in an airtight container at room temperature.

Tulip Leaves and Cookie Wedges

approximately 35 decorations of either shape

one-quarter recipe Vanilla Tulip Paste (page 1047)
1 teaspoon (2.5 g) unsweetened cocoa powder

1. To make Tulip Leaves trace template A in Figure 19–58; for Cookie Wedges use template B. Cut either template out of ¹/₁₆-inch (2-mm) thick cardboard (cake boxes work great for this). The templates as shown are the correct size for use in this recipe.

2. Use silicone mats or lightly grease the backs of even sheet pans, coat the pans with flour, and then shake off as much flour as possible.

3. Color 2 tablespoons (30 ml) of the Tulip Paste with the cocoa powder, mixing it until completely smooth. Place a portion in a piping bag and cut a small opening.

4. Spread the Vanilla Tulip Paste flat and even within the template on the prepared pans or silicone mats (see Figures 19–55 and 19–56, pages 1046 and 1047). Do not spread too many per pan or the last few will be too dark when you get to them. Pipe a straight line of cocoa-colored paste, in the center, down the full length of each cookie.

5. Bake the cookies at 425°F (219°C) for 4 to 5 minutes or until they just begin to turn brown in a few spots and around the edges. Keep the pan in the oven with the door open and remove the cookies one at a time. If making Tulip Leaves, quickly twist each leaf to make it curved. Hold it for one or two seconds, and it will be firm enough to keep its

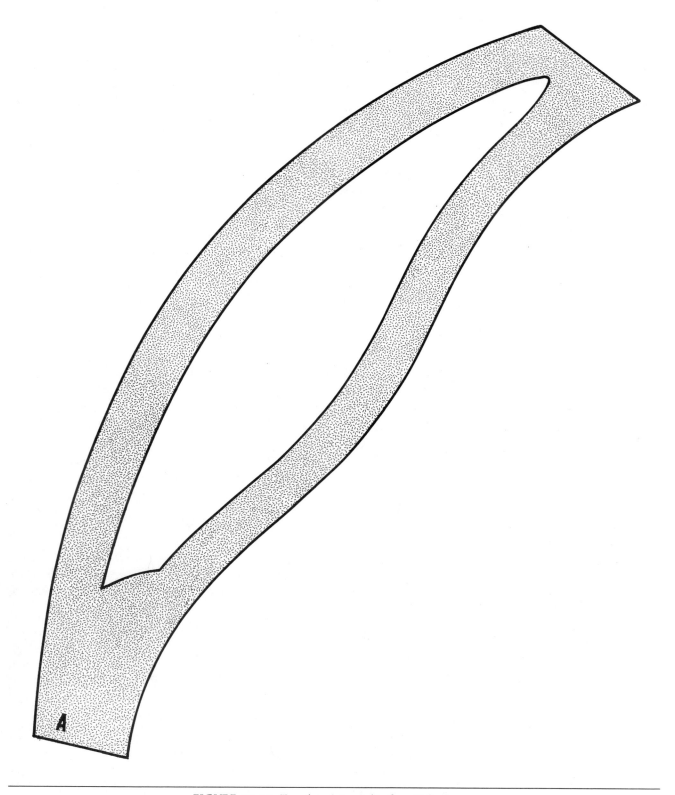

FIGURE 19–58 Template A is used to form Tulip Leaves

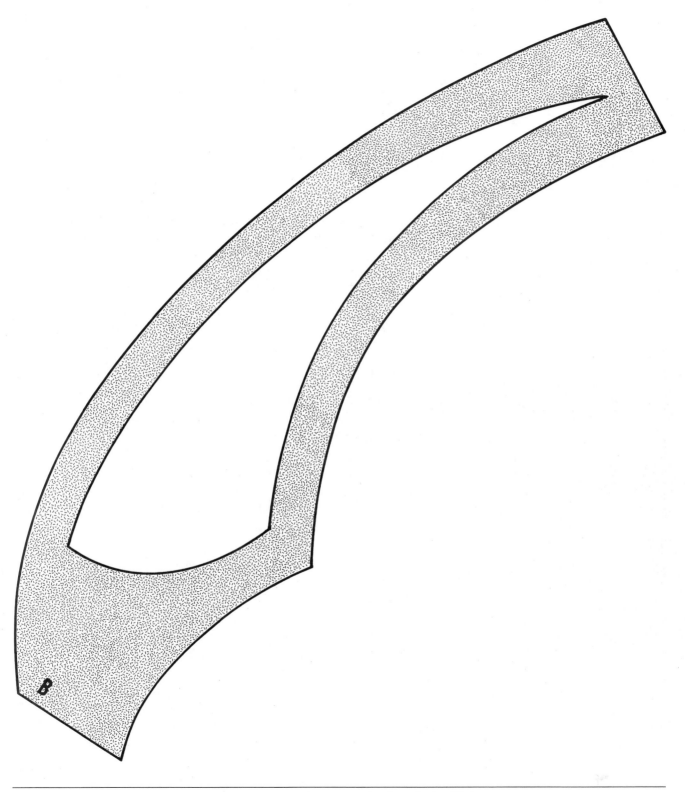

FIGURE 19–58 Template B is used to form Cookie Wedges

shape. For a slightly different look and a faster way to form them, place the leaves on top of a rolling pin at an angle almost parallel to the bias. If making Cookie Wedges, drape them over a rolling pin at a 45° angle after removing them from the oven.

 ## Cookie Butterflies

about 50 decorations

one-quarter recipe Vanilla Tulip Paste
   (page 1047)
1 teaspoon (2.5 g) unsweetened cocoa
   powder

NOTE: In addition to piping the dots on the wings you can use the cocoa-colored paste to pipe a body in the center of each butterfly. In this case you will need to color twice as much paste.

Making Cookie Butterflies is the easiest way of dressing up a dessert or pastry using Tulip Paste, because they require you to have very little contact with the hot cookies to form them—the V-shaped support box does the job for you. When a butterfly is placed next to an edible flower, mint sprig, or a piece of fruit, it not only gives the dessert height but adds a touch of elegance and beauty to the presentation. Cookie Butterflies should always be thin and fragile like a real butterfly. If the paste is spread out too thick the decorations look clumsy and the desired effect is lost.

1. To form the butterflies you will need a V-shaped molding box. If you do not have one, make a form following the directions for the Chalet Support Box on page 835. Or make a simplified version as follows: Begin with a 6-inch (15-cm) wide strip of corrugated cardboard. Make a cut lengthwise down the center of the strip, cutting only halfway through. Bend the cardboard into a V-shape, placing a strip of tape across the top at both ends to hold the proper angle. To hold the form upright as you work, secure it between the rows of an inverted muffin tin.

2. Make the Cookie Butterfly template (Figure 19–59). The template as shown is the correct size for use in this recipe. Trace the drawing and then cut the template out of $^1/_{16}$-inch (2-mm) thick cardboard (cake boxes are ideal).

3. Lightly grease the backs of clean, even sheet pans, coat with flour, and then shake off as much flour as possible, or use silicone mats, which do not need to be greased and floured.

4. Mix the cocoa powder into 2 tablespoons (30 ml) of the Tulip Paste, stirring until smooth. Place a portion in a piping bag.

5. Spread the plain Tulip Paste thinly and evenly within the butterfly template on the prepared pans or silicone mats (see Figures 19–55 and 19–56, pages 1046 and 1047).

6. Pipe three dots of cocoa-colored paste in descending size on each wing, with the largest dot at the bottom (see note).

7. Bake the butterflies, one pan at a time, at 400°F (205°C) for approximately 6 minutes or until the cookies begin to develop brown spots. Leave the pan in the oven with the oven door open, remove the cookies one at a time, selecting the cookie with the most brown spots first, and place them into the V-shaped form. Arrange the butterflies so that they are straight. If you have time, and your fingers are up to it, press the very end of the center of the butterfly against the box (between rounded ends) to make the front of the wings spread out at a slight angle. Remove the formed Cookie Butterflies once they have hardened (this only takes a few seconds) and repeat to form the remainder. It is a good idea to make a few more than you will need to allow for breakage.

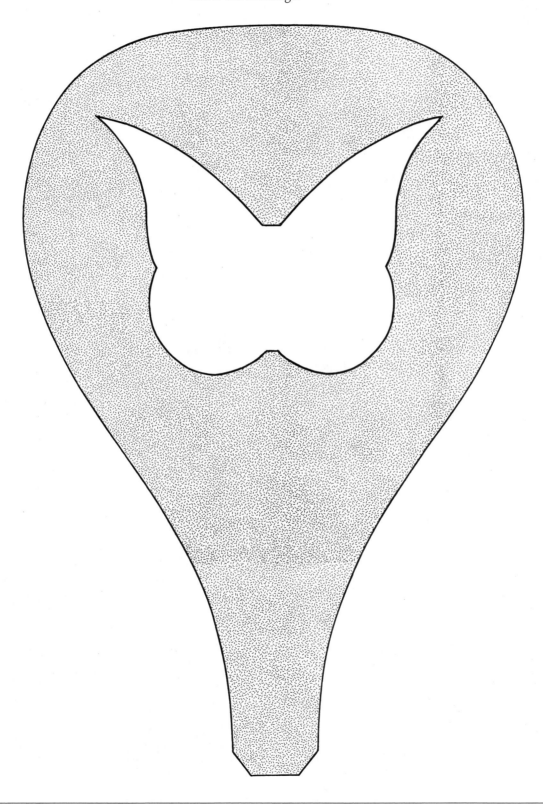

FIGURE 19–59 The template used to form Cookie Butterflies

Cookie Citrus Rinds and Cookie Figurines

decorations for 16 dessert servings

one recipe Vanilla Tulip Paste
   (page 1047)
1 tablespoon (18 g) finely grated
   citrus rind

NOTE: If the Cookie Rinds are not to be used until the following day after baking, you may eliminate the softening process. Instead, place them directly on sheet pans lined with baking paper, place another sheet of paper on top, and refrigerate overnight. The cold, damp air will soften them.

These long, curling, fanciful shapes are meant to resemble strips of citrus peel as they look when removed with a zester. You do not need to limit this decoration to make-believe citrus rind, however, as it certainly can be used (with or without the grated zest) to dress up a dessert anytime you feel like going a little wild with the presentation (which I think is a good idea every once in a while).

As you may have experienced, anything made from Tulip Paste is extremely brittle after baking, to the extent that items can sometimes seem to break for no reason at all. At the same time these products are very susceptible to moisture, and at the other end of the spectrum, if they are not stored properly (or in the case of filled items, if filled too long in advance) they become soft and collapse. While softening is normally considered a problem, it occurred to me to try to use it to my advantage, and I came up with the idea of shaping the softened spirals into these eye-catching decorations.

1. Use silicone mats if you have them or lightly grease the backs of five even sheet pans, coat with flour, and then shake off as much flour as possible.

2. Stir the citrus rind into the Tulip Paste and place a portion of the paste into a pastry bag with a no. 0 (1-mm) plain tip. Pipe out spirals about 6 inches (15 cm) in diameter. Do not close the spirals at the ends. Instead, pipe a wavy line approximately 6 inches (15 cm) long, extending from each spiral as shown in the illustration. Place six spirals on each of three sheet pans or silicone mats (Figure 19–60). This will give you two extra in case you break a decoration (which, unfortunately, is likely).

FIGURE 19–60 Piping Tulip Paste into spirals with extended wavy tails for Cookie Citrus Rinds

3. Pipe out a total of thirty-six 4-inch tall (10-cm) figurines on the remaining prepared sheet pans or silicone mats, using a design such as the one shown in Figure 17–21, third row second from the left, page 908, for example. (You need two per serving so, again, this gives you some extra.)

4. Bake at 400°F (205°C) for approximately 6 minutes or until the Tulip Paste has turned golden brown. Set aside to cool (see note).

5. Place a damp towel on the bottom of a sheet pan. Place a sheet of baking paper on top and weigh down the corners with forms or coffee cups to prevent the paper from curling up due to the moisture.

6. Very carefully transfer the baked spirals (not the smaller figurines) to the prepared pan. If any break as you move them do not discard the pieces at this point; they may still be usable unless they have broken in more than one place. Invert a second sheet pan on top as a lid.

7. Return to the 400°F (205°C) oven for 6 to 8 minutes or until the spirals remain soft and limp after they have cooled. Transfer to a sheet pan lined with baking paper. Repeat the softening procedure with the remaining spirals. Store the spirals in the refrigerator if they are not to be used within the next few hours. Cover the cookie figurines and store them in a warm dry place to keep them crisp.

8. Arrange the figurines and Cookie Rinds on top of dessert servings as specified in the individual recipes (see page 739, for example).

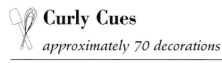

Curly Cues

approximately 70 decorations

one-half recipe Vanilla Tulip Paste (page 1047)
1½ teaspoons (4 g) unsweetened cocoa powder

NOTE: The cookies can alternatively be made without chocolate lines or you can reverse the colors: Spread Chocolate Tulip Paste within the template and pipe Vanilla Tulip Paste in a line down the center. This variety is a little tricky to bake since it is hard to judge when the cookies are done because the batter is dark to begin with.

*C*hances are you will initially be a bit frustrated when these thin, narrow cookie strips break in your hands, but do not give up. Your fingers will soon get used to the heat, and you will be able to wind the strips fast enough to keep them from breaking. And remember, if it was that easy, everyone would be making them!

Do not attempt to bake more than six to eight cookies at a time because they bake very fast, and you will not have time to form all of them before the last few get too dark. You can, however (as is true of any item made from Tulip Paste), spread the paste within the template ahead of time and have several pans ready to bake and form in succession. This is a good idea if you need to make quite a few decorations. In this case have several dowels ready, plan your work area, and include a place to put the formed cookies as you shape the remainder.

1. Trace the template in Figure 19–61 and then cut it out of ¹/₁₆-inch (2-mm) cardboard (cake boxes work great for this). The template as shown is the correct size for use in this recipe, but you will need to match the dotted lines to join the two halves as you trace it.

2. Use silicone mats or lightly grease the backs of even sheet pans, coat the pans with flour, and then shake off as much flour as possible. Have ready two dowels ½ inch (1.2 cm) in diameter and 16 inches (40 cm) long (in some cases wooden spoon handles are the appropriate size).

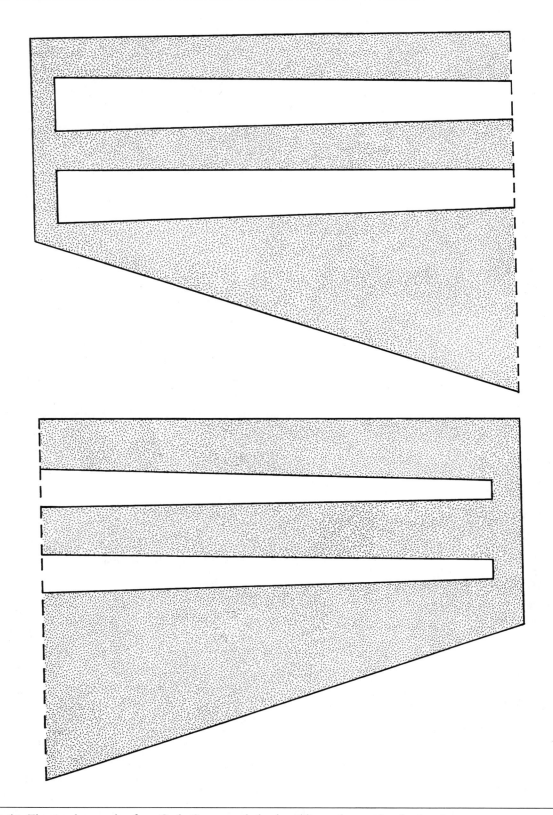

FIGURE 19–61 *The template used to form Curly Cues; match the dotted lines when tracing the drawing*

3. Mix the cocoa powder into 3 tablespoons (45 ml) of the Tulip Paste, stirring until it is completely smooth. Place a portion of the paste in a piping bag and cut a small opening.

4. Spread the Vanilla Tulip Paste flat and even within the template (see Figures 19–55 and 19–56, pages 1046 and 1047). Form six to eight cookies on each silicone mat or sheet pan. Pipe a straight line of the cocoa-colored paste in the center, down the full length of each cookie.

5. Bake one pan at a time at 400°F (205°C) for approximately 2 minutes or until one cookie begins to show a few brown spots. It takes a little experience to judge when to begin with the first cookie, and you have to move quickly at this point: If they are over-browned it is impossible to form them without breaking. However, if they are removed before they show any color at all, the cookies will not become crisp after they cool. Leave the pan in the oven with the door open.

6. Hold the dowel in one hand and quickly pick up the darkest cookie strip by the narrow end. Place the strip at a 45° angle to the dowel and quickly turn the dowel as you allow the cookie to wrap around the dowel and form a spiral (Figure 19–62). You can adjust the length and shape of the finished cookie by adjusting the angle at which the cookie falls on the dowel. For example, placing the cookie at close to a 90° angle to the dowel will produce a short, tightly wound cookie, similar to a telephone cord. Leave the cookie on the dowel for about 5 seconds, while holding both ends tightly against the dowel, before sliding it off. Or, if you are working with more than one dowel, place the dowel on the table with the ends of the cookie underneath and start to form the next cookie right away.

7. Form and bake the remaining cookies. The finished Curly Cues will keep for weeks if stored in a dry place.

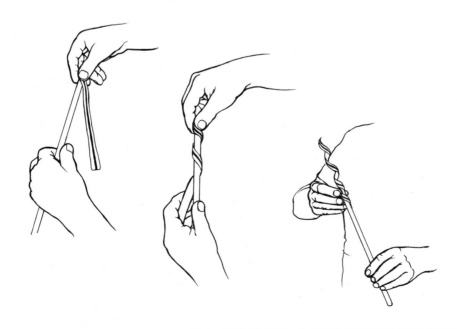

FIGURE 19–62 *Wrapping a soft Curly Cue around a dowel to shape it immediately after removing it from the oven and then pulling the cookie off the dowel after it has hardened*

Miniature Tulips

about 40 cookie shells

one-quarter recipe Vanilla Tulip Paste
(page 1047)
1 teaspoon (2.5 g) unsweetened cocoa
powder

The dots of cocoa-colored paste may be omitted if desired. Another way to form either of the small cookie shells is to use a lime or small lemon to press the cookie into the bottom of a small ladle (brown side down) instead of using a second form on top. If the fruit is a little too small, simply roll it around inside until the sides have been shaped. The baked cookies can also be draped over a lemon or lime (brown-side up) and then pressed into shape with your cupped hands if you have a good tolerance to the heat (see note 3 on page 1046).

1. Make the smaller template in Figure 19–54, page 1045. The template as shown is the correct size required for this recipe. Trace the drawing, then cut the template out of ¹/₁₆-inch (2-mm) thick cardboard (cake boxes work fine for this). Lightly grease the backs of clean, even sheet pans, coat with flour, and then shake off as much flour as possible (or if you have silicone mats use them instead; they do not need to be greased and floured).

2. Color 2 tablespoons (30 ml) of the Tulip Paste with the cocoa powder, mixing it in thoroughly. Place a portion of the cocoa-colored paste in a piping bag. Spread the plain Tulip Paste onto the prepared sheet pans (or silicone mats), spreading it flat and even within the template (see Figures 19–55 and 19–56, pages 1046 and 1047).

3. Pipe a small dot of the cocoa-colored paste in each petal of the tulip flowers.

4. Bake one pan at a time at 425°F (219°C) for approximately 5 minutes or until there are a few light brown spots on the cookies.

5. Leave the pan in the oven and remove the cookie shells one at a time. Working quickly, form them by pressing each cookie gently between two small forms as shown in Figure 13–5, page 674, example on the left (see note below). Center the cookie over the form, brown-side down, center another form on top, and press the center of the cookie into the form to make a tiny cup. It is easiest to work with two sets of forms at a time. As you finish forming the second cup, the first should be firm enough to remove and set aside. Repeat to form the remaining Tulips. Reserve until time of service. The cookie shells can be kept for several days at this point if stored in an airtight container at room temperature.

Miniature Tulip Crowns

about 40 cookie shells

Follow the instructions for Miniature Tulips, using the template in Figure 14–10, page 717. For a different look, try replacing the dots with lines piped from the middle of the cookie through the center of each petal, or just leave them plain.

Wedding Cake Assembly and Decoration

There are so many different types and variations of wedding cakes that the topic can easily fill a book all by itself. The following is a very basic guide for assembling a simple, traditional cake, a starting point from which you may create your own interpretation.

Some of the cakes I've seen recently are a bit overdone in my opinion, including one with a waterfall cascading down through the various tiers, and another where the top tier was turning and blinking like a Christmas tree! This is not my idea of a wedding cake, but I must admit I have made some strange ones myself. After seeing some of my Marzipan figures, one customer insisted on having me decorate all five tiers of the cake with nearly two dozen Marzipan lions, tigers, elephants, and monkeys instead of flowers; the bride and groom were going on an African safari for their honeymoon. Another wanted Marzipan sailboats sailing around each layer (they had the ceremony at a yacht club). But the strangest of them all had to be the couple who requested two large pink Marzipan pigs (wearing running shoes!) on the top tier, one Marzipan cat hidden in some fresh flowers on the middle tier, and sixteen Marzipan crocodiles, nose-to-tail, encircling the bottom tier! Even after inquiring discreetly about this particular combination I never did fully understand its significance.

The classic wedding cake, of course, has none of this. The layers are typically separated and placed on a stand, usually with five tiers. The base is generally 18 inches (45 cm) in diameter, the top around 8 inches (20 cm), and each layer is between 4 and 5 inches (10–12.5 cm) in thickness. The cake is usually iced and decorated in white buttercream, with buttercream or Marzipan roses tinted in a shade to coordinate with the color scheme of the wedding.

If the bottom tier is made of a regular chocolate or light sponge cake, even the largest sizes can be baked whole, although to ensure they are fully cooked in the center you sometimes have to overbake the edges a little (this is usually not a problem because the cake must be trimmed to fit the cake stand anyway). With heavier cakes such as carrot, or the Queen of Sheba, for example, the larger sizes should always be baked in two or even three layers.

Assembly using a cake stand

1. Place the cake plates from the stand on top of corrugated cake cardboards (use the heavy, double-lined variety) and trace around them with a pen. If the stand you are using has supporting pillars going through the center, mark this spot on the cardboards also.

2. Draw a second line 1/8 inch (3 mm) inside the circles, using the cake plates as a guide (draw part of the way, move the plate, draw a bit more, etc., until you end up where you started).

3. Using a sharp utility knife, cut out the smaller circles. Cut a space for the center support(s), if applicable.

4. Cut the skin from the top of the sponges, cutting them even at the same time. Check the bottoms and cut off the crust if it is too dark (usually on the larger sizes).

5. Place your cut cardboards on top of the appropriate sponges and cut straight down, trimming the sides of the sponge to fit the cardboard exactly.

6. Cut the cakes into two or three layers. Place one layer on the cardboard, then fill and stack the layers. It is a good idea to brush the sponge with a mixture of Plain Cake Syrup (see page 10) and a liqueur that is complementary to the flavor of the filling as you layer the sponges and filling, to be sure that the cake will be moist. This is especially important if you cut each sponge into only two layers.

7. To make sure that the buttercream is smooth and free from any air bubbles, soften it (over hot water if necessary) and place in the mixer about 10 minutes before it is needed. Stir the buttercream, using the paddle attachment, on low speed.

8. Unless the buttercream is applied to the cakes in a very thick layer, it is impossible to do so without getting some cake crumbs in it. For this reason you must first apply a crumb layer or crumb coat of buttercream. Ice the top and sides of the cakes with a thin layer of buttercream just as carefully as if you were icing the final layer. Place the cakes in the refrigerator long enough to harden the buttercream and glue the crumbs in place.

9. Remove one layer at a time from the refrigerator and place on the corresponding cake-stand plate, attaching the cardboard to the plate with a piece of tape rolled into a loop, sticky side out.

10. Place on a cake-decorating turntable and ice the top and sides with buttercream in a perfectly even layer. This would have been quite difficult, as well as time-consuming, if the cake had been the same size as the cake plate. However, since the stand is slightly wider than the cake, it is easy to fill in the space and make the sides even simply by holding the spatula against the cake stand, straight up and down, while rotating the turntable. Ice all of the layers in the same manner. Because the turntable will be too large to follow this procedure for the smallest layer(s), turn the base of the turntable upside down and use the bottom as a base on which to place these layers.

11. If the layers are to be decorated with the classical drop-loop pattern (which can be done very quickly and simply or made as complicated as you wish), it is essential that the pattern come together evenly. You do not want the last loop to be one-quarter of the size of the others, especially if you are decorating the top following the pattern on the sides, in which case it will be even more evident. To prevent this from happening, check the pattern and the remaining space to be decorated when you are three-quarters of the way around, then either increase or decrease the size of the loops gradually and make them come out even. Or, evenly mark the top of edge of the cake very lightly before piping to show where the loops begin and end. These marks can be covered when you decorate the top.

12. The tops of the cakes are usually decorated with a simple pearl pattern piped around the edge (see Figure 19–6, page 983) and a rosette piped where the ends of each loop meet. The cakes can then be decorated with flowers, either buttercream (see page 981), Marzipan (see page 1034), or fresh (see page 1006).

13. If the cakes have to be transported to another location for the reception, which is usually the case, take great care because a wedding cake, as opposed to a regular cake, has the same circumference as the base it is placed on, and it is therefore very easy to ruin the piping on the sides, and all of your careful work, with one careless move. (In fact, I have heard it said that there are only two people trustworthy enough to deliver a wedding cake: the person who made it and the person who is paying the bill!) I place each layer in an oversized box with a double layer of heavy cardboard in the bottom and attach the cake-stand plate to the cardboard with loops of tape (in addition to sternly cautioning to the driver to look at what is up ahead so he or she doesn't have to break suddenly). While it is unlikely that you will be able to close the lids of the cake boxes, it is a good idea to try and cover the cakes to some degree, because any small particles blowing in the air will stick immediately to the soft buttercream and is impossible to remove without leaving a mark.

Stacked wedding cakes

This is a much easier and quicker method of making wedding cakes; also there is no cake stand to take a deposit on, or to check to see if all of the pieces were returned. And if the cake is decorated with fresh flowers, as is so popular now, making this type of wedding cake is not any more difficult than making any large cake.

1. Cut out corrugated cardboards slightly smaller than your sponge layers, using a sharp utility knife so you can cut precisely and evenly. It is essential that you use the thick grade of cardboard, not just to ensure proper support for the cake but to avoid having the cardboard warp. Cut out two extra cardboards, one about 1 inch (2.5 cm) smaller, and one 3 inches (7.5 cm) larger, than the piece cut for the base of the stacked cake.

2. Glue 5-inch (12.5-cm) round paper lace doilies all around the perimeter of the largest cardboard. They should protrude out beyond the cardboard just a little bit. Do not use staples to attach the doilies; they can very easily come loose and get into the cake. Glue the smaller extra cardboard in the center of the one covered with doilies. Set aside. You can, of course, place the cake on top of one of the cake plates from the traditional cake stand or on a suitable platter, and avoid having to make this base, but that takes away the convenience of not having to worry about getting the stand or platter back if the cake is being taken off-site.

3. Cut hollow, clear plastic pipes ½–¾ inch (1.2–2 cm) in diameter, into lengths slightly longer than the height of the cake layers. You need four to support each of the larger layers, and three to support each of the smaller sizes, using the dimensions given for the tiers earlier. Make certain that all of the pillars used for each layer are exactly the same height, or the cake will lean.

4. Fill, layer, and ice the cakes with the crumb layer as described in using a cake stand.

5. When the crumb layer is chilled, place the layers one at a time on the turntable, and ice the tops.

6. A nice way to decorate the sides of a stacked cake is to pipe vertical lines of buttercream on the sides, using a no. 5 (10-mm) flat star tip (see Figure 19–1, page 980), piping the strips next to each other, and making sure you cover the cardboard at the bottom at the same time; pipe from the bottom to the top. Another way is to leave about ¼ inch (6 mm) of space between the strips, and then go back and fill in the space later with a series of small dots spaced evenly from top to bottom, with the bottom dot covering the cardboard. Use the same plain tip to make the dots that you will use to make the decoration on the tops of the cakes.

7. Even off any buttercream that sticks up above the edge on the top. Do the same on the lower edge of the cake, holding the spatula at a 45° angle against the cardboard. Decorate the top of the layers with a pearl pattern piped with a no. 3 (6-mm) plain tip.

8. When all of the layers have been iced and decorated, place the bottom layer on the base made earlier, attaching it with loops of tape so it will not slide. Push the plastic pillars into the cake, spacing them evenly and placing them so that the next layer will fit securely on top. Stack the remaining layers with pillars in between in the same way. Decorate the cake with flowers as described earlier.

Portioning of wedding cakes

Even though you could stack enough cakes to serve a wedding party of 400 to 500 guests if the layers were supported properly, it would be a very expensive cake and is not really practical, since it would take a long time to serve. A better way is to make a smaller cake for tiered display and the cake-cutting ceremony, and make up the remainder of the servings from sheet cakes made with the same flavors of sponge, filling, and buttercream. The sheet cakes can be cut and plated ahead of time and be ready to serve from the kitchen. This is also a good thing to suggest to a customer with a regular sized wedding party of 100 to 200 people who is trying to reduce the cost.

Naturally both the price and the number of servings you can get out of a cake depend on what kind of cake it is and who is serving it. Chocolate Truffle Cake with Raspberries, for example, can be cut into smaller slices than a light sponge cake. In certain situations, you may want to indicate to the person who will be serving the cake the number of portions they should plan to get from each tier. The following table works well for estimating the number of servings for various layers. To be even more accurate you should also take into consideration what else is being served at the reception, whether it just cake and champagne, or a buffet dinner, or hors d'oeuvres. Depending on these factors:

- an 18-inch (45-cm) cake will serve 40 to 50 guests
- a 16-inch (40-cm) cake will serve 30 to 40 guests
- a 14-inch (35-cm) cake will serve 25 to 30 guests
- a 12-inch (30-cm) cake will serve 15 to 20 guests
- a 10-inch (25-cm) cake will serve 10 to 15 guests
- an 8-inch (20-cm) cake will serve 8 to 10 guests

You usually can not count the top tier (except on the bill), because it probably will be saved.

20

Sauces and Fillings

Sauces

  Apricot Sauce
  Bijou Coulis
  Blueberry Sauce
  Bourbon Sauce
  Calvados Sauce
  Caramel Sauce I
  Caramel Sauce II
  Cherry Sauce
  Chocolate Sauce
  Cointreau Pear Sauce
  Cranberry Coulis
  Crème Fraîche
  Hot Fudge Sauce
  Kiwi Sauce
  Kumquat Sauce
  Mango Coulis
  Mascarpone Sauce
  Melba Sauce
  Mousseline Sauce
  Nougat Sauce
  Orange Sauce
  Persimmon Sauce
  Pineapple Sauce
  Plum Sauce

  Pomegranate Sauce
  Raspberry Sauce
  Red Currant Coulis
  Rhubarb Sauce
  Romanoff Sauce
  Strawberry Sauce
  Sour Cream Mixture
    for Piping
  Vanilla Custard Sauce
  White Chocolate Sauce

Fillings

  Chantilly Cream
  Cherry Filling
  Chocolate Cream
  Chunky Apple Filling
  Classic Bavarian Cream
  Crème Parisienne
  Ganache
  Italian Cream
  Lemon Cream
  Lemon Curd
  Lime Cream
  Mazarin Filling
  Pastry Cream
  Quick Bavarian Cream

The old saying that a cook is judged by his or her sauces, albeit originally said with savory sauces in mind, can be just as true in the pastry kitchen and equally true of fillings. The sauce and filling can be as important as a pretty decoration on a cake. A refreshing red Raspberry Sauce with a dense slice of chocolate cake, rich Caramel Sauce on a warm apple tart, gooey Hot Fudge Sauce on poached pears and vanilla ice cream, Sabayon with a liqueur soufflé, or Strawberry Sauce with sour cream hearts to garnish a Valentine's dessert are all sauces that can really make the dessert something memorable.

Served on the side in a sauceboat, or presented on the plate and enhanced with a piped design, the sauce can add a tremendous amount to the presentation as well as to the flavor of the dessert. As discussed in Chapter 19, Decorations, the current fashion of making elaborate sauce paintings is extremely popular for both desserts and other courses. A particular sauce can also be used to change the feeling of a traditional dessert presentation and add more variety to your menu. For an exotic tropical presentation and a more sophisticated tone, try serving Mango or Papaya Sauce with a chocolate cake instead of the more mundane whipped cream or Crème Anglaise, whenever these fruits are plentiful and inexpensive.

Although many sauces, especially those made with puréed fruit, are quickly prepared, it is much better to have a little left over than to run out in the middle of the service. Many sauces (and fillings) should always be on hand as part of your general *mise en place*. The majority of the following sauces may be stretched by adding a little fruit juice, Simple Syrup, or even borrowing from another similar sauce, as long as this is done early enough and not done excessively. The most common and perfectly acceptable rescue technique is the old trick of reliquefying vanilla ice cream to make a quick Sauce Anglaise (any of the sauce that is left over should be discarded). Of course there is another old saying to keep in mind (paraphrased slightly): "As long as there is water in the tap, there is sauce on the menu."

As for fillings, what would a profiterole be without the Bavarian cream inside, or a bear claw without its nutty filling; and Ganache or Lemon Curd can go a long way toward dressing up and flavoring many other pastries and petits fours. A rich, moist filling can also come to your rescue in saving a slightly overbaked or stale sponge (the emphasis here is on slightly—don't expect a miracle if the sponge is really finished).

Just like sauces, different fillings can be used with the same shell to create a greater selection without increasing the work proportionately. Fill an assortment of tartlet shells with Mazarin Filling, Ganache, Pastry Cream topped with fresh fruit, and Caramel Walnut Filling. Garnish them appropriately and you will have four entirely different pastries. If these fillings are kept on hand (along with a supply of Short Dough), this can be done with very little effort.

Sauces

Dessert sauces can be generally categorized as follows, although there are many variations of each, as well as hybrids that combine two or more types. Thickeners are used to give the sauce a certain amount of viscosity. The emulsion process is one way to thicken some types of sauces, as is the process of reduction. By far, the most common way to thicken a dessert sauce is by using a thickening ingredient such as cornstarch, arrowroot, gelatin, or pectin.

Caramel Sauces

Caramel sauces are prepared by melting and caramelizing sugar to the desired color, and then adding a liquid to thin it to a saucelike consistency. For the most basic caramel sauce nothing else is added. For a richer caramel sauce, cream and/or butter are incorporated. Other flavorings are sometimes added, for example, a spirit such as Calvados.

Chocolate Sauces

Chocolate sauces are used extensively and may be either hot or cold, and either thin for masking a plate or very rich and thick as in a fudge sauce. A basic chocolate sauce is made from chocolate and/or cocoa powder, sugar, and water cooked together. Richer versions contain the addition of cream and/or butter.

Coulis

A coulis is made by puréeing fruits, berries, or vegetables or forcing them through a sieve. In the pastry kitchen the term is used for berry juices and fruit purées that are sweetened as needed, usually strained, and then served as sauces. These are neither thickened nor binded. Though the title has gained popularity only in the last ten years or so, it is actually very old and was used as long as 600 years ago to refer to strained gravy or broth served with savory dishes. It comes from the Old French word *coleis,* an adjective used for "straining, pouring, flowing, or sliding," which in turn came from the same Latin source as the English word *colander.* Fruit coulis may be prepared using raw or cooked fruits; the most well-known is raspberry coulis.

Custard Sauces

The foundational custard sauce is crème anglaise, also known as vanilla custard sauce (I refer to it as the "Mother Sauce" of the pastry kitchen). Not only can many other sauces be prepared from this base, such as chocolate or coffee-flavored custard sauces, but the ingredients and method of preparation for crème anglaise are the starting point for many other dessert preparations as well (see Figure 20–1, page 1082). Custard sauces are made by thickening milk, cream, or half-and-half with eggs. The desired flavoring is added—vanilla, in the case of crème anglaise.

Fresh Cream or Sour Cream Sauces

Crème fraîche, Devonshire cream, clotted cream, and sour cream are all used as dessert sauces (and toppings), sometimes thinned and/or sweetened. They most frequently accompany fresh fruit but are also served with warm baked fruit desserts such as an apple tart. These may be flavored with vanilla or a spice—for example, cinnamon. Fresh cream is used as a sauce both in the form of heavy cream that is lightly thickened by whipping and whipped cream (or chantilly cream), which is really more of a topping.

Sabayon Sauces

Sabayon sauces can be hot or cold and are made by thickening wine— marsala in the case of the Italian version zabaglione—by whipping it over heat, together with egg yolks and sugar. Sabayon sauces are served with fruit and with souffles. Sabayon is also served as a dessert by itself.

Starch-Thickened Sauces

Most fruit sauces are thickened with starch. In my recipes I generally use cornstarch, but arrowroot can be substituted. A lesser amount must be used however, to achieve the same results and should be added at the end to the hot liquid on the stove (after dissolving it in water or fruit juice). Conversely, cornstarch-thickened sauces should be brought to a quick boil to allow the starch to gelatinize and to eliminate the raw starch taste. In addition to starch-thickened fruit sauces, this method is used for sauces made of cream or milk and sauces based on spirits or liqueurs.

 ## Apricot Sauce

approximately 4 cups (960 ml) sauce

2 pounds, 8 ounces (1 kg, 135 g) pitted fresh apricots
3 cups (720 ml) water
3 ounces (85 g) granulated sugar
2 tablespoons (16 g) cornstarch
2 tablespoons (30 ml) water

NOTE: The yield of this recipe will vary depending in the ripeness of the apricots.

1. Cut the apricots into quarters. Place in a saucepan with the first measurement of water and the sugar. Bring to a boil, then cook over medium heat until the fruit is soft. This will take approximately 10 minutes, depending on the ripeness of the fruit.

2. Strain the mixture, forcing as much of the flesh as possible through the strainer with the back of a spoon or ladle. Discard the contents of the strainer. Pour the sauce back into the saucepan.

3. Dissolve the cornstarch in the remaining water. Stir into the sauce. Bring the sauce back to a boil and cook for about 1 minute to remove the flavor of the cornstarch. Store the sauce covered in the refrigerator. If the sauce is too thick, thin it with water to the desired consistency.

VARIATION
Apricot Sauce from Canned Apricots

4 cups (960 ml) sauce

2 pounds, 8 ounces (1 kg, 135 g) strained apricots canned in syrup
2 cups (480 ml) liquid from canned apricots
2 tablespoons (16 g) cornstarch
2 tablespoons (30 ml) water

With such a variety of fresh fruit available from all over the world today, I am opposed to using fruit from a can just because a particular fruit is out of season. However, apricots are one of the few exceptions. Their season is too short to take full advantage of this delicious fruit, and because Apricot Sauce compliments so many different desserts, it is welcome all year round.

Follow the directions in the preceding recipe, replacing the first measurement of water and the sugar with the liquid from the canned apricots and reducing the cooking time in step one to 1 minute.

Bijou Coulis

approximately 4 cups (960 ml) sauce

1 pound (455 g) fresh or frozen raw cranberries

Use the IQF type if you use frozen raspberries. (IQF stands for individually quick frozen. Frozen fruit given this designation does not have any added sugar.) If you must use raspberries frozen in sugar syrup, you may want to decrease the sugar in the recipe. The coulis should be tangy.

8 ounces (225 g) granulated sugar

1/2 cup (120 ml) water

1 pound (455 g) fresh or frozen
raspberries

1. Combine the cranberries, sugar, and water in a saucepan. Bring to a boil, then reduce the heat and simmer for approximately 10 minutes or until the cranberries begin to pop open. Remove from the heat.

2. Transfer the cranberries to a food processor. Add the raspberries and purée. Strain through a fine mesh strainer. Discard the pulp and seeds. If the coulis is too thick, thin with water. Store in the refrigerator.

Blueberry Sauce

*approximately 3 cups
(720 ml) sauce*

7 ounces (200 g) granulated sugar

1 1/2 cups (360 ml) cranberry juice

1 tablespoon (15 ml) lime juice

2 tablespoons (16 g) cornstarch

3 tablespoons (45 ml) rum

1 dry pint (480 ml) or 12 ounces
(340 g) blueberries

NOTE: Due to the large amount of pectin in blueberries, the sauce may set up too much. Reheat, stirring, until liquid and smooth again, then adjust with water or Simple Syrup, depending on the level of sweetness.

1. Place the sugar, cranberry juice, lime juice, cornstarch, and rum in a saucepan. Bring to a boil and cook for a few minutes.

2. Remove from the heat and stir in blueberries. Let cool. Store covered in the refrigerator.

Bourbon Sauce

*approximately 4 cups
(960 ml) sauce*

6 egg yolks (1/2 cup/120 ml)

4 ounces (115 g) granulated sugar

3/4 cup (180 ml) bourbon whiskey

1 tablespoon (15 ml) vanilla extract

1 1/2 cups (360 ml) heavy cream,
approximately

1. Whip the egg yolks and sugar together just to combine. Whisk in the bourbon. Place over simmering water and whisk constantly until the mixture has thickened to the ribbon stage. Remove from the heat and whip until cold. Add the vanilla.

2. Whip the heavy cream until thickened to a very soft consistency. Stir into the yolk mixture. Adjust the consistency as desired by adding more heavy cream to thin it or more whipped cream to make it thicker. Serve cold or at room temperature. Bourbon Sauce may be stored covered in the refrigerator for three or four days. If the sauces separates, whisk it to bring it back together.

Calvados Sauce

*approximately 3 cups
(720 ml) sauce*

2 pounds (910 g) tart cooking apples
2¹/₂ cups (600 ml) unsweetened
    apple juice
1 cup (240 ml) white wine
12 ounces (340 g) granulated sugar
one cinnamon stick
¹/₃ cup (80 ml) lemon juice
2 tablespoons (16 g) cornstarch
¹/₂ cup (120 ml) Calvados,
    approximately

NOTE: The leftover apple purée can be refrigerated or frozen and used in apple pie filling or served as applesauce.

1. Peel the apples, core, and cut into thin slices. Place in a heavy-bottomed saucepan with the apple juice, white wine, sugar, cinnamon stick, and lemon juice. Bring to a boil, then reduce the heat and cook slowly until the apples are very soft and begin to fall apart. Do not allow any more of the liquid to evaporate than is necessary.

2. Remove the cinnamon stick and purée the apple mixture. Strain through a fine mesh strainer (*étamé*). Reserve the solids for another use (see note).

3. Dissolve the cornstarch in a few tablespoons of the apple liquid and add this mixture to the remaining apple liquid. Bring to a boil and cook for a few seconds to eliminate the cornstarch taste.

4. Remove from the heat and pour into a storage container. Stir in the Calvados, adjusting the amount in accordance with the consistency and flavor desired.

 ## Caramel Sauce I

*approximately 4 cups
(960 ml) sauce*

2 pounds (910 g) granulated sugar
1 teaspoon (5 ml) lemon juice
1¹/₂ cups (360 ml) water,
    approximately

1. Place the sugar and lemon juice in a small, heavy-bottomed saucepan. Cook, stirring constantly with a wooden spoon, over medium heat until all of the sugar has melted. Continue to heat the sugar until it reaches the color desired.

2. Immediately remove the pan from the heat and carefully pour in the water. Stand back a little as you do this because the syrup may splatter.

3. Return to the heat and cook, stirring constantly, to melt any lumps if necessary.

4. Let the sauce cool completely, then add additional water as needed to thin to the proper consistency. You must wait until the sauce has cooled before judging the thickness, because it will vary depending on the degree to which you caramelized the sugar.

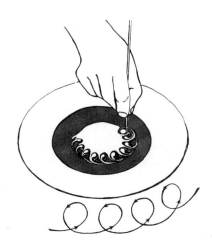

Caramel Sauce II

*approximately 3 cups
(720 ml) sauce*

1 pound (455 g) granulated sugar
$^1/_3$ cup (80 ml) water
$^1/_2$ teaspoon (2.5 ml) lemon juice
2 tablespoons (30 ml) glucose or light
    corn syrup
$1^1/_2$ cups (360 ml) heavy cream
2 ounces (55 g) unsalted butter

*T*his is a rich caramel sauce that is intended to be served hot. It will be quite thick when it has cooled, even to room temperature. If the sauce is to be used to mask a plate, for example, you should thin it with water to the desired consistency (or you can use Caramel Sauce I). Caramel Sauce II is perfect for serving with ice cream or apple or pear tarts.

1. Place the sugar, water, and lemon juice in a small saucepan. Bring to a boil. Brush down the sides of the pan with a clean brush dipped in water. Add the glucose or corn syrup. Cook over medium heat until the syrup reaches a golden amber color.

2. Remove the pan from the heat and add the heavy cream carefully. Stand back as you pour in the cream as the mixture may splatter. Stir to mix in the cream. If the sauce is not smooth, return the pan to the heat and cook, stirring constantly, to melt any lumps.

3. Add the butter (with the pan off the heat). Keep stirring until the butter has melted and the sauce is smooth.

Cherry Sauce

2 cups (480 ml) sauce

1 pound (455 g) fresh cherries or
    sweet canned cherries
8 ounces (225 g) granulated sugar,
    approximately
$1^1/_2$ cups (360 ml) red wine
grated zest from one lemon
2 tablespoons (16 g) cornstarch
1 teaspoon (5 ml) vanilla extract

NOTE: I like to use Bing cherries when I can get them, because their dark skin gives the sauce a rich color. If you use canned cherries, strain out the syrup and reserve for another use, such as Black Forest Cake, or discard. You may want to adjust the amount of sugar, depending on the type of cherries and wine used.

1. Pit the cherries and place them in a saucepan together with the sugar, wine, and lemon zest. Bring to a boil and cook over medium heat until the cherries are soft (canned cherries will only need to cook about 5 minutes). Purée the mixture, then strain. Discard the solids in the strainer.

2. Dissolve the cornstarch in a small amount of the puréed liquid. Stir into the remainder. Bring to a boil and cook for a few seconds. Remove from the heat and add the vanilla. Cherry Sauce can be served hot or cold.

Chocolate Sauce

*approximately 4¹/₂ cups
(1 l, 80 ml) sauce*

2 cups (480 ml) water
10 ounces (285 g) granulated sugar
¹/₂ cup (120 ml) glucose or light corn
syrup
4 ounces (115 g) unsweetened cocoa
powder, sifted
1 pound (455 g) sweet dark chocolate,
melted

*NOTE: As with Caramel Sauce I and II,
Chocolate Sauce is much thinner when it is hot;
if you plan to serve the Chocolate Sauce cold, let
it cool to room temperature first, then add water
if it is too thick. If the sauce has been refrigerated, warm it up to room temperature before
adjusting. The recipe as is makes a fairly thick
sauce when cold, ideal to cover a pear for example, but it is too thick to mask a plate without
adding water. On the other hand, if you want
the sauce to be thicker, incorporate additional
melted chocolate (warming the sauce first).*

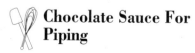 ## Bitter Chocolate Sauce

Chocolate Sauce For
Piping

*This is a versatile recipe that can be kept on hand to serve either hot or cold.
It is best suited to garnish a dessert—a slice of cake, a pastry, or poached
fruit, for example. If you serve the sauce as one of the main components of the
dessert, most notably with ice cream, use Hot Fudge Sauce (see page 1074)
instead.*

1. Combine the water, sugar, and glucose or corn syrup in a
saucepan. Bring to a boil and then remove from the heat.

2. Add enough of the syrup to the cocoa powder to make a soft
paste, stirring until the mixture is completely smooth. Gradually add
the remaining syrup to the paste.

3. Add the melted chocolate, and stir until combined. If necessary,
strain the sauce before serving.

*Replace 3 ounces (85 g) of the melted sweet dark chocolate with an equal
amount of melted unsweetened chocolate. Increase the water by ¹/₂ cup
(120 ml).*

*This sauce is used to pipe designs and decorate other sauces as part of many
dessert presentations (see page 998). To make the most attractive designs
and prevent the sauces from bleeding together, make the Chocolate Sauce the
same consistency as the other sauce you are using. Adjust the Chocolate Sauce
by adding water to make it thinner, or melted chocolate to thicken it (warm the
sauce first to prevent lumps).*

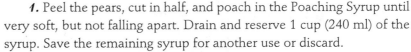

 ## Cointreau Pear Sauce

approximately 4 cups (960 ml) sauce

5 pounds (2 kg, 275 g) pears
   (approximately nine medium-sized)
two recipes Spiced Poaching Syrup
   (page 13)
2 tablespoons (30 ml) lemon juice
1/2 cup (120 ml) water
4 tablespoons (32 g) cornstarch
1/4 cup (60 ml) Cointreau liqueur
granulated sugar, as needed

1. Peel the pears, cut in half, and poach in the Poaching Syrup until very soft, but not falling apart. Drain and reserve 1 cup (240 ml) of the syrup. Save the remaining syrup for another use or discard.

2. Remove the pear cores and stems. Place the pears in a food processor together with the reserved syrup and purée until smooth. Strain the mixture and discard the contents of the strainer. Add the lemon juice to the purée.

3. Stir enough of the water into the cornstarch to dissolve it. Add the cornstarch mixture and the remaining water to the pear purée. Bring the mixture to a boil. Remove from the heat and stir in the Cointreau. Let cool. Add sugar to sweeten as needed, and/or thin with water if the sauce is too thick.

 ## Cranberry Coulis

3 cups (720 ml) sauce

12 ounces (340 g) fresh or frozen
   cranberries
8 ounces (225 g) granulated sugar
2 cups (480 ml) water

1. Combine the cranberries, sugar, and water in a saucepan. Bring to a boil, then reduce the heat and simmer for 10 minutes. The cranberries should be soft and have popped open.

2. Remove from the heat. Purée immediately and strain. Bring back to a quick boil, then let cool.

3. Skim off any foam that has formed on the surface. Store the Cranberry Coulis covered in the refrigerator but serve at room temperature. If the coulis is too thick after it has cooled, thin it with water.

 ## Crème Fraîche

2 cups (480 ml)

1 ounce (30 g) sour cream
2 cups (480 ml) heavy cream

1. Stir the sour cream into the heavy cream. Let stand at 80–90°F (26–32°C) for 24 hours. An oven with a pilot light, or the top of a stove with pilots, are possible places to maintain this temperature. Store covered in the refrigerator.

2. To thicken the cream, whip until you achieve the desired consistency.

Hot Fudge Sauce

4 cups (960 ml) sauce

5 ounces (140 g) unsweetened cocoa
    powder, sifted
6 ounces (170 g) light brown sugar
6 ounces (170 g) granulated sugar
1¼ cups (300 ml) heavy cream
8 ounces (225 g) unsalted butter
½ teaspoon (3 g) salt

*NOTE: This sauce must be served warm
because it becomes much too thick when cold or
even at room temperature. Reheat leftover sauce
over simmering water.*

1. Thoroughly combine the cocoa powder, brown sugar, and granulated sugar.

2. Place the cream, butter, and salt in a saucepan over low heat.
Melt the butter in the cream and bring the mixture to scalding.

3. Whisk in the sugar and cocoa mixture gradually to avoid lumps.
Cook over low heat, stirring constantly with the whisk, until the sugar
has dissolved and the mixture is smooth. Serve immediately or keep
warm over a hot water bath (bain-marie).

 ## Kiwi Sauce

*approximately 4 cups
(960 ml) sauce*

2 tablespoons (18 g) unflavored
    gelatin powder
⅓ cup (80 ml) cold water
2 pounds, 8 ounces (1 kg, 135 g) ripe
    kiwifruit (approximately twelve)
6 ounces (170 g) granulated sugar

*NOTE 1: If you would like to include some of
the distinctive black seeds in the sauce, strain
the purée through a chinois rather than an
étamé. Some of the pulp will come through as
well, making the sauce less smooth. You can get
around this to some extent by first straining all
of the seeds through a piece of cheesecloth and
then adding a few back in without adding any
pulp. The cheesecloth works well in this
instance because the pulp tends to stick to
the fabric.*

*NOTE 2: Kiwi Sauce will lose its brilliant
green color if the temperature goes too high.
Because of this, Kiwi Sauce is not thickened
with cornstarch as are the other fruit sauces in
this book.*

1. Sprinkle the gelatin over the cold water and set aside to soften.

2. Peel the kiwifruit. Process in a food processor just to purée. If the
fruit is processed for too long, many of the black seeds will break and
give the sauce a muddy appearance. Strain the purée through a fine
mesh strainer (*étamé*) (see note 1).

3. Add the sugar and softened gelatin mixture to the strained kiwi
juice. Heat the mixture to approximately 110°F (43°C), stirring constantly. Be careful not to overheat (see note 2). Remove from the heat
and, if necessary, continue stirring until all of the gelatin is dissolved.
Store covered in the refrigerator. If the sauce sets or becomes too thick
during storage, carefully warm it, stirring constantly, until it reaches the
desired consistency.

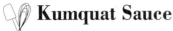

Kumquat Sauce

approximately 4 cups (960 ml) sauce

1 pound (455 g) kumquats
1½ cups (360 ml) water
2 tablespoons (16 g) cornstarch
2 cups (480 ml) fresh orange juice, strained (about six oranges)
8 ounces (225 g) granulated sugar

NOTE: Adjust the amount of sugar to taste depending on the sweetness of the citrus.

1. Slice the kumquats (do not peel them). Place the fruit and the water in a saucepan and bring to a boil. Cook until the kumquat slices have softened, about 5 minutes. Remove from the heat.

2. Add the cornstarch to a small amount of the orange juice and mix to dissolve. Mix this back into the remaining orange juice. Pour the mixture into a noncorrosive saucepan.

3. Purée the kumquat mixture and strain it into the orange juice, pressing as much of the liquid as possible through the strainer. Discard the contents of the strainer. Add the granulated sugar (see note). Bring the sauce to a boil, lower the heat, and cook for 30 seconds stirring constantly. Remove from the heat and let the sauce cool completely before using. If the sauce is too thick, thin it with water. Store covered in the refrigerator.

Mango Coulis

4 cups (960 ml) coulis

3 pounds, 8 ounces (1 kg, 590 g) ripe mangoes (five to six)
¼ cup (60 ml) lime juice, approximately
¼ cup (60 ml) orange juice, approximately

1. Use only perfectly ripe mangoes. They should yield easily to light pressure and have a pleasant, sweet smell. Unfortunately, the ripe fruits are also extremely difficult to peel. I have found the best way to overcome this is to slice off the two broader sides as close to the large flat seed as possible, then scoop out the flesh from these halves, and discard the skin. Cut and scrape the remaining flesh away from the seed.

2. Place the mango pulp in a food processor along with the lime and orange juices. Purée; then strain out the stringy fibers using a fine mesh strainer (*étamê*). Bring the purée to a quick boil. Adjust the flavor and consistency with additional lime or orange juice as desired. Store covered in the refrigerator.

Mascarpone Sauce

about 4 cups (960 ml) sauce

1 pound, 5 ounces (595 g) Mascarpone Cheese (page 9), at room temperature
3 tablespoons (45 ml) amaretto liqueur
1¼ cups (300 ml) half-and-half, approximately

NOTE: In a pinch you can make a quick version of mascarpone cheese by combining three parts soft cream cheese with one part sour cream, mixing just until smooth.

1. Thoroughly combine the cheese, liqueur, and half-and-half, mixing until completely smooth.

2. Adjust the amount of half-and-half as necessary to make the sauce thin enough to flow out when poured. Store covered in the refrigerator, but serve at room temperature.

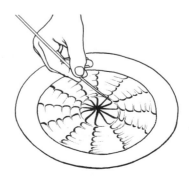

Melba Sauce

*approximately 4 cups
(960 ml) sauce*

1 pound, 12 ounces (795 g) fresh, ripe
    red raspberries or thawed IQF
    frozen raspberries
4 ounces (115 g) red currant jelly
3 tablespoons (24 g) cornstarch
granulated sugar, as needed
2 tablespoons (30 ml) kirschwasser

There are many versions of this classic sauce. The original was invented by Auguste Escoffier to compliment Peach Melba, a dessert he created for Dame Nellie Melba at a dinner given by the duke of Orléans in 1892 to celebrate her success in the opera Lohengrin, *although, actually, Melba Sauce was not used the first time Peach Melba was served. On the occasion of the special dinner Escoffier presented the ice cream and peaches inside a swan made of ice and topped the creation with spun sugar. It was not until the opening of the Carlton Hotel some eight years later that the dessert made it onto one of his menus where it was served with raspberry purée. The modern versions of Melba Sauce usually include either red currant jelly and/or kirsch liqueur.*

1. Purée the raspberries with the red currant jelly. Strain through a fine mesh strainer and discard the seeds. Measure, and add water if necessary to make 4 cups (960 ml) of juice.

2. Place the cornstarch in a saucepan. Add enough of the raspberry juice to liquefy the cornstarch. Stir in the remaining raspberry juice. Bring the sauce to a boil and sweeten with sugar if necessary. Remove from the heat and stir in the kirschwasser. Let cool and then thin with water if the sauce is too thick. Store covered in the refrigerator.

Mousseline Sauce

*approximately 4 cups
(960 ml) sauce*

3 ounces (85 g) granulated sugar
6 egg yolks (1/2 cup/120 ml)
1/3 cup (80 ml) boiling water
1 teaspoon (5 ml) vanilla extract
1 1/2 cups (360 ml) heavy cream,
    approximately

NOTE: In the recipes in this book Mousseline Sauce is usually flavored with a spirit or liqueur that is complimentary to a particular dessert. If you are serving this sauce with a dessert that does not specify a flavoring, you may want to add 1/4 cup (60 ml) of the liqueur or spirit of your choice.

1. Whip the sugar and egg yolks together just to combine. Whisk in the boiling water. Place the bowl over simmering water and thicken to the ribbon stage, whipping constantly. Remove from heat and whip until cool. Add the vanilla.

2. Whip the heavy cream until thickened to a sauce-like consistency. Combine with the yolk mixture. If needed, thin the sauce with a little heavy cream. If the sauce is too thin for your particular use, thicken by mixing in additional softly whipped cream. Store the Mousseline Sauce covered in the refrigerator for three to four days. If the sauce should separate, whisking will bring it back together.

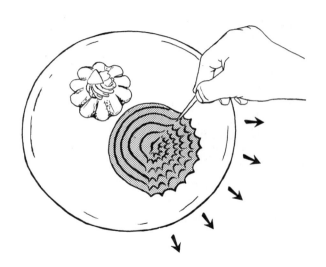

Nougat Sauce

4 cups (960 ml) sauce

3 ounces (85 g) granulated sugar
6 egg yolks (½ cup/120 ml)
⅓ cup (80 ml) boiling water
½ cup (120 ml) Nougat Flavoring
(recipe follows)
1¼ cups (300 ml) heavy cream

1. Whip the sugar and egg yolks just to combine. Whisk in the boiling water. Place the mixture over simmering water and heat, whipping constantly, until thickened to the ribbon stage. Add the Nougat Flavoring and remove from the heat.

2. Whip the heavy cream until it forms soft peaks. Combine with the egg yolk mixture. If the sauce is too thick, thin with a little additional water. Store covered in the refrigerator.

 Nougat Flavoring

1½ cups (360 ml)

1 pound (455 g) granulated sugar
1 teaspoon (5 ml) lemon juice
1 cup (240 ml) water
3 tablespoons (45 ml) amaretto
liqueur
1 tablespoon (15 ml) hazelnut liqueur

1. Place the sugar and lemon juice in a heavy-bottomed saucepan. Cook, stirring constantly, until the sugar reaches the light caramel stage.

2. Remove the pan from the heat and add the water. Be very careful; the hot caramel might splatter, so stand back. Place the pan back on the stove. Heat, stirring out any lumps, until the caramel is smooth. Let cool.

3. Add the liqueurs. Cover and store at room temperature.

 Orange Sauce

*approximately 4 cups
(960 ml) sauce*

4 cups (60 ml) strained fresh orange
juice (ten to twelve oranges)
5 tablespoons (40 g) cornstarch
2 tablespoons (30 ml) lemon juice
6 ounces (170 g) granulated sugar,
approximately

NOTE: When refrigerated overnight, the sauce will set to a jelly-like consistency. This occurs because of the large amount of natural pectin present in oranges. Forcing the sauce through a fine mesh strainer is usually all that is needed to make it smooth again, but if necessary, reheat to thin it.

1. Add enough orange juice to the cornstarch to make it liquid. Stir this into the remaining orange juice. Add the lemon juice and sugar, adjusting the taste by adding more or less sugar as needed, depending on the sweetness of the orange juice.

2. Heat to boiling in a stainless-steel or other noncorrosive pan. Lower the heat and cook for 1 minute while stirring constantly. Let cool completely. If the sauce is too thick, thin with water. Store covered in the refrigerator.

Bitter Orange Sauce

1. Follow the recipe for Orange Sauce with the following changes: Cut the peel of half of the oranges into about six pieces each and add these to the juice. It is not necessary to strain the juice now as directed. Follow the procedure for making the Orange Sauce, including the peels with the juice.

2. Set the sauce aside to allow the peels to macerate for 30 minutes. Strain to remove the orange peel as well as any pits or sediment.

Persimmon Sauce

about 2 cups (480 ml) sauce

1³/₄ cups (420 ml) strained persimmon pulp (see step one)
3 tablespoons (45 ml) lime juice
2 tablespoons (30 ml) orange juice, approximately
2 tablespoons (30 ml) honey
2 teaspoons (5 g) cornstarch

1. Hachiya persimmons have a slightly oblong shape and are pointed at the bottom end. They are very high in tannin and can be eaten raw only when fully ripe (the fruit should be almost jelly-like throughout). The smaller Fuyu persimmon is shaped like a tomato. It has very little tannin and can therefore be eaten raw before it is completely ripe and soft. This persimmon is easy to peel using a vegetable peeler. When either variety is very ripe and soft to the point of falling apart, just remove the stems, purée with the skin on, and then force the purée through a fine strainer.

2. Combine the persimmon pulp, lime juice, orange juice, and honey.

3. Add just enough water to the cornstarch to make it liquid. Add to the persimmon mixture and bring to a boil. Remove from the heat and thin with additional orange juice if desired.

Pineapple Sauce

about 3¹/₂ cups (840 ml) sauce

two medium-sized fresh, ripe pineapples (about 2 pounds/910 g each, unpeeled and including the crown)
3 tablespoons (24 g) cornstarch
8 ounces (225 g) granulated sugar, approximately
1 tablespoon (15 ml) lime juice
1 tablespoon (15 ml) light rum

1. Rinse, remove the crowns, peel the pineapples, and cut away the cores (save to use for pineapple drink, see page 481, if desired).

2. Dice 5 ounces (140 g) of the pineapple flesh into ¹/₄-inch (6-mm) pieces; reserve. Purée the remaining pineapple very fine in a food processor. Strain through a fine mesh strainer, pressing on the solids with a spoon to force out as much of the juice as possible. Discard the solids.

3. Dissolve the cornstarch in a small amount of the pineapple juice, then stir back into the remainder together with the sugar.

4. Bring the mixture to a boil and cook over medium heat, stirring constantly, for about 1 minute. Remove from the heat, stir in the diced pineapple, lime juice, and rum. Cool, then store covered in the refrigerator.

Plum Sauce

4 cups (960 ml) sauce

2 pounds, 8 ounces (1 kg, 135 g) fresh
   pitted plums
   or
2 pounds (910 g) drained canned
   pitted plums
3 cups (720 ml) water or liquid from
   canned plums
6 ounces (170 g) granulated sugar
3 tablespoons (24 g) cornstarch

1. Santa Rosa or Casselman plums are good choices when in season, but in any case use a red or purple variety of plum, which will give the sauce a pleasant pastel red color. Cut fresh plums into quarters.

2. Reserve ¼ cup (60 ml) of the water or canning liquid and place the plums in a saucepan with the remaining liquid and the sugar (if you are using canned plums packed in syrup, omit the sugar). Bring to a boil and cook over medium heat until the fruit is soft enough to fall apart, approximately 15 minutes for fresh plums, 1 minute for canned.

3. Remove from the heat and strain, forcing as much of the pulp as possible through the strainer using the back of a spoon or ladle. Discard the contents of the strainer.

4. Dissolve the cornstarch in the reserved liquid. Add to the sauce. Return the mixture to the saucepan and bring to a boil. Cook for 1 minute to remove the taste of the cornstarch. Serve hot or cold. When served cold the sauce may need to be thinned with water. Store covered in the refrigerator.

 ## Pomegranate Sauce

approximately 4 cups (960 ml) sauce

3 pounds (1 kg, 365 g) pomegranate
   seeds (approximately twelve
   medium-sized pomegranates;
   see note)
3 cups (720 ml) water
6 ounces (170 g) granulated sugar
3 tablespoons (24 g) cornstarch
1 cup (240 ml) grenadine

NOTE: Removing the multitude of seeds from each fruit can be quite time-consuming. If you are able to plan ahead, you can cut the time needed for this task nearly in half by freezing the pomegranates solidly and then thawing them before attempting to remove the seeds. For a more rustic looking sauce, reserve ½ cup (120 ml) of the seeds and add them to the sauce together with the grenadine.

1. Place the pomegranate seeds, water, and sugar in a heavy-bottomed saucepan. Bring to a boil and cook over medium heat for about 5 minutes. Remove from the heat.

2. Use a handheld food processor to break open the seeds, processing for only a few seconds—you should not pulverize the white seeds, just release the juice.

3. Strain through a fine mesh strainer (*étamé*), pressing hard with a kitchen spoon to extract as much of the juice as possible. Discard the solids in the strainer. (If you are only making a small amount, you can skip the food processor step and go straight to forcing the juice through the fine strainer with a spoon, but it takes longer.) Return the sauce to the pan, bring to a boil, and reduce by half.

4. Add just enough cold water to the cornstarch to make it liquid. Stir the mixture into the pomegranate juice. Bring back to a boil and cook for 10 to 15 seconds to eliminate the taste of the cornstarch. Stir in the grenadine. Cool and store covered in the refrigerator. If the sauce is too thick, thin it with water.

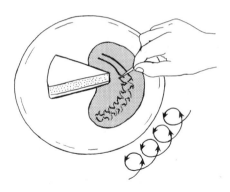

Raspberry Sauce

approximately 4 cups (960 ml) sauce

2 pounds (910 g) fresh ripe raspberries or thawed IQF frozen raspberries (see introduction to Bijou Coulis, page 1068)

3 tablespoons (24 g) cornstarch

2 ounces (55 g) granulated sugar, approximately

NOTE: *To make Blackberry Sauce, substitute blackberries for the raspberries.*

1. Purée the berries. Strain out the seeds using a fine mesh strainer. Measure and add water if necessary to make 4 cups (960 ml) of juice.

2. Place the cornstarch in a saucepan. Mix enough of the juice into the cornstarch to liquefy it, then stir in the remaining juice.

3. Heat the sauce to simmering. Add the granulated sugar, adjusting the amount as needed, depending on the sweetness of the berries.

4. Simmer the sauce for 1 minute. Cool and thin with water, if necessary. Store covered in the refrigerator.

Red Currant Coulis

4 cups (960 ml) sauce

2 pounds (910 g) fresh or frozen red currants (see note)

3/4 cup (180 ml) dry white wine

10 ounces (285 g) granulated sugar

NOTE: *If you use fresh currants, remove the stems before weighing the berries. If fresh are not available, use the IQF frozen berries (these do not contain sugar) and do not thaw before weighing. Once thawed, the juice separates from the berries and collects at the bottom.*

1. Combine the red currants, wine, and sugar in a saucepan. Bring to a boil and then remove from the heat.

2. Purée the mixture, strain through a fine mesh strainer, and discard the solids in the strainer.

3. Let the sauce cool, then thin with water if needed. Store the coulis covered in the refrigerator.

Rhubarb Sauce

4 cups (960 ml) sauce

3 pounds (1 kg, 365 g) fresh rhubarb stalks

1 1/2 cups (360 ml) water

1 pound, 8 ounces (680 g) granulated sugar

4 tablespoons (32 g) cornstarch

1. Wash the rhubarb. Trim both ends off each stalk, then cut across into 1/2-inch (1.2-cm) pieces. Place the rhubarb pieces in a saucepan together with the water and sugar. Cook over medium heat just until the rhubarb falls apart.

2. Place a strainer over a second saucepan. Strain the rhubarb mixture into the pan, pressing hard on the contents of the strainer with the back of a wooden spoon to force as much of the juice as possible into the pan. Discard the rhubarb in the strainer.

3. Stir enough cold water into the cornstarch to dissolve it, then stir into the rhubarb liquid. Bring the sauce to a boil and cook for about 1 minute to eliminate any cornstarch flavor. Cool to room temperature, then store covered in the refrigerator. If necessary, thin with water before serving.

Romanoff Sauce

*approximately 4 cups
(960 ml) sauce*

3 cups (720 ml) heavy cream
1 cup (240 ml) sour cream

1. Mix the heavy cream with the sour cream and whip them together until the mixture has thickened to the consistency of molasses.

2. If the sauce is not to be used immediately, adjust the consistency at serving time by whipping the sauce to thicken it or adding additional heavy cream to thin it. Store the sauce, covered, in the refrigerator.

Strawberry Sauce

*approximately 4¹/₂ cups
(1 l, 80 ml) sauce*

3 pounds (1 kg, 365 g) fresh ripe
   strawberries
2 tablespoons (16 g) cornstarch
4 ounces (115 g) granulated sugar

NOTE: When strawberries have white shoulders around the hull together with a little white on the tip (or nose), they are called "cat-faced." This usually occurs once a year when one of the growing regions gets hit with rain, forcing a cooler area to pick its berries before they are fully ripe. These immature berries are inexpensive but bland and without much color. If you have no choice but to use them, add a small amount of raspberry juice or Beet Juice (see page 3) to make the sauce more appealing.

1. Purée the strawberries. Strain through a fine mesh strainer. Measure and add water if necessary to make 4 cups (960 ml) of juice.

2. Place the cornstarch in a saucepan. Mix enough of the juice into the cornstarch to liquefy it, then stir in the remaining juice.

3. Heat the sauce to simmering. Add the sugar, adjusting the amount as needed, depending on the sweetness of the strawberries.

4. Simmer the sauce for a few minutes. Cool and thin with water, if necessary. Store covered in the refrigerator.

Sour Cream Mixture for Piping

heavy cream
sour cream

NOTE: The sour cream mixture and the sauce must have the same consistency for decorating. If the sour cream is too thick it will not blend with the sauce but break up into pieces instead. If it is too thin, it will run into the sauce, and you will not get clearly defined lines. The sauce, too, must be of the proper consistency to begin with: if it is too thin it cannot be decorated at all.

This is a much easier and quicker method than thickening the cream by whipping, and because such a small amount is actually eaten, the flavor of the sour cream is not noticeable. Instructions for using sour cream mixture in decorating are given on pages 998 to 1006.

1. Gradually stir enough heavy cream into sour cream until the mixture is approximately the same consistency as the sauce you are decorating.

2. Use as directed in the individual recipes. This mixture will keep for days in the refrigerator, but it may have to be thinned.

Vanilla Custard Sauce (*Crème Anglaise*)

*approximately 6 cups
(1 l, 440 ml) sauce*

12 egg yolks (1 cup/240 ml)
10 ounces (285 g) granulated sugar
1 quart (960 ml) half-and-half
one vanilla bean, split
   or
1 tablespoon (15 ml) vanilla extract

NOTE: The sauce can be made up much more quickly if you cook it directly over low heat. Of course, this is a little more tricky. Should you overheat and curdle the sauce, you can usually save it by adding 2 tablespoons (30 ml) heavy cream and processing in a blender, providing the sauce has only curdled and not scorched.

Vanilla Custard Sauce is prepared using the same basic method that is used to make the custard for vanilla ice cream. I use half-and-half, rather than milk, which is used classically, so that the chilled sauce can be frozen in an emergency to make ice cream. The resulting ice cream will not be quite as rich as usual but, as they say, "in a storm any port will do." You can do the opposite and thaw vanilla ice cream if you run out of Vanilla Custard Sauce (depending on the richness of the ice cream, you will need to either thin the ice cream a bit with some milk or half-and-half or thicken it with lightly whipped heavy cream). This sauce tastes especially nice with apple or pear tarts, and it can be flavored to compliment many different desserts. Like any heated mixture containing eggs, Vanilla Custard Sauce is a perfect breeding ground for bacteria, so follow strict sanitary guidelines.

The ingredients and technique used to make Vanilla Custard Sauce or Crème Anglaise are the beginning of many classical dessert preparations, as shown in Figure 20–1.

1. Combine the egg yolks and sugar in a mixing bowl. Whip until light and fluffy.

2. Bring the half-and-half to the scalding point with the vanilla bean, if used. Gradually pour the hot cream into the yolk mixture while stirring rapidly.

3. Place the mixture over simmering water and heat slowly, stirring constantly, until it is thick enough to coat the back of a spoon. Be very careful not to get it hotter than 190°F (88°C) or it will curdle.

Vanilla Custard Sauce (*Crème Anglaise*)
Ingredients: Egg yolks, granulated sugar, vanilla bean or extract, and half-and-half
Preparation: Egg yolks and sugar are whipped together until light and fluffy. Half-and-half is scalded with vanilla bean, if used. Scalded half-and-half is added to the egg yolks and sugar, and the mixture is thickened over simmering water. If vanilla extract is used, it is added after thickening.
If frozen, Vanilla Custard Sauce becomes **Vanilla Ice Cream**.

To Make						
↓	↓	↓	↓	↓	↓	↓
Crème Brûlée	**Pots de Crème**	**Crème Caramel**	**Pastry Cream**	**Bavarian Cream**	**Sabayon**	**Mousseline Sauce**
The half-and-half is replaced with heavy cream. The mixture is thickened further by baking in a water bath in the oven.	Whole eggs are added. The mixture is thickened further by baking in a water bath in the oven.	The yolks are replaced with whole eggs. The half-and-half is replaced with milk. The mixture is thickened further by baking in a water bath in the oven (caramelized sugar is first added to the bottom of the forms).	The yolks are replaced with whole eggs. The half-and-half is replaced with milk. Starch is added.	The yolks are replaced with whole eggs. The half-and-half is replaced with whole milk. Gelatin is added. After cooling, whipped cream is added and the mixture is thickened further in the refrigerator.	The half-and-half is replaced with wine. The vanilla is omitted.	The half-and-half is replaced with water. Whipped cream and liqueur are added after cooking. If frozen, it becomes **Basic Bombe Mixture**

FIGURE 20–1 A comparison of other desserts and dessert preparations in relation to Vanilla Custard Sauce (Crème Anglaise)

4. Immediately pour the custard into another container and continue stirring for a minute or so. Remove the vanilla bean and save for another use, or stir in the vanilla extract. Set the sauce aside to cool, stirring from time to time. When cold, store covered in the refrigerator. The sauce will keep this way for up to one week.

 ## White Chocolate Sauce

approximately 4 cups (960 ml) sauce

1 cup (240 ml) water
10 ounces (285 g) granulated sugar
½ cup (120 ml) glucose or light corn syrup
1 pound, 2 ounces (510 g) white chocolate

1. Combine the water, sugar, and glucose or corn syrup in a saucepan and bring the syrup to a boil. Remove from the heat and set aside to cool a bit.

2. Cut the white chocolate into small pieces so that it will melt quickly and evenly. Place in a bowl over a bain-marie and make sure the water is only simmering, not boiling. Stir the chocolate constantly until it is melted, never letting the chocolate get too warm on the bottom and sides of the bowl. (Ignoring these rules can cause the chocolate to become gritty and unusable.)

3. Add the melted chocolate to the warm sugar syrup and stir until combined. Before serving, adjust the consistency of the sauce as needed by adding additional melted chocolate to thicken it (warm the sauce lightly first) or water to make it thinner. White Chocolate Sauce may be served hot or cold. Store covered at room temperature for a few days or refrigerate for longer storage.

Fillings

 ## Chantilly Cream

6 cups (1 l, 440 ml) whipped filling

2 cups (480 ml) well-chilled whipping cream
1 teaspoon (5 ml) vanilla extract
1 tablespoon (15 g) granulated sugar

NOTE: Chantilly Cream must be refrigerated. It will break if left at room temperature for more than a short period of time.

Chantilly Cream takes its name from the chateau of Chantilly outside Paris, where the famous chef Vatel worked in the mid-1800s. The only difference between Chantilly Cream and sweetened whipped cream is the addition of vanilla in the form of either sugar, powder, or extract. Chantilly Cream should have a light and fluffy texture. If you do not have whipping cream, only manufacturing or heavy whipping cream, add 15 percent cold milk to the cream before whipping.

1. Chill the bowl and the whip attachment of an electric mixer. Pour the cream and the vanilla into the bowl. Start whipping at high speed. Add the sugar.

2. Keeping a watchful eye on the progress, continue whipping until stiff peaks form, or to the consistency specified in the individual recipes. Use as soon as possible.

🍴 Cherry Filling

*approximately 4 pounds
(1 kg, 820 g) filling*

2 pounds (910 g) drained sweet
    canned cherries (see step one)
3 cups (720 ml) liquid from canned
    cherries
Simple Syrup (page 11), if needed
2 tablespoons (30 ml) raspberry juice
2 ounces (55 g) cornstarch
2 ounces (55 g) pectin powder
2 ounces (55 g) granulated sugar

*B*ecause cornstarch will break down, making the filling watery after a few
days of storage, pectin powder is used in addition to cornstarch to offset this
problem. Use regular fruit-canning pectin rather than pure pectin for this recipe.

1. When you drain the juice from the cherries, press the cherries
firmly without crushing them. The liquid must be completely drained
off or the filling will be too runny. Measure the liquid; if there is not
enough, add Simple Syrup to make up the difference.

2. Add the raspberry juice to the cherry liquid. Dissolve the cornstarch in a small amount of the mixture before stirring into the remainder. Mix the pectin powder with the sugar. Blend into the cherry liquid
mixture.

3. Bring the sauce to a boil, stirring constantly. Cook over medium
heat until completely thickened, about 5 minutes.

4. Remove from the heat and add the drained cherries. Place a
piece of baking paper directly on the surface to prevent a skin from
forming as the filling cools. Store the filling covered in the refrigerator.

🍴 VARIATION
Fresh Cherry Filling

*approximately 4 pounds
(1 kg, 820 g) filling*

2 pounds (910 g) Bing or Lambert
    cherries
3 cups (720 ml) Plain Poaching Syrup
    (page 13)
2 tablespoons (30 ml) raspberry juice
1/4 cup (60 ml) lemon juice
2 ounces (55 g) cornstarch
2 ounces (55 g) pectin powder

1. Wash, remove the stems, and pit the cherries.

2. Cook the cherries in Poaching Syrup until tender, 4 to 5 minutes.
Strain, reserving the cherries and the syrup separately.

3. Combine the raspberry juice, lemon juice, cornstarch, and pectin
powder, and stir to dissolve the cornstarch. Add this mixture to the
reserved syrup.

4. Bring the mixture to a boil, stirring constantly. Cook over
medium heat until completely thickened, about 5 minutes.

5. Remove from the heat and add the drained cherries. Place a
piece of baking paper directly on the surface to prevent a skin from
forming as the filling cools. Store the filling covered in the refrigerator.

🍴 Chocolate Cream

*4 pounds, 6 ounces (1 kg, 990
g) or 9¹/₂ cups (2 l, 280 ml) filling*

5 ounces (140 g) sweet dark chocolate
2 ounces (55 g) unsweetened
    chocolate
1/2 cup (120 ml) Simple Syrup
    (page 11)
3 pints (1 l, 440 ml) heavy cream

1. Cut the chocolates into small pieces. Place in a bowl and melt
over simmering water. Remove from the heat and stir in the Simple
Syrup.

2. Whip the cream until is becomes slightly thickened. Be careful:
If you overwhip the cream it will break when you add the chocolate
(see note).

3. Place a small amount of the whipped cream in a bowl and
quickly fold in the chocolate mixture; do not whisk it in. Add the rest

NOTE: The Chocolate Cream is likely to break if the chocolate mixture is too hot; it should be approximately 110°F (43°C). The filling can also break if the cream does not contain at least 36 percent butterfat, but unfortunately this is somewhat harder to control.

of the cream and mix in. If the Chocolate Cream seems runny, stir it until the consistency becomes firmer.

Chunky Apple Filling

2 pounds, 12 ounces (1 kg, 250 g) or 5 cups (1 l, 200 ml) filling

3 pounds (1 kg, 365 g) Granny Smith, pippin, or Golden Delicious apples (about seven)
10 ounces (285 g) granulated sugar, approximately
¼ cup (60 ml) water
4 teaspoons (20 ml) lemon juice

1. Peel and core the apples. Chop approximately two-thirds of the apples into ½-inch (1.2-cm) pieces.

2. Place the chopped apples in a saucepan with the sugar, water, and lemon juice. Adjust the amount of sugar according to the tartness of the apples and your own taste. Stir to combine and cook over medium heat, stirring from time to time, until the mixture starts to thicken.

3. Chop the remaining apples into ¼-inch (6-mm) pieces and add them to the filling as it begins to thicken.

4. Continue cooking the filling until the apple chunks are soft and the filling has reached a jam-like consistency. Let cool at room temperature, then store covered in the refrigerator.

Classic Bavarian Cream

2 quarts (1 l, 920 ml); enough for sixteen individual 4-ounce (120-ml) or two 1-quart (960-ml) charlotte molds

8 egg yolks (⅔ cup/160 ml)
8 ounces (225 g) granulated sugar
2 tablespoons (18 g) unflavored gelatin powder
½ cup (120 ml) cold water
2 cups (480 ml) milk
one vanilla bean, split
    or
1 teaspoon (5 ml) vanilla extract
2 cups (480 ml) heavy cream

1. Whip the egg yolks and sugar until light and fluffy. Reserve.

2. Sprinkle the gelatin over the cold water and set aside to soften.

3. Bring the milk to the scalding point with the vanilla bean, if used. Gradually pour the hot milk into the yolk mixture while whipping rapidly. Return the mixture to the heat and bring back to the scalding point, stirring constantly. Do not boil.

4. Remove from the heat and stir in the reserved gelatin. Set aside to cool at room temperature, stirring from time to time.

5. Whip the cream to soft peaks. Remove the vanilla bean from the custard and save for another use, or add the vanilla extract, if used. When the custard has cooled to body temperature, slowly stir it into the cream.

6. Pour into molds or use as directed in the individual recipes.

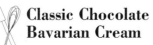

Classic Chocolate Bavarian Cream

*D*ecrease the gelatin to 4 teaspoons (12 g) and add 8 ounces (225 g) melted sweet dark chocolate when you stir in the gelatin.

Crème Parisienne (Chocolate Whipping Cream)

2 quarts (1 l, 920 ml) or 4 pounds, 8 ounces (2 kg, 45 g) cream

10 ounces (285 g) sweet dark chocolate
1 quart (960 ml) heavy cream
3/4 cup (180 ml) milk
3 ounces (85 g) granulated sugar

Crème Parisienne can be used for most of the recipes in this book that call for chocolate added to whipping cream, either as is or, if applicable, with gelatin added. This cream will not break (which can happen when you add warm melted chocolate to whipped cream that is too low in butterfat), because its fat content has been increased by whipping the cream with the chocolate already added. Crème Parisienne must be made at least 12 hours before it is to be whipped (or it will not whip up), but it can be stored in the refrigerator unwhipped for up to one week and used as needed. This can be a real time-saver if, for example, you are filling Chocolate Éclairs or a similar pastry every day.

1. Chop the chocolate into small pieces and reserve.

2. Bring the cream, milk, and sugar to a boil in a saucepan. Remove from the heat and stir in the chopped chocolate. Continue to stir until the chocolate is completely dissolved. Cool and refrigerate for at least 12 hours before whipping.

3. To use, whip as you would whipping cream.

Ganache

6 pounds, 4 ounces (2 kg, 845 g) or 9 1/2 cups (2 l, 280 ml) ganache

8 egg yolks (2/3 cup/160 ml)
8 ounces (225 g) granulated sugar
2 teaspoons (10 ml) vanilla extract
3 pounds, 8 ounces (1 kg, 590 g) sweet dark chocolate
1 quart (960 ml) heavy cream

NOTE: If a skin or crust forms on the top during storage, pour hot water on top of the Ganache, let it stand for 1 minute, then pour the water off. If needed, Ganache can be stored in the freezer for months. If the sugar has recrystallized, or if all of the sugar was not dissolved in the first place, heat the Ganache in a saucepan over low heat, stirring constantly, until all of the sugar crystals have dissolved, around 150°F (65°C).

In its most basic form Ganache is simply equal parts chocolate and cream by weight. Other ingredients such as butter and/or egg yolks can also be included together with flavorings if desired. It is a very rich mixture that has many different uses in the pastry kitchen. It can be used warm as a glaze, for filling and decorating cakes or pastries, or as the filling for a basic truffle. The ratio of chocolate to cream determines the consistency of the product after it cools. This recipe can easily be adjusted to individual needs: For a firmer Ganache add more chocolate; for a softer Ganache, decrease the amount. By not over-working the Ganache when adding flavorings or when softening it, you will preserve the rich, dark color. If you do want a lighter and fluffier Ganache, whip in air by first softening the Ganache over simmering water, then whipping at full speed for a few minutes.

1. Whip the egg yolks, sugar, and vanilla until light and fluffy.

2. Cut the chocolate into small pieces, place in a saucepan, and add the cream. Heat to 150°F (65°C), stirring constantly.

3. Stir the hot cream mixture into the egg yolk mixture and keep stirring for a minute or so to make sure the sugar is melted. If you plan to whip air into the Ganache, keep stirring on low speed until it is cold, then whip it for a few minutes until it is light and fluffy.

4. Let the Ganache cool and store it in airtight containers to use as needed. Ganache can be stored at room temperature for up to one week; it should be refrigerated for longer storage.

Italian Cream

7 cups (1 l, 680 ml) filling

2 cups (480 ml) heavy cream
2 teaspoons (10 ml) vanilla extract
one-quarter recipe Italian Meringue
   (page 591)

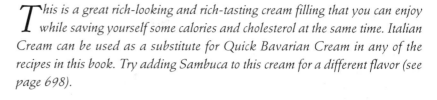

This is a great rich-looking and rich-tasting cream filling that you can enjoy while saving yourself some calories and cholesterol at the same time. Italian Cream can be used as a substitute for Quick Bavarian Cream in any of the recipes in this book. Try adding Sambuca to this cream for a different flavor (see page 698).

1. Whip the heavy cream and vanilla to soft peaks.

2. Fold the cream into the Italian Meringue. Refrigerate until needed. This filling should be used the same day it is made.

 ## Lemon Cream

7 cups (1 l, 680 ml) filling

3 cups (720 ml) lemon juice
$^1/_2$ cup (120 ml) orange juice
finely grated zest of six lemons
finely grated zest of two oranges
2 tablespoons (16 g) cornstarch
1 pound, 8 ounces (680 g) granulated
   sugar
12 eggs
6 ounces (170 g) unsalted butter
$^3/_4$ cup (180 ml) heavy cream

1. Combine the lemon juice, orange juice, lemon zest and orange zest. Set aside.

2. Mix the cornstarch into the sugar. Beat the eggs and the sugar mixture for a few seconds (just to combine) in a heavy saucepan made of stainless-steel or another noncorrosive material; do not use aluminum. Add the juice and zest mixture, then the butter and heavy cream.

3. Bring to the scalding point, stirring constantly, over medium heat; do not boil. Strain immediately. Use hot, as directed in individual recipes, or cool, then store covered in the refrigerator. Lemon Cream can be stored for two to three weeks.

 ## Lemon Curd

5 cups (1 l, 200 ml) filling

1$^1/_2$ cups (360 ml) lemon juice
finely grated zest of eight lemons
8 eggs
1 pound, 8 ounces (680 g) granulated
   sugar
12 ounces (340 g) unsalted butter

Lemon Curd makes an excellent flavoring or filling and can also be used as a sauce by thinning with additional lemon juice or with Simple Syrup. You will need approximately eight medium-sized lemons for the juice in the recipe.

1. Combine the lemon juice and zest.

2. Beat the eggs and sugar together in a heavy stainless-steel or other noncorrosive saucepan. Do not use aluminum. Add the lemon juice and zest and the butter.

3. Heat to boiling over low heat. Cook for a few seconds, stirring constantly, until the curd thickens. Strain immediately. Cool and use as needed. Lemon Curd will keep for weeks stored covered in the refrigerator.

Lime Cream

2 cups (480 ml) filling

1³/₄ cups (420 ml) freshly squeezed
    lime juice (approximately seven
    limes)
finely grated zest from three limes
3 eggs
8 ounces (225 g) granulated sugar
2 ounces (55 g) unsalted butter
¹/₄ cup (60 ml) heavy cream

Mazarin Filling

*4 pounds, 10 ounces
(2 kg, 105 g) filling*

1 pound, 14 ounces (855 g) Almond
    Paste (page 3)
6 ounces (170 g) granulated sugar
14 ounces (400 g) soft unsalted butter
2¹/₂ cups (600 ml) eggs
3 ounces (85 g) bread flour

NOTE: As with any uncooked filling that contains a large number of eggs, Mazarin Filling should be used right away to ensure the maximum volume in baked pastries.

Pastry Cream

6 pounds (2 kg, 730 g) custard

2 quarts (1 l, 920 ml) milk
two vanilla beans, split
    or
2 teaspoons (10 ml) vanilla extract
5 ounces (140 g) cornstarch
1 pound (455 g) granulated sugar
1 teaspoon (5 g) salt
6 eggs

1. Combine the lime juice and the grated zest. Set aside.

2. Beat the eggs and sugar together in a heavy noncorrosive saucepan, just long enough to combine (do not use an aluminum pan). Add the juice and zest mixture, the butter, and the heavy cream. Bring the mixture to the scalding point, stirring constantly over medium heat. Do not boil.

3. Remove from the heat and strain immediately. Set aside to cool.

4. Stored covered in the refrigerator, the Lime Cream can be kept for two to three weeks. Thin with water if necessary before using.

*M*azarin Filling is virtually the same as frangipane and one can be substituted for the other. It is an almond-based filling used in numerous European pastries and tarts. In addition to giving the paste a delicious flavor, the almonds absorb moisture, which helps baked goods made with this filling stay fresh longer than average.

1. Place the Almond Paste and sugar in a mixer bowl. Add the soft butter gradually while mixing on low speed, using a paddle.

2. After all of the butter has been incorporated and the mixture is smooth, mix in the eggs a few at a time, then mix in the flour. Store the Mazarin Filling in the refrigerator. Bring to room temperature to soften, then stir until smooth before using. Use as directed in the individual recipes.

*M*aking Pastry Cream is one of the basic techniques that anyone involved with cooking (pastry shop or otherwise) should master, because Pastry Cream has so many applications. In an emergency, it can be thinned and used as a sauce; it is a base for soufflés; it is a filling and flavoring for cakes; and it can be used as a topping for Danish or other pastries. In the pastry kitchen, there should always be a supply of Pastry Cream in the refrigerator.

Since Pastry Cream is made with cornstarch to stabilize the eggs, there is no danger of overheating and curdling it, as can happen, for example, with Vanilla Custard Sauce. Of course, you must still watch the heat and stir constantly to avoid burning it or having it lump.

1. Place the milk and the vanilla bean(s) (if used) in a heavy-bottomed saucepan. Bring to a boil.

2. Keeping an eye on the milk, mix the cornstarch, sugar, and salt in a bowl using a whisk. Gradually add the eggs, and mix until smooth.

One-quarter Recipe

1 pound, 8 ounces (680 g) custard

1 pint (480 ml) milk
one-half of a vanilla bean, split
   or
$^1/_2$ teaspoon (2.5 ml) vanilla extract
4 tablespoons (32 g) cornstarch
4 ounces (115 g) granulated sugar
$^1/_4$ teaspoon (1 g) salt
2 eggs

NOTE: If the heat is too high or you are stirring too slow at the point when the Pastry Cream reaches a boil, it will lump. If this happens, pass it through a strainer immediately, before it cools.

Quick Bavarian Cream

approximately 3 pounds, 12 ounces (1 kg, 705 g) or 9 cups (2 l, 160 ml) filling

$1^1/_2$ cups (360 ml) heavy cream
$^1/_2$ teaspoon (2.5 ml) vanilla extract
one-half recipe Pastry Cream
   (preceding page)

3. Slowly add about one-third of the hot milk to the egg mixture while whisking rapidly. Pour the tempered egg mixture back into the remaining milk.

4. Place over medium heat and cook, stirring constantly, until the mixture comes to a boil and thickens. Boil for a few seconds longer to make sure the raw starch taste has disappeared. Remove the vanilla bean(s), rinse and save for another use, or add the vanilla extract, if used.

5. Pour the custard into a bowl and cover with a piece of baking paper. When cooled, store in the refrigerator. If made and stored properly, Pastry Cream will keep fresh for up to four days. However, when it is that old it should only be used for pastries in which it will be baked.

*A*lthough not a classic Bavarian Cream, this is a timesaving version that uses Pastry Cream, a stock item in most pastry kitchens, as a prefabricated base. This eliminates the need for making a custard and waiting for it cool. If you do not have Pastry Cream on hand, you might want to make the Classic Bavarian Cream instead (see page 1085). If you are making Pastry Cream specifically to use in this recipe, make it far enough in advance so that it is thoroughly chilled before you combine it with the whipped cream, or you will risk breaking the cream.

1. Whip the heavy cream and vanilla to stiff peaks.

2. Fold the whipped cream into the Pastry Cream. Use as directed in the individual recipes.

Appendix A

Ingredients

Alcoholic Flavorings
Butter, Lard, and Margarine
Chocolate and Chocolate Products
Coffee
Cream and Milk
Eggs
Flour
Fruit
Herbs and Spices
Jellying Agents
Leavening Agents
Nuts
Rice
Salt
Sweeteners
Tartaric Acid
Tea
Thickeners
Tofu
Vanilla

Alcoholic Flavorings

Amaretto   A fruit-based liqueur from Italy. The primary flavor comes from sweet and bitter almonds.

Arrack   The fermented and distilled product of palm juice, raisins, and dates. Arrack has a very strong and distinctive aroma and is used in desserts and candies.

Brandy   Distilled from wine, brandy is classified by these labels: E—extra special, F—fine, M—mellow, O—old, P—pale, S—superior, V—very, and X—extra. V.S.O.P. means "very superior old pale."

Calvados   Apple brandy from France originating in the Normandy region. Known in America as applejack.

Chambord   A liqueur made from black raspberries and other fruits with herbs and honey.

Cognac   A type of brandy made in the vicinity of Cognac, a town in the Charente region of France.

Cointreau   A colorless French liqueur flavored with the peel of curaçao oranges and other oranges. In most cases it is interchangeable with Grand Marnier.

Crème de Cacao   A chocolate-flavored liqueur from France.

Crème de Cassis   A liqueur made from black currants.

Framboise (Raspberry Brandy)   A spirit distilled from fermented raspberry juice. Framboise is colorless and very strong. Framboise is classified as an eau-de-vie, as is any colorless spirit or brandy made from fruit juice. Framboise is also the French word for raspberry.

Frangelico   An Italian liqueur derived primarily from hazelnuts but flavored with berries and flowers as well.

Grand Marnier   A French liqueur made with oranges and aged cognac.

Kirschwasser   A colorless brandy distilled from the juice of a small black cherry found in the southern part of Germany. Also known as kirsch.

Madeira   A fortified sweet wine from the island of Madeira.

Maraschino   A liqueur made from the Amarasca cherry, it can be used as a substitute for kirschwasser.

Marsala   An Italian dessert wine originating from the Sicilian town of Marsala.

Rum   Rum is a spirit distilled from fermented sugarcane juice and/or molasses. The islands of the Caribbean Sea produce most of the world's rum supply. The lighter amber or golden-colored rums are produced for the most part in Puerto Rico and the Virgin Islands, while the heavier and darker varieties come primarily from the islands of Jamaica, Cuba, and Barbados. Sugarcane grown along the banks of the Demerara River in Guyana is used to make the strongest and darkest rum. Rum must be at least 60 proof by law (30 percent alcohol), but most brands are 80 proof, with the extreme being 151 proof rum, which is very convenient for flambé work since it will ignite without being heated. Rum is used extensively in the pastry shop.

The rum trade played an important role in shaping world events during Colonial times through the 1600s and 1700s as it developed in conjunction with the growth of sugar plantations in the West Indies. Starting in the 1600s, distilleries operating in New York and New England produced rum made from molasses that was imported from the West Indies. Rum became part of a trade cycle in which the profits from American rum were used to buy slaves in Africa, and the slaves were then traded in the West Indies for more molasses that became New England rum. During this era, rum was the prevailing alcohol of the poor in the Colonies, and it was not uncommon for some to enjoy it with breakfast, lunch, and dinner. By the year 1775 Americans were reportedly consuming an astonishing four gallons per person per year. This exorbitant consumption declined sharply with the decrease in sugar and molasses importation brought about by the passage of the Molasses Act and the Sugar Act, which virtually wiped out rum production in the Colonies. The heavy duties levied on imported molasses were an important factor in creating the unrest that ultimately led to the Revolutionary War.

Sambuca   Sambuca is a colorless, anise-flavored liqueur from Italy. *Sambucas Nigra* is the Italian name for the elder shrub, an attractive bush with honeysuckle-shaped leaves, clusters of tiny scented white flowers, and violet-black berries—elderberries. The name *sambuca* was given to the liqueur because elder was originally used as a flavoring agent. The traditional way of serving sambuca in Rome is flambéed with one or two dark-roasted coffee beans floating on top (referred to in Italian as *con la mosca,* "with the fly"). This is said to bring good luck. Sambuca has a sweet licorice taste and is very strong for a liqueur, 42 percent alcohol or 84 proof.

Whiskey   Made from distilled grain, usually rye, corn, wheat, or barley.

Butter, Lard, and Margarine

Butter   A good quality butter is made up of at least 80 percent fat and not more than 15 percent water. The remaining 5 percent is mineral matter, such as salt and milk solids. Because of its low melting point and wonderful aroma, butter is indispensable in the making of first-rate pastries, especially those made with buttercream and

puff pastry. In hot climates, a small amount of margarine must be added to the butter to make it workable. Two types of butter are used in cooking and baking: salted and unsalted, or sweet. All of the recipes in this book use sweet butter, but salted butter can be substituted if the salt in the recipe is reduced by approximately 1/5 ounce (6 g) for every 1 pound (455 g) of butter. You can not substitute salted butter, however, if there is little or no salt in the recipe or if the main ingredient is butter. Sweet butter should not be kept at room temperature for more than a day; it should be stored in the refrigerator or freezer.

Clarified Butter   Clarified butter is butter with the milk solids removed. It has a higher burning point than whole butter, which makes it preferable for frying. To clarify butter, melt it over low heat and let it bubble for a few minutes. Remove it from the heat and let it stand for about 10 minutes. Skim off all of the foamy solids on top and carefully spoon or pour the clear butterfat into a clean container. Discard the milky residue in the bottom of the pan.

Lard   Lard is almost 100 percent refined pork fat. The highest quality lard is pork leaf fat; lard from other sources must be labeled "rendered pork fat." Lard is excellent for frying and is unbeatable for making flaky pie dough because of its elasticity and shortening power. It can be kept for months if stored covered in a cool place.

Margarine   Margarine is made up of about 80 percent fat, 18 percent water, and 2 percent salt (unless it is unsalted). There are two types of margarine: oleomargarine, which is made from beef and veal fat with vegetable and/or other oils added, and vegetable margarine, which was created as a substitute for butter and is made from corn or soybean oil. Oleomargarine is made primarily for the baking industry and has been developed to meet various demands of baking professionals. Some oleomargarines are purposely made tough and with a high melting point; others cream well and are best in baked goods. If kept for a long time, margarine should be stored in a dark, dry place below 70°F (21°C).

Noisette Butter, or *Beurre Noisette*   This is the French term for "brown butter." To prepare *beurre noisette,* cook the butter over low heat until it reaches a light brown color and is fragrant. Be careful not to burn the butter.

Chocolate and Chocolate Products

(For information on chocolate production, see pages 880 and 881.)

Coating Chocolate   Coating chocolate can be dark, light, or white and is also referred to as confectionery coating, non-temp, and baker's chocolate; white coating chocolate is sometimes called "summer icing." Because there is no cocoa butter in coating chocolate (it has been replaced with other fats), it does not need to be tempered like real chocolate, so it is very convenient to use. Coating chocolate is used for ornaments and for decorating many items in the pastry shop. Products made entirely of coating chocolate may not be labeled as chocolate.

Cocoa Butter   Cocoa butter is the fat extracted from cocoa mass using a hydraulic press. Its uses include thinning chocolate, candy production, coating marzipan figures for shine and to prevent them from drying out rapidly, plus noncooking uses, including the manufacture of cosmetic creams and lotions.

Couverture   Couverture is a term used by some chocolate manufactures for their product. Although *couverture* is French for "coating" or "to coat," it is not the same as coating chocolate. Couverture can be dark, light, or white, and it often has a higher ratio of cocoa butter.

Sweet Dark Chocolate   Dark chocolate is cocoa paste finely ground and conched, with the addition of extra cocoa butter, sugar, and vanilla. Dark chocolate should contain a minimum of 20 percent total cocoa butter. Dark chocolate is used in fillings such as ganache and in a multitude of chocolate desserts. Tempered dark chocolate is used for decorations and coating candies and pastries.

Sweet Light Chocolate, or Milk Chocolate   Light chocolate or milk chocolate is made in the same way as dark chocolate with the addition of milk powder. Milk chocolate must contain at least 15 percent milk solids, 3 to 4 percent of which should be milk fat. The total fat content must be at least 25 percent, and the maximum sugar content is 50 percent. Light or milk chocolate is used in much the same way as dark chocolate.

Unsweetened Chocolate   Also known as cocoa block, bitter chocolate, and baking chocolate. Unsweetened chocolate is made from cocoa paste that has been finely ground and conched; the cocoa butter content should be at least 50 percent. Unsweetened chocolate is used as a flavoring and coloring agent for fillings, marzipan, mousses, and many other products; it is not eaten plain.

Unsweetened Cocoa Powder   Unsweetened cocoa powder is the finely ground product of the pressed cake that remains after the cocoa butter has been extracted from the cocoa mass. It should contain a minimum of 20 percent fat. There are two types of unsweetened cocoa powder: Dutch process, in which the powder is processed with an alkali, which gives it a smoother flavor and a bit darker color (this is the unsweetened cocoa powder used in this book); and natural unsweetened cocoa powder, which has not been treated and has a slight acid taste. Dutch process cocoa is easier to dissolve in liquid. Unsweetened cocoa powder is used in candy production, decorating pastries and cakes, and flavoring and coloring cake batters and cookies.

Note: Baking soda is commonly used as part of the leavening agent in cakes and other batters that contain unsweetened cocoa powder, because baking soda reacts with an acid. If you are using Dutch process unsweetened cocoa powder, which is neutral and will not react with baking soda, and the recipe does not contain any other acidic ingredient, substitute baking powder and double the measurement.

White Chocolate   White chocolate is not a true chocolate because it does not contain any cocoa solids. White chocolate should be made up of at least 15 percent milk solids (3 to 4 percent of which should be milk fat), a minimum of 20 percent cocoa butter, and a maximum of 55 percent sugar. It is used primarily in the production of candies but has become fashionable to use in mousses, ice creams, and cookies.

Coffee

Most of the civilized world is indebted to Northern Africa as the birthplace of the coffee bean, though the early history of coffee is clouded to the point where it is hard to say which appeared first, the coffee plant or mankind. The first coffee plants were discovered close to Kaffa in southwestern Ethiopia (coffee plants are still found growing wild in many countries today). The small red, seed-bearing coffee "cherries" are sweet and pleasant tasting and were eaten raw long before they were used to make the popular beverage we know today. Around 1000 A.D. the Arabs began making a drink by boiling the raw berries. Through experimentation they discovered that not only would extracting the seeds, or beans, from the cherries and using these alone make an improved drink, but by roasting and grinding the beans before immersing them in boiling water, the flavor was dramatically different and decidedly popular. Once this technique was in place, the consumption of coffee soon became widespread throughout the Islamic countries.

The name *coffee* does not, as one might assume, derive from the name Kaffa, where it was first discovered, but from the Arabic word *gahwah,* which was used for any beverage made from plant material, such as wine, for example. When coffee first reached Europe it was, in fact, known as "the wine of Arabia." Arabia served as a stepping-stone for coffee's universal popularity. In the sixteenth century coffee crossed from Egypt to Constantinople. History has it that it was the Turks who brought to the Western world the first real quality coffee, a great deal of which they left behind after they were defeated in the siege of Vienna during the war of 1683–1699. The enterprising Austrians not only quickly learned how to prepare the aromatic brew, but they also invented the croissant to go with it, in celebration of their victory over the Turks.

Until a little more than 200 years ago, the world was completely dependent on the Arabian region for its coffee supply. But, despite being fiercely protected by the Arabs, plants and fertile beans slipped out, first to the Dutch East Indies, producing the famous Java blend, and then little by little to the West Indies and various parts of Central and South America. Today, Brazil is by far the largest coffee producer in the world.

Coffee is the world's most prized agricultural commodity. The United States is the largest importer, consuming approximately half of the world's supply, but the per capita consumption here does not even come close to that in Scandinavia: In Sweden and Finland average annual consumption exceeds 12 kilos, or almost 27 pounds, of coffee per person. Coffee is an important ingredient in the baking industry; not only is it used as a flavoring agent in baked goods, but it is the drink that is most often consumed with our products, from breakfast pastries to mid-afternoon cakes or cookies, through after-dinner plated desserts.

Growing the beans and preparing them for market is in many ways similar to the production of chocolate. And not only do the flavors of coffee and chocolate marry wonderfully together in many dessert preparations, but wherever cocoa trees thrive, so does the coffee plant, or tree, since it too requires a moist, hot climate.

There are typically two coffee beans in each fleshy coffee cherry, or berry. Occasionally there is only one, in which case it is slightly larger and is called a peaberry. Among the many varieties of the genus *Coffea* that are known, only two species have a significant commercial importance in today's market: The Arabian coffee plant, *Coffea arabica,* and *Coffea robusta.* Arabica trees produce fruit six to eight weeks after flowering, while robusta takes up to one month longer. However, as its name suggests, robusta is heartier, being able to withstand extreme temperatures better, and robusta cherries stay on the tree after they ripen. The arabica cherries fall to the ground when ripe, making their cultivation more labor-intensive since the trees must be monitored and picked over several times.

Coffee trees produce bright white flowers with a wonderful fragrance much like jasmine. Like many members of the citrus family, and again like cocoa trees, the plants produce all of the growth stages simultaneously, from buds to ripe berries. During the last part of their development the berries change from green to amber and then become bright red. Depending on the species and the climate in which they are grown, the fact that the berries ripen at different times on the same tree means that the growers must pick the ripe berries at regular intervals every few weeks—an expensive undertaking—or use what is known as stripping, which means waiting until all of the berries on the tree are ripe before harvesting. This second method can produce contaminated fruit pulp.

Because only the small nuts (the coffee beans) are used, the outer layers, consisting of skin, pulp, mucilage, and parchment, must be removed once the berries are harvested. In what is known as the old method, the whole berries are allowed to dry out as the first step of their preparation, which can take up to twenty days, before the dry pulp is removed. This is not practical in climates with frequent rainfalls or high humidity. In the new method, known as the West Indian process, the berries are moved through a series of water tanks to first separate the ripe and unripe berries. They are then drawn into a pulping machine that crushes the flesh but leaves the parchment skin intact. The pulp is washed off in the next tank, but because the mucilage is not water-soluble, the beans are allowed to ferment slightly at this stage to dissolve the mucilage. The fermentation occurs in shallow water tanks, and the beans are stirred frequently during this time. The unwanted mucilage is then washed away in yet another series of water tanks. After the final washing is completed, the beans, still in their parchment, must be dried (the beans contain over 50 percent moisture). This can be done naturally by spreading the beans out on wicker work racks, or in special drying machines. The natural drying process is considered to produce a superior finished product. After drying, the beans are bagged and transported to processing centers, where they go through one final step to remove the parchment. The beans are then passed through a separator that removes any sand or dust and sorts them according to size. This is followed by careful hand-sorting of the better grades to pick out any undesirable beans. The beans are then packed into sacks.

Before they are ready to compete on the market, the coffee beans are roasted, a process that produces profound changes: The beans become larger and lighter, and they turn from gray green to brown in color. This last change occurs as a result of the conversion of the sugar in the bean into caramel as the beans are heated to between 400 and 450°F (205–230°C). The length of time for roasting varies and is determined by the desired color of the roast; around 30 to 35 minutes is the norm. The beans are turned constantly during roasting to prevent scorching. After roasting they are cooled rapidly. The roasting process develops *caffeol,* a volatile oil that is the main source of the distinctive aroma and flavor of the coffee beverage. The roasted beans are then blended, which is an important part of the coffee industry. The different formulas for various brands and companies are highly guarded secrets. Different beans are mixed to balance flavors. For example, pure mocha beans are a little too acid, while java are typically not acid enough. Just as a winemaker produces the desired product by blending different grape varietals and varying the amount of time allowed for aging, careful blending of different beans, combined with various degrees of roasting, produces the desired strength and flavor of the coffee beverage.

Cream and Milk

Cream   Cream is another name for the fat contained in whole milk. However, in modern dairies, instead of letting it rise to the surface on its own, it is skimmed off using a centrifugal method. Cream is produced and sold under many different names, mostly based on the fat content of the product.

Crème Fraîche   Crème fraîche is a cultured cream made by adding an acid-producing bacteria to pasteurized heavy cream. This produces a smooth, thick, yet pourable texture and a slightly tangy taste.

Half-and-Half   Half-and-half is a mixture of cream and whole milk in equal proportions containing between 10 and 18 percent butterfat.

Heavy Cream   Also called heavy whipping cream, this product should have at least 36 percent butterfat.

Light Cream   The butterfat content of light cream should be between 18 and 30 percent. This product is also known as coffee cream.

Manufacturing Cream   Not usually found in grocery stores, manufacturing cream is produced especially for the food industry. It is made with or without a stabilizer. Manufacturing cream should contain 40 percent butterfat, which, together with the stabilizer, should make it possible to add a slightly warm mixture, such as melted chocolate, to the cream without having it separate. Unfortunately pastry chefs have found out the hard way that this is not necessarily so, and I suspect that manufacturing cream sometimes comes out of the same spigot as whipping cream! In many of the recipes where whipped cream is added to a warm ingredient I add some egg white as a stabilizer for an extra precaution against separation (pasteurized egg whites should be used for this application).

Sour Cream   Sour cream must contain a minimum of 18 percent butterfat, and usually stabilizers and emulsifiers have been added. It is made commercially by adding a bacteria to pasteurized cream to produce lactic acid, and it is then left to culture for about two days. Sour cream can also be made by adding vinegar to pasteurized cream and letting it curdle. This produces an acidified sour cream instead of the usual cultured.

Whipping Cream   This form of cream should have between 30 and 36 percent butterfat. It is sometimes called light whipping cream.

Milk   Milk, in addition to being a nourishing beverage, is one of the most frequently used ingredients in the bakeshop. It contributes to the gluten structure in a bread dough and gives baked goods a nice crust, color, and flavor. Whole milk, fresh from the cow, contains almost 4 percent fat (usually referred to as butterfat) and 8 percent nonfat milk solids; the remaining 88 percent is water. When freshly drawn milk is left undisturbed for several hours, the fat portion will rise to the surface where it can be skimmed off to be used as heavy cream or for making butter. The remaining milk is very rich and would probably taste closer to what we know as half-and-half than the milk we are used to drinking. This raw milk, even if kept cold, has to be consumed within approximately 48 hours and cannot be sold since it has not been pasteurized.

Pasteurization is the process of heating the milk to 160°F (71°C) and holding it at that temperature for 15 seconds, which kills harmful bacteria. This process was invented by and named for Louis Pasteur, a French scientist who in the mid-1800s demonstrated that wine and beer could be preserved by heating them above 135°F (57°C). Milk is usually homogenized after being pasteurized, to ensure that the milk fat is evenly distributed throughout and will not rise to the surface as previously described. Homogenization is essentially achieved by forcing the milk through tiny holes, which breaks up the fat globules into small particles that remain dispersed throughout the liquid.

Milk is available for purchase in many varieties, the names of which, like cream, are based on the fat content of the product. Some of the names are confusing since different manufacturers and different states have their own particular names for certain grades. For example: extra-rich or premium milk, which has slightly more butterfat than regular whole milk, and low fat, which has a little more fat than skim or nonfat milk. There are also some variations in the middle, such as extra light, which falls between low fat and skim. Low fat, skim, light, or nonfat milk should not be substituted for whole milk in a pastry recipe in most cases.

Buttermilk   Buttermilk is made from sweet (or sour) milk after it has been churned to remove the fat. Commercially produced buttermilk, called cultured buttermilk, is made today by adding a bacterial culture to pasteurized skim milk; this converts the milk sugar to lactic acid and gives the buttermilk its characteristic slightly tart taste. Buttermilk is used in pastry recipes containing baking soda, which reacts to its acidity to produce carbon dioxide gas.

Dry Milk, or Milk Powder   Dry milk is produced when milk is rapidly evaporated by being forced through heated cylinders. Dry milk is usually made with skim milk, which gives it a very long shelf life and makes it an ideal substitute where it is impractical or impossible to get the fresh product. It is also used in some instances purely for the sake of convenience.

Evaporated and Condensed Milk   Evaporated milk is produced by heating whole milk to remove approximately 60 percent of the water content. It is then sterilized and canned. It can be reconstituted—made into whole milk again—by mixing it with an equal amount of water by volume. Condensed milk starts the same way, although it is usually not sterilized. It is also available as sweetened condensed milk, which contains 50 percent sugar.

Yogurt   Yogurt is made by adding a special bacteria to milk and holding it at a warm temperature, which causes the milk to ferment and coagulate and produces a tangy flavor. It has a thick custardlike consistency and is eaten plain as well as flavored with berries or other fruits. It is used in the pastry kitchen to prepare churned frozen yogurt and in fillings and sauces, usually in an effort to reduce the fat content of a particular recipe.

Eggs

Fresh Eggs   When eggs are called for in a recipe, the recipe is usually referring to eggs laid by domestic hens. However, eggs from turkeys, ostriches, or ducks can theoretically be used in baking; they are larger, but the basic composition is the same. Another variety of egg that is widely used is quail; they taste very much like chicken eggs, and their petite size makes them popular for hors d'oeuvre preparations.

There is no nutritional or flavor difference between white and brown eggs; the color variations come from different breeds of hens, and the choice is just a matter of personal preference.

Eggs are one of the two structural materials in baking (flour is the other), which makes them indispensable in a pastry shop. The list of uses for eggs is endless: When eggs are combined with flour they create a framework that supports and traps the air in cake batters; egg whites are needed for meringues, mousses, and soufflés; eggs are used to thicken custards; egg wash is used to glaze breads and pastries, and so on. Eggs also contain a natural emulsifier that contributes to smoother batters and creams.

Eggs require very gentle cooking; they start to thicken at just 145°F (63°C). In desserts where eggs are the main ingredient, such as crème caramel, sauce anglaise, and zabaglione, the mixture is cooked over, or in, a water bath to protect the eggs from too high a heat.

The average egg weighs about 2 ounces (55 g); the white is 1 ounce (30 g), the yolk is 2/3 ounce (20 g), and the shell is 1/6 ounce (5 g). All of the recipes in this book use 2-ounce (55-g) eggs (graded as large). If you use eggs of a different size, adjust the number in the recipe accordingly. Eggs are graded for freshness and quality as AA, A, or B; and by size as jumbo, extra large, large, medium, small, and peewee.

Eggs are most commonly sold in the shell. The only reason for not buying eggs in this form is to save the time it takes to crack and empty the shell, which can be significant in a busy bakery. Eggs are sold freshly cracked for the culinary industry in many countries today. Once cracked, however, whole eggs start to deteriorate and lose their whipping power very quickly. When cracked and separated, egg yolks start to form a skin almost immediately, so they must always be kept covered.

The shell of the egg is very porous, allowing the egg to absorb odors or flavors and to lose moisture, even before it has been cracked. Many commercially packaged eggs are coated with mineral oil to decrease moisture loss. It is essential to buy fresh eggs and keep them refrigerated; only those eggs needed for the day's work should be left at room temperature. Conversely, although fresh eggs are desirable, a *very* fresh egg, less than three days old, will not whip as high or increase sufficiently in volume during baking. If you are lucky enough to have a source for just-laid eggs, save them for your breakfast. You can determine the freshness of an egg by placing it in water mixed with 12 percent salt (for example, 1 pint water combined with 3 tablespoons plus 1 teaspoon salt). If the egg is not more than a few days old it will sink to the bottom; if the egg floats to the top, it has spoiled.

Bad eggs are very rare these days due to improved methods of storage and inspection, but it is still a good idea when cracking a large number of eggs to crack a half dozen or so into a small container before emptying them into the big batch. In this way, should you encounter a rotten egg, the entire batch will not be wasted. (On a similar note, you should never crack and add eggs directly over the mixer with the machine running, because if a piece of shell falls in, it will be impossible to retrieve it before it is broken and mixed into the other ingredients.) An egg that is merely sour can be used as long as it is to be baked. Although it will not contribute as much to the volume; the smell and taste of the sour egg will disappear with the heat.

Eggs and Sanitation   Because eggs contain a large amount of protein, they are an ideal breeding ground for bacteria, especially salmonella. Inadequate cooking or unsanitary use or storage of eggs can lead to food-borne illnesses. USDA guidelines state that pasteurization is complete when the egg is heated to 140°F (60°C) and ideally is held there for 2 to 3 minutes. (Pasteurization is defined as heating a liquid to a preset temperature for a specified period of time in order to destroy pathogenic bacteria.) Only fresh and freshly cracked eggs should be used in uncooked dishes. Frozen and precracked egg products should be reserved for use in dishes where they will be completely cooked, such as for baked items.

Storage of Eggs   Proper storage of eggs is of the utmost importance. Eggs will keep for up to four weeks in their shells if held at a temperature below 40°F (4°C).

They will loose quality rapidly if left at room temperature; in fact, eggs will age more in one day left at room temperature than in one week of refrigerated storage. Due to the porous nature of the shell, eggs should be stored away from strongly scented foods that might contaminate them.

Frozen Eggs   Frozen eggs are an excellent substitute for fresh and are very convenient to use. Thaw them slowly in the refrigerator one or two days before you plan to use them (although you can place them under cold running water to thaw in an emergency). Frozen egg whites and yolks can also be purchased separately. It is important to stir any thawed egg product thoroughly before using it.

Dehydrated Eggs   Eggs with the water removed are available in powdered form. They are used primarily by cake-mix and candy manufacturers and are not practical for use in batters that need volume, such as yeast doughs, cakes, and some pastries. Dried egg whites are more widely used in the pastry shop and with excellent results. These are especially useful and convenient for making meringue. Dried egg yolks can be used to make egg wash. Dried eggs, unlike most dehydrated products, are very perishable and must be stored in the refrigerator or freezer tightly sealed.

Flour

Flour is the other of the two structural materials used in baking (eggs are the first), and, like eggs, flour is a vital ingredient in the bakery: it simply would be impossible to make breads or pastries without it. Besides providing backbone and structure in baked goods, flour has four other important functions: generating a characteristic texture and appearance that is derived from the various strengths and types available; contributing to flavor, which comes from the different grains used; providing nutrition—flour contains proteins, carbohydrates, fats, minerals, and vitamins; and acting as a binding and absorbing agent, since upon coming in contact with a liquid, flour absorbs it instead of dissolving. By law, flour must contain no more than 15 percent moisture when it is sold, but it can absorb more moisture if it is not stored properly. (Wheat flour with a high water content does not keep well and will also lose some of its baking ability.) It is also possible for flour to dry out in high altitudes. These two factors are the reason you will often see the word *approximately* after the flour measurement for many of the doughs in this book since the amount required to reach a particular texture will vary with the amount of moisture in the flour.

Wheat Flours   Wheat flour, in a variety of different forms, is the flour used most often in the bakery. There are both "hard" and "soft" wheats. The hard wheats have a lower starch content and contain more of the proteins that will form gluten when the flour comes in contact with water and is kneaded. Flours made from hard wheats (bread flour) are used most often in making breads and in other yeast doughs. Soft wheat flour (cake flour) has a higher starch content and less protein; it is used alone or in combination with other flours in many recipes where a weaker gluten structure is desirable.

Wheat into Wheat Flour   Wheat is a very important cereal crop of the genus *Triticum* belonging to the grass family, *Gramineae*. Wheat was probably first cultivated in the Euphrates Valley nearly 9,000 years ago and has, ever since that time, played a significant role in the feeding of both people and animals. The most important species of wheat include common wheat, *Triticum vulgare*, used in bread; durum wheat, *Triticum durum*, used in pasta products; club wheat, *Triticum compactum*, used in cakes and pastries; and Polish wheat, *Triticum polonicum*. Most species of wheat have hollow stems and long narrow leaves. The heads of the plants contain twenty to one hundred flowers. Fertilization of the flowers is what produces the grain. The wheat plant can be grown in a wide range of environmental conditions but is best cultivated in temperate areas. Wheat cultivation has spread throughout the world through trade. The Spanish brought wheat to the Americas in 1519.

For thousands of years the sickle was the most common method used to harvest wheat, and threshing was done by beating to separate the kernels from the hulls. Mechanical inventions greatly advanced these processes in the nineteenth century. Wheat is usually stored on the farm after harvest in anything from simple pits and earthen containers to more sophisticated wood, steel, or cement storage structures. The wheat is next moved to the local elevator and then shipped to terminal elevators, which in turn supply the processors or ship to export locations. Because many different kinds of flour are made, wheat of different qualities is separated for delivery to mills that manufacture particular products.

The production process used to turn the grain into flour is called milling. The wheat kernel is made up of 83 percent endosperm, 14 percent bran, and 3 percent germ, which is the seed. The bran provides cover for the germ and endosperm and would serve as food for the seed if it were to grow into a strand of wheat. The process of milling is not done merely to pulverize the kernel but also to separate these three parts. If the kernel were simply to be finely crushed, it would essentially produce a very crude form of whole wheat flour which, although very uncomplicated to make, does not store well since it still contains the germ, which has a small percentage of fat and can therefore turn rancid. In the first step of the milling process the wheat is cleaned and tempered (warmed) and is then ground and broken before it is passed through a series of rollers to be ground into a finer consistency. The crushed wheat is then sifted through a series of screens with increasingly finer mesh. This product then goes through the pulveriser, which, using a series of sifters, separates the bran from the endosperm. The endosperm, still containing the germ, is then passed through more reducing rollers, which press the germ into flakes (possible because of its fat content) and small particles. The flattened germ and the endosperm can now be separated by sifting. Wheat germ oil is extracted from the wheat germ flakes, and the flakes are marketed separately from the flour. The resulting flour now has a greater shelf life since the germ has been removed. (In the commercial production of whole wheat flour some of the germ and the bran are ultimately recombined with the flour, bringing the composition close to that of the original wheat kernel.) The flour is then bleached and stored to mature; at this stage it is known as straight flour. Some manufacturers use potassium bromate to increase the yield (called bromating the flour), a controversial procedure that is banned in some areas. There is no nutritional difference between bleached and unbleached flour, although unbleached flour has a higher market value. It is more expensive because it takes longer (about two weeks) to mature. U.S. law requires that all flours not containing wheat germ must have niacin, riboflavin, thiamin, and iron added. After this is done the flour is labeled "enriched." This came about after the Depression. Eight ounces of wheat-based flour must contain 50 percent of the recommended daily allowance of the aforementioned additives. From this base various qualities of refined flour are produced, such as short patent flour, more commonly known as cake flour, which is high in starch and low in protein or gluten; medium patent flour, which uses about 90 percent straight flour, making it slightly higher in protein and lower in starch (this flour is known as all-purpose flour); and long patent flour, which yields a higher protein content and is known as bread flour.

All-Purpose Flour   All-purpose flour is a mixture of approximately equal parts hard and soft wheat flours. It is used in the kitchen rather than the bakeshop.

Bread Flour   Bread flour is a hard wheat (or hard patent) flour. It is very easy to dust into a thin film, making it ideal to use when rolling out and working with doughs. Bread flour is milled from wheat that is rich in protein. The wheat must be grown in areas with the appropriate amount of rainfall and in soil rich in nitrogen. Bread flour is pale yellow when first milled and turns off-white with aging. It feels slightly granular when rubbed between your fingers.

Cake Flour   Cake flour (soft patent) is made from soft wheat. The flour is chlorinated to further break down the strength of the gluten. It feels very smooth and can be pressed into a lump in your hand. The color is much whiter than bread flour. Because it contains less of the gluten-producing proteins, cake flour yields a more crumbly but lighter texture. It is used in making sponge cakes and other baked goods where a weaker gluten structure is preferable.

Pastry Flour   Pastry flour is another of the soft wheat flours. It is closer in color to bread flour, being off-white rather than true white like cake flour. It is close to all-purpose flour in gluten strength.

Whole Wheat Flour   Also known as graham flour, whole wheat flour is milled from the entire wheat kernel, including the germ and the bran; for this reason it is very nutritious. Whole wheat flour does not keep as long as white flour because of the fat contained in the wheat germ. Bread made from whole wheat flour is heavier than bread made with white flour, so most of the time a combination is used. Whole wheat bread dough takes less time to knead than bread made with white flour.

Nonwheat Flours   In addition to the many varieties of wheat flours, we also use flours milled from other plants. Each contributes its own distinctive taste, texture, and nutritional benefit; however, since these flours are lower in gluten content, they are combined with a percentage of wheat flour to assure proper leavening.

Barley Flour   This flour is seldom used in bread baking today, but in the past it was used extensively. To substitute barley flour for wheat flour, use half the amount by volume.

Buckwheat Flour   Buckwheat flour is made from the roasted seeds of the plant. Buckwheat is used most often in pancakes, especially for the popular buckwheat blini in Eastern Europe.

Corn Flour   Corn flour, not to be confused with cornstarch, is milled from either white or yellow corn. It is also produced as a by-product in the making of cornmeal. This flour does not contain any gluten. (Cornmeal is made from coarsely ground dried corn. It is sprinkled on top of English muffins, sourdough breads, and bread sticks to give them a crunchy crust.)

Potato Flour   Potato flour, also known as potato starch, is made from cooked, dried, ground potatoes. It is most frequently used as a thickening agent but can also be used in baking to reduce the gluten strength of bread flour, for example (in much the same way as cornstarch), since it does not contain any gluten.

Rye Flour   Rye flour is one of the best-tasting flours for making bread. It is divided into light, medium, and dark rye flours, as well as pumpernickel flour. As with wheat flour, these grades are determined by the part of the grain that the flour is milled from. The medium grade is the one most commonly used. Pumpernickel flour is made in much the same way as whole wheat flour: it is milled from the entire rye grain including the bran. Rye flour is almost always mixed with some wheat flour to give it added gluten strength and rising power in bread baking. A small amount of vinegar added to rye bread dough will help to bring out the rye flavor.

Soy Flour   Soy flour is made from the soybean rather than from a cereal grain. It is not commonly used in the pastry shop, but it is very nutritious and can be mixed with other flours in cakes for consumers with restricted diets.

Fruit

Apples   More than 20,000 varieties of apples are grown throughout the world, but only a dozen or so are sold commercially in the United States. Red Delicious, Golden Delicious, Rome Beauty, pippin, Jonathon, McIntosh, Stayman, Winesap, Gravenstein, Granny Smith, and Northern Spy are commonly found on the market. Apples are generally classified as eating apples, cooking apples, or all-purpose apples. Good choices for cooking are pippin, Granny Smith, and Golden Delicious. Apples are used in breakfast breads and pastries, tea cakes, apple charlotte, apple pies and tarts, and applesauce. In some recipes where the apples will be cooked into a filling, canned apples may be substituted for fresh. Apples are also used to make cider and brandy. For long storage apples should be kept in a cool place or in the refrigerator. They will keep for many months this way, especially the winter varieties. It is important, however, to check them frequently and remove any that have gone bad, for one rotten apple can indeed spoil the whole lot.

Apricots   Apricots are a stone fruit (drupe) and are part of the rose family, which includes, not surprisingly, peaches, plums, and nectarines. But it is surprising to note that this family also includes cherries, almonds, and coconuts. All have one seed (the kernel), which is enclosed in a stony endocarp called a pit. Almost all apricots sold in this country are grown in California. They are available fresh in the spring and summer months. Unfortunately, apricots are picked and shipped before they are ripe, as are peaches and plums, to protect them during transport. Ripe, plump, and juicy apricots simply would not travel very far without ending up bruised and damaged. Apricots are used in cakes, mousses, and fruit salads as well as in savory dishes. Apricot jam and apricot glaze are used extensively in the pastry shop. Dried apricots are often found in fruit cakes and tea breads. Apricot seeds are made into a kernel paste that is similar to almond paste but has a bitter aftertaste. The most common varieties of apricot are Royal, Blenheim, and Tilton. Ripe apricots are not good keepers. They should be stored in the refrigerator but will only last up to a week, depending on how carefully they were handled when they were picked.

Asian Pears   Asian pears are rapidly growing in popularity. Although they do look very much like a cross between an apple and a pear, which has led to the often used and misleading name of apple-pear, these are true pears also known as Oriental or Chinese pears. This delicious and very juicy fruit was first brought to the United States by Chinese gold miners during the gold rush. The trees are exceptionally attractive, producing bright white flowers in the spring, which contrast with its then leathery green leaves, and the leaves also give a cascade of fall colors later in the year. The culture of Asian pears is much the same as for European pear varieties, with the exception that Asian pears should be left to ripen on the tree. When ripe, the fruit is still quite firm to the touch and will not yield to slight pressure. The best indicator of ripeness is the ripe pear's sweet aroma. Asian pears are available on the market from late summer through the holiday season. They can be stored at room temperature for up to two weeks and in the refrigerator for much longer. The most common commercial variety is the Japanese *Nijisseiki,* also called Twentieth Century. Asian pears are excellent for cooking and poaching; however, they take much longer to cook than the common European pear.

Bananas   There are few plants that suggest the tropics as strongly as the banana, and indeed the plant thrives in the heat and humidity of this region. The banana plant's appearance is something like a palm: its giant leaves sweep out to 12 feet in length from what looks like a trunk but is actually the overlapping long stalks of the branches. Banana trees are so-called because their height can reach up to 30 feet; however, the banana is in fact the largest plant in the world without a woody trunk or stem. Although we usually picture bunches of bananas hanging down, they actually grow with the bottoms of the fruit pointing up toward the sun, in layer upon layer of semicircles, also known as "hands." Each hand contains ten to fifteen bananas, or fingers; there are approximately nine hands in a standard size bunch.

The yellow banana was one of the first plants to be cultivated, and one could easily argue that bananas are an ideal food in many ways: They are in plentiful supply and inexpensive all year long; they are no trouble to transport since they are shipped before they are ripe while still hard; they are easy to peel and can be digested by just about all ages; nutritionally they have more carbohydrate than any other fruit except the avocado; and unlike avocados, which are very high in fat and calories, bananas have only a trace amount of fat and are low in calories; and bananas also provide a substantial amount of potassium. Bananas are one of two fruits (pears are the other) that taste better when allowed to ripen off the tree. Therefore, bananas are shipped green, then ripened domestically in specially equipped warehouses. Costa Rica and Honduras rank as the two largest exporters of bananas to the United States. It is interesting to note that bananas are among the top three exports from such an unlikely place as Iceland. Here they are grown in greenhouses heated naturally by geysers that produce the ideal humidity for the plants to thrive. Once bananas have ripened, store them in a cool place. Refrigerate only if absolutely necessary; the skin will turn brown but the flesh will not be affected.

Red Bananas are becoming increasingly more available. These 4-to-6-inch-long bananas are so named because their skin turns a purplish red when they are ripe. Their flesh is sweeter and has a more pronounced yellow color than that of yellow bananas.

Finger Bananas (also known as "lady fingers") are the most esteemed bananas in the tropical countries. They are very small, only 3 to 4 inches in length, with a thin yellow skin; their flesh is soft and sweet. Unfortunately, we do not get to enjoy this delicacy as frequently as we do yellow bananas because the thin-skinned finger bananas do not transport as well.

Blackberries   Blackberries are available fresh through the summer and are also sold frozen or canned. Loganberries, boysenberries, and olallie berries are all hybrids of blackberries. Fresh berries are excellent for decorating and for use in fruit salads, tarts, and pies. Blackberries are very juicy, and they make a delicious and attractive sauce when puréed. They are also made into jam. To keep fresh berries from becoming crushed and molding prematurely, store them in the refrigerator spread out in a single layer on sheet pans. To freeze fresh berries, spread them out in a single layer, without crowding, and place in the freezer until frozen solid. Package the frozen berries in airtight bags or storage containers.

Black Currants   These very small berries should not be confused with dried currants (which are a variety of grape). Black currants are rarely available fresh in this country; however, they are very popular in Scandinavia and other parts of Europe such as Germany and France.

Black currants are always cooked before they are eaten because they are too bitter to eat raw. They are typically used in jams and are also used to make the French liqueur crème de cassis. Their dark color, which turns almost purple when mixed with other ingredients, gives cakes, mousses, or other desserts a very special look.

Blueberries   Blueberries grow wild in both Scandinavia and the United States. They are available fresh in the late spring and through the summer; they are also sold frozen and canned. Fresh blueberries are wonderful for adding color to fruit tarts and fruit salads. While not as desirable, frozen berries give a good result when used in muffins, tea cakes, pancakes, and other cooked products. Store or freeze blueberries as directed for blackberries. Do *not* thaw frozen blueberries before adding them to batters.

Cantaloupes   Cantaloupes, also called muskmelons, are a member of the melon family and are only sold and eaten fresh. Cantaloupes are available all year in this country as they are imported from Mexico throughout the winter. Cantaloupe flesh is very sweet and juicy, and in the pastry kitchen it is used mostly in fruit salads. Store ripe and/or cut melons in the refrigerator for no more than two to three days. Uncut melons may be left to ripen at room temperature. They will become softer and juicier, but their sweetness will not improve.

Carambolas (Starfruits)   This incredibly showy and unusual-looking fruit originated in Malaysia, but it now grows throughout the tropics and sparingly in Southern California and Florida. The carambola grows on small trees. The fruit is oblong in shape, varying in size from that of a small hen's egg to that of a medium-sized mango (2 to 5 inches), depending on where it is grown. Each fruit has five prominent ridges (you can find some rebels which have four or six) which, when sliced crosswise, reveal a striking star shape. This has given the fruit its alternate, and in this country more common, name: starfruit. Starfruits have a glossy yellow skin that turns from green to golden yellow when ripe. The interior flesh is a matching golden color and is rich in vitamins. Unfortunately, the fruit grown in the United States generally has a somewhat nondescript, dull flavor. The varieties grown in the tropics are eaten out of hand—skin, seeds, and all. They range in flavor from very sweet to refreshingly tart. In this country carambola is used mostly for decorative purposes, as a garnish for desserts, salads, or beverages. It is gaining in popularity in the pastry kitchen as an exotic alternative. The fruit will keep for up to two weeks in the refrigerator. The top of the ridges will turn brown, but this is not a problem since they are removed anyway. To use starfruit, wash, remove the skin on the very top of each ridge, using a vegetable peeler, and then slice across.

Cherimoyas   The cherimoya is the fruit of the annona tree and is native to the mountain regions of Peru and Ecuador. Today it is grown in many temperate climates, including, within the United States, Southern California, Florida, and to a lesser extent, Maui. This delicious fruit is sometimes referred to as a "custard apple" because the consistency of the pulp is soft and custardlike; the ivory flesh also contains black seeds that are not eaten. Cherimoyas are sure to amaze anyone experiencing this fruit for the first time: They are almost heart-shaped; their skin looks very much like a cross between an artichoke and a pineapple; and their flavor is a wonderful tropical combination of pineapple, mango, and banana. Cherimoyas are best eaten chilled, either cut into halves or quarters with the pulp scooped out using a spoon, or juiced and strained to make sorbet or ice cream. They should be purchased when they are still firm and left at room temperature to ripen. They can then be stored covered in the refrigerator for up to four days.

Cherries   Numerous varieties of cherries are grown all over the world. The most common sweet cherries for eating raw are Bing and Lambert. Bing cherries mature a few weeks before Lambert, and the Lambert is more elongated in shape, but both share the same rich flavor and dark, almost mahogany, coloring. Royal Anne (also known as Golden Bing) is a light (white) fleshed sweet cherry, not as popular because it does not ship well; its light skin shows even the slightest bruise. Sour cooking cherries include Montmorency, Morello, and the Amarasca cherry, which is used to make maraschino liqueur. Cherries are used in pies, tarts, cake fillings, and, of course, cherries jubilee. Cherries do not keep well and should always be stored in the refrigerator and left whole (with the stem and pit). Once pitted they will oxidize and start to deteriorate and spoil very quickly.

Coconuts   The coconut palm is grown throughout the temperate part of the globe. It has been called the "tree of life," as it produces everything that is needed to sustain life: Ropes and fishing nets are made from the fibers surrounding the shell, the leaves are made into mats and used as roofing material, the trunk is used as timber, the coconut flesh and liquid are very nourishing, the shells can be used to make bowls, and the tiny shoots of the palm can be prepared and eaten as a vegetable.

Although the name suggests otherwise, the coconut is not a nut but a drupe (stone fruit), belonging to the same family as plums, apricots, and peaches. Each coconut palm contains about 20 nuts, which take approximately one year to ripen. Since the trees flower and bear fruit continuously, the fruits can be harvested all year.

Fresh coconuts are relatively inexpensive and are available year round. In most grocery stores in this country "fresh" coconuts are almost exclusively marketed with their thick leathery skin and fibrous coating removed. In choosing a whole coconut, pick one that feels heavy for its size. You should be able to hear a sloshing sound from the liquid inside when you shake the coconut. To extract the meat, first puncture one or all three of the eyes on the end. Drain the milk, then, using a mallet or hammer, lightly tap the shell all around to loosen the meat inside. Break the coconut open using the same tool and remove the meat from the shell. Use a vegetable peeler to remove the brown skin from the meat.

Packaged coconut meat is available in many different forms: flaked, shredded, grated, and ground. Dried, unsweetened coconut that has been ground to the consistency of coarse cornmeal is called desiccated coconut; it is sometimes labeled as macaroon coconut. Unsweetened coconut milk, exported mainly from Thailand, is available canned. It is usually sold in grocery stores specializing in Asian food products or in the Asian food section of the supermarket. Before they have been opened, coconuts will keep in the refrigerator for up to a month, depending on how fresh they were at the time they were purchased. Once opened, the meat and the coconut milk should be used within a week's time or frozen for longer storage.

Coquitos   Coquitos are not your run-of-the-mill coconuts, though they do look just like a miniature version of coconuts, and they are related to the coconut palm. The small, cherry-sized coquitos, however, do not contain any milk. Coquitos are indigenous to South America where they were gathered by Indian tribes centuries ago. They can be eaten whole or cut in half; coquito halves make a great garnish for desserts that contain coconut. Cut just deep enough to penetrate and then break them in half for a natural look. Toasting coquitos lightly makes them less hard and more palatable; the meat should remain white. They can be stored whole at room temperature for several months if kept covered.

Cranberries   Wild cranberry vines are indigenous to North America. Today most of the cranberries grown commercially come from Massachusetts. Cranberries are very tart and are almost always sweetened. They are used in tea cakes, muffins, sauces, and preserves. Their bright red color adds a festive touch to many holiday desserts. Fresh cranberries keep for weeks in the refrigerator and freeze very well with little loss of flavor or texture.

Dates   Dates are the fruit of the date palm, previously grown mostly in Iraq for commercial purposes but more recently grown in California. Dates are very sweet—almost half sugar. They are most often sold dried and are available whole or pitted. Dates can be stuffed with fondant or marzipan and glazed with sugar to serve on a petits fours tray. They are also used in nut breads and muffins. Fresh dates are very perishable and must be kept refrigerated, although the dried variety may be stored at room temperature if well covered. Dates will have a more pleasant texture if stored in the refrigerator.

Dried Currants   Also called currant raisins and sometimes simply currants, dried currants are not, as you might expect, made from drying fresh black or red currants. Dried currants look like tiny raisins and are indeed made by drying Zante grapes. Dried currants are known as Corinth raisins in Europe, named for their place of origin in Greece. Currants are frequently used in baking and are often used to decorate cookies, especially gingerbread figures. Zante currants are the most common variety. Because currant raisins have their own distinct flavor, black raisins (although besides being much larger may look the same) should not be used as a substitute. Dried currants may be stored at room temperature for many months.

Feijoas   The feijoa not only bears delicious fruit, but it is an attractive addition to the garden. The leaves are dark green on top with a silvery hue underneath. In spring the shrub is full of white flowers that have scarlet stamens. The flower petals make a handsome addition to a plain green salad and can be used as a dessert garnish.

Provided the petals are removed with care, the remaining flower may still develop into a fruit. Mature, ripe feijoas are shaped like an elongated egg. Although the slightly acidic green skin is edible, it is generally peeled away and discarded. The off-white flesh has a delicious, very unusual, and complex flavor with hints of pineapple, guava, and eucalyptus. The feijoa is excellent in cream-based desserts, is a natural in salads, or can be enjoyed fresh eaten out of hand. Cut the fruit in halves or quarters and scoop out the flesh, including the small seeds (contained in the clover-shaped center surrounded by a jelly-like substance), which are edible as well.

Also referred to as a pineapple guava, and often confused with a guava, the drought-resistant feijoa belongs to the myrtle family and was named for the botanist Don da Silva Feijoa. The plants are native to South America, but today New Zealand is the largest supplier; California and Hawaii each produce a small crop as well. New Zealand feijoas are available from spring to early summer; those grown in this country can be found in the market from late fall through January and February. The ripe fruit should be stored in the refrigerator, where it will keep for several weeks.

Figs   The fig tree is a type of ficus that has been growing on the earth virtually since the beginning of time. They are cultivated extensively throughout the Mediterranean and closer to home in California. Figs are classified in botanical terms as a fruit receptacle, which means an inside-out flower. In addition to the fact that the fruit grows right where the leaves are attached to the branches without any visible flowering having taken place, figs are also unique in that they provide two crops annually. There are several hundred varieties in a wide range of colors and shapes from small, squat, and round to large and pear-shaped, and from almost white to dark purple or black. The most common commercial fig is the Brown Turkey variety, also referred to as Black Spanish. These are quite large with mahogany purple skin and juicy red flesh and are the first figs on the market each year. Mission or Black Mission figs are the most readily available and are the best overall for cooking. These have a dark pink interior. Kadota, the principal fig used for canning, are quite large with yellowish green skin and white to purple flesh inside. Smyrna from Turkey (known as Calimyrna when grown in California) are large, greenish, squat, extremely sweet figs that are available fresh but are mostly used for drying; these are the only figs that are not self-pollinating. Smyrna figs instead rely on a unique pollination method provided by a tiny wasp known as blastophaga, which lives inside the inedible figs that grow on the Capri fig tree. When the wasp larva mature they leave the Capri fig tree and look for another tree to serve as a nest in order to reproduce. Growers of Smyrna figs intervene just prior to the time this is to occur, placing baskets of Capri figs throughout their orchards. The female wasps work their way through the bottom of the Smyrna figs, carrying pollen on their wings and bodies. Once they discover that the inside of the Smyrna fig is not suitable for laying their eggs they retreat, leaving pollen behind.

Unripe figs can be ripened at room temperature; they should be placed away from direct sunlight and should be turned from time to time. Ripe figs may be stored in the refrigerator for up to three days. They bruise easily and should be arranged in a single layer covered with plastic.

Gooseberries   Gooseberries have never gained a foothold in the United States, partially due to the fact that the varieties native to this country are rather tart, small, and not as juicy as the European fruit, but also because federal and state laws (just as with red and black currants) regulate both interstate shipping and the areas where gooseberries can be grown, because the plants can serve as a host to White Pine Blister Rust. Gooseberries flourish in the northern parts of Europe where you would be hard put to find a garden without some variety. The gooseberry shrub is an attractive plant with beautiful spring flowers, colorful fruit, and bright green rounded foliage. There are dozens of varieties, producing different colors of fruit including white, yellow (amber), green, and red berries. The berries are translucent, revealing both the veins and seeds inside. These juicy fruits have been developed to perfection in England where the berries of some types reach 1½ inches in size. Gooseberries are excellent for use in jams, jellies, tarts, and pies. The berries also make a wonderful puckery ice cream. Gooseberries can be stored in the refrigerator for one week and may be frozen for many months.

Grapefruits   Grapefruits are divided into two groups: the pigmented or pink varieties, and the common grapefruit, also called white grapefruit. The fruit of both grow in grapelike clusters (hence the name) on one of the largest trees in the citrus family, which makes sense, since grapefruits are the largest of the commercially important citrus crops (the only citrus fruit that is larger than a grapefruit is the thick-skinned and elusive pummelo, which is the parent of the grapefruit we know today). The majority of the commercial U.S. crop is grown in the Indian River area of Florida. The grapefruits grown there are known to be of higher quality and larger size than those grown in the other principal growing areas of Texas, Arizona, and California. The popularity of grapefruit has gained rapidly for many years due to their health value and tangy refreshing flavor. Grapefruits are rich in vitamin C, one cup of freshly squeezed juice suppling the average daily requirement, and they are also low in calories. Grapefruits require a hotter climate than other citrus varieties, and even so, they take from one to one and one-half years to ripen fully. Grapefruits are available almost year-round. Grapefruits can be left at room temperature for about one week. The fruit is juicier when served or used warm rather than cool. Grapefruits will keep in the refrigerator for up to two months.

Grapes   Grapes are one of the oldest cultivated fruits. In the United States most of the commercial crop is grown in California, including grapes produced for wine making. Grapes range in color from pale green to dark red, almost black. Popular varieties include Thompson Seedless, Red Flame, Concord, and Champagne. Grapes are used in fruit salads and on fruit tarts. Grapes will keep for about one week stored covered in the refrigerator.

Honeydews   Honeydews are large, pale green melons with sweet, very juicy, light green flesh. They are used in the pastry kitchen in fruit salads and to make sorbet. Honeydews are shipped when they are hard (unripe) and then usually preripened before being sold. If the melon is very hard, leave it at room temperature for up to four days until it starts to soften slightly at the stem and bottom ends. While the flesh will become softer and juicier, it will not become any sweeter. Avoid honeydews that have a whitish tinge to the skin; they usually never ripen fully. Honeydews are available throughout the year. Ripe and/or cut melons should be refrigerated and used within two days.

Kiwifruit   Kiwis are native to China and were originally known as Chinese gooseberries. The commercial crop was primarily exported from New Zealand until fairly recently when they began to be cultivated successfully in California. Kiwis are oval with fuzzy brown skin, bright green flesh, and very small black seeds (which are eaten). Their colorful appearance has made them popular in recent years for decorating. Kiwifruit can be used in fruit salads, fruit tarts, sorbets, and sauces. See Figures 6–2 to 6–4, page 251, for a great way to peel kiwis. Firm kiwis can be ripened at room temperature but should be kept out of direct sunlight. Once ripe, they can be stored in the refrigerator for up to two weeks. Kiwis should not be stored next to other fruits because they are very sensitive to the ethylene gas emitted by them.

Kumquats   This small fruit—no bigger than a large olive—looks like a miniature oblong orange. Kumquats originated in China where the name means "golden orange." The fruit is eaten whole—peel, pits, and all. The unusual thing here, however, is that the peel is sweet and the flesh fairly tart. Kumquats are wonderful to use for decorating either fresh, pickled, or candied, and they are also used in salads and made into preserves. Fresh kumquats are readily available from November through March, but the fruit can hang on the tree for many months without negative side effects. The kumquat hybrids can be found in the market starting in September. These are sweeter and slightly larger than the bona fide version. Orangequat and Calamondin are the two most similar to kumquats. These two are also hardy, easy to grow, and the best suited for indoor cultivation of the entire citrus family. Store kumquats at room temperature for one week or so and in the refrigerator for four to six weeks.

Lady Apples   This beautiful, small, brightly colored apple (which is part of the crab apple family, since any apple tree that produces fruit two inches or less in diameter is classified as such) is one of many in a distinguished group known as "old apples." This group contains such well-known favorites as Northern Spy, Gravenstein, and Cox Orange (which is also known as Cox Orange Pippin). Some of these are still an important commercial resource, while others are only part of our childhood memories. In my case, I can remember the large Cox Orange tree I used to climb in order to reach the apples on the tallest branches, which had been left unpicked. Unfortunately for me, this was something I was not supposed to do, since in addition to being a delicious eating apple, Cox Orange apples are good keepers and can last well into the winter. The same is true for the Lady apple and its slightly larger hybrid, Lady Gala. Lady apples are not practical for cooking because of their small size, but for the same reason they are highly regarded for their decorative use, especially around the holidays. They are delightful to eat fresh and are sometimes pickled. Lady apples should be stored in the refrigerator well covered; they will keep this way for up to six weeks.

Lemons   Lemons originated in India and are a member of the citrus family. Today they are grown in the Mediterranean, the United States, Canada, South America, Asia, Australia, and Africa. Lemons, lemon juice, and lemon zest are all used frequently in dessert preparations as well as in other types of cooking, as lemon enhances many flavors, both sweet and savory.

Lemon juice is used not only as a flavoring agent but because of its acidic quality, it is also rubbed onto cut fruit to prevent oxidation (or it is used to make acidulated water for the same purpose). A few drops are used in caramelizing sugar to help prevent both recrystallization and premature darkening. Some lemon juice is added to egg whites when whipping meringue to increase the volume, and lemon juice is worked into the butter block to make it more elastic in making puff pastry. As a flavoring, lemon juice is almost as widely used as vanilla and chocolate in the pastry kitchen. Lemons are used in lemon curd and other fillings, fruit sauces, doughs, cakes, cookies, mousses, candies, sorbets and ice creams, candied citrus peels, and pies. Soaking lemons in hot water for about an hour before juicing them will increase the amount of juice that can be extracted. Rolling the fruit firmly against the table will also help. One medium lemon produces approximately 1/4 cup (60 ml) of juice and approximately 1 teaspoon of compacted, grated zest, weighing about 6 grams. Lemons will keep at room temperature for two weeks and can be stored in the refrigerator for up to six weeks well covered.

Limes   Limes are another member of the citrus family and are closely related to lemons. Limes are not used as extensively but can be substituted for lemons in many cases. Limes turn from green to yellow when fully ripe; however, immature green limes are the ones that have the desirable tart juice, and because of their bright green color, lime zest is often used as a garnish. Unlike lemons, limes should always be kept refrigerated; they will keep this way, well covered, for up to six weeks.

Lingonberries   Lingonberries look and taste a bit like small cranberries. Lingonberry preserves are a very popular condiment in Scandinavia. Fresh lingonberries are not usually available in the United States, but the preserves are sold in most grocery stores. Lingonberries are used as a topping, in sauces, in parfaits, and in mousses. In Sweden (and in my home in the United States) lingonberry preserves are traditionally served with dinner as an accompaniment to mashed potatoes. Lingonberries contain nature's own preservative, benzoic acid (also found in cranberries, prunes, and cinnamon), which makes it unnecessary to add any preservative, or even sugar, for storage, nor do they have to be refrigerated. This also makes it possible to market a product called *rårörda,* which is raw lingonberries simply crushed and minimally sweetened. Lingonberries ripen in September. It is a popular recreation for many families in Sweden to invade the forest at this time and harvest their plot of berries, the location of which is kept secret throughout the year. Lingonberries thrive in partly sunny openings in the woods and where moss is abundant.

Litchis   The litchi (also spelled "lychee") is most popular in China where it is eaten as a fruit, often chilled in syrup, dried and sold as "litchi nuts," and cooked in meat dishes. The fruit grows in bunches; each litchi fruit is about the size of an unshelled walnut and is enclosed in a brittle, brownish red bumpy skin. Inside is white flesh surrounding an inedible black pit. The flesh is juicy and has a sweet, almost perfumed, flavor and aroma. Fresh litchis are available in Asian markets in the summer and can be stored in the refrigerator for several weeks or may be frozen. Canned litchis are available in some stores. Litchis can be used in mousses, charlottes, ice creams, and sauces.

Mandarin Oranges   This small, somewhat flattened, variety of orange is distinguished by its loose easy-to-peel "kid glove" skin (although if the skin is too loose and puffy they should be avoided, because this is a sign the fruit is overripe and dry). Mandarins originated in China dating back as far as 2000 B.C. The tangerine member of the mandarin family was introduced to Europe early in the nineteenth century and reached America a few decades later. Mandarins and their hybrids are one of the most versatile fruits around, low in calories and high in both vitamins and minerals, and easy to section with your hands. Mandarins are divided into three classifications: the strictly Japanese satsumas; tangerines; and a range of various hybrids of the first two. Retailers (and also wholesalers) tend to generalize and market all of the smaller, deep orange-colored fruits that have a short neck and puffy skin as tangerines, including the satsumas (however, the larger tangelos, which have a distinctive nipple-shaped stem end, are usually identified correctly). The most popular mandarins for culinary use are the satsumas, and for good reason, since they are virtually seedless; these are the mandarins most frequently used for canning. The most common commercial variety in this country, however, is the tangerine, named for the city of Tangier. The hybrids tangor (a cross between a tangerine and an orange), temple, and murlott (also called a honey tangerine) are the best-known tangerine varieties. Also found in the complex hybrid category are the tangelos, which are a cross between a pomelo and a tangerine. Minneola and orlando are the most common types of these. The majority of the commercial mandarin crop is grown in Florida with California coming in a distant second. Mandarin oranges are available in varying degrees from November through May. Mandarins and all of their hybrids should be stored in the refrigerator, where they will keep for one or two weeks.

Mangoes   Mangoes grow on evergreen trees in tropical climates. They are widely used in India for cooking in chutneys and curries and to be eaten fresh. Different varieties of mango vary in color from yellow to green and red. When ripe, mangoes have a very strong and sweet fragrance. They are available fresh from spring to late summer and are also available canned. Mangoes have a large pit and are rather difficult to peel. The best method is to slice off the two broader sides as close as possible to the large flat seed, and then scoop out the flesh from these halves and discard the skin. See pages 632 and 633 for instructions on how to cut a mango "hedgehog" style, leaving the skin on. Mangoes are used in fruit salads, as a garnish, in ice cream, and in sauces. Fresh mangoes contain an enzyme that will inhibit gelatin from setting, but bringing the fruit pulp to a quick boil will neutralize the enzyme. Unripe mangoes can be softened and will become sweeter left at room temperature, away from direct sunlight, for a few days. To speed up the process, place two or more mangoes in a paper or plastic bag. Store ripe fruit covered in the refrigerator for up to one week.

Nectarines   Nectarines are one of the oldest fruits and are said to have grown more than two thousand years ago. They are part of the large stone fruit family, which includes plums, peaches, and cherries. The early commercially grown nectarines were small, softened fast, and did not travel well. Newer varieties contain part "peach blood" from crossbreeding in an attempt to get a larger and firmer fruit. However, a nectarine is not, as many believe, a hairless peach or a cross between a peach and a plum. Nectarines do share many characteristics of peaches and in most cases can be substituted for peaches. Follow the instructions given with peaches for ripening and storage.

Oranges   Oranges are probably second only to apples in their popularity. They are the most commonly used member of the citrus family for eating and cooking, and their sweet juice is a typical breakfast beverage. Oranges are grown commercially in the Unites States in Florida, California, Texas, and Arizona. Fresh oranges are available year-round. Oranges are an everbearing fruit (as are other types of citrus and also the coconut palm, cocoa tree, and coffee plant, to name a few), meaning that they produce both flowers and ripe fruit at the same time. Oranges are used in many of the same dessert preparations as lemons. Blood oranges are a variety of orange with red flesh, juice, and rind. Their distinctive color is nice in sorbets, fruit salads, and sauces. Bitter oranges, such as Seville, are used in marmalades and to make curaçao and Grand Marnier. Commercial oranges (and many other fruits) are almost always dipped in or sprayed with an edible wax to enhance their appearance and preserve freshness. Often an orange-colored vegetable dye is added to the wax. The colored wax is absolutely harmless, and there is no need to wash it off before using the fruit. Oranges will yield more juice if stored at room temperature, and they can be kept this way for up to two weeks. They can be stored about twice as long in the refrigerator. It is not necessary to wrap or cover oranges in either case as their sturdy skin offers enough protection.

Papayas   Papayas are a delicious tropical fruit, Mexican in origin, now grown in tropical climates all over the world. Their green skin turns yellow or orange when the fruit is ripe. Papayas are popular for breakfast and are used in ice cream, fruit salads, fruit tarts, and sauces. Papayas contain the enzyme papain, which aids in digestion (in fact, papayas were named "the tree of health" in the Caribbean because the fruit is so beneficial to people with stomach problems). Because of this enzyme, papayas can be used as a meat tenderizer, and for the same reason, raw papaya will inhibit gelatin from jelling. Bringing the fruit to a quick boil will kill the enzyme. Papayas that are about half yellow will ripen in approximately three days if left at room temperature. The process can be greatly accelerated by placing the fruit in a paper bag with a banana. Ripe papayas should be stored covered in the refrigerator. They will keep this way for up to one week, but their delicate flavor will fade after a time.

Passion Fruits   Although the name makes this fruit sound like an aphrodisiac, passion fruit was given its name by Spanish missionaries who said the appearance of the flowers had a significance to the Crucifixion. Passion fruits are about the size of an egg and have a hard, wrinkled skin when the fruit is ripe. The skin, which is almost like a shell, is not eaten. The flesh consists mostly of seeds, which can be eaten, or the flesh can be forced through a sieve to extract the juice. Passion fruit juice can be used in ice creams, soufflés, sauces, and beverages. Passion fruits are native to Brazil but are also grown now in California, Hawaii, Florida, Africa, India, and New Zealand. Ripe passion fruits can be stored in the refrigerator for about one week.

Peaches   Peaches, along with apricots, plums, and nectarines, are a stone fruit. There are both clingstone and freestone varieties. Red Haven is probably the most common peach sold. Peaches are very sweet and juicy when ripe, and they are one of summer's favorite fruits for ice creams and cobblers. Peaches are also often used to make jam. They need a warm climate with no frost and are grown in both North and South America, Australia, Africa, and many parts of Europe. Early settlers in America planted peach trees all along the Eastern seaboard, establishing the fruit so thoroughly in this country that botanists in the mid-eighteenth century assumed peaches to be native to the New World. Peach trees are thought to have originated in China and to have been introduced from there to the Middle East and Europe. Unfortunately, tree-ripened peaches do not travel very well, and the commercial crop is almost always picked and shipped hard and unripe. They will soften if left at room temperature (this can be accelerated by placing the fruit in a paper bag), but the flavor is never as good as that of the tree-ripened variety. Ripe peaches will keep four to five days if refrigerated.

Pears   Pears come in many sizes and colors from pale green to yellow, brown, and red. Some are best for cooking and others for eating raw. Popular varieties include Anjou, Bartlett, Bosc, Comice, and Seckel. One variety or another is available year-round. Pears are used in many desserts, such as the well-known pears belle hélène, as well as in tarts, charlottes, and ice creams, poached in wine, or served with cheese. Pears are also made into pear brandy and jam. Pears are harvested and shipped before they are ripe; the fruit actually develops a better flavor and texture if ripened off the tree. Pears served raw should be fully ripe. For baking and cooking, however, it is preferable to have them just a little underripe. Bosc pears should be used when they are hard, not soft. Comice and Anjou should be kept at room temperature. Do not store (mix) Comice pears with other kinds of fruit. Pears can be left at room temperature to ripen and then be transferred to the refrigerator for two or three days, or they can be refrigerated from the start, which will cause them to ripen more slowly. In either case, do not store in a sealed plastic bag. Pears will yield to light pressure when ripe.

Persimmons   There are two varieties of persimmons found in the United States: Hachiya and Fuyu. Hachiya, the persimmon most commonly found in stores, has a slightly oblong shape and is pointed at the bottom. The Hachiya persimmon is very high in tannin and can be eaten only when fully ripe (the fruit should be almost jellylike throughout). Instead of trying to peel the skin off the Hachiya, it is easier to cut it in half and use a spoon to scoop out the flesh; discard the stem, seeds, and skin. The smaller Fuyu persimmon is shaped like a tomato. It has very little tannin and can therefore be eaten before it is completely ripe and soft. This persimmon is easy to peel with a vegetable peeler. Both varieties are orange in color and available during the winter months. Persimmons are used in many traditional holiday recipes, the most popular being persimmon pudding. A too firm Fuyu persimmon can be ripened at room temperature in a few days. An unripe Hachiya is a different story, however, requiring as long as a few weeks to lose its astringent mouth-puckering tannin. To speed up the process, the fruit can be placed in a paper bag together with an apple; this will produce additional ethylene gas, which makes the fruit ripen. Another alternative is to expose the fruit to a small amount of alcohol (place the persimmons in a plastic container, place a few drops of alcohol on each of the leaflike sepals, and close the container tightly), which also encourages the fruit to produce more ethylene gas.

Physalis (Cape Gooseberries)   These rather unusual looking fruits are each surrounded by a loose, beige, ballooning, parchmentlike husk called a calyx. The seedy yellow berry inside is about the size of a cherry and has a sweet orange flavor, but with more acidity. There are two main varieties of physalis: the edible one discussed here (*physalis pruinosa*), also known by the names ground cherry and strawberry-tomato, and the ornamental variety (*physalis franchetii*), usually known as Chinese lanterns because of the bright orange-red lantern-shaped calyx that forms around the ripened berries. The ornamental physalis are often used in late fall floral arrangements. Cape gooseberries are great for pies and preserves (with their papery husk removed), but their price is usually prohibitive for this type of application. A better way to utilize these eye-catching berries is in decorating, with the attractive husk left on. Begin by snipping the husk open from the tip with a small pair of scissors. Either loosely spread the petals of the husk open like a flower about to bloom, or spread the petals of the husk all the way back to the stem and then dip the fruit into chocolate or fondant flavored with Cointreau or kirsch, to serve as a candy or unusual mignardises (another name for an assortment of petits fours). Cape gooseberries will keep fresh for many weeks stored in the refrigerator. If stored too long, however, the berry begins to dry up and eventually just the empty husk is left.

Pineapples   This handsome tropical fruit got its English name from its vague resemblance to a pine cone. In most European countries pineapples are known as *ananas,* derived from the Paraguayan word *nana,* meaning "excellent fruit." Pineapples are native to Central and South America. They did not reach Hawaii until 1790 when they were brought there by Captain James Cook. The Hawaiian Islands are now the biggest producers of pineapples in the world. Pineapple is one of the most widely eaten tropical fruits, probably second only to the banana and, like bananas, they are available all year. Pineapples generally grow one to a plant, growing out of the crown (the leafy part that is attached to the top when the fruits are marketed). The fruit develops from a bunch of small, lavender-colored flowers on a short stalk that grows from the center of leaves (the stalk becomes the core that runs vertically inside the mature pineapple). When developed, a pineapple is actually composed of many small hexagon-shaped fruits merged together, which can be seen from the pattern on the tough skin. The skin must be removed before the fruit is eaten. Being able to distinguish a sweet, ripe pineapple for harvest can be difficult, since the color is not a reliable indication, and is quite important since the starch in the fruit will no longer convert to sugar once the pineapple has been removed from the plant. Some sources say a good test is to see if a leaf will pull easily from the crown, but a sweet fragrance is probably the best indicator, just as it is in choosing a harvested pineapple in the market.

Pineapples, like many other tropical fruits, contain an enzyme (bromelain) that is beneficial to digestion but not to protein-based gelatin, where it will inhibit or prevent coagulation. The way around this is to use agar-agar or cornstarch for thickening, or simply to bring the fruit to a quick boil (which will destroy the enzyme) before using gelatin.

To remove the rind from a pineapple, begin by rinsing the fruit and twisting off the crown. The crown may be discarded or used for decorating. Cut off the base of the pineapple to make it level. Stand the fruit on end and remove the rind by cutting from the top to the bottom, following the curve of the fruit. Once all of the peel has been removed, you will see that the "eyes" follow a spiral pattern. Remove them by cutting spiral grooves that wind around the pineapple from the top to the bottom. This extra effort not only adds to the appearance but it saves a great deal of flesh that would be lost if you cut away enough of the entire surface to remove all of the eyes. Cut the pineapple crosswise into slices of the desired thickness and remove the core from each slice using a cookie cutter. Alternatively, cut the pineapple lengthwise into quarters, after removing the eyes, and slice the core off each quarter with a knife. A large part of the core can be eaten and makes a nice chewy treat. Pineapples will become softer and juicier (but not sweeter) if left at room temperature for a few days. Ripe pineapples should not be stored in the refrigerator longer than four to five days as the cold can damage the fruit.

Plantains   Plantains are closely related to the yellow banana but are considerably larger, averaging about 12 inches in length. They are left to ripen on the tree and change color from all green to all black (and become slightly wrinkled) when fully ripe. We usually see them in the market somewhere in between when their thick, slightly blemished skin has started to turn a reddish brown. Plantains are always cooked before they are eaten. Removing the peel from a raw plantain is quite a bit harder than removing the skin from a banana. If the plantains are to be boiled, do so with the skin on and it will then slip right off after cooking. Otherwise, use a sharp knife to cut off both ends so that part of the flesh is exposed. Cut lengthwise following the corner of one of the ridges without cutting into the pulp. Repeat with the adjacent ridge and use the edge of the knife to lift up the cut section of peel and pull it away in one piece. Repeat this procedure with each remaining segment of peel or until the remaining skin can be removed in one piece. Plantains are sometimes called "cooking bananas" and are used in Latin American countries in a way that is similar to the use of potatoes in the United States. Plantains should only be refrigerated if overripe. The exposure to cold interrupts their ripening cycle, and it will never resume, even if the fruit is returned to room temperature.

Plums   Plums are a drupe or stone fruit, meaning that they contain a pit. They are related to nectarines, peaches, and apricots and come in both cling and freestone varieties. Plums are far more diverse than some of these relatives however; in fact, there are so many varieties of plums (possibly up to two thousand) that sometimes even experts have trouble distinguishing between them. It will be less bewildering if you keep in mind that there are two main categories: Japanese and European. The Japanese varieties are medium to large and very juicy. They come in many different shades, of which only a few have a bluish or purple skin. Most of the European types of plum are blue or purple; they are usually smaller in size, round or oval, and have a firmer texture. In the United States about a dozen varieties are grown commercially. Plums are available from spring to early fall. Popular varieties include Santa Rosa, Casselman, Laroda, and Queen Ann. Prune plums are, as the name suggests, dried to make prunes. Plums are used in ice cream, cobblers, sauces, tarts, and fruit salads. Plums are also used to make brandy and jam. As with many other fruits, the ripening process for immature plums can be quickened by placing the fruit in a loosely closed paper bag and leaving it at room temperature for a day or two. Store ripe plums in the refrigerator for up to ten days.

Pomegranates   Pomegranate trees are often planted for ornamental use, and it is easy to see why: In spring their small carnation-like flowers bloom for two to three weeks; then in the early fall the fruit-bearing varieties produce large, bright red round fruit that are 3 to 5 inches in diameter and very showy. Pomegranates are grown widely, both in home gardens and commercially, in sub-tropical areas throughout Asia, the Mediterranean, and in Southern California, where they are in season from September to mid-December. The most common commercial variety of pomegranate is called "Wonderful."

The name *pomegranate* comes from the French, *pome grenate,* which is further traced back to the Latin, *pomum granatum,* meaning "apple with many seeds." Each round fruit contains hundreds of small edible seeds about the size and shape of a kernel of corn that in turn are made up of a smaller seed that is surrounded by translucent reddish pulp. The seeds are enclosed in pockets that are divided by a pale bitter-tasting membrane. Removing the seeds from these pockets without crushing their pulp is quite labor-intensive. If at all possible, freeze the pomegranates the day before they are to be seeded; when thawed, the seeds can be removed in nearly half the time.

Pomegranate seeds are eaten fresh sprinkled over a salad, used as a bright and unusual garnish, and added to many sweet dishes. For a quick, easy, and refreshing juice drink, roll a chilled pomegranate between your palms and the table to rupture the seeds inside, cut a small slit, insert a straw, and suck out the juice.

Grenadine, a very sweet red syrup used in cocktails, is made from pomegranates and gets its name from the French word *grenate* discussed above. Interestingly enough, this is also the origin of the word *grenade.* These small explosives not only have a similar round shape and a protruding fuse on top (which looks something like the stem end of the fruit) but they too are filled with tiny bursting pellets.

Whole pomegranates can be refrigerated for two to three months; the seeds and/or juice can be frozen for longer storage. Ten small to medium pomegranates, or 2 pounds, 8 ounces (1 kg, 135 g) of whole pomegranates, will yield approximately 2 quarts (1 l, 920 ml) of seeds.

Prickly Pears (Cactus Pears)   This unusual looking fruit is shaped like a common pear but has a thicker greenish purple skin that is full of thorns. The thorns are always removed, usually by singeing them off, before the fruit is shipped to market. The watermelon-like flesh inside has small black seeds throughout, which are not eaten. Prickly pears are very popular in many parts of the world, especially in the Mediterranean region. From Mexico all the way to South America they are known as cactus pears, which makes sense since they grow on several varieties of cactus. The fruit has become better known and available commercially in some areas only very recently. The low-calorie pulp is eaten raw, made into desserts, and stewed. Allow prickly pears to ripen at room temperature for a few days; they should be soft but not mushy. Store ripe fruit in the refrigerator.

Pumpkins   Pumpkins are not a fruit, but they are discussed here because they are used in a similar way in breads, pie fillings, and other baked goods. Pumpkins are a member of the winter squash family, which includes the well-known varieties acorn, butternut, and hubbard. There are hundreds of winter squash variations in sizes from the small acorn weighing about one pound to the giant pumpkin varieties that can reach over 200 pounds.

In contrast to the soft-skinned, young summer squashes, winter squashes are only harvested after they have reached maturity and their shells and seeds have grown hard and inedible. It is due to the protective property of their hard shells that winter squashes can be stored for many months after harvest. Unlike the other winter squash varieties, which are almost always prepared for consumption, over 90 percent of the pumpkins grown commercially in the United States are sold as jack-o-lantern pumpkins for Halloween. Most of these are the Connecticut Field variety, which are quite large and bright orange, making them well suited for carving, but they tend to be too stringy to eat. The much smaller sugar pumpkin is the one used almost exclusively for pies and other types of cooking. There are also miniature pumpkin varieties, about the size of an apple, that can be eaten whole after cooking; the better known of these are Jack Be Little and Munchkin. The flat, green pumpkin seeds are popular toasted as a snack or added to breads or cookies. With the exception of spaghetti squash, most winter squash varieties many be substituted for pumpkin for use in cooking, including the preparation of pumpkin pies. Store pumpkins in a cool dry place, but do not refrigerate more than one week or they will deteriorate more rapidly.

Quince   Quince have been growing in the Mediterranean for more than 4,000 years; the trees are said to have originated in Greece. The Romans used the flowers and the "golden apple" itself for many purposes, including scenting honey and perfume and as a symbol of love. The long-lived trees are popular in gardens throughout Europe, both for their fruit and for their decorative quality. Besides the flower show of pink and white in the spring, the leaves have a bright autumn hue when the weather begins to get cold, and the trees' twisted branches provide a spectacular silhouette in winter. Quince have never gained this kind of recognition in America, possibly because this yellow-skinned fruit, which looks something like a cross between an apple and a pear, has a rather astringent, bitter, acidic flavor and numerous hard seeds throughout. Because quince are high in pectin they are prized for making jellies and preserves, but they are also excellent in pies, tarts, and custards. The most popular commercial variety is the pineapple quince, but Champion is also a good choice. The fruit will keep for months stored in the refrigerator wrapped in plastic. Quince have strong sweet fragrance and help to keep the air fresh when placed unwrapped in a closet or cupboard. A few slices of raw quince can be added to a cookie jar as you would apple, to soften hard cookies.

Raisins   Raisins are dried seedless grapes. They are produced in abundance in California, almost exclusively from the Thompson seedless grape. Raisins are used in tea cakes, muffins, breads, cookies, candies, fruitcakes, and compotes. For many recipes, raisins should be soaked in water or spirits to plump them prior to use. This not only adds flavor but makes the raisins easier to slice through, enabling you to make a clean cut through a cake or pastry. And if the raisins are to be frozen (in an ice cream, for example), soaking them in alcohol will prevent them from freezing rock-hard. Raisins can be stored at room temperature for many months without becoming too dry or having the sugar crystallize on the surface, provided they are placed in an airtight container. If refrigerated they will keep for over a year.

Raspberries   Raspberries originated in Asia and Europe and grow wild in many parts of the United States. Raspberries are very popular for decorating and garnishing cakes, pastries, and tarts because of their uniform petite size and bright red color (although there are also black raspberries, which are not very common, as well as a hybrid golden raspberry). Raspberry sauce is used extensively in the pastry kitchen, and raspberries are also used in fruit salads, ice creams, and sorbets. Fresh raspberries, previously available only during the summer, are now obtainable year-round due to imports from New Zealand and Chile. The prices, of course, are higher when the fruit is imported. Frozen raspberries may be used to make sauce and sorbets. Store or freeze raspberries following the instructions given for blackberries.

Red Currants   Red currants originated in Europe and are very popular in Scandinavia and Germany. They grow in bunches like grapes on large bushes and are harvested in the early fall. Red currants are not as tart as black currants and can therefore be eaten raw. Fresh red currants are very pretty and look great as a garnish and in fruit salads. Unfortunately, they are not widely available fresh in the United States. It is actually illegal to grow red currants in many parts of the country, as the plants can harbor a parasite that kills the white pine tree. Red currants are used to make red currant jelly, which is used in Cumberland sauce, to fill cakes and pastries, and to make a glaze for fruit tarts. Berries are among the most perishable of all fruits, and red currants are no exception. Place them in a single layer on a pan or tray, cover, and store in the refrigerator; they will keep for up to two days.

Rhubarb   Rhubarb is actually a vegetable; however, it is mentioned here as it is often used like a fruit in pies and other desserts. Rhubarb grows in stalks that look something like overgrown red celery. Rhubarb is very tart and is almost always sweetened. It is quite juicy and will actually dissolve if overcooked. Rhubarb is used mostly in pies (sometimes combined with other fruits) and in cobblers.

Strawberries   Strawberries are one of the most popular fruits. The vines are found growing wild in many areas, but the berry grown commercially today is the result of much experimentation and crossbreeding. Strawberries are delicious served plain or with just a simple topping of cream and sugar. They are used in tarts, fruit salads, cakes, mousses, and strawberry shortcake. Fresh strawberries are available all year, although their flavor is at its peak in the summer. Frozen strawberries can be used in sauces and ice creams. Store or freeze strawberries as instructed for blackberries.

Tamarinds   Tamarinds, originally from the Asian and African rain forests, are cultivated today in the tropics and subtropics all over the world. They are also known as sour dates. Tamarind pods, which have a reddish brown hard shell, can grow up to 8 inches long; the pods hang in clus-

ters from the tall evergreen trees. The white flesh surrounding the black seeds turns light brown and dries up when the fruit is ripe. Tamarinds have a distinctive sweet-sour taste. Tamarinds can be obtained fresh beginning in the late fall and into the winter. They are also available throughout the year, either dried or as a sticky paste, in many grocery stores specializing in Asian foods. In addition to being used in various frozen desserts, tamarinds are most often used in Asian cooking and in the preparation of curries. Store tamarind pods in a plastic bag placed in the refrigerator.

Herbs and Spices

Angelica   Angelica is a monumental plant often growing to 6 feet and taller. It is a member of the parsley family native to Northern Europe, but today angelica can be found both cultivated and growing wild, along the Mediterranean and in North America. All parts of this strongly aromatic plant are edible: The leaves and roots are used for infusions such as tea and to flavor sweet wines and liqueurs, and both the stalk and roots are boiled in some countries and eaten as a vegetable; back in the seventeenth and eighteenth centuries so-called "angel water" derived from angelica was popular for washing the face. However, it is the celery-like candied stalks of angelica (unfortunately often spiked with too much green food coloring) that we know best. These are used to decorate cakes and pastries, and even though a bit old-fashioned today, their color makes a nice addition to fruitcakes and other holiday treats. Candied angelica will keep indefinitely if stored well wrapped in the refrigerator to prevent it from drying out.

Anise   Just like so many other aromatic herbs, anise is native to the Middle East. It is botanically related to caraway, cummin, fennel, and dill. The greenish brown comma-shaped seeds from this tall annual plant are used to flavor many confectionery dishes, as well as savory, and are also an important flavoring for liqueurs such as anisette, and apéritifs like ouzo, pastis, and Pernod. Anise oil has an antiseptic quality as well and is used to flavor toothpaste and to repel insects. An infusion made from anise seeds sweetened with honey is said to be a good digestion aid. Anise seeds should be bought whole and ground as needed. The seeds should be stored in a cool, dark place but, even so, they do not retain their scent very well, and it is best to purchase a small quantity at a time.

Caraway   This old spice originated in the temperate areas of Turkey and Iran and got its name from the Arabic word *karawyä*. Botanically a member of the parsley family, caraway looks very much like fennel, anise, or dill, with its umbrella-like flower clusters and long, feathery, bright green leaves. Each small dark seed has five lighter ridges. Caraway seeds have a strong aromatic warm taste. Their flavor is essential for many breads and sweet dishes, and caraway is used for savory dishes as well in many European countries, especially in the German-speaking areas and in Scandinavia. The seeds are high in protein and are well known for their digestive properties. They are good in combination with heavy dishes or those high in fat. Caraway has been used medicinally since early times, and the oil from the seeds is used in making the liqueur kümmel. Store the seeds in a dark, cool place to prevent them from losing their scent too soon. Legend has it that caraway seed was once added to chicken feed, supposedly because it would keep the chickens from wandering away (this was, of course, before the free-range chicken became fashionable).

Cardamom   Cardamom ranks as the third most expensive flavoring in the world, following saffron and vanilla. It is also one that you can hardly be faulted for misspelling, since the name of this ancient spice has had so many different variations—one dictionary lists seven, including "cardamony." Cardamom is a perennial shrub native to the Malabar Coast of India. The short flowering stems later carry small, yellowish green pods, each containing about twenty small seeds, which are black on the outside. Cardamom should be purchased in the pod and the seeds ground as needed since the seeds start to lose their essential oil as soon as they are removed from the pod. In addition to purchasing ground seeds or whole pods, ground pods are also available as a cost-saving commercial alternative. Store any of these varieties in a cool, dry place. Avoid using brown cardamom, an imposter which, though related to cardamom, has an inferior and overpowering flavor.

Cinnamon   The most widely used cinnamon today is the *Cinnamomun cassisa* variety that originated in Burma. The other type, *Cinnamomum zeylanicum,* is native to Ceylon, now called Sri Lanka. Both are derived from the bark of an evergreen laurel tree. This aged spice made its way to Europe through the ancient and dangerous spice route. Because of a then poorly prepared Chinese product, cassisa was once known as an inferior imitation of *Cinnamomum zeylanicum,* but today you would be hard put to tell the difference between the two in ground form. *Cinnamomum zeylanicum,* Ceylon cinnamon, has a slightly milder aroma and is lighter in color; the quills (the curled strips of bark) are easier to distinguish, being thinner and having a smoother, round appearance. Preparation and marketing of either kind is simple: thin shoots or young branches are cut when the bark is easy to separate from the wood and are then trimmed to about 4 inches long. A slit is cut on two sides of the bark, and the piece is carefully separated into two long strips, which are immediately placed back on the stick so that they will retain their shape. The pieces are then set aside for about 6 hours to let the bark ferment. In the next step, the thin outer skin is scraped off to expose the inner bark, which is the part we call cinnamon. The strips are dried for a short time and are then formed into quills, which, as they dry and contract, tighten into hard sticks. Cinnamon sticks will keep indefinitely in a dry place.

Cloves   Cloves are the dried, unopened, flowering buds of the clover tree, a handsome tropical evergreen related to the eucalyptus family. The tree grows to a height of approximately 40 feet. It takes seven years before the trees develop the flower buds that grow in small clusters and will turn into beautiful purple flowers, if they are not picked unopened to be used as a spice. Cloves take their name from the latin *clavus,* meaning "nail," and it is easy to see why, since they have a rounded head set atop a thinner, straight body. This very important spice is widely used to flavor desserts and confections. It originated in the Spice Islands (the Moluccas), a few small islands that had a monopoly on the world's clove supply for many years. In an effort to protect this standing, the Dutch, after driving the Portuguese from the region in the mid-seventeenth century, destroyed every clove tree except those on a single island. At this time clove had become a popular flavoring across Europe for use in savory dishes as well as sweet, but the price was considerable, due in part to the long and risky journey but also to the monopoly, since no sales were permitted unless the price reached a level set by the Dutch government. Today clove trees flourish in many tropical maritime climates and are grown as close to the United States as the island of Grenada in the West Indies. (The spice *clove* should not be confused with a "clove of garlic," which refers to a single segment of the garlic bulb.) Store cloves in an airtight container away from light.

Cumin Seeds   The seeds from this small annual look much like, and are often confused with, caraway seeds. Cumin, however, has a very distinctive warm and nutty flavor. The name comes from the Greek word *kúminon.* Cumin is widely used in Greece as well as throughout the Middle East. The spice is also popular in Europe, especially in Scandinavia and the Germanic-speaking countries, where it is often used to flavor breads. Kümmel, the caraway- and/or cumin-scented liqueur, takes its name from the Germanic word for cumin. The seeds come in three colors; the most common is amber, but white and black cumin seeds are also available. The latter have a peppery, more complex flavor. All are sold in seed or ground form. It is best to keep both on hand, since the seeds are difficult to grind finely. Store either one in an airtight container away from light. Cumin will keep fresh for up to six months.

Fennel Seeds   Fennel is a tall hardy plant with feathery leaves. It is native to the Mediterranean but has been used as an herb, spice, and vegetable throughout much of Europe since the time of the Roman Empire. Fennel was introduced to America by early European immigrants and today grows wild in many temperate climates along the roadside and in sunny meadows. There are two main types of fennel; the perennial (common fennel), also known as Roman fennel, is the source of the small, oval, greenish brown seeds sold either whole or in ground form. Fennel seeds are used in many different ethnic breads, crackers, sausages, and assorted savory dishes. The Florence fennel, also called finocchio, is an annual that looks very much like the common type but is smaller in size. It contains a swollen bulblike base and is cultivated throughout Southern Europe and in the United States. This type is used as a vegetable both raw and cooked, and its feathery foliage is used as a garnish much like fresh dill. Florence fennel has a light, sweet anise flavor and is sometimes erroneously labeled sweet anise. As is true with most spices and herbs, both ground fennel and fennel seeds should be stored in airtight containers in a cool, dry location.

Ginger   Ginger is the underground rhizome of an attractive perennial plant that produces leafy stems and pretty pink flowers. Ginger has a peppery sweet flavor and spicy aroma. It grows freely in most tropical and subtropical regions of the world. The cultivation of ginger originated in Asia and slowly made its way to Europe via the old spice route. The Spanish conquistadors introduced ginger root to the West Indies, where today its production is a flourishing industry, especially on the island of Jamaica, which is currently one of the two biggest producers of fresh ginger in the world along with the Malabar Coast of India. Mature ginger root is harvested when the stalks begin to whiten by simply unearthing the roots. The roots are then washed and scraped, leaving them a natural light taupe color. Mature ginger is peeled before it is used. Immature or spring ginger, as it is sometimes called, since it is only obtainable in the springtime, can be used without peeling because its skin is more tender; it also has a milder flavor and aroma than mature ginger. Fresh ginger root should have smooth shiny skin; dull and/or wrinkled skin indicates that the ginger is past its prime. Whole pieces of ginger root can be stored in the refrigerator for a week or so and frozen for much longer; ginger root should be tightly wrapped once peeled. Fresh ginger is used extensively in Asian cooking, where candied, preserved, and pickled forms are also utilized. Thin slices of pink pickled ginger, known as *gari* in Japan, are always served as an accompaniment to sushi. Dried ground ginger has a much less pungent bite than the fresh, and it should not be substituted if fresh ginger root is specified in a recipe. However, ground ginger is the type mostly widely used in the bakeshop, where it is employed to flavor cookies, spice breads, and a variety of sweets. Ginger, fresh or dried, tastes wonderful paired with many fruits and berries such as apples, pears, rhubarb, blueberries, and strawberries.

Mace   Mace is the fibrous bright red covering that enshrouds the nutmeg seed. The name is borrowed from the Greek word *markir,* an East Indian tree bark that is used as a spice. Mace is prepared for sale by being flattened and dried in the hot sun, during which time it takes on a yellowish tint. Mace is usually sold and used in a dried ground form, but it can also be obtained whole, in which case it is known as blade mace. Not surprisingly, the flavor of mace is similar to that of nutmeg although not as intense. Mace is not used as much for flavoring sweets as it is in savory dishes, where it is commonly found in pâtés and terrines. Mace should be stored in an airtight container in a dark, cool, dry place.

Nutmeg   Nutmeg is the kernel or pit from the fruit of the tropical, evergreen, nutmeg tree. The fruit has a red or yellow skin, is about 2 inches long, and resembles a cross between an apple and pear in shape. When mature, the outer flesh splits in two, exposing a red web of fibers that almost completely cover the small hard pit (when the red fibers are removed, dried and ground, they become the spice *mace*). Nutmeg is native to the Spice Islands. When the Islands were seized by the Dutch, they monopolized the sale of nutmeg, like so many other spices, and for a long time kept the trees from spreading by simply eradicating the spice from other islands. Eventually the cultiva-

tion of nutmeg was spread through enterprising traders, and today nutmeg can be found on many tropical and subtropical islands, including those in the West Indies. The nutmeg tree does not yield fruit (or the nuts contained within) until it is eight years old but will then continue to bear for half a century or so. Although the trees contain ripe fruit throughout the year, there are three major harvesting months, July, November, and March, with March being the largest harvest. This is the time that both nutmeg and mace are at their prime, while in the other two months one or the other is superior. After the flesh and mace are removed, the nutmeg pits are slowly dried until the kernel shrinks and rattles free inside the shell. The shells are then cracked, and the nuts are removed. The nuts are treated to protect them from insects and to ensure that they will not start to germinate when they are stored. If this is done properly, the nuts will keep indefinitely. Freshly ground nutmeg is far superior to the commercial preground variety. Nutmeg's sweet, spicy flavor and aroma has long been popular not just in the bakeshop but also in many savory dishes, where nutmeg is used to flavor vegetables and sauces, and nutmeg is, of course, considered a must in egg nog. A fashionable trend in the seventeenth century was for a gentleman to carry a small silver box containing a nutmeg and a grater, which were used to grate fresh nutmeg on top of hot chocolate. Store purchased ground nutmeg in an airtight container in a cool, dry location. If grinding (or grating) it yourself, do not prepare more than you need at one time.

Peppercorns   Pepper is the world's most important spice, and like salt, it was once used as a form of currency. It is native to India and India's Malabar Coast, where it grows wild. The smooth woody vines of the pepper plant (*Piper nigrum*) can climb 20 feet up tree trunks. Pepper is cultivated in many tropical regions, including Malaysia and parts of South America. One of the first spices to be merchandised by mankind, pepper was the most important commercial article traded between East India and Europe for hundreds of years. The Arabs profited from trades with the Roman Empire, and it is said that 3,000 pounds of this precious spice was part of the ransom demanded for Rome at the beginning of the fifth century. Ten centuries later, pepper most likely changed the course of history, given that the demands for it were so great that they inspired the many efforts by the Portuguese to find a way to reach India by sailing around Africa (they finely succeeded in 1498), to obtain the spice without having to pay the exorbitant prices that resulted from the overland route through the so-called Ottoman barrier on the way to Europe. Peppercorns are obtained from long grapelike clusters of about two dozen small berries each. These gradually turn from green to pink, and finally to red, as they ripen.

Green Peppercorns are harvested before they are ripe; they have a more mild, fruitier, but still peppery flavor compared with black pepper. Green peppercorns are difficult to obtain fresh and are usually sold packed in brine; freeze-dried are also available.

Black Peppercorns are picked when the berries are almost, but not quite, ripe. They are then dried until the skin shrivels and turns dark brown to black. Black pepper has the strongest flavor and is usually what is meant when one simply speaks of "pepper" in the kitchen. Because it loses its flavor rather quickly once it is ground, black pepper should always be freshly ground as needed. **White Peppercorns** are obtained by allowing the berries to ripen fully. The skins are then removed before they are dried, which produces smooth, slightly smaller peppercorns with a milder flavor.

Red Peppercorns (vine-ripened) are usually not found outside the country where they are grown.

Pink Peppercorns are not actually a pepper; they are the dried berries of a type of rose plant (the *Baies*). They are grown in Madagascar and imported through France, making them very expensive and something of a gourmet novelty.

Poppy Seeds   Poppy seeds are the dried, ripened seeds from the pod of the opium poppy, a tall annual with beautiful lilac or white colored flowers that is native to the Middle East. From the Middle East poppies spread to China some ten centuries ago and from there through the famous spice route to Europe, where today poppy seeds are immensely popular, especially in Germany and Scandinavia where they are used to flavor and decorate a multitude of baked goods. The crunchy texture and nutty flavor of the tiny seeds (one pound contains almost a million seeds) is also popular in many savory dishes in the Western kitchen, but even more so in Middle Eastern and Indian cuisines. The opium poppy is grown throughout the temperate regions of the world, illegally in most cases, to obtain the drug opium which has been used medicinally for thousands of years (opium did not become an abused narcotic until the nineteenth century when opium dens began to appear in China). Opium poppies are also cultivated legally to produce several important drugs, including Demerol, morphine, and codeine. The opiates are obtained from the thick juice that oozes out when an incision is made in the unripe seed capsule. Although poppy seeds come from the same pod, they are not narcotic. The majority of poppy seeds are bluish black, but pale yellow (also called white) and brown varieties are also available. Poppy seeds should be stored in a cool, dark place since they can become rancid.

Rosemary   The Latin name for rosemary, *Rosmarinus officinalis,* means "dew of the sea." This versatile aromatic herb is native to the Mediterranean area, where it grows wild thriving in the calcium-rich soil and dry climate. Its hardiness makes it a frequent addition to many home yards and gardens, where it will grow for many years with little attention. Rosemary is related to lavender, but unlike lavender it is evergreen, producing thin, dark green, needlelike leaves all year and pale blue flowers in the early summer. Although whole sprigs are sometimes used as a garnish, it is the redolent rosemary leaves that impart a delicious, yet very strong, flavor when this herb is used in cooking. Rosemary can easily overpower and dominate a dish and is most often used to flavor strong game dishes, poultry, and stews, and it is very often used with lamb. Rosemary is quite popular as a flavoring in bread in Italy and in some other countries as well. Rosemary is said to sooth the nerves, help digestion, and make the heart stronger. Herbal preparations containing rosemary are also made to stimulate hair growth. Keep dried rosemary in an airtight container away from light. Fresh sprigs of rosemary will keep for several days stored in a plastic bag in the refrigerator.

Saffron   Saffron is by far the most expensive of all spices. The saffron threads used for flavoring are the bright orange three-pronged stigmata, as well as a portion of the style that comes with it, of a small variety of purple crocus. The fact that they can only be harvested by hand, and that it takes around 75,000 flowers to produce one pound of saffron, explains the high price. Several varieties of this spice grow wild in the Mediterranean area of Europe; however, true cultivated saffron can best be distinguished by its large, loosely hanging stigmata. Saffron has been used since ancient times; it was introduced to Northern Europe by the Romans. Later, in the eighth century, the Muslims brought it west to Spain, which today is the largest producer. Saffron is indispensable for making Spanish paella, French bouillabaisse, and Milanese risotto, and it is used to a great extent in Middle Eastern cuisine, as well as in a number of European baked specialties such as the traditional saffron buns and breads. Saffron should always be purchased as threads, since the ground form can be easily adulterated with other yellow to orange food colorings such as safflower and marigold petals or ground turmeric. Ground saffron also loses its aroma more quickly. Store saffron in an airtight container protected from light. It will keep for up to six months.

Sesame Seeds   Sesame seeds come from a tall plant that originated in Africa. The plants are still widely grown there and throughout the Orient. The small, flat, oval seeds have a nutty flavor and come in both black and brown varieties in addition to the more commonly used ivory variation. Sesame seeds were brought to America by African slaves, and they became especially popular in the Southern United States. Today sesame seeds and sesame seed oil are used throughout the world and are very much associated with Chinese and other Asian cuisines. In the Middle East white sesame seeds are made into a paste called *tahini* and a confection called *halvah,* both of which are extremely popular there and in India. Sesame seeds are mostly used in or on top of cakes, cookies, breads, and rolls in Europe. Sesame seeds contain about 50 percent oil, so they can turn rancid very quickly. They can be kept in an airtight container in a cool, dark place for up to two months but should be refrigerated or frozen for longer storage.

Jellying Agents

Agar-agar   A natural vegetable substance extracted from Japanese seaweed, agar-agar can be purchased as a powder or in strips that look something like transparent noodles. It is odorless, colorless, and eight times stronger than gelatin. It is used when a very strong thickening agent is required: in some special meringues, pastries, jellies, and ice creams, for example. Since agar-agar is not protein-based like gelatin, it can be used as a thickening agent with raw tropical fruits that contain an enzyme such as bromelian or papain without it being necessary to boil the fruit first, as must be done when using gelatin.

Gelatin   Type B gelatin is derived from beef bones and/or calf skins. Culinary gelatin, known as type A, is made from pig skins. When dissolved, heated, and chilled, gelatin has the ability to turn a liquid into solid. As a general rule, 5 teaspoons (15 g) or 5 sheets of gelatin will set 1 quart (960 ml) of liquid to a firm consistency. This process is thermally reversible: The liquid will set at 68°F (20°C) and will melt at 86°F (30°C). Unflavored gelatin is available in both powder and sheet (leaf) form. Either can be substituted in equal weights.

When a recipe calls for powdered gelatin, the amount of liquid used to soften and dissolve the gelatin is generally specified. This is usually cold water but might also be wine, for example. The gelatin is sprinkled over the liquid and left for a few minutes to soften; it is then possible to heat the mixture in order to dissolve the granules.

Most brands of sheet gelatin weigh 1/10 ounce (3 g) per sheet. The gelatin sheets, like the powder, must also be softened in a liquid before they can be dissolved. However, sheets can be softened in virtually any amount of liquid as long as they are submerged. The amount of liquid need not be specified, because as they soften, the sheets will always absorb the same amount: 1½ ounces (45 ml) for every 9 grams (3 sheets). The sheets are removed once they are soft, without squeezing out the absorbed liquid. To substitute sheet gelatin in a recipe that calls for powdered, submerge the sheets in water, calculate the amount of liquid absorbed by each sheet, and figure that into your recipe. Then add the missing water to the gelatin sheets when you heat them to dissolve. For example: If the recipe instructs you to soften 2 tablespoons (18 g) of powdered gelatin in ½ cup (4 ounces/120 ml) of water, substitute six gelatin sheets (6 sheets at 3 grams each = 18 g), softened in enough water to cover. But, since you know that they will have absorbed only 3 ounces (90 ml) of the water, add 1 ounce (30 ml) more water.

To substitute powdered gelatin in a recipe that calls for gelatin sheets, use an equal weight of powder dissolved in as much water as the sheets would have absorbed. For example: If the recipe uses 6 sheets of softened gelatin, you would substitute 18 g of powdered gelatin, softened in the same amount of water that the sheets would have absorbed; in this case 3 ounces (90 ml).

After they are softened, either type of gelatin must be heated until it is completely dissolved. However, they must never be boiled, as boiling reduces the strength of the gelatin and causes a skin to form on the top, which is impossible to incorporate without creating lumps.

Raw papayas, pineapples, guavas, kiwis, mangoes, passion fruits, and figs, to list some of the most well known, all contain an enzyme that inhibits gelatin from setting by breaking down or dissolving the protein structure; their presence in a recipe can adversely effect the outcome where gelatin is used. However, the enzyme is destroyed if the fruit is heated to at least 175°F (80°C), so these fruits will gel normally if they are cooked first.

The strength or firmness of the set gelatin is measured using a tool called a Bloom Gellometer, which was invented by a French scientist named Bloom. It is a calibrated rod with markings from 50 to 300 bloom; 225 to 250 bloom is the most common. The tool is plunged into the set gelatin to obtain a reading.

The term *bloom* is also used in some cases to describe the process of softening the gelatin in a liquid before it is dissolved. This most likely has to do with the expansion of the gelatin as it absorbs the liquid. These two distinct meanings should not be confused.

Pectin   Pectin is naturally present in varying amounts in certain types of fruit. Apples, blueberries, cranberries, lingonberries, and most citrus fruits are particularly high in pectin. Pectin is used to thicken marmalades, jams, and jellies. Commercial pectin can be purchased in either a powdered or liquid form. A glaze made from pectin is popular for use on fruit tarts and pastries in Europe. However, a pure grade pectin (USP-NF) is required. It is not readily available but can be purchased from a chemical supplier or from the source listed in this book.

Leavening Agents

Ammonium Carbonate   Ammonium carbonate (or bicarbonate), also called hartshorn because it was originally produced from the hart's horns and hooves, is now made commercially and used mainly in cookies and short doughs to produce a longer lasting crisp texture. It can also be used in pâte à choux to give it an extra puff but can be used as a substitute for baking soda and baking powder only in cookies or doughs with very little moisture or in pastries baked at a high temperature. Ammonium carbonate reacts to heat, producing water, ammonia, and dioxide gas. It has a very strong odor that completely disappears above 140°F (60°C). It must always be stored in an airtight container or it will quickly evaporate. If ammonium carbonate is not readily available, it can be ordered from a laboratory or from the source listed in this book (a mixture of baking soda and baking powder in equal amounts may be substituted as a last resort).

Baking Powder   Baking powder is composed of one part sodium bicarbonate and two parts baking acid (generally cream of tartar, or phosphates in the case of single-acting baking powder) plus a small amount of starch to keep it from caking. When baking powder comes in contact with liquid and heat, it releases carbon dioxide gas, which causes the batter to expand and rise. Single-acting baking powders react and release gas only when they come in contact with a liquid. This makes them impractical for use in some recipes. Double-acting baking powders, the type most commonly used and the type used in the recipes in this book, react to both liquid and heat. Double-acting baking powder gives you the advantage of being able to delay baking the product. Provided the correct amount has been used, baking powder will not leave an aftertaste and should leave only small even holes inside the baked dessert rather than large air pockets. Generally speaking, the softer and more fluid the batter is, the more the baking powder will react. At high altitudes the amount of baking powder called for in a recipe must be decreased (see page 1131). Store baking powder covered in a cool place.

Cream of Tartar   Commercial cream of tartar used in baking is the acid potassium salt of tartaric acid that has been refined, bleached, and turned into a powder. Cream of tartar is used in manufacturing chemical leavening agents such as baking powder to release carbon dioxide; it is also used to inhibit recrystallization in candies and syrups and to help stiffen egg whites for meringues.

Potash (Potassium carbonate) Potash is a potassium compound that produces carbon dioxide when it comes in contact with an acid. It is an uncommon leavening agent, used mostly in cookies with spices and honey. It was obtained by leaching plant ash in the past, which is how it got its name.

Sodium Bicarbonate, or Baking Soda Sodium bicarbonate, or baking soda, when combined with an acid, produces carbon dioxide gas to inflate batters in the same way as baking powder. Baking soda starts to release gas as soon as it comes into contact with moisture, so products in which it is used should be baked as soon as possible after mixing. (This is especially true if baking soda is not used in combination with baking powder.) In addition to acting as a leavening agent, baking soda will darken the color of baked cakes and cookies, which can be an advantage in making gingerbread, for example. It will leave a strong alkaline flavor if too much is used, but in the case of gingerbread, the aroma is overshadowed by the strong spices. Store baking soda in an airtight container.

Yeast Yeast is one of the most essential ingredients for the baker. It is a living microorganism, actually a fungus, which multiplies very quickly in the right temperature range (78–82°F/25–27°C). In a bread dough the yeast feeds on the sugars (both the actual sugar added to the dough and the sugar produced from the wheat starch in the flour), fermenting them and converting the sugars to carbon dioxide and alcohol. As the bread bakes, the carbon dioxide is trapped within the dough, causing the bread to rise; the alcohol evaporates during baking. Besides the yeast naturally present in the air, there are three types available commercially: fresh (or compressed) yeast, dry yeast, and brewer's yeast. As the name implies, this last product is used mainly in the production of wine and beer; only fresh and dry yeasts are used in baking. All of the recipes in this book use fresh yeast. To substitute dry yeast for fresh, reduce the amount called for in the recipe by half. Fresh yeast should have a pleasant smell (almost like apple) and a cakey consistency; it should break with a clean edge and crumble easily. Fresh yeast can be kept up to two weeks in the refrigerator before it starts to lose its strength. Fresh yeast that is too old will begin to break down into a sticky, brown, foul-smelling substance and should not be used. To test yeast, dissolve a small amount in a mixture of ½ cup (120 ml) warm water, 2 teaspoons (10 g) of sugar, and 1 ounce (30 g) of flour: If the yeast is active it will expand and foam within 10 minutes. Fresh yeast can be frozen; however, it will lose about 5 percent of its strength. Frozen yeast must be thawed very slowly and then used the same day.

In working with yeast it is important that you pay close attention to the temperature of the product. Yeast fermentation is damaged in temperatures above 115°F (46°C), and the yeast is killed at 140°F (60°C). Yeast fermentation is slowed but not damaged at temperatures below 65°F (19°C) and is nonexistent at 40°F (4°C) or lower. Mixing the yeast directly into large amounts of sugar or salt will also damage or actually kill it.

Nuts

All nuts have a high oil content and, once shelled, should be stored tightly closed in a dark, cool place or in the freezer or they will become rancid and unusable very quickly.

Almonds There are two types of almonds: sweet almonds, which are available in markets and are used for cooking and eating, and bitter almonds, which contain prussic acid (toxic except in small amounts) and are used for flavorings and extracts. Almonds are widely used in the pastry shop as an ingredient in numerous breads and cookies, as well as being used to decorate many cakes, pastries, and Danish pastries. Almonds are available in a variety of forms—whole, sliced, slivered, or ground—and all of these can be purchased natural (skin on) or blanched (skin off). Almond extracts and flavorings are also widely used, and almonds are, of course, used to make almond paste and marzipan, two other important products in professional baking.

Almond Meal or Almond Flour is the name given to blanched almonds that are ground as fine as granulated sugar. This product can be purchased already prepared.

Apricot Kernels The soft innermost part of the apricot pit, the kernel, is used to make a paste similar to almond paste. Although it has an almondlike flavor, apricot kernel paste has a strong, bitter aftertaste.

Cashew Nuts The cashew tree is native to Brazil and the West Indies and belongs to the same family as the mango and pistachio. The tree produces fleshy applelike fruits, each with a single seed—the cashew nut—growing from the bottom as a hard protuberance. The nut is protected by a double shell (or actually three shells if you count the skin on the nut itself). The space between the inner and outer shells is filled with a toxic oily brown liquid called, appropriately enough, cashew nut shell oil. This oil is used to make resins and alkali-resistant flexible materials. Because small amounts of the oil are found on the inner shell and the kernel itself, the nuts are always heated before shelling to destroy the toxicity and avoid burns on the skin of the workers. Cashew nuts contain almost 50 percent fat and should therefore be stored covered in the refrigerator or freezer to prevent them from becoming rancid. As with all nuts, toasting greatly enhances their flavor. Although the pear-shaped apple itself is eaten by the natives, it is not favored as a fruit to eat out of hand for the most part. Instead, the rather tart, almost astringent, apples are used to make vinegar and a liqueur called Kajü. This name comes from the word *Caju,* which is the native name for the cashew.

Chestnuts Chestnuts are the seed of the chestnut tree, of which there are quite a few varieties. Chestnut trees are found in many parts of the world that have a temperate climate. The chestnuts (typically two or three) develop inside a prickly green husk and generally become ripe with the first frost around October. Each golden nut is enclosed in a thin brown membrane and then covered by a smooth mahogany-colored, leatherlike shell. The nuts are found fresh in the markets during the winter months and must be cooked and peeled before they are eaten. Just as they are in Europe today, chestnuts were once plentiful in the United States until a blight, transferred from a newly planted Far East variety, destroyed most of the trees early in this century. Though slowly on their way back, the chestnuts produced by the variety of chestnut tree found in this country are much smaller, although sweeter, than the better known Spanish variety, consequently most of the fresh chestnuts available are imported from Europe, and for the most part these come from Italy, where they are called *castagne.*

The chestnut harvest is one of the biggest events of the year in the mountain districts of Southern Europe, from the Pyrenees to the Alpine regions of France and Italy. Because cereal grains cannot be grown in these areas, chestnuts take the place of grain to a large extent, since chestnuts are mostly starch.

In addition to fresh in the shell or fresh vacuum-packed, chestnuts can be purchased dried, either whole or ground into flour; canned in brine; frozen; dehydrated; as a purée, either sweetened or unsweetened; and last, but certainly not when it comes to flavor, are the wonderful and luxurious *marrons glacés,* which are outrageously expensive but sensationally delicious—these are the ultimate in candied fruits or nuts. Fresh or cooked chestnuts should be kept in the refrigerator. The unsweetened purée should not be stored longer than a week, but marrons glacés will keep just about indefinitely. Nutritionally, chestnuts are a world apart from any other nut since they are mostly starch (carbohydrate) and are relatively low in fat and calories.

To remove the shells from fresh chestnuts, cut a small X on the flat side of each shell and either roast in a 375°F (190°C) oven for 10 to 15 minutes or cook in boiling water for 5 to 15 minutes, depending on whether or not the chestnuts will be given any further cooking. Chestnuts are easiest to peel while still warm. Sweetened chestnut purée is used alone as a filling and to flavor buttercream; whole candied chestnuts can be used to decorate cakes; chopped candied chestnuts can be added to candies and ice creams. Because fresh chestnuts are available in the winter months, chestnuts are often used in holiday desserts.

Coconuts *(see under fruits)*

Hazelnuts   Hazelnuts, also known as filberts in the United States, are grown throughout Europe; Turkey and Italy are the largest producers. The distinctive flavor is much improved by toasting, which is also the easiest way to remove most of the nut's skin (see note on pages 965 and 966). Hazelnuts are used in cakes, cookies, candies, and pastries; finely ground hazelnuts are used in linzer dough and in place of flour in some tortes. They are also used to make hazelnut paste, an important flavoring agent.

Macadamia Nuts   Macadamia nuts, grown mostly in Hawaii, have a delicious buttery flavor that is good in cookies and ice cream, where their taste is not overshadowed by the other ingredients. Because the shells are very difficult to crack, the nuts are almost always sold shelled and usually roasted as well. If you are able to find only roasted and salted nuts, thoroughly blanch and dry the nuts before using them in dessert recipes. Macadamia nuts can be substituted for other nuts in some recipes to give a dessert a tropical feeling.

Peanuts   Peanuts are actually a member of the legume family (as are beans, lentils, peas, and soybeans). They are also called goobers, goober peas, ground nuts, or grass nuts. The most common varieties are the Virginia and the Spanish peanut. Native to South America, the peanut plant was introduced to Africa by European explorers and reached North America with African slaves. Although they form underground, the edible part of the plant is not a tuber but seeds that are enclosed in a nutlike shell. Peanut farming in the United States began after the Civil War as a result of Southern farmers looking for a crop that would not be subject to the pests associated with cotton. The most famous researcher into the many uses for peanuts was George Washington Carver, whose discoveries helped establish peanut farming as a major industry. In the United States peanut butter is the most important peanut product, but very little peanut butter is consumed in other countries. About two-thirds of the peanut crop worldwide is used for oil. Peanuts are mostly used in cookies in the pastry kitchen and are also found, of course, in peanut brittle.

Pecans   Pecans (as well as walnuts) are indigenous to North America, and both are a type of hickory. Pecans are generally purchased already shelled, in halves or pieces. They are more expensive than most other varieties of nuts and are especially suitable for decorative purposes. Pecans are used in some candies and breakfast pastries and, of course, the American favorite, pecan pie.

Pine Nuts   Known as *pignolia* in Italy, pine nuts are the edible seed of the stone pine. Their rich flavor is increased by light toasting. Pine nuts are not used as much in baking as they are in other types of cooking. They are popular in savory dishes from Italy and the Mediterranean and are also used in Chinese preparations. Because pine nuts are quite high in oil and turn rancid very quickly, they should always be stored in the refrigerator or freezer. Pine nuts are good in cookies, and their petite, uniform size makes them attractive as a decoration on cakes as well.

Pistachios   Pistachios are popular for their distinctive green color and are usually used as a garnish on petits fours or candies and, of course, to make pistachio ice cream. Pistachios need hot, dry summers and cold winters. The largest share of the nuts are grown in the Middle East, although the United States, which has only been producing a commercial crop since 1976, is now the second largest producer in the world. The nuts have two shells: a red outer shell that is removed before packing and a thin inner shell, beneath which a thin skin surrounds the nut. The practice of dyeing the inner shell red is said to have been started by a New York street vendor, and the red color became so expected and associated with the nuts that at one time most pistachios were sold this way. Dyeing the shells is no longer so popular; less than 20 percent of the nuts sold today are dyed. When pistachios are purchased in the shell (the thin inner shell), the shells should be partially opened. If they are completely closed, it means the nuts were harvested before they were fully mature. To show off the green color to its fullest, remove the skins by blanching the nuts in boiling water, then pinching them between your fingers or rubbing them in a towel. Adding a pinch of salt to the water will also help to heighten the color.

Walnuts Walnuts are second only to almonds in their numerous uses in baking. Walnuts are used in many types of breakfast pastries and muffins, cookies, breads, brownies, ice creams, and tortes. Walnuts are always purchased shelled for use in commercial production, and these are available in halves for decorating, or in broken pieces at a less expensive price. Because of their high oil content, it is difficult to grind walnuts without having them turn into a paste. Grinding them with some of the granulated sugar in a recipe will help to alleviate this problem. Also because of the oil, it is preferable not to chop the nuts in a food processor; chop them by hand with a sharp knife instead. Be sure to store shelled walnuts in the refrigerator or freezer.

Rice

Rice is the most extensively utilized grain in the world; it serves as the principal food for more than half of the world's population, and since ancient times it has been the most commonly used food grain for a majority of the people in the world. Although it is not one of the most nutritious grains, consisting of over 80 percent carbohydrates, it still provides enough vitamins and minerals to mean the difference between survival and starvation in many Third World countries. A member of the grass family, *Gramineae,* rice can be grown successfully under climatic conditions ranging from tropical to temperate. When cultivated properly, rice produces higher yields than any other grain with the exception of corn; although the total area planted in rice is much smaller than that devoted to wheat, the rice crop feeds a far greater proportion of the world's population.

As it grows, the rice strand looks very much like wheat; its seed head, however, is completely different. The most common cultivation method is to flood the fields (rice paddies) that are planted with the appropriately named, and high yielding, aquatic rice. Rice plants require a steady supply of water, and therefore, in addition to flooding the fields through irrigation, rice is often planted during periods of excessive rainfall. Rice fields are kept flooded until just before harvest. Rice plants start from a single shoot and then develop many tillers and pointed, flat leaves. The plants grow from 2 to 6 feet tall and are usually self-pollinating. The kernel consists of bran layers, germ, and endosperm. More than 7,000 botanically different varieties of rice have been identified.

Rice is known to have been consumed almost 7,000 years ago in the Orient. It later spread to the Middle East and southern Europe, where it became a popular food during the Renaissance. Today the Italian arborio rice (the rice used to make risotto) is cultivated exclusively in the Po and Ticino valleys of Northern Italy. The United States is the leading exporter of rice but produces only about 2 percent of the total world crop. Most of this is grown in the Southern states and to a lesser extent in California. In most of the world rice is harvested by hand, using knives or sickles. The stalks are cut, tied in bundles, and left in the sun to dry. Different means are used to thresh the grain, ranging from using the weight of animals or tractors to threshing with various types of machines.

The most popular varieties of rice in this country are white long grain and white medium grain, but all rice is pale brown to begin with. Before it reaches the consumer it goes through a complex process, the first part being the threshing and milling, which strip the kernel of its husk, bran, and germ. Unfortunately, most of the nutritional fiber is lost as well, but this process does serve to increase the shelf life since (just as in removing the germ from wheat in making flour) it prevents the rice from becoming rancid.

There are three basic types of rice available for the commercial market: long, medium, and short grain. In the long grain category, regular milled white rice is the most common variety. Its kernel is about four times as long as it is wide. When cooked, this rice has a fluffy appearance and the grains separate easily. It is usually enriched with iron, calcium, and various vitamins to make up for the loss incurred in making the rice white; therefore, from a nutritive standpoint, the rice should not be parboiled or washed before it is cooked. Brown long grain rice is simply the entire unpolished grain with only the outer husk removed. Basmati rice is a highly aromatic long grain variety imported from the foothills of the Himalayas in India. Jasmine rice from Thailand is another fragrant long grain rice. Medium grain rice, besides being shorter and plumper, is also more moist and tender when cooked, although it is not as starchy as short grain rice. Medium grain rice has a tendency to become sticky as it cools. Short grain rice appears almost round and opal white. Although it does not contain gluten, it is known as glutenous rice in Japan and China. It is extremely starchy, which makes it easier to handle with chopsticks and therefore preferred in Asia. Converted or parboiled rice, generally known by the brand name Uncle Ben's, has been treated with pressurized steam to flush the minerals and vitamins out of the bran and concentrate them in the kernel. The rice is then dried before it is milled. This treatment also gelatinizes the starch, yielding a rice that is very fluffy after cooking with distinctly separate grains, which makes this a popular rice for use in culinary institutions using steam tables. Minute, instant, or quick rice is rice that has been completely or partially cooked before being dehydrated and packaged for the consumer. So-called wild rice is a completely different plant with very little relation to regular rice. Rice flour is prepared from broken rice grains and is used as a thickening agent. Rice flour does not contain any gluten and is therefore not used for baking bread. Raw rice grains should be stored in airtight containers in a cool, dry place. Stored this way, white rice will keep indefinitely.

Salt

Table salt has been valuable for centuries for seasoning and preserving food and has even at times through history been used as currency (the word *salary* comes from the word *salt*). The human body requires salt for regulating fluid balance. Common salt, sodium chloride, occurs naturally in pure, solid form as the mineral halite and in deposits of rock, or mineral, salts. Almost 80 percent of the total dissolved solids in ocean water are salt, and even greater amounts are found in inland saltwater lakes and seas. Salt is used more than any other mineral. When it is mixed with crushed ice it acts as a cooling agent and, conversely, when it is spread on icy streets it melts the ice. Today potassium iodine is often added to table salt (then called iodized salt) in order to supplement iodine intake in diets.

Salt plays a crucial role in almost all cooking and baking as a flavor enchancer, and in the case of bread it is used to retard yeast development, strengthen the gluten structure, and aid in browning. Salt is also used in cooking to intensify colors, such as when cooking green vegetables or blanching shelled pistachio nuts.

Salt is produced commercially by three methods: rock-salt mining; solar evaporation; and solution mining. Rock-salt mining occurs in salt domes or underground salt stratums. After the rock salt is brought to the surface, it is crushed into the desired commercial sizes. Solar salt is made by using the heat of the sun to evaporate water from the ocean or from inland salt lakes; solar salt is coarser than other varieties. In solution mining, water is forced into an underground salt deposit through a pipe. The brine is pumped to the surface through another pipe, is purified by the addition of chemicals, and is then condensed in a series of vacuum evaporators. The world's production of salt averaged 1,700 million metric tons annually in the 1980s and early 1990s. The United States is the world's largest salt producer. Kosher salt is a coarse-grained salt without additives that is excellent for use in cooking and as a table seasoning.

Sweeteners

Sugar and other sweeteners play many roles in baking, the most obvious one being to add a sweet flavor, but sugar also helps to give baked goods an attractive brown color, serves as a nutriment for yeast, makes doughs more tender and, to some extent, sugar acts as a preservative in the finished product. As described below, sugar and other sweeteners are available in numerous forms. (For information on sugar production, see pages 930 to 933).

AA Confectioners' Sugar   (*see Decorating or Sanding Sugar*)

Brown or Golden Sugar   Brown sugar is beet or cane sugar that is not fully refined. It contains molasses and many more impurities than granulated sugar. A mixture of granulated sugar and molasses can be used as a substitute for brown sugar in most recipes. Brown sugar is available to the professional in a variety of grades from light to dark brown; the darker sugars have a greater amount of impurities and a more bitter taste. Brown sugar contains a great deal of moisture and must be stored in airtight containers to keep it from drying out and hardening. If the sugar should become hard or lumpy, sprinkle a few drop of water lightly on top and warm it in a low oven, or place a slice of apple or bread in the sugar bin to add moisture.

Castor Sugar   Castor sugar is a granulated sugar that has been ground finer than regular table sugar, but not as fine as powdered sugar. It is actually the British equivalent of American powdered sugar. Castor sugar is used when it is necessary to use a sugar that will dissolve very quickly. The name originated from its association with the shaker-top container often used to store and dispense it.

Corn Syrup   Corn syrup is made from cornstarch that has been treated with enzymes to convert it to more simple compounds. It is used mostly in making candies and for sugar boiling because it keeps other sugars from recrystallizing. Corn syrup is also valuable for its ability to retain moisture in baked goods, and it is added to marzipan to improve elasticity. Corn syrup is available in both light and dark forms; the dark syrup contains added caramel color and flavorings and is not used as extensively. Although it is a liquid, a large amount of corn syrup or glucose is more easily (and less messily) measured by weight, by weighing it on top of one of the other ingredients in the recipe. Unless only a very small amount is required, measurements for corn syrup are given in both volume and weight throughout the book.

Decorating or Sanding Sugar   This is a coarse granulated sugar also known as AA confectioners' sugar. The larger crystals prevent it from dissolving easily, making it useful for decorating cookies and is often combined with sliced almonds on breakfast pastries. The sugar is also available tinted in various colors. It is excellent for sugar boiling and caramelizing because it contains few impurities.

Glucose   Glucose, as it is used in the pastry kitchen, is a viscous (44° Baumé) colorless syrup that is produced by partial hydrolycal decomposition, known as hydrolysis, which can be explained as the splitting of chemical bonds, using water. It is made from the starch in potatoes, wheat, rice, or corn. Glucose plays an important role in the confectionery industry, where its stabilizing effect is used to help prevent recrystallization when sugar is boiled to high temperatures, such as for cast, pulled, and blown sugar, for example; glucose also makes the boiled sugar more elastic. More than half of the glucose manufactured is used by the confectionery industry. Glucose should not be stored at temperatures above 68°F (20°C) because it will change from transparent to pale yellow in color. In most instances glucose can be replaced with light corn syrup.

Golden Syrup   Golden syrup is a by-product of sugar manufacturing that is refined to a greater extent than molasses. When the sugar, after many boilings, stops yielding crystals, the remaining syrup is clarified by filtering and is reduced. Golden syrup also goes through a decolorizing process, which gives it a milder flavor. It is composed of sucrose, dextrose, fructose, and a small amount of water. It is used in breads, cookies, and cakes.

Granulated Sugar   White granulated sugar is the most commonly used sugar variety and is what is meant when a recipe simply calls for sugar. It is produced for both cooking and table use. Granulated sugar is made from either sugar beets or sugarcane, and both varieties are slightly more than 99 percent pure sucrose. Granulated sugar is perfect for making cakes because the sugar granules are intentionally produced to be the right size for incorporating the proper amount of air into cake batters, and to melt and dissolve at the required speed and temperature during baking.

Honey   Honey comes from a natural source: it is the nectar collected by bees and deposited in their honeycomb. In addition to its sweetening power, honey also imparts the flavor of the flowers from which it was gathered. Honey is produced in practically every country in the world. Popular varieties include orange blossom honey from Spain, California, and Mexico; sunflower honey from Greece, Turkey, and Russia; rosemary honey produced in the Mediterranean countries; and clover honey, which is the honey most commonly used in America. The color of the honey will vary widely, depending on the source. Honey is available in four forms: comb honey, still in its waxy capsules; chunk honey, which contains both the filtered extracted honey and a piece of the honeycomb; extracted honey, the type most familiar for cooking and table use; and whipped or spun honey, which is extracted honey that is processed using controlled crystallization and has fine, easily spreadable crystals. Honey adds moisture to baked goods and gives a soft chewy texture to cakes and cookies. All honey will crystallize over time but is easy to liquefy by heating.

Invert Sugar   A chemically processed heavy syrup, sweeter than sugar, that will not crystallize. It is used mostly in icings and flavorings.

Loaf and Cube Sugar   Loaf sugar is used to make sugar sculptures. Sugar cubes are made by pressing damp, granulated sugar in molds, drying it, then cutting it into the desired shapes.

Malt Sugar or Syrup   Malt sugar is extracted from sprouted barley that has been dried and ground. It is used in yeast breads. Diastatic malt contains diastase, an enzyme that breaks down starch into sugars, which in turn provide food for the yeast during fermentation. Diastatic malt should not be used in products with a long fermentation, however, as too much of the starch will be broken down. Nondiastatic malt is processed using a higher temperature, which kills the diastase. When malt syrup or malt sugar is called for in the recipes in this book, you should use the nondiastatic formula. Malt sugar caramelizes at low temperatures and has a very distinctive taste. It is also excellent for retaining moisture in baked goods. In most cases you may substitute honey for malt sugar at a 2:1 ratio.

Maple Syrup   Made by boiling the sap of maple trees, this syrup has a wonderful rich flavor. It can be used in the pastry kitchen to make candies, flavor ice cream, make dessert sauces, and, of course, it is traditional in the United States to use it to top pancakes. The syrup is graded by color; the darker the syrup, the stronger the flavor. Maple syrup should be refrigerated after opening.

Molasses   Molasses is produced in the first stages of refining raw sugar. Used in breads and cakes, it adds a unique flavor and improves the shelf life. Molasses is available in three grades, light, dark, and blackstrap molasses. They are produced from the first, second, and third sugar boilings, respectively. Molasses may be labeled as sulfured or unsulfured, depending on whether or not sulfur was used in the sugar refining procedure.

Powdered Sugar   Also called confectioners' sugar, this sugar is produced by grinding granulated sugar to a powder. Its fineness is indicated by the number of ×s—6× is the standard while 10× is the finest. Starch is added to about 3% to prevent caking or lumping. Powdered and/or confectioners' sugar is used mostly for uncooked icings and decorating.

Turbinado Sugar   Although it is also known as "washed sugar," turbinado sugar actually goes through slightly fewer washing and refining procedures than regular granulated sugar. It retains a small amount of molasses both on the surface and in the crystal itself. It is about three times coarser than granulated sugar.

Tartaric Acid

Some tartaric acid is a natural constituent in most fruits, but the commercial product is extracted from grapes. Despite the somewhat poisonous-sounding name, tartaric acid is used for a number of purposes in cooking. Cream of tartar is made from it, and it is used to acidulate baking powder and ammonium carbonate. When used in sorbets and fruit desserts it augments the fruit flavor. It can be used whenever acidulated water or citric acid is called for (providing, of course, that the citrus flavor is not a necessary addition). Tartaric acid is not readily available but can be purchased or ordered from a drugstore in a granular form; it is quite inexpensive and lasts a very long time. Tartaric acid also acts as the catalyst for pectin glaze.

Tartaric Acid Solution   Mix ½ cup (120 ml) hot water and 4 ounces (115 g) tartaric acid until all of the granules are dissolved. Pour the liquid into a drop bottle.

Tea

Although second to coffee in commercial importance, tea ranks first as the most popular beverage in the world. The origin of tea and the infusion of dried tea leaves is a bit uncertain. Experts believe that the plant hails from a region in western China. An ancient legend has it that Shen-nung, a famous scholar and philosopher, in making a fire from the branches of the tea plant accidentally spilled some leaves into the boiling water he was preparing. The flavor proved to be so exhilarating that in a short time the preparation had become a common habit of the whole empire. The existence of tea was first recorded by Marco Polo, who spoke of the stimulating beverage and of the many teahouses in China. Tea was introduced to Europe in the sixteenth century by the Dutch East India Company and subsequently became very popular in England. The English implemented new growing areas in India in the Darjeeling and Assam valleys in the northeast part of the country, which would later become known as the world's premier tea-growing regions, and also on Ceylon (now Sri Lanka), an island that became well known for its Lipton Tea, produced by the famous tea baron Sir Thomas Lipton. Another Thomas, with the surname of Twining, also made his fortune in the tea business, having the foresight to realize just how popular tea was to become. Tea was (and still is) so enjoyed by the English that they developed a meal to go with it—high tea, which is always served at four o'clock, accompanied by biscuits (cookies) and tea cakes.

Tea also played a big role in American history: The taxation of tea led to the Boston Tea Party on December 16, 1773, when Colonists, opposed to the Tea Act of May

1773, dumped into the water over 300 chests of British tea valued at 9,000 pounds. The destruction intensified the controversy between Britain and its American Colonies and helped to trigger the War of Independence. America is also responsible for the invention of the tea bag and iced tea, both in 1904, the latter at the St. Louis World's Fair.

The tea shrub, of which there are many varieties, is a member of the camellia family. It needs rich loamy soil, and the best teas are produced at altitudes between 3,000 and 6,000 feet, since the plant grows slower in the cool air, yielding a better flavor. The cultivated tea plants are kept to about 3 feet in height and are constantly pruned to stimulate the growth of young shoots, or flushes as they called, which furnish the tender young leaves that are desired. The plants are pruned and picked regularly for about two years and are then cut down to about 1 foot or less to allow them to rest. Under proper conditions and care, the tea plant will bear for as long as half a century.

Tea leaves are handpicked by experienced workers, generally four significant times per year starting in April or May. This first picking, or flush, produces the finest and most expensive teas. The quality produced from the subsequent flushes becomes lower as the season progresses. The three major types of tea are black (fermented), oolong (semifermented), and green (unfermented). Green and black tea are made from the same plant. The main difference between them is that black teas are fermented.

In producing black tea, harvested leaves go through four main processes: withering, rolling, fermentation, and firing. Withering is accomplished by spreading the leaves out on bamboo or wire racks to dry. The purpose is to make the leaves soft and pliable for twisting in the rollers, which is done to break down the cell walls and release an enzyme that gives the tea its flavor. The "roll," or more accurately speaking, the mashed lumps, are then passed through a roll-breaker before the young leaves and stems are sifted through a wire mesh. The tea leaves are then spread out in a fermentation room where they oxidize, turning a copper color, and are allowed to ferment. Next comes the firing: The tea is spread out in a thin layer on broad, perforated metal bands, which move slowly while a current of hot air passes through them. This stops the fermentation and turns the leaves black. The dried and brittle tea leaves are then sifted through a series of sieves to determine the various grades. Tea grades refer to the size of the tea leaf. Orange pekoe has a fairly large leaf; if it includes the leaf bud as well, it is called flowery orange pekoe. Pekoe leaves are smaller; souchong leaves are round. Broken teas—tea leaves that have broken during processing—are graded as broken orange pekoe, and these make up the largest segment. Broken teas are further graded in descending size as broken pekoe; pekoe fannings; and dust, the last being the smallest leaf particles. Fannings are used to fill tea bags.

Oolong tea begins in the same way as black tea. Its fragrance, however, develops more quickly, and when the leaf is dried, it turns a coppery color around the edges while the center remains green. Oolong teas are fruity and pungent.

Green tea is produced like the others, except that the leaf is heated before rolling and the leaves are not fermented or made to oxidize. It remains green throughout processing, and the fragrance associated with black tea does not develop. Green teas are graded by age and style.

Although modern methods and equipment have taken over many of the tasks, tea leaves today are picked and to a great extent produced in much the same way as they were hundreds of years ago.

Some of the most famous teas are Darjeeling, produced in India; the Ceylon teas, from Sri Lanka, which have a smooth, flowery flavor; and Keemun, a dark China black tea that is also well known as English Breakfast tea. Various blended teas that have become popular are Irish Breakfast (made from Ceylon and Assam teas); Russian style, a China Congou that can contain other teas or flavorings; and Earl Grey, a black tea scented with bergamot (a citrus variation from the Mediterranian) or lavender oil.

India, China, Sri Lanka, Kenya, Indonesia, Japan, and the republic of Georgia are among the top producers of tea. Approximately 2.5 million metric tons of tea were produced annually in the early 1990s, and of this amount, India accounted for about one-third.

Thickeners

Arrowroot   Arrowroot is the powdered root of a plant called *Maranta arundinacea,* grown in the Caribbean. It is used to thicken glazes, fruit fillings, and puddings. Unlike cornstarch, arrowroot is not broken down by the acid in fresh fruits. Arrowroot thickens at a lower temperature than either cornstarch or flour, which is beneficial when you need to thicken a product that should not boil. It can be substituted for cornstarch in a lesser amount, and should be added at the end.

Cornstarch   Cornstarch is a fine, white powder derived from the endosperm of the corn kernel. It is used to thicken fruit fillings, glazes, and sauces. It becomes almost transparent once it has been dissolved and brought to a boil, making it more desirable for maintaining bright colors and giving an attractive appearance to foods than thickeners which become cloudy. To keep cornstarch from lumping, you must dissolve it in a cold liquid before adding it to any hot mixture. It will gelatinize at temperatures above 170°F (77°C) and will leave an unpleasant taste if it is not cooked long enough. Cornstarch is also added to cake batters to dilute the gluten strength of the flour because it is close to 100 percent starch. Foods thickened with cornstarch will start to soften and become more liquid after three to four days as the starch breaks down.

Potato Starch   Potato starch can be substituted for cornstarch and actually produces a better result. It gelatinizes at 176°F (81°C), leaves no unpleasant taste, and, when used as a thickener, does not break down, causing the product in which it is used to become watery. It can also be used to reduce the gluten strength of flour.

Tapioca Starch   Tapioca starch is derived from the root of the South American cassava plant. It is available in several forms, including quick-cooking granules, flakes, and pearls (also known as pellets). When cooked, this type of tapioca does not dissolve completely but instead the small particles become translucent and soft. The most widely used form of tapioca is tapioca flour, also called tapioca starch. It is used in the same way as arrowroot, cornstarch, and potato starch, but it is preferable for products that are to be frozen because it will not break down when thawed. Pearl tapioca must be soaked before cooking. It consists of small balls of dried tapioca starch and is used to make tapioca pudding, a custardlike dessert. Uncooked tapioca can be kept indefinitely if stored in a cool, dry place.

Tofu

Tofu is the Japanese name for bean curd. It is known as *dofu* in China, where it was apparently invented due to a culinary mistake around the second century B.C. This incredibly versatile food is a thick, creamy, cheeselike substance obtained from ground, cooked, and strained soybeans (of which there are more than a thousand varieties in a wide range of colors; however, the yellow soybean is one used to make tofu). The resulting soybean milk is curdled using heat and epsom salt. (Although rennet is commonly used to curdle dairy milk when making cheese, it will not work with soybean milk.) The curds are drained and processed in much the same way as when making cheese. Tofu has a bland and neutral flavor, and though it can be eaten on its own, it is generally added to other ingredients since it has the great ability to absorb the flavor of the food to which it is added. Tofu is used in every meal of the day in some cultures—from breakfast to dessert—fried, grilled, and poached. In the pastry kitchen it is used to make ice cream and as a substitute for some dairy products. Tofu is a dream come true for dieters and cholesterol counters. It is unique among high-protein foods as being low in calories and saturated fat and entirely free of cholesterol. Tofu is also an excellent source of calcium and other minerals.

Just as meringue can be used as a substitute for a portion of the whipped cream in some recipes, tofu can sometimes be used to replace cream cheese to create a lighter dessert. Using tofu in this manner requires a bit of experimentation. Begin by puréeing soft tofu and forcing the purée through a fine mesh strainer. The mixture may then need to be drained in a colander lined with cheesecloth, depending on the use. To get an idea of just how significantly the fat and calories can be lowered, consider that one pound of tofu has about 350 calories and 23 grams of fat (3.5 grams of saturated fat), whereas the same amount of cream cheese boasts about 1,600 calories and 160 grams of fat (100 grams of saturated fat).

Fresh tofu can be purchased in many forms, including soft or firm curds, packaged in water, or vacuum packed. All are highly perishable and should be kept refrigerated in water, and the water should be changed daily. In this way tofu can be kept for up to one week; it can be frozen for two to three months, but the texture becomes a bit chewy.

Vanilla

Vanilla, sometimes called "the orchid of flavor," is the most widely used flavoring agent in the pastry kitchen. Its uses are endless because its taste compliments just about any other flavor and improves many of them. Vanilla also has the distinction of being more expensive than any other flavoring or spice, with the exception of saffron. The expense is due in a large part to the fact that it can take up to one year, from blossom to cured vanilla bean, to produce a product of the highest quality.

Vanilla is the fruit of a tropical vine that is part of the orchid family. It requires a humid tropical climate and thrives around the equator from sea level to approximately 2,000 feet. The vine grows wild, climbing to the top of the tallest trees in the jungle, but as long as the vines can continue to grow upward they will not flower. For this reason the vines of *Vanilla planifolia,* the species most widely used for commercial cultivation, are pruned regularly and bent into loops to keep the beans within easy reach of the workers.

Clusters of buds are produced on the vines, taking many weeks to develop into orchids, which then bloom from early morning to late afternoon. If the flowers are not pollinated, they will drop from the plant by the early evening. Although a healthy vine will produce up to 1,000 flowers, only about 10 percent would be pollinated naturally. When grown commercially the flowers are therefore always hand-pollinated and, in the process, thinned to guarantee a good-quality bean. After pollination the flowers develop into long, thin, cylindrical-shaped green beans, which can reach a length of up to 12 inches although the more common size is around 8 inches. The beans are ready for harvest after approximately eight months.

There are different ways of curing the bean once it is harvested. The most common and ideal way is to use the sun to finish the ripening process. After a few days of storage the beans are spread out on blankets and left in the sun for several hours. The blankets are then folded over to cover the beans for the rest of the day, then wrapped around them and stored in airtight containers to sweat all night. This procedure is repeated for about two weeks until the beans have turned from green to dark brown. In the final step the beans are spread out on mats to dry every day for about two months. They are then stored indoors until they are dry enough to be packed and shipped.

According to history, the Spaniards stole vanilla cuttings from Mexico and planted them on the island of Madagascar. Madagascar had a monopoly on the crop for hundreds of years and today is, together with Mexico, the major producer of vanilla. The same species (sometimes referred to as bourbon vanilla from the name of one of the Madagascar islands) is grown in both Mexico and Madagascar. Tahiti is also an important growing area, producing a sweeter and more flowery-tasting bean.

Appendix B

Equipment

Adjustable Frame

Also known as a sheet pan extender. A 2-inch-high (5-cm) frame, usually placed around a baking pan, that adjusts to different widths and lengths.

Adjustable Ring

A 2-inch-high (5-cm) ring that typically adjusts from 6 to 14 inches (15–35 cm) in diameter. It is used to hold a filling while it sets, and it is useful for odd-size cakes.

Almond Mill

A commercial machine that was once indispensable in the bakeshop and still has many uses. It consists of two marble or granite rollers that turn at a low speed to prevent a buildup of heat from friction. The distance between the rollers can be adjusted as desired, depending on the usage. An almond mill will grind almonds as fine as flour, and its main function in the past was making almond paste by grinding almonds and sugar together. It is also useful for softening marzipan or almond paste that has dried or formed a crust.

Baba Molds

Small thimble-shaped baking forms used for making baba au rum pastries. The forms are usually made of aluminum and are 2¼ inches (5.6 cm) high, 2¼ inches (5.6 cm) across the top, and 2 inches (5 cm) across the bottom. (The traditional baba forms used in Europe are slightly taller and narrower, but they are not readily available in this country.)

Baguette Forms

Baking pans used for baguettes that are also known as French bread pans. They are made of several long half-spheres joined together side-by-side. The pans produce round loaves rather than loaves that are flat on one side. Some baguette forms are made of perforated metal to allow air to circulate around the loaves as they bake.

Bain-Marie

A hot-water bath used to protect delicate foods from heat that is too intense. A bain-marie is used in any of three ways: when food is to be placed over the hot water on the stove to cook a delicate sauce or to melt chocolate (such as with a double boiler); to keep cooked foods warm until serving, as in a steam table; or when the container holding the food is placed in the water to bake custards or other desserts in the oven, to provide them with constant, even heat and protect them from overcooking. It is important that foods cooked in a bain-marie are well surrounded by water, or they will cook at the oven temperature rather than that of the water.

Baker's Peel

A thin, flat wooden tool that is used like a shovel to move loaves of bread or pizzas in and out of the oven, when these items are set directly on the hearth. The blades of the peels are tapered in front and come in various sizes and shapes. The length of the pole or handle varies in accordance with the depth of the oven and can be up to 16 feet (4.8 meters).

Baker's Racks

They are metal racks available in several sizes that hold eight to twenty-four full-sized sheet pans. The racks are indispensable in a professional kitchen: Stationary racks are used for storage and for holding items during preparation, saving table space; portable racks are used for unloading deliveries and transporting goods to and from the walk-in, the work area, or the retail area. The rolling racks are available with locking wheels, and some models have adjustable shelves that can be raised to hold higher products.

Baking Paper

Also called parchment paper, or silicone-coated paper, baking paper is a specially treated nonstick paper that is used extensively in pastry and cake baking. The sheets of paper are 16 by 24 inches (40 × 60 cm) to fit full-sized sheet pans and are available in two thicknesses. The thicker paper is designed for multiple use.

Balloon Whisk

A whisk with a round (balloon) shape at the end. It is especially useful for incorporating the maximum amount of air into a batter.

Bannetons

Bannetons are coiled reed or willow baskets available in round, oval, or rectangular shapes. The baskets are used to imprint a rustic-looking beehive pattern on loaves of bread as they rise. The baskets are floured, the formed bread loaves are left to proof in the baskets, and the loaves are then carefully turned out onto a paper-lined sheet pan or a baker's peel to be transferred to the oven. As an alternative, you can use any type of woven basket approximately 8 inches (20 cm) in diameter and 3–4 inches (7.5–10 cm) deep. Be certain that the baskets have not been coated with any lacquer or paint, and cover the interior with a piece of cheesecloth before dusting with flour.

Baumé Thermometer

An instrument, also known as a saccharometer, syrup-density meter, hydrometer, or Baumé hydrometer, used to determine the concentration of sugar in a liquid as it effects the density. It is a thin glass tube with a graduated scale that ranges from 0 to 50°. The calibration on the scale refers to degrees of Baumé, named for the Frenchman Antoine Baumé. It is adjusted with weights at the bottom to read 0° Baumé in water that is 58°F (15°C). The mixture being measured must therefore be at or close to this temperature (tepid room temperature) for the reading to be accurate. The weights also allow the saccharometer to remain in a vertical position in liquid.

Another instrument with a very similar name—saccharimeter—also measures sugar concentration in a liquid but does so by measuring the angle through which the plane of vibration of polarized light is turned by the solution. The names of both instruments come from the Greek words *sakcharon* ("sugar") and *metron* ("measure").

Bear-Claw Cutter

A round cutter with multiple blades attached to a handle. It can be rolled along the edge of a Danish dough to cut the slits for bear-claw pastries.

Bread-Slashing Knife

A small, thin, sharp knife with a serrated or plain blade that is 4 inches (10 cm) long (or sometimes simply a blade without a handle), used to make cuts on the top of proofed breads just before the loaves are baked.

Brioche Pan

A round, fluted metal baking form with slanted sides. The small individual pans are $3^{1}/_{4}$ inches (8.1 cm) across the top, $1^{1}/_{2}$ inches (3.7 cm) wide on the bottom, and $1^{1}/_{4}$ inches (3.1 cm) high; larger forms are available in several sizes. In addition to being used for baking brioche, the pans can be used to mold charlottes and custards.

Bundt Pan

A tube-shaped cake pan that is rounded at the bottom and has a decorative pattern on the sides; this pan is very similar to a gugelhupf pan.

Cake Decorating Turntable

A rotating round disk on a heavy base, usually $4^{3}/_{4}$ inches (11.8 cm) high. The disc can be rotated with one hand while applying decorations or buttercream to a cake with the other hand.

Cake Knife

A very practical tool for the pastry kitchen, this is something of a cross between a knife and a metal serving spatula. The knife blade is $6^{1}/_{2}$ inches (16.2 cm) long, wide near the handle, and tapered to a point at the end. One side of the blade has a sharp edge and the other a serrated edge. It is designed to make it easy to cut and transfer cake slices without switching tools, but its size and shape lends it to many other applications as well.

Cake Rack or Cake Cooler

A cake rack looks like a grill and is designed so that air can circulate under, and also around, cooling breads or cakes. It is handy for icing pastries as well if a sheet is placed under the rack to collect the runoff.

Cardboard Cake Rounds and Sheets

These sturdy sheets can be made from regular cardboard or corrugated cardboard. They are available in several round sizes, as well as square and rectangular sizes that are designed to hold cakes baked in standard half- or full-sized sheet pans. The larger sizes are available in either single or double thickness; the thicker style is preferable because the sheets will lie flat. Finished cakes are placed on the sheets, in combination with a doily, to transport them from the bakery. The cardboard is also used to support cake layers or short dough cake-bottoms, making it much easier to move them during assembly and decorating.

Charlotte Molds

Metal forms used to make charlottes. The forms vary in size, but the classical style is plain, round, and flat on the bottom, with slightly slanted sides and heart-shaped ears.

Cheesecloth

A light, fine mesh gauze used in the pastry kitchen to strain sauces and to drain off the whey from cheese in making coeur à la crème, for example, or in draining yogurt.

Chef's Knife

An all-purpose knife with a tapered blade 8–14 inches (20–35 cm) long. It is used for chopping, mincing, and slicing.

Chinois

A rigid cone-shaped strainer made of perforated metal; also known as a China cap. In the pastry kitchen it is used to strain sauces or custards.

Chocolate Molds

Hollow molds used for making standing chocolate figures. The molds are made of two pieces that can be clamped together, leaving a small hole in the bottom to add melted chocolate. The molds can be made of plastic or metal and come in numerous sizes and special shapes such as animals, Santas, and Easter eggs. (See page 915 for information on using hollow chocolate molds.) In addition to hollow molds, there are also chocolate molds that consist of a flat plastic or metal tray with shallow indentations in various designs to produce solid chocolate figures that are flat on one side. These molds are also used to make other types of candy such as hard sugar candies.

Citrus Stripper

A small hand tool used to cut long, thin strips of citrus zest. The tool has a notch in the blade to remove the peel in uniform pieces, and it can also be used to make decorative patterns on vegetables or to score the skin on cucumbers.

Comb Scraper or Cake Comb

A plastic or metal scraper with a fluted or serrated edge. It is used to make a pattern on the surface of cakes or pastries.

Cone Roller

Also known as a *pizelle* cone roller, this is a wooden cone with a short round handle that is used to form warm *pizelle* (Italian wafer cookies), florentina, or tulip paste cookies into cones. In Scandinavia, tulip paste cookies made in this shape are called *krumkaka.*

Crème Brûlée Molds

Traditional crème brûlée dishes are made of ceramic, have a fluted pattern on the sides, and are $4^1/2$ inches (11.2 cm) in diameter and $3/4$ inch (2 cm) deep.

Croquembouche Molds

Cone-shaped molds that are flat on the very top, used to form the famous *pièce monté* the name comes from. The molds can be made of tinned or stainless-steel. Some have a small lip at the base on which to rest the first row of profiteroles as they are attached to one another around the form. Croquembouche molds come in sizes from 7 to 12 inches (17.5–30 cm) wide at the base and 10–20 inches high (25–50 cm).

Deep-Frying Thermometer

A thermometer specifically designed to read the temperature of hot fat for deep frying.

Deck Oven

A widely used oven in which a sheet pan holding the item to be baked, or the item itself (in the case of some breads, for example), is placed directly on the hearth (floor) of the oven. The inside of the oven is about 12 inches (30 cm) high; deck ovens do not have racks inside. Deck ovens are the oldest and most commonly used type of oven in commercial operations. They are made to hold from two to over sixteen sheet pans side-by-side (in the larger size oven the configuration of the pans is usually four across by four deep). Because two or more ovens are often placed on top of one another, they are also known as stack ovens. Deck ovens can be equipped with steam injectors.

Dipping Fork

A small fork, also known as a "dip stick," typically with two to four prongs but also available with different shapes on the end, such as round or oval rings, designed to hold various shapes of candies. Dipping forks are used for dipping pastries and candies into chocolate or icing.

Docker or Pricker

A tool that has spikes to prick doughs, eliminating air bubbles and preventing the dough from rising too much during baking. On one style the spikes protrude from a tube-shaped base attached to a handle, so it can easily be rolled over a large sheet of dough.

Dough Hook Attachment

A hook-shaped attachment for an electric mixer shaped in varying degrees of curl or curve. The straighter shape looks like a **J** and is known as a "sweet dough arm." On other doughs hooks the end can be curled in more tightly or around in a spiral shape. Dough hooks are used for kneading bread doughs and mixing other types of dough when the ingredients are to be combined without incorporating air. Dough hooks with a more pronounced curled shape do a more efficient job of mixing.

Dough Scrapers

Also called bench scrapers or "baker's helpers." Dough scrapers consist of a thin, rectangular, stainless-steel blade with a wooden or plastic handle; they can also be made from a solid piece of stainless-steel with one rolled long edge forming the handle. Dough scrapers are used to clean the top of a worktable and for cutting doughs and baked goods, such as cookies, into pieces. A soft plastic variation has one rounded side to facilitate scraping doughs or batters from the inside of a mixer bowl. This type is also handy for scraping dough off of a rolling pin because it can be bent to fit the curve of the pin.

Dowels

Also known as straight rolling pins. Dowels are cylindrical in shape from 16 to 20 inches (40–50 cm) long and $3/4$ to 2 inches (2–5 cm) in diameter; they do not have handles. Dowels can be made of hardwood or treated aluminum; wooden dowels are sometimes tapered at the ends. Small dowels are not intended for use in rolling out dough like a rolling pin but instead are used by rolling a sheet of dough around them to transfer it, or as a guide when cutting doughs, as you would use a ruler.

Drum Sieve

A circular wire strainer with straight sides about 4 inches (10 cm) high, usually with a wooden frame. The mesh is available in various sizes. The sieve is used to sift flour, powdered sugar, or nuts.

Eggs-in-Aspic Form

An oval metal form, 3¼ inches long and 2½ inches wide at the top (8.1 × 6.2 cm) with sloping sides, making it slightly narrower at the bottom. The form is primarily used in the garde-manger kitchen for the dish it was named for, but it is nice for molding custards and charlottes as well.

Étamé

A cone-shaped strainer with a soft, very fine mesh. An étamé is used in the pastry kitchen to strain sauces such as raspberry, for example, when it is desirable that the sauce is completely free of any tiny seeds.

False-Bottom Tart Pan

A tart pan with sides 1 inch (2.5 cm) high and a removable bottom. The most common size measures 11 inches (27.5 cm) in diameter. The pans are used for custard-based tarts and quiches that can not be inverted to unmold.

Fixative Syringe

A hand tool used to apply color to finished pieces in sugar work; also known as a hand sprayer. The syringe consists of two tubes, one slightly longer and thinner than the other, connected by a hinge. The tubes are bent at a 90° angle when the tool is in use; they fold flat for storage. The liquid coloring is sprayed (blown) on the sugar by submerging one end of the tool in the color and placing the other in your mouth. By blowing air into the syringe the color is sprayed in a very fine mist.

Flan Ring

A thin metal ring, usually made of tinned steel with rolled edges, that is about 1 inch (2.5 cm) high and comes in various sizes. It is placed on a sheet pan, which serves as the bottom, and is used to bake tarts.

Guéridon

A small serving cart on casters that is used in restaurants to cook food at the table. The carts have two or more burners and are most often used for flambé work.

Gugelhupf Pan

A tube pan with a rounded bottom and a decorative pattern on the sides. The typical size has just over a 1-quart (960-ml) capacity. It is used to bake gugelhupf, a type of coffee cake.

Hearth

The name used to refer to the floor of a deck oven. When instructions specify placing a loaf of bread directly on the hearth, it means the bread is to be set directly on the bottom of the oven without using a sheet pan. The bread is positioned in the desired area of the hearth by sliding it from a peel (the placement is critical since once the bread is placed on the hearth, it can not be moved until a crust has formed). Baking directly on the hearth makes a big difference in the taste and appearance of the bread. Because there isn't any pan, the bread dough is immediately hit with intense heat that creates a much more pronounced oven-spring and, in turn, a higher loaf with a better crust. If your oven does not have a hearth or ceramic bottom, baking stones or pizza stones can be purchased and used in the same way, but these are more suitable for home use since they will usually accommodate only a few loaves of bread. A second alternative is to cover an oven rack with 6-inch (15-cm) square terra cotta tiles, positioning the rack in the center of the oven. Just as with a baking stone or pizza stone, the tiles must be seasoned the first time they are used by heating and cooling them so they will not crack. Another way to create a hearth is to use refractory bricks (1½-inch/3.7-cm bricks used to build furnaces) in the same way. Once any of these homemade hearths are in place in your oven it is not necessary to remove them when the oven is used for other baking or roasting; the stones will actually improve the oven's performance and contribute to more even heating. To clean any of the hearth surfaces let them cool completely and then scrub with plain water. Do not use any soap.

Hotel Pan

A stainless-steel pan that is available in numerous standard sizes and depths. The pan has a lip all around so that it can be placed on top of a basin of hot water (bain-marie or steam table) to keep food warm. Hotel pans are also useful for marinating and storing food and for baking custards and soufflés in a water bath.

Loaf Pan

A rectangular metal baking form, also known as a bread pan. In the pastry kitchen, loaf pans are used for baking breads, pound cakes, and fruit cakes and for molding frozen desserts. They come in many sizes; a standard pan measures approximately 5 inches (12.5 cm) wide across the top, 9 inches (22.5 cm) long, and 3 inches (7.5 cm) high.

Marzipan Modeling Tools

A set of hand tools about 5 inches (12.5 cm) long, used to mark and form marzipan figures. The ends of the tools have a blunt, round, pointed, or engraved surface to make the various imprints. A professional set usually contains twelve tools. These are fairly expensive but are a necessary investment if you are making marzipan figures frequently. For occasional marzipan work, a set of small tools intended for use with modeling clay can be purchased at an art supply store at a considerably lower price.

Mazarin Forms

Small, round baking forms with slanted sides, typically 2½ inches (6.2 cm) in diameter on top, 1½ inches (3.7 cm) on the bottom, and 1¼ inches (3.1 cm) high.

Melon-Ball Cutter

A hand tool with hollow half-spheres on either end used to scoop out fruit into uniform balls. This tool can also be used to make small, elegant curled chocolate shavings.

Metal Bars

Aluminum or steel bars available in varying thicknesses and lengths. Two bars can be used as a guide to roll out candies and special doughs to a precise thickness; four bars can be used to hold a liquid such as boiled sugar or a candy filling within a small area, or in a certain shape, while it is setting up; a weight is placed against the outside of each bar to hold it in position. A metal bar can also be useful as a guide in making straight lines when using a trowel to create alternating lines of chocolate or batter on silicone mats or plastic strips. A typical bar is 18 inches (45 cm) long and 3/4 inch (2 cm) thick on all sides.

Muffin Pan

A metal baking pan with deep indentations or cups to hold and shape muffins as they bake. Pans for professional use come in standard full- and half-sheet-pan sizes usually holding two to four dozen muffins, depending on size.

Multiple Pastry Wheel

A tool with four or five pastry wheels connected, so that multiple strips of dough can be cut simultaneously. The distance between the wheels is adjustable.

Paddle Attachment

An attachment for an electric mixer used to beat and cream batters. Paddles are flat with two or three vertical bars inside a frame. A modified version that does not have any vertical bars (consisting of just a hollow frame) is sometimes known as a pastry knife and is used much like a dough hook for pie doughs or other doughs where less mixing is desirable.

Palette Knife

An elongated flexible spatula also known as an icing spatula. These spatulas have wooden or plastic handles and stainless-steel blades in lengths from 4 to 14 inches (10–35 cm); the width of the blade increases in proportion to the length, but the blade is always a long rectangular shape; the end of the blade can be straight or rounded. The most practical size for everyday use has a 10-inch blade that is 1 1/2 inches wide (25 × 3.7 cm) with a rounded tip. Palette knives have a multitude of uses in the pastry kitchen, including the application of icings and glazes and spreading batters into sheets and within templates.

Offset Palette Knives are available in the same configurations; these are also known as gooseneck spatulas. In these the blade is bent at almost a 90° angle about 2 inches (5 cm) from the handle and then bent again to become parallel to the handle. The advantage to this shape is the ability to spread a product very thin without the edge of a baking pan, the handle of the palette knife, or your hand getting in the way.

Pastry Bag

A cone-shaped plastic, nylon, or cloth bag that comes in lengths from 7 inches (17.5 cm) to over 20 inches (50 cm). When fitted with a piping tip, or pastry tip, it is used to pipe out batters and doughs. (See pages 21 to 23 for general information on using and caring for pastry bags; see pages 980 to 983 for information on using a pastry bag for decorating.)

Pastry Brush

A small flat brush from 1/2 to 2 inches (1.2–5 cm) wide used to apply a glaze, egg wash, chocolate, or melted butter. The brushes should be made with natural bristles such as boar rather than nylon.

Pastry Chef's Knife

A combination palette knife and serrated knife with a spatula-type handle and a blade that is 12 inches (30 cm) long and 1 3/8 inches (3.4 cm) wide with a rounded end. One edge of the blade is serrated and is used for cutting, and the other edge is smooth and is used as a palette knife. The wide blade facilitates cutting sponges into horizontal layers.

Pastry Cutters or Cookie Cutters

Professional pastry or cookie cutters come in round, oval, square, star, and heart shapes in sets of graduating sizes, in plain or fluted styles. Other cookie cutters, for both professional and home use, are available in a multitude of different shapes and sizes for special occasions and specific recipes.

Pastry Wheel

A sharp, round disk attached to a handle so that it can roll. Also known as a pizza cutter, it comes fluted or plain and is used to cut dough.

Perforated Sheet Pan

A metal baking sheet with tiny holes used to promote a crisp crust and ensure proper baking on the bottom of breads and rolls baked in a rack oven. The pans are used without baking paper and should be completely dry or the product will stick. The pans are not used in regular shelf-type ovens because the product could overbrown on the bottom.

Pie Weights

Small metal or ceramic pellets used to weigh down a dough or crust to prevent it from expanding too much during baking. Dried beans are a common substitution.

Pincers

A hand tool with two flat, springy arms that have a fluted pattern on the edges. They are available in different widths and shapes and are used for decorating the edges of pie crusts or to pinch a design on marzipan.

Piping Bag

A small paper cone, approximately 5 inches (12.5 cm) long, used for precise and delicate decorations and held by the fingers only. (See page 27 for instructions on making a piping bag; see page 984 for information on using a piping bag for decorating.)

Piping Bottle

A small plastic squeeze bottle with a narrow opening that is used in decorating. Piping bottles generally have a 1- to 2-cup (240–480-ml) capacity. (See pages 998 and 999 for more information.)

Piping Tip

Also known as a pastry tip, a piping tip is a small metal or plastic hollow cone that is fitted into a pastry bag. The tips come in many shapes and sizes. The most standard styles are either plain, producing a smooth edge, or star-shaped, making a fluted pattern. Other special tips are available for specific uses such as filling pastries or making buttercream decorations.

Plastic Strips

Flexible heavyweight sheets of acetate or polyurethane cut to the desired size for use in making chocolate containers or lining the sides of forms for chilled desserts. (The plastic strips are not ovenproof like baking paper and cannot be used as a substitute if the product is to be baked.)

Pots de Crème Forms

Small ceramic forms with tight-fitting lids used to bake and serve individual portions of custard. Each lid has a small hole to allow steam to escape.

Proof Box

A cabinet or room in which heat and humidity are controlled to create the correct environment for a yeast dough to proof (rise).

Pullman Pan

A baking pan used to make Pullman bread loaves. The pan has a sliding top so the loaf is enclosed on all four sides during baking. Pullman pans have a larger capacity than the average bread pan. The typical size measures 16 inches long, 4 inches high and across the base, and just slightly wider across the top (40 × 10 cm). Pullman bread slices are square and are used primarily for sandwiches or toast in commercial food establishments. Pullman loaves are named after Pullman railroad cars because of their resemblance to the car's long, boxy shape.

Rack Oven

A large convection oven holding one to four baker's racks at a time. The ovens are very expensive but save time by producing a large quantity of evenly browned breads, rolls, or other baked goods at once. The ovens come with racks specifically designed to fit each oven. The rack is rolled into the oven and locked onto an arm that rotates the rack during baking. Each rack holds about fifteen full-sized sheet pans. Rack ovens are usually equipped with steam injectors. Since the sheet pans do not come in con-

tact with the bottom of the oven, as they do in deck and rotating ovens, it is necessary to use perforated sheet pans so the product will brown on the bottom.

Ramekins

Shallow earthenware dishes in which single portions (e.g., individual soufflés) are baked and served. They are also used to mold chilled custard desserts. The most common size measures about 3 inches (7.5 cm) across and 1½ inches (3.7 cm) high and holds 5 ounces (150 ml).

Rectangular Fluted Pan

A metal baking pan generally used for tea cakes. The pans are rectangular on the top but slope down to a rounded, fluted design on the bottom. The typical size is 10 by 4¾ inches (25 × 11.8 cm) and 2 inches (5 cm) high. They are known in Germany as *rehrücken,* or saddle-of-venison pans.

Rolling Pins

Rolling pins are available in a wide array of sizes and are made from materials such as brass, plastic, marble, and porcelain in addition to wood, and there are even hollow rolling pins made of glass that are designed to be filled with ice to keep dough cold as it is rolled out. Some of these rolling pins are more suited for decorative use than actual production, especially in a professional kitchen. A solid cylinder made from hardwood, 12–16 inches long (30–40 cm) and 3–4 inches (7.5–10 cm) in diameter, is preferable. These are made in two styles; the more common has a steel rod and ball bearings inside with handles on both ends. The other very practical version has a removable wooden or treated aluminum dowel that is inserted through the center of the rolling pin and extends about 4 inches (10 cm) on either side to act as a handle; the dowel can also be used separately to hold dough sheets rolled around it to transfer them, or as a guide when cutting dough sheets. They are unbreakable.

French Rolling Pins are thin wooden cylinders about 18 inches (45 cm) long without handles. They are 2 inches (5 cm) in diameter at the center and are tapered from there toward each end; they are used for rolling out circular shapes.

Pastry or Pizza Rolling Pins, also called broom-handle or speed rolling pins, are intended for small pieces of dough. These rolling pins have only one handle, which is either suspended over the center, parallel to the pin and attached at a right angle to either end, or attached at a 90° angle from the same. Because only one hand is required when working with this type of pin, it leaves the other hand free to turn the dough. These rolling pins are made of wood and are 4–10 inches long (10–25 cm) and 2 inches (5 cm) in diameter.

Rotating Oven

This is also known as a revolving oven. Rotating ovens are large and bulky. The shelves that hold the sheet pans move around inside the oven like a Ferris wheel. The amount of space required makes them impractical, but on the positive side they eliminate the potential for hot spots because the products are in constant rotation. The modern version of the rotating oven is the smaller efficient rack oven.

Rubber Spatulas

These are also called bowl scrapers. They have a small, tapered rectangular blade made of rubber or nylon that is attached to a plastic or wooden handle. Typically one corner of the blade is square and the other is rounded. A typical size has a 12-inch (30-cm) handle and a blade that measures 2 by 3 inches (5 × 7.5 cm). One variation has a slightly cupped blade, which makes it easier to use the spatula to transfer food.

Salamander

A broiler with the heat source at the top or a heated thick metal disk suspended at the end of a metal rod, used to brown or caramelize food, for example, the sugar on top of a Crème Brûlée.

Savarin Forms

Small doughnut-shaped baking forms. The sizes vary, but a useful size is $3\frac{1}{2}$ inches (8.7 cm) in diameter, 1 inch (2.5 cm) deep, with a $1\frac{1}{4}$-inch (3.1-cm) hole. Savarin forms are used for making individual servings of savarins, as the name suggests, but can also be used for many other pastries and desserts.

Scales

Baker's Scales are also known as balance scales. These use an added weight counterbalancing system and have a sliding mechanism at the front that can be set from 1 to 16 ounces and in increments thereof. The counterweights come in 1-, 2-, 4- and 8-pound sizes. The advantage to using a balance scale is that it can accommodate a larger amount of product to be weighed since it is not limited to the capacity of a spring. This type of scale is not very accurate for measuring quantities less than 1 ounce, however. The product to be weighed is always placed on the left side of the scale and the weights are placed on the right, whether or not the scale bowl is used.

Electronic Scales are the most convenient and efficient type to use. They use a spring mechanism like the spring scale but have a digital readout that can be "zeroed," allowing you to weigh one ingredient on top of another without adding the desired measurements together, or to compensate for the weight of a container by placing the empty container on the scale, setting the readout back to zero, and then adding the product to be weighed. Electronic scales are by far the most expensive of the three types discussed here but will pay off in the long run by contributing to efficiency and reducing human error.

Spring Scales are best suited for portion control in a professional kitchen. They use a spring mechanism with a round dial and have one small, flat tray. Spring scales are available calibrated in ounces, pounds, or grams.

Sheet Pan

A metal baking sheet used in professional kitchens. The pan measures 24 by 16 inches (60 × 40 cm) and has 1-inch

(2.5-cm) sides. Half-sheet pans are 16 by 12 inches (40 × 30 cm); quarter-sized sheet pans measure 12 by 8 inches (30 × 20 cm). Half- and quarter-sized pans will fit the home oven.

Silicone Baking Mat

A thin (approximately $\frac{1}{8}$ inch/3 mm) soft, flexible sheet of a siliconized compound that withstands temperatures from −40° to over 550°F and has a nonstick surface. Silicone mats are used instead of baking paper and, if properly cared for, can be reused thousands of times. They are made in sizes to fit full or half-sheet pans. In addition to their use in baking, silicone mats are used for sugar work since they can tolerate high temperatures and do not need to be greased or oiled. Silicone mats should be washed using a soft, nonabrasive sponge or cloth and hot water or just wiped clean.

Silkscreen

A wide array of impressive patterns can be created using a silkscreen together with a silicone mat and ribbon sponge base. The material is tightly stretched inside a metal frame (unfortunately, you must purchase the frame with each pattern). The silkscreen is placed on top of a silicone mat, and a cocoa paste is spread on top using a special rubber trowel. When the silkscreen is lifted off, the pattern is duplicated in the thickness it was spread out (very thin) on top of the mat. Silkscreens must be handled and cleaned carefully since any small tear can prove fatal.

Skimmer

A flat, finely meshed (or with small holes) strainer attached to a handle, used to remove dirt or scum from a boiling liquid, to poach, and to deep fry.

Small Swedish Pancakes Pan (*Plättiron*)

A round cast-iron skillet measuring 9–10 inches (22.5–25 cm) in diameter. The skillet has five to seven $2\frac{1}{2}$-to-3-inch (6.2-to-7.5-cm) round depressions to form pancakes as they are cooking.

Springform Pan

A baking pan with removable sides, used mostly for baking cheesecakes. A clamp tightens the sides against the bottom.

Stainless-Steel Grill

These thin (about $\frac{1}{16}$-inch/2-mm) flat steel sheets, made to fit silicone baking mats, are available in many different patterns. After being placed on top of a silicone mat, tulip paste is uniformly and thinly spread on top, filling in the pattern. The grill is then removed, and the same procedure as when making ribbon sponges is followed (pages 277 and 278, steps two through five). Steel grills should be handled and stored with care to avoid bending them.

Steam Injector

A device available on some commercial ovens that sends steam into the oven during baking. The steam creates a moist environment that prevents a crust from forming too quickly on breads or rolls. The result is a thinner crust with a very crisp texture. The steam also makes breads and rolls shiny, much like the effect of using egg wash. (See pages 72 and 73 for more information.)

Sugar Basket Form

A form used as a guide to weave ropes of pulled sugar into a basket. The form has a $3/4$-inch (2-cm) thick wooden base with thirty-six removable $4^1/_2$-inch (11.2-cm) brass dowels. Six different shapes are drawn on the top of the base (including round, oval, diamond, and square), each with holes for the dowels that are individually drilled at the proper angle and distance for that particular shape. The dowels are inserted into the set of holes to form the desired shape, and then the sugar ropes are woven in and out around them. Once the sugar has hardened, the dowels are pulled out and are replaced with dowels made of sugar.

Sugar Pan

An unlined copper pan made especially for cooking sugar. The acidity of the copper causes some of the sugar to break down into invert sugar, which is more resistant to recrystallization. The sugar will also cook faster in this type of pan. A sugar pan has a small spout, which makes it easy to pour out the boiled sugar.

Sugar Thermometer

A thermometer specifically designed to measure the temperature of boiled sugar. Some have the names of the various sugar stages printed next to the corresponding temperature. Sugar thermometers made for professional use are protected by a metal casing that also serves to suspend the thermometer above the bottom of the pan.

Digital Thermocouple Thermometers, although still relatively expensive, are very convenient and precise. They are available with either built-in or plug-in probes for sugar cooking. The base, which provides a digital readout, is placed on the worksurface next to the stove, and a wire-type probe is clamped to the inside of the pan.

Table Brushes

Large brushes that are used to sweep excess flour or powdered sugar off the surface of a dough and from the table, as the dough is rolled out.

Tart Pan

A metal baking pan available in many shapes and sizes. The most frequently used tart pan is round, 11 inches (27.5 cm) in diameter, and 1 inch (2.5 cm) deep, but tarts are also made in square or rectangular shapes. Tart pans can be one solid piece or two pieces; the latter, called "false-bottom pans," simplify the removal of the baked tart. The pans have straight, usually fluted, sides.

Tartlet Pans

Pans used for making small, individual tarts that are usually filled with fruit or custard. Tartlet pans can be plain or fluted.

Template

A guide used to create a desired shape. It is sometimes used as a stencil to form a batter or paste. It can also be used to mask a certain portion of a product when applying a decoration; sifting powdered sugar over a doily on top of a cake is an example of using a template in this way.

Tread Rolling Pin

A decorating tool that creates a pattern of parallel lines when it is rolled over a sheet of dough or marzipan.

Trowel

Also known as a comb, this is a tool that is made for use in a professional pastry kitchen, in combination with a silicone baking mat, for the production of ribbon sponge sheets. The trowel comes with four to six interchangeable rubber blades with square notches in different patterns on each side. It is about 3 feet (90 cm) wide so it can cover the width of a full-sized mat in a single pass. In addition to square-notched trowels that create various striped designs, trowels are available with curved notches that create a sponge pattern that resembles ladyfingers piped side-by-side, to use for lining the sides of charlotte molds, and there are also trowels with triangular notches that create a pointed three-dimensional pattern on the surface of a sponge. A plastic trowel designed for applying glue can be purchased at a hardware store and used as a substitute for the professional square-notched tool but is not practical for mass production. (See page 276 for more information.)

Vegetable Peeler

This is sometimes called a fruit and vegetable peeler and also a potato peeler. There are several designs in different shapes. All consist of a blade that is slit in the center, allowing the peelings to pass through. The blade usually swivels within the frame and/or handle to follow the shape of the item being peeled.

Waffle Rolling Pin

A small tool shaped like a very thin rolling pin, about 13 inches (32.5 cm) long and 1 inch (2.5 cm) in diameter. The surface of the roller resembles a waffle iron and creates a decorative waffle pattern when rolled over dough. It is often used on marzipan.

Whip Attachment

An attachment for an electric mixer. As the name suggests, the whip attachment is used when it is desirable to incorporate a maximum amount of air into a thin mixture, such as when making a sponge batter or whipping cream; this tool is therefore almost exclusively used at high speed.

Zester

A hand tool used to cut the zest (the colored part of the rind without the white pith) from citrus fruits. About the size of a paring knife, a zester has five small holes at the end to remove the skin in small threads.

Appendix C

Conversion and Equivalency Tables

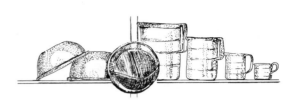

The Metric System
Precise Metric Equivalents
    Length
    Volume
    Weight
Precise Metric Conversions
    Length
    Volume
    Weight
Metric and U.S. Equivalents: Volume
    U.S. Volume Equivalents
Metric and U.S. Equivalents: Weight
Metric and U.S. Equivalents: Length
Temperature Conversions
Volume Equivalents of Commonly Used Products
Volume Equivalents for Shelled Eggs
Gram Weight of Commonly Used Products
Volume and Weight Equivalents for Honey, Corn
    Syrup, and Molasses
High-Altitude Adjustments for Cake Baking
Baumé Scale
    Baumé Readings for Sugar Solutions
        Relative to 2 Cups (480 ml) Water
Sugar Boiling Conversions

The Metric System

Accuracy of measurement is essential in achieving a good result in the pastry shop. Ingredients are therefore almost always weighed, or "scaled," to use the professional term. The few exceptions are eggs, milk, and water; for convenience, these are measured by volume at the rate of 1 pint to 1 pound, 1 liter to 1 kilogram, or, for a small quantity of eggs, by number. The system of measurement used in the United States is highly complicated and confusing compared to the simple metric system used just about everywhere else in the world. In the U.S. system, the number of increments in any given unit of measure is arbitrarily broken down into numbers that have no correlation to each other. For example, there are 12 inches in 1 foot, 32 ounces in 1 quart, 4 quarts in 1 gallon, 3 teaspoons in 1 tablespoon, and so on. Adding to the confusion is the fact that ounces are used to measure both liquids by volume and solids by weight; so if you see the measurement "8 ounces of melted chocolate," you do not really know if this means to weigh the ingredient or measure it in a cup. This can make a big difference in a particular recipe since 1 cup (8 liquid ounces) of melted chocolate weighs almost 10 ounces. The metric system, on the other hand, is divided into four basic units, one for each type of measurement:

- **Degree Celsius** is the unit used to measure temperature. The freezing point is 0°C and the boiling point is 100°C. Degree Celsius is abbreviated as °C throughout the text.

- **Meter** is the unit used to measure length and is divided into increments of centimeters and millimeters.
  10 millimeters = 1 centimeter
  100 centimeters = 1 meter

  Meters, centimeters, and millimeters are abbreviated as m, cm, and mm, respectively, throughout the text.

- **Liter** is the unit used to measure volume. A liter is divided into deciliters, centiliters, and milliliters.
  10 milliliters = 1 centiliter
  10 centiliters = 1 deciliter
  10 deciliters = 1 liter

Liters, deciliters, centiliters, and milliliters are abbreviated as l, dl, cl, and ml, respectively, throughout the text.

- **Kilogram** is the unit used to measure weight.
  1 kilo = 10 hectograms
  1 hectogram = 100 grams

The measurement of hectogram is rarely used in this country, and the kilo is instead divided into 1,000 grams. Kilograms and grams are abbreviated as kg and g, respectively, throughout the text.

The following approximate equivalents will give you a feeling for the size of various metric units:

- 1 kilo is slightly over 2 pounds
- 1 liter is just over 1 quart
- 1 deciliter is a little bit less than $1/2$ cup
- 1 centiliter is about 2 $1/2$ teaspoons
- 1 meter is just over 3 feet

Larger or smaller units in the metric system are always made by multiplying in increments of 10, making it a more precise system and much less confusing once you understand the principles. Nevertheless, many people who did not grow up using this method are reluctant to learn it and think it will be difficult to understand. Reading that there are 28.35 grams to 1 ounce looks intimidating, but it actually shows how the metric system can give you a much more accurate measurement. When measuring by weight any ingredient that is less than 1 ounce, use the gram weight for a precise measurement, or convert to teaspoons and/or tablespoons if necessary.

The equivalency tables in this chapter have been used to convert the measurements in this book and provide both the U.S. and metric measurements for all ingredients in the recipes. However, they do not precisely follow the conversion ratio; instead the tables have been rounded off to the nearest even number. For example, 1 ounce has been rounded up to 30 grams rather than 28.35, which is the actual equivalent; 2 ounces has been rounded down to 55 grams instead of 56.7 grams, and so on. As the weight increases, every third ounce is calculated at 25 g rather than 30, to keep the table from becoming too far away from the exact metric equivalent. Preceding these tables are the precise measurements for converting the various types of measure should you require them.

Precise Metric Equivalents

Length

1 inch	25.4 mm
1 centimeter	0.39 inches
1 meter	39.4 inches

Volume

1 ounce	29.57 milliliters
1 cup	2 dl, 3 cl, 7 ml (237 ml)
1 quart	9 dl, 4 cl, 6 ml (946 ml)
1 milliliter	0.034 fluid ounce
1 liter	33.8 fluid ounces

Weight

1 ounce	28.35 grams
1 pound	454 grams
1 gram	0.035 ounce
1 kilogram	2.2 pounds

Precise Metric Conversions

Length	To convert:	Multiply by:
	inches into millimeters	25.4
	inches into centimeters	2.54
	millimeters into inches	0.03937
	centimeters into inches	0.3937
	meters into inches	39.3701

Volume	To convert:	Multiply by:
	quarts into liters	0.946
	pints into liters	0.473
	quarts into milliliters	946
	milliliters into ounces	0.0338
	liters into quarts	1.05625
	milliliters into pints	0.0021125
	liters into pints	2.1125
	liters into ounces	33.8

Weight	To convert:	Multiply by:
	ounces into grams	28.35
	grams into ounces	0.03527
	kilograms into pounds	2.2046

In the tables that follow, metric amounts have been rounded to the nearest even number. These conversions should be close enough for most purposes.

Metric and U.S. Equivalents: Volume

U.S.	Metric
$1/4$ teaspoon	1.25 ml
$1/2$ teaspoon	2.5 ml
1 teaspoon	5 ml
1 tablespoon (3 teaspoons)	15 ml (1 cl, 5 ml)
1 ounce (2 tablespoons/$1/8$ cup)	30 ml (3 cl)
$1 1/4$ ounces	37.5 ml
$1 1/2$ ounces (3 tablespoons)	45 ml
$1 3/4$ ounces	52.5 ml
2 ounces (4 tablespoons/$1/4$ cup)	60 ml (6 cl)
3 ounces (6 tablespoons/$3/8$ cup)	90 ml (9 cl)
4 ounces (8 tablespoons/$1/2$ cup)	120 ml (1 dl, 2 cl)
5 ounces (10 tablespoons/$5/8$ cup)	150 ml (1 dl, 5 cl)
6 ounces (12 tablespoons/$3/4$ cup)	180 ml (1 dl, 8 cl)
7 ounces (14 tablespoons/$7/8$ cup)	210 ml (2 dl, 1 cl)
8 ounces (16 tablespoons/1 cup)	240 ml (2 dl, 4 cl)
9 ounces ($1 1/8$ cups)	270 ml (2 dl, 7 cl)
10 ounces ($1 1/4$ cups)	300 ml (3 dl)
11 ounces ($1 3/8$ cups)	330 ml (3 dl, 3 cl)
12 ounces ($1 1/2$ cups)	360 ml (3 dl, 6 cl)
13 ounces ($1 5/8$ cup)	390 ml (3 dl, 9 cl)

U.S.	Metric	U.S.	Metric
14 ounces (1³/₄ cups)	420 ml (4 dl, 2 cl)	6¹/₂ ounces	185 g
15 ounces (1⁷/₈ cups)	450 ml (4 dl, 5 cl)	7 ounces	200 g
16 ounces (2 cups/1 pint)	480 ml (4 dl, 8 cl)	7¹/₂ ounces	215 g
17 ounces (2¹/₈ cups)	510 ml (5 dl, 1 cl)	8 ounces	225 g
18 ounces (2¹/₄ cups)	540 ml (5 dl, 4 cl)	8¹/₂ ounces	240 g
19 ounces (2³/₈ cups)	570 ml (5 dl, 7 cl)	9 ounces	255 g
20 ounces (2¹/₂ cups)	600 ml (6 dl)	9¹/₂ ounces	270 g
21 ounces (2⁵/₈ cups)	630 ml (6 dl, 3 cl)	10 ounces	285 g
22 ounces (2³/₄ cups)	660 ml (6 dl, 6 cl)	10¹/₂ ounces	300 g
23 ounces (2⁷/₈ cups)	690 ml (6 dl, 9 cl)	11 ounces	310 g
24 ounces (3 cups)	720 ml (7 dl, 2 cl)	11¹/₂ ounces	325 g
25 ounces (3¹/₈ cups)	750 ml (7 dl, 5 cl)	12 ounces	340 g
26 ounces (3¹/₄ cups)	780 ml (7 dl, 8 cl)	12¹/₂ ounces	355 g
27 ounces (3³/₈ cups)	810 ml (8 dl, 1 cl)	13 ounces	370 g
28 ounces (3¹/₂ cups)	840 ml (8 dl, 4 cl)	13¹/₂ ounces	385 g
29 ounces (3⁵/₈ cups)	870 ml (8 dl, 7 cl)	14 ounces	400 g
30 ounces (3³/₄ cups)	900 ml (9 dl)	14¹/₂ ounces	415 g
31 ounces (3⁷/₈ cups)	930 ml (9 dl, 3 cl)	15 ounces	430 g
32 ounces (4 cups/1 quart)	960 ml (9 dl, 6 cl)	15¹/₂ ounces	445 g
33 ounces (4¹/₈ cups)	990 ml (9 dl, 9 cl)	16 ounces (1 pound)	455 g
34 ounces (4¹/₄ cups)	1 l, 20 ml	17 ounces (1 pound, 1 ounce)	485 g
35 ounces (4³/₈ cups)	1 l, 50 ml	18 ounces (1 pound, 2 ounces)	510 g
36 ounces (4¹/₂ cups)	1 l, 80 ml	19 ounces (1 pound, 3 ounces)	540 g
37 ounces (4⁵/₈ cups)	1 l, 110 ml	20 ounces (1 pound, 4 ounces)	570 g
38 ounces (4³/₄ cups)	1 l, 140 ml	21 ounces (1 pound, 5 ounces)	595 g
39 ounces (4⁷/₈ cups)	1 l, 170 ml	22 ounces (1 pound, 6 ounces)	625 g
40 ounces (5 cups)	1 l, 200 ml	23 ounces (1 pound, 7 ounces)	655 g
41 ounces (5¹/₈ cups)	1 l, 230 ml	24 ounces (1 pound, 8 ounces)	680 g
42 ounces (5¹/₄ cups)	1 l, 260 ml	25 ounces (1 pound, 9 ounces)	710 g
43 ounces (5³/₈ cups)	1 l, 290 ml	26 ounces (1 pound, 10 ounces)	740 g
44 ounces (5¹/₂ cups)	1 l, 320 ml	27 ounces (1 pound, 11 ounces)	765 g
45 ounces (5⁵/₈ cups)	1 l, 350 ml	28 ounces (1 pound, 12 ounces)	795 g
46 ounces (5³/₄ cups)	1 l, 380 ml	29 ounces (1 pound, 13 ounces)	825 g
47 ounces (5⁷/₈ cups)	1 l, 410 ml	30 ounces (1 pound, 14 ounces)	855 g
48 ounces (6 cups)	1 l, 440 ml	31 ounces (1 pound, 15 ounces)	885 g

U.S. Volume Equivalents

3 teaspoons	=	1 tablespoon
2 tablespoons	=	1 ounce
8 ounces (16 tablespoons)	=	1 cup
2 cups	=	1 pint
2 pints	=	1 quart
4 quarts	=	1 gallon

Metric and U.S. Equivalents: Weight

U.S.	Metric
¹/₂ ounce	15 g
²/₃ ounce	20 g
³/₄ ounce	22 g
1 ounce	30 g
1¹/₂ ounces	40 g
2 ounces	55 g
2¹/₂ ounces	70 g
3 ounces	85 g
3¹/₂ ounces	100 g
4 ounces	115 g
4¹/₂ ounces	130 g
5 ounces	140 g
5¹/₂ ounces	155 g
6 ounces	170 g

U.S.	Metric
32 ounces (2 pounds)	910 g
33 ounces (2 pounds, 1 ounce)	940 g
34 ounces (2 pounds, 2 ounces)	970 g
35 ounces (2 pounds, 3 ounces)	1 kg (1,000 g)
36 ounces (2 pounds, 4 ounces)	1 kg, 25 g
37 ounces (2 pounds, 5 ounces)	1 kg, 50 g
38 ounces (2 pounds, 6 ounces)	1 kg, 80 g
39 ounces (2 pounds, 7 ounces)	1 kg, 110 g
40 ounces (2 pounds, 8 ounces)	1 kg, 135 g
41 ounces (2 pounds, 9 ounces)	1 kg, 165 g
42 ounces (2 pounds, 10 ounces)	1 kg, 195 g
43 ounces (2 pounds, 11 ounces)	1 kg, 220 g
44 ounces (2 pounds, 12 ounces)	1 kg, 250 g
45 ounces (2 pounds, 13 ounces)	1 kg, 280 g
46 ounces (2 pounds, 14 ounces)	1 kg, 310 g
47 ounces (2 pounds, 15 ounces)	1 kg, 340 g
48 ounces (3 pounds)	1 kg, 365 g
49 ounces (3 pounds, 1 ounce)	1 kg, 395 g
50 ounces (3 pounds, 2 ounces)	1 kg, 420 g
51 ounces (3 pounds, 3 ounces)	1 kg, 450 g
52 ounces (3 pounds, 4 ounces)	1 kg, 480 g
53 ounces (3 pounds, 5 ounces)	1 kg, 505 g
54 ounces (3 pounds, 6 ounces)	1 kg, 535 g
55 ounces (3 pounds, 7 ounces)	1 kg, 565 g
56 ounces (3 pounds, 8 ounces)	1 kg, 590 g

U.S.	Metric
57 ounces (3 pounds, 9 ounces)	1 kg, 620 g
58 ounces (3 pounds, 10 ounces)	1 kg, 650 g
59 ounces (3 pounds, 11 ounces)	1 kg, 675 g
60 ounces (3 pounds, 12 ounces)	1 kg, 705 g
61 ounces (3 pounds, 13 ounces)	1 kg, 735 g
62 ounces (3 pounds, 14 ounces)	1 kg, 765 g
63 ounces (3 pounds, 15 ounces)	1 kg, 795 g
64 ounces (4 pounds)	1 kg, 820 g
65 ounces (4 pounds, 1 ounce)	1 kg, 850 g
66 ounces (4 pounds, 2 ounces)	1 kg, 875 g
67 ounces (4 pounds, 3 ounces)	1 kg, 905 g
68 ounces (4 pounds, 4 ounces)	1 kg, 935 g
69 ounces (4 pounds, 5 ounces)	1 kg, 960 g
70 ounces (4 pounds, 6 ounces)	1 kg, 990 g
71 ounces (4 pounds, 7 ounces)	2 kg, 20 g
72 ounces (4 pounds, 8 ounces)	2 kg, 45 g
73 ounces (4 pounds, 9 ounces)	2 kg, 75 g
74 ounces (4 pounds, 10 ounces)	2 kg, 105 g
75 ounces (4 pounds, 11 ounces)	2 kg, 130 g
76 ounces (4 pounds, 12 ounces)	2 kg, 160 g
77 ounces (4 pounds, 13 ounces)	2 kg, 190 g
78 ounces (4 pounds, 14 ounces)	2 kg, 220 g
79 ounces (4 pounds, 15 ounces)	2 kg, 250 g
80 ounces (5 pounds)	2 kg, 275 g

Metric and U.S. Equivalents: Length

U.S.	Metric
$1/16$ inch	2 mm
$1/8$ inch	3 mm
$3/16$ inch	5 mm
$1/4$ inch	6 mm
$3/8$ inch	9 mm
$1/2$ inch	1.2 cm
$3/4$ inch	2 cm
1 inch	2.5 cm
$1^{1/4}$ inches	3.1 cm
$1^{1/2}$ inches	3.7 cm
$1^{3/4}$ inches	4.5 cm
2 inches	5 cm
$2^{1/2}$ inches	6.2 cm
3 inches	7.5 cm
$3^{1/2}$ inches	8.7 cm
4 inches	10 cm
$4^{1/2}$ inches	11.2 cm
5 inches	12.5 cm
$5^{1/2}$ inches	13.7 cm
6 inches	15 cm
$6^{1/2}$ inches	16.2 cm
7 inches	17.5 cm
$7^{1/2}$ inches	18.7 cm
8 inches	20 cm
$8^{1/2}$ inches	21.2 cm
9 inches	22.5 cm
$9^{1/2}$ inches	23.7 cm
10 inches	25 cm
$10^{1/2}$ inches	26.2 cm
11 inches	27.5 cm
$11^{1/2}$ inches	28.7 cm
12 inches (1 foot)	30 cm

U.S.	Metric
13 inches	32.5 cm
14 inches	35 cm
15 inches	37.5 cm
16 inches	40 cm
17 inches	42.5 cm
18 inches ($1^{1/2}$ feet)	45 cm
19 inches	47.5 cm
20 inches	50 cm
21 inches	52.5 cm
22 inches	55 cm
23 inches	57.5 cm
24 inches (2 feet)	60 cm
25 inches	62.5 cm
26 inches	65 cm
27 inches	67.5 cm
28 inches	70 cm
29 inches	72.5 cm
30 inches ($2^{1/2}$ feet)	75 cm
31 inches	77.5 cm
32 inches	80 cm
33 inches	82.5 cm
34 inches	85 cm
35 inches	87.5 cm
36 inches (3 feet/1 yard)	90 cm
37 inches	92.5 cm
38 inches	95 cm
39 inches	97.5 cm
40 inches	1 meter
48 inches (4 feet)	1 meter, 20 cm

Temperature Conversions

Fahrenheit	Celsius	
32°F	0°C	(freezing point)
35°F	2°C	
40°F	4°C	(yeast is dormant)
45°F	6°C	
50°F	10°C	
55°F	13°C	
60°F	16°C	
65°F	19°C	
68°F	20°C	(gelatin sets)
70°F	21°C	
75°F	24°C	
80°F	26°C	(ideal temperature for yeast to multiply)
85°F	29°C	(lowest working temperature for tempered chocolate)
86°F	30°C	(gelatin dissolves)
90°F	32°C	(highest working temperature for tempered chocolate)
95°F	34°C	
100°F	38°C	(lowest working temperature for coating chocolate)
105°F	40°C	(working temperature for coating chocolate)
110°F	43°C	(highest working temperature for coating chocolate)
115°F	46°C	
120°F	49°C	

Fahrenheit	Celsius	
125°F	52°C	
130°F	54°C	
135°F	57°C	
140°F	60°C	(yeast is killed)
145°F	63°C	
150°F	65°C	
155°F	68°C	
160°F	71°C	
165°F	74°C	
170°F	77°C	
175°F	80°C	
180°F	82°C	
185°F	85°C	
190°F	88°C	
195°F	91°C	
200°F	94°C	
205°F	96°C	
210°F	99°C	
212°F	100°C	(water boils at sea level)
215°F	102°C	
220°F	104°C	
225°F	108°C	
230°F	110°C	
235°F	113°C	
240°F	115°C	(sugar syrup for Italian Meringue/soft ball stage)
245°F	118°C	
250°F	122°C	
255°F	124°C	
260°F	127°C	
265°F	130°C	
270°F	132°C	
275°F	135°C	
280°F	138°C	
285°F	141°C	
290°F	143°C	
295°F	146°C	
300°F	149°C	
305°F	152°C	
310°F	155°C	
315°F	157°C	
320°F	160°C	(sugar starts to caramelize)
325°F	163°C	
330°F	166°C	
335°F	168°C	
340°F	170°C	
345°F	173°C	
350°F	175°C	
355°F	180°C	
360°F	183°C	
365°F	185°C	
370°F	188°C	
375°F	190°C	
380°F	193°C	
385°F	196°C	
390°F	199°C	
395°F	202°C	
400°F	205°C	
405°F	208°C	
410°F	210°C	

Fahrenheit	Celsius
415°F	212°C
420°F	216°C
425°F	219°C
430°F	222°C
435°F	224°C
440°F	226°C
445°F	228°C
450°F	230°C
475°F	246°C
500°F	260°C
550°F	288°C

To convert Celsius to Fahrenheit   Multiply by 9, divide by 5 (Celsius $\times$ $^9/_5$), then add 32. Example: $190°C \times {}^9/_5 = 342 + 32 = 374°F$.

To convert Fahrenheit to Celsius   Subtract 32, multiply by 5, then divide by 9 (Fahrenheit $\times$ $^5/_9$). Example: $400°F - 32 = 368 \times {}^5/_9 = 204.4°C$.

Volume Equivalents of Commonly Used Products

1 pint water	1 pound
1 pound sliced almonds	6 cups (loosely packed)
1 pound bread flour (unsifted)	4 cups
1 pound cake flour (unsifted)	$4^1/_3$ cups
1 pound butter	2 cups
1 pound granulated sugar	$2^1/_4$ cups
1 pound powdered sugar	4 cups
1 pound brown sugar	$2^2/_3$ cups
1 pound unsweetened cocoa powder	$4^3/_4$ cups

Volume Equivalents for Shelled Eggs, Average Size

(these numbers are rounded for convenience and ease of multiplication)

Egg Whites

2	$^1/_4$ cup/60 ml
4	$^1/_2$ cup/120 ml
5	$^5/_8$ cup/150 ml
6	$^3/_4$ cup/180 ml
8	1 cup/240 ml
10	$1^1/_4$ cups/300 ml
12	$1^1/_2$ cups/360 ml
14	$1^3/_4$ cups/420 ml
16	2 cups/480 ml

Egg Yolks

3	$^1/_4$ cup/60 ml
4	$^1/_3$ cup/80 ml
6	$^1/_2$ cup/120 ml
8	$^2/_3$ cup/160 ml
9	$^3/_4$ cup/180 ml
10	$^7/_8$ cup/210 ml
12	1 cup/240 ml
16	$1^1/_3$ cups/320 ml

Whole Eggs

4	1 cup
16	1 quart

Gram Weight of Commonly Used Products

Item	Grams per Teaspoon	Grams per Tablespoon
ammonium carbonate	3.5	10
baking powder	4	12
baking soda	4	12
bread flour	2.5	8
butter	5	15
ground cinnamon	1.5	5
unsweetened cocoa powder	2.5	8
cornstarch	2.5	8
cream of tartar	2	6
granulated sugar	5	15
grated citrus zest	6	18
ground spices (except cinnamon)	2	6
malt sugar	3	9
mocha paste	4	12
powdered gelatin	3	9
powdered pectin	3	9
powdered sugar	3	9
salt	5	15

Volume and Weight Equivalents for Honey, Corn Syrup, and Molasses

Volume	Weight
1/4 cup/60 ml	3 ounces/85 g
1/3 cup/80 ml	4 ounces/115 g
1/2 cup/120 ml	6 ounces/170 g
2/3 cup/160 ml	8 ounces/225 g
3/4 cup/180 ml	9 ounces/255 g
1 cup/240 ml	12 ounces/340 g
1 1/4 cups/300 ml	15 ounces/430 g
1 1/3 cups/320 ml	1 pound/455 g
1 1/2 cups/360 ml	1 pound, 2 ounces/510 g
1 3/4 cups/420 ml	1 pound, 5 ounces/595 g
2 cups/480 ml	1 pound, 8 ounces/680 g
3 cups/720 ml	2 pounds, 4 ounces/1 kg, 25 g

High-Altitude Adjustments for Cake Baking

Since most recipes are developed for use at sea level (including those in this book), when baking at higher altitudes, where the atmospheric pressure is much lower, you must make some adjusts to produce a satisfactory result. Although some experimental baking has to be done to convert a sea-level recipe to a particular local condition and altitude, certain manufacturers will supply the rate of adjustment for some of their products.

At high altitudes the lower air pressure causes water to boil at a lower temperature. Thus more evaporation takes place while a cake is baking, because the liquid begins to boil sooner. This results in insufficient moisture to fully gelatinize the starch, which in turn weakens the structure. The lower air pressure also causes the batter to rise higher; however, it later collapses due to the lack of stabilizing starches.

It is necessary to make adjustments with cake baking starting at altitudes from 2,500 feet (760 meters). In general the changes consist of

- reducing the amount of baking powder or baking soda;

- increasing the amount of liquid, sometimes with additional eggs, egg whites, or yolks;

- increasing the flour; and

- using a higher baking temperature.

These changes are applied to a greater degree as the altitude gets higher. Although these changes help to protect the shape and consistency of the cake, they reduce its quality and flavor.

Adjustments for specific ingredients are as follows:

Leavening Agents   Baking powder or soda, and any other substitute that reacts with heat, must be reduced by 20 percent starting at 2,500 feet (760 meters) and gradually be reduced up to 60 percent at 7,500 feet (2,280 meters). For example, If a recipe calls for 10 ounces (285 g) of baking powder, only 4 ounces (115 g) should be used at 7,500 feet (2,280 meters). In a dark cake or muffin recipe that calls for both baking powder and baking soda together with buttermilk, it is best to change to sweet milk and use baking powder only (add the two amounts together) to save having to convert both leavening agents.

Eggs   At 2,500 feet (760 meters) add 3 percent more whole eggs, egg whites, or egg yolks. Progressively increase the amount of eggs until at 7,500 feet (2,280 meters) you are adding 15 percent more eggs. For example, if your recipe calls for 36 ounces (1 kg, 25 g) of eggs (which is 1 quart or 960 ml), you must use an additional 5.4 ounces (150 g) at the 7,500-foot (2,280-meter) level.

Flour   Beginning at 3,000 feet (915 meters), add 3 percent more flour, gradually increasing the amount up to 10 percent more at 8,000 feet (2,440 meters). For example, if your recipe calls for 40 ounces (1 kg, 135 g) of flour, you should use 1 1/4 ounces (35 g) more at 3,000 feet (915 meters).

Oven   Starting at 3,500 feet (1,065 meters), increase the baking temperature by 25 percent. For example, if your recipe says to bake at 400°F (205°C), you should increase the temperature to 500°F (260°C) at 3,500 feet (1,065 meters). The baking time should remain the same as at sea level, but you need to take care not to bake any longer than necessary to prevent the rapid evaporation that takes place at high altitudes.

Storage   Everything dries quicker in thin air, so to ensure maximum moisture and freshness, cakes should be removed from the pans, wrapped in plastic, and stored in the refrigerator as soon as they have cooled. It is actually preferable not to keep any sponges in stock at high altitudes; instead, make them up as you need them.

Baumé Scale

A French chemist, Antoine Baumé, perfected the saccharometer—also known by the names syrup-density meter, hydrometer, and Baumé hydrometer—an instrument that is used to determine the density of a liquid. A saccharometer is a thin glass tube with a graduated scale that ranges from 0 to 50° BE. The weights at the bottom of the saccharometer are precisely adjusted by the manufacturer so that it will read 0° BE when placed in water that is 58°F (15°C). Before using the instrument for the first time, it is a good idea to test it and, if necessary, compensate for any discrepancy, plus or minus, when using it. The weights at the bottom also allow the instrument to remain in a vertical position in the liquid. To use the saccharometer, a high narrow container, preferably a laboratory glass, must be filled with enough of the liquid to be measured for the saccharometer to float. The scale is read at the point where the instrument meets the surface of the liquid. For example, if the saccharometer settles at 28°BE, the density of the solution is 1.28, which means that 1 liter (33.8 ounces) of the solution will weigh 1 kg, 280 g (2 pounds, 13 ounces). The following table gives the Baumé readings for certain percentages of sugar solutions based on 2 cups

(480 ml) water and varying amounts of sugar when the mixture is brought to a boil to dissolve the sugar and the solution is then measured at room temperature (65°F/19°C). When measured hot, the BE° will read 3° lower. If the syrup is boiled for any length of time, these readings will no longer apply because the evaporation that will take place will increase the ratio of sugar to water.

Brix Scale   The Brix scale was invented by a German scientist named Adolf Brix; it is used for the same purpose as the Baumé scale—to measure the sugar content in a liquid. The Brix scale is calibrated to read 0.1° Brix at 68°F (20°C). A solution containing 20 grams of sucrose per 100 grams of liquid will read 20° Brix. The Brix scale is used only with pure sucrose solutions; it cannot be used with other solutions. The Brix reading is determined by using a hydrometer.

The Brix scale is used in the wine making industry to measure the sugar content in fresh or fermenting grape juice, by farmers in conjunction with other tools to measure the sugar to acid ratio in determining when to harvest fruits, and in the commercial fruit canning industry in the preparation of sugar syrups.

Baumé Readings for Sugar Solutions Relative to 2 Cups (480 ml) Water		
Water	**Granulated Sugar**	**Baumé at Room Temperature**
2 cups (480 ml)	5 ounces (150 g)	14° (sorbet syrup)
2 cups (480 ml)	6 ounces (170 g)	15°
2 cups (480 ml)	7 ounces (200 g)	17°
2 cups (480 ml)	8 ounces (225 g)	18° (baba syrup)
2 cups (480 ml)	9 ounces (255 g)	20° (candied citrus peel syrup)
2 cups (480 ml)	10 ounces (285 g)	21°
2 cups (480 ml)	12 ounces (340 g)	25°
2 cups (480 ml)	14 ounces (400 g)	27°
2 cups (480 ml)	1 pound (455 g)	28° (simple syrup)
2 cups (480 ml)	1 pound, 2 ounces (510 g)	29°
2 cups (480 ml)	1 pound, 4 ounces (570 g)	31°
2 cups (480 ml)	1 pound, 6 ounces (635 g)	32°
2 cups (480 ml)	1 pound, 8 ounces (680 g)	33°
2 cups (480 ml)	1 pound, 10 ounces (740 g)	34°
2 cups (480 ml)	1 pound, 12 ounces (795 g)	35° (liqueur candies)

Sugar Boiling Conversions

If you were to compare the sugar conversion tables in ten different cookbooks you would probably find ten different temperatures and almost as many names used to describe the same stage. Some charts have fourteen separate stages, which can really make your head spin! All of these names and stages are, in a way, misleading and unrealistic for use by anyone who does not have years of experience. For example, by the time you have tested and determined that the boiling sugar is at the crack stage, it has probably already reached hard crack. What is important is not what a particular stage is called and how to test for it, but what temperature is required for the sugar

syrup, based on what it is to be used for. I suggest you rely on an accurate sugar thermometer rather than your poor index finger and ignore all the different names; however, the testing procedures are listed in the following table should you want to use them.

Special thermometers for boiling sugar are calibrated according to the temperature range needed. Professional thermometers have a wire screen that protects the glass and should be stored hanging up, using the handle that is part of this screen. Although Centigrade is used more and more for measuring sugar in European countries, I have included the old Réaumur system here because it is still part of the scale on professional European thermometers.

Sugar Boiling Conversions				
Stage	**Fahrenheit**	**Celsius**	**Réaumur**	**Testing Procedure**
Thread	215-230°	102-110°	82-88°	Pull a little sugar between your thumb and index finger; shorter or longer threads will form depending on the temperature. (Pinch and open your fingers quickly to cool the sugar and prevent burns.)
Soft Ball	240°	115°	92°	Put your index finger in ice-cold water, dip it very quickly into the hot syrup, and immediately plunge it back into the ice water. The sugar will fall off your finger and you will be able to roll it into a ball.
Firm Ball	245°	118°	94°	Same as for soft ball stage, but the ball will be harder.
Hard Ball	250-260°	122-127°	97-101°	Same as for soft ball stage, but the sugar will be more resistant to forming a ball.
Small Crack	265-270°	130-132°	104-105°	Dip your finger into water and sugar as for the soft ball test; the sugar cannot be formed and will show small cracks.
Crack	275-280°	135-138°	108-110°	Same as for small crack stage, except that the sugar will break apart.
Hard Crack	295-310°	146-155°	116-123°	Test as for soft ball stage; the sugar will shatter in the ice water.
Caramel	320°	160°	128°	To test: check the color. Sugar turns from amber to golden brown to light brown.

Index